THE ROUTLEDGE HANDBOOK OF PUBLIC TAXATION IN MEDIEVAL EUROPE

Beginning in the twelfth century, taxation increasingly became an essential component of medieval society in most parts of Europe. The state-building process and relations between princes and their subject cities or between citizens and their rulers were deeply shaped by fiscal practices. Although medieval taxation has produced many publications over the past decades there remains no synthesis of this important subject.

This volume provides a comprehensive overview on a European scale and suggests new paths of inquiry. It examines the fiscal systems and practices of medieval Europe, including essential themes such as medieval fiscal theory and the power to tax; royal and urban taxation; and Church taxation. It goes on to survey the entire European continent, as well as including comparative chapters on the non-European medieval world, exploring questions on how taxation developed and functioned; what kinds of problems authorities encountered assessing their fiscal power; and the circulation of fiscal cultures and practices across cities and kingdoms. The book also provides a glossary of the most important types of medieval taxes, giving an essential definition of key terms cited in the chapters.

The Routledge Handbook of Public Taxation in Medieval Europe will appeal to a large audience, from seasoned scholars who need a comprehensive synthesis, to students and younger scholars in search of an overview of this critical subject.

Denis Menjot is Emeritus Professor of Medieval History at the Université Lumière-Lyon 2. With Pere Verdés Pijuan he directs the e-*Glossary of Medieval Taxation*. He has been president of the European Association of Urban History (2006–2008). He is president of the Société Française d'Histoire Urbaine and director of *Histoire Urbaine*, corresponding member of the Real Academia de la Historia. His previous publications include "Taxation and Sovereignty in Medieval Castile", in *Authority and Spectacle in Medieval and Early Modern Europe*, London, Routledge, 2017.

Mathieu Caesar is Associate Professor in Medieval History at the Université de Genève. He is the author of *Le pouvoir en ville. Gestion urbaine et pratiques politiques à Genève (fin XIIIe – début XVIe siècles)*, Brepols, 2011, and the editor of *Factional Struggles. Divided Elites in European Cities and Courts (1400–1750)*, Brill, 2017, and (with Franco Morenzoni), *La Loi du Prince*, vol. 1: *Les Statuts de Savoie d'Amédée VIII (1430)*, Turin, 2019.

Florent Garnier is Professor in Legal History at the University of Toulouse 1 Capitole. He is member of Commission scientifique du Comité pour l'Histoire Economique et Financière de la France. His previous publications include "Le fort portant le faible", *Déclarez vos revenus! Histoire et imaginaire d'un instrument fiscal (XVIIIe–XXIe siècle)*, O. Poncet and K. Weidenfeld (Études réunies par), Collection "Études et rencontres de l'École des Chartes", 57, Paris, 2019.

Pere Verdés Pijuan is currently Senior Scientist in the IMF-CSIC in Barcelona, Spain, where he directs the research group on "Taxation and public finances in the Crown of Aragon (13th–15th centuries)". He is director with Denis Menjot of the *Glossary of Medieval Taxation* and is part of the Steering Committee of the research network on taxation in the Hispanic kingdoms *Arca Comunis*. Since 2019, he has been director of the *Anuario de Estudios Medievales*.

This book received financial support from the Fonds General de l'Université de Geneve, the CIHAM, the Université de Toulouse 1 Capitole and the Spanish R+D+I project PGC-2018-100979-B-C22. It is also part of R+D+I projects PGC2018-097738-B-100, PID2021-126283NB-I00 and PID2021-123286NB-C21, funded by MCIN/ AEI/10.13039/ 501100011033/ and: "ERDF A way to make Europe"

THE ROUTLEDGE HANDBOOK OF PUBLIC TAXATION IN MEDIEVAL EUROPE

Edited by Denis Menjot, Mathieu Caesar, Florent Garnier and Pere Verdés Pijuan

LONDON AND NEW YORK

Cover image: French king Philip V (1293–1322) receiving tax, illumination by Robinet Testard from "Grandes chroniques de France" 1471.
© Tallandier / Bridgeman Images TAD1742772

First published 2023
by Routledge
4 Park Square, Milton Park, Abingdon, Oxon OX14 4RN

and by Routledge
605 Third Avenue, New York, NY 10158

Routledge is an imprint of the Taylor & Francis Group, an informa business

© 2023 selection and editorial matter, Denis Menjot, Mathieu Caesar, Florent Garnier and Pere Verdés Pijuan; individual chapters, the contributors

The right of Denis Menjot, Mathieu Caesar, Florent Garnier and Pere Verdés Pijuan to be identified as the authors of the editorial material, and of the authors for their individual chapters, has been asserted in accordance with sections 77 and 78 of the Copyright, Designs and Patents Act 1988.

All rights reserved. No part of this book may be reprinted or reproduced or utilised in any form or by any electronic, mechanical, or other means, now known or hereafter invented, including photocopying and recording, or in any information storage or retrieval system, without permission in writing from the publishers.

Trademark notice: Product or corporate names may be trademarks or registered trademarks, and are used only for identification and explanation without intent to infringe.

British Library Cataloguing-in-Publication Data
A catalogue record for this book is available from the British Library

ISBN: 978-0-367-90336-7 (hbk)
ISBN: 978-1-032-25847-8 (pbk)
ISBN: 978-1-003-02383-8 (ebk)

DOI: 10.4324/9781003023838

Typeset in Bembo
by Newgen Publishing UK

CONTENTS

List of contributors … vii

1 General introduction … 1
  Denis Menjot, Pere Verdés Pijuan, Florent Garnier and Mathieu Caesar

PART I
Medieval taxation … 13

2 History of taxation in medieval Europe: Sources, historiography and methods … 15
  Denis Menjot, Pere Verdés Pijuan and Mathieu Caesar

3 The right to tax and its justifications … 55
  Lydwine Scordia and Florent Garnier

4 Church taxation … 72
  Jordi Morelló Baget

PART II
Fiscal systems … 95

5 Crown of Aragon: Catalonia, Aragon, Valencia and Majorca … 97
  Mario Lafuente Gómez and Albert Reixach Sala

6 Kingdoms of Castile and Navarre … 120
  Pablo Ortego Rico and Íñigo Mugueta Moreno

7 Kingdoms of Sicily … 155
  Serena Morelli and Alessandro Silvestri

| 8 | Northern Italy: Cities and regional states
Patrizia Mainoni | 177 |

| 9 | The Church Lands (1200–1550)
Armand Jamme | 203 |

| 10 | Kingdom of France (with Brittany and Dauphiné)
Jean-François Lassalmonie | 224 |

| 11 | The Burgundian Low Countries
Marc Boone | 254 |

| 12 | Medieval German Holy Roman Empire
Laurence Buchholzer | 270 |

| 13 | Provence and Savoy
Mathieu Caesar and Michel Hébert | 294 |

| 14 | Kingdom of England
Maureen Jurkowski | 314 |

| 15 | The Scandinavian kingdoms
Thomas Lindkvist | 340 |

| 16 | Kingdom of Poland and the Grand Duchy of Lithuania
Piotr Guzowski and Urszula Sowina | 356 |

| 17 | Russia from the Mongol invasion to the death of Ivan the Terrible (1242–1584)
Pierre Gonneau | 372 |

| 18 | The Byzantine Empire
Anastasia Kontogiannopoulou | 389 |

| 19 | Muslim Worlds: Al-Andalus and the early Ottoman state
Ángel Galán Sánchez, Alejandro García-Sanjuán and Kate Fleet | 408 |

PART III
Glossary   **437**

Glossary   439

Index   479

CONTRIBUTORS

Marc Boone (Ghent 1955) was till 2021 full professor of medieval history at Ghent university. Member of the Royal Flemish Academy for Sciences and the Arts of Belgium, invited professor in Dijon, Paris (Sorbonne and EHESS), Milano. Francqui chair holder at the Université Libre de Bruxelles, former president of the European Association for Urban History, member of the Academia Europaea. He has published extensively on urban history, Burgundian history, financial history. At the occasion of his retirement a selection of his articles was edited: *City and State in the medieval Low Countries. Collected studies by Marc Boone*, Turnhout, Brepols, 2021.

Laurence Buchholzer is *maitresse de conférences* of medieval history at the University of Strasbourg. Her doctoral thesis on interurban relations in Franconia was published under the title: *Une ville en ses réseaux. Nuremberg à la fin du Moyen Âge*, Paris, Belin, 2006. Laurence Buchholzer is currently focusing her research on pragmatic literacy in German towns in the late Middle Ages (account books, tax books, administrative books, etc.), as well as on privileges and charters of urban liberties. She also coordinates research on university and knowledge history in Strasbourg in the nineteenth and twentieth centuries. Her affiliation research unit is the UR 3400 (ARCHE), University of Strasbourg.

Mathieu Caesar is Associate Professor in Medieval History at the Université de Genève. His research interests include late medieval urban societies, the Sabaudian principality and factional conflicts. He is also currently working on a new research on social and political downfalls during the fourteenth and fifteenth centuries. His books include *Le pouvoir en ville. Gestion urbaine et pratiques politiques à Genève (fin XIIIe-début XVIe siècles)*, Turnhout, Brepols, 2011; *Histoire de Genève*, t. 1: *La cité des évêques (IVe–XVIe siècle)*, Neuchâtel, Alphil, 2014. He his the editor of *Factional Struggles. Divided Elites in European Cities and Courts (1400–1750)*, Leiden, Brill, 2017; with Marco Schnyder, *Religion et pouvoir. Ordre social et discipline morale dans les villes de l'espace suisse (XIVe–XVIIIe s.)*, Neuchâtel, Alphil, 2014 and with Franco Morenzoni (ed.), *La Loi du Prince*, vol. 1: *Les Statuts de Savoie d'Amédée VIII (1430). Une œuvre législative majeure*, Turin, Deputazione Subalpina di Storia Patria, 2019.

Kate Fleet is the Director of the Skilliter Centre for Ottoman Studies, Newnham College, University of Cambridge. Her current research interests include various aspects of Ottoman commercial history and relations between the early Turkish republic and the Great Powers. Her books include *European and Islamic Trade in the Early Ottoman State: the Merchants of Genoa and Turkey* (Cambridge: Cambridge University Press, 1999), *A Social History of Ottoman Istanbul* (Cambridge: Cambridge University Press, 2010), together with Ebru Boyar and *Ottoman Economic Practices in Periods of Transformation: the Cases of Crete and Bulgaria* (Ankara: Türk Tarih Kurumu Basımevi, 2014), together with Svetla Ianeva. She has recently edited four volumes together with Ebru Boyar: *Ottoman Women in Public Space* (Leiden: Brill, 2016), *Middle Eastern and North African Societies in the Interwar Period* (Leiden: Brill, 2018), *Entertainment Among the Ottomans* (Leiden: Brill, 2019), and *Making a Living in Ottoman Anatolia* (Leiden: Brill, 2021). She is the editor of *The Cambridge History of Turkey: Byzantium-Turkey, 1071-1453* (Cambridge: Cambridge University Press, 2009) and, together with Suraiya N. Faroqhi, of volume II, *The Ottoman Empire as a World Power, 1453-1603* (Cambridge: Cambridge University Press, 2012). She is an Executive Editor of the *Encyclopaedia of Islam Three*.

Ángel Galán Sánchez is Professor of Medieval History at the University of Málaga. He has been "Post-doctoral Fleming Research Fellow" at the University of Edinburgh (1985–1986), Visiting Professor at the University of Lyon 2, Visiting Fellow at the Polish Academy of Sciences, the University of Paris IV, L'ÉHÉSS in Paris, the University of Roma Tre and the Escuela Española de Arqueología e Historia in Rome. In 2008 he founded Arca Comunis, a research network dedicated to the study of Fiscal Systems in the Middle and Modern Ages. The network houses research groups from Spain, France, Italy and Portugal. Author of a hundred works, he has mainly devoted himself to the study of Mudéjares y Moriscos in the Crown of Castile and the Tax System in Castile. Some of his works related to fiscal systems: *Haciendaregia y poblacion en el Reino de Granada* (1997, with R. G. Peinado), "An Old Society. "Mudejar Neighbors: New Perspectives" in A. Fábregas (ed), *The Nasrid Kingdom of Granada betwen East and West* (Brill, 2021). He is coeditor of *El alimento del Estado y la salud de la Res Publica. Origenes, estructura y desarrollo del gasto publico en Europa* (2013, with J. M. Carretero), *Siete siglos de fraude fiscal en Europa* (2020, with J. I. Fortea and J. Gelabert) or *El precio de la diferencia: mudejares y moriscos ante el fisco castellano* (2020 with A. Ortega and P. Ortego).

Alejandro García-Sanjuán earned a PhD in Medieval History from the University of Seville and is currently Professor of Medieval History at the University of Huelva (Spain). His major publications include *Till God Inherits the Earth. Islamic Pious Endowments in al-Andalus* (Brill, 2007), *Coexistence and Conflict. Religious Minorities in Medieval Iberia* (University of Granada, 2015, in Spanish), *The Islamic Conquest of Iberia and the Misrepresentation of the Past* (Marcial Pons, 2019, 2nd ed., in Spanish). More recently, he published *Jihad. The Rules of War in Classical Islamic Doctrine* (Marcial Pons, 2020, in Spanish) and co-edited with Hussein Fancy *What was the Islamic Conquest of Iberia? Understanding the New Debate* (Routledge, 2021).

Florent Garnier is Professor at the University of Toulouse 1 Capitole, his fields of research are Legal History, Medieval Taxation and Public Finances, Commercial law in Medieval and Modern times. Since 2013 he has been Member of the Commission scientifique du Comité pour l'Histoire Economique et Financière de la France and since 2015 Member of Director Commitee Thematic Network for Cooperative Research on the History of the Hispanic Fiscal Systems (13th–18th centuries). Some publications: *Un consulat et ses finances: Millau (1187-1461)*, Paris, C.H.E.F.F., 2006, 947 p.; *La famille et l'impôt*, L. Ayrault and F. Garnier (dir.), Collection "L'univers des normes", Presses Universitaires de Rennes, Rennes, 2009, 134 p.; *Histoire du discours fiscal en Europe*, L. Ayrault and F. Garnier (dir.) coll. "Finances publiques",

Bruxelles, Bruylant, 2014, 211 p.; Histoires du droit commercial, coll. "Corpus Histoire du droit", Paris, Economica, 2020; "Le boursier, le souquet et le consulat: droit et finances à Millau en 1441–1442", *Cultures fiscales en Occident du Xe au XVIIe siècle. Études offertes à Denis Menjot*, F. Garnier, A. Jamme, A. Lemonde and P. Verdés Pijuan (dir.), Études Médiévales Ibériques, vol. 17, Méridiennes, Presses Universitaires du Midi, Toulouse, 2019, pp. 143–152; "Le fort portant le faible", *Déclarez vos revenus! Histoire et imaginaire d'un instrument fiscal (XVIIIe–XXIe siècle)*, O. Poncet and K. Weidenfeld (Études réunies par), Collection "Études et rencontres de l'École des Chartes", 57, Paris, Ecole nationale des chartes 2019, pp. 131–142.

Pierre Gonneau is professor at Sorbonne Université (Paris) and *directeur d'etudes* at École Pratique des Hautes Études (Paris). His main publications are: *Des Rhôs à la Russie: Histoire de l'Europe orientale (730-1689)*, Paris, PUF, 2012; *La Russie impériale: l'empire des tsars, des Russes et des non-Russes (1689-1917)*, Paris, PUF, 2019; *Ivan le Terrible, ou le métier de tyran*, Paris: Tallandier, 2014; *Novgorod: histoire et archéologie d'une république russe médiévale (970-1478)*, Paris, CNRS, 2021.

Piotr Guzowski is professor at the University of Bialystok, Poland; he is an author of two books in Polish: *Chłopi i pieniądze na przełomie średniowiecza i czasów nowożytnych* (2008) [Peasants and money at the turn of the Middle Ages] and *Rodzina szlachecka w Polsce przedrozbiorowej. Studium demograficzne* (2019) [Noble Family in Pre-partition Poland. Demographic study] and co-editor of the volume: *Framing the Polish Family in the Past* (Routledge 2021). His main interest are connected with economic history, historical demography and environmental history. He is principal investigator in the project *Financial capacity of Jagiellonian states in in the comparative perspective*.

Michel Hébert is emeritus professor at the Université du Québec à Montréal, member of the Royal Society of Canada and foreign correspondent of the French Académie des Inscriptions et Belles-Lettres. He specializes in late medieval urban history and in the history of political representation. Among his recent works are *L'enquête générale de Leopardo da Foligno dans la viguerie de Draguignan (janvier-mars 1333)*, Paris, Éditions du Comité des travaux historiques et scientifiques, 2012; *Parlementer. Assemblées représentatives et échange politique en Europe occidentale à la fin du Moyen Âge*, Paris, Éditions de Boccard, 2014, which received the prix Gobert of the Académie des inscriptions et belles-lettres, and *La voix du peuple. Une histoire des assemblées au Moyen Âge*, Paris, Presses Universitaires de France, 2018. Most recently, he published, in association with Jean-Michel Matz, the *Journal de Jean Le Fèvre, chancelier des ducs d'Anjou et comtes de Provence (1381-1388)*, Rennes, Presses Universitaires de Rennes, 2020.

Armand Jamme is an *agrégé d'Histoire* doctor of the Sorbonne and a former member of the Ecole française de Rome. Director of Research at the CNRS since 2012, his work focuses on the rationalities specific to the government of populations, studied within the framework of the only power without equivalent in the Middle Ages, the papacy, between the twelfth and the sixteenth century. In this period, the West moved from an ideological structure in which the head of the Church was the head of all forms of cultural and political expression (theocratic model) to a time for balance, in which he was only one of the determinants of European historical evolution.

Maureen Jurkowski, Honorary Research Fellow in the History Department at University College London, is an archival historian specialising in the history of late medieval England.

She has worked on numerous research projects at various UK universities over the last 25 years; most notably, she spent six years cataloguing medieval and early modern taxation records for the "E 179 project" at The National Archives, London. In addition to many publications on other subjects, she is co-author of the reference handbook *Lay Taxes in England and Wales, 1188-1688* (London, 1998), an editor of fifteenth-century income tax records, and has written articles and essays on the taxation of both the laity and the clergy. Among other research papers she is preparing for publication are studies of the 1489 income tax and of clerical tax exemptions for malicious indictments by the laity.

A historian of Middle and Late Byzantine Period (7th–15th c.), Dr. **Anastasia Kontogiannopoulou** has written extensively about the economic and administrative organization of Byzantium during the Palaiologan Era (1261–1453) and various aspects of the economic, ecclesiastical and social life especially during the middle and late Byzantine period (7th–15th c.). She is the author of two books, and the editor of another one. She is published over twenty essays on various topics. She received her B.A in History (1995), M.A. and PhD in Byzantine History (1997 and 2003 respectively) from the Department of History and Archaeology, Aristotle University of Thessaloniki (Greece). She was Fellow of the Greek State Scholarships Foundation for Ph.D. (2000–2003) and post-doctoral research (2004–2005). She has worked in many research centers in Greece as Associate Researcher of Byzantine History and she has taught Byzantine History at the Hellenic Open University. She also has participated in Seminars of Byzantine History in Greece and France, as well as in many national and international Scientific Congresses. She has been appointed at the Research Centre for Medieval and Modern Hellenism of the Academy of Athens (KEMNE/Greece) since 2008. She is working concurrently on two projects. The first explores institutional and social aspects of late byzantine cities. The second explores gender roles and identities in Byzantium during the Palaiologan era (1261–1453). She also participates in the collective research project of KEMNE: "Social and Intellectual mobility of Modern Hellenism (1204–1821). Itineraries of persons, ideas, goods".

Mario Lafuente Gómez is *Profesor Contratado Doctor* at the University of Zaragoza where he teaches Medieval History. PhD in History at the University of Zaragoza (2009), he received the extraordinary award. His research interests are focused on war, power and public finance in the Late Medieval Crown of Aragon. He is the author of *Guerra en ultramar. La intervención aragonesa en el dominio de Cerdeña (1354-1355)*, Zaragoza, 2011; *Dos Coronas en guerra. Aragón y Castilla (1356-1366)*, Zaragoza, 2012; and *Un reino en armas. La guerra de los Dos Pedros en Aragón (1356-1366)*, Zaragoza, 2014. He has also published several papers and book chapters and is the editor of some books on Economic and Social History. He is a founding member (2015) of the *Iberian Association of Military History. 4th-16th Centuries* and the author of the chapter devoted to the Crown of Aragon in the volume *War in the Iberian Peninsula. 700-1600*, edited by Joao Gouveia Monteiro and Francisco García Fitz (Routledge, 2018).

Jean-François Lassalmonie was born in 1968. A former student of the École normale supérieure in Paris, he obtained his doctoral degree in medieval history from the University of Paris Sorbonne in 1996, after presenting a thesis on *La boîte à l'enchanteur. Politique financière de Louis XI (1461-1483)*, which was published in 2002. He devotes his research to the political and institutional history of the French royal state in the late Middle Ages, with special emphasis on finance. He is a master of conference in medieval history at the École normale supérieure since 1996. He acted as director of studies of the ENS History Department from 2008 to 2020.

List of contributors

Thomas Lindkvist, born 1949, Fil. Dr (Uppsala), Professor emeritus of medieval history at the University of Gothenburg. He has participated in several international and interdisciplinary projects and networks. His research interests include the agrarian social relations of medieval Sweden in a comparative Nordic perspective. He has studied the state formation in the Middle Ages: especially the transition from a predatory economy of the Viking Age to the medieval economy based upon appropriation of the internal resources. He has also contributed to the study of Christianization and the Swedish crusades in Finland. Recent research topics include the medieval iron production and its role in transforming medieval Sweden. Following a long interest in legal history, his most recent publication is a translation into English with introduction and commentary of the oldest provincial law codes of Sweden *The Västgöta Laws* (Routledge, 2021).

Patrizia Mainoni after teaching at the Università degli Studi di Milano, has been full professor of Medieval History at the Universities of Bari and Padua. She has taught quantitative methods applied to history, Economic and Social History of the Middle Ages, Medieval History, History of Women and of Gender Identity. Her research interests concern the relations between economy, politics and society during the twelfth–fifteenth centuries. She studies Mediterranean trade, manufacturing and guilds, fiscal and financial institutions in the communal and seigniorial periods (twelfth–fifteenth c.), and gender history. She is particularly interested in the history of taxation from the eleventh to the sixteenth century. She has published numerous volumes and essays in Italian and foreign publications and edited sources relating to the thirteenth–fourteenth centuries in Lombardy: *Mercanti lombardi fra Barcellona e Valenzia nel basso medioevo*, 1982; *Economia e politica nella Lombardia medievale. Da Bergamo a Milano fra XIII e XV secolo*, 1994; *Le radici della discordia. Ricerche sulla fiscalità a Bergamo tra XIII e XV secolo*, Milano 1997; *Politiche finanziarie e fiscali nell'Italia settentrionale (secoli XIII-XV)*, a cura di Patrizia Mainoni, 2001; *I Registri Litterarum di Bergamo (1363-1410). Il carteggio dei signori di Bergamo*, a cura di Patrizia Mainoni e di Arveno Sala, 2003; *"Con animo virile". Donne e potere nel Mezzogiorno medievale (secoli XI-XV)*, a cura di Patrizia Mainoni, 2010; *Comparing Two Italies. Civic Tradition, Trade Networks, Family Relationships between Italy of Communes and the Kingdom of Siciliy*, edited by Patrizia Mainoni and Nicola Lorenzo Barile, 2020.

Denis Menjot is currently Emeritus professor of Medieval History at the University Lumière-Lyon 2 after having been professor at the University of Strasbourg (1991–1996) and assistant professor at the University of Nice (1972–1990). His research interests include urban history, municipal and royal finance and taxation, power and social control in Medieval Castile. He is the author of numerous books and articles including *Fiscalidad y sociedad: Los murcianos y el impuesto en la baja edad media* (Murcia, 1986); *Les Espagnes médiévales* (Hachette, 1996); *Murcie castillane (1243-milieu du XVe): Une ville au temps de la frontière* (Casa de Velázquez, 2002; Spanish translation, 2009). He is co-author with Patrick Boucheron of *La Ville médiévale* (Le Seuil, 2003). He was the director (1996–2010) with Manuel Sánchez Martínez or an international team on Urban Taxation in the Mediterranean West in the Middle Ages (7 volumes of proceedings have been published). He is director with Pere Verdés Pijuan ot the *Glosary of Medieval Taxation*. He has been president of the European Association of Urban History (2006–2008). He is president of the Société Française d'Histoire Urbaine and director of *Histoire Urbaine* since 2007.

Serena Morelli is associate university professor of Medieval History at the Department of Literature and cultural heritages of University of Campany "Luigi Vanvitelli". She is member of the teaching staff of the Phd in *History and transmission of the cultural inheritances* and coordinates the laboratory "History, memory and image of the territory" at the same University. She has been fellow of the Istituto italiano di studi storici and of the Ecole francaise de Rome; and is member of the editorial boards of *Rives Méditerranéennes* and *Polygraphia*. Among the international research groups of which she was part, directed, as regard Soyhthern Italy, *Europange. Les processus de rassemblaments politiques: l'Europe angevine (XIIIe-Xv^e siècles)*, financed by ANR. Her research fields are the history of Southern history in the late medieval ages, with particular attention to fiscal polities, prosopography, administration history and lordships. Among her books: *Razionalità all'opera. I bilanci della Contea di Soleto nei domini del principe di Taranto Giovanni Antonio Orsini*, Giannini, Napoli 2020; *Per conservare la pace. I giustizieri nel Regno di Sicilia da Carlo I a Carlo II d'Angiò*, Liguori, Napoli, 2012.

Jordi Morelló Baget holds a PhD in Medieval History from the University of Barcelona (1998). Since the 1990s, he has been involved in various research projects at the Milà i Fontanals Institution (Barcelona-CSIC) and the University of the Balearic Islands, and more recently in the project directed by Ana Rodríguez at the CCHS-CSIC Institute of History (Madrid) *Petrifying Wealth. The Southern European Shift to Masonry as Collective Investment in Identity, c.1050–1300*. His main line of research is the study of the ecclesiastical taxation in the Crown of Aragon. He is a member of the *Grup de Recerca consolidat de la Generalitat de Catalunya* (Catalonia Regional Government Consolidated Research Group – *Renda feudal i fiscalitat a la Catalunya baixmedieval*) and of the "Arca Communis" [www.arcacomunis.uma.es/] research network. He is also contributing to the project *La desigualdad económica en las ciudades catalanas y mallorquinas durante la baja Edad Media a través de las fuentes del impuesto sobre la riqueza* (Economic inequality in Catalan and Majorcan cities during the late Middle Ages through the sources of wealth taxation) directed by Pere Verdés. He is the author of several books and editor of some others, as well as having published more than seventy articles in journals and collective works.

Íñigo Mugueta Moreno is Lecturer in Medieval History in the Department of Social and Education Sciences of the State University of Navarra, and Associate Lecturer in Medieval History in the Associated Center of the UNED (Universidad Nacional de Educación a Distancia) in Pamplona. He is also coordinator of Geography and History in the Master of Teaching in Secondary Education, in the State University of Navarra, and Advisor of the entrance exams to the University in Navarre. He is director of the GTLHistory Project (*Games to Learn History*), at the *I-Communitas* research institute. He did his doctoral thesis on finance and taxation in the kingdom of Navarra in the fourteenth century. He is the author of numerous scientific articles and books on medieval Navarra.

Pablo Ortego Rico (Madrid, 1984). PhD in History (Complutense University of Madrid, 2013) with Extraordinary Award. Since 2016 he has been Lecturer in Medieval History in the Department of Historical Sciences of the University of Malaga, where he was previously the beneficiary of a Juan de la Cierva postdoctoral contract. His research focuses on the study of the relationships between taxation, power and society within the framework of the state-building process in late medieval Castile, and on the analysis of the Castilian Mudejar religious minority between the thirteenth and fifteenth centuries. He is currently co-director of the Research Project *Building up a fiscal culture in Castile (13th–16th centuries): powers, negotiation and social articulation* (PGC2018-097738-B-I00), and Member of the Scientific Comittee of *Arca Comunis* (Network of Cooperative Research on the History of the Hispanic and European

Taxation). Author of more than fifty specialized publications, he has participated in twelve R&D projects and national and international research networks. Among his publications, the monographic volume *Poder financiero y gestión tributaria en Castilla: los agentes fiscales en Toledo y su reino (1429–1504)* (Madrid, Instituto de Estudios Fiscales, 2015) stands out.

Albert Reixach Sala (Santa Pau, 1986) is Juan de la Cierva – Incorporación postdoctoral researcher at the Department of History of the University of Lleida. Doctor in History at the University of Girona (2015) with extraordinary award, he was trained as PhD student at the Institució Milà i Fontanals of the Spanish National Research Council. He has also been lecturer and postdoctoral researcher at the University of Girona and visiting scholar at Ghent University and University of Paris 1 Panthéon-Sorbonne. He combines studies on several aspects of the society and economy of Late Medieval Crown of Aragon, with special attention to finances and local institutions. He has published two monographs on these issues, as well as several peer-reviewed journal articles and book chapters.

Lydwine Scordia is Senior Lecturer Habilitated to direct Research (HDR) at the Université de Rouen Normandy, her fields of research are Political and Financial History, thirteenth–sixteenth centuries (theory, bibliocal exegesis, theology, history, literature, illuminated manuscripts). Some publications: "Le roi refuse l'or de ses sujets. Analyse d'une miniature du *Livre de bonnes meurs* de Jacques Legrand", *Médiévales*, 46, 2004, pp. 109–130; "*Le roi doit vivre du sien*". *La théorie de l'impôt en France (XIIIe-XVe siècles)*, Paris, Institut d'Études Augustiniennes, Série Moyen Âge et Temps Modernes, 40, 2005, 539 p.; "*Rendez à César* et autres lemmes bibliques à connotation fiscale utilisés dans le discours politique des XIIIe et XIVe siècles", *La religion et l'impôt*, dir. Ludovic Ayrault et Florent Garnier, *La Lettre du Centre de Michel de L'Hospital*, 1, mars 2012, pp. 5–22; "L'enseignement fiscal de Louis XI au futur Charles VIII dans le *Rosier des guerres*", *Cultures fiscales en Occident du Xe au XVIIe siècle. Études offertes à Denis Menjot*, F. Garnier, A. Jamme, A. Lemonde and P. Verdés Pijuan (dir.), Études Médiévales Ibériques, vol. 17, Méridiennes, Presses Universitaires du Midi, Toulouse, 2019, pp. 105–113; "La conception fiscale du royaume de France à la fin du XVe siècle d'après le *Rosier des guerres*", *Les grandes œuvres fiscales*, dir. Christophe de la Mardière, *Revue européenne et internationale de droit fiscal*, 2019/3, pp. 289–300.

After obtaining his PhD in Medieval History, **Alessandro Silvestri** worked in various academic institutions such as the Birkbeck College, Trinity College Dublin, and Villa I Tatti | The Harvard Center for Italian Renaissance Studies. Currently, he is a Beatriu de Pinós fellow (MSCA-COFUND) at the Institución Milá y Fontanals de Investigación en Humanidades of Barcelona, the Humanities' section of the Spanish National Research Centre (CSIC). His area of research includes Sicily and the Crown of Aragon in the later Middle Ages, with a particular focus on topics such as bureaucracy, information management, archives, and finances. On those and other themes he published various book chapters and articles in various prestigious academic journals (such as *Journal of Medieval History*, *Accounting History Review*, and *Viator*), as well as a monograph entitled *L'amministrazione del regno di Sicilia Cancelleria, apparati finanziari e strumenti di governo nel tardo medioevo* (Viella, 2018).

Dr hab. **Urszula Sowina** is a professor at the Centre of History of Material Culture at the Institute of Archaeology and Ethnology, Polish Academy of Sciences in Warsaw. Chairwoman of the Commission of Urban History at the Committee on Historical Sciences of the Polish Academy of Sciences and member of the International Scientific Advisory Board of the

International Meetings of the Middle Ages in Nájera (Spain). She is the author of publications on the history of medieval and early-modern towns: sociotopography, layout, society, economics, history of material culture, water supply, legal systems, testaments and inventories of movable goods of the burghers of Cracow in the fifteenth–sixteenth centuries. She is the editor and co-author of the *The Historical Atlas of Polish Towns*, vol. 6: *Greater Poland*, fasc. 1: *Kalisz*, Toruń 2021. Among her most important publications are also: *Water, Towns and People. Polish Lands against a European Background until the Mid-16th Century*. Peter Lang Edition: Frankfurt am Main 2016, pp. 529 + ill. (Polish edition: *Woda i ludzie w mieście późnośredniowiecznym i wczesnowożytnym. Ziemie polskie z Europą w tle,* Warszawa 2009, pp. 488); *The Relations of the Town of Kraków and Its Patriciate with the Ruler and the Wawel Court from the 13th Century to the First Half of the 16th Century.* Studies in European Urban History (SEUH) 35: *La cour et la ville dans l'Europe du Moyen Âge et des Temps Modernes*, sous la dir. de Léonard Courbon et Denis Menjot, Brepols: Turnhout 2015, pp. 225–236; *Medieval Towns as a Research Problem in Polish Historiography over the Past Two Decades*. Documenta Pragensia, XXII/1: Städte im Mittelalter und in der Frühen Neuzeit als Forschungsthema in den letzten zwanzig Jahren. Praha 2013, pp. 495–511.

Pere Verdés Pijuan, PhD in Medieval History from the University of Barcelona, is currently Senior Scientist in the IMF-CSIC in Barcelona (Spain). Since 2008 he has been the principal investigator of R&D projects on taxation and public finances in the Crown of Aragon during the late middle ages that are funded by the corresponding Spanish Ministry and he is also one of the coordinators of the *Critical Glossary of Medieval Taxation* edited by the University of Lyon II and the IMF-CSIC. His major publications include *La ciudad en el espejo: hacienda municipal e identidad urbana en la Cataluña bajomedieval* (2010); *"Car les talles són difícils de fer e pijors de exigir". A propósito del discurso fiscal en las ciudades catalanes durante la época bajomedieval* (2012); *Fiscalidad urbana y discurso franciscano en la Corona de Aragón (s. XIV-XV)* (2015); *El mercado de la deuda pública en la Cataluña de los siglos XIV-XV* (2015); (with P. Orti) *The crisis of public finances in the cities of late medieval Catalonia (1350–1500)* (2016); (with J. Morelló et al.) *A study of economic inequality in the light of fiscal sources: the case of Catalonia (14th–18th centuries)* (2020).

1
GENERAL INTRODUCTION

Denis Menjot, Pere Verdés Pijuan, Florent Garnier and Mathieu Caesar

> In the Middle Ages, as in other times,
> finance was the basis of everything, conditioned everything and reflected everything
> ... men have lived and are living with financial and fiscal problems.[1]

In the long history of taxation in western Europe, the last three centuries of the Middle Ages, which are the focus of this book, are an essential stage because they were a period when public taxation – understood as a compulsory and generalised levy for the public good – began to be established. The legitimacy of taxation was also challenged and debated, and different types of taxation and management methods were experimented.

The very elaborate tax systems that had existed in the ancient world gradually disappeared during the Early Middle Ages in the political formations that had taken over from the Western Roman Empire.[2] Only in a few kingdoms, such as the Visigothic Kingdom of Toledo, and in the Carolingian Empire, did some remnants of classical taxation remain or were re-established, often in a transitory manner.[3] At the end of the first millennium, taxes were nearly unknown to the West, with a few rare exceptions, the most famous of which was the *Danegeld* levied in the Anglo-Saxon kingdoms originally to fend off the Scandinavian invasions and which continued until the eleventh century.[4] These few taxes were economically marginal. The princes and lords, who dominated both the land and the populace, levied heavy fees and tolls,[5] even appropriating in some cases the fiscal prerogatives of the ancient *fiscus*. However, these levies should not be confused with public taxes because they were raised for the particular interests of the lordships and not for those of the general community of the kingdom.

It was not until the thirteenth century that taxation in the strict sense began to reappear when princes and kings had become powerful enough to begin demanding financial support from all their subjects, and cities had grown and become autonomous enough to levy taxes within their boundaries to ensure their defence.[6]

This revival coincided, and was caused by, the recovery of Roman law during the twelfth and thirteenth centuries. Born out of its era and scholarly reflection, the tax issue then became part of the daily life of the lordships, the towns and the kingdoms. It resulted in a renewed production of documents that became more numerous and varied within different communities and institutions, both ecclesiastical and secular. Fiscal and financial documents, linked to other texts (such as charters, registers of deliberations and cartularies) thus contributed to the formation of a new "documentary landscape", in the abundance of scriptural texts and the proliferation of pragmatic writings.[7]

In the last centuries of the Middle Ages, western European monarchies, principalities and cities – chiefly the important city-states of central and northern Italy – were gradually implementing a fiscal system, that is to say, "a set of tax procedures and levies which combined in such a way that no source of income or wealth could escape the drain."[8] In the early stage, taxation was somewhat occasional and improvised, but a financial administration was put together, more or less coherent rules of management were established, and its methods of collection gradually became more efficient. During the fifteenth century, after three centuries of experiments, backtracking, aborted attempts and rejections, the tax[9] – at first levied exceptionally, irregularly even if frequently, often to help the king, the prince and the city defend the territory – steadily became an ordinary, regular levy, supposedly consented to by the entire population and concerning all subjects.

This evolution has been theorised by Richard Bonney and Mark Ormrod in what is known as "New Fiscal History", which revisited Schumpeter's interpretative model in four successive ideal types of state in Europe between Antiquity and the Modern Age, according to their fiscal regime: tribute state, domain state, tax state and fiscal state.[10] Our book focuses on the transitional period from the domain state – when the rulers relied on their own patrimonial and seigneurial revenues – to tax state when a large part of revenues were raised through taxation of all the subjects of the state. Without delving into the controversy about the validity of this model and its teleological vision,[11] what is important is that at different times in the monarchies, principalities, and in some large cities of central and northern Italy, a tax system was born that can be described as a state. A "state" that, despite the debates generated about the term, we can define according to the ideal parameters that Chris Wickham proposes: the centralization of legitimate enforceable authority (justice and the army), the specialization of governmental roles, the concept of public power, independent and stable resources for rules and a class-based system of surplus extraction and stratification.[12]

Originally created with the aim of covering clearly specified public expenditure, taxation eventually became instrumental to economic development – either supporting or hindering it – and to the acceleration or the obstruction of social dynamics and the genesis of administrative structures. Whether or not they were aware of it, the authorities played their part in the process, through careful orientation of the collection of private resources on the one hand, and the redistribution of the proceeds, on the other. Taxation was also a means for the monarch, the prince and the city-states to impose their power over a territory and its inhabitants and a means of control and integration of subjects, that is to say, it also held a political significance that extended well beyond finances. Furthermore it was the main area of contact between the central authority and the rest of the population. It was ultimately a foundation for the monarchical and princely states that rose to power across Europe in the Late Middle Ages.[13]

Monarchical or princely fiscal pressure also had repercussions on urban taxation, as the city administration could act as a levying agent for the state, which did not have the necessary apparatus at its disposal, and could take charge of the assessment and/or collection of a royal tax or participate in it. Hence urban communities – and not only the large Italian city-states – began to collect taxes granted by kings or princes during this period. Sometimes, these taxes added to the resources they derived from their domains, which varied greatly in importance. State finances had a growing influence on municipal finances, as towns could take advantage of the request for a subsidy to impose an additional levy on their inhabitants. The establishment and development of this municipal taxation seems to have followed the same evolution as that of the state taxation and often under the influence of the latter. Thus, in a lot of towns, there was no accounting or tax documentation prior to royal or princely demands. These systems were therefore closely linked, in some cases even competed, and their weight was added to the burden on the taxpayers.

In the Late Middle Ages, the fiscal panorama in western Europe was completed with the taxes collected by lords and by the Church. In the first case, we have to start from the fact that, during the last centuries of the medieval period, it was still not easy to distinguish between public and private power. Resources of a patrimonial and feudal nature continued to be paid to princes and monarchs, and many lords collected public taxes, either because they customarily had them, because they usurped them, or because they were granted them by sovereigns.[14] The Church, for its part, possessed its own taxation system that affected both laymen and, above all, clergymen. In a Christianised medieval Europe, all the faithful had to pay tithes and other taxes to the Church.[15] Yet in addition to this ecclesiastical taxation, the papal monarchy established its own system of taxation of the clergy in the course of the fourteenth century, the collection of which was rationalised across Christendom and which went hand in hand with the centralisation and substantial development of its administration.[16]

All the above-mentioned issues have generated an abundant mass of individual or collective publications and a flourishing of scientific meetings, in which the studies devoted to the beginnings of royal and urban systems of taxation are especially important. But there is still no comprehensive synthesis on a European scale that takes into account the monarchic and the municipal tax systems during the last three centuries of the Middle Ages; these have almost always been studied separately.[17] The research is still partially fragmented along national boundaries. The comparative studies are limited almost exclusively to the kingdoms of France and England during the last three centuries of the Middle Ages.[18]

In this context, this *Handbook of Public Taxation in Medieval Europe* aims to contribute to a comprehensive overview of public taxation systems on a European scale – not only of the major European states[19] – and to suggest new paths of inquiry, especially for a comparative history and the drawing up of a fiscal geography. At the origin of this book stands a group of seasoned scholars who have been working on medieval taxation in Europe for many years. Thus, the *Handbook* draws on our longstanding collaborative research in this field, which has led to the publication of many collective volumes and to the Online *Critical Glossary of Medieval Taxation*.[20]

To ensure coherence and to facilitate a comparative reading, we have written the *Handbook* as a collection of specially commissioned essays. We then brought together other historians specialised in these fiscal and financial issues in different European countries, most of whom had already worked together with one another and with the editors of this volume. We sent them an overarching text pointing out the various questions that we considered essential, but leaving them free to address other issues raised by their sources. This leaves the reader with the inevitably controversial task of testing the major theories through these multiple cases.

Our presentation is not intended to be exhaustive, but it focuses on certain questions and overlooks others. In this way, despite its unquestionable importance,[21] seigniorial taxation is only dealt with tangentially, as it would have been impossible to summarise the available information about the huge numbers of manors that made up the different territories analysed. Specifically, attention is paid to the resources of the royal domain, feudal and patrimonial in nature because, as has been mentioned, these incomes always constituted an important part of the monarchy's revenues.[22] Reference is also made to the public taxes that, for one reason or another, were collected by certain noblemen, whose domains were sometimes veritable states within the state.[23] With regard to ecclesiastical taxation, this is dealt with individually because its different taxes were omnipresent throughout the Christian west, although in some cases exactions transferred (or usurped) to the monarchies of different territories are also particularly documented. Nor must the growing fiscal pressure exerted by urban authorities over clergymen be overlooked, in view of the immense volume of wealth that they gradually amassed.[24]

Furthermore, this volume prioritises the study of taxation over that of finances or other collateral terms. However it is inevitable to refer to the different forms of public debt recorded in the territories studied at the end of the Middle Ages, as the authorities of the time found themselves obliged to constantly resort to credit and they linked their financing to the product of taxation. In this respect, especially interesting is the phenomenon of consolidated debt that is recorded in towns and cities in different parts of western Europe, and also the first examples of collective debt by larger territorial units.[25] A detailed study of it would however require a volume devoted solely to it, as is the case with the question of coinage. As we shall see, from the thirteenth century taxes paid to the prince by virtue of the privilege he possessed over the minting of coinage became widespread. They are alluded to, but not other means that the monarchy had to make the most of its power over the coinage; specifically, the repeated debasements that are recorded during the Late Middle Ages in virtually every part of Europe.[26]

On the contrary, taxation is dealt with broadly, without adopting the restricted concept of "tax" in its current juridical or economic meanings, as it is impossible to apply them *stricto sensu* to the Middle Ages. The reflections of different authors who have tackled the question of the different types of taxation in the medieval period are taken as a reference, beginning with Ch. Wickham. This author distinguishes between three ideal types of exaction: the tributes demanded by force at random, the rents from the land and what he calls taxation proper, that is, "resources extracted by rulers from their subjects (except those explicitly exempted) according to defined and more-or-less systematic criteria".[27] This volume focuses essentially on the second and above all the third category, although it also includes references to the first. In this respect, one must remember the warning given by S. Carocci and S. Collavini with respect to the continuity of exactions such as tribute and plunder until the Early Modern Age. According to these authors, the opposition between taxes and tributes should be played down, as very often both exactions could fulfil the same purpose, e.g., offering protection.[28]

In principle, the innumerable direct rents from the land are ruled out, but not other incomes of the *domain* that, as we have said, were paid to both kings and lay or ecclesiastical lords, and even cities. Not for nothing, the study positions itself in the transition between the *domain state* and the *tax state*, which did not complete until the Early Modern Age. As M. Ginatempo observes, within this *domain* we find different types of income, among which we can distinguish: patrimonial revenues proper (which, as well as the rents from the land, included the control of natural resources or monopolistic infrastructures), revenues arising from the administration of justice or from feudal sovereignty, and various exactions comparable to what Wickham defines as taxation. We are above all interested in this last group, which includes the provision of military services, the obligation to provide board and lodgings for the king or another authority, tolls and other levies on passage or markets, obligatory and arbitrary exactions (*pecha, questia, taille…*) and other vague "taxes".[29] Although it is not habitual, we must also remember that the monarchy (or the corresponding authority) occasionally extended its *domain* to other territories, outside the kingdom, thus obtaining various kinds of important resources. This happened in the case of the Mediterranean and Atlantic maritime powers, or when another territory was conquered where a different taxation system already existed, e.g., the Muslim territories in the Iberian Peninsula.

The new general taxation that, from the end of the thirteenth century, was established outside the *domain* is without doubt the volume's principal subject of study. This newly created tax regime, typical of the *tax state*, habitually corresponded to the definition of taxation made by Wickham, although some exactions paid to the public authorities are also documented for which it is not clear what the "more-or less-systematic criteria" was on which they were established; others constituted obligatory services (labour, military or of another kind), and others that we might call fees, paid to compensate for particular public services. In the first case, we are referring basically to certain subsidies, donations, aids or other demands made for various reasons and generically by monarchs to all their subjects, and distributed subsequently among the population by cities via locally based taxes.[30] As for the second case, the best known is the general mobilisation of the subjects for the defence of the territory or of the prince that, despite its initially personal nature, ended up being commuted for a financial compensation.[31] Lastly, of the fees, we can for example remember the ones paid for documents issued by the royal chancellery.

The rest of the taxes, collected by the monarchy or the cities, could be classified in different ways. Although it would correspond to the fiscal theory of the period, we do not believe that the use of fiscal concepts and categories inherited from Roman law (e.g. *munus*) is very operative when making comparisons.[32] Therefore, the authors of the volume have been recommended to use modern fiscal categories, among which we find the habitual distinction between direct and indirect taxes used by J. Favier in his classic study of 1971.[33] Beyond these two major categories, different methods of classification are resorted to that can sometimes overlap. In this way, within the direct taxes, one may distinguish between those that were levied on individuals or family units and the others that were levied more or less proportionally on wealth. Within the indirect ones, we find those that were levied on production, consumption, transactions, transportation and movement. Whether direct or indirect, the taxes could also be fixed or quota-based.

All these forms of taxation are of course merely for guidance when making comparisons between territories. Nevertheless, as we have mentioned, we must not forget that during the period studied exactions (tributes, rents, taxes, duties, grants…) cannot always be defined with certainty, that pigeon-holing them in the public or patrimonial realm is sometimes complicated and that their nature could evolve over time.[34]

Bearing in mind all these premises, the book is organised into three main sections. The first part, "*Medieval Taxation*" offers an introduction to general issues; its main purpose is to provide a framework for the second section.

Obviously, the first chapter presents the various types of sources available for the study, with the contributions and limitations of each, because our vision of taxation depends closely on the importance and complementarity of the documentation, the conservation of which also depends on the archival choices made in later periods. It also outlines the trends in historiography since the beginning of the twentieth century, presenting the questions, methods and conditions of production which have not evolved at the same pace in different European countries.[35] It concludes with an outline of the main current research directions.

The second chapter deals with the right to tax. In theory, the monarch was supposed to "live off his own", i.e., to live from the proceeds of his own seigneurial estates. However, as the royal functions expanded and the sovereign undertook defensive and offensive wars, it became clear that "his own" would not be sufficient to finance these undertakings, even with such expedients as forced loans, monetary mutation, or taxation of Jewish property. Theologians and jurists questioned taxation from the end of the thirteenth century. How did they justify the legitimacy of taxation and the right to tax? Tax theory and discourse were elaborated by drawing on various sources. The reception of the scholarly and political discourse must also be understood within the context, the power relations between the prince, the representative assemblies and the towns, as well as in practice. A fiscal "revolution" was thus underway.

The third chapter of this section is devoted to the only universal taxation in Christendom, that of the Church. As mentioned above, we have considered that this taxation should in some ways be included in the *Handbook* and that it should be dealt with in the first section of the book in order to avoid returning to it in the various chapters. The Church had to contribute everywhere to the needs of the kingdom in the form of subsidies and the secular authorities, kings and municipal councils taxed the clergy and thus a part of the ecclesiastical income was transferred to them.[36] Moreover, the modes of taxation and the procedures for the collection of this Church taxation served as models for other monarchies and territorial principalities, or at the very least influenced their tax systems to a greater or lesser extent.

The second part, "*Fiscal Systems*", is organised on a territorial basis, with each chapter presenting an overview for a chosen kingdom, a principality or some larger regions. As we have said, in the aim of being open and allowing comparisons, we have sought to be as wide-reaching as possible and not to limit ourselves to the main states: The kingdoms of France (with the principalities of Brittany and Dauphiné), England and Castile, the Crown of Aragon (kingdoms of Aragon, Valencia and Mallorca, and the Principality of Catalonia), the Holy Roman Empire, the Papal States, the Burgundian Low Countries, Italian cities-states and Southern Italy and Sicily. But we also include areas too often neglected in synthesis works, such as the kingdoms of Navarre and Russia, the Duchy of Savoy, the County of Provence, the Scandinavian kingdoms, and the Polish–Lithuanian Union. On the borders of Europe, we wanted to present the taxation of the Byzantine Empire, heir to Rome, and two Islamic states which, through their exchanges and contacts, had a certain influence on the neighbouring Christian kingdoms: Al-Andalus to the southwest and the Ottoman Empire to the southeast. Unfortunately, for reasons linked to the difficulties caused by the pandemic, the colleagues that we asked to write about the kingdoms of Portugal and Hungary were unable to complete their contributions.[37]

The chapters are intended to be deliberately concise syntheses, with a word count for each chapter of around 15,000–20,000 words, depending on the richness of scholarly works carried out, which, as the reader will see, vary considerably from one entity to another. They are not based on new archival research, but on a selection of existing publications in order to provide an overview of taxation on a European scale and to allow for comparisons. As a result, the bibliography proposed in each chapter is not exhaustive, but is limited to the most essential works selected by each author.

To the extent possible, the authors have sought to address all the multiple and complex aspects of tax systems.[38] Taxation is not only a matter of more or less sophisticated techniques. Its study cannot therefore be reduced to the various procedures used to levy taxes, but their knowledge is indispensable and fundamental because they reflect – and effectively influence – economic, social and political realities. Each author has therefore examined the taxation procedures: base (research and evaluation of the taxable matter, determination of the tax base) and liquidation (determination of the taxpayer's share by applying the tax rates to the tax base) and the collection methods: direct management and tax farming, without neglecting borrowing, which is nothing more than a disguised tax or an anticipated tax.

Taxation is not only characterised by the coverage of public expenditure according to the traditional "budgetary" concept – which must nevertheless be properly funded. Taxation is also a means of achieving, either in conjunction or in parallel, certain economic and/or social objectives in addition to purely financial ones. It is therefore a tool for policies and strategies that the authors have tried to identify, as well. According to a definition given by Jean-Claude Waquet and adopted by many authors, taxation is also characterised by its manifestation, *i.e.*, by the transformation of private resources into public resources via levy, and vice versa, by the transformation of public resources into private resources via redistribution.[39] The authors are therefore also interested in people: in the rulers and their choices, and in their dialogue with political society to ensure that taxes are accepted; in the finance men and their networks; but also in the taxpayers and their reactions to taxes (fraud, tax evasion or revolts).

Taxes appear under a profusion of different terms that give "the impression that the authorities do not know what tax to invent in order to seize wealth and thus meet the new needs of the kings".[40] The words change but the tax is reborn under another name. The study of tax vocabulary says a lot about the intentions and hesitations of the authorities, about the origins of the taxes and their transmission between territories or fiscal traditions. Apropos of these questions, the existence should be mentioned of some interesting studies that show us the possibilities of this avenue based on terms such as, for example, *vectigal, gabelle, ungeld* or *subsidio/auxilio/ayuda*.[41] With the aim of fostering more studies of this kind, the third part takes a practical turn, presenting a *"Glossary"* of roughly a hundred terms, with a selection of five to ten important terms for each territory covered in Part II. The definitions are generally concise. These terms will also become part of the online Glossary, consultation of which will enable the reader to reflect far more profoundly on these questions. To assist the reader, terms that appear in the glossary are marked with a ★ in the chapters of the first two sections.

This *Handbook* therefore aims to help fill a gap by offering a critical historical overview in a single volume, albeit divided by topic and country, of this "all-encompassing" subject. It is also conceived as a resource for young researchers who wish to embark on the study of finance and taxation, and for more experienced researchers in search of reference points and synthesis. It is intended for anyone studying the history of the state, socio-political history, economic history, history of societies and cultural history, for as Jean Favier wrote: "There is no historical research that does not touch on financial problems. There is no research on public finance without a broad understanding of political and social life."[42] We would add, quoting Joseph Schumpeter, that "The fiscal history of a people is above all an essential part of its general history [...] The spirit of a people, its cultural level, its social structure, the deeds its policy may prepare – all this and more is written in its fiscal history."[43]

Lastly, this *Handbook* shows that the taxation system established in the states and cities of the final centuries of the Middle Ages is at the origin of modern taxation, to which it has bequeathed many techniques and questions. Jacques Le Goff once wondered, "Was Europe born in the Middle Ages?" *Fiscal* Europe undoubtedly began to emerge in the fourteenth and fifteenth centuries.[44] This book aims to provide the historical perspective that is lacking in the numerous, multiple and often discordant discourses of economists, tax experts, political scientists and sociologists, because Europe, and fiscal Europe in particular, "will only come to fruition if it takes history into account."[45]

Notes

1 FAVIER, *Finance et fiscalité*, p. 11.
2 MIGEOTTE, *Les finances des cités grecques*; BRANSBOURG, "Fiscalité impériale et finances municipales", pp. 255–296; FRANCE, *Tribut. Une histoire fiscale*. For the rupture in fiscal systems between late Roman and early medieval Europe, WICKHAM, "The Other Transition", pp. 3–36; WICKHAM, *Framing the Early Middle Ages*.
3 CASTELLANOS, "The political nature of taxation"; DURLIAT, *Les finances publiques*; MAGNOU-NORTIER, *Aux origins de la fiscalité moderne*, which claims that the taxation system survived until the Carolingian Empire.
4 GREEN, "The Last Century of the Danegeld".
5 STOCLET, *Immunes ab omni teloneo,*
6 WICKHAM, "Lineages of western European taxation", pp. 25–42.
7 KELLER, GRUBMÜLLER, and STAUBACH (ed.), *Pragmatische Schriftlichkeit im Mittelalter*.

8 MUSGRAVE, *Fiscal Systems*. On the methodology of systems theory applied to financial history, see the presentation by WAQUET, *Le Grand-Duché de Toscane*, pp. 197–211.
9 To take one example, TRIANO MILÁN, "Proyectos para la implementación".
10 ORMROD, BONNEY, and BONNEY (ed.), *Crises, Revolutions*; BONNEY (ed.), *Economic Systems*; BONNEY (ed.), *Rise of the Fiscal State*.
11 For a critical analysis of this model, see CAROCCI and COLLAVINI, "The Costs of States", and for a more comprehensive historiographical discussion, see Chapter 1 (part I) of the present *Handbook*.
12 WICKHAM, *Framing the Early Middle Ages*, p. 57.
13 GENET, LE MENÉ (ed.), *Genesis of the Modern State*.
14 The seigneurial levies have been the subject of major works: BOURIN, MARTÍNEZ-SOPENA (ed.), *Pour une anthropologie*; FELLER (ed.), *Calculs et rationalités*.
15 LAUWERS (ed.), *La Dîme*.
16 FAVIER, *Les finances pontificales*.
17 Outstanding but limited exceptions: MENJOT and SÁNCHEZ MARTÍNEZ (ed.), *Fiscalidad de Estado*; GROHMANN, *"La fiscalità nell'economia europea"*; GINATEMPO, "Esisteva una fiscalità".
18 Examples: ORMROD, "The West European Monarchies"; GRUMMIT and LASSALMONIE, "Royal public finance"; see Chapter 2 of the present *Handbook*.
19 Like that of ORMROD, "The West European Monarchies".
20 In particular, MENJOT and SÁNCHEZ MARTÍNEZ (ed.), *La fiscalité des villes*; MENJOT, RIGAUDIÈRE, and SÁNCHEZ MARTÍNEZ (ed.), *L'impôt dans les villes*; MENJOT and SÁNCHEZ MARTÍNEZ (ed.), *El dinero de Dios*.
21 As shown by CAROCCI and COLLAVINI, "The Costs of States", pp. 138–141.
22 For example, in England during the 15th century: BRAYSON, "Deficit Finance".
23 For example, the principality of Taranto, in the kingdom of Naples: MORELLI, *Razionalità all'opera*.
24 MENJOT and SÁNCHEZ MARTÍNEZ (ed.), *El dinero de Dios*; MORELLÓ BAGET (ed.), *Financiar el reino terrenal*.
25 See, for example: BOONE, DAVIDS, and JANSSENS (ed.), *Urban public debts*; SÁNCHEZ MARTÍNEZ (ed.), *La deuda pública en la Cataluña bajomedieval*.
26 SPUFFORD, *Money and its Use*, pp. 291–320; FOURNIAL *Histoire monétaire*,
27 WICKHAM, "Lineages of western European taxation", pp. 26–27.
28 CAROCCI and COLLAVINI, "The Costs of States", pp. 141–146.
29 GINATEMPO, "Esisteva una fiscalità", pp. 295–296.
30 See, for example: MUGUETA, "Las demandas del rey de Navarra".
31 For example, this is the case of the French *arrière-ban*, the *cavalcade general* of Provence or the Catalan *usatge Princeps Namque*: CONTAMINE, *Guerre, État et société*, pp. 26–38; HÉBERT, "Aux origines des États de Provence"; SÁNCHEZ MARTÍNEZ, "Defensar lo principat de Cathalunya".
32 GARNIER, "L'impôt d'après quelques traités fiscaux"; MONTAGUT, "La doctrina medieval sobre el 'munus'".
33 FAVIER, *Finance et fiscalité*.
34 A curious example, in this respect, are some local indirect taxes that ended up being collected as capitations: GINATEMPO, *Spunti comparativi*, pp. 171–175; DÍAZ DE DURANA, *El dinero de la harina*.
35 Each author specifies in his or her chapter the state of the sources and the current status of the issue.
36 GENET and VINCENT (ed.), *État et Église*; MENJOT and SÁNCHEZ MARTÍNEZ (ed.), *El dinero de Dios*; MORELLÓ BAGET (ed.), *Financiar el reino terrenal*.
37 About these countries, see NÓGRÁDY, "A földesúri adó", RADY, "Fiscal and Military Developments"; NÓGRÁDY, "Seigneurial Dues", pp. 265–278; GONÇALVES, *Pedidos e empréstimos*; Magalhães Godinho, "A Formação do Estado", vol. I, pp. 123–173; CASTRO HENRIQUES, *State Finance*; DOMINGUEZ, *Fiscal Policy in Early Modern Europe*.
38 The system is an "object in its own right – a whole irreducible to the simple sum of its components ... a set of dynamically interacting elements, organised according to a purpose." J. de ROSNAY, *Le Macroscope*, quoted by WAQUET, *Le Grand-Duché de Toscane*, p. 205.
39 WAQUET, *Le Grand-Duché de Toscane*, pp. 175 and 180.
40 SCORDIA, *"Le roi doit vivre du sien"*, p. 165.
41 TURULL, "La recepción de *vectigalia*"; MAINONI, "Gabelle. Percorsi di lessici fiscali"; BUCHHOLZER, "Ungeld, Umgeld, Ohmgeld, Angal"; MUGUETA, "Las demandas del rey de Navarra".
42 FAVIER, *Finance et fiscalité*, p. 22.
43 SCHUMPETER, "The crisis of the Tax State", pp. 1 and 2.

44 Le Goff, *L'Europe est-elle née au Moyen Âge?*
45 Le Goff, *L'Europe est-elle née au Moyen Âge?*, p. 9.

Bibliography

Richard Bonney (ed.), *Economic Systems and State Finance*, Oxford, 1995.
Richard Bonney (ed.), *The Rise of the Fiscal State in Europe c. 1200–1815*, Oxford, 1999.
Marc Boone, Karel Davids and Paul Janssens (ed.), *Urban public debts: urban government and the market for annuities in Western Europe (14th–18th centuries)*, Turnhout, 2003.
Monique Bourin and Pascual Martínez-Sopena (edr.), *Pour une anthropologie du prélèvement seigneurial dans les campagnes médiévales (XIe–XIVe siècles)*: I. *Réalités et représentations paysannes*, II. *Les mots, les temps et les lieux*, Paris, 2004–2007.
Gilles Bransbourg, "Fiscalité impériale et finances municipales au IVe siècle", in *Antiquité Tardive*, 16, 2008, pp. 255–296.
Alex Brayson, "Deficit Finance during the Early Majority of Henri VI of England, 1436–1444. The 'Crisis' of the Medieval Engish 'Tax State'", in *The Journal of European Economic History*, 49/1, 2020, pp. 8–65.
Laurence Buchholzer-Remy, "Ungeld, Umgeld, Ohmgeld, Angal: discours sur une taxation indirecte (Haute-Rhénanie, Franche-Comté)", in *Cultures fiscales en Occident du Xe au XVIIe siècle. Études offertes à Denis Menjot*, ed. Florent Garnier, Armand Jamme, Anne Lemonde and Pere Verdés Pijuan, Toulouse, 2019, pp. 27–40.
Sandro Carocci and Simone M. Collavini, "The Costs of States. Politics and Exactions in the Christian West (Sixth to Fifteenth Centuries)", in *Diverging Paths? The Shapes of Power and Institutions in Medieval Christendom and Islam*, ed. John Hudson and Ana Rodríguez, Leiden, 2014, pp. 123–158.
Santiago Castellanos, "The political nature of taxation in Visigothic Spain", in *Early Medieval Europe*, 12/3, 2003, pp. 201–228.
Simonetta Cavaciocchi (ed.), *Fiscal Systems in the European Economy from the 13th to the 18th Centuries. Atti della "trentanovesima Settimana di Studi", Prato, 2007*, Firenze, 2008.
Philippe Contamine, *Guerre, État et société à la fin du Moyen Âge*, Paris, 1972.
José Ramón Díaz de Durana Ortiz de Urbina, *El dinero de la harina de las almas muertas de Vitoria (ca. 1420–1760)*, Vitoria, 2019.
Rodrigo da Costa Dominguez, *Fiscal Policy in Early Modern Europe: Portugal in Comparative Context*, New York-London, 2019.
Jean Durliat, *Les finances publiques de Dioclétien aux Carolingiens (284–889)*, Sigmaringen, 1990.
Jean Favier, *Finance et fiscalité au bas Moyen Âge*, Paris, 1971.
Jean Favier, *Les Finances pontificales à l'époque du Grand Schisme d'Occident, 1378–1409*, Paris, 1966.
Laurent Feller (ed.), *Calculs et rationalités dans la seigneurie médiévale: les conversions de redevances entre XIe et XVe siècles*, Paris, 2009.
Etienne Fournial *Histoire monétaire de l'Occident medieval*, Paris, 1970.
Jérôme France, *Tribut. Une histoire fiscale de la conquête romaine*, Paris, 2021.
Jérôme France, *Finances publiques, intérêts privés dans le monde romain*, Bordeaux, 2017.
Florent Garnier, "L'impôt d'après quelques traités fiscaux (XIVe–XVIe siècles)", in *Histoire du discours fiscal en Europe*, ed. Ludovic Ayrault and Florent Garnier, Brussels, 2014, pp. 64–114.
Jean-Philippe Genet and Bernard Vincent (ed.), *État et Église dans la genèse de l'État Moderne. Actes du colloque de Madrid, 1984*, Madrid, 1986.
Jean-Philippe Genet and Michel Le Mené (es.) *Genèse de l'État moderne. Prélèvement et redistribution. Actes du colloque de Fontevraud (1984)*, Paris, 1987.
Maria Ginatempo, "Spunti comparativi sulle trasformazioni della fiscalità in età post-comunale", in *Politiche finanziarie e fiscali nell'Italia settentrionale, secoli XIII-XV*, ed. Patrizia Mainoni, Milano, 2001, pp. 125–220.
Maria Ginatempo, "Esisteva una fiscalità a finanziamento delle guerre del primo '200?", in *1212–1214. El trieno que hizo a Europa*, actas de la XXXVII Semana de Estudios Medievales, Estella. 19 al 23 de julio de 2010, Pamplona, 2011, pp. 263–342.
Vitorino Magalhães Godinho, "A Formação do Estado e as Finanças Públicas", in *Ensaios e Estudos: uma maneira de pensar*, vol. I, Lisboa, 2009, pp. 123–173.
Iria Gonçalves, *Pedidos e empréstimos públicos em Portugal durante a Idade Média*, Lisboa, 1964.

Judith A. GREEN, "The Last Century of the Danegeld", in *English Historical Review*, 96, 1981, pp. 241–258.

Alberto GROHMANN, "La fiscalità nell'economia europea", *in Fiscal Systems in the European Economy from the 13th to the 18th Centuries. Atti della "trentanovesima Settimana di Studi", Prato, 2007*, ed. Simonetta CAVACIOCCHI, Firenze, 2008.

David GRUMMIT and Jean-François LASSALMONIE, "Royal public finance (c. 1290–1523)", in *Government and Political Life in England and France, c. 1300–c. 1500*, ed. Christopher FLETCHER, Jean-Philippe GENET and John WATTS, Cambridge, 2015, pp. 116–149.

Michel HÉBERT, "Aux origines des États de Provence: la 'cavalcade' genérale", in *CX Congrés National des Sociétés Savantes, Montpellier, 1985*, Paris, 1986, vol. III, pp. 53–68.

António Castro HENRIQUES, *State Finance, War and Redistribution in Portugal, 1249–1527*, tese de doutoramento em História, Universidade de York, 2008.

Hagen KELLER, Klaus GRUBMÜLLER and Nikolaus STAUBACH (ed.), *Pragmatische Schriftlichkeit im Mittelalter. Erscheinungsformen und Entwicklungsstufen*, Munich, 1992.

Michel LAUWERS (ed.), *La Dîme, l'Église et la société féodale*, Turnhout, 2012.

Jacques LE GOFF, *Le Moyen Âge et l'argent*, Paris, 1976.

Jacques LE GOFF, *L'Europe est-elle née au Moyen Âge?*, Paris, 2003.

Elisabeth MAGNOU-NORTIER, *Aux origines de la fiscalité moderne. Le système fiscal et sa gestion dans le royaume des Francs à l'épreuve des sources (V^e–XIe siècles)*, Paris, 2012.

Patrizia MAINONI, "Gabelle. Percorsi di lessici fiscali tra Regno di Sicilia e Italia comunale (secoli XII–XIII)", in *Signorie italiane e modelli monarchici (secoli XIII–XIV)*, ed. Paolo GRILLO, Rome, 2013, pp. 45–75.

Denis MENJOT and Manuel SÁNCHEZ MARTÍNEZ (ed.), *La fiscalité des villes au Moyen Age*, 4 vol., Toulouse, 1996–2002.

Denis MENJOT, Albert RIGAUDIÈRE and Manuel SÁNCHEZ MARTÍNEZ (ed.), *L'impôt dans les villes de l'Occident méditerranéen XIIIe–XVe siècle. Colloque tenu à Bercy les 3, 4 et 5 octobre 2001*, Paris, 2005.

Denis MENJOT and Manuel SÁNCHEZ MARTÍNEZ (ed.), *El dinero de Dios: iglesia y fiscalidad en el Occidente Medieval, siglos XIII–X*, Madrid, 2011.

Léopold MIGEOTTE, *Les finances des cités grecques aux périodes classique et hellénistique*, Paris, 2014.

Tomas DE MONTAGUT ESTRAGUÉS, "La doctrina medieval sobre el 'munus' y los 'comuns' de Tortosa", in *Libro Homenaje in memoriam Carlos Díaz Rementeria*, Huelva, 1998, pp. 475–489.

Serena MORELLI, *Razionalità all'opera. I bilanci della contea di Soleto nei domini del principe di Taranto Giovanni Antonio Orsini*, Napoli, 2020.

Jordi MORELLÓ BAGET (ed.), *Financiar el reino terrenal. La contribución de la Iglesia a finales de la Edad Media (s. XIII–XVI)*, Barcelona, 2013.

Iñigo MUGUETA MORENO, "Las demandas del rey de Navarra: vocabulario, discurso e identidades fiscales (1300–1425)", in *Anuario de estudios medievales*, 44/2, 2014, pp. 911–943.

Richard A. MUSGRAVE, *Fiscal systems*, New Haven and London, 1969.

Árpád NÓGRÁDY, "A földesúri adó és az adózás elve a késő középkori Magyarországon" [Seigneurial tax and the basis of taxation in late medieval Hungary], in *Gazdaság és gazdálkodás a középkori Magyarországon: gazdaságtör-ténet, anyagi kultúra, régészet*, ed. András Kubinyi, József Laszlovszky and Péter Szabó, Budapest 2008,

Árpád NÓGRÁDY, "Seigneurial Dues and Taxation Principles in Late Medieval Hungary" in *The Economy of Medieval Hungary*, Leiden, 2018, pp. 265–278.

Mark ORMROD, "The West European Monarchies in the Later Middle Ages", in *Economic Systems and State Finance*, ed. Richard BONNEY, Oxford, 1995, pp. 123–160.

Mark ORMROD, Margaret BONNEY and Richard BONNEY (ed.), *Crises, Revolutions and Self-sustained Growth: Essays in European Fiscal History, 1130–1830*, Stamford, 1999.

Martyn RADY, "Fiscal and Military Developments in Hungary During the Jagello Period", in *Chronica* (Szeged), 11, 2011, pp. 85–98.

Joseph Aloisius SCHUMPETER, "The Crisis of the Tax State", English translation by Wolfgang F. STOPLER and Richard A. MUSGRAVE, in *International Economic Papers*, 4, 1954.

Manuel SÁNCHEZ MARTÍNEZ (ed.), *La deuda pública en la Cataluña bajomedieval*, Barcelona, 2009.

Manuel SÁNCHEZ MARTÍNEZ, "Defensar lo principat de Cathalunya" pendant la seconde moitié du XIVe siècle: du service militaire à l'impôt", in *L'impôt dans les villes de l'Occident méditerranéen. XIIIe–XVe siècle*, ed. Denis MENJOT, Albert RIGAUDIÈRE and Manuel Sánchez MARTÍNEZ, Paris, 2005, pp. 83–122.

Lydwine SCORDIA, *"Le roi doit vivre du sien". La théorie de l'impôt en France (XIIIe-XVe siècles)*, Paris, 2005.

Peter SPUFFORD, *Money and its Use in Medieval Europe*, Cambridge, 1998.

General introduction

Alain STOCLET, "*Immunes ab omni teloneo*": *Étude de diplomatique, de philologie et d'histoire sur l'exemption de tonlieux au haut Moyen Âge et spécialement sur la Praeceptio de navibus*, Rome, Institut historique belge de Rome, 1999.
Charles TILLY, *The Formation of Nation States in Western Europe*, Princeton, 1975.
José Manuel TRIANO MILÁN, "Proyectos para la implantación de un impuesto único en Castilla en el siglo XV", in *Anuario de Estudios Medievales*, 51/2, 2021, pp. 913–938.
Max TURULL RUBINAT, "La recepción de vectigalia en la Cataluña medieval. De la tradición romana a la recopilaciones de época moderna", in *Initium*, 7, 2002, pp. 181–216.
Jean-Claude WAQUET, *Le Grand-Duché de Toscane sous les derniers Médicis*, Rome, 1990.
John WATTS, *The Making of Polities: Europe, 1300–1500*, Cambridge, 2009.
Chris WICKHAM, "The Other Transition: From the Ancient World to Feudalism", in *Past & Present*, 103, 1984, pp. 3–36.
Chris WICKHAM, "Lineages of western European taxation, 1000–1200", in *Corona, municipis i fiscalitat a la Baixa Edat Mitjana*, ed. Manuel SÁNCHEZ MARTÍNEZ and Antoni FURIÓ DIEGO, Lleida, 1997, pp. 25–42.
Chris WICKHAM, *Framing the Early Middle Ages. Europe and Mediterranean, 400–800*, Oxford, 2005.

PART I

Medieval taxation

2
HISTORY OF TAXATION IN MEDIEVAL EUROPE
Sources, historiography and methods

*Denis Menjot, Pere Verdés Pijuan and Mathieu Caesar**

Despite an abundance of sources held in national and municipal archives, medieval taxation has long failed to attract researchers, partly because financial and fiscal history – as Jean-Claude Waquet wrote in 1990 – is "unanimously respected for the state secrets it penetrates, for the arid language it uses, and above all for the boredom it instils and which is a clear sign of its distinction".[1] In recent decades, the field has drawn interest from many more scholars: historians, legal historians, philologists and sociologists, but to an unequal and varying extent by country, depending on scholars' conception of taxation and whether they adopt only the standpoint of the state (studying how it justifies the various levies, establishes and calculates tax and collects payments, with which resources and personnel), or also the taxpayer's standpoint (by examining the economic and social impact of taxation and the reactions it triggers).

Before looking at how scholars have written this history, and how their questions and methods have evolved over time, we should present the various sources available to them to write the history of taxation in the medieval West.

Source materials, their contributions and limitations

The sources available to the historian of medieval taxation are numerous, of widely varying importance and quite diverse depending on the states and cities, as illustrated in the chapters in the second part of this book.[2] Their chronological and geographical origins are more or less remote, and we cannot determine the precise chronology of the increase in quantities of financial and fiscal sources. However, from the thirteenth century onwards, they became more numerous, first in the southern part of Christendom (the cities of northern and central Italy, Catalonia and Languedoc). For the preceding period and for other regions, we must make do with furtive references in charters or chronicles, and a few exceptional artefacts such as the imperial tax roll of 1241–1242. England is the exception to this rule; it stands out due to the early publication of the Domesday Book (1085–1086) and the Pipe Rolls series (preserved since the early twelfth century).

Especially from the middle of the fourteenth century, with the well-known increase in the financial needs of princely and municipal authorities and their greater tax-levying capacity, there was substantial growth and diversification of financial and fiscal documents of all kinds in the kingdoms, principalities and cities of Europe.

This variety of sources reflects the magnitude of the new requirements that authorities of the era had to face. They had to define norms and rules for calculating, enforcing and collecting taxes, attempt to understand and evaluate the population's capacity to pay taxes, keep accounts, and oversee the work of tax officials. In some kingdoms, principalities and cities, efforts to resolve these issues generated an abundance of three essential types of sources: normative, fiscal and accounting.[3]

Normative sources

Taxation is governed by a set of legal norms.[4] Normative and regulatory documents are therefore the starting point for any analysis of taxation and fiscal management insofar as they lay the legal framework for the latter. These documents consist of royal or princely "laws" – such as the *Leges palatinae* promulgated by King James III of Majorca in 1337 – and ordinances that specify the powers of the financial officials, the process of publishing accounts, and the composition of the financial and fiscal rights and prerogatives granted to cities, such that royal privileges are also one of the normative sources of municipal law.

In addition, there are letters, charters, and registers of tax demands by royal and princely authorities. The preambles and statements justify the levy in the eyes of the taxpayers in order to obtain their consent, as was the case, for example, of the "cahiers" of *monedas* or *alcabalas* promulgated by the kings of Castile.[5] These documents describe the tax base and establish the methods for assessing and collecting tax, its duration, the time limits for payment, the persons exempted, the role of the city in tax collection, the circumstances in which the demand was made (ordinary taxation, concession by the state assemblies, result of bilateral negotiations with a city, etc.). In this way, they make known the monarchy's policy towards the town and shed light on the tax pressure in the kingdom.

Another source of law is the ordinances issued in fiscal matters by the assemblies of states: estates general, *Cortes*, *Corts*, *Parlements*, diets and provincial assemblies. A diachronic and synchronic analysis of the "cahiers" of the Cortes reveals, through the fiscal discourse, the financial positions and strategies of the central powers and the local elites.[6]

The decrees of municipal councils, recorded in the registers of ordinances and deliberations, are an essential normative element of municipal taxation. The purpose of these documents was to regulate the fiscal activity of the municipality. Some of the registers shed light not just on the decisions, but also on the deliberations, the legal and technical precautions taken to avoid fraud and abuse, the methods and deadlines for payment. In the case of extraordinary taxes, the duration of their collection and the allocation of the sums collected are specified. Some registers also contain petitions from tax farmers requesting a moratorium or a rebate, as well as any information about the public office of the treasurer. In the case of indirect taxes, they specify the rate or the amounts to be paid; for example, in Seville, the *cuadernos de condiciones* set out the terms for leases, along with the procedures and the duration of auctions.

The development and proliferation of offices for the collection of taxes (treasurers, tax collectors and receivers) also required a vast corpus of regulations to be drawn up. By studying these regulations, we learn about fiscal management methods and the concepts of medieval taxation and its oversight by the public authorities. The most striking sign of this is the establishment of carefully regulated chambers of accounts in many principalities and kingdoms.[7]

Tax documents

The purpose of these practical sources was to share the tax burden among taxpayers, to inventory the taxable matter and to estimate its value. In many towns, until a more or less late period, these documents were included in the general registers (known as ordinances or deliberation registers) of the town council. They consist of the registers of direct taxation: tax books/ *Steuerbücher*; books, handbooks or rolls for *taille*; *cherches de feux* (censuses), books of the *queste*, of the *vaillant* (in Lyon), of the *fogatge* in Catalonia, *padrones de monedas* and *padrones de pedidos* in Castile. These documents provide a list of those subject to tax in the various districts of the city, with their share and taxpaying contribution (i.e., households that had paid at least part of their tax) with the method of payment (in cash or in kind). In addition, there are lists of arrears, possibly with annotations indicating seizures for non-payment. These enable us to see the divergence between the tax levied and the tax actually collected; this gap reveals the difficulties in collecting the amounts due and therefore the rulers' greater or lesser capacity to impose their authority on their constituents and the latter's ability to resist.

A set of documents specific to the southern regions (cities of northern and central Italy, Languedoc, Catalonia and the Kingdom of Valencia) allows us to study direct taxation (of wealth) in greater detail, from knowledge of the taxable matter (the tax base), to the calculation of tax, to the collection of arrears.[8] These are books of property tax declarations (*estimi* in Italian cities, *manifests* in Catalonia, books of *peita* in the kingdom of Valencia), estimes and *compoix* (emblematic documents of the *langue d'oc* countries, countries where taxation, *taille réelle*, was based on property) and cadastres (*catasti* in the cities of central and northern Italy), which group together, by district, all (at least theoretically) of the persons who owned property in the tax territory of the city.

These documents were drawn up to allocate the tax burden based on an estimate of taxpayers' assets, or the community's contribution to the royal *taille* for the diocese, in addition to the amount of the community's own expenses. They record the first name and surname of the declarant, a list (starting with the dwelling house) of all his urban and rural properties, with their description, type, quality, names of adjacent property owners, and estimated value. Street names were rarely recorded. However, based on the sworn declaration of the inhabitants, these declarations failed to capture movable property and real estate possessions outside the city even though some *compoix* (known as *compoix cabalistes*) also enumerated movable goods. The value of the people's assets was converted into a fiscal value after applying various allowances and coefficients during a process called *allivrement*. The resulting tax base allowed the tax due to be calculated.[9]

For indirect taxation (i.e., tax on expenditure), non-accounting documentation was frequent. In some cases, lists of tariffs or surveys give us information on the tax rates applied at city gates, on toll bridges, or in river or sea ports. Substantial customs documentation is available throughout Europe and is a source for research on trade. Some indirect tax registers are extant, such as the *souquet* (tax on the resale of wine) registry from Millau and other towns in the Languedoc, the *rèves* registry in Provençal towns, and registries for the *gabelles* and excise duties in other European towns at different times. Toll and customs accounts reveal the rates of taxation on various taxed goods, but the goods are not always known when subject to tax-farming under a generic name such as the *almojarifazgo*, which the king of Castile levied on the city of Seville and surrounding territory.

Although most records of these tax-farmers have been lost (probably voluntarily by the tax-farmers themselves), other documents, such as the *cuaderno de arriendos* (tax farm book) in Seville, record the tax-farming process, but only in the second phase of the auction after the tender. Girona and other Catalan cities hold *llibres d'arrendaments* (farm books). This documentation takes us into the world of urban tax-farmers. In the archives of Catalan cities, there are *Manuals* that recorded the contracts for the leasing of *imposicions*, as well as *albarans*, which describe tax collection methods. In other cities, such as Geneva, notarised tax-farming contracts were not recorded in their own documentary series or in *ad hoc* registers, but in the minutes of the city councils.

We must also mention the registers of loans or public debt ledgers, which are numerous in Italian, Catalan and Valencian cities, and which show the creditors, the amount of the city's debts and the taxes on which they were secured, and therefore the interconnection between borrowing and taxation.

Accounting documents

Accounting sources are by far the most abundant materials available to historians of medieval taxation. These documents were created to record the amounts collected and disbursed and to oversee the work of the officials in charge of administering and handling traditional or new resources. The data they provide is not just quantitative. These sources are numerous and varied: "*états au vrai*", accounts of the treasurers-general, castellany accounts, accounts of royal officers, accounts of local treasurers, accounts of subsidies, tolls, etc.

The general accounts of kings and princes are quite diverse and often form discontinuous series. They were preserved very early in England (*Pipe Rolls*, from 1129) and in Flanders (*Gros Brie*, 1187), later in France, where the first existing royal accounts date from 1202–1203, and where the series only becomes quite substantial after 1328.[10] In the archives of Lille and Dijon, there are series of estate accounts for the House of Burgundy,[11] and in the archives of Barcelona, there are remarkable series for the Crown of Aragon, as well as in Pamplona for Navarre.[12] Central accounts are also extant for Savoy, Provence, Sicily and the Apostolic Chamber; those of the Popes of Avignon cover the largest geographical area, and that series is almost complete from 1316 to 1398. On the other hand, only one account for the Castilian monarchy survives, for the year 1429, and only a few remnants of estate accounts for the Duchy of Brittany, in which the first account of the treasury and general revenue, almost entirely preserved, dates from 1495–1496. In addition to the general accounts, there are narrower accounts concerning specific income streams or outlays, or particular financial bodies. One of the most voluminous extant series is that of the accounts of the *châtellenies* of the Savoy state. The most numerous extant documents are accounts of tolls and customs. Among these, we would cite the large series of customs accounts that records customs receipts on English wool beginning in 1275, on cloth from 1347, then on all flows through English ports from the end of the sixteenth century. We can also note the Sound Tolls Registers, which record the tolls collected by the king of Denmark at Elsinore, dating back to 1497, the *Aduanes del Mar* of Valencia, the Genoese *Carati Mari* or *Drictus Barberie,* and the land tolls of the Savoy state.

Towns used a whole series of ledgers: general accounts of the treasurers and receivers, with the sometimes evocative names such as "general ledgers", "small registers", "day ledgers", "accounts of common money", "manuals", "books of receipts and expenditure"; this list is not exhaustive.[13] Urban archives also contain partial and specialised accounts of the *taille* (drawn up with regularity in towns such as Périgueux or Saint-Flour), of *fouages*, of *questes*, of *imposicions*, of extraordinary taxes, of arrears… along with accounts of tolls, construction and repairs of fortifications, public works and roads, military expeditions, and the individual accounts of numerous municipal officers. This wide diversity undoubtedly reflected a desire to individualise each of the accounts, but it probably increased opacity of fiscal management and made auditing difficult for those lacking the necessary expertise.

Accounting documents are the largest and richest series of municipal sources, and their advent – or at least the beginning of a continuous series – is often the sign that a municipality had acquired substantial autonomy. Together with registers of deliberations, which they complete or sometimes replace, they form the basis of research on urban tax systems, since they reveal the names and amounts of tax revenues, whether or not they were allocated, the methods of taxation, the rate of levy, the tax base and rates, the collection techniques, the names of creditors, bidders and the competition for bids, and expenditure, thus making it possible to reconstruct municipal finances and taxation.

The various extant municipal general ledgers are held, often in large numbers, in the cities of the various European countries and, from the thirteenth century onwards, these are sometimes nearly complete series. In Italy, we note Piacenza (1170), Siena (1226), Genoa (1235) and Pavia (1246). In the north of the Kingdom of France, in Calais, extant sources include six annual municipal accounts prior to 1280, nine annual statements of debt (from 1263), statements of arrears, roles of *taille* and compulsory loans, weekly accounts of *maltôte* revenue, special accounts of expenditure and various rent deeds for 1255–1288. Ypres holds rolls of fines (1267–1268, 1280, 1280–1281) and an account for 1297–1298, Bruges ten complete accounts between 1281 and 1299, Douai a debt statement drawn up in 1295–1296, Arras an abridgement of two accounts (1241–1244). Provins holds a continuous series of accounts and debt statements from 1274. For Reims, two abridged accounts are extant for the years 1290–1291 and 1291–1292. In Paris, the first series of relatively homogeneous accounts of income and expenditure date from the years 1258–1261; these seem to coincide with the documents submitted for approval to the king's auditors. Further south, the oldest known account is that of the town of Najac in Rouergue and dates from 1258. The accounts of Millau also date from the second half of the thirteenth century, but only begin to form a series from 1356. In the Germanic areas, the earliest attested accounts are those of Osnabrück (1285) and Breslau (1299). They precede by far Aachen (from 1334), Duisburg (from 1348), Hamburg (from 1350), Lübeck, Zurich (from 1357), Basel (from 1360), Bern (from 1375), and Cologne (late fourteenth century). Copies of municipal accounts are found in Dortmund in a burgher's book from 1320, but in many cities the accounts were not kept in writing until the fifteenth century. In Castile, the first preserved general accounts date from 1368 in Seville, from 1391–1392 in Murcia – but only form a series in the first decades of the fifteenth – and in other cities they are only preserved from the middle of the fifteenth century, as in the Portuguese cities.

These urban accounts, like those produced by the princely and royal administrations, were drawn up less as management instruments than as a "methodical summary, for the purposes of verification and approval, of all the operations carried out during his mandate by the agent responsible for the receipt and handling of funds."[14] Their purpose was to balance out the transactions. The accounts were simple, distinguishing between revenue, often expressed in a rapid and general manner, and expenditure. The spending side was much more detailed, broken down into headings corresponding to the different sources or destinations of funds, as it was in the accountant's interest not to leave anything out. The register ends with a balance which makes it possible to establish the official's situation vis-à-vis the administration and to determine whether he is in debt or in credit, and to engage his responsibility, at least financially. Generally speaking, clarity and rationalisation characterise accounting registers – as well as tax registers – from the mid-fourteenth century. On the whole, they are well kept and contain few errors in calculation. However, accounting rationality did not always increase over time. In any case, the accounts are never uniform, even when they are not dummy collections made up of separate pages bound together in modern or contemporary times or ledgers filled in at different stages of the accounting and audit operations.

Unlike contemporary accounting systems, which are presented as a series of figures that can easily be computerised, the general accounts of medieval towns were rarely limited to simple "entries" of transactions. They were more than simple income and expenditure statements. The figures were inserted in a textual context with broad economic, social, technical, legal and political implications, which nevertheless became narrower in the last century of the Middle Ages with the professionalisation of record-keeping from both accounting and legal standpoints. Advances in accounting techniques in the administration led to a reduction in the informative quality of the registers. These could also contain "histories" written by the municipal administration itself, which was a reason for preserving these records.[15] For example, in Rodez, the municipal account books were enriched with descriptions of important events, and became the city's *livres de raison*, which no doubt explains their formal quality and their remarkably well-preserved condition.

In the best of cases, the accounts lend themselves to a serial history because they appear to be reliable sources for statistical analysis, even though we cannot ignore the discontinuity of many accounting series, which considerably limits the contribution of the remnants that have survived. However, in a study of municipal accounts in the Holy Roman Empire, Laurence Buchholzer-Rémy has clearly shown that the various accounting sources act as a system and that it is therefore impossible to consider any one of them as a faithful witness of the whole of urban financial activities.[16] It is therefore necessary to take an interest in the "writing project" that underlies the accounts, before any statistical or technical analysis, because the "family tree" of the account books thus describes very diverse origins. Written accounts are by no means "neutral records"; instead, they are "carefully controlled political texts".[17]

On the registers submitted for inspection by auditors or royal officials, dotted-line annotations indicate the auditing checks. Dijon, the seat of the Dukes of Burgundy, had account ledgers with wide margins to facilitate the checks carried out by princely or municipal officials and their use as archives. Conversely, a town such as Schaffhausen, under Habsburg control between 1330 and 1415, presented accounts that were almost devoid of any traces of revision or margin notes.[18] Margin notes can take several forms; they can be laconic, a simple sign indicating an accounting entry is accepted, rejected or pending; more developed, explaining the reason for refusals or requesting additional supporting documents; or very extensive, constituting a parallel "discourse" recorded in the margins of the accounting document, giving details on the hearing procedure or recording the discussions between the auditor and the accountant. In this case, the margin notes provide invaluable knowledge of financial policies and choices, auditing structures and mechanisms, but also for the study of the accountants and auditors responsible for final oversight.

In addition to these account registers, there are also supporting documents for the accounts. A large number of these have been preserved, for example, for the treasury, the household and the silver of the kings of France. In many Catalan towns, receipts were sometimes kept in special registers. In the light of more recent scholarship on administrative writing and "grey writings", these sources undoubtedly warrant being used more extensively, not only as a reservoir of information to supplement the richer documentary series, but also as an indication of administrative practices.[19]

Indirect and complementary tax sources

Historians of finance and taxation must not look only to accounting series and tax documents; taxation is not merely a technical and accounting topic. They must consult other sources held in the various collections of the royal, princely and municipal archives, which are not specifically devoted to financial and fiscal matters, but which are useful for understanding them.

Princely and royal archives hold documents from enquiries that were generally carried out in response to the "requests and complaints" of the populations affected by the struggles of the time. The number of such enquiries increased from the fourteenth century onwards, and they were carried out under the authority of the chambers of accounts (when they existed) or of the generals of finance and elected officials in the Kingdom of France.[20] They essentially dealt with requests to revise the number of "hearths" used to calculate the *taille*.

Judicial sources lay at the heart of tax litigation: trials, indictments by finance officers, letters of remission and petitions.[21] They also reveal the types of tax evasion and avoidance, the means of combating them and their limitations, and more generally, taxpayers' relationship to the state authorities.

Notarial documents are also useful: these include acknowledgements of debts, as well as contracts for the partial or whole transfer or assignment of debts. In addition, there are registers of loans or debt books which show the creditors, the amount of the town's debts and the taxes on which they were pledged, and therefore the interconnection between loans and taxes.

To these practical sources, we can also add theoretical and didactic texts that some authors describe as "erudite literature". Writing of exegetes, theologians, jurists and philosophers versed in the teachings of ancient authorities, manuals for confessors, essential for the study of the legitimacy of the right to tax, the vocabulary of taxation, theories of taxation in order to understand the fiscal "revolution" of the late Middle Ages. Treatises of government, such as that of Nikolaus Wurms (ca. 1400), are another type of document about accounts, which may shed light on them and provide data on the standard of account management and the types of registers to be established.[22] Mirrors of princes also sometimes provide valuable information on the tax practices that were considered lawful.[23]

Narrative sources must not be neglected, starting of course with the chronicles, which are often so rich in information about the men who had to deal with taxes, their collection, and the various forms of resistance, right up to the tax revolts.[24] Other sources, sometimes at the crossroads of genres – *ricordanze*, journals or memoirs – sometimes offer interesting material, such as the discourse on tax tyranny in the *Memoirs* of Philippe de Commynes[25] or the letters of Tuscan merchants such as Ser Lapo Mazzei or Francesco di Marco Datini.[26] And we should not forget the Italian world, so rich in *novellas* and *racconti* that offer colourful portraits of men of finance that undoubtedly merit further exploration?[27]

With regard to iconography, taxation is rarely depicted in secular manuscripts.[28] This is due in part to the difficulty of representing taxes, as well as the difficulty of representing the royal figure – Christlike by definition – without making it a predatory figure. Thus, we find mostly staged scenes of financial and accounting management, most often represented by officers seated at their benches with accounting books and coins. The famous illuminated registers of the Biccherna in Siena (the main institution for managing municipal finances) are undoubtedly a notable exception in terms of their richness.[29] As for sacred manuscripts, illuminators did not hesitate to depict taxes mainly through the New Testament tale of Saint Matthew the tax collector, or even portraying a counter, a chest or purses, although these images generally focus less on tax than on the vice of avarice or the proper/improper use of wealth.[30]

The materiality of sources and a new "documentary landscape"

Historians also need to make better use of the materiality of sources, of writing materials, as well as of the writings themselves: scrolls, registers, wax tablets or simple sheets. Armando

Petrucci's scholarship has shown how the study of writing practices sheds new light on society as a whole.[31]

Occasionally, a rare number of sources, such as the famous Stone of Justice of Perugia (1234), remind us that fiscal and accounting sources are also vectors of civic awareness and government propaganda.[32] Although most of the documents preserved do not reach the level of the Biccherna registers, the accounting archives and tax sources embody government and are an important vector of memory and civic awareness of municipalities or princely and royal offices. We should therefore pay attention to the ways in which tax writings were made, building on research about pragmatic writings, which have clearly shown that they are an open window on political and cultural history.[33]

Access to accounting and tax sources is not always easy as they are scattered across regional, municipal or notarial archives and libraries. However, some of them are now easier to consult thanks to digitisation, even though the latter is still limited, especially in municipal archives and compared to other sources such as chronicles, sermons and charters, and varies widely from one country to the next. Some collective initiatives are promoting better overall knowledge of urban fiscal documentation. This is the case of the *Index librorum civitatum* (https://stadtbuecher.de/), which lists the municipal books (*Stadtbücher*) of the medieval and modern periods of the Holy Roman Empire; the recataloguing of the 36,000 miscellaneous documents submitted to the Exchequer by royal tax collectors from ca. 1200 to ca. 1700; or the digitisation of numerous accounts of Savoyard castellanies and subsidies (thirteenth–fifteenth centuries).[34] Conversely, the cataloguing of certain other sources is sometimes lacking. This is the case of the *livros de receita e despesa*, which are only the subject of a separate series in certain Portuguese cities between the end of the fourteenth and the beginning of the sixteenth centuries (Viana, Vila do Conde, Porto, Lisbon, Ericeira, Montemor-o-Novo, Elvas and Loulé). The same holds true for similar sources in German cities. The *cuentas* series is too often a real catch-all in Spanish municipal archives.

The tax registers and urban accounts did not originate in an accounting "desert", as there had long been seigniorial or monastic censuses and accounts, cathedral *oeuvres*, and the cities undoubtedly benefited from the know-how of the merchant elites. However, the increased numbers of such documents coming down to us from the mid-thirteenth century in the cities, principalities and kingdoms cannot be attributed to better preservation or mere good luck.

This documentary situation results from the fact that durable writing materials were adopted for taxation matters at a later stage. It reflects the greater recourse to written materials under the influence of scholastic institutions and the requirements of Roman law, which had swept across the West since the beginning of the twelfth century. It can also be explained by the technical and cultural development and by the political and social transformations that affected Western Europe at the time and coincided with the genesis of taxation in states and cities and this shift from a system of exceptional taxes to ordinary ones.

The management of an increasingly complex tax system requires writing and the advent and gradual strengthening of an administration. However, it first implied the existence of a suitable writing material – paper – that was easier to handle and less expensive than parchment scrolls. The manufacture and use of paper, beginning in the thirteenth century in the Italian cities and the Spanish Levant, gradually spread throughout Christendom, stimulated by increased demand, favoured the multiplication of accounting and tax registers and the advent of more advanced accounting, even though parchment remained necessary until the end of the Middle Ages and beyond for the recording of documents intended to last, such as census books and many accounting registers, or even rolls.

The increased quantity of tax and accounting documents also corresponds to a new apprehension of reality and to another way of measuring it by quantifying it.[35] This is what Jacques Le Goff has described as a "counting obsession", which started at different periods depending on the country, but was noticeable everywhere from the end of the thirteenth century, with more clocks, *ars nova* music, and the merchant and monetary economy, particularly in Italy, where accounting benefited from the introduction of "Arabic" numerals at the beginning of the century, although the continued use of Roman numerals in no way prevented the development of increasingly sophisticated accounting procedures, as demonstrated Philip the Fair's household accounts and treasury journals.[36] This taste for figures also owed much to the early development of the ecclesiastical state apparatus and the rapid growth of papal taxation.

Moreover, it corresponded to an improvement in accounting techniques, rooted in a structural phenomenon: the management effort of states and urban communities to establish the tax base and to calculate and collect taxes. Collection and expenditure gave rise to an abundance of accounts and registers, as well as the simultaneous development of a staff of managers, more or less specialised and generally subject to more or less effective oversight, such as the authorising officers for payments.

In the fourteenth century, due to the crises caused by "misfortunes of the times", the diminishing resources of the royal domain had to be defended. This required more rigorous management, first of all, based more on writing, and the listing of people and property on which the levy was based,[37] and stricter accounting oversight; these trends led to new types of documentation. At the same time, as the population decreased, attempts were made to measure the population over time; *estimi*, *compoix*, cadastres, and *cherches de feux* bear witness to this new requirement to count *taxpayers*, not just the population, in an essentially fiscal aim.

The shift from a temporary and extraordinary tax with rudimentary management, which prevailed until the mid-fourteenth century, to a regular tax system produced a large volume of written documents in the Italian communes, Catalan and Languedoc towns to cope with the growing fiscal pressure, particularly for local defence (fortifications, armament, soldiers' pay and bribes paid to mercenaries to purchase their neutrality or departure) and the royal demands, which were becoming more numerous and burdensome. The towns acted as collection agents for the state, which did not have the necessary administrative resources. For example, in Valencia, there were no accounts or tax documents prior to the royal demands. Furthermore, it was often under growing pressure from taxpayers, who wanted to know how the taxes were levied and how the proceeds were used, that accounts and estimates were drawn up and kept in the cities of Mediterranean Europe.[38] The arrival of tradesmen on the political scene, along with their revolts demanding that the tax burden be shared according to the wealth of the inhabitants, gave rise to documents to establish the tax base and calculate tax, and registers to record the collection and spending.[39] For Jean-Louis Biget, "the appearance of tax and accounting registers in the fourteenth century thus corresponds to a form of relative 'democratisation' of the financial management of urban communities" in the south of France.[40] It also reflects the monarchy's concern to safeguard the yield of these levies. The gradual institutionalisation of the administrative fiscal management of towns is visible in the increase in the number of tax registers and account books. Its implementation coincided chronologically with the affirmation of monarchical power; "tax management was organised and regularised in towns in the context of the genesis of the modern state".[41]

These different sources are the materials used by historians to study taxation and fiscal management. We must now address the historiographical issues.[42] This will be the subject of the following section.

Historiographic milestones[43]

Like all history, the history of taxation is written – and rewritten – in different ways depending on the country and era. It is shaped both by the vicissitudes of state formation, traditions and various external influences, and by historians' lines of enquiry.

The history of finance and taxation in the Middle Ages boasts a long tradition, and encompasses scholarly works of varying quantity and quality, covering almost all countries and a large number of cities. These works address issues specific to the countries and the universities in which they were produced.[44]

However, for a long time, this history remained a marginal discipline, a mere chapter in the history of institutions or of the economy. Jean Favier's pioneering declaration in 1971, that "financial history is therefore the very opposite of a separate world [...] finance is at the basis of everything, shapes everything and reflects everything"[45] only very slowly made its way among historians of the Middle Ages.[46]

Nevertheless, the historiography has grown considerably and diversified over the last three decades. It reveals the importance of the subject and its complexity, the evolving challenges it faces, and the diversity of approaches. The field has not changed at the same pace in the different monarchies, principalities or cities, as will be seen in the different chapters of Part II. While there has been a sharp increase in the production of local scholarship, broader approaches are less frequent, national synthesis works are still quite rare, and transnational ones are almost inexistent.[47] Usually, monarchical, municipal and ecclesiastical taxation systems are studied separately, even though they are often interconnected and affect the same populations.[48] The international colloquium on taxation, organised more than fifty years ago, was something of an outlier in historiographic production for more than twenty years.[49]

As the introductory remarks to the contributions in the second part of this volume show, the historiography is very uneven in terms of quantity and quality of scholarship from one geographical area to the next and in terms of diversity of approaches. In the following pages, we wish only to present the main milestones of this very uneven historical production on medieval taxation since the beginning of the last century. The task is difficult because it is not possible to speak of a linear evolution, nor of a single scholarly perspective. Medieval (but also modern) taxation has been the subject of successive and varied historiographic contributions, both from history and from related disciplines (law, economics, sociology, etc.), which have no exact chronological limits and do not constitute watertight compartments.

Although it is not easy to establish a precise historiographic sequence for the history of taxation, it is possible to distinguish two main stages, before and after the 1980s. Before that, with a few exceptions, taxation was hardly more than a secondary subject in the study of broader issues. Afterwards, from the 1980s, taxes and public finance gradually drew special attention from historians and, for many of them, became a distinct subject of analysis for developing a general historical narrative.

Towards a history of taxation until the 1980s

During the period from the end of the nineteenth century to the 1980s, finance and taxation drew interest from only a few historians, even at the height of quantitative history in the 1970s and 1980s, when historians systematically used tax sources for their studies of demography,[50] economy and urban and rural societies, without always carrying out a thorough historical critique, which led to some misinterpretations. With a few remarkable exceptions which we will point out below, medieval historians, who had been trained in Latin, the study of diplomatic texts and palaeography, were not – or thought they were not – trained to study tax and accounting sources, which were considered too technical. These historians regarded these financial and tax issues as being of little concern to them.

In each country, taxation was still included in studies of monarchical, princely, municipal and even pontifical finances, approached from an administrative and institutional point of view, on the one hand, and on the other, with a few rare exceptions, in studies of the institutions themselves. Many of these older works are still used as references today, proof that the baton has not yet been passed.[51]

The institutional approach

The institutional approach is above all present in the writings related to the teaching of law in the law faculties of the late nineteenth and first half of the twentieth century. It is expressed in institutional history textbooks such as, for example in France, those of Adhémar Esmein, Paul Viollet, Léon-Louis Borrelli de Serres, Joseph Declareuil, Émile Chénon and François Olivier-Martin.[52] Therefore, legal historians focused on finances within the context of the construction of the monarchical state and from a royal and princely point of view. Amongst them, Viollet insists more on the importance of dialogue with the royal authorities and tax negotiations during the first half of the fourteenth century. The municipal dimension was more rarely addressed by these authors. Historians also approached finances from an institutional point of view. This is the case in France with Jean-Jules Clamageran, Adolphe Vuitry, Léon Say, Dupont-Ferrier, Ferdinand Lot and Robert Fawtier.[53]

Often more recent, the legal and institutional approach also has an important tradition in other European countries. For example, among the pioneers in this field, we find Georg von Below in Germany, Steel and McFarlane in Great Britain, Lyon and Verhulst in Northwestern Europe, Luis García de Valdeavellano and, above all, Josep Maria Font Rius in Spain. The latter devoted several studies specifically to the origins and evolution of Catalan municipal finances.[54] Subsequently, other scholars took up the flame. Among the most important of these, in Spain, we find Tomás de Montagut i Estragués, with his thesis on the king's *mestre racional* in the Crown of Aragon.[55]

This rich historiographic tradition has continued, particularly in urban history, since Georges Espinas's pioneering work at the turn of the twentieth century, which analysed the finances of the commune of Douai from an almost exclusively administrative and institutional point of view.[56] In this tradition, Albert Rigaudière undoubtedly stands out. He devoted a third of his monumental thesis to the finances of Saint-Flour.[57] In France, he directly inspired the thesis of his disciple, Florent Garnier, on the finances of Millau and, in Spain, he also exerted (together with Font Rius) a profound influence on Max Turull Rubinat's thesis dedicated to the Catalan town of Cervera.[58]

The economic and social approach

The development of economic history, especially in Germany with Georg von Below and in France with François Simiand, Ernest Labrousse and their followers and under the influence of the *Annales*, provided a framework for a new generation of scholarship, more focused on economic and social issues. However, in the field of tax history, the most important and stimulating theoretical contribution came from economist Joseph Schumpeter – also influenced by the writings of sociologist Max Weber – who put forward an explanatory model of development and political transformation in three stages: tribute state, domain state and fiscal state, on the basis of the state's financing capacity and financial resources.[59] Schumpeter paved the way for "fiscal sociology", which analyses the reproduction of the different fiscal systems and their effects on economic development and, consequently by loops of interconnections on the fiscal outcome and performance.[60]

Gabriel Ardant put forth another model in his theoretical work whose oversimplified title could suggest that it is mainly or solely concerned with sociology, whereas Book II deals with "taxes as a factor of progress or regression in the economy". On the contrary, Ardant insists on the impact of financial policies on economic infrastructures and how these in turn interfere with and orientate politics, and more broadly on the interaction between the state, finance, and the productive, political and social forces.[61]

Historical materialism has also left its mark on the study of taxation as a key factor in explaining both the transition from the Roman to the feudal world and the crisis of the late Middle Ages. For the former, the echoes of this historiographic current, initiated by Perry Anderson, continue to the present day with works by scholars such as British medievalist Chris Wickham.[62] For the latter, Guy Bois's thesis was a high point. He presents the crisis of feudalism as follows:

> The impasse was both political, institutional and moral. Upstream, a crisis in the mode of production; downstream, a centralised feudalism [and] an excessive levying of taxes, most of which fed into the seigneurial treasuries through multiple channels, an increased centralisation of taxation, combined with the hypertrophy of the state apparatus, with absolutism on the horizon.[63]

Royal or princely taxation is thus presented as an additional layer of taxation made possible by the alliance between the nobility and the 'state superstructure', the latter ensuring feudal domination while also reorganising feudalism. This is the vision adopted by Marxist historians or those influenced by historical materialism, such as Edward Miller or Rodney Hilton.[64]

The financial and technical approach

In this rich but broad historiographic context, some scholarship has addressed taxation as part of more general national or local research on finance. In these studies, the history of forms of taxation is based on three main focal points: firstly, an interest in the establishment and evolution of taxes; secondly, an analysis of taxes based on a modern taxonomy (i.e., ordinary/extraordinary or direct/indirect taxes); and thirdly, a presentation of the financial administration (or at least of certain institutions).

With regard to monarchies and principalities, scholarship has looked at the finances of a country or only one or several reigns. For England, the works of A.B. Steel, S.C. Mitchell, G.L. Harriss and M.C. Prestwitch stand out.[65] On the finances of the French monarchy, we should mention the work of M. Rey and J.B. Henneman, and, more recently, J. Kerhervé's thesis on the finances of the dukes of Brittany.[66] The Duchy of Burgundy has been the subject of several classic studies on ducal finances, such as that of A. Van Nieuwenhuysen.[67] In the Iberian Peninsula, M.A. Ladero published the first synthesis on Castilian royal taxation in 1973.[68] With regard to the Crown of Aragon, its abundant fiscal documentation attracted the attention of German Hispanists such as W. Kuchler, and Americans such as T.N. Bisson, followed by native historians such as J.A. Sesma or M. Sánchez.[69]

The exceptions are a few books focused on specific taxes, such as S. Moxó's research on *alcabalas* in the kingdom of Castile, Beresford's work on poll taxes in England, I. Gonçalves's research on *pedidos* and loans granted to the Portuguese monarchy (*pedidos e empréstimos*) in Portugal, and Ch. Samaran and G. Mollat's seminal book on pontifical taxation.[70]

For municipal taxation, with a few exceptions, we could cite Bernard Chevalier's comment in 1984 on the finances of the cities of the kingdom of France:

> the monographs that can be used are few and far between; they do not adhere to any standard analysis, thus, the presentation of the accounting aggregates varies too widely from one to the next to attempt the slightest totalisation or even the slightest valid comparison.[71]

Publications on urban finance and taxation are often strictly or predominantly 'budgetary' in nature, aiming at clarifying whether revenues covered expenditures and possibly explaining the reasons for the deficit and the means to overcome it; they also often focus on the administration and management of municipal finances.

The comprehensive approaches are the most numerous, oldest and most developed in Flanders and the Italian city-states. Of these, some are seminal works that represented a milestone in historiography. In 1934, Van Werveke was the first to include statistics in his study of Ghent's finances.[72] Clauzel's thesis on Lille marked a turning point in historiography, not because the author divided expenditure and revenue equally, but because he focused on expenditure foremost, claiming that "expenses command", and because he proposed a classification and a graphic representation.[73]

The cities of medieval Italy have long been celebrated for their advanced and technically complex financial institutions.[74] Since at least the 1930s, Italian historians have focused their efforts on understanding the mechanisms of wealth assessment (*estimi*) and tax collection, as well as the subtle interplay of public debt.[75] Among the important contributions to this historiographic segment are William Bowsky's study of Siena's finances from 1287 to 1355, Anthony Molho's study of Florentine finances from 1400 to 1433, Alberto Grohmann's study of direct taxation in Perugia, and Elio Conti's study of direct taxation in Florence.[76]

In the Germanic area,[77] Sander's thesis on Nuremberg was the first in-depth study of a municipal "budget" between 1431 and 1440 on the basis of municipal account books, followed by Fengler's on Greifswald and Kirchgässner's, which was the first book to be entirely devoted to the taxation of a city, Konstanz, between 1418 and 1460. Three other monographs subsequently left their mark on the history of urban finances: Josef Rosen's 147 pages on Basle's expenditures and 80 pages on its revenues; Martin Körner's long-term view of the structural and cyclical development of Lucerne's finances; and Andreas Ranft's overall budgetary approach, taking into account the main treasury and the autonomous beer and saltworks funds in Lüneburg.[78]

In the kingdom of France and neighbouring areas, the most striking research was that of Françoise Humbert on Dijon, a model for in-depth analysis of the entire structure of municipal finances and the trend in values over a long period, and Jean-Pierre Leguay's efforts to show how analysing the receivers' accounts could contribute to the study of one city, namely, Rennes.[79]

In the kingdoms of Castile and Aragon, almost always in very brief specialised works, finances are studied on the basis of one or a series of extant accounts, which are very rare before the mid-fifteenth century.[80] Special mention must be made of the studies initiated by the Toulouse medievalist Philippe Wolff on the city of Barcelona: the first by Y. Roustit, on the consolidation of long-term public debt, and the second by J. Broussolle, on indirect municipal taxes.[81]

Jean Favier, a French historian who studied at the École Nationale des Chartes, deserves special mention because of his writings, his teaching and his great influence on a whole generation of historians (not only French), whom he introduced to fiscal issues. His work on pontifical finances at the time of the Great Schism remains a benchmark on papal finances even today,[82] as is his manual *Finances et fiscalité au bas Moyen Age*, published in Paris in 1971. This book is an initial attempt at a general approach to taxation in Western Europe. Along with supporting documents, it focuses on the various types of fiscal and financial resources available to the authorities in the late Middle Ages, and on various issues related to their management. As a precursor of an autonomous and supra-national financial and fiscal history, it opens the way to comparative studies.[83]

The turn of the late twentieth century and new historiographic trends

These traditional historiographic trends have more or less continued to the present day. However, in the final years of the twentieth century, the growing interest in the issue of the origins of the modern state constituted a first turning point for the history of taxation in general and for the history of the medieval period in particular. The latter, partly derived from the former, is reflected in a novel self-proclaimed "New Fiscal History" historiographic trend. These new approaches undoubtedly gave a strong impetus to fiscal history, more specifically to the comparative history of taxation. This has resulted in the formation of large research groups and far-reaching collective projects and they inspired substantial scholarship.

Taxation and the genesis of the modern state

Only in the late 1960s did a shift occur with the transformation of political history. The latter began its profound mutation according to the concepts and methods of historical anthropology, which tended to "found a science of politics that envisages man in the form of *homo politicus*"[84] and also those of political sociology and political science. In this new political history that took shape during the 1970s and 1980s, the notion of power became central and the study of politics replaced the study of policy understood as the activities whereby men organise the city, the state and their governments. It is now a question of studying political institutions and regimes, as well as the forms, practices, discourses, symbolic representations, rituals and images that enable or attempt to legitimise them, as well as the political uses of social and cultural practices, the means of power, political actors, political forces, pressure groups and public opinion.[85]

This new political history developed in parallel with a growing interest in the origins of the modern state, which in the case of medieval history has its starting point in the seminal work of J. Strayer.[86] On a more general level, this question of origins received a decisive impetus from the Social Science Research Council, which, in the 1960s, launched a series of interdisciplinary studies devoted to the formation of nation-states in Western Europe. The eighth volume in this series, entitled *The Future of Europe*, coordinated by sociologist Ch. Tilly and published in 1975 under the title *The Formation of National States in Western Europe*,[87] places special emphasis on fiscal studies.

All these works, in addition to Ch. Tilly's book on the role of war in the formation of the tax systems that enabled the consolidation of the modern state,[88] led to taxation being regarded as an essential means of power, which played a predominant role in the formation and development of the monarchic and princely states in Western Europe. This idea was definitively reinforced in the framework of two other international undertakings with a clearly interdisciplinary and comparative aim: the CNRS's Action Thématique Programmée on the Genesis of the Modern State (1984–1986), coordinated by Jean-Philippe Genet,[89] and its four-year extension from 1989 in a more ambitious programme of the European Science Foundation, coordinated by Jean-Philippe Genet and Wim Blockmans. These two large-scale programmes made the issue of taxation a crucial theme by establishing the fundamental criterion for defining the modern state as being a "state whose material basis is a public tax accepted by political society".[90] These programmes gave rise to an impressive body of research, mostly collective books, relating to the genesis of the modern state in the various European nations over the long term from the twelfth/thirteenth century to the late eighteenth century. Among these, the establishment of state taxation from the thirteenth century became an important topic of study that holds an essential place in two volumes of synthesis works coordinated and published under the direction of Richard Bonney.[91]

The "New Fiscal History"

In addition to the gradual consolidation of taxation as a subject for historical study, the work of researchers – both those interested in the medieval period and those interested in other periods – has been marked in recent decades by the ideas of the so-called "New Fiscal History" (NFH),[92] led by Richard Bonney and Mark Ormrod. These ideas have undoubtedly given a strong impetus to fiscal history, and many scholarly works are based on or inspired by them. It is largely thanks to them that we can consider that financial and fiscal history has been able to become a discipline in its own right, independent of political, economic or institutional history, to which more researchers are now devoting their efforts. This does not mean that we should give up dialogue with other disciplines, quite the contrary. If there is one thing that characterises the NFH, it is its interdisciplinary vocation, as well as its aim to promote a comparative perspective on a fundamentally European or Western scale.[93]

In general, the main contribution of the NFH at the theoretical level is to have refined the classical model proposed by J.A. Schumpeter, by distinguishing four "ideal types" of state according to their fiscal makeup: the "tribute state", fuelled mainly by plunder and extortion; the "domain state", based on income from assets or the "domain"; the "tax state", capable of securing more than 50 percent of its revenues through general, albeit irregular but frequent, public taxation; and the "fiscal state", in which taxes are permanent and compulsory, and which has the political and institutional structures guaranteeing the government almost unlimited access to long-term borrowing.[94]

Taking this ideal characterisation as a reference, research on medieval taxation in recent decades has focused mainly on the process of transition from the "domain state" to the "tax state" in the last centuries of the Middle Ages. Although there were earlier manifestations, the importance of public taxation would gradually increase from the end of the thirteenth century onwards, mainly due to the needs of war. By the beginning of the Early Modern period, many territories in Western Europe had already reached the tax state and, as Ch. Tilly argues, this served to fuel the military competition that would eventually lead to the fiscal state in the late Early Modern period.

In recent years, this theory has been nuanced and even challenged by a number of historians, both of the Middle Ages and of other periods, although their interpretations of Bonney and Ormrod's theses do not always coincide. For example, Ginatempo warns against the temptation to trace the origins of the "tax state" to the late twelfth and early thirteenth centuries, when the "domain state" was still taking shape. In her view, this periodisation was also valid for the first Italian cities which, except in the exceptional case of Genoa and Venice, did not start to develop their tax systems before the end of the thirteenth century. Sandro Carocci and Simone Collavini criticise the NFH model firstly for its teleological vision, but also for its generalisation based on particular cases, in particular that of the very small minority of city-states in central

Italy or of centralised states. Its chronology needs to be refined in the various monarchies, as the domain state extends well beyond the fifteenth century and not only in the states of Central and Eastern Europe. In this sense, they emphasise the need to study seigniorial taxation and they relativise the difference between taxation and other forms of exaction, which continued until the Early Modern period.[95] Following Bonney and Ormrod in a thorough study, Alex Brayson also highlighted that "the political and economic limits of the medieval English 'tax state' had been reached, thus paving the way for a structural regression to a low-yield 'domain' state from the 1450s", showing that the evolution of tax regimes was not linear and could suffer backward steps, as Bonney and Ormrod pointed out.[96] Moreover, while Schumpeter believed that the "fiscal state" was the product of Western history, linked to the birth of the nation-state and democracy, recent works have shown that the characteristics of the "tax state" and the "fiscal state" can be found in other states, because societies do not necessarily go through the same stages to achieve the same results even though they have the same needs, and the formation of fiscal regimes can only be understood in terms of heterogeneous historicity that varies in time and space.[97] In sum, all these authors agree on the "hybrid" nature of tax systems and the need to adopt transnational, even global, perspectives in order to test the – arguably still useful – theories of NFH. As Ertman noted, "States were not closed laboratories for the development of fiscal systems. They were part of a transnational system of knowledge in which transfers of experience, successes, failures and emulation were important".[98]

An alternative tax theory approach

In a book on the Grand Duchy of Tuscany under the last Medici rulers, modernist historian Jean-Claude Waquet, proposes a new historical approach to public finance after devoting a long chapter to a critique of the foundations of the five main theories of public finance.[99] In his a definition that he calls "enlarged":

> finance transforms public resources into private, and private resources into public. It is broken down into a set of acquisition and transfer processes which, implemented by subjects who are themselves public or private, exert a reciprocal influence on each other.

He draws the conclusion that "finances are at the intersection of two strategies: one whereby the state acquires and uses its revenues, and one whereby individuals satisfy their own ends".

This new approach to finance went unnoticed by most medievalists for a long time because it was presented in a book whose title led them to believe that it did not concern them. However, it had important consequences and a definite influence on historiography, even if some historians had already integrated some of these ideas before J.C. Waquet theorised them. Let us list the main ones, which obviously do not apply to the medieval period alone. Contrary to the traditional "budgetary" conception of financial historians, the sole purpose of taxation was not to provide resources to cover expenses. The reconstitution of accounts and quantified analyses should therefore no longer be the main focus of research. Taxation is not only a matter of technique, but also a means of policy, and the characteristics of a tax system are more than ever the hallmark of a state's economic and social policy. Taxation is also characterised by its material effects, i.e., by the transformation of private resources into public resources via levies, and vice versa, by the transformation of public resources into private resources via redistribution.[100] Tax, expenditure and debt must no longer be considered separately but as a whole from the point of view of their overall impact. Redistribution must therefore be given a prominent place, whereas the literature on finance is more concerned with taxation. The individual becomes the *subject* of public finance and not just an *object*. We must therefore be interested in rulers and their choices, and in their dialogue with political society to ensure that taxes are accepted; in the finance men and their networks; but also in the taxpayers and their reactions to taxes (i.e., fraud, tax evasion or revolts). Less emphasis should be placed on calculations and more on discourse, on the information whose acquisition is essential for decision-making, and on communication to persuade and to discuss in order to obtain consent, rather than through coercion.

New paradigms, new research

Since the end of the twentieth century, scholarship on medieval taxation has grown much richer and more diversified (although not to the same extent from one country to the next) and become more internationalised, as the introductory historiographic presentations of each of the chapters in the second part show. This internationalisation, as well as the comparative and interdisciplinary orientation of the NHF, has also led to a change in the forms of research. Such research is increasingly carried out in teams as part of 'research groups' and/or programmes within universities or national and European organisations that bring together researchers from different disciplines: historians, legal and literary historians, economists or sociologists, in research that tends to favour spatial comparative or global approaches. There are countless collective research projects being initiated, supported and financed on new or renewed subjects.

Over the past thirty years, taxation studies have received an additional boost with the emergence of a number of institutions in the different European countries. As Bonney himself points out, this has been the case for the Comité pour l'Histoire Économique et Financière de la France (CHEFF). Founded under the aegis of the Ministry of Economy and Finance in 1986, this institution's purpose is

> to contribute towards a better understanding of the history of the state and its role in economic, financial, and monetary developments from the Middle Ages to the present day, to encourage academic publications on the subject, and to assist in their dissemination.[101]

To fulfil this role, in 1996, the CHEFF launched a collection dedicated to fiscal and financial history, which currently includes more than 170 works, including numerous studies devoted to taxation and finance in the late medieval period.[102] In Spain, the Instituto de Estudios Fiscales de Madrid, founded in 1960, was transformed in 2000 into an autonomous body of the Ministry of Finance with the aim of developing tax studies. Also in Spain, the research network *Arca Comunis* on the History of Hispanic Finance and Taxation (thirteenth–eighteenth centuries) and its relations with other European models was created in 2008.[103] The network has since published 15 books. If we add the programmes of the Institución Milà y Fontanals of the Consejo Superior de Investigaciones Científicas of Barcelona, we can see that research on both monarchical and urban taxation has made the most progress in the Iberian kingdoms over the last two decades[104] except for Portugal, which is still lagging behind despite some recent advances.[105]

We would also mention, for their comparative perspective on medieval (and modern) taxation, some weekly seminars, or "Settimane", organised in Prato by the Istituto Internazionale di Storia Economica "F. Datini" (founded in 1968). The most important of these is probably the one held in 2007, entitled *La fiscalità nell'economia europea (s. XIII–XVIII)*, although the issue of taxation was also dealt with to a greater or lesser extent in those of 1976, 1998 and 2015.[106]

The study of state taxation has also led to the development of work on municipal taxation, since the development of the latter is to a large extent conditioned by that of the former and, in any case, linked to it. A research programme devoted to urban taxation in the western Mediterranean in the late Middle Ages has helped stimulate research in this geographical area. Inaugurated in 1995 with a colloquium on the relationship between royal and municipal taxation in Western Europe at the end of the medieval period,[107] it continued for ten years under the leadership of D. Menjot and M. Sánchez; the results of the research and the annual proceedings were published in four volumes on *City Taxation in the Middle Ages* (Western Mediterranean) between 1996 and 2004. This programme was completed in 2005 with a colloquium organised in 2000 by the CHEFF, which published the proceedings, and another, published in 2006, on the relationship between royal and municipal taxation in the Hispanic kingdoms.[108]

Public debt warrants special mention because it is a subject closely related to both urban and 'state' taxation. Although it has been cultivated more by modernists (especially from an economic perspective), it has also been the subject of great attention by medievalists in countries where debt is of great importance, such as the city-states of Northern Italy,[109] the Burgundian Low Countries,[110] the Crown of Aragon.[111] All aspects have been analysed to a greater or lesser extent: forms of debt, methods of management, the geography of the market, creditors, the weight of debt, and the problems caused by debt. There are many other studies on the medieval period in research on public finance over the long term, and public debt is also present in monographs from other disciplines on the construction of the state.[112]

Many other collective studies have been conducted and published on expenditure and redistribution, Church and taxation, fiscal discourse and accounting, to name only a few. In the monarchies of the Western, Scandinavian (Denmark, Norway and Sweden), Slavic (Russia, Poland) and Byzantine worlds, fiscal systems and taxation are research topics closely linked with the political history and the origins and the development of states.

The main focal points of tax history: continuity and changes

Breaking with the traditional "budgetary" conception of financial historians, tax historians no longer consider that the sole purpose of taxation is to provide resources to cover expenditure. They no longer believe that taxation is only a technical subject. Instead, they view taxation as a policy tool, and the characteristics of a tax system are now, more than ever, seen as the distinguishing mark of a state's economic and social policy. Taxation is defined in tangible terms as the transformation of private resources into public resources by levying taxes, and vice versa, by the transformation of public resources into private resources through the redistribution of tax revenue.

This conception of taxation has resulted in more diverse and complex topics, but has not done away with the traditional questions, in particular the setting up of tax systems, the definition of their components, the administration and management of financial and fiscal resources, and the role of taxation in building the state. We should not be misled by the disruptive terminology sometimes used to attract attention, which could suggest that there has been a break in historiography. Most of the advances in this field build on the perspectives opened up in previous scholarship, even though sociological and anthropological currents have opened up new avenues.

From this abundant, diversified and increasingly interdisciplinary production, some major scholarly trends are emerging with new questions, a deepening or renewal of old questions, and the use of new methods. These trends can be grouped into five main categories.[113]

The power to tax: legitimacy, consent and resistance

A first set of scholarly works is organised around the power to tax: who holds sovereignty and therefore the right to tax? At what moment? Under what conditions? With what limits? What are the instruments available to monarchies, principalities and cities to establish a tax system?

Between the twelfth and fifteenth centuries, Western monarchs and princes needed to resort to taxation to meet their increasing financial needs. The traditional resources that they had inherited from their predecessors – land rents, seigniorial and feudal dues – were stagnant or diminishing because their rates and periodicity had been set by long-standing tradition and could not be increased by sovereigns to compensate for inflation aggravated by monetary changes. Taxes reappeared gradually, earlier or later depending on the country, as princes and monarchs became powerful enough to impose a levy on their subjects in exchange for (often illusory) protection. Along with the power to judge and to legislate, the power to tax is an integral part of sovereignty, but it requires legitimacy and, more than any other power, the consent of the population that is asked to contribute more and more. Exegetes, theologians and legal scholars, whether or not they belonged to the monarch's councillors, raised the issue of fiscal sovereignty, the need for taxation and the legal grounds of the power to impose it, debating the legitimacy of taxation and the conditions for tax collection, as well as the use of tax revenues, while the canonists of the mid-thirteenth century, such as Pope Innocent IV, laid the doctrinal foundations for an urban community's right to tax. By virtue of the corporative conception of the public good, urban communities had to obtain the prince's approval to create *gabelles* on consumption, but they could collect tax freely to meet the requirements of the *necessaria utilitas* recognised by civil law.[114]

Scholarly thought developed in universities before being disseminated in various ways, from *summae* – the *Summa de casibus poenitentiae*, written circa 1220–1221 by the Catalan Dominican friar Raymond of Penyafort, which quickly became well known and had considerable influence – to fiscal treatises[115] and works of political literature, such as Nicole Oresme's commentary on Aristotle's Politics (1371), not to mention handbooks for confessors, such as Martín Pérez's *Libro de las confesiones* (1316),[116] as well as sermons, "mirrors of princes" and wisdom treatises which purport to model the conscience of the king and provide him with teachings.[117]

In cities, contributing to the "*communis civium collecta*" – to borrow the term for "tax" used in a Cologne document from 1154 – was a duty for every burgher, confirmed in all urban laws, and a founding element of the urban community. Direct taxation was born at the same time as the urban community itself. The payment of a sum was recognition of the aid and protection that this urban community offered to taxpayers in return, and paying tax became a distinguishing factor for becoming a "citizen", as opposed to being a mere inhabitant of the city. Whoever does not pay or no longer pays tax loses this right; whoever resides long enough in the city and pays tax gains this right.

Alongside this theoretical debate on the legitimacy of fiscal sovereignty, researchers have been interested in the means used by monarchs to try to obtain the support of their subjects or at least their consent, since none of these rulers held absolute power or led an administration capable of imposing a tax by force.[118] None could decide arbitrarily to create a new tax or to define the rules for determining the tax base, tax rates or who would be subject to tax. Sovereigns were limited by their realm's historical traditions and its economic, social, political and administrative structures.

The installation and development of the monarchy's fiscal system did not go without any resistance from the country's political forces, namely the Church, the nobility and the towns, and the relations between the latter and the monarchy altered quite significantly throughout the fourteenth and fifteenth centuries.[119] Monarchies had to communicate to avoid conflicts and to obtain consent for the levying of taxes because taxation was an act that required consent from the representatives of political society, gathered together in assemblies. Kings summoned the Cortes, États Généraux, Parlements, diets, assemblies of regional states, most often to obtain consent for extraordinary taxation, but the representatives took advantage of these meetings to present petitions to the king because they know that if he approved them, they would become the law of the land. From the end of the thirteenth century, taxation became the main reason for the development of assemblies in all European monarchies and principalities.[120]

This need for consent explains the frequency of these assemblies, the evolution of their powers and their influence on sovereign's financial policy. While these assemblies were convened "to be able to consent, and not to be able to refuse, except in exceptional cases",[121] they were indispensable with their ritualised procedure in several stages. The monarchy's tools of negotiation, in addition to "threats, persuasion and the eloquence (of its representatives)",[122] included the granting of privileges, concessions and exemptions that favoured some taxpayers and penalised others. However, we should not forget the direct negotiations, which are not very well known, between representatives of the political forces and royal officers, particularly to attempt to reduce the amount of a subsidy or a levy, as well as the role of the town as an intermediary in the fiscal dialogue.[123]

Sovereigns cited war – the "just war" that theologians and jurists defined[124] – first and foremost, as grounds for their requests for exceptional subsidies, and thanks to war, their requests were accepted.[125] This may partly explain the lengthy conflicts, including the so-called Hundred Years' War, in the fourteenth and fifteenth centuries. In towns, too, the scourge of war – which hit Europe increasingly hard from the second half of the thirteenth century – led to the generalisation of taxation. In many of towns, the levying of taxes was made necessary "*Ad opus castri*" (for the work of defence), as stated in the oldest urban tax systems in Flanders; in Liège, from the last quarter of the thirteenth century, this levy was designated by the word "*firmitas*", which literally refers to its original function: financing the maintenance of the town's fortifications.[126] But in many towns, it was the repeated, pressing and often heavy royal demands, justified by military needs, which obliged the authorities to impose taxes, to distribute sums or to go into debt in order to satisfy them.

The tax initially imposed on an extraordinary basis would gradually – according to a chronology that has yet to be delineated in the various countries – become an ordinary and regular levy, supposedly enjoying popular consent, theoretically paid by the entire population and (again, theoretically) intended to guarantee the safety of the inhabitants and to serve the common good, i.e. to finance other expenses, for town infrastructure (paving streets, improving the water and sewage systems, building bridges) and for "social services" (education, public assistance, festivities and the functioning of a growing administration – all new expenses that also had to be funded).[127]

These arguments, but especially the forms of taxation and redistribution, gave rise to resistance.[128] As soon as an institutionalised power organises a coherent and centralised system of taxation, avoidance mechanisms appear through fraud, on the one hand (i.e. the 'illegal' diversion of the tax system to avoid paying), and through tax evasion, on the other hand (i.e. use of 'legal' loopholes to reduce the amount of tax paid), for example, by transferring property to the wife of the head of the household, or by going into arrears, which the wealthy did to avoid their obligations and which often resulted in a negotiated settlement with the tax authorities.[129] The authorities endeavoured to fight fraud and tax evasion through measures that were more or less coercive and were enforced to a greater or lesser extent: audits, fines, prison sentences or seizures.

Taxation also triggered revolts, of various frequencies and levels of violence, throughout the fourteenth and fifteenth centuries. These involved attacks on the property and/or persons of tax collectors, tax-farmers, municipal or royal officers, along with attacks on communal palaces and the destruction of tax and accounting documentation. Historians focus on the deformed image of these revolts as depicted in the sources (e.g., chronicles, municipal proceedings, tax rolls, trials or correspondence), publicised by the authorities that wrote them, and the prejudices transmitted by historiography since at least the nineteenth century. Historians also look at the traces left by these revolts on the imaginaries of the town and the state. They investigate the ultimate cause of these uprisings, for which the tax burden or corruption were often merely triggers or a means for certain segments of society to express their discontent on other issues, as well as their political and social aspirations. This explains the diverse profiles of the protagonists of these movements, given that they originally held very different social positions. Tax revolts soon expanded into protests over representation and inequality, thus becoming political revolts.[130]

Financial policies and strategies: modalities and stakes of the tax grab

With its multiple territorial, political, economic and social implications, taxation was one of the most visible fields of political action for princes, sovereigns and urban elites in the Middle Ages.[131] The choices made in terms of taxation reflected the taxable and therefore important economic activities of a town, but also the major political options of the elites.[132] For the latter, taxation was, of course, an issue of having the resources to cover expenditure for the general interest, but also of intervening in economic and social life by means of levies and redistribution.[133] The methods chosen to achieve these, sometimes contradictory, goals illustrate the social tensions within towns. Hence rulers' financial policies had to strike a balance between what was desired and what was possible. By looking at how authorities determined the type of tax, the tax base, the collection methods and expenditures, historians see with great precision the action of interest groups within a city and the relationship with higher authorities.[134] To specify these strategies, historians no longer limit themselves to a detailed study of taxation techniques; they also look at the redistribution of the tax revenue, which is just as essential.[135]

Indirect taxes on transactions, traffic and consumption were an important resource for monarchies and principalities, and by the fourteenth century at the latest, they had become the predominant tax method for a large majority of localities, even in towns where artisans' representatives had carved out a place for themselves in urban government, such as in the Flemish or Italian regions. It is no exaggeration to say that these taxes accounted for an average of 75–80 percent of urban revenues. However, these taxes were very unpopular and contested, as shown by the unflattering nicknames such as "*maletôte, ongeld, mala pecunia, ungeld*", by which they were often referred to, and the demonstrations of discontent by the "common people" towards them. These demonstrations show that contemporaries were quite aware that indirect taxes were fundamentally unfair, as they hit taxpayers according to their needs and not their means.

To explain why this form of taxation was predominant, we must take into account the fact that these excises were usually sold to the highest bidder. In addition, in Low Countries, as in Castile or in the Italian communes, the preference for taxation on consumption within the city walls often coincided with a hearth tax, whether or not it was proportional to farm income. The urban elites thus had the privilege of being among the least taxed in both cases, since urban excise duties did not affect them as much as the lower classes thanks to the production of their estates, while the latter, located outside the walls, escaped excessive taxation thanks to abatements, often according to their distance from the city.

Direct taxes, even if they were proportional to the taxpayer's ability to pay (as taxpayers often demanded), did not mean that the burden was distributed fairly. Estimates were, in fact, often crude and arbitrary, and abatements led to a personalisation of tax by establishing different taxes for craftsmen's workshops or commercial premises, setting caps on proportionality or providing various forms of tax relief, for example, for the exercise of a magistracy, or as in Saint-Flour, the marriage of the elder son.[136]

Public debt has been the subject of numerous studies, which have long highlighted its economic, political and financial importance in large Italian, Flemish, German, Rhineland, Catalan, Valencian and Provençal cities,[137] and more recently, in smaller towns such as Alzira, Gandia or Cullera in the Kingdom of Valencia, Vicenza or Bassano in Italy, Chartres in the Kingdom of France, and Cervera, Reus ou Sant Feliu de Guíxols in Catalonia, all of which carried a high level of permanent debt.

Scholarship has shown that short-term debt – attested from the second half of the twelfth century in the towns of central and northern Italy – gave way to consolidated debt that could take two forms: so-called perpetual annuities (hereditary or constituted: *censals, geldkauf, zinskauf*) and repayable only at the request of the borrower, and life annuities (*violaris, lybdind, leibgeding*). The interest that the towns had to pay on these debts absorbed a large, sometimes exorbitant, portion of their ordinary regional revenue by the late Middle Ages.

This public debt required a real system of taxation to be developed and implemented, allowing the payment of interest and ensuring that new loans could be granted. This is one of the reasons, if not *the* reason, for its emergence in Europe.[138] Public debt became a fundamental component of the tax system. Borrowing and taxation formed a dialectic that historians have attempted to study.[139] Above all, historians have shown how debt fuelled a vast transfer of wealth from the entire taxpaying population to the most privileged holders of debt securities, since interest payments were largely financed by taxes on consumption, as in Catalonia, whereas debt was at the genesis of state taxation.[140] Debt also allowed the savings of the city's inhabitants to be used, without them feeling that they were paying an additional tax, and attracted funds from outside the city, tying them to the city's financial interests. For annuity buyers, the prospect of acquiring a fixed income must have played a decisive role, as evidenced by the numerous and often long lists of annuity buyers in the accounts of most cities. In fact, rather than a lending operation, this new arrangement was presented as the purchase-sale of a periodic annuity (the interest), based on a determined set of goods (the assets and income of the municipality), for a price (the capital) proportional to the thing sold. On a social level, this approach also had the significant effect of binding a part of the urban elite to the princely policy.[141] By buying an annuity, the purchase price of which was used almost exclusively to pay taxes or fines to the prince, the burgher became a shareholder. The sale of annuities was thus an instrument of financial management leading not only to a redistribution of wealth within cities, but also between cities and finally between city and state. Astute contemporaries were well aware of the consequences of this consolidated debt, which was financed by all taxpayers but benefited only a small number of people.

Tax officials and finance men: tax administration and management

As taxes became regular and permanent, a specialised financial administration was set up to take charge of tax collection and the management of public funds and to make payments on the orders of the authorities. At the same time, more or less complex and effective management and auditing rules were put in place. As a result, a host of tax agents appeared; they were involved at different levels of the collection and redistribution of levies.

Historians have studied these different kinds of agents for two reasons. Firstly, because an administration is only as good as the people in it. Secondly, knowing about these agents is crucial for understanding the various interests around tax collection, the individuals or groups who benefited from this collection, and for grasping the rationale and stakes of the tax systems, mainly in the cities.

In monarchies and principalities, a new category of officials serving the prince appeared: receivers general, treasurers, principal farmers, and auditors of accounts.[142] Like all emerging categories, not much is known about these officials, especially as the documentation that has been preserved all too often provides only the names and positions of a few of them and only reveals those whose misappropriations were denounced or investigated by the chamber of accounts or an officer mandated by the royal administration. Scholarship has made famous some great financiers who, because they were close to the monarchs, have left more traces in the documentation, such as Jacques Coeur, Enguerrand de Marigny, and the two brothers Biccio and Musciatto Franzesi, to mention only the most famous in France. Researchers have focused on professional groups, such as the Jews in Castile and Aragon,[143] the Lombards in France, the Piedmontese in the Brabant cities,[144] and more recently on professional groups such as receivers and farmers at regional and local levels.[145]

The careers of certain officials, the indictments against some of them, the findings of investigations carried out by the chambers of accounts[146] — which were tasked with controlling all the accounting registers of the officials, who were forced to give an account of their management on a regular basis — all these elements raise the question of what was required of financial officials? Were they supposed to be honest and/or to be efficient? Did the king really want honest officials? Could he? Did he really care, even if it meant making them pay from time to time? Didn't he prefer efficient men, capable of getting rich, but also capable of providing the money he needed, especially for his wars? Were the exactions of finance officials tolerated as a necessary evil? If so, the issue was the level of royal agents. Was there not a difference in the recruitment of traditional royal agents, such as the court staff and bailiffs, and new officers, such as finance officials, whose numbers had swelled in the fourteenth century? Did the monarchy not take on as finance officers (accountants, treasurers or receivers) the individuals it could find? Men who had proven themselves, often parvenus. Wasn't forgiving some of the missteps of its accounting officers "the price to pay for maintaining the fragile balance between the prince's prodigality, the public interest and sovereign power, and above all for gaining acceptance for the construction of the state?"[147]

The world of the protagonists of tax negotiation in towns cities has recently been the subject of renewed attention from scholars: from municipal receivers and farmers, to treasurers of the specialised funds (for maintaining the city walls, managing the debt or arrears, etc.), to the assessors, collectors, auditors of the accounts, and guarantors.[148] All these individuals were practical, hands-on people, as shown by the vernacular language in which they kept their records and accounts. In towns, they ranged from members of large families to modest craftsmen who occasionally bid to become a tax-farmer for a few months to supplement their income. They were secondary protagonists in the various municipal tax systems and were part of the rank-and-file of what can be considered a real financial elite. Studying them helps us understand the evolution of political systems.

The study of these "tax practitioners", starting with the tax-farmers (who were numerous because the farm system was the preferred mode of collection for consumption taxes and a typical example of combinations of private and public strategies) has changed significantly over time. Historians have moved from the compilation of biographical records and prosopographical lists to sociological research, which is easier to carry out with access to notarial archives. They focus on geographical origin, social level, careers, level of monopolisation of financial positions, place in urban oligarchies, family, professional and political networks, what Pierre Bourdieu called "social capital". The number and especially the amount of the taxes that were auctioned to tax-farmers allow historians to specify the degree to which an individual, family or company held a monopoly, and to identify a group of specialists. The study of the various levels of participation in the tax negotiation (i.e., the number of taxes under contract, the duration of the contract, the amount of the auctions) makes it possible to determine whether tax-farmers used finance to gain access to political power or, on the contrary, whether they were a separate group from the dominant oligarchies which owed their fortune to their strategic position in the tax and financial systems, whether they were part of financial and/or commercial networks at local, regional or international level.

To deepen the study of relationships in the management of the taxes of monarchies, in addition to prosopography, the social network analysis and graph theory can be used.[149] This method consists of studying the relationships between individuals who interact and collaborate through bilateral or multilateral agreements of limited duration that generate a social network. Studying this social network is useful because it allows historians, on the one hand, to visualise the structures underlying these links and, on the other hand, to reveal the existence of significant opportunities that affect the access of these individuals to resources such as information, wealth or power.[150]

These various financial actors contributed to the formation and dissemination of tax and financial information that was essential for the authorities to make tax decisions, as they were the ones who were on the ground finding out about taxpayers and their ability to pay, collecting the amounts due, and they were the ones who put together the various documents mentioned above.[151]

State and municipal taxation

Since Bernard Chevalier began his joint study of state and municipal taxation,[152] there has been an increasing amount of scholarship focusing on the genesis of the two tax systems and their relationship with each other.[153] Were the two systems linked and competing, as Chevalier thinks in the kingdom of France or were they superimposed and articulated as Menjot thinks in the kingdom of Castile?[154]

Scholarship focuses on how the levies decided by the monarchy affected municipal finances and how municipalities were involved in collecting them. What role did they play in the negotiation of subsidies and the acceptance of taxes? To what extent was the tax burden of the monarchies responsible for the genesis and consolidation of the municipal fiscal and financial system?[155] To what extent did the early development of urban finances provide a valuable laboratory for princely finances?[156] Accounting and finance experts, originating from the merchant classes, were mainly located in towns. Lacking an adequate administration, sovereigns relied on urban administrations to collect taxes, especially wealth tax, because "in this matter, it is not the state power that holds the keys, but the urban power that has the tools and men to investigate, estimate and count".[157] The cities then provided the monarchies with the largest contingent of their finance officers, sealing another form of the close alliance between urban elites and the nascent modern state.

Scholars have shown that well-developed urban finances became an attractive prey for princes eager to increase their revenues. The struggle within the city between the patriciate and the artisans to extend control over urban revenues was thus mixed with the rivalry between the city and the kings to control and ultimately organise the levies for their benefit. Taxes were indeed "the roots of discord".[158]

Historians have also examined the relationship between the two fiscal systems "from the bottom up", i.e., starting with the municipality. They have studied the instruments adopted by municipalities to cope with the heavy subsidies demanded by the crown: raising traditional taxes, new taxes on consumption, and loans. They have therefore analysed the finances of communities before the introduction of a new royal tax in order to estimate the importance of its establishment and its weight, which varied according to whether or not the towns had the financial resources, particularly wealth assets. In towns where the documentation allows, historians then try to evaluate as precisely as possible the weight of the contributions paid to the prince/monarch: aid, subsidies, duties, forced donations, their evolution over time and their magnitude.[159] Whether royal/state taxation was administered by its own agents, or whether its management was transferred to municipal agents, historians examine oligarchies' involvement in the processes of leasing, collecting and transferring funds to the crown and the benefits they derived from it, and in general, the social transformations caused by royal taxation of towns.[160]

Tax revenues and tax burden: classical and news methods

The assessment of tax revenues and the share of each type of tax – as well as the expenditure – are recurrent questions in the work of historians. The limitations of the sources mentioned above, in particular the non-existence of complete general accounts and the dispersion of revenues in several different coffers, make this a complex, sometimes uncertain, exercise. In-depth critical analysis of the accounting sources is a prerequisite.

The analysis of the data raises methodological difficulties which historians have tried to resolve in various ways, none of which is entirely satisfactory. The conversion of the series into quantities of precious metals should be discarded, as these, like all commodities, are subject to inflation. Comparing with consumer products, whether or not they are included in the household basket, is also an unfeasible method because prices vary greatly from one period of the year to another. The solution of converting into a stable real currency seems to be the most usable method of calculating the percentages of income by tax or by region.

This quantitative approach requires statistical analyses.[161] To show trends in all budget items, or just a single item, an approach often used is to represent each item on a graph with cartesian coordinates, with an arithmetic or semi-logarithmic scale, the latter having the advantage of showing the multiplier from one year to the next. To make them more readable, some also include a trend line or, when there are not too many gaps, calculate moving averages, which smooths the curves and thus erases short-term variations. Vertical bar charts representing absolute or relative values are increasingly preferred. Each year is given its own bar, which is divided into as many items as are included in the classification, with the length of the divisions proportional to their magnitude. Readability is improved in two ways, either by isolating two bands, or by presenting the bands horizontally rather than vertically.[162]

Neither strip charts nor bar charts allow reasoning about both absolute and relative values. For this, matrix calculations and data matrix analysis software are necessary.[163] The latter software has the great advantage of building a histogram that allows reasoning both on the absolute figures for each item, calculated in rows (with the base of each column being proportional to the cumulative amount of expenditure for each financial year) and on the percentages of each item, calculated in columns.[164] Readability is greatly improved and items can be grouped together by main categories.

It is still very rare for medieval taxation scholars to venture beyond these elementary statistical analyses to calculate coefficients of correlation and linear variation, moving averages, standard deviations or to draw linear regression curves. They are reluctant to do so, claiming that the sources are incomplete, fragmentary and heterogeneous, whereas precisely one technique, correspondence factor analysis, offers a very powerful means of revealing spaces of relationships. Alain Guerreau has applied this method remarkably well to the analysis of the finances of the city of Dijon on the basis of the data provided by Françoise Humbert in her thesis.[165] He has shown the interest in combining classical and factorial analyses for the study of urban finances. The former "involves the concepts of equilibrium, hierarchy, self-regulation, gaps and shifts, discordances and oppositions, simultaneity and correspondence; factorial analyses, those of articulations, homology, symmetry, gaps and opposition". To date, this approach and the matrix analysis have not sparked emulation on a wide basis.

Conclusions

This overview of available sources and historiography, albeit incomplete, has traced the evolution in questions, approaches, methods and findings. It has highlighted the diversity of the types of sources and their importance, but also the uneven progress of research on both monarchical and princely taxation and on municipal taxation in European countries, which is only partly linked to the often-mentioned inadequacy of the documentation, but also due to a lack of interest and the influence of the historiographic legacy.

Taxation remains a field of study that has not been sufficiently explored. Some sources are still neglected or not fully examined, such as the voluminous registers of municipal deliberations in which tax issues hold a substantial place, or the archives of the chamber of accounts, which contain an abundance of interesting documents. Some questions deserve to be explored in greater depth, such as the economic and social impact of financial policies, the production of social identities, the two types of law that overlap and complement each other in cities, tax geography on a European scale, tax cultures, taxpayers' opinions of different levies, the relationship between taxation, state and society and the vocabulary of taxation.[166]

It would be advisable to go beyond the stage of case studies to propose common analytical frameworks, which some authors have begun to develop in research projects. Graphical representations should also be harmonised to allow comparisons across time and space. Without these efforts, the case descriptions will continue to stack up but without really advancing knowledge of taxation, which is only one component of tax systems and therefore of the financial policies and strategies of kings and urban authorities.

Notes

* Part 1 was written by Denis Menjot and Mathieu Caesar, parts 2 and 3 by Denis Menjot and Pere Verdès Pijuan.

1 WAQUET, *Le Grand-Duché de Toscane*, p. 137; our translation.

2 We have not aimed to be exhaustive, and the cases cited are given as examples. Above all, we have tried to highlight the variety of sources, the contributions and limitations of each, and the problems that arise from their use. The reader will find more details on extant sources in each of the articles in Part II.

3 BAUTIER and SORNAY, *Les sources de l'histoire économique*. For the sources of urban taxation in Western Mediterranean cities, see MENJOT and SÁNCHEZ MARTÍNEZ, *La fiscalité des villes*, vol. 1; COLLANTES DE TERÁN SÁNCHEZ (ed.), *Fuentes para el estudio de negocio fiscal*; KERHERVÉ, "L'historien et les sources financières".

4 However, it would be anachronistic to speak of a specifically fiscal law in the Middle Ages, as it is not possible to make a clear distinction between public and private.

5 LADERO QUESADA, *Legislación hacendística de la Corona de Castilla.*
6 HÉBERT, *Parlementer.*
7 CONTAMINE and MATTÉONI (ed.) *La France des principautés.*
8 On this type of source in the different territories of southern Europe in the Middle Ages and Early Modern period, see ABBÉ (ed.), *Estimes, compoix et cadastres* and RIGAUDIÈRE (dir.), *De l'estime au cadastre en Europe.*
9 For example, see RIGAUDIÈRE, *Le Livre d'estimes de 1380-1385.*
10 DUPONT-FERRIER, *Études sur les institutions*, vol. II, pp. 44–70 and 202–203. Some accounts have been published, for example: FAWTIER, *Comptes royaux, 1285-1314*; VIARD, *Les journaux du Trésor de Charles IV le Bel*; VIARD, *Les journaux du Trésor de Philippe VI de Valois*, followed by the *Ordinarium Thesauri of 1338-1339.*
11 MOLLAT and FAVREAU, *Comptes généraux de l'État bourguignon.*
12 For Navarre, CARRASCO and TAMBURRI, *Acta vectigalia regni Navarrae.*
13 In Seville, for example, in addition to books on cursive, there are *cuadernos de condiciones, cargo, cuaderno de arriendos, sumario del cargo,* and *libro de remembranzas.*
14 Definition given by GLÉNISSON and HIGOUNET, "Remarques sur les comptes ", p. 36. (our translation).
15 See MORSEL, "Sociogenèse d'un patriciat", pp. 83–106.
16 BUCHHOLZER-RÉMY, "Les comptes municipaux comme texte"; see also BUFFO, "Prassi documentarie e gestione", pp. 217–259.
17 See MORSEL, "De l'usage des sources" Our translation.
18 BECK "Les comptabilités de la commune de Dijon"; LANDOLT, *Der Finanzhaushalt der Stadt Schaffhausen.* The first income statement of 1396–1397 has 13 headings; the accounting year 1498–1499 has 38.
19 FOSSIER, PETITJEAN, and REVEST (ed.), *Écritures grises.*
20 Several of these enquiries have been published; DERVILLE, *Enquêtes fiscales de la Flandre wallonne.* vol. 1: TORCHET, *Réformation des fouages de 1426.*
21 CAESAR, "Juridical Uncertainty and Resistance", pp. 342–358.
22 ADRIAN, "Penser la politique dans les villes germaniques".
23 See below, "*The power to tax: legitimacy, consent and resistance*", and SANTAMARIA, "Comment roys et princes doivent diligamment entendre".
24 COHN *Lust for Liberty;* BOURIN, CHERUBINI, and PINTO (ed.), *Rivolte urbane e rivolte contadine*.
25 PHILIPPE DE COMMYNES, *Mémoires*, Book V, 19.
26 GUASTI (ed.), *Lettere di un notaro ad un mercante del secolo XIV.*
27 See below, MAINONI, "Northern Italy: Cities and regional states".
28 SCORDIA, *Le roi doit vivre du sien*; PRÉTOU, "L'imagerie de l'impôt", pp. 327–348.
29 TOMEI (ed.), *Le Biccherne di Siena.*
30 PRÉTOU, "L'imagerie de l'impôt dans la miniature occidentale", pp. 289–310
31 PETRUCCI, *Promenades au pays de l'écriture.*
32 See BARTOLI LANGELI, *Codice diplomatico del Comune di Perugia*, vol. 1, pp. 31–314.
33 CAMMAROSANO, *L'italia medievale*, pp. 174–193; CLANCHY, *From Memory to Written Record*; BECK, "Archéologie d'un document d'archives"; ANHEIM and THEIS (ed.); *Les comptabilités pontificales*; COQUERY, MENANT, and WEBER (ed.), *Ecrire, compter, mesurer.*
34 www.archinoe.net/console/ir_visu_instrument.php?depot=AD73&ir=CHATELLENIES [01/03/2022]
35 CROSBY, *The Measure of Reality;* BOMPAIRE, "Compétences et pratiques de calcul".
36 VIARD, *Les journaux du Trésor de Philippe IV le Bel.*
37 See ANHEIM, FELLER, JEAY, and MILANI (ed.) *Le pouvoir des listes.*
38 On the link between writing down accounts and socio-political struggles, see RIGAUDIÈRE, *Saint-Flour*, pp. 175–182; BRIAND, *L'information à Reims*, pp. 292–298. German historiography explains the changes in the form of some municipal accounts by urban revolts in the second half of the fourteenth and early fifteenth centuries; see BUCHHOLZER, "*Inter se computant in secreto*".
39 This was the case as early as 1296–1297, during the numerous "common" revolts in Ghent and other Flemish cities.
40 BIGET, *La fiscalité des villes*, conclusions, vol. 4, p. 316 (our translation).
41 BULST and GENET (ed.), *La ville, la bourgeoisie*, p. 9.
42 MATTÉONI, "L'impôt, l'État, la souveraineté…", pp. 195–218.
43 The bibliography cited in the endnotes includes only a selection of particularly representative works. For a more detailed bibliography, please refer to the bibliography at the end of each chapter in Part II.

44 GARNIER, "Fiscalité et finances médiévales".
45 FAVIER, *Finance et fiscalité*, p. 11.
46 For example, at the congress of the Comité des Travaux Historiques et Scientifiques (CTHS) held in Limoges in 1977, we read in the presentation that the two history departments that had organised it had agreed on the themes of the history of mentalities, the history of the Limousine, and, incidentally, the history of taxation, and the session on this theme attracted only a few participants.
47 With very few exceptions such as BONNEY (ed.). *Economic Systems and State Finance* and Ibid. *The rise of the fiscal state*.
48 They fill a chapter in *l'Histoire de l'Europe urbaine*, pp. 568–578.
49 *L'impôt dans le cadre de la ville et de l'État*.
50 The *Annals of Historical Demography* was founded in 1964.
51 For France, see the balance drawn up by FAVIER, "Histoire administrative et financière du Moyen Âge occidental", 1967–1968, pp. 355–360, 1968–1969, pp. 313–316 and 1969–1970, pp. 417–423; Id., "L'histoire administrative et financière du Moyen Âge depuis dix ans", pp. 427–503.
52 ESMEIN, *Cours élémentaire d'histoire du droit français*; VIOLLET, *Histoire des institutions*, especially volume 2, and volume 3; BORRELLI DE SERRES, *Recherches*; DOGNON, *Les institutions politiques*; DECLAREUIL *Histoire générale du droit français*; CHÉNON, *Histoire générale du droit français*; OLIVIER-MARTIN, *Histoire du droit français*, p. 708; Ibid., *Histoire des institutions politiques*, t. 3, pp. 447–448.
53 CLAMAGERAN, *Histoire de l'impôt en France*; VUITRY, *Etudes sur le régime financier*; SAY, *Dictionnaire des finances*; DUPONT-FERRIER, *Études sur les institutions financières*; LOT and FAWTIER, *Histoire des institutions*.
54 von BELOW, "Die älteste deutsche Steuer"; STEEL, "English Government Finance"; MCFARLANE, "Henry IV's government finance"; LYON and VERHULST, *Medieval Finance*; GARCÍA DE VALDEAVELLANO, *Curso de historia*; Josep María FONT RIUS, "La administración financiera", pp. 191–215
55 MONTAGUT, *El Mestre Racional a la Corona d'Aragó*; TURULL, *La configuración jurídica del municipi*.
56 ESPINAS, *Les finances de la commune de Douai*.
57 RIGAUDIÈRE, *Saint-Flour*.
58 GARNIER, *Un consulat et ses finances*; TURULL, *La configuració jurídica del municipi*.
59 SCHUMPETER, *The Crisis of the Tax State*.
60 BACKHAUS, "Fiscal Sociology".
61 ARDANT, *Théorie sociologique*, see the graph summarising Ardant's model in TILLY, *The Formation*, reprinted by WAQUET, *Le Grand-Duché*, pp. 144.
62 ANDERSON, *Passages from Antiquity*; WICKHAM, *Framing the Early Middle Ages*.
63 BOIS, *Crisis of Feudalism*, p. 364; Ibid., *La grande dépression médiévale*; the economic approach to the feudal system was theorised by KULA, *Economic Theory of the Feudal System*.
64 MILLER, "War, taxation"; HILTON, "Introduction".
65 STEEL, *The Receipt of the Exchequer*; MITCHELL, *Taxation in Medieval England*; HARRISS, *King, Parliament and Public Finance*; PRESTWITCH, *War, Politics and Finance under Edward I*.
66 REY, *Le domaine du roi*; HENNEMAN, *Royal Taxation*; KERHERVÉ, *L'Etat breton aux 14e et 15e siècles*.
67 VAN NIEUWENHUYSEN, *The Finances of the Duke of Burgund*.
68 LADERO QUESADA, *La hacienda real de Castilla en el siglo XV*.
69 KÜCHLER, *Die Finanzen der Krone Aragon*; BISSON, *Fiscal accounts*; SESMA MUÑOZ, *La Diputación del reino de Aragón*; SÁNCHEZ MARTÍNEZ, *La Corona de Aragón y el Reino Nazarí de Granada*.
70 MOXÓ, *Les alcabalas*; BERESFORD, *Lay subsidies and Poll taxes*; GONÇALVES, *Pedidos e empréstimos*; SAMARAN and MOLLAT, *La fiscalité pontificale en France*.
71 CHEVALIER, "Fiscalité municipale et fiscalité d'État en France", p. 144 (our translation).
72 VAN WERVEKE, *De Gentsche stadsfinanciën*.
73 CLAUZEL, *Finance and Politics*.
74 For a general overview of the fiscal history of Italian cities in the Middle Ages, see MAINONI, "Finanza pubblica e fiscalità", pp. 449–470 and *Politiche finanziarie e fiscali*.
75 The two pioneering books remain those of BARBADORO, *Le finanze della repubblica fiorentina* and LUZZATTO, *I prestiti della Repubblica di Venezia*.
76 BOWSKY, *The finance of the Commune of Siena*; MOLHO, *Florentine Public Finances*; GROHMANN, *L'imposizione diretta nei comuni*; CONTI, *l'imposta diretta a Firenze*.
77 For a brief but accurate of the taxation of German cities, see BUCHHOLZER, "L'impôt direct à Nuremberg", pp. 196–198.

78 SANDER, *Die reichsstädttische Haushaltung Nürnberg*; FENGLER, "Untersuchungen zu den Einahmen und Ausgaben der stadt Greifswald"; KIRCHGÄSSNER, *Das Steuerwesen der Reichsstadt Konstanz*; ROSEN, *Verwaltung und Ungeld in Basel*; KÖRNER, *Luzerner Staatsfinanzen*; RANFT, *Der Basishaushalt der Stadt Lüneburg.*

79 HUMBERT, *Les finances municipales de Dijon*, revenues are twice as important as expenses; LEGUAY, *La ville de Rennes.*

80 This is what emerges from the assessment presented by COLLANTES DE TERÁN SÁNCHEZ, "Los estudios sobre las haciendas concejiles", pp. 323–340. However, we should mention for their pioneering approach, LACARRA, "Le budget de la ville de Saragosse", pp. 381–384; PALACIOS MARTÍN and FALCÓN PÉREZ, "La hacienda municipal de Zaragoza", pp. 539–606; MENJOT, *Fiscalidad y sociedad*.

81 ROUSTIT, *La consolidation de la dette publique*, pp. 15–156; BROUSSOLLE, *Les impositions municipaux.*

82 FAVIER, *Les Finances pontificales.*

83 FAVIER, *Finance et Fiscalité.*

84 BALANDIER, *Anthropologie politique.*

85 This is the 1971 plea by LE GOFF, "L'histoire politique".

86 STRAYER, *On the Medieval Origins of the Modern State.*

87 TILLY (ed.), *The Formation of National States.*

88 TILLY, *Coercion, Capital, and European States.*

89 For the historiographic context of this programme, see MATTÉONI, "L'impôt, l'Etat, la souveraineté".

90 GENET, "The Genesis of the Modern State: Genesis of a Research Programme"; BÉGUIN and GENET, "Fiscalité et genèse de l'Etat".

91 BONNEY (ed.), *Economic Systems and State Finance*, "Introduction"; BONNEY (ed.), *The rise of the fiscal state.*

92 The term was introduced by HOFFMAN and NORBERG, *Fiscal Crises, Liberty*, Introduction, p. 2.

93 As already indicated, the point of departure for this trend comes from BONNEY (ed.), *Economic Systems and State Finance*; BONNEY (ed.), *The rise of the fiscal state*; ORMROD, BONNEY, and BONNEY (ed.), *Crises, Revolutions.*

94 Their notion of the "fiscal state" thus corresponds to what historians of early modern England (and elsewhere) have often called the "fiscal military state": that is, a political system where taxation is driven and determined primarily by the presence of war, and where the function and presence of the state tends significantly to subside during periods of truce and peace.

95 CAROCCI and COLLAVINI, "The Costs of States"; see also, GINATEMPO, "Esisteva una fiscalità".

96 BRAYSON, "Deficit Finance", pp. 8–65, p. 63. By the same author, see also the interesting reflections in *Fiscal Historiography: Towards a Collaborative Research Agenda.*

97 See the introduction, MONSON and SCHEIDEL (ed.), *Fiscal Regimes*; YUN CASALILLA and O'BRIEN, (ed.), *The Rise of fiscal states.*

98 ERTMAN, *Birth of the Leviathan.*

99 WAQUET, *Le Grand Duché de Toscane*. p. 175.

100 WAQUET, *Le Grand Duché de Toscane*, p. 192.

101 BONNEY, *What's New about the New French Fiscal History?*

102 For example, CONTAMINE, KERHERVÉ, and RIGAUDIÈRE, *L'impôt au Moyen Âge*. See other studies in the institution's catalogue: www.economie.gouv.fr/igpde-editions-publications/xixe-xxe-siecles/finances [01/03/2022].

103 Directed by Ángel GALÁN SÁNCHEZ at the University of Málaga, "*Arca Comunis*. Red interuniversitaria de investigación cooperativa de estudios sobre Historia de la Hacienda y la Fiscalidad hispana (siglos XIII-XVIII)", in *La historiografía medieval en España y la conformación de equipos de trabajo: los proyectos de investigación I+D+i*, Murcia, 2020, pp. 76–79; www.arcacomunis.uma.es

104 See the two exhaustive historiographical syntheses of LADERO QUESADA, "Estado, hacienda, fiscalidad y finanzas", LADERO QUESADA, "Lo antiguo y lo nuevo".

105 The assessment is less negative than that made in 2003 by DUARTE, "Fiscalidade Municipal Portuguesa", because particularly important have been the PhDs of HENRIQUES, "The Rise of a Tax State: Portugal" and DOMINGUEZ, *Fiscal Policy*.

106 CAVACIOCCHI (ed.), *La fiscalità nell'economia europea*. It retraces the evolution of taxation systems in Europe between the thirteenth and eighteenth centuries. Direct and indirect taxes, duties, levies, franchises, mandatory loans and public debt are all analysed, focusing attention on the dialectical relationship between the state and citizens, and on taxation as an instrument of power, diversified over

time and space. It follows another conference of the same institute, *Prodotto lordo e finanza pubblica*. See these other *settimane* at www.istitutodatini.it/collane/htm/atti.htm [01/03/2022].
107 Sánchez Martínez and Furió, *Corona, municipis i fiscalitat*.
108 Menjot, Rigaudière and Sánchez Martínez, *L'impôt dans les villes*; Menjot and Sánchez Martínez, *Fiscalidad de Estado*.
109 Ginatempo, *Prima del debito*.
110 Boone, "Stratégies fiscales et financières".
111 Sánchez Martínez, "Dette publique".
112 Examples include: Beguin (ed.), *Ressources publiques* and Stasavage, *States of Credit*.
113 We will cite here a few essential works, referring to the bibliography at the end of each chapter for specialised studies.
114 Isenmann, "Les théories du Moyen Âge", pp. 4–35; Scordia, "*Le roi doit vivre du sien*"; Verdés Pijuan, "Fiscalidad urbana", pp. 71–110. See also chapter 3.
115 Garnier, "L'impôt d'après quelques traités fiscaux".
116 See for example, Menjot, "L'impôt: péché des puissants".
117 Cf. Scordia, "L'enseignement fiscal de Louis XI".
118 Garnier, " Justifier le financement de la dépense ".
119 A Castilian example is Ortego Rico, "Monarquía, nobleza y pacto".
120 Watts, *The Making of Polities*, pp. 233–234.
121 Hébert, *Parlementer*, p. 433 (our translation).
122 Sánchez Martínez, "Negociación y fiscalidad", p. 143 (our translation).
123 Hébert, "Les chemins du dialogue" and Hébert, *Parlementer*.
124 Russell, *The just war*.
125 An example in France, Henneman, *Royal Taxation*; in England, Liddy, *War, Politics and Finance*.
126 Moreover, in the northern towns of the Kingdom of France, fines were often expressed not in money but in a number of bricks, a practice that reflects the fact that the original purpose of the fine was to contribute to the collective effort of building the walls.
127 Kempshall, *The Common Good*; Lecuppre-Desjardin and Van Bruaene (ed.), *De Bono Communi*; Collard (dir.), *Pouvoir d'un seul*.
128 Most recently, on these issues in the Iberian kingdoms, see Laliena Corbera, Lafuente Gómez and Galan Sánchez, *Fisco, legitimidad y conflict*; see also an example, Caesar, "Small towns and Resistance".
129 Garnier, Menjot, and Verdès Pijuan (ed.), "Introducción", *Fraude et evasion fiscale*.
130 Mollat and Wolff, *Ongles bleus*; Pezzolo, "Rivolte fiscali in Italia"; Verdès Pijuan and Reixach Sala "Contre l'impôt".
131 Fryde, "The Financial Policies".
132 Mainoni, *Politiche finanziarie*; Caesar, *Le pouvoir en ville*.
133 Genet and Le Mené (ed.), *Genèse de l'État moderne*.
134 Boone, "Strategie fiscali e finanziarie " and Collantes de Terán Sánchez, "Interessi privati", pp. 37–56 and 57–74.
135 Menjot and Sánchez Martínez, *La fiscalité des villes*, vol. 3 *La redistribution*; Galán Sánchez and Carretero Zamora (ed.), *El alimento del Estado*.
136 Rigaudière. *Saint-Flour*.
137 Some especially evocative works: Furio, "Deuda publica"; Id., "La dette dans les dépenses municipales", pp. 321–350; Ginatempo, *Prima del debito*; Sánchez Martínez (ed.), "Dette publique".
138 Stasavage, "Why Did Public Debt Originate in Europe?"
139 Ginatempo, *Prima del debito*; Boone, Davids, and Janssens (éds.), *Urban public debts*; Sánchez Martínez, *La deuda pública*.
140 Sánchez Martínez, *El naixement de la fiscalitat d'Estat*
141 Boone, "Plus deuil que joie", pp. 3–25.
142 *Les serviteurs de l'État*; Galan Sánchez and Garcia Fernández, *En busca de Zaqueo*; García Fernández and Vítores Casado (ed.), *Tesoreros, "arrendadores"*; Garnier, *Un consulat et ses finances*; pp. 339–521. Montagut Estragués, *El Maestro Racional*.
143 Ladero Quesada, *Judíos y conversos de Castilla*.
144 Kusman, *Usuriers publics et banquiers du Prince*.
145 Ortego rico, *Poder financiero y gestión tributaria*.
146 *Les Chambres des comptes*; Feller (ed.), *Contrôler les agents du pouvoir*, pp. 191–209.

147 Mattéoni, "Vérifier, corriger, juger", p. 67 (our translation).
148 Among the most recent examples, Menjot, "Protagonistas"; Ortega Cera, "El arrendamiento de rentas".
149 Degenne and Forsé, *Introducing Social Networks*; Requena Santos, *Análisis de redes sociales*.
150 For an excellent use of this method see Ortego Rico, "Arrendadores mayores y arrendadores menores", pp. 99–116, using two software packages for social network analysis, Ucinet and Netdraw.
151 Garnier, "Le roi, l'emprunt et l'impôt", pp. 157–184, which outlines a research programme on tax information.
152 Chevalier, "Fiscalité municipale et fiscalité d'État en France".
153 Among others, Ormrod, "Urban communities and royal finance", pp. 45–60; Sánchez Martínez (ed.), *Fiscalidad real y finanzas urbanas*; Menjot and Sánchez Martínez (ed.), *Fiscalidad de Estado y fiscalidad municipal*.
154 Chevalier, "Fiscalité municipale et fiscalité d'État en France"; Menjot, "Système fiscal étatique et systèmes fiscaux municipaux", pp. 21–52.
155 *La gènesi de la fiscalitat municipal*.
156 Chevalier, "La fiscalité urbaine en France", pp. 61–78.
157 Rigaudiere, "Les origines médiévales de l'impôt", p. 287.
158 Mainoni, *Le radici della Discordia*.
159 Sánchez Martínez and Hebert, "La part du prince", pp. 295–320.
160 Boone, "Stratégies fiscales et financières", pp. 235–253.
161 However, lacking the basic knowledge of the semiology of graphics, see Bertin, *La graphique*; Vergnault-Belmont, *L'œil qui pense*, historians, either out of habit or because they are not at ease with mathematics, frequently use charts that illustrate more than they demonstrate, and are ultimately less useful than a simple table of figures.
162 This is the method used in the book edited by Bonney, *Economic Systems and State Finance*, all graphics are harmonised in this way.
163 AMADO online https://paris-timemachine.huma-num.fr/amado/
164 This is the method used by Menjot, "Le système fiscal de Murcie...", pp. 473–475.
165 Guerreau, "Analyse statistique des finances municipales de Dijon", pp. 5–34; *Notes statistiques sur les jardins de Saint-Flour*, pp. 341–357.
166 Such as the vocabulary of taxation in Critical Glossary of Medieval Taxation (http://www.medieval-fiscal-glossary.net/) *Glossaire de fiscalité médiévale* or the pioneering work of semantic analysis of economic and financial vocabulary based on French texts from 1355-1405 in Ancelet-Netter, *La dette, la dîme et le denier*.

References

Jean-Loup Abbé (ed.), *Estimes, compoix et cadastres: histoire d'un patrimoine commun de l'Europe méridionale*, Toulouse, 2017.
Dominique Adrian, "Penser la politique dans les villes allemandes à la fin du Moyen Âge. Traités de gouvernement et réalités urbaines", in *Histoire urbaine*, 38, 2013, pp. 175–194.
Dominique Ancelet-Netter, *La dette, la dîme et le denier: une analyse sémantique du vocabulaire économique et financier au Moyen Âge*, Villeneuve d'Ascq, 2010.
Perry Anderson, *Passages from Antiquitty to Feudalism*, London, 1974.
Étienne Anheim and Valérie Theis (ed.), *Les comptabilités pontificales*, Mélanges de l'École française de Rome. Moyen-Âge, 118/2, 2006.
Étienne Anheim and Laurent Feller, Madeleine Jeay, and Giuliano Milani (ed.), *Le pouvoir des listes au Moyen Âge – II. Liste d'objets/listes de personnes*, Paris, 2020.
Gabriel Ardant, *Théorie sociologique de l'impôt*, t. 2, Paris, 1965.
Gabriel Ardant, *Histoire de l'impôt*, 2 vol. Paris, Fayard, 1971–1972.
Gabriel Ardant, *Histoire financière de l'antiquité à nos jours*, Paris, 1976.
Ludovic Ayrault and Florent Garnier, *La famille et l'impôt*, Rennes, 2009.
Ludovic Ayrault and Florent Garnier (dir.), *Passé et présent du discours fiscal en Europe*, Bruxelles, 2014.
Jürgen Backhaus, "Fiscal sociology: What for?", *American Journal of Economics and Sociology*, 2002, pp. 55–77.

Georges BALANDIER, *Anthropologie politique*, Paris, 1967.
Bernardino BARBADORO, *Le finanze della repubblica Fiorentina. Imposta diretta e debito pubblico fino all'istituzione del Monte*, Florence, 1929.
Attilio BARTOLI LANGELI, *Codice diplomatico del Comune di Perugia*, vol. 1, Perugia, 1983.
Robert-Henri BAUTIER, Janine SORNAY, *Les sources de l'histoire économique et sociale du Moyen Âge*, 4 vol., Paris, 1968–1984.
Patrice BECK, "Les comptabilités de la commune de Dijon", *Comptabilités* [Online], 2, 2011, http://journals.openedition.org/comptabilites/371 [01/03/2022].
Patrice BECK, *Archéologie d'un document d'archives. Approche codicologique et diplomatique des cherches des feux bourguignonnes (1285–1543)*, Paris, 2006.
Katia BÉGUIN (ed.), *Ressources publiques et construction étatique en Europe. XIIIe–XVIIIe siècle*, Paris, 2015.
Katia BÉGUIN and Jean-Philippe GENET, "Fiscalité et genèse de l'Etat: remarques introductives", in *Ressources publiques et construction étatique en Europe. XIIIe-XVIIIe siècle*, Paris, 2015, pp. 3–15.
Georg von BELOW, "Die älteste deutsche Steuer", in Ibid., *Probleme der Wirtschaftsgeschichte. Eine Einführung in das Studium der Wirtschaftsgeschichte*, Tübingen, 1920, pp. 622–662.
Georg von BELOW, *Die landständische Verfassung in Jülich und Berg bis zum Jahre 1511*, 3 vol., Düsseldorf, 1885–1891.
Maurice Warwick BERESFORD, *The Lay Subsidies: The Poll Taxes of 1377, 1379, and 1381*, Canterbury, 1963.
Jacques BERTIN, *La graphique et le traitement graphique de l'information*, Paris, 1977.
Jean-louis BIGET, "La gestion de l'impôt dans les villes (XIIIe–XVe siècle): Essai de synthèse", in *La fiscalité des villes au Moyen Âge*, vol. 4: *La gestion de l'impôt*, ed. Denis MENJOT and Manuel SÁNCHEZ MARTÍNEZ, Toulouse, 2004, pp. 311–336.
Thomas N. BISSON, *Fiscal Accounts of Catalonia under the Early Count-Kings, 1151–1213*, Berkeley and Los Angeles, 1984.
Guy BOIS, *Crise du féodalisme. Économie rurale et démographie en Normandie orientale du début du XIVe siècle au milieu du XVIe siècle*, Paris, 1976.
Guy BOIS, *La grande dépression médiévale, XIVe et XVe siècles. Le précédent d'une crise systémique*, Paris, 2000.
Marc BOMPAIRE, "Compétences et pratiques de calcul dans les livres de changeurs français (XIVe–XVe siècles)", in *Écrire, compter, mesurer. Vers une histoire des rationalités pratiques*, ed. Natascha COQUERY, François MENANT, and Florence WEBER, Paris, 2006, pp. 143–162.
Richard BONNEY, "What's New about the New French Fiscal History?", in *The Journal of Modern History*, 70, 1998, pp. 639–667.
Richard BONNEY (ed.), *Economic Systems and State Finance*, Oxford, 1995.
Richard BONNEY (ed.), *The rise of the fiscal state in Europe, c. 1200–1815*, Oxford, 1999.
Marc BOONE, "*Plus dueil que joie*. Les ventes de rentes par la ville de Gand pendant la période bourguignonne: entre intérêts privés et finances publiques", in *Bulletin trimestriel du Crédit Communal de Belgique*, 176, 1991, pp. 3–25.
Marc BOONE, "Stratégies fiscales et financières des élites urbaines et de l'Etat bourguignon naissant dans l'ancien comté de Flandre (XIVe-XVIe siècle)", in *L'argent au Moyen Âge: idéologie, finances, fiscalité, monnaie (Actes du XXVIIe congrès de la Société des Médiévistes de l'Enseignement Supérieur, Clermont-Ferrand, 30 mai-1er juin, 1997)*, Paris, 1998, pp. 235–253.
Marc BOONE, Karel DAVIDS and Paul JANSSENS (ed.), *Urban public debts: urban government and the market for annuities in Western Europe (14th-18th centuries)*, Turnhout, 2003.
Léon-Louis BORRELLI DE SERRES, *Recherches sur divers services publics du XIIIe au XVIIe siècle*, Paris, 1895.
Patrick BOUCHERON, Denis MENJOT, with Marc BOONE, *Histoire de l'Europe urbaine*, vol. 2: *La ville médiévale*, Paris, 2011.
Monique BOURIN, Giovanni CHERUBINI and Giuliano PINTO (ed.), *Rivolte urbane e rivolte contadine nell'Europa del Trecento: un confronto*, Florence, 2008.
William M. BOWSKY, *The finance of the Commune of Siena, 1287–1355*, Oxford, 1970.
Alex BRAYSON, "Deficit Finance during the Early Majority of Henry VI of England, 1436–1444. The 'Crisis' of the Medieval Engish 'Tax State'", in *The Journal of European Economic History*, 49/1, 2020, pp. 9–73.
Alex BRAYSON, "Fiscal Historiography: Towards a Collaborative Research Agenda", https://thefiscalhistorycommunity.blogspot.com/2020/08/fiscal-historiography-towards.html [01/03/2022].
Julien BRIAND, *L'information à Reims aux XIVe et XVe siècles*, Unpublished PhD Thesis, 2012.
Jean BROUSSOLLE, "Les impositions municipaux de Barcelone de 1328 à 1462", in *Estudios de Historia Moderna*, 5, 1955, pp. 1–164.

Laurence BUCHHOLZER, "L'impôt direct à Nuremberg: de son établissement à son encaissement (XIIIᵉ-XVᵉ siècles)", in *Cahiers d'histoire*, 44/2, 1999, pp. 196–198.

Laurence BUCHHOLZER, "Ungeld, Umgeld, Ohmgal, Angal: discours sur une taxation indirecte", in *Cultures fiscales en Occident du Xe au XVIIe siècle. Etudes offertes à Denis Menjot*, ed. Florent GARNIER, Armand JAMME, Anne LEMONDE, and Pere VERDÉS PIJUAN, Toulouse, 2019, pp. 27–40.

Laurence BUCHHOLZER "La textualité des comptes municipaux au prisme de l'historiographie allemande", in *Les comptes et les choses. Discours et pratiques comptables du XIIIᵉ au XVᵉ siècle en Occident (principautés, monarchies et mondes urbains)*, t.1, ed. Anne LEMONDE, Rennes, PUR, 2022.

Laurence BUCHHOLZER, "Les comptabilités municipales en terres d'Empire. Un bilan historiographique", *Comptabilités* [Online], 13, 2020, http://journals.openedition.org.scd-rproxy.u-strasbg.fr/comptabilites/4271 [01/03/2022].

Jean BROUSSOLLE, "Les impositions municipaux de Barcelone de 1328 à 1462", in *Estudios de Historia Moderna*, 5, 1955, pp. 1–164.

Paolo BUFFO, "Prassi documentarie e gestione delle finanze nei comuni del principato di Savoia-Acaia (Moncalieri, Pinerolo, Torino, fine secolo XIII-prima metà secolo XIV)", in *Scrineum Rivista*, 11, 2014, pp. 217–259.

Mathieu CAESAR, *Le pouvoir en ville. Gestion urbaine et pratiques politiques à Genève (fin XIIIᵉ-début XVIᵉ siècles)*, Turnhout, 2011.

Mathieu CAESAR, "Juridical Uncertainty and Resistance to royal taxation and rural revolts in late medieval France: the case of Beauvoir-sur-Mer and Bois-de-Céné (1480)", in *Journal of Medieval History*, 43/3, 2017, pp. 342–358.

Mathieu CAESAR, "Small towns and Resistance to Taxation in Late Medieval Savoy", in *Cultures fiscales en Occident du Xᵉ au XVIIᵉ siècle. Etudes offertes à Denis Menjot*, in ed. Florent GARNIER, Armand JAMME, Anne LEMONDE, and Pere VERDÉS PIJUAN, Toulouse, 2019, pp. 325–334.

Paolo CAMMAROSANO, *L'italia medievale. Struttura e geografia delle fonti scritte*, Rome, 2016.

Sandro CAROCCI and Simone M. COLLAVINI, "The Costs of States. Politics and Exactions in the Christian West (Sixth to Fifteenth Centuries)", in *Diverging Paths? The Shapes of Power and Institutions in Medieval Christendom and Islam*, ed. John HUDSON and Ana RODRÍGUEZ, Leiden, 2014, pp. 123–158.

Juan CARRASCO PÉREZ et al. (ed.), *Acta vectigalia regni Navarrae. Documentos financieros para el estudio de la Hacienda Real de Navarra. Serie I, comptos reales, registros*, 17 vol., Pamplona, 1999–2009.

Simonetta CAVACIOCCHI (ed.), *La fiscalità nell'economia europea secc. XIII-XVIII. Atti della "Trentanovesima Settimana di Studi" 22–26 aprile 2007*, Florence, 2008.

Emile CHÉNON, *Histoire générale du droit français public et privé, des origines à 1815*, 2 vol., Paris, 1926–1929.

Bernard CHEVALIER, "Fiscalité municipale et fiscalité d'État en France du XIVᵉ à la fin du XVIᵉ siècle, deux systèmes liés et concurrents", in *Genèse de l'État moderne: Prélèvement et redistribution: actes du colloque de Fontevraud, 1984*, ed. Jean-Philippe GENET and Michel LE MENÉ, Paris, 1987, pp. 137–151.

Bernard CHEVALIER, "La fiscalité urbaine en France, un champ d'expérience pour la fiscalité d'Etat", in *Corona, municipis i fiscalitat a la Baixa Edat Mitjana*, ed. Manuel SÁNCHEZ MARTÍNEZ and Antoni FURIÓ, Lleida, 1997, pp. 61–78.

Jean-Jules CLAMAGERAN, *Histoire de l'impôt en France*, Paris, 1867.

Michael T. CLANCHY, *From Memory to Written Record. England 1066–1307*, Oxford, 1993.

Denis CLAUZEL, *Finances et politique à Lille pendant la période bourguignonne*, Dunkerque, 1982.

Samuel Kline COHN, *Lust for Liberty the politics of social revolt in medieval Europe, 1200–1425. Italy, France, and Flanders*, Cambridge, 2006.

Antonio COLLANTES DE TERÁN SÁNCHEZ (ed.), *Fuentes para el estudio de negocio fiscal y financiero en los reinos hispánicos (siglos XIV-XVI)*, Madrid, 2010.

Antonio COLLANTES DE TERÁN SÁNCHEZ and Denis MENJOT, "Hacienda y fiscalidad concejiles en la Corona de Castilla en la Edad Media", in *Historia, instituciones, documentos*, 23, 1996, pp. 213–254.

Antonio COLLANTES DE TERÁN SÁNCHEZ, "Ciudades y fiscalidad", in *Actas del VI coloquio internacional de historia medieval de Andalucía: las ciudades andaluzas, siglos XIII-XVI (Estepona, 1990)*, ed. José Enrique LÓPEZ DE COCA CASTAÑER and Angel GALÁN SÁNCHEZ, Malaga, 1991, pp. 129–149.

Antonio COLLANTES DE TERÁN SÁNCHEZ, "Los estudios sobre las haciendas concejiles españolas en la Edad Media", in *Anuario de Estudios Medievales*, 22, 1992, pp. 323–340.

Antonio COLLANTES DE TERÁN, "Interessi privati e finanze pubbliche: comportamenti delle oligarchie urbane dei grandi regni ispanici (secoli XIV–XV9", in *Cheiron*, 24, 1995, pp. 57–73.

Franck COLLARD (ed.), *Pouvoir d'un seul et bien commun (VIe–XVIe siècle)*, in *Revue française des idées politiques*, 32, 2010, pp. 227–413.

Natascha COQUERY, François MENANT, and Florence WEBER, (ed.), *Écrire, compter, mesurer. Vers une histoire des rationalités pratiques*, Paris, 2006.

Philippe CONTAMINE and Olivier MATTÉONI (ed.), *La France des principautés: les chambres des comptes, XIVe et XVe siècles. Colloque tenu aux Archives Départementales de l'Allier, Moulin-Yzeure, 6–8 avril 1995*, Paris, 1996.

PHILIPPE CONTAMINE and OLIVIER MATTÉONI (ed.), *Les Chambres des comptes en France aux XIVe et XVe siècles. Textes et documents*, Paris, 1998.

Philippe CONTAMINE, Jean KERHERVÉ, and Albert RIGAUDIÈRE (ed.), *L'impôt au Moyen Âge, l'impôt public et le prélèvement seigneurial fin XIIe-début XVIe siècle*, 3 vol., Paris, 2002.

Elio CONTI, *l'imposta diretta a Firenze nel Quattrocento (1427–1494)*, Rome, 1984.

Alfred W. CROSBY, *The measure of reality: Quantification and western society, 1250–1600*, Cambridge, 1997.

Joseph DECLAREUIL, *Histoire générale du droit français des origines à 1789*, Paris, 1925.

Alain DEGENNE and Michel FORSÉ, *Introducing social networks*, London, 1999.

Alain DERVILLE, *Enquêtes fiscales de la Flandre wallonne (1449–1549). 1: L'enquête de 1449*, Lille, 1983.

Paul DOGNON, *Les institutions politiques et administratives du pays de Languedoc, du XIIIe siècle aux guerres de religion*, Paris, 1895.

Rodrigo da Costa DOMINGUEZ, *Fiscal Policy in Early Modern Europe: Portugal in Comparative Context*, New York-London, 2019.

Luís Miguel DUARTE, "Fiscalidade Municipal Portuguesa (estado da questão)", in *El món urbà a la Corona d'Aragó del 1137 als decrets de Nova Planta*, ed. Salvador CLARAMUNT RODRÍGUEZ, vol. 3, Barcelona, 2003, pp. 231–244.

Gustave DUPONT-FERRIER, *Études sur les institutions financières de la France à la fin du Moyen-Âge*, 2 vol., Paris, 1930–1932.

Adhémar ESMEIN, *Cours élémentaire d'histoire du droit français à l'usage des étudiants de première année*, Paris, 1892 (11th ed., 1912).

Études sur la fiscalité au Moyen Age, Actes du 102e Congrès National des Sociétés Savantes: Limoges, 1977. Section de philologie et d'histoire jusqu'à 1610, vol. 1, Paris, 1979.

Thomas ERTMAN, *Birth of the Leviathan: building states and regimes in medieval and early modern Europe*, New York, 1997.

Georges ESPINAS, *Les finances de la commune de Douai des origines au 15e siècle*, Paris, 1902.

Jean FAVIER, *Les Finances pontificales à l'époque du Grand Schisme d'Occident, 1378–1409*, Paris, 1966.

Jean FAVIER, "Histoire administrative et financière du Moyen Âge occidental", in *École pratique des hautes études. 4e section, Sciences historiques et philologiques. Annuaire*, 1966, pp. 323–329; 1968, pp. 355–360; 1969, pp. 313–316; 1970, pp. 417–423; 1971 pp. 449–454.

Jean FAVIER, "L'histoire administrative et financière du Moyen Âge depuis dix ans", in *Bibliothèque de l'École des Chartes*, 126, 1968, pp. 427–503.

Jean FAVIER, *Finances et fiscalité au bas Moyen Age*, Paris, 1971.

Robert FAWTIER, *Comptes royaux, 1285–1314*, 3 vol., Paris, 1953–1956.

Georg FENGLER, *Untersuchungen zu den Einnahmen und Ausgaben der Stadt Greifswald im 14. und beginnenden 15. Jahrhundert*, Greifswald, 1936.

José María FONT RIUS, "La administración financiera en los municipios catalanes medievales", in *Historia de la Hacienda española (épocas antigua y medieval)*, Madrid, 1982, pp. 291–315.

Edmund B. FRYDE, "The Financial Policies of the Royal Governments and Popular Resistance to them in France and England, c. 1290–c. 1420 ", in *Revue belge de Philologie et d'Histoire*, 57–4, 1979, pp. 824–860.

Arnaud FOSSIER, Johann PETITJEAN and Clémence REVEST (ed.), *Écritures grises. Les instruments de travail des administrations (XIIe-XVIIe siècle)*, Paris-Rome, 2019.

Antoni FURIÓ, "Deuda publica e intereses privados. Finanzas y fiscalidad municipales en la Corona de Aragón", in *Edad Media. Revista de historia*, 2, 1999, pp. 35–80.

Antoni FURIÓ, "La dette dans les dépenses municipales", in *La fiscalité des villes au Moyen Âge (Occident méditerranéen). 3: La redistribution de l'impôt*, ed. Denis MENJOT and Manuel SÁNCHEZ MARTÍNEZ, Toulouse, 2002, pp. 321–350.

Angel GALAN SÁNCHEZ and Ernesto GARCIA FERNÁNDEZ (ed.), *En busca de Zaqueo: los recaudadores de impuestos en las épocas medieval y moderna*, Madrid, 2012.

Angel GALÁN SÁNCHEZ and Juan Manuel CARRETERO ZAMORA (ed.), *El alimento del Estado y la salud de la Res Publica: Orígenes, estructura y desarrollo del gasto público en Europa*, Madrid, 2013.

Ernesto García Fernández and Imanol Vítores Casado (ed.), *Tesoreros, "arrendadores" y financieros en los reinos hispánicos: la Corona de Castilla y el Reino de Navarra, siglos XIV–XVII*, Madrid, 2012.

Luis García de Valdeavellano, *Curso de historia de las instituciones españolas. De los orígenes al final de la Edad Media*, Madrid, 1952.

Florent Garnier, *Un consulat et ses finances: Millau (1187–1461)*, Paris, 2006.

Florent Garnier, "Fiscalité et Finance Médiévales: Un État de La Recherche", in *Revue Historique de Droit Français et Étranger*, 86/3, 2008, pp. 443–452.

Florent Garnier, "Justifier le financement de la dépense au Moyen Âge", in *El alimento del Estado y la salud de la Res Publica: Orígenes, estructura y desarrollo del gasto público en Europa*, ed. Angel Galán Sánchez and Juan Manuel Carretero Zamora, Madrid, 2013, pp. 51–72

Florent Garnier, " L'impôt d'après quelques traités fiscaux (XIVᵉ–XVIᵉ siècles)", in *Passé et présent du discours fiscal en Europe*, ed. Ludovic Ayrault and Florent Garnier, Bruxelles, 2014, pp. 64–114.

Florent Garnier, "Le roi, l'emprunt et l'impôt: considérations pour une histoire de l'information fiscale et financière au bas Moyen Âge", in *XLI Semana de Estudios Medievales, 2014, Estados y mercados financieros en el Occidente cristiano (siglos XIII–XVI)*, Estella, 2015, pp. 157–184.

Florent Garnier, Denis Menjot, and Pere Verdès Pijuan, "Introduction. Fraude et evasion fiscale au Moyen Âge et à l'époque moderne", in *Baetica. Estudios de Arte, Geografía e Historia*, 36–37, 2015, pp. 7–10.

Jean-Philippe Genet and Michel Le Mené (ed.), *Genèse de l'État moderne: Prélèvement et redistribution: actes du colloque de Fontevraud, 1984*, Paris, 1987.

Jean-Philippe Genet, "La genèse de l'État moderne: genèse d'un programme de recherche", in *A génese do estado moderno no Portugal tardo-medievo: séculos XIII–XV*, ed. Maria Helena da Cruz Coelho and Armando de Carvalho Homem, Lisboa, 1999, pp. 21–51.

Maria Ausiliatrice Ginatempo, "Spunti comparativi sulle trasformazioni della fiscalità in età post-comunale", in *Politiche finanziarie e fiscali nell'Italia settentrionale, secoli XIII–XV*, Milano, 2001, pp. 125–220.

Maria Ausiliatrice Ginatempo, *Prima del debito. Finanziamento della spesa pubblica e gestione del deficit nelle grandi città toscane (1200–1350 ca.)*, Florence, 2000.

Maria Ausiliatrice Ginatempo, "Esisteva una fiscalità a finanziamento delle guerre del primo '200?", in *1212–1214. El trieno que hizo a Europa, actas de la XXXVII Semana de Estudios Medievales, Estella. 19 al 23 de julio de 2010*, Pamplona, 2011, pp. 263–342.

Jean Glénisson and Charles Higounet, "Remarques sur les comptes et sur l'administration financière des villes françaises entre Loire et Pyrénées (XIVᵉ-XVIᵉ siècles)", in *Finances et comptabilité urbaines du XIIIe au XVIe siècle: colloque international, Blankenberge, 6–9-IX-1962*, Bruxelles, 1964, pp. 31–67.

Iria Gonçalves, *Pedidos e empréstimos públicos em Portugal Durante a Idade Média*, Lisbon, 1964.

Iria Gonçalves, *As Finanças municipais do Porto na segunda metade do século XV*, Porto, 1987.

Alberto Grohmann, *L'imposizione diretta nei comuni dell'Italia centrale nel XIII secolo. La Libra di Perugia del 1285*, Rome, 1986.

David Grummit and Jean-François Lassalmonie, "Royal public finance (c. 1290–1523)", in *Government and Political Life in England and France, c.1300–c.1500*, ed. Christopher Fletcher, Jean-Philippe Genet, and John Watts, Cambridge, 2015, pp. 116–149.

Annalisa Guarducci (ed.), *Prodotto lordo e finanza pubblica. Secoli XIII–XIX. Atti della "Ottava Settimana di Studi", 3–9 maggio 1976*, Florence, 1988.

Cesare Guasti (ed.), *Lettere di un notaro ad un mercante del secolo XIV / ser Lapo Mazzei*, 2 vol., Florence, 1880.

Alain Guerreau, "Analyse statistique des finances municipales de Dijon au XVᵉ siècle: observations de méthode sur l'analyse factorielle et les procédés classiques", in *Bibliothèque de l'école des chartes*, 140/1, 1982, pp. 5–34.

Alain Guerreau, "Notes statistiques sur les jardins de Saint-Flour au XIVᵉ siècle", in *Les cadastres anciens des villes et leur traitement par l'informatique*, ed. Jean-Louis Biget, Jean-Claude Hervé, and Yvon Thébert, Rome, 1989, pp. 341–357.

Yolanda Guerrero Navarrete, José Antonio Jara Fuente, Juan Carlos Padilla Gómez, José Sánchez Benito, and Ana Concepción Sánchez Pablos, "Fiscalidad de ámbito municipal: en las dos Castillas (siglos XIV y XV): estado de la cuestión", *Medievalismo*, 11, 2001, pp. 225–277.

Gerald Leslie Harriss, *King, parliament, and public finance in medieval England to 1369*, Oxford, 1975.

Michel Hébert, *Parlementer: assemblées représentatives et échange politique en Europe occidentale à la fin du Moyen Âge*, Paris, 2014.

Michel HÉBERT, "Les chemins du dialogue: aller aux Etats dans la Provence des XIVe et XVe siècles" in *Cultures fiscales en Occident du Xe au XVIIe siècle. Etudes offertes à Denis Menjot*, ed. Florent GARNIER, Armand JAMME, Anne LEMONDE, and Pere VERDÉS PIJUAN, Toulouse, 2019, pp. 81–92.

J. B. HENNEMAN, *Royal Taxation in Fourteenth-Century France: The Development of War Financing, 1322–1356*, Princeton, 1971.

J. B. HENNEMAN, *Royal Taxation in Fourteenth-Century France: The Captivity and Ransom of John II, 1356–1370*, Philadelphia, 1976.

António Castro HENRIQUES, "The Rise of a Tax State: Portugal, 1367–1401", in *e-Journal of Portuguese History*, 12/1, 2014.

Rodney H. HILTON, "Introduction" in *The Transition from Feudalism to Capitalism*, ed. Rodney H. Hilton, London, 1976, pp. 9–30.

Jean-Claude HOCQUET, "Cité-Etat et économie marchande", in *Systèmes économiques et finances publiques*, ed. Richard BONNEY, Paris, 1996, pp. 67–86.

Philip T. HOFFMAN and Kathryn NORBERG (ed.), *Fiscal crises, liberty, and representative government, 1450–1789*, Stanford, 1994.

Françoise HUMBERT, *Les finances municipales de Dijon du milieu du XIVe siècle à 1477*, Paris, 1961.

Eberhard ISENMANN, "Les théories du Moyen Âge et de la Renaissance", in *Systèmes économiques et finances publiques*, ed. Richard BONNEY, Paris, 1996, pp. 3–36;

Matthew S. KEMPSHALL, *The Common Good in Late Medieval Political Thought*, Oxford, 1999.

Jean KERHERVÉ, *L'Etat breton aux 14e et 15e siècles. Les Ducs, l'Argent et les Hommes*, 2 vol., Paris, 1987.

Jean KERHERVÉ, "L'historien et les sources financières de la fin du Moyen Âge", in *Le Médiéviste devant ses sources: Questions et méthodes*, ed. Claude CAROZZI and Huguette TAVIANI-CAROZZI, Aix-en-Provence, 2004, pp. 185–206.

Bernhard KIRCHGÄSSNER, *Das Steuerwesen der Reichsstadt Konstanz 1418–1460*, Konstanz, 1960.

Martin KÖRNER, *Luzerner Staatsfinanzen 1415–1798: Strukturen, Wachstum, Konjunkturen*, Luzern, 1981.

Winfried KÜCHLER, *Die Finanzen der Krone Aragon während des 15. Jahrhunderts (Alfons V. und Johann II)*, Aschendorff, 1983.

Witold KULA, *Théorie économique du système féodal. Pour un modèle de l'économie polonaise, XVIe–XVIIIe siècle*, Paris-La Haye, 1970.

David KUSMAN, *Usuriers publics et banquiers du Prince. Le rôle économique des financiers piémontais dans les villes du duché de Brabant (XIIIe-XIVe siècle)*, Turnhout, 2013.

L'impôt dans le cadre de la ville et de l'État. Colloque international, Bruxelles, 1966.

La gènesi de la fiscalitat municipal (segles XII–XIV), Revista d'historia medieval, 7, 1996.

JOSÉ MARÍA LACARRA, " Le budget de la ville de Saragosse au XVe siècle: dépenses et recettes", in *Finances et comptabilité urbaines du XIIIe au XVIe siècle. Colloque international, Blankenberge 6.–9. IX. 1962. Actes*, Bruxelles, 1964, pp. 381–384.

Miguel Ángel LADERO QUESADA, *La hacienda real de Castilla en el siglo XV*, La Laguna, 1973.

Miguel Ángel LADERO QUESADA, *Fiscalidad y poder real en Castilla (1252–1369)*, Madrid, 1993.

Miguel Ángel LADERO QUESADA, *Legislación hacendística de la Corona de Castilla en la Baja Edad Media. Selección y transcripción*, Madrid, 1999.

Miguel Ángel LADERO QUESADA, *La hacienda real de Castilla 1369–1504*, Madrid, 2009.

Miguel Ángel LADERO QUESADA, "Estado, hacienda, fiscalidad y finanzas", in *La historia medieval en España. Un balance historiográfico (1968–1998)*, Pamplona, 1999, pp. 457–504.

Miguel Ángel LADERO QUESADA, "Lo antiguo y lo nuevo de la investigación sobre fiscalidad y poder político en la Baja Edad Media hispánica", in *Estados y mercados financieros en el occidente cristiano (siglos XIII-XVI)*, Pamplona, 2015, pp. 13–54.

Carlos LALIENA CORBERA, Mario LAFUENTE GÓMEZ, and Angel GALÁN SÁNCHEZ (ed.), *Fisco, legitimidad y conflicto en los reinos hispánicos (siglos XIII-XVII): homenaje a José Ángel Sesma Muñoz*, Zaragoza, 2019.

Oliver LANDOLT, *Der Finanzhaushalt der Stadt Schaffhausen im Spätmittelalter*, Ostfildern, 2004.

Jean-François LASSALMONIE, *La boîte à l'enchanteur. Politique financière de Louis XI*, Paris, 2002.

Élodie LECUPPRE-DESJARDIN and Anne-Laure VAN BRUAENE (ed.) *De Bono Communi. The discourse and practice of the common good in the European City (13th-16th c.)*, Turnhout, 2010.

Jacques LE GOFF, "L'histoire politique est-elle toujours l'épine dorsale de l'histoire", republished in *Ibid., L'imaginaire médiéval*, Paris, 1985, pp. 333–349.

Jean-Pierre LEGUAY, *Les comptes des miseurs de la ville de Rennes au XVe siècle*, Rennes, 1968.

Les serviteurs de l'État au Moyen Âge. XXIXe congrès de la Société des Historiens Médiévistes de l'Enseignement Supérieur Public (Pau, mai 1998), Paris, 1999.

Christian LIDDY, *War, Politics and Finance in Late Medieval English Towns: Bristol, York and the Crown, 1350–1400*, Woodbridge, 2005.

Ferdinand LOT and Robert FAWTIER, *Histoire des institutions françaises au Moyen Âge*, 2 vol., Paris, 1957–1958.

Gino LUZZATTO, *I prestiti della Repubblica di Venezia, sec. XIII–XV. Introduzione storica e documenti*, Padua, 1929.

Bryce LYON and Adriaan VERHULST, *Medieval Finance. A Comparison of Institutions in Northwestern Europe*, Brugge, 1967.

Kenneth Bruce MCFARLANE, "Henry IV's government finance: council, parliament, finance", in Id., *Lancastrian Kings and Lollard Knights*, Oxford, 1972, pp. 78–101.

Patrizia MAINONI, "Finanza pubblica e fiscalità nell'Italia centro-settentrionale tra XIII e XV secolo", in *Studi storici. Rivista trimestrale*, 40, 1999, pp. 449–470.

Patrizia MAINONI, *Le radici della discordia. Ricerche sulla fiscalità a Bergamo tra XII e XV secolo*, Bergamo, 1997.

Patrizia MAINONI, *Politiche finanziarie e fiscali nell'Italia settentrionale (secoli XIII–XV)*, Milan, 2001.

Jean-Claude MAIRE-VIGUEUR, "Les rapports ville-campagne dans l'Italie communale: pour une révision des problèmes", in *La ville, la bourgeoisie et la genèse de l'Etat moderne (XIIe–XVIIIe siècles). Actes du colloque de Bielefeld (29 novembre–1er décembre 1985)*, ed. Neithard BULST and Jean-Philippe GENET, Paris, 1988, pp. 21–34.

François OLIVIER-MARTIN, *Histoire du droit français des origines à la Révolution*, Paris, 1948.

Olivier MATTÉONI and Patrice BECK (ed.), *Classer, dire, compter: discipline du chiffre et fabrique d'une norme comptable à la fin du Moyen Âge: colloque des 10 et 11 octobre 2012 organisé par l'IGPDE*, Paris, 2015.

Olivier MATTÉONI, "L'impôt, l'Etat, la souveraineté. Retour sur l'enquête 'La genèse de l'Etat moderne'", in *Penser l'ancien droit public. Regards croisés sur les méthodes des juristes (III)*, ed. Nicolas LAURENT-BONNE and Xavier PRÉVOST, Paris, 2021, pp. 195–218.

Olivier MATTÉONI, "Vérifier, corriger, juger. Les Chambres des comptes et le contrôle des officiers en France à la fin du Moyen Âge", in *Revue historique*, 309, 2007, pp. 31–70.

Denis MENJOT, *Fiscalidad y sociedad. Los murcianos y el impuesto en la baja edad media*, Murcia, 1986.

Denis MENJOT, "Le système fiscal de Murcie (1264–1474)", in *Finanzas y fiscalidad municipal. V Congreso de Estudios Medievales*, Avila, 1997, pp. 473–475.

Denis MENJOT, "L'impôt: péché des puissants. Le discours sur le droit d'imposer dans la *Libro de las Confesiones* de Martín Pérez (1316)", in *Derecho y justicia: el poder en la Europa Medieval*, ed. Nilda GUGLIELMI and Adeline RUCQUOI, Buenos-Aires, 2008, pp. 117–134.

Denis MENJOT, "Système fiscal étatique et systèmes fiscaux municipaux en Castille (XIIIe s.-fin du XIVe s.)", in *Fiscalidad de Estado y fiscalidad municipal en los reinos hispánicos medievales*, ed. Denis MENJOT and Manuel SÁNCHEZ MARTÍNEZ, Madrid, 2006, pp. 21–52.

Denis MENJOT, "Taxation and Sovereignty in Medieval Castile", in *Authority and spectacle in Medieval and early Modern Europe. Essays in honor of Teofilo F. Ruiz*, ed. Yuen-Gen LIANG and Jarbel RODRÍGUEZ, London and New-York, 2017, pp. 84–103.

Denis MENJOT, "Protagonistas del negocio fiscal: arrendatarios, fieles y fiadores en Murcia (1364–1427)", in *Poder, fisco y sociedad en las épocas medieval y moderna: a propósito de la obra del profesor Miguel Ángel Ladero Quesada*, ed. Ángel GALÁN SÁNCHEZ and Eduardo AZNAR VALLEJO, Madrid, 2018, pp. 339–359.

Denis MENJOT and Manuel SÁNCHEZ MARTÍNEZ (ed.), *La fiscalité des villes au Moyen Âge (France méridionale, Catalogne et Castille)*, vol.1: *Étude des sources*, vol.2: *Les systèmes fiscaux*, vol. 3: *La redistribution de l'impôt*, vol. 4: *La gestion de l'impôt*, Toulouse, 1996–2004.

Denis MENJOT and Manuel SÁNCHEZ MARTÍNEZ (ed.), *Fiscalidad de Estado y fiscalidad municipal en los reinos hispánicos medievales*, Madrid, 2006.

Denis MENJOT, Albert RIGAUDÈRE, and Manuel Sánchez Martínez (ed.), *L'impôt dans les villes de l'Occident méditerranéen. XIIIe-XVe siècle*, Paris, 2005.

Edward MILLER, "War, taxation and the English Economy in the late thirteenth and early fourteenth centuries", in *War and economic development*, ed. Jay Murray WINTER, Cambridge, 1975.

Sydney Knox MITCHELL, *Taxation in Medieval England*, New Haven, 1951.

Anthony MOLHO, *Florentine Public Finances in the early Renaissance, 1400–1433*, Cambridge, 1971.

Michel MOLLAT and Robert FAVREAU, *Comptes généraux de l'État bourguignon entre 1416–1420*, 2 vol., Paris, 1965–1966.

Michel MOLLAT and Philippe Wolff, *Ongles bleus, Jacques et Ciompi. Les révolutions populaires en Europe aux XIVe et XVe siècles*, Paris, 1970.

Andrew MONSON and Walter SCHEIDEL (ed.), *Fiscal Regimes and the Political Economy of Premodern States*, Cambridge, 2014.

Tomás de MONTAGUT I ESTRAGUÉS, *El Mestre Racional a la Corona d'Aragó (1283–1419)*, Lleida, 1987.

Joseph MORSEL, "De l'usage des sources en Histoire médiévale", in *Ménestrel* (www.menestrel.fr/ spip.php?rubrique1026&lang=fr&art=fr#1005) [01/03/2022].

Joseph MORSEL, "Sociogenèse d'un patriciat. La culture de l'écrit et la construction du social à Nuremberg vers 1500", in *Histoire urbaine*, 35, 2012, pp. 83–106.

Salvador de MOXÓ, *La alcabala, sus orígenes, concepto y naturaleza*, Madrid, 1963.

Íñigo MUGUETA, *El dinero de los Evreux. hacienda y fiscalidad en el Reino de Navarra: 1328–1349*, Pamplona, 2008.

Mark ORMROD, "The English Crown and the Customs, 1349–1363", in *Economic History Review*, XL, 1987, pp. 27–40

Mark ORMROD, "The West European Monarchies in the later Middle Ages", in *Economic Systems and State Finance*, ed. Richard BONNEY, Oxford, 1995, pp. 123–160.

Mark ORMROD, "England in the Middle Ages", in *The rise of the fiscal state in Europe, c. 1200*–1815, ed. Richard BONNEY, Oxford, 1999, pp. 19–52.

Mark ORMROD, "Urban communities and royal finance during the later Middle Ages", in *Corona, municipis i fiscalitat a la Baixa Edat Mitjana*, ed. Manuel Sánchez MARTÍNEZ and Antoni FURIÓ, Lleida, 1997, pp. 45–60.

Mark ORMROD, Margaret BONNEY, and Richard BONNEY (ed.), *Crises, Revolutions and Self-sustained Growth: Essays in European Fiscal History, 1130-1830*, Stamford, 1999.

Ágatha ORTEGA CERA, "El arrendamiento de rentas regias como modalidad de préstamo. Una aproximación a los principales grupos financieros de la Castilla de los Reyes Católicos", in *En la España Medieval*, 2020, pp. 177–204.

Pablo ORTEGO RICO, "Arrendadores mayores y arrendadores menores. La configuración de redes socioeconómicas a través de la gestión de la Hacienda Real a fines del siglo XV: algunos ejemplos", in *En busca de Zaqueo: los recaudadores de impuestos en las épocas medieval y moderna*, ed. Angel GALAN SÁNCHEZ and Ernesto GARCIA FERNÁNDEZ, Madrid, 2012, pp. 99–116.

Pablo ORTEGO RICO, *Poder financiero y gestión tributaria en Castilla: los agentes fiscales en Toledo y su reino (1429–1504)*, Madrid, 2015.

Pablo ORTEGO RICO, "Monarquía, nobleza y pacto fiscal: lógicas contractuaes y estrategias de consenso en torno al sistema hacendístico castellano (1429–1480) ", in *Pacto y consenso en la cultura política peninsular (siglos XI al XV)*, ed. José Manuel NIETO SORIA and Oscár VILLAROEL GONZÁLEZ, Madrid, 2015, pp. 123–162.

Pere ORTÍ GOST and Pere VERDÉS PIJUAN (ed.), *El sistema financiero a finales de la Edad Media: agentes, instrumentos y métodos*, Valencia, 2020.

Bonifacio PALACIOS MARTÍN and María Isabel FALCÓN PÉREZ, "Las haciendas municipales de Zaragoza a mediados del siglo XV (1440–1472)", in *Historia de la hacienda española (épocas antigua y medieval). Homenaje al Profesor García de Valdeavellano*, Madrid, 1982, pp. 539–606.

Luciano PEZZOLO, "Rivolte fiscali in Italia tra tardo medioevo e prima età moderna" in Florent GARNIER, Armand JAMME, Anne LEMONDE, and Pere VERDÉS PIJUAN (ed.), *Cultures fiscales en Occident du Xe au XVIIe siècle. Etudes offertes à Denis Menjot*, Toulouse, 2019, pp. 357–364.

Philippe de COMMYNES, *Mémoires*, ed. Jean DUFOURNET, 3 vol., Paris, 2007.

Michael PRESTWITCH, *War, Politics and Finance under Edward I*, London, 1972.

Pierre PRÉTOU, "L'imagerie de l'impôt dans la miniature occidentale à la fin du Moyen Âge. entre refus fiscal et rachat spirituel", in *El dinero de Dios: iglesia y fiscalidad en el Occidente Medieval, siglos XIII–XV*, ed. Denis MENJOT and Manuel SÁNCHEZ MARTÍNEZ, Madrid, 2011, pp. 289–310.

Andreas RANFT, *Der Basishaushalt der Stadt Lüneburg in der Mitte des 15. Jahrhunderts. Zur Struktur der städtischen Finanzen im Spätmittelalter*, Göttingen, 1987.

Félix REQUENA SANTOS (ed.), *Análisis de redes sociales: Orígenes, teorías y aplicaciones*, Madrid, 2003.

Maurice REY, *Le domaine du roi et les finances extraordinaires sous Charles VI (1388–1413)*, Paris, 1965.

Maurice REY, *Les finances royales sous Charles VI: les causes du déficit, (1388–1413)*, Paris, 1965.

Albert RIGAUDIÈRE, *L'assiette de l'impôt direct à la fin du 14e siècle: Le Livre d'estimes des Consuls de St.-Flour pour les années 1380–1385*, Paris, 1977.

Albert RIGAUDIÈRE, *Saint-Flour, ville d'Auvergne au bas Moyen âge: étude d'histoire administrative et financière*, Paris, 1982.

Albert Rigaudière, "Les origines médiévales de l'impôt sur la fortune", in *L'impôt au Moyen Âge: l'impôt public et le prélèvement seigneurial, fin XIIe - début XVIe siècle; colloque tenu à Bercy les 14, 15 et 16 juin 2000*, ed. Philippe Contamine, Jean Kerhervé, and Albert Rigaudière, vol. 1, Paris, 2002, pp. 227–288.

Albert Rigaudière, *De l'estime au cadastre en Europe: le Moyen Âge*, colloque des 11, 12 et 13 juin 2003, Paris, 2006.

Josef Rosen, *Verwaltung und Ungeld in Basel 1360–1535. Zwei Studien zu Stadtfinanzen im Mittelalter*, Stuttgart, 1986.

Yvan Roustit, "La consolidation de la dette publique à Barcelone au milieu du XIVe siècle", in *Estudios de Historia Moderna*, 4, 1954, pp. 15–156.

Frederick H. Russell, *The just war in the Middle Ages*, Cambridge, 1975.

Charles Samaran and Guillaume Mollat, *La fiscalité pontificale en France au 14e siècle*, Paris, 1905.

Manuel Sánchez Martínez, *La Corona de Aragón y el Reino Nazarí de Granada durante el siglo XIV: las bases materiales y humanas de la cruzada de Alfonso IV (1329–1335)*, PhD, Universidad de Barcelona, 1974.

Manuel Sánchez Martínez (ed.), *Finanzas y fiscalidad en la Edad Media*, in *Anuario de Estudios Medievales*, 22, 1992.

Manuel Sánchez Martínez, *El naixement de la fiscalitat d'Estat a Catalunya: segles XII-XIV*, Vic, 1995.

Manuel Sánchez Martínez and Antoni Furió (ed.), *Corona, municipis i fiscalitat a la Baixa Edat Mitjana*, Lleida, 1997.

Manuel Sánchez Martínez (ed.), *Fiscalidad real y finanzas urbanas en la Cataluña medieval*, Barcelona, 1999.

Manuel Sánchez Martínez and Michel Hébert, "La part du prince: Contributions et transferts au roi dans les dépenses des villes des pays de la Couronne d'Aragon et de Provence", in *La fiscalité des villes au Moyen Âge (Occident méditerranéen). 3: La redistribution de l'impôt*, ed. Denis Menjot and Manuel Sánchez Martínez, Toulouse, 2002, pp. 295–320.

Manuel Sánchez Martínez, "Negociación y fiscalidad en Cataluña a mediados del siglo XIV: las Cortes de Barcelona de 1365", in *Anuario de Estudios Medievales*, 61, 2005, pp. 123–164.

Manuel Sánchez Martínez, "Dette publique, autorités princières et villes dans les Pays de la Couronne d'Aragon (14e–15e siècles)", in *Urban Public Debts. Urban Government and the Market for Annuities in Western Europe (14th-18th centuries)*, ed. Marc Boone et al., Turnhout, 2003, pp. 27–50.

Manuel Sánchez Martínez, Antoni Furió and José Angel Sesma Muñoz, "Old and New Forms of Taxation in the Crown of Aragon (13th-14th Centuries)", in *La fiscalità nell'economia europea secc. XIII-XVIII. Atti della "Trentanovesima Settimana di Studi" 22–26 aprile 2007*, ed. Simonetta Cavaciocchi, Florence, 2008, pp. 99–130.

Manuel Sánchez Martínez (ed.), *La deuda pública en la Cataluña bajomedieval*, Barcelona, 2009.

Paul Sander, *Die reichsstädttische Haushaltung Nürnberg: Dargestellt auf Grund ihres Zustandes von 1431 bis 1440*, Lepizig, 1902.

Jean-Baptiste Santamaria, "'Comment roys et princes doivent diligamment entendre a la conduite et gouvernement de leurs finances'. Portrait du prince en maître des comptes à la fin du Moyen Âge", in *Ce que compter veut dire: culture de cour, gouvernement princier et pratiques comptables (Europe occidentale, XIIIe–XVIIIe siècles)*, ed. Béatrice Touchelay, *Compatbilité(S). Revue d'histoire des comptabilités*, 11, 2019.

Léon Say, *Dictionnaire des finances*, 2 vol., Paris, 1889–1894.

Joseph A. Schumpeter, "The crisis of the Tax State", in *Joseph A. Schumpeter: The Economics and Sociology of Capitalism*, ed. Richard Swedberg, Princeton, 1991, pp. 99–140.

Lydwine Scordia, *'Le roi doit vivre du sien'. La Théorie de l'impôt en France (XIIIe-XVe siècles)*, Paris, 2005.

Lydwine Scordia, "L'enseignement fiscal de Louis XI au futur Charles VIII dans le Rosier des guerres" in *Cultures fiscales en Occident du Xe au XVIIe siècle. Etudes offertes à Denis Menjot*, ed. Florent Garnier, Armand Jamme, Anne Lemonde, and Pere Verdés Pijuan, Toulouse, 2019, pp. 105–113.

José Ángel Sesma Muñoz, *La Diputación del reino de Aragón en la época de Fernando II*, Zaragoza, 1977.

David Stasavage, *States of Credit: Size, Power, and the Development of European Politics*, Princeton, 2011.

David Stasavage, "Why Did Public Debt Originate in Europe?", in *Fiscal Regimes and the Political Economy of Premodern States*, ed. David Monson and Walter Scheidel, Cambridge, 2014, pp. 523–533.

Anthony B. Steel, "English Government Finance, 1377–1413", in *English Historical Review*, 51, 1936, pp. 577–597.

Anthony B. Steel, *The Receipt of the Exchequer, 1377–1485*, Cambridge, 1954.

Joseph Reese Strayer, *On the Medieval Origins of the Modern State*, Princeton, 1970.

Charles Tilly (ed.), *The Formation of National States in Western Europe*, Princeton, 1975.

Charles Tilly, *Coercion, Capital, and European States, AD 990–1990*, Cambridge, Mass., 1990.

Romain TELLIEZ, "Le contrôle des agents du pouvoir: une priorité pour la royauté? (en France à la fin du Moyen Âge)", in *Contrôler les agents du pouvoir*, ed. Laurent FELLER, Limoges, 2004, pp. 191–209.

Alessandro TOMEI (ed.), *Le Biccherne di Siena. Arte e finanza all'alba dell'economia moderna*, Rome, 2002.

Yann TORCHET and Hervé TORCHET, *Réformation des fouages de 1426. Diocèse ou évêché de Cornouaille*, Paris, 2001.

Béatrice TOUCHELAY (ed.), *Histoire des villes à travers leur comptabilité à la fin du Moyen Âge*, Compatbilité(S). Revue d'histoire des comptabilités, 12, 2019.

Max TURULL RUBINAT, *La configuració jurídica del municipi baix-medieval. Règim municipal i fiscalitat a Cervera entre 1182–1430*, Barcelona, 1990.

Max TURULL RUBINAT, "Finances i fiscalitat municipals a Catalunya durant la Baixa Edat Mitjana", in *L'Avenç*, 130, 1990, pp. 60–65.

André VAN NIEUWENHUYSEN, *Les finances du duc de Bourgogne, Philippe le Hardi (1384–1404)*, Bruxelles, 1984.

Hans VAN WERVEKE, *De Gentsche Stadsfinanciën in de Middeleeuwen*, Bruxelles, 1934.

Pere VERDÉS PIJUAN, *'Per ço la vila no vage a perdició': la gestió del deute públic en un municipi català (Cervera, 1387–1516)*, Barcelona, 2004.

Pere VERDÉS PIJUAN, "Fiscalidad urbana y discurso franciscano en la corona de Aragón (s. XIV-XV)", in *Fiscalità e religione nell'Europa cattolica: idee, linguaggi e pratiche (secoli XIV-XIX)*, ed. Massimo Carlo GIANNINI, Rome, 2015, pp. 71–110.

Pere VERDÉS PIJUAN and Albert REIXACH SALA, "Contre l'impôt", forthcoming in *Histoire Urbaine*, 2023.

Françoise VERGNEAULT-BELMONT, *L'œil qui pense. Méthodes graphiques pour la recherche en sciences de l'homme*, Paris, 1998.

Jules VIARD, *Les journaux du Trésor de Charles IV le Bel*, Paris, 1917.

Jules VIARD, *Les journaux du Trésor de Philippe VI de Valois*, Paris, 1899.

Paul VIOLLET, *Histoire des institutions politiques et administratives de la France*, 4 vol. Paris, 1890–1912.

Adolphe VUITRY, *Études sur le régime financier de la France avant la Révolution de 1789*, 2 vol., Paris, 1878–1883.

Jean-Claude WAQUET, *Le Grand-Duché de Toscane sous les derniers Médicis: essai sur le système des finances et la stabilité des institutions dans les anciens États italiens*, Rome, 1990.

Jean-Claude WAQUET and Denis MENJOT (ed.), *Transazioni, strategie e razionalità fiscali nell'Europa medievale e moderna*, Rome, 1996.

John WATTS, *The making of polities: Europe, 1300–1500*, Cambridge, 2009.

Chris WICKHAM, *Framing the Early Middle Ages: Europe and the Mediterranean, 400–800*, Oxford, 2005.

Bartolomeo YUN CASALILLA and Patrick O'BRIEN, (eds), *The Rise of fiscal states: a global history, 1500–1914*, 2012.

Karl Zeumer, *Die deutschen Städtesteuern, insbesondere die städtischen Reichssteuern im 12. und 13. Jahrhundert. Beiträge zur Geschichte der Steuerverfassung des Deutschen Reiches*, Leipzig, 1878.

3

THE RIGHT TO TAX AND ITS JUSTIFICATIONS

Lydwine Scordia and Florent Garnier

In the second half of the fifteenth century, the German theologian Gabriel Biel attempted to define the many terms for "charges (*praestationes*) imposed on the people by lords": "tribute (*tributum*), ground rent (*census*), levy to pay soldiers (*stipendium*), commodities tax (*gabellum*), toll (*pedagium*), safe-conduct tax (*guidagium*), duty on trading (*assisum*), thelony (*teloneum*), tallage (*tallia*), general aid (*collecta*), exaction (*exactio*)."[1] He remarked that "but all too often, one tax was mistaken for another". This comment confirms that semantic confusion abounded between different fiscal levies. In every context and space, in this instance the Latin West, taxation raised philosophical and political issues which theologians and jurists were still striving to resolve in the 1480s.

In the late thirteenth century, when the prince "lived off his own", namely revenues generated from his domain, the issue of the legitimacy of taxation began to be raised. Fiscal thinking focused on public taxation, "a charge made without consultation to pay for expenditure which is of public benefit"[2] by the prince as the overlord of a territory, whether this *princeps* be a king, prince, duke, or doge. The same questions were addressed to him: What gives him the right to tax his subjects (*causa efficiens*) and for what purpose is the money intended (*causa finalis*)? What form will the tax take (direct, indirect), and will it be on people or property (*causa materialis*)? Is there an upper limit on the tax (*causa formalis*)? The Aristotelian principle of the four causes helped the medieval world to define fiscal theory (*Analytica posteriora*, II, 11). It filled thousands of folios in works by theologians and jurists tasked by those in power from the late thirteenth century onwards with developing learned arguments for the right to tax. Thinking around taxation intensified in the 1280s – i.e. several decades before the Hundreds Years' War – against the backdrop of a strengthening of the powers of the *princeps* (justice, law, taxation). In 1337, when war broke out between the kingdoms of France and England, the theory was developed. The war did not prompt fiscal thinking, but facilitated the practical implementation of regular and permanent modern taxation. There were no objections to the taxation of his subjects by the prince in a certain number of instances, but the question which arose was whether this same prince could perpetuate the levy of taxes irrespective of the circumstances. This became the crux of the matter.

The extensive historiography of taxation in Europe reveals the complexity of the topic and the development of challenges to it. In the last fifty years, research has tended to favour

DOI: 10.4324/9781003023838-4

spatial, comparative or global approaches. Historians and jurists have been involved in major research programmes focusing on the modern state, taxation in towns, and the vocabulary of taxation.[3] Jean-Philippe Genet has emphasised the fiscal aspect in defining the characteristics of the modern state as an original socio-political structure: "a modern State is a State whose material basis is public taxation accepted by public society (on a wider territorial scale than the city-state) and which involves all subjects."[4] The medieval period is presented as the era of "the emergence of global theories" of taxation (Eberhard Isenmann). In the last twenty years, monographs, often based on PhD theses, and articles have placed an emphasis on the origins of taxation, the theory of taxation, the fiscal policy of principalities, and works about taxation.[5] These studies tend to favour approaches which are either conceptual and political, financial and economic, or administrative and prosopographic.[6] Relationships between the prince and cities have attracted particular attention in a variety of spaces. In the kingdom of France, there were "concurrent and connected tax systems" (Bernard Chevalier). In the Crown of Aragon, the existence of a municipal taxation system has been analysed. The concept occupies a key role in research in Europe in the 2000s.[7]

In order to understand the fiscal revolution of the late Middle Ages, it is necessary to examine the writings of exegetes, theologians, jurists and philosophers versed in the teachings of ancient authorities (the Bible, Aristotle, the Church Fathers, the Compilations of Justinian, etc.); this explains the range of fiscal vocabulary employed, which they have attempted to adapt to their own times. This method of referring back to Antiquity requires researchers to draw on ancient sources, and medieval commentaries, together with their political re-uses in treatises intended for princes in the closing centuries of the Middle Ages. This plethora of sources culminated in the establishment of a centuries-old corpus shaped by the *causa impositionis*. Scholars of the humanities/philosophers, theologians and jurists did not approach the issue of taxation in the same way, but drew on the same authorities and thus produced interwoven commentaries. They all shared the aim of establishing the legitimacy of taxation on the basis of the common good and public utility in order to allow those in power to introduce fair and equitable taxation policies.

The Paris Faculty of Theology established a reputation as an incubator for political thought due to the high calibre of its speculative thinking and its renowned masters, but also because France engaged with taxation at an early date, thus explaining the intensity of the debates which took place there. The issues discussed in Latin attracted the most able masters and students of the Latin West, and this was a contributory factor in the dissemination of the right to tax.

Arguments around taxation were based on the scholastic model of *pro et contra*, a form which was prevalent in universities (faculties of Humanities, Theology and Law) and the councils of princes. The European space of the *ius commune* was therefore permeated by stimulating scholarly debate; every principality, at its own pace, drew inspiration for the introduction of taxation from it, and its opponents criticised it in order to lend authority to their challenges. Justification for taxation made the shift from political treatise to pragmatic writings and princely ordinances in line with the spatial and chronological context. Modern taxation was not a foregone conclusion: it was the product of the diverse circumstances prevailing in the Latin West, characterised by fiscal ebb and flow. Modern princes stimulated and reaped the benefits of "a decisive acceleration of the dynamics introduced or tested on a small scale in the Middle Ages".[8] As in other fields, it is helpful to think in terms of a continuum which extends beyond the medieval period, since debate around taxation did not end in 1500, even though the foundations for the legitimacy of the right to tax had been established.

The idea of permanent taxation, which was debated in the thirteenth century, was revolutionary. However, it did not draw a line under the past; the principle that the prince must "live off his own" was retained (1). But thinking about taxation had now gained traction and was literally subjected to questioning through the process known as *quaestio* (2). A theory of taxation was developed and was also informed by the implementation of fiscal policies, which in turn sparked further debate and justifications (3).

The prince must "live off his own"

Until the thirteenth century, the prince "lived off his own" (1). Political literature abounds with examples of warnings to princes against seizing their subjects' money (2). The development of powers, the rediscovery of Aristotle and the Code, and the context of the times introduced changes which radically altered the financial balance in principalities (3).

Living within one's means

The only prevailing financial theory in the Middle Ages (and even beyond) stated that the *princeps* must "live off his own", i.e. from revenues generated from his domain relating to ownership of the land (*cens*, sale of foodstuffs, etc.) and to the seigneurial system (banalities, *corvée*, etc.). The role of the *princeps*, as feudal lord and *minister Dei*, was to defend his country and its inhabitants and to dispense justice (*pax et ordo*). His sphere of action was limited and revenues from his domain were sufficient for the exercise of this conservative government: the prince lived within his means. His role was gratuitous, i.e. free, and he could not impose tax on those whom he served. In return, a vassal owed his lord help and counsel (*auxilium et consilium*).

Feudal custom limited the financial *auxilium* owed to the lord to four circumstances: paying the lord's ransom, financing his departure on Crusade, the cost of knighting his first-born son, and providing a dowry for his eldest daughter. These four events, which were based on custom, and therefore legitimised by longstanding tradition, did not require negotiation with his vassals or their consent. This ad hoc (extraordinary) assistance was fundamentally personal, in the sense that it related to people (the lord, his son, and daughter). It was not directly associated with defending a space. It was also limited by the fact that two of these events (the elevation of his son to the rank of knight, and his daughter's marriage) could not be repeated. Seigneurial taxation was not therefore permanent.

The challenge facing the prince was to attempt to legitimise a levy on a new category of people, his subjects, and thus to move beyond a framework defined by feudal relationships. This new legitimisation of taxation must benefit an entity which extends beyond the physical person of the prince: the *res publica*.

Demonstrating the virtue of the prince

The literature of "mirrors for princes", so called because it offers the reader a virtuous image of a prince, addresses financial matters at some length. Anxious that the exercise of power was inherently open to abuse, these *artes gubernandum* aimed to shape the conscience of a ruler, to ensure that he did not cross the line from prince to tyrant. The authors of these mirrors were often members of mendicant orders. They shored up their treatises with Bible references to curse the prince (Ezekiel 34. 2) and praise the Good Shepherd (Genesis 29. 7; John 10. 2–4; Jeremiah 23. 1–4). Vices and virtues were illustrated by *exempla*. The deadly sin of avarice tended to be mentioned with increasing frequency in the thirteenth century as it was the root of all evil (1 Timothy 6. 10). As slaves of money themselves, princes enslaved their subjects.

Princes were advised to use their wealth for the benefit of their people and thus demonstrate the virtue of liberality.[9]

In order to persuade them, authors cited the counter-example of Rehoboam son of Solomon (1 Kings 12. 1–24 and 2 Chronicles 10. 1–19), who refused to reduce taxes and lost ten twelfths of his kingdom. The Bible teems with financial references and metaphors which were used to provide foundations for fiscal thinking. It was the quintessential Book, a model for all things, and a fount of words for learning to think: scholars conceptualised the issues of their day in the language of the Vulgate, but many of the verses were ambiguous.[10]

Political and theological approaches converged to curb a prince's ability to tax his subjects except in a small number of instances, and it was therefore possible for them to scrutinise the use to which sums paid were put. These blockers relate to regular levies in the form of a direct tax, whose use was not universally apparent or understood.

Finding the means to pursue one's **ars gubernandi**

Several factors played a part in upsetting the financial balance in France in the thirteenth century and brought the issue of taxation to the fore. Until this point, the prince had been pursuing a policy of living within his means and favouring the *aurea mediocritas*, but in the twelfth and thirteenth centuries, the scope of his *ars gubernandi* was expanding, which led him to seek out the financial means to implement his policy. A whole raft of causes prompted this change of direction which marked the beginning of the fiscal revolution.

The first cause was related to a change in the politics of the feudal system as the Capetian prince attempted to assert his authority over his lords, whom he believed to be neglecting their duties as protectors and dispensers of justice. This more authoritarian and interventionist prince was inevitably drawn into costly wars. The domain grew and he was forced to develop an administration. The second cause was associated with cultural expansion in the twelfth and thirteenth centuries and the rediscovery of an extensive body of arguments both in ancient philosophy (the Aristotelian corpus) and juridical sources (civil and canon law), which offered the prince a conceptual framework with which to justify his sovereignty over all of his subjects on the basis of his *summa potestas*. A third cause undermined the prince's finances. At the turn of the thirteenth and fourteenth century, revenues from the royal domain declined due to the economic climate and transfer of property by the prince to various lords to secure their loyalty. This was particularly obvious in France where income from the royal domain accounted for 80 percent of income in 1202–1203, 50 percent in 1330, 2.8 percent in 1461, and 2 percent in 1483, when Louis XI died. Management of the royal domain caused controversy: within the kingdom, the prince was accused of squandering the domain to justify taxation; outside the kingdom, the dukes of Burgundy were boasting of living off their domains and not taxing their subjects.

Political change was gathering pace and fuelling the financial imbalance. But where could the money required be found? There were several possibilities: coin debasement, borrowing, or sale of offices. But these all had their limitations and provoked criticism. The remaining option was taxation, but it was restricted to certain feudal situations and was considered sinful.

The decision to implement a fiscal policy implied defining the taxable group. Should citizens be taxed like in Athens or Rome on the basis of their membership of the community? Or should membership of the community be conditional on paying tax? Medieval admiration for Antiquity prevailed and members of the community were taxed. Intense thinking about community was fostered in the thirteenth century by the Aristotelian definition of a *koinônia* created for good, and Cicero's emphasis on the bonds between the members of a *res publica*, united in law by consent and connected by communion in matters of utility. Can we therefore deduce that *all* inhabitants of a kingdom, principality or town had to support the common good of the *res publica*? The three-way division of roles in society (praying, fighting, working) exempted the first two orders who contributed to the common good in specific ways from paying tax. However, princes were successful in levying *décimes* (tenths), a tax on clergy revenues, in order to pursue crusades. These tended to become annual in the early thirteenth century and even to extend beyond the strict *causa finalis* of the crusade. Taxation of the clergy was one of the great debates of the day. Henry Plantagenet and Philip the Fair based their reasoning on the fact that the clergy, who like the laity enjoyed the protection of a prince, had to submit to his law as members of the community. The issue in debates was not the ecclesiastical tax on the clergy, but tax levied by the public power on all members of the body of the kingdom, without referring back to the spiritual power. A prince who attempts to obtain the financial means to pursue political ends must justify his role and define the scope of *regimen* to increase the number of both lay and ecclesiastical taxpayers. The reign of Philip the Fair represented a decisive phase in the assertion of the royal right to tax. He established "new relationships – in the sphere of legal theory at least – between the king and these new taxpayers whose duty to take part in the defence of the realm also forced them to share in the expenses of the *res publica*."[11] The Prince also attempted to make the nobility pay by offering a tax exemption in exchange for a contribution (free gift). The conjunction of blockers, both philosophical (service role) and religious (damnation), with developments in the art of *regimen* explains why the debate around taxation was so intense.

The nature of the debates: challenges to taxation

Fiscal debate developed in scholarly circles in scholastic form (1). Theologians and jurists exploited a number of themes which were enablers (providence, treasury, necessity, etc.) to potentially outweigh blockers and provide a framework for taxation (2). However, this legitimisation of public levies did not spell the end of the theory of a prince living "off his own" with its roots in the domain, as is demonstrated by the absence of illuminations depicting the prince levying taxes (3).

The scholastic form of inquiry into taxes

Taxation was challenged in academia in the last twenty years of the thirteenth century. Masters carried out their own inquiries in the form of *quaestiones disputatae*. The scholastic method of disputation from opposing positions (*disputatio*) allowed them to distinguish between different cases and to find a well-balanced solution. Philosophers, theologians and jurists (with expertise in both canon and civil law) implemented this method. Each group had its preferred themes, but they were all motivated by ideals of justice and peace. The scholastics had all studied the same sources, although they each favoured certain authors, and structured their thinking by transposing Aristotle's methodology into the tax arena. Taxation was deemed fair or unfair on the basis of the answers to four causes: *causa efficiens* (Who is imposing it?), *causa finalis* (For what purpose will the tax be used?), *causa materialis* (Who and what will bear the burden of the tax?), and *causa formalis* (What will be the extent of this tax?).

In the years 1280–1300, eminent masters had to respond to questions on the legitimacy of tax on laity and clergy. These debates were held primarily in the Faculty of Theology in Paris, during solemn sessions called quodlibetal questions (*quaestiones disputatae de quodlibet*). During these gatherings open to all, the *magister* was subjected to open questions on any topic (*de quolibet*), posed by students or masters alike (*a quolibet*). The structure of quodlibetal questions allowed listeners to follow the development of the master's thinking *in vivo*, during an inquiry in which the authorities were referenced in evidence *pro* and *contra*, before the *magister* delivered a learned and well-balanced answer. Some examinations of political philosophy clearly reflected issues of interest during the reign of Philip IV.

The Franciscan master Richard de Mediavilla offers a good example of these debates, as he had to answer two questions, one on the taxation of clergy (1286), and the other on the taxation of the laity (1287): "Can the clergy be forced to pay for expenditure made for the common good?"[12] (*Quodlibeta*, II, 30) and "Are subjects obliged to pay new *tailles* to their temporal lords which are for the sole utility of their lords?"[13] (*Quodlibeta*, III, 27). The Franciscan supported his answer on the taxation of the clergy and laity primarily with judicial authorities: 30 percent civil law, 70 percent canon law for the clergy, and 30 percent civil law, 46 percent canon law for the laity. In canon law, he drew on causes 11, 16 and 23 of Gratian's *Decretum*, which address the relationship between the church and temporal power, and the titles of the *Decretals* compiled by Raymond of Pennafort referring to the legitimacy of direct taxes (*tributum, census, collecta, tallia, exactio,* etc.) and indirect taxes (*pedagia, guidagia* and *salinaria*) according to the status of people and property. The theologian drew less heavily on civil law (*Corpus juris civilis*). In his question on the taxation of clergy, he cited three laws from the *Code* outlawing the levy of taxes on goods in a city-state except if the need arose and if ordered by the prince. He also cited three excerpts from the *Digest* relating to the legislative power of the emperor and his fiscal monopoly. Absolutist principles are absent from the Franciscan's arguments and from the writings of theologians and legal scholars more broadly.[14] Taxation does not legitimise the *dominium* of the prince over property (constitution Bene a Zenone). Jurisconsults only recognised the power over public order of an emperor and, by implication, a prince; subjects owned their property. Theologians and legists sought out other authorities to substantiate the *pro* side of their answers.

This appeal to the same authorities did not produce uniform responses. Jurists were more specifically interested in the connection between the right to tax and the right to expropriate, which boiled down to the sensitive issue of the *dominium* of the prince (*causa efficiens*); theologians, for their part, were interested in the compatibility of fiscal power and the official function (*causa finalis*). It is not meaningful to contrast theologians who by definition inhabited a more otherworldly realm, with jurists firmly grounded in reality; the former were able to cite a *casus* (a brief account of a real event) and the latter were not averse to speculating about principles.

These scholars, theologians and jurists were pragmatists who had to develop solutions and eventually train graduates to take up positions in the prince's council and chancellery. The influence of their writings extended far beyond the walls of the university. The quodlibetal questions and *consilia* were read, retranscribed and used in a very wide range of circles.

Enablers to thinking about taxation: providence, treasury and necessity

Taxation was rejected because it was associated either with excessive exercise of power (tyranny), or with defeat and the payment of tribute by the vanquished. It was not, therefore, applicable to free men. Overcoming these obstacles was a matter of urgency, as the prince no longer had the financial means to govern, and can be explained primarily by the exaltation of political power. Masters valorised the power of the prince as a fiscal authority (*causa efficiens*) able to determine the fair use of tax (*causa finalis*). At the end of the thirteenth century, certain biblical exegetes removed the stigma attached to the exercise of power by an individual and overlooked the sinful origin of royalty (Deuteronomy 17; 1 Samuel 8). They glossed the divine origin of all power which justified the payment of tax to a prince who worked for peace and justice: *Pay to all what is owed to them: taxes to whom taxes are owed* (Romans 13, 1–7). Several enablers were deployed: providence, a treasury and necessity.

Exegesis of Genesis 41 provided the basis for the valorisation of princely power. A prince must exercise the cardinal virtue of prudence by listening to wise counsellors (Joseph in this instance) who advise him to build up reserves and to levy a tax of one fifth in anticipation of famine. Nicholas of Gorran, a Dominican, stated this explicitly: it is the role of the king "to be the providence of his subjects".[15] If he works for the good of his subjects, the prince can exceed his power and exercise it fully. If necessity dictates, and for public utility, the prince can legitimately levy taxes on his subjects, *quintam partem*. This new exegesis throws two key notions into relief: prudence and necessity. A prudent prince foresees and provides as he is able to interpret situations of necessity. These commentaries were compatible with the extremely wide diffusion of the teachings of Aristotle, for whom political power was natural to man and beneficial to his essence as it was directed towards the common good of the city-state.

Princes were even advised to build up a treasury in anticipation of future threats (Richard de Mediavilla). This legitimisation of a treasury was at odds with a number of Bible verses exhorting men not to store up treasures on earth but to place themselves in the hands of Providence without worrying about tomorrow (Matthew 6. 19 and 34). Members of mendicant orders (Dominicans and Franciscans), who were committed to poverty, were particularly attached to this idea. Thus, extolling the virtues of prudence in a ruler justified building up a treasury and levying taxes. The arguments of the Franciscan master decouple the levying of tax from an effective cause and make it conditional on a foreseeable cause. This development, which associates necessity and war to the point of assimilating them, contains the seed of permanent taxation.

The concept of necessity, which is central to an understanding of fiscal theory, was first glossed from a theological and liturgical perspective on the basis of verses from Mark 2, 23–27. Necessity constituted a departure from normal law. Necessity took on a fiscal meaning at the Third Lateran Council (1179). Canon 9 recalls the fiscal immunity of the church, except in instances of necessity for the common benefit and when the resources of the laity prove to be insufficient. Canon 46 of the Fourth Lateran Council IV (1215) reiterates this exception and specifies that it is the responsibility of the Pope to verify the case for public utility. The principle of *necessitas non habet legem* is taken up by Gratian in the *Decretum* and *Decretals*. An example which illustrates the influence of canonical thought in the resolution of a temporal financial crisis is English clerical resistance to the tax imposed by Henry III in 1225. Pope Honorius III invited the clergy to support the king via taxation as he was in a situation of need vis-à-vis public utility. Papal influence on fiscal theory should not be overlooked; the pope justified public taxation 1225, but also opposed it in the 1290s.

Necessity was a constant reference point both for feudal aid and the imposition of taxes. Jacques de Révigny drew on the argument of necessity and public utility to justify taxation in wartime. Philippe de Beaumanoir discussed their necessity in *Coutumes de Beauvaisis* (1279–1283). Whereas custom should prevail in peacetime, war increases the legislative powers of the king, who can do "many things" as "they are justified in times of necessity". But the bailiff of Vermandois went a step further when he included in the concept of necessity "[fear] of future war" (§ 1510) and equated a foreseeable war with war that had been declared. In the Crown of Aragon in the late fourteenth century, the usage of *Princeps namque* shifted from military service to the payment of a sum of money. It became a "new fiscal burden" with the peculiarity of being a non-negotiable form of taxation imposed at the will of the prince alone.[16] Thus the *defensio regni* tended to monopolise the end purpose of the tax. It paved the way for an urgent necessity obvious to all which authorised the prince to take action.

Necessity, stated or imputed, as interpreted by the prince, opened up a large number of avenues, but it only allowed for an ad hoc political initiative as it was based on exceptional circumstances. Canon law addressed this at length by stating that necessity (circumstantial) placed law (permanent) temporarily in abeyance. The adage *cessante causa, cessat effectus*, which has its origins in canon law, was used to gain acceptance for extraordinary fiscal policy by guaranteeing that it would not be permanent and announcing a return to ordinary revenue. Against the backdrop of the wars of the late thirteenth and early fourteenth centuries, theologians and jurists reflected on the notion of a foreseeable and permanent necessity. This issue posed a genuine semantic challenge as necessity and permanence are antinomic. Should necessity be understood in terms of funding for urgent expenditure or for the regular operation of a political community? Ernst Kantorowicz has drawn attention to *consilium* 98 of Oldradus de Ponte.[17] In the early fourteenth century, the jurist *in utroque jure*, working at the Curia in Avignon, offered a solution by developing the notion of *necessitas in habitu*, as distinct from *necessitas in actu*. This culminated in the concept of annual necessity and, as a consequence, *perpetua necessitas*. Like Richard de Mediavilla in 1287, he advised the prince to set aside reserves in his coffers to pay soldiers and meet any other potential needs. He emphasised the regular requirements associated with justice and the defence of the realm.

The "time of necessity" was decoupled from the present time and projected into a foreseeable future. The argument for necessity, focusing on the defence of the realm and war, lifted all temporal and moral impediments as the prince was acting for the common good. Approximately a century before taxation became permanent as a result of the royal ordinances of Charles VII (1439 and 1445), the theoretical justification was in place. Only a *princeps prudentissimus*, who was therefore by definition provident, could decree necessity as a superior lord and thus trigger the levy of taxes. The theologico-judicial argument reveals a future vision of the art of *regimen*, in a much less conservative and more dynamic form.

The dissemination of fiscal theory

Masters strove to surround the levy of taxes with *sine qua non* conditions, but thereby legitimised it. Scholarly thinking developed within university circles was disseminated in different ways ranging from the *summae* of confessors to fiscal treatises and political literature. However, no illuminated *ars gubernandi*, with a single exception, depicts the prince levying tax.

The fiscal debate was referenced in the *summae* of confessors. The institutionalisation of annual confession, which was made compulsory by the Fourth Lateran Council, prompted a flurry of manuals of casuistry to allow priests to help the faithful conduct an examination of conscience. The summae compiled the *rationes* of theologians and the *jura* of decretalists and civil lawyers. The most famous examples (Raymond of Pennafort and John of Freiburg) contain huge swathes of material from the proliferation of fiscal thinking developed by university faculties. Thus in 1317, Astesanus of Asti, draws attention to Richard de Mediavilla's quodlibet III, 27, citing the passage relating to the lawfulness of tolls, *De pedagiis*.[18] Members of mendicant communities were the primary authors of summae and treatises on good government for pastoral reasons (confession) and political reasons, as they were directly threatened with taxation of the clergy (a state tax).

Mirrors for princes played a role in the dissemination of fiscal teaching. *De regimine principum*, intended for the future king, Philip IV, was a huge success throughout the Latin West until the sixteenth century at least. This *ars gubernandi* (1278), bristling with Aristotelian and theological references was swiftly translated into French (1282), and the translation by Henri de Gauchi provided the basis for translations into Italian, English, Castilian, and Hebrew. Self-government (*ethiqua*), government of the family (*oeconomica*) and of the city-state (*politica*) are each described in turn. In the latter case, *regimen* is celebrated as an art and a science, and a specific place is reserved for prudence, a cardinal and political virtue (*rex sagittator*). Giles of Rome continued to advocate the theory of the domain ("living off one's own") as the only source of lawful revenue. However, he advised princes to use speculative and monopolistic practices inspired by Aristotle to raise money.

Various "fiscal treatises" written by jurists between the early fourteenth century and the first half of the sixteenth century were brought together in the sixteenth century in the *Tractatus universi iuris*.[19] They shed light on a common fund of principles and solutions. Treatises, *consilia* and other *quaestiones* broadly justify rather than challenge taxation. Jurists made the power to levy taxes an attribute of the *summa potestas* of the *princeps*. Its identification with kings, lords and even city-states raised further questions according to the type of levy made. For Petrus de Ubaldi, a city-state's ability to raise a levy was sanctioned by the *causa finalis*, and its acknowledged autonomy.[20] In the second half of the fifteenth century, in his treatise *De gabellis, tributis et vectigalibus*, Giovanni Bertachini also mentioned different circumstances for city-states. Those which held a *merum imperium* could set their own taxes. This was the case for the city-states of Tuscany and Lombardy. Other towns could only introduce new *gabelles* with authorisation from the prince. During this period, Francesco Lucani stated in his *Tractatus de collectis* that the *princeps solus imponere collectas pro publica utilitate*.

Theologians and jurists placed a number of parameters around taxation (the status of the people and property taxed, types of expenditure, frequency, etc.) but this theoretical legitimisation was not reflected in iconography. The fiscal power now attributed to the *usus principis* did not permit depictions of the prince as a tax collector. Until the fifteenth century, and even later, the only permitted image was of a king distributing alms to the needy. Irrespective of the period, and even after the introduction of modern taxation, medieval iconography banned any depiction of the prince levying tax or touching coins. However, some illuminations are potentially misleading, such as the work preserved in a late manuscript, *Le Livre des bonnes meurs* by Jacques Legrand, which features a miniature of subjects holding out a dish full of gold coins to a king. The king's body language and the text on the opposite page certainly do not suggest that he is levying tax. The picture actually shows the king rejecting his subjects' money. An exemplary prince "lives off his own". He is liberal, i.e. he distances himself from worldly goods. To accept money would imply that he was receiving a salary or looking after his own interests.[21]

To our knowledge there is only one illumination in existence showing the king levying tax, even metaphorically. The *Livre des trois âges*, a political poem written for Louis XI in 1483 by his physician and astrologer, Pierre Choinet, reviews his reign in verse and images. It celebrates peace and prosperity in the kingdom. One of the illuminations represents a pastoral scene in which a shepherd (the king) is shearing a sheep (the people). Shearing wool represents the levy of taxes. The basket full of wool is the royal treasury. The pastoral metaphor and the quatrain clearly endorse royal taxation. The first line approves permanent taxation ("it is good to shear sheep once a year"), but the next three lines criticise the policy of Louis XI who levied *taille* several times a year, in what are described as "*crues de tailles*" (a phrase which suggests overflowing rivers and excess). Choinet presents a rule intended for the successor to the "universal spider": "without skin, wool cannot grow on flesh". In other words, too much taxation kills taxation. Although the reality of the Hundred Years' War and its repercussions were causing princes to levy annual taxes, it was still forbidden to depict the prince as a tax collector.

Taxation practices (thirteenth to fifteenth centuries)

Fiscal theory brought a new dimension to government by a prince, but the relationship was not linear as the art of governing involves taking into account the context and reality of a society permeated with customs and privileges. The scholarly focus on the ruler (*causa efficiens*) conceals to some extent those being ruled who will have to pay the tax (*causae materialis et formalis*) and who are interested in the *causa finalis*. Was obedience the only right available to them? Fiscal practice was based on compromise (1) and challenges which brought about changes in the right to tax (2), until the burning desire for peace led to the introduction of permanent taxation (3).

Fiscal dialogue: negotiating taxation

Bible verses entreat those who are governed to obey and to pay tax; they also set out the terms of this obedience. A ruler must exercise good government based on peace and justice and more broadly on anything which is not contrary to God. The authoritative conception of power does not preclude recourse to the community, which must approve matters affecting it (Godefroid de Fontaines) – *quod omnes tangit ab omnibus approbare debet* (what touches all must be approved by all). This maxim drawn directly from imperial Roman law was captured by canon law in a decretal of Innocent III (1198–1216).[22] It influenced the procedure of political assemblies. It also featured for the first time in the convocation of parliament by Edward I in November 1295.[23] The majority of these assemblies convened by a prince, be they permanent or occasional depending on the principality, addressed the issue of public taxation. Although they had different names (parliament, assembly, estates, cortes), these gatherings were attended by representatives of political entities mandated on behalf of all to enter "into a negotiation with the prince ruling the territory on all aspects of the pursuit of the common good". These *parliaments* (a word with its etymology in the notion of "parler ensemble" or talking together) were tasked with negotiating the terms of the tax imposed by the prince (apportionment, level, duration, etc.). In other words, they revealed the exchanges and transaction "between princes who never have absolute power and subjects who never radically challenge their remit".

The governor and the governed often used the same arguments for public utility, which were bandied between them: just cause, clear necessity, defence of the country and political love. This latter theme, which already featured in the scholarly debates of theologians, tended to become increasingly common in fiscal debate.[24] The prince loves his people like a father and protects them from danger, and this is why he levies taxes; his subjects pay their tax because they love the prince on account of his good works. This love is a political virtue which Giles of Rome advised princes and subjects to learn and cultivate as part of the art of governing and being governed. Whether it be real or forced, this political love belongs to the rhetoric of the fiscal *regimen*. Love and taxation were inextricably associated during the Estates General in 1484. They had assembled to attempt to restore more moderate taxation after the terrible reign of Louis XI, and the chancellor, Guillaume de Rochefort, devoted his opening speech to the love which the young Charles VIII already felt for his subjects, and his firm belief that he could count on the love of representatives for the benefit of the *res publica*. Royal letters and preambles to ordinances demonstrate the emergence of the love theme in fiscal argument.

Discourse also highlights how theory adapted to the realities of the context. The prince overuses the *causa necessitatis* and emphasises the affective approach to *regimen*. He transposes scholarly notions of the "common good" and "public utility" into a metaphor of the living body of which all clergy and laity in the kingdom are limbs. The theorisation of taxation is amplified by contact with reality. Fiscal decisions are accompanied by politico-affective justifications and, more practically, by compensations. These bilateral agreements demonstrate a dialogue between governor and governed and form part of the history of the right to tax. This raises the question of why these populations finally agreed to pay tax: was it for the prince, the good of the community, or of the principality? Notions of *res publica*, and of the State were still highly theoretical and conceptual. Rulers had to find an argument which was easy to understand and could set in motion the introduction of taxation. However, not all parliaments were in agreement and some assemblies which opposed the idea also attempted to change the right to tax.

Opposition to taxation

Just as heresies had helped to shape Christian dogma during the Council of Nicaea, so opposition to taxation helped to move fiscal theory forward. Once the conditions for fiscal legitimacy were established, it was to be anticipated that this would enable malcontents to frame their objections. The governed were particularly interested in the form the tax would take and the purpose for which it would be used.

The prince was accused of using war as a pretext for levying tax and then misappropriating it for his own ends, or worse still, committing the country to a war in order to obtain a tax levy *sub colore justiciae*.[25] The soul of such a prince was in peril of damnation and he would lose his territory as his subjects would surrender to any foreign prince. During his conflict with the king of France, Pope Boniface VIII reminded Philip IV that he had to protect his subjects and not inflict the heavy burden of taxation on them and risk losing their love, and consequently their obedience. Gratian's *Decretum* authorised taxation of clergy in the event of necessity and for public utility if funding from lay people was insufficient, subject to a papal assessment of this utility. The demands of Philip IV did not meet these criteria: the king believed that he could pronounce on their necessity without reference to the pope. The loss of the love of the people became one of the main themes of opposition to taxation.

Princes who invented wars to raise taxes were accused of tyranny if they did not return the money. The theme of restitution was associated with sins against one's neighbour which the casuists had outlined in their *summae confessorum*. Lords had to return the money raised if they levied a tax without reason or for a pointless cause (purchasing clothes, building castles). If restitution was impossible, reparation had to be made in the form of compensation. This was not only essential for salvation, but was also a form of commutative justice. The casuistry of restitution accompanied the introduction of modern taxation. Philip IV was forced to return the subsidy of 1313 levied for a campaign against the Flemish which never took place as a truce was signed.[26] In 1329, Philip VI returned tax levied in anticipation of a future conflict, as he had made a commitment to do so if war did not break out.[27]

Subjects did not have to pay an unfair tax. They could refuse to pay and even depose a prince who refused to revoke it. The theory of taxation also conversely included conditions for just disobedience vis-à-vis princes. In 1314, Philip IV asserted his right to tax and his intention to levy new subsidies. Leagues of nobles, prelates and cities were formed in the kingdom and swore an oath of allegiance. Louis X was forced to sign charters guaranteeing that the king would not levy any taxes without "*evidens utilitas*" and "*emergens necessitas*".

When a tax was levied without its beneficiary having *potestas indicenci*, jurists agreed to accept that the taxpayer had committed tax evasion but that this did not constitute a sin. Following in the footsteps of Balde, Giovanni Bertachini examined fraud in connection with the *gabelle*. In the early fourteenth century in the south of France, Pierre Antiboul described various fraudulent practices. They all referred to attempts to avoid tax in an urban context.

With the expansion of taxation on assets and a growing desire to better understand its nature and value, *malitia* increased among clergy and laity.

Opposition was more overt when the prince was politically weak as a result of military defeats. Assemblies in the period 1355–1357 attempted to force the king of France to accept control of the monarchy by a council or the Estates General. In December 1355, shortly before the Battle of Poitiers, the Estates announced that they would agree to pay the *gabelle*, but stipulated that its use would be controlled by a council. Positions hardened after the defeat at Poitiers (19 September 1356) and the imprisonment of John II of France (John the Good). Meetings of the Estates General in 1356 and 1357 culminated in the Great Ordinance (28 December 1357). The king could not levy tax without the approval of the Estates General, 36 *réformateurs* were appointed to control the royal finances. The issue of tax was at the heart of reform programmes.

Hostility aroused by excessive numbers of officials was another aspect of fiscal opposition. This criticism was repeatedly mentioned in political treatises and the reform ordinances. Unanimous criticism was levelled at the vicious circle created by an overcrowded administration which required funds to pay the wages of finance officials. The king himself criticised the repercussions of these excessive numbers. The Cabochien ordinance of 26–27 May 1413, promulgated by Charles VI against a backdrop of civil war, included articles hostile to the proliferation of administrative officials. Their number was felt to be even more excessive as the war dragged on. A government bursting at the seams with officials, which was persecuting the poor people while the prince was unable to restore peace, was denounced as tyrannical.

From a tax for war to a tax for peace

War did not prompt thinking about tax, but indirectly contributed to the introduction of permanent taxation. Paradoxically, it was a desire for peace, rather than the defence of the realm which led to the acceptance of modern taxation. Here too, France blazed a trail for fiscal innovation, ahead of other principalities.

The ransom of three million gold ecus payable to England led John II to sign three financial ordinances on 5 December 1360. Every household had to pay a direct tax (*fouage*) until the ransom was settled. This fiscal measure was supplemented by the creation of a new gold currency, the franc. The name conjured up the historic freedom of the Franks, as if in anticipation of the liberation of the kingdom from its enemies. The *fouage* levied by the legitimate authority (*causa efficiens*) for a just cause (*causa finalis*) did not spark any opposition in principle, but there was criticism of the apportionment of the levy. The number of households had decreased significantly and tax officials had not taken this into account.

Against the backdrop of the reconquest of the kingdom, Charles V commissioned Évrart de Trémaugon, a doctor *in utroque jure*, to write a summa to take stock of the various ancient issues (the lines of demarcation between spiritual and temporal power) and current issues (tax). The master decided to present it in the form of a dialogue (*disputatio*) between a "learned cleric" and a "wonderfully gifted" knight. The *Somnium Viridarii* was completed in 1376 and translated into French as *Le Songe du Vergier* (1378). The cleric opened the debate with a polemical question about taxation[28]: "How can the king of France be absolved of tyranny neither other secular princes who burden their subjects with *tailles* and *fouages*, *gabelles* and imposts and other aids which it is impossible to bear". The knight's answer summarises the conditions of fiscal power based on Richard de Mediavilla's quodlibetal question (1287), which he transcribes without referencing it. This intertextuality between two texts written approximately a century apart demonstrates the importance of magisterial thinking. Although it was legitimised by a late thirteenth-century Franciscan monk via *Le Songe du Vergier*, Charles V nevertheless decided to abolish *fouage* on his deathbed (1380). Did the prince still doubt his power to levy tax? Fiscal law took into account political and financial parameters and also incorporated other factors which it is more difficult to evaluate, but which are equally important, such as the conscience of the prince and the "psychology of the tax".[29]

Ultimately, it was not the defence of the realm which gave birth to the modern taxation, but the desire for peace. War and internal conflicts between factions led to a proliferation of armed men, including mercenaries, who far exceeded the military aid of lords. Armies, which were paid to take part in conflicts, were dismissed without pay when conflicts temporarily came to an end. The tax revolution was brought about by the violence meted out to civilian populations during truces by armed bands of *routiers* and *écorcheurs*. The problem was particularly severe in France as the Hundred Years' War had taken place on French soil.

Unable to win the war or sign the peace, the Valois and Lancastrian kings were accused of letting armed men operate unchecked and profiting from this. It was the responsibility of the prince to stop these injustices and maintain an army. Although his fiscal monopoly was secure – public taxation took priority over taxes owed to a lord – the prince still shared the military function with the lords. A solution gradually emerged, tying the fiscal revolution into the military revolution. In 1445, an ordinance from Charles VII established a standing army (15 companies of between six and 700 men), under the sole authority of the king. These soldiers would receive a wage financed by taxation. A permanent army, even in peacetime, led to permanent taxation. The *causa finalis* of modern taxation was identified due to the return of peace. On the strength of his desire for peace and his victories in the battlefield, Charles VII announced that *aides* (introduced in 1439) and *taille* (introduced in 1445) would be extended without the consent of the estates as the meetings were too expensive and the debates too protracted.

Henceforth, princes would increase the *taille* (Louis XI) or decrease it (Louis XII), but these changes only affected the level of the tax and not its nature. This raised the question of whether the fiscal revolution would be permanent. Following the death of Louis XI (August 1483), the council of guardians of the young Charles VIII decided to cut the *taille* by a quarter and announced a meeting of the Estates General. From January to March 1484, 284 delegates from across the kingdom, representing every social group for the first time (including peasants), aired their fiscal grievances in Tours. At the end of the talks, the three estates confirmed their attachment to the theory of the royal domain, but agreed, under the current circumstances, to pay a "gift and octroi" of 1,200,000 *livres* for two years instead of the *taille*, and a gift of 300,000 "by way of "gift and octroi" for the happy accession of the king to the Crown. The Estates viewed this financial aid as a gift freely granted by the deputies, but a provisional one, which therefore challenged the ordinance of 1445. The right to tax did not follow a straight trajectory but oscillated between an intangible attachment to the theory of the domain, which was reiterated until 1789, and a fiscal policy which was regularly presented as a temporal necessity.

In conclusion: legacy and heirs

Fiscal theory has its origins in the use of ancient sources adapted by scholastics (argument) and economic factors which sparked new debates. Theologians (quodlibetal questions) and jurists (*casus et consilia*) addressed the theme of taxation by drawing on the same fund of theologico-juridical authorities. The right to tax belongs in the field of medieval political science with all its standards and diverse practices. Looking beyond chronological and spatial differences, permanent and regular modern taxation cut its ties with past ideas and sparked a number of revolutions.

The first revolution relates to the beneficiary. Taxation was initially associated with personal aid under the feudal system, then with the *princeps*, as the interpreter of what constituted necessity for the common good (city-state, kingdom, Crown, *res publica*, State, etc.). Medieval Aristotelian thought privileged the survival of the whole over the parts; benefit for a single person was associated with tyrannical behaviour. The organic metaphor designates the prince as the head or heart able to lead (head) or bring life (heart) to the whole body. By placing the emphasis on incarnation, Christianity further accentuated the role of the *princeps* as servant and agent of the common good. This was evident in arguments for taxation which stressed the *summa potestas* of the prince and drew on the vocabulary of affect. It is quite clear that the prince both symbolises and embodies the kingdom, the Crown and the *res publica*. Subjects have not paid tax for the state entity, an overly abstract concept, but have accepted the taxation required to guarantee peace and justice. They have also accepted that the prince should build up financial reserves. In 1523, Francis I created the *Trésor de l'Épargne*, a central treasury into which all general revenues were to be deposited. The choice of name signalled the royal intention to be a provident prince.

The second departure from the past imposed a philosophical revolution on the medieval population. "Living off one's own" meant living from the land, the basis and symbol of wealth. The land and not money yielded fruit by its ability to reward man's labour manyfold. The monetarisation of modern taxation placed the emphasis on money (chrematistic), as the source of the prince's wealth, and not on the management of the domain (economic).

The third break with tradition was semantic. Theologians and jurists made necessity, which was by definition temporary, a factor of permanence. This argument was mainly deployed as a *causa finalis* for fiscal initiatives. It does not imply that the prince introduced uniform legislation. Whether it be in the context of assemblies or communities, the prince and the governed debated the fiscal burden and reached compromises and exceptions while reaffirming that the only financial theory was that the prince must live off his own. Tax which was levied regularly was no longer extraordinary in nature, but was still considered to be temporary for administrative purposes (a semantic fiction).

The pages devoted by Jean Bodin to different ways of filling the national treasury in the *Six Livres de la République* demonstrate that the epistemological rift between the Middle Ages and modern times was not fully effective. This work of political philosophy, written in French (1576), was soon widely disseminated in printed form and in 1586, Bodin made the decision to translate it into Latin. It was in this form that the volume was glossed in university circles. After discussing the domains of the Republic (VI, 1), chapter 2 of the last book addresses "The Treasury" (VI, 2, *De aerario*). Bodin, who was steeped in theological, juridical and historical culture, sprinkled his synthesis with ancient and medieval references and contemporary references to Henri II and his four sons, four years after the St Bartholomew's Day Massacre.

Bodin explained that since money was the sinews of war, in order to preserve the Republic, it was necessary "to be fully aware of it" in three respects: firstly, to seek "honest ways to provide funds for the finances", then to specify their use "for the benefit and honour of the republic", and thirdly, to save a proportion of them. After citing the counter-example of Sparta, which conquered Greece with the help of its treasury but lost it by resorting to borrowing, Bodin declares that "war is not underpinned by debt" and that there are seven ways to fill the treasury. The initial allusion to Cicero (*nervi Reipublica pecunia*) and the reference to Lacedaemonian history reveal that for Bodin, the treasury was intimately associated with war.

The domain is the primary means, ranked in first place and most extensively discussed, as it is "the most honest and sure of all". Revenue from the domain means that the prince is not forced to "burden his subjects with taxes or seek ways of confiscating their property".

Traditional theory contrasting the royal domain and taxation is mentioned. Taxation is only the seventh and last resort. It should only be implemented when every other avenue has failed and there is "an urgent need to provide for Republic" in which case "charges and taxation of subjects are very fair, as there is nothing fairer than necessity". Bodin adopts the standard pronouncements of the Middle Ages when he places excessive emphasis on necessity. The rest of the chapter is less clear-cut, as the tax which has been justified is immediately restricted in wartime. Bodin specifies that in peacetime it would be "expedient to impose it in the form of loan". He then adds a time parameter to classify the three means of raising money from subjects: "extraordinary, ordinary and a third sort which combines elements of the other two, which is called *deniers casuels*" (i.e. occasional). However, the levy must cease when the objective has been achieved. Bodin adopts medieval thinking on the right to tax, including the belief held by certain princes that each must pay their share. He developed in particular the idea of a state bank, something which had been in existence in other countries since the Middle Ages (Italy, Spain, the Netherlands, etc.). In municipal finances in the fourteenth and fifteenth century, there was already recourse to loans, and the balance was tipping in favour of perpetual annuities which were connected to taxation. State credit was structured at various levels (local, regional et national). In sixteenth-century France, state debt grew. Credit and taxation informed the thinking of theorists of the State and economy from the sixteenth to the eighteenth centuries.

Notes

1 Biel, *Collectorium circa quattuor libros Sententiarum*, IV, di. 15, q. 5.
2 Chevalier, "Fiscalité municipale et fiscalité d'État", pp. 135–152, to p. 139; Rigaudière, "L'essor de la fiscalité royale", pp. 323–391; Isenmann, "Les théories du Moyen Âge", in *Systèmes économiques et finances publiques*, dir. Richard Bonney, Paris, 1996, pp. 4–35.
3 Rigaudière, "Rétrospective" et "Perspectives", pp. 27–30 and pp. 685–688; Chevalier, "Fiscalité municipale et fiscalité d'État", pp. 137–151; Chevalier, "Genèse de la fiscalité urbaine en France", pp. 21–38. Chevalier, "La fiscalité urbaine en France", pp. 61–78.
4 Genet, "La Genèse de l'Etat Moderne: Genèse d'un programme de recherche", p. 23 sq.
5 Scordia, "Le roi doit vivre du sien".
6 Favier, "Histoire administrative et financière", *Annuaire de l'E.P.H.E.*, 1967–1968, pp. 355–360, 1968–1969, pp. 313–316 and 1969–1970, pp. 417–423; "L'histoire administrative et financière" B.E.C., 126 (1968), pp. 427–503. Garnier, "L'impôt d'après quelques traités fiscaux", pp. 64–114. Grummit and Lassalmonie, "Royal public finance", pp. 116–149.
7 *La fiscalità nell'economia europea. Sec. XIII–XVIII.*
8 Béguin and Genet, "Fiscalité et genèse de l'Etat: remarques introductives", p. 15.
9 *Le Livre de l'information des princes*, fol. 11rb., 70ra and 75rb.
10 Scordia, "Rendez à César et autres lemmes bibliques", pp. 5–22.
11 Rigaudière, "L'essor de la fiscalité royale", pp. 323–391.
12 Richard de Mediavilla, *Quodlibeta*, II, 30, ms. lat. 14305, f° 181vb–183va. Scordia, "Transcription et traduction d'une question quodlibétique", pp. 21–51.
13 Richard de Mediavilla, *Quodlibeta*, III, 27, Paris, BNF, ms. lat. 14305, f° 194vb–195rb.
14 Rigaudière, "L'essor de la fiscalité", pp. 527–529.
15 Nicolas de Gorran, ms. BnF, lat. 15560, ff. 105 va–105vb. Scordia, "L'exégèse de Genèse 41", pp. 93–119.
16 Sánchez Martínez, *Pagar al rey en la Corona de Aragón*, pp. 209–210.
17 Kantorowicz, *Les deux corps du roi*, pp. 850–854; McManus, "The Consilia and Questiones", pp. 85–113.
18 Astesanus d'Asti, *Summa de casibus conscientiae*, livre I, titre 31, article 4, Paris, fol. 36d–38a.
19 Garnier, "L'impôt d'après quelques traités fiscaux", pp. 64–114.
20 *Tractatus*, f° 96, b, 1–4 et 96 v, a, 4.
21 Scordia, *"Le roi doit vivre du sien"*, pp. 171–197.

22 Congar, "*Quod omnes tangit bet*", 36, pp. 210–259; Gouron, "Aux origines médiévales de la maxime *quod omnes tangit*", pp. 277–286; Gaines Post, "A Romano-Canonical Maxim", pp. 197–251.
23 Hébert, *Parlementer*, pp. 98–103, p. 1 and p. 3 (for quotes).
24 Scordia, "*Subjectio, subventio et dilectio* ", pp. 75–96.
25 Ullmann, *The Medieval Idea of Law*, p. 186.
26 Brown, "Reform and Resistance, pp. 109–137.
27 Brown, "Taxation and morality ", Vol. 8, No. 1, pp. 21–22.
28 Évrart de Trémaugon, *Le Songe du Vergier*, pp. 229–232.
29 Bercé, "Pour une histoire institutionnelle et psychologique de l'impôt moderne", p. 161.

References

Gabriel Biel, *Collectorium circa quattuor libros Sententiarum*, ed. Wilfrid Werberck and Udo Hoffman, 5 vol., Tübingen, 1973–1977.
Katia Béguin and Jean-Philippe Genet, "Fiscalité et genèse de l'État: remarques introductives", in *Ressources publiques et construction étatique en Europe. XIIIe-XVIIIe siècle*, Paris, 2015.
Yves-Marie Bercé, "Pour une histoire institutionnelle et psychologique de l'impôt moderne", in *Genèse de l'État moderne. Prélèvements et redistribution*, ed. Jean-Philippe Genet and Michel Le Mène, Paris, 1987.
Elizabeth A.R Brown, "Taxation and morality in the Thirteenth and Fourteenth Centuries: Conscience and Political Power and the Kings of France", in *French Historical Studies*, Vol. 8, No. 1, 1973, pp. 1–28.
Elizabeth A.R. Brown, "Reform and Resistance to Royal Authority in Fourteenth Century France: The Leagues of 1314–1315", in *Politics and Institutions in Capetian France*, London, 1991, pp. 109–137.
Bernard Chevalier, "Fiscalité municipale et fiscalité d'état en France du XIVe à la fin du XVIe siècle. Deux systèmes liés et concurrents", in *Genèse de l'état moderne. Prélèvements et redistribution*, ed. Jean-Philippe Genet and Michel Le Mené, Paris, 1987, pp. 135–152.
Bernard Chevalier, "Genèse de la fiscalité urbaine en France", in *La Gènesi de la fiscalitat municipal (segles XIIe-XIVe), Revista d'Historia medieval*, 7 (1996), pp. 21–38.
Bernard Chevalier, "La fiscalité urbaine en France, un champ d'expérience pour la fiscalité d'État", in *Colloqui Corona, municipis i fiscalitat a la baixa Edat Mitjana*, Lleida, 1997, pp. 61–78.
Pierre Choinet, *Le Livre des trois âges*, facsimilé du Smith-Lesouëf 70 de la BnF, ed. Lydwine Scordia, Rouen, PURH, 2009.
Yves-Marie Congar, "*Quod omnes tangit ab omnibus tractari et approbari debet*", in *Revue d'Histoire du Droit Français et Étranger*, 36, 1958, pp. 210–259.
Jean Favier, "Histoire administrative et financière du Moyen Âge occidental", in *Compte rendu annuel de la conférence à l'École pratique des Hautes Études (IVe section), Annuaire de l'E.P.H.E.*, 1967–1968, pp. 355–360, 1968–1969, pp. 313–316 and 1969–1970, pp. 417–423 and "L'histoire administrative et financière du Moyen Âge depuis dix ans", in *B.E.C.*, 126 (1968), pp. 427–503.
La fiscalità nell'economia europea sec. XIII–XVIII, Trentanovesima Settimana di Studi (Istituto Internazionale di Storia Economica F. Datini), Prato, 2008.
Antoni Furio, "La dette dans les dépenses municipales", in *La fiscalité des villes au Moyen Âge (Occident méditerranéen) 3. La redistribution de l'impôt*, Toulouse, 2002, pp. 321–350.
Florent Garnier, "Justifier le financement de la dépense au Moyen Âge", in *El alimentado del Estado y la salud de la res publica: origenes, estructura y desarrollo del gasto público en Europa*, Madrid, 2013, pp. 51–72.
Florent Garnier, "L'impôt d'après quelques traités fiscaux (XIVe–XVIe siècles)", in *Histoire du discours fiscal en Europe*, ed. L. Ayrault and F. Garnier, Brussels, 2014, pp. 64–114.
Genèse de l'Etat moderne. Prélèvement et redistribution, ed. J.-Ph. Genet and M. Le Mené, Paris, 1987.
Jean-Philippe Genet, "La Genèse de l'Etat Moderne: Genèse d'un programme de recherche", in *A Génese do Estado Moderno no Portugal tardo-medievo (seculos XIII–XV). Ciclo de conferências (1996–1997)*, ed. M. H. da Cruz Coelho and A. L. de Carvalho Homen, Lisbonne, 1999.
Jean-Philippe Genet, "France, Angleterre, Pays-Bas. L'État moderne", in *Histoire du monde au XVe siècle*, ed. Patrick Boucheron, Paris, 2009, pp. 135–154.
André Gouron, "Aux origines médiévales de la maxime *quod omnes tangit*", in *Histoire du droit social, Mélanges en hommage à Jean Imbert*, ed. Jean-Louis Harouel, Paris, 1989, pp. 277–286.
David Grummitt and Jean-François Lassalmonie, "Royal public finance (c. 1290–1523)", in *Government and Political Life in England and France, c. 1300–c. 1500*, edited by Ch. Fletcher, J.-Ph. Genet and J. Watts, Cambridge, 2015, pp. 116–149.

Michel Hébert, *Parlementer. Assemblées représentatives et échange politique en Europe occidentale à la fin du Moyen Âge*, Paris, 2014.

Eberhard Isenmann, "Les théories du Moyen Âge sur les finances publiques", in *Systèmes économiques et finances publiques*, ed. R. Bonney, Paris, 1996, pp. 3–37.

Ernst Kantorowicz, "Mourir pour la patrie", *Mourir pour la patrie et autres textes*, Paris, 1984.

Ernst Kantorowicz, *Les deux corps du roi*, Princeton, 1957, transl., Paris, 1989.

Brendan McManus, "The Consilia and Questiones of Oldradus de Ponte", in *Bulletin of Medieval Canon Law*, 23, 1999, pp. 85–113.

Denis Menjot, "L'impôt: Péché des puissants. Le discours sur le droit d'imposer dans le *Libro de la confesiones* de Martin Pérez (1316) ", in *Derecho y justicia: el poder en la Europa medieval. Droit et justice: le pouvoir dans l'Europe médiévale*, ed. N. Guglielmi and A. Rucquoi, 2008, pp. 117–133.

Renzo Pomini, *La causa impositionis nello svolgimento strorico della dottrina finanziaria*, Milan, 1951.

Gaines Post, "A Romano-Canonical Maxim, *Quod omnes tangit*", in *Bracton and Early Parliaments. Traditio*, 4, 1946, pp. 197–251.

Albert Rigaudière, "L'essor de la fiscalité royale du règne de Philippe le Bel (1285–1314) à celui de Philippe VI (1328–1350)", in *Europa en los umbrales de la crisis (1250–1350), XXI semana de estudios medievales, Estella'94* , Pamplona, 1995, pp. 323–391.

Albert Rigaudière, "Rétrospective" et "Perspectives", in *Penser et construire l'Etat dans la France du Moyen Âge (XIIIᵉ–XVᵉ siècle)*, Paris, 2003.

Albert Rigaudière, "Donner pour le Bien Commun et contribuer pour les biens communs dans les villes du Midi français du XIIIᵉ au XVᵉ siècle", *De Bono Communi, The Discourse and Practice of the Common Good in the European City (13th-16th c.), Studies in European Urban History*, 22, Turnhout, 2010, pp. 11–53.

Amable Sablon du Corail, *La guerre, le prince et ses sujets. Les finances des Pays-Bas bourguignons sous Marie de Bourgogne et Maximilien d'Autriche (1477–1493)*, Turnhout, 2019.

Manuel Sánchez Martínez and Pere Orti, "La Corona en la génesis del sistema fiscal municipal en Catalunya (1300–1360)", *Corona, municipis i fiscalitat a la baixa edat mitjana*, Lérida, 1997, pp. 233–278.

Manuel Sánchez Martínez, *Pagar al rey en la Corona de Aragón durante el siglo XIV (Estudios sobre fiscalidad y finanzas reales y urbanas)*, Anejos del Anuario de Estudios Medievales 50, Barcelona, 2003.

Lydwine Scordia, "Les sources du chapitre sur l'impôt dans le *Somnium Viridarii*", in *Romania*, 117, 1999, pp. 132–142.

Lydwine Scordia, "L'exégèse de Genèse 41, les sept vaches grasses et les sept vaches maigres: providence royale et taxation vertueuse (XIIIᵉ–XIVᵉ siècles)", in *Revue des Études Augustiniennes*, 46, 2000, pp. 93–119.

Lydwine Scordia, "Le roi refuse d'accepter l'or de ses sujets. Analyse d'une miniature du *Livre de bonnes meurs* de Jacques Legrand", in *Médiévales*, 46, 2004, pp. 109–130.

Lydwine Scordia, *"Le roi doit vivre du sien". La théorie de l'impôt en France (XIIIᵉ-XVᵉ siècle)*, Paris, 2005.

Lydwine Scordia, "Transcription et traduction d'une question quodlibétique (1286) du franciscain Richard de Mediavilla sur la taxation des clercs par les pouvoirs civils", in *Études franciscaines*, 2/1, 2009, pp. 21–51.

Lydwine Scordia, "Le bien commun, argument *pro et contra* de la fiscalité royale, dans la France de la fin du Moyen Âge", in *Revue Française d'Histoire des Idées Politiques*, 32, 2010, pp. 293–309.

Lydwine Scordia, "*Subjectio, subventio et dilectio*: les devoirs des sujets envers le prince dans la *Postille* de Nicolas de Lyre", in *Nicolas de Lyre, franciscain du XIVᵉ siècle, exégète et théologien*, ed. Gilbert Dahan, Paris, 2011, pp. 75–96.

Lydwine Scordia, "*Rendez à César* et autres lemmes bibliques à connotation fiscale utilisés dans le discours politique des XIIIe et XIVe siècles", in *La religion et l'impôt*, ed. Ludovic Ayrault and Florent Garnier, *La Lettre du Centre de Michel de L'Hospital*, 1, March 2012, pp. 5–22.

Walter Ullmann, *The Medieval Idea of Law as represented by Lucas de Penna. A Study in Fourteenth-century Legal Scholarship*, London, 1946.

Pere Verdés Pijuan, "Fiscalidad urbana y discurso franciscano en la corona de Aragón (s. XIV-XV)", *Fiscalità e religione nell'Europa catòlica. Idee, linguaggi e pratiche (secoli XIV–XIX)*, ed. Massimo Carlo Giannini, Rome, 2015, pp. 71–110.

Pere Verdés Pijuan, "La teoría del gasto público en la corona de Aragón: el *Dotzè del crestià* (1385)", *El alimento del Estado y la salud de la Res Publica: orígenes, estructura y desarollo del gasto público en Europa*, ed. Ángel Gálan Sánchez and Juan Manuel Carretero Zamora, Madrid, 2014, pp. 73–96.

4
CHURCH TAXATION

Jordi Morelló Baget

Introduction: state of the question

Church taxation is a complex subject that can be tackled from different angles, and one of them, incidentally unavoidable, is that of the relations between Church and state. Such a relationship has gradually been repositioned in the context of the genesis of the modern state, according to a line of work begun quite a few decades ago and resumed more recently.[1] With a view to being able to clarify the aspects common to ecclesiastical taxation and royal finances, historians usually give priority to the upper echelons, whether of the relations between the papacy and monarchies – in the international sphere – or between the Church and the king – in the internal framework of each kingdom –, and so one rarely gets to the bottom of the whole framework, the taxpayers themselves. Be that as it may, the fiscal contribution of the clergy to the development of the modern state is a crucial fact that has still not been sufficiently highlighted. Consider the growing numbers of the clerical population, and the enormous wealth that the Church amassed in each kingdom, both being affected to a greater or lesser extent by the expansion of the so-called tax state.

One must remember, however, that from an organizational point of view the Church was a conglomerate made up of different entities. On this point, there are numerous studies from the administrative point of view on the different ecclesiastical economies (of parishes, cathedral chapters, monasteries/convents and commanderies or priorates of military orders). Nevertheless, it is rather uncommon to tackle the subject of fiscal provisions, even when inventories or accounts generated due to these payments are made use of.

Moreover, we have the valuable considerations of legal historians on the creation of a fiscal doctrine, with regard, also, more directly to the taxes the clergy paid;[2] and although the law referring to the forms of payment of a whole series of exactions is quite well known, attention has rarely been paid to its application, to the dialectic established between the law and the practices of taxation.

If we limit ourselves to the study of pontifical taxation, there is a series of general works that continue to be unavoidable points of reference.[3] Nevertheless, in recent decades new contributions have been made. Without doubt, this has made it possible to broaden the study framework, due not only to the work of medieval historians but also to that of other scholars working on situations inherited from the Middle Ages. Particularly, one ought to point out the renewed study of the collectorates,[4] as well as other studies focused on the contribution of the Church to the demands of kings.[5] Some of these studies incorporate prosopographical analyses of the Church collectors,⁶ which could be extended to the secular agents who took part in the administration of the ecclesiastical taxes paid to finance royal undertakings. This is a reflection of the high degree of collaboration that existed between the Church and monarchies, aside from some episodes of confrontation and even famous conflicts, such as the one that arose between Pope Boniface VIII and Philip IV of France in the early fourteenth century.⁷

In the sphere of heuristics and the publication of sources, some countries are in a better situation than others. Firstly, the exploitation of Vatican sources is still of prime importance. Besides the accounts registers of the *Collectoriae* or of the collection of certain taxes (tenths★, annates★, procurations★…), there are other series of a financial nature, like the *Introitus et exitus*. Publication of these volumes should be continued. All these Vatican sources, including the registers of *Supplicationes*, provide a great deal of interesting information on the subject of taxation in its peripheral dimension, not just from the point of view, therefore, of the papacy's central finances or of the issues related merely to benefices.⁸ There are also many fiscal sources in other Church archives (cathedral and diocesan, for example) of which better use could be made.

Other published sources come from national archives. In Great Britain, following in the footsteps of Lunt, there is a remarkable tradition of the study of clerical taxation, which is also based on the greater effort made in the publication of primary sources. In this respect, there is a project promoted since the 1990s under the aegis of the History Department of the University of York (the E 179 project), creating an online database catalogue of the records of taxation of the medieval and early modern clergy of England and Wales, based on the series of documents in the National Archives.⁹

As we are now well into the digital age, mention must also be made of the creation of some websites, like the one promoted by Professor Denton in his database hosted by the Humanities Research Institute at Sheffield University containing the valuation of the English and Welsh parish churches and prebends listed in the ecclesiastical taxation assessment of 1291–1292.¹⁰ It would be an example to follow by other countries where exceptional documentation for later periods is also conserved. Based on inventories of this kind, the distribution – albeit in relative terms – of clerical wealth can be mapped; more generally, the study of certain fiscal inventories allows us to gain greater knowledge of the geography of the clergy (and of benefices) in each territory.¹¹

Apart from the publication of sources and their exploitation, it is extremely important to know what forms of exaction were prevalent in each period and how frequently they were established, along with other factors that play a part in taxation (reasons or justifications put forward in each case, forms of administration and collection, the agents intervening, etc.). On this point, different authors do not always offer clear information about one basic aspect, knowing how to distinguish between the levies paid by the clergy with respect to the other exactions that were passed on to the vassals of the Church; of course, depending on the sources used, such discernment is not always easy to make. Moreover, there is a long history of considering the exactions paid to the Church to be "ecclesiastical taxation", which can sometimes generate confusion with the taxation imposed on the clergy. We could refer, for example, to the matter of the tithe, but that only affects the core subject of the present exposition tangentially.¹²

Logically, every author tends to prioritize their respective geographical area, as well as certain ages or periods; on this point, there is notably a huge number of studies referring to the period of the Avignon Papacy – with its continuation in the period of the Schism – made above all by French historians, which has doubtlessly been to the detriment of the periods before and after the fourteenth century. Moreover, one would like to see a greater effort made to compare the different realities studied, something that at times is difficult to undertake even between neighbouring regions due to the use of different vocabulary, coinage or other particularisms.

The ultimate end of all these studies would be that of being able to assess the full extent of the impact of taxation with regard to the different categories of taxpayers, along with the analysis of the problems deriving from it (insolvency, forms of opposition and methods of repression); there is certainly a long way to go in this field.

In short, starting from a great variety of approaches to the different realities studied, it is difficult, although not impossible, to attempt to discern common patterns in a global phenomenon: that of the gradual conversion of clergymen to taxpaying subjects. Albeit in general terms, it is possible to detect similar evolutionary trends, if not surprising parallels, wherever the clergy found itself affected by the expansion of different types of taxation, the length and breadth of Christendom subject to the Roman papacy.

In this exposition, through the power of synthesis, we shall see first how Church taxation was specifically expressed, before going on to see to what extent the clergy was affected by the other forms of taxation developed in the late Middle Ages. We shall conclude by referring to the system of benefices, which served as a basis for contribution to the principal ecclesiastical taxes, and to the evolution of Church taxation after the Council of Constance.

Ecclesiastical taxation in its early stages of development

Although it may seem an obvious thing to say, ecclesiastical taxation was actually created by the Church, and it should therefore be distinguished from forms of taxation emerging in other spheres. However, this picture is complicated from the moment when part of this ecclesiastical taxation began to be set aside for the benefit of monarchies or other secular bodies. Be that as it may, it is a good idea to begin our study with the taxes created at the behest of the papacy.

The birth of clerical taxation: papal tenths

The beginnings of clerical taxation can be traced to the period of the first crusades, with the establishment of income taxes. The earliest examples of clerical taxation are recorded with reference to the First Crusade, although they are isolated cases. From then on, two different pathways began to develop, depending on whether it was a case of establishing general taxes – demanded of all subjects, including clergymen – or those specific to the clergy. For the moment, we shall deal with the latter.

A first landmark would be the contribution called for by Pope Clement III in 1188, in the encyclical addressed to the bishops to oblige the clergy of their respective bishoprics to contribute to the recovery of the Holy Land. In France and England, that contribution had to be subsumed under a general tax – the Saladin tithe – but in other lands, like Poland, the papal order was complied with by the imposition of a tenth★ (10 per cent of declared income) on the clergy in that kingdom. "Thus originated papal taxation of the clergy for the crusade."[13] From then on, other taxes on the clergy in the whole of Latin Christendom are recorded: the "fortieth" ordained by Innocent III in 1199 to some extent began the series of the thirteenth century; this tax was discussed in councils, both provincial and diocesan, and it was the clergy itself who had to be assessed for the purpose of having to pay, in this case, one-fortieth of their incomes. Other taxes established in the years 1208 and 1209 were no longer imposed to meet the needs of the Holy Land, but to fight heresy in the south of France and northern Italy (Lombardy), but they only affected the clergy in those regions.

More papal exactions followed, such as the twentieth established in 1215 in accordance with the measures taken at the Fourth Council of the Lateran – the pope himself, Innocent III, and his cardinals contributed with a tenth. His successor, Honorius III, organized the collection of another twentieth; to this end, commissioners were sent in 1218 to different parts of Christendom with full powers to direct the collection. The practice of setting aside part of the money collected for other purposes was consolidated with this pope and his immediate successor, Gregory IX, as was the case with the tenth★ established in 1229, in the context of the long-standing war with the German emperor. As a result of the Council of Lyon in 1245, another twentieth was proclaimed for the Holy Land – in France and England it was commuted for a tenth★ – to be collected for a period of three years; in 1262 Urban IV ordered the collection of a hundredth for five years (equivalent to one year's twentieth).

"The pontificate of Gregory X proved to be the high point of papal taxation of the clergy for the crusade."[14] The papal tenth★ of 1274 – decreed at the Second Council of Lyon for a period of six years – signals a decisive moment in terms of organization: 26 collectorates for the whole of Roman Christendom were established for the purpose, with a collector general in charge of each district with the power to appoint deputy-collectors. This imposition was the first in the series of the famous *Rationes decimarum*, collection registers referring to different regions of Italy and the Iberian Peninsula.[15]

In short, the taxes established for – or with the pretext of – the crusades shaped the model of taxation of ecclesiastical income; the tenth★ was the option eventually imposed, to the detriment of other percentages used up to then. As it was a proportional tax, before it could be collected an assessment of the income of each contributing subject had to be made. In England, the first known valuations (1217, 1229) were simple estimates made by the clergy itself, but it was after the Valuation of Norwich (1254–1257), made for the collection of three papal tenths★, when processes to verify these estimates were introduced. Later, the valuations made in 1291 for the sixth papal tenths★ imposed by Pope Nicholas IV became the basis for all clerical taxation until the Anglican Reform, well into the sixteenth century. In other kingdoms the initial processes of assessment are far less well known; in Portugal, it is considered that the *taxatio* made for the collection of a tenth★ granted to the king in 1320 could have served as a matrix of reference for subsequent contributions.[16]

Right from the start, various types of exemption were considered in the contribution of tenths★ for different reasons: in the case of the military orders, because they were already contributing to the crusades with their armies (bear in mind, moreover, that those organizations began to regularly collect sums of money to send to their overseas domains for the defence of the Holy Land); cardinals were also considered to be exempt because of the services they provided to the pope. At the same time, exemptions of the monastic orders proliferated, especially the mendicants, out of consideration for their real or presumed poverty. All these exemptions would subsequently be extended to other clerical contributions. In any case, the granting of exemptions would always be at the mercy of whoever was pope at the time – until the moment when monarchs also intervened and began to use these exemptions for their own ends. The clergymen charged with collecting taxes were also usually exempted from payment.

The expansion of papal taxation during the Avignon Papacy

During the Avignon period (1309–1378), the "papal monarchy" demanded the creation of its own system of taxation, which went hand in hand with the process of centralization and the great development of bureaucracy and accounting that the pontifical administration underwent in that period.[17] According to a certain point of view, the papacy became the prototype for a primitive expression of the modern state, as, among other things, it equipped itself with the first rationalized tax collection system.[18] In this way, it would have stolen a march on the development of the different feudal states, serving as a model for other territorial taxation systems. Furthermore, mutual influences have been observed between both taxation systems (papal and monarchic), as Jacques Verger noted with respect to the two-way transfer of organizational models.[19]

The fact is that, in the first half of the fourteenth century, we witness a considerable increase in the papacy's ability to tax "ecclesiastical temporalities", based more than anything on the spread of reservations of benefices.[20] Pope John XXII (1316–1334) was the principal promoter of that taxation system, which apparently spread unopposed by the clergy. Below, I shall refer to the exactions imposed *in partibus* (in the different territories of Christendom), ignoring, therefore, the others that had to be paid in the curia itself.

During the Avignon Papacy, a tax closely associated with benefices started to become more important: annates★ ("First Fruits"). This form of taxation constitutes the symbol par excellence of pontifical taxation and it is to a large extent the reason for the consolidation of the collectorate system during the Avignon Papacy. Dating back hundreds of years, as a feudal tax on succession, the first papal reservations were made in the thirteenth century. It was, however, not until the beginning of the following century that this type of taxation became more widespread. John XXII regularized its payment through the bull *Si gratanter advertitis* (1316). Initially limited to the vacant benefices at the papal court, this levy spread rapidly to all those who had been conferred by the Holy See.

The annate★ was equivalent to the first year's profits (net income) of the benefice; in this respect, it was a highly onerous imposition, although it only had to be paid once, even if the benefice fell vacant more than once in the course of the same year. The major benefices (of bishops and abbots) were exempt from paying it, as these were already paying the so-called services (common and lesser) in the curia.[21] Annates★ and common services were, however, different kinds of payments.

With regard to the method of payment, at the Council of Vienne (1311) it was stipulated that annates★ had to be paid at the same rate as the tenth, and the rule was clearly defined under John XXII. The receiver would be paid according to that rate, leaving the difference for the beneficed priest (the remainder after subtracting the tax from the total value of the revenue that could actually be obtained from the benefice in question). The opposite could however also be the case – making the difference payable instead of the tax – either of them being the collector's choice in theory. If the benefice was not taxed at the rate of the tenth, it had to be evaluated, in which case half of this valuation would be payable. The benefices whose annual incomes did not exceed six silver marks or ten Touraine pounds would be exempted from payment.

To know which benefices were subject to taxation, all the conferrals of benefices signed by the pope were taken from the registers of *Supplicationes*; the declaration of the benefice's income, the annual value, frequently expressed as *secundum taxationem decime,* was prescribed in these pleas. In the period of the Schism, annates★ eventually accounted for on average a quarter of the money raised by the pontifical collectors.

Annates★ could occasionally be brought into line with vacancies★ (*fructus medii temporis*), which implied the appropriation of the incomes of the benefice for the entire period it remained vacant; it is possible, however, that they may have ended up being calculated like the annates★.[22] Through the bull *Ex debito* (1316) the cases were codified that had to be included in the expression "vacancies *in curia*", and through successive ordinances new additions were incorporated. There were popes – the case of Benedict XIII – who deliberately kept some benefices vacant for the purpose of being able to have supplementary revenues.

Another means of obtaining revenue were spolia on the property of deceased bishops and abbots.[23] Originally, this was the right to remove the contents of the house of a bishop who had just died. The first spolia confiscated by popes, from 1262 at least, were those of clergymen who died intestate in Rome. With John XXII, the papacy also began to collect spolia from those who died outside the curia. In 1362, Urban V decreed the first general reservation; from then on, this exaction was gradually extended in line with the increase in the number of benefices reserved for apostolic conferral. It was applied to the movable goods of the deceased, which, once the relevant inventory had been made, were sold to the highest bidder for the purpose of obtaining cash for the Apostolic Camera, although the most highly prized goods (books and jewellery) were usually kept apart and sent to the curia.

Another type of tax was by way of the reservation of procurations*, based on the exemptions granted to bishops from the obligation to make periodic visits to their dioceses. Amid the dangers of the plague and the wars of the fourteenth century, prelates chose to request papal licences for the visits to be made through proxies; in return for these licences, the papacy began to receive part of the corresponding procurations* and later it was even able to entrust the papal collectors themselves with this task, as Innocent VI decreed in 1355, it being possible to take, depending on the case, half or full procurations*.

Through a bull of Urban V in 1369, reservations became widespread. In some regions (not so in the territories professing obedience to Rome), the receipt of procurations* was practically regularized until the early fifteenth century, and it eventually brought in a third of the total raised by the collectors of Avignon during the Schism.[24]

Throughout the fourteenth century, the papacy also claimed extraordinary subsidies* – frequently called "charitable"[25] – to pay for the Church's expenses, that is, those of the papacy. The history of these subsidies* – like virtually everything that has been mentioned here – goes back a long way due to the donations made for different reasons.[26] Subsidies* *pro necessitatibus Ecclesie Romane* flourished in the course of the twelfth and thirteenth centuries as a result of the schisms and then the war against the Hohenstaufen dynasty;[27] and in the fourteenth century, as a result of the new crisis that arose with Louis of Bavaria and the wars in Italy.

With regard to tenths*, due to the frequent grants made to monarchs, the papacy tried to at least keep hold of those it was able to collect in the Italian Peninsula. In Latium, to cite a well-known case, a total of 22 papal tenths* are recorded in the period from 1274 to 1400, by then at the height of the Schism.[28] After the sexennial tenth* of 1274, there is a second sexennial in 1313, likewise allocated to the crusade, and three more triennial ones for the war against the Turks beginning in 1343. The triennial one of 1357 was *in subsidiorum guerrarum Romane Ecclesie,* while others refer to the needs of the Apostolic Camera. A total of 68 annual contributions are recorded in 126 years, covering, therefore, more than half of the period.

In short, the Avignon popes did not stint in their efforts to successfully increase their fiscal sources of revenue through the series of rights that I have just mentioned. According to P. Partner, "some of these rights could reasonably be called taxes";[29] annates*, of course, could be, as well as tenths* and subsidies* – when they were distributed according to the rates of the taxes on benefices; the rest were either appropriations (vacancies*, spolia) or tributes (procurations*).[30]

All the forms of taxation noted so far, and yet other kinds of obligations (such as the taxes paid by some monasteries depending directly on the Holy See), had to be gathered by the different collectors who had gone to each territory. In the fourteenth century, the collectorates became permanent; by the middle of the century there were 31 collectorates distributed all over Europe, almost half of them (15) in France,[31] six in central and northern Europe, four in Italy (in the period of the Schism this rose to more than 20), four in the Iberian Peninsula, two in the British Isles and one in Cyprus. Everything was centralized in the Apostolic Camera, the body that administered the papal finances, where the collectors had to go to account for their management. To do this, the collector handed over a copy of the *Liber rationum*, written in the first person, from which a smaller notebook was drafted, the *Compotus brevis*, for the purpose of facilitating control of these accounts. The deputy-collectors also kept their own accounts in the context of the demarcations to which they were assigned. Although the task of collection could be entrusted to bishops, they were more usually cathedral canons, recruited from among the clergy in the region where they went to carry out their business (or if they were foreigners, they would normally receive a benefice in the area of their collectorate).

In sum, the expansion of this taxation is yet another example of how the papacy acted as a supranational body, draining towards the pontifical court large sums of money collected the length and breadth of Latin Christendom.[32] The medieval Church – having become the de facto largest corporation of the period – functioned, according to certain English-speaking historians, as a Europe-wide "multinational" company.[33] Nor can we overlook the transformation of pontifical Avignon into an important financial hub, in which numerous bankers and businessmen were present, who also took part in the fiscal machinery of the papacy; hence also the role played by the papacy in the development of the financial systems of the period, closely associated with the creation of its own system of taxation. Everything would change in the conciliar period, when, besides putting an end to the Schism, papal taxation was reformed completely, as we shall see below.[34]

Other areas of development of ecclesiastical taxation

Leaving aside the papal sphere, we must not forget that other fiscal realities existed at inferior levels, as well as in other areas of ecclesiastical jurisdiction. Bishops, for example, could demand a series of payments from the clergy in their diocese, some of them customary like the *cathedraticum*, which could be made effective when synodal assemblies were held, the reason why it also came to be known by the name of the *synodaticum*. There were also exactions received in the form of spolia (on the property of deceased clergymen). We have already mentioned visitations with regard to papal reservations; their origins are also very old, being the ecclesiastical version of the right of refuge or hospitality, so they were initially paid in kind. This right could be exercised by both bishops and archbishops, and also by archdeacons/archpriests, each one in his respective jurisdictions or group of dependent parishes. Prelates could also impose extraordinary collections to pay for situations of need.

The different levies imposed by bishops on their diocesan subordinates are examples of the relationship of personal dependence on their person. Considered heterogeneous taxation, as it was made up of an amalgam of archaic rights, and accepted due to its traditional nature, in the opinion of V. Tabbagh it wouldn't be a proper fiscal system.[35] In any case, it cannot be denied that much of the fiscal system created by the papacy borrowed some of these rights from taxation based on appropriation (via the mechanism of the reservation); put another way, the pontifical taxation system did not come out of nowhere, it appropriated pre-existing practices, although it took them to the highest level of efficiency and systematization.

As has already been said, the payment of procurations★ was closely associated with the bishops' mandatory visits to the parishes in their dioceses, which they could either make in person or through delegates; papal legates could also demand procurations★ for the same reason, that is, with a view to managing the travelling expenses of themselves and their retinues;[36] indeed, long before they appropriated episcopal procurations★, popes made use of them when they travelled to other provinces.[37]

Here too we ought to refer to contributions demanded by the general chapters of some religious orders from their respective communities, although none of this seems to bear comparison with the taxation developed within the military orders. The Hospitallers of Saint John of Jerusalem, for instance, created a complex fiscal network based on its organizational structure, of which the commandery was the basic unit of administration. The contributions were distributed among the different districts (commanderies or priorates) according to the patrimony and the productive capacity of each body, the principal exaction paid being those called "*responsiones*", along with annates★, vacancies★ and extraordinary subsidies★. This system of taxation therefore has many features in common with the system of papal Avignon; what is more, bearing in mind that such a system of payments was regulated definitively from the middle of the fourteenth century onwards, the influence of Avignon seems to have been decisive. The Hospitallers' system of taxation reached overload in the fifteenth century due to the heavy investments the order had to make in the defence of Rhodes against the Turkish threat.[38]

The taxation of the clergy by secular authorities

Despite being protected by clerical privilege, throughout this period clergymen were also affected, more or less directly, by secular taxation, in which they were required to take part ever more frequently. We thus witness a gradual definition of the fiscal status of the clergy, whose theoretical immunity would progressively be eroded due to increasing pressure from kings and municipal councils.

The fiscal status of clergymen: between immunity and taxation

As is well known, the persons under the sole jurisdiction of the Church were subject to its laws. Implicit in clerical privilege was the enjoyment of certain legal and jurisdictional prerogatives, as well as the defence of fiscal exemption. Together with the invocation of "ecclesiastical freedoms", this privilege was used as a shield against the interference exercised by lay authorities.

From the sphere of canon and civil law a fiscal right was gradually drafted, with diverging or even opposing points of view, to do with the fiscal submission of clergymen: if they had to contribute, in which taxes, for what reasons, in what way? Here we can only remember a few aspects of the controversy centred on the clergy, to serve as a complement to what is explained in the chapter by Scoria & Garnier in the present book.

The maxim *necessitas non habet legem* could also be applied to the situation of clergymen with regard to taxation, in the sense of being able to justify a temporal infringement of ecclesiastical freedoms. Necessity would be invoked above all in wartime and, more specifically, in relation to the defence of the kingdom. In the continual warfare of the fourteenth century, this argument became almost permanent.

Common utility, based on the Thomist notion of the common good, also began to be a reason put forward. This principle was applied more on a local level, in order to justify the participation of the clergy in municipal taxation. According to Henri de Gand, a jurist of the late thirteenth century, clergymen were part of the city, and given that they made use of the common things and benefited from them, they ought to contribute whenever the occasion arose (in the upkeep of the walls, for example).

Generally speaking, attempts were made to maintain everything that had been established in the Third and Fourth Councils of the Lateran (1179, 1215), limiting the contributions of the clergy only to cases of need or public utility, due to insufficiency of laymen and or papal consultation.

Regardless of the reasons put forward in favour (or against), the question of jurisdictional protection continued to be the main obstacle standing between the Church and laymen; clergymen were not obliged to obey the laws or ordinances of laymen unless it was by order of their hierarchical superiors, whether bishops or the pope himself, all of them acting as the staunch defenders of ecclesiastical jurisdiction and freedoms. Boniface VIII insisted – through the famous bull *Clericis laicos* (1296) – on the papal authorization that clergymen who granted any subsidies* had to have, on pain of excommunication, for any kings too who demanded such payments. Aside from the confrontations, in practice it was necessary to reach compromise solutions. The key question was having an authorization from the pope and/or with the consent of the clergy itself.

Contributions due to the needs of the kingdom: alternation between tenths and subsidies

The right to tax was, with regard to the clergy at least, a matter reserved for popes (and, to a lesser extent, to other hierarchs of the Church as well). Kings, no matter how much they tried, did not have the power to tax the clergy legitimately; if they did, conflict was assured.

With respect to the papal blessing, the famous dispute between Boniface VIII and the king of France in the early fourteenth century is paradigmatic, a dispute that also had fiscal undertones, which, unlike what is usually believed, was not resolved so favourably for the interests of the French king; thus, according to J. Denton, when it came to asking the churchmen of the kingdom for help, it was still necessary to consult the papacy, something that in France remained unchanged until the reign of Francis I.

Aside from the tour de force between the pope and lay princes, the idea began to take hold of also having the consent of the clergy, as had originally been stipulated at the Third Council of the Lateran (1179). Clergymen's assemblies became the favourite place, even in those early days, for dealing with royal demands for help.

Therefore, in order to achieve the involvement of the clergy in the general taxation of the kingdom, there were two possible avenues for each monarch to pursue, resorting to the papacy, or to the assembled representatives of the kingdom's clergy. Naturally, tenths* correspond to the first avenue, although it was not always easy to obtain them; for this, it was necessary to make full use of all the persuasive force of diplomacy in the legations dispatched to the curia, or, better still, to attempt to place influential prelates close to the pope. Needless to say, in this respect the kings of France had things easier than others as they had to deal with a papal court highly influenced by French cardinals.

In the second case, the holding of a provincial council was taken advantage of (in theory, kings could not directly convoke these assemblies, unless they resorted to ecclesiastic authority). The importance these assemblies were gaining in the discussion and granting of subsidies* to the monarchy is more than borne out in some kingdoms; in England, there was not just one body representing the English clergy but two, the convocations of the provinces of York and Canterbury, which throughout the Middle Ages acted separately. In the Crown of Aragon, grants to the king could initially be ratified in the framework of a single province, as is attested to in the reign of James I (1213–1276), something that changed as a result of the creation (in the early fourteenth century) of the province of Zaragoza, segregated from that of Tarragona, since the conciliar assemblies of both provinces almost always functioned separately when it came to approving subsidies* to the Crown.

The starting point for clergymen contributing to royal demands was the general levies established in the twelfth century for the crusades. The first case arose in 1165 when, in answer to the call made by Pope Alexander III, King Louis VII of France asked his subjects, both laymen and clergy, for a proportional contribution based on income. A similar contribution was demanded by Henry II of England in his continental domains. Other "crusades taxes" followed in 1185 and 1188 – in this latter case, the so-called Saladin tithe, by which a tenth* of the value of the annual income of each contributing subject had to be paid. Apart from the general nature of these impositions, the degree of clergy's involvement in the organization of the collection was notable; parishes began to act as collecting centres – the money had to be kept in boxes locked with different keys and then handed over to the bishop of the diocese. The bishops were to gather the money in the manner decided by themselves and the king. Some members of the military orders (Templars and Hospitallers) could also take part at this stage, in parallel with the well-known role that they went on to play – the former especially – as bankers of the crusades.

There were further attempts to impose a general levy for the Holy Land in France and England in 1201, in the Empire too – in Swabia (1207) at least – and later (1221) in the kingdom of Sicily, where the Emperor Frederick II proceeded to tax clergymen and laymen differently (the former with a twentieth, which would be added to that which was already being collected at the behest of the pope). There followed other contributions granted to princes: thus, for example, in 1248 Louis IX of France, instead of the general twentieth, imposed a tenth* with which he raised nearly 750,000 Touraine pounds. After his second expedition to Tunis, he was able to benefit from another three-year tenth* granted by Clement IV in 1267. Not only did these grants of clerical taxes begin to multiply everywhere, they could also be used for other purposes, with papal approval. In Castile, for example, from the start the aim was not to allocate the product of tenths* or other extraordinary provisions to distant lands overseas, but to finance the continuation of the war against the Muslims in the Peninsula.[39]

Throughout the thirteenth century, therefore, kings were used to addressing the clergy of their kingdoms to demand from them subsidies* for the defence of the kingdom, when not putting forward other justifications. These sums – generally granted in the context of ecclesiastical assemblies – were donated ex gratia, that is, voluntarily. The amounts payable were the result of a negotiation with the bishops, who immediately proceeded to distribute them among the different episcopal demarcations and then within each bishopric, in this case being able to take into account, to a greater or lesser degree, the levels of income of the clergy (as in the case of tenths*). Subsidies* could also be granted in the form of loans, whose repayment was not always assured.

Later, as a result of the institutionalization of the general assemblies, in the fourteenth century the ecclesiastical order was asked to give the Crown other kinds of help together with the other representatives of the kingdom. These other contributions were usually passed on to the vassals of the Church. This dynamic could have led to the creation of a general system of taxation – outside the royal administration – in which the involvement of the clergy was also desired; in the Crown of Aragon, the universal introduction of the new taxes established by the Diputación del General – an institution emanating from the parliament to handle the administration of the donations granted to the king – brought with it the protest of the clergy of Catalonia, whose members feared they would be subjected to a double imposition, as they were already paying tenths* for similar reasons.[40]

Throughout the fourteenth century, therefore, we witness a proliferation of royal demands affecting the ecclesiastical order based on the alternation of tenths* and subsidies*. In France, the collection of tenths* intensified especially during the first half of the fourteenth century; according to Causse, from the middle of the century onwards, this tax went into decline, given that one sees a growing recourse to subsidies* authorized by the papacy. In England continuous papal tenths* were imposed by the papacy from 1305 to 1336, more often than not in favour of the king. With the start of the Hundred Years War, Edward III managed to impose other provisions on the clergy as well as papal tenths★. Later, in the period between 1377 and 1422 – corresponding to the reigns of Richard II, Henry IV and Henry V – as many as 60 grants are recorded in the form of half tenths★ by the province of Canterbury, as against the 40 by the less wealthy province of York, all of this combined with a few special subsidies★.[41]

In the Crown of Aragon an early period of the coexistence of both avenues (first half of fourteenth century) was followed by another one with a preponderance of tenths★, in this case justified primarily by the subjugation of Sardinia, in continual revolt since its military occupation in 1323. Given that the king of Aragon had acquired the island as a fief from the Holy See, the popes generally kept a third of the money raised for themselves.[42] Resorting to the tenth★ became a habitual measure of the Aragonese monarchy until the change of dynasty in 1410; thus, in the period from 1349 to 1410, fifteen papal grants are recorded, generally for short periods of one, two or three years. Out of a total of 61 years, tenths★ were collected in 41 of them.[43] In Portugal one also observes a series of at least seven tenths★ for the period 1312–1377.[44]

In all parts, the tenth, without ceasing to be an extraordinary tax, became an almost regular form of taxation for monarchs until the early years of the fifteenth century, or, more to the point, until the end of the Schism, when the political and religious outlook changed significantly.

That regularity made it possible to have an approximate estimate of the money that could be raised annually from each tenth: in the case of England, based on the valuation of 1291, this sum has been put at about 16,000 pounds sterling.[45] In Portugal, a tenth★ collected in the kingdom as a whole – taking as a reference the valuation of 1320 – could raise (in the local currency) as much as 60,000 pounds a year.[46] In the Crown of Aragon, in accordance with the first estimates made in the early fourteenth century, it was considered that a tenth★ brought in no more than 18,000 Barcelona pounds a year (= 32,727 Aragonese florins).[47] In France, the tenths★ obtained by the last Capetian king (Charles IV) and the first Valois one (Philip VI), amounted to almost 200,000 Touraine pounds effectively raised per year.[48] These figures, although disparate due to the use of different currencies, reveal the different potential of the clergy in each realm.

Other ways of transferring ecclesiastical income

Besides what has been said in relation to tenths★ and subsidies★, papal grants of annates★ are also recorded to some kings; nevertheless, as a result of the increase in papal reservations, the possibility of continuing to benefit from this ecclesiastic revenue gradually vanished. Nor was the pathway of confiscation, without asking for the pope's blessing, ruled out; some monarchs, the king of Aragon for instance, went on to appropriate the incomes of benefices that were vacant or in the hands of cardinals and other absentee (foreign) clerics, something comparable to actions carried out by the English monarchy in the 1370s. What is more, with the advent of the Schism (1378), King Peter the Ceremonious went even further by appropriating all the rights that the Apostolic Camera received in his kingdoms, something that would be repeated in 1416 with the first kings of the Trastámara dynasty. Both episodes were concluded with the restitution to the papacy of those rights, but not of the money the Crown had already received.

Furthermore, we witness a successive introduction of rights of amortization over the property that was being transferred to the Church, which fully concerns the sphere of real immunity, and more specifically, the problem of mortmain. Once it had been transferred, that property could not be returned to lay hands – due to its inalienable nature – while it also ceased to contribute in royal taxes. For the purpose of being able to make up for this loss of taxable material, some kings began to enact laws of amortization, for example the well-known statute of Edward I in 1279, which prohibited these alienations on pain of the confiscation of the property.[49] As these prohibitions, despite their reiteration, were futile, sooner or later a choice was made to introduce taxes levied on those transfers (or settlements in return for obtaining the corresponding royal privilege of amortization). From what we know about some kingdoms, the taxes were usually quite high, of the order of one-third of the value of the property transferred. To administer everything that this involved – the inspection of the transfers, the making of inventories and the collection of the corresponding taxes of amortization – ad hoc offices could be created, like the one that began to function in Valencia, in the Crown of Aragon, in the fifteenth century.[50]

Lastly, we can refer to some more specific methods of transferring ecclesiastical income. Since the thirteenth century, if not before, some monarchies fought to be able to have a share in the ecclesiastical tithe; this is the case of the Castilian *tercias*, initially an object of appropriation until they were institutionalized in 1247 – when they at last gained the pope's blessing; much later (1421) they became a permanent resource, and always with the theoretical justification of the war against the Muslims. The *tercias* were the equivalent of two-ninths of the tithe (22.22 per cent) and they were also paid in other territories in the Iberian Peninsula, such as the kingdoms of Portugal, and in Valencia in the Crown of Aragon, where it was called the *terç-delme*.[51]

In sum, the examples noted so far illustrate the various ways that could be used in different periods or moments with a view to achieving a greater transfer of ecclesiastical income to the royal coffers, transitorily in some cases, more lasting in others. The only denominator common to this entire amalgam of contributions is that they were revenue of ecclesiastical origin. The underlying fact was how to take advantage of the enormous wealth accumulated by the Church or the religious institutions – in property, incomes and patrimony – wealth obtained thanks to donations in the form of alms and other gifts by laymen, beginning with the kings themselves. Taxation became a means of diverting that wealth into lay hands or, rather, for the benefit of nascent states, which over time became the principal beneficiaries of the transfer of ecclesiastical revenue.

Much to its regret, the clergy became a fiscal subject of the state. However, we are talking about a group whose jurisdictional subjection – to the papacy or the kingdom – continued to be the object of controversy for centuries in Catholic Europe. This problem would be more or less resolved in practice through the growing tutelage exercised by monarchs over the Church in their kingdoms, including the extension of royal patronage to a greater number of ecclesiastical benefices. Not included in this were the new Protestant states, separated from Rome religiously and fiscally, where the resolution of the problem was unquestionably more drastic.

The other front open: municipal taxation

We are not too sure if the contribution of the clergy was a problem posed within the framework of the state, prior to becoming a burning issue in urban communities,[52] or whether it was the issues raised locally that pointed the way forward by monarchies later.[53] Whatever it was, it is clear that municipal authorities also made an effort to achieve the greatest possible participation of the clergy in their taxes, which meant sooner or later opening up another fiscal front from where it would also be possible to advance in the erosion of clerical exemption. The late medieval period was crucial for the beginnings of urban ecclesiastical taxation.

The clergy's fiscal situation in towns and cities was very variable and fluctuating depending on the local circumstances, starting with the unequal number of churchmen and religious institutions in every town or city.[54] In all parts conflicts arose over the participation of the clergy – the secular above all – in municipal taxation, in the thirteenth century and even more so in the fourteenth, right at the time when the municipal taxation system was crystallizing. The clergy's stiff opposition to the demands of the local authorities indeed seems fairly logical, bearing in mind that it was already subject to other ecclesiastical taxation. All these disputes had to be resolved through agreements or by way of judicial rulings. Although the solutions adopted in each locality present a very varied casuistry, this does not mean we cannot point to some common patterns.[55]

To start with, the clergy had to contribute in all kinds of local exactions governed by common utility. This principle was embodied above all when it came to financing public works in the general interest, such as roads, bridges, and above all the walls. Moreover, emphasis was placed on continuing to subject to taxation all the properties whose ownership had been transferred to clergymen or religious institutions (in application of the principle *res transit cum onere suo*). On the contrary, it was necessary to impose levies on property in mortmain ("dead hands") as an amortization. The patterns of wealth in the late fourteenth century began to include the assets of clergymen, either because this was what had been agreed between churchmen and councillors, or because the property in question had not paid a right of transfer. Another way was to establish global sums on account of what it was considered the clergy's contribution to communal taxation should be, and to leave the resulting internal share-out in ecclesiastical hands.

With regard to indirect taxation, the problems posed were different. In theory, clergyman did not have to contribute in impositions (or *sisas*) if they did not consent to it. Excluded from this were the *clericos negotiatores*, who would contribute for the goods they bought and sold, and not for the goods they might have purchased for their own use or consumption. However, the municipal authorities had to take numerous measures to try to put a stop to the fraud committed by churchmen; for example, with regard to the smuggling of wine.

There were also disputes that began over the fiscal treatment of tonsured clerics (simple clergymen in minor orders), particularly numerous in some cities, due to the fraud they committed taking advantage of that condition.[56]

Over time many of these disputes were resolved, as to a greater or lesser extent churchmen were made to pay municipal taxes. Nevertheless, they were always treated in a different way, since they were normally allowed to pay less than the rest of the taxpayers, and only in certain cases.

The continuity of the taxation of benefices

Now that the main characteristics of ecclesiastical taxation and churchmen's contributions to secular demands have been expounded, it only remains for me to refer to two general questions that we should bear in mind to gain a full understanding of the relationship between taxation and the Church in the late Middle Ages. The first question is the foundations on which the principal ecclesiastical exactions to which I have referred were laid, the benefice system. The second question is how these exactions – developed during the Avignon papacy – evolved after the Council of Constance.

The taxation of ecclesiastical benefices

The principal common denominator of many of the taxes mentioned up to now – the main ones at least – was the taxation of benefices. In fact, the expansion of ecclesiastical contributions took place in parallel with that of the benefice system.[57] In this way, the benefice, understood in a very broad sense, became the key piece in the maintenance of the taxation system developed within the Church.

To proceed to the collection of tenths★ or other income taxes, it was necessary to tax benefices. The tenth★ was the result of the sum of all the incomes declared by each clergyman under oath. Beyond what was decreed at the Second Council of Lyon (1274) and the general instructions contained in the papal bulls of authorization, there is no record of a precise rule referring to how to conduct these assessments. In principle, all kinds of ecclesiastical income had to be taken into account, both from the benefice (tithes, oblations and other parish income) and from the Church domains, hence the distinction established between spiritualities and temporalities.[58] This gave rise to recording seigniorial income, such as that received by the monasteries and the highest-ranking churchmen. Over time, it was more common, and it must even have been more practical, to take as a value of reference the price of the leases made on those incomes, at times opting to establish an average estimate of several years' returns; in Portugal, for the tenth★ levied in 1320, the last ten years' income had to be taken into account;[59] in the Crown of Aragon, in the mid fifteenth century, the incomes of the years immediately preceding were evaluated (in some cases, of the last four years).[60] The expenses of, or taxes on the benefice had to be discounted from the total amount of income. The "rate" was, therefore, the net income, on the basis of which, since it was a tenth, the corresponding quota (10 per cent) had to be applied. The crux of the matter would be declaring numerous charges in order to obtain maximum relief, although not everything was validated by the supervising agents. In short, such estimates of the levels of ecclesiastical wealth were merely approximate; considered, for taxation purposes, to be *veros valores* (true values), they in fact fell quite some way short of the actual value of the incomes received.[61]

The taxes calculated for each contributor gave rise to the drafting of specific registers (tax books), while the collection proper was noted down in other books designed to monitor the payments that were being made in accordance with the stipulated periodicity (in the case of tenths★, it was usually two payments a year).[62] In many cases it was no longer even necessary to make a note of the holders of each benefice. This was because, strictly speaking, it was not the clergymen who were taxed, it was the benefices, regardless of the changes taking place with regard to the holders. Moreover, as the taxes remained virtually unchanged, it was enough to make serialized copies of previous registers with just the odd change here and there.

Throughout the period, there was a steady rise in the number of items assessed in parallel with the incorporation of new benefices, above all of newly established chaplaincies, which proliferated particularly in the towns and cities. To give just one well-documented example, the number of benefices taxed in the bishopric of Barcelona increased by almost 60% between 1347 and 1457.

The clergy taxed in each bishopric ranged from the simple curate (a clergyman without cure of souls) to the bishop, who was usually taxed the most, followed by the cathedral canons and parish rectors. Monastic establishments, both male and female, could be taxed globally or according to the post or office held, beginning with the principal dignitaries (abbots/priors). Foreign clergymen and establishments could also be registered, although exclusively for the incomes they received in that particular bishopric. This means that some would be taxed in several dioceses according to the different locations of their incomes or benefices; and the same thing could happen within each diocese, even more so in a period with a high incidence of pluralism, the accumulation of several benefices by the same holder. Nor were hospitals completely excluded from these valuations, even if it was only for the benefices attached to their chapels. This picture tended to diversify with the incorporation of other religious administrations or those associated with pious foundations (alms, masses and anniversaries) and even of bodies with lay members (confraternities, sacristies, works factories).

In all, this fiscal documentation reveals very diverse situations at different levels, between bishoprics or within each diocese. As opposed to the principal ecclesiastical dignitaries, whose higher taxes are the reflection of the substantial incomes they received, there was, at the other extreme, a number of clergymen on very low incomes. And the same contrast existed between the wealthiest monastic houses and other religious establishments with very low levels of income. It is of course true that the poorest were exempt from paying any taxes. Thus, according to the rules established by Pope Boniface VIII in 1301, secular clerics whose income was lower than seven florins a year were exempted from paying the tenth, a figure that in France would be set at seven Touraine pounds; in England, in the early fourteenth century a minimum contribution of three marks was being applied, increased later (fifteenth century) to 12; with respect to the Crown of Aragon, this minimum was established (1333) at 20 Barcelona pounds, as long as they were clergymen who personally resided there and did not possess other benefices.[63]

Along with the principle of proportionality (of share-outs made "in such a way that the better off should support the poorer"), in some countries, as in England, ways were also sought to incorporate the unbeneficed clergy as taxpayers, stipendiary mass-priests who received their payment not from endowments of property, but from stipends, although they were assigned lower quotas. Thus, in the four experimental poll taxes levied between 1377 and 1381, by taxing individual members of the clergy, attempts were made to ensure that no one escaped paying.

As has already been mentioned, tenths★ could also be used as a value of reference for the collection of annates★. With respect to the subsidies★ distributed according to proportional quotas, it was also necessary to resort to the tax registers of benefice inventories. In this case, the type of levy applied depended on the amount payable in the context of the diocese, once the overall sum had been shared out among all those in the province. Those subsidies★ could also be distributed, based on a limited number of quotas differentiated by categories of taxpayers, as can be observed in England (late fourteenth century), despite continuing to take as the principal reference the valuation of 1291.

Tenths★ remained immutable for a long time, which eventually led to a growing disparity with respect to real incomes. There was, however, always the possibility of making isolated discounts or other kinds of settlements. Over time, it became necessary to start taking more general measures, like those introduced in France in the 1360s and 70s, consisting in establishing reductions to half the value of the tenth★ (from then on, tenths★ began to count the same as the earlier twentieths). Fifty per cent reductions are also recorded in the Crown of Aragon in the first half of the fifteenth century. These measures must have been applied in response to the clergy's complaints and the widespread discontent due to the high level of fiscal pressure that by then they were under on several fronts.

With regard to the collection of procurations★/visitations, whether those paid to the bishops or those reserved by the papacy, it was necessary to draft another kind of register. In theory, the tax only concerned parish rectors; in this case, the payments were usually of quite uniform amounts, taking as a reference the rates established in Pope Benedict XI's bull *Vas electionis* (1336).

Changes and continuity after the fiscal reforms of Constance

The Council of Constance (1414–1418) put an end not only to the Western Schism but also, in part at least, to the Avignon taxation system, and the resulting increase in fiscal pressure that it had entailed. Important fiscal reforms were undertaken at it, reconfiguring the system under other parameters, and putting an end to certain abuses of authority.⁶⁴

On one hand, certain limits were placed on the collection of new tenths★, which from then on could only be established due to universal needs of the Church. Subsidies★ could only be charged if the prelates in each kingdom or province had consented to them. Two of the exactions that had become the most unpopular and abusive for the clergy, spolia and papal reservations of procurations★, were abolished. The papacy also completely renounced vacancies★, so after 1418 no further general reservations of that exaction were made.

As for annates★, although voices advocating their elimination were also raised, it was decided to keep them, but it was in the context of the different concordats established with the "nations" of Christendom where all the issues raised were eventually outlined, in both the beneficial and the fiscal order. In any case, there was a tendency to limit their receipt, it being decreed, among other things, that benefices of less than 24 florins in value should not pay. The practice was also ratified according to which they had to be paid in accordance with the *taxatio* established for tenths★.⁶⁵

The later Council of Basel was, on this point, more categorical; by a decree published in 1435, both the annates★ and the services paid by prelates were abolished. However, as this decree was never applied, annates★ continued to be paid throughout the fifteenth century, and some new taxes were even implemented, like the *quindennia* (half annate★). This tax, introduced generally by Pope Paul II in 1469, had to be paid every 15 years on the incomes of the benefices attached to the ecclesiastical corporations.⁶⁶ In the early modern period this exaction continued to play a certain role: King Henry VIII, after becoming the head of the Church of England, appropriated this papal tax and incorporated it into the purview of a new official: the Treasurer of First Fruits and Tenths.

To sum up, it is undeniable that the conciliar era brought about certain changes that tended to ease fiscal pressure on the clergy, even if it was only at the request of the pope. However, previous dynamics were soon restored, and fiscal grants for the benefit of secular monarchies were again made. In Castile the alternation of subsidies★ and tenths★ continued initially, but later on the tendency prevailed of converting tenths into subsidies★ *a un tanto alzado* (in return for a specific sum), while in the Crown of Aragon they moved swiftly from subsidies★ consented to by the clergy – at the beginning of the conciliar period – to subsidies★ authorized by the papacy, and once again, in the second half of the fifteenth century, to the introduction of new tenths★. Both types of payments served to finance the war against the infidel – in the war in Granada and later North African expeditions. In Portugal, extraordinary royal taxation led to general "requests", entailing the disappearance of tenths★ as a specific tax granted by the pope.⁶⁷ In England, besides continuing the practice initiated in the previous century with poll taxes on the unbeneficed clergy – five are recorded in the fifteenth century – other income taxes in the form of tenths★, and even forced loans in the sixteenth century, were resorted to; more often than not they were provisions granted by the clergy in the manner of subsidies★.

We have previously referred to the fossilization of taxes on benefices and the subsequent reductions made in some kingdoms. It was in this later period when global revisions of the assessments of ecclesiastical incomes began to be recorded. The first example is here in the Crown of Aragon, in what was the drafting of the so-called *veros valores* due to the major operation carried out after 1444 after the subsidy★ granted by Pope Eugene IV to King Alfonso the Magnanimous.⁶⁸ In Castile a similar operation took place in the period of the collection of the tenth★ of Calixtus III (*c.* 1458), which constitutes the most immediate precedent of the "establishment of true values" that would continue to be made throughout the sixteenth century.⁶⁹ In England, the *valor ecclesiasticus* of 1535 was the result of the first survey made since

1291 in order to properly assess a new annual tax of 10 per cent from all benefices. The *Valor* gave the government a solid understanding of the scale of the wealth of the church as a whole, and more particularly of the monasteries, some of which – the poorest ones – were dissolved the following year.[70] These generalized instances of bringing the taxes on benefices up to date were operations promoted by monarchs – with or without the backing of the papacy – at a time when they had already become the principal beneficiaries of the different taxes levied on the clergy, either subsidies⋆ or tenths⋆.

Furthermore, in some kingdoms, clergymen's assemblies could have experienced a certain boom when intervening in the processes of negotiating the new royal demands or subsidies⋆, at least with a view to obtaining reductions or other compensations.[71] It was therefore at the end of the Middle Ages when the fiscal activity of these assemblies began to be far better known with regard to the distribution of these subsidies⋆ or also to the establishment of apportionments to pay for other kinds of expenses (embassies, lawsuits, credit obligations).

The resurgence of clergymen's assemblies likewise connects with the gradual configuration of national Churches, theoretically more docile and more influenced by the power of princes. In any case, the submission of the clergy to state taxation would not have been possible without collaboration between the Church's ruling classes and the monarchical power, and, especially, without the role played by the bishops, who to a large extent became agents of the monarchy – in the context of the process of the clericalization of the machinery of government.[72] The fact is that ecclesiastical taxes went on to become an inevitable part of the fiscal policies introduced by monarchies, and of the resulting finances developed by the early modern state.

With the dawn of modernity, there were no radical changes. It was rather a case of the maintenance of the medieval legacy, at least with regard to the trends and dynamics hitherto developed. Apparently, the new forms of taxation introduced later – a field of study that is perfect for modern scholars specializing in tax affairs – were quite unoriginal, as they were more than anything derived from, or subsequent developments of, what already existed. In general terms, we are therefore speaking of a survival of benefice taxation as it had gradually been shaped in the centuries considered here.

Notes

1 GENET and VINCENT, *Etat et Eglise dans la genèse de l'Etat Moderne*; BARRALIS, BOUDET, DELIVRÉ and GENET, *Église et État, Église ou État?*
2 For a broader approach, see the study of BIN, *L'influence de la pensée chrétienne*.
3 Like the works of Samaran and Mollat and Favier noted into the bibliographical appendix. Others refer to the study of the collectorates, such as those of KIRSCH, *Die päpstlichen Kollektorien in Deutschland*; LUNT, *Accounts rendered by papal collectors*; José TRENCHS, *Aragón y la Cámara Apostólica*.
4 Schuchard for Germany; Le Roux for France (see bibliographical appendix).
5 Tello, for the Crown of Aragon (see bibliographical appendix).
6 For a general approach, see VONES-LIEBENSTEIN, "El método prosopográfico", pp. 351–364.
7 A conflict that also had a fiscal background; see DENTON, "Taxation and the conflict", pp. 241–264.
8 Apart, of course, from other initiatives on the series of papal bulls and other editions (or reissues) of chancellor documentation.
9 See WATT, "Taxation of the clergy in England", pp. 1–10; JURKOWSKI, "The History of Clerical Taxation", pp. 53–81.
10 www.dhi.ac.uk/taxatio/ [25 January 2022]
11 A good example of geospatial analysis, carried out within the framework of an Atlas of Medieval Christianity Project, is that of Meunier, which includes a map on the distribution of the amount on the tenth of 1313 throughout France (MEUNIER, "L'imposition des églises paroissiales", pp. 1–11).

12 Of course, there are numerous works devoted to the study of the tithe everywhere, but those carried out as a comparison between territories are scarce; see, in that sense, that of Hernández, "El diezmo y las catedrales en España e Anglaterra", pp. 81–111. More generally, see the volume directed by Lauwers, *La dîme, l'Église et la société féodale*.

13 According to Cazel, "Financing the Crusades", p. 135. See also Housley, *The italian crusades*; Housley, *The Avignon papacy and the crusades*; Baloup and Sánchez, *Partir en croisade*.

14 Again, according to Cazel, "Financing the Crusades", p. 138.

15 The series *Rationes decimarum Italiae* contains various volumes with some more modern reissues. In the case of the Crown of Aragon and Navarra, the edition corresponds to the collection of the last two years of the six-year tenth: see Rius, *Rationes decimarum Hispaniae*.

16 Boissellier, *La construction administrative d'un royaume*, p. 117.

17 Apart from the classical study of Renouard, *Les relations des papes d'Avignon*, see *Aux origines de l'État Moderne* and the dossier "Les comptabilités pontificales".

18 According to the point of view of G. Mattingly, noted in Prodi, *El soberano pontífice*, p. 13, n. 5.

19 Verger, "Le transfert de modèles d'organisation", pp. 32–39.

20 This was the new financing mechanism created to replace the taxes that had fallen under secular control as a result of the Bonifacian crisis, according to Watts, *The making of Politicies*, p. 163.

21 In this regard, see Clergeac, *La curie et les bénéfices consistoriaux*; Hoberg, *Taxae pro communibus servitiis*.

22 According to Genequand, "Des florins et des bénéfices", vacants and annates were interchangeable from a financial point of view.

23 In this field, the main reference study if that of Williman, *Records of the papal right spoil*.

24 Favier, *Les finances pontificales*, pp. 235–237.

25 They would be equivalent, to some extent, to the "graceful" subsidies given by the clergy to secular princes.

26 Actually, the tenths also came under the same consideration as *pro Terre Sancte* subsidies.

27 See Jamme, "Interférences et individuations fiscales", p. 41.

28 Battelli, "Le decime pontificie del Lazio", pp. 71–78.

29 Partner, "The Papacy and the Papal States"p. 359); on the other hand, it is a general trend to refer to these levies in different ways (either as taxes, rights, rents…), that is, without paying attention to greater subtleties.

30 This would more or less correspond to the tripartite classification postulated by Jean Favier, for whom the "procurationes" were distributions by legal categories. On the other hand, we put aside the censuses satisfied by some monasteries directly dependent on the Holy See.

31 However, in the French and Provençal area the number of collectors was changing; see Le Roux, "Mise en place des collecteurs et des collectories", pp. 53–54.

32 The outflow of capital outside the kingdom began to be viewed with concern by some monarchs, who were able to take measures to try to stop it.

33 Ekelund *et alii*, *Sacred Trust*; Witham, *Marketplace of the Gods*.

34 As it is well known, the return of the popes to Italy gave rise to the configuration of new finances based, above all, on the territorial resources obtained from the Italian papal lands, as well as on the development of new sources of income of a spiritual nature (sale of offices, indulgences).

35 Tabbagh, "Le prélèvement épiscopal sur les bénéfices", p. 667.

36 By way of example, see Sáez, "El cardenal Gil Álvarez de Albornoz", pp. 231–254.

37 See, for example, Graboïs, "Les séjours des papes en France au XIIe siècle", pp. 5–18.

38 Sarnowsky, "The Rights of the Tresaury", pp. 267–275; Bonneaud, "La crise financière des Hospitaliers", pp. 501–534; and Bonet, "Obligaciones y contribuciones de los hospitalarios", pp. 281–313.

39 See Ladero, *Fiscalidad y poder real en Castilla*, p. 204; Goñi, *Historia de la bula de la cruzada*.

40 More specifically, the problem arose with the purchases of cloths made by clergymen; see Morelló, "El clero de Catalunya davant els impostos del General", pp. 169–279.

41 In this regard, see Rogers, "Clerical Taxation under Henry IV", pp. 123–144.

42 On the succession of tenths and other ecclesiastical contributions at the time of King Peter the Ceremonious, see Tello, *"Pro defensione regni"*; and for the subsequent period, Morelló, "La contribución de la Iglesia a las arcas del rey", pp. 167–190).

43 In fact, it would not be 61 years but 52, if we do not count the years 1379–87, corresponding to the period of seizure of the rights of the Apostolic Chamber by the Aragonese monarch.

44 Apart from the works of Boissellier, see Farelo, "Payer au roi et au pape", pp. 55–106.

45 JURKOWSKI, "The History of Clerical Taxation", p. 56).
46 BOISSELLIER, *La construction administrative d'un royaume*, p. 42.
47 Such forecast later was reduced (1375) to 30,000 florins; MORELLÓ, "El clero de Catalunya davant els impostos del General", p. 194. Regarding the effective collection of the tenths at this time, see TELLO, *"Pro defensione regni"*.
48 GENEQUAND, "Des florins et des bénéfices", p. 6.
49 RABAN, *Mortmain legislation and the English Church*.
50 In this regard, see PALAO, *La propiedad eclesiástica*.
51 The list about forms of withholding ecclesiastical income does not end here, but could continue with the first fruits, usuries and uncertain pious causes, indulgences (alms from crusades), "responsiones" of the military orders ....
52 As postulates RIGAUDIÈRE, "Le clerc, la ville et l'impôt", pp. 21–69.
53 According to BILLEN and BOONE, "Taxer les écclesiastiques", pp. 251–272).
54 In general terms, the number of religious could be between 5–10 per cent of the urban population.
55 Among the most recent contributions, see also those of BUCHHOLZER-REMY, "Participation ou exemption fiscale", pp. 273–288); VERDÉS, "La contribución eclesiástica", pp. 131–168.
56 There were frequent cases of lay people who resorted to the clerical jurisdiction in order not to have to pay the municipal contributions.
57 Some authors refer to an explosion of the papal taxation on benefices; LEVILLAIN (dir.), *Dictionnaire historique de la papauté*, p. 410.
58 See especially DENTON, "The Valuation of the Ecclesiastical Benefices", pp. 231–241.
59 BOISSELLIER, *La construction administrative d'un royaume*, p. 117.
60 MORELLÓ, "Searching the 'Veros Valores'", pp. 207–225.
61 The real value of ecclesiastical benefices often remains obscure, according to JURKOWSKI, "'I Believe in miracles'", pp. 141–142.
62 Initially, the fact of making tax books had implications that do not occur in those regions where only collection books are kept; in this regard, see MOREROD, "La taxation décimale", pp. 331–332.
63 JURKOWSKI, "The History of Clerical Taxation", p. 63; JURKOWSKI, "Monastic History in Clerical Taxation Records", p. 10; CAUSSE, *Église, finance et royauté*, v.1, p. 244; MORELLÓ, "La contribución del clero de la Corona de Aragón", p. 98.
64 In this regard, the work of STUMP, "The Reform of Papal Taxation", is fundamental.
65 Not in vain, in France, due to the reductions made between 1363 and 1374 on the decimal rates, there had been a tendency to prioritize the collection of the subtractions before the rate.
66 This was intended to compensate for the interruption of those benefices in the payment of annates, since, being ascribed perpetually to such legal entities, it did not give arise to vacant or new provisions.
67 BOISSELLIER, *La construction administrative d'un royaume*, p. 116, n. 130).
68 MORELLÓ, "Acerca de la contabilización de los 'veros valores'", pp. 289-321; VALLDECABRES and VALLDECABRES (ed.), *Declaracions fiscals del clero valencià* ([25 January 2022]; see also KÜCHLER, *Les finances de la Corona d'Aragó*, p. 211 y sig.
69 PERRONE, "The Road to the Veros Valores", pp. 143–165.
70 Preserved in 22 manuscript volumes, it has been the subject of numerous studies based on the edition of CARLEY and HUNTER, (ed.), *Valor ecclesiasticus temp. Henrici VIII*.
71 PERRONE, *Charles V and the Castilian Assembly of the Clergy*.
72 In England, the divorce with Rome did not bring a relief – in fiscal terms – for the taxpaying clergy, but quite the opposite; see SCARISBRICK, "Clerical Taxation in England", pp. 41–54. SHEILS, "Modernity, Taxation and the Clergy", pp. 745–755.

References

Isabel R. ABBOTT, "Taxation of Personal Property and of Clerical Incomes, 1399 to 1402", in *Speculum*, XVII/4, 1942, pp. 471–498.
Aux origines de l'État Moderne. Le fonctionnement administratif de la Papauté d'Avignon, Rome, 1990.
Ludovic AYRAULT and Florent GARNIER (coords.), *La religion et l'impôt. Actes du colloque de Clermont-Ferrand, 6 et 7 avril 2006" / La Revue*, 1, mars 2012.
Daniel BALOUP and Manuel SÁNCHEZ MARTÍNEZ (ed.), *Partir en croisade à la fin du Moyen Âge. Financement et logistique*, Toulouse, 2015.

Christine Barralis, Jean-Patrice Boudet, Fabrice Delivré and Jean-Philippe Genet (dir.), *Église et État, Église ou État? Les clercs et la genèse de l'État moderne. Actes de la conférence organisée à Bourges en 2011 par SAA et l'université d'Orléans en l'honneur d'Hélène Millet*, Paris, 2014.

Ursmer Berlière, *Les collectories pontificales dans les ancients diòceses de Cambrai, Thérouanne et Tournai au XIV siècle*, Rome, 1929.

Prim Bertran Roigé, "La fiscalitat eclesiàstica en els bisbats catalans (1384–1392). Tipologies impositives i diferències territorials", in *Acta Historica et Archaeologica Mediaevalia*, 18, 1997, pp. 281–300.

Fabrice Bin, *L'influence de la pensée chrétienne sur les systèmes fiscaux d'Europe occidentale*, Paris, 2006.

Stéphane Boissellier, *La construction administrative d'un royaume. Registres de bénéfices ecclésiastiques portugais (XIII-XIVe siècles)*, Lisboa, 2012.

Pierre Bonneaud, "La crise financière des Hospitaliers de Rhodes au quinzième siècle (1426–1480)", *Anuario de Estudios Medievales*, 42/2, 2012, pp. 501–534.

John Caley and Joseph Hunter (ed.), *Valor ecclesiasticus temp. Henrici VIII auctoritate regia institutus*, 6 vol., London, 1810–1834.

Bernard Causse, *Église, finance et royauté: la floraison des décimes dans la France du Moyen Âge*, 2 vol., Paris-Lille, 1988.

Fred A. Cazel, "Financing the Crusades", in *A history of the crusades. 6: The impact of the crusades on Europe*, ed. Kenneth M. Setton, Madison, 1989.

Adiren Clergeac, *La curie et les bénéfices consistoriaux. Étude sur les communs et menus services, 1300–1600*, Paris, 1911.

James Hutchinson Cockburn, *Papal collections and collectors in Scotland in the Middle Ages*, Edinburgh, 1926.

Herbert S. Deighton, "Clerical Taxation by Consent, 1279–1301", in *The English Historical Review*, LXVIII/267, 1953, pp. 161–192.

Jeffrey H. Denton, "The Valuation of the Ecclesiastical Benefices of England and Wales in 1291–2", in *Historical research*, LXVI/161, 1993, pp. 231–241.

Jeffrey H. Denton, "Taxation and the conflict between Philip the Fair and Boniface VIII", in *French History*, 11/3, 1997, pp. 241–264.

Robert B. Ekelund *et alii*, *Sacred Trust: the medieval Church as an economic firm*, Oxford, 1996.

Mário Farelo, "Perspetivas de trabalho em torno da fiscalidade apostólica em Portugal (1309–1377)", in *Populaçao e Sociedade*, 31, 2019, pp. 24–47.

Jean Favier, *Les finances pontificales à l'époque du grand schisme d'Occident (1378–1409)*, Paris, 1966.

Jean Favier, "Temporels ecclésiastiques et taxation fiscale: le poids de la fiscalité pontificale au XIVe siècle", in *Journal des Savantes*, 2, 1964, pp. 102–127.

Andrea Gardi, "La fiscalità pontificia tra Medioevo ed età moderna", in *Società e Storia*, IX, 1986, pp. 509–557.

Philippe Genequand, "Des florins et des bénéfices: l'appareil fiscal pontifical au temps de la première modernisation des États (XIIIe-XIVe siècle)", in *Memini*, 24, 2018. Doi:10.400/memini.1126

Jean-Philippe Genet and Bernard Vincent (ed.), *Etat et Eglise dans la genèse de l'Etat Moderne. Actes du colloque de Madrid, 1984*, Madrid, 1986

José Goñi, *Historia de la bula de la cruzada en España*, Vitoria, 1958.

Aryeh Graboïs, "Les séjours des papes en France au XIIe siècle et leurs rapports avec le développment de la fiscalité pontificale", in *Revue d'Histoire de l'Eglise de France*, 49, 1963, pp. 5–18.

José Julián Hernández Borreguero, "El diezmo y las catedrales en España e Inglaterra hacia finales de la Edad Media", *Hispania Sacra*, LXV (julio-diciembre 2013), pp. 81–111. doi:10.3989/hs.2013.037

Hermann Hoberg, *Taxae pro communibus servitiis. Ex libris obligationum ab anno 1295 usque ad annum 1455*, Città del Vaticano, 1949.

Norman Housley, *The italian crusades: the papal-angevin alliance and the crusades against christian lay powers, 1254–1343*, Oxford, 1982.

Norman Housley, *The Avignon papacy and the crusades, 1305–1368*, Oxford, 1986.

Maureen Jurkowski, "Monastic History in Clerical Taxation Records", in *Monastic Research Bulletin*, 15, 2009, pp. 2–16.

Maureen Jurkowski, "The History of Clerical Taxation in England and Wales, 1173–1663: The Findings of the E 179 Project", in *The Journal of Ecclesiastical History*, 67/1, 2016, pp. 53–81. Doi:10.1017/S0022046915001608

Johann Peter Kirsch, *Die päpstlichen Kollektorien in Deutschland während des XIV. Jahrhunderts*, Paderborn, 1894.

Winfried Küchler, *Les finances de la Corona d'Aragó al segle XV (Regnats d'Alfons V i Joan II)*, València, 1997.

Miguel Ángel Ladero, *Fiscalidad y poder real en Castilla (1252–1369)*, Madrid, 1993.

Michel LAUWERS (ed.), *La dîme, l'Église et la société féodale*, Brepols, 2012.

Amandine LE ROUX, *Les collecteurs pontificaux dans le royaume de France (1316–1521)*, San Marino, 2008 [doctoral thesis from the Università di San Marino].

Amandine LE ROUX, "La fiscalité pontificale en Languedoc sous Jean XXII", in *Cahiers de Fanjeaux*, 45, 2009, pp. 237–254.

Amandine LE ROUX, "Mise en place des collecteurs et des collectories dans le royaume de France et en Provence (1316–1378)", in *Lusitania Sacra*, XXII, 2010, pp. 45–62.

Amandine LE ROUX, *Servir le pape, le recrutement des collecteurs pontificaux dans le royaume de France et en Provence de la papauté d'Avignon à l'aube de la Renaissance (1316–1521)*, 3 vol., Paris, 2010 [doctoral thesis from the Université de Paris-Ouest Nanterre la Défense].

"Les comptabilités pontificales", in *Mélanges de l'École française de Rome: Moyen Âge*, 118/2, 2006.

Philippe LEVILLAIN (dir.), *Dictionnaire historique de la papauté*, Paris, 1994.

William E. LUNT, *Papal Revenues in the Middle Ages*, 2 vol., New York, 1934 (reimp. 1965).

William E. LUNT, *Financial relations of the Papacy with England to 1327*, Cambridge, 1939.

William E. LUNT, *Financial relations of the Papacy with England, 1327–1534*, Cambridge, 1962.

William E. LUNT, *Accounts rendered by papal collectors in England (1317–1378)*, Philadelphia, 1968.

Alison K. MCHARDY, *Cerical Poll-Taxes in the Diocese of Lincoln, 1377–1381*, Lincoln, 1992.

José Luis MARTÍN RODRÍGUEZ, "El poblamiento de Portugal según "Collectoriae" vaticanas del siglo XIV: diócesis de Lisboa y Coimbra", in *Revista da Facultade de Letras*, 13, 1996, pp. 123–148.

Denis MENJOT and Manuel SÁNCHEZ MARTÍNEZ (ed.), *El dinero de Dios. Iglesia y fiscalidad en el Occidente medieval (siglos XIII-XV)*, Madrid, 2011.

Hugo MEUNIER, "L'imposition des églises paroissiales et des établissements monastiques d'après le compte de décimes de 1329", in *Atlas Archéologique de Touraine*, dir. Elisabeth ZADORA-RIO, Tours, 2014, pp. 1–11.

Guillaume MOLLAT and Charles SAMARAN, *La fiscalité pontificale en France au XIV siècle (période d'Avignon et du Grand Schisme d'Occident)*, Paris, 1905 (reimpr. 1968).

Jordi MORELLÓ BAGET, "Acerca de la contabilización de los "veros valores" en la Corona de Aragón y la gestión, del subsidio eclesiástico de 1443 (a partir de las cuentas de un notario barcelonés)", in *De l'autel à l'écritoire. Genèse des comptabilités princières en Occident*, dir. Thierry PÉCOUT, Paris, 2017, pp. 289–321.

Jordi MORELLÓ BAGET, "En torno a la disyuntiva décima/subsidio en Castilla y la Corona de Aragón durante la baja Edad Media", in *Hispania*, 77/257, 2017, pp. 643–671. doi: 10.3989/hispania.2017.017

Jordi MORELLÓ BAGET (ed.), *Financiar el reino terrenal. La contribución de la Iglesia a finales de la Edad Media (s. XIII–XVI)*, Barcelona, 2013.

Jordi MORELLÓ BAGET, "Searching the 'Veros Valores' of Some Religious Centres of Barcelona (About the Ecclesiastical Subsidy of 1443)", in *Religione e istituzioni religiose nell'economia europea (1000–1800). Atti della XLIII Settimana di Studi*, Prato, 2012, pp. 207–225.

Marcel PACAUT and Olivier FATIO (ed.), *L'hostie et le denier. Les finances ecclésiastiques du haut Moyen Âge à l'époque moderne*, Genève, 1991.

Francisco J. PALAO, *La propiedad eclesiástica y el juzgado de amortización en Valencia (siglos XIV a XIX)*, Valencia, 2001.

Peter PARTNER, "The Papacy and the Papal States", in *The Rise of the Fiscal State in Europe, c.1200–1815*, ed. Richard BONNEY, Oxford, 1999.

Sean PERRONE, "The Road to the Veros Valores. The Ecclesiastical Subsidy in Castile, 1540–42", in *Mediterranean Studies*, VII, 1998, pp. 143–165.

Sean PERRONE, *Charles V and the Castilian Assembly of the Clergy. Negotiations for the Ecclesiastical Subsidy*, Leiden-Boston, 2008.

Stefan PETERSEN, *Benefizientaxierungen in den Peripherie: Pfarrorganisation – Pfrundeneinkommen – Klerikerbildung im Bistum Ratzeburg*, Göttingen, 2001.

Paolo PRODI, *El soberano pontífice. Un cuerpo y dos almas: la monarquía papal en la primera Edad Moderna*, Madrid, 2010 [original version: Bolonia, 2006].

Sandra RABAN, *Mortmain legislation and the English Church, 1279–1500*, Cambridge, 1982.

Rationes decimarum Italiae nei secoli XIII e XIV, Città del Vaticano, 1932–2005.

Yves RENOUARD, *Les relations des papes d'Avignon et de compagnies commerciales et bancaires des 1316 à 1378*, Paris, 1941.

Albert RIGAUDIÈRE, "Le clerc, la ville et l'impôt dans la France du Bas Moyen Âge", in *Fiscalità e religione nell'Europa cattolica. Idee, linguaggi e pratiche (secoli XIV-XIX)*, ed. Massimo Carlo GIANNINI, Roma, 2015, pp. 21–69.

José Rius (ed.), *Rationes decimarum Hispaniae (1279–80)*, 2 v., Barcelona, 1946–1947.

Alan Rogers, "Clerical Taxation under Henry IV, 1399–1413", in *Bulletin of the Institute of Historical Research*, XLVI/114, 1973, pp. 123–144.

Emilio Sáez, "El cardenal Gil Álvarez de Albornoz y el impuesto de las procuraciones en Emilia-Romaña", in *Italica*, 14, 1980, pp. 231–254.

Jürgen Sarnowsky, "The Rights of the Tresaury: the Financial Administration of the Hospitallers on Fifteenth-Century Rhodes, 1421–1522", in *The Military Orders. Welfare and Warfare*, vol. II, ed. Helen Nicholson, Aldershot, 1998, pp. 267–275.

John J. Scarisbrick, "Clerical Taxation in England, 1485 to 1547", in *Journal of Ecclesiastical History*, 11, 1960, pp. 41–54.

Christiane Schuchard, *Die päpstlichen Kollektoren im späten Mittelalter*, Tübingen, 2000.

William Sheils, "Modernity, Taxation and the Clergy: the Disappearance of Clerical Taxation in Early Modern England", in *La fiscalita nell'economia europea secc. XIII-XVIII. Atti della Trentanovesima Settimana di Studi, 22–6 aprile 2007*, ed. Simonetta Cavaciocchi, Florence, 2008, pp. 745–755.

Phillip H. Stump, "The Reform of Papal Taxation at the Council of Constance (1414–1418)", in *Speculum*, 64, 1989, pp. 69–105.

Vicent Tabbagh, "Le prélèvement episcopal sur les bénéfices séculiers de la France septentrionale aux XIVe et XVe siècles", in *L'impôt au Moyen Âge. L'impôt public et le prélèvement seigneurial fin XIIe-début XVIe siècle. I. Le droit d'imposer. Actes du Colloque tenu à Bercy les 14, 15 et 16 juin 2000*, dir. Philippe Contamine, Jean Kerhervé and Albert Rigaudière, Paris, 2002.

Esther Tello, *"Pro defensione regni": Corona, Iglesia y fiscalidad durante el reinado de Pedro IV de Aragón (1349–1387)*, Roma, 2020.

José Trenchs, *Aragón y la Cámara Apostólica bajo Benedicto XII (1334–1342)*, Barcelona, 1971 [unpublished doctoral thesis].

Rafael Valldecabres and Teresa María Valldecabres (ed.), *Declaracions fiscals del clero valencià en 1444*, Valencia, 2018 (http://mural.uv.es/ravallro/TOT.pdf).

Pere Verdés Pijuan, "La contribución eclesiástica a la fiscalidad municipal en Cataluña durante la época bajomedieval", in *Financiar el reino terrenal. La contribución de la Iglesia a finales de la Edad Media (s. XIII-XVI)*, dir. Jordi Morelló Baget, Barcelona, 2013, pp. 131–168.

Jacques Verger, "Le transfert de modèles d'organisation de l'Église à l'Etat à la fin du Moyen Age", in *Etat et Eglise dans la genèse de l'Etat Moderne. Actes du colloque de Madrid, 1984*, ed. Jean-Philippe Genet and Bernard Vincent, Madrid, 1986, pp. 32–39.

Ursula Vones-Liebenstein, "El método prosopográfico como punto de partida de la historiografía eclesiástica", *Anuario de Historia de la Iglesia*, 14, 2005, pp. 351–364.

Hellen Watt, "Taxation of the clergy in England and Wales, c. 1180–1664: an introduction to the E 179 project and database", in *Clergy, Church and society in England and Wales, c. 1200–1800*, ed. Rosemary C. E. Hayes and William J. Shiels, York, 2013, pp. 1–10.

John Watts, *The making of Politicies: Europe, 1300–1500*, Cambridge, 2009 (translated into Spanish: Valencia, 2016).

Daniel Williman, *Records of the papal right spoil (1316–1412)*, Philadelphia, 1988.

Larry Witham, *Marketplace of the Gods. How Economics explains Religion*, Oxford, 2010.

PART II
Fiscal systems

5
CROWN OF ARAGON
Catalonia, Aragon, Valencia and Majorca

Mario Lafuente Gómez and Albert Reixach Sala

Introduction

By the end of the eleventh century, the north-eastern area of the Iberian Peninsula was divided in two different social formations. On the one hand, there lay Christian society, whose main features had developed during the High Middle Ages, and which, since the end of the first millennium, had been undergoing an intensive process of social change similar to that observed in other territories of the northern Iberian Peninsula and Europe. On the other hand, in the same area, we find a fully consolidated and organised Islamic society which was formed around a series of political entities that functioned, for all intents and purposes, as sovereign states that shared a similar attachment to the same community of believers.

The Crown of Aragon was a composite monarchy that emerged in the first of the two aforementioned social formations.[1] Its origins date back to 1137, with the dynastic union between the sovereign powers of the Kingdom of Aragon and the County of Barcelona, the former represented by Queen Petronila and the later by Count Ramon Berenguer IV, who, in turn, exercised his authority over three other Catalan counties (Girona, Osona, and Cerdanya). This singular initial configuration became more complex due to the Crown's territorial expansion during the rest of the Middle Ages, with the milestones of the conquest and feudal colonisation of the kingdoms of Majorca (1229) and Valencia (1238). In addition, from the end of the thirteenth century, the kings of Aragon expanded their dominions through the incorporation of various territories in the western Mediterranean and, especially, the islands of Sicily and Sardinia, (along with Corsica during certain stages) and, by the 1440s, Naples and much of the southern Italian Peninsula.

In the following pages, we will offer an interpretative synthesis of the origins and evolution of the taxation system that developed between the twelfth and fifteenth centuries in the peninsular territories of the Crown of Aragon. We will leave the Crown's overseas possessions aside, as they will be the main subject of study of other chapters. The study of taxation in the Crown of Aragon has a consolidated historiographical tradition, starting with the European projects on the genesis of the Modern State that emerged in the 1980s. More specifically, it has drawn the attention of several research teams based in the main cities of the former Iberian dominions of the Aragonese kings (Barcelona, Valencia, Zaragoza, and City of Majorca).[2] In recent years,

DOI: 10.4324/9781003023838-7

progress in the analysis of unpublished sources has been accompanied by a constant dialogue with other historiographic traditions, such as that of Castile and France.[3]

Following these authors, we will take into consideration three different areas of taxation. The first is made up of royal and manorial estates, which comprised the rents, rights and taxes levied by the monarch and the different seigneurial powers. We will pay special attention to the House of Aragon, which tended to extend its fiscal pressure beyond its strict jurisdictional domains in its aim to encompass the whole of society. Secondly, we will focus on general taxation, also known as State taxation, an expression that designates the tax system which, from the end of the thirteenth century, developed from the estates that met in the parliaments of the core territories of the Crown. In the mid-fourteenth century, this system came under the direction of commissions of deputies – the *Diputaciones del General* –[4] which were independent of royal power. Finally, we will shift our attention to the municipal sphere. We consider this to be a particularly significant context, since its analysis allows us to verify the scope of the transformations that took place in the two previous areas and, at the same time, gain insight into the role that various social forces played at different times.

In this chapter, except for very specific mentions, we will not deal with the ways in which the Church contributed to the monarchy's demands, nor with the transfer of fiscal mechanisms that the Crown had obtained through the delegation of the Roman Curia. All of these aspects will be addressed from a comparative perspective in the fourth chapter of this book.

Royal and seigneurial taxation

The seigneurial powers that coexisted in the northeast of the Iberian Peninsula benefited from several sources of tax revenue within their domains. However, with the passage of time, the Crown developed the ability to levy taxes on the inhabitants of all the territories under its suzerainty. During the central decades of the fourteenth century, some of these taxes became general in scope and, eventually, gave rise to a true system of general taxation, which we will analyse later.

The demands of kings and feudal lords within their domains

Royal and seigneurial taxation in the territories of the Crown of Aragon was based on the *pecha** (Aragon), the *qüestia** (Catalonia) and the *peita** (Valencia). It was a direct tax which was, in principle, paid by commoners on a yearly basis. It had developed from the old feudal fees that lords imposed on their peasants through the capitation system, which underwent important changes from the end of the twelfth century. The main novelty was the conversion of the tax into a collective obligation, so that local governments began to negotiate and distribute the amounts that their lords demanded. In Aragon, this change meant a transition from the system of *pechas capitales* (per capita *pechas**, levied on fiscal units) to that of *pechas tasadas* (appraised *pechas**, levied on communities), which became the most widespread at the end of the thirteenth century. In Catalonia, the transition from one system to the other took place mainly within the framework of the royal domain, where the *qüestia** was levied collectively since the twelfth century, while in Valencia, the *peita** was a similarly collective tax after its implementation in the second half of the thirteenth century.[5]

Along with the *pechas*, *qüesties* and *peites**, which were collected collectively through direct taxes, there were other taxes levied on commerce and other types of economic activities. In the Crown of Aragon, these levies received different names, often related to the places of collection (*portazgos*, *pontajes*), the taxed products (*carnerajes*), the form of measurement (*mesuratges*) or simply to the act of transportation (*peajes/peatges*★) or the legal status of the transportation itself (*lezdas/lleudes*★). This scheme was under the control of the local bailiffs until the end of the thirteenth century, when it switched to the control of the general bailiffs. Furthermore, this mosaic of taxes was complicated by all kinds of recurrent alienations.[6]

The exercise of manorial rights also resulted in the imposition of other exactions by both the lords and the sovereigns, although their application throughout the territory was much more heterogeneous and their yield quantitatively lower. Some of these taxes were levied collectively, following the procedure applied in the case of the *pechas*, *qüesties* and *peites*★ during the thirteenth century. We find this pattern, for example, in the *cenas de presencia y de ausencia*, which communities, especially smaller ones, paid to their lords as a redemption of the old feudal obligation that compelled them to provide them with accommodation and maintenance.[7] Similarly, Islamic and Jewish communities (*aljamas*) were obliged to pay an annual tribute to their lords. In the case of the Jewish communities under royal jurisdiction, there is evidence that they regularly paid *qüesties* or *peites*★ and *cenas de presencia y de ausencia*, on top of constant subsidies and other demands, as well as a regular tax called *protección* (protection) between the mid-fourteenth century and 1410.[8] As for the Muslim communities, which were especially important in the kingdoms of Aragon and Valencia and the southwestern part of Catalonia, documents reveal the payment of the right of *cena* together with other extraordinary contributions, coinciding especially with periods of war.[9]

War transforms royal taxation into taxes of general scope

The strengthening of the monarchy that accompanied the transformation of the feudal system in the Crown of Aragon during the thirteenth century entailed the expansion of the sovereigns' powers throughout the entire spectrum of social relations. This implied the metamorphosis of some of the traditional seigneurial demands, which gradually turned into benefits obtained through taxation. War played a decisive role in this process.

The first examples of demands linked to periods of war were the *redención de hueste* or *redempció d'host*, which were levied by the monarchy in Aragon, Catalonia, and Valencia, along with the custom called *Princeps namque*, which was found exclusively in Catalan territory.

The appropriation of the right to military service by the nobility, including the monarch, had been regulated within the framework of local legislation during the eleventh and twelfth centuries, although, in practice, its execution was usually carried out through the bartering of personal service in exchange for a financial contribution. Over time, these different normative traditions were integrated, at the initiative of the Crown, in a process that accelerated in the middle of the thirteenth century, when the monarchy promoted the approval of charters that allowed the military mobilisation of all its subjects and vassals in both the kingdoms of Aragon (1247) and Valencia (1271). However, the significance of these charters did not lie in their literal application, but rather in the expansion of taxation through the exchange of military service for an economic contribution. In this way, the *redención de hueste* constituted a very important resource for the funding of the armies of the monarch from the middle of the thirteenth century until the third quarter of the following century.[10]

In Catalonia, the *Princeps namque* is documented since the twelfth century. This was a figure of customary law (*usatge*) that allowed the sovereign to demand the military mobilisation of all his subjects and vassals in the case of an attack or invasion of their own territory. From the second half of the thirteenth century, the *Princeps namque* became another source of income, since, as we have seen when referring to the *redempció d'host*, military service was frequently commuted for the payment of a previously negotiated sum.[11]

As we have just seen, both the *redención de hueste* and the *Princeps namque* aimed at obtaining economic resources to support the monarch's armies. This need triggered the main fiscal innovations promoted by the monarchy since the end of the twelfth century. These royal efforts materialised in the demand for *monedajes**, a formula that involved the levying of a direct tax on the income of commoners, and *bovatges**, which were collected especially in Catalonia. Both solutions date from the reign of Peter II (1196–1213) and were consolidated in the reign of James I (1213–1276). Among the arguments used by the monarchy to justify its demands were the preservation of internal peace, the need to finance the war against Muslims, financial aid for the marriage of certain women of the royal family and, above all, the preservation of the value of the currency. This last argument was decisive in legitimising the tax, since the payment of *bovajes** and *monedajes** was presented as a way of guaranteeing that the sovereigns would not carry out currency devaluations.[12] Both taxes continued to form part of the exactions required by the monarchy throughout the thirteenth century in situations of special need, as shown by the demands for *bovatges** in Catalonia and *monedajes** in Aragon.[13]

The apparent territorial specialisation of the *bovajes** and the *monedajes** was not as strict as it may seem, since both taxes were required in both territories. It is true, however, that the former was never well received in Aragon, while the latter was similarly unpopular in Catalonia.[14] It is also worth highlighting the different evolution of both these taxes. The *bovaje** declined in Catalonia from the 1300s, because of the general franchises obtained by the population of royal and ecclesiastical domains (*Corts* of Barcelona, 1300) and the privileges later issued for the benefit of ecclesiastical manors,[15] whereas the *monedaje** consolidated into an ordinary direct tax in Aragon. During the reign of James II (1291–1327) the *monedaje** became a direct tax, collected every seven years, and levied on all solvent commoner households that owned more than 70 Aragonese shillings (*sueldos*). The actual collection amounted to 7 shillings per household.[16]

Starting in the last two decades of the thirteenth century, the demand for *monedajes** and *bovajes** was accompanied by demands for other economic services of a general nature. Their amount and scope used to be the subject of intense negotiations with the estates gathered in the *Cortes* or Parliaments which, as they emphasised, granted donations *non ex obligatione seu debito, sed solum ex providentia et mere voluntate*.[17] Among the more recurrent formulas, we find the *gabelas sobre la sal* and certain types of *herbajes*, although the most relevant fiscal instruments at this time were, without doubt, the *sisas** *generales*, which were approved at the end of the century in the context of the serious conflict that arose between the kings of Aragon and a powerful coalition made up of the Franco-Angevin dynasty and the Papacy. In Aragon, a *sisa general* was approved by the *Cortes* of Zaragoza in 1290,[18] while, in Catalonia, the same was done in 1292 by the *Corts* held in Barcelona.[19]

In the 1320s, a fiscal system based on indirect taxes on trade and the trafficking of goods was progressively introduced in the Crown of Aragon. It was first applied in cities and was considered to be an essential instrument for meeting the Crown's extraordinary taxation needs. It later became the core of the general taxation approved in the assemblies and managed by the commissions of deputies or the territorial councils. The triggering factor for this process was the need to finance the Crown's military campaigns in the Mediterranean, specifically on the island of Sardinia, from 1321, and from 1356 in the War of the Two Peters, which was fought mainly in the Iberian Peninsula. To guarantee the material endowment of their armies, the monarchs resorted to various sources of financing. Some of them were of a non-fiscal nature, such as the sale of patrimony, with the consequent reduction of the royal domain, but above all the Crown engaged in the request for extraordinary economic services.

The funding of the Sardinian campaigns by fiscal means has been studied in depth by several authors.[20] According to the conclusions proposed by M. Sánchez on the first campaign, which started in 1321, the negotiations gave rise to a major fiscal cycle that was common to all the Crown states, together with Sicily and Majorca. This initiative levied a sum of three and a half million of Barcelonese *sous* (shillings), territorially distributed in the following manner: Catalonia, 35.4 per cent; Aragon, 31.7 per cent; Valencia, 22.0 per cent; Sicily, 5.7 per cent; and Majorca, 5.2 per cent.[21]

The collection of indirect taxes through *sisas*★ experienced a decisive boost in the mid-1340s, in the context of the fiscal cycles aimed at financing the reintegration of the Kingdom of Majorca into the Crown. This fiscal pressure was especially manifest in Catalonia, where Peter IV obtained large donations. In the case of the settlements under royal jurisdiction, these quantities were raised through long-term credits, a practice that the king favoured. In the Kingdom of Valencia indirect taxation (*sisas*★) experienced a similar boost, while, in Aragon, the crown imposed the collection of direct taxes.[22]

Just a decade later, the military expedition aimed at quelling the rebellion of the Judge of Arborea in Sardinia motivated the continued strengthening of indirect taxation. In this context, the collection of the economic services ran through the same channels that had preferably been used since the 1320s. Therefore, the indirect taxation in the royal estates of Catalonia and Valencia was, again, noteworthy, while in Aragon direct taxation continued to prevail.[23]

This model of economic organisation for the military endowment of a great Mediterranean expedition was lastly experienced in the biennium of 1354–1355. From then on, negotiations returned to the assembly, as had happened in the late thirteenth century. Thus, we switch from a system based on economic cooperation between the royal domain and ecclesiastical manors and the military mobilisation of the feudal aristocracy to a model based on the participation of the diversity of entities that composed each of the three estates of the realm. This transformation materialised between 1356 and 1364, during the war against the Crown of Castile and coincided with the creation of the *Diputaciones del General*, institutions that emerged in parallel to represent the estates of Aragon, Valencia, and Catalonia. The main function of these *Diputaciones* was precisely to manage the outcoming product of extraordinary taxation and, more specifically, a new indirect, customs-based tax of a general scope significantly called *generalidades*★.[24]

Old resources for a new stage (c. 1380–late fifteenth century)

These transformations culminated in a general tax system to which we will pay attention in the next section. In parallel, from the 1380s the Crown continued to request occasional extraordinary contributions. These demands came into conflict with the privileges of the estates and municipalities. Therefore, the monarchy chose to combine negotiation with different forms of pressure. This wave of exactions began in the last decades of the reign of Peter IV and continued with his children and, later, with the new Trastámara dynasty. The extraordinary and controversial nature of these requests has led to the suggestion that they could be interpreted as a "new tax system", although most of the methods had distant precedents.[25]

In addition to the occasional recuperation of some taxes of seigneurial origin, the monarch's demands usually revolved around three different mechanisms. Firstly, the *coronatges*, which were donations that were linked to the accession to the throne, followed by the *maridatges*, requested on the occasion of the wedding of princesses and, more rarely, the *novella cavalleria*, which was associated with the knighting of the king's sons. Between the end of the thirteenth and the middle of the fourteenth centuries, these subsidies were always linked with the payment of the *qüèstia*★, whereas from 1356 they became extraordinary requests, first levied on the Crown's domains and later, on those under ecclesiastical jurisdiction. More specifically, Peter IV and his children requested five *coronatges* and five *maridatges*, and, under the rule of the House of Trastámara, we can document one *coronatge* and five *maridatges*.[26]

Secondly, the king's retinue and other members of the royal family demanded complementary contributions under different pretexts that usually materialised in *redenciones de penas* or the purchasing of privileges and freedoms by communities. This practice has been defined as a form of "concealed taxation" and, from the analysis of specific towns, scholars have been able to ascribe a polyhedric character to these types of contributions.[27]

Finally, during the reigns of Alphonse the Magnanimous (1416–1458) and John II (1458–1479), major cities like Barcelona and Valencia granted various loans to both kings. In these operations, such cities would transfer to the monarch the money collected through the selling of *censales* (perpetual annuities), and, in turn, he would repay them with the assignment of yields from the royal patrimony until the maturity date. The contributions of the city of Valencia are particularly noteworthy, especially during the reign of King Alphonse the Magnanimous.[28]

In conclusion, after years of an intense tax burden related to the conflicts over the control of the western Mediterranean and against Castille, war had ceased to be the main driver of the Crown's tax machinery and, consequently, the royal administration was forced to return to alternative practices. Nevertheless, the Crown continued to develop certain taxation instruments that were specially adapted to war. Three of them were of major economic and social significance: the *quema*, the *derecho de italianos* and the *derecho de alemanes y saboyanos*. These were three forms of indirect taxation that applied to the value of the different goods that were introduced into the Crown of Aragon by subjects of the king of Castile (*quema*), from the northern Italian states (*derecho de italianos*), and by subjects of the German emperor and the duke of Savoy (*derecho de alemanes y saboyanos*). The rationale behind these taxes was the need to compensate for the attacks on trade committed by Castilian, German and Italian subjects and organisations. The *quema*, which was the oldest, was imposed from the first third of the fourteenth century and represented between 1.25 and 2.5 per cent of the merchandise's value.[29] The *derecho de los italianos* came into practice in 1403 and entailed a fee of a 1.25 per cent;[30] while the *derecho de alemanes y saboyanos* was introduced in 1420 and rose to a fee of 1.66 per cent.[31] Furthermore, the Crown claimed its rights on the booty resulting from war. In this case the fee was of one fifth of the collected booty and was therefore known as the *quinto real*.[32] Other fees were occasionally imposed, as in the case of early fourteenth century Valencia, when the Crown chose to demand a seventh part of the booty (the so-called *setmo*).[33]

General taxation

As we have just pointed out, the War of the two Peters had a decisive impact on the transformation of the taxation related to the funding of royal armies. The military requirements saw the development of the taxation and funding schemes of the *Diputaciones* of the three main territories of the Crown of Aragon (Aragon, Catalonia, and Valencia), whose structures endured until the eighteenth century. We will now see their common origins and subsequent evolution.

Into general taxation: the War of the two Peters (1356–1366)

The conflict with Castile was certainly a decisive milestone. Unlike previous conflicts, which were never a threat to the Crown's core peninsular territories, the war took on an eminently defensive nature. This fact impacted the thinking of its funding: from then on, the economic and military organisation of the king's armies became a common concern for the oligarchies of the three estates. Therefore, the defence of the land began to centre around the *Cortes,* whether territorial (those celebrated separately in each of the Crown's territories) or general (those that gathered the representatives of the three estates of Aragon, Catalonia, Valencia, and Majorca). Under these circumstances, the economic contributions related to the defence of the Crown's territorial integrity were extended to the whole of the social body, and every estate therefore had to assume part of the tax burden.

This transformation began in the Aragonese *Cortes* of Cariñena (1357). Its taxation policies were replicated in the *Corts* of Valencia (1357–1358) and the Catalan *Corts* of Cervera (1359). From then on, the parliaments took control of almost every aspect of their management through the election of specialised boards of deputies. Similarly, this same context saw the creation of the aforementioned *generalidades**, a customs tariff with a protectionist intention that was approved in the General *Cortes* of Monzón of 1362–1363. In principle, this tax was meant to be collected on the outer borders of the Crown's territory, but not long after its inception it was revised and levied autonomously in each of the Crown's peninsular states.[34] This decision was taken in the Aragonese *Cortes* of Zaragoza of 1364, the Valencian *Corts* of Cullera-Valencia of 1364–1365 and the Catalan *Corts* of Barcelona of 1365. In these parliaments, the oligarchies of each of the Crown's territories adapted the tax to their own economic dynamics and thereby developed autonomous tax structures that were under the control of independent boards of deputies. The constant financial needs of the *Diputaciones*, usually linked to their permanent indebtedness, implied the survival of the new tax beyond the end of the war. Thus, the *generalidades** came to be, in due time, the basis of each of the Crown states' treasuries.[35]

Because of the consolidation of these fiscal structures, from the second half of the decade of 1360, the majority of the contributions that were meant to fund foreign wars had to be approved by the assembly and were managed, in turn, by each *diputación*. Broadly speaking, the continuation of the Sardinian campaigns from 1366 lay behind the demands for the majority of royal subsidies. These were paid in the form of loans, which were presented before the *Cortes* that took place in the second half of the fourteenth century, that is, the *Cortes* under the reign of Peter IV, in 1368, 1373, 1376, 1379–1380 and 1383–1394, and under his son's reigns in 1393 and 1396. In most of these cases, the contributions granted were levied principally through the aforementioned *generalidades** and, less importantly, with hearth taxes, which were distributed among the different communities according to the jurisdiction they fell under and the number of homes in each of them.[36]

Under the rule of the House of Trastámara the balance between the power of the estates and the Crown changed considerably. In this new scenario, the famous Italian campaigns of Alphonse the Magnanimous (1416–1458), together with his conflicts against the king of Castile, did not seemingly entail a direct fiscal pressure on the *Diputaciones* of the Crown's peninsular territories.[37] In any case, we are still in need of global studies on the evolution of general taxation from the end of the fourteenth century.

The development of the Diputaciones del General *in Aragon, Catalonia, and Valencia (c. 1360–end of the fifteenth century)*

Starting with Aragon, the evolution of the taxation system run by the *Diputación* went as follows: the *Cortes* of Zaragoza of 1364 adapted the conditions approved in the General *Cortes* of Monzón of 1362–1363 to the specifics of the Aragonese territory. They established a general tax of 5 per cent of the value of all the goods that left the kingdom and, conversely, liberalised the entry of all products besides wine, which was taxed at three shillings (*sueldos*) per load.[38] The success of this system relied on Aragonese exportations of wool and cereal and did not affect the cloth trade, which was dominated by Catalan and Bearnese merchants who were also heavily invested in the local credit market. In the following decades, the *generalidades*★ and the specifics of their collection were constantly adjusted to the fiscal needs of the Crown and the *Diputación*, but always taking into account their possible impact on the market. In the *Cortes* of Zaragoza of 1413–1414, the exports of wool, wheat and livestock were specifically taxed. This laid the basis for the taxation system until 1449, when its overall workings were reorganised.[39]

The custom tariffs were collected through a network of collecting points located both in border towns and in the main urban centres in the kingdom's interior. To make the process of collection more agile, the territory was dived into several administrative districts, called *sobrecollidas*, which were assigned to an officer, known as *sobrecollidor*. Under their supervision, the tax collectors (*collidores*), together with other employees, were in charge of the collection itself. Additionally, the pressing needs of the Crown's treasury led the deputies to adopt a system based on the leasing of these taxes, which left their management in the hands of large investors, in exchange for the payment of a sum previously agreed upon in the *Cortes*. This solution was applied regularly between the end of the fourteenth and the middle of the fifteenth centuries, although the chronic indebtedness of the *Diputación* and other conjunctural problems deteriorated the profitability of these investments.[40]

In Catalonia, the taxes that were under the control of the *Diputació del General* were based on two main points: the *generalitats dels draps*, which were levied on the production and trade of textiles, and the *drets d'entrades i eixides*, which were taxes on the import and export of all kinds of goods and were levied in different border enclaves, both inland and maritime. Among the taxes on textiles, there was a distinction between the *bolla de plom*, which was levied on the manufacture of fabrics according to their quality, and the *dret del segell de cera*, a general tax of 10 per cent on the value of resales and a 5 per cent tax on consumption-oriented purchases. The *drets d'entrades i eixides* taxed a general amount *ad valorem* of 0.8 per cent, although this sum varied to favour the imports of some products or to penalise the export of others. All of these figures were introduced in the *Corts* of Tortosa of 1365, following the precedent of the aforementioned *Cortes* of Monzón of 1362–1363 and, starting in the 1380s, were subject to various adjustments. From then on, despite the seeming stability of the different taxes, some tariffs were modified. The doubling of the basic tax rate for the *drets d'entrades i eixides* throughout the fifteenth century is especially noteworthy.

The deputies did not only intervene in the tax rates, they also experimented with different forms of management. Nevertheless, around 1390, the formula that survived until the beginning of early modernity was effectively consolidated. It consisted of the triennial lending of the tariffs (*drets d'entrades i eixides*) for the whole of Catalonia, in parallel with the *bolla de plom* and the *segell de cera dels draps*, which were based around roughly thirty collection areas. The *generalitats dels draps* offered a potential income that ascended to over 50,000 pounds (*lliures*) during the first half of the fifteenth century. However, in other circumstances the deputies considered the direct appointment of collectors to be more profitable, as happened regularly in the extensive collection area led by the city of Barcelona from 1431 until the early sixteenth century.[41]

The Kingdom of Valencia followed a similar path to that of Catalonia. The *Corts* of 1388–1389 saw the development of a double taxation system: firstly, on textiles, with the tax known as *tall del drap*, and secondly on foreign trade, with the exactions known as *tretes*. The *tall del drap* was levied on the production, circulation, and sale of different types of clothes and, in 1404, became a form of ordinary income for the *Diputació*. It experienced changes in the types of clothes that were subject to taxation and their tax rates until 1432, when the tax rate was set at

8.75 per cent. It was levied on three large circumscriptions that contained minor subdivisions within them.[42]

The Diputaciones del General *resort to debt from the decade of the 1360s*

In any case, the development of the *generalidades** was not exclusively the result of the monetary demands of the monarchy or the protectionist interest of the oligarchy. From the beginning of the whole process, in the decade of the 1360s, another factor played a decisive role in the birth of the tax. We are referring to the indebtedness of the *Diputaciones*, prompted by the need for a rapid response to the fiscal demands of the second half of the War of the Two Peters. In effect, the Aragonese, Catalan, and Valencian *Diputaciones* had to face structural indebtedness and, therefore, were forced to maintain the fiscal system they had implemented in the 1360s. Only in this way were they able to ensure the income necessary to satisfy the promised interest.

This strategy was adopted first in Catalonia, where the *Corts* held in Tortosa in 1365 decided to issue public annuities (*censals*), which were assigned to the whole of the *General*, the political community formed by the inhabitants of the Principality. At that time, a considerable number of the economic services granted to the monarchy were financed through long-term loans, whose return was linked directly to the collection of the aforementioned *generalitats** and other taxes controlled by the *Diputació*. Debt repayment was secured by the political community as a whole and can therefore be understood as public debt and the basis of a genuine system of state taxation. Far from being a one-off solution, this type of bond emission became a staple of the fiscal practices of the *Diputació* of Catalonia during the following decades and the whole of the fifteenth century. During the first third of the fifteenth century, the *Diputació*'s debt varied between 290,000 and 460,000 pounds (*lliures*), while the average interest decreased until it oscillated between 6.25 per cent and 4.54 per cent.[43]

The *Diputación del General* of Aragon started to issue public debt securities starting from the *Cortes generales* held in Monzón in 1376. As in Catalonia, the reliance of the *Diputación* on these forms of credit was practically absolute from the very beginning. Therefore, the *Diputación* assembled a complex administrative system that funnelled the collection of the aforementioned *generalidades** (a form of customs duty) towards the repayment of the interests on its debt. This system was supposed to generate a surplus, enabling it to pay for both the institution's expenses and the interest on its debt, but the constant increase of its indebtedness placed it under the threat of bankruptcy. In this context, the deputies adopted three successive remediation plans between 1398 and 1488. In all three cases, the deputies' strategy was based on amortising part of the previous loans through the obtention of new long-term loans at a lower interest rate. Additionally, the *Diputación* occasionally imposed new customs fees, collected indirect general taxes, and cut back on spending that was deemed superfluous. Nonetheless, at the end of the Middle Ages, the *Diputación*'s total debt was close to 450,000 pounds (*libras*).[44]

Regarding the Kingdom of Valencia, the first debt emission based on perpetual annuities (*censals*) took place in 1390 and, as in Catalonia and Aragon, continued throughout the rest of the Middle Ages and the early modern period.[45] Nevertheless, unlike in the case of Aragon, the Valencian *Diputació* was never under special pressure with regard to the payment of capital interest, since the repayment of loans was not usually postponed beyond six or seven years, at least during the first quarter of the fifteenth century. In this way, in 1418, the capital obtained through the sale of *censals* reached the sum of 110,000 pounds, which, with an interest rate of 7.14 per cent, resulted in an interest payment of 8,000 pounds *per annum*. In this context, the total amount of interests paid by the Valencian *Diputació* amounted to 10,000 pounds *per annum*.

This sum, although quite considerable, was far from the 20,000 pounds that the *Diputació* paid in the 1480s.⁴⁶

Municipal taxation

From the twelfth century on, the communities of the peninsular territories of the Crown of Aragon began to assume the levying and managing of the taxes that were paid by their inhabitants under different circumstances.⁴⁷ As of the 1350s, their powers were reinforced with the diffusion of mid- and long-term debt and the general consolidation of regular taxation.

The origins of municipal taxation (twelfth–mid fourteenth centuries)

Independently of their juridical status, the inhabitants of a specific town or village had collective needs to be met, such as the maintenance of communal infrastructure – churches, bridges, or roads – as well as the obligation to fulfil their lord's demands. Thus, from the end of the twelfth century, we can document the distribution of common expenses in towns like Lleida or Zaragoza.⁴⁸

To better understand these fiscal strategies, we need to stress a basic difference between the towns and cities of Aragon and those of Catalonia, Valencia, and Majorca. The former, as was the case in Castile, enjoyed the income generated by the possession of real estate, which was known as *bienes de propios*. In contrast, in the latter, these formulas were non-existent. In Catalonia, Valencia, and Majorca the primary forms of a town's shared treasury, an intrinsic element for the formal recognition of communities, had to rely on the payment of taxes by their inhabitants and, more occasionally, on loans granted by the local elites or by city-dwelling Jews. These contributions of the inhabitants were usually materialised through taxes proportional to their wealth, known in due time as *tallas* or *talles*. Their levying was the first form of taxation at the local level, with consequences that went further than the strictly economic: these taxes contributed to the continuing development of permanent bodies of local government and representation both in Catalonia and Aragon.⁴⁹

Besides the needs of the community itself, the monarchs' requests were decisive in the process of consolidation of municipal taxation: these demands fomented a change in the perception of local contributions, from individual to collective and, therefore, managed by local councils or *universitates*. We can observe this trend in Teruel, where, at the beginning of the thirteenth century, the representatives of the community took on the responsibility of collecting the *pecha**. Along the same lines, in the Kingdom of Valencia, the rudimentary local administrations became, shortly after the Christian conquest, authentic tax agencies at the service of the Crown.⁵⁰

The need to distribute the contributions arising from the *qüestia**, *peita** and *pecha** among the whole community, according to its inhabitants' patrimonies, resulted in the progressive implementation of certain organisational structures.⁵¹ We can see evidence of this in cities such as Zaragoza (1180), Lleida (1200), Barcelona (1226), City of Majorca (1237), and Valencia (1246 and 1252). Therefore, with the monarch's authorisation, and notwithstanding an important degree of autonomy, the communities developed techniques to rate goods, according to the information collected through wealth registers known as *llibres del manifest, de estimes,* or *de vàlues,* in Catalonia and Valencia.⁵²

As we have seen, at the end of the thirteenth century, the monarch authorised the implementation of the first types of indirect taxes on the consumption and trade of various goods. It was, however, an extraordinary resource, with a limited validity and usually tied to the funding of public works or other local needs. This was the case of Barcelona at the end of Peter III's (1276–1285) rule, when the king gave permission to the city's representatives to introduce a *sisa* to fund the construction of the city's wall without the intervention of royal officers. In the following year's difficult scenario, this tax was generally levied in the entirety of the royal and ecclesiastical domains of Catalonia, thus anticipating the first experience of a general tax in the Principality in the *Corts* of 1289 and 1292. In this same period, we find similar concessions in some Valencian and Aragonese towns and, from 1300, in Majorca, Ibiza and Menorca. Even considering the fact that these later concessions were not approved in the assemblies, as had happened in the previous decades, they did share the goal of contributing to the military campaigns of the monarchy or to other defence-related expenditures.[53]

Beginning in the 1320s and 1330s, the successive Mediterranean expeditions of the monarchs and members of the royal family served to accelerate this process. We can find direct documentary evidence of this in the royal towns of Catalonia and, more generally, Valencia, though not in Aragon, where the Crown's demands were usually fulfilled through direct taxation.[54] In the context of the conquest of Sardinia in 1321–1322, the main towns of Catalonia were authorised to levy *imposicions** on a wide variety of products and activities. This experience was repeated in the following decade, in 1340, to combat the threat of the Marinid Sultanate in Northern Africa, and it was later on expanded to all of the communities under royal jurisdiction.

The consolidation of municipal taxation (c. 1350–1500)

In spite of the considerable fiscal experience of the towns and cities of the Crown of Aragon, and despite the differences and similarities between its territories, the systems of municipal taxation were not considered to be consolidated until the decade of the 1350s.[55] The decisive turning point was, in broad strokes, the constant recurrence to debt by the local administrations in the decades of the 1340s and 1350s. In order to match the constant demands of the Crown, credit became a more systematic recourse, since the gathering of *tallas* and indirect taxes was always a slower process. Finally, the emission of public debt bonds, instead of contracting short-term loans, implied the prolongation of exactions until they became permanent.

The determining effect of the reliance on credit: from short-term loans to the emission of public debt

From the thirteenth century onwards, the city councils had had to ask for loans to meet fiscal demands and other urgent necessities. Yet, the rise of royal contributions and subsidies from 1330 on revealed the need for relying on mid- and long-term loans, usually through professional bankers (*canviadors* or owners of *taules de canvi*).[56] Likewise, in the 1330s, and, to a greater extent in the 1340s, many Catalan municipalities began to issue lifelong and perpetual annuities, known as *violaris* and *censals*.[57] This was the case of Cervera before 1332, and Girona between 1342 and 1343. In the same period, under the auspices of the monarchy, this kind of emission became generalised in many royal towns and cities in Catalonia. In all of these places, the recurrence to these instruments started as a short-term measure for the payment of royal contributions and subsidies.[58] However, from 1353 on, with the uninterrupted cycle of donations linked to the wars in the Mediterranean, the royal towns and cities resorted to the sale of new annuities (*violaris* and *censals*) *en masse*, so as to satisfy their commitments to the private *taules de canvi* or directly to royal officers. In that situation, the short-term amortisation of loans became impossible and, therefore, the fiscal resources under the control of the municipal governments were necessarily regularised and consolidated.

Let us finally take a look at the origins of the indebtedness of local administrations in the whole of the Crown's territory. Debt emissions in the 1340s in Catalonia were followed, in the subsequent decades, by the first emission of *censals* in the Kingdom of Valencia, with some isolated early cases in Castelló de la Plana in 1350, Alzira in 1351, Alpont in 1352, the city of Valencia itself in 1356, and Gandia in 1359. In the case of Majorca, the first operations of this type are documented in Palma in 1355.[59] In Aragon, we find some sporadic news of the sale of annuities by some rural communities such as Fraga, la Fresneda, Monroyo and Calatayud in the 1320s–1340s, though it is worth noting that the city of Zaragoza did not take part in this kind of debt operation until 1364.[60]

Indebtedness grew rapidly as the result of an intense period of fiscal pressure related to the war against Castille (1356–1366), followed by new royal expeditions, internal conflicts against some of the Crown's main vassals and especially the defensive efforts against the recurrent threat of invasion by mercenaries from beyond the Pyrenees. Furthermore, the reliance on lifelong and perpetual annuities became generalised among towns and cities, both in royal and seigneurial jurisdictions, and even in small rural communities.[61] The multiplication of debt securities in the financial markets allowed for the progressive decrease of interest rates in the late fourteenth century and the beginning of the following century until it reached between 5 and 3 per cent. This, however, did not spare several towns and cities from financial turmoil.[62] In some of these places, bankruptcy was avoided through an increase in the rates of indirect taxation and a further reduction in interest on debt.[63] In the specific case of Barcelona, the city relied on the creation of a public bank guaranteed by the wealth of all of its citizens: the *Taula de Canvi*.[64]

As we have already stated, the first debt sales by the government of the city of Valencia took place in 1356. These sales took the form of *censals* with an interest rate of 7.14 per cent. In addition to the emission of a small number of *violaris*, the sale of *censals* was more common, with an interest rate of 8.33 per cent until 1400, when it was reduced to 7.69 per cent. The government adopted a number of measures to redeem part of the owed annuities and constituted an ephemeral public bank (*taula de canvi*), but indebtedness continued to grow in the fifteenth century.[65]

The enormous demands of the period from 1350 to 1370 were also felt in City of Majorca, where the basis for the credit market changed from short-term loans to *violaris* and finally to *censals morts*. From 1359 onwards, the monarch promoted a number of different reforms aimed at containing expenditure and debt rescheduling, though they failed to produce lasting results due to the rise of new increasing monetary needs.[66]

In the Kingdom of Aragon this type of financial instruments were present in private markets. Nevertheless, their expansion into municipal councils did not begin until the 1360s.[67] In the city of Zaragoza the long-term debt interest which had been issued in previous tax years (mainly *censales* at 10 per cent interest rate) did not make an impact on the local treasury until the years comprised between 1368 and 1374. In the fifteenth century, the interest rates paid by the city council went from an average of 9.16 per cent in 1410 to 6.67 per cent in 1470.[68] Other towns in Aragon went through periods of financial turmoil because of the indebtedness resulting from the sales of *censales*.[69]

The evolution of municipal treasuries

As we have previously stated, the first sales of perpetual and lifelong annuities in the central years of the 1350s made the debt irredeemable and forced the perpetuation of the *imposicions*★, *ajudes* and *sisas*★, which were taxes levied on the consumption and circulation of various products. In the case of Catalonia, this process was forged in the contributions that were granted in the royal parliaments of 1353 and 1356. These parliaments established the rates and figures which would serve as reference in the coming years for the royal towns and cities of Catalonia and, later on, to those under the jurisdiction of lay and ecclesiastical lords. Finally, during the war against Castile, the "municipalisation" of indirect taxes was consolidated by consigning their yields to the payment of the interests produced by the sale of annuities (*censals*). The aforementioned phenomenon was not limited to Catalonia, but also affected the royal towns of the Kingdom of Valencia. In the General *Cortes* of Monzón of 1362–1363, the monarch granted several privileges that conferred practically absolute powers to the municipal authorities to decide on these exactions.[70] Thus, during this decisive stage, between the mid-1350s and the 1360s, a regular apparatus of indirect taxation was defined and established, which represented the core of the income of the Catalan and Valencian municipalities. In Aragon these resources had traditionally been discarded, but an important first step was taken in the *Cortes* of Zaragoza of 1364: a royal concession approved the levying of indirect taxes to complement the income produced by the council's own patrimony and, therefore, became a precedent for the diversification of the fiscal policies of some municipal councils. In the city of Zaragoza, the local government decided to collect municipal *sisas** in 1386 to deal with the growing importance of long-term debt. In other Aragonese towns, indirect taxes (known as *sisas**, *ayudas* or *arcas*) were consolidated in the first half of the fifteenth century.[71]

Broadly speaking, the systems of indirect taxation of the 1350s and 1360s was based on different exactions, which were levied, on the one hand, on the consumption and distribution of basic food products (cereals, meat, wine, and fresh fish) and, on the other hand, through *ad valorem* rates on the commercialisation and circulation of a wide range of merchandise (and even real estate transactions and financial products), together with the circulation of people and goods. Without a doubt, the *sisas** levied on basic foodstuffs provided the highest returns, since they taxed both the operators at the markets and, more intensely, the final consumers. Regarding the taxes levied on the circulation of people and goods, we can distinguish between those which were levied on entering a city through land (known as *barres* in several Catalan towns) and those which, in large costal ports, taxed the goods that came by sea.

In most Catalan and Valencian towns, the *imposicions** or *sisas** became permanent from the mid-1350s onwards, while in Aragon they did so in the mid-1360s. They were usually collected through individual annual leases (or for periods of a few months in large cities such as Barcelona or Valencia). In the absence of a reasonable offer, they were also collected through the *ad hoc* appointment of collectors.[72] In fact, the need to maximise this form of income contributed to the development of a complex systems of direct collection, known as *bulletí*. We can document this process in cities such as Manresa, Vic or Cervera in the second half of the fifteenth century, or in Valencia in the sixteenth century. Thus, there were various strategies to improve the yield of the *imposicions**, as shown in the case of Barcelona.[73] In general terms, the rates of the most lucrative exactions (meat, flour, and wine) were increased through surcharges, which were sometimes tendered separately (*anadiments* or *afegitons*). From time to time, the local governments also promoted capitations related to these basic products and created some new minor taxes. Lastly, from the early fifteenth century on, we see the beginning of a new process that culminated in the sixteenth century: the formation of municipally controlled monopolies over foodstuff such as wheat, meat, and wine. In this way, the local councillors ensured a regular source of income through a tax structure that they controlled more closely, compared to the *imposicions**, which were leased to private agents.[74]

As a result of all these dynamics, from the mid-fourteenth century onwards direct taxation proportional to personal wealth was relegated, in many urban centres, to an extraordinary resource. In large cities such as Barcelona and Valencia, the apportionment of direct taxes became residual and even disappeared, since they were strongly rejected by the local populace and were deemed as technically difficult to collect. Even so, in towns such as Girona, Valls, and Reus, from the mid-fourteenth century and until modern times, *talles* continued to be levied under different circumstances. Depending on the *causa impositionis*, local governments levied different types of *talles*: some were proportional to each taxpayer's wealth, while other were related to wealth brackets (known as *mans*) or, more occasionally, consisted of simple capitations. In other places, such as the town of Cervera, the continuity of the royal *qüestia*★ until the eighteenth century justified the levying of an annual *talla*.[75] In Castelló de la Plana and Alcoi, together with other Valencian towns, we can observe a similar tendency, in both cases related to the levying of the *peita*★.[76] In the towns and cities of the Kingdom of Aragon, *tallas* were also regularly paid throughout the fifteenth century.[77]

Furthermore, starting in the 1350s, some communities began to experiment with fiscal forms that were different from traditional direct taxation and indirect levies on the consumption and circulation of goods. These taxes were meant to be levied on various sources of income, which included agricultural production, but also wages, profits in manufacturing and trade, and profits in the form of property-related income. Following the model of seigneurial tithes, they were known as *redelmes*, together with other names that depended on their exact rate: *desè* (10 per cent), *onzè* (9.09 per cent), *dotzè* (8.33 per cent) or *vintè* (5 per cent), among other variants. The first cases are documented in Roussillon in the 1340s and, in the following decades, they spread mainly throughout villages and rural towns in Catalonia. In Aragon we also find isolated indications of similar taxes (*rediezmos* or *oncenos*) in the fifteenth century; not so, at the moment, in the kingdoms of Valencia and Majorca. One of the main purposes of the *redelmes* was to deal with the growing indebtedness of local corporations, as well as meeting specific communal needs.[78]

Conclusions

The evolution of royal and seigneurial taxation in the Crown of Aragon, between the twelfth and fifteenth centuries, was closely related to the transformations experienced by feudal society and its forms of domination. The strengthening of royal power, common to other areas of the medieval West, resulted in the consolidation of a series of seigneurial levies which, within the framework of the royal domains, were regularised during the thirteenth century. These were, on the one hand, the taxes known as *pechas*, *qüesties and peitas*★, which were levied on local communities, and, on the other hand, a large series of transit tariffs on all types of products and consumer goods. At the same time, other seigneurial exactions were consolidated in the royal estates, thus providing the royal coffers with increasingly stable income. The *cenas* and the taxes levied on the Jewish and Muslim *aljamas* were especially noteworthy.

The superior authority of the monarchy over the rest of the seigneurial powers also promoted an irreversible trend towards the expansion of the Crown's tax-collecting capacity. The triggering factor and legitimising element of this process was, above all, war, insofar as it allowed to appeal to legal reasons that were difficult to refute, such as the need to defend territorial integrity and, consequently, the very structure of society. On these bases, the monarchy made demands based on the obligation of military service, such as the *redención de hueste* and the custom of *Princeps namque*, which was exclusive to Catalonia. The attempts to collect taxes on a general scale from the beginning of the thirteenth century were even more relevant. This effort took different forms, but the Aragonese *monedajes*★ and the Catalan *bovatges*★ stand out. However, their scope was soon limited by the resistance of the ruling groups.

During the first half of the fourteenth century the fiscal demands of the monarchy increased due to the continuous wars in the Mediterranean. This pressure was mostly applied on the communities under royal jurisdiction and, to a lesser extent, on ecclesiastical domains. In this context, indirect taxes were gradually imposed, especially in Catalonia and Valencia, until a fundamental change took place at the difficult juncture of the War of the Two Peters (1356–1366). At that time, three commissions of deputies, one for each of the Crown's peninsular territories, appropriated the power to manage the economic services that the estates' assemblies granted to the king and decided, in parallel, to apply a fiscal system based on the collection of *sisas*★, customs tariffs or taxes on textile (*generalidades*★). This system was perpetuated due to the incessant fiscal pressure of the monarchy on the *Cortes*, but also because of the deputies' decision to resort to long-term debt. The need to pay interests implied that the indirect taxes under the control of the *Diputaciones* had to become permanent. Therefore, these institutions became true governing bodies in Aragon, Catalonia, and Valencia.

The monarchy, for its part, continued to benefit from this solid fiscal structure, although with a very limited ability to intervene. For this reason, in order to increase their sources of income without necessarily relying on the *Cortes*, the Crown developed different fiscal alternatives from the end of the fourteenth century onwards. In this sense, the sovereigns recovered exactions with a feudal origin, such as the *coronajes* or *maridajes*, requested loans from the councils of the largest cities in their territory, promoted the collection of new indirect taxes (*quema, derechos de italianos y alemanes*), and experimented with resources that were not strictly fiscal, such as the sales of privileges or the granting of royal pardons.

Regarding municipal taxation, during the central decades of the fourteenth century, the structures that had already been in existence since the twelfth century underwent important transformations. These were triggered by the constant fiscal pressure of the monarchy, which was caused by successive wars. Urban and rural communities had to constantly borrow money and ended up resorting to medium or long-term loans. Thus, the sale of annuities as a form of public debt reinforced the role of indirect taxes on the commercialisation and consumption of various products as the cornerstone of the taxation system of most towns and cities. Until the mid-fourteenth century, local finances were based on proportional taxes on wealth and, in some cases, the communal ownership of property. However, from 1360 onwards, the emergence of the combination of *imposicions*★/*sisas*★ led to the definitive consolidation of municipal treasuries. Local governments acquired decisive powers in the economic sphere by having the capacity to decide on the level of indebtedness of the community and the strategies adopted to face pending expenses or new needs. These measures became the object of frequent debates and conflicts, both with the nobility and the clergy, on the one hand, and the middle and lower strata of urban society, on the other.[79] Beyond that, the municipalities became the institutions most capable of levying taxes, investing money, and redistributing wealth at a local level. Thus, the management of municipal finances and other related activities, such as the purchase of annuities, the arrangement of loans, and the leasing of indirect taxes, became important areas of economic activity from the last third of the fourteenth century onwards.

Notes

1 CORRAO, "Stati regionali e apparati burocratici", pp. 99–143; SABATÉ, "¿Qué es un imperio en la Edad Media?", pp. 19–36.

2 Currently, the research teams focused on the study of taxation in the Crown of Aragon during the Middle Ages are organised around three research groups: *Renda feudal i fiscalitat a la Catalunya baixmedieval* (Barcelona, IMF-CSIC), *Cultures i Societats de l'Edat Mitjana* (València, Universitat de València) and *Centro de Estudios Medievales de Aragón* (Zaragoza, Universidad de Zaragoza).

3 SÁNCHEZ, FURIÓ and SESMA, "Old and New Forms of Taxation", pp. 99–130; CATEURA, "Transformaciones fiscales y financieras", pp. 165–182.

4 With respect to the words cited in their original form in the text, we have adopted the following criteria. Terms related to Catalonia and the kingdoms of Valencia and Majorca are in Catalan, while those linked to the kingdom of Aragon are in Spanish. Terms referring to the whole of the Crown of Aragon are expressed in their different forms, although, when simplification is needed, we have chosen the Spanish form.
5 LALIENA, "La metamorfosis del Estado feudal", pp. 67–98, specifically pp. 89–90; LALIENA, "El impacto del impuesto", pp. 561–604; SÁNCHEZ, "Tributos negociados: las *questie*/subsidios", pp. 65–99; BAYDAL, *Guerra, relacions de poder i fiscalitat negociada*, pp. 108–138.
6 ORTI, *Renda i fiscalitat en una ciutat medieval*, pp. 397–401, 445–446; RIERA, *La Corona de Aragón*, pp. 155–250.
7 MIQUEL, "La cena de presència", pp. 277–334.
8 MORELLÓ, "En torno a la presión fiscal", pp. 293–348; RIERA, "La *protecció*, un impost sobre les aljames", pp. 95–137.
9 BOSWELL, *The Royal Treasure*, pp. 195-258; LEDESMA, "La fiscalidad mudéjar en Aragón", pp. 3–17; LÓPEZ PÉREZ, "Las repercusiones económicas de la guerra de los Dos Pedros", vol. 1, pp. 211–228; LAFUENTE, *Un reino en armas*, pp. 155–162; GUERSON, "Death in the Aljama of Huesca", pp. 35–63.
10 BAYDAL, "Peites, qüesties, redempcions d'exèrcit i subsidis", vol. 1, pp. 259–286, mainly pp. 264–265; LAFUENTE, *Un reino en armas*, pp. 152–155.
11 Ferrer MALLOL, "La organización militar en Cataluña", pp. 119–222, specifically pp. 156–162; SÁNCHEZ, "*Defensar lo principat de Cathalunya*", pp. 171–211; VERDÉS, "La contribución del Consell de Barcelona", pp. 81–104, specifically pp. 87–88.
12 BISSON, *Fiscal Accounts of Catalonia*, pp. 122–150; LALIENA, "La metamorfosis del Estado feudal", pp. 82–87.
13 ORTI, "La primera articulación del Estado feudal", pp. 967–998, mainly pp. 978–990; LALIENA, "La metamorfosis del Estado feudal", pp. 82–85.
14 LALIENA, "La metamorfosis del Estado feudal", pp. 85–86.
15 ORTI, "La primera articulación del Estado feudal", pp. 993–994.
16 ORCÁSTEGUI, "La reglamentación del impuesto del monedaje", pp. 113–121.
17 SÁNCHEZ, "La evolución de la fiscalidad regia", pp. 393–428.
18 *Acta Curiarum Regni Aragonum. I. Cortes de los reinados de Alfonso II*, vol. 2, pp. 417–418.
19 *Corts, parlaments i fiscalitat a Catalunya*, pp. 19–25.
20 LAFUENTE, "La conquista y colonización de Cerdeña", pp. 105–145, mainly pp. 119–122.
21 SÁNCHEZ, "Contributi finanziari di città e ville", pp. 317–352.
22 BAYDAL, *Els orígens de la revolta de la Unió*, pp. 189–230; LAFUENTE, "La incidencia de la fiscalidad real extraordinaria", pp. 153–177, mainly pp. 164–166.
23 LÓPEZ BONET, "Repercusiones fiscales en Mallorca", t. II, vol. 2, pp. 529–551; SÁNCHEZ, "Las Cortes de Cataluña en la financiación de la guerra", pp. 364–365; LAFUENTE, *Guerra en ultramar*, pp. 150–152; BAYDAL, "L'aportació fiscal valenciana", pp. 21–60.
24 SESMA, "Las transformaciones de la fiscalidad real", t. I, vol. 1, pp. 231–292; LAFUENTE, *Un reino en armas*, pp. 162–210.
25 SÁNCHEZ, "La última ofensiva de Pedro el Ceremonioso", pp. 1453–1469.
26 REDONDO, "Coronatges i maridatges a la Corona d'Aragó", pp. 61–93.
27 SABATÉ, "L'augment de l'exigència fiscal", pp. 423–465.
28 VERDÉS, "La contribución del Consell de Barcelona", pp. 97–98; KÜCHLER, *Les finances de la Corona d'Aragó*, pp. 334–466; GARCÍA MARSILLA, "Avalando al rey", pp. 377–390; GARCÍA MARSILLA, "El impacto de la Corte en la ciudad", pp. 291–308, specifically pp. 303–306.
29 SESMA, "Zaragoza, centro de abastecimiento", pp. 125–158; DIAGO, "La *quema*. Trayectoria histórica de un impuesto", pp. 91–156.
30 FERRER MALLOL, "Els italians a terres catalanes", pp. 393–467, specifically pp. 394–425.
31 LÓPEZ ELUM, "Las relaciones comerciales de la Corona de Aragón", pp. 47–57.
32 ACIÉN, "El quinto de las cabalgadas", pp. 39–52; FERRER MALLOL, "Corso y piratería entre Mediterráneo y Atlántico", pp. 255–322, mainly, pp. 310–313.
33 FERRER MALLOL, "La tinença a costum d'Espanya", pp. 1–102, specifically p. 29.
34 SESMA, "La fijación de fronteras económicas", pp. 141–163; SESMA, "Fiscalidad y poder", pp. 447–463; SESMA, "Fiscalidad de estado y comercio exterior", pp. 459–467.
35 SESMA, "Las generalidades del reino de Aragón", pp. 395–396.

36 Sánchez, "La consolidació de la nova fiscalitat", pp. 110–112; Lafuente, "La fiscalidad extraordinaria en la financiación de las guerras", pp. 113–146, mainly pp. 129–144.
37 Riera, "La Diputació del General de Catalunya", pp. 152–249, specifically pp. 176–177, 204–209, 222; Küchler, *Les finances de la Corona d'Aragó*, pp. 158–192; Sáiz, "Nobleza y expansión militar de la Corona de Aragón", pp. 729–780, specifically pp. 733–744.
38 Sesma, "Fiscalidad de estado y comercio exterior", p. 462.
39 Sesma, "Fiscalidad de estado y comercio exterior", pp. 464-467; Sesma, "Las generalidades del reino de Aragón", pp. 413–414.
40 Sesma, "La burbuja censualista", pp. 215–241, specifically pp. 228–229; Sesma, "Trayectoria económica de la hacienda", pp. 171–202, specifically p. 194.
41 Berthe, *Les finances de la "Generalitat"*; Sánchez, "La nova fiscalitat d'Estat", pp. 60–68, mainly pp. 65-66; Sánchez, "La consolidació de la nova fiscalitat", pp. 99–117; Orti, "Les finances de la Diputació", pp. 119–137.
42 Muñoz, "Las Cortes valencianas", pp. 463–483, mainly pp. 475–480.
43 Sánchez, "Las primeras emisiones de deuda pública", pp. 219–258; Sánchez, "Barcelona, mercado de la deuda pública", pp. 413–441; Orti, "Les finances de la Diputació", pp. 126–130.
44 Sesma, "La burbuja censualista", pp. 215–241. De la Torre, "The first issue of annuities".
45 Muñoz, "Las Cortes valencianas", p. 480.
46 Viciano, "Deute públic i renda censalista", pp. 925–953, mainly pp. 931–932.
47 Sánchez, Furió and Sesma, "Old and New Forms of Taxation", pp. 107–113.
48 Turull, Orti and Sánchez, "La génesis de la fiscalidad municipal", pp. 115–134, specifically pp. 117–120; *Colección diplomática del Concejo de Zaragoza*, vol. 1: años 1119–1276, doc. 20 (1180).
49 Turull, "Universitas, commune, consilium", pp. 637–677; Laliena, "El impuesto antes del impuesto", pp. 67–91, specifically pp. 81–86.
50 García and Sáiz, "De la peita al censal", pp. 307–336.
51 See the previous subchapter on royal taxation.
52 Turull and Morelló, "Estructura y tipología de las "estimes-manifests"", pp. 271–326; Furió, "Avant le cadastre", pp. 200–231.
53 Sánchez, Furió and Sesma, "Old and New Forms of Taxation", pp. 112–113; Mira and Viciano, "La construcció d'un sistema fiscal", pp. 135–148, specifically, pp. 141–142. With regard to Aragon: *Acta Curiarum Regni Aragonum. I. Cortes de los reinados de Alfonso II*, vol. 2, pp. 415–418; Tomás, "Pueblas y mercados en Ribagorza", pp. 65–122, specifically pp. 99–100 and 121.
54 Sánchez and Orti, "La Corona en la génesis del sistema", pp. 242–260; Mira and Viciano, "La construcció d'un sistema fiscal", p. 143; García, "La génesis de la fiscalidad municipal", pp. 149–170, specifically pp. 158–163.
55 Sánchez and Orti, "La Corona en la génesis del sistema", pp. 233–233; García, "La génesis de la fiscalidad municipal", p. 161.
56 García Marsilla, *Vivir a crédito*, pp. 233–241; Guilleré, *Girona al segle XIV*, vol. I, pp. 249–255; Reixach, *Finances públiques i mobilitat social*, pp. 75–77, 222–237.
57 Sánchez, "Dette publique, autorités princières et villes", pp. 27–50.
58 Furió, "Deuda pública e intereses privados", pp. 35–79; Verdés, "El mercado de la deuda pública", pp. 243–271.
59 Baydal, *Els fonaments del pactisme valencià*, p. 698; Furió, "El deute públic municipal", pp. 71–136; Cateura, *El crèdit i el sistema financer*, p. 15, 456.
60 Lafuente, "Anhelos de transparencia", pp. 147–184, specifically p. 152; Diago, "Haciendas municipales en el reino de Aragón", pp. 335–356; Laliena, "Crisis tempranas de la deuda municipal", pp. 147–173.
61 Orti, "Una primera aproximació als fogatges", pp. 747–773; Reixach, "Presión fiscal y endeudamiento", pp. 415–454.
62 Sánchez ed., *La deuda pública en la Cataluña bajomedieval*. On the difficult management of public debt in some towns: Verdés, *Per ço que la vila no vage a perdició*; Morelló, *Fiscalitat i deute públic*, pp. 873–892; Martí, "Governar el deute en temps de crisi", pp. 129–179.
63 Orti and Verdés, "The Crisis of Public Finances", pp. 199–221.
64 Orti, "Les finances municipals de la Barcelona", pp. 257–282, specifically pp. 272–281; Miquel, "The Taula de Canvi of Barcelona", pp. 236–253.
65 García Marsilla, *Vivir a crédito*, pp. 243–280.
66 Cateura, *El crèdit i el sistema financer*, pp. 18–21.

67 ABELLA, "La deuda pública en los municipios aragoneses", pp. 47–64.
68 LAFUENTE, "Anhelos de transparencia", p. 152; LAFUENTE, "La deuda pública en el municipio de Zaragoza", pp. 213–231, specifically pp. 216–223.
69 SESMA, "La burbuja censualista", pp. 215–241; LALIENA, "L'endettement des communautés paysannes", pp. 201–212.
70 VERDÉS, "Sobre la regalia d'establir imposicions", pp. 545–578.
71 LAFUENTE, "Agentes económicos y acción institucional", pp. 43–66, specifically pp. 45–52; LAFUENTE, "Anhelos de transparencia", pp. 152–156.
72 GARCÍA MARSILLA, "Los agentes privados del fisco", pp. 139–154; DE LA TORRE, "Grandes negocios urbanos", pp. 187–210.
73 VERDÉS, "La gestión de los impuestos indirectos", pp. 173–189; MIQUEL, *La guerra civil catalana*, pp. 188–239, 249–323, 337–363.
74 MORELLÓ, "Agli albori dell'istituzionalizzazione del microcredito", pp. 391–425, specifically 407–423. About the specific case of the kingdom of Aragon, see the bibliography included in: IRANZO, "Abastecimiento urbano, fiscalidad y política frumentaria", pp. 206–250.
75 MORELLÓ, ORTI, REIXACH and VERDÉS, "A study of economic inequality", pp. 259–281; VERDÉS, "El principio de la *causa impositionis*", pp. 93–104.
76 MIRA and VICIANO, "La construcció d'un sistema fiscal", pp. 135–148; FURIÓ, VICIANO, ALMENAR, RUIZ and CHISMOL, "Measuring economic inequality", pp. 169–201.
77 FALCÓN, "Finanzas y fiscalidad", pp. 239–274.
78 MORELLÓ, "Els impostos sobre la renda", pp. 903–968; VERDÉS, "Onzens, dotzens i similars", pp. 417–461.
79 VERDÉS, "Car les talles són difícils de fer", pp. 129–153.

References

Juan ABELLA SAMITIER, "La deuda pública en los municipios aragoneses en los siglos XIV y XV", in *Anuario de Estudios Medievales*, 39/1, ene-jun 2009, pp. 47–64.

Manuel Pedro ACIÉN ALMANSA, "El quinto de las cabalgadas: un impuesto fronterizo", in *Hacienda y comercio, II Coloquio de Historia Medieval Andaluza*. Sevilla, 1982, pp. 39–52.

Acta Curiarum Regni Aragonum. I. Cortes de los reinados de Alfonso II a Alfonso IV (1164–1328), eds. Guillermo TOMÁS FACI, Carlos LALIENA CORBERA, Zaragoza, 2020, vol. 2.

Vicent BAYDAL SALA, "Peites, qüesties, redempcions d'exèrcit i subsidis. La naturalesa i l'evolució dels principals tributs reials directes a la Corona d'Aragó des de Jaume I fins a Alfons el Benigne (1213–1336)", in *Jaume I. Commemoració del VIII centenari del naixement de Jaume I*, ed. María Teresa FERRER I MALLOL, Barcelona, 2011, vol. 1, pp. 259–286.

Vicent BAYDAL SALA, *Els fonaments del pactisme valencià. Sistemes fiscals, relacions de poder i identitat col·lectiva al regne de València (c. 1250–c. 1365)*, Unedited PhD, Barcelona, Universitat Pompeu Fabra, 2011.

Vicent BAYDAL SALA, *Els orígens de la revolta de la Unió al regne de València (1330–1348)*, València, 2013.

Vicent BAYDAL SALA, *Guerra, relacions de poder i fiscalitat negociada: els orígens del contractualisme al regne de València (1283–1330)*, Barcelona, 2014, pp. 108–138.

Vicent BAYDAL SALA, "L'aportació fiscal valenciana a les campanyes sardes de 1353–1355)", in *Renda feudal i fiscalitat a la Catalunya baixmedieval. Estudis dedicats a Manuel Sánchez Martínez*, ed. Pere ORTI, Jordi MORELLÓ and Pere VERDÉS, Barcelona, 2018, pp. 21–60.

Maurice BERTHE, *Les finances de la "Generalitat" de Catalogne (1392–1479)*, Diplôme d'Études Supérieures d'Histoire, Toulouse, Université Toulouse-2, 1958.

Thomas N. BISSON, *Fiscal Accounts of Catalonia under the Early Count-Kings (1151–1213)*, Berkeley, 1984.

John BOSWELL, *The Royal Treasure: Muslim Communities under the Crown of Aragon in the Fourteenth Century*, New Haven – London, 1977, pp. 195–258.

Pau CATEURA BENNÀSSER (ed.), *El crèdit i el sistema financer del regne de Mallorca (segles XIV–XV)*, Palma, 2009.

Pau CATEURA BENNÀSSER, "Transformaciones fiscales y financieras del reino de Mallorca en la Baja Edad Media. Una revisión historiográfica", in *Fisco, legitimidad y conflicto en los reinos hispánicos (siglos XIII–XVII): homenaje a José Ángel Sesma Muñoz*, ed. Carlos LALIENA, Mario LAFUENTE and Ángel GALÁN, Zaragoza, 2019, pp. 165–182.

Ángel CANELLAS LÓPEZ (ed.), *Colección diplomática del Concejo de Zaragoza*, vol. 1: *Años 1119–1276*, Zaragoza, 1972.

Pietro Corrao, "Stati regionali e apparati burocratici nella Corona d'Aragona (sec. XIV e XV)", in *XVIII Congrès d'Història de la Corona d'Aragó*, ed. Rafael Narbona, València, 2005, pp. 99–143.

Corts, parlaments i fiscalitat a Catalunya: els capítols del donatiu (1288–1384), eds. Manuel Sánchez Martínez, Pere Orti Gost, Barcelona, 1997.

Máximo Diago Hernando, "Haciendas municipales en el reino de Aragón durante el siglo XIV. El caso de Calatayud y su Comunidad de aldeas", in *Fiscalidad de Estado y fiscalidad municipal en los reinos hispánicos medievales*, eds. Manuel Sánchez Martínez, Denis Menjot, Madrid, 2006, pp. 335–356.

Máximo Diago Hernando, "La *quema*. Trayectoria histórica de un impuesto sobre los flujos comerciales entre las coronas de Castilla y Aragón (siglos XIV y XV)", in *Anuario de Estudios Medievales*, 30/1, 2000, pp. 91–156.

Maria Isabel Falcón Pérez, "Finanzas y fiscalidad de ciudades, villas y comunidades de aldeas aragonesas", en *Finanzas y fiscalidad municipal, V Congreso de Estudios Medievales*, Ávila, 1997, pp. 239–274.

Maria Teresa Ferrer i Mallol, "Els italians a terres catalanes (segles XIII–XV)", in *Anuario de Estudios Medievales*, 10, 1980, pp. 393–467.

Maria Teresa Ferrer i Mallol, "La tinença a costum d'Espanya en els castells de la frontera meridional valenciana (segle XIV)", in *La frontera terrestre i marítima amb l'Islam*, Barcelona, 1988, pp. 1–102.

Maria Teresa Ferrer i Mallol, "La organización militar en Cataluña en la Edad Media", in *Conquistar y defender. Los recursos militares en la Edad Media Hispánica*, ed. Miguel Ángel Ladero Quesada, Madrid, 2001, pp. 119–222.

Maria Teresa Ferrer i Mallol, "Corso y piratería entre Mediterráneo y Atlántico en la baja Edad Media", in *La Península Ibérica entre el Mediterráneo y el Atlántico, siglos XIII–XV*, Sevilla-Cádiz, 2006, pp. 255–322.

Antoni Furió, "Deuda pública e intereses privados. Finanzas y fiscalidad municipales en la Corona de Aragón", in *Edad Media. Revista de Historia*, 2, 1999, pp. 35–79.

Antoni Furió, "Avant le cadastre. Les libres d'estimes du royaume de Valence au bas Moyen Âge", in *Estimes, compoix et cadastres. Histoire d'un patrimoine commun de l'Europe méridionale*, ed. Jean-Loup Abbé, Toulouse, 2017, pp. 200–231.

Antoni Furió, "El deute públic municipal al regne de València en la baixa edat mitjana. Un assaig de quantificació", in *El País Valenciano en la Baja Edad Media. Estudios dedicados al profesor Paulino Iradiel*, eds. David Igual, Germán Navarro, València, 2018, pp. 71–136.

Antoni Furió, Pau Viciano, Luis Almenar, Lledó Ruiz, Guillem Chismol, "Measuring economic inequality in Southern Europe: the Iberian Peninsula in the 14th–17th centuries", in *Disuguaglianza economica nelle società preindustriali: cause ed effetti – Economic inequality in pre-industrial societies: causes and effects*, Florence, 2020, pp. 169–201.

Juan Vicente García Marsilla, "La génesis de la fiscalidad municipal en la ciudad de Valencia (1238–1366)", in *Revista d'Història Medieval*, 7, 1996, pp. 149–170.

Juan Vicente García Marsilla, *Vivir a crédito en la Valencia medieval: De los orígenes del sistema censal al endeudamiento del municipio*, València, 2002.

Juan Vicente García Marsilla, "Avalando al rey: Préstamos a la Corona y finanzas municipales en la Valencia del siglo XV", in *Fiscalidad de Estado y fiscalidad municipal en los reinos hispánicos medievales*, eds. Manuel Sánchez Martínez, Denis Menjot, Madrid, 2006, pp. 377–390.

Juan Vicente García Marsilla, "El impacto de la Corte en la ciudad: Alfonso el Magnánimo en Valencia (1425–1428)", in *El Alimento del Estado y la salud de la Res Pública. Orígenes, estructura y desarrollo del gasto público en Europa*, eds. Ángel Galán Sánchez, Juan Manuel Carretero Zamora, Madrid, 2013, pp. 291–308.

Juan Vicente García Marsilla, "Los agentes privados del fisco. Las sociedades arrendatarias de impuestos en la Valencia medieval", in *Inversors, banquers i jueus. Les xarxes financeres a la Corona d'Aragó (s. XIV-XV)*, eds. Pau Cateura, Lluís Tudela, Jordi Maíz, Palma de Mallorca, 2015, pp. 139–154.

Juan Vicente García Marsilla, Jorge Sáiz Serrano, "De la peita al censal. Finanzas municipales y clases dirigentes en la Valencia de los siglos XIV y XV", in *Corona, municipis i fiscalitat a la baixa edat mitjana*, Lleida, 1995, pp. 307–336.

Alexandra Guerson, "Death in the Aljama of Huesca: the Jews and the Royal Taxation in Fourteenth-Century Aragon", in *Sefarad*, 75, 2015, pp. 35–63.

Christian Guilleré, *Girona al segle XIV*, Barcelona-Girona, 1993, vol. I, pp. 249–255.

María Teresa Iranzo Muñío, "Abastecimiento urbano, fiscalidad y política frumentaria: el mercado del trigo en Huesca en el siglo XV", in *Una economía integrada. Comercio, instituciones y mercados en Aragón, 1300–1500*, eds. Carlos Laliena, Mario Lafuente, Zaragoza, 2012, pp. 206–250.

Winfried KÜCHLER, *Les finances de la Corona d'Aragó al segle XV (regnats d'Alfons V i Joan II)*, Valencia, 1997, pp. 334–466.

Mario LAFUENTE GÓMEZ, *Guerra en ultramar. La intervención aragonesa en el dominio de Cerdeña (1354–1355)*, Zaragoza, 2011.

Mario LAFUENTE GÓMEZ, *Un reino en armas. La guerra de los Dos Pedros en Aragón (1356–1366)*, Zaragoza, 2014, pp. 155–162.

Mario LAFUENTE GÓMEZ, "Agentes económicos y acción institucional: la reestructuración fiscal del concejo de Zaragoza entre las décadas de 1360 y 1380", in *Agentes de los sistemas fiscales en Andalucía y los reinos hispánicos (siglos XIII–XVIII): un modelo comparativo*, eds. Mercedes BORRERO, Juan CARRASCO, Rafael G. PEINADO, Madrid, 2014, pp. 43–66.

Mario LAFUENTE GÓMEZ, "Anhelos de transparencia. Inspección y reforma de la gestión municipal en Zaragoza a finales del siglo XIV (1391–1400)", in *Consumo, comercio y transformaciones culturales en la baja Edad Media: Aragón, siglos XIV–XV*, eds. Carlos LALIENA, Mario LAFUENTE, Zaragoza, 2016, pp. 147–184.

Mario LAFUENTE GÓMEZ, "La fiscalidad extraordinaria en la financiación de las guerras de Cerdeña por la Corona de Aragón (1320–1410)", in *Commercio, finanza e guerra nella Sardegna tardomedievale*, eds. Olivetta SCHENA, Sergio TOGNETTI, Roma, 2017, pp. 113–146.

Mario LAFUENTE GÓMEZ, "La deuda pública en el municipio de Zaragoza en la Baja Edad Media: el concejo de la ciudad y la corporación de propietarios de La Almozara", in *La crisi baixmedieval a la Corona d'Aragó (1350–1450)*, eds. Lluís TUDELA, Pau CATEURA, Palma, 2019, pp. 213–231.

Mario LAFUENTE GÓMEZ, "La conquista y colonización de Cerdeña por la Corona de Aragón. Historiografías nacionales, investigaciones recientes y renovación interpretativa", in *RiMe. Rivista dell'Istituto di Storia dell'Europa Mediterranea*, 6/I, junio 2020, pp. 105–145.

Carlos LALIENA CORBERA, "La metamorfosis del Estado feudal. Las estructuras institucionales de la Corona de Aragón en el periodo de expansión (1208–1283)", in *La Corona de Aragón en el centro de su Historia. 1208–1458. La monarquía aragonesa y los reinos de la Corona*, ed. José Ángel SESMA MUÑOZ, Zaragoza, 2009, pp. 67–98.

Carlos LALIENA CORBERA, "Crisis tempranas de la deuda municipal en el Bajo Aragón: Monroyo 1346", in *De la escritura a la Historia (Aragón, siglos XIII–XV)*, eds. José Ángel SESMA MUÑOZ, Carlos LALIENA CORBERA, Zaragoza, 2014, pp. 147–173.

Carlos LALIENA CORBERA, "El impacto del impuesto sobre las economías campesinas de Aragón en vísperas de la Unión (1277–1283)", in *Dynamiques du monde rural dans la conjoncture de 1300*, eds. Monique BOURIN, François MENANT, Lluís To FIGUERAS, Roma, 2014, pp. 561–604.

Carlos LALIENA CORBERA, "L'endettement des communautés paysannes en Aragon à la fin du Moyen Âge: 1340–1460", in *La fabrique des sociétés médiévales méditerranéennes: les Moyen Âge de François Menant*, ed. Diane CHAMBODUC DE SAINT PULGENT and Marie DEJOUX, Paris, 2018, pp. 201–212.

Carlos LALIENA CORBERA, "El impuesto antes del impuesto en el reino de Aragón a comienzos del siglo XIII: fisco, reforma y legitimidad", in *Fisco, legitimidad y conflicto en los reinos hispánicos (siglos XIII-XVII): homenaje a José Ángel Sesma Muñoz*, eds. Carlos LALIENA, Mario LAFUENTE and Ángel GALÁN, Zaragoza, 2019, pp. 67–91.

Mª Luisa LEDESMA RUBIO, "La fiscalidad mudéjar en Aragón", in *Actas del V Simposio Internacional de Mudejarismo: Economía*, Teruel, 1991, pp. 3–17.

José Francisco LÓPEZ BONET, "Repercusiones fiscales en Mallorca de las sublevaciones sardas en la segunda mitad del siglo XIV", in *La Corona d'Aragona in Italia (secc. XIII–XVIII), XIV Congreso de Historia de la Corona de Aragón, Sassari, 1995*, t. II, vol. 2, pp. 529–551.

Pedro LÓPEZ ELUM, "Las relaciones comerciales de la Corona de Aragón con los alemanes y saboyanos. 'Dret alemà y saboyà' (1420–1694)", in *Saitabí*, 26, 1976, pp. 47–57.

María Dolores LÓPEZ PÉREZ, "Las repercusiones económicas de la guerra de los Dos Pedros en las aljamas musulmanas aragonesas: el caso de Escatrón y Alborge", in *De mudéjares a moriscos: una conversión forzada. Actas del VIII Simposio Internacional de Mudejarismo*, Teruel, 2002, vol. 1, pp. 211–228.

Albert MARTÍ ARAU, "Governar el deute en temps de crisi: Castelló d'Empúries (1386–1421)", in *Anuario de Estudios Medievales*, 40/1, enero-junio 2010, pp. 129–179.

Laura MIQUEL MILIAN, *La guerra civil catalana i la crisi financera de Barcelona durant el regnat de Joan II (1458–1479)*, Unedited PhD, Girona, Universitat de Girona, 2020.

MIQUEL MILIAN, Laura, "The Taula de Canvi of Barcelona: success and troubles of a public bank in the fifteenth century", in *Journal of Medieval Iberian Studies*, 2021, 13/2, 2021, pp. 236–253.

Marina MIQUEL VIVES, "La "cena de presència" a la Corona d'Aragó a mitjan segle XIV", in *Estudios sobre renta, fiscalidad y finanzas en la Cataluña bajomedieval*, ed. Manuel SÁNCHEZ MARTÍNEZ, Barcelona, 1993, pp. 277–334.

Antoni José MIRA, Pau VICIANO, "La construcció d'un sistema fiscal: municipis i impost al País Valencià (segles XIII–XIV)", in *Revista d'història medieval*, 7, 1996, pp. 135–148.

Jordi MORELLÓ BAGET, "Els impostos sobre la renda a Catalunya: redelmes, onzens i similars", in *Anuario de Estudios Medievales*, 27, 1997, pp. 903–968.

Jordi MORELLÓ BAGET, *Fiscalitat i deute públic en dues viles del Camp de Tarragona. Reus i Valls, segles XIV-XV*, Barcelona, 2001, pp. 873–892.

Jordi MORELLÓ BAGET, "En torno a la presión fiscal sobre las aljamas de judíos de Tarragona: Del pago de subsidios a la contribución en *coronatges y maridatges*", in *Sefarad*, 71/2, 2011, pp. 293–348.

Jordi MORELLÓ BAGET, "Agli albori dell'istituzionalizzazione del microcredito sui cereali: l'insediamento delle *Arcas di Misericordia* e dei *pósitos* municipali nel Basso Medioevo ispanico", in *I Monti frumentari e le forme di credito non monetarie fra Medioevo ed Età Contemporanea*, ed. Ippolita CHECCOLI, Bologna, 2015, pp. 391–425.

Jordi MORELLÓ BAGET, Pere ORTI GOST, Albert REIXACH SALA, Pere VERDÉS PIJUAN, "A study of economic inequality in the light of fiscal sources: the case of Catalonia (14th-18th centuries", in *Disuguaglianza economica nelle società preindustriali: cause ed effetti – Economic inequality in pre-industrial societies: causes and effects*, Florence, 2020, pp. 259–281.

Rosa MUÑOZ POMER, "Las Cortes valencianas y el cambio de las estructuras fiscales en el tránsito del siglo XIV al XV", in *Anuario de Estudios Medievales*, 22, 1992, pp. 463–483.

Carmen ORCÁSTEGUI GROS, "La reglamentación del impuesto del monedaje en Aragón en los siglos XIII–XIV", in *Aragón en la Edad Media*, 5, 1983, pp. 113–121.

Pere ORTI GOST, "Una primera aproximació als fogatges catalans de la dècada de 1360", in *Anuario de Estudios Medievales*, 29, 1999, pp. 747–773.

Pere ORTI GOST, *Renda i fiscalitat en una ciutat medieval: Barcelona, segles XII–XV*, Barcelona, 2000.

Pere ORTI GOST, "La primera articulación del Estado feudal en Cataluña a través de un impuesto: el bovaje (ss. XII–XIII)", in *Hispania*, LXI/3, 209, 2001, pp. 967–998.

Pere ORTI GOST, "Les finances municipals de la Barcelona dels segles XIV i XV: Del censal a la Taula de Canvi", in *El món del crèdit a la Barcelona medieval*, ed. Manuel SÁNCHEZ MARTÍNEZ, Barcelona, 2007 (= *Barcelona. Quaderns d'Història*, 13), pp. 257–282.

Pere ORTI GOST, "*Les finances de la Diputació del General de 1380 a 1462*", in *Història de la Generalitat de Catalunya: Dels segles medievals a l'actualitat, 650 anys*, ed. Maria Teresa FERRER I MALLOL, Barcelona, 2011, pp. 119–137.

Pere ORTI GOST, Pere VERDÉS PIJUAN, "The Crisis of Public Finances in the Towns of Late Medieval Catalonia (1350–1500)", in *Le crisi finanziarie: Gestione, implicazione sociali e conseguenze nell'età preindustriale*, Atti Settimane di Studi e altri Convegni, Florence, 2016, pp. 199–221.

Esther REDONDO GARCÍA, "Coronatges i maridatges a la Corona d'Aragó (segles XIV i XV): el procediment administratiu dels subsidis extraordinaris", in *Renda feudal i fiscalitat a la Catalunya baixmedieval. Estudis dedicats a Manuel Sánchez Martínez*, eds. Pere ORTI, Jordi MORELLÓ and Pere VERDÉS, Barcelona, 2018, pp. 61–93.

Albert REIXACH SALA, *Finances públiques i mobilitat social a la Catalunya de la baixa edat mitjana: Girona, 1340–1440*, Madrid, 2018.

Albert REIXACH SALA, "Presión fiscal y endeudamiento en las comunidades rurales del noreste catalán durante la Guerra con Castilla (1356–1366)", in *Edad Media. Revista de Historia*, 21, 2020, pp. 415–454.

Antoni RIERA MELIS, "La Diputació del General de Catalunya, 1412–1444. El desenvolupament d'una administració autonòmica medieval en un context conflictiu", in *Acta Historica et Archaelogica Mediaevalia*, 30, 2010, pp. 152–249.

Antoni RIERA MELIS, *La Corona de Aragón y el reino de Mallorca en el primer cuarto del siglo XIV*, Madrid, 1986, pp. 155–250.

Jaume RIERA SANS, "*La protecció*, un impost sobre les aljames de jueus reials (1346–1410)", in *Renda feudal i fiscalitat a la Catalunya baixmedieval. Estudis dedicats a Manuel Sánchez Martínez*, eds. Pere ORTI, Jordi MORELLÓ and Pere VERDÉS, Barcelona, 2018, pp. 95–137.

Flocel SABATÉ CURULL, "L'augment de l'exigència fiscal en els municipis catalans al segle XIV: elements de pressió i de resposta", in *Corona, municipis i fiscalitat a la baixa edat mitjan*, Lleida, 1995, pp. 423–465.

Flocel SABATÉ CURULL, "¿Qué es un imperio en la Edad Media? La Corona de Aragón como punto de discusión", in *Expériences impériales. Les cultures politiques dans la péninsule Ibérique et au Maghreb, VIIIe-XVe siècles*, ed. Yann DEJUGNAT, Bordeaux, 2020, pp. 19–36.

Jorge SÁIZ SERRANO, "Nobleza y expansión militar de la Corona de Aragón: la nobleza valenciana en las guerras del rey (1420–1448)", in *Anuario de Estudios Medievales*, 33/2, 2003, pp. 729–780.

Manuel SÁNCHEZ MARTÍNEZ, "Contributi finanziari di città e ville della Catalogna alla conquista del regno di Sardegna e Corsica (1321–1326)", in *Medioevo. Saggi e Rassegne*, 20, 1995, pp. 317–352.

Manuel SÁNCHEZ MARTÍNEZ, "La evolución de la fiscalidad regia en los países de la Corona de Aragón (c.1280–1356)", in *XXI Semana de Estudios Medievales, Europa en los umbrales de la crisis: 1250–1350*, Pamplona, 1995, pp. 393–428.

Manuel SÁNCHEZ MARTÍNEZ, "La última ofensiva de Pedro el Ceremonioso: las demandas para el jubileo de 1386", in *Aragón en la Edad Media*, 14–15, 1999, Homenaje a la profesora Carmen Orcástegui Gros, pp. 1453–1469.

Manuel SÁNCHEZ MARTÍNEZ, "La nova fiscalitat d'Estat", in *El naixement de la Generalitat de Catalunya*, eds. Manuel SÁNCHEZ MARTÍNEZ, Carme BERGÉS, Cervera, 2003, pp. 60–68.

SÁNCHEZ MARTÍNEZ, Manuel, "*Defensar lo principat de Cathalunya* en la segunda mitad del siglo XIV: de la prestación militar al impuesto", in *Pagar al rey en la Corona de Aragón durante el siglo XIV. Estudios sobre fiscalidad y finanzas reales y urbanas*, Barcelona, 2003, pp. 171–211.

Manuel SÁNCHEZ MARTÍNEZ, Pere ORTI GOST, "La Corona en la génesis del sistema fiscal municipal en Cataluña (1300–1360)", in *Pagar al rey en la corona de Aragón durante el siglo XIV. Estudios sobre fiscalidad y fiananzas reales y urbanas*, Barcelona, 2003, pp. 379–425.

Manuel SÁNCHEZ MARTÍNEZ, "Dette publique, autorités princières et villes dans les Pays de la Couronne d'Aragon (14e-15e siècles)", in *Urban Public Debts. Urban Government and the Market for Annuities in Western Europe (14th-18th centuries)*, eds. Marc BOONE et al., Turnhout, 2003, pp. 27–50.

Manuel SÁNCHEZ MARTÍNEZ, "Tributos negociados: las questie/subsidios de las villas catalanas en la primera mitad del siglo XIV", in *Anuario de Estudios Medievales*, 38/1, 2008, pp. 65–99.

Manuel SÁNCHEZ MARTÍNEZ, Antoni FURIÓ, J. Ángel SESMA MUÑOZ, "Old and New Forms of Taxation in the Crown of Aragon (13th–14th Centuries)", in *La fiscalità nell'economia europea (sec. XIII–XVIII). XXXIX Settimana di Studi dell'Istituto Internazionale di Storia Economica «Francesco Datini» di Prato*, ed. Simonetta CAVACCIOCCI, Prato, 2008, pp. 99–130.

Manuel SÁNCHEZ MARTÍNEZ (ed.), *La deuda pública en la Cataluña bajomedieval*, Barcelona, 2009.

Manuel SÁNCHEZ MARTÍNEZ, "Las primeras emisiones de deuda pública por la Diputación del General de Cataluña (1365–1369)", in *La deuda pública en la Cataluña bajomedieval*, ed. Manuel SÁNCHEZ MARTÍNEZ, Barcelona, 2009, pp. 219–258.

Manuel SÁNCHEZ MARTÍNEZ, "La consolidació de la nova fiscalitat a Catalunya (1359–1380)", in *Història de la Generalitat de Catalunya: Dels segles medievals a l'actualitat, 650 anys*, ed. Maria Teresa FERRER I MALLOL, Barcelona, 2011, pp. 99–117.

Manuel SÁNCHEZ MARTÍNEZ, "Barcelona, mercado de la deuda pública emitida por la Diputación del General de Cataluña (1371–1374)", in *A l'entorn de la Barcelona medieval: Estudis dedicats a la doctora Josefina Mutgé i Vives*, eds. Manuel SÁNCHEZ MARTÍNEZ et al., Barcelona, 2013, pp. 413–441.

José Ángel SESMA MUÑOZ, "Las generalidades del reino de Aragón. Su organización a mediados del siglo XV", in *Anuario de Historia del Derecho Español*, 46, 1976, pp. 395–396.

José Ángel SESMA MUÑOZ, "Trayectoria económica de la hacienda del reino de Aragón", in *Aragón en la Edad Media*, 2, 1979, pp. 171–202.

José Ángel SESMA MUÑOZ, "La fijación de fronteras económicas entre los estados de la Corona de Aragón", in *Aragón en la Edad Media*, 5, 1983, pp. 141–163.

José Ángel SESMA MUÑOZ, "Fiscalidad y poder. La fiscalidad centralizada como instrumento de poder en la Corona de Aragón (siglo XIV)", in *Espacio, tiempo y forma. Revista de la Facultad de Geografía e Historia de la UNED*, 4, 1989, pp. 447–463.

José Ángel SESMA MUÑOZ, "Las transformaciones de la fiscalidad real en la baja Edad Media", in *El poder real en la Corona de Aragón (siglos XIV–XVI)*, XV Congreso de Historia de la Corona de Aragón, Zaragoza, 1997, t. I, vol. 1, pp. 231–292.

José Ángel SESMA MUÑOZ, "Zaragoza, centro de abastecimiento de mercaderes castellanos a finales del siglo XIV", in *Aragón en la Edad Media*, 13, 1997, pp. 125–158.

José Ángel SESMA MUÑOZ, "Fiscalidad de estado y comercio exterior en Aragón", in *Acta historica et archaeologica mediaevalia*, 22, 2001, pp. 459–467.

José Ángel Sesma Muñoz. "La burbuja censualista y las crisis financieras en Aragón. Ajustes y medidas de rescate para evitar la bancarrota (siglos XIV–XV)", in *Estados y mercados financieros en el Occidente cristiano (siglos XIII–XVI)*, Pamplona, 2015, pp. 215–241.

Guillermo Tomás Faci, "Pueblas y mercados en Ribagorza", in *Crecimiento económico y formación de los mercados en Aragón en la Edad Media (1200–1350)*, eds. J. Ángel Sesma Muñoz, Carlos Laliena Corbera, Zaragoza, 2009, pp. 65–122.

Sandra de la Torre Gonzalo, "Grandes negocios urbanos de finales del siglo XIV: el arrendamiento de ingresos fiscales de Zaragoza", in *Consumo, comercio y transformaciones culturales en la baja Edad Media: Aragón, siglos XIV– XV*, eds. Carlos Laliena, Mario Lafuente, Zaragoza, 2016, pp. 187–210.

Sandra de la Torre Gonzalo, "The first issue of annuities by the Diputación of the kingdom of Aragon (1376–1436): raising capital and sovereign debt in the Middle Ages", in *Journal of Medieval History*, DOI: 10.1080/03044181.2022.2102061

Max Turull Rubinat, Pere Orti Gost, Manuel Sánchez Martínez, "La génesis de la fiscalidad municipal en Cataluña", in *Revista d'història medieval*, 7, 1996, pp. 115–134.

Max Turull Rubinat, "*Universitas, commune, consilium*: sur le rôle de la fiscalité dans la naissance et le développement du Conseil (Catalogne, XIIe–XIVe siècles)", in *Exceptiones iuris: Studies in Honor of André Gouron*, ed. Bernard Durand and Laurent Mayali, Berkeley, 2000, pp. 637–677.

Max Turull Rubinat, Jordi Morelló Baget, "Estructura y tipología de las *"estimes-manifests"* en Cataluña (siglos XIV–XV)", in *Anuario de Estudios Medievales*, 35/1, 2005, pp. 271–326.

Pere Verdés Pijuan, "*Per ço que la vila no vage a perdició*". *La gestió del deute públic en un municipi català (Cervera, 1387–1516)*, Barcelona, 2004.

Pere Verdés Pijuan, "La gestión de los impuestos indirectos municipales en las ciudades y villas de Cataluña: el caso de Cervera (s. XIV–XV)", in *La fiscalité des villes au Moyen Âge (Occident méditerranéen). 4. La gestion de l'impôt*, eds. Denis Menjot, Manuel Sánchez Martínez, Toulouse, 2004, pp. 173–189.

Pere Verdés Pijuan, "Sobre la regalia d'establir imposicions i barres a Catalunya: la convinença de Sant Joan Despí (1370)", in *Initium*, 10, 2005, pp. 545–578.

Pere Verdés Pijuan, "*Car les talles són difícils de fer e pijors de exigir*. A propósito del discurso fiscal en las ciudades catalanas durante la época bajomedieval", in *Studia Historica, Historia medieval*, 30, 2012, pp. 129–153.

Pere Verdés Pijuan, "El mercado de la deuda pública en la Cataluña de los siglos xiv-xv", in *Estados y mercados financieros en el Occidente cristiano (siglos XIII-XVI). Actas de la XLI Semana de Estudios Medievales de Estella (15–18 de julio de 2014)*, Pamplona, 2015, pp. 243–271.

Pere Verdés Pijuan, "La contribució del Consell de Barcelona a les demandes de la Corona, 1387–1462", in *Barcelona. Quaderns d'Història*, 23, 2016, pp. 81–104.

Pere Verdés Pijuan, "'Onzens, dotzens' i similars a Cervera durant el segle XV: els intents de crear un nou impost sobre la renda", in *Renda feudal i fiscalitat a la Catalunya baixmedieval. Estudis dedicats a Manuel Sánchez Martínez*, eds. Pere Orti, Jordi Morelló and Pere Verdés, Barcelona, 2018, pp. 417–461.

Pere Verdés Pijuan, "El principio de la *causa impositionis* en las tallas municipales de Cataluña", in *Cultures fiscales en Occident du Xe au XVIIe siècle 2. Études offertes à Denis Menjot*, eds. Florent Garnier, Armand Jamme, Anne Lemonde, Pere Verdés, Toulouse, 2019, pp. 93–104.

Pau Viciano, "Deute públic i renda censalista al país Valencià en el segle XV. Una proposta d'interpretació", in *Anuario de Estudios Medievales*, 48/2, 2018, pp. 925–953.

6
KINGDOMS OF CASTILE AND NAVARRE[1]

Pablo Ortego Rico and Íñigo Mugueta Moreno

Introduction

The two political spaces analysed in this chapter (kingdoms of Castile and Navarre) dig their medieval roots in the Christian kingdoms formed in the north of the Iberian Peninsula between the eighth and the tenth centuries. The Kingdom of Castile (or Castile and León) was the successor of the small Kingdom of Asturias, which emerged in the northwest of the Iberian Peninsula in the eighth century; it came to be known as the Kingdom of León after its territorial consolidation north of the Douro River in the tenth century. Its eastern frontier march, bordering with the valley of the Ebro, was the County of Castile, a *de facto* independent polity from the tenth century. For its part, the Kingdom of Pamplona (known as Kingdom of Navarre from 1162 onwards) was formed in the ninth century in the western Pyrenees, north of the Ebro, and became the dominant Christian polity in the Iberian Peninsula during the reign of Sancho III (1004–1035). After the death of this monarch in 1035, the territories that he had controlled through inheritance (Kingdom of Pamplona and counties of Aragón and Ribagorza) or marriage (County of Castile) were distributed among his children.

Ferdinand I, one of Sancho III's children, inherited the County of Castile, and was elevated in 1037 to the throne of León. This was the beginning of a complex political entity (Kingdom of Castile and León), that even in the eleventh and twelfth century was prone to territorial fragmentation, in relation to a patrimonial conception of the *regnum*. As such, the death of some monarchs was followed by territorial distributions between their children, for instance after the death of Ferdinand I in 1065 or Alphonse VII in 1157. In the latter case, this distributive policy lead to the coexistence of two separate kingdoms, each with their own ruler and areas of expansion to the south, between 1157 and 1230: the Kingdom of León, which covered the western regions of the Iberian Peninsula, except for Portugal, which became politically independent in 1139; and the Kingdom of Castile, which bordered with the Kingdom of Aragón to the east and the region of La Mancha to the south.

In the second half of the twelfth century, the Kingdom of Navarre – heir of the former Kingdom of Pamplona and again an autonomous polity from 1134, after a period during which it was under the control of the kings of Aragón – could not expand to the south, as it shared no frontier with Muslim-held territories. Meanwhile, Castile and León was gradually becoming the hegemonic power in the Iberian Peninsula, expanding to the south with the conquest of large territories at the expense of al-Andalus. In addition, in 1230 Ferdinand III (1217–1252) merged for good the formerly separated kingdoms of Castile and León into the

Crown of Castile, and conquered the valley of the Guadalquivir (which includes a large proportion of modern Andalucía) and Murcia, in the south of the Iberian Peninsula. The only Muslim-held polity to remain independent in the Iberian Peninsula was the Nasrid emirate of Granada, which controlled the Mediterranean coast of the southeast from 1246 to its conquest by the Catholic Monarchs in 1492. In this way, between the thirteenth and fifteenth centuries, Navarre was barely 12,000 km^2 in size, compared to the approximately 350,000 km^2 held by the Crown of Castile from 1230 onwards.[2]

This is a very brief account of the process that led to the political consolidation of the two kingdoms the fiscal history of which between the twelfth and the fifteenth centuries is examined in this chapter. As pointed out by previous works, the analysis of the royal and municipal fiscal systems of Castile and Navarre presents a privileged perspective of the process of state construction in these kingdoms, which became especially intense in the thirteenth and fourteenth centuries, and of the political, social and economic relationships in the cities, which supported and stimulated many of the fiscal developments witnessed by the period.

Royal and municipal fiscal systems in Castile have been paid sustained historiographical attention since the late 1960s, and the general features of taxation from the thirteenth century onwards, and its evolution over time, are well understood.[3] Regional differences have been outlined, and the political and socio-economic impact of taxation in each region has been assessed, especially during the fifteenth century, when the sources are especially abundant.[4] In Navarre, the fiscal records of the *Cámara de Comptos* have been used for historical research from the seventeenth century, but it was only in the 1970s that they were regarded as interesting in themselves, in works that analysed the administration of the kingdom.[5] In addition, from the early 1990s a series of targeted projects have improved our understanding of the rents received by monarchs and cities, and of their management.[6] In the early twenty-first century these studies have received an additional boost with the emergence of the research network *Arca Comunis* (founded in 2008), which revolves around the study of Iberian and European fiscal systems.[7]

Therefore, there is enough of a critical mass of research about both fiscal systems for a global and comprehensive explanation of their emergence and evolution between the twelfth and sixteenth centuries to be attempted, despite the artificial nature of the periodisation criteria used and the inevitable feeling of teleology that always hoovers over a study of these characteristics. In this regard, in order to make explanations easier and guide readers with no specialist knowledge about the geographical and chronological coordinates of the work, the chapter is divided into three parts, in which thematic, chronological and spatial criteria converge: the first addresses the origins and initial steps of royal fiscal systems in each territory (twelfth–thirteenth centuries); the second deals with the process of construction and expansion of state fiscal systems, beginning with Castile, from the mid-thirteenth century and, from the fourteenth century, also Navarre; finally, the third examines birth and evolution of urban taxation, from its origins to the fifteenth century. Each part begins with a brief introduction that broadly outlines the evolution of fiscal systems in each context, and emphasises the similarities and differences of Castilian and Navarre taxation, helping the reader to digest the detailed analysis of each kingdom's taxation separately.

The origins of royal taxation: from feudal rights to taxation in the "King's demesne"

After the disappearance of the Visigothic Kingdom of Toledo in the aftermath of the Muslim invasion in 711, the "public" conceptualisation of power lost ground to emerging political and social structures marked by feudal and seigniorial relations. In this context, the services and resources demanded by the political authorities that emerged to the north of the rivers Douro and Ebro between the eight and eleventh centuries (Kingdom of Asturias-León, County of Castile and Kingdom of Pamplona) were inextricably linked to the exercise of feudal power, the scope of which varied from region to region. These royal services were similar to those perceived by other lay and ecclesiastical lords. The ultimate consequence of this was the rupture with Visigothic, Roman-inspired, public forms of taxation,[8] the raising of domanial tributes and the absence of "taxes" imposed by a sovereign "public" authority.[9]

Many of the royal rents, the payment of which predated the twelfth century, dug their roots in military services, documented in the County of Castile from the tenth century and in the Kingdom of Castile and León, united under the rule of Ferdinand I, from 1037 (*castellaría/ mena* or obligation to contribute to the construction and repair of fortresses;[10] *anubda* or participation in border surveillance duties).[11] Most of these services to the king or other lords were turned into cash payments later, as it happened, for instance, with the obligation to join military expeditions led by the king, which from a certain date could be replaced by a payment in cash. Other services, common to all the territories under consideration despite their different nomenclature (*infurción*, *marzazga* and *martiniega*★ in Castile and León, *pechas*★ in Navarre), also point to an early stage of taxation, and are linked to old domanial economic rights posed to peasant communities by feudal lords. Although some of these services were turned in the twelfth and thirteenth centuries into tributes paid in recognition of the "king's authority" (*señorío del rey*), their collection was also the prerogative of other lords. Finally, other feudal-seigniorial duties referred to the obligation to provide the king and other lords (and their entourages) with food and lodging, although by the early thirteenth century these were generally paid in cash.

The ability of the crown to tax the whole population in its dominions crystallised, first in Castile and later in Navarre, in the imposition of tributes over the minting of coinage. This led to compensatory payments after the kings renounced their prerogative to alter coinage, which only they could issue in virtue of the *ius regalium* (*moneda forera*★ in Castile and León, *monedaje*★ in Navarre). The fact that these tributes taxed all the vassals in the kingdom was the forerunner of the new forms of taxation that were to emerge thereafter. In Castile, taxes became increasingly linked to the principle of territoriality, which was supported by the extension of the superior authority of the king over the whole territory of the kingdom during the thirteenth and fourteenth centuries, although some remnants of former taxation models survived. In Navarre, the principle of territoriality was only applied to taxation at a later date, and it was not until the early fourteenth century that attempts were made to impose territorial taxes to complement the *monedaje*★.

First attempts to build a royal fiscal system in Castile and León (twelfth to mid-thirteenth century)

In late medieval Castile, old tributes (*pechos y derechos ciertos*) were residues of early practices adopted by the royal fiscal system before the mid-thirteenth century. However, their implementation was a significant milestone in the process of construction and extension of royal power during the twelfth and the first half of the thirteenth centuries.[12] The generalisation of these taxes in both the original territory of the kingdom north of the Douro and the areas conquered from the mid-eleventh century onwards (*Extremaduras* or territories situated beyond the Douro, *Transierra* or territories south of the Central System to the Tagus River), in which domanial tributes were eased off, laid the foundations of the fiscal function of the crown. This fiscal function was likely encouraged by the small weight of land that belonged to the king's personal patrimony and their associated direct rents. On the other hand, the early emergence of a royal fiscal system in Castile and León may also be associated with the notion of *imperium*, which monarchs like Alphonse VII, crowned as *Imperator totius Hispaniae* in 1135, reformulated from a feudal perspective during the eleventh and twelfth centuries to express their hegemony over other Christian powers in the Iberian Peninsula and consolidate their internal position.

However, the first significant steps for the construction of a royal fiscal system were taken during the reigns of Alphonse VIII of Castile (1158–1214) and Alphonse IX of León (1188–1230), after the separation of both kingdoms in 1157. Economic growth, internal colonisation processes and urbanisation, and increased money circulation made it easier to channel revenue to cover the monarchy's expenses. The crowns' growing need of resources was framed by conflict between Castile and León, aristocratic strife and military campaigns against the Almohads, which were particularly intense during the reign of Alphonse VIII (Christian defeat at Alarcos in 1195 and victory in Navas de Tolosa in 1212).[13]

The royal tributes (*pechos y derechos*) imposed during this period include cash payments to substitute for the military obligation to join the king's host, such as the *fonsadera*, turned into a monetary payment during the reign of Alphonse VI (1065–1109) and paid by freemen who did not participate in the war as *milites*;[14] *yantares*, *conduchos* and *hospedajes*, which reflected the obligation to feed and accommodate the king or lord and their entourage, which were also turned into cash payments gradually;[15] and *infurciones*, *marzazgas*, and *martiniegas**, direct tributes paid in cash by non-privileged social groups in recognition of the king's authority.[16]

The royal *marzazga*, which was paid each March – it is attested in the reign of Alphonse VII (1126–1157) but it became widespread during that of his grandson Alphonse VIII (1158–1214) – and the *martiniega**, paid in the day of Saint Martin, were neither exclusive nor equivalent, but had shared characteristics. The kings collected them in the northern territories, but they also became extensive to the regions to the south of the Douro (*Extremaduras*) and those to the south of the Central System conquered by Alphonse VI in 1085, in the valley of the Tagus (former Muslim kingdom of Toledo). At the same time, they are the most characteristic expression of the expansion of royal ordinary taxation beyond the territories over which the king exercised his direct seigniorial dominion (*realengo*) in the final decades of the twelfth century and the opening decades of the thirteenth century.[17] By the late thirteenth century, these were still important tributes; in 1292 "royal rents" in Castile and León, which included *martiniegas** and other similar tributes, amounted to 40 per cent of the monarch's regular revenue.[18]

The earliest general contributions to cover the whole kingdom are also dated to the twelve and thirteenth centuries. These services were linked with the obligation of economic *auxilium/servitium* to the king. The best documented was the extraordinary royal *petitum* or *pedido* demanded by Alphonse VII as early as 1136. This demand became increasingly frequent from 1157 and, especially in Castile, from 1170.[19] This early form of *pedido* – perhaps a direct tribute – disappeared when Alphonse X (1252–1284) began requesting extraordinary contributions from the *Cortes*, but continued until the end of the Middle Ages in northern territories that operated according to specific constitutional settings (*Allendebro*, Lordship of Vizcaya) and some seigniorial estates, in this case as a rent collected by the lords of the estate.[20] Also related to the economic *auxilium* to the king in war contexts are the obligatory loans requested by Alphonse IX of León to the councils in 1202 and 1204, and later by Ferdinand III in 1248 to fund the conquest of Seville, which were, in theory, returned afterwards.[21]

To these sources of revenue we must add the tolls imposed on goods (*portazgos*) in cities and villages, which, according to Alphonse X's *Partidas*, were a royal monopoly. These tolls are a symptom of the growing importance of internal trade during the twelfth and thirteenth centuries, which was further stimulated by the foundation of fairs and markets. Their returns for the monarchy, however, waned from the thirteenth century onwards, owing to the large number of total or partial exemptions in place and of the concession of this right to ecclesiastical and municipal institutions. These grants were especially common in newly conquered territories, like Andalusia and Murcia, or those in which supply was problematic. They were also awarded to settlements that hosted important merchant communities or were near the frontier, like in the Cantabrian region or the Castilian frontier with Aragón and Navarre. Despite this, and Alphonse X's attempts to eliminate barriers to internal trade, the royal ledger for 1292 still lists over forty *portazgos*. However, the concession of these fees to ecclesiastical, municipal and seigniorial fiscal systems was common practice between the twelfth and the fourteenth centuries.[22]

The *moneda* joined existing taxes in the early thirteenth century (in León from 1202, at the latest, and in Castile perhaps as early as 1197).[23] Originally, this rent was conceived as a compensation for the king's commitment to leave the purity, weight and legal value of coinage unaltered. By the reign of Alphonse X (1252–1284), the *moneda* had become a recurrent payment (under the name *moneda forera**), collected every seven years with no need of endorsement from the kingdom's parliamentary assembly (*Cortes*). This tribute was also collected after the crowning of a new monarch, which reset the seven-year count to zero. In addition to its longevity, the tribute survived until 1724, the importance of the *moneda forera** was that it became the base for the calculation of the services granted by the *Cortes* from 1269 onwards. It was also a direct tax that affected all non-privileged vassals of the realm. Initially, this wealth tax amounted to 1 *maravedí* per taxpayer (*pechero*), and it was later raised (fourteenth and fifteenth centuries) to 6 *maravedíes* in León and 8 *maravedíes* in Castile. Finally, only the king was entitled to the *moneda*, and its collection led to important synergies with the local contexts through which it was channelled, opening the door for the royal authority to make itself felt in many political spaces.[24]

The fiscal function of the Castilian crown was reinforced by the progressive identification, in the late twelfth and the early thirteenth centuries, of some of these economic rights (*yantar*, *fonsadera*, and *moneda*, in addition to the judicial function) with the elements that defined the "king's authority" (*señorío del rey*). This was conceived as a superior political-jurisdictional form of legitimacy that belonged to the king and extended over the whole *regnum*, which was beginning to be regarded as a transpersonal entity. In the same way, the expansion of the "king's authority" would explain the generalisation during this period of the expression "king's *fiscus*" to define the services and rents to which the public authority that the king represented was entitled.[25]

Therefore, the "king's authority" legitimised the collection of royal tributes and stood above the "seigniorial domain" that, in different ways, various political figures (including the king in the *realengo* estates) exercised over the territories that they administered. This is, for instance, the case with the "seigniorial domain" of the Church (*abadengo*), that of lay lords (*solariego*), and that observed in some seigniorial estates created in the twelfth century north of the Douro, where vassals were entitled to elect their lords (*behetrías*).[26] Tributes rooted in primitive forms of royal taxation and other taxes converged in the territories ruled under either of these forms of "seigniorial authority", sometimes as a result of royal concessions to the respective lords and others as a derivation of the "domanial authority" over the land. This is reflected in the *Libro Becerro de las Behetrías* (1352), which records the multiple royal and seigniorial rents raised north of the Douro, many of which were of considerable antiquity.[27]

However, in newly conquered and colonised territories, like the valley of the Guadalquivir and Murcia, which were annexed by Castile and León in the 1230s and 1240s, the monarchs were free to impose a less heterogeneous, and sometimes more solid, fiscal system. For this, the crown took direct control of Islamic tributary forms and structures, which were grounded on a mercantile and urban economy, and therefore, had greater potential for centralisation. This also happened after the conquest of Toledo in 1085 and the adoption of rights over commercial activities formerly held by Muslim sovereigns, which were merged in the late twelfth century in the so-called *almojarifazgo*★ (after the Arabic *al-musrif*).[28]

Similarly, the political organisation of the territories conquered and colonised in the eleventh and twelfth centuries between the Douro and the Tagus, and in the thirteenth century in the valley of the Guadalquivir, increased the kings of Castile's leverage to raise revenue. Most of these territories were put under the direct seigniorial authority of the king (*realengo*) with formulas such as "*comunidades de villa y tierra*", predominantly south of the Douro, and with the imposition of the royal domain also over the great Muslim cities now under Christian rule, like Toledo (1085), Córdoba (1236), Murcia (1243) and Seville (1248). These cities, like others in the kingdom, were governed by autonomous councils and were endowed with their own territory (*alfoces*), over which they had jurisdiction as the king's delegates. The exceptions to this policy were large properties, generally rural in nature, granted as seigniorial estates (*abadengo*) to major ecclesiastical figures such as the Archbishop of Toledo in the valley of the Tagus, or the military orders of Santiago, Calatrava and Alcántara from the mid-twelfth century in the region of La Mancha and the valley of the Guadiana. In these territories, the payment of seigniorial rents over land, as well as the exaction of ecclesiastical rents continued throughout the Middle Ages.[29]

The gradual crystallisation of a rich royal patrimony in Navarre (twelfth–thirteenth centuries)

During the thirteenth century, the Navarre crown essentially lived off the wealth inherited from previous monarchs, while increasing the royal assets through purchase, donation and exchanges, and reorganising said assets to increase the efficiency of revenue collection systems.

Kings Sancho VI (1150–1194) and Sancho VII (1194–1232) initiated the "unificación de *pechas*★", that is, the reorganisation of the tributes due by all vassals in the kingdom.[30] In the northern regions of the kingdom – more sparsely populated and dominated by Atlantic landscapes – the "*pechas*★ *encabezadas*", paid by the household, were predominant, while in the southern and central regions – more densely populated and marked by Mediterranean landscapes – the most common type were *pechas*★ imposed as a fixed payment on whole communities.[31] In contrast to old services paid in kind with a wide variety of goods, the unification of *pechas*★ reduced the available payment methods to coin, wheat, barley and oats. The large amounts paid in concept of *pechas*★ and their conversion into annual fees paid by the largest villages in the centre and the south of the kingdom has led to a debate around whether the "unificaciones de *pechas*★" can be regarded as a true fiscal reform, substituting direct taxes for servile rents. In any case, widespread attempts to abandon the (servile) social condition of *pecheros* indicates that the *pecha*★ retained shameful connotations in Navarre.

In the early thirteenth century, Sancho VII acquired numerous properties in the south of the kingdom, where he lived, often at the expense of noble families.[32] His purchases and exchanges allowed him to greatly increase his income, in the absence of extraordinary tributes of any kind. He left his heirs a kingdom in which his landed estates and *solariegas* rents accounted for approximately 75 per cent of the king's revenue (in the vicinity of 23,000 pounds of *dineros sanchetes*), in a normal year, that is, a year in which no extraordinary revenue was forthcoming.[33] This fiscal potential likely conditioned the emergence of new sources of taxation in Navarre.

The first tentative steps to collect extraordinary tributes were taken by the new monarchs from the French dynasty of Champagne. Theobald I and Theobald II collected the earliest *monedajes*★ in 1244 and 1264, after negotiating new conditions for minting coinage, a royal right contained in the *Fuero General de Navarra*.[34] The occasional ecclesiastical *rediezmo* of 1268, which taxed ecclesiastical rents and properties with one tenth of their value, began being raised in this same context with the authorisation of the Church.[35] Thenceforth, the only fiscal demands until 1329 were extraordinary exactions (euphemistically referred to as "grants") on Jewish communities,[36] and those negotiated with the clergy on a few occasions, for instance in 1305.[37]

Finally, the tolls became an important source of revenue in Navarre from the first half of the thirteenth century at the latest, and their regulation seems to have gone a good way back. For instance, the charter of the neighbourhood of San Cernin, in Pamplona, recognised in 1229 its residents exemptions from tolls. Therefore, the known Late Medieval tolls must have been set up by Sancho VII and Theobald I, since several lawsuits dated to 1254 record the complaints filed by the neighbourhood of San Cernin and the town of Estella against the tolls imposed by these monarchs.[38]

The toll system took shape during the thirteenth and fourteenth centuries, forming a network of branches in which royal officials, known as *"guardas del peaje"*, supervised external trade, collecting import (*peajes*) and export duties (*sacas*), and ensuring that no *"cosas vedadas"* were exported, that is, goods the export of which was occasionally forbidden (precious metal, weapons, cereal or horses). These offices were situated at the ends of the most important communication routes: the Way of St. James between Saint-Palais (Lower Navarre) and Los Arcos; the Cantabrian route, with several entry points in Tudela; the wine route, to the Basque Country through Bernedo and Laguardia; and the eastern route, to Aragón, which left the kingdom through Sangüesa.[39]

It is estimated that in the first half of the fourteenth century tolls accounted for 15 per cent of the total ordinary revenue of the Crown (approximately 2,500 pounds of *dineros sanchetes*). Concerning custom duties, we have details about the toll post in Sangüesa in 1363, which applied a wide range of fees, from 3 per cent to 16 per cent.

In contrast, indirect taxation does not seem to appear in Navarre prior to the fourteenth century, when we hear about municipal *sisas*★ for the first time. However, there were other small and local indirect taxes on consumption known as *leztas*★, which applied to a limited array of relevant products in each market, being regulated by the local charters from the twelfth century onwards. These indirect taxes were succeeded by trade duties on grain (known as *chapiteles*) which gradually emerged in different towns.[40] Other forms of fiscal revenue appeared in the thirteenth century, such as those linked to the administration of royal justice: fees for the use of scribes offices and for the use of the royal seal.[41]

The construction of a fiscal system for the State

Although at different paces and with different intensity, the fiscal systems analysed here underwent significant transformations during the thirteenth and fourteenth centuries. Change, which was always grounded on the previous systems, began crystallising in Castile and León during the mid-thirteenth century and in Navarre during the mid-fourteenth century. In structural terms, they are related to economic factors such as the development of craft and commercial activity, and to political factors, such as the funding of external or internecine wars, the expansion of the royal power over the whole *regnum*, and the distribution of revenue among the political forces that were an integral part of the crowns' structure (especially noble lineages, but also cities and the Church).

In the case of Castile, fiscal innovations were also supported by the development of Roman-inspired legal principles that recovered and fitted the notion of the *res publica* within the prevailing feudal system, which often made for an uneasy coexistence. Similarly, the dissemination of the principle of nature bonded the whole population and their "natural lord" (the king) through taxes, in a kingdom whose process of territorialisation was pretty much complete by the early fourteenth century. These ideas gradually undermined feudal relationships, although these did not disappear completely and continued populating political language and practices.

In this way, the royal fiscal systems in both Castile and Navarre, despite their significant qualitative and quantitative differences, similarly combined the old and the new. During the thirteenth and fourteenth centuries, the traditional rents inherited from previous centuries were joined by new tributes, monopolies and royal rights; indirect taxation over internal and external trade and consumption; and, especially, direct tributes and other services, based on the duty of *auxilium* to the king, the collection of which was authorised by the *Cortes*, whose role as representative body of the estates, and the voice of fiscal consent, consolidated in the thirteenth century.

"Fiscal revolution" and the strengthening of royal power in Castile (ca. 1250–ca. 1350)

Castile was one of the earliest kingdoms in the medieval West to develop, from the mid-thirteenth century, a state fiscal system, although this always operated in parallel to other taxation models such as the ecclesiastical, the seigniorial and the municipal. On the foundations of the pre-existing taxation, the Crown's fiscal system took a significant quantitative and qualitative leap ahead with the imposition of new taxes in the whole kingdom after Castile and León became a single Crown for good in 1230.

This process received a vigorous boost during the reign of Alphonse X (1252–1284), especially between 1265 and 1280, when the custom system was reorganised; the first general tax on transhumant flocks was created; personal taxes on religious minorities were increased; and the model for extraordinary contributions passed by the *Cortes* (*servicios**) was set up. At the same time, with papal permission, the monarchy increased its share of ecclesiastical rents, which are examined in detail in Chapter 4 in this volume (from 1247, two ninths of ecclesiastical tithes – *tercias reales*, ecclesiastical subsidies and crusade indulgences). The collection of these items, justified by the struggle against the infidels and the protection of the Church by the Crown, continued over time and made substantial contributions to the royal coffers.[42]

In a second phase, following a period (1282–1325) in which some of the fiscal innovations put forward by Alphonse X faced some resistance, his great-grandson Alphonse XI gave the last touches to the Crown's new fiscal system during his effective rule (1325–1350). The royal rights over salt mines consolidated in 1338, and taxes on transhumant flocks in 1343 (*servicio y montazgo*). In parallel, the collection of a general and indirect tax over sales and consumption (*alcabala**) began in 1342, following a temporary authorisation by the *Cortes*.[43]

The development of this new fiscal model was related to structural economic conditions inherited from the twelfth century. For instance, the intensification of trade (stimulated by the monarchs with the foundation of fairs and markers, the limitation of barriers to internal trade as early as the second half of the thirteenth century, and the regulation of external trade), and the increase of money in circulation that came with an increasingly widespread exchange economy. On the other hand, foreign policy initiatives, and the increase in royal expenses that they entailed, also contributed to the expansion of royal taxation. Important among these were Alphonse X's aspiration to the imperial title from 1256 onwards and, especially, the cost of war.

The intense military activity of these decades allowed Castile to consolidate its victories over Islam in the south of the Iberian Peninsula, organise the defence against the Marinid invasions from North Africa from 1275, and sustain a struggle to control the Strait of Gibraltar that lasted until the mid-fourteenth century, when the Muslims in the Iberian Peninsula were reduced to the Nasrid emirate of Granada.[44] Granada, which became a vassal state of Castile in 1246, made periodical payments in gold (*parias*) to buy peace, a practice begun in the Iberian Peninsula in the mid-eleventh century. The *parias* were negotiated in the truces signed by the emirs and the Castilian kings, which were periodically renovated until 1482, with the beginning of the war that was to end in the conquest of the emirate.[45]

However, the war against the infidel, in itself, does not explain everything, although it was the main stimulus for the development of taxation. The increasing fiscal range of the Crown is also related to political aspects such as the rearrangement of power relations between the Crown and other political agents (nobility, cities and the Church). This process rested on Roman-inspired ideas that were at the foundations of the superiority of the king's public authority (the royal *potestas*) over feudal-estate relations. This attempt to strengthen royal power was further encouraged by the revitalisation, during the reign of Alphonse X, of the idea of *imperium* and for the constitution of a universal law to eventually supersede the existing legal fragmentation. These moves towards legal unification resulted in very relevant juridical initiatives, such as the major compilation of universal laws commissioned by Alphonse X (*Siete Partidas*), which explicitly established that the king could act as an emperor in his own kingdom; or an attempt to determine legal hierarchies (*Ordenamiento de Alcalá*, 1348); the latter contributed to reinforce the authority of the kings and their legislative function, which was generally exercised during the meetings of the *Cortes*.[46]

In turn, the advance of royal taxation awoke the interest of other agents, especially the nobility, to have a share in the growing revenue through the perception of military salaries, known as *tierras* and *soldadas*. The end of the major territorial conquests in the mid-thirteenth century had cut short the economic expectations of the aristocrats (booty and land) who had supported the king's campaigns. For this reason, as well as individual motivations and circumstances, the Castilian nobility sought to participate in the new fiscal system and became its main beneficiary, despite its initial resistance.

In conclusion, the expansion of the fiscal powers of the Castilian monarchy is one of the key drives in the process of consolidation of royal power from the mid-thirteenth century onwards, and, to a large extent, one that shaped the future political structure of the kingdom. The trend was for royal power to grow and for the king to have increasing leverage, but not without resistance and setbacks, in what was anything but a smooth linear process. In addition, the sources of revenue tried during this period were to become, with adjustments, the basis of the monarchy's tributary system thereafter, as many of these items of taxation were to survive until the end of the *Ancien Régime*, in the nineteenth century. For this reason, the fiscal innovations of the period 1250–1350, although originally adopted to address a very specific set of problems, were in the long run proven revolutionary, despite the fact that their promoters could not even imagine their future projection and that their implementation, tentative and temporary at first, was occasionally seriously compromised.

The control over regalías

Some of these fiscal innovations are related with the full exercise of *regalia*, or exclusive rights that the Castilian monarchs held in virtue of the *ius regalium*. Many of these rights are already attested in the twelfth century, although they expanded during the thirteenth and fourteenth centuries because of the new Roman-inspired conceptualisation of the royal authority that the Castilian Crown promoted. Among the king's most important exclusive attributions was the issuing of money. We cannot go into details here, but it is worth mentioning that, between 1265 and the stabilisation of currency in 1480, the Crown recurrently tinkered with the purity and weight of money, especially bullion coinage. This was an expediency measure to reap immediate profits, despite causing inflation and economic damage to the kingdom, as often denounced by the *Cortes*.[47]

Other royal prerogatives (judicial fees, ownership over property whose owner was not known or died without heir, one fifth of the booty taken from Muslims) did not yield large returns. More significant were chancellery fees charged for the issuing of documents, even as late as the final years of the thirteenth century less.[48] For their part, royal monopolies over mining and the exploitation of the coastline were consolidated between the thirteenth and the fourteenth centuries, although a few instances in which the Crown surrendered these rights are attested. The only rights over fisheries (*pesquerías*) that raised substantial revenue were those over tuna-fishing in the Atlantic coast of Andalusia (*almadraba*), although this monopoly was granted to the powerful lineage of the Guzmán between 1299 and 1368.[49]

Mining resources belonged to the Crown, and these were initially leased out for substantial fees, for instance the iron mines (*ferrerías*) in Vizcaya, Guipúzcoa and other Atlantic regions, the exploitation of which intensified between 1257 and 1292.[50] However, Alphonse XI's liberalising policies and donations led to a reduction of the profits yielded by *ferrerías*, but which does not reflect a decrease in iron production.[51] The mercury mines of Almadén-Chillón, exploited in equal partnership by the Crown and the military order Calatrava from 1249, were fully surrendered to the masters of the order in 1282, and became one of the organisation's main sources of income.[52]

Royal rights over the exploitation of coastal and interior saltpans were made effective as early as the reign of Alphonse VIII of Castile. They were leased out during the reign of Ferdinand III, and the price of salt was fixed, while mechanisms to control wholesale salt transactions in monopolistic warehouses (*alfolíes*) were put in place. Later, Alphonse X reinforced this royal right with the support of Roman law, as reflected in the *Partidas*. In this way, by 1292 saltpans accounted for 6 per cent of fixed royal revenue.[53] In 1338, frequent fraud and the large number of agents that benefitted from saltpans, moved Alphonse XI to pass a set of regulations which emphasised the royal ownership of all saltpans and *alfolíes*, fixed prices and created obligatory salt quotas for cities, towns and villages. This system, however, failed from 1351, and free transactions and traditional fraud control systems were resumed, although the areas in which the salt extracted in each production area was to be commercialised and retailed was put in place (except in Andalusia). This taxation model was still in operation in the fifteenth century, when saltpans and *alfolíes* amounted to 3–3.5 per cent of the king's ordinary revenue.[54]

Royal taxation over good transit: almojarifazgos and customs; servicio y montazgo over transhumant livestock

Fiscal reforms implemented from the mid-thirteenth century also involved the creation, in some cases, and the consolidation, in others, of indirect taxes on the external and internal circulation of goods. Concerning taxes on exterior trade, the monarchs followed the example set by the former Muslim rulers of their new conquests. In these regions, urban trade did not slacken during the Andalusi period, and many of their tributary regimes continued under the Christian rule. In this way, the *almojarifazgos*★ collected in Toledo in the twelfth century, and in the southern territories (especially Seville, Córdoba, and Murcia) after their conquest in the 1230s and 1240s, embraced a set of indirect taxes brought together under the principle of unified treasury and lease.

The extremely complex array of tributes included in each territory's *almojarifazgo** comprised a wide diversity of concepts, which varied from city to city.[55] In any case, the most important component of the *almojarifazgo** were the custom duties over exterior trade, which generally rose to 10 per cent of the value of all imported products; exchanges with the emirate of Granada were taxed with 15 per cent of their value, an additional tribute known as *diezmo y medio diezmo de lo morisco*, which was collected during truces with the Nasrid kingdom and which was made independent from the *almojarifazgos** applied by each custom district from the final third of the fourteenth century.[56]

Over time, the rents raised by each *almojarifazgo** became disaggregated with the lease of specific items, or with the cession of some of these items to municipalities and cities, for instance Toledo and Seville.[57] Seville's was the most profitable *almojarifazgo** of the kingdom, as it taxed the active Andalusian maritime trade. In this case, the rent was assimilated to a complex custom office, which charged custom duties divided into a number of categories (*renta de Berbería, almonaima* and *cuenta de mercaderes, partido de las mercaderías* and *rentas menudas*). This came in addition to a 10 per cent tax over the production of olive oil in the districts of El Aljarafe and La Ribera, a continuation of the Islamic tithe on agricultural production which, in the fifteenth century, was leased out separately. Finally, in 1498 the custom offices of all southern coastal *almojarifazgo**s that belonged to the Crown were included in the *almojarifazgo** *mayor de Sevilla* as a way to rationalise the management of custom offices and improve their performance.[58]

On the other hand, in 1268 Alphonse X used existing precedents to begin charging custom duties in territories that were not included in the *almojarifazgo** districts. The general rate was 10 per cent on imports and the same percentage over all exports that exceeded imports in value. The aim of this reform was to outline external trade; create royal officials (*alcaldes de saca*) to control contraband and the export of banned goods (precious metal, coin, horses, weapons); even out the balance of trade; protect strategic economic sectors; and, especially, profit from the development of international trade and the increasingly neat definition of land borders with neighbouring kingdoms, where custom offices were set through which goods had to pass obligatorily. This involved the creation of the "tithes of the sea" (*diezmos** *de la mar*) in the Cantabrian coast, which were consolidated after the foundation of the *Hermandad de la Marina de Castilla* in 1296 (this *Hermandad* was constituted by coastal councils interested in commercial activity); the *diezmo** *de la mar* was later also extended to coastal harbours in Galicia). In addition, during the reign of Alphonse XI a series of custom offices were set up in overland routes with the kingdoms of Aragón and Valencia to tax legal imports and exports with a general rate of 10 per cent. However, no similar custom offices were created in the border with Portugal during the fourteenth and fifteenth centuries.[59]

The collection of these overland and maritime customs continued in the second half of the fourteenth and through the fifteenth centuries into the Early Modern Age, although some ended up in the hands of aristocratic houses, like the *diezmos** *de la mar*, which were ceded to the lineage of the Velascos in 1469.[60] Overall, the royal customs offices were a significant source of income, which accounted for approximately 12 per cent of ordinary royal revenue between 1429 and 1465.[61]

However, external trade was not the only target of taxes on the circulation of goods. The great development of Castilian stock-keeping between 1230 and 1260, and the organisation in 1273 of the *Mesta*, an organisation created to settle lawsuits between shepherds and their masters and to defend the sector, soon led the monarchy to also tax this economic activity, with the argument that the flock owners and the shepherds that brought them through the droveways (*cañadas*) enjoyed the royal protection. As early as 1261, Alphonse X got the *Cortes* to pass a special *servicio*★ over transhumant flocks, collected like a custom fee in specific checkpoints, in exchange for the exemption over tolls (*montazgos*), excepting only those collected by the military orders in their demesnes. After 1269, this *servicio*★, the management of which was leased out, was turned into an annual fixed-rate tax, in kind or its cash equivalent, over the number and types of animals; this did not yet involve the disappearance of many local *montazgos* collected by lords and councils in their barren lands.

In 1343, perhaps yielding to the financial pressures posed by the war against Islam (campaign of Algeciras), Alphonse XI merged all rents over transhumant stock-keeping intro a single tax, which comprised various items, and appropriated all *montazgos* in the kingdom for the Crown. The new tax was called *servicio y montazgo*★, and its management was leased out for several years at a time, in periods beginning in the day of Saint John (24 June). From that moment onwards, the collection of the tax was centralised in the passes in the Central System and other regions through which the flocks had to transit.[62] The *servicio y montazgo*★ was an important tax in the Late Middle Ages, not so much for the amount of revenue that it raised in and by itself, but because it had a direct impact on other economic sectors. In the fifteenth century, the lease only amounted to 2.5 per cent of ordinary income, although it was a relatively safe rent.[63]

Head tax over Jewish and Muslim minorities

Other taxes consolidated by Alphonse X affected the Jewish and free Muslim communities (*Mudéjares*), which were burdened with specific head taxes (*cabeza de pecho*). The origin of these tributes may date back to figures like the *iudaica* and similar items, which are sporadically attested from the last third of the twelfth century.[64] These tributes were justified by the protection that the king granted religious minorities as their personal lord, the foundation of religious tolerance towards these groups, which paid in this way the "price" for keeping their faith.

The head tax imposed on *Mudéjares* (*cabeza de pecho de los moros*) was low and varied from place to place. In many instances, these sources of revenue were ceded to municipal and seigniorial treasuries (*haciendas señoriales*) in the fourteenth and fifteenth centuries. The head tax on the Jewish community, in contrast, yielded much more substantial returns, as reflected by the 4,320,000 *maravedíes* demanded by Alphonse X from the Jewish community after the execution for fraud of his treasurer, Çag de la Maleha, in 1280. Although the heavy economic burden that this head tax posed on the Jewish communities led the Crown to moderate the tribute, the collection of the *pecho de los judíos* – distributed among local communities by a commission of Jewish elders – was there to stay. Later, during the fourteenth and fifteenth century, the revenue yielded by this figure decreased, although Alphonse XI demanded economic *servicios*★ to the Jewish communities to fund the war against the Muslims.[65]

The beginnings of extraordinary donations granted by the Cortes: the servicios

The formulation and generalisation, from the mid-thirteenth century, of extraordinary donations (*servicios*★) granted by the *Cortes* was perhaps the most relevant step in the configuration of a state fiscal system in Castile. The amounts granted in these early *servicios*★ were calculated, taking as a given number of *monedas foreras*. On the other hand, the early *servicios*★ were not only relevant for the revenue they afforded, but because they were to become a recurrent expedient thenceforth. But they were also important because they totally redefined the political relationship between the monarch and the kingdom. The fact that they had to be endorsed by the assembly that represented the estates of the realm, something that never changed, opened communication channels with the political community, especially with the cities and towns whose representatives sat at the *Cortes*. This greatly reinforced the role of the assembly as institutional instrument and stage for consensus, in application of the Roman-law principle of *Quod omnes tangit, ab omnibus debet approbari*, and laid the ground for a legitimating rhetoric that justified a fiscal system based on the idea of "commonwealth" (*pro del regno*).[66]

The origin of *servicios*★ can perhaps be tracked back to 1258, when the *Cortes* granted Alphonse X a double *moneda forera*★ to meet the costs of his imperial aspirations (the so-called *fecho del Imperio*), after the death of his relative Emperor Conrad IV Hohenstaufen. However, the first explicit reference to the concession of a *servicio*★ by the *Cortes* dates to 1269, within the context of the ongoing reform of the Crown's financial sources. The nobility opposed, arguing that the *servicio*★ undermined their privileges, since it also affected their vassals. This argument, along with others that similarly rejected the political and fiscal innovations implemented by Alphonse X, was used by the nobility to justify their revolt against the king from 1271 to 1274.[67]

Once this resistance was overcome, the concession of extraordinary *servicios*★ by the *Cortes* was resumed in 1274, in relation to the final fruitless attempts of Alphonse X to be crowned emperor, the need to pay for military operations against the Marinid invasion in 1275, and the costs of war in the frontier with Granada.[68] Later, Sancho IV (1284–1295) and Ferdinand IV (1295–1312) turned these *servicios*★ into a recurrent source of income. The revenue so collected was used to fund the conquest of various strongholds, like Tarifa (1292), to meet diplomatic costs and, especially, to pay the salaries (*tierras*) of members of the nobility and knights who were entitled to some of the revenue collected from 1297 to 1312.

However, the concession of *servicios*★ slowed down or was limited to specific territories during the minority of Alphonse XI (1312–1325), as a result of the complaints expressed by the *Cortes* and corporations of cities (*Hermandades*) organised for the defence of their common interests, as well as of the disputes that divided the king's tutors. Afterwards, during Alphonse XI's effective rule (1325–1350) and that of his successor Peter I (1350–1369), the collection of *servicios*★ continued to meet the costs of the 1327 and 1350 campaigns against Granada and of the defence of the Andalusian frontier, a circumstance that the Crown took full advantage of to consolidate its authority.[69]

Extraordinary *servicios*★ also contributed to define a new relational framework between the monarchy and cities, which often asked through the *Cortes* to be able to control their collection. *Servicios*★ involved direct taxes calculated on the basis of the wealth of taxpayers (*pecheros*) (regrettably, the amounts paid by each taxpayer is not always clearly reflected in the record at this early stage). For instance, between 1275 and 1279, taxpayers with 10 *maravedíes* worth of assets paid 10 *sueldos*. After 1286, taxpayers in León went on to pay 1 *maravedí* for each 10 *maravedíes* in assets, except those whose wealth ranged from 5 to 10 *maravedíes*, which only paid half a *maravedí*. Those below the minimum threshold were exempt and were labelled as "fiscal poor". The rate of this tax was higher in Castile: 8 *maravedíes* for taxpayers that owned landed and movable property worth 60 *maravedíes*. During the reign of Alphonse XI, exemptions were granted to men that kept horses, the children of those who kept horses up to 16 years of age, *hidalgos*, knights armed at the king's expense, crossbowmen, and the dwellers of castles in the frontier with Granada. Therefore, exemptions from *servicios*★ and also from *moneda* were thenceforth to become a recognition of noble status.[70]

The beginnings of the royal ad valorem tax on consumption: alcabalas

The donations granted by the *Cortes* are also associated with one of the most significant fiscal innovations adopted during the rule of Alphonse XI: the generalisation of an *ad valorem* tax over sales and consumption called *alcabala*★ (after the Arabic *al-qabala*). The precedents for this tax are multiple: the imposition of a tax of 1/11 on the returns of loans and sales to Jews and Muslims in 1253; the indirect taxes imposed by Jewish communities to meet the *cabeza de pecho*; *alcabalas viejas*, collected with royal permission by some municipalities to cover their costs in the final third of the thirteenth and the early fourteenth centuries; some impositions on commodities (linen and cotton, cloth, captives) included in the *almojarifazgos*★; and, extraordinary 1 per cent taxes (*sisas*★) on sales attested as early as 1293 to pay for the war against Granada.

On these foundations, in 1333 Alphonse XI demanded a general tax on sales with which to fund the war against infidels and the frontier castles in Andalusia, where the threat of Muslim attacks was acutely felt and the monarch had greater room for manoeuvre. He reiterated his petition in 1338, and the representatives of cities expressed their consent. The extension of this tax to other territories took place in 1342 when, as a way to meet the costs of the siege of Algeciras in the context of the war against Nasrids and Marinids for the control of the Strait of Gibraltar, the king negotiated with the *Cortes* the temporary collection of *alcabalas*★ in the whole kingdom. In 1345, this tax was prorogued for six years, after the king committed not to request other extraordinary services during this period.

Therefore, in origin the *alcabala*★ was the method adopted to collect some of the *servicios*★ granted by the *Cortes*, and demanded the approval of the assembly that represented the estates of the realm. The *Cortes*' acquiescence was probably favoured by Alphonse XI's promotion of urban oligarchies, which during his rule gained control over many municipal governments through the constitution of closed assemblies (*regimientos*) with the king's support. By 1348, the details of the tax were explicitly established: the initial rate of 3.33 per cent was kept by Peter I (1350–1369) when he resumed the extraordinary and temporary collection of *alcabalas*★. Afterwards, his step-brother Henry II Trastámara (1369–1379) increased the rate to between 5 and 10 per cent, and consolidated the tax: it was requested again in 1366 to the *Cortes* that proclaimed him king to face the costs of the war that ultimately saw the elevation of the Trastámara dynasty to the throne, after the murder of Peter I in 1369.[71]

Consolidation of the Castilian royal fiscal system and innovations in taxation (1369–1504)

The arrival of the Trastámara dynasty in 1369 did not arrest the process of gradual consolidation of the Castilian fiscal system. Much to the contrary, Henry II (1369–1379) and his successors John I (1379–1390) and Henry III (1390–1406) continued moving forward with, and expanded, the previous reforms. This strengthening of the Royal Treasury (*Hacienda Real*) responded to the financial needs faced by these monarchs, largely related to the conflicts connected with the projection of the Hundred Years' War on the Iberian Peninsula (civil war between Peter I and Henry II in 1366–1369; John I's war against Portugal from 1381 to 1385; and, English invasion of Galicia in 1386). In addition, it is worth recalling that these episodes coincided with the worse years of the Crisis of the Late Middle Ages, after the Black Death epidemic of 1348, and resulted in the increase of the fiscal pressure, which probably peaked during the reign of John I.

Internally, the new dynasty gave new impetus to previous policies, which were to define the balance of power between monarchy, nobility and urban councils.[72] First, Henry II granted numerous seigniorial demesnes to the members of the nobility who had helped him to the throne. His successors endorsed this policy and continued rewarding political services with demesnes; as a result the extent of "seigniorial estates" grew at the expense of *realengo*. From then on, the leading noble families, which had been renovated after the civil war and which also included the king's relatives, began deploying new strategies of political action. Especially of note among these are their involvement in the fiscal system, the exercise of seigniorial authority, the display of their political influence in the royal court, and the formation of factions which competed to steer the king's will.[73] On the other hand, the *Cortes* consolidated their role as channel for the political expression of cities and forum for fiscal negotiation, consent and complaint. In addition, municipal governments further developed the process of oligarchisation originally promoted by Alphonse XI, and drew increasingly closer bonds with the Crown, which was able to intervene in urban contexts with new instruments, such as the dispatch of royal keepers to the cities (*corregidores*).[74]

The "centralised monarchy" built by the first members of the Trastámara dynasty, between 1369 and 1406, was endowed with new institutional and bureaucratic instruments to improve the exercise of royal power, including the fiscal system. The head managers of tributary resources were the *contadores mayores de Hacienda*, who were ultimately responsible for supervising income and organising expenditure. Under them, an extensive network of revenue agents and tax farmers collected the actual taxes according to the regulations and conditions outlined in the appropriate tax legislation (*cuadernos de rentas*); this system reached maturity in the first half of the fifteenth century.[75] Expenditure was centralised in four territorial treasurers (León, Castile, Toledo and Andalusía) in 1371; these figures disappeared in the 1440s. However, in reality their work controlling outlays was parallel to that of other specific treasurers and the head collectors of each district, whose prominence increased over time.[76]

The sums distributed were calculated as annual fixed amounts over an ordinary rent (*situados*), awarded as a royal privilege for life (*juros de por vida*) or as an hereditary grant (*juros de heredad*). The beneficiaries of these rents were generally members of the nobility (from the late fourteenth century, especially those who paid political or military services to the Crown), ecclesiastical institutions and, further down the line, members of urban oligarchies. This consolidated the insertion of these political forces in the framework of the monarchy and their links with the Crown. However, during the reigns of John II and Henry IV, these grants became an increasingly heavy burden for the royal coffers. For this reason, from 1480 the Catholic Monarchs began to reduce these grants in order to gradually disembarrass the Royal Treasury (*Real Hacienda*).[77] Aside from royal grants, the head accountants (*contadores mayores*) also controlled the payment (*libranzas*) of the state's ordinary and extraordinary expenses (royal house, bureaucracy, justice), military salaries (garrisons, salaries of the "king's vassals" in the shape of *tierras*, *acostamientos* or *sueldos*), and diplomatic costs, among others. Finally, income and outgo were audited by the *contadores mayores de cuentas*.[78]

There were few significant novelties in the typology of fiscal items during this period, although the management of some changed and others became ordinary sources of revenue. From 1369, a series of minor old rents, and especially the new taxes placed under the royal jurisdiction between 1250 and 1350 (saltpans and *alfolíes*, *almojarifazgos**, custom duties, *servicio y montazgo** and *tercias reales*), became ordinary rents.

The most significant change before 1406 refers to the *servicios** granted by the *Cortes*, obligatory loans and *alcabalas**. From 1369 to 1406 the *Cortes* granted a minimum of 28 extraordinary donations, the concession and collection of which included two well-differentiated items, which increased the yield and compensated for the debasement of coinage, a recurrent phenomenon between 1369 and 1400. These components were a given number of *monedas* (direct tribute) and the simultaneous collection of *alcabalas** (indirect tax) for a limited period of time. The collection of *monedas*, which was totally or partially leased out to financial companies, was managed around the community and calculated on the basis of each taxpayer's wealth. The collection of *alcabalas** was also outsourced; their rate initially fluctuated between 5 and 10 per cent, until it was eventually fixed at 10 per cent in the late fourteenth century.[79] In 1386–1387,

John I requested specific services from Jews and Muslims, and from at least 1388 also a direct tribute on these communities (*servicio y medio servicio*), the regular collection of which continued annually through the fifteenth century, until the expulsion of the Jews in 1492 and the forced conversion of *Mudéjares* in 1502.[80]

However, in some circumstances the resources approved by the *Cortes* were insufficient to meet the Crown's military and diplomatic expenses. For this reason, the monarchy ramped up the request of obligatory loans to councils (*empréstitos*), which were in theory to be paid back with the returns of the *servicios**. This increased the fiscal pressure on taxpayers in a recessive economic context. Henry II demanded two loans (1373 and 1375) to recover the royal donations with which he rewarded foreign military support during the civil war (Beltrán Duguesclin) and compensated the kings of Aragón and Navarre for their participation in the conflict. For his part, John I made recurrent use of forced loans on councils (1381, 1383, 1384) to fund his aspirations to the throne of Portugal, aborted in 1385 after his defeat to João de Avis at Aljubarrota. A new loan, requested in 1386, was used after the English invasion of Galicia to compensate the Duke of Lancáster and to make him give up his pretensions to the Castilian throne. After this, the Crown arrested the creation of a system of "sovereign credit" and systematically relying on loans, but these petitions had created a precedent, and the practice was resumed at times of crisis, for instance in 1429 in the context of the war with Aragón.[81]

The fact that the Crown pulled the brakes on the creation of a "sovereign credit" system may be related to the most significant novelty in the monarchy's fiscal structure during the reign of Henry III (1390–1406). In 1400, the king imposed his full jurisdiction on the ordinary collection of *alcabalas**, with a 10 per cent rate, bypassing thenceforth the authorisation of the *Cortes*, which endorsed this tax for the last time in 1398. This was a major success in the process of extension of the fiscal sovereignty of the Crown to the whole kingdom, and lay the foundations for a strong "fiscal state", at a much earlier date than in other Western European polities: in the fifteenth century, *alcabalas** were often leased out alongside the *tercias reales*, and accounted for 80 per cent of the Crown's ordinary revenue.[82]

In parallel to this, Henry III also sought to change the structure of the *servicios** awarded by the Cortes. Already as early as the 1380s, John I had requested additional, non-refundable sums from the councils (referred to by different names – *servicios*/pedidos*) to complement *monedas* and *alcabalas**. After the *alcabala** was made an ordinary source of revenue, the next step was to reform the collection of the donations awarded by the *Cortes*, following earlier developments. From 1398 onwards, the *servicios** passed by the assembly included a certain number of *monedas* and a global amount to be divided among the councils (*pedido*) according to population censuses (for instance, the one carried out in 1409); these soon became obsolete, leading to significant discrepancies between real population and tax allocation. Afterwards, the councils began collecting the tribute among its resident citizens according to wealth-based tax brackets. Therefore, the collection system of the *pedido* increased the fiscal prerogatives of municipalities, which was another step towards the integration of councils in the political structure of the monarchy and their cooperation with the Crown.[83]

During the fifteenth century, the *Cortes* awarded *pedidos* and *monedas* very frequently. Despite their gradually decreasing yield in gold and silver equivalents, they compensated for the shrinking returns of ordinary revenue during the reigns of John II (1406–1454) and Henry IV (1454–1474), and the also decreasing proportion of ordinary sources of revenue that was not burdened by royal grants (*situados*). Conversely, the number of these royal grants grew to reward services and cement loyalties in contexts of internal political strife, a recurrent feature in Castile between 1406 and 1480. In this way, in the period 1406–1476, the *Cortes* passed *pedidos y monedas* as many as 33 times, although some of these spread out the collection of the donation over more than one year. In order to justify their financial requests, the Crown appealed to grave issues that affected the "commonwealth" of the kingdom, understood as a political community. Often, these issues had to do with the war against Granada, which saw several periods of intense activity between 1406 and 1462 (1407–1408, 1410, 1431, 1455–1457 and 1462), the cost of the defence of the frontier, and other conflicts such as the war with Aragón in 1429–1430. Other recurrent argument included diplomatic costs and expenses that aimed to stifle conflict among the aristocratic factions that fought to control the levers of royal power during the reigns of John II and Henry IV.[84]

The decreasing yield of ordinary rents was compounded by the active intervention of the nobility in the collection of ordinary and extraordinary royal tributes in the territories put under seigniorial jurisdiction by members of the Trastámara dynasty. The extension of "jurisdictional demesnes" – at least half the population of Castile lived under this form of jurisdiction by the end of the Middle Ages – contributed to revitalise aristocratic *haciendas* in parallel to the consolidation of the monarchy's fiscal system. In this way, the nobility continued receiving traditional rents derived from the direct exploitation of their property and other seigniorial tributes (e.g. leasing out of offices and services; tolls on the transit of people, livestock and goods; justice administration fees; and, a wide variety of services related to rural vassalage), while, from the fifteenth century, also collecting royal rents such as the *alcabalas*★ and the *servicios*★ granted by the *Cortes*. In many instances this was, in fact, an usurpation of royal prerogatives, while in others it was done with the more or less tacit consent of John II or Henry IV. Both monarchs used the cession of rents as a bargaining chip to ensure the loyalty of the nobility and integrate the high aristocracy in the monarchy's government structures. As such, these rents, along with *juros* and other payments against the royal coffers granted by *libranza*, turned the Crown's fiscal system into the main rent-seeking mechanism for the high Castilian nobility during the fifteenth century.[85]

The Crown's fiscal system retained many of its previous features after the political crisis of 1465–1480, begun in 1465 with the deposition, in effigy, of Henry IV and closed with Isabella I's victory in the War of the Castilian Succession (1474–1480) and her consolidation in the Castilian throne alongside her husband Ferdinand II of Aragón. However, their joint reign, which lasted until 1504, witnessed highly significant novelties, as the Catholic Monarchs needed resources to fund costly enterprises such as the final war against Granada (1482–1492) and the wars with France for the control of Naples and Roussillon (1495–1497 and 1501–1503).

First, between 1476 and 1498 the monarchs did not appeal to the *Cortes* for donations (*pedidos* and *monedas*), owing to the operational problems that their complex collection system entailed and the large number of exemptions in existence. Between 1478 and 1498, *servicios*★ were replaced by an ordinary contribution renewed every three years and the occasional imposition of extraordinary tributes. The new tax was negotiated with the *Hermandad general* (an association of cities united, under the Crown's patronage, for the defence of their mutual interests and security), and was generally collected as an *ad valorem* (*sisas*★) tax over the sale of everyday consumer goods. This revenue was used to partially fund standing military forces (*capitanías* of the *Hermandad*) that participated in the war against Granada.[86] However, in 1500 the monarchs again requested *servicios*★ from the *Cortes*, taking advantage of the experience gained with the collection of the contributions to the *Hermandad*. The management of these renewed *servicios*★ was thenceforth delegated on urban councils,[87] which, in addition, were often made responsible for the collection of the *alcabalas*★ from 1495 onwards. Municipal involvement in the management of *alcabalas*★, the Crown's main ordinary source of revenue, was implemented by a system called *encabezamiento*, which implied the payment of a fixed amount negotiated by the council and the Crown for a given period of time. In exchange, the council managed the collection of *alcabalas** in its jurisdiction autonomously, creating opportunities for profit for the municipal coffers and giving councils a greater degree of control over local taxation.⁸⁸

All these novelties ran in parallel with the increasingly intensive exploitation of extraordinary sources of revenue (crusade bull and ecclesiastical subsidies), the imposition of new tributes on the Jewish and Muslim communities (payment of a gold *castellano* per household from 1482), and substantial private loans from individuals and corporations to fund the war in Granada.⁸⁹ The monarchy's inability to return many of these loans drove it to issue long-term public debt bonds from 1489 onwards (*juros de prestido*, later called *juros al quitar*); the initial annual interest rate was between 9.09 and 10 per cent, and it was to be met with the returns of ordinary royal taxes.⁹⁰ This was in addition to the numerous rents collected in the Kingdom of Granada after its conquest in 1492, which are analysed in detail in Chapter 19 in this volume. In this way, by 1500 the fiscal system built by the Castilian monarchy combined the old and the new with the adoption of new features that were to remain in place into the Early Modern Age.

Moving ahead of the patrimonial stage in Navarre (fourteenth and fifteenth centuries)

As previously noted, the *Hacienda* of the Kingdom of Navarre benefitted from the accumulation of royal property, the reform and rationalisation of landed rents (*pechas**), and the profits yielded by custom duties. In addition, in contrast with Castile, which embarked in large-scale exterior endeavours, Navarre was not only geographically cornered, having no opportunity for territorial expansion, but since 1234, the kingdom was ruled by foreign dynasties: the Counts of Champagne (1234–1274); the kings of France (1274–1328); and the Counts of Evreux (1328–1425). As a result, Navarre was in a peripheral geographical position with regard to the centres of power that controlled it (Champagne-Paris-Evreux).

Meanwhile, the French Crown would not (or could not) involve the kingdom of Navarre in major or excessively costly political projects. In general, they were content with collecting the rents yielded by the royal estates and other royal prerogatives, and it was only in 1328 that Navarre witnessed the first steps to create an autonomous political project that sought to generate fiscal resources in the kingdom. Especially from 1350, Charles II "the Bad" squeezed the kingdom's resources to fund his far-reaching political ambitions in France.

On the other hand, while in Castile political projects were defended with legal arguments and an ambitious legislation based on Roman law was being deployed, in Navarre the *Fuero General* was heavily conditioned by the power of the nobility, which constrained the monarchy to a pact-based policy and saw any measure to increase royal power with suspicion. To make matters worse, the absenteeism of the new monarchs from the Champagne made for a poor bargaining position, forcing Theobald I and Theobald II to accept the model of monarchy imposed by the aristocracy. In addition, these groups complained against the policy followed by former monarchs, who had increased the royal patrimony at the expense of the nobility. In terms of taxation, all of this resulted in a monarchy with very limited means to raise revenue.

The creation of new extraordinary taxes

Extraordinary taxes only appear in Navarre from 1328 onwards, with the arrival of the Evreux dynasty to the throne and the separation of Navarre from the French Crown, which had shown little fiscal interest in the kingdom. Having no immediate fiscal precedents, the first Evreux monarchs, Joanna II and Philippe III (1328–1349), resorted to coinage (*monedaje**, called *subsidio**) to enable the collection of two direct quota-based taxes (8 *sueldos* per *fuego*) in all the territories of the kingdom. In addition, in 1338 they also imposed a feudal donation to meet the costs of the marriage of Princess María with Peter IV of Aragón. This contribution, framed as a *pedido*, fell exclusively on peasants, as the towns and the nobility were made exempt. Other economic demands (called *subvenciones*) only affected the Jews and the clergy (in the latter case after a process of negotiation).[91]

The foundations of the fiscal system that was to remain in place in Navarre until the second half of the fifteenth century, when the system collapsed as a consequence of the civil war, were laid out during the reign of Charles II (1351–1387). The system was based on the collection of direct taxes that were managed by the royal administration (*ayudas*★, later called *cuarteles*★), and a major indirect annual tax, the *imposición*★ (later called *alcabala* or *alcabalas*★), which from 1363 taxed (5 per cent) all commercial transactions undertaken in the kingdom's markets.[92]

During the first half of Charles II's reign, direct taxes became increasingly common, and the collection of an annual donation of 40,000 florins, distributed among cities and towns according to population, became a regular feature. Afterwards, cities and towns made up for the expense by applying a flat-rate tax on all the inhabitants (except for the poor and landless). From 1377 onwards, the amount to be paid by each city was no longer calculated on the basis of population, but according to the book of *fuegos* of 1376; the rates were not reviewed until 1427–1428. In this way, each city knew how much to pay in each quarterly *cuartel*★ (10,000 florins) and annual *ayuda*★ (40,000 florins). The change of name from *ayuda*★ to *cuartel*★ took place when the Crown began requesting more than one *ayuda*★ per year; in the new system, *ayudas*★ were negotiated and granted by *cuarteles*★, that is, in multiples of 10,000 florins, fetching as much as 80,000 florins in a single year in 1431. The consolidation of this system, which was grounded on the principle of fiscal solidarity, brought about the end of the former direct, quota-based, *ayudas*.★[93]

The annual collection of *cuarteles*★ and *alcabalas*★ survived until the end of the Middle Ages, when new items were added to the system in specific circumstances, such as the *donativo*, collected by the last kings of Navarre, Juan de Albret and Catherine de Foix (1484–1516).

Negotiation-legitimacy before the kingdom and the relationship between the king and the Cortes

Until 1328 the royal fiscal system of Navarre was partial, "*forera*", imposed and not-negotiated. It was partial because it did not reach all regions and all social groups; "*forera*" because it based its legitimacy on the legal charts or *fueros* in force; and imposed because it fell upon groups that possessed no bargaining power. Therefore, until 1328 the King of Navarre collected only tributes over which he had legal rights. For this reason, the first extraordinary tax imposed upon the kingdom (*monedaje*★) was based on the royal prerogative to issue coinage.

Beginning in 1328, the new monarchs Joanna II and Philipp III tried to negotiate new sources of revenue with the *Cortes*, and the outlines of this negotiation are well known. In 1329, Philipp III offered to issue good coinage in exchange for a *monedaje*★ of 8 *sueldos* per *fuego*. The *Cortes* accepted this without demur, until the king notified the sort of coin that he intended to strike. Apparently, the kingdom's representatives were not happy with it, and this led them back to the negotiation table. The king was granted a second *monedaje*★ in 1330, this time in exchange for not issuing the intended series. The payment of the *monedaje*★ was made extensive to the whole kingdom (*subsidio*★ *imposito*) and only the nobility was exempt. The city of Tudela claimed for its universal aristocratic character to be recognised and revolted against the *monedaje*★, although this only led to a harsh repression and a 4,000 pounds penalty.[94]

In 1338, a new *ayuda*★ was requested to meet the costs related to the marriage of Princess María with King Peter IV of Aragón. The idea was to pay for the substantial dowry promised by the Navarre king with a donation; a donation, however, that the kingdom was not willing to grant. At this point, separate negotiations began with each social estate: Muslim and Jewish communities were forced to hand over a *subsidio*★ *imposito*, because they had no leverage to negotiate with the king. The common, for their part, was also compelled to pay a *subsidio*★ *imposito*, which was in fact a *pedido* or feudal donation established in the *Fuero General de Navarra*. Finally, the men from the "good towns" could negotiate a small "*servicio concedido al rey*", the denomination of which clearly flagged the voluntary nature of the payment.⁹⁵

However, as noted, it was during the reign of the bellicose and active Charles II that the Navarre fiscal system really took off. The new monarch began exploring new ways to increase his revenue from the early years of his reign. He used the *forero* tax in several occasions and resorted to both *monedaje*★ (at the beginning of his rule) and *pedidos* (in 1359, 1365 and 1371, although only the earliest one was labelled as such). He also exacted taxes from the clergy, for instance the *primicias* collected in 1357 and 1370–1371, and the ecclesiastical *rediezmo* of 1363.⁹⁶

At the same time, *ayudas*★ became increasingly frequent, joined in 1363 by the *imposición*★.⁹⁷ All these taxes had to be approved by the *Cortes*, which periodically reminded the monarch of his role and of the exceptional character of these donations. At any rate, as far as we know the *Cortes* did not reject a single royal petition until the crisis caused by the war in 1450, although the assembly always had enough leverage to negotiate amounts and collection methods. However, the rhetoric of negotiation was upheld, and the monarch always justified his requests, as recorded in the ledgers of the Kingdom of Navarre. Almost invariably, Charles II used war as an argument – "to succour the king"; "for the war in Normandy"; "in defence of the realm"; "for the men-at-arms"; "succour and aid"; "the king's obvious need" – in addition to other scenarios grounded in the Navarre legislation and fiscal tradition, such as royal marriages and the issue of coinage.⁹⁸

After Charles II's tentative beginnings – in 1363, this monarch collected a direct donation (15 *sueldos* per *fuego*); the first indirect tax (*veinteno*); an ecclesiastical *rediezmo*; and a *pedido* that fell on the peasants – the annual collection of *ayudas*★ and *imposiciones*★, later known as *cuarteles*★ and *alcabalas*★, gradually consolidated. In this way, Charles II managed to move from partial and *foreros* taxes (which affected only part of the population or depended on the existence of a specific norm), to a stable collection system involving two consolidated tributes, one direct and the other indirect. In this process, the *Cortes* acted more as a help than as an obstacle, because Charles II handled them with ease, and they invariably endorsed his proposals. This notwithstanding, in order to develop a system that suited his needs, even this forceful monarch had to follow the rules of fiscal rhetoric and legitimising arguments and to resort to a wide variety of fiscal typologies. In contrast, the Prince of Viana was forced to admit in 1448 that no taxes could be collected in Navarre without the authorisation of the *Cortes*.⁹⁹

The development of municipal taxation

The crystallisation of royal taxes in Castile and Navarre affords only a partial understanding of the development of fiscal systems in these two kingdoms, because the urban expansion of the eleventh to the thirteenth centuries and the financial needs of cities and towns also sparked the creation of important revenue-raising mechanisms. In this case, however, the differences between Castile and Navarre are substantial, in terms of fiscal autonomy, pace and scope. Despite this, analogous taxation mechanisms were implemented in both kingdoms, such as the indirect taxes (*sisas*★) authorised by the monarchs in specific circumstances or the extension of direct taxation to the whole urban population. Also similar was the cooperation of monarchies and cities in the collection of subsidies approved by the *Cortes*, and the belated and limited emergence of consolidated forms of public urban debt.

In Castile, the regular collection of municipal tributes and the fiscal autonomy of cities crystallised very gradually, in a process that began in the eleventh century and was only complete by the fifteenth century. In addition, in many ways the creation of urban fiscal systems ran parallel to the formation and consolidation of the royal fiscal system, which took advantage of the fiscal management mechanisms created by cities and towns to collect its own tributes. It is worth recalling that in *realengo* areas urban councils acted as the king's delegates, administering the territory under their jurisdiction (*tierra* or *alfoz*), and this also applied to the management and collection of many royal taxes between the late eleventh and the late fifteenth centuries. However, the autonomy of Castilian municipalities to raise their own taxes was limited, although it only increased over time, being subject to royal authorisation. On the other hand, when the economic foundations of council institutions were laid out, the Crown tended to reserve the most substantial sources of revenue for itself. In conclusion, although royal and municipal *haciendas* formed distinct structures and managed very uneven resources – in Castile, the scales fell clearly in favour of the royal coffers, which captured much more substantial resources – the systems were interrelated and supported one another in their development.[100] In contrast with the fiscal autonomy achieved by Castilian cities, especially from the thirteenth century onwards, the small size of Navarre made it easier for the Crown to control taxation, also in cities, until at least the second half of the fifteenth century. Examples of taxes directly administered by the cities are hard to come by, in what is a substantial difference with Castile.

The construction of the fiscal autonomy of Castilian municipalities

The origins of municipal taxation in Castile and León can be traced back to the eleventh century, when the *concilium* (council) was constituted as the government institution of cities and towns. Between then and the early thirteenth century, the funds raised by the councils were used to meet military and defensive needs (construction and repair of city walls and fortresses); to fund the construction and maintenance of infrastructures (road, bridges) and water supply systems; and to pay the salaries of the first municipal officials (*aportellados*). At this early stage, the sources of revenue were multiple and facilitated, following royal concessions, the emergence of incipient local fiscal structures, although we cannot yet speak of a stable urban treasuries (*haciendas urbanas*).[101]

The earliest municipal sources of revenue include royal rents ceded temporarily or indefinitely, in whole or in part, by the monarchs; direct contributions imposed by the municipalities on non-exempt citizens to fund public and defensive works, following the principle of communal responsibility; fines or *caloñas* imposed for infractions, surrendered by the king, totally or partially, in favour of councils from the late eleventh century; part of the booty taken in raids against the Muslims, which was especially important in cities and towns near the frontier; and, tolls for goods and livestock, likewise surrendered by the Crown, like the older *portazgos** over goods and *montazgos* over livestock. From the early thirteenth century, cities also collected the rents yielded by real estate ceded to the council, in addition to administering the *realengo* territories (*alfoces/tierras*) in delegation of the king.[102]

Like with the royal fiscal system, the reign of Alphonse X (1252–1284) was a key milestone in the construction or urban fiscal systems in Castile. However, the Crown never sought to harmonise local fiscal structures, which were always characterised by variety and their local peculiarities, even if many councils had similar sources of revenue.[103] In this context, the number of *realengo* cities and towns that were made exempt from some traditional tributes to the Crown multiplied, exemptions that also extended over certain social groups, like urban knights. On the other hand, Andalusian cities conquered in the first half of the thirteenth century in Andalusia and Murcia were endowed with additional resources to meet their defensive needs – which were greater for their proximity to the frontier – and the construction of public works. Finally, from 1269 onwards the councils cooperated in the collection of the *servicios** granted by the *Cortes*, putting their administrative structures at the service of the Crown. This only increased their mutual interdependence and geared up the integration of councils in the political structures of the monarchy.[104]

In this way, from the second half of the thirteenth century onwards, municipal *haciendas* comprised a wide typology of sources of income, which varied according to local-specific factors (location; size; level of political development and ruling system; commercial activity and productive structure; degree of autonomy from the Crown; relationship with the Crown; defensive needs; internal social relations).[105] For instance, in Seville and Murcia Alphonse X authorised a new annual direct tax on wealth (*derecho de vecindad*), divided into several tax brackets; this tax was to disappear in the early fourteenth century. More widespread was the ownership of real estate, and the associated rents, by councils, particularly in the fourteenth and fifteenth centuries. In this regard, two types of assets must be distinguished: first, lands open to collective use, called *bienes comunales* (communal woodland and grazing areas) and the rents derived from their use (*derecho de montaracía*, for the upkeep of these estates; fines for infractions; *montazgos* or tolls for livestock); second, *bienes de propios* (graze land, agricultural estates and, to a lesser extent, urban buildings, shops and infrastructures), which were generally leased out to private lessees.

Part of the judicial fines and financial penalties for forms of economic wrongdoing defined in local charters also began going to councils in the second half of the thirteenth century; this was linked to the council's jurisdiction over the city/town and the territory (*alfoz/tierra*) that defined its fiscal space. In the thirteenth and fourteenth centuries, in cities like Murcia, Córdoba, Seville, Úbeda, Valladolid and León these judicial rents were joined by tributes on gambling houses (*tafurerías*) or gambling-related penalties. Councils also continued benefitting from occasional or permanent assignations from the royal rents,[106] and extraordinary tributes, the payment of which corresponded to all citizens proportionally to their wealth (*repartimiento*).

Taxpayers of *repartimientos* were generally divided into wealth brackets, and paid according to their movable and landed wealth. The returns from these contributions were used to meet specific expenses that ordinary revenue could not cover, and became a recurrent feature. In some cities, like Segovia and Soria, this direct tax became the council's main source of revenue during the fourteenth and fifteenth centuries; in fifteenth-century Madrid, Cuenca and Zamora, ordinary or extraordinary direct *repartimientos* accounted for half of municipal revenue in those years in which it was collected. In any case, the distribution and relative importance of these direct taxes were very uneven. It is of note that, in general, taxpayers from the city's territory paid considerably larger sums than the actual city-dwellers.[107] In addition to these direct contributions, cities also resorted to more or less voluntary loans in times of need, for instance in Burgos during the fifteenth century.[108]

However, the most important novelty from the second half of the thirteenth and the early fourteenth century, once the public perception of traditional tributes was fully consolidated, was the increased ability of many councils to charge tolls and indirect taxes on the circulation of goods and on commercial transactions in the city and its territory. These new tributes were a direct consequence of the vitality of economic exchange, although in many cases the city's full residents *vecinos* were exempt, for instance from good transit fees, or were entitled to pay lower rates. These taxes, authorised by the Crown, included *portazgos*★ and *rodas* over the transit of goods, or *almotacenazgos* to the south of the Central System; the *almotacenazgos* taxed commercial activities that were under the authority of the *almotacén*, an official inherited from the Andalusi period, whose task it was to supervise market operations and impose fines for breaching the city's economic regulations. In the south of the Iberian Peninsula, the *almotacenazgo* also included fees for the use of weights and measures, the control of which by many councils was authorised by the monarchy between the mid-thirteenth and the late fourteenth century. In the remaining cities, the use of weights and measures led to a widespread form of council tax (by the fifteenth century it was collected by most cities) known under many names (*peso del rey*, *peso del concejo*, *peso y cuchares*, *renta de las medidas*).[109]

Like the monarchy, some cities also made an early use, with royal permission, of municipal *alcabalas*★ and *sisas*★ as *ad valorem* taxes on transactions involving staples (wine, cereal and meat) in the city. In the late thirteenth and early fourteenth centuries, cities like Murcia, Burgos, Oviedo, Valladolid and León used this revenue to cover expenses like the construction and maintenance of the city walls. In Burgos, for instance, the so-called *alcabala vieja* was still in place in the fifteenth century and was outsourced, along with other rents under the control of the council from the second half of the fourteenth century, such as tolls over goods coming in or going out of the city (*portazgo*★, *barra*, *menusel*), the rent of meat and the fee for the weighting of flour.[110] During the fourteenth and fifteenth centuries, the collection of municipal *sisas*★ became widespread, and on some occasions these taxes even became ordinary sources of revenue; indirect taxation was, therefore, one of the main sources of fiscal revenue for Castilian cities.[111]

In Córdoba and Seville, on the other hand, the monarchs reserved for themselves the lion's share of urban *almojarifazgos*★, but ceded those of the *tierra* to the council. In Seville, the rural *almojarifazgo*★ was the greatest source of revenue for the council, and included a number of different tributes and rents: *portazgo*★; toll fees; tithes on certain products (tiles, bricks, kitchen wares); the *alcabala*★ over the first sale of some goods; monopolies on salt and soap; fees for the use of weights and measures; and rents for the exploitation of commercial and industrial buildings, among others.[112]

In addition, in the late thirteenth century, some cities exploited real estate that belonged to the council (*bienes de propios*) such as shops, baths, industrial facilities (mills, kilns, tanneries, pottery workshops, etc.), and shops that went out for lease. However, in Andalusia the Crown initially reserved the control of urban commercial spaces inherited from the Andalusi period (*alcaicerías*) for itself, or leased out the exploitation of shops and warehouses used to store consumer goods. By the fifteenth century, at any rate, these spaces were as a rule in council hands, and many cities and towns in Castile promoted the construction of public cereal warehouses (*alhóndigas*, *mesones* and *almudíes*).

In a similar way, most urban councils held in the fifteenth century the monopoly over the sale of staples (meat, fish, wine). Concerning meat, and less often fish, in addition to owning the boards on which it was cut, the urban supply was leased out for brief periods of time (generally a year) to private contractors known as *obligados*. It was different with salt, which was commercialised within the framework of the royal monopoly, except in Andalusia and Murcia, where the Crown ceded the exploitation of some saltpans to local authorities, for instance in Seville.[113]

Finally, from the mid-fifteenth century many cities also began administering money-changing tables and public scribes. Both elements fell to the royal jurisdiction and, although from 1333 to 1350 they were put under the direct administration of the monarchy by Alphonse XI, his son Peter I ceded their control to the councils in 1351. Similarly, some councils began charging fees for transactions carried out through intermediaries (*correduría*). These sources of revenue are related more or less directly with the development of urban economies and with the extension of the jurisdictional powers of cities, as a delegation of royal authority.[114]

In order to manage this growing number of sources of revenue, which in the second half of the thirteenth and first half of the fourteenth centuries became more stable and systematic, the administrative structure of many councils began including specialists in fiscal administration (*mayordomos*) that remained outside royal control, which emphasised municipal fiscal autonomy even further. The increasing institutionalisation of municipal *haciendas* ran parallel to the reorganisation of urban powers and the redefinition of their relationship with the monarchy. Many cities fell under the control of closed oligarchic governments (*regimientos*) constituted by king-appointed knights. The prerogatives of these *regimientos*, which were promoted by Alphonse XI from the 1330s and proliferated in the final years of the Middle Ages, included the administration of local taxation. The fiscal function of councillors (*regidores*), in addition to ensuring the payment of their salaries, could guarantee the political support of municipal elites to the monarchy and their cooperation in the collection of royal taxes. The mechanisms put in place to organise the collection of the *servicios*★, and later the *pedidos*, approved by the *Cortes* and collected with the aid of urban censuses, could also act as a stimulus for the imposition of *repartimientos* or local contributions to meet extraordinary council expenses. In general, the crystallisation of oligarchic municipal governments drove the local fiscal systems towards models that benefited the elite, which were often made exempt from the extraordinary direct payments exacted in the form of *repartimientos*.[115]

The period from 1369 to 1474, between the ascension of the Trastámara dynasty to the throne and the death of Henry IV, did not bring substantial changes to the urban taxation systems in Castile, the main outline of which was defined in the preceding period. This was a period of consolidation and expansion of existing elements, with a greater legal and institutional definition, a closer integration of royal and local fiscal systems, and a tighter control of local taxation by *regimientos*. Similarly, the pressure posed by the Crown to exact loans, advances and contributions from the councils for the war resulted in many cases in the cession to some cities of rights, assets and rents that other cities already controlled.

This did not prevent a gradual deterioration of many local *haciendas* during the fifteenth century, a result of the increase in the volume of expense, including the costs of judicial lawsuits; the payment of salaries to *regidores*, *corregidores* and municipal officials; the purchase of land and buildings; the construction of public works; the repair of city walls; and, the organisation of public festivities. After 1475, the Catholic Monarchs tried to improve municipal finances by increasing revenue and curbing expenses, authorising extraordinary *repartimientos* and the temporal exaction of new local *sisas*★, which were also used to collect the contributions to the *Hermandad* from 1478 to 1498 and, after 1500, the new *servicios*★ passed by the *Cortes*.[116] The debate around the convenience of imposing direct and regressive taxes that took into account the wealth of taxpayers, which was implicit in the *repartimiento* model, or indirect taxes, like the *sisa*★, on staples, turned in many cities and towns into a political issue. This confronted the political ideology of the oligarchy represented in the *regimiento* (which was generally in favour of direct taxation) and the urban common (*común*) and its representatives (often in favour of indirect taxes). In any case, in contrast with the Crown of Aragón, resorting to consolidated municipal credit systems and the issue of "public debt" supported by municipal revenue was rarely regarded as a valid option to improve council finances. One exception is Burgos, which in 1475 authorised the issue of public debt on the back of the local *portazgo*★ (*doblamiento de la barra*), which was bought by the city's political and mercantile elite.[117]

The limited fiscal autonomy of towns in Navarre

The earliest references to urban municipal autonomy in Navarre are disperse and unclear, although they reveal a widespread local fiscal practice, the collection of the *tallas*, attested in Olite (1244), Estella (1258), Pamplona (1287), Viana (1301)[118] and the charter of Tudela.[119] It is also known that, in Viana, the *talla* involved mechanisms of fiscal solidarity (*por sueldo et por libra*, that is, the tax was calculated according to wealth), and that this was not uncontroversial. However, In Navarre the royal records are much richer than local archives, so the internal mechanisms of the royal fiscal system are much better understood. In addition, the small size of the kingdom enabled the Navarre kings to keep a much tighter grip on the administration of taxation, leading to the stunted growth of municipal fiscal systems and the belated, and underdeveloped, emergence of municipal public debt.

As a result, until the mid-fourteenth century the king continued receiving payment for rents to which towns were entitled, as clearly established in their urban charters: rents for the leasing out of real estate, occasional indirect taxes on specific goods (*leztas**), and the returns of extraordinary petitions that the king had the right to impose on the rest of the kingdom. For internal expenses, towns relied on *tallas*, which could include mechanisms of fiscal solidarity to distribute the burden more equitably among their citizens.

In 1333, however, a new tax, the *sisa**, was created during a period of famine caused, at least partially, by grain hoarding. The regulations of the *sisa**, the collection of which was resumed between 1351 and 1355, gave shape to an indirect form of taxation that is not fully understood, but which at least endowed the councils with resources to meet the expenses that they were now assuming, for instance the control of hoarding, prices, and weights and measures.[120] The *sisa** was suppressed in 1355, and from 1363 the collection of the royal *imposición** became the norm, which also superseded fiscal practices that preceded the imposition of the *sisa**. In addition the administration of the *imposición**, direct at first, leased out *in toto* later and, eventually, divided into a large constellation of tax-farming arrangement (by which time the tax was known as *alcabalas**,[121] borrowing the Castilian name), meant that in Navarre *imposiciones** did not end up in local coffers, in contrast with what was usual practice in the Crown of Aragón. The consequences of this are significant, for it was largely the revenue derived from the *imposiciones** what enabled Aragonese councils to appeal to credit (normally to meet the kings demands). In Navarre, the administration of both direct (*ayudas** or *cuarteles**), and indirect taxes (*imposiciones** or *alcabalas**) staid in the Crown's hands, either through royal officials or leases.

Municipal fiscal systems in Navarre did not begin to truly develop until the late fifteenth century, with the cession of the *imposición** to a number of towns, such as Tudela (1469) and Pamplona (1474), in the context of the civil war. However, it is worth pointing out that throughout the second half of the fifteenth century the Kingdom of Navarre was divided into two factions, and that traditional administrative structures were on the verge of collapse. This is the background of the concession, by John II, of an exemption over *cuarteles** and *alcabalas** to the town of Tudela (1469), in exchange for the provision of 50 men-at-arms for the king's retinue, which was a way to conceal an *encabezada* payment (paid for by towns with their own internally-raised resources).[122] In order to meet this expense, and since no indirect royal taxes were any longer being collected in Tudela, the council began imposing new municipal taxes, such as the *echas* or *cugidas*; the butchers' rents; the *tallo* on pork fat; the rents on fish (salted fish, *tallo* on fresh fish and the *cornado*, also on fresh fish); the bakers' tribute; the *carapito*; the *foranías*; a tribute on hearths; the *correduría de oreja*; the *correduría* rents; the butchers' *corambres*; and the *blanca*.[123]

Finally, we must point out that public debt in Navarre during the Middle Ages was limited, as far as we know, to the town of Tudela, and this only because of the town's exceptional fiscal position vis-à-vis the rest of the kingdom after John II's concession. The earliest bonds (*censales*, issued in 1499 and 1507), offered an interest of 5 per cent. In any case, the issue of municipal public debt in Navarre was a late and isolated phenomenon, limited to the town of Tudela.[124]

Conclusions

The study of the evolution of fiscal systems in Castile and Navarre until the late fifteenth century allows us to conclude that both Crowns built a solid fiscal base, and that these were, despite the shared nomenclature (*alcabalas**, *sisas**, *monedaje*/moneda forera**, *servicios**), very different from one another.

Between 1250 and 1350, the Castilian Crown increased its fiscal muscle by creating new tributes and sources of revenue, which were later consolidated during the Trastámara period (1369–1504). This lay the foundation of a strong "fiscal state" by the end of the Middle Ages, with the wherewithal and the sovereignty to capture most of its resources without consent from other agents. During the fifteenth century, the Castilian Crown's tributary system rested on ordinary indirect taxes, in some cases inherited from the Andalusi system (especially *alcabalas** on consumer goods, which became an ordinary tax in 1400, and custom duties on foreign trade). These tributes were under royal jurisdiction, and no negotiation with other political agents (*Cortes*, cities, the Church) was thus necessary. In addition to these ordinary rents, extraordinary resources, increasingly frequent and substantial, were negotiated with the cities through the *Cortes* (*servicios**) or with the Church. From the late fifteenth century, credit and public debt also became an integral part of the system. For their part, the Navarre monarchs built, from 1350 onwards, a fiscal system based on a combination of their extensive patrimonial properties (including traditional rents, or *pechas**, and custom duties) and new direct (*cuarteles**) and indirect (*alcabalas**) taxes, which were still subject to negotiation with the kingdom's other political forces, in a stark contrast with Castile.

These differences were the result, first, of a different conceptualisation of royal power in both kingdoms. Beginning with Alphonse X, Castile adopted and developed a Roman-inspired notion of monarchy that led to the expansion of the "king's sovereignty" (*señorío del rey*) to increasingly wide spheres. Much later, in the fifteenth century, the Crown also deployed absolutist principles that gradually strengthened the king's authority, but not without the strong political opposition of other agents, which allowed the nobility to share many of the profits yielded by the fiscal system without having to resort to a pact-based juridical framework. In contrast, from 1234 the Navarre Crown acted "in absentia", and was therefore weak against the leading members of the nobility, which were notoriously bellicose and rebellious, especially given the pact-based (in a legal sense) notion of power that prevailed in the kingdom.

On the other hand, the different size of Castile and Navarre was also a factor in the administration of the fiscal system. In Navarre, the Crown tried to administer both urban and rural rents directly, and the dimensions of the kingdom made this possible. This was achieved through the creation of an efficient and well-staffed accountancy system. While the Navarre kings controlled directly every single item of royal taxation, in Castile, from the thirteenth century onwards, cities assumed the collection of a growing number of royal tributes, either as delegates of the Crown or after the monarchy surrendered said tributes in their favour. This brought cities into the structure of the State, within which they acted as intermediaries, especially after the configuration of oligarchic urban governments (*regimientos*) that began in the mid-fourteenth century. In exchange, cities were largely autonomous in terms of taxation, in stark contrast with the "total centralisation" of Navarre, where towns enjoyed little fiscal autonomy until the second half of the fifteenth century. At the same time, the outsourcing of tax collection became increasingly sophisticated in Castile, often involving the leasing out of royal tributes to financial companies for a fixed sum.

Finally, the different pace at which Castile and Navarre reached fiscal maturity is probably explained by the uneven expenditure needs of both monarchies and the limitations that the internal political balance in each kingdom posed to the creation of new tributes, as well as their economic structure. Although both fiscal systems appear to be well developed and consolidated by the second half of the fourteenth century, tributes that applied to the whole kingdom emerged much earlier in Castile than in Navarre. If the "Castilian fiscal revolution" unfolded between 1250 and 1350, with Alphonse X and Alphonse XI as main catalysers, the "great leap ahead" in Navarre did not happen until 1350–1377. Except for a few isolated incidents, Navarre was unburdened by external conflicts until the reign of Charles II (1349–1387), and its kings could afford to live of the rich patrimony accrued by Sancho VI and Sancho VII. In contrast, for Castile, the thirteenth and fourteenth centuries were a period marked by war, both internal and external, which hovered up enormous resources. Therefore, financial needs – especially military expenses – were a much more pressing concern for Castilian than for Navarre kings, at least until 1350. This forced them to try new formulas to increase their revenue, increasingly dependent on consumption and commercial activity. These causes sufficiently explain the different evolution of tributary systems in both kingdoms, and their different tax rates.

Notes

1 This work is part of the following Research Projects: "Sistemas fiscales y construcción estatal: Castilla, centros y periferias (1250–1550) (PID2021-126283NB-I00), "La construcción de una cultura fiscal en Castilla: poderes, negociación y articulación social (ca. 1250–1550)" (PGC2018-097738-B-100) and "Circuitos financieros, crecimiento económico y guerra (siglos XV–XVI)" (UMA18-FEDERJA-098). Part of Castile, by Pablo Ortego Rigo. Part of Navarra, by Íñigo Mugueta Moreno.
2 Ladero Quesada, *La formación medieval de España*; Monsalvo Antón, *La construcción del poder real*; Carrasco Pérez, "Reino de Navarra".
3 Ladero Quesada, *La Hacienda Real*; Ladero Quesada, *Fiscalidad y poder real*; Ladero Quesada, "Lo antiguo y lo nuevo"; Ladero Quesada, "Estado, hacienda, fiscalidad y finanzas"; Menjot, "Taxation and sovereignty".
4 Menjot, *Fiscalidad y sociedad*; Ortego Rico, *Poder financiero*; Rubio Martínez, *El reinado de los Reyes Católicos*; Triano Milan, *La llamada del rey*; Vitores Casado, *Poder, sociedad y fiscalidad*; Bello León and Ortego Rico, *Los agentes fiscales*.
5 Zabalo Zabalegui, *La administración*.
6 Ramírez Vaquero, "Estado de las investigaciones"; Ramírez Vaquero, "Hacienda y poder real"; Mugueta Moreno, "Estrategias fiscales".
7 Galán Sánchez, "*Arca Comunis*".
8 Valverde Castro, "Monarquía y tributación"; Castellanos, "The political nature of taxation".
9 Monsalvo Antón, *La construcción del poder real*, pp. 68–71.
10 Alvarado Planas, "La castellaría".
11 González de Fauve, "La anubda y la arrobda".
12 Monsalvo Antón, *La construcción del poder real*, pp. 101–110.
13 Estepa Díez, "La construcción"; Monsalvo Antón, *La construcción del poder real*, pp. 101–110.
14 Estepa Díez, "En torno a la 'fonsadera'".
15 Loring García, "Del palacio a la cocina"; Guglielmi, "Posada y yantar".
16 Ladero Quesada, *Fiscalidad y poder real*, pp. 31–50.
17 Estepa Díez, "Organización militar"; Estepa Díez, "La construcción", pp. 78–79; Ladero Quesada, *Fiscalidad y poder real*, pp. 33–36.
18 Hernández, *Las rentas del rey*, vol. 1, p. LXXXII.

19 Sánchez Albornoz, "Notas para el estudio"; Estepa Díez, "La construcción", pp. 71–72; Monsalvo Antón, *La construcción del poder real*, pp. 104–105.
20 Ladero Quesada, *Fiscalidad y poder real*, p. 51.
21 Grassotti, "Alfonso IX"; Grassotti, "Un empréstito".
22 González Mínguez, *El portazgo*; Ladero Quesada, *Fiscalidad y poder real*, pp. 129–137 and 284–286.
23 Sánchez Albornoz, "¿Devaluación monetaria".
24 Ladero Quesada, *Fiscalidad y poder real*, pp. 52–55.
25 Estepa Díez, "La construcción", pp. 85–86.
26 Estepa Díez, "Formación y consolidación".
27 Estepa Díez, "La behetría".
28 Hernández, *Las rentas del rey*, vol. 1, pp. CXXXI–CXXXIII. *Vid. almojarifazgo* in glossary.
29 de Ayala Martínez, *Las órdenes militares*; Porras Arboledas, "La hacienda".
30 Mugueta Moreno, "Pecha" in *Glosario Crítico de Fiscalidad Medieval* (http://gcfm.imf.csic.es).
31 Fortún Pérez de Ciriza, "Colección de fueros"; Fortún Pérez de Ciriza, "Una reforma fiscal"; Fortún Pérez de Ciriza, "Los Fueros".
32 Fortún Pérez de Ciriza and Martín Duque, "Relaciones financieras"; Mugueta Moreno, "¿Un capbreu".
33 Mugueta Moreno, *El dinero*.
34 Carrasco Pérez, "El impuesto".
35 Felones Morrás, "Contribución al estudio"; Mugueta Moreno, "La fiscalidad real"; Mugueta Moreno, "Rediezmo" in *Glosario Crítico de Fiscalidad Medieval* (http://gcfm.imf.csic.es).
36 Miranda García, "El precio".
37 Mugueta Moreno, "Subvención (1)" and "Subvención (2)" in *Glosario Crítico de Fiscalidad Medieval* (http://gcfm.imf.csic.es).
38 Mugueta Moreno, "Peajes" and "Sacas" in *Glosario Crítico de Fiscalidad Medieval* (http://gcfm.imf.csic.es).
39 Martín Duque, "Peaje de Pamplona"; Carrasco Pérez, "Documentos"; Grocin Gabas, "Peajes navarros"; Llansó, "Peaje de Pamplona".
40 Mugueta Moreno, *El dinero*, pp. 230–236; Mugueta Moreno, "Lezta" in *Glosario Crítico de Fiscalidad Medieval* (http://gcfm.imf.csic.es).
41 Carrasco Pérez, "Notariado y Hacienda"; Carrasco Pérez, *Dinero y deuda*.
42 Nieto Soria, *Iglesia y poder*; Nieto Soria, *Iglesia y génesis*; Ladero Quesada, *Fiscalidad y poder real*, pp. 185–208.
43 Ladero Quesada, *Fiscalidad y poder real*; Menjot, "L'établissement", pp. 149–172; Ladero Quesada, "Fiscalidad regia".
44 O'Callaghan, *The Gibraltar Crusade*.
45 Melo Carrasco, "En torno".
46 Menjot, "Taxation and sovereignty", pp. 84–89.
47 Ladero Quesada, "Monedas y políticas"; Ladero Quesada, "La política"; Castán Lanaspa, *Política económica*; MacKay, *Moneda, precios y política*.
48 Ladero Quesada, *Fiscalidad y poder real*, pp. 48–50 and 84–86.
49 Ladero Quesada, "Las almadrabas".
50 Hernández, *Las rentas del rey*, vol. 1, pp. CXXX–CXXXI; Ladero Quesada, *Fiscalidad y poder real*, pp. 95–99.
51 Ladero Quesada, *La Hacienda Real*, p. 182; Díez de Salazar, *Ferrerías de Guipúzcoa*; Vitores Casado, "Agentes económicos".
52 Ladero Quesada, *Fiscalidad y poder real*, pp. 96–99.
53 Pastor de Togneri, "La sal"; Hernández, *Las rentas del rey*, vol. 1, p. CXXVIII; Estepa Díez, "La construcción", pp. 79–80.
54 Ladero Quesada, "La renta"; Ortego Rico, "Las salinas".
55 Ladero Quesada, *Fiscalidad y poder real*, pp. 137–140.
56 Fernández Arriba, "Un aspecto".
57 Ladero Quesada, *Fiscalidad y poder real*, pp. 140–151.
58 Ladero Quesada, *La Hacienda Real*, pp. 122–145; Bello León, "La cuenta"; González Arce, *El negocio*.
59 Ladero Quesada, *Fiscalidad y poder real*, pp. 151–168; Menjot, "Économie"; Diago Hernando, "Introducción".

60 Salas Almela, *La más callada revolución*, pp. 31–105; Franco Silva, "Los condestables".
61 Ladero Quesada, *La Hacienda Real*, pp. 97–113; Ladero Quesada, "Fiscalidad y génesis", p. 102; Ladero Quesada, "Las aduanas".
62 Ladero Quesada, *Fiscalidad y poder real*, pp. 119–127.
63 Ladero Quesada, *La Hacienda Real*, pp. 149–166.
64 Estepa Díez, "La construcción", pp. 80–82.
65 Hernández, *Las rentas del rey*, vol. 1, pp. CXXXIII–CXLIV; Ladero Quesada, *Fiscalidad y poder real*, pp. 71–81.
66 Nieto Soria, "Fundamentos".
67 Ladero Quesada, *Fiscalidad y poder real*, pp. 55–57 and 300–303.
68 O'Callaghan, "The Cortes".
69 Arias Guillén, *Guerra y fortalecimiento*, pp. 237–268; Ladero Quesada, *Fiscalidad y poder real*, pp. 58–68.
70 Ladero Quesada, *Fiscalidad y poder real*, pp. 69–71.
71 Ladero Quesada, "Los primeros pasos"; Ladero Quesada, *Fiscalidad y poder real*, pp. 169–183; Arias Guillén, *Guerra y fortalecimiento*, pp. 246, 260–261 and 265–267.
72 Menjot, "Le consentement fiscal".
73 Quintanilla Raso, *La nobleza señorial*.
74 Monsalvo Antón, *La construcción del poder real*, pp. 412–423.
75 Ladero Quesada, *Legislación hacendística*.
76 Torres Sanz, *La administración central*, pp. 213–234; Cañas Gálvez, *Burocracia y cancillería*, pp. 124–139; Ladero Quesada, *La Hacienda Real*, pp. 446–459 and 467–477.
77 Gálvez Gambero, *Endeudamiento y financiación*.
78 Ladero Quesada, *La Hacienda Real*, pp. 467–477.
79 Ladero Quesada, *La Hacienda Real*, pp. 408–420, 459–460; Menjot, "L'incidence", pp. 330–334.
80 Ladero Quesada, *La Hacienda Real*, p. 416; Ladero Quesada, "Las juderías"; Ortego Rico, "La imagen".
81 Olivera Serrano, "Empréstitos"; Gálvez Gambero, "La deuda", pp. 4–9.
82 Ladero Quesada, *La Hacienda Real*, pp. 57–90.
83 Ladero Quesada, "Política económica"; Ladero Quesada, *La Hacienda Real*, pp. 416–418 and 422; Menjot, "La fiscalité royale"; Triano Milán, *La llamada*, pp. 243–339; Romero Martínez, *Fisco y recaudación*; Ortego Rico, "Pedido regio".
84 Triano Milán, *La llamada*, pp. 79–98, 131–141; Ortego Rico, "Guerra y paz".
85 Quintanilla Raso, "Haciendas señoriales"; Ortego Rico, "Monarquía, nobleza".
86 Ladero Quesada, *La Hermandad*; Triano Milán, *La llamada*, pp. 431–586; Ortego Rico, "La 'contribución'".
87 Carretero Zamora, *Cortes*, pp. 61–126.
88 Ortego Rico, *Poder financiero*, pp. 487–576.
89 Ladero Quesada, *Castilla*, pp. 201–224; Ortego Rico, "Mudéjares castellanos".
90 Gálvez Gambero, "Reforma".
91 Mugueta Moreno, "Las demandas"; Mugueta Moreno, "Subvención", in *Glosario Crítico de Fiscalidad Medieval* (http://gcfm.imf.csic.es).
92 Mugueta Moreno, "Estrategias fiscales", pp. 219–264.
93 Ramírez Vaquero, "Patrimonio"; Monteano Sorbet, *Los navarros*, pp. 271–325.
94 Mugueta Moreno, *El dinero*, pp. 417–460.
95 Mugueta Moreno, *El dinero*, pp. 468–481.
96 Mugueta Moreno, "Estrategias fiscales", pp. 219–264.
97 Ongay, *El registro*; Ongay, "El mercado"; Ongay, "Los Arcos".
98 Ramírez Vaquero, "La irrupción".
99 Fuentes Pascual, *Catálogo del Archivo*, p. 172.
100 Menjot, "Système fiscal"; Menjot and Collantes de Terán Sánchez, "La génesis", pp. 53–54, 57; Menjot and Collantes de Terán Sánchez, "Hacienda y fiscalidad"; Ladero Quesada, *La Hacienda Real*, pp. 687–688; Collantes de Terán Sánchez, "Alfonso X", p. 265.
101 Menjot and Collantes de Terán Sánchez, "La génesis", pp. 55–57.
102 Menjot, "Système fiscal", pp. 22–23; Menjot and Collantes de Terán Sánchez, "La génesis", pp. 58–61; Ladero Quesada, *La Hacienda Real*, pp. 687–688.
103 Collantes de Terán Sánchez, "Alfonso X", pp. 254–255 and 266–267.

104 MENJOT, "Système fiscal", pp. 33–39.
105 GUERRERO NAVARRETE, "Impuestos"; SÁNCHEZ BENITO, "Las haciendas", pp. 407–408.
106 LADERO QUESADA, *La Hacienda Real*, pp. 700–709 and 733–737.
107 MENJOT, "La fiscalité directe"; MENJOT, "Les enjeux"; COLLANTES DE TERÁN SÁNCHEZ, "Alfonso X", p. 262; GUERRERO NAVARRETE, "Impuestos", pp. 364–365.
108 GUERRERO NAVARRETE, "Impuestos", pp. 362.
109 LADERO QUESADA, *La Hacienda Real*, pp. 710–713; COLLANTES DE TERÁN SÁNCHEZ, "Alfonso X", pp. 258–259.
110 GUERRERO NAVARRETE, "Impuestos", pp. 360–362; PARDOS MARTÍNEZ, "La renta".
111 LADERO QUESADA, *La Hacienda Real*, pp. 718–721; COLLANTES DE TERÁN SÁNCHEZ, "Alfonso X", pp. 262–263.
112 COLLANTES DE TERÁN SÁNCHEZ, "Les impôts", pp. 465–467, 469–470 and 480–482; MENJOT and COLLANTES DE TERÁN SÁNCHEZ, "La génesis", pp. 61–72; LADERO QUESADA, *La Hacienda Real*, pp. 721–723; GONZÁLEZ ARCE, *Un patrimonio*.
113 LADERO QUESADA, *La Hacienda Real*, pp. 714–718.
114 LADERO QUESADA, *La Hacienda Real*, pp. 713–714 and 731–733.
115 LADERO QUESADA, *La Hacienda Real*, pp. 691–692 and 696–698; MENJOT, "Système fiscal", pp. 30–32; GUERRERO NAVARRETE, "Impuestos", pp. 369–370.
116 LADERO QUESADA, *La Hacienda Real*, pp. 724–731; SÁNCHEZ BENITO, "Las haciendas", pp. 408–413 and 425–426.
117 GUERRERO NAVARRETE, "El 'juro'".
118 CARRASCO PÉREZ, "Fiscalidad".
119 Eloísa RAMÍREZ VAQUERO, "Finanzas municipales", p. 426.
120 MUGUETA MORENO, "Estrategias fiscales", pp. 219–264.
121 CARRASCO PÉREZ, "Las imposiciones"; MUGUETA MORENO, "El desafio fiscal".
122 RAMÍREZ VAQUERO, "Finanzas municipales", pp. 413–432.
123 CARRASCO PÉREZ, "Sobre la hacienda".
124 RAMÍREZ VAQUERO, "Finanzas municipales", pp. 429–430.

References

Javier ALVARADO PLANAS, "La castellaría en la Edad Media castellana: análisis histórico-jurídico", in *Boletín de la Facultad de Derecho*, 8–9, 1995, pp. 15–30.
Fernando ARIAS GUILLÉN, *Guerra y fortalecimiento del poder regio en Castilla*, Madrid, 2013.
Juan Manuel BELLO LEÓN, "La cuenta de mercaderes y las rentas menudas del Almojarifazgo Mayor de Sevilla a finales del siglo XV", in *Historia. Instituciones. Documentos*, 43, 2016, pp. 31–70.
Juan Manuel BELLO LEÓN and Pablo ORTEGO RICO, *Los agentes fiscales en la Andalucía Atlántica a finales de la Edad Media: materiales de trabajo y propuesta de estudio*, Murcia, 2019.
Francisco de Paula CAÑAS GÁLVEZ, *Burocracia y cancillería en la corte de Juan II de Castilla (1406–1454). Estudio institucional y prosopográfico*, Salamanca, 2012.
Juan CARRASCO PÉREZ, "Sobre la hacienda municipal de Tudela a finales de la Edad Media", in *Historia de la Hacienda Española (épocas Antigua y Medieval). Homenaje al Profesor García de Valdeavellano*, Madrid, 1982, pp. 129–169.
Juan CARRASCO PÉREZ, "Documentos para el estudio de las aduanas bajomedievales: el peaje de Pamplona de 1358", in *Cuadernos de Estudios Medievales*, 8–9, 1983, pp. 109–155.
Juan CARRASCO PÉREZ, "Fiscalidad y finanzas de las ciudades y villas navarras", in *Finanzas y fiscalidad municipal. V Congreso de Estudios Medievales*, León, 1997, pp. 327–352.
Juan CARRASCO PÉREZ, "Reino de Navarra", in *Historia de las Españas Medievales*, dir. Juan CARRASCO, Josep Maria SALRACH, Julio VALDEÓN and María Jesús VIGUERA, Barcelona, 2002, pp. 175–206 y 345–362.
Juan CARRASCO PÉREZ, "Las imposiciones en las Buenas Villas del reino de Navarra: Tudela a mediados del siglo XV", in *Príncipe de Viana*, 65/233, 2004, pp. 789–806.
Juan CARRASCO PÉREZ, "El impuesto del monedaje en el Reino de Navarra (ca. 1243–1355): fiscalidad, demografía, historia monetaria", in *Príncipe de Viana*, 72/252, 2011, pp. 55–162.
Juan CARRASCO PÉREZ, "Notariado y Hacienda Pública en el reino de Navarra. El devengo de los sellos del rey (1294–1414)", in *Príncipe de Viana*, 74/257, 2013, pp. 111–191.

Juan Carrasco Pérez, *Dinero y deuda. Crédito judío en las villas navarras del Camino de Santiago. 1266–1341*, Pamplona, 2019.

Juan Manuel Carretero Zamora, *Cortes, monarquía, ciudades. Las Cortes de Castilla a comienzos de la época moderna (1476–1515)*, Madrid, 1988.

Guillermo Castán Lanaspa, *Política económica y poder político. Moneda y fisco en el reinado de Alfonso X el Sabio*, Valladolid, 2000.

Santiago Castellanos, "The political nature of taxation in Visigothic Spain", in *Early Medieval Europe*, 12/3, 2003, pp. 201–228.

Antonio Collantes de Terán Sánchez, "Alfonso X y los Reyes Católicos: la formación de las haciendas municipales", in *En la España Medieval*, 13, 1990, pp. 253–270.

Antonio Collantes de Terán Sánchez, "Les impôts municipaux indirects ordinaires et extraordinaires de Séville", in *La fiscalité des villes au Moyen Âge (Occident méditerranéen). 2. Les systèmes fiscaux*, ed. Denis Menjot and Manuel Sánchez Martínez, Toulouse, 1999, pp. 463–483.

Estebal Corral García, *El mayordomo de concejo en la Corona de Castilla (siglos XIII-s. XVIII)*, Madrid, 1991.

Carlos de Ayala Martínez, *Las órdenes militares hispánicas en la Edad Media (siglos XII–XV)*, Madrid, 2007.

Máximo Diago Hernando, "Introducción al estudio del comercio entre las Coronas de Aragón y Castilla durante el siglo XIV: las mercancías objeto de intercambio", in *En la España medieval*, 24, 2001, pp. 47–101.

Luis Miguel Díez de Salazar, *Ferrerías de Guipúzcoa (siglos XIV-XVI). Aspectos históricos e institucionales de la industria siderometalúrgica vasca*, San Sebastián, 1983, 2 vols.

Carlos Estepa Díez, "Formación y consolidación del feudalismo en Castilla y León", in *En torno al feudalismo hispánico. I Congreso de Estudios Medievales*, Ávila, 1989.

Carlos Estepa Díez, "Organización militar, poder regio y tributaciones militares en la Castilla plenomedieval", in *Brocar*, 20, 1996, pp. 135–176.

Carlos Estepa Díez, "La behetría y el poder regio", in *Los señoríos de behetría*, ed. Carlos Estepa Díez and Cristina Jular Pérez-Alfaro, Madrid, 2001, pp. 47–64.

Carlos Estepa Díez, "La construcción de la fiscalidad real", in *Poder real y sociedad. Estudios sobre el reinado de Alfonso VIII (1158–1214)*, ed. Carlos Estepa Díez, Ignacio Álvarez Borge and José María Santamaría Luengos, León, 2011, pp. 65–94.

Carlos Estepa Díez, "En torno a la 'fonsadera' y las cargas de carácter público", in *Studia historica. Historia medieval*, 30, 2012, pp. 25–41.

Román Felones Morrás, "Contribución al estudio de la Iglesia navarra del siglo XIII: el libro del rediezmo de 1268, I. Estudio y valoración", in *Príncipe de Viana*, 43/165, 1982, pp. 129–210.

Elena Azucena Fernández Arriba, "Un aspecto de las relaciones comerciales entre Castilla y Granada: el diezmo y medio diezmo de lo morisco en la segunda mitad del siglo XV", in *Historia. Instituciones. Documentos*, 13, 1986, pp. 41–62.

Luis Javier Fortún Pérez de Ciriza, "Una reforma fiscal en el Noroeste de Navarra (1192–1193)", in *Historia de la Hacienda española (épocas Antigua y Medieval). Homenaje al profesor García de Valdeavellano*, Madrid, 1982, pp. 235–259.

Luis Javier Fortún Pérez de Ciriza, "Colección de fueros menores y otros privilegios locales de Navarra", in *Príncipe de Viana*, 43/165-166-167, 1982, pp. 273–346 y pp. 951–1036; 46/175, 1985, pp. 361–488.

Luis Javier Fortún Pérez de Ciriza, "Los Fueros menores y el señorío de realengo en Navarra (ss. XI-XIV)", in *Príncipe de Viana*, 46/176, 1985, pp. 637–639.

Luis Javier Fortún Pérez de Ciriza and Ángel J. Martín Duque, "Relaciones financieras entre Sancho el Fuerte de Navarra y los monarcas de la Corona de Aragón", in *Príncipe de Viana*, 63/227, 2002, pp. 863–869.

Alfonso Franco Silva, "Los condestables de Castilla y la renta de los diezmos de la mar", in *En la España medieval*, 12, 1989, pp. 255–284.

Francisco Fuentes Pascual, *Catálogo del Archivo Municipal de Tudela*, Pamplona, 1947.

Ángel Galán Sánchez, "*Arca Comunis*. Red interuniversitaria de investigación cooperativa de estudios sobre Historia sobre la Hacienda y la fiscalidad (siglos XIII-XVIII)", in *La historiografía medieval en España y la conformación de equipos de trabajo: los proyectos de investigación I+D+i*, Murcia, 2020, pp. 76–79.

Federico Gálvez Gambero, "Reforma y consolidación de un activo financiero. Los juros al quitar en la tesorería de lo extraordinario de Juan y Alonso de Morales (1495–1504)", in *En la España Medieval*, 38, 2015, pp. 99–134.

Federico GÁLVEZ GAMBERO, "La deuda pública en la Corona de Castilla en época Trastámara (ca. 1369–1504)", in *Journal of Medieval Iberian Studies*, 2021, pp. 96–118.

José Damián GONZÁLEZ ARCE, *El negocio fiscal en la Sevilla del siglo XV. El almojarifazgo mayor y las compañías de arrendatorios*, Sevilla, 2017.

José Damián GONZÁLEZ ARCE, *Un patrimonio concejil ingente: el almojarifazgo de los pueblos de Sevilla (siglos XIII–XV)*, Murcia, 2020.

María Estela GONZÁLEZ DE FAUVE, "La anubda y la arrobda en Castilla", in *Cuadernos de Historia de España*, 49–50, 1964, pp. 5–42.

César GONZÁLEZ MÍNGUEZ, *El portazgo en la Edad Media. Aproximación a su estudio en la Corona de Castilla*, Bilbao, 1989.

Hilda GRASSOTTI, "Alfonso IX y el origen de los empréstitos", in *Cuadernos de Historia de España*, 69, 1987, pp. 217–224.

Hilda GRASSOTTI, "Un empréstito para la conquista de Sevilla", in *Cuadernos de Historia de España*, 45/46, 1967, pp. 191–247.

Maria Carmen GROCIN GABAS, "Peajes navarros. Pamplona (1354)", *Príncipe de Viana*, 48/182, 1987, pp. 789–843.

Yolanda GUERRERO NAVARRETE, "Impuestos y contribuyentes en los concejos de la meseta Norte", in *Finanzas y fiscalidad municipal. V Congreso de estudios medievales*, León 1997, pp. 353–394.

Yolanda GUERRERO NAVARRETE, "El 'juro y deuda de la doblería' en Burgos durante el reinado de los Reyes Católicos", in *Expresiones del poder en la Edad Media. Homenaje al profesor Juan Antonio Bonachía Hernando*, ed. María Isabel DEL VAL VALDIVIESO, Juan Carlos MARTÍN CEA and David CARVAJAL DE LA VEGA, Valladolid, 2019, pp. 595–604.

Nilda GUGLIELMI, "Posada y yantar. Contribución al estudio del léxico de las instituciones medievales", in *Hispania*, 101, 1966, pp. 5–40 and 102, 1966, pp. 165–219.

Francisco J. HERNÁNDEZ, *Las rentas del rey. Sociedad y fisco en el reino castellano del siglo XIII*, Madrid, 1993, vol. 1.

Miguel Ángel LADERO QUESADA, "Las juderías de Castilla según algunos servicios fiscales del siglo xv", in *Sefarad*, 31/2, 1971, pp. 249–264.

Miguel Ángel LADERO QUESADA, "Las aduanas de Castilla en el siglo XV", in *Rivista internazionale di storia della banca*, 7, 1973, pp. 83–110.

Miguel Ángel LADERO QUESADA, *Castilla y la conquista del reino de Granada*, Granada, 1987.

Miguel Ángel LADERO QUESADA, "La renta de la sal en la Corona de Castilla (Siglos XIII-XVI)", in *Homenaje al profesor Juan Torres Fontes*, Murcia, 1987, vol. 1, pp. 821–838.

Miguel Ángel LADERO QUESADA, "La política monetaria en la Corona de Castilla (1369–1497)", in *En la España medieval*, 11, 1988, pp. 79–124.

Miguel Ángel LADERO QUESADA, "Fiscalidad regia y génesis del Estado en la Corona de Castilla (1252–1504)", in *Espacio, Tiempo y Forma. Serie III, Historia Medieval*, 4, 1991, pp. 95–136.

Miguel Ángel LADERO QUESADA, "Los primeros pasos de la alcabala castellana, de Alfonso X a Pedro I", in *Anuario de Estudios Medievales*, 21, 1992, pp. 785–802.

Miguel Ángel LADERO QUESADA, "Las almadrabas de Andalucía (siglos XIII–XVI)", in *Boletín de la Real Academia de la Historia*, 190/3, 1993, pp. 345–354.

Miguel Ángel LADERO QUESADA, *Legislación hacendística de la Corona de Castilla*, Madrid, 1999.

Miguel Ángel LADERO QUESADA, "Estado, hacienda, fiscalidad y finanzas", in *La historia medieval en España. Un balance historiográfico (1968–1998)*, Pamplona, 1999, pp. 457–504.

Miguel Ángel LADERO QUESADA, "Monedas y políticas monetarias en la Corona de Castilla (siglos XIII a XV)", in *Moneda y monedas en la Europa medieval (siglos XII–XV)*, Pamplona, 1999, pp. 129–178.

Miguel Ángel LADERO QUESADA, *La Hermandad de Castilla. Cuentas y memoriales (1480–1498)*, Madrid, 2005.

Miguel Ángel LADERO QUESADA, *La Hacienda Real de Castilla (1369–1504). Estudios y documentos*, Madrid, 2009.

Miguel Ángel LADERO QUESADA, *La formación medieval de España. Territorios, regiones, reinos*, Madrid, 2014.

Miguel Ángel LADERO QUESADA, "Lo antiguo y lo nuevo de la investigación sobre fiscalidad y poder político en la Baja Edad Media hispánica", in *Estados y mercados financieros en el occidente cristiano (siglos XIII–XVI)*, Pamplona, 2015, pp. 13–54.

Miguel Ángel LADERO QUESADA, "Política económica de Enrique III de Castilla. 1391–1406", in *Diez estudios sobre Hacienda, política y economía en Castilla. 1252–1517*, Madrid, 2021, pp. 73–91.

María Isabel LORING GARCÍA, "Del palacio a la cocina: estudio sobre el conducho en el Fuero Viejo", in *En la España Medieval*, 14, 1991, pp. 19–44.

Joaquim LLANSÓ, "Peaje de Pamplona (1362)", in *Príncipe de Viana*, 48/181, 1987, pp. 331–436.

Angus MACKAY, *Moneda, precios y política en la Castilla del siglo XV*, Sevilla, 2006.

Ángel J. MARTÍN DUQUE, "Peaje de Pamplona (1351)", in Ángel J. MARTÍN DUQUE, Javier ZABALO ZABALEGUI and Juan CARRASCO PÉREZ, *Peajes Navarros. Pamplona (1351), Tudela (1365), Sangüesa (1362), Carcastillo (1362)*, Pamplona, 1973, pp. 13–79.

Fermín MIRANDA GARCÍA, "El precio de la fé. Rentas de la Corona y aljamas judías en Navarra (siglos XII–XIV)", in *Príncipe de Viana*, 210, 1997, pp. 51–65.

Diego MELO CARRASCO, "En torno al torno al vasallaje y las parias en las treguas entre Granada y Castilla (XIII–XV): una posibilidad de análisis", in *Medievalismo*, 22, 2012, pp. 139–152.

Denis MENJOT, "L'incidence sociale de la fiscalité directe des Trastamares de Castille au XIVe siècle", in *Historia. Instituciones. Documentos*, 5, 1978, pp. 329–372.

Denis MENJOT, "La fiscalité royale directe en Castille sous les premiers Trastamare. Remarques sur l'évolution d'une pratique financière dans un cadre urbain (1374-début du XVe siècle)", in *Actes du 102e. Congrès National des Sociétés Savantes (Limoges, 1977) section de Philologie et d'Histoire jusqu'à 1610. Vol.1, Études sur la fiscalité au Moyen Age*, Paris, 1979, pp. 91–108.

Denis MENJOT, "Économie et fiscalité: les douanes du royaume de Murcie au XIVe siècle", in *Les Espagnes médiévales. Aspects économiques et sociaux. Mélanges offerts à Jean Gautier Dalché*, Paris, 1983, pp. 333–348.

Denis MENJOT, *Fiscalidad y sociedad: los murcianos y el impuesto en la Baja Edad Madia*, Murcia, 1986.

Denis MENJOT, "L'établissement du système fiscal étatique en Castille (1268–1342)", in *Génesis medieval del Estado Moderno. Castilla y Navarra (1250–1379)*, ed. Adeline RUCQUOI, Valladolid, 1987, pp. 149–172.

Denis MENJOT, "La fiscalité directe dans les systèmes financiers des villes castillanes", in *La fiscalité des villes au Moyen Âge (Occident méditerranéen). 2. Les systèmes fiscaux*, ed. Denis MENJOT and Manuel SÁNCHEZ MARTÍNEZ, Toulouse, 1999, pp. 223–257.

Denis MENJOT, "Le consentement fiscal: impôt royal et forces politiques dans la Castille de la fin du Moyen Age", in *Colloque L'impôt public et le prélèvement seigneurial en France, Paris-Bercy, juin 2000*, Paris, 2002, pp. 202–220.

Denis MENJOT, "Système fiscal étatique et systèmes fiscaux municipaux en Castille (XIIIe s.-fin du XVe s.)", in *Fiscalidad de Estado y fiscalidad municipal en los reinos hispánicos medievales*, ed. Denis MENJOT and Manuel SÁNCHEZ MARTÍNEZ, Madrid, 2006, pp. 21–51.

Denis MENJOT, "Les enjeux de la fiscalité directe dans les systèmes financiers et fiscaux des villes castillanes aux XIVe et XVe siècles", in *La fiscalità nell'economia europea. Secc. XIII-XVIII. Atti della Trentanovesima Settimana di Studi (20–26 aprile 2007)*, ed. Simonetta CAVACIOCCHI, Florence, 2008, pp. 699–730.

Denis MENJOT, "Taxation and sovereignty in medieval Castile", in *Authority and Spectacle in Medieval and Early Modern Europe. Essays in Honor of Teófilo F. Ruiz*, ed. Yuen-Gen LIANG and Jarbel RODRIGUEZ, New York, 2017, pp. 85–102.

Denis MENJOT, Antonio COLLANTES DE TERÁN SÁNCHEZ, "La génesis de la fiscalidad municipal en Castilla: primeros enfoques", in *Revista d'Història Medieval*, 7, 1996, pp. 53–80.

Denis MENJOT, Antonio COLLANTES DE TERÁN SÁNCHEZ, "Hacienda y fiscalidad concejiles en la Corona de Castilla en la Edad Media", in *Historia, Instituciones, Documentos*, 23, 1996, pp. 213–254.

Fermín MIRANDA GARCÍA, "El precio de la fé. Rentas de la Corona y aljamas judías en Navarra (siglos XII–XIV)", in *Príncipe de Viana*, 210, 1997, pp. 51–65.

José María MONSALVO ANTÓN, *La construcción del poder real en la Monarquía castellana (siglos XI-XV)*, Madrid, 2019.

Peio J. MONTEANO SORBET, *Los navarros ante el hambre, la peste, la guerra y la fiscalidad. siglos XV y XVI*, Pamplona, 1999.

Íñigo MUGUETA MORENO, *El dinero de los Evreux. Hacienda y fiscalidad en el reino de Navarra (1328–1349)*, Pamplona, 2008.

Íñigo MUGUETA MORENO, "Estrategias fiscales en el reino de Navarra (1349–1387)", in *Iura Vasconiae*, 6, 2009, pp. 197–243.

Íñigo MUGUETA MORENO, "El desafío fiscal: fuentes navarras sobre el negocio fiscal y financiero (1362–1512)", in *Fuentes para el estudio del negocio fiscal y financiero en los Reinos Hispánicos (siglos XIV–XVI)*, dir. Antonio COLLANTES DE TERÁN, Madrid, 2010, pp. 119–147.

Íñigo Mugueta Moreno, "Las demandas del rey de Navarra: conceptos, discurso e identidades fiscales (1300–1425)", in *Anuario de Estudios Medievales*, 44/2, 2014, pp. 911–943.

Íñigo Mugueta Moreno, "La fiscalidad real sobre el clero en el reino de Navarra en el siglo XIV", in *Cultures fiscales en Occident du Xè au XVIIè siècle: études offertes à Denis Menjot*, dir. Floran Garnier, Armand Jamme, Anne Lemonde and Pere Verdés Pijuán, Toulouse, 2019, pp. 209–225.

Íñigo Mugueta Moreno, "¿Un capbreu o censier entre la documentación real de Teobaldo I? Orígenes de la contabilidad real navarra", in *Contabilidad, finanzas públicas y cultura de Estado en la Corona de Aragón (siglos XIV–XVI)*, ed. Mario Lafuente Gómez and María Teresa Iranzo Muñío, Salamanca, 2021.

José Manuel Nieto Soria, *Iglesia y poder real en Castilla. El episcopado. 1250–1350*, Madrid, 1988.

José Manuel Nieto Soria, *Iglesia y génesis del Estado Moderno en Castilla (1369–1480)*, Madrid, 1993.

José Manuel Nieto Soria, "Fundamentos de legitimación impositiva en el origen de las asambleas representativas de Castilla", in *Fisco, legitimidad y conflicto en los reinos hispánicos (siglos XIII-XVII)*, ed. Carlos Laliena Corbera, Mario Lafuente Gómez and Ángel Galán Sánchez. Zaragoza, 2020, pp. 93–114.

Joseph F. O'Callaghan, "The Cortes and Royal Taxation during the Reign of Alfonso X of Castile", in *Traditio*, 27, 1971, pp. 387–398.

Joseph F. O'Callaghan, *The Gibraltar Crusade: Castile and the Battle for the Strait*, Philadelphia, 2011.

César Olivera Serrano, "Empréstitos de la Corona de Castilla bajo la dinastía Trastámara (1369–1474)", in *Hispania*, 51, 1991, pp. 317–327.

Nelly Ongay, "Los Arcos: Notas sobre la vida económica en 1366", in *Príncipe de Viana*, 50/188, 1989, pp. 533–548.

Nelly Ongay, "El mercado de Estella en 1366", in *Príncipe de Viana*, 46/175, 1985, pp. 449–512.

Nelly Ongay, *El registro del venteno en Tudela (1362)*, Mendoza, 1997.

Pablo Ortego Rico, "Guerra y paz como fundamentos legitimadores de la exacción fiscal: siglos XIII-XV", in *Guerra y paz en la Edad Media*, ed. Ana Arranz Guzmán, María del Pilar Rábade Obradó and Óscar Villarroel González, Madrid, 2013, pp. 93–107.

Pablo Ortego Rico, "Monarquía, nobleza y pacto fiscal: lógicas contractuales y estrategias de consenso en torno al sistema hacendístico castellano (1429–1480)", in *Pacto y consenso en la cultura política peninsular (siglos XI al XV)*, ed. José Manuel Nieto Soria and Óscar Villarroel González, Madrid, 2013, pp. 123–162.

Pablo Ortego Rico, "Las salinas de Atienza, Medinaceli y Molina de Aragón en la Baja Edad Media: propiedad, comercio y fiscalidad", in *Historia. Instituciones. Documentos*, 40, 2013, pp. 207–249.

Pablo Ortego Rico, "Pedido regio y repartimientos en Castilla: aproximación a partir del ejemplo del arzobispado de Toledo (1399–1476)", in *Baetica. Estudios de Arte, Geografía e Historia*, 36–37, 2014–2015, pp. 119–156.

Pablo Ortego Rico, "La «contribución» de la Hermandad en Castilla la Nueva: modelos tributarios y poderes concejiles", in *Chronica nova*, 41, 2015, pp. 271–319.

Pablo Ortego Rico, *Poder financiero y gestión tributaria en Castilla: los agentes fiscales en Toledo y su Reino (1429–1504)*, Madrid, 2015.

Pablo Ortego Rico, "La imagen de la minoría islámica castellana a través de las fuentes fiscales a fines de la Edad Media", in *Edad Media. Revista de historia*, 17, 2016, pp. 33–66.

Pablo Ortego Rico, "Mudéjares castellanos y fiscalidad real a fines del Medievo: élites, reparto, conflicto y fraude", in *El precio de la diferencia: mudéjares y moriscos ante el fisco castellano*, ed. Ángel Galán Sánchez, Ágatha Ortega Cera and Pablo Ortego Rico, Madrid, 2019, pp. 51–114.

Julio A. Pardos Martínez, "La renta de alcabalda vieja, portazgo y barra... del concejo de Burgos durante el siglo xv (1492–1502)", in *Historia de la hacienda española (épocas antigua y medieval). Homenaje al Profesor García de Valdeavellano*, Madrid, 1982, pp. 607–680.

Reyna Pastor de Togneri, "La sal en Castilla y León. Un problema de alimentación y del trabajo y una política fiscal (siglos x-xiii)", in *Cuadernos de Historia de España*, XXXVII–XXXVIII, 1963, pp. 42–85.

Pedro Andrés Porras Arboledas, "La hacienda de las órdenes militares en la Baja Edad Media castellana", in *Estudios en homenaje a Don Claudio Sánchez Albornoz en sus 90 años*, Madrid, 1983, vol. 4, pp. 535–555.

María Concepción Quintanilla Raso, "Haciendas señoriales nobiliarias en el reino de Castilla a fines de la Edad Media", in *Historia de la hacienda española (épocas antigua y medieval). Homenaje al Profesor García de Valdeavellano*, Madrid, 1982, pp. 767–798.

María Concepción Quintanilla Raso, *La nobleza señorial en la Corona de Castilla*, Granada, 2008.

José María Sánchez Benito, "Las haciendas de los concejos en la submeseta Sur (siglos XIV y XV)", in *Finanzas y fiscalidad municipal. V Congreso de estudios medievales*, Ávila, 1997, pp. 395–430.

Eloísa Ramírez Vaquero, "Patrimonio de la corona e ingresos fiscales en Navarra en el S. XV", in *Huarte de San Juan. Geografía e Historia*, 2, 1995, pp. 73–98.

Eloísa Ramírez Vaquero, "Hacienda y poder real en Navarra en la Baja Edad Media. Un esquema teórico", in *Príncipe de Viana*, 60/216, 1999, pp. 87–118.

Eloísa Ramírez Vaquero, "Estado de las investigaciones sobre la Hacienda de Navarra", in *Medievalismo*, 12, 2002, pp. 163–195.

Eloísa Ramírez Vaquero, "Finanzas municipales y fiscalidad de Estado. Tudela en la transición al siglo XVI", in *Fiscalidad de Estado y fiscalidad municipal en los reinos hispánicos medievales*, ed. Denis Menjot and Manuel Sánchez Martínez, Madrid, 2006, pp. 413–432.

Eloísa Ramírez Vaquero, "La irrupción de las imposiciones extraordinarias en Navarra: para qué y sobre quién", in *La fiscalità nell'economia europea. Secc. XIII-XVIII. Atti della Trentanovesima Settimana di Studi (20–26 aprile 2007)*, ed. Simonetta Cavaciocchi, Florence, 2008, vol. 1, pp. 217–231.

Adelina Romero Martínez, *Fisco y recaudación: impuestos directos y sistemas de cobro en la Castilla Medieval*, Granada, 1999.

Amparo Rubio Martínez, *El reinado de los Reyes Católicos en Galicia: actividad económica y fiscalidad regia*, Santiago de Compostela, 2016.

Luis Salas Almela, *La más callada revolución. Conflictos aduaneros, nobleza y Corona en Castilla (1450–1590)*, Madrid, 2020.

Claudio Sánchez Albornoz, "¿Devaluación monetaria en León y Castilla al filo de 1200?", in *Homenaje a J. Vicens Vives*, Barcelona, 1965, vol. 1, pp. 607–617.

Claudio Sánchez Albornoz, "Notas para el estudio del *petitum*", in *Estudios sobre las instituciones medievales españolas*, México, 1965, pp. 483–519.

David Torres Sanz, *La administración central castellana en la Baja Edad Media*, Valladolid, 1982.

José Manuel Triano Milán, *La llamada del rey y el auxilio del reino: del pedido regio a las contribuciones de la Santa Hermandad (1403–1498)*, Sevilla, 2018.

María del Rosario Valverde Castro, "Monarquía y tributación en la Hispania visigoda: el marco teórico", in *Hispania Antiqua*, 31, 2007, pp. 235–252.

Imanol Vitores Casado, "Agentes económicos e instituciones públicas en la configuración del mercado del hierro vasco (siglos XIV–XVI): poder, crédito y finanzas", in *En la España medieval*, 40, 2017, pp. 191–247.

Imanol Vitores Casado, *Poder, sociedad y fiscalidad en el Señorío de Vizcaya durante la Baja Edad Media*, Bilbao, 2020.

Javier Zabalo Zabalegui, *La administración del Reino de Navarra en el siglo XIV*, Pamplona, 1972.

Javier Zabalo Zabalegui, "Peaje de Pamplona (1355)", in *Príncipe de Viana*, 46/176, 1985, pp. 675–722.

7
KINGDOMS OF SICILY*

Serena Morelli and Alessandro Silvestri

Introduction

The establishment of the *Regnum Sicilie* (Kingdom of Sicily) dates back to 1130, when Antipope Anacletus II (1130–1138) appointed the Norman count Roger as King of Sicily (1130–1154). In the following years, Roger further expanded his influence across Southern Italy, where he already controlled Apulia and Calabria. By the end of the 1130s, the Kingdom of Sicily included both the island and the entire southern mainland, which the Norman monarchs governed through a governmental central apparatus based in Palermo and various administrative branches in the localities. After the Swabian dynasty of the Hohenstaufen inherited the realm in 1198, King Frederick II (1198–1250 as King of Sicily; 1220–1250, as Holy Roman Emperor) further strengthened its administrative and financial institutions, which crucially influenced the governmental structures of the following centuries.

Supported by Papacy, in 1266 Charles of Anjou defeated Manfred of Sicily (1258–1266), the last Swabian monarch, and conquered the *Regnum Sicilie*, establishing his court in Naples. However, the Angevin rule over the entire realm was temporary. In 1282, on occasion of the so-called Sicilian Vespers, Sicily rebelled against Charles and offered the Crown to Peter III of Aragon (1276–1285), whose wife Constance was a daughter of Manfred of Sicily. Sicily thus became a member of the Crown of Aragon, and later an independent polity under a cadet branch of the Catalan-Aragonese dynasty of Barcelona (1296–1409), before returning under the direct Aragonese rule in 1409, under Martin I of Aragon (1396–1410). Although the Angevin monarchs faced various political troubles and internal political conflicts, in particular from the 1340s onwards, they maintained their control over the Southern Italian mainland until 1442, when Alfonso V of Aragon (1416–1458) "the Magnanimous" conquered Naples. Despite being both members of the Crown of Aragon and later of the early-modern Spanish Empire, Southern Italy and Sicily – respectively known as *Sicilia citra farum* and *Sicilia ultra farum* – remained two distinct polities, with separate governmental apparatuses and fiscal systems.

The two polities that emerged in the southern mainland and in Sicily after the Sicilian Vespers inherited the previous Norman-Swabian institutional framework, which the new Angevin and Aragonese rulers respectively adjusted according to their political and financial needs. As a result, they established original systems of government, and further developed their financial and central administrative institutions, also incorporating traditions and practices from the French and Iberian areas. On the other hand, their fiscal structures followed different paths, for they adapted to the characteristics of each of them: the southern mainland and Sicily were diverse in size and population, marked by distinct political, social, and financial dynamics, as well as variously integrated into the economic and commercial environment of the Mediterranean. Unsurprisingly, those two fiscal systems – despite a few common aspects – remained different even after the Aragonese conquered southern Italy in 1442, as well as after both the realms became constituent components of the Spanish Empire in the early sixteenth century.

As a result of this historical process, the study of taxation in the late-medieval kingdoms of Sicily is related to two distinct historiographies, which discussed the tax related-matters by adopting various historiographical approaches and by relying on different – quantitatively and qualitatively – archival sources. Ludovico Bianchini's *Della storia delle finanze del regno di Napoli* (1835) is still today the only monograph on the subject. It describes the operation of the Neapolitan financial administration and fiscal system from the Norman age to the early Nineteenth century. Although this work lacks a theoretical interpretation in terms of development of the realm's fiscal structures, it remains a valuable source of information for current historians. As for late-medieval Sicily, the only overview on its fiscal system is an essay by Giuseppe di Martino, which is merely descriptive but useful.[1]

More broadly, the history of taxation in Southern Italy and Sicily has been mostly practiced by scholars who did not make fiscal structures and taxes into their main objects of inquiry. Instead, they used taxation as a tool of analysis for developing broader political, social, and economic investigations over those areas. Some scholars suggested that fiscal policies were tools through which foreign dynasties exercised their authority over their dominions. For instance, in the context of the Italian *Risorgimento*'s historiography, Michele Amari discussed the fiscal oppression that afflicted Sicily during the Angevin rule, which unsurprisingly led to the revolt of the Vespers for expelling the foreign dynasty.[2] Following a similar approach, more than one century later Carmelo Trasselli ideologically stated that Alfonso V, of the Trastámara dynaty, permanently undermined the Sicilian finances and economy by brutally exploiting its fiscal resources for decades.[3]

By pursuing a non-ideological approach to research, since the late 1960s other historians adopted new methodologies, which originated from both various scholar environments (i.e. the English and the French academia), and different research fields, such as economic history. In so doing, Mario Del Treppo analysed the fiscal policies of the fifteenth-century Crown of Aragon – which included both the two kingdoms of Sicily – in the context of their trans-Mediterranean commercial network, with a main focus on the Kingdom of Naples under Alfonso the Magnanimous (1442–1458).[4] On the other hand, David Abulafia, Henri Bresc, Stephen Epstein, and Eleni Sakellariou investigated taxation in connection to their broader inquiries over the backwardness of Southern Italy and Sicily.[5] Moreover, in the context of a recent new wave of studies focused on urban history, a few scholars examined the fiscal systems at the local level, both in terms of contribution to the Crown's income and of funding the municipalities' administrations.[6]

Through working on those different strands of investigation, scholarship thus renewed traditional topics of research and explored a new set of themes, among which it is worth mentioning: the relationship between ordinary and extraordinary taxation; the criteria which defined the distribution of the tax burden among taxpayers; the emergence of a significant variety of revenues, such as those originating from public debt and compulsory loans; the role of merchants and bankers in funding the Crown.

While discussing the lordships of the southern Italian mainland, Sandro Carocci analysed the aristocratic tax system of the twelfth and thirteenth centuries, with a particular stress on the tolls on rural communities.[7] At the same time, both Southern Italian and Sicilian historians have examined – although only partially – ecclesiastical taxation and tolls, among which the so-called papal *decima*, i.e. an amount corresponding to one tenth of the incomes each diocese owed to the Pope.[8]

Drawing upon the above-mentioned literature on taxation and fiscal policies of Southern Italy and Sicily, five historiographical axioms seem to emerge. Firstly, after the common Norman-Swabian age, the two kingdoms of Sicily followed similar, but at the same time different fiscal patterns, which reflected their own specific socioeconomic environments. Second, to understand fully the development of their fiscal policies is fundamental to analyse them on a Mediterranean scale, as clearly attested, for instance, by the Crown of Aragon's influence on its Italian realms. Third, war played a crucial role for the development of taxation in the *Mezzogiorno*, as well as for the emergence of systems of regular direct taxation. Fourth, rather than a mere governmental tool solely managed by the monarchs, taxation evolved into a sphere of negotiation and compromise between the Crown and his subjects, whether they were aristocratic factions, urban oligarchies, or ecclesiastical bodies. Fifth, the urban network played a growing role in influencing the fiscal strategies of the monarchy, as the most part of southern Italian and Sicilian incomes directly originated from their demesnial cities and towns.

Although historians increasingly focused on the study of taxation, the critical gaps in documentation significantly influenced the development of research, both in connection to chronologies and subjects. Therefore, further investigation is still needed on various aspects of the history of taxation in both the southern mainland and Sicily. For instance, because of the destruction of the medieval archives of Naples, southern Italian scholars barely touched the second half of the fourteenth century, which needs to be further explored. Sicilian historiography, on the other hand, mainly investigated the island's fiscal policy during the late-thirteenth and fourteenth century, mostly neglecting the huge amount of fifteenth-century archival records – preserved in both the archives of Palermo and Barcelona – de facto unexplored from the 1450s onwards. Concerning urban history, despite few exceptions (e.g. the archives of Aquila in Abruzzo and Palermo in Sicily), the massive archival losses of municipal and feudal records hindered the analysis of taxation at the urban and local level, with just few studies investigating the development of fiscal systems and the management of customs and duty tolls in towns and urban lordships.

This chapter examines public taxation in Southern Italy and Sicily between the twelfth and the early sixteenth century. On the one hand, it explores the various fiscal strategies their rulers pursued in those two territories to raise income – e.g. by relying more on direct taxes rather than indirect imposts, or vice versa. On the other hand, it analyses how those strategies developed to meet the growing financial needs of monarchs, finally leading to the emergence of systems of ordinary direct taxation for supporting the enormous costs of war during the mid-fifteenth century. At the same time, urban taxation will be discussed to understand more clearly the fiscal policies of the two kingdoms of Sicily, which both mostly relied on the profits from demesne municipalities.

For practical reasons, after discussing the emergence of taxation in the Norman and Swabian *Regnum Sicilie*, this essay examines the following fiscal developments of the two kingdoms of Sicily in distinct sections, with specific subsections focused on the fiscal strategies at the urban level and on their interactions with central governments.

The origins of the fiscal system in the *Regnum Sicilie* (1130–1250)

The emergence of royal taxation: the Norman Age

As soon as Roger II of Hauteville became the first monarch of the new Kingdom of Sicily (1130–1154), he established an innovative administrative system which incorporated the previous governmental traditions of Muslim Sicily, as well as of the Byzantine and Lombard territories in Southern Italy. Although a few scholars regarded the new kingdom – and its administrative organization – as a precursor of the early-modern political and institutional systems, it should be considered as an example of feudal monarchy. Far from being stable, the Kingdom of Sicily's institutions and administrative practices frequently changed after their establishment, with King Roger II only recognized as a *primus inter pares*.[9] Nonetheless, exploiting his pre-eminent position, the monarch strategically expanded his authority and influence over the various territorial lordships and powers of Southern Italy. In so doing, he built a new set of institutional and feudal relationships with a group of lords who previously possessed the same prerogatives of the monarch, thus becoming the main landowner of the kingdom. By taking direct control of all the revenues arising from the management of lands, waters, woods, pastures, and so on, King Roger II extended the royal possessions and prerogatives, increasing at the same time the realm's income – the latter, remains difficult to determine due to lack of records. However, the process that led to the full acknowledgement of the royal rights was not a straight development, but the result of a slow and turbulent transformation, with phases of political uncertainty – such as in the last decades of the Norman rule – which led to the emergence of territorial powers equipped with significant political and fiscal autonomy.

To strengthen his authority and consolidate his power, Roger II promoted the reformation of the institutional apparatus of the Kingdom. Following the Assise of Ariano (1140), organs and officers specialized in the management of financial and political affairs were established both at the center and in the peripheries. Through managing royal demesne and de facto operating as a treasury, the already existing *dohana de secretis* collected various revenues from indirect taxation, such as from circulation and sale of goods. Moreover, a network of territorial officers, such as the *iusticiarii* (justiciaries) and the *camerarii* (chamberlains), raised revenues from the *auditorium* and other royal taxes.[10] On behalf of chamberlains, a group of officers known as *baiuli* (bailiffs) administered taxes at the local and urban level. They collected incomes from the *iura fisci* (customs and excise tolls), such as the *ius buczerie* and the *ius anchorage* – which respectively concerned butchery and anchorage – and the *ius statere*, which pertained to measurement and weight of goods. Despite being variously called, those tolls were similar across the entire kingdom, except for a few local variations. Interestingly, the position of *baiulus* was usually farmed out for a fee ranging between fifteen and forty *onze*, according to the length of the office (two or more years).

Even the first attempts to organize systems of direct taxation emerged within this feudal world. However, nothing remotely like the Domesday Book was ever produced in the *Regnum Sicilie*. The earliest document concerning taxation is the *Catalogus Baronum*, which dates back at least to 1167 (the first surviving copy is of the early fourteenth century).[11] The *Catalogus* lists the fiefs of the Kingdom of Sicily and the military services the feudal lords owed to the monarch in terms of *militi* (soldiers) serving in the Duchy of Apulia and the Principality of Capua. The *Catalogus* was probably part of a broader inquiry on the military forces of the kingdom; however, it is also possible that Calabria and Sicily did not raise military levies. More broadly, the *Catalogus* was a crucial resource of fiscal knowledge for the Crown during a period in which royal taxation was still occasional.

Feudal lords were only sporadically required to provide the *servitium pecuniarum*★ (i.e., the payment of a certain amount of money) which was probably due alongside the *servitium personarum*★, namely one man for each fief with an annual income of 20 *onze*. Owners of allodial lands had to pay an *adiutorium*★ or subsidy, which was levied periodically, and was somehow like the military duty paid to feudal lords. Moreover, King William I of Sicily (1154–1166) decreed that lords, laymen and clergymen could ask the *adiutoria*★ from their own vassals, according to criteria that varied from one place to another.[12] In essence, during the Norman age taxation was marked by a certain degree of confusion, with different and variously called systems of tax collection and, at the same time, distinct types of taxes sharing similar denominations.

The reforms under Frederick II of Hohenstaufen (1220–1250)

The age of the Swabian sovereign Frederick II marked a significant turning point for the Kingdom of Sicily, for it led to the reorganization of the realm's administrative framework and to the emergence of a clear fiscal strategy. In particular, the *Dohana* experienced a process of systematic development, aimed at precisely defining the sovereign rights.[13] The *colletta*★ emerged as a general direct taxation to be imposed as the equivalent of the military service provided by feudal lords. Through the Constitution of Melfi (1231), the monarch finally defined the procedures for income collection, also establishing the four specific circumstances in which the direct taxes could be raised: the knighting of the monarch, the marriage of his heirs, the payment of a ransom for the king's imprisonment, and waging war. Despite the fact that *collette*★ were extraordinary revenues (i.e. irregularly perceived), from 1223 onwards they became de facto annual incomes. The amount raised from this form of direct taxation varied considerably and depended on the political and financial needs of the moment: for instance, the Crown collected 102,000 *onze* in 1238, and 60,800 *onze* in 1242. From an administrative point of view, a group of officers raised the *colletta*'s★ revenues – which amounted to two *tarì* per person – with the *iusticiarii* and several tax collectors respectively operating at the provincial level and in the various towns of the realm. It should be noted that, at the end of his reign, Frederick II abolished this form of direct taxation due to its unpopularity; however, his successor Conrad I (1250–1254) reintroduced it as soon as he took the throne in order to support his growing financial needs.

Between 1220 and 1231, Frederick II also intervened on indirect taxation (excise and customs duties, as well as various local taxes), with the specific purpose of restoring royal rights and privileges. In so doing, he created new royal monopolies (e.g. on salt) and established the so-called *fundaci*, i.e. warehouses for goods, thanks to which royal officers regularly collected duties on customs and storage.[14] Indeed, the reforms of the various royal duties and levies should be analysed in connection with the development of the overall economic system of the kingdom. Focusing on commerce, the monarch hoped to enhance the kingdom's resources, preventing at the same time local powers and feudal lords from exercising any influence on the management of economic affairs. The following measures were introduced: revision and equalization of tariffs for Sicilian subjects and foreigners, but with various exceptions (e.g. the Venetians); reduction of the *ius exiture* (an export tax on goods) for the realm's inhabitants, at least for some foodstuffs (e.g. oil, cheese and salted meats); free trade within the Kingdom for agricultural products such as *victualia* and *ligumina*, as well as flax, but with the obligation of transferring the twelfth part of the harvest to the Crown.[15]

The goals of Frederick II appear even more evident by examining his policy on the grain's production and trade. He aimed to increase demand for foodstuffs from foreign merchants, and encourage internal production at the same time. In addition to establishing new fairs, the monarch reduced the customs duties and lowered the tax rates due for loads of grain to be exported: to a fifth of the value in Sicily and to a seventh of the value in the rest of the kingdom. Furthermore, to ensure royal control over the routes of grain trade, in 1239 Frederick II decreed that grain could be exported by sea only from a list of official ports, located in both Sicily and the southern mainland, with royal officers (*portulani*), supervising trade on behalf of the Crown.[16] The Swabian also forbade circulation of foreign currency, imposed the new imperial silver *denarii* as the exclusive currency for internal transactions, allowing the use of gold only in the trade and business with Venetians. Whether the economic interventionism and fiscal policies of Frederick II had a positive impact on the kingdom or instead weakened the dynamism of the *Mezzogiorno*'s elites is hard to determine due to the lack of documentary evidence.[17]

Indeed, although Fredrick II relied on the administrative structures previously established by the Normans, he used a different approach in managing the kingdom's incomes. The Swabian monarch pursued a more focused strategy aimed at strengthening the rights of the Crown, which can be described as a real fiscal policy, later followed also by his successors Conrad and Manfred. In the period between the collapse of the Swabian rule and the advent of the Angevin domination, the Kingdom of Sicily's fiscal system raised annual revenues ranging from 200,000 to 250,000 *onze*. Those profits, for instance, were significantly higher than those raised by the kingdoms of France and England during the same century. According to the calculations of William A. Percy, whereas Louis IX of France (1226–1270) annually collected about 100,000 *onze*, Henry III of England (1216–1272) received 60,000 *onze*.[18]

The Angevin taxation in the Kingdom of Sicily *citra farum*: towards the strengthening of fiscal procedures (1266–1442)

The Angevin rule began in 1266 after the battle of Benevento and the defeat of King Manfred of Sicily. During the following 150 years, seven sovereigns and two branches of the Angevin dynasty controlled the southern mainland of the kingdom – the island of Sicily became independent in 1282 – thus crucially influencing the development and management of taxation, which experienced two main stages: a first phase (1266–1343), which ended on a positive note, and a second phase during which the financial situation gradually deteriorated to the point that not even the sale of Avignon to the Holy See between 1349 and 1350 for 80,000 florins restored the finances of the Angevin Kingdom of Sicily.

The first phase of the Angevin rule (1266–1343)

Once he established his authority over the Kingdom of Sicily, Charles I of Anjou opted for preserving the previous fiscal organization, facilitating at the same time the institutionalization of the administrative developments already in progress. In so doing, he precisely defined the number and size of the fiscal districts of the realm: if eleven justiciaries (*iusticiarii*) managed the collection of direct taxes, five *secrezie* and *portolanati* became responsible for levying indirect taxation and raising its revenues, respectively from customs and excise duties and various other levies, and from royal ports. Although Charles I roughly maintained the types of taxes of the previous ages, he replaced the *colletta*★ with the so-called *subventio generalis*★ (general subsidy), a direct taxation to be paid by those invested with demesne possessions and rights. Such a fiscal strategy allowed the sovereign to raise significant revenues from his subjects – de facto, whenever it was needed – for funding the expansion across the Mediterranean and in the Balkan, as well as for waging war against Sicily.

As discussed by William A. Percy, the total tax revenue of 1282 increased by almost 50 per cent compared to the immediately preceding years. Whereas on occasion of the *subventio*★ of 1276 Charles I raised about 60,000 *onze*, in 1282 he raised about 107,891 *onze*. From the outbreak of the War of the Sicilian Vespers (1282) to the end of the century, Southern Italian subjects were asked to pay 44,500 *onze* a year through a general subsidy, in addition to various other donations.[19] Although the Swabian fiscal system was preserved, the growing financial needs of the Angevin monarchs led to invisible, but significant transformations, which clearly emerge by examining the letters and orders the Angevin rulers sent to their territorial officers in the late thirteenth century. Firstly, the request of the subsidy became annual; second, the government regularly prepared the so-called *cedule taxationis*, which listed the amounts of taxes due by each city of the kingdom; third, early methods for assessing wealth and assets of those individuals living in the royal demesne were introduced, later evolving into a practice known as *apprezzo*; finally, a new group of officers known as *erarii* was entrusted with money collection on behalf of the provincial justiciars.[20]

These Angevin innovations emerged within a context in which the monarchs had the right to raise money for military support from its subjects/vassals. However, the nature of the subsidy remained extraordinary. In order to lower the tension with their subjects, the Crown promoted the *Ordinanze e i Capitoli di San Martino* (1282), which re-established previous legislation.[21] It was decreed that the *subventio*★ could only be raised in the following, extraordinary cases: the defence of the kingdom or liberation of the king, not more than 50,000 *onze*; the knighting of the king, as well as of his sons and relatives, not more than 12,000 *onze*; weddings of the royal family, not more than 15,000 *onze*. Despite these restrictions – it should be pointed out – in the following years the Angevin monarchs continued to raise annual subsidies.

On occasion of general subsidies, the tax rate was determined according to the size of each town, with each *fuoco* (hearth) required to pay one *augustale* or one half of an *augustale* (according to different interpretations). Interestingly, once the overall amount to be paid for each province was established, the royal court did not accept further modifications. If, for various reasons, the monarch granted fiscal reductions to a *universitas* (urban community), the loss of revenue was immediately distributed among the surrounding towns. In practice, the latter bore the burden of the fiscal reduction granted to another *universitas*, so that the treasury could receive the exact amount previously established for each province. In 1277 the revenue oscillated between the amount of 3,505 *onze* for Calabria and the amount of 9,304 *onze* for the Terra di Lavoro. Those sums, it should be noted, remained roughly the same until the mid-fourteenth century, because the *cedule taxationis* were never updated.[22]

The development of direct taxation at the end of the thirteenth century took place in a context that was extremely flexible and, to an extent, rather ambiguous. Unsurprisingly, if several requests for money pertained to direct taxation, those requests did not necessarily regard general subsidies. For example, in 1295–1296 the town of Lucera paid an overall amount of 899 *onze*, of which 400 for the general subsidy, 333 for a traditional donation to the king, and 166 for the militia of Charles I of Hungary, nephew of Charles II of Anjou (1289–1309). In the following years, the amount paid by Lucera further increased: in 1298–1299, 1,225 *onze* (400 for the *subventio*★, 500 for the fleet, 200 for the army, 125 for the siege of Castellabate), and in 1299–1300, 1,530 *onze* (500 for the *subventio*★, 500 for the fleet, 500 for the army, and 30 to pay the money collectors).

Moreover, the Crown benefited from other types of taxation, such as the *relevio*★ and the *adoa*★ (or *adoha*), which were both of Norman-Swabian origins. On the one hand, the *relevio*★ was a direct tax the heir of a deceased feudal lord had to pay to succeed and legally acquire a fief. It corresponded to half the fief's incomes in the year before the death of the feudal lord;

during the reign of Charles I, this taxation generated roughly 2,000 *onze* a year. On the other hand, the *adoa*★ was the sum of money feudal lords paid for replacing their military service. Interestingly, as a result of the military escalation of the fourteenth century, the revenues from the *adoa*★ remarkably increased: from 6,000 *onze* in 1316 to 8,000 *onze* in 1341, and 20,135 *onze* under Queen Joanna II of Anjou-Durazzo (1414–1435).

As discussed above, five *secrezie* and *portolanati* were vested with the authority to raise revenues from indirect taxation in their territorial districts. In carrying out their tasks, these magistracies – but a single officer usually administered both – collected a broad range excise and customs duties pertaining to the Crown. They ranged from the various sums raised by *capitani* and *baiuli* at the urban level to the tolls managed by the *magistri passuum* and *dohanerii*, which collected their profits from those merchants who crossed the realm's borders. The *secrezie* were usually farmed out to merchants or wealthy individuals in exchange for immediate incomes.[23] For instance, under Charles I, the *secrezia* of Apulia was farmed out for 2,400 *onze* in 1272 and for 9,550 *onze* in 1279–1280; the *secrezia* of the provinces of Principato, Abruzzo, and Terra di Lavoro was farmed out for 1,750 *onze* in 1270.[24]

Because of the broad variety of taxes managed by each *secrezia*, it is difficult to assess precisely the overall income the Crown received from indirect taxation. However, the existing archival sources give some interesting clues on those incomes. Whereas in 1324 the *secrezia* of Apulia raised 16,500 *onze*, four years before the same *secrezia* farmed out the *gabella* on salt for 3,000 *onze*.[25] Also in the case of the above-mentioned *ius exiture*, the profits of the monarchs significantly varied, depending on the period and the geographical area. For example, in Apulia the toll to export 100 *salme* of wheat was 20 *onze* in 1283 and 10 *onze* in 1288; in 1299, the same toll increased to 30 *onze*.[26] This financial practice allowed the Angevin monarchs to collect rapidly huge amounts of money that could be used for their most immediate needs, whether they concerned waging war, or paying off debts, such as the huge debt the Crown had with the Papacy because of the War of the Sicilian Vespers, which in 1293 amounted to 93,340 *onze* – the debt was fully paid off only in 1340.[27]

The crisis of the Angevin fiscal system during the second half of the fourteenth century

If the outbreak of the Sicilian Vespers War in 1282 had produced the systematization of the Angevin fiscal structures, also leading to a significant increase of the kingdom's incomes, the incessant internal conflicts of the following century – after the death of Andrew of Hungary in 1345, husband of Queen Joanna I of Naples (1343–1382) – dramatically deteriorated the operation of the fiscal administration. Unsurprisingly, in such a critical situation the newly established financial office of the *camera summarie* – composed of officers experienced in financial and fiscal affairs – took on the crucial task of monitoring attentively the multiple incomes and expenditures of the realm.[28]

Therefore, from the mid-fourteenth century onwards the Angevin monarchs could not more rely on the regular revenues from the *subventio generalis*★. To meet their most urgent political and military needs, they were instead forced to depend on other occasional direct incomes, variously called *donativi* and *collette*★. In so doing, the Angevin kings vested various officers (such as *erarii*, *rationales*, treasurers, etc.) with the authority to raise the revenues from these direct taxes across the provinces of the realm, for the justiciaries were no more involved in those matters.

In addition to the decline of the direct taxation's profits, other factors contributed to the collapse of the kingdom's incomes. On the one hand, a number of demesne towns were granted various "fiscal exceptions" – namely, exemptions from paying taxes – intended to alleviate the economic and social consequences of plague and warfare. On the other hand, the Crown invested several feudal lords with the right of autonomously managing taxation in their lordships, in exchange for their political and military support. In this regard, it is worth mentioning the exceptional case of the Principality of Taranto. Originally managed by members of the Angevin dynasty – such as Philip I and Philip II of Taranto – this Principality encompassed various fiefs and towns in Apulia and possessed an institutional apparatus that mirrored the governmental structures of the Angevin Kingdom of Sicily. Because of its economic resources, this Apulian lordship benefitted from substantial tax revenues, which its princes managed almost independently thanks to the significant fiscal autonomy granted to them by the Crown. In the following century, the fiscal autonomy of the Principality of Taranto further increased, while prince Giovanni Antonio Orsini equipped his lordship with a network of officers (*collectores*) in charge of raising income from various taxes, such as the *fundaci**, due for storage of goods. Moreover, the prince established administrative districts led by a group *erarii*, in charge of collecting the profits from direct taxes.[29]

Indeed, the emergence of powerful lordships equipped with broad fiscal autonomies such as the Principality of Taranto was one of the Angevin "legacies" the new Aragonese monarchy had to face alongside the collapse of the revenues from taxation during the second half of the fifteenth century.

The reign of the Aragonese monarchs in Naples: aspects of the tax state

In 1435 Queen Joanna II of Anjou-Durazzo (1414–1435) died heirless. The Queen's indecision in choosing her successor led to a war between the pretenders to the Neapolitan throne. After a seven-year conflict, in 1442 Alfonso V of Trastámara – who had been appointed as legitimate heir 1420 – finally defeated René and conquered the realm. The new sovereign immediately tackled the problem of restoring the fiscal structures of the Kingdom, which had collapsed during the war of succession (1435–1442). In so doing, Alfonso sent a number of ad hoc officers to the various provinces of the realm in order to inquire into the financial frauds committed in the previous years, as well as into the legitimacy of all those incomes and fiscal rights paid on demesne resources. Those officers were also entrusted with the retrieval of all those revenues which had not been collected during war.

More importantly, by relying on the local parliamentary assembly, in 1443 Alfonso crucially reformed the fiscal system of the realm. In so doing, he transformed the once extraordinary direct taxation into an ordinary practice. In particular, the Aragonese introduced in Naples a hearth tax (*focatico**) – called general taxation (*tassa generale*) since 1449 – which lasted for the entire Aragonese rule, but for a brief experimental period under his successor. The amount due for the *focatico** changed according to the population of the kingdom, which the personnel of the *camera summarie* assessed every three year. As decreed in 1443, a tax of one ducat had to be paid for each hearth. However, Alfonso promoted periodical reviews of tax rates: for instance, on occasion of the parliament of 1456, it was established that two ducats were to be paid for each hearth. In exchange for this increase of taxation, the monarch granted more judicial autonomy to his feudal lords.

This new form of taxation led to a huge increase in tax revenue: the expected revenue for 1443 was 345,000 ducats and in 1456 it rose to 460,000 ducats. From an administrative perspective, the authorities established five fiscal districts – which increased to six under King Ferrante of Naples (1458–1494) – each of them under the administration of a tax collector known as *percettore regio*, who replaced the justiciaries and all the other officers in charge of collecting incomes from direct taxation and toll duties.[30] Finally, it should be noted that the hearth tax did not fully replace the occasional subsidies (*collette**), for throughout the fifteenth century various forms of ordinary and extraordinary taxes coexisted. The monarch always maintained the right to organize *collette** according to the specific circumstances already established in the thirteenth century.

Another important aspect of the fifteenth-century fiscal policy of Southern Italy concerns the management of salt, which the Crown controlled as a monopoly. If it is true that, on some occasions, monarchs freely accorded to each hearth a *tomolo* of salt – corresponding to 40 kilograms – as a reward for the payment of the *focatico**, it is also true that, more often, each hearth had to pay a variable amount of money to purchase salt. The combination of this salt tax with the *focatico** is known as *funzioni fiscali*.[31] However, with the purpose of increasing royal revenues, King Ferrante of Naples temporarily abolished the system of the *funzioni fiscali*, preferring to collect revenues from the towns' *datia* and excise duties: in practice, each municipality was asked to pay sums due for the *colletta** with the incomes from urban taxation. This new royal strategy – it should be noted – is probably to be connected to the various problems the *universitates* faced while preparing the above-mentioned *apprezzi*, such as heated contrasts among the municipalities' political factions, or the fact that several citizens deceived the authorities about their incomes. The existing sources attest that in 1485, by farming out all the kingdom's revenues (i.e. from the *focatici**, *tratte*, customs and excise duties, etc.), the Crown raised about 800,000 ducats – in addition to other extraordinary incomes. Although the urban elites supported the reform of King Ferrante, this fiscal strategy was adopted only on three occasion (1481–1482, 1482–1483, and 1484–1485). Although the reasons that led the monarch to abolish his reform remain unclear, it is possible to assume that he did not want to excessively rely on an uncertain source of income such as indirect taxation.

In addition to the incomes from direct taxation, the Aragonese monarchs also benefited from increasing revenues from various demesnial rights and tolls, which were administered in strict connection with the overall economic and commercial strategies of the Kingdom – for instance, this is the case of the protectionist policy for the grain trade, the reduction of taxes on exports, and the preservation of levies on imports. However, among the various developments of royal rights, the new customs duties for sheep (*Dogana delle pecore*) and the reform of the border posts (*passi*) seem to be the most important innovations.[32] On the one hand, further developing the previous Angevin organization, Alfonso the Magnanimous increased the revenues from the transhumance of cattle, which moved from Abruzzo to the province of the Capitanata (in the northern area of the actual Apulia). Those revenues rapidly became the linchpin of indirect taxation for the Crown, as they grew from 18,168 ducats in 1443 to about 100,000 ducats in 1450, to the detriment of several barons, who were deprived of important sources of income.[33] On the other hand, both the Aragonese sovereigns significantly renovated the system of the *passi* of the realm in order to increase their income and favouring trade at the same time. In the late thirteenth century, Charles I of Anjou had established the so-called *magistri passuum*, who were responsible for overseeing imports and exports through borders. However, because of the emergence of large feudal lordships, a few barons had created several illegal *passi*, which obstructed circulation of goods both along the borders and within the Kingdom, thus damaging the Crown's revenues. In order to fully restore royal jurisdiction, Alfonso the Magnanimous entrusted the *rationales* of the *camera summarie* with the task of raising the revenues from the *ius passorum** and supervising trade along frontiers; moreover, in 1466 King Ferrante of Naples abolished all the illegal *passi*. If from 1282 to the mid-fifteenth century the *passi* had increased from 25 to 208 (including both royal and feudal *passi*), in 1471 there were only nine *passi* at the borders of the Kingdom. Unlike the previous Angevin monarchs, both Alfonso and Ferrante promoted reforms and fiscal policies which were fully integrated into the broader economic system of the Kingdom of Sicily *citra farum*. Therefore, through pursuing this strategy, they significantly increased royal revenues, facilitating at the same time trade within the realm.[34]

It is worth noting that despite the various interventions of the Aragonese rulers on excise, customs and trade duties, incomes from direct taxation remained significantly higher in comparison to those from indirect taxation. As discussed by Mario del Treppo, in 1444 and 1458 indirect revenues respectively corresponded to 24 per cent and 31 per cent of overall income of the realm, respectively about 200,000 ducats and 150,000 ducats. Under King Ferrante, whereas in 1483 the royal treasury raised 427,564 ducats from the *funzioni fiscali* (*focatico*★ and mandatory payments due for the distribution of salt) – corresponding to 66 per cent of the total income – it raised 220,881 ducats (34 per cent) from excise and customs duties.[35] These significant differences among the two types of royal incomes, alongside the collection of taxes and levies of a city nature and the continuous conflict on the forms of taxation and distribution of the fiscal burden at the urban level, characterized the entire fiscal history of Southern Italy.

Urban taxation in the Kingdom of Sicily *citra farum*

When discussing urban taxation in Southern Italy, it is crucial to analyse two intertwined questions: on the one hand, the influence of the royal systems of direct taxation on the procedures of tax collection at the urban level; on the other hand, the management of municipal taxes, which were levied on the basis of the local *statuti* and often derived from local customs.

Direct taxation at the urban level

It was the responsibility of each municipality distributing among its citizens the royal demands for direct taxation. This distribution took place according to the criteria established in the *apprezzo* by a tax committee, which the provincial justiciar appointed for each *universitas* under his jurisdiction. Indeed, the *apprezzo* was the result of negotiation between the tax committee's members (two noblemen, two *populares*, and two members of the lower classes), whose interests differed significantly. Unsurprisingly, the aristocratic elites frequently opposed the compilation of the *apprezzo*, because they did not want to pay the largest share of royal demands. Whether on some occasions – such as in Raiano, Roccabotte and Pescara in Abruzzo – the aristocratic factions simply refused to pay the amounts determined in the *apprezzo*, in other circumstances they reacted violently. For instance, in 1331 the nobles of Angri set fire to the buildings of the *populares*, after the aristocratic attempt of taking control of the committee failed. In 1342, the nobility of Monopoli rejected the tax committee's decisions and produced autonomously its own *apprezzo*. Therefore, to circumvent these problems, the non-aristocratic classes of the *universitas* often sought the Crown's support. For example, in 1329 the *universitas* of Atri petitioned the king for electing a tax committee solely composed of foreign officers.

At the same time, however, the Crown was mostly interested in receiving the incomes expected. This explains why King Robert of Anjou (1309–1343) – as well as King Ferrante of Naples in the following century – often allowed the *universitates* to pay their taxes with the proceeds of the *datia* (excise tolls), as the towns of Castellammare and Amalfi respectively did in 1325 and 1333.[36] This fiscal procedure highlights the difficulty of making a precise distinction between direct and indirect taxation. The forms and methods used for distributing the tax burden also had important political and institutional repercussions. On the one hand, it involved the *universitates*' need for financial and fiscal autonomy and, on the other, the necessity to organize a regular and functional system of tax collection.

The monarchy and municipalities' goals did not necessarily contrast with each other. Unsurprisingly, Kings and urban communities often agreed on various solutions, as exemplified by the *Libro Rosso* of Molfetta, namely the book of the town's privileges. This *libro* clearly shows the continuous bargaining between the *universitas* and the monarchs, with the town's representatives constantly concerned with obtaining reductions of taxes and, at the same time, with keeping updated the list of taxpayers. As decreed by Queen Joanna II in 1415, the citizens of Molfetta were required to rely on the *apprezzo* for the payment of royal subsidies, and "*per testas seu capita hominum*" ("per head or per capita of people") for other types of levies, including local taxation (e.g. for repairing walls).[37]

The case of Molfetta was not an exception, but the result of a slow and complex development affecting the entire kingdom. In order to adjust their urban fiscal systems, from the early fourteenth century onwards several Southern Italian towns had autonomously developed their own *catasti*, which described the properties of their citizens and the taxes due for those properties. In so doing, the town authorities had intended to control the management of the local fiscal procedures and to influence the distribution of the tax burden among their citizens, even when it concerned the *subventiones generales*★. Not by chance, these demands were often paid through raising incomes via indirect taxation at the urban level.

Despite the Aragonese reforms, during the second half of fifteenth century a few urban communities continued to use the traditional systems of taxation, as in the case of the seven *universitates* of the county of Soleto – which paid their taxes to Giovanni Antonio Orsini, prince of Taranto and constable of the kingdom. Therefore, in 1456 Soleto, Cutrofiano, and Zollino still paid taxes in the form of subsidies; two years later, only Zollino remained tied to the previous form of tax collection.[38]

Situations such as these reveal that the introduction of new fiscal system could generate significant opposition at the urban level. As already discussed for the Angevin period, demesne towns continued to play a crucial role in organizing the distribution of the tax burden among their citizens, as well as in establishing the forms of payment (e.g. relying on the incomes from customs and excise duties), also extending their authority to the surrounding territories.

The management of indirect taxation

This general system of direct taxation was connected to the *universitates*' fiscal organization, which in turn relied on a set of indirect duties and taxes. As previously discussed, during the Swabian and Norman ages the *baiuli* were responsible for collecting these indirect excise tolls, which often derived from local fiscal customs. The *baiuli* were originally royal officers entrusted with the management of the *regalia*, a set of privileges and rights pertaining to sovereigns. However, during the second half of the thirteenth century – concurrently to the emergence of the municipalities' governmental structures – the *baiuli* evolved into officers in charge of administering various urban possessions and rights, namely collective resources such as lands for pasture, woods, waterways, and so on. Whereas the *baiuli* became representatives of the urban communities, the captains (*capitanei*) later emerged instead as the officers operating in the municipalities on behalf of monarchs.[39]

Because of the heterogeneous political landscape of Southern Italy before the establishment of the Norman rule, municipalities developed such a variety of traditions and customs that it seems almost impossible to outline a systematic synthesis of urban taxation. Nevertheless, historians have agreed that the Angevin age marked a crucial turning point, for the Southern

Italian *universitates* acquired increasing political and administrative autonomy between the late thirteenth and the early fourteenth century.[40] This process also led to the preparation of municipal statutes which, once approved by the Angevin monarchs, gave full legitimacy to various urban traditions and customs, as well as to the management of all those rights and possessions pertaining to communities. At the same time – and even more evidently in the following Aragonese age – taxation and fiscal policies at the urban level emerged as crucial tools of interaction and negotiation between the Crown and municipalities.

In this regard, the management of the municipal *datia* is a significant example of this process. Although the monarchs had the right to approve the *datia*, as well as of administering contracts and determining prices, the *universitates* could autonomously establish new taxes for their ordinary and extraordinary needs.[41] In Manfredonia, for example, during the fifteenth century local authorities further developed the previous Angevin system of municipal *datia* to pay the royal imposts, according to the practice analysed above. In so doing, they raised significant revenues from indirect taxation, as in the case of excise duties on consumption and on commerce of goods, which from the countryside arrived in the port of the city; moreover, another amount was due when loading carts or transferring grain and barley onto ships. If more revenues were needed, the corpus listing the Manfredonia's excise and custom duties could be modified, for example, in order to change the tolls' rates or to include new duties, such as a levy on fishing.[42] Moreover, as a result of farming out revenues, customs duties enriched political society which was already wealthy enough to be able to pay for the right to levy duties and excise and, at the same time, encouraged urban development in an intensive and mutually beneficial dialogue between local ruling elites and the monarchy.

The case of the city of L'Aquila is even more interesting, because it attests the difficult relationships between a municipality and its territorial district, which included small villages and communities. For instance, in 1476 the city town council decided to distribute the royal demands through assessments on properties. However, because of the frequent pressures and protests by those sections of the local society who felt damaged – in particular, those people living in the rural area (*contado*) surrounding L'Aquila – the fiscal policy was subject to continuous modifications, in particular with reference to the number of taxable hearths.[43]

More broadly, the strategy of transferring a significant part of the tax burden on those who lived in the *contadi*, outside the city walls was common among several southern Italian urban centers, such as Capua, Lecce, and Sessa Aurunca. In practice, the urban fiscal policies also resulted from the continuous negotiation between municipalities and their rural areas, which aimed to preserve their old fiscal customs. In turn, this ongoing bargaining process – similarly to the Angevin age – influenced the interventionist fiscal policy of the Aragonese.

Taxation in Catalan-Aragonese Sicily

From the prevalence of indirect taxation to the donativum

Unlike the southern mainland, Sicily had been within the sphere of influence of the Crown of Aragon since the late thirteenth century, when the island rebelled against Charles I of Anjou in 1282 and offered the Crown to Peter III of Aragon (1276–1285). Although during the Angevin age (1266–1282) Sicily had massively contributed to various *regie subventiones*, supplying the *Regnum Sicilie* with roughly one-fourth of its entire income, Charles I did not have enough time to exercise any significant influence over Sicily's fiscal policy, which was further developed only during the following Aragonese age. Firstly, King Peter III ideologically used taxation as a tool to strengthen his own position, with the explicit purpose of freeing his new subjects from the Angevin fiscal oppression. Second, by referring to previous legislation, his successor James I of Sicily (1285–1295) decreed that the general subsidy or *colletta*★ could only be raised on four circumstances: collecting up to 15,000 *onze* in case of defensive war or internal rebellion, and of ramson of the king or of his heirs; and no more than 5,000 *onze* for the knighting of the sovereign or his brothers and heirs, as well as for the marriage of the king's sister, daughters, and heirs. For example, in 1285–1286 the admiral Roger of Lauria raised 11,506 *onze* on behalf of the monarch with the specific purpose of equipping the royal fleet and facing the Angevin menace.[44]

However, Sicilian monarchs only occasionally relied on the incomes from direct taxation – e.g. the *colletta*★ only raised in the Val di Noto for equipping the fleet (1322)[45] – even when the island became independent under Frederick III of Sicily (1296–1337) and led an expensive defensive war against the Angevin. On the one hand, the Crown relied on the revenues from various feudal levies such as the above-mentioned *adoa*★.[46] On the other – more importantly – they received substantial profits thanks to the excise income (*gabelle*★ or *cassie*) from royal demesne, mostly customs duties and tolls on production and consumption of various products (e.g. meat, silk, wood, etc.).[47]

In each demesne town, a *vicesecrezia* farmed out the relevant fiscal revenues to private individuals in exchange for immediate and higher profits; more rarely, they resorted to direct management of tolls (*in credencia*). The revenues, net of expenses, were later transferred to a central officer known as *magister secretus*, who managed various incomes, among which also the taxes levied on Jews, such as the *gisia*. Probably established under the Islamic rule (from the Ninth to the Eleventh century) the *gisia* originally was a poll tax, later evolving into a collective tax to be paid by the Jewish community of each *universitas* of the realm. The sum each hearth was required to pay amounted to 3 *tarì* during the fourteenth century and to an import between 1.10 and 2 *tarì* during the following century.[48]

To increase his income, Frederick III reformed the already existing *gabelle*★ and introduced new tolls. The book of the new *gabelle*★ of Palermo (1312) is exemplary of this process. It lists seventeen tolls, regulating different goods and services, such as the all-embracing *cabella dohane maris*, which obliged all the foreigners who exported goods by sea to pay a toll of 3 per cent of their value – but no tax was paid on gold and other luxury articles. The same 3 per cent rate was due for those goods merchants exported by sea from Palermo, but for the Catalan and the Genoese traders, who only paid a toll of 1 per cent. Other *gabelle*★ concerned specific products, such as those on livestock (*cabella platee someriorum*) or on potteries (*cabella figulorum*). In 1320, with the specific purpose of waging war against the Angevin, the Crown introduced a special 3 per cent toll over imports and exports (*cassia propter guerram*) in several Sicilian municipalities.[49]

The incomes of Sicilian monarchs constantly decreased during 1300, because of the substantial alienations of the demesne's resources, and of demographic decline, which also damaged exports. Whereas in 1278–1279 the Palermo's tolls generated about 6,300 *onze* a year, between 1326 and 1328 their profits ranged from 4,700 to 5,700 *onze*. However, if the indirect taxation's revenues significantly reduced, those from direct taxation did not do better. Although Sicilian monarchs increased the hearth tax to 3.15 *tarì*, due to demographic decline, the *collette*★ made less income than in the past. For instance, the town of Terranova provided the Crown with 400 *onze* in 1277 and 340 *onze* in 1337–1338.[50]

In search of revenues to supplement the losses of both direct and indirect taxation, monarchs increasingly relied on the profits from grain exports (*ius exiturae*★), which Henri Bresc vividly described as a "fiscalité parallèle". Those incomes resulted from the sale of licenses for exporting grain (*tratte*★): a duty of one *tratta*★ for a *salma* of wheat, and half *tratta*★ for the same quantity of barley and legumes. Although those revenues significantly changed from year to year, depending on the amount of exports and on the cost of *tratte*★ – at that time, between 3 and 4 *tarì*[51] – they were fundamental for Sicilian finances, as they provided the Crown with about 10,000 *onze* per year.[52]

Starting with the 1330s, Sicily experienced a devastating civil war between baronial factions, which lasted until 1362, with its sovereigns in the role of passive spectators of the massive occupation of the royal demesne and its resources by aristocracy. Royal incomes thus further collapsed, to the extent that the Palermo's *gabelle*★ were farmed out for just 1,800 *onze* in 1375–1376 and 1,700 *onze* in 1376–1377[53] – roughly one third of the previous profits. The situation was even worse with reference to direct taxation, to the extent that it is uncertain if the Crown actually enjoyed the meagre revenues of *collette*★. For instance, the *magister iusticiarius* Blasco II Alagona – as stressed in his own will – administered in person the royal subsidies for waging war against the Crown's rebels, who unsurprisingly were the leading families (Chiaromonte and Palizzi) of the rival baronial faction.[54]

The economic problems of Sicily persisted after the restoration of royal authority in 1392, when Martin I (1392–1409), nephew of the John I of Aragon (1387–1396), took the throne. Because of the severe opposition he faced, the new sovereign was forced to raise *collette*★ almost every year, both for funding his invading army, and for obtaining support from the local ruling classes, which enjoyed parts of those incomes. For instance, in 1392 King Martin I granted Francesco Guerra Ventimiglia with 150 *onze* to be paid from the incomes of the *colletta*★ raised in Alcamo, Gibellina, Partanna, and Vicari.[55] Sicilian monarchs even used the indirect taxation's profits to fund direct taxation, also establishing ad hoc *gabelle*★ – as they did in Catania and Randazzo – and taxes (e.g. a 5 per cent tax over harvests).

The fiscal pressure over the realm only decreased after King Martin I crushed rebels and secured his power. On occasion of the Syracuse parliament (1398), he reduced the hearth tax to 3 *tarì* and abolished all the grants to be paid on the incomes of *collette*★ and *tratte*★ (i.e., licenses for exporting grain and legumes). In 1402, the monarch even confirmed that the subsidies could only be raised on the four above-mentioned circumstances, as established by his predecessors. Although Martin I did not strictly follow those limitations – *collette*★ were raised in 1401–1402, 1402–1403, 1404, 1406, and 1407 – the direct taxation's load remained moderate. For instance, the subsidy of 1404 only aimed to collect 2,400 *onze* for building 12 galleys against piracy. Rather than relying on the incomes from direct taxes, the Crown was strategically exploiting the substantial profits from indirect taxation. On the one hand, thanks to the reacquisition of the royal demesne, the *vicesecrezie* and the newly independent *secrezie* of Catania, Messina, and Palermo had notably increased their incomes (e.g. between 1400 and 1409, Palermo raised an average of 3278.½ *onze*). On the other hand, after stopping the massive concession of free *tratte*★ in favour of royal supporters, the revenues from grain exports had constantly grown, to the extent that in 1407–1408 the Crown received an amount of 11,696.½ *onze*.[56]

Following the sudden death of King Martin (1409) and of his homonym father and heir (1410), Sicily experienced a new civil war (1410–1412), which led to the collapse of its fiscal system and occupation of royal lands and resources. The new monarch Ferdinand I of Trastámara (1412–1416) promoted the reconstruction of the realm's financial base, encouraging retrieval of royal demesne, and launching several inquiries over the management of its resources, whether they concerned the *secrezie* or grain exports. This strategy resulted in the initial grow of incomes from indirect taxation. However, in the following years these incomes again reduced due to stagnation of the grain exports and to the several demesne alienations – also including entire *universitates* – through which Alfonso the Magnanimous was waging war in the southern mainland. Between 1437 and 1442, whereas the ordinary revenues from indirect taxation only represented about 15 per cent of the treasury's income – the *magister secretus'* incomes were almost entirely pawned – those from direct taxation (16,090 *onze*) were roughly 20 per cent.[57] Indeed, although the *collette*★ were raised almost annually from the mid-1430s onwards, their load was not excessive compared with the other components of the Crown of Aragon, for Alfonso enjoyed substantial profits from alienation of Sicilian demesne and its resources (e.g. in 1440–1441, 10,600 *onze*, i.e. 58 per cent of the treasury's incomes).[58]

The growing importance of direct taxation went *pari passu* with its development. From an occasional contribution, it became regular taxation, resulting from a bargaining process between the Crown and the Sicilian parliament.[59] In practice, the latter granted Aragonese monarchs an agreed amount of money known as *donativum*★ (donation) – to be collected in annual instalments (*tande*) – in return for approval of their demands. For example, in 1446 and 1452 Alfonso the Magnanimous received two donations of 150,000 and 300,000 florins of Aragon, respectively to be paid in 6 and 12 years, with the specific purpose of recovering alienations of Sicilian demesne.[60] But for few exceptions, his successors could autonomously determine how to use those revenues. For instance, Ferdinand II of Aragon (1479–1516) used the donations' revenues – from 100,000 florins (1488) to 300,000 florins (1502) for a three-year period – for waging war in the Iberian Peninsula and Italy. Thanks to the *donativum*★ – extraordinary donations could be raised, if needed – direct taxation therefore became a regular income on which Aragonese monarchs could rely on for allocating their growing expenses, in addition to the usual incomes from the *secrezie* and grain exports (roughly 100,000 *salme* a year since the 1470s).[61]

According to the fully standardized procedure of 1506, the ecclesiastical parliamentary estate paid one fifth of the donation, and the aristocratic and the demesnial branches two fifths each one. The representatives (*deputati*) of each estate agreed upon the amounts due by each ecclesiastical institution, as well as demesnial and feudal urban centers, which in turn paid according to their population and properties: respectively, a hearth tax of 2,45 and 1,88 *tarì*. Finally, various tax collectors travelled across the island to raise revenues which, through a network of bankers, were later transferred to the royal treasury of the Kingdom of Sicily.[62]

The emergence of urban taxation

Rather than depending on direct taxation, Sicilian monarchs mostly relied on the incomes from indirect taxes levied in the royal demesne, which included the main urban centers of the island (i.e. Catania, Messina, and Palermo). Thanks to the revenues generated by the *gabelle*'s★ profits, the island's urban network massively contributed to the general income of the kingdom. Sicilian municipalities de facto funded the military and administrative system of the island, significantly contributing to various other payments (for instance, salaries and grants). Not by chance, Sicilian *universitates* played a key role in the development of the island's taxation since the establishment of the Aragonese rule, crucially influencing the mechanisms of fiscal policy at the urban level and in particular the management of the royal *gabelle*★. The various town councils periodically submitted the list of their *gabelle*★ and relevant regulation to the monarch, who examined and later approved them in the form of a privilege. The *gabelle*★ thus resulted from negotiation between the Crown and their subjects and were regularly reformed according to the changing political and economic circumstances. For instance, the above mentioned new *gabelle*★ of Palermo (1312) replaced the previous list of *gabelle*★, which in turn were later modified on several occasions.[63] The update of royal *gabelle*★ became even more frequent during the fifteenth century, when Alfonso the Magnanimous used them as a tool of patronage, namely granting their management to and distributing their incomes among local aristocracy and urban elites in exchange for political and militarily support.

Alongside the *gabelle** administered by royal officers such as *secreti* and *vicesecreti*, the *universitates* autonomously managed and farmed out various municipal *gabelle** – albeit the monarch's approval was mandatory – through which they funded their own administrations at least since the early fourteenth century. For example, in 1319 Frederick III granted the *universitas* of Palermo three *gabelle** or *cassie* on carbon, slaves, and handmaids, which served the purpose of raising money for paying the salaries of the city's bailiff and judges. In 1423 and in 1433, the *universitas* of Palermo farmed out the *gabella buchirie* (i.e., on butchery) in order to raise the incomes needed for repairing the city walls.[64]

The growing fiscal autonomy of which Sicilian urban centers enjoyed during the later middle ages seems even more evident if we look at direct taxation. As thoroughly discussed by Fabrizio Titone, the *universitates* could independently establish how to raise the amounts due on occasion of *collette** and later of parliamentary donations. In short, for raising the incomes needed, town councils preferred to farm out the *gabelle** of the forthcoming years in advance, or to adopt ad hoc excise taxes on essential needs (e.g., on foodstuff), such as the infamous *maldinaru*, which in turn could be farmed out, as it happened in Nicosia (1374) and in Catania (1454). Through following this strategy, political ruling elites – who de facto represented the wealthiest members of urban society – levied indirect taxes on goods to the entire community, regardless the income of citizens. More rarely, town councils agreed to raise incomes via direct taxation, which was based on various criteria of proportionality, as it happened, for instance, in Sciacca in 1437, and in Palermo in 1442. However, current research does not allow us to clearly understand the methods through which town councils assessed the wealth and assets of their citizens.[65]

Conclusion

Through analysing taxation in the kingdoms of Sicily *citra* and *ultra farum*, this chapter has shown that the emergence and subsequent transformations of the fiscal systems of those two realms followed various complex developments. Despite originating from the common administrative apparatus of the Norman-Swabian *Regnum Sicilie*, the two kingdoms of Sicily established different fiscal structures and methods of money collection which reflected their distinct economic, political, and social backgrounds. At the same time, however, those two countries followed similar patterns of fiscal change, which started with the long-term and expensive war following the Sicilian Vespers. The latter, in both Southern Italy and Sicily, is to be considered as the spark that triggered the development of more organized financial structures, and led to the emergence of a network of officers entrusted with fiscal matters both at the center and in the localities. However, as discussed above, direct taxation remained for long time an extraordinary income on which the sovereigns could theoretically rely only within the limits established by legislation. If it is true that both Southern Italian and the Sicilian monarchs often circumvented those restrictions and raised *subventiones** almost annually, it is also true that they often received meagre revenues from those money collections, in particular because of the fourteenth-century political instability and of the demographic decline which affected both those countries.

Indeed, the age of Alfonso the Magnanimous marked a turning point for the fiscal development of the two kingdoms of Sicily. After becoming constituent components of the Crown of Aragon, both these policies introduced regular systems of direct taxation, which resulted from agreements between the monarchs and local parliaments. Following the parliamentary model of the Iberian territories of the Catalan-Aragonese union, in both the Italian realms the fiscal policy became a critical terrain of negotiation at the highest level of the political spectrum.[66]

In turn, the fifteenth-century fiscal transformation had a significant impact on the relationships between the Crown and their Southern Italian and Sicilian municipalities, for the urban network substantially contributed to royal incomes in both the kingdoms of Sicily. Urban ruling classes thus acquired a growing role in both the political and the financial spheres, crucially influencing the distribution of the tax burden among the *universitates* and the administration of the *datia*, as well as autonomously shaping – more or less relying on royal support – their own fiscal systems. As discussed above, many heated debates occurred in the town councils between the various urban social classes and interests groups, in order to establish the criteria of distribution of the fiscal load at the urban level: namely, if relying on the incomes from indirect taxation or on taxes on the basis of wealth. In this regard, the Southern Italian municipalities also experienced the standardization of the procedures aimed at assessing the wealth and assets of citizens – a theme that still needs to be explored with reference to Sicilian *universitates*.

Within this common pathway towards the establishment of direct taxation on a regular basis, the two kingdoms of Sicily were marked by significant differences in terms of fiscal structure of their overall incomes, though the lack of records does not allow us to analyse in details the matter during the thirteenth and fourteenth century. The rulers of Southern Italy had traditionally relied on the revenues from the various forms of direct taxation, whether they raised taxes through *subventiones generales*★ and *collette*★ – as they did during the Norman-Swabian and later Angevin age – or through the *focatico*★ during the fifteenth century. In this regard, Mario Del Treppo suggested that, in Naples, the Aragonese received 69 per cent of their revenues from direct taxes.[67] On the contrary, Sicilian monarchs received the most part of their revenues from the royal demesne, thanks to the excise income from the *secrezie* and to the profits from the *tratte*★ and grain trade. As discussed by Stephen Epstein with a focus on the fifteenth century, the different fiscal structure of those two realms originated from two intertwined reasons: on the one hand, the amount of population living in the demesne of the southern mainland and Sicily – respectively, 20 per cent and 50 per cent – and on the other, the fact that the island possessed the largest demesne compared to the southern mainland.

At the same time, it should be noted, the two kingdoms of Sicily followed different policies in the management of the grain trade, and in administering the fiscal rights from the *ius exiture*★ and from the sale of the *tratte*★, which variously contributed to their incomes. The strategies the monarchs applied over the centuries adapted to external and internal factors, such as the levels of grain production and demand, demographic trends, as well as the various political relationships with other polities. If one looks at Sicily after the Vespers, for instance, the monarchs lowered the cost of the grain *tratte*★ to preserve "their existing share of the foreign markets", and to receive constant revenues from customs duties. This development attracted new commercial partners, such as Pisa and Venice, for replacing those – such as Genoa and Florence, or even Southern Italy – with whom trade had been banned.[68] The variability of grain prices also affected the Angevin Kingdom of Sicily where, after 1282, Apulia replaced Sicily as the largest grain producer of the southern mainland. Here, the prices of wheat and barley did not only respond to variations in agricultural productivity, but also to changes in internal demand.[69] Given the importance of grain trade in both Southern Italy and Sicily, its revenues were an important but unpredictable source of fiscal income, which could significantly change from time to time.

Through following different fiscal strategies and relying on variously structured sources of income, in the course of the fifteenth century both Southern Italy and Sicily established systems of direct taxation on regular basis. Nevertheless, the Aragonese sovereigns did not fully dismiss the previous extraordinary procedures for raising incomes, or reject other various methods for collecting revenues (e.g. demesne alienations or "compulsory loans"), thus still exploiting their monarchical prerogatives and rights on all those circumstances in which they urgently needed monies – for instance, for waging war in Italy and in the Mediterranean. Although the two kingdoms of Sicily were experiencing their own development towards the emergence of the fiscal state, they were indeed in a phase of transition, during which the Crown could rely on a various set of tools and methods to raise incomes, which were typical of both the "domain" and the "tax" state.[70]

Notes

[*] Serena Morelli authored pp. 158–167, and Alessandro Silvestri pp. 167–171. The authors jointly wrote the Introduction and the Conclusion. Note that in both the kingdoms of Sicily, the basic unit of currency was the golden *onza*, which was actually never coined. However, smaller coins such as the *tarì* and the *grani* circulated. Therefore, one *onza* represented 30 *tarì*, and 1 *tarì* was equivalent to 20 *grani*.

1. See respectively BIANCHINI, *Della storia delle finanze* and DI MARTINO, *Il sistema tributario*.
2. AMARI, *La guerra del vespro siciliano*, vol. 2, ch. 4.
3. TRASSELLI, "Sul debito pubblico in Sicilia", pp. 71–112.
4. DEL TREPPO, *I mercanti catalani*.
5. See respectively ABULAFIA, *The Two Italies*; BRESC, *Un monde méditerranéen*; EPSTEIN, *An Island for Itself*; SAKELLARIOU, *Southern Italy in the Late Middle Ages*.
6. See, for instance, TERENZI, *L'Aquila nel regno*, ch. 4, § 1; AIRÒ, "Et signanter omne cabella", pp. 165–214; TITONE, *Governments of the Universitates*, ch. 4.
7. CAROCCI, *Signorie di Mezzogiorno*, ch. 10.
8. See for instance: TOOMASPOEG *Decimae Il sostegno economico* and MOSCONE, "L'ufficio della Collettoria di Sicilia", vol. 1, pp. 323–351.
9. MATTHEW, *The Norman Kingdom of Sicily*, ch. VIII.
10. On the origins and development of the Norman administration and on the dohana de secretis in particular, see TAKAYAMA, *The Administration of the Norman Kingdom of Sicily*, as well as bibliography therein mentioned, as well as MARTIN, "L'organisation administrative et militaire du territoire", pp. 71–121.
11. JAMISON, *Catalogus baronum*; as well as JAMISON, "The Administration of the County of Molise", pp. 1–34.
12. CAROCCI, *Signorie di Mezzogiorno*, pp. 182, on the meaning of auditorium, see *ibidem*, p. 421.
13. BARILE, "«Isti hodie sunt secreti»", pp. 113–138.
14. MARTIN, "Monopolii", *sub voce*; and MARTIN, "Le città demaniali", pp. 179–195.
15. POWELL, "Medieval Monarchy and Trade", pp. 420–524.
16. ABULAFIA, *Frederick II. A medieval emperor*, p. 333.
17. PETRALIA, "Ancora sulla 'politica economica'", pp. 207–227.
18. PERCY, *The revenues of the Kingdom of Sicily*, p. 2, and p. 247.
19. PERCY, *The revenues of the Kingdom of Sicily*, pp. 41–87, pp. 261–264 and pp. 265–268; CAGGESE, *Roberto d'Angiò*, p. 613.
20. MORELLI, "Note sulla fiscalità diretta", vol. 1, pp. 389–413: pp. 399–400.
21. TRIFONE, *La legislazione angioina*, pp. 50–58; TRIFONE, *Les registres d'Honorius IV*, docs. pp. 96–98.
22. PERCY, *The revenues of the Kingdom of Sicily*, pp. 195–202, 262–264; MOSCATI, "Ricerche e documenti sulla feudalità", pp. 1–15.
23. On taxation, see: YVER, *Le commerce et les marchands*, pp. 45–49; about officers, see instead: CADIER, *Essai sur l'administration*, pp. 23–34.
24. MARTIN, "Fiscalité et économie étatique", p. 613.
25. CAGGESE, *Roberto d'Angiò*, vol. 1, p. 625; the amounts collected by secreti and portolani during Charles'reign: PERCY, *The revenues of the Kingdom of Sicily*, pp. 155–171.
26. YVER, *Le commerce et les marchands*, p. 115. For more estimates, see PERCY, *The revenues of the Kingdom of Sicily*, pp. 147–154.
27. LEONARD, *Histoire de Jeanne Ire*, vol. 1, p. 56 s.
28. DELLE DONNE, *Burocrazia e fisco a Napoli*.
29. MORELLI, *Razionalità all'opera*.
30. DEL TREPPO, "Il regno aragonese", p. 113.
31. Concerning the role of the Neapolitan parliament: Pietro GENTILE, "Finanze e parlamenti nel regno di Napoli", pp. 185–231; RYDER, *The Kingdom of Naples*, pp. 214–215.

32 Dalena, *Passi porti e dogane*.
33 Marino, *Pastoral Economics*; Del Treppo, "Il regno aragonese", pp. 116–127.
34 Sakellariou, *Southern Italy*, pp. 142–143, pp. 165–176, and pp. 459–470, including the list of toll franchises granted by the monarchs.
35 Del Treppo, "Il regno aragonese", pp. 119–121.
36 Caggese, *Roberto d'Angiò*, pp. 398–405, as well as Camera, *Memorie storico diplomatiche*, vol. 1, p. 458.
37 Magrone, *Libro Rosso*, doc. 19, pp. 114–116, and doc. 21, pp. 119–121.
38 Morelli, *Razionalità all'opera*, pp. 102–106.
39 Galasso, *Il regno di Napoli*, pp. 407–455; Bulgarelli, "I beni comuni ", pp. 119–138.
40 Caravale, "La legislazione statutaria", pp. 167–200.
41 Faraglia, *Codice diplomatico sulmonese*, doc. CXXXI, pp. 162–165; Caggese, *Roberto d'Angiò*, p. 404.
42 Airò, "Et signanter omne cabella", pp. 191–203.
43 De Matteis, *L'Aquila e il contado*; Terenzi, *L'Aquila nel Regno*, pp. 357, 368–376, 453–461.
44 On the estimate of hearth tax, see Marrone, "Sovvenzioni regie, riveli, demografia", pp. 27–29.
45 Di Martino, *Il sistema tributario*, p. 26, note 1. The subsidies received by the Sicilian monarchs between 1282 and 1392 are listed in in Bresc, *Un monde méditerranéen*, vol. 2, p. 795.
46 Epstein, *An Island for Itself*, p. 376. Other feudal levies included the *ius relevi* and the *ius decime et tareni*, i.e. taxes respectively due on occasion of inheritance of fiefs and of feudal transactions.
47 For an overview on the use and development of the term of gabella in medieval Italy, see Mainoni, "Gabelle. Percorsi di lessici fiscali", pp. 45–75.
48 On the Jews' fiscal contribution, see Bresc, *Arabi per lingua*, ch. 4, and Simonsohn, *The Jews in Sicily*, vol. 18, ch. 4.
49 Peri, *La Sicilia dopo il Vespro*, pp. 103–104.
50 Bresc, *Un monde méditerranéen*, vol. 2, pp. 794–796, and Epstein, *An island for Itself*, pp. 376–377.
51 Cancila, "I dazi sull'esportazione", pp. 409–443.
52 Bresc, *Un monde méditerranéen*, vol. 2, p. 796, and Epstein, *An Island for Itself*, pp. 377–378.
53 Sardina, *Palermo e i Chiaromonte*, p. 259.
54 Giuffrida, *Il cartulario della famiglia Alagona*, doc. XXVIII (21.10.1355), p. 48.
55 Marrone, "Sovvenzioni regie, riveli, demografia", p. 45, note 61.
56 Bresc, *Un monde méditerranéen*, vol. 2, pp. 841–843, and pp. 850–853.
57 Silvestri, *L'amministrazione del regno di Sicilia*, pp. 271–286.
58 Silvestri, *L'amministrazione del regno di Sicilia*, p. 280, and Epstein, *An Island for Itself*, p. 381.
59 Pasciuta, *'Placet Regie Maiestati'*.
60 Bresc, *Un monde méditerranéen*, pp. 853–854.
61 Ligresti, "Parlamento e donativi in Sicilia", pp. 437–459, and Giuffrida, *La finanza pubblica*, ch. 5 and 6.
62 Cancila, *Fisco, ricchezza, comunità*, pp. 240–246.
63 Dentici (ed.), *Fisco e società nella Sicilia aragonese*, ch. 1.
64 De Vio (ed.), *Felicis et fidelissime urbis panormitanae*, pp. 78–79.
65 Titone, *Governments of the Universitates*, ch. 4.
66 Küchler, *Les finances de la Corona d'Aragó*, ch. 3.
67 Del Treppo, "Il regno aragonese", p. 117.
68 Epstein, *An Island for Itself*, pp. 384–386, and pp. 271–272.
69 Percy, *The revenues of the Kingdom of Sicily*, pp. 147–154; Yver, *Le commerce et les marchands*, pp. 97–126.
70 On the concept of "domain state" and "tax state", see Ormrod, Bonney and Bonney, *Crises, Revolutions and Self-sustained Growth*. On Southern Italy, see Bulgarelli, "Domain state e tax state", pp. 781–813.

References

David Abulafia, *The Two Italies: Economic Relations between the Norman Kingdom of Sicily and the Northern Communes*, Cambridge, 1977.
David Abulafia, *Frederick II. A medieval emperor*, New York-Oxford, 1988.
Anna Airò, "Et signanter omne cabella et dacii sono dela detta università. Istituzioni, ambiente, politiche fiscali di una 'località centrale': Manfredonia nel sistema territoriale di Capitanata tra XIII e XVI secolo", in *Storia di Manfredonia*, vol. 1, *Il Medioevo*, ed. Raffaele Licinio, Bari, 2008, pp. 165–214.

Michele AMARI, *La guerra del vespro siciliano, o Un periodo delle istorie siciliane del sec. XIII*, Paris, 1843.
Nicola BARILE, "«Isti hodie sunt secreti»: la duana de secretis fra tradizione sveva e continuità angioina", in *Periferie finanziarie angioine. Istituzioni e pratiche di governo su territori compositi (sec. XIII-XV)*, ed. Serena MORELLI, Rome, 2017, p 113–138.
Henri BRESC, *Un monde méditerranéen: économie et société en Sicile 1300–1450*, Rome, 1986.
Henri BRESC, *Arabi per lingua, Ebrei per religione. L'evoluzione dell'ebraismo siciliano in ambiente latino dal XII al XV secolo*, Messina, 2001.
Antonino GIUFFRIDA (ed.), *Il cartulario della famiglia Alagona di Sicilia. Documenti 1337–1387*, Palermo-São Paulo, 1978.
Ludovico BIANCHINI, *Della storia delle finanze del regno di Napoli*, Naples, 1859.
Alessandra BULGARELLI LUKACS, "*Domain state* e *tax state* nel regno di Napoli (secoli XII–XIX)", in *Società e Storia*, 106, 2004, pp. 781–813.
Alessandra BULGARELLI LUKACS, "I beni comuni nell'Italia meridionale: le istituzioni per il loro management", in *Glocale. Rivista molisana di storia e scienze sociali*, 9–10, 2015, pp. 119–138.
Léon CADIER, *Essai sur l'administration du royaume de Sicile sous Charles Ier et Charles II d'Anjou*, Paris, 1891, pp. 23–34.
Romolo CAGGESE, *Roberto d'Angiò e suoi tempi*, Florence, 1921 (anastatic reprint, Bologna, 2001).
Matteo CAMERA, *Memorie storico diplomatiche dell'antica città e ducato di Amalfi*, Salerno, 1876.
Orazio CANCILA, "I dazi sull'esportazione dei cereali e il commercio dei grani nel regno di Sicilia", in *Nuovi quaderni del Meridione*, 28 (1969), pp. 409–443.
Rossella CANCILA, *Fisco, ricchezza, comunità nella Sicilia del Cinquecento*, Rome, 2001.
Sandro CAROCCI, *Signorie di Mezzogiorno. Società rurali, poteri aristocratici e monarchia (XII-XIII secolo)*, Rome, 2014.
Romolo CAGGESE, *Roberto d'Angiò e suoi tempi*, Florence, 1921 (anastatic reprint, Bologna, 2001).
Mario CARAVALE, "La legislazione statutaria dell'Italia meridionale e della Sicilia", in Mario CARAVALE, *La monarchia meridionale. Istituzioni e dottrina giuridica dai Normanni ai Borboni*, Roma-Bari 1988, pp. 167–200.
Pietro DALENA, *Passi porti e dogane marittime dagli angioini agli aragonesi. Le* Lictere passus *(1458–1469)*, Bari, 2007.
Roberto DELLE DONNE, *Burocrazia e fisco a Napoli tra XV e XVI secolo. La Camera della Sommaria e il* Repertorium alphabeticum solutionum fiscalium regni Siciliae Cisfretanae, Florence, 2012.
Angiola DE MATTEIS, *L'Aquila e il contado. Demografia e fiscalità secoli XV-XVIII*, Naples, 1973.
Mario DEL TREPPO, *I mercanti catalani e l'espansione della Corona d'Aragona nel secolo XV*, Naples, 1972 (or. edn. 1968).
Mario DEL TREPPO, "Il regno aragonese", in *Storia del Mezzogiorno*, vol. 4, Rome, 1986, pp. 89–201.
Rosa Maria DENTICI BUCCELLATO (ed.), *Fisco e società nella Sicilia aragonese: le pandette delle gabelle regie del XIV secolo*, Palermo, 1983.
Michaelis DE VIO (ed.), *Felicis et fidelissime urbis panormitanae selecta aliquot privilegia*, Palermo, 1706.
Giuseppe DI MARTINO, *Il sistema tributario degli aragonesi in Sicilia*, Palermo, 1990 (or. edn. 1938–39).
Stephan R. EPSTEIN, *An Island for Itself: Economic Development and Social Change in Late Medieval Sicily*, Cambridge, 1992.
Nunzio F. FARAGLIA, *Codice diplomatico sulmonese*, Lanciano, 1888.
Giuseppe GALASSO, *Il regno di Napoli. Il Mezzogiorno angioino e aragonese (1266–1494)*, Torino, 1992.
Pietro GENTILE, "Finanze e parlamenti nel regno di Napoli dal 1450 al 1457", in *Archivio storico per le provincie napoletane*, 38, 1913, pp. 185–231.
Antonino GIUFFRIDA, *La finanza pubblica nella Sicilia del '500*, Caltanissetta-Rome, 1999.
Evelyn M. JAMISON, "The Administration of the County of Molise in the Twelfth and Thirteenth centuries", in *The English Historical Review*, 44, 1929, pp. 529–559, and 45, 1930, pp. 1–34.
Evelyn M. JAMISON (ed.), *Catalogus baronum*, Rome, 1972.
Winfried KÜCHLER, *Les finances de la Corona d'Aragó al segle XV (Regnats d'Alfons V i Joan II)*, Valencia, 1997 (or. edn. Münster, 1983).
Emile LEONARD, *Histoire de Jeanne Ire reine de Naples, comtesse de* Provence, Paris, 1932–1937.
Domenico LIGRESTI, "Parlamento e donativi in Sicilia nella prima metà del Cinquecento", in *Siculorum Gymnasium*, nuova serie, 50, 1997, pp. 437–459.
Domenico MAGRONE, *Libro Rosso. Privilegi dell'Università di Molfetta*, Trani, 1899.
Patrizia MAINONI, "Gabelle. Percorsi di lessici fiscali tra Regno di Sicilia e Italia comunale (secoli XII–XIII)", in *Signorie italiane e modelli monarchici (secoli XIII–XIV)*, ed. Paolo GRILLO, Rome, 2013, pp. 45–75.

John A. Marino, *Pastoral Economics in the Kingdom of Naples*, Baltimore-London, 1988.

Antonino Marrone, "Sovvenzioni regie, riveli, demografia in Sicilia dal 1277 al 1398", in *Mediterranea ricerche storiche*, 24, 2012, pp. 23–56.

Jean M. Martin, "L'organisation administrative et militaire du territoire", in *Potere, società e popolo nell'età sveva (1210–1266). Atti delle seste giornate normanno-sveve, Bari-Castel del Monte-Melfi, 17–20 ottobre 1983*, Bari, 1985, pp. 71–121.

Jean M. Martin, "Le città demaniali", in *Federico II e le città italiane*, ed. Pierre Toubert and Agostino Paravicini Bagliani, Palermo, 1994, pp. 179–195.

Jean M. Martin, "Fiscalité et économie ètatique dans le royaume angevin de Sicile à la fin du XIII siècle", in *L'État angevin. Pouvoir, culture et société entre XIII et XIV siècle*, Rome, 1998, pp. 601–648.

Jean M. Martin, "Monopolii", in *Enciclopedia federiciana*, Rome, 2005, sub voce.

Donald Matthew, *The Norman Kingdom of Sicily*, Cambridge, 1992.

Serena Morelli, *Razionalità all'opera. I bilanci della contea di Soleto nei domini del principe di Taranto Giovanni Antonio Orsini*, Naples, 2020.

Serena Morelli, "Note sulla fiscalità diretta e indiretta nel regno angioino", in *Territorio, culture e poteri nel Medioevo e oltre. Scritti in onore di Benedetto Vetere*, ed. Carmela Massaro and Luciana Petracca, Galatina, 2011, vol. 1, pp. 389–413.

Ruggero Moscati, "Ricerche e documenti sulla feudalità napoletana nel periodo angioino", in *Archivio storico per le province napoletane*, 61 (n.s. 22), 1936, pp. 1–15.

Marcello Moscone, "L'ufficio della Collettoria di Sicilia e la struttura istituzionale della chiesa palermitana. Da un inedito conto della decima della metà del Trecento", in *Dall'Archivio Segreto Vaticano. Miscellanea di testi, saggi e inventari*, Vatican City, 2006, vol. 1, pp. 323–351.

Mark Ormrod, Margaret Bonney and Richard Bonney (ed.), *Crises, Revolutions and Self-sustained Growth: Essays in European Fiscal History, 1130–1830*, Stamford, 1999.

Beatrice Pasciuta, *'Placet Regie Maiestati'. Itinerari nella normazione del tardo medioevo*, Turin, 2005.

William A. Percy, *The revenues of the Kingdom of Sicily under Charles of Anjou, 1266–1285, and their Relationship to the Vespers*, unpublished doctoral thesis, Princeton University, 1964.

Illuminato Peri, *La Sicilia dopo il Vespro: uomini, città e campagne, 1282–1376*, Rome-Bari, 1982.

Giuseppe Petralia, "Ancora sulla 'politica economica' di Federico II nel *Regnum Siciliae*", in *Dentro e fuori la Sicilia. Studi di storia per Vincenzo d'Alessandro*, ed. Pietro Corrao and Ennio Igor Mineo, Rome, 2009, pp. 207–227.

James M. Powell, "Medieval Monarchy and Trade. The Economic Policy of Frederick II in the Kingdom of Sicily (a Survey)", in *Studi Medievali*, s. 3, 3, 1962, pp. 420–524.

Alan Ryder, *The Kingdom of Naples under Alfonso the Magnanimous. The making of a modern state*, Oxford-New York, 1976.

Eleni Sakellariou, *Southern Italy in the Late Middle Ages: Demographic, Institutional and Economic Change in the Kingdom of Naples, c.1440–c.1530*, Leiden & Boston, 2012.

Patrizia Sardina, *Palermo e i Chiaromonte: splendore e tramonto di una signoria. Potere nobiliare, ceti dirigenti e società tra XIV e XV secolo*, Caltanissetta-Rome, 2003.

Alessandro Silvestri, *L'amministrazione del regno di Sicilia. Cancelleria, apparati finanziari e strumenti di governo nel tardo medioevo*, Rome, 2018.

Shlomo Simonsohn, *The Jews in Sicily*, vol. 18, *Under the rule of Aragon and Spain*, Leiden-Boston, 2010.

Hiroshi Takayama, *The Administration of the Norman Kingdom of Sicily*, Leiden-New York, 1993.

Pierluigi Terenzi, *L'Aquila nel regno. I rapporti politici fra città e monarchia nel Mezzogiorno tardomedievale respectively*, Bologna, 2015.

Fabrizio Titone, *Governments of the Universitates. Urban Communities of Sicily in the Fourteenth and Fifteenth Centuries*, Turnhout, 2009.

Kristjan Toomaspoeg (ed.), *Decimae Il sostegno economico dei sovrani alla Chiesa del Mezzogiorno nel XII secolo*, Rome, 2009.

Carmelo Trasselli, "Sul debito pubblico in Sicilia sotto Alfonso V d'Aragona", *Estudios de Historia Moderna*, 6, 1956, pp. 71–112.

Romualdo Trifone, *Les registres d'Honorius IV (1281–1285)*, Paris, 1901.

Romualdo Trifone, *La legislazione angioina*, Naples, 1921.

Jacques Yver, *Le commerce et les marchands dans l'Italie méridionale au XIIIe et au XIVe siècle*, New York, 1968, pp. 45–49.

8
NORTHERN ITALY
Cities and regional states

*Patrizia Mainoni**

Any summary of taxation in communal and post-communal Italy should begin by remarking on the geopolitical context that fostered this particular urban development. The north-central macro region of Italy, comprised of modern-day Piedmont, Liguria, Lombardy, Veneto, Emilia Romagna, Tuscany and Umbria, is characterized by great environmental diversity, from the mountains of the Alps and the Apennines to the Po Valley and the shores of the Tyrrhenian and Adriatic seas. The Italy of the age of Communes roughly corresponds to the Kingdom of the Lombards (north of Rome), which was conquered by Charlemagne and called *Regnum Ytalie*. In the early Middle Ages, the *civitates* (cities) were largely governed by their bishops, with or without imperial appointment. In Liguria, as in Tuscany and Veneto (except for Venice, which had developed later and more independently), Carolingian counts and marquises retained their authority. With the demographic and economic growth that took place after the year 1000, the government of bishops and counts was supported by urban elites who, at the end of the eleventh century, gradually started taking over the government of cities (called Communes) through their representatives (*consules*). Political arrangements in each *civitas* varied in terms of timeframes and characteristics, precisely because they developed independently from each other. The full autonomy of the Communes was facilitated by the absence of the Germanic emperors from Italy, especially at the beginning of the twelfth century. The situation changed towards the middle of the century when Frederick I was elected emperor. He wanted to bring the Communes under the control of the empire, specifically Milan, which was aggressive towards its neighbouring cities. By the end of the conflict, this internal political crisis had triggered the replacement of the *consules* with a foreign *podestà* from allied cities. The new war led by Frederick II, emperor and king of Sicily, which ended with the sovereign's death (1250), was very costly and caused later conflict between the Communes and between the *partes* (factions). This gave rise to the first appearance of the *signori*, who arose from urban society as guarantors of peace, representing the victory of their faction. During the first half of the fourteenth century, various *signori* (the Visconti, Della Scala, Gonzaga, Da Carrara, Este and so on) consolidated their power in Lombardy, in Emilia and in Veneto, while the Tuscan towns and Bologna remained republics. The Visconti of Milan and the commune of Florence extended their dominion over numerous towns, establishing the most extensive and lasting regional or multi-city *signorie*. Gian Galeazzo Visconti acquired a huge and disjointed set of lands, which was largely lost after his death (1402). The Italian political framework remained fragmented because there were areas such as Piedmont, where the Savoy dynasty left a lot of autonomy to small towns and to bigger communities such as Turin, Pinerolo, Chieri, as well as small states, consisting of one or two medium-sized towns, like the lordships of the Gonzaga of Mantua and the Este of Ferrara and Modena. Venice, on the other hand, started conquering its own large state between Veneto and Lombardy in 1402.[1]

Even in the most fortunate cases (Genoa, Venice, Siena, Florence, Bologna and very few other cities), what we know about taxation is dependent on the state of the surviving documentation. While city historians writing in the eighteenth and early nineteenth centuries paid attention to medieval tax issues because they could link them to institutions that were still in existence or of recent memory, these issues became less compelling after the unification of Italy. At the beginning of the twentieth century, the main focus of research on the history of economics and finance was on public finance in the communes of Genoa, Florence and Venice. These were studied particularly in order to clarify the origins of the permanent 'public debt,' which was considered the precursor of modern systems of public finance. At the end of the nineteenth century, Heinrich Sieveking, a German historian of the positivist school who was mainly interested in the history of commerce, collected extensive documentation on the finances of Genoa. His work, although somewhat outdated, is still a point of reference because, until recently, it was not followed by much subsequent research on Genoese taxation. On the other hand, Florence, with its impressive documentation and the economic and financial pre-eminence of its merchant companies, became the subject of a more up-to-date volume by Bernardino Barbadoro thirty years later. This work is still fundamental. Less attention was paid at the time to the other Tuscan city-states (Pisa, Siena and Lucca), while an eloquent study by Gino Luzzatto confirmed Venice as exceptional for its advanced financial organization.[2] Emphasis, however, was placed not so much on the systems of taxation as on the methods used to finance public spending through loans and interest-bearing and negotiable debt securities.

During the second half of the twentieth century, discussion focused on property surveys (*estimi* and *catasti*), which are among the richest tax records in terms of demographic, economic and social information due to the variety of data that they contain, although little attention was paid to tax systems themselves.[3] Analysis of financial and tax issues owes much to the contribution of a fierce group of Anglo-American and French scholars, including Bowsky (for Siena), de La Roncière (for Florence), Molho (for Florence's 'public debt'), Knapton and Mueller (for Venice).[4] The explosion of the amount of research on Tuscany, especially on Siena and Florence, resulted in a focus on these two cities, which came to be regarded as the general models for the financial systems of the Communes.

New interest in the formation of the regional states (during the fourteenth and fifteenth centuries) shifted the focus from the dominant cities to subject cities and lands, providing an opportunity to highlight how tax practices change perspective when viewed from the centre rather than from the Communes, which were then considered the periphery.[5] The fiscal history of the Venetian state was reconsidered based on the fifteenth-century relationship between Venice and the cities of the *Terraferma*.[6]

Today, the systems used in tax collection have become the way to understand the reasons behind decisions on tax policy. Contributions have multiplied, making it difficult to summarize the latest scholarship. Regions such as modern-day Piedmont, which up until recently had been overlooked in this respect, have been taken into account.[7] Drawing on the robust historiographical tradition of case studies of individual towns, recurring themes include the *estimo*, the property assessments used for direct taxation and for forced loans, and the gradual organization of the "public" debt, meaning the loans obtained by city governments through various means. For Tuscany, Maria Ginatempo compared the "Florentine model" with those of other Tuscan towns, highlighting the diverse financial and tax decisions made before direct tax on citizens was abandoned.[8]

The period prior to the mid-thirteenth century, which has been substantially neglected, is currently being re-evaluated through a re-reading of twelfth-century documents and legal sources, which bring tax practices to the forefront.[9] Scholars are paying more attention to the political climate of taxation between the thirteenth and fourteenth centuries, while the social mechanisms of taxation have proved useful for understanding the problems of the late communal age, as is particularly evident in the case of the *estimi*.[10] On the other hand, there is a lack of research on indirect taxation, merchant duties and *gabelle* on consumer goods, which has only partially been filled by specialized publications of primary sources and studies at the regional level.[11] Tax relations with the *contadi* (rural districts) have a well-established historiographical tradition due to their extensive political significance, but there is still work to be done in this area on the nature and management of local taxes. Taxation in the *signorie* also remains to be explored, especially concerning its relationship with the communal taxation eventually still in existence[12]

The construction of the communal tax system in the twelfth century

The tools used for taxation were undergoing full-scale evolution towards the mid-twelfth century, when city populations were increasing and communal institutions were developing. At that time, the Communes were a work in progress that did not have access to all possible income. Extraordinary *collecte*, *fodra* or *datia* and charges levied on the inhabitants of an area were already in existence, but provisions of money and services in the countryside (*onera rusticana*) often remained in the hands of lords or bishops. Even when supported by city governments, the bishop and the cathedral, the count or the marquis often continued to receive the revenue from tolls, *telonea*, *pedagia*, *ripatica*, market rights, and gate taxes★, all of which were rising dramatically due to commercial development.

The *fodrum*★, owed to the emperor when he travelled to Italy (in the tenth to twelfth centuries), was also collected by bishops through imperial licenses. It is not possible to assess the impact of the occasional royal *fodrum*★, which was paid in kind. In some cases, in the first half of the twelfth century, agreements were made with cities and small communities for monetary payment. The fact that a limit was set in these cases indicates that it was a possibility, especially between the eleventh and early twelfth centuries.[13] The system for collecting the *fodrum*★ had to be based on the *focatico* (the hearth), that is, by family (people living together in the broad sense). The actual method used to impose it is still very poorly documented. In an economically homogenous society in which the *milites* and the clergy were exempt (at least partially), there would not have been great disparities in the amount collected, especially in the countryside. In twelfth-century Arezzo, the imperial *fodrum*★ was collected at the rate of 26 *denarii* per hearth in the smaller towns and 12 *denarii* in cities. The Communes also demanded the *fodrum*★ (or *colletta*), especially from their subject villages. During the first half of the twelfth century, Bologna levied a fixed annual hearth tax on the *rustici* of its countryside, which was added to any extraordinary *collecta*★. At the beginning of the twelfth century, Milan asked its countryside for the *fodrum*★, grain supplies and carting services. The situation had to change with the growth of the twelfth and thirteenth centuries. During the thirteenth century the *focatico* was divided so as to no longer burden the poor to the same extent as the wealthy (e.g. the statutes of Pistoia).[14] There were also direct taxes on the countryside based on the ability to work (*iuvaticum*, *zappatici* and *bracciatici*), based on individual persons and on possession of oxen.

Around the middle of the twelfth century, a remarkable attempt was made to reinstate the tax practices and government rights that the Communes had gradually acquired as they took over from previous rulers (bishops and counts). The initial attack was launched by the bishops and immediately afterward by the emperor, Frederick I. The battlefield was the law, supported by canon law, which was in the process of being formed, and by analysis of Justinian's *Corpus Iuris*, which was at the basis of imperial sovereignty. It began by settling the theoretical underpinnings of the church tithe (*decima*) and, on the imperial side, by claiming those rights that, at the time, were considered *iura regalia*.[15] As far as church taxation was concerned, the nature of the *decima* was examined. It was a tax for maintaining churches and for poor relief, which also concerned the inhabitants of towns. Sara Menzinger has suggested that this tax, which was levied on agricultural products, may have provided the model that inspired the *estimi* of the communes. Canonists questioned whether the *decima* should be levied on landed property or on individuals; in some cases, the levy fell on both categories, such that merchant profit was included within the *decima*.[16]

For his part, Frederick Barbarossa argued that tax revenue, along with many other rights, like minting coins, belonged to the emperor. The emperor's involvement was based on explanations that imperial jurists had developed to justify the sovereign's demands (Roncaglia 1158). The content of the imperial *iura* was not completely clear. We have more writings on what was recognized as *regalia*, but the contemporary Genoese chronicler Caffaro placed the demand for market rights (that is, taxes on trade) at the top.[17] Once again, Sara Menzinger has proposed that the tax theories developed by jurists in support of Emperor Frederick I and the contemporary reflection on the nature and legality of taxes in canon law may have directly impacted the development of city tax practices due to the active role played by jurists in communal governments. Civil law, which was also being developed, adopted the positions taken by canon law in seeking to define the different types of levies. Frederick I also took a stand on the bishops' claims, especially after the truce of 1177, confirming and reconciling the *iura*. As a result, the bishops' dispute with the Communes was prolonged for decades. By the peace of Constance, which ended the war (1183), the emperor officially granted the Communes the rights that they were already exercising.

It was not until the thirteenth century that legal thought classified two broad categories of taxes, ordinary and extraordinary, which could, in turn, impact property, individuals, or both. The distinction between ordinary and extraordinary income is the only distinction used in medieval political/financial language. Ordinary income, characterized by its predictability, could be assessed in advance. This was much rarer in the case of extraordinary income. Ordinary income was primarily comprised of indirect taxes, but its boundary with extraordinary taxes, both incoming and outgoing, seems somewhat vague, except for judicial proceeds and direct urban taxes, which were part of the latter. The need to better define taxes, as well as their later conceptual organization, indicates the new importance of taxation in the early age of Communes.

The financial needs of a twelfth-century commune should have been rather limited. Wars were conducted by citizen armies, the *milites* fought with their own horses, and the impressive public works policies that characterized the thirteenth century had not yet begun. But this was not the case in the Communes that were engaged in aggressive external expansion, such as Pisa and Genoa. It was, however, the unpredictable and protracted war against Frederick I that tested the nascent financial capabilities of the Communes. The emperor's involvement in Italy thus acted as a catalyst for the process of forming tax structures, forcing cities to deal with the reality of unexpected and heavy expenses. The severity of the levy imposed by the imperial *podestà* on the Communes defeated during the first phase of the war (1158–1177), the payment of a *subsidium* to the emperor by his allied cities, the cost of ambassadors between the Communes and for the peace of Constance, the taxes paid to Frederick I and to his successor Henry VI, produced a real upheaval in tax practices. City rulers had to take out loans with the wealthiest citizens, often making personal pledges with regard to them, and resort to extraordinary direct taxation. The coexistence of these two systems characterizes communal finance everywhere.[18] Between the mid-twelfth century and the beginning of the thirteenth century, surveys of the assets on which taxes were regularly paid were carried out in Pavia, Verona, Piacenza and Genoa. This demonstrates that there was no written document concerning duties and direct taxes in cities and in the countryside, for example the *curaria* (market duty), *collecta*★ or *colta*, *fodrum, iugaticum/boateria, albergaria* (the lord's right to hospitality), etc.

Various Communes were able to assess their citizens' assets for financial and tax purposes. In 1162, Pisa required its inhabitants, both male and female, to declare all of their property, moveable and immovable, in writing and under oath. It was then assessed through a fairly complex procedure.[19] Similar surveys took place in Genoa in 1165 and in 1167 to levy a *collecta*★ on property.[20] Whether the aim was to require a direct tax, as is certain for Genoa, or a forced loan, as in Pisa, is irrelevant, because both cases show how the idea of appraising property for the purposes of financial demands was anything but unusual at the time. The *libra* or *estimum*★ appeared in Siena and Lucca in the following two decades, and in Florence and Venice in the early thirteenth century. It is not a matter of dating the 'introduction' of the *estimo* precisely. The earliest mentions of it, however, coincide with Emperor Frederick I's presence in Italy, when the financial commitments of the Communes expanded through the use of extraordinary contributions. Already, contemporary documentation contains two terms to define the assessment of wealth, *per libram* and *ad estimum*, which referred to the two methods of assessment. The criterion for tax declarations in the twelfth century (for which we have only Pisa's description and there is no guarantee that it was applied in the same way everywhere) was, however, certainly different from what was used in the inventory of *mansi* and mills drawn up in Milan by order of Frederick I (1167). That inventory was to be used to levy a fixed tax on every Milanese land unit, not to assess the assets of individuals. In the countryside, charges, which included personal services, remained a local issue and, despite the force of custom, a disjointed and changing reality, especially after the growth of cities in the area at the expense of the local lords. An example is the exchange of the *albergaria* owed to the *domini* of the land with the *iugaticum*, granted by the commune of Piacenza to the hamlet of Monticelli.[21]

Extraordinary direct taxation

After the conflict with the emperor ended, tax innovations (and problems) tended to be essentially the same throughout communal Italy due to the movements of the *podestà* from one city to another. It is therefore possible to see a relatively homogeneous tax system starting in the thirteenth century. In some cities, once the needs of war disappeared, the internal political system degenerated into open conflict precisely because of taxes. The emerging political party, called the Popolo (*pars populi*), called for a more equitable distribution of tax burdens. Problems arose when longstanding privileges were impacted and objective inventory criteria were adopted. If wealth assessment methods were already in place in almost every commune in central-northern Italy, as is shown by numerous records, in some cases the question of the *estimo*, or the addition of more inclusive criteria for it, triggered violent clashes. Generally, the conflict was due to the *milites*, who, in return for military service on horseback and compensation for weapons and mounts, enjoyed income from the city and, above all, tax exemptions.[22] In Milan, the privileges of the high clergy and their vassals were challenged (1198). After a war between the *pars militum* and the *pars populi*, an *estimum*★ was finally drafted in 1220–1224, and immediately redrafted in 1225. In 1240, under the pressure of a new war against Emperor Frederick II, an analytical inventory of property and debt/credit was established, based on declarations that were thoroughly checked by communal officials. The *estimo* remained in force, albeit with changes, for decades.[23] The dispute between *pars militum* and *pars populi* that exploded in Milan due to the abolition of exemptions for the *milites* and clergy was not, however, a widespread phenomenon. The rules for the *estimum*★, as far as we know, differed from city to city, including self-declarations or estimates of assets carried out by commissions appointed by the Councils, which were more sensitive to partisan logic. This explains why, in many cases, there is no evidence of conflict.[24] When sources have been preserved, the more analytical inventories, or *catasti*, like those of Bologna, reveal the socio-economic structure of their communities.

Assessments of assets were useful tools not just in levying taxes and forced loans, but in many situations, such as the seizure of the property of *banditi*. The process of making entries into a register, as in the thirteenth-century examples that have survived, was part of a new administrative culture based on writing and on the gradual development of administrative practices. During the mid-thirteenth century, the idea was solidified that contributing financially to the good of the community according to one's personal situation was a civic obligation. In the second half of the century, when the incentive to immigrate had run out, enrolment in the *estimo* became proof of citizenship.[25] For a good part of the thirteenth century, the *estimo* (or *libra*) was the political manifestation of communal taxation. This was perhaps less because of the tax revenue it generated and more due to its explicit reference to the principles of equity, justice, and of membership in a community, all of which emerged during the time of the *podestà* and the *popolo* as the basis of civil coexistence. From the middle of the thirteenth century, however, direct taxation was made to fall mainly on the countryside, where calls for taxation had previously focused. During the 1230s and 1240s, when the war against Emperor Frederick II raised the level of spending, the *fodrum* was aggressively demanded from rural communities in Lombardy, which were forced to collectively borrow from *domini* and from wealthy citizens, a situation which was destined to become pervasive.[26]

The taxation of ecclesiastical property was a separate problem. The war against Frederick I had collapsed the protection of bishops by imperial diplomas; the *estimo* of Church property also became a bitter battleground, this time with the Papacy. When peace negotiations began with the emperor, ecclesiastical property was subjected to *onera et exactiones*, prompting the intervention of Pope Alexander III. The glossators, based on the *Corpus Iuris*, believed that the Church's assets could be taxed, albeit within certain limits. The dispute flared up more severely during the papacy of Innocent III (d.1216) because the property of bishops and monasteries had been subjected to new *collectas et tallias*. Despite Innocent III's strict prohibition, the issue remained essentially unresolved and intertwined with local politics while, as seen above, canon law was developing tax theory under the twofold pressure of Justinian *Codex* and ecclesiastical taxation.[27]

In the second half of the thirteenth century, the *estimo* was not the only basis for direct taxation: in the towns of Piedmont and Lombardy which had fallen under the rule of Charles of Anjou, before and after his conquest of Sicily (1268), other systems of assessment were put into place that divided taxpayers into three classes based on property. They were taxed using a fixed progressive (but not proportional) hearth tax, so that those with greater wealth paid less than those placed in the lower tier. This demonstrates a clear rejection of the *estimum*★ *ad libram*, which best reflected actual wealth, as is quite evident in Piacenza, where the tiers were structured in great detail so as not to burden the merchant-banking elite, who were encouraged to finance the king. The connection with the lordship of Charles of Anjou is shown by the fact that, after this experience, the three tiers were re-proposed during the brief rules of Charles II and of Robert of Anjou. Although the Angevin hearth taxes were joined by a demand for other revenue, like the salt tax, tolls and duties, their reappearance suggests the continuing vitality of tax practices that were favoured due to their support by the wealthier classes and their simplicity of implementation.[28]

The *estimo* or *libra* from the thirteenth to the fourteenth centuries

The *estimo* was therefore a cornerstone of tax issues in the city-states. It reflected the relationship between the interests of the various social groups and is the best known manifestation of them. Those who did not own property were nevertheless registered in the *estimo* under reference numbers. Urban and rural *estimi* were differentiated. The urban *estimo* was divided up by city gates and also, in larger towns, by smaller districts, neighbourhoods, or parishes. Only the *miserabiles* were excluded.

There has been much discussion among contemporary historians about the methods used for the *estimo* during the late Middle Ages. If, in the earlier period of the age of Communes, the amount to be paid, on an extraordinary and exceptional basis, could be established in proportion to declared assets, especially in cities (as with the Genoese *colletta* of the 1160s and probably the Milanese *fodri* in the early thirteenth century), the direct relationship with declared wealth may have ceased towards the middle of the thirteenth century, as it did in Perugia (although it is impossible to generalize or provide dates). Instead, the *colletta* was demanded based on an abstract figure assigned to each payer. The two terms *estimum** and *libra* therefore became essentially synonymous: levying the *estimum ad libram* meant taxing on the basis of financial capacity to pay, as assessed by commissions. In northern Italy, the term *estimum** was more widespread, while *libra* was used in central Italy and *talea** in Piedmont. An assessment of assets was still the basis, but the sum of the required tax was redistributed when the need for spending grew. This practice, which sped up the collection procedure, was already in use for the direct taxation of the countryside *contadi*, where it probably originated. In the event of necessity, several successive *collette* or *fodri* could be levied and the coefficient used with respect to the estimated figure could be varied in *denari* (or *soldi* and *denari*) *per lira* (or 100 *lire*) of the *estimo* (e.g. 2 *denari per lira* of the *estimo*, 6 *denari per lira*). In the north the commissions that allocated the *estimo* or *allibramento* were smaller. In central Italy they were larger and were appointed on a geographical basis, but they were always reflections of the Councils where the wealthiest member prevailed. The criteria for allocating the *estimo* figure, the assets to be exempted (the home, the debts), the possible inclusion of a personal component, (especially in small villages, such as men of working age), and the possibility of deductions, were all variables that were decided through extensive negotiations.[29]

At the end of the thirteenth century, the civil tension that had accompanied the introduction of new assessment systems in some cities seemed to have died out in the presence of intolerance for direct taxation itself. The mechanism for allocating the *estimo* figure was complex and theoretically equitable, but its purpose was to establish how much the citizen would have to pay. In the case of Bologna, studied by Massimo Vallerani, the arbitrary nature of the assessments seems to have grown at the beginning of the fourteenth century, together with political use of the allocation of *estimo* figures. The last *estimo* for the city of Bologna was drawn up in 1329, and then it disappeared until 1385.[30]

In the early fourteenth century, the major Tuscan city-republics abandoned the direct taxation of citizens in favour of *prestanze*, or forced loans, while it continued in the countryside. Smaller towns, like Arezzo and Borgo San Sepolcro, continued to implement the *datia*, i.e.

direct, extraordinary taxes.[31] The base used to calculate the *prestanze* and, for low incomes, to pay the tax, was still the *estimo*, which was periodically revised.[32] The phase of consolidation of "debt" in the city-states of Florence, Pisa, Siena and Lucca has been clarified by Maria Ginatempo's comparative studies, which stressed that a turning point took place in Siena towards the end of the thirteenth century and in Florence around 1315.[33] In Florence, direct taxation resumed under the short-lived *signorie* of the fourteenth century. Siena, which at the end of the thirteenth century had ceased demanding taxes from its citizens, began a detailed survey of property in 1316–1318 called the *Tavola delle Possessioni* (tables of possessions), to be used as the basis for the *prestanze*. The drafting of the Sienese *catasto* was a result of the strong ideological impact of the communal government of "the Nine", which commissioned the famous fresco "The Allegory of Good Government" for the Council hall in Siena's Palazzo Pubblico (1338–1339).

In northern Italy, the *estimo* remained the basis for extraordinary direct taxation. In the second half of the thirteenth century as in the early fourteenth century, it is clear that in Lombardy, Bologna and Veneto, forced loans, which were not necessarily repayable, were alternated with the *colletta*, *fodro* and *taglia*★: the choice between them depended on the party in power. Rural communes and citizens would go into debt in order to pay them, as was highlighted by Paolo Gabriele Nobili's work on Bergamo.

The definitive consolidation of the *signoria* of the Visconti over Lombardy during the first half of the fourteenth century confirmed the *talea*★ (the term that had replaced *fodrum*, which had been used during the communal period) as the most suitable tool to support aggressive territorial expansion. In 1355, at the height of a phase of economic growth, the Visconti ordered an analytical survey of property with consistent criteria throughout the state, the first known of its kind in central-northern Italy. The legislation for the *estimo* was completed in 1361 with other provisions that included the assets of the clergy and a census of businesses, hotels, taverns, shops and bakeries, etc. The artisan component of wealth was therefore specifically targeted. After the total was decided by the government, the *taglie*★ were assigned to individual towns and communities. Each area then divided its share among those listed in their registers. The *estimo* thus had to be calculated according to common guidelines, but was based on rules that each community worked out independently and submitted for central approval.

It was not just a matter of roughly dividing up the tax burden, but of confirming or denying privileges and exemptions through the criteria used for assessment.[34] The city of Milan, capital of the state, is an eloquent example. In 1389 Gian Galeazzo Visconti established new legislation for the *estimo*, but it was applied with some discretion, leading to a puzzle in 1394 when civic administrators asked which of three recent *estimi* should be used as the basis for allocation of a *taglia*★. The prince replied that the fairest was the one based on the legislation of 1389, while he excluded another of the three because it had included the dotal assets of widows and, especially, those of exempt individuals. The subjectivity of the choices made in compiling the *estimo* was exacerbated after the death of the first duke (1402), when new criteria followed one after another, changing the rules from time to time to favour landowners and merchant-artisans.[35]

A frequent cause for dispute was the taxation of *cives* who bought farms in the countryside but did not reside there and those who settled elsewhere while holding on to their property in their place of origin. Although they might have to pay taxes, they were not listed as citizens, while communities were required to answer even for individuals who were absent. The conflicting interests of the merchants/landed aristocracy and the smaller communities are reflected in various princely decrees issued between 1339 and 1347, valid throughout the state. After initially leaning in favour of absent owners, the Visconti decided to give in to pressure from the communities. Gian Galeazzo Visconti, however, seeking support from the wealthiest classes, repealed the legislation in force in 1389 and returned to the first decree, which favoured citizen property holders and damaged rural communities. The question, which was also discussed by the celebrated jurist Bartolo da Sassoferrato (1314–1357) along the lines later adopted by the lord of Milan, was not limited to the Visconti, nor did the problem arise only with regard to the *cives*. It also concerned women's property when wives were originally from another district.[36] In the case of the Visconti, a strongly interventionist tax system was implemented during the fourteenth century, which was followed by an era of greater community autonomy in the fifteenth century, but was impacted by a disparity of treatment between *cives* and *districtus*.

The gabelle from the thirteenth to the fourteenth centuries

The *gabelle* or *dazi* were the backbone of ordinary revenue from the second half of the thirteenth century, both in the major republican city-states, where in some cases they financed the public debt, and in city-states under a *signoria*, where the extraordinary direct tax continued to be paid based on the *estimo*. Despite its apparent simplicity, indirect taxation is the most difficult sector to analyse because it is impossible to date the introduction of the asset items and because of the plurality of taxes and their continuous transformations. Although some fiscal institutions remained in existence under the same names for a long time and up to the first half of the eighteenth century, it would be unadvisable to conclude that, in hindsight, they provide evidence of modernity. These "containers" may refer to taxes that had taken on very different meanings over time. It should be noted that the multiplication of the *gabelle* in the second half of the thirteenth century was accompanied by strong pressure on extraordinary direct tax.

During the thirteenth century, the appearance of new "indirect" taxes throughout Europe was supported by demographic growth and was a response to the growing financial needs of sovereigns, which pushed cities to find sources of income alternative to the *collette*.[37] Based on the uncertain dates available, the appearance of *gabelle* in the Communes of north-central Italy received a strong stimulus after the end of the conflict with Frederick II and with the presence of Charles of Anjou in Italy, even before the conquest of the kingdom of Sicily (1268). The cities were divided between Guelph and Ghibelline factions, with immense financial and military mobilization and a renewal of internal and mutual aggression. Unlike *ripatici* (mooring rights), tolls and market rights, which had been, at least in theory, granted by the emperor, these new taxes were created by the urban communes.[38] Subsequently, there is evidence of the collection of duties in smaller towns and in the countryside, collected by the dominant city but partly left to local control, highlighting the fact that this phenomenon occurred simultaneously throughout the Italian communes.[39] The exponential multiplication of taxes that accelerated towards the end of the thirteenth century is by no means a foregone conclusion. Siena issued an initial codification of regulations for *gabelle* in 1273, but they continued to increase in number and, towards the end of the thirteenth century, the lists had to be continuously updated. This gives the impression that new duties were being introduced in this period in response to the pressures of necessity.

In Tuscany and Bologna, the term *gabelle* meant all taxes, including direct taxes, and excluding those based on the *estimo*. In the Po Valley, indirect taxes were generally called *datia* (in the northeast they were also referred to as *theloneum* or *tholoneum*). A division between taxes on commercial transit and taxes on consumption is useful but artificial, because the same goods could be taxed several times before reaching the end buyer. As for taxes on the movement of goods, the customs duties in a given area, especially at bridges and river ports, were only managed by the towns when they had control over that area (and not all of them were under such control). Tolls, like merchant duties in general, did not affect every commodity indiscriminately. To encourage resupplies, wheat, beans and other foodstuffs could be exempt, and higher duties were levied on competing products. In port cities, customs duties were paid by merchants, who were often foreigners, and therefore they did not impact the *cives*. Foreigners often owed heavier duties or additional fees.[40] Merchant tax rate schedules are rich economic/ taxes sources, but they are multi-layered texts and their interpretation is problematic, even if they reflect the economic importance of cities. The *gabella* of Bologna, in its late thirteenth-century form, had a very complex structure, an indication of the city's commercial importance at the time. The duty, as seen in the oldest rate schedules, was calculated based on the quantity of the goods.[41] A tax that was widespread everywhere was the *gabella delle porte* or gate tax★ collected upon entering a town before the goods were put up for sale. Twelfth-century texts also included payments in kind.[42] Peasants who brought their products into the city had to pay the gate tax★. Two amusing short stories by Franco Sacchetti describe attempts to smuggle eggs and meat by deceiving the tax collectors.[43]

It seems that around the beginning of the fourteenth century, the gate tax★ was divided into several types of taxes, as in Milan, where it was distinguished from merchant duties and limited to raw materials and consumer foodstuffs. In Florence, too, the fourteenth-century gate tax★ was separated from merchant duties, but in 1338 they were collected together and it became the most profitable tax.[44] The duty on merchandise was calculated *ad valorem* by quantity and type of goods. For some raw materials or products, duties could be paid separately to increase the yield. These manoeuvres of merchant duty reflect government attitudes towards commercial interests. In Milan in the 1320s the duty was doubled. The Visconti heavily taxed trade and production in Milan and its district, but in the 1340s, once the political situation had settled, merchants were favoured by the forced concentration of routes through the city. In the fifteenth century the duty on merchandise was lightened by currency devaluation because the Milanese rate schedule, the most extensive of communal Italy, was not updated until the end of the fifteenth century.[45]

The second sector, which came after transit taxes chronologically, are the so-called *gabelle* "on consumption", meaning primarily food consumption (wine, *macina*★ or milling, salt, bread, meat) but also various activities (a *gabella* on contracts, on dowries, on *baratteria*/gambling). The reality is more complex, because the same kinds could fall under several categories, or be collected together, like Florence's taxes on *macina*★ (milling) and on flour.[46] In an abundant but substantially homogeneous panorama, the kinds of duties and percentages of duties varied over time. If a duty is mentioned at a certain moment, except for the large *gabella* on wine★, salt, meat and bread, it is impossible to know whether it was collected consistently. The contrast with the *estimo* is clear: if the latter was paid by those enrolled in lists and only on an extraordinary basis, the new *gabella* impacted everyone's consumption. The levy of the *gabella* is therefore radically different than what was paid based on the *estimo* because it increased the cost of living. Asking for a direct tax or to increase the *gabelle*, especially those relating to daily spending, was a choice that had an extensive impact of which governments were fully aware. While drawing up the *estimo* could spark discussions and disputes, the *gabelle* triggered popular revolts, as in Venice in 1266 over the *macina*★, in Milan in 1302 over the salt *gabella*, and in Cremona over the burden of the salt *gabella*★ and the brutality used to collect it.[47]

Many taxes were first introduced provisionally to meet increasing needs. This is demonstrated by Verona's statutes of 1276, which show the *tholonea* on a certain number of edible and industrial goods. For some foodstuffs it said that the amount to be paid would only be decided on later. The rubrics of the Veronese statutes of 1327 concerning the same assets as the 1276 statutes demonstrate a more organized structure. Contemporary contracts from Milan, the earliest that have survived for this city, date back to this second phase, showing some duties being contracted out. It is thus possible to conclude that, after an experimental period, with the persistence, indeed the growth of the deficit at the end of the thirteenth and first third of the fourteenth centuries, the overall structure of *gabelle* in northern Italy was settling in as a type of contract and also as an administrative system.

The nature of the duties was linked to local structures of demand and varied from city to city. The profitability of individual items could avoid the consequences of a drop in demand caused by demographic crises by increasing the prices of goods, changing tax rates and reorganizing the duty. The amalgamation of several commodities and the addition of *addizionali* (surcharges) were common phenomena. Ancient public rights or those of the *signorie*, like rights on butchers or mills, were replaced by specific levies. The term *dazio della carne* (meat tax) covered animals which were taken into town for butchering; the sale of live, working animals was subject to another levy. The *dazio sul pane* (bread tax), especially on white bread, a kind of luxury, concerned only bread sold ready, but there was also a duty on the baking of bread in the public oven, because most of the population made bread at home. In the countryside, the levy of the main duties on foodstuffs was collected *en bloc*. Communities tried, when possible, to collect their own duties in order to manage them independently.

One of the most hated duties, because it affected the price of bread, was the *macina** (or milling *gabella*), a tax on the milling of wheat brought by private individuals to the mills. It was present throughout central and northern Italy under various names and could be combined with a tax on flour, as was the case in Florence. In the *contadi* it was transformed into a direct tax, based on the calculation of *bocche* (mouths). The *macina** was also levied where there was no lordly right to the mills, as was the case in Lombardy. While the *macina** was present in general, its application was irregular because it was repeatedly reduced or abolished by agreement. The *imbottati* or *imbottature* (on hay, wheat and wine, but not always together) was a direct tax found throughout north-central Italy from about the end of the thirteenth century. It was calculated on the spot at the time of harvest and was collected from the producers whether the products were sent to the market or not.[48] The salt *gabella**, which will be discussed below, impacted individuals, but in various cases it was also based on the *estimo*.

Along with the salt *gabella**, the best documented and most profitable duty was the wine duty. The wine duty was paid wholesale when it entered the city, and retail when it was sold in jugs at taverns. This duty provided one of the most substantial sources of income in the most populous cities such as Milan, Venice, Florence and Siena. In the second half of the thirteenth century, the communes in Lombardy held a monopoly on taverns, appointing tavernkeepers to manage them with obvious aims of social and financial control. At the beginning of the fourteenth century, when direct management had been abandoned, a duty was levied on consumption *per boccale* (by the tankard). For example, in Venice, which was a large market for the import and export of wines from everywhere, wine was subject to an entry and exit duty from at least the thirteenth century. Taverns were authorized in limited numbers and tavernkeepers could only buy wine from the Commune's warehouse. The retail duty on wine could be as high as 40 per cent of the price.[49]

During the thirteenth century a *gabella* on notarial contracts was introduced in Tuscany and in Bologna. In Tuscany, the *gabella* on contracts certainly offered on of the most profitable categories. In Siena, where it already existed, it was reformulated around 1289. In Bologna, it was differentiated by type of contract (dowries, property sales). Under the Visconti, during the tax reform of 1355 which aimed at taxing all types of income, notaries were required to register all financial agreements with a special office, causing a general protest. The imposition of this requirement, its reintroduction around 1393 (limited to dowries) and its subsequent abolition in 1402 on the death of the first duke, demonstrate how the public registration of contracts, unlike the *gabelle* on food consumption, impacted the interests of landowners and merchant-bankers. A lucrative but ethically questionable arrival, which appeared in the second half of the thirteenth century, was the *baratteria*, or license for gambling dens.[50] Due to the fact that it authorized gambling, it was often repealed. In one example, it is possible to see the specific motivation behind the introduction of a duty: the early fourteenth-century duty on *plaustri ferrati* (wagons with iron wheels) in Cremona, Milan and Verona was to be used to pay for the maintenance of new urban paving.

The salt *gabella** is a unique case due to its hybrid nature as a business, sales monopoly, obligation to purchase and a direct tax. The transformation from a state monopoly to a personal tax occurred towards the end of the thirteenth century. In the Po Valley, which depended on imports, the salt tax was more burdensome than in regions with direct access to salt flats, like Siena. The introduction of the salt *gabella** by Charles of Anjou in his domains in Piedmont, for the sale of salt from his salt flats (1259), provided the model for organization in the Communes. The obligation to purchase, however, arose from a later policy of supply of salt from Venice, which wanted to establish itself as the only distributor for the entire Po Valley. The sale of salt, often, but not everywhere, calculated as a distribution tax (*onus, talea salis*), was organized by compelling the collection of certain quantities that were calculated based on a set of parameters decided by the cities from time to time, and in which the *estimo* played a key role. Managed directly by the *signori*, under the Visconti and the Sforza salt traffic was part of the state's ordinary income. The impact of the burden, which was also extended to citizens based on the *estimo* (Milan and perhaps other cities excluded), became particularly unbearable in the 1360s and 1370s when penalties were introduced for failure to collect. In Veneto, the obligation seems to have been burdensome only for the countryside, while in the city salt was still sold under a monopoly regime. In the countryside around Florence it was levied based on the *estimo*, but in the city it was limited to a monopoly, as in Lucca. In Siena, on the other hand, the regulations of 1305 suggest that the aim was fair distribution at a controlled price. In the mid-fourteenth century, Siena transformed the salt tax into a direct tax, both for its citizens and for the inhabitants of the countryside; the salt tax was levied based on *estimo* until 1434, when it went back to the system of the early fourteenth century.[51]

One may wonder how much taxes "on consumption" impacted the poorest inhabitants, who had to shop at the market, did not enjoy exemptions like monasteries and hospitals, did not receive yield in kind and could not accumulate supplies. In the city, the application of ceiling prices in times of famine and ration policies for keeping the market supplied aimed at keeping the prices of essential goods under control. Taxation that was too burdensome would thus have had the opposite effect. In her extensive survey, Maria Ginatempo noted that in Florence, in the second half of the fourteenth century, urban consumption was probably more heavily taxed than in the second half of the fifteenth century. This observation can be extended to the cities of the Visconti state. In the second half of the fourteenth century, demographic decline due to the succession of plague epidemics and the cost of wars to expand regional states combined to increase the tax burden throughout north-central Italy.[52]

The administration of such a large set of taxes involved transforming the systems used to manage it. In the thirteenth century, direct management by tax collectors appointed by the commune prevailed. The communes wanted to keep their income under control, even if it took a long time to collect the taxes. Regimes ruled by the *Popolo* often turned to the religious orders of the Humiliati or the Cistercians to manage city finances and also to act as tax collectors.[53] With the multiplication of the *gabelle*, offices called *Gabelle* were established throughout north-central Italy to oversee the administration of duties (in Cremona, Bologna, and Siena, etc.).

Management of salt was also conducted by a special *Gabella* (in Venice, the *Camera del Sale*), which was independent of the office that administered the other taxes. The *Gabella del Sale* is documented in all Lombard communes (Novara, Pavia, Brescia, Milano, Como, Bergamo and Cremona) at the beginning of the fourteenth century. Towards the beginning of the new century, the use of religious orders became inadequate to control an increasingly complex mechanism, in which tax collectors had obtained the right to use force. In Florence after 1340 the prevailing farming system often was abandoned for direct management.[54]

With tax farming, a subcontractor undertook to pay the agreed levy, often in several instalments. The revenue was thus secure, but less than with direct management. The risk was borne by the tax farmer, especially in times of internal crisis and war, when it was sometimes impossible to collect a duty. Except in the case of the salt *gabella*★, which took care of itself, and the *Arti* (guilds) in Tuscany, which often took on the contracts for duties that concerned them, tax farmers were companies of financiers composed, for the minor *gabelle*, of persons of modest social standing. The abandonment of direct management of contracts led to the introduction of forms of protection for tax farmers and for their hated employees, the tax collectors who physically carried out the collections. In Visconti Milan, this development is represented by the transformation of the office of the duty judge, a commune official who appeared towards the end of the thirteenth century. A Milanese contract from 1329/1330 states that the judge must be appointed by the tax farmers and paid by the commune: he was no longer the non-partisan official of the communal tradition. Tax farmers also had the right to be assisted by numerous *offitiales* chosen by them, with the permission to carry arms. In the fourteenth century, duties were still considered a resource belonging to the community, the proceeds of which were voluntarily given to the ruling class or to the prince. In Piedmont, tax farmers came from the town aristocracy.[55]

In the State of Milan, as in Tuscany after the Florentine state was established, the prince or the Signoria were wholly or almost entirely entitled to the proceeds of ordinary taxation. In the Venetian state of the *Terraferma*, on the other hand, the towns remained free to decide which taxes to levy and how to collect their own duties, while in towns under Visconti rule the intervention of the lord's officials was invasive even before the mid-fourteenth century.[56]

The 'public debt': linking the obligation to contribute, State credit and private investment

The "public debt" continues to be the focus of much attention because it testifies to the intertwining of the political-financial and the economic-social. Loans could constitute an obligation, trigger lucrative interest mechanisms, and take on the character of "non-returnable" taxes, thus becoming direct taxes. Their impact, or *gravezza*, was ambiguous in some large communes (Venice, Genoa, Florence, Siena and Lucca) because there was a duty to contribute but also a repayment of revenue, which meant that the "public debt" was often inextricably linked to taxes. Thus this issue cannot be neglected.

Urgent needs were met by borrowing money from the richest citizens and from merchant companies, including foreign companies. In the twelfth century, it is evident that voluntary loans secured by taxes and state revenue accompanied the demand for an extraordinary direct tax. The collateral offered to creditors depended on the resources available. In 1140–1150, Genoa assigned customs duties, the public counters of *bancherii* (bankers) and mooring rights (assignments known as *compere*) to aristocratic citizens. Onerous mortgages were also used, as in 1154, when the Genoese government was in debt for a large sum, 15,000 lire, with various creditors, including the commune of Piacenza.[57] In Venice in 1164, the income from the

Rialto, i.e. public rights and customs duties, was pledged for a loan granted by the doge and by a few other *cives*.[58] In the same years, the consuls of Pisa (1162) pledged the salt monopoly, mooring rights (*ripatico*) and the iron mines. Mid-twelfth-century contracts in Genoa, Venice and Pisa demonstrate a great availability of financial and tax resources, much greater than those of land-locked communes. It was this availability that enabled Genoa and Venice to choose a path other than direct taxation in the following century: asking the *cives*, instead of paying the *collecta*★, to subscribe to forced loans on the basis of the *estimo*. The issue of forced loans, which were repayable but did not generate interest, was not uncommon in the communes of the thirteenth century, as were attempts to impose a monopoly on the sale of certain goods. What distinguished Genoa and Venice was the decision, which was certainly taken gradually, not to exhaust the operation by repaying every single debt item and by recovering the pledged income items, but to implement a complex mechanism of long-term interest loans, supported by solid availability of income. This system was perfected towards the middle of the thirteenth century.

In twelfth-century Genoa assets were pledged to creditors/contractors for many years and the duration of the *compere* risked getting out of control. In 1165–1167, the city decided to resort to a direct tax (*collecta*★) based on the *estimo*, applying a rate of 2.5 per cent on registered property. Subsequently, the two methods, *compere* and *collette*, were applied together until the *compere* was organized on a permanent basis in the second half of the thirteenth century.[59] Citizens subscribed forced loans whose yield (8–10 per cent) was financed by the allocation of income directly administered by the *participes* (majority shareholders). The set of assets, which could not always be redeemed, was reorganized several times. When Simone Boccanegra took power (1339), there was also an attempt to abolish the *compere* and return to direct taxation. In the fourteenth and fifteenth centuries, the shares, which involved a large number of *cives*, were transferable and could even be transmitted through inheritance, thus becoming an investment rather than an obligation. At the beginning of the fifteenth century, a further consolidation of the *compere* with the resurgence of the "public debt" (Banco di San Giorgio, 1407), meant that it was the Banco that made financial policy choices for the Genoese government. The Banco's shares were offered on the free market and enjoyed considerable success as an investment by non-*cives*, especially those from Lombardy.[60]

Venice, which had almost double the population (perhaps 100,000 inhabitants by the end of the thirteenth century) and greater institutional strength than Genoa, followed a linear path towards financial organization in which direct tax played a completely marginal role for centuries. Genoa, which collected large customs revenues, did not have Venice's hold over the exclusive Adriatic markets or its strict control over maritime activity, as only Venetian *cives* had the right to trade by sea. In this city as well, there may have been an initial mixed path with forced loans/direct taxation, which ended with the abandonment of the *decimum*, the direct tax that disappeared after the twelfth century. When the Venetian "public debt" was organized in a stable manner (1262), the land customs, maritime customs and the *Fondaco dei Tedeschi* to control traffic from Germanic countries were all active. Venice collected very profitable gabelles such as the duty on wine★ (documented from at least 1263), on commercial brokering (*mesetteria*) and probably others, with offices in the Rialto. The salt trade was destined to become a major source of revenue.[61] Citizens were obligated to buy *imprestiti* (government bonds) based on the *estimo*; however, merchant capital was not included in the assessment. The *imprestiti* yielded 5 per cent interest. Before 1363 the loans were periodically repaid; even when the debt was recognized as non-redeemable, Venice kept it under control, periodically redeeming the *imprestiti* in order to raise the market value of the shares, which depended on demand. In fact, speculators bought at low prices on the *imprestiti* market which then yielded a lot in proportion. The Republic therefore preferred the path of a two-way relationship with its *cives*, whose interests were one with those of the State, meaning that it could count on robust tax revenues. In the fourteenth century, *imprestiti* were also sold to non-citizens, offering both a good investment and, in the case of foreign *signori*, a public demonstration of alliance and political support.[62]

The third great Mediterranean port, Pisa, should be added to the "classic" Genova–Venice combination. Pisa's mercantile development had taken place even earlier. It is necessary to note that in this case as well, when its citizens were required to declare their assets in 1162, perhaps to impose a forced loan, the city turned to the *datia* (direct tax). During the thirteenth century, Pisa's mixed system, which combined a strong capacity for customs revenue with forms of direct taxation and interest-free loans, did not develop in the direction taken by Genoa and Venice. The debt of the Commune was unified only in the mid-fourteenth century, when forced bonds with interest were already being issued. By that point, however, the Pisan political situation had deteriorated and the Commune was overly indebted.[63]

In Siena and Florence, forced loans with interest appeared at the end of the thirteenth century without immediately launching the debt consolidation process, which followed fifty years later. It is no coincidence that the decision to forgo direct taxation coincided with the manufacturing, banking and commercial expansion of Florence. Large merchant companies had arisen and engaged in transnational operations of enormous magnitude with a high availability of liquid capital to invest. Financing the "debt" was therefore another opportunity for the wealthy. Shares of the *Monte* were negotiable only with the authorization of the Commune.[64] Unlike Venice and Genoa, where it was primarily customs-commercial revenues that supported the loans, interest from the Tuscan *prestanze* were paid for by the gabelles that impacted their own citizens as producers and consumers, and by intense commerce. The importance and nature of forced loans multiplied, as general forced *prestanze* deductible from direct taxes, without interest, accompanied by interest-bearing *prestanze* levied on groups of wealthy citizens, became the basis of the Florentine tax system. This system was almost exclusively founded on income-producing *prestanze*, but only for those in the upper portion of the *estimo*.

The organization of the *Monti* (in Florence, Siena, Lucca and Pisa), the financial offices responsible for managing the public debt, did not occur before the mid-fourteenth century; however, direct taxation remained in place for the countryside as well as for citizens with a low *estimo*. Interest was paid not by pledging tax assets as in Genoa, but by transferring the proceeds from the *gabelle*. In Florence, before the demographic-economic collapse of the plague, citizens had enthusiastically subscribed shares in the *Monte*. This was no longer the case in the fifteenth century, when a good part of those listed in the *estimo* tried to evade the obligation to purchase shares. As Anthony Molho observed, many *prestanziati* preferred to pay less but lose their money or sell their right to purchase the shares to third parties.[65] The mandatory direct tax, however, also maintained its symbolic significance in Florence. In 1378, among the demands made to the city government by the Ciompi was the abolition of the *Monte* system and the return to direct taxation. Siena, whose merchant-banking companies had arisen prior to those in Florence, did not develop manufacturing of international significance and derived most of its income from taxing the countryside. It is thus understood that, in Siena, the abandonment of taxes on its citizens was not perceived as definitive. During the fourteenth century, the city followed a prudent policy, managing debt with non-transferable securities and not excluding the possibility of liquidating them.[66]

A recently highlighted aspect is the fact that, at least from the fourteenth century, "public debt" securities became a part of family property. Purchased as pensions for widows and assigned to daughters as dowries, as they changed hands they no longer had the appearance of the financial-fiscal obligation that had driven their issue, but became similar to the voluntary *censi* contracts present in other European areas, especially in Barcelona and Valencia.[67] All city-states resorted to both direct tax and voluntary and compulsory credit. The main crux of the issue, which separates the few communes capable of bearing a permanent public debt from those that were unable to do so, is the security of the payment of large-scale and long-term interest payments. In Venice, Genoa and Florence the public debt was a secure resource to be used when needed. During the thirteenth century, the Lombard, Venetian and Emilian communes (Milan, Como, Cremona, Bergamo, Bologna and Vicenza) also imposed forced loans, which in some cases involved a large part of their citizens, by issuing interest-free bonds. These bonds could be used to deduct the *fodri*, or repaid (*charte debiti*). The extraordinary direct tax that was allocated based on the *estimo* nevertheless remained the main resource and the purpose of the commune's financial manoeuvres was to pay off the debt.[68] During periods of crisis, such as between the thirteenth and fourteenth centuries, the repayments themselves were anything but guaranteed.

In the first half of the fourteenth century, before the formation of the multi-city *signorie*, expanded forms of financial participation based on the use of packages of revenue were tested in the communes of Lombardy and Veneto. As early as the last twenty years of the thirteenth century, the salt duty, the most profitable duty, was the item that was sold most often to secure the loans granted by chains of lenders.[69] In Verona in 1337–1339, as a pledge for a large loan to the Della Scala lords, a series of duties and public rights were assigned to a consortium of hundreds of citizens who continued to collect the revenues for centuries.[70] There were attempts to provide the city finances with greater resources and to involve wealthy *cives*, but the evolution towards permanent debt, probably inspired by that of Genoa, was blocked by the scarcity of the revenue required to recover the assets, to pay the interest and to keep the debt under control. In the cities of northern Italy it does not seem that there was any possibility of transforming floating public debt into consolidated and transferable debt (with the exception of an attempt in Milan in the mid-fifteenth century during a brief republican government). Even the issue of debt securities was abandoned at the beginning of the fourteenth century. The albeit high fiscal resources available, against the territorial ambitions and military expenses of the *Signori*, which absorbed much more than the revenue from the *gabelle*, did not guarantee the repayment of debt unless it was granted privately, especially by the large banks, such as those of the Borromeo and the Medici.

In Milan, however, after the break following the fall of Duke Ludovico Sforza "il Moro", during the rule of the last duke, Francesco II Sforza (d.1535), there was a modest consolidated public debt based on the proceeds from ordinary revenue. In Bologna, too, a first consolidated public debt appeared at the end of the fourteenth century, which was better organized during the first half of the fifteenth century.[71] As Giacomo Todeschini observed, these were now interest-bearing deposits in the state coffers, with a clear shift toward voluntary purchase, which was now severed from the fiscal and compulsory traits that had characterized the communal era.[72]

The fifteenth century: changes in direct taxation in Florence, Venice and Milan

If the fourteenth century was marked by a surge in taxation in the second half of the century, the first half of the next century experienced a trend towards ordinary forms of taxation due to the wars that accompanied the formation of the regional states. In early fifteenth-century Florence, the obligation to contribute to public finances according to one's abilities was based on various types of taxation. Forced loans that were interest-bearing (*a rendere*) but not redeemable made up most of the city's income; other categories of direct taxation were less common, such as those without payment of interest. Outright taxes (*a perdere*), demanded only in certain periods of war, were aimed at the repurchase of the shares. They were true taxes which everyone had to pay, but they were the only taxes paid by taxpayers with a low *estimo* coefficient. The coefficient, as was customary, was established by commissions appointed from time to time and divided by neighbourhood. Due to criticisms that the *estimi* were based on arbitrary assessments, a proposal was made in 1422 to introduce a *catasto* in Florence similar to the *estimo* of Venice, which was based on analytical declarations that would provide a complete picture of citizens' assets. After objections and postponements, the stimulus of the war against the Duke of Milan and the increase of *prestanze*, a reform began in 1427. The *catasto* used homogeneous criteria and included the entire Florentine state. It was updated in 1431 and 1433. The declarations also included movable assets, which was why it was opposed by Florence's ruling class, made up of great banker-merchants. The use of the *catasto* was therefore quite brief before a return to the commissions, which cautiously assessed commercial wealth.[73] Interest from *prestanze* dropped drastically. The new succession of wars in the middle of the century multiplied the number of extraordinary demands. Florence's cautious foreign policy during the second half of the fifteenth century, however, alleviated what had become, in effect, direct taxes. At the end of the fifteenth century, after the expulsion of the Medici, direct tax (*decima*) was reintroduced for citizens and *comitatini* (inhabitants of the countryside), but only for real property.[74]

By the first half of the fifteenth century, the Republic of Venice had conquered a large part of the Po Valley (the so-called *Terraferma*), transforming into a large territorial state. In the city, the impact of direct taxation remained moderate, relying on substantial revenue from customs and consumer duties, as well as the revenue from the salt trade, which alone made up 17 per cent of annual revenue.[75] Ordinary needs could have been met, but the republic was faced with heavy military expenses, the long war against Milan, and the Turkish advance in the Adriatic. Venice granted financial autonomy to the cities that became part of the *Terraferma*. Verona, Vicenza, Brescia and Bergamo could administer their own income and tax their district, much more than under the previous Visconti rule. Towards the middle of the fifteenth century, however, Venice introduced a breakdown by *carati*, distinguishing the cities from their territories, to monitor the balance of power from above and more equitably distribute the taxes that the cities tended to pass on to the countryside. Direct taxation was also introduced, initially only in case of need, as with the *dadia delle lance*. In 1463, the government decided to levy the *decima*, a direct tax on real estate both in the city and in the *Terraferma*, and the *tansa*, a tax on trade and manufacturing, aimed particularly at those who were not registered for the *estimo*. The *decima* was based on the *estimo* declarations, the *tansa* on assessments performed by commissions. Thus, in the second half of the fifteenth century, a mixed system of forced loans and direct taxation was created. The contribution of the cities of the *Terraferma* was negligible until the sixteenth century, when the Turkish threat forced Venice to increase taxes there as well.[76]

The State of Milan often resorted to forced loans demanded of groups of citizens with the highest income recorded on the *estimo*. In exchange for credit, the lenders, generally wealthy merchant-bankers and public officeholders, obtained lucrative treasury assignments in the State's cities and the right to manage trade over monopolies such as the salt trade.[77] The loans were accompanied by *taglie*★ and *subsidia* levied on towns. There was an attempt to impose ordinary direct taxation, which was never completed. In 1426–1427 during the war against Venice, Duke Filippo Maria levied a fixed monthly payment that was referred to as a *tassa* (*tassa mensualis*), a general monthly *taglia*★ based on the *estimo*. This experiment ended around 1428. The duke's support for commercial and manufacturing interests, however, encouraged collection methods that did not penalize merchant profits. In 1433, the duke issued detailed legislation for the *estimo* based on the model of the contemporary Florentine *catasto* and the Venetian declarations.[78] Filippo Maria also introduced new types of ordinary direct taxation that concerned only the countryside and did not interfere with the urban economy. The most lasting and significant innovations, which came about in the 1440s, were the *taxa equorum* (the "horse tax" or the allocation of military quarters) and the *carreggio* (the obligation to provide service with wagons) both levied on the countryside only, using the same criteria in all countryside *distretti*.[79] The initiative introduced further inequality with the cities, because it accentuated the tendency to pass levies on to the countryside, where agricultural production was already subject to the *imbottati*. From the first half of the fifteenth century to the mid-sixteenth century, there was therefore a clear development of forms of ordinary revenue that came from taxation from which the cities were exempt.

The levy of the *taglie*★ in cities and communities, very frequent in the Visconti state during the fourteenth and early fifteenth centuries, lessened in the second half of the fifteenth century. The frequent use of private credit and the succession of taxes aimed at particular categories (the feudal lords, the clergy) can explain the reluctance on the part of the Sforza to make use of general *taglie*★ which, regardless of the controversy that they caused, would have impacted precisely those who were able to contribute more via taxes and loans. The inability to return to the heavy extraordinary taxes on the *estimo* as implemented under the Visconti, in addition to the loss of the cities of Bergamo and Brescia, helps explain the greater financial difficulties encountered by the Sforza (1452–1535). The dukes, especially Galeazzo Maria and Ludovico *il Moro*, sold many tax revenues from the countryside to courtiers and *fideles*. The State of Milan followed the evolution that occurred in the other Italian regional states during the second half of the fifteenth century with some delay, because the direct tax on assets became an ordinary tax only with the very slow drafting of the *catasto* by the will of Emperor Charles V of Habsburg from 1536–1537, which was slowed down by heated controversies.[80] The persistent hostility to forms of analytical assessment of properties, such as the Tuscan *catasto*, is therefore understandable.

Maria Ginatempo has calculated that, during the second half of the fifteenth century, direct taxes, including those on consumption, salt and *imbottati* comprised 35 per cent of total revenue in Florence, against almost 50 per cent in the states of Milan and Venice. Under the Sforza, as shown in the accounts of 1463, 47 per cent of revenue consisted of an accumulation of direct taxes on the countryside *contadi*: salt, the horse tax (15 per cent), the *imbottati* and the *macina*★.[81] The fifteenth-century trend towards ordinary direct taxation, however, unites both the republican and princely states. The public debt was concentrated in the hands of the nascent citizen-patricians, financed by a multitude of direct and indirect taxes. By the end of its existence, even the Sforza duchy of Milan was able to guarantee income from its shares.

Up to this point, overall figures have been avoided because, until the sixteenth century, such figures were based on chronicle sources that cannot be verified or substantiated. The monetary currency referred to here is the gold coin. In 1343, the ordinary income of the Republic of Venice, before the formation of the State of the *Terraferma*, was about 250,000 ducats per year, becoming 1,100,000 ducats around 1432, as in the second half of the century.[82] Around 1340, the ordinary income of the Republic of Florence was about 300,000 florins per year. In 1470, the estimated ordinary income of the State of Florence amounted to about 256,000 florins.[83] At the time of greatest expansion of the State of Milan at the end of the fourteenth century, Gian Galeazzo Visconti, duke of Milan, probably had access to ordinary financial resources of around 900,000 gold florins. On the other hand, these resources seem to have halved during the rule of Duke Filippo Maria, during the war waged against Milan by Venice and Florence (422,000 florins). The Sforza's income during the 1460s and 1470s, with a state that was much reduced territorially compared to the previous period, amounted to 500,000 ducats per year. Towards the 1490s, under Ludovico *il Moro*, it likely rose to 600,000 ducats including, however, extraordinary taxation and forced loans, which were largely levied during the crisis of the late fifteenth century.[84]

Ordinary tax revenues, however, constituted only part of a much greater spending capacity, financed by loans in their various forms. Around 1330, in years of particular need, Florence's revenue could be almost doubled by *prestanze*. The revenue of 1470 should include the yield from *prestanze*, which were levied in amounts that varied depending on the year, but were of decidedly more limited importance than during the fourteenth century and the first half of the fifteenth century. The importance of debt also decreased in fifteenth-century Venice in favour of direct taxation. In the Visconti-Sforza State of Milan, heavy indirect taxation and frequent extraordinary taxation, *taglie*★ and *subsidia*, forced loans with or without interest, private loans and the sale of revenues, enabled an ambitious as well as a financially disastrous policy of expansion in the fourteenth to fifteenth century.

Conclusions

The acquisition of existing tax assets as well as more complex forms of direct taxation of citizens were part of the political and economic evolution of cities in the twelfth century. The capacity to collect taxes became a fundamental aspect of the full freedom enjoyed by the Communes and, later, by the multi-city *signorie*. Compared with transalpine cities, some urban centres reached considerable size and military power in the thirteenth century. Urban concentration and the governance of large districts explains their financial wealth and the tight control they exercised over resources.[85] The cities' income was uneven, however, because it depended on the possession of ports, rivers, transit routes, mines, as well agricultural production and manufacturing.

The types of taxation and the methods of collection that were implemented were not based solely on technical needs, but also depended on government choices. The turning points have been highlighted, while recognizing the limits of what we can actually know from the information available. We have observed that the tax system followed a broadly synchronous chronological trend throughout the Italian cities of the thirteenth to fifteenth centuries, but the groundwork had been prepared by their common origin as part of the *regnum Ytalie* and by the presence of Church institutions in the field of taxation (*decima*). The circulation of the office of the *podestà* during the thirteenth century facilitated the transmission of methods, as in the case of the *estimo*. Academic discussions on the right of taxation engaged both secular and canon jurisprudence, providing governments with the tools needed to overcome the impasse that developed around the question of legitimacy, as seen when the *signori* demanded the *taglie*★ and extraordinary *subsidia*, which had to be periodically justified.

In the long run, the most significant issue was who and what to tax. In the time of the Communes, however, the strong sense of civic membership justified the sacrifices demanded so that loans and taxes came to be considered a necessary evil. In the *signorie*, however, the detachment between citizens and taxes in the second half of the fourteenth century occurred earlier than in the republican states. The tax burden imposed by the Visconti on the cities in their domain largely facilitated the Venetian victory in the *Terraferma*. All of the states took on debt, but their ability to obtain loans that did not turn out to be yet another tax was linked to the certainty with which they were able to pay at least the interest. Where there were insufficient means, the use of credit too onerous and the expenses out of control, the sale of revenue was an alternative, as adopted under the Sforza in the fifteenth century. Venice, Genoa, Florence and

Siena were certainly exceptional city-republics and thus they do not represent the full range of cases, which current research has shown to be more nuanced and complex and which should include princely cities and states. Despite the implementation of financial and tax policies that were different from those found in republican states, both princely states and republics had quite a few points in common, changing over the course of centuries.

Notes

* Translated from the Italian by Katy Ferrari.
1. Demographic overview in GINATEMPO and SANDRI, *L'Italia delle città*. At the height of their population at the end of the thirteenth century, the cites of present-day Piedmont were small (about 5,000 inhabitants in Asti, Moncalieri, Turin, Pinerolo and Vercelli), the cities of present-day Liguria, Lombardy and Emilia-Romagna were large or very large (Milan 150,000, Genoa, Piacenza, Cremona, and Bologna 40,000–50,000 inhabitants); in Veneto, with the exception of Verona, Padua and Venice (40,000–100,000 inhabitants), the urban population was smaller. In Tuscany, Florence had reached its maximum development (100,000 inhabitants), perhaps double the population of Siena and Pisa. On the origin of the Communes, WICKHAM, *Sleepwalking*.
2. SIEVEKING, *Genueser Finanzwesen*; BARBADORO, *Le finanze*; BISCARO, "Gli estimi"; Gino LUZZATTO, *Il debito pubblico*.
3. The most significant works include HERLIHY and KLAPISCH-ZUBER, *Les Toscans*. An extensive bigliography of census sources is found in ALFANI and BARBOT, *Ricchezza, valore, proprietà*.
4. Scholarship multiplied throughout the second half of the twentieth century, especially on Tuscan cities. Enrico Fiumi was the first to analyze the complex mechanisms of assesment of wealth (FIUMI, "L'imposta diretta"); MOLHO, *Florentine Public Finances*; MOLHO, *Firenze nel Quattrocento*; DE LA RONCIÈRE, "Indirect Taxes"; BOWSKY, *The Finance*; CONTI, *L'imposta diretta*; GROHMANN, *L'imposizione diretta*; CAMMAROSANO, "Il sistema fiscale". On Venice: KNAPTON, "Le dinamiche delle finanze pubbliche"; MUELLER, *The Venetian Money Market*.
5. *Lo Stato territoriale fiorentino*; MAINONI, *Le radici della discordia*.
6. Among Michael Knapton's many contributions regarding taxation of the *Terraferma*: KNAPTON, "Il fisco nello Stato veneziano"; KNAPTON, "Venice and the *Terraferma*"; on the modern era PEZZOLO, *Il fisco dei veneziani*.
7. For a bibliography prior to 2000, see the appendix to *Politiche finanziarie e fiscali*. Among the recent works concerning modern-day Piedmont: CENGARLE, "Il distretto fiscale di Vercelli"; GRAVELA, "Comprare il debito della città"; BUFFO, "Prassi documentarie e gestione delle finanze"; GRAVELA, "Un mercato esclusivo". See also chapter 9 (Part II) in the present publication.
8. GINATEMPO, *Prima del debito*; GINATEMPO, "Spunti comparativi".
9. MAINONI, "A proposito della 'rivoluzione fiscale'"; CONTE and MENZINGER, *La Summa Trium Librorum*; MENZINGER and VALLERANI, "Giuristi e città"; MENZINGER, "Pagare per appartenere".
10. VALLERANI, "Il valore dei *cives*".
11. An exception is GINATEMPO, "Spunti comparativi."
12. For example: LAZZARINI, "Prime osservazioni"; MAINONI, "Fiscalità signorile".
13. BRÜHL, *Fodrum, Gistum*.
14. FIUMI, "L'imposta diretta"; BOCCHI, "Le imposte dirette"; MAINONI, "A proposito della 'rivoluzione fiscale'", p. 35; MAIRE VIGUEUR, *Cavalieri e cittadini*; SCHARF, "Fiscalità e finanza"; NOBILI, "Alle origini della fiscalità".
15. Medieval legal thought, as opposed to today's reasoning, held that the right to enforce and the right of sovereignty (of the king, of the feudal lord) did not merge together. The problem is discussed in VOLANTE, *La concezione patrimoniale*.
16. MENZINGER, "'Una Scienza Arcana'".
17. *Gli Annali di Caffaro (1099-1163)*, p. 96.
18. VIOLANTE, *Le origini del debito pubblico* and VIOLANTE, *Imposte dirette e debito pubblico nel basso medioevo*.
19. *Statuti inediti della città di Pisa*, pp. 4–5.
20. CAMMAROSANO, "Le origini della fiscalità", pp. 238–239.
21. FIUMI, *L'imposta diretta*; MAINONI, "A proposito della 'rivoluzione fiscale.'"
22. MAIRE VIGUEUR, *Cavalieri e cittadini*, pp. 175–267.
23. GRILLO, "L'introduzione dell'estimo", pp. 11–38.

24 Buffo, "Prassi documentarie"; Gravela, "Contare nel catasto. Valore delle cose e valore delle persone negli estimi delle città italiane (secoli XIV–XV)," in *Valore delle cose*, pp. 271–294.
25 *Credito e cittadinanza*; *Cittadinanze medievali*.
26 Nobili, *Alle origini della* città, pp. 93–107.
27 Ronzani, "*Ecclesiastica libertas*", pp. 367–382.
28 Mainoni, "Il governo del re"; Rao, "Gli Angiò e la gestione".
29 See in particular Fiumi, "L'imposta diretta"; summary and bibliographic references in Ginatempo, "Spunti comparativi," pp. 154–155; Grillo, "L'introduzione dell'estimo"; also useful Ammannati, De Franco and Di Tullio, *Misurare la diseguaglianza*.
30 Vallerani, "Fiscalità e limiti dell'appartenenza"; Vallerani, "Il valore dei *cives*."
31 Scharf, *Borgo San Sepolcro*, pp. 95–150.
32 Conti, *I catasti agrari*, p. 4.
33 Ginatempo, *Prima del debito*, pp. 57–65.
34 Mainoni, "*Viglaebium opibus primum*", pp. 246–260; De Angelis Cappabianca, *Voghera alla fine del Trecento*.
35 Mainoni, "Fiscalità signorile" pp. 126–129; Del Bo, "Mercanti e finanze statali".
36 Volante, "La concezione patrimoniale", p. 353; Kirshner, "Nascoste in bella vista".
37 For the Crown of Aragon, Sánchez Martínez, "La evolución de la fiscalidad".
38 Analytical background in Ginatempo, "Spunti comparativi"; Mainoni, "Indici delle istituzioni".
39 Scharf, *Borgo San Sepolcro*, pp. 98–113.
40 For example Frangioni, *Milano e le sue strade*.
41 *Statuti di Bologna del 1288*, vol. I, pp. 124–126.
42 Of great interest is the *Breve recti mercati* (1173–1184) of Verona (*Le carte del Capitolo*, vol. II, pp. 241–245; 249–250).
43 Franco Sacchetti, *Le Trecento Novelle*, no. 146 and 147.
44 Giovanni Villani book XI, chapter 92 (1338).
45 Mainoni, "Finanza e fiscalità", pp. 35–38.
46 Giovanni Villani, book XI, chapter 92 (1338).
47 Pezzolo, "La costituzione fiscale", p. 120; Mainoni, "La gabella del sale", pp. 65–69; Grillo, "Rivolte antiviscontee".
48 Bowsky, *Le finanze*, pp. 162–167; Ginatempo, "Spunti comparativi". For the *imbottato*, pp. 167–171. In later cases, the amount of the *imbottato* could be contracted *en bloc*.
49 Mainoni, *Le radici*, pp. 59–66; for Venice (1318) Knapton, *Le dinamiche*, p. 493; Costantini, "Le coesistenze", chapter VIII.
50 Frescura Nepoti, "Natura ed evoluzione", p. 158; Rizzi, *Ludus/ludere*, pp. 67–69.
51 Mainoni, "La gabella del sale"; in general Hocquet, *Il sale*; Ginatempo, *Prima del debito*, appendix 2.
52 De La Roncière, "Indirect Taxes". The possible chronology is in Ginatempo, *Prima del debito*, pp. 93–97.
53 Zanoni, *Gli Umiliati*; Grillo, "I religiosi".
54 Mainoni, "La gabella del sale", pp. 67–69; De La Roncière, "Indirect Taxes", pp. 183–185.
55 Mainoni, "Finanza", pp. 32–33; Gravela, "Un mercato esclusivo".
56 On the State of Florence from the viewpoint of a subject community, Scharf, *Borgo San Sepolcro*. The tax bibliography regarding the Venetian *Terraferma* owes much to the pioneering research of Michael Knapton: for an initial overview Knapton, *Il sistema fiscale*, pp. 19–30.
57 *Gli Annali di Caffaro*, p. 95 and p. 100.
58 Luzzatto, *Il debito pubblico*, p. 14.
59 Cammarosano, *Le origini della* fiscalità, pp. 238–239.
60 Molho, *Tre città-stato*, pp. 190–191; Felloni, "Cenni storici", pp. 9–11; Miner, "Profit and Patrimony".
61 Luzzatto, *Storia economica*, p. 100, and pp. 103–104.
62 Mueller, *The Venetian Money Market*, pp. 455–461.
63 Violante, *Economia, società*, chapter 3; there is no extensive research for the following period: a good synthesis in Ginatempo, *Prima del debito*, pp. 132–136.
64 Pezzolo, "Tradizione e innovazione", p. 26.
65 Molho, *Florentine Public Finances*, pp. 68–69.
66 Ginatempo, *Prima del debito*, pp. 94–131.

67 MINER, *Profit and Patrimony*.
68 GRILLO, "L'introduzione dell'estimo"; NOBILI, "Alle origini della fiscalità".
69 MAINONI, "Finanza", p. 25.
70 MUELLER, *The Venetian Money Market*, p. 456.
71 CARBONI, *Il debito della città*, pp. 78–79.
72 DE LUCA, "Debito pubblico"; TODESCHINI, "Finanza e usura".
73 The essential analysis is still CONTI, *L'imposta diretta*, pp. 8–10, and all of chapter 4.
74 PEZZOLO, "Pas de dette", pp. 140–141.
75 For Venetian public finance, see the specific contributions starting in vol. II of *Storia di Venezia dalle origini*. For the *Terraferma*: KNAPTON, *Il fisco*; PEZZOLO, *Il fisco*. For Ventitian "denunce": *L'anagrafe e le denunce*.
76 PEZZOLO, "Pas de dette".
77 DEL BO, "Mercanti e finanze statali".
78 MAINONI, "Fiscalità signorile".
79 COVINI, "'*Alle spese di Zoan villano*'".
80 A synthesis of the issue and historiographical information in CHITTOLINI, "Notes sur la politique fiscale"; CAPRA, "The Italian States".
81 GINATEMPO, *Spunti comparativi*, table 2.
82 PEZZOLO, *Una finanza*, table 4, pp. 38–40.
83 GINATEMPO, *Prima del debito*, pp. 123–125, with data that also refers to the previous era and to the other major Tuscan cities; CONTI, *L'imposta diretta*, p. 24.
84 LEVEROTTI, "La crisi".
85 Important discussion in STASAVAGE, *States of Credit*; WICKHAM, *Sleepwalking*.

References

Guido ALFANI and Michela BARBOT, *Ricchezza, valore, proprietà in età preindustriale*, Venice 2009.
Francesco AMMANNATI, Davide DE FRANCO and Matteo DI TULLIO, *Misurare la diseguaglianza economica nell'età preindustriale: un confronto fra realtà dell'Italia centro-settentrionale*, Dondena Working Papers, Working Paper No. 65, September 2014, www.dondena.unibocconi.it.
Gli Annali di Caffaro (1099–1163), ed. Gabriella AIRALDI, Genoa, 2002.
Bernardino BARBADORO, *Le finanze della Repubblica fiorentina. Imposte dirette e debito pubblico fino all'introduzione del Monte*, Florence 1929.
Gerolamo BISCARO, "Gli estimi del comune di Milano nel secolo XIII", in *Archivio Storico Lombardo*, 45, 1928, pp. 343–495.
Francesca BOCCHI, "Le imposte dirette a Bologna nei secoli XII e XIII", in *Nuova Rivista Storica*, 57, 1973, pp. 278–279.
Carlrichard BRÜHL, *Fodrum, Gistum, Servitium Regis*, 2 vol., Köln-Graz, 1968.
Paolo BUFFO, "Prassi documentarie e gestione delle finanze nei comuni del principato di Savoia-Acaia (Moncalieri, Pinerolo, Torino, fine secolo XIII-prima metà secolo XIV)," in *Scrineum Rivista*, 11, 2014, pp. 217–259.
Paolo CAMMAROSANO, "Il sistema fiscale delle città toscane", in *La Toscana nel secolo XIV. Caratteri di una civiltà regionale tardo medioevo*, Pisa 1988, pp. 201–213 (reprinted in *Studi di storia medievale. Economia, territorio, società*, Trieste 2009, pp. 243–254).
Paolo CAMMAROSANO, "Le origini della fiscalità pubblica delle città italiane," in *Studi di storia medievale. Economia, territorio, società*, Trieste, 2009, pp. 229–242.
Carlo CAPRA, "The Italian States in the Early Modern Period", in *The Rise of Fiscal State in Europe, c.1200–1815*, ed. Richard BONNEY, Oxford, 1999, pp. 417–442.
Mauro CARBONI, *Il debito della città. Mercato del credito, fisco e società a Bologna fra Cinque e Seicento*, Bologna 1995.
Le carte del Capitolo della cattedrale di Verona, 2 vol., ed. Emanuela LANZA, Rome, 2006.
Federica CENGARLE, "Il distretto fiscale di Vercelli sotto Gian Galeazzo (1378–1402): una proposta di cartografia informatica", in *Vercelli nel secolo XIV*, ed. Alessandro BARBERO and Rinaldo COMBA, Vercelli, 2010, pp. 377–410.
Giorgio CHITTOLINI, "Notes sur la politique fiscale de Charles Quint dans le duché de Milan: le '*nuovo catasto*' et les rapports entre ville et campagne", in *The World of Emperor Charles V*, ed. Willem Pieter BLOCKMANS and M. E. H. Nicolette MOUT, Amsterdam, 2004, pp. 143–160.

Jean Claude Hocquet, *Il sale e la fortuna di Venezia*, Rome, 1990.

Emanuele Conte and Sara Menzinger, *La Summa Trium Librorum di Rolando da Lucca (1195–1234). Fisco, politica, scientia iuris*, Rome, 2012.

Elio Conti, *L'imposta diretta a Firenze nel Quattrocento*, Rome 1984.

Elio Conti, *I catasti agrari della Repubblica Fiorentina e il catasto particellare toscano (secoli XIV–XIX)*, Rome, 1966.

Massimo Costantini, "Le coesistenze: le strutture dell'ospitalità" in *Storia di Venezia dalle origini alla caduta della Serenissima*, vol. V: *Il Rinascimento. Società ed economia*, Rome, 1996.

Charles-Marie de La Roncière, "Indirect Taxes or 'Gabelle' at Florence in the fourteenth Century: the Evolution of Tariffs and Problems of Collection", in *Florentine Studies. Politics and Society in Renaissance Florence*, ed. Nicholas Rubinstein, London, 1968, pp. 140–192.

Laura De Angelis Cappabianca, *Voghera alla fine del Trecento. Fiscalità signorile, demografia, società*, Milan, 2004.

Giuseppe De Luca, "Debito pubblico, mercato finanziario ed economia reale nel Ducato di Milano e nella Repubblica di Venezia tra XVI e XVII secolo", in *Debito pubblico e mercati finanziari*, pp. 119–146

Beatrice Del Bo, "Mercanti e finanze statali nel ducato di Milano in età visconteo-sforzesca", in *Il governo dell'economia. Italia e Penisola Iberica nel basso Medioevo*, ed. Lorenzo Tanzini and Sergio Tognetti, Rome, 2014, pp. 131–153.

Statuti di Bologna del 1288, ed. Gina Fasoli and Pietro Sella, 2 vol., Vatican City, 1937.

Storia di Venezia dalle origini alla caduta della Serenissima, 12 vol. Rome, 1991–2002.

Credito e cittadinanza nell'Europa mediterranea dal Medioevo all'Età Moderna, ed. Ezio Claudio Pia, Asti, 2014.

L'anagrafe e le denunce fiscali di Legnago (1430–32). Società ed economia in un centro minore della pianura veneta del Quattrocento, ed. Bianca Chiappa, Sandra Della Riva and Gian Maria Varanini, Verona, 1997.

Giuseppe Felloni, "Cenni storici", in *Inventario dell'archivio del Banco di San Giorgio (1407–1805)*, 4, *Debito pubblico*, 1, Genoa, 1989, pp. 9–11.

Enrico Fiumi, "L'imposta diretta nei comuni medievali della Toscana", in *Studi in onore di Armando Sapori*, vol. I, Milan-Varese, 1957, pp. 327–353.

Luciana Frangioni, *Milano e le sue strade*, Bologna, 1982.

Santa Frescura Nepoti, "Natura ed evoluzione dei dazi bolognesi nel secolo XIII", in *Atti e memorie. Deputazione di storia patria per le province di Romagna*, 31, 1980–1981, pp. 137–163, p. 158.

Paolo Gabriele Nobili, *Alle origini della città. Credito, fisco e società nella Bergamo del Duecento*, Bergamo, 2012.

Paolo Gabriele Nobili, "Alle origini della fiscalità comunale. Fodro, estimo e prestiti a Bergamo fra fine XII e metà XIII secolo", *Reti Medievali* 11/1, 2010, pp. 45–78.

Maria Ginatempo and Lucia Sandri, *L'Italia delle città. Il popolamento urbano tra Medioevo e Rinascimento (secoli XIII-XVI)*, Florence, 1990.

Maria Ginatempo, *Prima del debito. Finanziamento della spesa pubblica e gestione del deficit nelle grandi città toscane (1200–1350 ca.)*, Florence, 1997.

Maria Ginatempo, "Spunti comparativi sulle trasformazioni della fiscalità nell'Italia post-comunale", in *Politiche finanziarie e fiscali nell'Italia settentrionale (secoli XIII–XV)*, ed. Patrizia Mainoni, Milan, 2001, pp. 125–222.

Marta Gravela, "Contare nel catasto. Valore delle cose e valore delle persone negli estimi delle città italiane (secoli XIV–XV)", in *Valore delle cose e valore delle persone dall'Antichità all'Età moderna*, ed. Massimo Vallerani, Rome, 2018, pp. 271–294.

Marta Gravela, "Comprare il debito della città. Élite politiche e finanze comunali a Torino nel XIV secolo", in *Quaderni Storici* 49, 2014, pp. 743–773.

Marta Gravela, "Un mercato esclusivo. Gabelle, pedaggi ed egemonie politiche nella Torino tardomedievale," in *Reti Medievali Rivista*, 19/1, 2018, DOI: 10.6092/1593-2214/5614.

Paolo Grillo, "L'introduzione dell'estimo e la politica fiscale del Comune di Milano nel secolo XIII", in *Politiche finanziarie e fiscali nell'Italia settentrionale (secoli XIII-XV)*, ed. Patrizia Mainoni, Milan, 2001, pp. 11–38.

Paolo Grillo, "Rivolte antiviscontee a Milano e nelle campagne fra XIII e XIV secolo", in *Rivolte urbane e rivolte contadine nell'Europa del Trecento. Un confronto*, ed. Monique Bourin, Giuliano Pinto and Giovanni Cherubini, Florence, 2008, pp. 197–216.

Paolo GRILLO, "I religiosi al servizio dello stato (comuni e signorie, secoli XIII–inizio XIV)", in *La mobilità sociale nel Medioevo italiano.3. Il mondo ecclesiastico*, ed. Sandro CAROCCI and Amedeo DE VINCENTIIS, Rome, 2017, pp. 313–336.

Alfredo GROHMANN, *L'imposizione diretta nei comuni dell'Italia centrale nel XIII secolo. La* Libra *di Perugia del 1285*, Rome, 1986.

David HERLIHY and Christiane KLAPISCH-ZUBER, *Les Toscans et leurs familles*, Paris, 1978.

Statuti inediti della città di Pisa dal XII al XIV secolo, ed. Francesco BONAINI, Florence, 1870.

Julius KIRSHNER, "Nascoste in bella vista: donne cittadine nell'Italia tardo-medievale", in *Cittadinanze. Forme di appartenenza nel mondo medievale*, ed. Sara MENZINGER, Rome, 2017, pp. 195–228.

Michael KNAPTON, "Le dinamiche delle finanze pubbliche", in *Storia di Venezia. Dalle Origini alla caduta della Serenissma*, vol. III: *la formazione dello stato patrizio*, Rome, 1997, pp. 475–528.

Michael KNAPTON, "Il fisco nello Stato veneziano di Terraferma fra '300 e '500: la politica delle entrate", in *Il sistema fiscale veneto. Problemi e aspetti (XV–XVIII secolo*, ed. Giorgio BORRELLI, Paola LANARO and Francesco VECCHIATO, Verona, 1982, pp. 15–58.

Michael KNAPTON, "Venice and the *Terraferma*", in *The Italian Renaissance State*, ed. Andrea GAMBERINI and Isabella LAZZARINI, Cambridge, 2012, pp. 132–155.

Michael KNAPTON, "Il sistema fiscale nello stato di Terraferma nei secoli XIV–XVIII. Cenni generali", in *Venezia e la Terraferma. Economia e società*, Bergamo, 1989, pp. 19–30.

Michael KNAPTON, "Il fisco nello Stato veneziano di terraferma tra '300 e '500: la politica delle entrate", in *Il sistema fiscale veneto. Problemi e aspetti, XV–XVIII secolo*, ed. Giovanni BORELLI, Paola LANARO and Francesco Vecchiato, Verona, 1982, pp. 15–57.

Isabella LAZZARINI, "Prime osservazioni su finanze e fiscalità in una signoria cittadina: i bilanci gonzagheschi fra Tre e Quattrocento", in *Politiche finanziarie e fiscali nell'Italia settentrionale (secoli XIII–XV)*, ed. Patrizia MAINONI, Milan, 2001, pp. 87–124.

Franca LEVEROTTI, "La crisi finanziaria del ducato di Milano alla fine del Quattrocento", in *Milano nell'età di Ludovico il Moro*, Milan, 1983, vol. II, pp. 585–632.

Lo Stato territoriale fiorentino (secoli XIV–XV). Ricerche, linguaggi, confronti, ed. William J. CONNELL and Andrea ZORZI, San Miniato 1996,

Gino LUZZATTO, *Il debito pubblico a Venezia dagli ultimi decenni del XII secolo alla fine del XV*, Varese-Milan, 1963 (initially published under a different title in 1929 and later rewritten).

Gino LUZZATTO, *Storia economica di Venezia dall'XI al XVI secolo*, Venice, 1995.

William M. BOWSKY, *The Finance of the Commune of Siena (1287–1355)*, Oxford, 1970.

Patrizia MAINONI, *Le radici della discordia. Ricerche sulla fiscalità a Bergamo tra XIII e XV secolo*, Milan, 1997.

Patrizia MAINONI, "A proposito della 'rivoluzione fiscale' nell'Italia settentrionale del XII secolo", in *Studi Storici*, 1, 2003, pp. 5–42.

Patrizia MAINONI, "*Viglaebium opibus primum*. Uno sviluppo economico nella Lombardia del Quattrocento", in *Metamorfosi di un borgo. Vigevano in età visconteo-sforzesca*, ed. Giorgio CHITTOLINI, Milan, 1992, pp. 193–266.

Patrizia MAINONI, "Fiscalità signorile e finanza pubblica nello stato visconteo-sforzesco", in *Estados y mercados financieros en el Occidente cristiano (siglos XIII–XVI), XLI Semanas Estudios Medievales Estella*, Pamplona, 2015, pp. 105–156.

Patrizia MAINONI, "Il governo del re. Finanza e fiscalità nelle città angioine (Piemonte e Lombardia al tempo di Carlo I d'Angiò)" in *Gli Angiò nell'Italia nord-occidentale (1259–1382)*, ed. Rinaldo COMBA, Milan, 2006, pp. 103–137.

Patrizia MAINONI, "Finanza e fiscalità nella prima metà del Trecento" in *La congiuntura del primo Trecento in Lombardia (1290–1360)*, ed. Paolo GRILLO and François MENANT, Rome, 2019, pp. 19–42.

Patrizia MAINONI, "La gabella del sale nell'Italia del nord, secoli XIII–XIV", in *Politiche finanziarie e fiscali nell'Italia settentrionale (secoli XIII–XV)*, ed. Patrizia MAINONI, Milan, 2001, pp. 39–86.

Jean-Claude MAIRE VIGUEUR, *Cavalieri e cittadini. Guerra, conflitti e società nell'Italia comunale*, Bologna. 2003, pp. 259–261.

Sara MENZINGER (ed.), *Cittadinanze medievali: dinamiche di appartenenza a un corpo comunitario*, Rome 2017.

Sara MENZINGER, Massimo VALLERANI, "Giuristi e città: fiscalità, giustizia e cultura giuridica tra XII e XIII secolo. Percorsi di ricerca", in *I comuni di Jean-Claude Maire Vigueur. Percorsi storiografici*, ed. Maria Teresa CACIORGNA, Sandro CAROCCI and Andrea ZORZI, Rome, 2014, pp. 201–234.

Sara MENZINGER, "Pagare per appartenere. Sfere di interscambio tra fiscalità laica in Francia meridionale e nell'Italia comunale (XII secolo)", in *Quaderni Storici*, 49, 2014, pp. 673–708.

Sara MENZINGER, "'Una Scienza Arcana.' *Res* e *persona* nelle teorie fiscali basso-medievali", in *Valore delle cose e valore delle persone dall'Antichità all'Età moderna*, ed. Massimo VALLERANI, Rome, 2018, pp. 209–240.

Jeffrey MINER, "Profit and Patrimony. Property, Markets, and Public Debt in Late Medieval Genoa", in *Business History Review*, 94/1, 2020, pp. 73–94.

Anthony MOLHO, *Florentine Public Finances in the Early Renaissance, 1400–1433*, Cambridge Mass. 1971.

Anthony MOLHO, *Firenze nel Quattrocento*, vol. I, *Politica e fiscalità*, Rome, 2006.

Reinhold MUELLER, *The Venetian Money Market. Banks, Panics and Public Debt, 1200–1500*, Baltimore and London, 1997.

Maria Nadia COVINI, "'*Alle spese di Zoan villano*': gli alloggiamenti militari nel dominio visconteo-sforzesco", in *Nuova Rivista Storica*, 76, 1992, pp. 1–56.

Gian Paolo G. SCHARF, *Borgo San Sepolcro a metà del Quattrocento. Istituzioni e società (1440–1460)*, Florence, 2003.

Gian Paolo G. SCHARF, "Fiscalità e finanza pubblica ad Arezzo nel periodo comunale" in *Archivio Storico Italiano*, 2006, pp. 215–266.

Luciano PEZZOLO, *Il fisco dei veneziani: finanza pubblica ed economia tra XV e XVII secolo*, Verona, 2003.

Luciano PEZZOLO, "La costituzione fiscale dello Stato veneziano," in *Il Commonwealth veneziano tra 1204 e la fine della Repubblica*, ed. Gherardo ORTALLI, Oliver Jens SCHMITT and Ermanno ORLANDO, Venice, 2015, pp. 109–129.

Luciano PEZZOLO, "Tradizione e innovazione. I debiti governativi nell'Italia del Rinascimento," in *Debito pubblico e mercati finanziari in Italia, secoli XIII–XX*, ed. Giuseppe DE LUCA and Angelo MOIOLI, Milan, 2007, pp. 15–30.

Luciano PEZZOLO, "Pas de dette sans impôts. Les relations entre la politique fiscale, les institutions et la situation politique en Italie entre 1350 et 1700", in *Ressources publiques et construction étatique en Europe*, ed. Katia BÉGUIN and Jean-Philippe GENET, Paris, 2015, pp. 131–148.

Luciano PEZZOLO, *Il fisco dei Veneziani: finanza pubblica ed economia tra XV e XVII secolo*, Venice, 2003.

Luciano PEZZOLO, *Una finanza d'ancien régime. La Repubblica veneta tra XV e XVIII secolo*, Naples, 2006.

Riccardo RAO, "Gli Angiò e la gestione delle finanze in Piemonte e in Lombardia", in *Périphéries financières angevines. Institutions et pratiques de l'administrations de territoires composites (XIIIe–XIVe siècle). Periferie finanziarie angioine. Istituzioni e pratiche di governo su territori compositi (sec. XIII–XIV)*, ed. Serena MORELLI, Rome, 2018, pp. 271–290.

Alessandra RIZZI, *Ludus/ludere. Giocare in Italia alla fine del medioevo*, Treviso-Rome, 1995.

Mauro RONZANI, "*Ecclesiastica libertas - ecclesiastica immunitas* dal Lateranense III al Lateranense IV", in *Il Lateranense IV. Le ragioni di un concilio*, Spoleto, 2017, pp. 367–382.

Franco SACCHETTI, *Le Trecento Novelle*, ed. Michelangelo ZACCARELLO, Florence, 2014.

Manuel SÁNCHEZ MARTÍNEZ, "La evolución de la fiscalidad regia en los países de la Corona de Aragón (c.1280–1356)", in *Europa en los umbrales de la crisis (1250–1350)*. XXI *Semana Estudios Medievales Estella*, Pamplona, 1994, pp. 393–428.

Heinrich SIEVEKING, *Genueser Finanzwesen 1. Genueser Finanzwesen vom 12. Bis.14. Jahrhundert*, Freiburg 1898 and *Genuese Finanzwesen 2. Die Casa di S. Giorgio*, Freiburg, 1899 (translated into Italian as *Studio sulle finanze genovesi nel Medioevo e in particolare sulla Casa di S. Giorgio*, in *Atti della Società Ligure di Storia Patria* 1905, part I, pp. XIII–257 and 1906, part II, pp. VII–364).

David STASAVAGE, *States of Credit: Size, Power and the Development of European Polities*, Princeton, 2011.

Giacomo TODESCHINI, "Finanza e usura: i linguaggi dell'economia pubblica come retoriche della disuguaglianza sociale (XII–XV secolo)", in *Estados y mercados financieros en el Occidente cristiano (siglos XIII–XVI)*, XLI *Semanas Estudios Medievales Estella*, Pampluna, 2015, pp. 83–104.

Massimo VALLERANI, "Il valore dei *cives*. La definizione del valore negli estimi bolognesi del XIV secolo", in *Valore delle cose e valore delle persone dall'Antichità all'Età moderna*, ed. Massimo VALLERANI, Rome, 2018, pp. 241–270.

Massimo VALLERANI, "Fiscalità e limiti dell'appartenenza alla città in età comunale. Bologna fra Due e Trecento," in *Quaderni storici*, 147, 2014, pp. 709–742.

Cinzio VIOLANTE, "Le origini del debito pubblico e lo sviluppo costituzionale del Comune" (republished in *Economia, società, istituzioni a Pisa nel basso medioevo. Saggi e ricerche*, Bari 1980).

Cinzio VIOLANTE, "Imposte dirette e debito pubblico nel basso medioevo" (republished in *Economia, società, istituzioni a Pisa nel basso medioevo. Saggi e ricerche*, Bari 1980).

Raffaele VOLANTE, "La concezione patrimoniale dell'imposta nel diritto comune", in *Quaderni fiorentini per la storia del pensiero giuridico moderno*, 49, 2020, pp. 349–374.

Chris WICKHAM, *Sleepwalking into a new World. The Emergence of Italian Communes in the Twelfth Century*, Princeton, Oxford 2015.

Luigi ZANONI, *Gli Umiliati nei loro rapporti con l'eresia, l'industria della lana ed i Comuni nei secoli XII e XIII*, Milan 1911 (reprint Rome, 1970).

9
THE CHURCH LANDS (1200–1550)

Armand Jamme

If the development of a tax system is necessarily linked to the confirmation of State power, it is clear that papal taxation in the Church's Lands could only occur based on the expansion and retraction of papal authority. Pope Innocent III has always been seen as the founder of a "Papal State",[1] but many of his predecessors had acted as if they were, and his successes were not long lasting. The trigger was apparently the death of Henry VI, Holy Roman Emperor, which caused the Staufer's dream of uniting Italy and Germany to finally collapse. However, it took the popes more than half a century to remove the Hohenstaufen dynasty from the political scene, as their subjects frequently switched loyalties from one side to another: the political position of the towns and the nobility was based therefore on specific agreements negotiated with the sovereign or his representatives. The communities wanted to have a direct relationship with the central authority, without intermediaries, while State powers everywhere were expanding and thus relied on administrations, statutes and ordinances with collective functionalities.

When Frederick II died in 1250, the Church Lands included three provinces, in addition to Campagna and Sabina, which had ancient links with Rome: the Patrimony of St Peter in Tuscany, created by Innocent III to unite scattered lands primarily west of the Tiber (as he was not able to annex the whole of Tuscany), and two provinces formerly governed in the name of the emperor, the Duchy of Spoleto and the March of Ancona. In the 1270s, the pope expanded his authority northwards, firstly beyond the Alps, since he obtained the restitution by the king of France of the Comtat Venaissin, following the Treaty of Paris (1229), and then beyond the Apennines, where Romagna was ceded by the king of Germany, the exarchate of Ravenna having been under the virtual control of Rome since the Byzantines.[2] Thereafter, the expansion of the Church came to a halt. In the fourteenth century, papal acquisitions were marginal with the exception of Avignon, since Benedict XII refused to buy the Dauphiné. The challenge for the pope at that time was to make his Italian subjects obey him, which only Cardinal Albornoz really managed to do from 1353 onwards, in transforming the Church Lands into a principality.[3] However, Albornoz's model was short-lived. Many communes reverted to de facto independent status, negotiating their submission, while *condottieri* and relatives of the pontiffs carved out their own small State within these lands during the Great Schism and the conciliar crisis. The authority of these new lords in the March of Ancona and in Romagna alternatively ebbed and flowed during the second half of the Quattrocento, until the political ambitions of Cesare Borgia eliminated them all.[4] Therefore, it was not until the reign of Julius II that papal domination ultimately reached a level in central Italy somewhat comparable to that of the Albornozian period. The climax of the territorial development of the Church came shortly afterwards, when the contiguous territories of Parma and Piacenza were united into a province called Gallia Cispadana, which came under the authority of the papacy and lasted until 1545.[5]

Interest in the finances of these vast territories is relatively recent, even if at the turn of the nineteenth and twentieth centuries, a few historians produced studies still essential for research, particularly regarding the fifteenth century.[6] The works of J. Delumeau, M. Monaco, P. Partner and D. Waley in the 1950s should be considered pioneering.[7] For a long time, historians were more focused on questions pertaining to the finances of the papacy, sometimes to point out its agreements with bankers, rather than considering the impact of taxation on its territories. Ostensibly on the fringes of the institution, the Church Lands only began to interest scholars when it became accepted they played an important role in the financing of papal programs.[8] Hence the analysis of territorial taxation developed from the sixteenth century onwards, and for the century that preceded it[9]... not without some controversies based on the academic split between medievalists and modernists. For example, W. Reinhard in 1984 stated that the sixteenth and seventeenth centuries were the great period of development of the territorial tax system, in contrast with earlier times when the Church Lands could have been "an oasis without taxes"! Still today it is considered that the territories under the pope's control contributed more or less half of the Church's total revenue circa 1500. This idea may have been reinforced by the sources themselves, since from the fifteenth century onwards, the clerks of the Camera divided the revenues into two groups, spiritual and temporal, even though this classification was far from reality, as already noted by W. Reinhard.[10] For earlier centuries, the Church Lands were reputed to be of no financial benefit to the pope. Occasional works focusing on specific provinces or pontificates are also useful for questions of long-term analysis.[11] In this compartmentalised historiographical sketch, it should be pointed out that the fine synthesis authored by A. Gardi in 1986 is still inescapable.[12]

For the fourteenth to sixteenth centuries, the study of territorial taxation is facilitated by the conservation of the registers of provincial treasuries and assorted tax collectors. These documents are, for the most part, preserved in the Vatican archives as well as the Archivio di Stato of Rome. The loss of almost all the account registers of the twelfth and thirteenth centuries makes it impossible to fully grasp the differences between the imperial and papal tax systems. Similarly, the gaps in the series of accounts of the fourteenth and fifteenth centuries make it difficult to perceive possible harmonisation policies between different provinces, some of which were formerly subject to the pope, and others being of more recent acquisition. Therefore, a large part of the questions concerning papal territorial taxation cannot be addressed without making extensive use of the rich archives held in Italian communes.[13]

The development of State taxation on Church Lands necessarily included different tax experiments developed by communes, sometimes modified by the various uprisings and revolts against their own tax systems, which were created by the ruling class. Between the multiplication of taxes on trade, on consumption and the introduction of direct taxation based on property assessment, they also involved alternative choices according to changes in their political regime. Historiography has identified an overall shift from episcopal government to communal regime, then to a lord (*signore*), before ultimately falling under the domination of the pope; this general trend experienced particular scansions everywhere.[14] The debates over urban fiscal policies then entered into correspondence with both the taxation policies and the financial challenges of the central power, which seems to have generally avoided conflict with cities on that matter. Yet the question concerning the urban fiscal methodologies in the conception of the new pontifical taxes is still a frontier of research, even though the fiscal policies of the cities and the pontifical power undoubtedly influenced each other long before modern times.

For historians, two periods should be considered in the history of these territories. The first occurred when these lands were merely an appendix of apostolic sovereignty, which was based on spiritual and ecclesiastical foundations. The second began when they became a necessary condition of that sovereignty. In the thirteenth and fourteenth centuries, income from Church Lands was apparently not essential to papal government of Christendom. However, during the fifteenth and sixteenth centuries, there was a sharp contraction in ecclesiastical resources, albeit not at all irreversible,[15] and taxation in these territories played a key role in supporting papal finances. Therefore, the transition between these two periods would have taken place during the Great Schism, which undermined the roots of the medieval papacy! In fact, a real diachronic study of papal fiscal policies would modify such an analysis. If what really changed the condition of the pope's subjects was the transformation of central power into a sort of "Fiscal-Military State" – a model in which economic development was based on maintaining strong armed forces, as well as forcing the citizens into a regime of high taxation[16] – then it will be necessary to revise these conclusions, as the transition did not actually take place during the Schism and therefore cannot be "softly" connected to the political context of the mid-fifteenth century.[17]

From the twelfth to fourteenth centuries: Towards a decline in general taxation?

Historians see the *cens** as one of the primary foundations of territorial taxation during Innocent III's times, as it is generally considered that the letters he addressed in 1200 to the communes of Fermo, Ancona, Osimo, Fano, Iesi and Pesaro (all in the March of Ancona) are representative of the forms of submission expected by the papacy. These letters limit financial obligations to the payment of a *procuratio* to nuncios and papal legates when present in the province, and to an annual *pensionem* (only fixed for Fano and Iesi at 50 and 40 pounds, respectively), which was to be taken half from the city, half from the diocese, at the rate of 9 *denarii* for each hearth, *ut more vestro loquamur* (as specified in the text), *exceptis clericis, militibus, iudicibus, advocatis, tabellionibus et his qui nullas possessiones habere noscuntur, qui non consueverunt affictum prestare*,[18] which is obviously a very strange manner to determine a *cens*.* On the basis of these letters, historians therefore view the payment of *cens** and procurations* (derived from an imperial *fodrum*, which would be the obligation to provide hospitality to the emperor and his representatives[19]) as the basis of pontifical territorial taxation.[20]

Taking into consideration the porosity and polysemy of the medieval fiscal lexicon, it seems appropriate to again take up the question, starting with documents that earlier studies had neglected: the administrative inquiries carried out in the decades following the problematic transfer of sovereignty over the Duchy of Spoleto and of the March of Ancona.[21] In 1232, the Bishop of Beauvais Milon de Châtillon, rector of those two provinces, entrusted a certain Teodino with an inquiry into the rights of the Church in two districts of the Duchy: the Valnerina and the Mountain of Spoleto. He focused on the defence and restoration of the rights of the Church, which intended to succeed the Empire without revolutionising the forms of political authority. The enquiry showed that the rector's representatives demanded, sometimes by subjecting the inhabitants who resisted predation, the payment of *fodrum, banna, follias, salariis, adiutoria de festis* and *albergarias*.[22] For all the witnesses, paying the *fodrum* was an act of recognition of political domination. The findings of this document are confirmed by another survey carried out in the spring of 1263 in the northern part of the Patrimony of St Peter: in

Acquapendente, the sovereign's representatives collected the *focaticum* and half the revenues coming from judicial matters and from the tolls levied at the Porta della Ripa.[23] Both of these surveys provided consistent evidence, despite the diversity of the terms used, on the reality of tax collection, and we note that none of the witnesses mentioned the slightest payment of a *cens*★!

The *fodrum* in the Duchy of Spoleto was called *focaticum* in the Patrimony and *affictus* in the March of Ancona. This appears to be the primary tax: the person or institution that collected it each year was the lord, according to all testimony. Several witnesses provided its basis: *XXVI lucensium per quodlibet focum; XXVI denariorum per focularem*.[24] It was therefore not a right of lodging, but a hearth tax★ paid by both the communities under the pope's lordship and by those dependent on other lords.[25] This tax constituted the first general and ordinary tax paid by the populations of central Italy, despite the fact some historians fail to acknowledge it occurring until 1531.[26] It was no longer the sign of sovereignty, even if it was originally due to the emperor, but only, especially after the famous Peace of Constance (1183), political domination.[27] In September 1217, when the podestà of Spoleto granted the right to build a new *castrum*, the beneficiaries agreed to *anuatim dare per unumquemque focularem XXVI lucenses pro fodero*. These examples were numerous until the end of the thirteenth century.[28] Through the distribution of this tax, one can clearly see the usurpations by the communes of the emperor's rights. From this, obviously follows the need for the dominated communities to *exhibere foculares* to their lord, as Frederick II even recalled in a diploma of June 1244.[29] Indeed, many were exempted on these lists of taxable hearths: in Acquapendente, for example, the *focaticum* was not paid by *militibus et a nobilibus hominibus, a iudicibus, sacerdotibus, notariis, medicis, iaculatoribus, orfanis et viduis sine regimine, et ab hominibus qui non haberent valentiam LX sol. et ab hominibus, qui non sunt consueti dare seu solver*.[30] Those exemptions were probably not of papal origin. Even at the end of the thirteenth century, a French pope like Martin IV was fully aware that the *affictus* was of imperial origin, as he noted in a *rescriptum* relating to Urbino.[31]

As lord, the pope also received the entirety or part of the *banna* and *follias*, the fines imposed locally by his judge for any breach of the statutes, and the *salaria* paid for the initiation of any legal case. The communities of the Spoleto Valley had to provide wheat and spelt as aid for Christmas and Easter. They also had to provide for the maintenance of the representatives of the *dominus*, whose title fluctuated (the witnesses mention bailli, *nuncius* and *procurator*), and of the judge if there was one. Some communities were subject to *albergarias* or *procurationes*,★ which for the Church meant the cost of hosting the prelates visiting the benefices under their jurisdiction.[32] Finally, since this was an obligation that entailed costs, the summons to parliament and military operations must be mentioned. The acts of submission of the municipalities, large and small, to the pope or the emperor only stated their duty, without additional details, since it differed according to the various circumstances. The cities were responsible for managing and organising military service, by requiring the communities they dominated to contribute,[33] using for that the hearth tax★ lists they had. The delays caused by such a system explain why the powers tried to commute the obligation for military service into a monetary contribution, such as Frederick II did in the Duchy in June 1244, *ita tamen quod loco exercitus faciendi dent pecunia in ea proportione taxanda qua taxantur alia castra et villas pro modo et facultatibus suis*, as well as his stubborn opponent, the Cardinal Raniero Capocci, who in March 1248 delegated to his notary and close confidant the obligation to collect the money *pro stipendiis militum que habemus et habere intendimus*.[34]

Is it possible, in the absence of any account registers, to assess the importance of all those taxes? An undated document entitled *Proventus et reditus de Ducatu* has been preserved, produced in the 1230s, before Frederick II and his son Enzo took over much of the province.[35] The area considered by the description extends from Terni to Assisi, passing through Foligno, without however mentioning Spoleto. For the 33 communities concerned, the payment of the *fodrum* is the first tax mentioned, except for the cities of Assisi and Foligno, which were visibly exempt. The description then records the aid due for Christmas and Easter, paid by all the communities except Assisi, Foligno and Terni. Then it mentions the *banna* and *follias*, collected at a third, two-thirds or in full, then any toll revenue, which was collected in the same way. Finally, some *castra* were required to supply wheat and spelt, sometimes in large quantities. These levies were already and by far much more burdensome in the countryside than in the cities. The difference is even glaring if we compare the city of St Francis, which paid no taxes, with Cannara, which lies immediately at its feet in the plain, and had to pay 16 pounds and 16 cents for the *fodrum*, 10 pounds for the Nativity, 7 pounds for the Resurrection, which gave the rector all the income from the *banna* and *follias*, plus 100 *rasengas* of wheat and 100 *rasengas* of spelt per year… That the mendicant friars had a preference for towns from the outset is very easy to see!

These fiscal inequalities suggest relations were already strained in the twelfth century between representatives of the imperial power (the dukes of Spoleto and the margraves of Ancona) and the large towns: the competition for the control of the territory between these powers appears to have been intense, especially for the virgin spaces which could be allotted and for the small *castra*… which sometimes appealed to the emperor to get out of these conflicts![36] By taking over the Duchy and the March, the papacy inherited a system of relations already split by the privileges accorded and the politico-territorial ambitions of the towns.[37] From this perspective, the struggle against the Staufer had even more devastating effects than ever: for more than thirty years, the ambitions of the great cities had been brought out into the open, starting with Rome, which entered into competition with the pope, including on the fiscal level since the city claimed the right to the collection of the *focaticum* in a large part of Campagna and Patrimony. Passing from one loyalty to another, the cities obtained confirmation of their tax exemptions, limited their military obligations, while at the same time expanding their territories. The final victory of the pope was thus achieved at the expense of his authority, and with a clear decrease in the resources collected by the provincial administrations.[38]

After the Angevin victory, a wide-ranging tax collection effort involved new administrative inquiries leading to the compilation of new books describing the rights of the Church… but all of which have been lost.[39] For the last decades of the thirteenth century, it is therefore the communal documentation that allows us to understand the evolution of papal taxation. This must be taken in consideration with the few extant extracts of accounts and reports preserved. The whole of this documentation clearly highlights the old differences in the tax systems of each province, which developed until the fourteenth century as independent States, a fact that ultimately explains the specificities of the tax lexicon already noted.[40]

The only account book preserved in its entirety, relating to the March of Ancona in 1279–1280, shows mainly judicial receipts.[41] There were only two taxes, the *fitto* (as this account is written in Tuscan) paid by the communities and the *procuragione* paid by clerics. The amount of the *fitto* at that time appears to have remained stable, as shown by the receipts kept by the communes. The date of this general stabilisation, however, remains unknown. Around 1360, a notary working for the Duke of Spoleto explained that originally the *focularia* had been paid by each *domus in qua fiebat fumen seu ignis*, at the rate of 26 *denarii* per year; the amount of the tax varied from one year to another since it resulted from the number of hearths that *tunc erat* in each community. Then it was decided that the communities should pay a fixed sum *incommutabiliter* on the 1st of May.[42] The sources seem to distinguish between these two phenomena: the granting of privileges by the pope or the emperor to certain communities, thus exempting them from presenting their lists of households,[43] and the general granting of this same favour to all communities. This stabilisation of the *affictus* cannot be observed in the Patrimony of St Peter due to gaps in the documentation. But in the end, all this explains the evolution of the lexicon used by the notaries, who henceforth established an equivalence between *focaticum/fodrum* and *cens*,★ as such an evolution amounted to the payment of a flat fee. As for the *procuragione inposta per messer lo Marchese*, it only concerned monasteries, priories, collegiate churches and diocesan clergy in the March,[44] whereas in the Patrimony its basis was very different, since it was paid both by communities, like Orvieto and Viterbo, which each paid 100 pounds, and by the clergy. It was probably for this reason, that the term was used in the plural in that province.[45]

The local communities were also responsible for the rector's representative, a *castellanus* or a *podestà*, who was entitled to receive room and board, which was an important charge when their *familia* was large. The payment of these wages was not, strictly speaking, a revenue since these sums did not reach the provincial treasury. However, they were part of the resources available to be used for governing, as shown by the list drawn up by the administration of the March in 1283, which lists the salaries each community had to pay and which exceeded 4,800 pounds a year.[46]

Finally, the nobles and communes were liable for military service. Waley's statistics emphasise the extent of their noncompliance,[47] but his results were impacted by the documentation extant, where absolutions abound following the payment of a fine. The communal archives of the March also show communities that went well beyond their obligations![48] Probably influenced by the Angevin victory, the military contribution took on the name of "taille" in the March, which was governed from 1272 by a servant of the Angevin king, Foulque de Puyricard.[49] "Imposed by the rector" during the provincial parliament who distributed the burden, the *tallia militum* was then regularly required in this province. And just like military service, it was both recurrent and variable. The rector fixed the amounts (the texts sometimes mention a duplicate *tallia*★) and the deadlines, in the same way that he used to establish the total number of horsemen that each community had to provide.[50] The parliament probably decided on the distribution of the *tallia*★ among all of the communities, which either had to develop their taxes on trade and consumption or levy a *colletta* on landed property to fulfil their obligations. In the March of Ancona, the *tallia*★ was a substantial tax. The receipts preserved in Fabriano show that between 1278 and 1281, the commune paid more than 2,000 pounds.[51] The difference is very clear with the Duchy of Spoleto, which maintained the system of direct service, i.e., a maximum of eight days of service per year within the province, and also with the Patrimony, where the levy (which had to be authorised by the pope) brought in a total of less than 2,000 pounds per year for the whole province around 1299.[52]

The sources therefore reveal very different fiscal realities from one province to another… which the annexations of the Comtat Venaissin and Romagna (in 1274 and 1279, respectively) certainly increased. In the Comtat, the first surviving account books suggest a total absence of tax revenues in the thirteenth century. The pope was merely a large landowner who dispensed justice,[53] and nothing is known about the military service commitment theoretically duty-bound by the communities. In Romagna, the communities were required to pay the *affictus fumantie*, according to an ostensibly variable rate,[54] and military service was often replaced by a financial contribution.[55] They also had to receive and pay the representatives appointed locally by the rector. There is no record of *procurationes*,★ however. To a certain extent, the fiscal status of the Comtat Venaissin seems to have been quite similar to those of the Duchy of Spoleto, and the one of the March, of Romagna. The diversity of these tax systems in the papal territories did not really pose a problem for governing, as it was a time – we should remember – when the bulk of their resources came first and foremost from the exercise of justice. Nevertheless, it does raise questions about a possible policy of harmonisation, since the popes chose to endow each of these provinces with the same government structure (i.e., a rector, a treasurer and judges).

From the first decades of the thirteenth century, in order to overcome the continual protests of the communities against the government of rectors, the papacy tended to convert all or part of its rights of jurisdiction and lordship into a *cens*.* Rieti, for example, was obligated in 1198 to pay 13 sous and 30 denarii for *justiciis* and half of the *placitis et bannis et forefactis et de sanguine et de plaza et scorta et passagio et ponteis*, but Honorius III gave up all his rights in the town in 1226 in exchange for the payment of a *cens** of 30 pounds.[56] This change was easy to implement since the communities were not previously obliged to pay any *cens*,* and it simplified the administrative task for both the towns and the central power, although it modified the nature of the relationship with the lord-sovereign, who by consequence became more removed. During the thirteenth century, these conversions of rights into taxes multiplied.[57] In addition, they may have been a way for the pope to fight against the corruption of his own officers. In June 1299, Boniface VIII decided that Bettona, a small commune of the Duchy, which was fed up with repeated controversies with the rector over the payment of *banna* and *salaria*, and over the tolls and the Christmas and Resurrection aids, would pay an annual *cens** of 100 pounds to the Apostolic Chamber.[58] Lordship rights, taxes and levies were thus converted into a *cens** more sizeable than in Rieti, in spite of an inverse demographic ratio between the two communities.

In the course of the thirteenth century, other forms of conversion into a *cens** appeared, sometimes to end as well recriminations of the subjects against the rectors. At the beginning of the 1290s, Nicholas IV granted some forty small- and medium-sized communities of the March the right to appoint their own podestà, in exchange for a fee ranging from 16 to 150 pounds.[59] The pope also levied some *cens** on gardens, houses, lands, rights and estates that had been confiscated for rebellion, and then passed these goods on to private individuals, communes, lords or churches.[60] He thus took the typical papal licence of surrendering the use of Church goods to its most faithful sons, which occurred even in the ritual of coronation.[61] Being originally a usufruct fee for prerogatives belonging to the Church, these *cens** only became a recognitive form of pontifical sovereignty over time, by losing their "raison d'être".[62]

Such a policy created a direct relation between the pope and his subjects at the expense of the provincial administration. It therefore served the particularism of these communities. Moreover these conversions into a *cens** deepened the inequalities between the communities of the same province and undoubtedly weakened the rectors, who lost much of their authority, their resources and of course the right to appoint their own representative in many places. Did this development lead to an increase of judicial penalties, or even to new taxes? It is difficult to give a clear answer. The forms of nomination to the rectorate do not mention any new taxing powers[63]... perhaps of course, because the receipt of existing taxes was not working, as the register of the treasurer in the Patrimony in 1304–1306 shows. Revenues from justice and leasing accounted for 64 per cent of revenues. But if taxes only provided 26 per cent, it was also because their collection rate was very low: the *focatico* brought in 519 pounds in twenty months, whereas the annual revenue should have been around 1,500 pounds![64]

Residing beyond the Alps, the papacy initially lost interest in its Italian lands, whose government was entrusted to Gascon officials who did little to alter the existing balance. However, the report addressed to the pope in 1320 provides a less calamitous picture of the revenues in the Patrimony than the register of 1304–1306.[65] The resumption of provincial government, entrusted by John XXII to energetic rectors, allowed for the compilation of extremely precise accounts during the decades 1320–1330. This rich documentation, now preserved for all the provinces, confirms numerous elements suggested by the incomplete sources of the thirteenth century (diversity of provincial tax systems, weakness of taxation in some of them), as well as the originality of the solutions found by this pope to increase resources, while posing some methodological problems.

In the oldest province under the control of the papacy, Campagna, taxation always played a marginal role, or even none at all in certain years. In 1320 the actual tax revenue was limited to the procurations★ paid after the arrival of a new rector; but in 1324 the account shows no tax revenue at all.[66] In the Patrimony, the register of 1318–1320 mentions three taxes: the procurations,★ paid exclusively by the clerks, the *tallia*★ and the *focatico*, then bringing in 390, 339 and 219 florins, respectively. These represented only 18.6 per cent of the revenues. In the register for 1320–1322, the tax share of resources rose to almost 29 per cent due to a sharp drop in the revenues from justice.[67] In the Duchy of Spoleto, taxation was limited to the payment of a hearth tax,★ a gift to the rector (sometimes called *procuratio*★) and aids for Christmas and Easter, which amounted to between 200 and 300 florins. Here too, the bulk of the revenue came from justice.[68] The first surviving account register for Romagna, in 1325, shows only the collection of a hearth tax,★ which nevertheless yielded 2,880 pounds, and of some *cens*★ paid by ecclesiastical institutions. In the absence (apparently) of a levy, taxation represented only 19.3 per cent of annual revenues.[69] As for the Comtat Venaissin, the records show that under John XXII, the treasurer did not actually collect any taxes at all.[70]

These findings may nevertheless be revised by the rich documentation produced in the March of Ancona. Indeed, the report of an auditor specially commissioned from Avignon in 1324 has been preserved. He had access to all the registers, some of which are now lost. This report provides an accounting synthesis for the years 1321–1324, which opens a window on a writing system that is far more diversified than one might assume today when consulting the so-called general accounts that have been preserved. The composition of the revenues seems exceptional: in this report, there are the *cens*★ paid by the communes for their right to elect the podestà, the *affictum*, a subsidy★ paid by the clergy, a subsidy★ paid by the Jews, in addition to the *tallia*★ paid by the communities. The pontiff also granted the rector various tenths levied in the provinces of central Italy, amounting to 22,241 florins, plus a subsidy★ of more than 20,000 florins coming directly from Avignon.[71] If we remove the exogenous elements, taxation in the March now represents almost 30 per cent of revenues. What is remarkable is that the pope did not surmount the challenge of provincial resources by doubling the *tallia*★, as some rectors did in the thirteenth century, but rather by increasing taxes on clerics and non-Christians. The objective was clearly to avoid additional burdens on the faithful communities in the war against the rebels… and perhaps also to minimise the criticisms of the Franciscans concerning the wealth of the Church! This report nevertheless raises questions about the allegedly "general" character of the accounts kept for all these provinces.

The rich provincial documentation of the first half of the fourteenth century also gives us the opportunity to understand the behaviour of the population in regard to taxation, which may help explain the various provisions adopted by the popes. In the March in 1321–1324, the *cens*★ yielded only 2,350 pounds per year on average, while theoretically they should have yielded 2,900 pounds. For the *affictus*, which should have yielded 1,556 pounds, the results were even more disappointing, falling from 972 livres in 1321, climbing to 1,264 in 1322, but going down to 832 in 1323 and even 713 in 1324.[72] The secondary role of taxation in provincial revenues may have been justified by the collective behaviour of the subjects regarding existing taxes. To what extent did this attitude also explain why the rectors frequently levied heavy financial penalties against the communities? The question remains open. It is clear, however, that the complaints of the subjects, as shown by both rectoral and papal constitutions, mainly concerned the functioning of justice: in the decades 1270–1350, they rarely mention taxation, which remained weak or even non-existent at the time.

It is understandable that in these conditions, to ensure the normal functioning of the institutions and eventually to fight against rebellions, the pope had to be constantly concerned about his subjects and often had to provide his rectors with external resources. However, not all pontiffs believed that the provinces should not be living off their own revenue: during the decades 1330–1340, there was a sharp decline in the authority of the provincial rectors, with the exception of the Comtat Venaissin of course, because they were less financially supported by the Roman curia. Many communes in central Italy fell into the hands of "tyrants", much less out of rejection of papal taxation – contrary to what many historians affirm (!) – than because of the inefficiency of the provincial government.

The bumpy development of a State tax system

The subjects' perception of papal taxation changed in the second half of the fourteenth century. As shown in the account of Guillaume de Bénévent, treasurer of the wars of Cardinal Albornoz from 1355 to 1359, the conquest of the Italian cities was only possible due to financing coming from Avignon.[73] Yet with the deterioration of the French political situation following the battle of Poitiers (1356), Avignon's financial resources fell sharply. Even after the annexation of Bologna in 1360 and after the death of the Spanish cardinal in 1367, the war continued in central Italy: in addition to "internal" conquests (Todi and Perugia in 1371), "external" operations against the Visconti and their allies were undertaken. This context, marked by the continuity of conflict for more than twenty-five years, was at the origin of a fiscal revolution that profoundly modified the nature of the relations between the pope and his subjects. This topic is still ignored by the historiography, which favours a schismatic break, and then oppose Avignon's governing of these provinces and regimen of a State in the Quattrocento. In fact, under Albornoz's leadership, the government of the former provinces of central Italy entered resolutely into a State dimension. Historical interpretation has long been bogged down in the wrong direction, perhaps because most of the account registers for this period have been lost. However, the municipal archives preserve a very large number of receipts, which compensate for the loss of the registers and reveal the forms of this fiscal revolution brought about by the functioning of the costly powerful State model built by Albornoz and his successors.[74]

In 1355 in the parliament of Fermo, Albornoz imposed a *tallia*★ on all of the communities of the March that recognised his authority. This was a recurrent levy, regularly assessed every four months until at least 1376. In 1367, for example, the receipts referred to "the twelfth year of the levy", a statement which underlines the understanding by contemporaries of a change in the tax system. The payment, however, did not exempt the same communities from other charges (i.e., for building fortresses, port repairs, indemnities paid to mercenary companies, war against the Visconti, etc.). In short, even after having instituted the annual payment of the *tallia*★ (without requiring yearly a parliamentary approval), the cardinal continued to demand new taxes to meet specific needs. However, while these new "subsidies" requested in parliament became established, the annual tax burden borne by the communities continued to rise. In Rocca Contrada, a medium-size town in the March, it was about 1,300 ducats between 1955 and 1360, varied between 1,000 and 1,900 ducats between 1361 and 1370, and then reached 1,900 to 2,400 ducats between 1370 and 1375. In twenty years, according to the receipts preserved in the archives, this community paid the papal treasurers more than 30,000 ducats![75] The Albornozian legations subjected the communities to a real "State shock" marked by fiscal pressure that appears to have been out of control.

The same phenomena can be seen in the Duchy of Spoleto, which previously enjoyed an extremely favourable tax regime. From 1359 to 1360, the receipts kept in Assisi, Cascia,

Gubbio, Spello and Spoleto changed in nature. They are less often about *affictus* and aids than about subsidies (*ex causa concordie societatis, pro guerra Bononie*) brought to the cardinal, who did not use them for the Duchy.[76] At the same time, the rector began to collect sums to be used in the province *pro exercitu*.[77] Finally, more than ten years after the March of Ancona, a levy of a *tallia*★ in four terms was decreed, starting on 1 June 1366, with quite a high annual amount (1,938 ducats for Gubbio, 1,400 for Assisi and 1,080 for Spoleto[78]) and according to tried and tested logistics: on 4 July 1373, the syndic of Gubbio was issued a receipt "for the first term of the eighth year". For all the communities, the expense of the *tallia*★ represented a sum substantially greater than the eight days of military service previously required! In addition to this tax, extraordinary levies were also exacted (for the war against Perugia, for the construction of fortresses, for the war against the Visconti…), the amounts of which became increasingly onerous. A comparison between the March and the Duchy demonstrates a movement towards some uniformity and its consistency in the fiscal obligations of the pope's subjects. Gubbio, for example, paid 4,883 florins to the papal treasurers in the one-year period, between March 1374 and March 1375[79] – a uniformity reinforced by the *incameramento* of communal finances, that is to say, their control by an agent of the Apostolic Chamber, after the conquest of each town.

The same changes can be seen in the only surviving accounts for this period, namely the Patrimony of St Peter. *Focaticum* and *tallia*★ were still levied according to the old system, but here as well the proceeds from the subsidies soared: 4,763 florins in 1359–1360, 8,819 the following year, 8,896 thereafter, and finally the enormous sum for the year 1363–1364, which undoubtedly included many arrears, of 10,986 florins and 6,764 ducats.[80] All this data support the idea that the Italian lands of the Church had been transformed into a Fiscal State, or even a Fiscal-Military-State, during the 1360s, since it was henceforth the receipt of tax proceeds that kept the government solvent as it engaged in multiple conflicts.

Perhaps unexpectedly, a similar process was developed simultaneously in the Comtat Venaissin, from 1355 onwards, as the Comtat was also liable to taxation as a result of the wars in Provence and France. C. Faure thought about a lexical confusion in an imposition he considered unique each year,[81] whereas there were both a *tallia*★ and subsidies, which were approved by the provincial parliament and paid by the clergy, the nobles and the communities. The Comtat Venaissin did not require, unlike in Italy, the maintenance of a permanent army and the construction of countless citadels. As a result, fiscal pressure in that province did not reach a comparable level to central Italy until the Great Schism, which gradually enabled the provincial parliament to assert itself politically into the equation by managing the process of levying taxes and thus acquire real political authority.[82]

In central Italy, the Albornozian State model provoked, even during Albornoz's lifetime, numerous revolts against some of the cardinal's officers and relatives, and even involved entire regions. Communities and barons of Campagna rose up in 1366 to secure various exemptions, taking into account their contributory capacities.[83] The increasing fiscal pressure during the pontificate of Gregory XI, as his representative in Perugia pointed out,[84] raises the question of the relevance of a distant government of the State that the pope claimed. Between October 1375 and May 1376, barons, towns and castles, encouraged and supported by Florence, hoping to end the pope's political power in Italy, switched into rebellion, sometimes only for a few months if they were able to obtain increased autonomy and additional tax privileges through negotiations. It is clear, however, that with the so-called War of the Eight Saints and after the Great Schism, the State model built by Albornoz and his successors disappeared: the vicarial court, its chancery, the general treasury, all were swept away in the wars and ubiquitous policies of Urban VI.

The ephemeral recuperations of Boniface IX, and then of Martin V, were indeed developed on a provincial basis.[85] It came down to a regional definition of authority, guided by a Roman curia that had absorbed the State structures within it... without totally forgetting the experiences of the Albornozian model, which remained a political reference for several centuries. During the Schism, the innumerable erections of towns and their territories in vicariate for sometimes ridiculous fees created new fiscal entities, increasing the inequities between the various subjects of the pope. As is well known, the decades 1380–1440 were the height of the "lordship phenomenon" in central Italy, when many communities passed under the control of a few families and *condottieri* who sometimes enjoyed exorbitant privileges.[86] It is clear that, during the first half of the Schism, at least, the pope of Avignon was able to obtain *tallia*★ and subsidies with a good proportion in the Comtat Venaissin, whereas the Roman pope was quite incapable of doing so in his vast Italian provinces.[87] By the time the Schism ended in 1429, a commission of cardinals concluded that papal revenues had fallen to a third of the level prior to 1378.[88] Partner's fanciful analyses may be confusing,[89] but the sources prove the cardinals at the end of the pontificate of Martin V were right, as this collapse in revenues, contrary to what is often believed, was not solely the result of the fall of ecclesiastical taxation throughout Europe.

From the 1420s onwards, account registers are once again available for all of the Italian provinces. They show that the administration of resources was now decentralised. However, the provincial treasurers could only collected some of the revenues they had previously raised. After the Schism, the fall of judicial revenues was confirmed; the resources now consisted essentially on taxes. But there was a *Dogana del bestiame* that sold permits for access to pastures, a *Dogana delle tratte* collecting taxes on the grain trade, some *Salarie* managing the sale of salt, etc. The disappearance of an autonomous State structure also favoured the spread of fiscal discrepancies and inequalities between the various provinces. In Campagna, the main revenue remained the *focaticum*, although no contribution was apparently paid by the clergy. In the Patrimony, the treasurer levied a subsidy,★ which was a synthesis of the old *focaticum*, the *tallia*★ and the procurations,★ according to A. Anzilotti. Its establishment, necessarily negotiated with the provincials, was more probably exchanged with the suppression of the three previous impositions. Paid by laymen and clerics, the Jews contributing through a specific tax, this regular subsidy★ did not prevent the imposition of extraordinary subsidies to pay *condottieri*, for example. In the March of Ancona, on the contrary, the fiscal dialogue with taxpayers was unable to develop. The treasurer always collected the *cens*,★ the *affictum*, the *tallia*,★ a subsidy★ from the clerics and from the Jews, and some *cens*★ for vicariates. In the Duchy, most communities paid a *tallia*★ or subsidy in 1425, sometimes discounted. The following registers show that the clergy and the Jews also paid a subsidy.★[90] After the Schism, some elements of the Albornozian fiscal policy had survived despite the collapse of papal authority, but not its logics.

The confusions and equivalences made by notaries in the fifteenth century complicate the historical analysis, as K. Bauer has pointed out,[91] and only a series of detailed studies would make it possible to grasp the complex evolution of the tax system during that time. Scattered vestiges of the fiscal system built in the Albornozian period are easily identified, but forms of involution, returning to previous processes, can also be found.[92] Until 1425, the distribution of these subsidies would have been carried out according to the number of taxable hearths, then Martin V would have opted for the *allivment*. This change may have been motivated by the low yield of the tax. Partner has shown that Martin V only collected one-third of the subsidies theoretically owed by his subjects.[93] But the forms of distribution seem to have been discussed on both provincial and community bases throughout the century.

The most important fiscal phenomenon in the fifteenth century was the development of indirect taxation. In order to avoid officially increasing taxes on the towns, which had been at the root of numerous revolts, the popes of the Quattrocento developed alternatives. The reconquest of the cities, and therefore the *incameramento* of the communal finances, gave the Apostolic Chamber the balance of the communal budgets, but also permitted it to develop the tax systems that the cities had been able to build up... which, in the case of Rome, whose demographic and economic development was very strong, proved particularly profitable. To a certain extent, the development of papal taxation in the fifteenth century was therefore inspired by urban methods, since it multiplied indirect taxation on taxpayers. Profitable levies now impacted the grain trade, pigs, transhumance, and increasingly salt, which was sold at forced prices,[94] generating then specific institutions. This fiscal policy was promoted by the Roman Apostolic See, as early as the Great Schism if we consider the *Dogana del bestiame*,[95] and was also verified in the curia, since there too the cost of the acts increased and specific institutions were created to manage these resources: the revenues of the *Dateria* continued to grow and finally literally exploded between 1480 and 1525, as it rose from 40 to 162,000 ducats per year.[96] This reorientation of the entire fiscal policy of the Apostolic See provoked the dispersal of accounting methods noted by M. Caravale,[97] in contrast to the concentration of management around provincial treasurers which characterised preceding centuries.

During the course of the Quattrocento, there was then a reversal in the ratio between direct and indirect taxation. Total revenues certainly increased, but as the *bilanci* of 1451, 1481 and then 1525 show,[98] the net income from provincial treasuries was clearly low compared to the resources provided through taxation of commercial activities and consumption, to which was added revenue from the alum discovered in Tolfa, which was entirely devoted to the crusade.[99] Partner thought that the total income had increased considerably compared to the Avignon period, but this is not really the case, especially if one considers the 50,000 ducats due to the exploitation of the alum. The resources derived from the Church's Italian lands were not superior to those received in 1371–1375.[100] Even in a time of great financial need, such as during the crusade of 1461–1462, the pope only managed to raise 471, 694 florins, whereas Gregory XI's revenues in a more difficult period like the harsh year 1374–1375 exceeded officially 480,000 florins.[101]

An analysis of cash flows suggests a rapid rebuilding of papal finances during the fifteenth century, but also a cap, since Clement VII's annual budget was around 450,000 florins. The basis of revenues was nonetheless radically different. The income from ecclesiastical institutions throughout Christendom (annates and common services) now constituted only one-ninth of the papacy's total revenues. The reconquest of the cities had been completed and the territory itself even enlarged by a new province in 1521, the Gallia Cispadana (formed with the districts of Parma and Piacenza ceded by the king of France), but all the Papal State provided only about a quarter of total revenue.[102] Once again, it fell to Rome, as earlier during the eleventh and twelfth centuries,[103] to provide the Apostolic See with the bulk of its resources (more than half), which came in the form of taxes on trade, consumption and acts issued by the curia, and through the sale of offices and the payment of judicial compositions of all kinds.[104] After the collapse of the system of ecclesiastical taxation built during the thirteenth and fourteenth centuries, and contrary to a myth developed in the historiography on the basis of the distinction made by papal accountants between spiritual and temporal revenues, it was not the Church State that ensured the functioning of the pontifical monarchy. It contributed significantly, but the bulk of papal resources came from Rome itself, due to a clever system of taxing practically everything that could be taxed, from exchangeable and consumable goods to privileges and acts. From a financial point of view, the Church State was still a secondary element of papal power in the first decades of the fourteenth century, even though it had become politically indispensable for the full manifestation of its authority.

The recurrent wars in Italy modified the earlier balances without revolutionising the logic of territorial taxation. To soften the image of his taxation, the pope frequently "returned" to certain communities part of the sums due, in the form of rebates or charitable donations.[105] He sought not to appear as a mere tax collector! The protective and therefore benevolent dimension of his government, called for by Christian ideology, was to be perceived through these accommodations that he conceded to his subjects. Defending the independence of papal sovereignty during the conflict between the French and the Imperials did not lead to a complete revision of his fiscal policy. As usual, the papacy embarked on a race for expedients, increasing the rate of indirect taxes, developing the sale of offices, and also creating, from 1526, the Monte della Fede for the management of public debt, precisely in order to avoid increasing taxation.[106] Of course, this was a loan of 200,000 ducats in return for the delivery of perpetual and transferable securities earning an annual interest of 10 per cent guaranteed by the *gabelles* on the trade of goods entering in Rome. Such a measure also meant that in the long term there would be a reduction of the overall revenue collected by the Apostolic Chamber.

The sack of Rome in 1527 and the recurrence of conflicts allowed the papacy to implement previously conceived tax strategies, but innovations henceforth would be rare. In 1529, Clement VII decreed a new *tassa dei cavalleggeri* to pay for mounted troops and a tax of 0.5 per cent on the value of all real estate, both ecclesiastical and secular. But this did not end practices of the past, since in 1531 he demanded a subsidy* of one ducat per hearth, levied according to the traditional method and *secundum facultates personarum*, always insisting on his functions of authority and protection ("*taxamus et moderamus*").[107] His policy was continued with less caution by Paul III, who in 1536 renewed this "*sussidio focatico*", still accompanied by a double tithe on the clergy and a twentieth on the Jews,[108] while maintaining the property tax that was expected to be applied with a specific tariff in Rome.[109] But when in the following year, the pope, still short of money, decided to raise again the price of salt,[110] creating the seeds of discontent, a revolt took place throughout the papal territory, from the Gallia Cispadana to the Roman Campagna, passing through Rimini, Senigallia and Perugia.

The *Guerra del sale*, which was particularly harsh in Perugia,[111] consolidated the authority of the pope in the State, and even opened the way for additional indirect taxes. It also forced the papacy to better consider the opinion of its subjects. It seems indeed impossible to separate the method of taxation used to establish a new subsidy* in 1543 from this important revolt. Presented as an extraordinary tax of 300,000 ecus over three years to compensate for the non-increase in the price of salt and other contributions, it was instituted only after approval by the representatives of each province, who demanded the removal of exemptions, since even the officers of the Chamber and the cardinals had to pay it. At the same time, secular and regular clerics were taxed (10 per cent and 25 per cent on the value of their income, respectively!) and the twentieth of the property belonging to Jews was also levied, so that all subjects contributed to the taxation.

The carefully negotiated creation of this subsidy* suggested that its extraordinary character was merely rhetorical. The manner of revenue distribution, involving the subjects aimed to convince them and proved to be a highly effective political tool… until Marcel II in 1555 decided to extend it automatically! Thus, the *sussidio triennale* became a regular and typical imposition of the Papal State in modern times. As A. Gardi has already noted, the success of this tax served as a model for the establishment of other taxes, such as the *quattrino* on meat in 1553, the *foglietta* on wine at the time of Sixtus V, the tax on galleys in 1588, and even extraordinary subsidies such as that of 1557, which was supposed to be levied on real estate long before being transformed into a repartition tax.[112]

Conclusion

It is clear that the development of the Church of Rome's taxation in these territories was confusing, ambiguous, marked by phases of expansion and shrinkage, and by influences, which are for now totally undervalued, of fiscal models inherited from the Empire and created by the cities. This complexity was reinforced by the duality of the authority over lay and ecclesiastical subjects, who were very early invited to support doubly (as a member of the ecclesiastical institution and as a subject of the temporal leader) the government of these provinces. This complexity was also increased by provincial identities, based on specific privileges and even lexicons. It must be noted the abundance of terms denoting the same or similar fiscal practice. This complexity was also the result of the conception that the papacy had over time, both in its own territories and in its role as head of the Church. For a long time, the provinces were considered a set of goods and rights belonging to the Church of Rome, which was their owner and therefore claimed the right to collect the fruits of this ownership. Hence this ability to transform a series of seigniorial rights, impositions and property rights or sovereignty rights into rents, simplified the collection of money, but at the price of an obvious negation of any intermediary State structure. This complexity resulted from political factors, from the successive crises the Apostolic institution underwent from the thirteenth to the fifteenth centuries, before a progressive absolutisation of pontifical authority transformed the pope into the head of a State (and not of States), imposing his will beyond the realm of particular towns and provinces.

Long-term analyses do not always confirm the historical conclusions anticipated by previous historians. In fact, it appears that around the year 1200, the big cities of the new and old provinces of central Italy already entered a process of "defiscalisation". The large communes often constituted protected areas after having negotiated with the central authority the form of their submission. The impressive number of groups exempted from paying the hearth tax★ says everything about the power of the urban elites prior to 1200. The only binding tax to which urban societies seemed to be subjected to at that time was, as for the nobles, the blood tax, i.e., military service. Inheriting this very unequal tax system, the pontiff could only benefit from the imposition of taxation on the small communities. In the course of the thirteenth and fourteenth centuries, there was a succession of opposite movements, phases of abandonment marked by concessions of lands, rights and taxes, and attempts to reconstitute the old prerogatives though various surveys and archives, according to the political logics prevailing in the curia and provincial administration. But the division of the territory contributed to multiplication of fiscal approaches as well as divergences.

With the appearance of a State perspective in the years following the Albornozian conquest, marked by the levying of general subsidies and the application of an elaborate fiscal policy in the March to all the provinces (in short, just like for the famous constitutions), the communities were subjected over a few years to a real "fiscal revolution". Its effects on the economy and the government of these towns are still unknown (with the exception of Gubbio). It is probably not an exaggeration to say this fiscal "hype" explains the importance of the 1375–1376 revolt and the deconstruction of the Albornozian State model in the years during and following the Schism.

The challenging and slow reconstruction of pontifical authority during the fifteenth century based on better negotiated fiscal relations with the subjects, favoured the introduction of simplifications (deletion of certain taxes), and the development of indirect taxation of goods. But this policy, on a provincial basis, proved insufficient to deal with a long-lasting war between the Imperials and the French. The development of taxpaying capacity therefore became a necessity again. In the first half of the sixteenth century, increases in taxes led finally to a new revolt. This led to the resumption of patient negotiations with the subjects in order to establish a secure taxation system, the *sussidio triennale*, emblematic marker of the papacy's fiscal policy in modern times.

Notes

1 WALEY, *The Papal State*; SOMMERLECHNER (ed.), *Innocenzo III*.
2 NOBLE, *The Republic of Saint Peter*.
3 Recently PIRANI, *Con il senno e con la spada*.
4 CAROCCI, "Città e governo papale" *nel Quattrocento*".
5 CASTIGNOLI, *Storia di Piacenza*; BERTINI, *Storia di Parma*.
6 FUMI, *Inventario e spoglio… Città di Castello*; Id., *Inventario e spoglio… Perugia e Umbria*; Id., *Inventario e spoglio…Marca*; Anzilotti, *Cenni sulle finanze*.
7 DELUMEAU, *Vie économique*; MONACO, *La situazione de la Reverend*; PARTNER, *The Budget*; in his book cit. n.1, D. Waley updates one of his previous articles under the chapter *The Financial Utility of The Papal State* (pp. 252–275).
8 Since Klemens Bauer, who saw in the construction of a State an economic necessity for the popes, who established in the sixteenth century a tax system with few exemptions, based therefore on a clear desire of standardization of the condition of its subjects, an analysis that still has its defenders ("Studi per la storia delle finanze" and "Die epochen der Papstfinanz"), but his work remained little debated after its publication.
9 CARACCIOLO, "I bilanci dello Stato ecclesiastico"; CRISTOFARI MANCIA, *Il primo registro*; CARAVALE, *La finanza pontificia*; ID., "Entrate e Uscite"; STUMPO, *Il capitale*.
10 REINHARD, "Finanza pontificia e Stato", p. 356; ID., "Finanza pontificia, sistema beneficiale".
11 PARTNER, *The Papal State*; REYDELLET-GUTTINGER, *L'administration pontificale*; ESCH, *Bonifaz IX*; THEIS, *Le Gouvernement pontifical*.
12 GARDI, "La fiscalità Pontificia". Of no use is the contribution of P. Partner in the book directed by BONNEY, (*The Rise of the Fiscal State*), in which the author fails to make a clear distinction between collection of revenues and taxation.
13 JAMME, "De la banque à la Chambre?"
14 See GINATEMPO, *Prima del debito*; MAINONI, *Politiche finanziarie*.
15 During Philipp II's reign a system of levies on Spanish churches comparable to that of the fourteenth century was rebuilt (GIANNINI, *L'oro e la tiara* and ROSA, "La 'scarsella di nostro signore'").
16 FILIOLI URANIO, "El Estado pontificio".
17 As Paolo Prodi thought. For him, strangely, the army only became a papal concern around the time of the peace of Lodi! (cf. *Il sovrano pontefice*, pp. 111–114).
18 THEINER, *Codex diplomaticus*, vol. 1, no. 43, pp. 35–36.
19 WALEY, *The Papal State*, p. 258; PARTNER, *The Lands of Saint Peter*, pp. 126, 144, 195, 199; GARDI, "La fiscalità Pontificia", p. 522. There is no explanation for these interpretations. The thirteenth century sources are very clear on the fact that the *fodrum* was in central Italy a hearth tax and not a right of lodging.
20 PETRUCCI, "Innocenzo III e i comuni", pp. 34–35; GARDI, "La fiscalità Pontificia", p. 521.
21 See ERMINI, "Caratteri della sovranità", pp. 761–793.
22 *Le Liber censuum de l'Église romaine*, pp. 534–536.
23 THEINER, *Codex diplomaticus*, 1, no. 273, pp. 146–147.
24 *Ibidem* and SANSI, *Documenti storici inediti*, p. 270.
25 FABRE, *Le Liber Censuum*, vol. 1, pp. 450–452.
26 MONACO, *La situazione della Reverenda*, p. 45.
27 The agreement of 1207 between Belforte and Camerino specified that these 26 *denarii* per hearth *dare teneamur usque ad adventum imperatoris vel eius certi numptii qui de plano erunt* (*Il libro rosso del comune di Camerino*, no. 9, pp. 33–36).
28 SANSI, *Documenti storici inediti*, p. 345, 349; sometimes the rate was lower (*Documenti del comune di Cagli*, vol. 1, no. 9); see also the table of fiscal duties of the communities subject to Camerino (BIONDI, *Il libro rosso*, p. 9).
29 SANSI, *Documenti storici inedita*, pp. 285–287.
30 THEINER, *Codex diplomaticus*, 1, no. 273, pp. 146–147.

31 *Ibidem*, no. 423, p. 264.
32 *Le* Liber *Censuum*, vol. 1, pp. 534–536.
33 The statements of account of 23 *milites* sent by Osimo in the papal army in 1234 has been preserved (*Il libro rosso del comune di Osimo*, no. 127–130); see also an agreement made by Fabriano (*Il libro rosso del comune di Fabriano*, no. 31).
34 SANSI, *Documenti storici inediti*, pp. 285–287, and *Il libro rosso del comune di Iesi*, no. 122); other cases, *ibidem*, no. 98 and in BALDETTI, *Documenti di Cagli*, no. 164.
35 *Le* Liber Censuum, vol. 1, pp. 450–452.
36 Thus the privilege of Frederick Barbarossa granted to Monte San Vito in 1177 (CARLETTI, *Il libro rosso di Iesi*, no. 114).
37 Basically there was not a clear difference in the forms of submission that the provincial government wanted from the communities and the submission that the more powerful communes asked to those which were subject to them (see *Il libro rosso di Fabriano*, no. 23; *Il libro rosso di Camerino*, no. 7; BALDETTI, *Documenti di Cagli*, no. 158).
38 Since the major cities were sometimes granted an impressive number of *castra* formerly under the jurisdiction of the Church, a stabilisation of the *affictus* and a limited military service; see for other tax privileges of those times, THEINER, *Codex diplomaticus*, p. 114, 115, 117, 119, 126, 136, 137, etc.
39 Because the collection of fees was often conflictual (*Il libro rosso di Iesi*, no. 176); on these investigations, see JAMME, "L'enquête et ses desseins".
40 Without mentioning here the intra-provincial specificities: in the north and the centre of the March, the communes readily used the term *collecta fumantium* (*Il libro rosso di Osimo*, no. 23; *Il libro rosso di Iesi codice 2*, no. 102), whereas the term *affictus* seems to be used more in the south (BIONDI, *Il libro rosso di Camerino*, p. 9). In Osimo in 1226, the latter specifically referred to the tax paid to the sovereign: new citizens were exempted for five years from *collectas et guaitas et omnia alia dacia comunis, preter affictum domini pape et inperatoris* (*ibidem*, no. 114).
41 See a detail study in JAMME, "Comptabilité provincial".
42 REYDELLET-GUTTINGER, *L'administration pontificale*, p. 133.
43 For an example, see *Il libro rosso di Fabriano*, no. 6.
44 PALMIERI, *Introiti ed Esiti*, 1889, p. 41.
45 See the extracts from the account of the treasurer Bonsignore di Gregorio (1290–1293 in THEINER, *Codex diplomaticus*, 1, no. 491, p. 317 et seq.) and the book of Rinaldo Malavolti from 1299 (FABRE, *Un registre caméral*, pp. 177–195).
46 JAMME, "Una delle fonti".
47 WALEY, *The Papal State*, pp. 279–281.
48 *Il libro rosso di Fabriano*, no. 128, 138.
49 The term was used by Frederick II in 1230 and by Onorius III with the meaning of *exactio insolite*, especially when ecclesiastics were the victims (!), and then of *collecta*. It was only from the 1270s onwards that it became common in central Italy and gave even its name to a league of cities (NALDINI, "La *tallia militum*").
50 In 1265 Clement IV reminded his legate in the March *quod de XV militibus impositis nuper Callensibus, eis V duximus remittendos* (*Les registres de Clément IV*, no. 991).
51 *Il libro rosso di Fabriano*, no. 130–136, 139.
52 This is probably why the communes of the Tiber valley replied to the rectors who often asked for military aid that their request had to be presented to the council of the city, which would examine them according to their merit. For Waley (*The Papal State*, pp. 283–285), this was a form of insubordination… that perhaps wasn't! See for the Patrimony the book of Rinaldo Malavolti summarised by Fabre, "Un registre cameral", pp. 177–195). It should be remembered that in 1300 a constitution of Boniface VIII limited impositions in this province to the *focatico* and the procurations, only when the rector visited the communities!
53 The list of grievances against the rector presented by three ambassadors of the communities sent to Boniface VIII concerns almost exclusively the abuses of the judicial officers (THEIS, *Le gouvernement pontifical*, p. 153).
54 In 1288, Imola, who was taxed on the basis of 2,000 hearths, obtained a reduction to 1,500 (PINI, *La popolazione*, Bologna, 1976).
55 In Romagna, military service would have been commuted to *tallia* around 1287, according to WALEY, *The Papal State*, p. 292. But no doubt that the payment of contributions *pro stipendia militum* existed

long before: in 1281, barely two years after the annexation of the province, the letter appointing new rectors mentioned their right of *inpositas exigendi* (RUDOLPH, *Das Kammerregister*, no. 29a).

56 THEINER, *Codex diplomaticus*, vol. 1, p. 29, and Archivio di Stato di [from now AS] Rieti, Diplomatico, no. 1.
57 The accounts sometimes keep a record of this mutation, as the register of the treasurer of Sabina in 1284, which specifies for the 100 pounds paid by Terni: *pro censu seu afficto, salario et pedagiis* (THEINER, *Codex diplomaticus*, vol. 1, p. 283).
58 *Ibidem*, p. 356.
59 For a total amounting to 1824 pounds (JAMME, "Una delle fonti della *Descriptio*", app. 2, pp. 500–501.
60 As shown by the book of Rinaldo Malavolti for the Patrimony and the account registers of the Duchy (REYDELLET-GUTTINGER, *L'administration pontificale*, p. 69).
61 When he throws coins to the crowd and says "What I have, I will give you" (PARAVICINI BAGLIANI, *Il trono di Pietro*, p. 19). This is undoubtedly how the papacy lost the entire legacy of the famous Countess Matilda in less than a century (see THEINER, *Codex diplomaticus*, p. 45, 47, 65, 79, and GOLINELLI, *L'ancella di san Pietro*).
62 As a collection of rectoral letters shows (PARAVICINI BAGLIANI, "*Eine Briefsammlung*", no. 16–18, 59), the rectors of the Duchy had some difficulty in obtaining the full amount due.
63 Forty-eight letters of nomination preserved between 1216 and 1305 were consulted, which insist above all on *justicia* and *disciplina*, even if the rector is given the power to *precipiendi, ordinandi, disponendi, statuendi et faciendi sicut expedire videris*.
64 And for the tallia, it had only brought in 1,761 livres in 20 months, whereas its revenue should have exceeded 2,000 livres in 12, if we compare this register (WALEY, "An account-book", pp. 18–19) with the book of Rinaldo Malavolti of 1299.
65 ANTONELLI, "*Una relazione del vicario*", pp. 465–467.
66 Archivum Apostolicum Vaticanum [from now AAV], *Intr. et Ex. 39, fol. 57–99; Intr. et Ex. 69, fol. 134–160*.
67 ASV, *Intr. et Ex. 21, fol. 1–22, and 39, fol. 1–31*.
68 REYDELLET-GUTTINGER, *L'administration pontificale*, pp. 69–71.
69 ASV, *Collect.* 201, fol. 3–37; confirmed by an account register for the year 1327 which shows comparable proportions, i.e., 15 per cent of the revenues (*Intr. et Ex. 77, fol. 18-31v*).
70 With the exception of the subsidy demanded from the Jews, see the very precise study of papal revenues in THEIS, *Le gouvernement pontifical*, pp. 420–440, ID., "Jean XXII et l'expulsion", pp. 41–77.
71 About this report JAMME, "From Administrative Control", pp. 156–159.
72 ASV, *Intr. et Ex. 46, fol. 1–12v*.
73 ASV, *Collect.* 387, fol. 97 et v. See BATTELLI, "Le raccolte documentarie", pp. 463–507.
74 JAMME, "Lo Stato della Chiesa".
75 For the 156 receipts preserved for the years 1355–1376 see VILLANI, *Regesti di Rocca, passim*.
76 ASAssisi, Perg. no. 241, 341; ASCSpello, Perg no. 27, 28; ASGubbio, Perg. no. 19–21 (as well for this city, the detailed study of LUONGO, *Gubbio nel Trecento*, pp. 494–507).
77 ASAssisi, Perg. no. 244, 340–341; ASGubbio, Perg. no. 25–26.
78 ASGubbio, Perg. no. 27–28, 30–31, 35, 38, 40–41, 43; ASSpolète, Perg. no. 245/1–2, 248; ASAssisi, Perg. no. 294–295, 342–343, 390.
79 ASGubbio, Perg. no. 46, the distribution of the subsidy being still based on the number of hearths in a community and its territory.
80 AAV, *Collect.* 176, fol. 1–54.
81 FAURE, *Étude sur l'administration*, p. 135.
82 ZERNER, "Du bon gouvernement"; BUTAUD, "La perception de l'impôt".
83 FALCO, "I communi della Campania", p. 235 and pp. 242–243.
84 CASINI BRUNI, *Lettere di Gerardo du* Puy; GLÉNISSON, "Les origines de la révolte"; LUONGO, *Gubbio nel Trecento*, pp. 513–514.
85 See ESCH, *Bonifaz IX*, and PARTNER, *The Papal State*.
86 See MAIRE VIGUEUR (ed.), *Signorie cittadine* (above all the papers of Jean-Claude Maire Vigueur and Francesco Pirani, pp. 105–172 and 509–547).
87 See FAVIER, *Les Finances pontificales*, pp. 167–194.
88 HALLER, *Concilium Basiliense*, vol. 1, pp. 173–174.
89 One must deplore the many errors of P. Partner in his "The Budget of the Roman Church", p. 259, since he considers Gregory XI's income varied between 200 and 300,000 florins, whereas a receipt

for the year 1374–1375 (THEINER, *Codex diplomaticus*, pp. 556–557) states that it exceeded 480,000 florins; the same problem applies to the resources of the Italian provinces at the death of Albornoz, which are said to have been 86,000 florins for him, whereas the original document clearly states 126,000 (edited in JAMME (ed.), *Le Souverain*, p. 258).
90 For all that see CARAVALE, "Le entrate pontificie".
91 BAUER, "Studi per la storia", p. 367 and pp. 380–381; but the problem predates the fifteenth century!
92 In this sense only, the statement of Gardi ("La fiscalità Pontificia", p. 530) that, as the territory was reconquered, the tax system of the thirteenth and fourteenth centuries was reconstituted, is valid.
93 PARTNER, *The Papal State*, p. 116.
94 With Calixtus III, a system of forced assignment at a fixed price of a certain quantity of salt according to the number of inhabitants was definitively put in place, which under Sixtus IV brought in more than 30,000 ducats per year.
95 MAIRE VIGUEUR, *Les pâturages de l'Eglise*.
96 CANZONERI, *La storia e il diritto*; FABBRICATORE, "La Dataria apostolica".
97 CARAVALE, "Le entrate pontificie", pp. 73–75.
98 Ed. respectively by CARAVALE, "Entrate e uscite", BAUER, "Studi per la storia", and MONACO, *La situazione de la Reverenda*. The first two do not constitute any kind of *bilancio* or budget, possibly preventive, as K. Bauer, P. Partner and M. Caravale have thought. They were compiled from the reports drawn up by the clerks of the Chamber responsible for examining the accounts of various treasurers and collectors, hence their incompleteness (JAMME, "Logique administrative").
99 WEBER, *Lutter contre les Turcs*, and ID., "L'alun de la croisade?"
100 The list of 1481 shows a "normal" income of 160,000 florins, whereas in March 1371, Pierre d'Estaing estimated it at 190,000 florins (JAMME, "Instructions et avis", p. 78).
101 For both figures see GOTTLOB, *Aus der Camera apostolica*, pp. 260–261, and THEINER, *Codex diplomaticus*, pp. 556–557.
102 At the beginning of the sixteenth century, the main novelty was the leasing of provincial treasuries and customs according to M. Caravale (*La finanza pontificia*, pp. 9–46). But this practice probably originated in the last decades of the fifteenth century.
103 When the city was the paradise of bankers (see VENDITTELLI, *Mercanti-banchieri romani*).
104 GENSINI (ed.), *Roma capitale*, Pisa, 1994.
105 JAMME, "Logique administrative", p. 179 and p. 189.
106 MONACO, "Il primo debito pubblico"; PALERMO, "Finanza, indebitamento e sviluppo".
107 As early as 1523, Adrian VI had thought to raise a subsidy of half a ducat per hearth, including the Comtat Venaissin, together with a twentieth on the Jews and a tenth on the clergy (CARAVALE, *La finanza pontificia*, pp. 51–57; GARDI, "La fiscalità Pontificia", pp. 533–534).
108 CARAVALE, *La finanza pontificia*, pp. 53–58; GARDI, "La fiscalità Pontificia", p. 535.
109 As in the past, the commune preferred to compromise with the authorities to avoid taxation by paying 8,000 ducats (PECCHIAI, *Roma nel Cinquecento*, pp. 62–63).
110 CARAVALE, *La finanza pontificia*, p. 73.
111 BONAINI (ed.), "La guerra del sale"; CARAVALE, "Lo Stato pontificio", pp. 251–253.
112 See the clever analysis of GARDI, "La fiscalità Pontificia", p. 537 et seq.

References

Mercurio ANTONELLI, "Una relazione del vicario del Patrimonio a Giovanni XXII", in *Archivio della Società romana di storia patria*, 18, 1895, pp. 447–467.
Antonio ANZILOTTI, "Cenni sulle finanze del Patrimonio di San Pietro in Tuscia nel secolo XV", in *Archivio della Società romana di storia patria*, 42, 1919, pp. 349–399.
Ettore BALDETTI (ed.), *Documenti del comune di Cagli*, vol. 1: *La « città antica » (1115–1287)*, Ancona, 2006.
Clemens BAUER, "Die epochen der Papstfinanz. Ein Versuch", in *Historische Zeitschrift*, 1928, pp. 457–503.
Clemens BAUER, "Studi per la storia delle finanze papali durante il pontificato di Sisto IV", in *Archivio della Società romana di storia patria*, 150, 1927, pp. 319–400.
Giuseppe BERTINI (ed.), *Storia di Parma*, vol. 4: *Il ducato farnesiano*, Parma, 2014.
Francesco BONAINI (ed.), "La guerra del sale, ossia il racconto della guerra sostenuta dai Perugini contro Paolo III nel 1540, tratto dalle memorie inedite di Girolamo di Frolliere", in *Archivio storico italiano*, 16/2, 1851, pp. 403–476.

The Church Lands (1200-1550)

Richard BONNEY, *The Rise of the Fiscal State in Europe (1200–1815)*, Oxford, 1999.

Germain BUTAUD, "La perception de l'impôt et le recouvrement des arrérages en Comtat Venaissin (fin XIVe-début XVe siècle)", in *La fiscalité des villes au Moyen Âge*, vol. 4: *La gestion de l'impôt*, ed. Denis MENJOT and Manuel SÁNCHEZ MARTÍNEZ, Paris, 2004, pp. 221–238.

Emanuele CANZONERI, *La storia e il diritto della Dataria apostolica*, Naples, 1969.

Alberto CARACCIOLO, "I bilanci dello Stato ecclesiastico fra XVI e XVIII secolo: una fonte e alcune considerazioni", in *Mélanges en l'honneur de F. Braudel*, Toulouse, 1973, vol. 2, pp. 99–103.

Mario CARAVALE, "Entrate e Uscite dello Stato della Chiesa in un bilancio della metà del Quattrocento", in *Per Francesco Calasso. Studi degli Allievi*, Rome, 1978, pp. 167–190.

Mario CARAVALE, *La finanza pontificia nel Cinquecento: le province del Lazio*, Naples, 1974.

Mario CARAVALE, "Le entrate pontificie", in *Roma capitale (1447–1527)*, ed. Sergio GENSINI, Pisa, 1994, pp. 73–106.

Mario CARAVALE, "Lo Stato pontificio da Martino V a Gregorio XIII", in *Lo Stato pontificio da Martino V a Pio IX*, Torino, 1978 (*Storia d'Italia*, diretta da G. Galasso, 14), pp. 1–371, 251–253.

Sandro CAROCCI, "Città e governo papale nel Quattrocento", in *Vassalli del papa. Potere pontificio, aristocrazie e città nello Stato della Chiesa (XII–XV sec.)*, Roma, 2010, pp. 99–159.

Marcella CASINI BRUNI, *Lettere di Gerardo du Puy al Comune di Orvieto (1373–1375)*, Perugia, 1970.

Piero CASTIGNOLI (ed.), *Storia di Piacenza*, vol. III: *Dalla signoria viscontea al principato farnesiano (1313–1545)*, Piacenza, 1997.

Maria CRISTOFARI MANCIA, *Il primo registro della Tesoreria di Ascoli (20 agosto 1426–30 aprile 1427)*, Rome, 1974.

Jean DELUMEAU, *Vie économique et sociale de Rome dans la seconde moitié du XVIe siècle*, 2 vol., Paris, 1957–1959.

Giuseppe ERMINI, "Caratteri della sovranità temporale dei papi nei secoli XIII e XIV", in *Scritti storico-giuridici*, ed. Ovidio CAPITANI and Enrico MENESTÒ, Todi, 1997, pp. 761–793.

Arnold ESCH, *Bonifaz IX und der Kirchenstaat*, Tübingen, 1969.

Ersilia FABBRICATORE, "La Dataria apostolica: il dicastero della grazia concessa", in *Nuovi Annali della Scuola Speciale per Archivisti e Bibliotecari*, 21, 2007, pp. 63–90.

Paul FABRE, "Un registre caméral du cardinal Albornoz en 1364", in *Mélanges d'Archéologie et d'Histoire*, 7, 1887, pp. 129–195.

Giorgio FALCO, "I communi della Campania e della Marittima nel Medio Evo", in *Archivio della Società romana di storia patria*, 49, 1926, pp. 127–302.

Claude FAURE, *Étude sur l'administration du Comtat Venaissin du XIIIe au XVe siècle (1229–1417)*, Paris – Avignon, 1909.

Jean FAVIER, *Les Finances pontificales à l'époque du Grand Schisme d'Occident (1378–1409)*, Paris, 1966.

Fabrizio FILIOLI URANIO, "El Estado pontificio como Fiscal-Military State: consideraciones economicas, financieras y sociales sobre el armamento de galeras en los siglos XVI y XVII", in *Tiempos modernos* 33, 2016/2, pp. 346–376.

Luigi FUMI, *Inventario e spoglio dei registri della Tesoreria apostolica di Città di Castello, dal R. Archivio di Stato in Roma*, Perugia, 1900.

Luigi FUMI, *Inventario e Spoglio dei registri della tesoreria apostolica di Perugia e Umbria dal R. Archivio di Stato di Roma*, Perugia, 1901.

Luigi FUMI, *Inventario e spoglio dei registri della Tesoreria apostolica della Marca*, in *Le Marche*, 4, 1904, pp. 1–7, 109–118, 282–298.

Andrea GARDI, "La fiscalità pontificia tra Medioevo ed età moderna", in *Società e storia*, 9, 1986, pp. 509–557.

Sergio GENSINI (ed.), *Roma capitale (1447–1527)*, Pisa, 1994.

Massimo CARLO GIANNINI, *L'oro e la tiara. La costruzione dello spazio fiscale italiano della Santa Sede (1560–1620)*, Bologna, 2003.

Maria GINATEMPO, *Prima del debito. Finanziamento della spesa pubblica e gestione del deficit nelle grande città toscane*, Florence, 2000.

Giulio BATTELLI, "Le raccolte documentarie del cardinale Albornoz sulla pacificazione delle terre della Chiesa", in *Scritti scelti. Codici-Documenti-Archivi*, Rome, 1975, pp. 463–507.

Jean GLÉNISSON, "Les origines de la révolte de l'État pontifical en 1375. Les subsides extraordinaires dans les provinces italiennes de l'Église au temps de Grégoire XI", in *Rivista di storia della Chiesa in Italia*, 5, 1951, pp. 145–168.

Paolo GOLINELLI, *L'ancella di san Pietro: Matilde di Canossa e la Chiesa*, Milan, 2015.

Adolf GOTTLOB, *Aus der Camera apostolica des XV. Jahrhunderts*, Innsbruck, 1889.

Johannes HALLER, Concilium Basiliense, *Studien und dokuments zur Geschichte der Jahre 1431–1437*, 8 vol., Basle, 1896–1910.
Il libro rosso del comune di Camerino, ed. Ilaria Biondi, Spoleto, 2014.
Il libro rosso del comune di Fabriano, ed. Attilio Bartoli LANGELI, Erminia IRACE and Andrea MAIARELLI, Fabriano, 1998.
Il libro rosso del comune di Osimo, ed. Maela CARLETTI and Francesco PIRANI, Spoleto, 2017.
Armand JAMME, "Comptabilité provinciale, écriture du crime et modèles de "disciplinement" dans les Terres de l'Église (XIIIe–XVe s.)", in *Monuments ou documents? Les comptabilités, sources pour l'histoire du contrôle social*, ed. Aude WIRTH-JAILLARD, Aude MUSIN, Nathalie DEMARET, Emmanuel BODART, and Xavier ROUSSEAUX, Brussels, 2015, pp. 45–79.
Armand JAMME, "De la banque à la Chambre? Les mutations d'une culture comptable dans les provinces de l'Etat pontifical (1270–1430)", in *Offices, Ecrit et Papauté (XIIIe–XVIIe s.)*, ed. Armand JAMME and Olivier PONCET, Rome, 2007, pp. 97–251.
Armand JAMME, "From Administrative Control to Fighting Corruption? The Procedural Steps of the Accounts Auditing in the Papal State (Thirteenth to Sixteeenth Cent.)", in *Accounts and Accountability in Late Medieval Europe. Records, Procedures and Sociopolitical Impact*, ed. Ionutz EPURESCU-PASCOVICI, Turnhout, 2020, pp. 145–164.
Armand JAMME, "Instructions et avis du cardinal Pierre d'Estaing sur le gouvernement des Terres de l'Eglise (1371)", in *Hommes, cultures et sociétés à la fin du Moyen Âge. Liber discipulorum en l'honneur de Philippe Contamine*, ed. Patrick GILLI and Jacques PAVIOT, Paris, 2012, pp. 69–105.
Armand JAMME, "L'enquête et ses desseins dans l'Etat pontifical aux XIIIe et XIVe siècles", in *Quand gouverner c'est enquêter. Les pratiques politiques de l'enquête princière (Occident, XIIIe–XIVe siècles)*, ed. Thierry PÉCOUT, Paris, 2010, pp. 257–284.
Armand JAMME (ed.), *Le Souverain, l'Office et le Codex. Gouvernement de la cour et techniques documentaires dans les* Libri officiariorum *des papes d'Avignon (XIVe - XVe siècle)*, Rome, 2014.
Armand JAMME, "Lo Stato della Chiesa, un ignoto Fiscal-Military State nel Trecento? Il problema della documentazione", in *Le fonti della fiscalità nell'Italia medievale*, special issue of the journal *Documenta* (to be published in 2022).
Armand JAMME, "Logique administrative, fraude et népotisme: l'examen des comptes d'un trésorier pontifical de la Marche d'Ancône en 1486", in *Cultures fiscales en Occident du Xe au XVIIe siècle. Etudes offertes à D. Menjot*, ed. Florent GARNIER et al., Toulouse, 2019, pp. 165–194.
Armand JAMME, "Una delle fonti della *Descriptio Marchiae*? L'ignoto registro del tesoriere fiorentino Rinaldo Campana (1283–84)", in *Incorrupta monumenta Ecclesiam defendunt. Studi offerti a S. Pagano*, ed. Andreas GOTTSMANN, Pierantonio PIATTI, and Andreas REHBERG, Rome, 2018, vol. 2, pp. 479–501.
Le Liber censuum de l'Église romaine, ed. Paul FABRE and Louis DUCHESNE, 4 vol., Paris 1905–1952.
Les registres de Clément IV (1265–1268), ed. Edouard JORDAN, Paris, 1893–1945.
Alberto LUONGO, *Gubbio nel Trecento. Il comune popolare e la mutazione signorile (1300–1404)*, Rome, 2016.
Patrizia MAINONI, *Politiche finanziarie e fiscali nell'Italia settentrionale*, Milano, 2021.
Jean-Claude MAIRE VIGUEUR, *Les pâturages de l'Eglise et la douane du bétail dans la province du Patrimonio (XIV–XV siècles)*, Rome, 1981.
Michele MONACO, *Il primo debito pubblico pontificio: il Monte della fede (1526)*, In *Studi romani*, 1960, pp. 553–569.
Michele MONACO, *La situazione de la Reverenda Camera Apostolica nell'anno 1525. Ricerche d'Archivio*, Rome, 1960.
Lamberto NALDINI, "La *tallia militum societatis tallie Tuscie* nella seconda metà del sec. XIII", in *Archivio Storico Italiano*, 78, 1920, pp. 75–113.
Thomas NOBLE, *The Republic of Saint Peter. The Birth of the Papal State 680–825*, Philadelphia, 1984.
Luciano PALERMO, "Finanza, indebitamento e sviluppo economico a Roma nel Rinascimento", in *Debito pubblico e mercati finanziari in Italia secoli XIII–XX*, ed. Giuseppe DE LUCA and Angelo MOIOLI, Milan, 2007, pp. 83–100.
Gregorio PALMIERI, *Introiti ed Esiti di papa Niccolò III (1279–1280)*, Rome, 1889.
Agostino PARAVICINI BAGLIANI, "Eine Briefsammlung für Rektoren des Kirchenstaates (1250–1320)", in *Deutsches Archiv für Esforschung des Mittelalters*, 35, 1979, pp. 138–208.
Agostino PARAVICINI BAGLIANI, *Il trono di Pietro. L'universalità del papato da Alessandro III a Bonifacio VIII*, Rome, 1996.
Peter PARTNER, "The Budget of the Roman Church in the Renaissance period", in *Italian Renaissance Studies. A tribute to the late Cecilia M. Ady*, ed. Ernest F. JACOB, London, 1966, pp. 256–278.

Peter PARTNER, *The Lands of Saint Peter: the Papal State in the Middle Ages and the early Renaissance*, London, 1972.

Peter PARTNER, *The Papal State under Martin V. The administration and Government of the Temporal Power in the Early Fifteenth Century*, London, 1958.

Pio PECCHIAI, *Roma nel Cinquecento*, Bologna, 1948.

Enzo Petrucci, "Innocenzo III e i comuni dello Stato della Chiesa. Il potere centrale", in *Società e istituzioni dell'Italia comunale: l'esempio di Perugia (secoli XII–XIV)*, Perugia, 1988, vol. 1, pp. 91–136.

Antonio Ivan PINI, *La popolazione di Imola e del suo territorio nel XIII e XIV secolo*, Bologna, 1976.

Francesco PIRANI, *Con il senno e con la spada, il cardinale Albornoz e l'Italia del Trecento*, Rome, 2019.

Paolo PRODI, *Il sovrano pontefice. Un corpo e due anime: la monarchia papale nella prima età moderna*, Bologna, 1982.

Wolfgang REINHARD, "Finanza pontificia e Stato della Chiesa nel secolo XVI e XVII", in *Finanze e Ragion di Stato in Italia e in Germania nella prima età moderna*, ed. Aldo DE MADDALENA and Hermann KELLENBENZ, Bologna, 1984, pp. 353–387.

Wolfgang REINHARD, "Finanza pontificia, sistema beneficiale e finanza statale nell'età confessionale", in *Fisco, Religione, Stato nell'età confessionale*, ed. Hermann KELLENBENZ and Paolo PRODI, Bologna, 1989, pp. 459–504.

Chantal REYDELLET-GUTTINGER, *L'administration pontificale dans le Duché de Spolète (1305–1352)*, Florence, 1975.

Mario ROSA, "La 'scarsella di nostro signore'. Aspetti della fiscalità spirituale pontificia in età moderna", in *Società et Storia*, 10, 1987, pp. 817–845.

Gerald RUDOLPH, *Das Kammerregister Papst Martins IV. 1281–1285 (Reg. Vat. 42): Untersuchung und kritische Edition*, Rome, 2004.

Achille SANSI, *Documenti storici inediti in sussidio allo studio delle memorie umbre*, Foligno, 1879.

Jean-Claude MAIRE VIGUEUR (ed.), *Signorie cittadine nell'Italia comunale*, Rome, 2013.

Andrea SOMMERLECHNER (ed.), *Innocenzo III. Urbs et Orbis*, 2 vol., Rome, 2003.

Enrico STUMPO, *Il capitale finanziario a Roma fra cinque e seicento. Contributo alla storia della fiscalità pontificia in età moderna (1570–1660)*, Milano, 1985.

Augustin THEINER, *Codex diplomaticus dominii temporalis Sanctae Sedis*, 3 vol., Rome, 1861.

Valérie THEIS, "Jean XXII et l'expulsion des juifs du Comtat Venaissin", in *Annales HSS*, 2012, pp. 41–77.

Valérie THEIS, *Le Gouvernement pontifical du Comtat Venaissin (vers 1270–vers 1350)*, Rome, 2012.

Marco VENDITTELLI, *Mercanti-banchieri romani tra XII e XIII secolo: una storia negata*, Rome, 2018.

Virginio VILLANI, *Regesti di Rocca Contrada, II. Secoli XIV–XVI*, Ancona, 1997.

Daniel WALEY, *The Papal State in the Thirteenth Century*, London, 1961.

Daniel WALEY, "An account-book of the Patrimony of Saint Peter in Tuscany 1304–1306", in *Journal of Ecclesiastical History*, 6, 1955, pp. 18–25.

Benjamin WEBER, "L'alun de la croisade? Etapes et difficultés de la mise en place d'un monopole pontifical sur l'alun de Tolfa (1461–1471)", in *Cahiers de recherches médiévales et humanistes*, 25, 2013, pp. 597–619.

Benjamin WEBER, *Lutter contre les Turcs. Les nouvelles formes de la croisade pontificale au XVe siècle*, Rome, 2013.

Monique ZERNER, "Du bon gouvernement en société rurale: pour ou contre la taille, deux débats aux trois Etats du Comtat Venaissin au début du XVe siècle", in *La société rurale et les institutions gouvernementales au Moyen Âge*, ed. John DRENDEL, Montreal, 1995, pp. 89–101.

10
KINGDOM OF FRANCE (WITH BRITTANY AND DAUPHINÉ)

Jean-François Lassalmonie

This chapter deals with public taxation in the kingdom of France at the three levels of the royal state, principalities and towns. Sources comprise legal and regulatory texts by king, princes or town authorities, and most of all, evidence issued by their agents in the process of tax raising and management. The latter is of two kinds: papers preparatory to collection, such as direct tax distribution rolls, lists of taxpayers, and municipal inventories of their wealth; and accounts of the use of the sums collected. Royal fiscal sources are mostly stored in the National Archives (*Archives Nationales*) and National Library (*Bibliothèque nationale de France*) in Paris, but they are much fragmentary, as a result of the 1737 blaze at the Chamber of Accounts, where they were held before 1789, and the sales or destructions of the Revolution.[1] Likewise, many princely fiscal sources, at first stored in the principality's Chamber of Accounts, were transferred to the royal Chamber in Paris when the land entered the king's domain. Brittany's subsisting fiscal sources are mainly held in the departmental repositories (*archives départementales*) of Ille-et-Vilaine or Loire-Atlantique, and Dauphiné's in those of Isère or Drôme. Urban fiscal sources are stored in city repositories (*archives municipales*) or, sometimes, public libraries (*bibliothèques municipales*).[2] In any case, all kinds of sources are fragmentary, due to the combined hazards of neglect, fire, thefts and wars over the centuries.

Modern studies on medieval French public taxation begin with three brilliant *amateurs*. Jean-Jules Clamageran was a Republican lawyer who wrote a remarkable history of French taxes under the Second Empire, before he became an ephemerous Finance Minister of the Third Republic.[3] Adolphe Vuitry was a Bonapartist lawyer and academician who acted as Finance Subsecretary under the Second Republic, then as governor of the *Banque de France* and Minister President of the State Council during the reign of Napoléon III, and who published a distinguished history of French royal finance after the fall of the imperial regime.[4] Colonel Léon-Louis Borrelli de Serres retired from the army after he was injured in a fall from his horse and devoted himself to a meticulous research on royal medieval administration at the turn of the nineteenth and twentieth centuries.[5] The task was then carried on by historians trained in the positivist methods of the *École des Chartes*. Gustave Dupont-Ferrier studied extensively the new royal taxes and fiscal administration which emerged in the fourteenth and fifteenth centuries,[6] while Alfred Spont and Paul Dognon concentrated on the specific features of Languedoc.[7]

In the middle of the twentieth century, foreign scholars joined in. American historians Joseph Reese Strayer, then Elizabeth A. R. Brown and John Bell Henneman, investigated the transition from feudal aid to modern taxation at the turn of the thirteenth and fourteenth centuries, and the first stages of the new fiscal system in the eve and early phase of the Hundred Years War.[8] On the French side, in the second half of the twentieth and beginning of the twenty-first centuries, Maurice Rey and the author devoted their doctoral theses to royal finance under Charles VI and Louis XI, while those of Jacques Vidal and, later, David Sassu-Normand carried on research on royal taxation in Languedoc.[9] With regard to cities, Bernard Chevalier, Albert Rigaudière and ultimately Florent Garnier scrutinized urban taxation and its relation to royal finance, while Southern France was involved in a comprehensive international research program on the fiscal systems of Western Mediterranean towns led by Denis Menjot and Manuel Sánchez Martínez.[10] As for the great principalities of the realm, Jean Kerhervé's doctoral thesis gave an extensive overview of the virtually independent duchy of Brittany's tax system and financial administration,[11] while taxation in Dauphiné was studied by Vital Chomel, Isabelle Vernus-Moutin and, more recently, Anne Lemonde.[12] At the turn of the twentieth and twenty-first centuries, the Economy and Finance Ministry historical committee (*Comité pour l'histoire économique et financière de la France*, CHÉFF), established in 1988, gave a strong impulse to research in French financial history, including the Middle Ages, through an active policy of colloquiums and publications.[13]

In the last decades, research on medieval taxation has benefited from wider trends of Middle Ages historiography. National and European programs on the origins of the modern states put emphasis on the importance of taxes at the core of this new kind of political frame, the modern state being defined as "a state whose material base lies on a public tax system agreed by the political society".[14] The last criterium echoes another trend of recent research, which highlighted the importance of dialogue between the prince and his subjects. The idea that taxation, and more generally, state authority is not imposed from the top, but negotiated with the community (or at least, the elites) is central in recent historiography. Combined with a further trend which focuses on communication issues as part of the art of government,[15] it led to renewed interest for representative assemblies and their rhetoric.[16] The history of taxation is also a history of ideas, which was illustrated by Lydwine Scordia's works on fiscal ideology in late medieval France.[17] A last major trend of recent research, following the pioneering works of anthropologist Jack Goody and medievalist Michael Clanchy, focused on the so-called "revolution of writing", the long-term progress of literacy which allowed the development of ever more various uses of writing in Western societies from the twelfth century on. It renewed medievalists' interest for accountancy, a practice first reborn in ecclesiastical estates, then devised for their own purposes both by Italian merchants-bankers and by nascent fiscal administrations.[18]

As a whole, since the middle of the past century, research on medieval public finance has shifted from a mainly legal and institutional approach to a more comprehensive one, which seeks to take into account all the actors of the political process of taxation – not only the prince and his agents, but the taxpayers, as well as the non-taxpayers (the clergy and nobility) who form the core of political society. Historians currently deal with social history (the groups and networks who support, resign themselves to, or oppose taxation) and even more with cultural history in the broadest sense (communication, ideas, knowledges and know-how). Meanwhile, as a likely consequence of the decline of Marxist historiography after the 1970s, the economic approach of fiscal history has been neglected, and the efforts that had been made (not only by Marxist historians) to estimate the actual weight of taxation on production and trade[19] have not been carried on. On the other hand, it is still uncommon to write fiscal history from the taxpayers' viewpoint, as the bulk of the sources are a product of the fiscal institution. Finally, a more technical area for research to come may focus on taxation basis, especially with respect to royal or princely direct taxation.[20]

Royal taxation

French royal taxation was born between the twelfth and fourteenth centuries, gradually taking shape along a process which was neither regular nor linear, with accelerations, hesitations and regressions. Building up the royal tax system was an essentially political process, closely linked to the spatial expansion of royal authority over the kingdom, as was already noticeable under Philip Augustus; in the fourteenth century, the tax administration was often the first royal service to settle in seigniorial lands outside the king's domain.

A prehistory of royal taxation (twelfth and thirteenth centuries)

In the twelfth century, the resources of the Capetian kings were drawn from their domain, their regalian rights and their feudal rights. Like every lord, they collected a variety of customary dues in their own lands in central northern France around Paris, fixed or variable, in cash or kind, from peasants, merchants and Jews. Another source of income was the exercise of seigniorial justice by royal local agents, the provosts (*prévôts*). The French kings also got benefits from minting, not as much from the difference (called *seigneuriage*) between the cost of producing coins and the legal value they assigned to them than from the payments Louis VI (1108–1137) and his successors negotiated with the towns of the royal domain in exchange for their pledge not to debase their money. Those sums were collected every three years through an indirect *taille* on wine and bread in most cities, including Paris. More generally, the *taille*★, a seigniorial arbitrary tax then either direct or indirect, was the main contribution of the towns of the royal domain to the king's revenues. In Compiègne the triennial money tax was a *fouage*★ imposed on hearths, and this kind of levy also existed in the duchy of Normandy, where it was maintained by Philip Augustus after the conquest of 1204. The "king's Jews" of the royal domain also paid him a specific *taille*★ in exchange for the protection and privileges he granted them. The French monarchs got another regular income, either in kind or cash, from exercising their right of hospitality (*gîte*) over a few bishoprics, abbeys and some tens of localities in the royal domain. They also found an occasional revenue in the right of regalia (*régale*) they held upon a part of the bishoprics and abbeys of the kingdom, which enabled them to perceive their income from the death of the prelate to his replacement. As for the nobility, the kings could claim two kinds of feudal revenue from their direct vassals: the *relief*, a tax on succession to the fief, and the *aide aux quatre cas* vassals owed their feudal lord when he was ransomed, departed for crusade, had his eldest son knighted or married his eldest daughter. Yet the kings of the twelfth century could hardly obtain those dues outside the royal domain. All these revenues were generally levied by the provosts. Beginning in the 1170s, the monarchy tended to ensure its income by leasing the charge of provost and the collection of the customary taxes to local businessmen for a fixed sum.[21]

The reign of Philip II Augustus (1180–1223), and especially the "decisive decade" of 1190–1203 (J. Baldwin), was a first turning point in the exercise of royal power. The king's financial organization was reformed and accounting regulations were set up, yet the taxation system remained grossly unchanged. The bailiffs (*baillis*), who appeared in the last years of Louis VII (1137–1180), progressively took in charge the administration of the domain as medium-rank royal officers above the provosts-farmers, and the collection of the different kinds of revenue was divided between the two levels with variations over time. Some steps were taken to improve royal income, but they proved to be isolated and ill-fated. From 1180 to 1182, Philip Augustus seized the king's Jews' precious goods, then cancelled the debts Christians owed them, but ordered debtors to pay one fifth of the sums to himself, and finally expelled Jews from the domain while confiscating their real properties. Such one-time measures deprived the king of regular income on his Jews, though, and in 1198 he allowed them to come back. In the meanwhile, Philip had levied in 1188 the *Dîme saladine*, a tithe (*décime*) on his vassals, both lay and clerical, who wouldn't join him in the Third Crusade, but he had to step back in front of Church opposition. As a result, the estimated doubling of royal resources under Philip Augustus was not due to fiscal innovation, but to the extension of his domain to rich lands in northern France and Normandy.[22]

The next steps took place in 1225, when an assembly of the French Church granted Louis VIII (1223–1226) a five-year tithe on its income, at the pope's request, to finance a crusade against Cathar heretics in Languedoc, and in 1248, when Louis IX (1226–1270) was preparing for the Seventh Crusade. The king, who already benefited from a new triennial tithe granted by the First Council of Lyon in 1245, raised an aid for the crusade on the towns of his domain, thus treating them as vassals. It was the first time the monarchy succeeded in mobilizing urban wealth at a significant level: in the royal account for Ascension Term 1248, the income from the cities exceeded the revenues from the countryside. In the second half of the thirteenth century, the last Capetian kings resorted to both new sources of income. As soon as 1252, the cities were solicited again to give so-called "grants" or "loans" for other matters of war or peace, the term "aid" being reserved for crusades. Meanwhile, the papacy granted new multi-year tithes to Louis IX and his successors, not only for the last Holy Land crusades, but also for the so-called "crusade" against the excommunicated king of Aragon in 1284 and 1289. Yet such resources remained extraordinary, that is, not regular.[23]

The second half of the thirteenth century also saw the genesis of the king's Chamber of Accounts out of a section of the *Curia regis* which, from the 1250s on, specialized in auditing the accounts of whoever handled the king's money. The new institution, definitely organized in 1320, was soon imitated in principalities across the kingdom.[24] Yet, it primarily asserted itself as the guardian of royal domain and though it strongly helped fixing and enforcing harmonized accountancy rules,[25] its role in shaping a modern taxation system remained marginal.

In quest of modern taxation: trial and error (from Philip the Fair to John the Good)

The reign of Philip IV the Fair (1285–1314) was the second major turning point in building up royal authority. The growth of administration, as well as a new policy conceived at the scale of the whole kingdom or the international level, required means the king's ordinary sources of income definitely couldn't match. New regular revenues had to be found.

On several occasions throughout his reign, Philip the Fair attempted to raise a feudal aid beyond his direct vassals, for his own knighthood in 1285, for his daughter's wedding in 1308 and for his sons' knighthood in 1313. Each time, his requests to rear vassals or towns were faced with protests of breaking customary rules, making it clear that the enlargement of the circle of contributors wouldn't rely on feudal law. From 1294 on, the king pretended to raise tithes on the French Church, with the consent of assemblies of the clergy, but without the pope's authorization, which led to a first clash with Boniface VIII, who considered the grant of such taxes to be a pontifical prerogative. At the same time, Philip the Fair resorted to altering his money, which provided him huge revenues for a time, but caused economic perturbations, social unrest and widespread resentment, eventually earning him the infamous reputation of "king counterfeiter". After 1300, he renounced such a hazardous policy and the income from royal mints dropped dramatically.

Meanwhile, an effort was made among the theologians and legal experts who supported royal power to promote the idea that the king could legitimately raise taxes on all his subjects, not only feudal aids on his direct vassals. This ideological undertaking exploited the resources of Roman law, rediscovered in the twelfth century and widely spread and studied throughout Western Europe since then. From the reign of Louis IX, it was admitted that "the king is emperor in his realm", so the model of the Roman *princeps*, as described in the *Corpus juris civilis*, could be applied to him. Although some adages in the *Corpus* could be read as giving the prince an unlimited right of taxation, most experts in Roman law (*légistes*) insisted this right could only be exercised when it was justified by the common interest (*utilitas publica*) of the kingdom, especially in case of urging necessity (*imminens necessitas*) such as the defence of the realm (*tuitio regni, defensio regni*). Yet these statements had to migrate from theory to reality: the context of tensions or open war either with England or Flanders, which fills Philip's reign, would then be invoked to ask for his subjects' financial contribution.

In 1292, the king made a first attempt at indirect taxation by ordering a sales tax of one *denier* per pound (0.4 per cent) in the whole kingdom. He faced general opposition: the lords refused its collection on their lands, the towns rebelled or negotiated its substitution for a fixed sum (*composition*), and a chronicler called it a *maltôte* (ill-raised), which became a synonym for unfair tax in late medieval French. Then the king turned to direct taxation, this time seeking his direct vassals' consent, often by granting them a portion of the sums collected. Various formulas were tested in Languedoc: at first a fixed tax on hearths in 1294, then a 1.5 per cent tax on personal property in 1295. This same year, a 1 per cent tax on real estate was ordered on the lays and clerks of the whole kingdom. In 1296, it became a one-fiftieth tax and was renewed from year to year. There was some grumbling, but the king instructed his agents not to raise the tax on unwilling lords' lands, and the towns often negotiated its replacement by a flat payment in the North or a fixed hearth tax in the South.

The French defeat at Courtrai opened a new stage in 1302, as Philip the Fair proclaimed any layman had to take up arms for the defence of the kingdom as a member of the *arrière-ban*. In practice, he allowed commoners to pay a tax proportionate to their real and personal wealth instead of serving in the army. This new way of justifying taxation was, in fact, the generalization of a practice that already provided the king with soldiers paid by some communities since the beginning of his reign. It also removed direct taxation from the noblemen who "used to bring not their money, but their arms" to the defence of the state, as one of their representatives would remind the Estates General of 1484. Yet Philip the Fair was well aware that the new tax, which was raised again in 1303 and 1304, wouldn't be easily accepted. Not only did he preach conciliation to his agents and make concessions, but in 1304 he negotiated the agreement of local assemblies of towns or nobility to the new levy. This same year, peace in Flanders put a temporary end to war taxation.

Ten years later, when he prepared a new campaign against the Flemish, the king gathered in Paris an assembly of the clergy, nobility and towns of the whole kingdom, as he had done in 1302 during his conflict with Boniface VIII, and in 1308 when he attacked the Templars. This time, his purpose was financial as well as political: the towns pledged him an aid for the campaign to come. Shortly thereafter, Philip the Fair summoned all his subjects to the army, then allowed commoners to pay a tax instead and clerks and noblemen to negotiate a payment with his commissioners. But a truce with Flanders compelled the king to repeal the tax just before his death in 1314, and rebel aristocratic leagues forced his son Louis X (1314–1316) to condemn it as "illicit".

The French kings of the first half of the fourteenth century were eager to know the number of hearths of the local communities, because they wished to divide the total amount of direct taxes between them on this basis. On the other hand, they were less interested in detailed information on individual wealth, which, for obvious reasons, the communities were reluctant to give them when they registered such sensible data. After Philip the Fair's attempts to access it, as in Languedoc in 1301, his successors preferably let communities divide freely their collective share between taxpayers. The monarchy at least tried to rely on its own verified lists of hearths, instead of depending on those of the lords or communities. In 1303, Philip the Fair planned to "put all the hearths of the realm in writing", but a general inventory of the parishes and hearths of the royal domain (at the time, most of the realm) was not carried out before 1328, and this enormous, yet partial and undetailed work was made obsolete by the Black Plague of 1348. Such a large-scale undertaking was too difficult to keep updated and was never renewed, although Charles VIII intended to do so in 1491.[26]

The events of 1314 inaugurated a new period in which the king negotiated taxes with various kinds of local assemblies, instead of attempting to impose them upon a reluctant political society. The hostility of the early fourteenth-century lords towards the very principle of the royal right of taxing their men may explain that Philip the Fair's sons tended to deal with towns, seeking to convince them the required subsidy was necessary to the defence of the realm. In a renewed context of tensions and wars with England or Flanders, the last Capetians and the first Valois Philippe VI (1328–1350) engaged in an endless series of negotiations with individual cities, local or large regional assemblies, first to get their agreement to a tax, then to define its shape. This decentralized dialogue between king and communities eventually formalized in two ways. On the one hand, it led to the constitution of local Estates, which took a regular shape by the middle of the century. On the other hand, the monarchy progressively developed a privileged relationship with the main towns in each region of the kingdom, which generally enjoyed representation in the local assembly and were distinguished as the "good towns".[27]

In the short run, though, such a multilateral process made it impossible to lay down a general taxation system. At least, Philip the Fair and his sons were able to establish two export taxes. In 1305, the king forbade almost all exportations, but provided that derogations would be granted by the new service of *ports et passages*; in 1321, the Chamber of Accounts of Paris set the tariff of derogation fees, which were called *droit de haut passage*. Then in 1324, Charles IV instituted a more liberal regime for fabric pieces or farming and fishing goods, which could be freely exported, but would pay a specific export tax to the *ports et passages* agents, the *droit de rève*. Such was the fiscal frame of the French monarchy when it entered the Hundred Years War. Some regional tendencies began to emerge from local diversity: when Philip VI summoned the *arrière-ban* and raised a tax instead of military service in 1337, most Northern towns negotiated a flat payment, while most Southern cities opted for a fixed tax on hearths.

In the early 1340s, as the war entered an active and costly phase, Philip VI inaugurated a new fiscal policy. First, he turned to indirect taxation. Between 1337 and 1340, he reinstated the *rève* he had abolished in 1333. In 1340, some local assemblies in the North granted him a 4 *deniers* per pound (1.7 per cent) sales tax; in 1343, he obtained its extension to the whole kingdom from the Estates General of Paris. From the 1330s on, the sales tax formula was also favoured by Northern towns, which tended to rely on it to gather the flat sums they pledged to the king. In 1341, Philip VI unilaterally established a tax on salt (*gabelle du sel*★), which was given a permanent administration in 1343, in a still rare assertion of his right of taxation. Second, as the king was faced with urging financial needs, he sought to save time by dealing with a general assembly, as Philip the Fair had done in 1314. From 1343 on, he gathered the Estates General every few years. Those of 1346 were divided for the first time for practical reasons: the Estates of Languedoil convened in Paris and the Estates of Languedoc in Toulouse. This practice would become current and reinforce the affirmation of different fiscal traditions in the North, which favoured sales taxes, and the South, where the tax on hearths (*fouage*★) became the ordinary formula from 1342 on. Yet general assemblies only gave their consent to the principle of a subsidy to the king for the defence of the realm: Philip VI still had to send commissioners to negotiate its actual shape and rate with the clergy, nobility, towns and communities at the local level. Nevertheless, the taxation system was in progress: after the defeat at Crécy in 1346 and the fall of Calais in 1347, the aid agreed by the Estates General at the end of the year was negotiated at the local level in only three months and brought unprecedented revenues in the king's coffers.[28]

Yet, as they found it increasingly uneasy to obtain funds from the Estates without submitting to their control to any degree, Philip VI and his son John the Good (1350–1364) resorted to an alternative source of income by altering the value of the money. Such a policy, which reminded the public opinion of Philip the Fair, was widely unpopular because of the economic and social perturbations it caused in an already destabilizing context of war and plague. In his 1355 *Treaty on money* of Aristotelian inspiration, Nicole Oresme, who later became a counsellor of Charles V, insisted that money belonged to the community and provided the claim for good money with a theoretical basis.[29]

The first assertion of royal taxation: John the Good and Charles V

When the long truce imposed by the Black Plague on English and French came to an end this same year, John the Good convoked the Estates General of Languedoil in Paris to ask for new subsidies. The assembly's demands, exacerbated by the new defeat at Poitiers and the captivity of the king in 1356, degenerated in a political crisis which reached its climax in 1358, with revolution in the capital and anti-seigniorial insurrection in the northern campaigns. Dauphin Charles eventually capitalized on the fears of the aristocracy and upper bourgeoisie to reverse the political situation and put an end to the parliamentary experiment. From 1358 on, against the general tide of Western Europe, he laid the foundations of an authoritarian model where fiscal policy was decided by the prince and his counsellors, then implemented by his officers, while the representative assemblies were left apart or asked for a formal consent. This was notably the case in Languedoc, where the Estates had not been compromised in the troubles of the mid-1350s. Negotiations between the king and the elites of the kingdom actually went on, but they were limited by the assertion of the royal right of taxation as well as the stabilization of the tax system.

In 1360, after peace was made with England through the harsh Treaty of Brétigny, King John went back to France and opted for monetary stability and tax-based finance. While in Compiègne, on December 5th, he simultaneously created a good gold coin of long posterity, the franc, and took up fiscal measures from the Estates General of Languedoil of 1355–1358 or former ones to design a whole set of indirect taxes. The sales of goods would be taxed along three categories: one fifth on salt, one thirteenth on the wholesale of wine and other alcoholic drinks, one fourth on their retail, and twelve *deniers* per pound (5 per cent) on any other merchandise. Salt and wine had, for a long time, been identified as the most profitable taxable items. The ordinance labelled all three taxes "aids", but they were also called *gabelles*★ in the fourteenth century; only in the fifteenth century was the latter name reserved for salt tax. The initial purpose was to face the king's enormous ransom, but after a few years their income was allotted to other expenses. The Ordinance of Compiègne may be seen as the birth certificate of French modern taxation, as it fixed its frame after seventy years of trial. In the early 1360s, a compensation tax was also instituted on the export of goods outside the area where aids were levied, as the king couldn't tax their sale; it was soon called *imposition foraine*★. All merchandise leaving the kingdom would pay the new tax in addition to the earlier rights of *rève* and *haut passage*, which were ultimately considered as pertaining to the domain.

Then in 1363, at John the Good's request, the Estates General of Languedoil gathered in Amiens and reinstated the *fouage*★ to raise an army for the defence of the realm – not against the English, but the Great Companies of dismissed mercenaries who plundered and ransomed towns and countryside. The royal fiscal system was now complete with direct and indirect taxation. When Charles V (1364–1380) resumed war against Edward III in 1369, he just had to get regional assemblies, then the Estates General of Languedoil to vote its strengthening. The Estates of Languedoc complied for their part at every stage from 1360, providing one fifth or so of the king's extraordinary revenues.[30] As taxation became regular, in many regions local assemblies asserted themselves as direct partners for royal officials. The land of Rouergue at first sent deputies to the Estates General of Languedoc to discuss and vote taxes, then set up Estates of its own in the late 1350s and early 1360s at the instigation of towns. The new assembly was in charge not only of granting taxes, but of distributing their burden between communities; only in case of dissent would royal authorities arbitrate on distribution matters.[31]

Along with taxes came a new public service: as soon as 1355, the Estates General of Languedoil mandated *élus* (officials "chosen" by the assembly) to organize the collection of the subsidies on a regional scale, and generals to supervise the management of the funds at the central level. After 1358, they became royal officers at king's appointment, providing the middle and upper ranks of the new administration of aids. In the fourteenth century, the districts the *élus* were responsible for were often dioceses; they ultimately were called *élections*. There, those key fiscal actors presided over the division and levy of direct taxes; monitored the *greniers à sel* (salt warehouses), run by the *grenetiers*, which had the monopoly of salt sale and *gabelle*★ collection in most of the kingdom; leased the raising of other indirect taxes to farmers; and ultimately watched over the pay-out of all the tax revenues to the district *receveur*. They also judged causes concerning the new taxes, whose appeals went to the Court of Aids of Paris, established in the late 1360s and definitely organized in 1390; specific Courts of Aids were set in Montpellier for Languedoc and Rouen for Normandy. Except for its judicial section, which remained the "Justice of Aids", the aids administration was renamed "extraordinary finance" in the fifteenth century, as opposed to the "Treasure" or "ordinary finance" based on royal domain traditional income. Indeed, the new tax system, also referred to as "aids for the war", was officially supposed to last no longer than the exceptional circumstances that motivated it. Up to the very end of the Middle Ages, the French monarchy would have to cope with the deep-rooted idea that "the king must live on its own", that is to say, on the revenues from the Crown's estates and traditional rights.[32]

The birth of permanent royal taxation in the 1360s was made possible by the consent of the elites, satisfied with good money and, as for churchmen and noblemen, with their exemption from *fouage*★, as well as the resignation of town and country commoners, faced with the threat of Great Companies. It provided Charles V with the secured and abundant income all his predecessors since Philip the Fair had desperately sought, allowing him to invest heavily in permanent armed forces. Those means, together with Constable Bertrand du Guesclin's cautious tactics, permitted to recapture most of French territories under English control from 1369 to 1378.

Yet in 1380 Charles V, on his deathbed, suppressed the *fouage*★, which had been denounced many years earlier as unfair and oppressive by his own think tank of private learned counsellors, and whose increasing burden had provoked riots in Languedoc towns in 1378–1379. Such an *in extremis* move suggests that the king's Christian conscience was still uncomfortable with the policy of permanent taxation he had practiced throughout his reign, relying on Roman law or Aristotelian justifications about the common good of the kingdom. Shortly thereafter his brothers, having assumed power on behalf of his minor son Charles VI, abolished the aids under the pressure of public opinion. But the needs of the royal state couldn't be matched by ordinary finance alone, and the aids were restored as soon as 1382–1383 despite new urban riots throughout the kingdom.

In 1384, direct taxation was revived in the supposedly more lenient form of *taille★*. Its global amount was decided by the king, then departed in successive stages down to homesteads. The final stage was in the hands of parish assemblies, who had to fix each taxpayer's personal contribution according to its wealth (as recorded in registers in southern France). Most of all, the new direct tax was raised only to face casual needs, military or other: there were fourteen nationwide levies of *grandes tailles★* in the thirty years 1384 to 1413, left apart regional levies in march territories. Some progress was made in Languedoc, where the royal *élus* gave up the unreliable lists of hearths in 1404 to divide more fairly the fiscal contributions of the dioceses between their communities on the basis of taxpayer's wealth. But for lack of regular *taille★*, indirect taxation remained the only stable source of fiscal income. Though the royal government resorted anew to money devaluation from 1385 on, Charles VI could no more afford a powerful permanent army.[33]

The process sped up in the early fifteenth century, due to the ill king's inability to rule, rivalries between princely factions and the Lancastrian offensive. Political division between Armagnacs and Burgundians, along with decades of degradation of royal finance and army, led to civil war, then to the disaster of Agincourt in 1415 and plunged France in a crisis even deeper than in the 1350s, culminating in the 1418 Burgundian massacre of Armagnac central state elites in Paris, the 1420 Treaty of Troyes and the breakup of the kingdom.

The second assertion of royal taxation: Charles VII

Faced with the collapse of the French royal state, Dauphin Charles had to recapture means for action, and finance was the key. In early 1418, Queen Isabeau had proclaimed once more the abolition of aids, giving the final blow to what still remained of fiscal income. What's more, the territories under Charles' obedience – the so-called "Kingdom of Bourges" – didn't stretch out to such rich and populated lands as Normandy and Île-de-France, now under English or Burgundian hands. The Dauphin, then King Charles VII (1422–1461), had to turn to the Estates, either regional or general (for Languedoil, in fact reduced to central France south of Loire, and Languedoc), to ask for subsidies just as the first Valois kings had done.

In 1423, the Estates of Languedoil restored the aids for three years, but this was only the first step in a long march towards their definitive rebirth. The Kingdom of Bourges engaged in the testing of a wide range of taxes to collect the granted subsidies, either direct (*taille★*, capitation) or indirect (*barrage*). The king had little initiative in this versatile fiscal policy, which basically reflected the hesitations of the assemblies in their quest for the less harmful formula. Only in 1436 would the Estates of Languedoil re-establish the aids for good, followed one year later by Languedoc. Yet the *élus* and their *élections* weren't restored in the southern province: they were replaced by diocese commissioners.[34]

Whatever their shape, the subsidies granted seemed impressive. Yet they were delusive. From 1417 on, France endured a monetary crisis which proved much worse in the Kingdom of Bourges than in the English and Burgundian area. From 1419 to 1422, the devaluation in Dauphin-controlled mints reached unprecedented levels. Then Charles VII's money incompletely recovered, and the following years to 1436 still registered many up-and-down monetary mutations, contrasting with northern France's relative stability. In the first times of his government the penniless Dauphin's monetary policy was a matter of political survival as he sought desperately needed income. In a letter to his servants in Languedoc, Charles admitted in 1422 that the necessities of the war against the English enemies and Burgundian rebels had compelled him to devalue so much his money that it had become "practically worthless".

Furthermore, war destructions and plunders, economic disturbances, fiscal experiments and a weakened state authority combined their effects to affect tax collection: the sums which came in the coffers were far from matching the amounts voted in assemblies. As a result, his hardly paid soldiers went back to the practices of the Great Companies. Their ruthlessness earned them the sad name of *Écorcheurs* (Skinners), but they often capitalized on their reputation to "negotiate" with local communities a tribute called *patis* (or *appatis*) in exchange for sparing them. The *patis* were the consequence of the collapse of royal taxation in a war context, but at the same time they became a de facto tax system that outcompeted the legal one. Thus, Charles VII's efforts to give *patis* an appearance of legality, after failing to stop them, were a lesser-evil policy which secured in the long run the defence of the Kingdom of Bourges, while waiting for better times.

The decisive turning point happened after Charles VII's consecration in Reims in 1429, the French–Burgundian reconciliation at the Treaty of Troyes in 1435 and the joint reconquest of Paris in 1436. In 1439, the Estates General of Languedoil recognized the levying of *tailles** as a royal prerogative. They nevertheless were supposed to convene again the following year, but the breakout of the princely rebellion of the Praguerie prevented the meeting: Charles VII overcame the revolt and never convoked them anymore. The assembly's crucial acknowledgement, immediately recorded in a royal ordinance, laid the legal basis for the restoration of Charles V's authoritarian model. This reassertion of the king's fiscal monopoly was echoed in 1444 by Charles VII's formal abolition of his captains' right to raise *patis* on their own, ending two decades of forced tolerance.

Languedoc was theoretically not concerned by the ordinance of 1439 and still convened each year to vote taxes, as did some local Estates in various parts of Languedoil. Yet their actual ability to question the amounts requested would gradually decrease, even if some space for negotiation on any other topic would remain. In 1443, the Estates of Languedoc obtained that the aids would be replaced by an annual fixed payment to the king, the "equivalent of aids", to be levied through specific taxes on retail sales that the assembly would design itself. Some local Estates in western Massif Central, although those lands were part of Languedoil, even managed to avoid the implementation of aids until the early 1450s and then opted for an "equivalent", this time in the form of a direct tax raised with the *taille**. In dealing with these matters, Charles VII showed patience and flexibility as he was anxious that local elites support, or at least don't oppose, his fiscal plans.

Then, the monarchy launched an ample administrative reform. From 1443 to 1447, the distinction between ordinary and extraordinary finance that had prevailed before 1418 was re-established, with a separate administration in charge of each one. At the head of both services, the competences of officers in charge of expenditure orders, accountancy, control and litigation were more distinctly drawn. At the regional level, the key role of *élus* was reasserted outside Languedoc. The purpose of the reform, in the medieval spirit, was to revive the past good rules: this was the reason for the restoration of the administration of ordinary finance (or Treasury) in 1443, as the king intended to improve the management of his domain. Yet it brought innovation, as both financial services were largely decentralized within the frame of three supra-regional *charges*: Outre-Seine-et-Yonne (mainly Île-de-France and Champagne), Languedoil and Languedoc. The directors of each administration (the treasurers of France for ordinary finance, the generals of finance for extraordinary finance), besides formally running their service in common, would each directly head one of the three *charges*. In the same way, a chief accountant of extraordinary finance, the receiver general of finance, and his assistant, the controller general, were instituted within each *charge*; yet the central accountant of ordinary finance, the changer of Treasure, and his assistant, the clerk of Treasure, were still in charge of the whole of the kingdom. The institutions of French royal finance, so reorganized, thereafter adapted to territorial expansion with the multiplication of *charges*, but their frame remained unchanged until the sixteenth century.

Meanwhile, Charles VII took the occasion of a five-year truce with Henry VI in 1444 to set up the major military and fiscal reform he was thinking of for years. In 1445, he restored a royal permanent cavalry, organized in *compangies d'ordonnance* whose tactical units, the "lances", were headed by men-at-arms (*gens d'armes*). A specific direct tax was created to finance it: the *taille des gens d'armes*, whose global amount was divided between the northern *élections* and southern dioceses according to the number of lances each one was supposed to pay for. Once again, the French monarchy justified the *taille des gens d'armes* with the threat its own soldiers, not the English, posed to the people of the kingdom. Still in 1451, Charles VII recalled that the military and fiscal reform had been devised to "avoid the great plundering which was done on our poor people by our soldiery, who then held the countryside in our kingdom and lived without rules". Not only did the reforms meet the adhesion of the Church and the nobility, who escaped direct taxation and, as for the latter, was offered better prospects of military careers, but beyond the upper estates of society, they also enjoyed the consent, or at least the resignation of the non-privileged bulk of the Frenchmen, who considered it to be the price for the return to safety.

In the following years, Charles VII supplemented his permanent forces with cavalry and infantry reserves (*francs-archers*, 1448), feudal reserves reorganized after the royal cavalry model (*ban et arrière-ban*, 1448), and garrison troops (*mortes-payes*, 1450). Each component of the army had its own secured source of financing: the *taille des gens d'armes* provided for the permanent cavalry, the newly created *taille du roi* and indirect taxes for the artillery as well as the reserves when on duty and any other wartime temporary force, while indirect taxation also covered civilian expenses. This well-devised financial and military apparatus allowed Charles VII to take back Normandy (1449–1450), then Gascony (1451 and 1453) from a weakened England, putting a victorious end to the Hundred Years War. The reconquest of Normandy, though devastated, and the subsequent reduction of the royal army, then led to fiscal relief. As soon as 1452, the *taille du roi* was abolished and Normandy had to support one third of the lances, easing the burden of the remaining of the kingdom.[35]

Fiscal abuse and normalisation: Louis XI and Charles VIII

Although Louis XI (1461–1483) took the opposite view to Charles VII on every field of politics, he maintained the financial and military institutions as reshaped in the 1440s. The new king's caution was highlighted in the fiscal reforms he launched in Normandy and Languedoc between 1462 and 1464. In each case, the king empowered the lively regional assembly to collect taxes but bound the reform to an obligation of result, and as soon as he realized the aim wouldn't be achieved, he ended the experiment. On the other hand, in 1462 Louis XI abolished the 5 per cent aids in the *charge* of Languedoil and replaced them with two different taxations systems. The countryside would pay instead a special direct tax in addition to the *taille des gens d'armes*, and the towns a new 5 per cent tax on a range of goods tighter than the former aids taxation basis, the less lucrative items being exonerated. The urban part of the reform was then extended to Paris and Rouen in 1465, and its rural part to the *charge* of Outre-Seine-et-Yonne the following year.

In 1465, Louis XI was faced with the War of the Common Good, an aristocratic rebellion which denounced the king's fiscal oppression (though it was still to come) and pledged to abolish taxation. Louis XI overcame it at the cost of huge concessions, then devoted himself to the reinstatement of royal authority, both by reconstituting a royal party among the aristocracy at great expense, and by developing the army. As a result, fiscal pressure began to increase in the second half of the 1460s, and the rise accelerated after feuds with Duke of Burgundy Charles the Bold gave way to open war after 1470. It concentrated on direct taxation, as Louis XI got into the habit of adding one or more *crues de taille** (supplements) in the course of the year, as he encountered new charges, to the *principal* (original amount). One of them, the *crue* for the king's affairs, became a regular supplement to the *taille des gens d'armes*, levied with the latter at least from 1468 on: it became the main instrument of the rise in direct taxation.

In Languedoc, Louis XI agreed in 1464 that the total of the *aide* (the country's contribution to the nationwide *taille**) and the equivalent of aids would amount to a flat sum. At this time, the *aide*, as such defined, actually represented the portion of the *taille** of the kingdom that the country was supposed to bear, that is, about one tenth. But as the *taille** began to inflate, the Estates of Languedoc were faced with the growing difference between the tenth they owed and the fixed *aide*. They filled the gap with a supplement to the *aide**, which was soon called *octroi** (grant): it formed the variable (and quickly, the major) part of direct taxation in the country. Meanwhile, two "general searches" were run throughout Languedoc to update the lists of hearths, the first one by royal commissioners in 1464 after the failed fiscal experiment, and the second by Estates officials with royal assent from 1480 to 1482. The latter is unfortunately the less documented, but it was much more detailed than the former and provided the basis for dividing direct taxation between the dioceses until the French Revolution.

The death of Charles the Bold in 1477 didn't end Burgundian Wars, as Louis XI competed with Archduke Maximilian of Habsburg to grab the duke's lands until the second Treaty of Arras in 1482. In addition to the yearly "*crue* for the king's affairs", Louis XI began to raise in 1478 a monthly "*crue* for the cartage of artillery" for the duration of campaigns. Then in 1480, the king launched an ambitious military reform, replacing the *francs-archers* with a permanent infantry partly recruited among Swiss mercenaries, and creating a large mobile camp to host his army, the King's War Camp. The highly expensive new forces as well as the artillery were financed by a new permanent supplement to the *taille**, the "*crue* instead of the *francs-archers*", which absorbed the *crue* for artillery cartage.

Louis XI also increased indirect taxation on wine and salt. On the one hand, in 1474 he instituted a new tax on wine exported to Burgundy, as well as every merchandise exchanged between kingdom and principality. The one *écu* per *queue* of wine (about 15 per cent) tariff was also applied to other taxable goods, the *queue* of wine therefore being used as a standard value. On the other hand, the king resorted to *crues* on salt taxes, first at a local level after 1465, then in the whole kingdom except Languedoc in 1471, and again in the early 1480s. By that time, the fiscal pressure hit its peak: the amount of taxes had more than tripled, and that of direct taxes almost quadrupled, over the past twenty years.[36]

A reaction was unavoidable after Louis XI died in 1483. The Estates General of 1484 regained control over royal taxation. They voted a two-year "grant and voluntary gift", whose yearly amount was supposed to be that of Charles VII's last *taille**, promoted as a canon for reasonable taxation, along with a one-time supplement to cover coronation costs. The two subsidies put together amounted to about 40 per cent of Louis XI's last *taille**. The Estates General were to convene again to vote taxes for 1486, but the informal regents, Anne and Pierre de Beaujeu, got young King Charles VIII (1483–1498) to order at first the levy for 1485 of "the same sum" they had voted for in 1484, implicitly including the coronation grant, and subsequently to raise a supplement on his own. This second step was a quick retrieval of the royal right of taxation, and the two levies were continued in 1486 without summoning the Estates General.

From then on, the *taille*★ (which soon recovered his name) was divided between the *principal*, supposedly representing its normal amount, and the *crue*, a supplement reputedly dictated by adverse circumstances. The episodic aristocratic rebellions of the "Foolish War", new war against Archduke Maximilian and conquest of unfriendly Brittany provided such circumstances from 1485 to 1491. Until 1487, the *principal* remained at the level of the sums granted by the Estates General while the *crue* rose, but from 1488 on, the *principal* itself integrated both *principal* and *crue* of the previous year.

In 1491, Charles VIII assumed effective power while peace was restored. From then on, the amount of *taille*★ was stabilized for the remaining of the reign with the exception of two huge *crues*, the first of which was ordered in 1492 to cover past deficits. It didn't suffice anyway, and from 1491 on, the king raised in advance the first terms of the next *taille*★, so he entered each new year having already spent a part of the receipts supposed to make for the year's expenses. In 1493, it was estimated the king's cumulated arrears already represented the amount of Charles VII's last *taille*★. This didn't prevent Charles VIII from launching the first Italian War (1494–1497). The king ordered a last huge *crue* in 1494 to finance military preparations, presuming the revenue of the Kingdom of Naples would thereafter restore his finance. But the conquest of Naples in 1495 brought no cornucopia, and as Charles VIII refused to raise taxes, he broke with long-time principles of royal financial policy as soon as 1494. He resorted to borrowing (an expedient all his predecessors had used) at an unprecedented level, not only within his kingdom, but with foreign bankers for the first time since Philip the Fair, and allowed the sale of domain properties with a buy-back clause, as the domain was legally inalienable; yet, such an infringement of the Crown's rights deterred purchasers. When Charles VIII unexpectedly died in 1498, the monarchy's arrears only slightly exceeded those of 1493, but this result was due to massive indebtment.[37]

The French monarchy left the Middle Ages with an efficient taxation system, but Louis XI's oppressive policy revived moral impediments to the full use of this tool; thus, Charles VIII's refusal to balance his finance through tax increase. Such qualms were to endure until Francis I; only then would royal taxes rise again, to reach the records of Louis XI's late years in the more prosperous France of the middle of the sixteenth century.[38]

Princely taxation

The Burgundian principality, which laid across both kingdom and Empire, and turned into a de facto independent state, will not be addressed here, as its fiscal sources are so abundant and its historiography so rich that it would have oversized this chapter. Although many other French principalities, whether royal apanages or not, developed institutions on the royal model, they enjoyed limited autonomy and were hardly able to set up a tax system of their own: their rulers could, at best, get a share of royal taxes. Only the duchy of Brittany asserted itself as another independent state, complete with princely taxes. Dauphiné is another special case, as it fell under royal authority in 1349 but was located outside France, so royal taxes didn't apply to it: it remained a peripheral principality, a personal possession of the king or the heir to the throne, with a separate tax system. Thus, the present section will focus on these two polities.

Duchy of Brittany

Although Philip Augustus installed in Brittany the Capetian dynasty of the House of Dreux in 1213, and in spite of the duchy's occupation (1373) and aborted confiscation (1378) by Charles V, the dukes (to whom the kings of France only recognized the title of count before

1297) maintained the independence of their principality until Charles VIII's conquest and marriage with Duchess Anne in 1491.

Up to the mid-fourteenth century, the dukes' resources classically came from their seigniorial, feudal and regalian rights. They consisted in fixed rents on tenures, profits from the domain or from ducal banalities (especially mills, ovens and fish drying facilities), light indirect taxes on the circulation and retail of merchandises (*coutumes*), judicial fines, sealing and registration fees, taxes on property mutations (*lods et ventes*) also in use in the royal domain, and feudal rights on vassals such as the *bail* which allowed the duke to perceive a fiefdom's revenue during the minority of a vassal, or the *rachat* which, from 1276 on, alternatively entitled the duke to one year of the fief's income at the death of a vassal. The revenues of the domain were centralized until the second third of the thirteenth century by a seneschal in each of the eight *baillies* of the duchy. By the end of the century, they had lost their financial functions to five *grands receveurs*, who disappeared in the first half of the fourteenth century. Domain resources were then handled at the local level of castellanies (or groups of castellanies) by *receveurs ordinaires*, directly accountable to the central administration. They collected some resources, but leased most others to farmers, especially domain and banal facilities profits, *coutumes*, and even seal and register fees. From the mid-fifteenth century, the *receveurs ordinaires* themselves were more and more replaced by farmers. Finally, in spite of the shortfalls this practice happened to cause it in the long run, the ducal state leased all domain revenues to general farmers in 1485.

In 1303, Brittany contributed to Philip the Fair's direct tax on hearths, an exceptional episode which remained isolated. Like the Hundred Years War in the kingdom, Brittany's War of Succession (1341–1364) led to the birth of the ducal modern taxation system. In 1345, Duke Charles of Blois ordered the levy of a local hearths tax on Nantes and its vicinity; such war subsidies of various geographical extension became usual in the following years in the zone under the duke's control. Meanwhile, in the areas occupied by the English supporters of his opponent John of Montfort, regular *patis* were raised on the parishes.

After his final victory in Auray in 1364, the new Duke John IV of Montfort (1364–1399) laid the ground for a comprehensive fiscal system. In 1365, he negotiated with each of his main vassals the right to tax the import, export and retail of merchandise, especially in the ports under episcopal lordship. Afterwards, he gathered the Estates of Bretagne in Vannes to ask for the first regular peacetime *fouage** to be raised in the whole duchy, in order to clear past war debts and ensure the principality's financial independence from the king of France. From then on, direct taxation would always be consented by the Estates, or at least by a session of the ducal council extended to bishops and barons, as general assemblies also including town representatives were still exceptional in the second half of the fourteenth century.

The first Montfort duke also reorganized the direction of ducal finance by merging the charges of Treasurer and *receveur général* by 1367. The office then underwent sporadical splits in two charges, at first on a geographical basis, as was already the case under Charles of Blois, for the western Celtic-speaking half of Brittany (*Bretagne bretonnante*) and the eastern French-speaking half (*Bretagne gallo*), between 1379 and 1398, and later on an institutional basis, for Ordinary (domain) and Extraordinary (other), at various short times between 1410 and 1451. From then on, the unified office got ever more authority, especially under the powerful and competent Treasurer Pierre Landais (1460–1485). From 1446 on at least, the Treasurer and *receveur général* was assisted by a general controller on the French model. John IV's reign was also crucial for the institutionalization of the section of the *Curia ducis* which audited ducal accounts since the 1260s into a Chamber of Accounts. No later than 1369, he established it in Vannes, where it remained until the end of the Middle Ages, and after his return from exile in 1379, he emancipated it from the ducal council and provided it with proper officers.

Both indirect and direct taxes set in 1365 were supposed to be temporary, and in return for prelates and magnates' support, the duke made fiscal concessions. Tax income was shared with ecclesiastic and lay lords, who were exempted from import and export duties and, until the early fifteenth century, put in charge of collecting the *fouage** in their lands. Ports also enjoyed import–export tax exemption or relief, and after 1379 many towns were exonerated from *fouage**. This policy couldn't fully neutralize aristocratic opposition to ducal authority, encouraged by the king of France: in 1395 the duke of Burgundy, who then ruled the kingdom, arbitrated that all indirect taxes would be abolished in the duchy. Only after the House of Blois-Penthièvre, the Montfort dukes' archenemies, was brought down in 1420 would the ducal fiscal system freely develop.

The frequency of *fouages** then quickly became annual. In the long run, *fouages** became ever heavier from John IV to the end of independence, except for a pause in the 1450s in the aftermath of the Hundred Years War, but the tendency was reversed after the French conquest of 1491, as the king was careful to ensure the Bretons accepted his domination. The *fouage** was levied by special *receveurs* under the appointment and authority of a *receveur général*. Unlike their French colleagues, they were temporary officials named for each individual *fouage**; only after 1460 were they often the same from year to year. The *receveur général du fouage** was generally the Treasurer and *receveur général* of the duchy; he had to give an advance of the sums to be collected, and so were local *receveurs*, so they were recruited among wealthy ducal officers or businessmen. The collection area of the *receveurs* progressively stabilised in the frame of dioceses, or parts of dioceses.

The first lists of hearths were probably compiled by the local administration. In the 1390s, complaints about their obsolescence led John IV to order local update inquiries. In 1426, John V launched a general reformation of hearths: justice officers, domain *receveurs* and *receveurs des fouages** consulted local notables and visited parishes to make new lists. At the same time, the hearth was officially defined as a grouping of three homesteads, thus separating the fiscal unit from the family residence unit. Some progress was made in estimating taxpayer's capacity in the course of the century: while John V's local investigators merely wrote it down as a fraction of a standard *fouage** of 20 *sous* per hearth (an already outdated rate at the time), the mixed updating commissions of local officers and members of the Chamber of Accounts who operated in the second half of the century described family structure, sources of income, rent charges, land area and cattle with their mode of possession.

Beginning in the 1380s, many ducal and seigniorial towns (whose number varied between 20 and 40) were exempted from *fouages**, but from the 1420s on, they were asked instead for an "aid of towns" which became regular under Duke Francis I (1442–1450), and was in fact a parallel *fouage** granted by the Estates with the general one. Yet the aid of towns was much lighter than the *fouage**, and its stability between 1460 and 1480 sharply contrasted with the doubling of the latter, a result of Treasurer General and great merchant Pierre Landais' policy as well as an illustration of the political pact between the ducal state and the cities, who contributed in other ways to the finance and defence of the principality. Like the *fouage**, the aid of towns was levied by temporary special *receveur général* (generally the Treasurer) and local *receveurs*.

The indirect taxes were collected by local farmers under the control of the domain *receveurs ordinaires* until the early fifteenth century, then by general farmers at the diocese level. The main one was the tax on wine (in fact, on any alcoholic drink), called *pipage* in the fourteenth century and *impôt* in the fifteenth century: in 1483, it made for 80 per cent of indirect taxes income, and a quarter of the ducal state's overall receipts. It was voted every year by the Estates, and its rate increased in the long run, though at a lesser degree than the *fouage**. By 1430, distinct tariffs were instituted for Breton and foreign wines, the latter being charged twice as much as the former. The *traites*★ were perceived on land exportation through the French border by as many farmers as there were kinds of merchandise. The *devoirsd' entrée et issue*★ were charged on goods entering or leaving ports. A general tariff was edicted in 1397 and revised in 1422, then remained unchanged until the sixteenth century: it standardized local rates and allowed merchandises to be taxed only in the first port. The *brefs de Bretagne* (writs) were a ducal ship insurance against confiscation by local lords in case of coastal shipwreck. They appeared in the mid-thirteenth century as a regalian right exercised by the duke, and were inserted one century later in the new fiscal frame as a navigation tax. In 1454, their tariff was proportionated to ships tonnage. They were delivered by port officials under the authority of the domain *receveurs ordinaires* until the institution of an ad hoc general farm in 1483. Lastly, the "County and Provostry of Nantes" was a conglomerate of old and new rights on the land, sea and river circulation of goods around the mouth of the Loire, the most important items being salt imported by sea and wine going down the river. It was handled by the most prosperous farm of the duchy, generally held by Italian companies, which also took in charge the local delivery of *brefs* in the mid-fifteenth century.

Duke John IV sought to ensure Brittany's independence from France with the English support and built its taxation system with the help of his English treasurer Thomas of Melbourne. Yet the fiscal frame, primarily relying on a direct *fouage*★ and an indirect tax on wine, was inspired by the French royal model, as was the Chamber of Accounts. The complementary taxes on the circulation of merchandises and "sea tax system" (J. Kerhervé) were more a consequence of the duchy's geography than an imitation of the English model. So designed, the fiscal system of the Montfort dukes, once stabilized in the 1420s, proved well suited to the principality: its efficiency allowed them to proportionately raise as much, if not more income from Brittany as the Valois kings from the rest of France in the second half of the fifteenth century. Only the actual demographic and economic disproportion between the two polities doomed the duchy's independence.[39]

Dauphiné de Viennois

Before the last independent Dauphin de Viennois, Humbert II, "transported" in 1349 his Empire principality (on which the Emperor renounced his sovereignty in 1378) to the king of France, the resources of dauphins were of classical seigniorial and regalian nature. They primarily consisted of land revenue from the domain, profits from low justice exercised by the castellans and high justice exercised by the *juges mages* (upper judges), circulation taxes and sealing and registration fees. The only distinctive feature of Dauphiné was the relative importance of indirect taxes on the transit of merchandise (called *péages* and *grandes gabelles*★), which were the second source of the dauphin's income, reflecting the animation of trade roads along the Rhône and Durance valleys. Yet they remained far behind the seigniorial revenues collected by the dauphin's castellans within the domain districts, called castellanies. In addition, the dauphin could ask for a direct feudal aid, but in 1341, Humbert II formally abolished direct taxation. He was then preparing the cession of his principality and sought to preserve it from fiscal oppression in the future.

From 1350 on, the dauphin was the eldest son of the king of France, or the king himself if he had no son, but in most cases the king was the actual ruler of Dauphiné. The dauphin was first of all a French royal prince who never lived in the principality; the exception of Dauphin Louis, from 1447 to 1456, was a disguised exile. The absent prince (in fact, the king) was represented by a governor, who ruled the country with the assistance of the Council of Dauphiné. The principality thus became a personal, and most commonly informal, possession of the French king, which remained distinct from the kingdom.

The French domination had two almost immediate consequences on the local tax system. On the one hand, the farms regime was introduced as soon as the 1350s in the collection of both castellanies revenues and circulation taxes. On the other hand, as he couldn't order by himself the levy of a direct tax, Dauphin Charles I (later King Charles V) convoked a number of prelates, lay vassals and town deputies in 1357 to ask them for a "subsidy" after the disaster in Poitiers. This precedent laid a frame for direct taxation in the country: it had to be consented, relied on hearths like the French *fouage*★ and represented the participation of Dauphiné to the war effort of the neighbouring kingdom. Other subsidies followed at an irregular pace, about every five years in the first decades. They were due by resident commoners above a fixed wealth limit, whose list was established by castellans in the domain, that is, in most of the country; elsewhere, the lords gave only the number of their taxable men and would levy themselves the corresponding sum. As for towns, some contributed and others didn't.

The still sporadic subsidies didn't give birth to a special administration: they were collected in the existing districts of Dauphiné, castellanies and *mandements*, by ordinary officials and transferred to the Treasurer of the country, an officer established in 1355, who sent to the king what was not reserved for local expenses. Yet they introduced in the country the French distinction between "ordinary finance" based on the domain and "extraordinary" concerning the whole of Dauphiné, which consisted here of the subsidy alone. At the same time, the old Bench of Accounts, after an eclipse, was revived in 1367 by Charles V under the French name of Chamber of Accounts, then reformed in 1384 on the royal model. As soon as 1383, it compiled in a register rigorous lists of hearths for all the country, whose update in 1392–1393 took the form of a judicial investigation, so that the subsequent registers of hearths of 1393–1394 gave a legal basis to subside levying. From then on, the lists could only be altered through a new "revision of hearths" enquiry, granted by the grace of the dauphin at communities' request. The first to ask for it was the town of Romans in 1405; many others followed. By the end of the fourteenth century, the levying was made so efficient a subsidy could bring in about one tenth of the extraordinary revenues in the kingdom of France.

On the other hand, the first assemblies which agreed subsidies were no more than extended versions of the traditional dauphin's feudal council, where prelates, magnates and towns were occasionally summoned to give their individual consent, not the collective agreement of the three orders of the principality, as Dauphiné was still a patchwork of political bodies with no sense of common identity. In 1367, Charles V encouraged the emergence of a representative assembly, but it didn't take shape before 1388. From then on, the Estates of Dauphiné (as they were named in 1391) became the collective partner of the king and his governor in negotiating fiscal matters as well as others.

In the early fifteenth century, the deteriorating political situation of the French monarchy made more frequent the king or dauphin's requests for what was now called "free grants". In 1407, the purpose of the "grant" was the purchase of Valentinois and Diois by Dauphin Louis, head of the Armagnac faction, but instead he used it in the French civil war in spite of the vain opposition of the assembly. Afterwards, the rhythm of "free grants" accelerated until 1426 as to become practically annual, while the Estates enjoyed greater autonomy. A global sum was voted, then divided by the estimated number of hearths to fix the amount owed by each taxpayer. But economic depression caused local communities to ask for revisions of the lists of solvable hearths: the latter ultimately became less numerous than insolvable hearths, and the tendency ever aggravated after 1410. As a whole, the number of solvable hearths fell by 40 per cent between the 1390s and 1420s.

To compensate the loss, towns were urged to contribute to "free grants" according to the actual number of their hearths instead of negotiating a more lenient flat sum; then Dauphin

Louis II helped the Estates and local communities to include the numerous allodial land tenants (*alleutiers*) of the country in the lists of taxable hearths. On the other hand, from 1426 on, unsolvable hearths were put together to constitute fictive taxable ones: the hearth, which until then had been an actual family homestead, turned into a fiscal abstraction. To avoid confusion, the true hearth was therefore called *bellue* ("spark", as a reference to the home fireplace), while its former name *feu* (hearth) was applied to the new fiscal unit. This innovation was then promoted by Dauphin Louis II, during his residence in Dauphiné and later during his reign as King Louis XI, as well as Charles VII during his taking hand of the country in the meantime. The general revisions of hearths of 1457–1461 and 1474–1476 completed the overall spread of the fiscal hearth, which, depending on the local degree of prosperity, aggregated eight to twelve insolvable homesteads. In the 1440s, the dauphin also urged exonerated towns to renounce their privilege: Valence submitted. As a result, the decrease of solvable hearths was ultimately ceased after 1461.

Dauphin Louis was interested in defending the basis of the direct tax, rather called "aid" in the late fifteenth century, as he favoured from the start what would be his preferred fiscal instrument when on the French throne. He asked for higher amounts than former dauphins, and sometimes dispensed himself of the vote of the Estates. When he was king, the aid of Dauphiné unavowedly became the contribution of the country to the *taille*★ of the realm. In 1473, another step was made towards the French model with the institution of a general to head regional finance. Yet direct taxation still represented a lesser part of the overall receipts of Dauphiné than was the case in France or Brittany, and fiscal pressure was much lighter than on the western bank of the Rhône. At the end of the Middle Ages, the Alpine principality actually took its part of the charges of the kingdom and its direct taxation had developed under French influence, but its integration to the royal fiscal system was still far from complete.[40]

Tax and the city

The historiography of medieval France urban taxation is mainly monographical, and few attempts were made to provide syntheses at a national scale.[41] In addition, research proved more dynamic regarding southern cities than northern ones.[42] Such historiographical imbalance reflects the unequal richness of sources across the country, which is not incidental: it is the consequence of different fiscal choices made in the South and North, which produced more detailed evidence in the former area.

In the twelfth century, French towns, whether they had or not a formal autonomous status, found their first resources in the concession or usurpation of seigniorial indirect taxes as well as the direct collections by charitable associations which often preceded the northern *communes* and southern consulates.[43] When the regional princes or the king began to sporadically request their financial support in the thirteenth century, the towns raised direct *tailles*★ (or *collectes*) on their inhabitants; in the North, where they could access a financial market centred in Arras[44], some borrowed money or even sold lifetime and perpetual rents, like Calais.[45] In Provins, short-term loans represented the first source of income until 1290; in addition, a few lifetime rents were sold, but they disappeared by 1278. Véronique Terrasse thinks the reason was plausibly the lack of permanent resources to meet long-term obligations; in Artois, the count prohibited such sales in 1290.[46] Yet the trend was not general: life annuities were still a burden for Amiens in 1382.[47] In any case, the reimbursement of loans and the payment of rents required regular municipal revenues. As there was no permanent direct taxation, northern towns began to develop indirect *assises* or *accises*★ (also called *maltôtes* in the fourteenth century)[48] on the transit and sales of merchandise, whose introduction required the king or prince's agreement,[49] and whose collection was leased to farmers.[50] As soon as 1259, Amiens was granted such a tax by Saint Louis to face its debts.[51]

In Languedoc, although the first documented case of direct taxation of the inhabitants of a town dates back to as early as 1158, even before the first Italian examples, such initiatives remained rare throughout the thirteenth century. Those early cases were based on a taxation of movable and immovable property, depending on its value accordingly to the system of *allivrement*, or proportionate calculation *"per solidum et libram"*. Such a practice, already in use in Montpellier in 1204,[52] was adopted by many cities in the middle of the century and promoted by Alphonse of Poitiers, Saint Louis' brother and count of Toulouse, in 1260.[53] In 1263, Alphonse therefore ordered the assessment of urban household heads' property as a liable basis for taxation, and the setting of lists of taxpayers with their taxable wealth, called *livres d'estime*: Toulouse was probably the first city to comply by 1264. In 1270, *allivrement* became compulsory for all direct taxes raised in Languedoc towns above a said level.[54] In practice, inventory of private wealth was taken in charge by *consulates* (municipal authorities), so that such information remained under the cities' control, and the enquiry relied on owners' declarations to ensure their goodwill. The technique then progressively spread south of a line from Dijon to Bordeaux, mostly in *langue d'oc* countries.[55] Within this area, in the fourteenth century most towns held fiscal registers under the various names of *livre d'estime*, *compoix*, *vaillant* or later *nommées*.[56] Such information enabled them to refine fiscal techniques by calculating individual contributions on the basis of combined criteria, taking into account each taxpayer's household, property and revenue. *Cadastres*, where information wasn't arranged by taxpayer but by place, didn't appear before the late fifteenth century: the *cadastre* of Toulouse dates from 1478.[57]

Alphonse of Poitiers' measures were part of a larger Capetian response to urban unrest due to fiscal matters. The fact that the levies were decided, calculated and implemented by the same elites who monopolized town government raised suspicion among lower-rank taxpayers (who belonged to the intermediate levels of urban society, such as shopkeepers and craftsmen, as the poorer were exonerated) that their taxation was unfair and devised to favour the rich. This led to inner political conflicts and to the prince or king's intervention, on behalf of keeping peace. By 1260, at the very same time his brother promoted *allivrement* in the South to make direct taxes less arbitrary,[58] in the North Louis IX regulated municipal finance within the royal domain in order to end abuses, ordering towns to request his permission before any loan or indirect taxation, and to hold an accountancy which would be controlled by his masters of accounts.[59] Not only was the king asserting his authority upon his towns' finance, but his ordinances were the starting point of the slow emergence of municipal accountancy, which had practically not existed as long as the cities had no elaborate taxation system:[60] the oldest conserved town accounts are those of Arras (1241) in the North and Najac (1258) in the South,[61] and early accounts were often private papers of municipal magistrates in charge of collections.[62] Yet Louis IX's decisions were short-lived: tens of accounts from towns in Île-de-France, Picardy and Normandy were controlled by royal agents from 1260 to 1265, then the effort was ceased.[63]

Urban accountancy generalized only in the fourteenth century,[64] and its control would remain in the hands of municipal commissions (although a royal official attended them)[65] except when financial bankruptcy would cause the prince or king to intervene. In the meanwhile, the end of the thirteenth century was critical for towns finance as growing indebtment in the North could no more be matched by indirect taxation in a context of economic downturn, prompting the raising of municipal *tailles** whose unfairness angered everywhere ordinary taxpayers against the oligarchy of northern *échevinages* as well as southern consulates, while their collection still wasn't efficient enough to cover charges.[66] By 1280, northern royal bailiff Philippe of Beaumanoir described a situation very similar to that of 1260. "Rich" urban rulers escaped their own direct taxation while grieving the "poor", prompting them to revolt; to avoid such breakdown of public peace, the lord of the city had to impose a fair share of the burden.[67] Saint Louis and Alphonse's policy didn't reach its goal: in Languedoc, urban elites circumvented the supposedly neutral *allivrement* system by understating their declared wealth and developing complex calculation rules to their own benefit.[68] From the second half of the thirteenth century on, control of fiscal information, either through *livres d'estime* or accounts, would be the key to fair taxation and the core of conflicts about town government between urban oligarchy and lower *bourgeoisie*.[69]

Then the wars in Gascony, Flanders and ultimately the Hundred Years War made Philip the Fair and his successors' requests more frequent and heavier. As soon as 1293, many towns pledged to Philip the Fair a flat sum instead of the newly instituted royal *maltôte* and raised it as a municipal direct tax. The practice came into common use in the first half of the fourteenth century: cities negotiated their contribution with royal commissioners, then freely chose the way they would levy it.[70] Yet the new direct taxation was also used by cities to meet their own needs: in Provins it was combined with loans in a transitory phase beginning in 1293, before becoming the first source of municipal revenue in the 1310s.[71]

In Languedoc, the growing requests of the king prompted towns to develop a municipal direct taxation in order to collect the contribution they formally pledged him by contract until Charles VII. While each city designed its own rules and procedures, many common features emerged, which in fact were characteristic of a wider area spreading from Provence to the Kingdom of Valencia. The nobility and clergy resisted the consulates' efforts, backed by the monarchy, to impose the general tax on them; the taxpayers were commoner heads of hearths, and their contribution consisted of both a capitation, the *personal* or *capage*, and a tax calculated, according to a sliding scale, on the estimated value of their taxable properties, when it exceeded a cap. Such a regressive tax formula, which benefited the rich elites who held municipal power, again fuelled suspicion and anger among other taxpayers and provoked urban troubles that culminated in the 1370s, as in Montpellier in 1379, as Charles V's demands got heavier.[72] Protesters claimed for the original proportionate taxation formula, which they deemed to be perverted by the secrecy of wealth estimation procedures and the complex set of calculation rules that included various criteria for abatements. In the fourteenth and fifteenth centuries, direct taxation was the pillar of Languedoc municipal tax systems, so the registers where taxpayers were listed, and their taxable wealth assessed, became ever more sophisticated. The idea that fairly made *livres d'estime* would ensure fiscal justice as a tool of balanced distribution of the tax burden was expressed in the name many Languedoc towns gave them from the 1350s on: *compoix* (counterweight).[73] Yet, only in the course of the fifteenth century would some progress be made toward more equity, as wealth estimation commissions would be named by larger assemblies, and estimation rules better publicized.[74]

Meanwhile, the 1340s marked a turning point, as Philip VI, faced with Edward III's mounted offensives deep into the kingdom, organized a defensive strategy based on local strongholds and ordered the restoration or creation of urban fortifications.[75] As the king couldn't pay for it, he allowed towns to raise ad hoc taxes. The new royal policy, which put on the cities a part of the costs of the defence of the realm, was to endure to the end of the Middle Ages. As a result, the fiscal urban experiments of the thirteenth and early fourteenth centuries entered, in the second half of the century, in a phase of institutional stabilization and technical improvement which provided every town with a coherent tax system.[76]

From the 1340s on, it was well admitted that whilst the cities remained free to raise every kind of taxes for their own purpose, they couldn't levy taxes to fortify without the *octroi*★ (grant) of such right by the king, who therefore asserted himself as the source of legitimate taxation for the defence of the realm. So did the duke in Brittany.[77] At first this right was granted for one to three years, but in the course of time, its renewals applied to ever longer periods, up to a decade. Sometimes, the grant ultimately became permanent.[78]

Most towns asked for indirect taxes, which were often called *cloison*★ or *clouaison* (enclosing) duties in the North. They were generally raised on everyday consumer products, either at the gates of the city when those entered or quit it (the taxes were then usually named *droit de barrage*, or barrier duty), or in shops and markets when they were sold at retail – sometimes in both cases. Depending on the nature of the item, their amount was defined either as a proportion of its value or as a fixed sum per weight, capacity or length unit. The raising was organized either by kind of item or by place of collection, and leased to farmers. Taxes on wine were, by far, the most common and profitable. They were levied on retail through the universally spread technique of *appetissement* (called *souquet* in the South and *billot* in Brittany), the reduction by about one tenth of the quantity of wine delivered to the buyer. Salt was the second widespread pillar of urban indirect taxation, through an additional duty granted by the king in his local warehouse over royal *gabelle*★. Cereals, flour and bread were also taxed in many cities, as were a great variety of other items according to local economic features: Dijon's tariff included fifty-two products in 1358.[79]

The towns more occasionally resorted to direct *tailles*★ (also called *comu*, or common, in *langue d'oc*)[80] when it was necessary to raise important amounts in a short time, especially to build up their first fortification in the 1340s.[81] In the whole kingdom, the opportunity of defence taxation was also used by municipal authorities, backed by the monarchy, to get noble and clerical townsmen to contribute willy-nilly, in one way or another, to the *taille* for the fortifications which protected them too, although they always refused to pay the common tax and enjoyed a special treatment.[82]

The development of a regular fiscal system prompted the *échevins* or consuls to specially entrust one of them, or at least a member of the municipal elite, with the management of the sums collected, under a variety of titles such as receiver, clerk, treasurer, purser, *clavaire* (keeper of the keys), *greffier* (secretary), *argentier* (money manager), or *miseur* (expender) in fifteenth-century Brittany.[83] He had to keep a record of his receipts and expenses, which led to the generalization and progressive rationalization of municipal accountancy. Yet it was not unified everywhere: separate accounts could be held for distinct sources of income, or expenditure items, such as fortification and other city expenses.[84]

The birth of urban taxation systems in France was tightly linked to the contemporary assertion of the king's own fiscal frame. In 1360, as John the Good instituted a global royal tax system, all rival levies which might endanger its collection were forbidden and the cities were legally deprived of their resources. In 1367 Charles V had to concede them a portion of the indirect *aides* he collected on urban sales, but this measure reduced royal income; municipal taxation was eventually restored.[85] In the end of the fourteenth century, the Chamber of Accounts of Paris compelled the towns to ask the king permission to levy municipal *tailles*★, whatever their purpose, completing the assertion of the royal origin of urban taxation.[86]

Royal and municipal taxation then found an equilibrium, which was to last until the Wars of Religion in the second half of the sixteenth century. The king never refused the *octroi*★ of taxes required by the cities. Meanwhile, the towns became more reluctant to raise direct taxes as the king's fiscal frame relied ever more on *taille*★ from the 1440s on, and avoided the borrowing practices that had ruined many northern cities in the late thirteenth century. Thus, they favoured indirect taxation which, in the fifteenth century, almost always made for the two thirds of municipal income at the very least. The complementarity of royal and municipal tax systems at the end of the Middle Ages was only one aspect of the privileged relationship the French monarchy developed in the fourteenth and fifteenth centuries with its "good towns".[87]

From the late twelfth to the late fifteenth century, the development of public taxation in the kingdom of France at the three levels of the royal state, principalities and towns was a largely intertwined process. The gradual emergence of royal taxes went along with the progress of Capetian authority until the late thirteenth century. Then, the new assertiveness of the monarchy, leading to more frequent wars, sped up the state's fiscal genesis, opening an era of experiments and dealings with the political society. The early crushing defeats of the Hundred Years War then acted as a catalyst, giving way in the mid-fourteenth century to a comprehensive, permanent tax system firmly under the king's control. It thereafter followed the fortunes of royal authority, collapsing in the early fifteenth century before being restored, with some adjustments, in the middle of the century.

The assertion of the king's fiscal monopoly prevented principalities from developing a tax system of their own, except for Brittany and Dauphiné, which both imitated the royal model in the second half of the fourteenth century. Towns also experienced a stage of slow emergence of municipal taxes for their own limited purposes, that was hastened, from the late thirteenth century on, by the growing demands of the king or regional prince, and ultimately gave way, in the mid-fourteenth century, to a comprehensive fiscal system, both imposed and granted by the king, to fortify themselves as their contribution to the defence of the kingdom.

In this process, fundamental choices were made, which could be termed as a fiscal policy. To begin with, royal finance wouldn't rely on credit, and especially, not on the capital and expertise of Italian bankers: the Tuscan brothers Albizzo and Mucciatto Guidi dei Franzesi ("Biche" and "Mouche" in French sources), main lenders as well as financial and monetary advisers of Philip the Fair from 1290 to 1307, remained an exception.[88] Only short-term credit would be used as an advance on tax income to meet urging needs. It wouldn't depend on money mutation, either, and kings would explicitly link regular taxation to good money. Both choices were made, after trial, by Philip the Fair, and only in critical times would his successors depart from them. Then, while raising both indirect and direct taxes, Charles V put emphasis on the latter as the most efficient way to adjust revenues to needs, a choice later reasserted by Charles VII and Louis XI, and followed by Brittany as well as Dauphiné. Northern towns also turned away from credit in the late thirteenth century, but from the mid-fourteenth century on, cities everywhere relied primarily on indirect taxation, though they also raised municipal *tailles*★ and developed, in the South, sophisticated assessments of their basis.

Such choices had political and social implications. As for royal taxation, Jean-Jules Clamageran stressed long ago that *taille*★ better fitted the open countryside, where sales easily evaded *aides*★ farmers' supervision, whilst indirect taxation better fitted closed towns, where the concentration of trade made it more efficient. Louis XI tended towards focusing the former on the countryside and the latter on cities, a worthwhile policy for urban taxpayers at a time of stable *aides*★ and growing *tailles*★. In return, the spared towns would be in a condition to meet the king's casual demands for loans and subsidies, such as in wartime.[89] Moreover, when the city had to find funds at once to meet royal requests or face any urging need, it borrowed them from its rich elite, who was then paid off with interest on a new levy to come, at the expense of other taxpayers; thus, such advances were an opportunity of short-term profit for the urban oligarchy.[90] The recruitment of most of the monarchy's tax officials among the urban business community[91] obviously influenced its fiscal policy toward towns. As for municipal taxation, Bernard Chevalier stressed that the cities' emphasis on indirect duties, at the very same time the monarchy made the opposite choice, was dictated by the concern that royal and urban levies wouldn't thwart each other.[92] On the other hand, municipal *tailles*★ were mostly raised on the inhabitants of the town, whilst a fair part of indirect taxes were paid by peasants from the countryside coming into town for their business, shopping and taking meal and drink in inns,[93] as well as buying their compulsory portion of salt at the royal warehouse and being charged with the city's surtax.[94]

Yet in a Christian society were kings and princes received their power from God and were accountable to him, their fiscal policy also dealt with faith and morality. How to reconcile taxation, still a new and unaccustomed action, with their crucial duty of justice? In 1305, Philip the Fair asked Pope Clement V for spiritual help, as he felt guilty about the taxes he had raised and thought he had sinned by altering coinage,[95] which may be the ultimate reason why he renounced money mutations. Charles V similarly abolished the *fouage*★ on his deathbed in a dramatic about-turn, Charles VII consulted theologians in 1455 on the eventuality of not paying the royal domain's creditors (an idea he finally abandoned),[96] and Charles VIII refused to raise taxes during the Italian Wars. Only Louis XI never made such concerns apparent, though his immoderate donations to saints and churches may have been an unavowed redeeming transfer of ill-got richness. Beyond the earthly aims and stakes of medieval taxation, its religious and ethical dimension also took part in its shaping.

Notes

1 NORTIER, "Le sort des archives dispersées", pp. 460–537.
2 Since the late twentieth century, many townships (*communes*) have federated into syndicates (*communautés de communes*) which share common services; in some cases their archival repositories and libraries have merged.
3 CLAMAGERAN, *Histoire de l'impôt en France*.
4 VUITRY, *Études sur le régime financier* (the study actually ends in 1380, due to the author's death).
5 BORRELLI DE SERRES, *Recherches sur divers services publics* (the study actually ends with the fifteenth century, due to the author's death).
6 DUPONT-FERRIER, *Études sur les institutions financières*.
7 SPONT, "La taille en Languedoc", pp. 365–384 and 478–513; SPONT, "L'équivalent aux aides", pp. 232–253; SPONT, "La gabelle du sel", pp. 427–481; SPONT, "La taille en Languedoc … (conclusion)", pp. 482–494; DOGNON "La taille en Languedoc", pp. 340–346; DOGNON, *Les institutions politiques*.
8 STRAYER and TAYLOR, *Studies*; STRAYER, "Pierre de Chalon", pp. 334–339; STRAYER, "Italian Bankers", pp. 113–121; STRAYER, "Notes", pp. 399–421; BROWN, "*Cessante causa*", pp. 565–587; BROWN, "Taxation and Morality", pp. 1–28; BROWN, "Customary Aids", p. 1, pp. 91–258; BROWN, *Customary Aids*; BROWN, "Unctus ad executionem justitie", pp. 145–168; HENNEMAN, *The Development of War Financing*; HENNEMAN, *The Captivity and Ransom of John II*.
9 REY, *Le domaine du roi*; REY, *Les finances royales*; LASSALMONIE, *La boîte à l'enchanteur*; VIDAL, *L'équivalent des aides*; SASSU-NORMAND, *Pro defensione et tuitione regni*.
10 CHEVALIER, "Fiscalité municipale et fiscalité d'État", pp. 137–151; CHEVALIER, "La fiscalité urbaine en France", pp. 61–78; CHEVALIER, "Genèse de la fiscalité", pp. 21–38; RIGAUDIERE, *Saint-Flour*; RIGAUDIÈRE, "Le financement", pp. 19–95; GARNIER, *Un consulat*; GARNIER, "Le roi, l'emprunt et l'impôt", pp. 157–184; *La fiscalité des villes au Moyen Âge*; *L'impôt dans les villes de l'Occident méditerranéen*.
11 KERHERVÉ, *L'État breton*.
12 CHOMEL, "Ressources domaniales", pp. 179–192; VERNUS-MOUTIN, *La taille en Dauphiné*; VERNUS-MOUTIN, "Les états du Dauphiné", pp. 113–122; VERNUS-MOUTIN, "Recherches sur la réalité de la taille", pp. 145–154; LEMONDE, "Taille réelle et taille personnelle", pp. 279–292.
13 Among others, RAUZIER, *Finances et gestion d'une principauté*; *L'impôt au Moyen Âge*; LASSALMONIE, *La boîte à l'enchanteur*; *L'impôt dans les villes de l'Occident méditerranéen*; *De l'estime au cadastre. Le Moyen Âge*; GARNIER, *Un consulat*; *Monnaie, fiscalité et finances au temps de Philippe le Bel*.
14 GENET, "La genèse de l'État moderne", p. 3.
15 Communication issues also include fiscal and financial information: on this topic, GARNIER, "Le roi, l'emprunt et l'impôt", especially pp. 175-183.
16 HÉBERT, *Parlementer*; for a regional case study, QUÉRÉ, *Le discours politique des états de Languedoc*.
17 SCORDIA, *Le roi doit "vivre du sien"*; on taxation in legal literature, GARNIER, "L'impôt", pp. 67–113.
18 *Classer, dire, compter*; *De l'autel à l'écritoire*.

19 Contamine, "Guerre, fiscalité royale et économie", pp. 266–273; Charbonnier, "Les trois fiscalités en Auvergne", pp. 271–281; Dubois, "Le commerce de la France", pp. 15–29.
20 Lemonde, "Taille réelle et taille personnelle", pp. 279–292.
21 Baldwin, *The Government*, pp. 44–51 and 158–161; Sivéry, *Les Capétiens et l'argent*, pp. 13–16 and 103–105.
22 Baldwin, *The Government*, pp. 51–54 and 160; Sivéry, *Les Capétiens et l'argent*, pp. 100, 111 and 128–129.
23 Causse, *Église, finance et royauté*, vol. 1, pp. 189–190, 193–199 and 222–230; Sivéry, *Les Capétiens et l'argent*, pp. 140–146 and 166–169.
24 Jassemin, *La Chambre des Comptes de Paris*; *La France des principautés*; Prévost, *Le personnel de la Chambre des Comptes de Paris*.
25 *Classer, dire, compter*.
26 Chevalier, "La fiscalité urbaine en France", p. 77; Rigaudière, "L'essor de la fiscalité royale", p. 578 and 587; Rigaudière, "De l'estime au cadastre", p. 9.
27 Chevalier, *Les bonnes villes*.
28 Essential synthesis in Rigaudière, "L'essor de la fiscalité royale", pp. 323–391; Lassalmonie "L'imposition foraine", pp. 763–766.
29 Belaubre, *Histoire numismatique*, pp. 88–94; Demurger, *Temps de crises*, pp. 24–26; Autrand, *Charles V*, p. 264.
30 Contamine, *Guerre, État et société*, pp. 136–137, n. 3.
31 Garnier, "Les états du Rouergue", pp. 172–179.
32 Scordia, *Le roi doit "vivre du sien"*.
33 Belaubre, *Histoire numismatique*, pp. 94–95 and 106; Demurger, *Temps de crises*, pp. 32–34; Autrand, *Charles V*, pp. 426–429, 671–672, 677–683, 825–828 and 851; Lassalmonie, "L'imposition foraine", pp. 766–768; Larguier, "Construction d'un système fiscal", p. 353.
34 Dupont-Ferrier, *Études sur les institutions financières*, vol. 1, pp. 26–27 and 37; Larguier, "Construction d'un système fiscal", p. 353.
35 Contamine, *Guerre, État et société*, p. 250, 546, 631, 634 and pp. 290–292, 304–305, 337, 348–349, 367–370; Contamine, "Lever l'impôt en terre de guerre", pp. 11–39; Contamine, *Charles VII*, pp. 95–97, 270 and 320–322; Belaubre, *Histoire numismatique*, pp. 107–113; Lassalmonie, *La boîte à l'enchanteur*, pp. 27–30 and 34–36.
36 Lassalmonie, *La boîte à l'enchanteur*; Larguier, "Construction d'un système fiscal", pp. 353–354.
37 Lassalmonie, "Les finances de la monarchie française", pp. 3–141; Chevalier, *Du droit d'imposer*, pp. 33–47; Chevalier, "Le financement de la première guerre d'Italie", pp. 41–66.
38 Lassalmonie, "Les finances de la monarchie française", p. 95; Chevalier, "Le financement de la première guerre d'Italie", p. 59.
39 Kerhervé, *L'État breton*.
40 Chomel, "Ressources domaniales", pp. 179–192; Vernus-Moutin, *La taille en Dauphiné*; Lemonde, *Le temps des libertés en Dauphiné*, pp. 72–73, 160–199 and 293–314.
41 The classic *Histoire de la France urbaine*, published in 1980, devotes only a few pages to the topic (pp. 293–301), which were not updated in the 1998 revised and completed edition (pp. 284–293); the following notes refer to the first edition.. The only available syntheses to date are Rigaudière, "Le financement des fortifications", pp. 19–95; Chevalier, "Fiscalité municipale et fiscalité d'État", pp. 137–151; Chevalier, "La fiscalité urbaine en France", pp. 61–78; Chevalier, "Genèse de la fiscalité urbaine", pp. 21–38; Garnier, "Le roi, l'emprunt et l'impôt", pp. 157–184; and at a regional level, Larguier, "Construction d'un système fiscal", pp. 347–355.
42 Significantly, the major works on urban finance in the past half century are doctoral theses about Southern cities: Rigaudière, *Saint-Flour* and Garnier, *Un consulat*.
43 Chevalier, "Genèse de la fiscalité", pp. 27–30.
44 *Histoire de la France urbaine*, p. 299; Chevalier, "Genèse de la fiscalité urbaine", p. 32.
45 Chevalier, "Genèse de la fiscalité", pp. 30–32.
46 Terrasse, *La commune de Provins*, pp. 338–354.
47 Dufour, "Situation financière des villes de Picardie", p. 593.
48 Chevalier, "Genèse de la fiscalité", p. 35.
49 Chevalier, "Genèse de la fiscalité", p. 32.
50 Chevalier, "La fiscalité urbaine en France", p. 73.
51 Dufour, "Situation financière des villes de Picardie", pp. 592–593.

52 Chevalier, "La fiscalité urbaine en France", p. 74.
53 Larguier, "Construction d'un système fiscal", pp. 347–350.
54 Wolff, Les "estimes" toulousaines, pp. 25–26.
55 Chevalier, "La fiscalité urbaine en France", pp. 75–76. Albert Rigaudière stressed that *livres d'estime* "never really passed" a Venice-Milan-Lyon-Bordeaux axis (Rigaudière, "De l'estime au cadastre", p. 4), although he had previously studied those of Dijon, north of this line (Rigaudière, "Connaissance, composition et estimation du *moble*", p. 41, preliminary note). Mâcon, between Lyon and Dijon, also had *livres d'estime* (Guerreau, "Rentes des ordres mendiants", p. 956). Dijon may have been the northernmost case.
56 Chevalier, "La fiscalité urbaine en France", pp. 74–75; Rigaudière, "De l'estime au cadastre", pp. 15–16. In Lyon, the registers were called *livre du vaillant* in the fourteenth century and *nommées* in the fifteenth century (*ibidem*). On this topic, see *Les cadastres anciens*; *De l'estime au cadastre* (especially Rigaudière, "De l'estime au cadastre", pp. 3–22, an essential synthesis); and *Estimes, compoix et cadastres*.
57 Wolff, Les "estimes" toulousaines, p. 43; Chevalier, "La fiscalité urbaine en France", p. 75; Catalo and Molet, "Le parcellaire du cadastre", pp. 192–200.
58 Wolff, Les "estimes" toulousaines, p. 24.
59 Chevalier, "Genèse de la fiscalité", p. 33; Sivéry, Les Capétiens et l'argent, p. 146.
60 Chevalier, "Genèse de la fiscalité", p. 26.
61 Chevalier, "Genèse de la fiscalité", p. 26; Larguier, "Construction d'un système fiscal", p. 349.
62 Chevalier, "La fiscalité urbaine en France", p. 68.
63 Chevalier, "Genèse de la fiscalité", p. 26 and 33.
64 Chevalier, "Genèse de la fiscalité", p. 26.
65 Chevalier, "Genèse de la fiscalité", p. 37. A regional synthesis: Rigaudière, "Le contrôle des comptes urbains", pp. 207–242.
66 Rigaudière, "Le financement des fortifications", pp. 22–23; Chevalier, "Genèse de la fiscalité", p. 34.
67 *Histoire de la France urbaine*, p. 301.
68 Larguier, "Construction d'un système fiscal", p. 351.
69 Wolff, Les "estimes" toulousaines, pp. 24–26; Chevalier, "La fiscalité urbaine en France", pp. 67–68.
70 Rigaudière, "L'essor de la fiscalité royale", p. 378 and 383.
71 Terrasse, *La commune de Provins*, pp. 346–348 and 350.
72 Challet, "Montpellier 1379", pp. 377–400. For a wider contextualisation, see a classic synthesis: Mollat and Wolff, *Ongles bleus*.
73 Rigaudière, *Saint-Flour*, vol. 2, p. 822, n. 188; Rigaudière, "De l'estime au cadastre", p. 16, n. 46. This author notes another possible etymology: "movable asset", from the latin *compendium*. This would, then, highlight the growing importance of the taxpayer's wealth in the assessment of his fiscal capacity, ultimately leading to the *cadastre* (Rigaudière, "De l'estime au cadastre", pp. 16–17).
74 Larguier, "Construction d'un système fiscal", pp. 350–352.
75 Rigaudière, "Le financement", pp. 20–21.
76 Chevalier, "Genèse de la fiscalité", p. 22 and 35–36.
77 Rigaudière, "Le financement", p. 50.
78 Rigaudière, "Le financement", pp. 46–48; Chevalier, "Genèse de la fiscalité", pp. 35–36.
79 Rigaudière, "Le financement", pp. 49–56; Chevalier, "Fiscalité municipale et fiscalité d'État", pp. 145–146; Chevalier, "Genèse de la fiscalité", p. 36 and 38.
80 Garnier, *Un consulat*, p. 673.
81 Rigaudière, "Le financement", pp. 56–57.
82 Rigaudière, "Le financement", pp. 60–64.
83 *Receiver*: Chevalier, *Tours*, p. 90 (Tours); Favreau, *La ville de Poitiers*, vol. 2, p. 580 (Poitiers); Rigaudière, *Saint-Flour*, vol. 1, pp. 161–163 (Saint-Flour). *Clerk*: Terrasse, *La commune de Provins*, pp. 268–270 (Provins). *Treasurer*: Bochaca and Micheau, "Le recouvrement de la taille", p. 161 (Saint-Émilion). *Purser (boursier)*: Garnier, *Un consulat*, pp. 347–461 (Millau). *Clavaire*: Larguier, "Perception et gestion de l'impôt", pp. 149–150 (Narbonne). *Greffier*: Desportes, *Reims*, p. 509 (Reims, where there were two). *Argentier*: Guilbert, *Les institutions municipales*, p. 175 and 179 (Montreuil-sur-Mer). *Miseur*: Leguay, *La ville de Rennes*, pp. 21–31 (Rennes); Denmat-Léon, *Administrer en comptant* (Nantes and other Breton cities). In Rennes, the *miseur* belonged to the local merchant elite; he was named by the ducal power in the early fifteenth century, and later elected by an assembly of notables (Leguay, *La ville de Rennes*, pp. 24–28). The title might change over time: Paris

had a clerk in the thirteenth and fourteenth centuries (CAZELLES, *Nouvelle histoire de Paris*, p. 203), a receiver in the fifteenth century (FAVIER, *Nouvelle histoire de Paris*, p. 432); the little town of Cordes in Albigeois had a purser in the fourteenth century and a treasurer in the fifteenth century (PORTAL, *Histoire de la ville de Cordes*, p. 333).

84 CHEVALIER, "La fiscalité urbaine en France", pp. 69–71; CHEVALIER, "Genèse de la fiscalité urbaine", p. 37.
85 CHEVALIER, "Fiscalité municipale et fiscalité d'État", p. 142.
86 CHEVALIER, "Genèse de la fiscalité", p. 36.
87 CHEVALIER, "Genèse de la fiscalité", pp. 37–38.
88 STRAYER, "Italian Bankers", pp. 113–121; FAVIER, *Philippe le Bel*, pp. 18–19, 116 and 212.
89 LASSALMONIE, *La boîte à l'enchanteur*, pp. 127 and 246–247.
90 CHEVALIER, "Fiscalité municipale et fiscalité d'État", p. 148.
91 CHEVALIER, "La fiscalité urbaine en France", p. 78.
92 CHEVALIER, "Genèse de la fiscalité", p. 37.
93 It is highly doubtful that municipal taxation of wine intended to deter alcoholism, as anachronistically suggested in the *Histoire de la France urbaine*, p. 297.
94 CHEVALIER, *Tours, ville royale*, p. 100.
95 BROWN, "Taxation and Morality", pp. 17–18; BROWN, *"Unctus ad executionem justitie"*, pp. 148–149 and p. 168, n. 75.
96 LASSALMONIE, *La boîte à l'enchanteur*, p. 56.

References

Françoise AUTRAND, *Charles V le Sage*, Paris, 1994.
John Wesley BALDWIN, *The Government of Philip Augustus. Foundations of French Royal Power in the Middle Ages*, Berkeley-Los Angeles-London, 1986.
Jean BELAUBRE, *Histoire numismatique et monétaire de la France médiévale (de la période carolingienne à Charles VIII)*, Paris, 1986.
Michel BOCHACA and Jacques MICHEAU, "Le recouvrement de la taille à Saint-Émilion d'après le compte de Ramon Fortz, trésorier de la ville (1470–1471)", in *La fiscalité des villes au Moyen Âge (Occident méditerranéen)*, ed. Denis MENJOT and Manuel SÁNCHEZ MARTÍNEZ, vol. 4, Toulouse, 2004, pp. 161–172.
Léon-Louis BORRELLI DE SERRES, *Recherches sur divers services publics du XIIIe au XVIIe siècle*, 3 vol., Paris, 1895–1909.
Elizabeth [Atkinson Rash] BROWN, *"Cessante causa* and the Taxes of the Last Capetians. The Political Applications of a Philosophical Maxim", in *Studia Gratiana*, 15, 1972, pp. 565–587.
Elizabeth [Atkinson Rash] BROWN, "Taxation and Morality in the Thirteenth and Fourteenth Centuries: Conscience and Political Power and the Kings of France", in *French Historical Studies*, 8, 1973, pp. 1–28.
Elizabeth [Atkinson Rash] BROWN, "Customary Aids and Royal Fiscal Policy under Philip VI of Valois", in *Traditio*, 30, 1974, pp. 191–258.
Elizabeth [Atkinson Rash] BROWN, *Customary Aids and Royal Finance in Capetian France: the Marriage Aid of Philip the Fair*, Cambridge (Mass.), 1992.
Elizabeth [Atkinson Rash] BROWN, *"Unctus ad executionem justitie*: Philippe le Bel, Boniface VIII et la grande ordonnance pour la réforme du royaume (du 18 mars 1303)", in *Le roi fontaine de justice. Pouvoir justicier au Moyen Âge et à la Renaissance*, ed. Silvère MENEGALDO and Bernard RIBÉMONT, Paris, 2012, pp. 145–168.
Les cadastres anciens des villes et leur traitement par l'informatique. Actes de la Table ronde de Saint-Cloud, 31 janvier-2 février 1985, ed. Jean-Louis BIGET, Jean-Claude HERVÉ and Yvon THÉBERT, Rome, 1989.
Jean CATALO and Henri MOLET, "Le parcellaire du cadastre de 1478", in *Toulouse au Moyen Âge. 1000 ans d'histoire urbaine (400-1480)*, ed. Jean CATALO and Quitterie CAZES, Portet-sur-Garonne, 2010, pp. 192–200.
Bernard CAUSSE, *Église, finance et royauté. La floraison des décimes dans la France de la fin du Moyen Âge*, Paris-Lille, 1988.
Raymond CAZELLES, *Nouvelle histoire de Paris. De la fin du règne de Philippe Auguste à la mort de Charles V, 1223–1380*, Paris, 1972.

Vincent CHALLET, "Montpellier 1379: une communauté au miroir de sa révolte", in *La comunidad medieval como esfera pública*, ed. Oliva HERRER and Hipólito RAFAEL, Sevilla, 2014, pp. 377–400.

Pierre CHARBONNIER, "Les trois fiscalités en Auvergne au milieu du XVe siècle", in *Études sur la fiscalité au Moyen Âge. Actes du CII*e *congrès national des sociétés savantes (Limoges, 1977)*, Paris, 1979, vol. 1, pp. 271–281.

Bernard CHEVALIER, *Tours, ville royale, 1356-1520. Origine et développement d'une capitale à la fin du Moyen Âge*, Louvain-Paris, 1975.

Bernard CHEVALIER, *Les bonnes villes de France du XIV*e *au XVI*e *siècle*, Paris, 1982.

Bernard CHEVALIER, "Fiscalité municipale et fiscalité d'État en France du XIVe à la fin du XVe siècle. Deux systèmes liés et concurrents", in *Genèse de l'État moderne. Prélèvement et redistribution. Actes du colloque de Fontevraud, 1984*, ed. Jean-Philippe GENET and Michel LE MENÉ, Paris, 1987, pp. 137–151.

Bernard CHEVALIER, "Du droit d'imposer et de sa pratique. Finances et financiers du roi sous le règne de Charles VIII", in *Représentation, pouvoir et royauté à la fin du Moyen Âge*, ed. Joël BLANCHARD, Paris, 1995, pp. 33–47.

Bernard CHEVALIER, "La fiscalité urbaine en France, un champ d'expérience pour la fiscalité d'État", in *Corona, municipis i fiscalitat a la Baixa Edat Mitjana. Col·loqui, Lleida, 22–24 juni de 1995*, ed. Manuel SÁNCHEZ MARTINEZ and Antoni FURIÓ DIEGO, Lleida, 1996, pp. 61–78.

Bernard CHEVALIER, "Genèse de la fiscalité urbaine en France", in *Revista d'història medieval*, 7, 1996, pp. 21–38.

Bernard CHEVALIER, "Le financement de la première guerre d'Italie", in *L'impôt au Moyen Âge. L'impôt public et le prélèvement seigneurial en France, fin XII*e*-début XVI*e *siècle. Colloque tenu à Bercy les 14, 15 et 16 juin 2000*, ed. Philippe CONTAMINE, Jean KERHERVÉ and Albert RIGAUDIÈRE, vol. 1, Paris, 2002, pp. 41–74.

Vital CHOMEL, "Ressources domaniales et subsides en Dauphiné (1355–1364)", in *Provence historique*, 25, 1975, pp. 179–192.

Jean-Jules CLAMAGERAN, *Histoire de l'impôt en France, depuis l'époque romaine jusqu'à 1774*, 3 vol., Paris, 1867–1876.

Classer, dire, compter. Discipline du chiffre et fabrique d'une norme comptable à la fin du Moyen Âge. Colloque des 10 et 11 novembre 2012, ed. Olivier MATTÉONI and Patrice BECK, Paris, 2015.

Consensus et représentation. Actes du colloque organisé en 2013 à Dijon, ed. Jean-Philippe GENET, Dominique LE PAGE and Olivier MATTÉONI, Paris-Rome, 2017.

Philippe CONTAMINE, *Guerre, État et société à la fin du Moyen Âge. Études sur les armées des rois de France, 1337–1494*, Paris-La Haye, 1972.

Philippe CONTAMINE, "Guerre, fiscalité royale et économie en France (deuxième moitié du XVe siècle)", in *Proceedings of the Seventh International Economic History Congress*, ed. Michael Walter FLINN, Edinburgh, 1978, t. 2, pp. 266–273.

Philippe CONTAMINE, "Lever l'impôt en terre de guerre: rançons, appatis, souffrances de guerre dans la France des XIVe et XVe siècles" in *L'impôt au Moyen Âge. L'impôt public et le prélèvement seigneurial en France, fin XIIe-début XVIe siècle. Colloque tenu à Bercy les 14, 15 et 16 juin 2000*, ed. Philippe CONTAMINE, Jean KERHERVÉ and Albert RIGAUDIÈRE, vol. 1, Paris, 2002, pp. 11–39.

Philippe CONTAMINE, *Charles VII. Une vie, une politique*, Paris, 2017.

Cultures fiscales en Occident. Études offertes à Denis Menjot, ed. Florent GARNIER, Armand JAMME, Anne LEMONDE and Pere VERDÉS PIJUAN, Toulouse, 2019.

De l'autel à l'écritoire. Genèse des comptabilités princières en Occident (XIIe–XIVe siècle), ed. Thierry PÉCOUT, Paris, 2017.

De l'estime au cadastre. Le Moyen Âge. Colloque des 11, 12 et 13 juin 2003, ed. Albert RIGAUDIÈRE, Paris, 2006.

Alain DEMURGER, *Temps de crises, temps d'espoirs, XIV*e*–XV*e *siècles* (Nouvelle histoire de la France médiévale, 5), Paris, 1990.

Aurore DENMAT-LÉON, *Administrer en comptant: les miseurs dans les villes bretonnes à la fin du Moyen Âge*, doctoral thesis in progress, Sorbonne University, Paris.

Pierre DESPORTES, *Reims et les Rémois aux XIV*e *et XV*e *siècles*, Paris, 1979.

Paul DOGNON, "La taille en Languedoc de Charles VII à François Ier (à propos d'un article récent de M. Spont)", in *Annales du Midi*, 3, 1891, pp. 340–346.

Paul DOGNON, *Les institutions politiques et administratives du pays de Languedoc du XIII*e *siècle aux guerres de religion*, Toulouse, 1896.

Henri DUBOIS, "Le commerce de la France au temps de Louis XI. Expansion ou défensive?", in *La France de la fin du XV*e *siècle. Renouveau et apogée. Tours, 3–6 octobre 1983*, ed. Bernard CHEVALIER and Philippe CONTAMINE, Paris, 1985, pp. 15–29.

Charles Dufour, "Situation financière des villes de Picardie, sous Saint Louis", in *Mémoires de la Société des Antiquaires de Picardie*, 15, 1858, pp. 583–691.

Gustave Dupont-Ferrier, *Études sur les institutions financières de la France à la fin du Moyen Âge*, 2 vol., Paris, 1930–1932.

Estimes, compoix et cadastres. Histoire d'un patrimoine commun de l'Europe méridionale, ed. Jean-Loup Abbé, Toulouse, 2017.

Jean Favier, *Nouvelle histoire de Paris. Paris au XVe siècle, 1380–1500*, Paris, 1974.

Jean Favier, *Philippe le Bel*, Paris, 1978.

Robert Favreau, *La ville de Poitiers à la fin du Moyen Âge. Une capitale régionale* (Mémoires de la Société des Antiquaires de l'Ouest, fourth series, 15) Poitiers, 1978.

La fiscalité des villes au Moyen Âge (Occident méditerranéen), ed. Denis Menjot and Manuel Sánchez Martínez, 4 vol., Toulouse, 1996–2004.

La France des principautés. Les Chambres des Comptes aux XIVe et XVe siècles. Colloque tenu aux Archives départementales de l'Allier, à Moulins-Yzeure, les 6, 7 et 8 avril 1995, ed. Philippe Contamine and Olivier Mattéoni, Paris, 1996.

Florent Garnier, *Un consulat et ses finances: Millau (1187–1461)*, Paris, 2006.

Florent Garnier, "L'impôt d'après quelques traités fiscaux (XIVe–XVIe siècle)", in *Histoire du discours fiscal en Europe*, ed. Ludovic Ayrault and Florent Garnier, Paris, 2014, pp. 67–113.

Florent Garnier, "Le roi, l'emprunt et l'impôt: considérations pour une histoire de l'information fiscale et financière au bas Moyen Âge", in *Estados y mercados financieros en el Occidente cristiano (siglos XIII–XVI). XLI Semana de Estudios Medievales, Estella, 15–18 de julio de 2014*, Estella, 2015, pp. 157–184.

Florent Garnier, "Les états du Rouergue aux XIVe et XVe siècles: institutionnalisation d'un dialogue et expression d'un consensus", in *Consensus et représentation. Actes du colloque organisé en 2013 à Dijon*, ed. Jean-Philippe Genet, Dominique Le Page and Olivier Mattéoni, Paris-Rome, 2017, pp. 163–191.

Jean-Philippe Genet, "La genèse de l'État moderne. Les enjeux d'un programme de recherche", in *Actes de la recherche en sciences sociales*, 118, 1997, pp. 3–18.

Alain Guerreau, "Rentes des ordres mendiants à Mâcon au XIVe siècle", in *Annales. Économie, sociétés, civilisations*, 25/4, 1970, pp. 956–965.

Jean Guilbert, *Les institutions municipales de Montreuil-sur-Mer*, Arras, 1954.

Michel Hébert, *Parlementer. Assemblées représentatives et échange politique en Europe occidentale à la fin du Moyen Âge*, Paris, 2014.

John Bell Henneman, *Royal Taxation in Fourteenth-Century France. The Development of War Financing, 1322–1356*, Princeton, 1971.

John Bell Henneman, *Royal Taxation in Fourteenth-Century France. The Captivity and Ransom of John II, 1356–1370*, Philadelphia, 1976.

Histoire de la France urbaine, ed. Georges Duby, vol. 2, *La ville médiévale des Carolingiens à la Renaissance*, ed. Jacques Le Goff, Paris, 1980; revised and completed edition, *La ville en France au Moyen Âge*, Paris, 1998.

L'impôt au Moyen Âge. L'impôt public et le prélèvement seigneurial en France, fin XIIe-début XVIe siècle. Colloque tenu à Bercy les 14, 15 et 16 juin 2000, ed. Philippe Contamine, Jean Kerhervé and Albert Rigaudière, 3 vol., Paris, 2002.

L'impôt dans les villes de l'Occident méditerranéen. Colloque tenu à Bercy les 3, 4 et 5 octobre 2001, ed. Denis Menjot, Albert Rigaudière and Manuel Sánchez Martínez, Paris, 2003.

Henri Jassemin, *La Chambre des Comptes de Paris au XVe siècle, précédée d'une étude sur ses origines*, Paris, 1933.

Jean Kerhervé, *L'État breton aux 14e et 15e siècles. Les ducs, l'argent et les hommes*, 2 vol., Paris, 1987.

Gilbert Larguier, "Perception et gestion de l'impôt à Narbonne au XVe siècle", in *La fiscalité des villes au Moyen Âge (Occident méditerranéen)*, ed. Denis Menjot and Manuel Sánchez Martínez, vol. 4, Toulouse, 2004, pp. 145–160.

Gilbert Larguier, "Construction d'un système fiscal: le cas du Languedoc", in *Cultures fiscales en Occident. Études offertes à Denis Menjot*, ed. Florent Garnier, Armand Jamme, Anne Lemonde and Pere Verdés Pijuan, Toulouse, 2019, pp. 347–355.

Jean-François Lassalmonie, "Les finances de la monarchie française sous le gouvernement des Beaujeu (1483–1491)", in *Études et documents*, 6, 1994, pp. 3–141.

Jean-François Lassalmonie, *La boîte à l'enchanteur. Politique financière de Louis XI*, Paris, 2002.

Jean-François Lassalmonie, "L'imposition foraine, un impôt ambigu (XIVe–XVe siècles)", in *L'impôt au Moyen Âge. L'impôt public et le prélèvement seigneurial en France, fin XIIe–début XVIe siècle. Colloque tenu* à Bercy les 14, 15 et 16 juin 2000, ed. Philippe CONTAMINE, Jean KERHERVÉ and Albert RIGAUDIÈRE, Paris, 2002, vol. 3, pp. 763–815.

Jean-Pierre LEGUAY, La ville de Rennes au XVe siècle à travers les comptes des miseurs, Paris, 1969.

Anne LEMONDE, Le temps des libertés en Dauphiné. L'intégration d'une principauté à la Couronne de France (1349–1408), Grenoble, 2002.

Anne LEMONDE, "Taille réelle et taille personnelle à la fin du Moyen Âge", in Cultures fiscales en Occident. Études offertes à Denis Menjot, ed. Florent GARNIER, Armand JAMME, Anne LEMONDE and Pere VERDÉS PIJUAN, Toulouse, 2019, pp. 279–292.

Michel MOLLAT and Philippe WOLFF, Ongles bleus, Jacques et Ciompi. Les révolutions populaires en Europe aux XIVe et XVe siècles, Paris, 1970.

Monnaie, fiscalité et finances au temps de Philippe le Bel. Journée d'études du 14 mai 2004, ed. Philippe CONTAMINE, Jean KERHERVÉ and Albert RIGAUDIÈRE, Paris, 2007.

Michel NORTIER, "Le sort des archives dispersées de la Chambre des Comptes de Paris", in Bibliothèque de l'École des Chartes, 123/2, 1965, pp. 460–537.

Charles PORTAL, Histoire de la ville de Cordes, Tarn (1222–1799), Albi, 1902.

Danièle PRÉVOST, Le personnel de la Chambre des Comptes de Paris de 1320 à 1418, unpublished doctoral thesis, University of Paris I, 2000.

Sylvie QUÉRÉ, Le discours politique des états de Languedoc à la fin du Moyen Âge, 1346–1484, Montpellier, 2016.

Jean RAUZIER, Finances et gestion d'une principauté au XIVe siècle. Le duché de Bourgogne de Philippe le Hardi (1364–1384), Paris, 1996.

Maurice REY, Le domaine du roi et les finances extraordinaires sous Charles VI, 1388–1413, Paris, 1965.

Maurice REY, Les finances royales sous Charles VI. Les causes du déficit, 1399–1413, Paris, 1965.

Albert RIGAUDIÈRE, Saint-Flour, ville d'Auvergne à la fin du Moyen Âge. Études d'histoire administrative et financière, 2 vol., Paris, 1982.

Albert RIGAUDIÈRE, "Le financement des fortifications urbaines en France du milieu du XIVe à la fin du XVe siècle", in Revue historique, 273, 1985, pp. 19–95.

Albert RIGAUDIÈRE, "Connaissance, composition et estimation du moble à travers quelques livres d'estime du Midi français (XIVe–XVe siècles)", in Les cadastres anciens des villes et leur traitement par l'informatique. Actes de la Table ronde de Saint-Cloud, 31 janvier-2 février 1985, ed. Jean-Louis BIGET, Jean-Claude HERVÉ and Yvon THÉBERT, Rome, 1989, pp. 41–81.

Albert RIGAUDIÈRE, "L'essor de la fiscalité royale, du règne de Philippe IV le Bel (1285–1314) à celui de Philippe VI (1328–1350)", in Europa en los umbrales de la crisis (1250–1350). XXI Semana de Estudios Medievales. Estella, 18 a 22 de julio de 1994, ed. Juan CARRASCO PÉREZ, Pamplona, 1995, pp. 323–391.

Albert RIGAUDIÈRE, "Le contrôle des comptes urbains dans les villes auvergnates et vellaves aux XIVe et XVe siècles", in La France des principautés. Les Chambres des Comptes aux XIVe et XVe siècles. Colloque tenu aux Archives départementales de l'Allier, à Moulins-Yzeure, les 6, 7 et 8 avril 1995, ed. Philippe CONTAMINE and Olivier MATTÉONI, Paris, 1996, pp. 207–242.

Albert RIGAUDIÈRE, "De l'estime au cadastre dans l'Occident médiéval: réflexions et pistes de recherches", in De l'estime au cadastre. Le Moyen Âge. Colloque des 11, 12 et 13 juin 2003, ed. Albert RIGAUDIÈRE, Paris, 2006, pp. 3–22.

David SASSU-NORMAND, Pro defensione et tuitione regni. La fiscalité des rois de France en Languedoc au XIVe siècle (sénéchaussée de Carcassonne et confins), unpublished doctoral thesis, Lumière Lyon 2 University, 2013.

Lydwine SCORDIA, Le roi doit "vivre du sien". La théorie de l'impôt en France (XIIIe–XVe siècles), Paris, 2005.

Gérard SIVÉRY, Les Capétiens et l'argent au siècle de Saint Louis. Essai sur l'administration et les finances royales au XIIIe siècle, Villeneuve-d'Ascq, 1995.

Alfred SPONT, "La taille en Languedoc de 1450 à 1515", in Annales du Midi, 2, 1890, pp. 365–384 and 478–513.

Alfred SPONT, "L'équivalent aux aides en Languedoc de 1450 à 1515", in Annales du Midi, 3, 1891, pp. 232–253.

Alfred SPONT, "La gabelle du sel en Languedoc au quinzième siècle", in Annales du Midi, 3, 1891, pp. 427–481.

Alfred SPONT, "La taille en Languedoc de 1450 à 1515 (conclusion)", in Annales du Midi, 3, 1891, pp. 482–494.

Joseph Reese STRAYER and Charles Holt TAYLOR, Studies in Early French Taxation, Cambridge (Mass.), 1939.

Joseph Reese STRAYER, "Pierre de Chalon and the Origins of the French Customs Service", in Festschrift Percy Ernst Schramm zu seinem 70. Geburtstag, ed. Peter CLASSEN and Peter SCHEIBERT, Wiesbaden, 1964, vol. 1, pp. 334–339.

Joseph Reese STRAYER, "Italian Bankers and Philip the Fair", in *Action and Conviction in Early Modern Europe. Essays in Memory of E. H. Harbison*, ed. Theodore K. RABB and Jerrold E. SEIGEL, Princeton, 1969, pp. 113–121.

Joseph Reese STRAYER, "Notes on the Origins of English and French Export Taxes", in *Studia Gratiana*, 15, 1972, pp. 399–421.

Véronique TERRASSE, *La commune de Provins (1152–1355). Histoire institutionnelle, administrative et sociale*, unpublished doctoral thesis, École des Hautes Études en Sciences sociales, Paris, 2000.

Isabelle VERNUS-MOUTIN, *La taille en Dauphiné, du "transport" de 1349 à la révision générale de 1474–1476*, thèse pour le diplôme d'archiviste-paléographe de l'École nationale des Chartes, Paris, 1988 (unpublished; summary in *Positions des thèses de l'École des Chartes*, Paris, 1988, pp. 199–208).

Isabelle VERNUS-MOUTIN, "Les états du Dauphiné et l'impôt (v. 1349–v. 1476)", in *Violence et contestation au Moyen Âge. Actes du CXIV^e congrès national des sociétés savantes (Paris, 1989)*, Paris, 1990, pp. 113–122.

Isabelle VERNUS-MOUTIN, "Recherches sur la réalité de la taille dans le bailliage des Montagnes du Dauphiné à la fin du Moyen Âge", in *Pierres de mémoire, écrits d'histoire: pages d'histoire en Dauphiné offertes à Vital Chomel*, ed. Alain BELMONT, Grenoble, 2000, pp. 145–154.

Jacques VIDAL, *L'équivalent des aides en Languedoc*, Montpellier, 1960.

Adolphe VUITRY, *Études sur le régime financier de la France avant la Révolution de 1789*, 3 vol., Paris, 1878–1883.

Philippe WOLFF, *Les "estimes" toulousaines des XIVe et XVe siècles*, Toulouse, 1956.

11
THE BURGUNDIAN LOW COUNTRIES

Marc Boone

Introduction – The Low Countries: a patchwork of territories and powers

In 1384, the first Duke of Burgundy – a branch of the reigning French royal dynasty of Valois – came to power in the Low Countries. In 1369, Duke Philip the Bold had married Margaret of Male, the only daughter and sole heir of Louis of Male, the last count of the House of Dampierre. Margaret was to inherit the Counties of Flanders and Artois (and some principalities outside the Low Countries, such as Franche-Comté). After Louis of Male's death, Philip became the ruler of these territories, which were to a very large part held in fealty from the French crown. Philip's marriage strategy laid the foundations of possible further expansion. In Cambrai in 1385, his son (who would later become Duke John the Fearless) and his daughter Margaret married the children of the Count of Hainault and Holland-Zeeland from the Bavarian Wittelsbach dynasty, while his younger son Anthony of Burgundy became regent (and heir-apparent) of the Duchy of Brabant. Dynastic serendipity, purchase and conquests resulted in Philip's grandson, Duke Philip the Good, ruling over an impressive set of principalities, which apart from both Burgundies (duchy and county) were mainly situated in the former Low Countries (roughly speaking, the present-day states of Belgium and the Netherlands and large portions of Northern France).[1] Among these were the Duchies of Brabant, Limburg and Luxemburg, the Counties of Flanders, Artois, Hainault, Holland-Zeeland and Namur, and the city of Malines. The dukes' territories encompassed several episcopal territories, the prince-bishoprics of Liège and Utrecht, and the bishoprics of Cambrai, Tournai and Thérouanne. These remained ecclesiastic enclaves in the Low Countries, although the dukes succeeded in exerting a certain control over these territories (which were economically landlocked by the dukes' principalities) as they managed to have strong influence over the appointment of the bishops. Historians have labelled the Burgundian duke's territories a "state", but this description has been much disputed, and a more appropriate term might be "composite monarchy", the concept used to refer to the territorial complex ruled over by the dukes' Habsburg successors.[2]

Nevertheless, what remains crucial when evaluating the fiscal policy in the territories united in the hands of the Valois dukes is their institutional intervention, directly inspired by the practices they had witnessed at work in the French royal institutions. More precisely in the royal Courts of Accounts (*Chambre des comptes*), a model they imposed on their territories as soon as they were able to do so. In 1386, Duke Philip the Bold established the court of accounts of

Lille, which became competent for Flanders and Artois (later on also for Hainault and Namur). The court of accounts of Dijon (competent for both the Duchy and the County of Burgundy) was reorganized in the same year, and following the same principles, his second son Anthony established a court of accounts for Brabant in Vilvoorde in 1404 (it would soon be transferred to Brussels and also become competent for Limburg and Luxemburg). In 1446, Duke Philip the Good organized a court in The Hague for the Counties of Holland and Zeeland.[3]

Further generations of dukes and their Habsburg successors added other principalities mainly in the eastern and northern parts of the Low Countries (Utrecht, Friesland, Groningen, Drente, Gelre and Overijssel) to their territories. The institutional links of Flanders and Artois to the French crown were definitively cut in 1529 (Treaty of Cambrai), so that finally in 1548 the imperial "Burgundian Circle" became the seventeen provinces under Habsburg rule. Of course, the various principalities had developed formal financial institutions and practices long before the Burgundian dukes and their Habsburg heirs unified the territories in a personal union. The different Courts of Accounts (between 1474 and 1477, Duke Charles the Bold temporarily unified these into a single chamber in Mechlin) not only dealt with the development of the duke's finances, but also incorporated the archives produced by their respective precursors in each of the principalities. Researchers at the French CNRS have published a comprehensive overview of the literature and the inventories of sources that are essential to understand how the Burgundian administration incorporated and handled the archives that were mainly produced from the twelfth century onwards in the different principalities.[4]

Apart from this unifying process brought about by the Valois Dukes of Burgundy, a second general aspect of the Low Countries is essential to understand the history of taxation in the medieval period. The Low Countries were, alongside Northern and Central Italy, among the most urbanized parts of Western Europe. Of the approximately 2,6 million people living in the Low Countries at that period, one in three lived in a town. The most populated principalities were Flanders, Brabant, Hainault, Holland and Liège. According to the model developed by Jan de Vries to calculate urban density, circa 1500, the southern Low Countries reached a density comparable to 80 per cent of the highest density in Western Europe (i.e. Venice and its hinterland), whereas in comparison Paris and its region attained little more than 50 per cent. Another indication: circa 1500, approximately 150 towns in Europe had 10,000 inhabitants or more, and at least twenty-five of these were located in the Low Countries.[5] Contrary to other medieval European cityscapes, the Low Countries' principalities developed in a relatively small space, which prevented a flourishing of city-states comparable to the big cities in Northern and Central Italy, and prevented any city emerging as a capital city, at the top of the urban hierarchy as happened with Paris or London. The subsequent commercial metropolises – Arras in the twelfth-thirteenth century, Bruges in the fourteenth-fifteenth century, Antwerp in the sixteenth century and finally Amsterdam in the seventeenth century – became dominant in their region. In turn, they fulfilled the role of nodal point for international trade and domestic industrial trade, though they always had to count on the complementary roles fulfilled by other cities.[6]

From the point of view of fiscal history, these circumstances gave rise to two fundamental features: first, the cities developed a proper financial and fiscal system in order to answer their own needs, and second, their bargaining power in relation to any central princely government was such that the representative institutions played a fundamental role in establishing fiscal policies by any ruler.[7] In this respect, the former Burgundian Low Countries were quite exceptional as the Estates (General) and the Estates of each principality succeeded in retaining the right to assemble on their own initiative and thus to remain master of their agenda. By the end of the fifteenth century, they had even become fiscal agents of their own, leading up to what has been labelled a "financial revolution" typical of the Dutch Republic as it emerged from the rebellion against Spain in the sixteenth century.[8]

In what follows, we will discuss urban and princely financial and fiscal organization and practices separately, although they were clearly interconnected to a large extent,[9] notably because the creation of public debt at the municipal and principality levels linked local and "state" finances. Even more: the staff working in the princely courts of accounts and from which the princes recruited their fiscal agents very frequently came from the urban commercial and social elites, which enabled a transfer of financial and fiscal techniques from city to "state".[10]

Urban fiscal policies and practices

Given the importance of urbanization in the history of the Low Countries, it comes as no surprise that the study of urban history, and more precisely of urban finances, has held a crucial place on the research agenda. After all, financial accounts were part of the best-kept urban archives given their eminent political relevance. Of course, the grand tradition of urban history goes back to the days of one of the leading historians of his era, Henri Pirenne (1862–1935), but continues to dominate historical research agendas until today.[11] In the decades following Pirenne's pioneering work, the study of urban finances became an important topic especially concerning the large cities of Flanders and Brabant. Their role in history had already been "rediscovered" as an aspect of romanticism in the nineteenth century, a period in which several source-editions were inspired by the desire to revive the old glorious history of the cities.[12] Several important monographs set the tone and influenced further research also in the other former principalities of the Low Countries.[13] A special role in promoting the study of urban finances was played by the cultural activities of the "Crédit communal de Belgique", a bank founded in 1860 to provide funding for local authorities. Since 1962, a committee for history "*pro civitate*" has been active and was financed by the bank. Between 1963 and 1999, this committee published one hundred volumes, mainly proceedings of colloquia and PhD theses on urban history with a clear focus on financial history. The history and functioning can be reconstructed through the introductions to the first and last of the colloquia, held in Blankenberge in 1962 and Spa in 1999, respectively.[14] In 1996, Crédit communal de Belgique merged with the French bank Crédit local de France to form Dexia, and this merger ended this remarkable example of patronage.[15]

The early results of this research sparked great interest in urban financial history in many ways: a series of studies were published using cities' accounts as the main source. To give just two examples: the study of public works, or the study of the way "representative" institutions operated.[16] Although no direct sources on this fundamental aspect of urban agency were preserved, the latter study was possible because each city kept a record of the travel expenses of its representatives. This information was extracted from the chapters on missions and embassies available in each account. It enabled the researchers to study how, when and why these representatives had met. The same approach was applied to nearly all the principalities of the former Low Countries.

The accounts of the cities in the Middle Ages are of a similar nature: a simple bookkeeping, listing the revenues, followed by the expenditures and closing with a balance indicating clearly whether the year ended with a surplus or a deficit. All accounts were made on a yearly basis, and had to be presented to the inhabitants each year as part of the ceremony of renewal of the bench of aldermen. However, a gradual trend toward uniformity became visible after the court of accounts of the Dukes of Burgundy began to audit the copy each city was required to deliver to its archive.¹⁷ The remarks formulated by the masters of the court of accounts resulted in a more streamlined version of the accounts.¹⁸ Of course, some of the cities – and foremost Ghent and Bruges, which had embodied the resistance and revolt against the centralizing policy of the dukes – refused as long as possible to fulfil the requirement to deposit a copy of their accounts with the court. In the long run, they, too, had to give in, which resulted in the fact that the archives of the courts of accounts hold the most complete collection of urban accounts in the Low Countries.

In the highly urbanized Low Countries, city finances were the backbone of the extraordinary receipts the princes could hope to tap into for their own treasury. The *aides*★ or *beden*, as they were called in French and Dutch (the two administrative languages of the Burgundian principalities), were the subject of lengthy negotiations between the representatives of the Estates, to a large extent dominated by the elites of the cities. The prince and his subjects agreed to an overall sum, and the amount each city (and each territory of the countryside) had to pay was specified in a repartition table. For the County of Flanders, this list (known as the Transport of Flanders) came into existence as a result of the Franco–Flemish conflicts at the beginning of the fourteenth century and the financial settlement of the fine to be paid to the French crown.¹⁹ It remained unchanged for a long time, but was nevertheless adapted to the changing circumstances (economic development or depression and the loss of territory after heavy flooding). Such changes occurred, for instance, in 1408 after an elaborate inquiry by a specific commission, composed of representatives of the prince and of his subjects.²⁰ Within each city, funds were mainly raised through indirect taxation: the so-called excises (in the vernacular, these taxes were often designated in terms that clearly show they were not quite "popular": *ongeld*★ *maletôte*), which on average made up easily 80–85 per cent of the cities' annual income. Traditionally, the prince had to confirm the city's right to levy these indirect taxes (and to change or adapt the tax rate when required); in return, the prince received a certain sum of recognition (the patent or *octroi*★). The excises had a direct impact on the consumption and economic activities in the cities. The most important ones were those levied on the consumption of products for which no substitution was possible: wine and beer, grain, peat (the most important source of energy in the medieval Low Countries), or feedstock imports for the city's economy. In the Low Countries, wool remained very important given the size of the traditional drapery industry, though the quantities varied among different sources of origin: indigenous wool, English or Spanish wool. The consumption of meat and fish was also subject to excises levied in the specific hall or market place where these commodities were presented to the general public. The excises were normally farmed out to a collector or a consortium of collectors who made a public offer and thereby ensured that the city would dispose of a guaranteed income. Once a specific excise was assigned to them, the collectors had to organize the recovery of the taxes themselves; this often took place at the cities' gates, where it was relatively easy to watch what entered or left the city. Of course, the incentive for these collectors was the potential to collect more than what they had agreed to pay to the city's receiver, so that they could make a personal gain on the whole operation. Sometimes, no collectors put in bids or they made bids that the city could not accept, hence forcing the city to take charge itself. However, this remained quite exceptional and occurred only in moments of acute crisis. The normal way of collecting indirect taxes was by farming them out. An analysis of the farmers of the excises of Ghent in the Burgundian period has made clear that a group of wealthy farmers had set itself up almost in a professional way; they belonged to or had ties with some of the cities' wealthiest families, thus linking the management of the cities' most important source of income to their own private interests.²¹ Contemporary observers were well aware of the socially discriminating aspects of indirect taxation.²² People paid taxes on their consumption, while their individual purchasing power was of course very different, although the tax to be paid on a given quantity, of let's say beer or wine, remained the same for everyone. Already in the early fourteenth century, an anonymous Ghent Franciscan friar wrote a vivid description of the social and political unrest that was sweeping over both city and county. The author was very aware of how much the social inequalities reinforced by this fixation on indirect taxation fuelled the great tradition of unrest that would later mark so heavily the history of the towns of Flanders, Brabant and Liège over the fourteenth century.[23] In the course of the preceding thirteenth century, however, when cities were politically in the firm grip of the traditional patriciate, a certain tradition of direct taxes had been present. These were similar to the *tallia*, a tax that took into consideration taxpayers' wealth to a certain extent and was therefore much more "proportional" than the indirect taxes. Direct taxation did show up exceptionally in later centuries, but revealingly, only in the context of crisis when pressure on the cities' finances was such that all sources of income had to be tapped. Many examples came to the foreground during the wars the cities of Flanders (and to some extent of other principalities) waged against the Habsburg heir to the Dukes of Burgundy, Archduke Maximilian of Austria, in the years 1482–1492.[24] The paradox remains, however, that when the representatives of the middling groups (the guilds and professional organizations of workers and petty businessmen) had successfully gained power by joining the ruling benches of the aldermen – and they did so from the early fourteenth century onward – they maintained the indirect taxes as the most important source of income for the cities. Undoubtedly, the forces of tradition and the restricting bureaucratic processes of collecting and bookkeeping were responsible for this. And of course, even within the dominant model of indirect taxation, choices could be made to shift taxation across the various consumer goods, allowing the consumption patterns of specific groups within the city to be targeted and thus making fiscal policy possible. Opting for heavier taxation of wine instead of the more popular beer revealed a clear intention to tax the wealthier consumers of wine more heavily. In specific circumstances, such as the enormous fine the city of Ghent had to pay to the Duke of Burgundy after it had lost the war against him in 1453, all possible indirect taxes were temporarily imposed and invented (such as a tax of 2.08 per cent on the wages of household staff, to be paid by their employers, or a tax of 1.67 per cent on housing rents), which often proved to yield little or no revenue. Others were more successful: for example, an indirect tax on the export of textiles (1.67 per cent of the value of linens, 2.5 per cent of the value of woollens) or on the sale of houses (3.33 per cent of the value), which had the effect of harming the city's most important export industry.

This does not mean that all forms of direct taxation were completely absent in the cities. In the thirteenth century, as said, reminiscences of *tallia*-like taxes can be found in the sources; from the early fourteenth century onward, however, a clear overall preference for indirect taxation is perceptible. These remained rather primitive in form and never reached a level comparable to the *estime*-like sources available for many cities in southern parts of Europe. A specific variant of direct taxation emerged in the Low Countries cities, as they imposed a levy on the goods that by marriage, migration or death of a burgher vanished from the city (the so-called *issue** or *exuwe* taxation). It oscillated around 10 to 12 per cent of the value of immovable goods and 15 per cent of movable goods. In a city like Ghent, this tax represented roughly 6 to 10 percent of the total revenue of the city, far behind the yield of the indirect taxation.

When cities had to make ends meet, they were of course incited to contract loans, which resulted in the creation of a sizeable public debt. Given the central position of the Low Countries in the commercial and industrial networks of North-western Europe and their economic power, this proved not to be an insurmountable problem. Several groups of moneylenders are identified and succeeded one another. In the twelfth and thirteenth centuries, financiers from Arras (at that moment still a Flemish city before the County of Artois was separated from Flanders in 1237) were dominant.[25] The emergence of Bruges as the nodal point of international commerce in North-western Europe implied that the Italian merchants, active and present in Flanders from the 1270s onward, dominated the money market.[26] Several generations of Italian merchants and moneylenders succeeded each other, and they all had close ties with both the cities and the princes. In the fourteenth centuries, these Italian moneylenders came from the regions of Piedmont and Lombardy (the cities of Asti and Chieri are often mentioned), hence the general denomination of "Lombard", meaning any foreign moneylender, preferably of Italian origin.[27] As these Italian merchants and brokers also lent money to the princes in increasing numbers, we will look at their role when dealing with the princely finances.

Princely taxation

Like all medieval princes, the Dukes of Burgundy were able to mobilize the money of their subjects without having to comply with the latter's expectations as long as their demands stayed within the boundaries of the existing rules concerning the *aides*★. These encompassed the so-called feudal cases: the oath of chivalry of the heir-apparent, the financing of a crusade, the dowry of the eldest daughter, imprisonment (and thus ransom) of the ruler. Of course, the dukes (and before them the counts and dukes of each principality) had the princely demesne, consisting of the landownership by the reigning dynasties, at their disposal. Our knowledge of its composition and organization goes back to the twelfth century.[28] But of course, the demesne had developed over the centuries, incorporating new sources of income (such as tolls, rights on land reclamation, rights on wasteland, exploitation of peat extraction), reflecting the growth of the economy, as new activities created new flows of money. Despite the traditional cry that the prince should be able to live on his own income, the profits from the princely demesne and traditional sources of income did not cover all the princely needs, especially since the expenses the prince had to face tended to expand in an almost uncontrollable way.[29] The logic of "state-formation" pushed the dukes to enlarge their territories at the expense of rival powers, which resulted – not always but quite often – in warfare or at least military operations. These implied a very heavy cost and had a profound impact on the economy of the ruler's territories, while also colliding with the commercial logic guiding the wealthy merchants' actions.[30] The duke was therefore forced to negotiate additional *aides*★ with his subjects. This reinforced the need to negotiate with the latter's representatives in the context of the Estates in order to obtain extra money. The Estates encompassed the traditional three estates (the clergy, nobility and third estate), although in the context of the highly urbanized Low Countries, the representatives of the Third Estate (in the County of Flanders the so-called Members of Flanders, dominated by the three big cities, Ghent, Bruges and Ypres) were predominant. This does not preclude the fact that, from time to time, the clergy was also summoned to contribute to a general *aide*.[31]

The various dukes did, of course, try to impose fixed taxation on their subjects, often inspired by French royal policy, such as the demand for a *gabelle*-like taxation on the production and consumption of salt, but they never succeeded in gaining acceptance for permanent taxation.[32] On the contrary: their plans met with so much resistance that the situation often degenerated into rebellion, if not open warfare, with their own subjects. Ghent's war against Duke Philip the Good in 1449–1453, for instance, was provoked by the duke's proposal to impose a *gabelle* on salt. While the first two dukes, Philip the Bold and John the Fearless, were still successful in obtaining massive "grants" from the royal French treasury, their successors were no longer in this position, and therefore had to increase the fiscal pressure on their subjects.[33] But the population was not inclined to give in to the ducal demands, not even when the authoritarian

Duke Charles the Bold tried to impose, at the start of his reign in 1468, a general direct levy on all the Burgundian territories. This taxation had to be developed using the hearth taxes as a model, as these already belonged to the fiscal traditions dating back to pre-Burgundian periods in several principalities, such as Brabant, Hainaut and Luxemburg.[34] It required registration of all inhabitants of all the principalities and resulted in a very partial registration, since the project did not turn out the way the duke had hoped, as the elites of mainly the large cities were able to thwart the project.[35] They repeated this feat in the sixteenth century, when the Duke of Alba, representing King Philip II of Spain, also tried – in vain – to impose a permanent direct tax inspired by a more equitable distribution of the fiscal burden upon his subjects in the Low Countries.[36]

Having established courts of accounts in different principalities, the Dukes of Burgundy had an efficient organization to control their financial agents and subjects and to keep the necessary archives, creating a living memory of the finances of their lands. They did not, however, dispose of an instrument comparable to a modern budget, although they did make use of what was called an "*état au vrai*" (a projection of presumed revenues, based on past experiences); some of these have been preserved from the reign of Duke Philip the Good onward.[37] Nevertheless, the political construction in the former Low Countries by the Valois Dukes of Burgundy held one major trump card: the central organization of the princely finances, controlled and guided by the courts of accounts, which acted as a permanent auditor. The action of the courts resulted, as for the accounts produced by each city, in a gradual uniformization of the practices and even of the visual aspects of bookkeeping. In the County of Holland, for instance, the illustrated accounts characteristic of the Counts of the Bavarian dynasty (1349–1433) made room for the sober Burgundian conciseness: no more illustrated entries, but sober headlines and everywhere marginal notes revealing the intervention of the masters of the courts of accounts.[38] The almost obsessive zeal with which the masters controlled and added marginal notes, obliging the receivers to specify and justify expenses and financial transactions, conceals widespread corruption and collusion. This course of events turned the Burgundian fiscal administration into a giant with feet of clay. As the prince's income did not allow a well-paid and sufficiently numerous corps of civil servants to be established, the latter were far too often induced into arrangements in the informal sphere and often brought to the brink of corruption. Time and again, complaints were formulated and officials brought to trial, but in the end the same ruffians returned to business, revealing how certain families and interest groups had succeeded in infiltrating official positions, a type of practice that did not build taxpayers' trust.[39]

The responsibility for collecting the ducal income was in the hands of a group of "private" receivers and administrators who often farmed their positions.[40] At their head stood "general receivers" on various levels: the general receivers in each of the principalities (or group of principalities; Flanders and Artois, for instance, were merged into the hands of one receiver general), coordinated by a general receiver of all finances ("*receveur général de toutes les finances*"), who ultimately oversaw the finances in both the ducal territories in Burgundy proper and in the Low Countries (the so-called "*pays de l'au-delà et de l'au-deça*"). The sources they produced are exceptionally well preserved and count among the best and most complete collections of princely archives, some of them were the subject of carefully-chosen editions so as to allow the outside world an impression of their intrinsic value.[41] Another set of publications of accounts on the principality level has been published for the Counties of Holland and Zeeland in the pre-Burgundian period.[42]

Given the practical difficulties of transporting and transferring considerable sums of money over large distances, the general receivers had to act on each level with the balance that each local or regional receiver could present. Local receivers made sure their own expenses were met first, so that in the best case only a positive surplus balance could be sent to a "higher" level. The result is accounts filled with expected revenues and payments that were carried forward or transferred to other local receivers, the so-called "assignats".[43] In such circumstances, an overall view of what was at one's disposal was almost impossible to obtain. However, there was little doubt that the dukes were among the wealthiest rulers of their time, although if this wealth is measured taking into account different parameters (such as the number of inhabitants, the area under consideration, etc.) and especially the ability to levy taxes, the Kings of France were richer.[44] The Dukes of Burgundy, however, won the image battle as their wealth was much more concentrated and was propagated by the exceptional splendour of their court. They therefore appeared to be wealthier and were considered more trustworthy by the financiers of their time, first and foremost Italian bankers, observing the deeds of the dukes from their offices in Venice, Florence, Milan, etc. The most important risk factor remained the instability of their fiscal revenues.

Under the Dukes of Burgundy, a new generation of Italian bankers, mostly of Tuscan origin, came to the foreground and replaced the traditional "Lombards". The Rapondi family from Lucca, for instance, was decisive as financiers for the policies of the first Burgundian dukes, Philip the Bold and John the Fearless. The Rapondi also financed the city of Bruges, for instance, by advancing the city's contribution to an *aide* for the duke; in order to guarantee their reimbursement, they obtained impressive rights over the city's excises.[45] They also facilitated the transfer of important sums of money, always a delicate operation in a period characterized by endemic warfare. The Rapondi had representatives in both Bruges and Paris, and arranged the ransom for the duke's heir (the later Duke John the Fearless), taken prisoner by the Ottoman Turks after the defeat of Nicopolis in 1396. No wonder that a statue – lost due to the effects of the French Revolution – of Dino Rapondi, the most influential member of the family, even adorned the dukes' "Sainte Chapelle" in Dijon. While the economy grew, as did the Burgundian control over ever larger territories, the financial needs of the dukes grew in step. Under Philip the Good and his son Charles the Bold, the even bigger Florentine bank of the Medici, represented in Bruges among others by Tommaso Portinari (now mainly remembered as patron of some of the most important artists of his time), took over the role of principal financier of the ducal policies.[46] To convince his financiers to continue to lend him large sums of money, parts of the ducal demesne and the duke's tax revenues were temporarily farmed out: Portinari could, for instance, count on the sizeable revenue of the Calais toll on the import of English wool into the Burgundian territories.

Having failed to establish a system of unquestioned and fixed taxation (as the King of France had done), the ducal finances remained vulnerable, and continued to depend on the goodwill of their subjects, who had to concede *aides**, and/or on the calculations of their lenders. Duke Charles the Bold had to live with these limitations and had to face the limits of his financial wherewithal in a rather abrupt way. The moment of truth came after he had established a professionalized army without having enough financial backing and an efficient tax system to support it. The result was that his army abandoned him at some critical moments. According to the much-quoted statement by the chronicler Philippe de Commynes, who had left Charles the Bold and joined his rival King Louis XI of France, the territories of Duke Philippe the Good looked like the heavenly "*terres de promission*" ("the promised land") because the duke had taxed his subjects in a very reasonable way. Of course this statement allowed its author to mark the difference with the next duke, Charles, whose reign witnessed a very impressive surge of taxation and with whom his personal relationship deteriorated quickly insofar as he left the duke and took sides with the French king.[47] Historiography may have greatly nuanced de Commynes' views, they nevertheless point to the lower levels of taxation under Duke Philip and to a general, albeit very unbalanced, sharing of wealth.[48] The dukes had to live on credit, and while on several occasions they pledged their most valuable jewels as collateral, the establishment of a permanent public debt became one of the characteristics of the period, linking private wealth and savings to a political project (i.e. the formation of a centralized "state"), with a substantial transfer of tax income as a side effect.

Public debt: a driver of political and fiscal innovation?

The important role played mostly by Italian bankers present from the late thirteenth century onward in the commercial hubs of the former Low Countries has already been mentioned, since they lent money to both cities and princes. But another source of credit emerged foremost in the cities, and its importance increased over time because it presented a direct link with any fiscal policy of both the city and "state". The savings held by most wealthy individuals, members of the political and artisanal elites within the cities, allowed them to invest part of their money in annuities with the demesne of city and prince as collateral. Two types of annuities were on the market: inheritable annuities, with a piece of land or house as collateral, and life annuities, with one or two individuals as life beneficiaries. Rich individuals – mainly wealthy burghers and a remarkable number of clergymen with whom this was a popular form of investment – who bought an annuity advanced a certain sum to the city (or the prince) and received in exchange a fixed yearly sum, a rent on their investment. In principle, the payments were unlimited in the case of inheritable annuities, but of course limited by the life expectancy of the buyer in the case of life annuities. Although the payment was theoretically perpetual in the case of heritable annuities, they tended to become redeemable quite soon, thus being very similar to other credit arrangements. In the case of a life annuity, the contract was terminated when the beneficiary (or beneficiaries; a life annuity on two or even more lives was possible) passed away. Many cities even paid an incentive bonus to anybody reporting the death of a life annuity holder. The arrangement, which allowed for money to be lent and unproductive accumulative capital to be invested, was compliant with the Church's strict rules concerning credit. Long neglected as a rather primitive form of handling credit in an effort to circumscribe ideological obstacles to banking, the exceptionally well-documented sale of annuities by the Brabantine city of Mechlin opened the way to a more diversified approach. It demonstrated how the sale of annuities and the fact they allowed for a concentration of financial resources in the hands of an urban elite could be used in innovative ways: as current accounts to make various types of payments, as investments in banking operations by the towns' moneychangers, and finally, as transfers to third parties involving sophisticated banking techniques.[49]

The long-term city debts under various arrangements were first attested in the twelfth century in the large Northern Italian communes. Genoa and Venice were the forerunners, not surprisingly given their strong commercial backbone and the financial strength of their political and economic elites. Gradually, a consolidated public debt emerged as an essential element of communal strength. These Italian practices may have been a source of inspiration for what was to happen in the former Low Countries and in different principalities that were to become Burgundian territory from the late fourteenth century onward. The Counties of Artois and Flanders and the Duchy of Brabant were among the first, as the early development of their economies and the surpluses produced in the agrarian economy (the crucial element for explaining the development and growth of urban societies) had created a certain accumulation of wealth, leading to a search for different ways to fructify that wealth. Moreover, these same regions had established early financial contacts with Italian-based financiers.[50] Annuities were the most popular financial tool to achieve this; their use is attested in the Low Countries from the thirteenth century onward: in 1228 the city of Tournai had issued life annuities; Arras, a major financial centre in the thirteenth century, followed soon in 1241 if not earlier; as did Calais (in 1263), Douai (1270), Ghent (1275) and Bruges (1283). At that time, the city of Bruges had a capital debt in life annuities already amounting to more than six times the city's annual income. This fact illustrates how important public debt had become to the city's finances.[51] Over the centuries, the sale of annuities with both the city's and the prince's demesne as collateral became the principal element of a consolidated public debt. For cities, the way this system operated had major consequences for internal fiscal policy, while also strongly influencing the relationship between towns and the prince. Internally speaking, the system was responsible for a massive shift in income as the benefits of the sale of annuities went to those with enough income to be able to invest by buying annuities, while the cost was financed by the city's most important source of income: indirect taxes or excises. We have demonstrated the effects and agency at work with the example of the massive sale of annuities by the city of Ghent after its defeat against Duke Philip the Good of Burgundy in 1453. The income the city generated in the short term by selling these annuities was needed to pay the enormous fine that the duke had imposed. While the private investors, both inside and outside the city, who bought the annuities thus linked their private financial interests to the success of the central authorities, the urban communities as a whole had to face the corresponding expenditures and to take on the burden of the debt.[52] All taxpayers, who paid indirect taxes equally regardless of their individual purchasing power, saw how their collective financial efforts helped make even richer those who were already wealthy enough to invest in annuities… a fine example of fiscal techniques as a tool to transfer income.

When cities sold annuities, they put up their own demesne and income as collateral. In the context of the Low Countries' cities, and again with the Counties of Flanders and Holland-Zeeland and the Duchy of Brabant as forerunners, a system of political representation had developed in the context of the Third Estate's meetings. Contrary to most of their counterparts elsewhere in Europe, they managed to act in a way that remained quite independent from the prince, with whom the representatives were locked in an almost constant dialogue and negotiation. What was typical for the Low Countries and made them definitely different from other European experiences is the fact that the rulers never succeeded in obtaining the exclusive right to call their meetings, let alone to determine their agenda.[53] It should therefore not come as a surprise that such deep-rooted political cooperation also fostered financial cooperation among the members of the Third Estates, in the first place the dominant urban representatives. The system of not just a single city putting up collateral for the sale of annuities, but a whole principality, has long been seen as a new development of the sixteenth century, centring on the then-booming province of Holland. In fact, James Tracy has even described the shift to collective public debt to finance a common policy (first and foremost, war) a "financial revolution".[54] Recent research has modified this view both from a geographical standpoint (in the Iberian Peninsula, the practice of selling annuities at the initiative of representative institutions can be attested from the fourteenth century onward) and a chronological one. In the extremely demanding circumstances of the "civil war" waged essentially by the cities of Flanders (and to a lesser extent Brabant and Holland) against Maximilian of Austria, the idea and practice of pledging collective resources to provide satisfactory assurance to potential creditors found its way.[55] This assurance concerned mainly these cities' own rich citizens, who had endorsed the financial and fiscal strategy of their cities. It was – and therefore the idea of a "financial revolution" keeps its full relevance – a necessary step toward a true "republican" experiment in the course of the Low Countries' revolt against the Habsburg king of Spain, Philip II, not only built on political ideals but also on the control of the financial power generated by the efficient and leading urban economies.[56]

As such, the history of the financial and fiscal realities of the Burgundian Low Countries illustrates how several interconnected elements gave rise to a unique financial construction under the supervision of the creative urban forces. Among these elements, we should stress the presence of a dense and efficient urban network, well connected to international trade flows and steered by its successive economic centres over a period stretching from the thirteenth to the sixteenth centuries: Arras, Bruges, Antwerp and finally Amsterdam. These were central places and hubs where the most advanced financial techniques of their time were available and permeated into broader layers of society. Another important factor remains the agency of an ambitious dynasty of the Valois Dukes of Burgundy and their Habsburg successors, who unified the territories and endowed them with new centralizing financial institutions, thus reducing transaction costs. However, they never succeeded in imposing a permanent fiscal system on their subjects, whose ruling elites and representatives remained both an inevitable interlocutor and an indispensable financier of their policies.

Notes

1. BLOCKMANS and PREVENIER, *The Promised Lands*.
2. In her recent synthesis, LECUPPRE-DESJARDIN, *Le royaume inachevé des ducs de Bourgogne* uses the notion "la grande principauté de Bourgogne" (English version in press with Manchester University Press: *The illusion of the Burgundian state*). On the discussion: BOONE, "Yet Another Failed State?", pp. 105–120. For the application of the notion of "composite state", see also: STEIN, *Magnanimous Dukes and Rising States*.
3. BOONE, "L'État bourguignon, un État inventeur", p. 141.
4. BAUTIER and SORNAY, *Les sources de l'histoire économique*, 1984; BAUTIER and SORNAY, *Les sources de l'histoire économique*. In principle a separate volume (volume II) is planned concerning the ecclesiastic principalities and the civic and seigneurial archives, the complexity and lack of finances throw a shadow over this extremely useful enterprise.
5. BLOCKMANS, DE MUNCK and STABEL, "Economic Vitality", pp. 26–29.
6. A recent overview inspired by the New Institutional Economics theory: GELDERBLOM, *Cities of Commerce*.
7. BLOCKMANS, *Medezeggenschap*. pp. 182–212. A translation to English is being prepared: *Voice. Political participation in Europe before 1800* (Routledge).
8. TRACY, *A Financial Revolution in the Habsburg Netherlands*.
9. See also a general overview in BOONE, "Systèmes fiscaux dans les principautés à forte urbanisation des Pays-Bas méridionaux", pp. 657–683.
10. The literature on this personnel is quite abundant, as a starting point the classic work remains: BARTIER, *Légistes et gens de finances au XVe siècle*.
11. See the introduction and state of art in BLONDÉ, BOONE and VAN BRUAENE, *City and Society in the Low Countries* (a French version with Claire Billen as co-editor under the title: *Faire société au Moyen Âge*).
12. This was particularly the case for the city of Ghent, with editions of the accounts of the fourteenth century, the period of the "Van Artevelde's", editions of the accounts of the other leading Flemish cities Ypres and Bruges followed soon, they were (and are) the result of the publishing strategy by the Royal Commission for History of Belgium, see for Ypres (the accounts from 1267 till 1329): http://commissionroyalehistoire.be/pdf/A37ComptesVilleYpres_1267_1329_G_Des_MarezEtE_De_Sagher/tI_1909/titrePreface_XXIIIp_p292.pdf (consulted on Sept. 14, 2020). For Bruges, the accounts from 1280–1319): http://commissionroyalehistoire.be/pdf/electronInd/StadsrekeningBrugge.pdf (consulted on Sept. 14, 2020).
13. Dating from Pirenne's days a classic monograph remains ESPINAS, *Les Finances de la Commune de Douai*. The classic example of the study of the finances of the biggest of all medieval cities, Ghent, remains VAN WERVEKE, *De Gentsche stadsfinanciën*, to be completed for the Burgundian period by BOONE, *Geld en macht* and RYCKBOSCH, *Tussen Gavere en Cadzand*. A similar approach, but clearly more focused on the economic context, concerns the Brabantine city of Louvain: VAN UYTVEN, *Stadsfinanciën en*

stadsekonomie te Leuven and concerning the other leading city of Brabant: DICKSTEIN-BERNARD, *La gestion financière d'une capitale*. On the smaller cities of Brabant: PEETERS, *De financiën van de kleine*. In the County of Holland, concerning the city of Leiden: MARSILJE, *Het financiële beleid van Leiden*.

14 *Finances et comptabilité urbaines* and *Destruction et reconstruction de villes*.
15 On this and the tradition of urban history in Belgium: BILLEN and BOONE, "L'histoire urbaine en Belgique", pp. 3–22. The only remaining echo of this activity is the *pro civitate* committee in the context of both Belgian royal academies promoting the study of urban history, the president of which is the author of these lines.
16 An example of the first (public works): SOSSON, *Les travaux publics*; references for the studies and editions concerning the assemblies: see note 7.
17 On the way the Burgundian Court of Accounts functioned, the literature is abundant; an overview is given in SANTAMARIA, *La chambre des comptes de Lille,* pp. 256–259.
18 BLOCKMANS, "Le contrôle par le prince des comptes urbains", pp. 287–343.
19 VAN WERVEKE, "Les charges financières", pp. 81–93.
20 BUNTINX, "De enquête van Oudenburg", pp. 75–137.
21 BOONE, "Marché libre, rendement collectif et intérêts privés, un trio infernal?", pp. 159–175.
22 BILLEN, "A la recherche d'un prélèvement fiscal équitable", pp. 871–880.
23 BOONE, "Le comté de Flandre dans le long XIVe siècle", pp. 17–47.
24 SABLON DU CORRAIL, *La guerre, le prince et ses sujets*.
25 Concerning this early financial history: see again BIGWOOD, *Le régime juridique et économique du commerce de l'argent*.
26 See BROWN and DUMOLYN, *Medieval Bruges*.
27 Again the literature is abundant, an overview in KUSMAN, *Usuriers publics et banquiers du Prince*.
28 In a comparative perspective drawing on examples from Flanders, Normandy, France and England: LYON and VERHULST, *Medieval finance*.
29 On the theoretical basis and justification of princely finances: SCORDIA, *"Le roi doit vivre du sien"* and LEYTE, *Domaine et domanialité publique*.
30 BLOCKMANS, "Voracious states and obstructing cities", pp. 218–250.
31 See BILLEN and BOONE, "Taxer les ecclésiastiques", pp. 273–288.
32 BOONE, "Les ducs, les villes et l'argent des contribuables", pp. 323–341.
33 Duke Philip's finances are until now the only ones to have been studied systematically; see VAN NIEUWENHUYSE, *Les finances du duc de Bourgogne. Économie et politique,* and VAN NIEUWENHUYSE, *Les finances du duc de Bourgogne. Le montant des ressources*. A specific study on the "aides" levied in Flanders: ZOETE, *De beden in het graafschap Vlaanderen*. To this, one should add the study of the finances of Mary of Burgundy by Sablon du Corrail, see note 24.
34 In all principalities, these had given birth to elaborate overviews and tax registrations; see the editions and studies (the sources are unique information for demographic studies) in the series of the Royal Commission for History, by CUVELIER, *Les dénombrements de foyers*; ARNOULD, *Les dénombrements de foyers*; PETIT (†) and WEBER, *Les aides et subsides*. With regard to this kind of document: ARNOULD, *Les relevés de feux*. In the County of Holland, similar registration of levies on parcels within the cities were used as basis for a tax in favor of the count, for instance: GOUDRIAAN *Het Goudse hofstedengeldregister*.
35 See partial editions: DE SMET, "Le dénombrement des foyers en Flandre en 1469", pp. 105–150 and concerning the French-speaking part of the County of Flanders: DERVILLE, *Enquêtes Fiscales*.
36 CRAEYBECKX, "La portée fiscale et politique du 100e denier", pp. 343–374.
37 ARNOULD, "Une estimation des revenus et dépenses de Philippe le Bon", pp. 131–219 and ARNOULD, "Le premier budget du duc Charles de Bourgogne (1467–1468)", pp. 226–271; SORNAY, "Les états prévisionnels des finances ducales au temps de Philippe le Bon", pp. 35–94.
38 BOS-ROPS, *Graven op zoek naar geld,* pp. 248–253.
39 See the publication in note 10, and several examples in KRUSE, "Les malversations commises par le receveur general", pp. 283–312 and several contributions to the issue "La face noire de la splendeur".
40 A study of the personnel of the ducal demesne at the start of the Burgundian period: SOENS, *De rentmeesters*.
41 A first series of publications concern the years 1416–1420 (chosen because for these years accounts on all levels, general accounts for Burgundy, for Flanders-Artois and for the "recette générale de toutes les finances" are available: MOLLAT and FAVREAU, *Comptes généraux de l'État bourguignon*. A second series reflects the fundamental reforms by Duke Charles the Bold: GREVE, LEBAILLY, FLAMMANG, BESSEY and HAMEL, *Comptes de l'argentier de Charles le Téméraire*.

42 The editions were prepared by the "Holland 1300–1500" Workgroup supervised by Dick E.H. DE BOER, D.J. FABER, Huub P.H. JANSEN and Jan W. MARSILJE; final editing by Michel J. VAN GENT. They concern the years 1358–1361 and 1393–1396. In addition to accounts connected to the court officials and the dijkgraafsrekeningen of the Grote Waard, accounts issued by lower-level civil servants have also been published for the years 1393–1396. The classic printed editions were published in the years 1980–1997, they are also available online: see https://en.huygens.knaw.nl/resources/de-rekeningen-van-de-grafelijkheid-van-holland-uit-de-beierse-periode/?noredirect=en_GB (consulted on Oct. 7 2020).

43 An excellent introduction to how this has to be interpreted is offered in Sablon du Corrail's book on the finances of Mary of Burgundy (see note 24).

44 LASSALMONIE, "Le plus riche prince d'Occident?", pp. 63–82.

45 LAMBERT, *The City, the Duke and their Banker*.

46 BOONE, "Apologie d'un banquier médiéval", pp. 31–54 and VERATELLI, *A la mode italienne*.

47 De Commynes himself had many (financial and other) connections with Flemish cities, and his testimony has to be interpreted in that sense: BOONE, "Philippe de Commynes et le monde urbain", pp. 201–224.

48 VAN UYTVEN, "La Flandre et le Brabant", pp. 281–317, reprinted in his *Production and Consumption*.

49 KUSMAN and DEMEULEMEESTER, "Connecting regional capital markets", pp. 94–95.

50 See above the literature mentioned in notes 25, 27 and 28.

51 TRACY, "On the dual origins", pp. 16–21.

52 BOONE, "'Plus deuil que joie'", pp. 3–25 and BOONE, "Stratégies fiscales et financières des élites urbaines", pp. 235–253.

53 See the recent comparative survey by BLOCKMANS, *Medezeggenschap*, pp. 182–212. An English version is being prepared: *Voice. Political participation in Europe before 1800* (Routledge).

54 See above note 8.

55 See HAEMERS, *For the common good*, passim and HAEMERS, *De strijd om het regentschap*, pp. 160–166 and finally a specific answer by the same author to the image of the "financial revolution" of Tracy: HAEMERS, "A financial revolution in Flanders?", pp. 135–160 (see note 49).

56 On the original character of what happened in the Low Countries: see again DAVIDS and LUCASSEN, *A miracle mirrored* (especially the chapter by Marjolein 't Hart and Peter Spufford).

References

Maurice-Aurélien ARNOULD, "Une estimation des revenus et dépenses de Philippe le Bon en 1445", in *Acta Historica Bruxellensia. III Recherches sur l'histoire de finances publiques en Belgique*, 3, 1974, pp. 131–219.

Maurice-Aurélien ARNOULD, "Le premier budget du duc Charles de Bourgogne (1467–1468)", in *Bulletin de la commission royale d'histoire*, 150, 1984, pp. 226–271.

Maurice-Aurélien ARNOULD, *Les relevés de feux*, Turnhout, 1976 and 1985.

Maurice-Aurélien ARNOULD, *Les dénombrements de foyers dans le comté de Hainaut (XIVe-XVIe siècle)*, Bruxelles, 2006.

John BARTIER, *Légistes et gens de finances au XVe siècle. Les conseillers des ducs de Bourgogne Philippe le Bon et Charles le Téméraire*, Bruxelles, 1955.

Robert-Henri BAUTIER and Janine SORNAY, *Les sources de l'histoire économique et sociale du Moyen Âge. Les États de la maison de Bourgogne. Vol. I: Archives des Principautés du Nord. 2. Les principautés du Nord*, Paris, 1984.

Robert-Henri BAUTIER and Janine SORNAY, *Les sources de l'histoire économique et sociale du Moyen Âge. Les États de la maison de Bourgogne. Vol. I: Archives centrales de l'État bourguignon (1384–1500). Archives des principautés territoriales. 1. Les principautés du Sud. 2. Les principautés du Nord (supplément), comté de Hollande et Zélande et duché de Gueldre (par Michel VAN GENT)*, Paris, 2001.

Georges BIGWOOD, *Le régime juridique et économique du commerce de l'argent dans la Belgique du Moyen Âge*, Bruxelles, 1921.

Claire BILLEN, "A la recherche d'un prélèvement fiscal équitable. Pratiques, discours et porte-parole dans les Pays-Bas méridionaux (XIIIe-XIVe siècles)", in *La fiscalità nell'economia europea secc. XIII-XVIII. Fiscal systems in the European economy from the 13th to the 18th centuries*, Atti della 39a Settimana di Studi, Fondazioni istituto internazionale di storia economica F. Datini Prato, ed. Simonetta CAVACIOCCHI, Florence, 2008, pp. 871–880.

Claire Billen and Marc Boone, "L'histoire urbaine en Belgique: construire l'après-Pirenne entre tradition et renovation", in: *Città & Storia*, V-1, 2010, pp. 3–22.

Claire Billen and Marc Boone, "Taxer les ecclésiastiques. Le laboratoire urbain des Pays-Bas méridionaux (XIIe-XVIe siècles)", in *El dinero de Dios. Iglesia y fiscalidad en el occidente medieval (siglos XIII-XV)*, ed. Denis Menjot and Manuel Sánchez Martínez, Madrid, 2011, pp. 273–288.

Claire Billen, Bruno Blondé, Marc Boone and Anne-Laure Van Bruaene, *Faire société au Moyen Âge. Histoire urbaine dans des anciens Pays-Bas, 1100–1800*, Paris, 2021.

Frans Blockmans, "Le contrôle par le prince des comptes urbains en Flandre et en Brabant au moyen âge", in *Finances et comptabilité urbaines du XIIIe au XVIe siècle. Colloque international Blankenberge 6-9-IX-1962*, Bruxelles, 1964, pp. 287–343.

Wim Blockmans, "Voracious states and obstructing cities: an aspect of state formation in preindustrial Europe", in *Cities & the Rise of States in Europe, A.D. 1000 to 1800*, ed. Charles Tilly and Wim P. Blockmans, Boulder, 1994, pp. 218–250.

Wim Blockmans and Walter Prevenier, *The Promised Lands. The Low Countries under Burgundian Rule, 1369–1530*, Philadelphia, 1999.

Wim Blockmans, *Medezeggenschap. Politieke participatie in Europa voor 1800*, Amsterdam, 2020.

Wim Blockmans, Bert De Munck and Peter Stabel, "Economic Vitality: Urbanisation, Regional Complementarity and European Interaction", in *City and Society in the Low Countries, 1100–1600*, ed. Bruno Blondé, Marc Boone and Anne-Laure Van Bruaene, Cambridge, 2018, pp. 22–58.

Bruno Blondé, Marc Boone and Anne-Laure Van Bruaene, *City and Society in the Low Countries, 1100–1600*, Cambridge, 2018.

Marc Boone, *Geld en macht. De Gentse stadsfinanciën en de Bourgondische staatsvorming (1384–1453)*, Gent, 1990.

Marc Boone, "'Plus deuil que joie'. Les ventes de rentes par la ville de Gand pendant la période bourguignonne: entre intérêts privés et finances publiques", in *Bulletin trimestriel du Crédit Communal*, 1991, 45, #176, pp. 3–25.

Marc Boone, "Stratégies fiscales et financières des élites urbaines dans les anciens Pays-Bas face à l'état burgundo-Habsbourgeois", in *L'argent au moyen âge. Actes du XXVIIIe congrès de la Société des Historiens Médiévistes de l'Enseignement Supérieur Public, Clermont-Ferrand 30 mai – 1 juin 1997*, Paris, 1998 (*Publications de la Sorbonne, série histoire ancienne et médiévale n° 51*), pp. 235–253.

Marc Boone, "Apologie d'un banquier médiéval: Tommaso Portinari et l'Etat bourguignon", in *Le moyen âge*, CV, 1999/1, pp. 31–54.

Marc Boone, "Les ducs, les villes et l'argent des contribuables: le rêve d'un impôt princier permanent en Flandre à l'époque bourguignonne", in *L'impôt au moyen âge. L'impôt public et le prélèvement seigneurial en France, fin XIIe début XVIe siècle. II. Les espaces fiscaux, Colloque tenu à Bercy les 14,15 et 16 juin 2000*, ed. Philippe Contamine, Jean Kervhervé and Albert Rigaudière, Paris, 2002, pp. 323–341.

Marc Boone, "Le comté de Flandre dans le long XIVe siècle: une société urbanisée face aux crises du bas Moyen Age", in *Rivolte urbane e rivolte contadine nell'Europa del Trecento: un confronto*, ed. Monique Bourin, Giovanni Cherubini and Giuliano Pinto, Florence, 2008, pp. 17–47.

Marc Boone, "Systèmes fiscaux dans les principautés à forte urbanisation des Pays-Bas méridionaux (Flandre, Brabant, Hainaut, Pays de Liège) au bas moyen âge (XIVe-XVIe siècle)", in *La fiscalità nell'economia europea secc. XIII-XVIII. Fiscal systems in the European economy from the 13th to the 18th centuries, Atti della 39a Settimana di Studi, Fondazioni istituto internazionale di storia economica F. Datini » Prato*, ed. Simonetta Cavaciocchi, Florence, 2008, pp. 657–683.

Marc Boone, "Philippe de Commynes et le monde urbain", in: *1511–2011. Philippe de Commynes. Droit, écriture: deux piliers de la souveraineté*, ed. Joël Blanchard, Geneva, 2012, pp. 201–224.

Marc Boone, "L'État bourguignon, un État inventeur ou les limites de l'invention", in *La Cour de Bourgogne et l'Europe. Le rayonnement et les limites d'un modèle culturel*, ed. Werner Paravicini, Torsten Hiltmann and Frank Viltart, Ostfildern, 2013, pp. 133–156.

Marc Boone, "Marché libre, rendement collectif et intérêts privés, un trio infernal? Les fermiers des assises de la ville de Gand à la fin du Moyen Âge", in *Memini. Travaux et documents. Des communautés aux États. Mélanges offerts à Michel Hébert*, vol. 19–20, 2015–2016, pp. 159–175.

Marc Boone, "Yet Another Failed State? The Huizinga-Pirenne Controversy on the Burgundian State Reconsidered", in *Re-Reading Huizinga: Autumn of the Middle Ages, a Century Later*, ed. Peter Arnade, Martha Howell and Anton Vander Lem, Amsterdam, 2019, pp. 105–120.

Marc Boone, *City and State in the Medieval Low Countries. Collected studies by Marc Boone*, Turnhout, 2022.

Jami A.M.Y. Bos-Rops, *Graven op zoek naar geld. De inkomsten van de graven van Holland en Zeeland, 1389–1433*, Hilversum, 1993.

Andrew Brown and Jan Dumolyn (ed.), *Medieval Bruges, c. 850–1550*, Cambridge, 2018.

Willy Buntinx, "De enquête van Oudenburg. Hervorming van de repartitie van de beden in het graafschap Vlaanderen", in *Bulletin de la Commission Royale d'Histoire*, 139, 1968, pp. 75–137.

Jan Craeybeckx, "La portée fiscale et politique du 100e denier du duc d'Albe", in *Acta Historica Bruxellensia. I Recherches sur l'histoire de finances publiques en Belgique*, 1967, pp. 343–374.

Joseph Cuvelier, *Les dénombrements de foyers en Brabant (XIVe-XVIe siècles)*, Bruxelles, 1912–1913.

Karel Davids and Jan Lucassen (ed.), *A miracle mirrored. The Dutch Republic in European Perspective*, Cambridge, 1995.

Alain Derville, *Enquêtes Fiscales De La Flandre Wallonne: 1449–1549*, Lille, 1983.

Destruction et reconstruction de villes, du moyen âge à nos jours. Actes du 18e colloque international Spa, 10-12.IX.1996, Bruxelles, 1999.

Claire Dickstein-Bernard, *La gestion financière d'une capitale à ses débuts: Bruxelles, 1334–1467*, Bruxelles, 1977.

Georges Espinas, *Les Finances de la Commune de Douai des Origines au XVe Siècle*, Paris, 1902.

Finances et comptabilité urbaines du XIIIe au XVIe siècle. Colloque international Blankenberge 6-9-IX-1962, Bruxelles, 1964.

Oscar Gelderblom, *Cities of Commerce. The institutional foundations of international trade in the Low Countries, 1250–1650*, Princeton, 2013.

Koen Goudriaan e.a., *Het Goudse hofstedengeldregister van ca. 1397 en andere bronnen voor de vroege stadsontwikkeling van Gouda*, Hilversum, 2000.

Anke Greve, Émilie Lebailly, Véronique Flammang, Valérie Bessey and Sébastien Hamel (ed.), *Comptes de l'argentier de Charles le Téméraire, duc de Bourgogne, 1468–1475, Vol. 1–5*, Paris, 2001–2014.

Jelle Haemers, *For the common good. State power and urban revolts in the reign of Mary of Burgundy (1477–1482)*, Turnhout, 2009.

Jelle Haemers, *De strijd om het regentschap over Filips de Schone. Opstand, facties en geweld in Brugge, Gent en Ieper (1482–1488)*, Gent, 2014.

Jelle Haemers, "A financial revolution in Flanders? Public debt, representative institutions, and political centralization in the county of Flanders during the 1480s", in *Economies, Public Finances and the Impact of Institutional Changes in Interregional Perspective: The Low Countries and Neighbouring German Territories (14th–17th Centuries)*, ed. Remi Van Schaïk, Turnhout, 2015, pp. 135–160.

Holger Kruse, "Les malversations commises par le receveur général Martin Cornille à la cour de Philippe le Bon d'après l'enquête de 1449", in *Revue du Nord*, 77, 1995, pp. 283–312.

David Kusman, *Usuriers publics et banquiers du Prince. Le rôle économique des financiers piémontais dans les villes du duché de Brabant (XIIIe-XIVe siècle)*, Turnhout, 2013.

David Kusman and Jean-Luc Demeulemeester, "Connecting regional capital markets in the late medieval Low Countries. The role of Piemontese bankers as financial pathfinders and innovators in Brabant, Guelders, Flanders and Hainaut (c. 1260–1355)", in *Economies, public finances and the impact of institutional changes in interregional perspective. The Low Countries and neighbouring German territories (14th–17th centuries)*, ed. Remi Van Schaïk, Turnhout, 2015, pp. 94–95.

Bart Lambert, *The City, the Duke and their Banker. The Rapondi family and the Formation of the Burgundian State (1384–1430)*, Turnhout, 2006.

Jean-François Lassalmonie, "Le plus riche prince d'Occident?" in *La Cour de Bourgogne et l'Europe. Le rayonnement et les limites d'un modèle culturel*, ed. Werner Paravicini, Torsten Hiltmann and Frank Viltart, Ostfildern, 2013, pp. 63–82.

Élodie Lecuppre-Desjardin, *Le royaume inachevé des ducs de Bourgogne (XIVe-XVIe siècles)*, Paris, 2016.

Guillaume Leyte, *Domaine et domanialité publique dans la France médiévale (XIIe-XVe siècles)*, Strasbourg, 1996.

Bryce Lyon and Adriaan Verhulst, *Medieval finance. A comparison of financial institutions in Northwestern Europe*, Bruges, 1967.

Jan W. Marsilje, *Het financiële beleid van Leiden in de laat-Beierse en Bourgondische periode, 1390–1477*, Hilversum, 1985.

Michel Mollat and Robert Favreau, *Comptes généraux de l'État bourguignon entre 1416 et 1420*, Paris, 1965–1976, 3 vol.

Jean-Paul Peeters, *De financiën van de kleine en secondaire steden in Brabant van de 12de tot het midden der 16de eeuw: het voorbeeld van Diest, Nijvel, Tienen, Zoutleeuw, Vilvoorde, Aarschot, Zichem, Geldenaken, Halen, Hannuit, Landen en Gembloers*, 3 vol., Bruxelles, 1980.

Roger PETIT (†) and Jean-Pol WEBER, *Les aides et subsides dans le Luxembourg de 1360 à 1565. Contribution à l'étude du développement de la fiscalité dans une principauté territoriale*, 4 tomes, Bruxelles, 2013.

Wouter RYCKBOSCH, *Tussen Gavere en Cadzand. De Gentse stadsfinanciën op het einde van de middeleeuwen (1460–1495)*, Gent, 2007.

Amable SABLON DU CORRAIL, *La guerre, le prince et ses sujets. Les finances des Pays-Bas bourguignons sous Marie de Bourgogne et de Philippe le Beau (1477–1506)*, Turnhout, 2019.

Jean-Baptiste SANTAMARIA, *La chambre des comptes de Lille de 1386 à 1419. Essor, organisation et fonctionnement d'une institution princière*, Turnhout, 2012.

Lydwine SCORDIA, *"Le roi doit vivre du sien". La théorie de l'impôt en France (XIIIe-XVe siècles)*, Paris, 2005.

Jan DE SMET, "Le dénombrement des foyers en Flandre en 1469", in *Bulletin de la Commission Royale d'Histoire*, 99, 1935, pp. 105–150.

Tim SOENS, *De rentmeesters van de graaf van Vlaanderen. Beheer en beheerders van het grafelijk domein in de late middeleeuwen*, Bruxelles, 2002.

Janine SORNAY, "Les états prévisionnels des finances ducales au temps de Philippe le Bon", in *Actes du 109e congrès national des sociétés savantes, Dijon, 1984, Histoire médiévale*, t. II, pp. 35–94.

Jean-Pierre SOSSON, *Les travaux publics de la ville de Bruges, XIVe-XVe siècles. Les matériaux. Les hommes*, Bruxelles, 1977.

Robert STEIN, *Magnanimous Dukes and Rising States. The Unification of the Burgundian Netherlands, 1380–1480*, Oxford, 2017.

James D. TRACY, *A Financial Revolution in the Habsburg Netherlands: Renten and Renteniers In the County of Holland, 1515–1565*, Berkeley, 1985.

James D. TRACY, "On the dual origins of the long-term urban debt in medieval Europe", in *Urban Public Debts. Urban government and the Market for Annuities in Western Europe (14th–18th centuries)*, ed. Marc BOONE, Karel DAVIDS and Paul JANSSENS, Turnhout, 2003, pp. 16–21.

Andrée VAN NIEUWENHUYSE, *Les finances du duc de Bourgogne Philippe le Hardi (1384–1404). Economie et politique*, Bruxelles, 1984.

Andrée VAN NIEUWENHUYSE, *Les finances du duc de Bourgogne Philippe le Hardi (1384–1404). Le montant des ressources*, Bruxelles, 1990.

Raymond VAN UYTVEN, *Stadsfinanciën en stadsekonomie te Leuven van de XIIe tot het einde der XVIe eeuw*, Bruxelles, 1961.

Raymond VAN UYTVEN, "La Flandre et le Brabant: 'terres de promission' sous les ducs de Bourgogne?" in *Revue du Nord*, 43, 1961, pp. 281–317.

Raymond VAN UYTVEN, *Production and Consumption in the Low Countries, 13th–16th Centuries*, Aldershot, 2001.

Hans VAN WERVEKE, *De Gentsche stadsfinanciën in de middeleeuwen*, Bruxelles, 1934.

Hans VAN WERVEKE, "Les charges financières issues du traité d'Athis de 1305", in *Revue du Nord*, 32, 1950, pp. 81–93.

Federica VERATELLI, *A la mode italienne. Commerce du luxe et diplomatie dans les Pays-Bas méridionaux, 1477–1530. Edition critique de documents de la Chambre des comptes de Lille*, Villeneuve d'Ascq, 2013.

Antoon ZOETE, *De beden in het graafschap Vlaanderen onder de hertogen Jan zonder Vrees en Filips de Goede (1405–1467)*, Bruxelles, 1994.

12
MEDIEVAL GERMAN HOLY ROMAN EMPIRE

*Laurence Buchholzer**

During the period between 1970 and 2010, a few German and Anglo-Saxon historians wrote brief overviews on taxation and public finances in the medieval German Empire, for the purpose of comparison across Europe.[1] They all stressed that taxation in German countries differed considerably from the English and French systems, especially at the imperial level.[2] Seen from the modern state building perspective often used, the German tax system appears to be an enigma, and possibly archaic and inefficient. In the German Holy Roman Empire, the concept of the state was not undisputable, even in modern times,[3] and the transition from a domain economy (*Domänenstaat, Domain state*) to direct taxing of subjects by the State (*Steuerstaat, Tax State*) or to the finance State (*Finanzstaat*) did not occur.[4] Empire-wide taxation remained extraordinary; it had to be approved by the Empire's states (*Reichsstände*) and justified by absolute necessity. Therefore, the supposedly gravediggers of the general imperial taxation system, i.e. princes and their territories,[5] on the one hand, and free and imperial cities[6] on the other, might be in the line of fire when looking for the initiators of the fiscal State, which itself was still in its infancy at the end of the Middle Ages.[7]

The rare syntheses produced were developed on top of an endless number of dissertations (*Inaugural-Dissertation*) completed with an institutional perspective at the end of the nineteenth century throughout Germany. Early twentieth century, developments in economic history provided some framework for a new breed of studies, more focused on issues concerning taxing techniques or the contribution of taxes to budgets. Many of those early works still serve as references nowadays, which is evidence that the baton was not passed in the second half of the twentieth century nor at the beginning of the twenty-first.[8] Apart from the significant and numerous contributions brought about by Eberhard Isenmann, the taxation field has been shunned from the 1950s till now, to the benefit of studies on bookkeeping or debt.[9] The fascination for accounting has, however, shed light on the outcome of direct and indirect taxation and their respective shares in the budget of free or imperial cities during the fifteenth century. Yet, resuming investigations on well-known taxes such as the *Bede** may not be useless.

As the publication of new sources proves quite limited,[10] the study of taxation in the Empire's lands struggles to overcome the highly institutional approach inherited from the nineteenth century, which overly compartmentalizes the Imperial tax system, that of the princely states and the one for the free and imperial cities. Outside the German-speaking world, the few works published in French or English give the reader an overview of the taxation system in free and imperial cities as well as insights into the imperial taxation during the fifteenth and sixteenth centuries, including the Common Penny (*Gemeiner Pfennig★*).[11] Nevertheless, some aspects of imperial taxation have never been heard of. While international research is familiar with the Burgundian "cherche de feux", the Florentine *catasto* and other southern estimations, what do we really know about the German tax books (*Steuerbücher*)? What about investigations,[12] expert legal opinions on the most appropriate forms of taxation, the exemption of clerics,[13] or tax revolts?[14] The vacuum in international scientific research about these issues still fuels the belief that taxation and the royal or territorial management of finances in the Empire were poorly developed; yet archives portray a quite different reality and show that fiscal experiments and reflections, even though unfinished, were abundant during the fifteenth century.

In any case, there are reasons to hope for scholarly renewal in the field if leading figures of the new German economic history grant medieval taxation matters some attention.[15] The ever-increasing digitization of the nineteenth century's works makes it easier to access old and scholarly publications that were scattered all over the place. Such a process helps to better grasp the context of some statements, and even to question historiographical myths. The *Index Librorum Civitatum civitatum* project[16] that endeavours to list municipal books (*Stadtbücher*) of medieval and modern times, holds out the promise of better overall knowledge of urban fiscal documentation. Hence, developing a history of fiscal pragmatic writing becomes possible.[17] Modernists, who specialize in the modern State, are leading the way so that medievalists may "find things to say about taxation excluding the State".[18] The starting point could be the social and material practices associated with levying and paying taxes, the geographical and social patterns outlined by these practices, the symbolic communication used, the resulting conflicting interactions, forms of political or administrative construction, etc.[19]

Dealing with the imperial taxation from the eleventh century to the 1530s in just a few pages is nothing but impossible gamble; covering such a wide topic in a single glance without any centralizing and standardizing tendency is not an easy task. Tax, meant as a compulsory levy that must, in the Empire, be (more or less directly) agreed to and justified, is an expression of power. As a matter of fact, the number of powers concerned is huge. The 1521 Worms Matrikel (*Matrikul*)[20] provides an idea, which is both moving and highly fictional; it is all about 420 fragments of the Empire: 7 electors, 3 archbishops, 45–47 bishops, 31 lay princes, including three from the Pays Welches (Dukes of Meuse, Savoy, Chalon), 65 prelates, 13 or 14 abbesses, 4 bailiwicks (*Balleien*) of the Teutonic Order, 137–140 counts and lords, 84–85 free cities, imperial cities, and quasi-autonomous towns. So many "little powers" which had a say about the Empire's tax demands that were, moreover, set by only some *happy few* who held the highest positions in the hierarchy (*Stände*). So many "little powers" which themselves levied taxes on their urban and rural subjects and could be confronted with taxpayer reactions and demands, individually or in the framework of the *Landstände* (territorial states).[21] So many "little powers" that were built, among other things, through taxation that forms the link between those who demand, those who collect and those who pay.

It is also worth noting that our view of the taxation system being considered is closely linked to records kept. Yet, in the case of the German Empire, actual tax writings (tax books/ *Steuerbücher*, tax ordinances/*Steuerordnungen*, etc.) appeared not until the middle of the fourteenth century at best. As for preceding periods, only vague mentions in charters or chronicles, and a few exceptional wrecks, such as the 1241–1242 imperial tax list serve as existing written traces left. This situation results from the late use of writing on perennial media in the taxation field, and archive conservation choices made during medieval and modern times. It definitely impacts our interpretation of the fifteenth-century documents. Given the lack of detailed information on earlier times, and before presenting the following overview in two parts, one of which is entirely devoted to tax experiments in the fifteenth century, it may be appropriate to tone down any novelty effect projected.

Tax development in the German empire from the eleventh century to the fourteenth century

Endowed with imperial dignity starting with the coronation of Otto I (962) and favoured by some dynastic continuity, the Ottonians (936/962–1024), followed by the Salians (1024–1125), were subsequently able to retain control over the vast Carolingian imperial domain (*Reichsgut*) as well as the military, fiscal and monetary sovereign rights. By virtue of the personal ties binding them to the Ruler, grandees, who were members of the imperial aristocracy, owed him advice, troops for the Roman expedition and other wars, as well as resources for the court upkeep. In return, they could expect graces and honours. Indeed, the Ottonians and Salians created and granted numerous market-operating and coinage rights. They granted immunities, forests, lucrative sovereign rights such as tolls and *teloneum* taxes or allocated counties.[22] In spite of their retained link with the higher authority, lay and especially ecclesiastical grandees were granted rights that increased their powers (*Herrschaften*).

The devolution of sovereign rights provided the Empire's aristocracy with means required to implement a fiscal policy that ended up gaining greater autonomy during the Investiture Controversy (1075–1122). The resulting financial means for bishops could be seen in the eagerness they displayed in transforming their cities during the eleventh century. The lifetimes of Bishop Benno II of Osnabrück (1068–1088) and of Archbishop Adalbert of Hamburg-Bremen (1043–1072) are reminiscent of monumental constructions, including churches, castles and fortifications, made possible through "new burdens and demands with regard to the country and the people".[23] At the end of the eleventh century and even more so in the twelfth century, the German Empire entered a process of power feudalisation, which got enhanced by the development of topographical lines and ministeriality (*Ministerialität*). During the twelfth century, local potentates began to levy in their rural and urban territories a fee similar to the land tax, known at that time only through scarce mentions in charters (see *Bede**).[24]

In addition to castles and rural manors, counts, dukes, or simple lords founded localities (*Märkte*) which soon turned urban (*Stadt*), such as those founded by Henry the Lion in Bavaria (Munich) or the ones by the Zähringers in the Upper Rhineland (Bern, Freiburg im Breisgau, Freiburg, etc.). In Munich, for example, the new dukes Wittelsbach established their rule over the city, after 1180. The dukes of Bayern-Landshut took up residence there in 1255. They granted the community of citizens a stopover right and a monopoly on the salt trade routes. Despite the municipal rights they were granted in 1279 and 1294, the citizens remained under the high jurisdiction of the duke who levied an annual city tax (*Stadtsteuer*) of 600 pounds and could request military assistance.

Under the aegis of bishops, cities began their demographic and space development at the end of the eleventh century. In Speyer, Worms, Mainz, Cologne, Strasbourg, Basel, or Augsburg, by virtue of the privileges and sovereign rights granted to them by the Ottonians and Salians, bishops and archbishops levied taxes on trade, on transport, and on the consumption of wine or flour (*Ungeld**). Between the end of the eleventh century and the middle of the thirteenth century, sworn urban communities and municipalities got structured in these episcopal cities. As they were dominated by ministerials (*Ministerialen*) and affluent merchants, they demanded and obtained from their lord/bishop to be collectively responsible for the direct manorial tax (*Gewerf, Bede**). Thanks to privileges and municipal rights, they defined themselves as peace and special rights areas; they were granted rights on markets, tolls, currency, customs, banishment, etc., initially on a temporary basis. In Cologne, for example, as of 1154, there was a communal property tax, designated as the *communis civium collecta*, the proceeds of which had to be allocated to the construction of the city walls. In 1180, the city received definitive confirmation of that: it could henceforth levy taxes and duties to build and maintain its defence. In Cologne, and elsewhere, such a tax law soon found its expression in the oath of citizenship, in which every citizen promised to pay taxes and defend the city. The oldest preserved oaths thus reveal the "original" tax obtained by the municipality, such as the *Ungeld*★ in Basel or the *Gewerf* in Colmar.[25]

Despite the strengthening of nobility, ecclesiastical and even communal influences when the Staufen dynasty came to power, they still enjoyed the substantial income drawn from the imperial domain (*Reichsgut*), an extensive family estate and all sorts of sovereign prerogatives (customs, coinage, mining rights, authority and taxation levied on the Jews, etc.).[26] Frederick II was the richest ruler in Europe in the thirteenth century.[27] However, such affluence was essentially based on revenues from the Kingdom of Sicily, as there was not any public taxation imposed on all subjects in the German Empire. Yet, on his arrival in Germany, Frederick II (1212/1220–1254) embarked on a policy of reasserting royal power. In episcopal cities, he and his son (Henry [VII]) interfered in emerging conflicts between bishops and communities, through ecclesiastical advocate offices (*Vogtei*, powers conferred on a layman to exercise protection, judicial and military functions that an ecclesiastical lord could not perform). In Constance or Augsburg, half of the main manorial fee (*Ungeld*★ or *Bede*★) eventually went to them in their capacity as advocates. However, the Staufens supported the emancipation of the municipalities from ecclesiastical powers. In Mainz, for example, after two privileges granted by the emperor in 1236, the archbishop had to guarantee freedoms to the citizens, including exemption from tax and military duties, as well as customs relief. In Speyer, when the conflict between the bishop, the community and the cathedral chapter came to an end, the bishop acknowledged the independence of the council and renounced his right to levy taxes. In the thirteenth century, Cologne, Regensburg, Mainz, Speyer, Strasbourg, and Worms gradually took their first steps towards becoming free cities (*Freie Stadt*) which, in theory, would cease to be indebted to their former lord and which, while recognizing a link with the Empire, would not feel obliged to pay taxes to the king, nor even to provide any military aid.[28]

In the Staufen patrimonial lands and those subjected to imperial tax, Frederick II and his son regained direct authority over provost jurisdictions and ecclesiastical advocate offices by taking them over from subordinates or by obtaining them in fief in ecclesiastical domains. The Ruler, thus, became the lord protector and Justiciar of the local population (*Schutzherr, Gerichtsherr*). As such, he could grant them privileges such as the right to build a fortification or a town, with funding coming from temporary concessions of the *Ungeld*★ or *Bede*★. The royal cities (*Königsstädte*) were reclaimed by the royal and imperial authorities, who aimed to develop those places into efficient military, economic and administrative centres. The administration of justice, defence, and finance was performed by a *Schultheiss*, an officer appointed by the king and often chosen from the ranks of the imperial ministerials.[29] Thus, in the Upper Rhineland, it was on his *Schultheissen* of Brisach, Colmar, Sélestat or Kaysersberg that King Frederick II imposed the obligation to recognize privileges of exemption from the *teloneum* obtained by the Cistercian abbey of Pairis. In the towns where these men were in office, they had to stop collecting "any kind of exaction" (*ab ipsis aliquid genus exactionis*) on Cistercian goods at the sale and purchase.[30] Some officers, holding the title of *advocatus provincialis* or *procurator*, were entrusted with higher administrative functions, as was the case with Wolfelin of Haguenau, *Schultheiss* of the town, who became *Prokurator* in charge of administering the imperial property and tax revenues of the whole of the royal Lower Alsace until his disgrace in 1237.

In return for imperial favours and protection, all the localities taken under the Empire's wing in the years 1215–1230 paid the sovereign an annual tax in money (called *precaria* in a 1241–1242 list).[31] Historians refer to it, for want of a better term, as the *Reichsstadtsteuer*★ or *Reichssteuer*, with the ambiguity that it did not consist of taxation on all inhabitants of the Empire.[32] This direct tax payable by towns and villages of the Empire, including Jewish communities (*Judensteuer*★), provided one of the regular revenues of the king over the long term. The amounts required, though variable in the thirteenth century and distributed by each community among its members, levelled off at the beginning of the fourteenth century for several hundreds of years. However, the overall revenue drawn from these taxes tended to decrease due to pledges (*Verpfändung*) affecting town and cities (on this notion, see p. 277 below) or because these tax revenues were allocated to third parties in exchange for loans or services provided.

Imperial cities were submitted to further financial and fiscal obligations. In return for the protection of the king and the Empire, they were obliged to be faithful, and to provide advice, assistance, and honours. Well known in the fifteenth century thanks to narratives, those obligations were probably established in the twelfth century in royal cities and in the thirteenth century in localities that had turned imperial.[33] Communities were required to provide lodging for the king and his court when they stayed within their walls or nearby. As the king toured the kingdom following his coronation, communities honoured him with gifts (*Schencke*), silver cups, wine vats, oats, or fish. Quantities or values appeared to be set by custom. When the imperial cities of the Grand Bailiwick of Alsace celebrated the arrival of the Ruler together, they also appeared to follow fixed distribution criteria.

Even though the German monarchy seemed concerned with taking stock of its revenues and regularly levying taxes on imperial cities around 1230–1240, adverse tendencies such as exemptions and concessions, emerged. While the imperial tax could be temporarily allocated to the urban communities themselves – for a duration required to build a fortification or recover from a fire outbreak – the concessions made to princes proved to have serious consequences. The Constitution in favour of ecclesiastical princes (*privilegium in favorem principum ecclesiasticorum*, 26 April 1220) and secular princes (1231, confirmed by Frederick II in 1232) granted them numerous sovereign rights. To the former, Frederick II confirmed the abandonment of the right of spoil and the *jus regalium*. He extended the coinage and customs rights and promised that nobody could interfere in territories to impose new tolls or currencies,[34] or to build castles, towns, and markets. To the latter, the secular princes (*Landesherren, domini terrae*), Henry (VII) recognized all the attributes of territorial sovereignty (*Landeshoheit*), which limited the royal power to the estate lands of the reigning dynasty and to a few remnants of the imperial fiscal system. However, the princely power was limited by the statute of 1232; reforms could not be carried out without the advice and consent of the *meliores et majores terrae*. The peace edict (*Mainzer Reichslandfriede*) of 1235, issued in Latin and German – which was a first – further qualified the princely power as it pointed out that any legitimacy derived from the king. Without his consent, princes could not create new tolls, *teloneum* taxes or duties on the markets. This text is the first to show the term *Ungeld*★, referring to an indirect tax that developed throughout towns and cities to fund urban fortifications. The Ruler claimed to be the great authorizer of this tax, as for other customs, coinage or conduct duties.[35]

However, the troubles arising from the excommunication and deposition of Frederick II and the Interregnum (1250–1273) gave princes *de facto* greater fiscal latitude. In the fourteenth century, the Habsburgs' main revenues in their Austrian territories (excluding Tirol and Anterior Austria) came from sovereign duties, such as the tolls of Linz, Stein, Gmünd and their lucrative duties on salt trade, coinage, and the annual direct taxes paid by the Jews and towns (*Judensteuer*★, *Stadtsteuer*). In 1359, in return for renouncing a monetary mutation, Duke Rudolf IV introduced a 10 per cent *Ungeld*★ on wine and beer sold in Austrian drinking establishments. This indirect tax soon became the main source of income for Austrian dukes, until they resorted to extraordinary territorial taxes (*Landsteuer*), which were demanded on behalf of "country necessity".[36]

At the end of the nineteenth century, ecclesiastical chronicles reported the pressure exerted by lords who mercilessly squeezed populations. They hinted at the existence of rates that varied according to the estate and social status, and stealthily revealed that tax lists were used (*tabulas exactionum*).[37] According to the Dominican *Annales Basileenses*,[38] Bishop Conrad of Lichtenberg imposed in 1274 an *exactionem magnam* such as none of his predecessors had ever dared to demand. Those who previously owed 1, 2, 3 or 4 sous in terms of land tax consequently owed one or two livres, while, as before, the "wealthy" and knights were exempted. Fleeing the popular clamour in Strasbourg (*clamorem pauperum*) provoked by the move, the bishop is said to have renewed his tax demands in Rouffach and Soultz. Over there, and after being shown the *tabulas exactionum*, he transformed amounts initially formulated in livres into marks, taxed some people at more than fifty silver marks, spared neither widows nor nuns, thus provoking an exodus and tax evasion outside the bishopric of Strasbourg. Such princely tax moves clashed with the first communal taxes in episcopal and royal cities. Therefore, a few years earlier, the Strasbourg municipality was accused, by the bishop, of "illegitimate exactions". In 1261, the manifesto by Bishop Walther of Geroldseck, which hastened the war with the Strasbourg bourgeoisie, accused the municipality of having decided on a new *Ungeld*★ on the milling without any approval from the bishop and the chapter. The *Mahlungeld* was allegedly taken "illegitimately against God, to the great detriment of the people (*Volk*) of Strasbourg and the rural people (*Landleute*), rich and poor". The bishop denounced its systematic nature and contrasted it with his virtuous tax practices, which consisted of imposing taxes "only when they were necessary for the city, so that our common citizens are not impoverished while the most powerful people grow wealthier".[39]

These tax conflicts should not overshadow the fact that many tax agreements already existed. Over the thirteenth century, in many towns, even seigneurial ones, communities obtained privileges creating some forms of subscriber taxes or ceding the temporary right to levy seigneurial taxes for their benefit (*Bede*★, *Ungeld*★), or even the possibility of raising their own taxes. For example, in 1275, the citizens and the council of the town of Guebwiller agreed to set the annual tax (*Gewerf*) at 40 silver marks, payable between Saint Martin's Day and Christmas. The lord of the town, Abbot Berthold, pledged not to ask for more. In return, the citizens pledged their allegiance and obedience to the abbey and acknowledged the abbey's rights.[40]

The Interregnum had marked a decline in the sovereign rights and tax assets placed in the hands of the Ruler, and when Rudolf of Habsburg (1273–1291) came to power, he tried to restore them. He pursued a claiming policy (*Revindikationenpolitik*), which was based on consensus and the frequent participation of the princes in court meetings. However, due to the lack of archives and financial administration, the reinstatement of property and rights to the crown domain remained limited. It was only successful in places where royal and estate interests were most closely intertwined, in Swabia, Alsace and the Rhineland. To this end, Rudolf established grand bailiffs (*Reichslandvogten*).[41] These men, chosen from among the king's followers, were responsible, among other things, for regional peace (*Landfrieden*), supervision of monasteries and the Jews, surveillance of customs and collection of imperial taxes (*Reichsstadtsteuer*★ and *Judensteuer*★). The fiscal and financial potential of the so-called imperial cities (*Reichsstädte, civitates imperii*) did not escape the Ruler. He integrated them fully into his policy, as he relied on the *Schultheißen*. In addition to the renewed collection of annual taxes from the imperial cities (*Reichsstadtsteuer***), the Ruler appeared to increase the number of extraordinary taxes. For year 1274, the *Chronique de Colmar*, as well as the 2nd Swabian continuation of the *Kaiserchronik*, mentioned a "new exaction" and "a general land tax" (*generalis precaria*). This tax may have been levied beyond the imperial cities, which in that year also owed a *Hofsteuer**; it could correspond to a wealth tax of a 3 per cent rate. Despite the *jus subcollectandi* obtained by many imperial cities, Rudolf is said to have tried again in 1284–1285 to introduce a graduated direct tax on estates, the Thirtieth Penny (*Dreizigsten Pfennig, Zwanzigster Pfennig**). He allegedly backed down after revolts in Colmar, Haguenau, Frankfurt, Wetzlar, etc. The texts concerning such developments are difficult to interpret, though. In 1284, the epic of "Fake Frederick" (II), Tile Kolup, was played out. He claimed to regain his throne and received support and subsidies from several cities,[42] but ended up at the stake in July 1285. It is possible that payments demanded in 1284–1285 were judicial fines (*Besserung*), just like the 1,300 marks mentioned in a Colmar charter of 18 June 1285 and obviously paid by means of an extraordinary tax levy in the town. In any case, in 1290, imperial cities reverted to the ordinary services of the *Stadtsteuer* without further ado.

Despite the royal claiming policy throughout the German Empire, albeit at very different rates, local potentates started the long process of transforming heterogeneous sets of rights (*Adelsherrschaften*) in sovereign territories. One of the vectors of the transformation was taxation. However, there were significant territorial and regional differences. Thus, assemblies gradually organized by order and playing roles in fiscal matters (*Landstände*) emerged at the beginning of the fourteenth century in many places but not in some territories, particularly ecclesiastical ones. Moreover, since the *Landstände* were established out of negotiations and agreements, they did not have the same socio-political composition everywhere.[43]

In the south-eastern part of the Kingdom of Germany, one of the principalities whose construction was most advanced in the period spanning the thirteenth century to the early fourteenth century was that of the dukes of Bavaria, the Wittelsbachs. They took over the inheritance of several extinct lines and recovered their advocate offices or imperial fiefs. They imposed a higher authority on independent nobility powers (*Adelsherrschaften*), thanks to the high justice and the peace legislation (*Landfriedengesetzgebung*, from 1244 onwards). They structured administrative areas, relied on ministerials to manage their rights and estates and on clerics to keep records; they took up residence in Munich and Landshut and formed a council attended by nobles and officers. However, taxation heterogeneity dragged on until the fourteenth century, despite those signs of territorialization. The duchy of Bavaria-Landshut or Bavaria-Munich was not subjected to any general tax applying to all its inhabitants. Taxes inherited from land or communal powers, on a subscribing basis, fixed, and frequently called *Steura, stiura*, appear in 1291–1294 records of the *Vitztum* of Upper Bavaria. They were collected in May and autumn but differ in terms of how they were levied in towns, cities, countryside, and districts (*Gerichte*). These taxes, which were collected from different groups of people with different dependence relationships, were paid into ducal coffers, and eventually became regular. They were recorded, together with the expected general amounts, in "urbariums" and "salbücher" (*Salbücher, Urbare*), just like those also kept for the Habsburg territories.[44] In addition to these consolidated old manorial dues, there were extraordinary tax demands, such as the *Notbede* (necessity land tax) demanded by Duke Ludwig on the occasion of his daughter's marriage to the Landgrave of Hesse in 1292, or the tax levied in 1295 in the bishopric of Regensburg to settle ducal debts. Whether in the form of new land taxes, defence levies or requisitions inspired by feudal aid to the four cases, these tax levies became ever more prominent in the fourteenth century. There were several reasons for this, including the increased financial needs of a structuring territorial power, greater recourse to writing and to the conservation of the writing, and the advent of territorial state assemblies (*Landstände*). Did these states reflect local developments or broad European trends? Did they result from general judicial meetings, court meetings (*Hoftagen*), knightly meetings (*Rittertage*), regional peace meetings (*Landfrieden*), feudal obligations (*Schutz und Schirm* on the one hand, *Rat und Hilfe* on the other), credit commitments (granted in particular by citizens and towns)? Perhaps all at the same time; in any case, their advent was obviously associated with tax issues. In Upper Bavaria, the *Schneitbacher Urkunde* (1302) granted the states the right of assembly and consent to taxation, on the occasion of a general tax levy (*gemain stewr*). In that year, the nobles of Upper Bavaria granted the duke the right to levy a cattle tax on their own subjects, on the one hand, and on the "Sires" on the other. In Lower Bavaria, the *Ottonische Handfeste* (1311) granted by Duke Otto III (1290–1312) confirmed the privileges of the nobility in exchange for their consent to a tax, payable, in different ways, by them and their dependents.

As local powers grew stronger, it became clear that the king could not live solely on his own any further. From the time of Ludwig of Bavaria (1314–1347) and Charles IV (1347–1378, Emperor in 1355), the rulers chose to fill in deficits by means of pledges and credit. The pledge (*Verpfändung*), which meant giving up an income, a tax, or even a city, in exchange for a predefined sum of money paid in advance by the pledgee, was a response to the lack of cash flow that prevailed during that period.[45] The practice made it possible to establish ties with the pledgees or to make payments for services, while at the same time maintaining the possibility of a return to the Empire that the trend towards hereditary fiefs could not guarantee any more. The possibility of repurchasing granted to the cities ensured the Ruler of valuable capital contributions. In the reign of Charles IV, according to estimates by A. Nuglisch, out of 130,000 guilders of annual revenues from the German fiscal system, the pledges provided 63,000 guilders and almost 40,000 guilders came from regular revenues (such as the proceeds of the *Stadtsteuer* and ordinary levies on Jews). The rest came from extraordinary taxes levied on imperial cities and the Jews (17,000 guilders), monies collected during the two Roman expeditions and gifts presented to the emperor and his court when they visited imperial cities.[46]

Obviously, the share of the pledges (*Verpfändung*), which kept growing until Sigismund, went hand in hand with the use of extraordinary taxation. Charles IV subjected the imperial cities to it to secure the support of electors for the election of his son Wenceslas. He likewise used fines (*Strafgeld*). Claiming the imperial cities had not responded to his requests for military levies for the war against the Wittelsbachs, he demanded heavy monetary payments from the cities of Upper and Lower Swabia, Franconia, Alsace and the Wetterau. They paid a total of 195,200 fl, which was almost the amount he paid to acquire the Margraviate of Brandenburg. The cities that were approached on this occasion did not necessarily collect these sums through taxation. Thus, Augsburg paid 36,000 guilders to the sovereign in 1373 by issuing and selling life annuities, at 1 guilder for 7 guilders.

Eventually, the imperial finance administration was privatized as the pledge practice increased and the royal domain decreased. Given that the exercise of kingship required a substantial property base (*Hausmachtkönigtum*), power remained in the hands of the most powerful princely dynasties who could afford the running costs of the kingdom, i.e. the Luxemburgs, the Wittelsbachs or the Habsburgs. Royal power shifted to the heart of principalities which controlled the administration of the Empire. From the little known about them, the chamberlains (*Kammermeister*) and officers of the chamber had territorial links under the reign of Rupert of Palatinate as well as under the Luxembourgs. They came from the small imperial nobility and were among relatives of the king's council members. They managed the revenues without necessarily discriminating between assets of the empire and the dynasty. Approaches to tax collection were not uniform. Because imperial tax revenues (*Stadtsteuer* or *Judensteuer**) were frequently allocated to a third party, the monies did not systematically move to the chamber, far from it. The records of the chamber under Rupert of Palatinate reveal that only half a dozen cities paid the St Martin tax directly to him. Furthermore, a large part of the royal finances went unofficially through urban creditors from Nuremberg or Augsburg. During the reign of Charles IV, Nuremberg received the imperial tax of the Swabian and Franconian towns as a deposit. As the hidden capital of the Empire under the Luxemburgs, the city which was governed by men who lent money to the king, retained its function as a deposit place for imperial taxation over the long term.[47]

Tax experiments of the fifteenth and early sixteenth centuries

In 1356, the Golden Bull proclaimed after the imperial coronation of Charles IV (1347–1378, emperor in 1355) designed the way forward for the Empire. It definitively granted the election right to seven electors whose principalities would not be shared any more.[48] The precedence of these princes also applied to the court meetings (*Hoftage*) where they served and advised the king. After the defeat of the urban leagues in the war opposing them to the princes (1st Town War 1388–1389), the definition of the fiscal policy, as well as other royal affairs, fell primarily under the authority of the king and the electors. The formation of the imperial states (*Reichsstände*) gradually took shape from the top of the social and political hierarchy. After the college of electors, the college of princes grew stronger. It took another century (1489) for the free and imperial cities – which were only invited at the pleasure of the king and higher states – to be structured into a collegiate body, and for the running or the imperial diets (*Reichstag*) to develop some organization.

In this princely-led Empire, plagued by numerous wars during the fifteenth century, funding for political and military actions became critical. Yet in the Holy Roman Empire, it was still all about extraordinary situations. Genuine ideas were expressed, and fierce debates took place in royal/imperial assemblies. Between 1420 and 1430, two proposals for extraordinary fiscal financing coexisted. One was a tax fictitiously presented as a military contribution, based on subsidiarity, and therefore mediated by the direct members of the Empire (the Matrikel, *Reichsmatrikel*); the other was a general imperial tax in money levied upon the subjects of the Kingdom (the *Reichssteuer*). The first option prevailed thanks to developments in the fifteenth and early sixteenth centuries. However, both approaches were in place in 1422 when the Hussite taxes were established.

The Hussite War (1419–1436) brought about the *Hussengeld*. In the first instance, the tax was referred to by means of periphrases.[49] From 1428 onwards, and even more so in 1431, this general tax was referred to by the compound word *Hussengeld* or *Hussensteuer**, a term that appeared both in words used in imperial assemblies and in the account books of free and imperial cities that passed on the imperial demand to their populations.[50]

Five crusades against the Hussites took place between 1420 and 1436. They mobilized the imperial forces in a way that was even more imperative as the confrontations took place in the king's patrimonial territories and in the eastern regions of the kingdom (Bohemia, Bavaria, Franconia, Austria, Silesia, Saxony, Brandenburg). Talks of a Germany-wide tax dated back to a time as early as the 1422 Nuremberg imperial assembly.[51] According to statements by two diplomats from Strasbourg, rumours had it that sometimes the princes, and in other cases the king who "needed money", were behind the plan. The states that met in Nuremberg in 1422 were reminded of their duty of obedience to the king and the armed service they had to perform "against the unbelievers in Bohemia". They needed to consider the situation that was "of unprecedented gravity and severity". However, the argument soon became that of the defence of Christianity, the common good, the preservation of the king and the Empire. By virtue of their military service duty (*Dienst*), electors, bishops, dukes and secular princes, lords, counts, knights, and squires, as well as imperial and free cities were called upon to provide the necessary troops for war and for urgent expeditions, such as the defence of the Karlstein Castle, which required an estimated 6,000 cavalrymen and 38,000-foot soldiers. For that purpose, a first Empire Matrikel[52] was issued. Entitled "Levy for Daily War in Bohemia", it listed the military contributions of imperial members, in descending hierarchical order (from electors to free and imperial cities), in *Gleven*, *Schutzen* or equipped horses.[53] Letter exchanges that followed this first request admitted of some approximations. Prelates, counts, lords, knights, squires, towns, female convents, and secular clerics might have been forgotten or not explicitly listed for the levy. Therefore, they were called upon to agree to a new kind of contribution. To fund the maintenance of the troops in their "ordinary war" against the Hussites for one year, a matter which "concerns the whole of Christendom", "every man in the kingdom" had to be taxed and had to obey the demand for levy on pain of disgrace or property and fiefs confiscation. A direct tax, the 100th penny (*Hundertster Pfennig*), agreed upon by some members of the Empire, was imposed on those who did not contribute by virtue of the Matrikel. In fact, the Margrave of Baden, and the Counts of Öttingen were given full imperial powers to carry out the levy in their areas of authority. The tax was to be levied at a rate of one hundredth on unearned incomes, ground rents, revenues and benefits of prelates, abbots, abbesses, counts, lords, knights, and squires. For citizens and peasants, it was applicable to movable and immovable property. Special requirements affected the Jewish population, who were obliged to pay a tax on their property, the third penny (*dritter Pfennig*, 33.3 per cent).[54]

The collection was not up to expectations; indeed, potential taxpayers shied away. As early as December 1, Pope Martin V announced that the contributions for the ordinary war against heretics had not been properly established at the Nuremberg assembly. The principle of ex-gratia payments should have prevailed for clerics. As for the cities, sometimes they negotiated not to provide the ordinary war aid due for a year in exchange for a replacement amount, sometimes they deferred the military aid requested.[55]

The repeated defeats against the Hussites, however, added a new meaning to the first abortive attempt at general money taxation. To strengthen and better equip the army of the Empire, the 1427 imperial assembly meeting in Frankfurt decided to tax the members of the Empire for the war against the Hussites.[56] In the absence of Sigismund, the papal legate was the driving proposal force. The underlying model was that of papal taxation, and the general direct tax was again presented as a necessity on behalf of Christianity. The tax ordinance of 1427 reveals a complex combination, varying from estate to estate. It mixed capitation, estate tax, income tax, personal tax, and a special tax for Jews, to cover everyone. Electors and princes could contribute as they wished. Squires, knights, lords, and counts owed a personal tax, graduated according to their dignity, between 3 guilders for squires and 25 guilders for counts. For non-noble laymen, their estates were charged according to two brackets: half a guilder for 200 to 1,000 guilders of estate, one guilder if above. As for the ecclesiastical profits and annuities of clerics or religious people, they were subjected to an income tax (*Ertragssteuer*, 5 per cent, 1 guilder per 20 guilders). Any less wealthy Christian, cleric or layman, man, or woman, who falls below the threshold of 200 guilders in estate, was subjected to a capitation of one *Groschen boh*. Religious people without income or property had to pay a capitation of two *Groschen boh*. As for the Jews, throughout the Empire, they were liable to a heavier capitation fee of one guilder, in line with the *Güldener Opferpfennig*★. There is literature providing guidance on the intended collection procedures. The clergy had to pay the money in episcopal cities. For the laity, territorial towns, manorial villages, or free and imperial cities were collection points. The nobles had to deposit the money with a diocesan commission. From the diocesan coffers and the coffers set up in cities, the money was transferred to five depositing and accounting places, managed by commissions of 6–8 people: Cologne, Erfurt, Salzbourg, Breslau (Wroclaw), Nuremberg. A central commission in Nuremberg, consisting of six representatives of the electors and three representatives of the imperial cities, oversaw the whole process and was responsible for payments to the armies in liaison with the military high command.

Members of the empire who were not present or not consulted, especially from the cities, quickly protested the new tax. Both the demand for a tax in money, instead of the usual provision of military aid, and the way it was collected were seen as problematic. Several cities agreed, however, on the condition that they would keep control of the collection procedures. The cities of the Swabian Urban League and Frankfurt chose to equip troops and send them to the desired location. Strasbourg seemed to be coping with the cash levy. Nuremberg paid almost 420 Rhenish guilders.[57] The index of a register summarizes the content of the exchanges between the main cash office in Nuremberg and potential contributors. The following is a selection of their answers. Duke Charles of Lorraine wanted to give nothing for the war but what he had already offered. The Duchess of Mecklenburg was prepared to do her utmost in this matter… The Count of Öttingen "will send his money to Nuremberg immediately". Cities such as Freiburg i. Br. and Brisach could not contribute because of war conditions at home. Frankfurt said it wanted to equip troops rather than provide money. Trient pointed out the novelty of the taxation, which, moreover, concerned Germany and not the "Pays welches" … Görlitz, which had spent everything in soldiers against heretics, could not further give money. Regensburg had collected the money in safekeeping with a trusted man in Nuremberg and would pay it out when others had paid their dues … As one may guess, the amounts collected in 1428–1430 did not match the efforts deployed. However, in several imperial cities, the terms *Hussensteuer*★ and *Hussengeld* gained ground. In 1431, when the Nuremberg imperial assembly established a matrikel and required a one-year military contribution for the defence of the border with Bohemia at the rate of one man in arms for every 25 adult male inhabitants, several towns introduced a direct tax in money, which they called *Hussengeld*. The Nuremberg Magistrate seemed to have been inspired by the 1427 tax procedures. He levied an extraordinary direct tax (*Anschlag*) not only on the citizens, but also on the rural subjects of the Waldstromer Council and Forestry Office. The cash tax was to be paid to the district masters within three days in towns and three weeks in rural areas. This expeditious implementation reveals the smooth running of the tax administration, which had experience of direct taxation through the *Losung*★, and a first population count carried out in 1430 for work on the city's ditches.[58] The amounts required were set according to the estate possessed, with the value of movable property being estimated in money by taxpayers. Seven brackets were set: from the holders of little estates valued less than 50 guilders who owed 2 sch.d.h., to wealthier owners of more than 1,000 guilders in estate, who owed 4 guilders. Each taxpayer paid the money based on a tax oath and a self-assessment. The contribution was made "according to one's conscience", so the amounts paid individually were not recorded.

Over the years, the imperial expeditions against the Hussites were funded by the tax measures of 1422, 1427 and 1431. Again, in 1434 in Basel, consideration was given to how to cover war costs. The annual income of the clergy was subjected to half a tithe (*Zwanzigster Pfennig* or *Zwanzigster*★).[59] As far as the laity were concerned, a tax ordinance was drawn up and combined capitation for the less well off and income taxation for the others. It was never acted upon. The principle of a general Empire tax was set aside until the 1470s. The wars against the Turks, combined with a growing reform tendency,[60] revived plans for a general imperial tax payable in money. Projects came and went in rapid succession but were neither approved nor implemented. In all sides, there were opponents, who rejected the projects on specific points or positions of principle, including the lack of fairness between the states, the people's supposed fear of being subjected to an "everlasting tribute as was the case in France",[61] the fear that the Empire or the taxed members would be impoverished, the fear of a headlong rush to war, the non-necessity, failure to respect the secrecy of each person's wealth and poverty, monetary shortage, etc. As a result of these projects, free and imperial cities, which were vital contributors, were more systematically invited to the Empire's assemblies and eventually formed a college when the Empire's Diet was institutionalized in 1495. In addition, the town councils (*Städtetage*) which were held among the free and imperial cities from 1471 onwards to better reconcile their positions shed new lights on tax plans. In 1471, at the Diet of Regensburg, and again in 1474 at the Diet of Augsburg, an ambitious project for a war tax against the Turks was discussed; it combined military aid based on a matrikel (*kleine Hilfe*, 10,000 men on horseback and on foot) and monetary aid (*Grosse Hilfe*, supposed to provide for the upkeep of 60,000 men), in the form of a common penny throughout the Empire or a tenth penny on the estate. The preamble to the 1474 text shows the extent to which theoretical thinking on taxation was informed by Roman law and scholastic moral economy, i.e. taxation must be general and rely on all states to be fair. Tax burdens should be carried according to individual capacities and demands should be tailored to needs. However, there was a long way to go from the principle to the reality. In September 1471, 43 towns directly represented at the Frankfurt assembly declined the granting of the tenth penny. The Rhenish cathedral chapters (Cologne, Mainz, Trier) and the Count of Palatinate joined the refusal front. In 1471, as well as in 1474, the project never materialized. This was also the case in 1486 with a proposed estate tax in connection with the Hungarian War, and in 1492 with a hearth tax ordinance.[62]

The Common Penny (*Gemeiner Pfennig**) was the last concrete attempt to levy a general direct tax throughout the Empire. It arose from the meeting of the states and the first imperial diet (*Reichstag*), the Diet of Worms (from 2 February 1495).[63] While King Maximilian wanted to fund the war against the Turks and the campaign against Charles VIII in Italy, the imperial states, which supported constitutional reform, demanded a quid pro quo, and tied the tax to structural political changes. To guarantee lasting peace (*Ewiger Landfrieden*) and to provide for the maintenance of the Imperial Court of Justice (*Reichskammergericht*), the definition of a common penny (*Gemeiner Pfennig**) was agreed upon, and the principle of this was adopted on 7 August 1495. The ordinance[64] envisaged a universal tax much less ambitious than the 1471–1492 plans; it was due annually for a period of only four years. Every man or woman over 15 years of age in the Empire, noble, cleric or layman, had to contribute. A capitation tax of 1/24 guilder – the equivalent of half a day's wage for a construction journeyman, and therefore a rather modest tax – was charged to the less well off (*armer Volk, gemain person*).[65] The head of the fiscal hearth was required to collect it for the members of the household, including the household staff. For the sake of some semblance of fiscal fairness, the taxes varied according to one's estate. Those whose fortune exceeded 500 Rhineland guilders had to pay ½ guilder; above 1,000 guilders, the payment was one guilder, to which a free contribution could be added.[66] In any case, taxpayers were required to estimate their estates by considering not only real estate assets but also unearned incomes and profits. Princes, prelates and counts could give more out of grace and charity (*Standessteuer*, tax according to rank). The Jews were still subjected to the heavy one-guilder personal tax, irrespective of their ages, which was only mitigated by the possibility of a community distribution.

Despite its moderate weight and the room left for voluntary payment, the *Gemeiner Pfennig** faced opposition. Leading princes such as the dukes of Upper and Lower Bavaria, the Count of Palatinate, imperial knights, or the Confederates[67] refused to contribute to the tax. The *Gemeiner Pfennig*★ was established by imperial states that did not represent the full spectrum of the society or the entire political landscape of the German Empire. It also implied setting up a direct link between the Ruler, who was the collector, and the inhabitants of the Empire. However, many territorial forces were committed to subsidiarity and full authority over their subjects. Elsewhere, authorities were prepared to contribute only if the territorial states agreed. Many knights of the empire grumbled about a "forced" tax, which they thought was undue for those already contributing as soldiers. The late appointment of the masters of the imperial treasury in April 1497 did not ease the situation. It was not until that year that the collection became effective. The operation was to be deployed by commissions within the parish, then supervised in each territory (*Land*) by a commissioner; all the money was supposed to reach the treasury chamber in Frankfurt which was under the control of the king and six treasury masters representing the members of the Empire (electors, princes, prelates, counts and barons, knighthoods, free cities, and imperial cities). However, each one implemented it with its own means, i.e. municipal or pulpit announcements, collections by parish priests or neighbourhood leaders in the cities.[68] The Ruler received the money directly from his estate lands and from several northern entities. The *Buch der Gebrechen*,[69] which recorded issues faced, shows how little information the senior officers received. It also shows that beyond the principle of a universal tax or the – modest – amounts demanded, issues of competence and power were at stake. The protests or refusals to pay resulted less from the *Gemeiner Mann* rebelling against the imperial or taxing authority than from issues of orders given by lords or officers. The link is very clear in cases where competences and rights were intertwined. In 1497, the authority that claimed to raise the *Gemeiner Pfennig*★ in these circumstances asserted a new power and set a precedent that other lords were quick to reject. Thus, the bishopric of Heidelberg, the Dominican convents of Wimpfen and Heidelberg, and the monastery of Schönau opposed the levying of the Common Penny by the *Hochstift* of Worms on their citizens. In the territory of the imperial city of Ulm, the city authorities faced strong resistance, because the Empire knighthood and the Bavarian dukes had ordered their subordinates not to pay the *Gemeiner Pfennig*★ to the cities. The small nobility appeared to be even more determined in refusing to allow another lord to collect the money – even though this would be paid into the Frankfurt imperial coffers – as its seigneurial authority was wavering in the face of the assertion of princely or urban territories. The fact that the rights over many people and areas were not homogeneous provoked a refusal from those who did not want to lose authority over their constituents. Conversely, those who had the power to enforce the collection, based on even limited seigneurial land or ban rights, put new pawns on the chessboard. The imperial city of Nuremberg, which had already built up a homogeneous territory, recorded few refusals, apart from the imperial villages of Sennfeld and Gochsheim, which claimed to be under the protection of the Hennebergs – members of the Franconian knighthood. Records show only three rebels, who were in an area where the Franconian knights had rights and did not subject their subordinates to the *Gemeiner Pfennig*★. It should also be noted that the 1497 collection was an opportunity for the Nuremberg authorities to get to know the population fairly better. Whereas the registers of ordinary direct taxation, i.e. the *Losung*★ registers, merely recorded the taxpayer's oath taking, the *Reichssteuerregister* provides entries according to districts and commanderies in the city, or captaincies and *Orten* in the territory, with the name of the head of the hearth, the amount paid if a taxpayer's estate exceeded 500 guilders and the number of people who paid the capitation. Although still limited when compared to the data recorded in the princely tax lists of Ansbach or Kulmsbach, probably because the principle of self-assessment based on one's own conscience prevailed, this information already represents an important step away from the secrecy which was usually offered to the Nuremberg taxpayer.

Eventually, between 1497 and 1499, ecclesiastical powers and free and imperial cities (15,807 guilders in total for the cities) were the ones that mainly paid the Common Penny. Among others, the Bishop of Würzburg delivered 2,878 guilders to the imperial treasury in Frankfurt; the principality of Ansbach-Kulmbach gave 2,850 guilders; Nuremberg and its territory, 2,326 guilders; Ulm and Strasbourg, around 1,100 guilders; Cologne and Lübeck, around 1,000 guilders each. The electors who paid include the Archbishop of Mainz. In total, the campaign yielded about half of the expected 300,000 guilders (63,377, and then 93,377 guilders). Little of this money went to the maintenance of the new imperial institutions (10,000 guilders for the *Reichskammergericht*). This experiment with a direct and universal imperial tax was the last, despite some attempts in the sixteenth century to fund the war against the Turks.[70]

Was the episode a fiscal failure? The response from members of the Empire was not insignificant, and though the amounts collected did not meet the objectives set, the same was true of taxes using matrikels. The *Gemeiner Pfennig** seems to have failed because it was seen as a potential "permanent ground rent". However, the political impact must also be considered. Collection issues, far from being incidental as they led to an increase in the collector's power, aggravated the state of fragile local balances in all the *non-clausum* territories of the German Empire.[71] And there were many of them ... There was some contradiction in promoting perpetual peace in the Empire, on the one hand, and fuelling the fire for a few pennies on the other: much ado about nothing... because the amounts collected could not guarantee the running of the new central imperial institutions. The Empire and the imperial states (*Reichsstände*) therefore reverted to the traditional feudal system without a direct fiscal link between the Ruler and most of the inhabitants of the Empire. The imperial matrikel system, and later the *Römermonat* system, prevailed.

The term *Reichsmatrikel* developed in the second half of the sixteenth century. However, the principle of listing the imperial forces and what they were to provide in terms of contingents and/or replacement tax for imperial aid (*Reichshilfe*) preceded the use of the concept. The Matrikel was introduced at a time when the Empire states and diets were not yet established, and it was far from clear that all the forces listed were "liable for the Empire's army". In the context of the Empire institutional reform starting in the second quarter of the fifteenth century, enrolment in the Matrikel meant a duty to contribute, largely established by higher states (ruler, electors, and princes); conversely, the Matrikel confirmed that those enrolled had a direct link with the Empire (*Reichsunmittelbarkeit*), which was sought even by those who did not wish to contribute to the extent of what was demanded.

The matrikels drawn up in 1422[72] and 1431 to assemble and maintain the troops needed for the war against the Hussites required, on behalf of the Empire, forces that until then owed feudal service to the king and those that had or had had a seigneurial relationship with him. It took the argument of compelling necessity (*inevitabilis necessitas*) and of safeguarding Christianity to legitimize such a procedure. In 1422, 1431, 1456, 1467, 1471 and 1480, there were successive requests for military aid that used the imperial Matrikel to fund wars to defend Christianity, first against the Hussites and then against the Turks. After the *Gemeiner Pfennig** in 1495–1499, the diets returned to using matrikels in 1505, 1507, 1510 and 1521.[73] The register drawn up at the Diet of Worms in 1521 took on a referential value because it was linked to the Italian imperial coronation project (which turned out to be the last one). It went hand in hand with establishing a money equivalent of military contributions, the *Römermonat* or "Roman Month". It corresponded to the amount required for the monthly maintenance of a soldier during the imperial coronation expedition, estimated at 4 guilders per infantryman and 12 per horseman. The alternative cash tax, a principle already accepted and negotiated by the members of the Empire, became a supplementary tax that could be added to the military aid. The amounts given were henceforth also expressed in Roman months. Thus, Charles V requested 73 ½ Roman months during his reign. Nevertheless, the imperial states fought throughout the sixteenth century to ensure that the contribution of armed men prevail. They succeeded in making imperial taxes (*Reichssteuern*) conditional on their consent and participation; the taxes remained extraordinary and defined for a given expenditure. In 1555, in Augsburg, the decision was made once and for all that the collection of taxes should not be carried out by imperial administrative bodies, but by those who consented, namely the princes and the free and imperial cities. The matrikel principle let the imperial states determine the basis of what they paid as imperial "service". They became intermediaries with obligations between the Ruler and the inhabitants of the Empire. Within their territories, princes could set up their own collection procedures and collect funds that went far beyond imperial demands. Estates in princely territories (*Landstände*), if any, nevertheless demanded a proper tax request, a consent process, and control over the use of the money, which was still often granted by princes in the sixteenth century.[74] As a result, the setting up of a matrikel was also a territorial issue, as the situation in the Anterior Austria (*Vorderösterreich*) shows, among other examples. In 1445/46, Duke Albrecht VI of Habsburg introduced a general contribution (*Landschatzung*) to fund the Zurich War. He then drew up for the first time a list of required forces which mentioned councillors, rural nobles, as well as offices (*Ämter*) and towns by geopolitical entities. The list was then used as a basis for convening estates assemblies and levying territorial taxes. The country states became truly structured in 1469 at the Neuenburg assembly; the list, which was reorganized, mentioned the forces of the territory according to three curiae (prelates, knights, country = *Landschaften*), which had now been formalized.[75]

As much as the history of imperial fiscal experimentation can be told in a linear fashion, it is difficult to account for the countless fiscal practices and experiments carried out by cities or territorial lords. The city of Cologne resorted to a direct property tax only once (1371), but it repeatedly introduced new customs duties and indirect taxes on wine, beer, bread, spices, etc. In the end, there were more than 150 different excise duties, of which wine taxation took the lion's share and accounted for about 10 per cent of the municipal revenue. Each stage, from the arrival of the wine by ship to its consumption, was an opportunity to levy taxes; one excise tax was levied on imports, another was a duty on corks, etc. The taxation of beer between 1370 and 1513 took six different forms, which were largely combined: a production tax (*Bierpfennig*), a tax on consumption in drinking establishments (*Malzpfennig*), a tax on domestic consumption (*Bürgermalzpfennig*, from 1414 onwards), a tax paid by professional brewers (*Brauermalzpfennig*), a customs duty on imported beers, and then in 1471 a *Keuteakzise*[76] on dark beers (*Rotbier*, without hops).

Similar ingenuity was used to broaden the tax base and make larger parts of the urban population contribute while respecting differences in status. In the small imperial city of Colmar, the council introduced a tax that was meant to be "common" in 1424. It was payable by the citizens and peasants, clerics, and nobles. A complex combination was devised, which combined indirect cash taxation on individual wine consumption and on wheat for milling. The wealthier people were taxed on the possession of steeds, horses, and valets, according to their estate. As for corporation members deprived of a horse, they were required to purchase basic commodities for the community. However, the implementation did not withstand a revolt.

With this maze of fiscal demands from the territories and cities, it may be difficult to identify the key moments of fiscal innovation. Nevertheless, the search for new fiscal means seems to have been intense in the years 1470–1500. In 1476, twenty or so towns consulted on their tax system by the Fribourg municipal secretary testified to the inventiveness of this period and the proliferation of war taxes (*Reissteuer*). In Meran, a city under the control of the Duke of Austria, in addition to the ordinary city tax (*Stadsteuer*) of 121 marks per year, the inhabitants provided two extraordinary subsidies in a year, one by fiscal hearth, the other in the form of a graduated capitation according to their estate, on behalf of the necessity of war.

Rather than multiplying case studies, Georg Vogeler has chosen to take an original approach to taxation in German territories, which we can follow here, knowing that an equivalent for cities is still missing.[77] At the territorial level, recording taxes in books and registers started between 1350 and 1535, whereas initially generic amounts or tax lists were kept only on loose sheets or rolls.[78] These books seem to reveal processes if attempts are made to list, describe, date and locate them. Georg Vogeler has identified 677 of them devoted to extraordinary taxes and dating from before 1535, while 16 are known only in the form of copies and 83 attested but not preserved. The inventory reveals enormous discrepancies, for example between the single copy of the Landgraviate of Thuringia and the 133 books of the Duchy of Bavaria-Landshut. At the top of the list are the Duchy of Gelderland in the Netherlands (163), followed by the Duchy of Bavaria-Landshut (133), the Duchy of Brunswick-Luneburg (57), the Duchy of Mecklenburg (44) and the Habsburg territories (39); many territories have only one or two volumes, if any. The earliest territories to keep tax lists on loose sheets like Tirol were not the quickest to create and keep books. However, this documentary form attests to an overall, cumulative fiscal management (it groups together several geographical areas and/or the taxes paid by different members of a territory – clergy, nobility, towns, flat countries, etc.). Political entities that kept books the most, used older volumes as a reference within a serial administrative practice. Yet, as seen with the few names mentioned above, they are very few. In the imperial territories of the Late Middle Ages, fiscal administration was in its infancy. Everywhere, bookkeeping did not start until after 1350, and the real development of the *Steuerbücher* took place in the second half of the fifteenth century, with 226 books for 1451–1475 and 168 in the last quarter of the century (/677), with a peak in 1480 before a slump. The discrepancies are also seen at regional level. The presence and preservation of tax books occurred earlier and was more significant in western areas such as the Duchy of Gelderland. In the Duchy of Bavaria-Landshut, which is the second-largest territory in terms of the number of books preserved, there are only 14 documents before 1450, and 124 books in the second half of the fifteenth century. The eastern and north-eastern territories joined the move even later. Out of 44 books, the Duchy of Mecklenburg only has three dating back to a time before 1450. A careful external and internal serialized critique provides a blueprint for the standard territorial *Steuerbuch*. It is oblong and consists of 18 sheets of paper organized in one or two sections. Introduced by *Item*, entries are organized line by line, in the vernacular. They mention the taxpayer's name, with an amount opposite the name. The headings include amounts, but totals are rare. For whoever is familiar with French or Italian tax books, the portrait painted is striking for its economy of language: the introductory remarks are brief and do not contain long discourses legitimizing the power of the prince and even less so the fiscal role of the states. The *Steuerbücher* do not elaborate much on the nature of the tax either. The rate is rarely specified, and the same is true for the tax bases. The traces of use refer to two processes, i.e. collection and counting.

Of all the territorial entities making up the German Holy Roman Empire (excluding cities), the large number of powers that have kept only one or two books shows the extent to which, apart from the consolidated manorial and property taxes, the authorities only approached taxation in extraordinary and transitory forms, even in their written practices. The increased presence of tax books at the end of the fifteenth century may not be seen as an immediate reflection of an increase or acceleration of tax demands at that time. However, it does point to several mixed phenomena being at play in the second half of the fifteenth century: increased use of extraordinary taxation to meet unmet financial needs; officers who were more accountable to the supervisory authority or to the assemblies of states; and exceptional cases in which more regular management is used for extraordinary situations, etc.

At the end of the Middle Ages, and at least until the seventeenth century, the powers in the German Holy Roman Empire, including the royal and imperial powers, devised forms of taxation that remained limited in time, occasional and complex, to identify what the various social actors could each agree to. Urban populations as well as territorial or imperial assemblies maintained the idea that spending and its related tax demands must be necessary, that there may be other means of finding money, that "frugality is the best tax"; this accounts for the flexibility of the framework. Tax was not envisaged to become institutionalized; this can be seen in the fact of not preserving tax books, using sparingly written document, or fearing an *ewigen Tribut*, as mentioned during imperial assemblies. It remained often associated with oaths, self-declaration, or payment "according to one's conscience". It was a matter related to circumstances and context: "Where treasure is small and the country rich, little must be demanded of the prince and more of the country, and vice versa", according to the conclusions of the Diet of 1510. Given such pragmatism, there has probably been too little examination of practices, concrete methods of collection, actors involved in collections, or routes for the money collected. Do these records depict lasting structures, lines of conflict, as the *Gemeiner Pfennig*'s* collection unveiled? Flexibility and illegibility, whether voluntary or produced by the geographical interweaving of powers in the Empire, characterizes the powers and spaces considered. Ultimately, the epistemological challenge lies in refraining from forcing an interpretation when it comes to giving an account of it.

Notes

* I would like to thank Komi Adogli (Faculté des sciences historiques, Université de Strasbourg) for the translation and the research centre UR3400/ARCHE for its financial support.
1 BULST, "Impôts et finances publiques", pp. 65–76; ISENMANN, "The Holy Roman Empire in the Middle Ages", pp. 243–280; ISENMANN, "Medieval and Renaissance Theories", pp. 21–52. See in the same book: ORMROD and BARTA, "The Feudal Structure", pp. 73–75; ISENMANN, "Prinzipien", pp. 153–184; ROWAN, "Imperial Taxes and German Politics", pp. 203–217.
2 ISENMANN, "Reichsfinanzen und Reichssteuern", pp. 1–76 and 129–218; SCHMID, "Reichssteuern", pp. 153–198.
3 With additional references, RENAULT, *La permanence de l'extraordinaire*.
4 SCHUMPETER, "La crise de l'État fiscal"; OESTREICH, "Ständetum und Staatsbildung", pp. 277–289; KRÜGER, *Finanzstaat Hessen*.
5 DROEGE, "Die finanzielle Grundlagen", pp. 145–161.
6 About towns and taxation, ISENMANN, *Die deutsche Stadt* [2nd expanded edition 2012, first edition Stuttgart, 1988]; FUHRMANN, "Die Bedeutung direkter und indirekter Steuern", pp. 801–818.
7 Numerous studies on taxation during the Modern Period, see RENAULT, *La permanence de l'extraordinaire*; RAUSCHER, "Systèmes fiscaux, dettes et emprunts", pp. 81–100; SCHWENNICKE, "Ohne Steuer kein Staat".
8 e.g.: BRENNECKE, *Die ordentlichen direkten*; ZEUMER, *Die deutschen Städtesteuern*; KIRCHGÄSSNER, *Das Steuerwesen der Reichstadt Konstanz*.
9 SAHM, *Theorie und Ideengeschichte*; ISENMANN, "Reichsstadt und Steuern im Spätmittelalter"; *Steuern, Abgaben und Dienste*; REINER, *Zum Teufel*; SCHOMBURG, *Lexikon der deutschen Steuer*.
10 *Das Steuerbuch der Stadt Ingolstadt von 1463*; *Die Steuerbücher der Stadt Konstanz*; *Das Reichssteuerregister von 1497 der Reichsstadt Nürnberg*; *Das Reichssteuerregister von 1497*, 1985; *Das Reichssteuerregister von 1497*, 1988.
11 ROWAN, "The Common Penny", pp. 148–164; BLICKLE, "Gemeiner Pfennig und Obrigkeit (1495)", pp. 180–193; SCHMID, *Der Gemeine Pfennig von 1495*; ISENMANN, "Reichsfinanzen und Reichssteuern".

12 Scott, *Die Freiburger Enquete von 1476*.
13 Buchholzer-Remy, "Participation ou exemption fiscale des clercs", pp. 251–272; Le Roux, "Les comptabilités collectorales en terres d'Empire".
14 Renault, *La permanence de l'extraordinaire*; *Stimme der ewigen Verlierer?*
15 *Methods in Premodern Economic History*.
16 https://stadtbuecher.de/
17 This way was initiated for accounting or tax books of the German territorial states. See Vogeler, "Financial and Tax Reports", pp. 1775–1784; Vogeler, "Tax Accounting", pp. 235–254; Mersiowsky, *Die Anfänge territorialer*.
18 Renault, *La permanence de l'extraordinaire*, p. 17.
19 Vogeler, "Teil 1: Überlieferung und hilfswissenschaftliche Analyse", pp. 165–295 (see p. 166), Vogeler, "Teil 2: Funktionale Analyse und Typologie", pp. 57–204.
20 The "Reichsmatrikul" of 1521 is edited in *Deutsche Reichstagsakten*, Jüngere Reihe [RTA, JR], 2, 1896, pp. 424–442 and in *Quellensammlung*, pp. 313–317. Duhamelle, "Reichsmatrikel".
21 See Duhamelle, "Landtag".
22 In the eleventh century, from Henry II to Henry IV, 54 counties were granted to bishops as compensations for service provided to the king (*Königsdienst*). Such governing procedure of the Empire lasted as long as the Ruler was seen as the Lord's anointed, but it came to a halt with the conflict between Henry IV, the papacy and part of the imperial church.
23 Weinfurter, *Das Jahrhundert der Salier*, p. 70.
24 von Below, "Die älteste deutsche Steuer", pp. 622–662; Bosl, "Schutz und Schirm, Rat und Hilfe", pp. 43–52; Erler, "Bede", col. 346–348; Thier, "Bede", pp. 494–496; Isenmann, *Die deutsche Stadt*, p. 173; Schomburg, *Lexikon*, p. 36.
25 Erler, *Bürgerrecht und Steuerpflicht*; *Neubürger im späten Mittelalter*.
26 See Glossary, Judensteuer, Güldener Opferpfennig, Judenkrönungsgeld; Suchy, "Vom *Güldenen Opferpfennig*", pp. 114–129.
27 Ormrod and Barta, "The Holy Roman Empire", pp. 73–75.
28 Except in a few cases. See Isenmann, *Die deutsche Stadt*, pp. 111–113; Moraw, "Reichsstadt, Reich und Königtum", pp. 385–424 and p. 412.
29 Zeilinger, *Verhandelte Stadt*.
30 Finsterwalder, *Elsässische Stadtrechte III*, pp. 26–31. The levying of these indirect taxes was apparently linked to the construction of fortifications in several of these localities.
31 *Constitutiones, Monumenta Germaniae Historica*, 3, ed. Jakob Schwalm, 1904–1905, pp. 1–5; Isenmann, "Reichssteuerverzeichnis von 1241", p. 640; Zeumer, *Die deutschen Städtesteuern*; Kirchner, "Die Steuerliste von 1241", pp. 64–104; Vogeler, "Tax Accounting", pp. 238–239.
32 Becker, *Geschichte der Reichslandvogtei im Elsass*; Landwehr, *Die Verpfändung*; Schubert, *König und Reich*; Sehring, *Die finanziellen Leistungen*.
33 *Civitas imperii* is an expression occasionally used for Vienna and Lübeck, for example, during the reign of Frederick II. The denomination got widespread after 1273.
34 Monnet, "Des villes allemandes", pp. 20–68, see p. 49.
35 M.G.H., *Constitutiones* 2, pp. 241–247 (latin), n° 196, pp. 248–263 (German). See Buchholzer, "Ungeld, Umgeld, Ohmgeld, Angal", pp. 27–40; B. Tlusty, "Full Cups, Full Coffers", pp. 1–28; Angermeier, "Landfriedenspolitik", pp. 167–186.
36 Lackner, "Finanzwesen der Herzogen", pp. 284–300. Innkeepers and tenants of drinking establishments paid the tax, but made up for the loss of revenue by passing it on to consumers. They kept prices unchanged but adjusted on capacity measures. Extraordinary territorial taxes that were levied from 1390 onwards went along with the formation and consultation of states which gradually took shape from 1402 onwards in Austria, but only emerged during the second half of the fifteenth century in former Austrian territories.
37 Many of these early lists are only known through mentions. The first preserved lists of taxpayers were drawn up in the Tirol around 1274–1277. They are entitled *steura* (taxes), provide the day of taxation, the names and tax amounts. That of Imst for 1275 bears *dabit* "has given". It was probably used to draw up a statement of outstanding dues.
38 See M. G. H., *Scriptores*, vol. 17 [MGH SS, 17], ed. Georg Heinrich Pertz, Hannover, 1861, pp. 193–202 and 196.
39 *Urkundenbuch der Stadt Strassburg*, ed. Wilhelm Wiegand, vol. 1, Strasbourg, 1879, n° 471, pp. 355–356.

40 ZEILINGER, *Verhandelte Stadt*.
41 In the north and east, royal domain property was entrusted to the Dukes of Saxony and Brunswick and to the Margrave of Brandenburg. Rudolf's power did not extend much beyond the Cologne-Erfurt line. However, he sought to assert the imperial status of the cities of Goslar, Dortmund and Lübeck.
42 *MGH SS*. 17, p. 254, p. 211 ff. The statement is based primarily on analyses by Karl Zeumer who generalized from a few cases. ZEUMER, *Die deutschen Städtesteuern*. Zeumer also mentions an attempt to tax merchants at 1/8 of their capital in 1279; KRIEGER, *Rudolf von Habsburg*, pp. 189–191; MARTIN, *Die Städtepolitik*, pp. 159–164.
43 Thus, in the fifteenth and sixteenth centuries, there were territorial estates (*Landstände*) consisting of three colleges (clerics, nobles, towns), or two (nobles and towns) or four (clerics, counts, knights, towns). It was possible for these estates to include representatives of the farming community, although this was very rare.
44 HÄLG-STEFFEN, "Habsburgisches Urbar", in *Dictionnaire historique de la Suisse (DHS)*, version of 10.10.2007, Online: https://hls-dhs-dss.ch/fr/articles/008954/2007-10-10/, [Accessed 31 December 2020]; *Das Habsburgische Urbar*, ed. Rudolf MAAG, 2 vol., 1894–1904; PARTSCH, *Die Steuern des Habsburger Urbars*.
45 LANDWEHR, *Verpfändung der deutschen Reichsstädte*.
46 NUGLISCH, *Das Finanzwesen*. See also NUGLISCH, "Das Finanzwesen", pp. 145–167. A. Nuglish estimates that the gifts Sigismund received from cities after his coronation amounted to 25,000 guilders.
47 The history of the depository banks, operating upstream of the treasury chamber in Frankfurt, is yet to be written. The imperial circles established in the sixteenth century took over the collection of imperial taxes, among other functions. In 1557, there were also two masters of the Imperial Penny, one in Leipzig for the imperial taxes of Upper and Lower Saxony, the other in Augsburg (which combined the tax revenues of the Upper and Lower Rhine circles, Franconia, Swabia and Bavaria). In theory, the contents of their coffers were delivered to the depository cities (*Legstädte*) of Regensburg, Augsburg, Nuremberg, and Leipzig. Prior to the existence of these institutions, the role of Nuremberg seems to have been established as early as the reign of Charles IV, but the list of other locations appears to be evolving, as evidenced by the locations of the *Reichssteuer* in the fifteenth and early sixteenth centuries. See RENAULT, *La permanence de l'extraordinaire*, pp. 45–50; von STROMER, *Oberdeutsche Hochfinanz*.
48 In hierarchical order, the Archbishop of Mainz, the Archbishop of Cologne, the Archbishop of Trier, the Elector of Bohemia, the Elector of Palatinate, Saxony, and Brandenburg.
49 *Deutsche Reichstagsakten*, Ältere Reihe [DRTA, ÄR], vol. 8: *Deutsche Reichstagsakten unter Kaiser Sigmund*, zweite Abtheilung, 1421–1426, ed. Dietrich KERLER, Gotha, 1883, p. 146 and ff.; *Deutsche Reichstagsakten*, Ältere Reihe, vol. 9: *Deutsche Reichstagsakten unter Kaiser Sigmund*, Dritte Abtheilung, 1427–1431, ed. Dietrich KERLER, Gotha, 1887, p. 151 and 591.
50 Among the municipal revenues of the year 1431, the *Baumeisterbücher* of Augsburg reported the collection of almost 194 golden guilders for the *Hussengeld*. BMB 35, Folio 14r, ed. Simone WÜRZ (26.04.2019), in *Digitale Edition der Augsburger Baumeisterbücher*, ed. Jörg ROGGE, unter informationswissenschaftlicher Mitarbeit von Radoslav Petkov, Michael Haft, Christiane Dressler und Torsten Schrade. https://lod.academy/bmb/id/bmb-bm-037r/1
51 DRTA, ÄR, 8, n° 135, p. 146.
52 DRTA, ÄR, 8, n° 145, pp. 156–166, before 30 August 1422.
53 Literally, spears. *Gleven* are cavalry units consisting of one equipped rider, with full armour, spear and weapon, and several jacks (1 to 4). *Schutzen* are units of shooters.
54 DRTA, ÄR, 8, n° 234, p. 274.
55 DRTA, ÄR, 8, n° 159, p. 181; ROWAN, "Imperial Taxes and German Politics", pp. 203–217; WERMINGHOFF, "Die deutschen Reichskriegssteuergesetze", pp. 1–111; ISENMANN, "Reichsfinanzen und Reichssteuern".
56 DRTA, ÄR, 9, n° 76, pp. 91–110.
57 On all the above, see DRTA, ÄR, 9, including Nos. 100, 102, 103 and 105, Nos. 208–215. The great variety of answers comes out of lists of those who paid or did not pay paid the *Hussensteuer*⋆ between 1428 and 1430; MORAW, "Der ‚Gemeine Pfennig'", pp. 130–42 and 136–138. There are not any general tax or accounting records for 1422 and 1427. But the authorities listed in the registers may have kept tax books related to this general tax demand. The city of Augsburg, for example, kept a special tax register for the *Hussitensteuer*.
58 Concerning the *Losung*, see BUCHHOLZER, "L'impôt direct à Nuremberg", pp. 195–217. Records of the *Losung* were kept for 1430. In October 1427, the council of Nuremberg ordered the contribution

of the entire population over 12 years of age for work on ditches. It was possible to personally carry out the chore or to pay a replacement fee of 20 *heller*/day. The list of contributors/taxpayers was set out in a special book, the *Grabenbuch* (1430). The names of house owners were listed, together with the number of people (aged above 12 years) living in the houses. The contribution was required for 10 years. The 1430 Grabenbuch thus mentions 15,488 people. See Paul SANDER, *Die reichsstädtische Haushaltung Nürnbergs*, Leipzig, 1902, pp. 346–347.
59 DRTA, 11, n° 144, pp. 277–279.
60 ROWAN, "Imperial Taxes and German Politics", pp. 214–214, based on ISENMANN, "Reichsfinanzen und Reichssteuern", pp. 131–154. The author reviews several expert opinions, such as that of Archbishop Jacob von Sirck of Trier to the other ecclesiastical electors in 1452–1453, or the opinions of the lawyer Martin Maier.
61 ISENMANN, "Reichsfinanzen und Reichssteuern".
62 DRTA, ÄR, 22, 2, 1999, n° 123a, pp. 810–813. The 1471 ordinance also provided for the taxation of income from ground rents, unearned incomes, capital, and labour. That of 1474 was even more complex and ambitious. See ISENMANN, "Reichsstadt und Steuern", pp. 26–30 and 154–190.
63 See SCHMID, *Der Gemeine Pfennig*; ISENMANN, "The Holy Roman Empire", pp. 243–280; ISENMANN, "Reichsfinanzen und Reichssteuern", pp. 190–218; MORAW, "Der Gemeine Pfennig", pp. 130–142.
64 See DRTA, Mittlere Reihe, *Deutsche Reichstagsakten unter Maximilian I*, vol. 5, ed. Heinz ANGERMEIER, 2 tomes, Göttingen, Vandenhoeck & Ruprecht, 1981, dedicated to the Diet of Worms in 1495, and *Deutsche Reichstagsakten unter Maximilian I*, vol. 6, ed. Heinz GOLLWITZER, Göttingen, Verlag Vandenhoeck & Ruprecht, 1979, for 1496–1498. The text of the ordinance can be found in ZEUMER, *Quellensammlung*, pp. 294–296.
65 1/24 Rhenish guilder, i.e. 10.5 pennies (252/24). Twenty-four people together would therefore give one guilder. This was low compared to other taxes. See BLICKLE, "Gemeiner Pfennig und Obrigkeit", pp. 180–193, here p. 192. Peter Blickle compares the payment per hearth in Weingarten in 1495, i.e. 1/5 fl, with what the monastery of Weingarten raised per month and per hearth to finance the war against Duke Ulrich of Wurttemberg in 1519, i.e. ½ guilder per month.
66 Accordingly, estates of more than 1,000 guilders or annuities of more than 50 guilders were only moderately taxed. Studies of the *Gemeiner Pfennig* registers, e.g. Nuremberg, show that additional voluntary contributions were not significant.
67 ZÄCH, "Gemeiner Pfennig", in *Historisches Lexikon der Schweiz (HLS)*, Version vom 23.11.2006. Online: https://hls-dhs-dss.ch/de/articles/013767/2006-11-23/, [10.12.2020].
68 Central registers do not exist, but various registers of the *Gemeiner Pfennig* (lists of taxpayers and amounts) have been kept at the local level. For example, for Mecklenburg, the principality of Ansbach-Bayreuth, Nuremberg. ENGEL, *Das Mecklenburgische Kaiserbederegister* and note 12. See also ROWAN, "The Common Penny", pp. 148–164, about the (often sketchy or incomplete) lists that exist in Frankfurt, i.e. 96 entities out of the 327 that constitute the empire.
69 *Buch der Gebrechen*, ca 1497, Stadtarchiv Frankfurt, Reichssachen-Nachträge 2449, Lagerort Kasten I, 2. The issues outlined concern mainly the south-west of Germany. However, the book also includes data on the Archbishopric of Worms, the Teutonic Order, the Bishopric of Fulda, Isenburg-Büdingen and the imperial cities.
70 ISENMANN, "Reichsfinanzen und Reichssteuern", pp. 195–198; ROWAN, "The Common Penny (1495–1499)", pp. 151 and 167.
71 https://saintempire.hypotheses.org/publications/glossaire/territorium
72 See RTA VIII, no. 145, register drawn up at the Diet of Nuremberg in July 1422.
73 SCHMIDT, *Der Städtetag in der Reichsverfassung*, p. 404 and ff.
74 In Bavaria, for example, the state assemblies met 33 times between 1514 and 1579, then only 6 times between 1579 and 1612, before being interrupted until 1669.
75 SPECK, *Die vorderösterreichischen Landstände*.
76 *Akzise* was the locally used term. In the more southern parts of the Empire, the term *Ungeld* or even *Böser Pfennig* was used. In Cologne, taxes did not suffice to cover the city's expenses in the fifteenth century; the city, therefore, made extensive use of life and perpetual annuities. See von MÜLLER, "Zwischen Verschuldung und Steuerreebellion", pp. 100–113, here 111–112.
77 VOGELER, "Spätmittelalterliche Steuerbücher".
78 The *Tiroler Raitbücher*, which are accounting books, mention tax amounts, starting from 1288. There are detailed but isolated lists giving names of taxpayers and amounts for Tirol and for the period 1274–1277. For the year 1286, the parish of St Columban in Cologne has a parchment scroll with an

organization by areas, streets, houses, names, tax dues and tax revenues. It was handled by two separate people, one of whom wrote down the names and verified the payment, the other of whom indicated the balance due.

References

Heinz ANGERMEIER, "Landfriedenspolitik und Landfriedenzgesetzgebung unter den Staufern", in *Probleme um Friedrich II*, ed. Josef FLECKENSTEIN, Sigmaringen, 1974, pp. 167–186.

Joseph BECKER, *Geschichte der Reichslandvogtei im Elsass. Von ihrer Errichtung bis zu ihrem Übergang an Frankreich 1273–1648*, Strasbourg, 1905.

Georg von BELOW, "Die älteste deutsche Steuer", in Georg von BELOW, *Probleme der Wirtschaftsgeschichte. Eine Einführung in das Studium der Wirtschaftsgeschichte*, Tübingen, 1920, pp. 622–662.

Peter BLICKLE, "Gemeiner Pfennig und Obrigkeit (1495)", in *Vierteljahresschrift für Sozial- und Wirtschaftsgeschichte*, 63, 1976, pp. 180–193.

Karl BOSL, "Schutz und Schirm, Rat und Hilfe als Voraussetzung von Steuer, Abgabe und Dienst im Mittelalter", in *Steuern, Abgaben und Dienste*, ed. Eckart SCHREMMER, Stuttgart, 1994, pp. 43–52.

Adolf BRENNECKE, *Die ordentlichen direkten Staatssteuern Mecklenburgs im Mittelalter*, Diss. Marburg, 1901.

Laurence BUCHHOLZER-REMY, "L'impôt direct à Nuremberg: de son établissement à son encaissement (XIIIe-XVe siècles)", in *Cahiers d'histoire*, 1999/2, 44, pp. 195–217.

Laurence BUCHHOLZER-REMY, "Participation ou exemption fiscale des clercs dans les villes de Haute-Allemagne (xive-xve siècle)", in *El Dinero de Dios. Iglesia y fiscalidad en el occidente medieval (siglos XIII-XV)*, ed. Denis MENJOT and Manuel SÁNCHEZ MARTÍNEZ, Madrid, 2011, pp. 251–272.

Laurence BUCHHOLZER-REMY, "Ungeld, Umgeld, Ohmgeld, Angal: discours sur une taxation indirecte (Haute-Rhénanie, Franche-Comté)", in *Cultures fiscales en Occident du Xe au XVIIe siècle. Études offertes à Denis Menjot*, ed. Florent GARNIER, Armand JAMME, Anne LEMONDE and Pere VERDÉS PIJUAN, Toulouse, 2019, pp. 27–40.

Neithard BULST, "Impôts et finances publiques en Allemagne au XVe siècle", in *Genèse de l'État moderne. Prélèvement et redistribution, Actes du Colloque à Fontevraud 1984*, ed. Jean-Philippe GENÊT and Michel LE MENÉ, Paris 1987, pp. 65–76.

Das Reichssteuerregister von 1497 der Reichsstadt Nürnberg (und der Reichspflege Weißenburg), ed. Peter FLEISCHMANN, Nuremberg, 1993.

Das Reichssteuerregister von 1497 des Fürstentums Brandenburg-Ansbach-Kulmbach unterhalb Gebürgs, ed. Gerhard RECHTER, Nuremberg, 1985.

Das Reichssteuerregister von 1497 des Fürstentums Brandenburg-Ansbach-Kulmbach oberhalb Gebürgs, ed. Gerhard RECHTER, Nuremberg, 1988.

Das Steuerbuch der Stadt Ingolstadt von 1463, ed. Rainer FUNK, Ingolstadt, 1969.

Die Steuerbücher der Stadt Konstanz, ed. Peter RÜSTER, vol. 1–3, Sigmaringen, 1959–1966.

Georg DROEGE, "Die finanzielle Grundlagen des Territorialstaats in West- und Ostdeutschland an der Wende vom Mittelalter zur Neuzeit", in *Vierteljahrschrift für Sozial- und Wirtschaftsgeschichte*, 53, 1966, pp. 145–161.

Christophe DUHAMELLE, "Reichsmatrikel", in *Glossaire des mots de l'Empire*, ed. Christophe DUHAMELLE, online, https://saintempire.hypotheses.org/publications/glossaire/reichsmatrikel [5 February 2021].

Christophe DUHAMELLE, "Landtag", in *Glossaire des mots de l'Empire*, ed. Christophe DUHAMELLE, online, https://saintempire.hypotheses.org/publications/glossaire/reichsmatrikel [5 February 2021].

Adalbert ERLER, *Bürgerrecht und Steuerpflicht im mittelalterlichen Städtewesen. Mit besonderer Untersuchung des Steuereides*, 2. ed., Francfort/Main, 1963 [1. ed., 1939].

Adalbert ERLER, "Bede", in *Handwörterbuch zur deutschen Rechtsgeschichte [HRG]*, ed. Adalbert ERLER and Paul Wilhelm FINSTERWALDER, *Elsässische Stadtrechte III, Colmarer Stadtrechte*, Heidelberg, 1938, n° 21 et 26, pp. 26–31.

Bernd FUHRMANN, "Die Bedeutung direkter und indirekter Steuern in ausgewählten Städten des Deutschen Reichs (Römischen Reichs) vom 14. bis ins 17. Jahrhundert", in *La fiscalità dell' economia europea secc. XIII-XVIII*, ed. Simonetta CAVACIOCCHI, Florence, 2008, pp. 801–818.

Franziska HÄLG-STEFFEN, "Habsburgisches Urbar", in *Dictionnaire historique de la Suisse (DHS)*, version of 10.10.2007, Online: https://hls-dhs-dss.ch/fr/articles/008954/2007-10-10/, [Accessed 31 December 2020].

Eberhard Isenmann, "Reichsfinanzen und Reichssteuern im 15. Jahrhundert", in *Zeitschrift für historische Forschung*, 7, 1980, pp. 1–76 and 129–218.
Eberhard Isenmann, "Medieval and Renaissance Theories of State Finance", in *Economic Systems and State Finance*, ed. Richard Bonney, Oxford, 1995, pp. 21–52.
Eberhard Isenmann, "Reichssteuerverzeichnis von 1241", *Lexikon des Mittelalters*, Munich, Zürich, 1977–1999, 7, 640.
Eberhard Isenmann, "The Holy Roman Empire in the Middle Ages", in *The Rise of the Fiscal State c. 1200-c. 1815*, ed. Richard Bonney, Oxford, 1999, pp. 243–280.
Eberhard Isenmann, "Prinzipien, Formen und Wirtschaftliche Auswirkungen von Besteuerung – Steuergerechtigkeit und Steuergleichheit im 15. Jahrhundert (Deutschland und Italien)", in *La fiscalità dell' economia europea secc. XIII-XVIII*, ed. Simonetta Cavaciocchi, Florence, 2008, pp. 153–184.
Eberhard Isenmann, *Die deutsche Stadt im Mittelalter 1150–1550: Stadtgestalt, Recht, Verfassung, Stadtregiment, Kirche, Gesellschaft, Wirtschaft*, Vienne, Cologne, 2014 [2nd expanded edition 2012, first edition Stuttgart, 1988].
Eberhard Isenmann, "Reichsstadt und Steuern im Spätmittelalter", in *Reichsstadt und Geld, 5. Tagung des Mühlhäuser Arbeitskreises für Reichsstadtgeschichte, Mühlhausen 27 Februar bis 1. März 2017*, ed. Michael Rothmann and Helge Wittmann, Petersberg, 2018.
Ekkehard Kaufmann, Ruth Schmid-Wiegand, vol. 1, Berlin, 1971, col. 346–348.
Bernhard Kirchgässner, *Das Steuerwesen der Reichstadt Konstanz 1418–1460. Aus der Wirtschafts- und Sozialgeschichte einer oberdeutschen Handelsstadt am Ausgang des Mittelalters* (=Diss. Jur. Freiburg i.Br. 1952), Constance, 1960.
Gero Kirchner, "Die Steuerliste von 1241. Ein Beitrag zur Entstehung des staufischen Königsterritoriums", in *Zeitschrift für Rechtsgeschichte Germ.*, N.F. 70, 1953, pp. 64–104.
Karl-Friedrich Krieger, *Rudolf von Habsburg*, Darmstadt, 2003.
Raphael Matthias Krug, *"Es ist doch zem Jungsten ein end daran": Die Augsburger Steuerbücher im Spätmittelalter (1346–1430) als Medium städtischer Verwaltung*, University Augsburg, 2006.
Kersten Krüger, *Finanzstaat Hessen 1500–1567. Staatsbildung im Übergang vom Domänenstaat zum Steuerstaat*, Marburg, 1980.
Christian Lackner, "Finanzwesen der Herzogen von Österreich in der zweiten Hälfte des 14. Jahrhunderts", in *Unsere Heimat, Zeitschrift des Vereins für Landeskunde von Niederösterreich*, Jahrgang 63/1992, Heft 4, pp. 284–300.
Götz Landwehr, *Die Verpfändung der deutschen Reichstädte im Mittelalter*, Köln/Weimar/Wien, 1987.
Amandine Le Roux, "Les comptabilités collectorales en terres d'Empire, des ressources documentaires pour l'étude des pratiques de l'écrit, d'une histoire institutionnelle et culturelle de la fiscalité pontificale", in *Comptabilité(s), Revue d'histoire des comptabilités*, 13, 2020.
Thomas Michael Martin, *Die Städtepolitik Rudolfs von Habsbourg*, Göttingen, 1976.
Mark Mersiowsky, *Die Anfänge territorialer Rechnungslegung im deutschen Nordwesten. Spätmittelalterliche Rechnungen, Verwaltungspraxis, Hof und Territorium*, Stuttgart, 2000.
Methods in Premodern Economic History. Case Studies from the Holy Roman Empire, c. 1300-c.1600, ed. Ulla Kypta, Julia Bruch and Tanja Skambraks, Palgrave Macmillan, 2019.
'Mit dem Zehnten fing es an'. Eine Kulturgeschichte der Steuer, ed. Uwe Schulze, Munich, 1986 [reprint 1992].
Pierre Monnet, "Des villes allemandes au XIIIe siècle", *Villes d'Allemagne au Moyen Âge*, ed. Pierre Monnet, Paris, 2004, pp. 20–68.
Peter Moraw, "Reichsstadt, Reich und Königtum im späten Mittelalter", in *Zeitschrift für Historische Forschung*, 6, 1979, pp. 385–424.
Peter Moraw, "Der ‚Gemeine Pfennig'. Neue Steuern und die Einheit des Reiches im 15. und 16. Jahrhundert", in *"Mit dem Zehnten fing es an". Eine Kulturgeschichte der Steuer*, ed. Uwe Schulze, Munich, 1986 [reprint 1992], pp. 130–142.
Achatz von Müller, "Zwischen Verschuldung und Steuerreebellion. Die mittelalterliche Stadt an den Beispielen Florenz und Köln", in *'Mit dem Zehnten fing es an'. Eine Kulturgeschichte der Steuer*, ed. Uwe Schulze, Munich, 1986 [reprint 1992], pp. 100–113.
Neubürger im späten Mittelalter. Migration und Austausch in der Städtelandschaft des alten Reiches (1250–1550), ed. Rainer C. Schwinges, Berlin, 2002.
Adolf Nuglisch, *Das Finanzwesen des Deutschen Reiches unter Kaiser Karl IV*, Inaugural-Dissertation, Strasbourg, 1899.
Adolf Nuglisch, "Das Finanzwesen des Deutschen Reichs unter Kaiser Sigmund", in *Jahrbücher für Nationalökonomie und Statistik*, ser. 3, vol. 21, 1901, pp. 145–167.

Gerhard OESTREICH, "Ständetum und Staatsbildung in Deutschland", in Gerhard OESTREICH, *Geist und Gestalt des frühmodernen Staates*, Berlin, 1969, pp. 277–289.

W. M. ORMROD and János BARTA, Chap. "The Feudal Structure and the Beginning of State Finance", "2.8. The Holy Roman Empire", in *Economic Systems and State Finance*, ed. Richard BONNEY, Oxford, 1995, pp. 73–75.

Gottfried PARTSCH, *Die Steuern des Habsburger Urbars*, Zürich, 1946.

Quellensammlung zur Geschichte der deutschen Reichsverfassung, ed. Karl ZEUMER, Tübingen, 1913.

Peter RAUSCHER, "Systèmes fiscaux, dettes et emprunts: le cas de la monarchie des Habsbourg (XVIe-XVIIIe siècle)", in *Ressources publiques et construction étatique en Europe* XIIIe-XVIIIe *siècle*, ed. Katia BEGUIN, Paris, 2015, pp. 81–100.

Sahm REINER, *Zum Teufel mit der Steuer! 5000 Jahre Steuern – ein langer Leidensweg der Menschheit*, Wiesbaden, 2012 [enlarged edition 2018].

Rachel RENAULT, *La permanence de l'extraordinaire. Fiscalité, pouvoirs et monde social en Allemagne aux* XVIIe-XVIIIe *siècles*, Paris, 2017.

Steven ROWAN, "The Common Penny (1495–1499) as a Source of German Social and Demographic History", in *Central European History*, 10/2, 1977, pp. 148–164.

Steven ROWAN, "Imperial Taxes and German Politics in the Fifteenth Century: An Outline", in *Central European History*, 13, 1980, pp. 203–217.

Reiner SAHM, *Theorie und Ideengeschichte der Steuergerechtigkeit*, Berlin, 2019.

Peter SCHMID, "Reichssteuern, Reichsfinanzen und Reichsgewalt in der ersten Hälfte des 16. Jahrhundert", in *Säkulare Aspekte der Reformationszeit*, ed. Heinz ANGERMEIER, Munich, Vienne, 1983, pp. 153–198.

Peter SCHMID, *Der Gemeine Pfennig von 1495. Vorgeschichte und Entstehung, verfassungsgeschichtliche, politische und finanzielle Bedeuntung*, Göttingen, 1989.

Georg SCHMIDT, *Der Städtetag in der Reichsverfassung. Eine Untersuchung zur korporativen Politik der freien und Reichsstädte in der ersten Hälfte des 16. Jahrhunderts*, Stuttgart, 1984.

Walter SCHOMBURG, *Lexikon der deutschen Steuer- und Zollgeschichte. Abgaben, Dienste, Gebühren, Steuern und Zölle von den Anfängen bis 1806*, Munich, 1992.

Ernst SCHUBERT, *König und Reich. Studien zur spätmittelalterlichen deutschen Verfassungsgeschichte*, Göttingen, 1979.

Joseph A. SCHUMPETER, "La crise de l'État fiscal", in Joseph A. SCHUMPETER, *Impérialisme et classes sociales*, Paris, 1984 [*Die Krise des Steuerstaats*, Leipzig, 1918].

Andreas SCHWENNICKE, *"Ohne Steuer kein Staat." Zur Entwicklung und politischen Funktion des Steuerrechts in den Territorien des Heiligen Römischen Reichs (1500–1800)*, Francfort, 1996.

Tom SCOTT, *Die Freiburger Enquete von 1476. Quellen zur Wirtschafts- und Verwaltungsgeschichte der Stadt Freiburg im Breisgau im fünfzehnten Jahrhundert*, Freiburg i. Breisgau, 1986.

Walter SEHRING, *Die finanziellen Leistungen der Reichsstädte unter Ruprecht von der Pfalz*, Diss. Phil. Greifswald, 1916.

Dieter SPECK, *Die vorderösterreichischen Landstände. Entstehung, Entwicklung und Ausbildung bis 1595/1602*, 2 vol., Fribourg/Brisgau, 1994.

Steuern, Abgaben und Dienste vom Mittelalter bis zur Gegenwart. Referate der 15. Arbeitstagung der Gesellschaft für Sozial- und Wirtschaftsgeschichte vom 14. bis 17. April 1993 in Bamberg, ed. Eckart SCHREMMER, Stuttgart, 1994.

Stimme der ewigen Verlierer? Aufstände, Revolten und Revolutionen in den österreichischen Ländern (c.1450–1815), ed. Peter RAUSCHER and Martin SCHEUTZ, Vienne-Munich, 2013.

Wolfgang von STROMER, *Oberdeutsche Hochfinanz 1350–1450*, Teil 1–3, Wiesbaden, 1970.

Barbara SUCHY, "Vom *Güldenen Opferpfennig* bis zur *Judenvermögensabgabe*. Tausend Jahre Judensteuer", in *Mit dem Zehnten fing es an. Eine Kulturgeschichte der Steuer*, ed. Uwe SCHULTZ, Munich, 1993, pp. 114–129.

Andreas THIER, "Bede", in *HRG*, ed. Albrecht CORDES, Heiner LÜCK, Dieter WERKMÜLLER and Ruth SCHMIDT-WIEGAND, vol. 1, 2nd revised edition, Berlin, 2008, pp. 494-496.

B. Ann TLUSTY, "Full Cups, Full Coffers: Tax Strategies and Consumer Culture in the Early Modern German Cities", in *German History*, 32, 1, 2014, pp. 1–28.

Georg VOGELER, "Spätmittelalterliche Steuerbücher deutscher Territorien, Teil 1: Überlieferung und hilfswissenschaftliche Analyse", in *Archiv für Diplomatik*, 49, 2003, pp. 165–295, "Teil 2: Funktionale Analyse und Typologie", in *Archiv für Diplomatik*, 50, 2004, pp. 57–204.

Georg VOGELER, "Tax Accounting in the Late Medieval German Territorial States", in *Accounting, business and financial history*, 15, 2005, pp. 235–254.

Georg Vogeler, "Financial and Tax Reports", in *Handbook of medieval studies. Terms-methods-trends*, ed. Albrecht Classen, Berlin, New York, 2010, pp. 1775–1s784.

Stefan Weinfurter, *Das Jahrhundert der Salier 1024–1125*, Ostfildern, 2008.

Albert Werminghoff, "Die deutschen Reichskriegssteuergesetze von 1422 und 1427 und die deutsche Kirche", in *Zeitschrift der Savigny-Stiftung für Rechtsgeschichte Kanonistische Abteilung*, 36, 1915, pp. 1–111.

Benedikt Zäch, "Gemeiner Pfennig", in *Historisches Lexikon der Schweiz (HLS)*, Version vom 23.11.2006. Online: https://hls-dhs-dss.ch/de/articles/013767/2006-11-23/, [10.12.2020].

Gabriel Zeilinger, *Verhandelte Stadt. Herrschaft und Gemeinde in der frühen Urbanisierung des Oberelsass vom 12. bis 14. Jahrhundert*, Ostfildern, 2018.

Karl Zeumer, *Die deutschen Städtesteuern, insbesondere die städtischen Reichssteuern im 12. und 13. Jahrhundert. Beiträge zur Geschichte der Steuerverfassung des Deutschen Reiches*, Leipzig, 1878.

13
PROVENCE AND SAVOY

Mathieu Caesar and Michel Hébert

Savoy and Provence, whose territories lie on the left bank of the Rhône river, over and across the southern Alps and reaching to the Mediterranean Sea, share a common history in the post-Carolingian era, forming the Kingdom of Arles in the tenth century. Loosely incorporated into the Holy Roman Empire, the two principalities diverged in their later evolution. Whereas the Counts of the House of Savoy maintained their control over the northernmost parts of the kingdom and the Piedmontese lands south of the Alps, the County of Provence fell under the lordship of the Counts of Barcelona, who would later become Kings of Aragon. By marriage and inheritance, the County of Provence was transferred to the French Angevin dynasty, through Charles I of Anjou (in 1246) and his offspring. Moreover, from the year 1266, the Angevin Counts of Provence were also crowned Kings of Sicily, although after the revolution of the Sicilian Vespers (1282), their actual dominion was reduced to the southern lands of the Italian peninsula (often incorrectly referred to as the Kingdom of Naples). The medieval county (more exactly, the Counties of Provence and Forcalquier) included the present-day French departments of the Bouches-du-Rhône, Var, Alpes-de-Haute-Provence, Alpes-Maritimes and parts of Vaucluse, in the vicinity of the influential papal Avignon (1309–1376).[1] The County and then Duchy (from 1416) of Savoy, meanwhile, grew out by incorporating various territories. Around the mid-fifteenth century, the principality included approximately the present-day French departments of Ain, Savoie and Haute-Savoie, Nice with its *arrondissement*, most of francophone Switzerland, the Valle d'Aosta and part of Piedmont.[2] Most of these territories were able to keep a certain degree of autonomy, which affected their taxation and relations with the prince over these matters.

Separated by the Principality of Dauphiné, which would be incorporated into the Kingdom of France in 1349, Savoy and Provence shared a common destiny, in that they were in many ways subject to the influence of the powerful French monarchs, their neighbours, albeit remaining politically independent until 1481 (Provence) or well into the modern era (Savoy). Their fiscal systems, distinct as they were, shared some common grounds, due mostly to the dominant role of Roman law and the political influence of Mediterranean polities, Iberian dominions or Italian city-states.

The Sabaudian financial administration developed considerably starting from the reorganization, partially inspired by the English model, and promoted by Count Pierre II during the 1250s,[3] whereas the combined Angevin and Catalan models, in addition to Church practices, influenced the development of the Provençal taxation and accounting systems.[4] For both territories, historians dispose of various types of accounts that are among the richest and best-preserved series for medieval Europe. The accounts of the general treasurers, the castellany rolls (in Savoy) and local treasurers (*clavarii*) accounts (in Provence), the accounts for the subsidies★ granted to the prince, the toll accounts and the proceedings of the assemblies of Estates are the most important and relevant series for a study of Sabaudian and Provençal princely taxation.[5]

In spite of – and in part because of – this abundance of archival material, historians have often used these sources solely as a reservoir of information for specific purposes, with limited attention to fiscal issues. Moreover, the fragmentation of medieval Savoy into three modern states (France, Italy and Switzerland) adds historiographical national – and sometimes even regional/local – cleavages.[6] Fortunately, some pathbreaking research has been undertaken during the past two decades: the castellany account rolls,[7] the war finances[8] and tolls[9] in Savoy, as well as the central and local accounting practices in Provence[10] have been examined in a renewed perspective. Unfortunately, these account-based studies tend to focus on limited financial or administrative issues. Much work remains to be done on taxation proper. Similar remarks apply to urban taxation, which has attracted little research interest with regard to the extant sources.[11] One must still leaf through studies on single cities to grasp information, and little has been done on a comparative level.[12]

Princely taxation

Across the Western world, the development of public forms of taxation under princely authority emerged from the lack of sufficient resources from traditional lordship and demesne at the turn of the fourteenth century. Additional revenue came through extraordinary subsidies★ and renewed forms of aid mostly related to the context of public warfare, resulting in a remarkable growth in institutionalized state taxation. In Provence and in Savoy, however, subsidies★ were but a supplementary form of taxation which contributed to the growth of princely revenue and to the institutionalization of its management. Traditional lordship and demesne revenues remained an essential resource for princely finances throughout the entire Middle Ages.

Provence

In Provence, in coping with the insufficiency of traditional revenue, the granting of war subsidies★ led to an early and remarkable development of political representation in the second half of the fourteenth century. Growing needs of princely households in the fifteenth century, however, gave rise to new forms of levies founded upon and nurturing a rising affirmation of princely regality.

Lordship and demesne

Founded upon a superior lordship nominally linked to the Holy Roman Empire but in fact independent from any form of actual control, the Counts of Provence in the Middle Ages collected various types of feudal revenues.[13] Traditional ownership rights provided various sources of income based either on people or on land (annual *census*). The coinage monopoly allowed the counts to benefit from minting practices and currency debasing. Economic duties included potentially profitable income from local commercial traffic (*lesda*★), or tolls and port dues established either on the Rhône river or on the busy overland routes connecting the thriving Northern and Central Italian cities to Avignon and beyond, to the French Languedoc and Iberian kingdoms.[14] Saltworks, in coastal cities such as Berre and Hyères, and taxation based on the salt trade (*gabella**) provided substantial profits and were closely monitored by watchful public officers.[15] Special levies applied collectively to urban or rural communities, either for the traditional lodging privilege (*fodrum*, known in Provence as *alberga**) or the strictly regulated military tax (*cavalcata**), both hearth taxes founded on local censuses.[16] Jews were also subject to a special tax (*tallia judeorum*), independently administered and collected by their own communities.[17]

Two additional public resources accounted for substantial revenue. The first ensued from the comital power to adjudicate. Considering that judicial sentencing was overwhelmingly rendered through fining, local and regional accounts testify to the significance of such income in the public treasury, accounting for as much as 20 to 30 per cent of total revenue.[18] The second ensued from the feudal aids levied on the four customary occasions, that of the knighting of a son, the marriage of a daughter, the payment of the lord's ransom and his crusading aid, as well as fifth and sixth locally specific forms of aid, for the count's visit to the emperor his overlord and for the purchase of a valuable piece of feudal land. Such aids were levied approximately two dozen times in the first half of the fourteenth century.[19]

Undoubtedly, these seigneurial and feudal assets were carefully managed. General surveys, such as those conducted by Count Charles of Anjou in 1252[20] or by Kings Charles II in 1297–1299[21] and Robert in 1333–1334,[22] could list in an orderly manner and assess the value of all the public holdings through an organized network of regional bailiwicks (*vicaria* and *bajulia*). Special decrees, such as that of Brignoles (1297), organized the collection, transmittal and maintenance of the princes' income through the institution of local (*clavarius*) and general (*thesaurarius*) treasurers.[23] In these same years was established a regional exchequer court (*curia camere*) based on similar institutions founded in contemporary Sicily and Catalonia.[24] The earliest assessment that can be made, through partial accounts and public inquiries, reports a cumulative income of approximatively 6,000–8,000 pounds around 1250, an indetermined part of which being provided by taxation strictly speaking.[25]

Public utility and early war subsidies

In spite of such careful provisions and the existence of a well-organized bureaucracy, traditional public income suffered from a threefold limitation. First, feudal income was related to personal ties and, for a good part, could only proceed from the count's vassals whose number varied according to historical tradition, personal status and the nature of each income category. Second, it was strictly dependent on customary tariffs that could not be adjusted to specific and rising needs. Third, in accordance with traditional principles of fiscal freedom, providing that princes should rely on their own estates, no new income (*novitas*) was lawful, if not expressly consented by subjects.

This last principle ("no taxation without representation") was by no means specific to medieval Provençal lands, emerging as it did from the English Magna Carta (1215) and numerous freedom charters granted in western medieval policies from the thirteenth century onward. But the road to political representation was not immediately opened. Arguably, the first (at the very least, the first well-documented) levy to overreach the above-mentioned limitations was the general subsidy* required by King Charles II in 1292.[26] Pressing financial needs related to a planned military campaign against the Aragonese kingdom, in the general context of the enduring rivalries opposing French and Angevin princes to their Iberian counterparts in the Western Mediterranean, prompted King Charles to call for a special form of aid, referred to as a subsidy* and based on clear references to the Romano-canonical notion of necessity (*necessitas*).

Through this argument, traditional limitations could be overridden, most notably the conventional exemptions of nobles and clergymen, and the levy could be considered truly general (*subsidium generale**). Acceptance, however, was tied to the uncoerced (theoretically, at least) nature of the tax and numerous chancery writs were issued to guarantee the non-prejudicial character of such a non-obligatory (*non ex debito*), freely consented (*ex gratia*) contribution from all three estates of society (nobility, clergy, and urban or rural communities). This important turning point marks the first establishment of a form of general and mandatory public taxation.

Political representation, closely tied to the granting of consent, was to appear almost simultaneously. Some early assemblies of the three Estates were convened, in 1286 and in 1302, for various reasons. But the first convocation directly related to the granting of consent for a military subsidy* was called in 1307 and, from then on, such assemblies became increasingly frequent. It should be noted that these early subsidies* were always granted separately by representatives of the three orders of society and that their gracious character was acknowledged by the granting of appropriate letters stating, as in one example dating from 1320, that an absence of princely recognition would be nothing less than absurdly indignant, ungrateful and injurious. These important milestones were but the first steps toward the establishment of a full-fledged tax system in the mid-fourteenth century.[27]

The emergence of a public tax system

The beginning of the Hundred Years War (1337–1453) opposing the French and English crowns, in conjunction with internal feudal rivalries and with repeated attempts to maintain and strengthen the Angevin hold on the Kingdom of Naples, created a state of almost permanent warfare in the County of Provence. The spread of mercenary armies – in 1357, 1361 and 1374, for instance – forced the mustering of local troops, far beyond the limited return of the traditional *cavalcata**. Furthermore, the dynastic crisis and civil war following the death of Queen Joanna I (1382–1387) and the organized plundering of the aristocratic bandit Raymond de Turenne (1390–1400) led to a permanent state of war that subsided only in the first decades of the fifteenth century.[28] The effect of these disruptions on the emergence of a public tax system was paramount. The convening of a great assembly of the three Estates in Aix-en-Provence in the autumn of 1359 was a true landmark in these developments. The assembly, acting as fully representative of the body politic and designating itself for the first time as the general council of the three Estates (*consilium generale trium statuum*), raised what might be considered the very first general, or "national", army, to be paid for by newly-instated taxes based on the traditional territorial districts. Such taxes were to be proportional to the general population, founded on the true numbers of hearths without distinction of social or clerical status. They would substitute for the traditional feudal levies. They would be collected by elected treasurers and their revenue would be managed by an elected committee formed by members of the three Estates, to the notable exclusion of any royal officer. The Estates were to be convened on a regular basis, from then on, to maintain regular supervision of the new tax system.[29]

The significance of such innovations can hardly be overstated. They established a public fiscal system, parallel to and independent from the traditional royal income and treasury. They freed tax collection from traditional limitations and, most importantly, they firmly tied the administration of public taxation to the institution of new and efficient forms of political representation.[30] The system, however, was not immediately and thoroughly instated, nor was it easily recognized by the sovereign princes. Over the following century, frequent reminders were made of the obligation of consent to any form of new taxation by the body of an elected assembly.[31] But all in all, it proved itself efficient in the long run. The Estates met over a hundred times in the years 1350–1450, granting new subsidies* in most if not all occasions.[32] They obtained in exchange a right to petition their kings on a variety of subjects on the basis of a quid pro quo, trading financial aid for graceful government in a manner very similar to that which developed in contemporaneous England or Aragon. At the height of their activity in the mid-fifteenth century, the average annual subsidy* granted by the Estates reached approximately 40,000 florins, a significant part of a princely revenue otherwise (and quite unfortunately) hardly measurable. These amounts, naturally, weighed heavily on town finances, and it will be shown hereafter to which degree they contributed to the development of municipal tax systems.

New forms of taxation

The newly established public tax system, being under the control of the Estates, however productive in revenue, did not directly favour the princes' financial situation. As early as the first quarter of the fifteenth century, the Angevin kings sought to gain some fiscal autonomy by a series of innovative measures, all sharing a common intent, to bypass or override the popular control on public revenue.[33] The first and by far the most effective measure consisted in the massive development of public credit by resorting to the abundant financial resources of the Italian merchants established in Avignon. By discounting the product of the anticipated public subsidies* and enabling these creditors to collect the local revenue in the form of a public debt, the princes not only received lump sums of money when required, but most importantly, they could have these sums managed by their own treasurers, thereby causing the disappearance of the institutional framework (collectors, treasurers, auditors) established by the Estates in the previous decades.[34] This in turn resulted in a marked decline in the convening of the Estates. From the years 1450 until the end of the century, they were seldom assembled and their functions were in large part replaced by face-to-face negotiations between princely officers and singular towns whose bargaining power was, obviously, far diminished.

Other imaginative means of collecting revenue were introduced in the course of the fifteenth century. In 1441, King René of Anjou established general customs duties of 6 per cent on the value of all incoming and outgoing merchandises to and from the County of Provence, by land or by sea. Having caused a general outcry, for not being submitted to the consent of the Estates, and probably also because the collection of such duties was hard to enforce, this measure was almost immediately dismissed. Some other initiatives, while not pertaining to taxation strictly speaking, constitute an assortment of measures intended to line the princes' coffers and, as such, they complement an ever-evolving public tax system. These parafiscal levies fall into two different categories. First, in line with the enduring practice of solemn pageants celebrating the first or triumphant entries of kings and princes into their prominent cities and towns, some members of the royal family occasionally took advantage of this custom and of the accompanying gifts offered by the "joyous" subjects to tour the country and collect their gracious offerings. In the case of the tours organized by and for Queen Margaret of Anjou in 1434 and Prince John of Calabria in 1443, it is a fact that not only were the offerings directly proportional to the visited towns' populations, but also that previous negotiations with princely officers had greatly contributed to the fixing of these amounts.[35] The same can be said of the visitations of specially mandated commissioners for the reformation of justice. Touring the Provençal towns in 1447 and again in 1449, these officers, disinclined to enter into the hardships of a true process of reformation, negotiated (sometimes prior to their arrival) the payment of lump sums, again proportional to the towns' populations, in exchange for the granting of letters of general pardon.[36] Such initiatives, without doubt, constituted forms of special taxation and their effect, combined with that of the granting of subsidies*, weighed heavily on the local finances and the urban tax systems. All in all, having emerged from the necessities of warfare and territorial defence in the fourteenth century, public taxation in the following and more peaceful decades was generally justified by more encompassing and abstract arguments, such as the state of the royal household or the king's honour. Out of an *imminens necessitas* had emerged a state of *perpetua necessitas*, the cornerstone of the building of a modern state so brilliantly brought to light by the ground-breaking works of Gaines Post and Ernst Kantorowicz.[37]

Savoy

During the second half of the twelfth century, the County of Savoy became a territorial principality largely established around the passes of the western part of the Alps.[38] The Mont-Cenis and the Grand-Saint-Bernard were the two main passes controlled by the House of Savoy, positioning the principality as a crossroad between Italy and Northern Europe. Princely taxation developed foremost exploiting this situation: taxation, in the form of a dense network of tolls, brought not only new fiscal resources, but also became a way of establishing political power and territorial control. Starting from the 1330s–1350s, the growth of princely taxation was above all the result of ad hoc subsidies*.

Tolls and the promotion of a road network

The counts actively promoted the creation of a dense network of roads and toll stations by providing road maintenance and security for merchants. The Sabaudian princes also had an active policy of acquiring the various fiscal rights controlling these roads from the families or ecclesiastic institutions which possessed them.[39] Although some of these fiscal rights were ancient, and some roads probably never ceased to be used (likewise for taxation imposed on people, merchandise and livestock), the twelfth century certainly marked a turning point with the creation of new tolls and the aforesaid policy of concentration of these rights into the hands of the Sabaudian princes. By the beginning of the fourteenth century, most of these tolls on the main commercial roads were controlled by the Count of Savoy. During this period, the sources increasingly use the word *pedagium* – a term which slowly replaced the ancient term *theloneum* and marked the transition toward a fiscal system mainly controlled by the prince and for which the justification relied on road maintenance and the protection of merchants from thieves.[40]

A toll station was often a quite complex mix of different rights and taxes levied on people, goods and livestock. It was quite rare to have a unique form of taxation, a single *pedagium*.[41] Some of the main stations – such as Saint-Maurice, Savigliana, Rivoli, Chambéry and Montmélian – had a "great toll" (taxing the international trade crossing Savoy) – and a "small toll" (taxing the internal commerce, normally goods bought or sold within the principality). In many cases, other indirect taxes could be added, e.g., the *pontonagium* (a tax paid for the use and maintenance of a bridge) and other various forms of indirect taxation bearing different names (*gabella**, *leyda**, etc.). In many instances, special indirect taxes were levied according to the nature of the goods circulating. Such specific taxes, for instance, could be levied on wood, salt, meat, and wine at many tolls. Nice, which, along with some neighbouring valleys, became Sabaudian territory in 1388, granted access to the Mediterranean trade and a *gabella** on salt provided substantial revenues during the first half of the fifteenth century.[42]

Forms of collection also varied, and no general trend is discernible. In some cases, the local castellan could be in charge of collecting the toll and keeping the accounts, and in other cases, a special officer (a *péager*) with his own accounts was appointed and salaried by the prince. In order to ensure a quick and sure revenue, the prince could also decide to lease out a toll to a farmer. And in some cases, customs could be enfeoffed to some regional noble families or temporary ceded to communes for some important financial needs.

Given the complexity of the network and the accounting system, it is extremely difficult to evaluate the importance of toll revenues for the princely finances. They appear to be important during the twelfth and thirteenth centuries especially. At the beginning of the fourteenth century, tolls accounted for some 25 per cent of the general treasurer's revenues.[43] However, it should be stressed that this treasurer never centralized all revenues; he only collected some fiscal revenue and the surplus coming from castellanies.

Many tolls clearly declined in importance from the fourteenth century. Once again, it is extremely difficult to offer clear explanations for the swift variations of these revenues – which could be often significant from year to year – and for long-term trend changes. During the twelfth century, the road of the Mont-Cenis was busily occupied by the transit of Italian merchants heading for the Champagne fairs. And the Valaisan route – which also benefited from the Simplon pass – became increasingly used during the thirteenth century due to the growth of the Milanese economy. The decline of northern fairs and the development of maritime trade certainly contributed to the gradual loss of importance of toll revenue. Changes on a more regional scale should also be taken into account. The Valaisan route certainly suffered from the evolution of the wool industry in Milan and Lombardy.

The growth of subsidies

On both sides of the Alps, the count regularly received substantial direct tax income from urban and rural communities, as well. In Piedmont, the direct form of taxation was the annual *culmagium* or *focagium*. The *culmagium* had normally been negotiated with the prince and could therefore vary from one town to another.[44] North of the Alps, the annual direct tax levied by the prince was the taille (*tallia*★ or *talliagium*). The taille could be, according to the legal status of the people, *accensata* (an annual fix amount) or levied *ad misercordiam* – the amount was determined by the prince according to his needs.[45] While in the Italian part of the principality, these annual direct taxes were levied until the fifteenth century, in the territories north of the Alps, many communes succeeded in being freed from the taille★, often with the granting of written freedom charters (*franchises*). However, the tax was replaced by a new one: the *teysia domorum*, based on the length of house façades on the public street.[46]

By the middle of the thirteenth century, these regular resources provided by tolls and various direct and indirect taxes became increasingly insufficient to cover the growing needs of the prince. Thus ever more frequently, the counts raised extraordinary contributions from their subjects.[47] These subsidies★ clearly originated from the feudal aid. During the 1260s–1290s, many castellans in the Bresse, Valle d'Aosta and the Chablais collected extraordinary taxes levied for the purchase of new territory and for the marriage of the count's daughter.[48] Until the 1330s, the practice was certainly still embryonic, and if one takes the extant subsidy★ accounts as an indicator of the importance of these forms of taxation, it was not until the 1350s that their levy became regular and general.

Quite interestingly, during the last decades of the thirteenth century, several terms were used to refer to subsidies★: *subsidium*, as well as *auxilium*, *donum* and, most frequently, *complainta*. With the later generalization of the subsidies within the whole county, the term *subsidium*★ prevailed (along with *donum*).[49] By the middle of the fourteenth century, direct taxation had become the largest source of revenue for unforeseen expenditures.[50] As for many other European princes, war needs had come to put the heaviest stress on Sabaudian finances.[51]

It is difficult to know how and to what extent the first subsidies* were discussed and granted by local communities and cities. It is nevertheless certain that by the last quarter of the fourteenth century, the granting of a subsidy* was usually negotiated with the Estates, and the reasons justifying the subsidies* became more numerous.[52] In addition to the "customary" aids – which in Savoy included the crusade, the count's ransom, the daughter's dowry, the knighting of his eldest son and expenses linked to a visit to the Emperor – war and the defence of the county soon became the most frequent grounds invoked for such levies. During the fifteenth century, in some cases, occasional large and unavoidable expenses could also justify the request of a subsidy*. It is important to underline, however, that until the end of the fifteenth century, the prince could not avoid justifications nor rounds of negotiation with the Estates. Although extraordinary (*i.e.*, negotiated), the subsidies* were levied regularly – on average every two or three years – and requests for a subsidy* were very seldom refused.

The subsidy* was generally established at a fixed sum per hearth, 1 or 2 florins, but at a local level, communities levied the required amount according to the wealth of the taxpayers. Quite rapidly, from the 1330s, the principle of the "*divite pauperem adiuvante*" was recognized. By 1372, subjects who were under the dominion of lords owning rights of high justice (they were "mediated subjects") were taxed at a lower rate, usually half or two-thirds of the tax.

The collecting of subsidies* could be the task of the castellan or of special officers. Payments were generally made to the general treasurer.[53] During the period 1340–1380, with some to-ing and fro-ing, many Sabaudian communes earned the right to negotiate fixed amounts and gained the freedom to collect the subsidy* in their own way. Thus, at a local level, for citizens, princely fiscality could take the form of direct or indirect taxation according to these local policies. The prince usually granted a *lettre reversale*, stating that the subsidy* had been granted by special grace as a gift (*donum*). This was not entirely fictional; cities could not avoid the payment, but they could always negotiate the amount. The necessity to discuss the grant and the rate of the subsidies* prompted the development of the Estates, which were mainly (but not only) a product of the princely fiscal pressure. From a Sabaudian perspective, it is difficult to distinguish clearly between seigneurial and state taxation and to consider *dona* as a pure feudal levy, as "*la vraie originalité du prélèvement féodal*".[54]

Urban taxation

Far from being comparable to such urbanized regions as the Low Countries or Northern and Central Italy, Provence and Savoy nonetheless hosted a number of small- to mid-sized towns resting upon dense networks of late ancient and early medieval bishoprics and at the crossroads of commercial transit roads, across and around the Alps. Early freedom charters, in both polities, eased the establishment of autonomous, if not entirely independent, town governments and the rise of commercial and industrial activities favoured rapid increases in population. When struck by the double scourge of wartime and epidemics, from the early fourteenth century, these partly depopulated towns were still well enough organized to cope with new and increased fiscal levies arising simultaneously from their own defence needs and from the overreaching demands of princely authorities.

Provence

Local taxation, in Provence, is closely tied to the existence of recognized communities, in accordance with the Roman legal definition of the *universitas*, authorizing, among other attributes, the possession of a treasure chest, as a repository for commonly owned cash assets. Such a statute did not require the granting of a charter. It therefore applied to large cities and towns, as well as to more humble villages, unless occasionally disputed by some backward-leaning feudal lords (as was the case for the Arles archbishop's town of Salon-de-Provence or the Knights Hospitallers' burgh of Manosque). In the early and poorly documented times of the High Middle Ages, very loosely structured communities could levy occasional taxes to cover such expenses as the building and maintenance of public ramparts, streets or fountains. These taxes could be informally collected on a weekly basis (*tallia dominicalis**) and, if proportional to the taxpayers' assets, the value of these holdings could be registered by such means as the cutting of tally-sticks or the engraving of signs on lintels above the entrance of individual houses.[55] Such practices, of course, bear witness to very basic tax systems meeting only the elementary needs of scarcely populated towns.

The growth of urban populations, from as early as the twelfth century, and the increasing pressure of the princely needs in subsequent times, entailed rising financial needs and, as a result, the organizing of well-developed tax systems geared to the finding of revenue and the setting of equitable tax bases, which in turn led to new institutional and administrative developments.[56]

The search for revenue

Taxes are traditionally categorized as direct or indirect and the former, in turn, may be fixed or proportional. There is evidence for each of these categories and various mixes thereof in the late medieval urban tax systems. Choices were made in accordance to various factors that can only be explained by a thorough understanding of local circumstances and practices. Fixed personal taxes, based on hearths (*foci*), family or housing units, rested upon their heads (*capagium*) and could provide as much revenue as there were taxable hearths. Proportional taxes (*tallia**) were based on fortune and could, in turn, be founded on capital or, less frequently, on income. Generally qualified as "penny and pound" (*ad solidum et libram*) taxes, deemed more equitable than fixed taxes, these levies were commonly practiced in Provence as early as the mid-thirteenth century, as was the case, for instance, in Tarascon in 1265 for the financing of armed troops.[57] Their origin, under Italian influence emerging from Roman legal tradition, can be traced as far as the mid-twelfth century in neighbouring Montpellier.[58]

Indirect taxes, on the other hand, were founded on the commercial exchange of essential commodities, such as wheat, wine or meat, fish and poultry products. Under different names (*reva, gabella**, *soquet*), they were established *ad valorem* and could also be named after the applied rate (*dezenum, vintenum* and so on). They appeared later than their direct counterparts, possibly not earlier than the early fourteenth century (1319 in Marseilles, for instance) but they came in general use in the following decades.[59]

Implementing such taxes was a matter of policy involving, in many cases, quite elaborate strategies. Considering the fact that indirect taxes were easier to raise but less equitable than their direct counterparts and that fixed taxes were also less equitable than proportional taxes, urban elites managing such socially sensitive issues generally combined two or more categories when compelled to raise higher than usual revenues to meet extraordinary needs. Such strategies, often deemed to favour the more affluent, fostered division and occasional rebellion, as happened in Toulon in 1396 or in Manosque in 1400. In Draguignan in 1406, a lengthy quarrel opposed, first, popular forces and local elites who had established an indirect tax and, in a second stage, these elites and the corporation of butchers, with the latter complaining that the tax had been specifically established on meat products. As can be seen by this example, no single strategy could be applied and such variables as local supply, organized labour forces or the provision of currency had to be taken into account.

The setting of a tax base

However difficult, the setting of equitable tax bases was a matter of constant thinking and specifications concerning both the defining of the tax-paying citizenry and the evaluation of taxable assets. Although it was generally recognized that each and every citizen, owning local property and making his principal residence in a given town was forced to contribute to the common tax burden, customary exemptions claimed by clerks and nobles, by royal officers and moneyers were frequently questioned. While most of these exemptions were judged unacceptable by royal decrees, the struggle against ever-renewed claims was a most frequent matter of concern for town governments, arguing that a town population should always be considered as a single body (*una communitas, unum corpus*). Conversely, and for charitable purposes finding their origin in Roman legal tradition, beggars (*mendicantes*) were systematically tax exempt. Such individuals were not necessarily true beggars, but rather citizens owning less than a given amount, generally five or ten pounds, of capital assets. Thus regarded, fiscal mendicancy could apply to a very substantial portion of the population, up to 45 per cent in a list drafted in Tarascon in 1392.[60]

The evaluation of assets went a long way from the primitive engraving of house lintels. Early lists, aside from distinguishing sufficient and mendicant hearths, could provide a lump assessment of the total value of one's properties, as was the case in Sisteron in 1327.[61] As fiscal pressure and resistance thereto developed in the course of the fourteenth century, such lists expanded into far more refined cadastral registers (*allibramentum, liber libre*). Such censuses, more complete and better qualified, occasionally added goods and chattels, including livestock, to land property. They could include land income and annuities. In addition, they might assess the value of land property according not only to the type of farming (farmland, pasture or vineyard), but also to the territorial location and the financial burdens weighing on them.[62] A model of such refined assessments and calculations is provided by the huge multi-volume cadastre of the towns and villages of the neighbouring pontifical Comtat Venaissin in 1414, foreshadowing the celebrated Florentine *catasto* of 1427.[63]

The institutionalization of tax collecting

Such complexities and refinements undoubtedly called for the development of an appropriate administrative machinery. It is reasonable to assume that issues related to the establishment and collecting of rising levels and new forms of taxation from the late thirteenth century greatly contributed to the institutionalization of town and village governments.[64] The granting, by princely authority, of representative councils starting in the years 1290–1300 to Avignon, Aix-en-Provence, Tarascon and a score of minor towns, although referring to such commonplace arguments as public utility and the common good, can readily be related to the sequels of the general subsidy* of 1292 and to internal rivalries concerning either the proportionality of taxes or noblemen's participation in common levies, as was the case in Aix in 1292 or in Saintes-Maries-de-la-Mer in 1307.[65]

More specifically, the distribution of the tax burden was entrusted to ad hoc appraisers (*estimatores, allibratores, talliatores*) and its collection was managed by varying numbers of citizens who might pay themselves with a fixed percentage of the revenue collected. At the higher level of the city government, a treasurer (*clavarius*) held the keys to the public chest and maintained a written account of receipts and expenditures,[66] whereas committees of auditors (*auditores computorum*) would control the legality of financial transactions and report to the general council. As for indirect taxes, their collection was leased out to affluent citizens, generally notaries or merchants, through public auctions.

Without surprise, the rise of urban taxation was directly related to war needs, as early as the mid-fourteenth century, not only to cope with the princely demands negotiated through the assembly of the Estates hereabove mentioned, but also, and most importantly through the years 1350–1400, to finance the costly town defences, be it the maintenance of fortifications or the payment of armed troops. Budget headings of these categories could amount to 60 or 70 per cent of total expenditures, even reaching 90 per cent in extremely perilous situations.[67]

Savoy

Savoy was mostly a rural and Alpine principality. During the second half of the fifteenth century, it had only two cities of more than 10,000 inhabitants: Mondovì and Geneva.[68] However, some Sabaudian territories, particularly Piedmont and the Pays de Vaud, developed a quite dense network of small towns.[69] Many cities hold series of accounts and other registers, such as the Piedmontese *catasti* (inventories of taxable properties and goods), pertaining to the taxes levied on their citizens.[70]

Sabaudian towns, both north of the Alps and in the Piedmont, developed a fiscal system mainly based on ordinary indirect taxation, combining taxes on sale and circulation. The right to perceive indirect taxes was generally regulated by the concession of early freedom charters or later concessions by the prince. Cities normally levied an array of taxes over merchandises sold at the weekly city market, known in many places as the *leyda*★.[71] Towns located at commercial crossroads where princely tolls were collected could benefit from the traffic. Thus, for example, by the end of the thirteenth century, the commune of Villeneuve in the Chablais collected three main taxes: a *rivagium* (on merchandises using the lake harbour), a tax on bales of various goods, and a third tax, a toll for the maintenance of roads.[72] Similarly the commune of Geneva made substantial profit taxing merchandise sold during its international fairs in the two town *Halles*.[73]

Wine taxes certainly constituted one of the main sources of revenue for many communes. Called *commun* in Faucigny and Savoie, *trezenum* in the Bresse, *longuellum*★ in the Pays de Vaud or *introgium vini* in Geneva, once again the variety of names is a sign of the differences of taxes applied to the wine sold in or entering the city.[74] Since communes were not free to establish new indirect taxes without the consent of their lord – usually the Sabaudian prince, or the bishop for episcopal cities such as Geneva and Lausanne – many of these taxes remained extraordinary.

Most of the time, at least during the fourteenth century, such rights were temporary and granted to finance a specific issue that could not be faced with the ordinary revenues of the town. But it was in fact frequent to have cities, well into the fifteenth century, constantly renewing some of their fiscal privileges – and paying for them.

Possibly linked with the crisis of international fairs in Geneva, the decline of international traffic across the Alps forced financial hardships on some cities and prompted a search for new fiscal income. Thus, for example, Geneva and Chambéry introduced new indirect taxes on the meat sold by the city butchers, often facing great resistance from the latter. The commune of Geneva also introduced *gabelles*★ on salt and wine entering the city.[75] As for the prince, indirect taxes, whether ordinary or extraordinary, were never enough to cover unexpected expenses and direct taxation was, at times, a necessity.

Sabaudian Piedmont presented a diverse and complex situation with its dense network of small towns and rural communities. Some of these cities, notably Mondovì and Vercelli, controlled a rural district, the *contado*.[76] In many centres, direct taxation (*talea*, not to be confused with the princely *tallia**) appeared from the middle of the thirteenth century, but it remained an extraordinary means for communal finances (and often a highly unpopular one). Until the fifteenth century, indirect taxation constituted the main fiscal revenue, the basis of the communal finance.[77]

Similar patterns can be observed north of the Alps. From the end of the thirteenth century (and increasingly during the first half of the fourteenth century), many communes levied direct taxes proportional to the wealth of their citizens. The different names given to the direct tax reflect regional differences within the Sabaudian principality: *collecta*, *commune* (Bresse), *tallia** or *leva* (Chablais, Geneva and Chambéry), *gietum* (Pays de Vaud). The fact that these were extraordinary resources does not imply that they were infrequent. On the contrary, between 1350 and 1450, many communes could collect direct taxes on average every two to four years. Most of the time, the right had been granted by the Count of Savoy, justified by the need to build and maintain urban fortifications. Especially since the second half of the fourteenth century, these taxes were often introduced to cope with the subsidies* required by the prince.[78]

Conclusion

Princely fiscal demands, in Provence and in Savoy as well as in most West European polities at the turn of the fourteenth century, were closely related to the new requirements of war financing.[79] Limited as they were by traditional restrictions, the princes were dependent on new sources of revenue, mainly in the form of war subsidies*. Extraordinary by nature, such subsidies* were subject to an obligation of consent, in accordance with widely acknowledged principles of freedom and property. In Provence, more than in its northern neighbours' dominions, this in turn brought about the development of an institutionalized form of political representation, through the assembly of the three Estates, which might be explained by a noteworthy Catalan influence, as well as by the relative weakness of an absent or distant princely authority. Similar trends are also discernible in Savoy, although less remarkable, at least from an institutionalization standpoint. Estates were slower to take place and the assemblies (especially those summoned on fiscal grounds) concerned almost exclusively the cities.

In both polities, the granting of subsidies* was but one of a number of traditional or newly instated forms of taxation, many of which were directly associated with commercial traffic, such as a network of tolls in Savoy or the attempted establishment of custom duties in Provence. Unfortunately, in Provence, extant records are far from sufficient to allow quantitative assessments of the total amounts of revenue, let alone their composition or long-term trend. In Savoy, the difficulty lies elsewhere: the number of extant accounts is almost overwhelming, and scholars must still undertake significant archival work to draw some conclusions.

Urban fiscal systems grew out of and developed mainly from the need to fortify towns and to meet increased princely demands.[80] However, it would be a simplification to reduce princely taxation to a form of pressure with a negative impact on communal freedoms. In many cases, towns were able to negotiate, thereby maintaining or increasing their autonomy. During the second half of the fourteenth century, Provençal as well as Sabaudian towns gained new fiscal resources to build or renovate city walls. Henceforth, new taxes and new forms of collection applied not only to urban territories, but more often than not to entire castellanies (in Savoy) or *vigueries* and *baillies* (in Provence). Thus, towns were given fiscal authority over the countryside and increased their character as local centres of power.[81] In the end, the history of late medieval fiscal systems in these two polities cannot be reduced to a purely linear growth of princely taxation leading to increased fiscal centralization.

Notes

1 BARATIER, *Atlas historique*.
2 A short overview with essential bibliography is BARBERO, "The feudal principalities", pp. 177–196.
3 CASTELNUOVO and GUILLERÉ, "Les finances et l'administration de la Maison de Savoie", pp. 33–125.
4 PÉCOUT, *De l'autel à l'écritoire*.
5 For a detailed inventory of these series: BAUTIER and SORNAY, *Les sources de l'histoire économique et sociale*.
6 RAVIOLA, ROSSO and VARALLO, *Gli spazi sabaudi*.
7 See especially: GAULIN and GUILLERE, "Des rouleaux et des hommes", pp. 51–108; GUILLERE, "Dernières recherches", pp. 327–354 and CASTELNUOVO, "The Rolls, the Prince, and their Depositories", pp. 183–202. About the early rolls, see two digital projects: Castellanie (www.castellanie.net/) and GEMMA (http://ressourcescomptables.huma-num.fr/).
8 GUILLERÉ, BIOLZI and MACHERAT, *Les sources du financement de la guerre*; BIOLZI, "Les guerres d'Amédée VII de Savoie", pp. 127–143; BIOLZI, "Military Recruitment and Funding in Savoy", pp. 45–68.
9 MORENZONI, *Marchands et marchandises*.
10 COULET, "La chambre des comptes de Provence", pp. 199–232; COULET, "La Chambre des comptes de Provence sous le règne du roi René", pp. 211–222; BONNAUD, "Le processus d'élaboration et de validation des comptes de clavaire", pp. 241–253; BONNAUD, "Les officiers comptables des comtés", pp. 269–288; PÉCOUT, "Les registres dits rationnaires", pp. 59–106: PÉCOUT, "Comptabilité urbaine, comptabilité du prince".
11 BAUTIER and SORNAY, *Les sources de l'histoire économique et sociale*.
12 CAESAR, "Small Towns and Resistance to Taxation", pp. 319–327; HÉBERT, "Le système fiscal des villes de Provence", pp. 57–81, is a notable exception.
13 General surveys of late medieval Provençal history might be found in BOURRILLY and BUSQUET, *La Provence au Moyen Âge*; AURELL, BOYER and COULET, *La Provence au Moyen Âge* and, in the general Mediterranean context, LÉONARD, *Les Angevins de Naples*.
14 ROSSIAUD, *Dictionnaire du Rhône médiéval*; TAVIANI, "Le commerce dans la région aixoise", pp. 255–285.
15 VENTURINI, "La gabelle du sel", pp. 105–115.
16 These rights are thoroughly analyzed by BARATIER, *Enquêtes sur les droits et revenus de Charles Ier d'Anjou*, pp. 53–110; HÉBERT, "L'enquête de 1319–1320 sur la cavalcade en Provence", pp. 357–384.
17 SHATZMILLER, "La perception de la *tallia judeorum*", pp. 221–236; COULET, "La *tallia judeorum* en Provence", pp. 439–445; COULET, "La communauté des Juifs de Provence", pp. 55–73.
18 LAVOIE, "Les statistiques criminelles et le visage du justicier", pp. 3–20; BONNAUD and PARADIS, "Les crises du XIVe siècle", pp. 9–25; HÉBERT, "La justice dans les comptes de clavaires de Provence", pp. 205–220.
19 A partial list can be found in BARATIER, *La démographie provençale*, pp. 19–20.
20 BARATIER, *Enquêtes*, pp. 235–414.
21 PÉCOUT, *L'enquête générale*.
22 Published under the direction of PÉCOUT, under the general heading of *L'enquête générale de Leopardo da Foligno*.
23 HÉBERT, "L'ordonnance de Brignoles", pp. 41–56.
24 COULET, "La chambre des comptes de Provence", and COULET, "La Chambre des comptes de Provence sous le règne du roi René".
25 BARATIER, *Enquêtes*, pp. 207–229. The provençal pound counts for 240 provençal or royal *denarii*.
26 HÉBERT, "Le subside de 1292 en Provence", pp. 343–367.
27 HÉBERT, "Une identité mise en scène", pp. 183–194.
28 HÉBERT, "L'armée provençale en 1374", pp. 5–27; HÉBERT, "La cristallisation d'une identité", pp. 151–164; HÉBERT, "Les États de Provence", pp. 181–197.
29 HÉBERT, "Guerre, finances et administration", pp. 103–130.
30 A Catalan influence on these developments can hardly be dismissed. See SÁNCHEZ MARTÍNEZ, *El naiximent de la fiscalitat d'Estat*, pp. 119–134; SÁNCHEZ MARTÍNEZ, "La convocatoria del usatge *Princeps namque*", pp. 79–107.

31 Hébert, "Les États de Provence et le contrôle de l'impôt", pp. 67–77.
32 Hébert, *Regeste des États de Provence*.
33 Hébert, "*Cum peccuniis indigeamus*", pp. 103–120.
34 Hébert, "Crédit public, fiscalité et représentation", pp. 3–22.
35 Hébert, "Dons et entrées solennelles", pp. 267–283.
36 Hébert, "Réforme de la justice et impératifs financiers", pp. 479–502.
37 Post, *Studies in Medieval Legal Thought*; Kantorowicz, *The King's Two Bodies*.
38 Sergi, *Potere e territorio* and Ripart, *Les fondements idéologiques du pouvoir*.
39 A useful mapping is Mariotte and Perret, *Atlas historique français*, pl. xxviii/1.
40 On the alpine tolls, Daviso di Charvensod, *I pedaggi delle Alpi occidentali*, is still useful, although the statistical data are problematic.
41 Some of these toll stations have been studied. See in particular, Chomel and Ebersolt, *Cinq siècles de circulation internationale;* Duparc, "Un péage savoyard", pp. 145–188; Gravela, "Un mercato esclusivo", pp. 231–259; Morenzoni, *Marchands et marchandises*; and Morenzoni, *Sur les routes des Alpes*.
42 Bergier, "Port de Nice", pp. 857–866; Boyer, "Les comptes de Jean Maleti", pp. 1–48.
43 Castelnuovo and Guilleré, "Le crédit du prince", p. 155. We also lack a good and comprehensive study on the princely finances. The necessary starting point is still Chiaudano, *Il bilancio sabaudo* and *La finanza Sabauda*.
44 Comba, *La popolazione in Piemonte*, pp. 10–34.
45 Anex, *Le servage au Pays de Vaud*, pp. 120–137 and 329–332; Carrier and Mouthon, *Paysans des Alpes*, pp. 99–134 and Panero, "Un tributo bassomedievale", pp. 783–798.
46 Prévité Orton, *The early history of the House of Savoy*, pp. 448–447 and Champoud, *Les droits seigneuriaux*, pp. 124–125.
47 On the subsidies, especially in rural context, see H. Gelting, "La communauté rurale", pp. 17–34 and Carrier, "Local Communities", pp. 205–228. Information can also be found in regional and demographic studies. See in particular, Bouquet, "Quelques remarques sur la population du comté de Savoie", pp. 49–80; Comba, *La popolazione*, pp. 11–13 and Dubuis, *Le jeu de la vie et de la mort*. On cities, see the next point.
48 Cf. Chiaudano, *La finanza*, p. 128; Tallone, *Parlamento*, vol. 8, pp. xlvii–xlviii and Mariotte-Löber, *Ville et seigneurie*, p. 60 n. 12. Other examples in the accounts of the castellanies of Bâge (ADCO, B6740), Saint-Triviers-de-Courtes (ADCO, B9941 and B9941), Pont-de-Vaux (ADCO, B9155 and B9156), Bourg-en-Bresse (ADCO, B7081), and Conthey et Saillon (ASTo, SR, Inv. 69, f. 41r, r. 4).
49 Similar evolution for the neighboring Dauphiné, see Anne Lemonde, "Complainte", in *Glosario Crítico de Fiscalidad Medieval* (www.imf.csic.es/index.php/fuentes-documentales/fuentes-documentales-gcfm).
50 Indirect extraordinary taxation, besides some attempts in 1331 (cf. Anex-Cabanis, *Les sources du droit du canton de Vaud*, pp. 33–34 and Brossard, *Cartulaire de Bourg-en-Bresse*, p. 28), never became a way to cover unforeseen expenditures.
51 See note 5 above for bibliography.
52 On subsidies and the Estates, see Tallone, *Parlamento Sabaudo*; Koenigsberger, *Estates and Revolutions*, pp. 19–79; Tappy, *Les États de Vaud* and Caesar, *Le pouvoir*, pp. 145–159.
53 An inventory of the numerous extant subsidy accounts: Bautier and Sornay, *Les sources de l'histoire économique*, vol. 1, pp. 416–450. The accounts of the general treasurer (cf. Bautier and Sornay, *Les sources de l'histoire économique*, vol. 1, p. 313) provide invaluable lists of the communities, nobles, and ecclesiastical institutions that paid a *subsidium*.
54 Genet, "L'État Moderne", p. 263.
55 Baratier, *La démographie provençale*, p. 16.
56 The upcoming developments proceed largely from Hébert, "Le système fiscal des villes de Provence", to which I refer here once and for all.
57 Hébert, "L'élection des chevaliers", pp. 81–102.
58 Gouron, "L'invention' de l'impôt proportionnel", pp. 245–260.
59 Droguet, *Administration financière et système fiscal à Marseille*.
60 Hébert, *Tarascon*, p. 57.
61 Laplane, *Essai sur l'histoire municipale*, pp. 153–201.
62 Busquet, *Études sur l'ancienne Provence*, pp. 141–172; Coulet, "Les villages provençaux", pp. 117–130; Stouff, "Les livres terriers d'Arles", pp. 307–340.

63 ZERNER, *Le cadastre*; HERLIHY and KLAPISCH-ZUBER, *Les Toscans et leurs familles*.
64 The Catalan case has been well studied by TURULL RUBINAT, "Gobierno municipal", pp. 507–530.
65 GIORDANENGO, "*Qualitas illata per principatum tenentem*", pp. 261–301 [p. 275]; AMARGIER, "Autour de la création du conseil de communauté", pp. 437–448.
66 See for example SMAIL, "The general taille of Marseille", pp. 473–486; ROUX, "Bertrand Roquefort", pp. 107–140.
67 GALLO, "*Quia talis tractatus longus esset et sumptuosus*", pp. 137–160; GUÉNETTE, "Une ville aux prises avec la guerre", pp. 429–442; DROGUET, "Une ville au miroir de ses comptes", pp. 171–213.
68 Geneva was formally an independent episcopal city whose bishop had the imperial immediacy. However, the city had strong ties with Savoy and the princes exercised some rights within the city (cf. CAESAR, *Le pouvoir*).
69 LEGUAY, "Un réseau urbain médiéval", pp. 13–64. For Piedmont, see GINATEMPO, "La popolazione", pp. 31–79.
70 See n. 7 above.
71 On Piedmontese market towns, NASO, "Il platea mercati", pp. 99–118. For urban centers north of the Alps, see reference in n. 28 and in subsequent notes.
72 THÉVENAZ, *Ecrire pour gérer*, pp. 60–74.
73 CAESAR, *Le pouvoir*, pp. 226–228.
74 CAESAR, "*Gabelle cedunt in minori dampno*", pp. 833–849; VAILLANT "Le commun du vin", pp. 1–5. MOREL, *La vie à Châtillon-en-Dombes*, pp. 172–182. BRONDY, *Chambéry*, pp. 61 and 104; COMBA, *Vigne e vini*.
75 CAESAR, *Le pouvoir*, pp. 228–233.
76 BARBERO, "Signorie e comunità rurali", pp. 411–510; NEGRO, *Scribendo nomina et cognomina*; GRAVELA, "Comprare il debito della città", pp. 743–773; BUFFO, "Prassi documentarie", pp. 217–259; BARBERO, "Fiscalità e finanza pubblica", pp. 1–48.
77 DAVISO DI CHARVENSOD, "I catasti", pp. 41–74; DAVISO DI CHARVENSOD, *I più antichi catasti*; DAVISO DI CHARVENSOD, "I più antichi catasti", pp. 66–102 and COMBA, *Storia di Torino*, pp. 261–264.
78 MOREL, *La vie à Châtillon-en-Dombes*, pp. 144–172 and 184–190; ANEX-CABANIS, *Les sources du droit*, p. 165, 190 and 296–297; DÉGLON, *Yverdon*, pp. 102–103, 133, 248 and 292–293; BRONDY, "Population et structure sociale", pp. 323–343; THÉVENAZ, *Écrire pour gérer* and CAESAR, *Le pouvoir*, pp. 221–260.
79 For a comparative point of view, see in particular RIGAUDIÈRE, "L'essor de la fiscalité royale", pp. 323–391; HARRISS, *King*.
80 For a general overview, see BUTAUD, "Le coût de la guerre", pp. 235–265.
81 CAESAR, "Les villes et le contrôle des espaces périurbains", pp. 167–180; HÉBERT, "'Bonnes villes' et capitales régionales", pp. 527–542.

References

Paul AMARGIER, "Autour de la création du conseil de communauté aux Saintes-Maries-de-la-Mer en 1307", in *Bulletin philologique et historique*, 1965, pp. 437–448.
Danielle ANEX, *Le servage au Pays de Vaud (XIIIe-XVIe siècle)*, Lausanne, 1973.
Danielle ANEX-CABANIS, *Les sources du droit du canton de Vaud. Droits seigneuriaux et franchises municipales*, B/2: *Bailliage de Vaud et autres seigneuries vaudoises*, Basle, 2001.
Martin AURELL, Jean-Paul BOYER and Noël COULET (eds.), *La Provence au Moyen Âge*, Aix-en-Provence, 2005.
Édouard BARATIER, *La démographie provençale du XIIIe au XVIe siècle, avec chiffres de comparaison pour le XVIIIe siècle*. Paris, 1961.
Édouard BARATIER et al., *Atlas historique: Provence, Comtat Venaissin, principauté d'Orange, comté de Nice, principauté de Monaco*, Paris, 1969.
Édouard BARATIER, *Enquêtes sur les droits et revenus de Charles Ier d'Anjou en Provence (1252–1278)*, Paris, 1969.
Alessandro BARBERO, "Signorie e comunità rurali nel Vercellese fra crisi del districtus cittadino e nascita dello stato principesco", in *Vercelli nel secolo XIV: atti del quinto congresso storico vercellese*, ed. Alessandro BARBERO and Rinaldo COMBA, Vercelli, 2010, pp. 411–510.

Alessandro BARBERO, "The feudal principalities: the west (Montferrato, Saluzzo, Savoy and Savoy-Acaia)", in *The Italian Renaissance State*, ed. Andrea GAMBERINI and Isabella LAZZARINI, Cambridge, 2012, pp. 177–196.

Alessandro BARBERO, "Fiscalità e finanza pubblica a Vercelli fra stato visconteo e stato sabaudo (1417–1450)", in *Vercelli fra Quattro e Cinquecento. Atti del settimo Congresso storico vercellese*, ed. Alessandro BARBERO and Claudio ROSSO, Vercelli, 2018, pp. 1–48.

Robert-Henri BAUTIER and Janine SORNAY, *Les sources de l'histoire économique et sociale du Moyen Âge. Provence, Comtat Venaissin, Dauphiné: États de la maison de Savoie*, vol. 1, Paris, 1968.

Jean-François BERGIER, "Port de Nice, sel de Savoie et foires de Lyon. Un ambitieux projet de la seconde moitié du XVe siècle", in *Le Moyen Âge*, 69, 1963, pp. 857–866.

Roberto BIOLZI, "Les guerres d'Amédée VII de Savoie: coûts et administration militaire (1378–1391)", in *Le Moyen Âge*, 121, 2015, pp. 127–143.

Roberto BIOLZI, "Military Recruitment and Funding in Savoy: Piedmont and Chablais, Late-Thirteenth to Mid-Fourteenth Century", in *Accounts and Accountability in Late Medieval Europe. Records, Procedures, and Socio-Political Impact*, ed. Ionuţ EPURESCU-PASCOVICI, Turnhout, 2020, pp. 47–72.

Jean-Luc BONNAUD, "Le processus d'élaboration et de validation des comptes de clavaire en Provence au XIVe siècle", in Kouky FIANU and De Lloyd GUTH (eds.), *Écrit et pouvoir dans les chancelleries médiévales: espace français, espace anglais*, Louvain-la-Neuve, 1997, pp. 241–253.

Jean-Luc BONNAUD, "Les officiers comptables des comtés de Provence et Forcalquier et leurs comptes (XIVe-XVe siècles)", in *De l'autel à l'écritoire. Genèse des comptabilités princières en Occident*, ed. Thierry PÉCOUT, Paris, 2017, pp. 269–288.

Jean-Luc BONNAUD and Bruno PARADIS, "Les crises du XIVe siècle et la gestion d'un État: les revenus de la justice en Provence", in *Annales du Midi*, 123, 2011, pp. 9–25.

Jean-Jacques BOUQUET, "Quelques remarques sur la population du comté de Savoie au XIVe siècle d'après les comptes de subsides", in *Revue historique vaudoise*, 71, 1963, pp. 49–80.

Victor-Louis BOURRILLY and Raoul BUSQUET, *La Provence au Moyen Âge (1112–1482)*, Paris-Marseille, 1924.

Jean-Paul BOYER, "Les comptes de Jean Maleti, receveur-général du comte de Savoie et les terres neuves de Provence au début du XVe siècle", in *Recherches régionales. Alpes-Maritimes et contrées limitrophes*, 16, 1976, pp. 1–48.

Réjane BRONDY, "Population et structure sociale à Chambéry à la fin du XIVe siècle, d'après les documents fiscaux", in *Mélanges de l'École française de Rome. Moyen-Age, Temps modernes*, 86/2, 1974, pp. 323–343.

Joseph BROSSARD, *Cartulaire de Bourg-en-Bresse*, Bourg-en-Bresse, 1882.

Paolo BUFFO, "Prassi documentarie e gestione delle finanze nei comuni del principato di Savoia-Acaia (Moncalieri, Pinerolo, Torino, fine secolo XIII-prima metà secolo XIV)" in *Scrineum Rivista*, 11, 2015, pp. 217–259.

Raoul BUSQUET, *Études sur l'ancienne Provence. Institutions et points d'histoire*, Paris, 1930.

Germain BUTAUD, "Le coût de la guerre et de la défense dans les villes au bas Moyen Âge: l'exemple de la France du Midi et de l'Italie", in *La fiscalité des villes au Moyen Âge (Occident méditerranéen). 3. La redistribution de l'impôt*, ed. Denis MENJOT and Manuel SÁNCHEZ MARTÍNEZ, Toulouse, 2002, pp. 235–265.

Mathieu CAESAR "La défense de la ville et le poids de la guerre dans les finances communales de Genève aux XIVe-XVe siècles", in *Études savoisiennes*, 13–14, 2004, pp. 45–68.

Mathieu CAESAR, "*Gabelle cedunt in minori dampno*. Les politiques fiscales de la Communauté de Genève entre rupture et continuité (fin XIVe-début XVIe s.)", in *Fiscal Systems in the European Economy from the 13th to the 18th Centuries*, ed. Simonetta CAVACIOCCHI, Florence, 2008, pp. 833–849.

Mathieu CAESAR, *Le pouvoir en ville. Gestion urbaine et pratiques politiques à Genève (fin XIIIe – début XVIe s.)*, Turnhout, 2011.

Mathieu CAESAR, "Les villes et le contrôle des espaces périurbains. Les cas de Genève et des villes de la principauté savoyarde aux XIVe et XVe siècles", in *Aux marges de la ville. Paysages, sociétés, représentations*, ed. Sophie BOUFFIER, Claude-Isabelle BRELOT and Denis MENJOT, Paris, 2015, pp. 167–180.

Mathieu CAESAR, "Small Towns and Resistance to Taxation in late Medieval Savoy", in *Cultures fiscales en Occident du XIe au XVIIe siècle. Études offertes à Denis Menjot*, ed. Florent GARNIER, Armand JAMME, Anne LEMONDE and Pere VERDÉS PIJUAN, Toulouse, 2019, pp. 319–327.

Nicolas CARRIER, "Local Communities and Fiscal Reform in Late Medieval Savoy: Lords, Peasants, and Subsidies", in *Accounts and Accountability in Late Medieval Europe. Records, Procedures, and Socio-Political Impact*, ed. Ionuţ EPURESCU-PASCOVICI, Turnhout, 2020, pp. 205–228.

Nicolas CARRIER and Fabrice MOUTHON, *Paysans des Alpes: les communautés montagnardes au Moyen Âge*, Rennes, 2010.

Guido CASTELNUOVO, "The Rolls, the Prince, and their Depositories: The Archiving of Late Medieval Financial Accounts Reconsidered (Savoy, Mid-Fourteenth to Mid-Fifteenth Century)", in *Accounts and Accountability in Late Medieval Europe. Records, Procedures, and Socio-Political Impact*, ed. Ionuț EPURESCU-PASCOVICI, Turnhout, 2020, pp. 183–202.

Guido CASTELNUOVO and Christian GUILLERÉ, "Le crédit du prince: l'exemple savoyard au bas Moyen Âge", in *Crédit et société. Les sources, les techniques et les hommes (XIVe-XVIe s.)*, ed. Jean-Marie CAUCHIES, Neuchâtel, 1999, pp. 151–164.

Guido CASTELNUOVO and Christian GUILLERÉ, "Les finances et l'administration de la Maison de Savoie au XIIIe siècle", in *Pierre II de Savoie "Le petit Charlemagne" († 1268)*, ed. Bernard ANDENMATTEN, Agostino PARAVICINI BAGLIANI and Eva PIBIRI, Lausanne, 2000, pp. 33–125.

Philippe CHAMPOUD, *Les droits seigneuriaux dans le pays de Vaud: d'après les reconnaissances reçues par Jean Balay de 1403 à 1409*, Lausanne, 1963.

Mario CHIAUDANO, *Il bilancio sabaudo nel secolo XIII*, Turin, 1927 and *La finanza Sabauda nel sec. XIII*, 3 vol., Turin, 1933–1938.

Vital CHOMEL and Jean EBERSOLT, *Cinq siècles de circulation internationale vue de Jougne: un péage jurassien du XIIIe au XVIIIe siècle*, Paris, 1951.

Rinaldo COMBA, *La popolazione in Piemonte sul finire del medioevo*, Turin, 1977.

Rinaldo COMBA (ed.), *Vigne e vini nel Piemonte medievale*, Cuneo, 1990.

Rinaldo COMBA (ed.), *Storia di Torino*, vol. 2: Turin, 1997.

Noël COULET, "La *tallia judeorum* en Provence après la Peste Noire", in *Provence historique*, 35, 1985, pp. 439–445.

Noël COULET, "Les villages provençaux, la queste et le cadastre", in *La société rurale et les institutions gouvernementales au Moyen Âge*, ed. John DRENDEL, Montréal, 1995, pp. 117–130.

Noël COULET, "La communauté des Juifs de Provence à la fin du XIVe siècle. Nouveaux documents sur la *tallia judeorum*", in *Revue des études juives*, 155, 1996, pp. 55–73.

Noël COULET, "La chambre des comptes de Provence", in *Les Chambres des comptes en France aux XIVe et XVe siècles*, ed. Philippe CONTAMINE and Olivier MATTÉONI, Paris, 1998, pp. 199–232.

Noël COULET, "La Chambre des comptes de Provence sous le règne du roi René", in *René d'Anjou (1409–1480). Pouvoirs et gouvernement*, ed. Jean-Michel MATZ and Noël-Yves TONNERRE, Rennes, 2011, pp. 211–222.

Maria Clotilde DAVISO DI CHARVENSOD, "I più antichi catasti del Comune di Chieri", in *Bollettino storico-bibliografico subalpino*, 39, 1937, pp. 66–102.

Maria Clotilde DAVISO DI CHARVENSOD, *I più antichi catasti del comune di Chieri: 1253*, Turin, 1939.

Maria Clotilde DAVISO DI CHARVENSOD, "I catasti di un comune agricolo piemontese del XIII secolo", in *Bollettino storico-bibliografico subalpino*, 54/1, 1956, pp. 41–74.

Maria Clotilde DAVISO DI CHARVENSOD, *I pedaggi delle Alpi occidentali nel Medio Evo*, Torino, 1961.

Roger DÉGLON, *Yverdon au Moyen Âge (XIIIe-XVe siècle). Étude de la formation d'une commune*, Lausanne, 1949.

Alain DROGUET, "Une ville au miroir de ses comptes: les dépenses de Marseille à la fin du XIVe siècle", in *Provence historique*, 30, 1980, pp. 171–213.

Alain DROGUET, *Administration financière et système fiscal à Marseille dans la seconde moitié du XIVe siècle*. Aix-en-Provence, 1983.

Pierre DUBUIS, *Le jeu de la vie et de la mort. La population du Valais (XIVe-XVIe s.)*, Lausanne, 1994.

Pierre DUPARC, "Un péage savoyard sur la route du Mont-Cenis aux XIIIe et XIVe siècles: Montmélian", in *Bulletin philologique et historique*, 1, 1960, pp. 145–188.

Alexandra GALLO, "*Quia talis tractatus longus esset et sumptuosus*. Argumenter les finances de guerre à Sisteron en 1391", in *Provence historique*, 58, 2008, pp. 137–160.

Jean-Louis GAULIN and Christian GUILLERÉ, "Des rouleaux et des hommes: premières recherches sur les comptes de châtellenies savoyards", in *Études savoisiennes*, 1, 1992, pp. 51–108.

Michael H. GELTING, "La communauté rurale, rouage de l'administration fiscale: l'exemple de la Maurienne (XIVe-XVe siècle)", in *Le Alpi medievale nello sviluppo delle regione contermini*, ed. Gian Maria VARANINI, Naples, 2004, pp. 17–34.

Jean-Philippe GENET, "L'État Moderne: un modèle opératoire?" in *L'État Moderne: Genèse, bilans et perspectives*, ed. Jean-Philippe GENET, Paris, 1990, pp. 261–281.

Maria Ginatempo, "La popolazione dei centri minori dell'Italia centrosettentrionale nei secoli XIII-XV. Uno sguardo d'insieme", in *I centri minori italiani nel tardo Medioevo. Cambiamento sociale, crescita economica*, ed. Gian Maria Varanini and Federico Lattanzio, Florence, 2018, pp. 31–79.

Gérard Giordanengo, "*Qualitas illata per principatum tenentem*. Droit nobiliaire en Provence angevine (XIIIᵉ-XVᵉ siècle)", in *La noblesse dans les territoires angevins à la fin du Moyen Âge*, ed. Noël Coulet and Jean-Michel Matz, Rome, 2000, pp. 261–301.

André Gouron, "L'invention' de l'impôt proportionnel au Moyen Âge", in *Comptes rendus des séances de l'Académie des Inscriptions et Belles-Lettres*, 138, 1994, pp. 245–260.

Marta Gravela, "Comprare il debito della città. Élite politiche e finanze comunali a Torino nel XIV secolo", in *Quaderni storici*, 147/3, 2014, pp. 743–773.

Marta Gravela, "Un mercato esclusivo. Gabelle, pedaggi ed egemonia politica nella Torino tardomedievale" in *Reti Medievali Rivista*, 19/1, 2018, pp. 231–259.

Maryse Guénette, "Une ville aux prises avec la guerre: Brignoles à la fin du XIVᵉ siècle", in *Provence historique* 40, 1990, pp. 429–442.

Christian Guilleré, "Dernières recherches sur les comptes de châtellenies savoyards", in *Le gouvernement des communautés politiques à la fin du Moyen Âge: entre puissance et négociation: villes, finances, État: actes du colloque en l'honneur d'Albert Rigaudière, Paris, 6–8 novembre 2008*, ed. Pierre Bonin, Florent Garnier, Corinne Leveleux-Teixeira and Anne Rousselet-Pimont, Paris, 2011, pp. 327–354.

Christian Guilleré, Roberto Biolzi and Sylvain Macherat, *Les sources du financement de la guerre en Savoie (1308–1354): les comptes des guerres avant les trésoriers des guerres*, Chambéry, 2019.

Gerald L. Harriss, *King, Parliament and Public Finance in Medieval England to 1369*, Oxford, 1975.

Michel Hébert, "Le système fiscal des villes de Provence (XIVᵉ-XVe siècles)", in *La fiscalité des villes au Moyen Âge (Occident méditerranéen). 2. Les systèmes fiscaux*, ed. Denis Menjot and Manuel Sánchez-Martinez, Toulouse, 1999, pp. 57–81.

Michel Hébert, "Guerre, finances et administration: les États de Provence de novembre 1359", in *Le Moyen Âge*, 83, 1977, pp. 103–130.

Michel Hébert, *Tarascon au XIVᵉ siècle. Histoire d'une communauté urbaine provençale*, Aix-en-Provence, 1979.

Michel Hébert, "L'armée provençale en 1374", in *Annales du Midi*, 91, 1979, pp. 5–27.

Michel Hébert, "L'élection des chevaliers: un épisode de recrutement militaire en Provence au XIIIᵉ siècle", in *Cahiers des études anciennes*, 4, 1983, pp. 81–102.

Michel Hébert, "Les États de Provence et le contrôle de l'impôt (XIVᵉ-XVᵉ s.)", in *Razo. Cahiers du Centre d'Etudes Médiévales de Nice*, 9, 1989, pp. 67–77.

Michel Hébert, "Les États de Provence à l'époque de la dédition niçoise (1382–1388)" in *1388. La dédition de Nice à la Savoie*, Paris, 1990, pp. 181–197.

Michel Hébert, "La cristallisation d'une identité: les États de Provence, 1347–1360" in *Événement, identité et histoire*, ed Claire Dolan, Québec, 1991, pp. 151–164.

Michel Hébert, "Dons et entrées solennelles au XVe siècle: Marguerite de Savoie (1434) et Jean d'Anjou (1443)", in *De Provence et d'ailleurs. Mélanges offerts à Noël Coulet. Provence historique*, 49, 1999, pp. 267–283.

Michel Hébert, "Le subside de 1292 en Provence", in *L'impôt au Moyen Âge. L'impôt public et le prélèvement seigneurial, fin XIIᵉ – début XVIᵉ siècle. Vol. 2, Les espaces fiscaux*, ed. Philippe Contamine, Jean Kerhervé and Albert Rigaudière, Paris, 2002, pp. 343–367.

Michel Hébert, "L'ordonnance de Brignoles, les affaires pendantes et la continuité administrative en Provence sous les premiers Angevins", in *Information et société en Occident à la fin du Moyen Âge*, ed. Claire Boudreau, Kouky Fianu, Claude Gauvard and Michel Hébert, Paris, 2004, pp. 41–56.

Michel Hébert, "La justice dans les comptes de clavaires de Provence: bilan historiographique et perspectives de recherche", in *La justice temporelle dans les territoires angevins aux XIIIᵉ et XIVᵉ siècles. Théories et pratiques*, ed. Jean-Paul Boyer, Anne Mailloux and Laure Verdon, Rome, 2005, pp. 205–220.

Michel Hébert, "'Bonnes villes' et capitales régionales: fiscalité d'État et identités urbaines en Provence autour de 1400", in *L'impôt dans les villes de l'Occident méditerranéen (XIIIᵉ-XVᵉ siècle)*, Paris, 2005, pp. 527–542.

Michel Hébert, *Regeste des États de Provence, 1347–1480*, Paris, 2007.

Michel Hébert, "L'enquête de 1319–1320 sur la cavalcade en Provence", in *Quand gouverner c'est enquêter. Les pratiques politiques de l'enquête princière (Occident, XIIIᵉ-XVᵉ siècles)*, ed. Thierry Pécout, Paris, 2010, pp. 357–384.

Michel Hébert, "Crédit public, fiscalité et représentation en Provence au milieu du XVᵉ siècle", *Provence historique*, 60, 2010, pp. 3–22.

Michel Hébert, "Réforme de la justice et impératifs financiers. Commissaires royaux et villes de Provence (1447–1449)", in *Le gouvernement des communautés politiques à la fin du Moyen Âge*, ed. Pierre Bonin, Florent Garnier, Corinne Leveleux-Teixeira and Anne Rousselet-Pimont, Paris, 2010, pp. 479–502.

Michel Hébert, "*Cum peccuniis indigeamus*: politiques fiscales et expédients financiers dans la Provence de René d'Anjou", in *René d'Anjou (1409–1480). Pouvoirs et gouvernement*, ed. Jean-Michel Matz and Noël-Yves Tonnerre, Rennes, 2011, pp. 103–120.

Michel Hébert, "Une identité mise en scène. Les premières assemblées représentatives dans les comtés de Provence et de Forcalquier (XIIIᵉ-début XIVᵉ siècle)", in *Identités angevines. Entre Provence et Naples, XIIIᵉ-XVᵉ siècle*, ed. Jean-Paul Boyer, Anne Mailloux and Laure Verdon, Aix-en-Provence, 2016, pp. 183–194.

David Herlihy and Christiane Klapisch-Zuber, *Les Toscans et leurs familles. Une étude du catasto florentin de 1427*, Paris, 1978.

Ernst Kantorowicz, *The King's Two Bodies. A Study in Mediaeval Theology*, Princeton, 1957.

Helmut G. Koenigsberger, *Estates and Revolutions: Essays in Early Modern European History*, Ithaca, 1971.

Édouard de Laplane, *Essai sur l'histoire municipale de la ville de Sisteron*, Paris, 1840.

Rodrigue Lavoie, "Les statistiques criminelles et le visage du justicier: justice royale et justice seigneuriale en Provence au Moyen Âge", *Provence historique*, 29, 1979, pp. 3–20.

Jean-Pierre Leguay, "Un réseau urbain médiéval: les villes du comté, puis du duché de Savoie", in *Bulletin du Centre d'Études Franco-Italien*, 1979, pp. 13–64.

Émile-G. Léonard, *Les Angevins de Naples*, Paris, 1954.

Jean-Yves Mariotte and André Perret, *Atlas historique français: le territoire de la France et de quelques pays voisins*, vol. 3: La Savoie, Paris, 1979.

Ruth Mariotte-Löber, *Ville et seigneurie: les chartes de franchise des comtes de Savoie, fin XIIᵉ siècle-1343*, Annecy, 1973.

Octave Morel, *La vie à Châtillon-en-Dombes d'après les comptes de syndics: 1375–1500*, vol. 1, Bourg-en-Bresse, 1921.

Franco Morenzoni, *Marchands et marchandises au péage de Villeneuve de Chillon: (première moitié du XVe siècle)*, Lausanne, 2016.

Franco Morenzoni, *Sur les routes des Alpes – Religieux, marchands et animaux dans la Suisse occidentale (XIIIᵉ-XVᵉ siècles)*, Turnhout, 2019.

Irma Naso, "Il platea mercati. Il piccolo comercio in centri urbani dell'Italia nord-occidentale (secoli XIII-XV)", in *El mercat. Un món de contactes i intercanvis*, ed. Flocel Sabaté Curull, Maite Pedrol, Lleida, 2014, pp. 99–118.

Flavia Negro, *Scribendo nomina et cognomina. La città di Vercelli e il suo distretto nell'inchiesta fiscale sabauda del 1459–60*, Vercelli, 2019.

Francesco Panero, "Un tributo bassomedievale gravante su servi e liberi: la *taglia* in Savoia e in Piemonte (secoli XII-XV)", in *"Quei maledetti Normanni". Studi offerti a Errico Cuozzo per i suoi settant'anni da Colleghi, Allievi, Amici*, ed. Jean-Marie Martin and Rosanna Alaggio, Ariano Irpino, vol. 2, 2016, pp. 783–798.

Thierry Pécout (ed.), *De l'autel à l'écritoire. Genèse des comptabilités princières en Occident*, Paris, 2017.

Thierry Pécout, *L'enquête générale de Leopardo da Foligno*, 9 vol., Paris, 2008–2017.

Thierry Pécout (ed.), *L'enquête générale de Charles II en Provence (1297–1299)*, Paris, 2018.

Thierry Pécout, "Les registres dits rationnaires de la Chambre des comptes de Provence. La question d'une comptabilité générale sous la première maison d'Anjou", *Bibliothèque de l'École des chartes*, 174, 2018–2019, pp. 59–106.

Thierry Pécout, "Comptabilité urbaine, comptabilité du prince: modèles et interactions en Provence (XIIIᵉ-début XIVᵉ s.)", *Comptabilité(s)*, 12 (2019) [online].

Gaines Post, *Studies in Medieval Legal Thought. Public Law and the State, 1100–1322*, Princeton, 1964.

Charles W. Prévité Orton, *The early history of the House of Savoy: 1000–1233*, Cambridge, 1912.

Blythe Alice Raviola, Claudio Rosso and Franco Varallo (eds.), *Gli spazi sabaudi. Percorsi e prospettive della storiografia*, Rome, 2018.

Albert Rigaudière, "L'essor de la fiscalité royale, du règne de Philippe le Bel (1285–1314) à celui de Philippe VI (1328–1350), in *Europa en los umbrales de la crisis (1250–1350). XXI semana de estudios medievales, Estella '94*, Pamplona, 1995, pp. 323–391.

Laurent RIPART, *Les fondements idéologiques du pouvoir des comtes de la maison de Savoie (de la fin du Xe au début du XIIIe siècle)*, PhD Dissertation, University of Nice, 1999.

Jacques ROSSIAUD, *Dictionnaire du Rhône médiéval. Identités et langages, savoirs et techniques des hommes du fleuve (1300–1550)*, 2 vol., Grenoble, 2002.

Paul ROUX, "Bertrand Roquefort et les comptes trésoraires de la ville d'Hyères en 1397–1398", in *Recueil de mémoires et de travaux publiés par la Société d'histoire du droit et des institutions des anciens pays de droit écrit*, 9, 1979, pp. 107–140.

Manuel SÁNCHEZ MARTÍNEZ, *El naiximent de la fiscalitat d'Estat a Catalunya (segles XII-XIV)*, Girona, 1995.

Manuel SÁNCHEZ MARTÍNEZ, "La convocatoria del usatge *Princeps namque* en 1368 y sus repercusiones en la ciudad de Barcelona", in *El temps del Consell de Cent, I. L'emergència del municipi, segles XII-XV*, ed. Manuel ROVIRA I SOLÀ and Sebastià RIERA I VIADER, Barcelona, 2001, pp. 79–107.

Giuseppe SERGI, *Potere e territorio lungo la strada di Francia*, Napoli, 1981.

Joseph SHATZMILLER, "La perception de la *tallia judeorum* en Provence au milieu du XIVe siècle", in *Annales du Midi*, 82, 1970, pp. 221–236.

Daniel Lord SMAIL, "The general taille of Marseille, 1360–1361: a social and demographic study", in *De Provence et d'ailleurs*, pp. 473–486.

Louis STOUFF, "Les livres terriers d'Arles du XVe siècle", in *Les cadastres anciens des villes et leur traitement par l'informatique*, ed. Jean-Louis BIGET, Jean-Claude HERVÉ and Yvon THÉBERT, Rome, 1989, pp. 307–340.

Armando TALLONE, *Parlamento Sabaudo*, 13 vols., Bologna, 1928–1946.

Denis TAPPY, *Les États de Vaud*, Lausanne 1988.

Huguette TAVIANI, "Le commerce dans la région aixoise au milieu du XIVe siècle (1348–1349) à travers un fragment de compte de péage d'Aix-en-Provence", in *Annales du Midi*, 74, 1962, pp. 255–285.

Clémence THÉVENAZ, *Écrire pour gérer. Les comptes de la commune de Villeneuve autour de 1300*, Lausanne, 1999.

Max TURULL RUBINAT, "Gobierno municipal y fiscalidad en Cataluña durante la Baja Edad Media", in *Anuario de historia del derecho español*, 76, 2006, pp. 507–530.

Pierre VAILLANT, "Le commun du vin dans les villes du Dauphiné et du Faucigny aux XIIIe et XIVe siècles d'après les chartes de franchises", in *Le Vin au Moyen Âge: production et producteurs*, Grenoble, 1978, pp. 1–5.

Alain VENTURINI, "La gabelle du sel des comtes de Provence des origines sous Charles Ier d'Anjou jusqu'à la fin du règne de Jeanne Ière. État de la question", in *Le roi, le marchand et le sel*, ed. Jean-Claude HOCQUET, Lille, 1987, pp. 105–115.

Monique ZERNER, *Le cadastre, le pouvoir et la terre. Le Comtat Venaissin pontifical au début du XVe siècle*, Rome, 1993.

14
KINGDOM OF ENGLAND

Maureen Jurkowski

The main focus of this chapter will be the development and evolution of English royal taxation from the Norman conquest of 1066 to the end of the reign of the first Tudor king, Henry VII, in 1509. The origins of the system that began to develop in the early thirteenth century lay in the need for England's kings to raise extraordinary sums of money to fight their increasingly frequent wars of conquest and defence, and the dawning realisation that the traditional feudal levies that they had imposed on their vassals since the eleventh and twelfth centuries would not yield what was required. By the mid-thirteenth century it had become evident that the king could only demand such heavy exactions with the consent of his greater subjects, who were seen to be representative of their tenantry – hence the concurrent development of "great councils" into "parliaments" of lords and commons. Except in national defence emergencies, when it was acknowledged that the king had the right to force their hand, he could only procure grants of subsidies and other taxes in this way; the price of his subjects' assent was his reciprocal agreement to redress their complaints against his rule. His relationship with the clergy evolved similarly at roughly the same time: by 1280 the clerical provinces of Canterbury and York were meeting in separate convocations to make their own grants of taxation, again in exchange for the remedy of grievances. Indeed, the main purpose of both parliaments and convocations was always the granting of supply to the king. To a certain extent, therefore, the history of taxation parallels the development of these representative assemblies – a theme explored in important monographs by the historians Gerald Harriss and John Maddicott.[1]

Key to the establishment of England as a strong monarchical state in the two centuries following the Conquest had been its development of an efficient central administration, at the heart of which were the secretarial office of Chancery, financial office of Exchequer and the common law courts of justice. The creation and preservation of their administrative records on parchment rolls – continually augmented and kept for future reference – were fundamental to all three, as were the local officials supporting them, such as the unpaid tax collectors appointed to collect taxes on an ad hoc basis.[2] The rich archives of the royal Exchequer in particular provide historians with the tools necessary to understand the workings of the government's finances and public taxation system. They attest also to both the ambition and practical success of the English medieval crown in drawing its subjects into the public and collective enterprise of taxation.

In the first half of the twentieth century, when the taxation records from the royal Exchequer became available for public scrutiny at the Public Record Office (now The National Archives) in London, it was largely American scholars who took the lead in their systematic examination and analysis. Sidney Knox Mitchell consulted the great rolls of the Exchequer ("the pipe rolls") for his survey of taxation in the twelfth and thirteenth centuries. The doyen of parliamentary lay taxation, James Willard, spent years mining the series of miscellaneous documents subsidiary to the tax collectors' accounts (series E 179) which culminated in the publication of his authoritative history of the subject, as well as a useful guide to Exchequer sources on taxation. Finally, the painstaking researches into papal taxation of William Lunt, drawing upon papal, episcopal and royal archival sources, underpins all subsequent work on the taxation of the English and Welsh clergy.[3] The next generation of taxation historians – most notably Mark Ormrod, Jeffrey Denton and Alison McHardy – all benefitted from the pioneering work of these scholars.

A university-based research project carried out at The National Archives between 1995 and 2013 has made its own contribution by re-cataloguing the 36,000 documents (dating from *c.* 1200 to *c.* 1700) that comprise the E 179 series, correcting previous errors and adding newly-discovered items from unsorted miscellanea. Now entered into an online database that links each item with a specific tax grant or imposition and provides indexes of the properties taxed, this new research tool allows scholars to interrogate and analyse these records remotely.[4] In offering direct evidence of the assessment and collection processes, these records elucidate the recurrent problems faced by both royal governments and taxpayers throughout the middle ages (and beyond) in the continual striving towards fair and effective taxation of the kingdom's inhabitants. These problems will be at the forefront of the broadly chronological analysis of both lay and clerical taxation presented below.

First, two preliminary points about the scope of the coverage should be made. Although the medieval kingdom extended geographically beyond England into lands over which its kings claimed lordship – namely, Ireland, Wales, Gascony and other French territories – these states lay largely outside the system of parliamentary taxation established in the thirteenth century. Generally speaking, their residents paid taxes to English kings only in their capacity as feudal lords, chiefly because sovereign representative bodies comparable to the English parliament had been either slow to develop or were lacking entirely there.[5] Hence they figure only briefly in this history, with the exception of the Welsh clergy who paid clerical taxes as part of the province of Canterbury.

Similarly, a paucity of record sources means that the subject of municipal taxation can only be treated separately from royal taxation in a cursory fashion. From an early date the largest towns paid a negotiated annual "fee-farm" (*firma burgi*) to the king in lieu of the revenues due to him from tolls, rents and borough court profits. We know only the total amounts paid – not how they were assessed or collected – and that some fee-farms had to be reduced in the later middle ages because of economic decline. By the same token, payments of early occasional taxes (*dona* or "aids") to the crown were recorded, but not how they were raised.[6] Only a few extant early borough *tallage*★ rolls, moreover, provide evidence of urban taxes imposed by seigniorial lords; most such rolls relate to the royal *tallages*★ discussed below.[7] Finally, in the early thirteenth century, cities and boroughs began to purchase royal licences for permission to collect specific types of tolls (for periods of years) in order to finance public works projects such as the paving of roads (*pavage*), building of walls (*murage*), and erection of bridges and port defences (*pontage* and *quayage*). While evidence is plentiful of the granting of these licences, accounts for the tolls collected – such as the *murage* and *pavage* account of 1256 from Shrewsbury recording weekly receipts of about 20*s*. (£1) at the town's three gates – are more scarce. In fact, most large municipal building works were funded by bequests in testamentary wills and other charitable donations.⁸ All other urban taxes were those levied by the royal government, discussed below.

Early land taxes: *gelds* and *carucages*

The eleventh-century Old English, pre-Conquest kings levied a general land tax known as a *geld** – originally devised as tribute to placate Danish invaders – to meet their extraordinary expenditure. The unit of assessment in most of the south was the "hide" – generally understood to be the basic unit of land sufficient to support a very large family group, varying in size according to the fertility of the soil and prevailing local customs. In Kent it was the "sulung", and in the north the "carucate" (or ploughland) – i.e., the amount of land that could be ploughed by one team of oxen in a year. In East Anglia, uniquely, a set rate of £10 was levied on each hundred (an administrative unit estimated at 100 hides) to which each vill contributed. The few surviving "*geld** rolls" record the number of hides in each hundred liable to pay (usually at the rate of 2*s*. per hide), together with hides that were waste or otherwise exempt.⁹

William I (the Conqueror) imposed *gelds** at least three times, levying one in 1084 at 6*s*. per hide to increase its yield, on the basis of outdated pre-Conquest assessments. Following a *geld** inquisition in 1086, meant to discover "lost hides" that had long evaded payment, William ordered the comprehensive survey of his new kingdom known as the "Domesday Book". Although its primary purpose appears to have been to assess the kingdom's resources, it was clearly used, at least partly, to collect future *gelds**. Unsurpassed in its scope and thoroughness, the Domesday survey compared the present ownership of lands, estates and towns with that in the reign of Edward the Confessor. Having divided the country into seven or eight circuits, assessment was made by commissioners from the nobility whose principal interests were in other counties, in order to ensure their impartiality. Initial assessment was based on written accounts provided by tenants-in-chief to county sheriffs. Local officials and six jurors of each village then checked this information against the *geld** rolls in the commissioners' presence, and more detailed, local information was collected, when disputed claims were heard. Finally, the survey was standardised and abbreviated.¹⁰

William's successors continued to levy *gelds**: his son William II levied it at a double rate in 1096, Henry I imposed *gelds** annually for at least part of his reign, and Stephen also levied them, but was generous with grants of exemption. Henry II collected a *geld** in 1156 but had to pardon about 20 per cent and allowed much as waste, due to the civil war in Stephen's reign. Details of the last known collection, in 1162, were entered onto the "pipe rolls".¹¹ By the end of the twelfth century it had been replaced by a similar land tax: the *carucage**.

The first *carucage** was an emergency measure based on an outdated *geld** assessment levied in 1194 at 2*s*. per ploughland for the ransom demanded by Emperor Henry VI to release Richard I (the Lionheart), captured in 1193 on his return from the Third Crusade. The new assessment made for the *carucage** levied at 5*s*. per carucate in 1198 was based on the oaths of local officials (overseen by a knight and clerk in each county) as to the number of cultivated carucates in each vill, by what form of tenure they were held, what their value was and who held them. It provoked follow-up enquiries by royal justices in eyre, who suspected underassessment, and many landholders made fines in lieu of divulging further details of their holdings. Large landowners again paid fines to avoid assessment when John levied a *carucage** in 1200, using the plough team itself as the unit of assessment, and in fact, few, if any, of the subsequent *carucages** levied in the early years of Henry III's rule were fully assessed. Little is known of the *carucage** of 3*s*. per hide levied in 1217, but a few assessment rolls survive for the *carucage** of 2*s*. per plough levied in 1220. They reveal that in Wootton hundred in Oxfordshire the overall hundred totals were merely apportioned among the vills, while religious houses, some northern barons, and the men of Cornwall instead paid lump sums. The yield was a disappointing £2,671 1s.8½d. The final *carucage**, granted in 1224 by bishops and abbots when Bedford castle was under siege by the rebellious baron Falkes de Bréauté, raised at least 3,500 marks by levying half a mark on their demesne lands and 2s. on the lands of their free tenants and villeins, but the manner of assessment is unknown.[12]

Feudal taxes: tallages, scutages and feudal aids

Two other types of taxes levied in the twelfth and thirteenth centuries – *tallages** and *scutages** – were feudal in origin and of French derivation. Manorial lords had imposed *tallages** on their unfree tenants at will since before the Conquest, levying amounts agreed between lord and tenant, not based on assessed values, generally once per year. The royal *tallage** that developed in the second half of the twelfth century was, by contrast, an occasional imposition on the free men of the king's boroughs and tenants of his rural demesne negotiated by royal officials working in circuits of several counties.

Henry II levied *tallages** in 1168, 1173, 1174, 1177 and 1187, sometimes in conjunction with *scutages** for his military campaigns. In 1194 a *tallage** partly paid the ransom of Richard I and he levied four more in successive years. King John levied four *tallages** from 1203 to 1206, assessed by his justices in eyre and collected by the sheriffs, and again, at higher rates, in 1210 and 1214. Henry III collected *tallages** fourteen times, most often to pay debts, and with frequency between 1237 and 1269, when parliament withheld consent to *fractional taxes**. At least twelve *tallages** were imposed on the Jews between 1210 and 1278, especially during Henry III's reign, when he demanded large sums from them.

*Tallages** were otherwise abandoned after 1268 because they were not as lucrative as the *fractional taxes** levied by Henry and his successor Edward I. But as impositions that required no consent they were revived in 1304, in the face of new resistance to *fractional taxes** after 1297, which they were adapted to resemble. Both lands and moveable goods were valued in London in 1304, if not elsewhere, although some taxpayers fined in lieu of assessment. In 1312 Edward II imposed a *tallage** at two rates: a tenth on landed revenue and a fifteenth on moveable goods. When Edward III proposed a similar *tallage** in 1332, parliament granted him a tax on moveable goods instead. He promised not to levy *tallages** again and they were duly abolished by an act of 1340.[13]

*Scutage** – known by 1100 – was a payment to commute military service due to the king by his tenants-in-chief (i.e., vassals holding land directly from him) when required to do so. Its origins lay in the association of landholding with military obligation, whereby their lands were valued in knights' fees, each fee being the amount of land considered adequate to support one knight on military service. When the king issued a summons for the feudal host, he expected each tenant-in-chief to appear personally at the appointed time and place with his full complement of knights. Levied after a campaign on those who had not answered the summons or served, *scutage** reimbursed the king for the cost of hiring replacements.

It became over time an increasingly unpopular and ineffective tax. The inherent inflexibility of the arrangements created difficulties, as the inflation that began in the late twelfth century and continued until about 1260 produced a corresponding rise in military wages and the costs of plate armour and warhorses, affecting not only the mercenaries to be hired but also those tenants-in-chief willing to perform their military obligations in person. The original quota of knights' fees for which tenants-in-chief were liable became increasingly unrealistic, and the subdivision of individual fees with the passing of generations made further complications. *Scutage*★ rates rose to compensate for the shortfall, doubling from 10*s*. per knight's fee in 1189 to 20*s*. by 1195, and to 40*s*. by the mid thirteenth century.

By way of compromise, both John and Henry III reduced the nominal knights' fees for which each tenant-in-chief owed service or *scutage*★ (the "*servitia debita*") in lieu of higher *scutage* rates. Kings abused their right to levy *scutage*★: it became an arbitrary way of raising revenue (sometimes) long after the campaign which it justified. As a result, evasion, delays and resistance by those liable to pay led to diminishing returns and the practice evolved where fines were taken at the outset from those unwilling to serve before the host was summoned in lieu of paying *scutage*★ later. By the end of Henry III's reign fining in advance occurred regularly.[14] In 1279 Edward I instituted the practice of double-charging, by collecting both advance fines for his Welsh campaign of 1277 and levying a *scutage*★ on his tenants-in-chief of 40*s*. per fee on their original number of fees. Although hotly disputed, it formed a precedent on which Edward II and Edward III drew when levying *scutages*★ in 1285, 1305, 1314, 1319 and 1337 for their Welsh and Scottish campaigns. By 1337 there were six *scutages*★ in the process of collection, and in 1340 Edward III agreed to abandon *scutage*★ collections and pardon all sums owed for them, in return for a parliamentary tax grant. One further attempt to levy a *scutage*★ by Richard II in 1385 proved to be the last.[15]

The third of the early feudal taxes was the *feudal aid*★, an obligatory contribution required from vassals to assist their feudal lord in exigent circumstances. It persisted as a form of taxation into the later middle ages, but by then required parliamentary sanction. From the twelfth century, it was customary in two sets of circumstances. According to a legal treatise attributed to the jurist Ranulf de Glanville, a lord could exact a *feudal aid*★ to pay the expenses of knighting his eldest son or marrying his first-born daughter. The exactions had to be reasonable and moderate, according to the size of the vassal's fee, so that he should not lose the property needed to maintain his position. The basis of assessment of these *aids* evolved over time and kings increasingly abused the rules for levying them.

Henry I levied an *aid* to marry his daughter Matilda to Emperor Henry V in 1110 as a *geld*★, at the rate of 3*s*. per hide, whereas his grandson Henry II collected another to marry his daughter Matilda to the duke of Saxony in 1168 in the form of a *scutage*★ of one mark per knight's fee, but he also took gifts ("*dona*") from both prelates holding land by military service and sheriffs, and a *tallage*★ from royal demesne tenants.[16] In 1235 Henry III levied a *scutage*★ of two marks per fee to marry his sister Joan to the Emperor Frederick II as an *aid*, justified by her father King John's failure to levy such a tax, and in 1245 Henry collected an *aid* of 20*s*. per fee to marry his eldest daughter Margaret, although the wedding did not take place until 1251. Edward I did not let the death in 1291 of Alfonso III of Aragon, intended husband of his eldest daughter Eleanor, deter him from levying the *aid* granted in 1290 for their marriage twelve years later to pay his Scottish military expenses. An *aid* to knight the future Edward II was levied in 1306 as a thirtieth and twentieth on moveable goods. Even more unusually, Edward III raised an *aid* in 1333 to marry his sister Eleanor to Reginald, count of Guelders, by sending begging letters to 295 members of the higher clergy, who contributed £1,320.

Edward III's highly contentious *aid* to knight his son Edward, the Black Prince, in 1346 provoked anger and violent resistance. Without parliamentary approval, he attempted to charge double *scutage*★ rates on not only his own military tenants, but also those of other lords. While it eventually raised over £9,000, Edward had to agree to halve the rate of future *aids* by statute. Henry IV's *aid* of 1401 for the marriage of his daughter Blanche to Rupert, duke of Bavaria, proved something of a fiasco, with the collection much delayed and loans necessary to meet the expenses. When, in 1504, Henry VII attempted to levy two *aids* for knighting his eldest son Arthur (died 1502) and marrying his daughter Margaret to James VI of Scotland in 1503, parliament placated him with a subsidy of £30,000, in lieu of a fresh assessment of knights' fees. The subject of *feudal aids*★ was not raised again until the seventeenth century.[17]

Fractional taxes, 1166 to 1332

Slowly but inexorably *fractional taxes*★ on moveable goods eclipsed *gelds*★ and feudal taxes. Both easier to assess and more profitable to levy, they were arguably the first truly national taxes even if their origins as "aids" to support the crusading states in the Holy Land were international and ecclesiastical in inspiration. Imposed by Henry II in 1166, at the suggestion of the French king Louis VII, the first *fractional tax*★ levied 2*d*. on each pound (£) of all revenue or moveable goods for one year, and 1*d*. in each of the next four years. Individuals possessing only a house, or a trade, were charged 1*d*. – all proceeds to be stored in locked chests inside parish churches. The surviving ordinance for an "aid" imposed for the Holy Land in 1185, based on a tax levied in Palestine in 1183, suggests that it was collected by the international military orders and charged complex, graduated rates in England and Henry II's French domains.

We know much more about the "*Saladin tithe*" of 1188 levied in response to Saladin's victory at Hattin, in order to fund a third crusade, led by Henry II and Phillip II of France. Levied at three or four times the rate of the previous two, a tax of one tenth of rents and moveable goods for one year was collected in each parish in the presence of the parish priest and rural dean, a Knight Templar, a Knight Hospitaller, a royal servant and clerk, the baron's servant and clerk, and the bishop's clerk. If anyone was deemed to have paid less than they ought, four or six jurors from the parish declared on oath the amount that he should have paid, to be added to the total due. All laymen and clergy (crusaders excepted) had to pay, on pain of imprisonment, but many resisted. The chronicler Gervase of Canterbury estimated the yield at £70,000 from Christians and £60,000 from Jews – almost certainly an exaggeration. Henry died before he could take the cross; his son Richard I used the proceeds for his crusade in 1190. It was another "aid" that raised the bulk of the funds needed for the 100,000 marks needed to ransom the captive Richard in 1193, plus an additional £5,000 tribute, in the form of a fourth from the rents of all laymen and clergy for one year and a fourth of their moveable goods. Four collections had to be made, including one of gold and silver plate from churches. Even though Emperor Henry VI raised his demand by 50,000 marks, enough of the money was paid to the imperial representative in London to effect Richard's return in March 1194. The remainder was pardoned by Duke Leopold on his deathbed.

In a reign marked by war with France and baronial rebellion, only twice did John levy *fractional taxes*★ – both times encountering resistance. The seventh that he imposed on the goods of earls and barons in 1203 was a punitive tax for allegedly deserting him in Normandy. Assessed by the king's justiciar and the archbishop of Canterbury, little is known of the actual levy. When John desperately sought funds in 1207 to recover his lost Norman lands – after the seven *scutages*★ levied between 1199 and 1206 – his council agreed to a thirteenth, levied as an aid of 1*s*. in the mark on rents and moveable goods, paid by both laymen and clergy. Royal justices carried out the assessment, on the oaths of every man, as to the value of his rents and goods. Despite evasion, concealment of goods and outright refusal to pay, over £57,425 was reportedly received, some of it from the penal fines of defaulters and lump sums paid by the higher clergy in lieu of assessment.

Henry III did not levy his first *fractional tax*★ until 1225, when his minority government looked to the precedent of 1207 for a tax that could raise great sums to respond to the threat to Gascony posed by Louis VIII's conquest of Poitou. A "great council" of over sixty leading bishops, abbots, earls and barons debated the justiciar Hubert de Burgh's proposal of a fifteenth on moveable goods for at least a week before agreeing to levy it in exchange for the king's confirmation and reissue of the Great Charter (*Magna Carta*) of 1215 and Charter of the Forest of 1217. Both charters listed fundamental liberties and privileges which King John and his son had been forced to concede to rebel barons – key concessions that would be demanded time and again in future tax grants. It was at this juncture that the reciprocal nature of the tax granting process began to be established. It was also a seminal moment in the evolution of the great council into a representative "community of the realm" and forum for granting royal taxation, created from the consequences of Richard's capture and John's disloyalty to him and early death, leaving a minor son.

The careful assessment process for the 1225 levy also furnished a precedent for future *fractional taxes**. Commissioners (termed "justices") were appointed in each county to oversee the assessment. They chose four knights of each hundred to assess and collect the tax in the neighbouring hundred, but not their own. All landowners, both lay and clerical, including merchants in cities and boroughs, were liable to pay, but the poor were excused after complaints. Taxpayers had to swear as to the number, quantity and value of their goods, and those of their two nearest neighbours, with disputes settled by a jury of local men. The assessment of the goods of the nobility was made, however, on the oaths of their reeves or sergeants. Exempt from assessment were books, church and chapel ornaments, horses, jewels, plate, utensils, the contents of larders, cellars and haybarns and grain bought to provision castles. Merchants were not liable for tax on arms, riding horses, domestic utensils or the contents of their larders and cellars for their own consumption or use, while villeins were not taxed on arms which they were sworn to carry, utensils, flesh, fish, drink, hay or forage for their own consumption or use. Surviving assessments suggest that considerable effort was made to obtain accurate valuations, but members of some religious orders paid lump sums in lieu of assessment. Total receipts were estimated in the 1230s at 86,758 marks, 2*d*. (about £58,500).[18]

The fortieth levied by Henry III in 1232 to pay debts incurred during his Gascony campaign is notable for establishing a two-step assessment process by local jurors, supervised by knights and reeves. For the first time a minimum threshold of liability for taxpayers – which was to fluctuate thereafter – was set (at 40*s*.) and the clergy were not assessed for the goods on the lands attached to their churches (spiritualities). Accordingly, the yield was estimated by the Exchequer at only 24,712 marks 7*s*.5*d*. (about £16,400). The assembly in which the thirtieth levied by Henry III in 1237 was granted was the first that was officially designated as a "parliament". The tax was not meant to fund a military campaign, but to repay debts incurred through maladministration and the marriage of Henry's sister. It was agreed only after the king admitted three new barons to his council and re-confirmed the charters, as in 1225. He also had to stipulate expressly that granting an aid for non-military purposes would not serve as a precedent. It yielded only 33,811 marks 2*s*.1*d*. (about £23,000).

After 1237 parliaments and councils were reluctant to grant taxes for several decades because of their opposition to Henry III's government, specifically refusing to do so in 1242, 1244, 1254, 1257 and 1258. Only after the defeat of the baronial reform movement in 1265 did grants resume – the first being the twentieth on goods voted in 1269 to finance a crusade by Prince Edward, levied only after representatives of the commons gave their consent, and yielding nearly £31,500. In 1275 the laity granted Edward I a fifteenth on goods to pay his crusading debts, but the "first national tax for war" in his reign was the thirtieth on goods voted in 1283 by the laity and clergy, in two separate parliaments, for his conquest of Wales. In 1290 a parliament which sat for four months granted him a fifteenth on goods for expenses incurred in Gascony, to be paid over two years, probably on condition that he expel the Jews. In

January 1291 the levy was extended to Wales and in October 1291 to Ireland, where the clergy were also asked for a tenth. Some fifteen assessment rolls survive from Wales, but no enrolled account. In Ireland the tax was collected only with great difficulty; as late as 1299 it had yielded only £4,796. Henceforth (from 1300), the king negotiated with individual communities in Wales and Ireland for subsidies.[19]

The rate of these intermittent tax grants escalated rapidly in the war-plagued years of 1294 to 1297. Philip the Fair's formal confiscation of Gascony in May 1294, quickly followed by the outbreak of rebellion in Wales and formation of a Franco–Scottish alliance in October 1295, initiated a crisis. In March 1296 Edward invaded Scotland, expeditions were sent to Gascony in 1294, 1295 and 1296 and the English coast was threatened with invasion. As a result, grants of *fractional taxes*★ became at first annual, and then regular, occurrences until the early years of Edward III's reign. The *fractional tax*★ granted in 1294 contained the important innovation of a double rate. Taxpayers in urban areas and the royal ancient demesne paid the higher rate of a sixth, since they were believed to possess greater wealth than those in rural communities, who paid only a tenth.

For this reason, differential rates became the norm for most future *fractional taxes*★. An eleventh and seventh, e.g., was levied in 1295, and a twelfth and eighth in 1296, when treasure in the form of coins became a taxable item and it remained so thereafter. The crisis year was 1297 when Edward led an unpopular expedition to Flanders and his demands for further heavy taxation faced serious opposition. Both the barons and the clergy – the latter by then taxed separately on their spiritual income – had become weary of the financial burdens under which they had been placed by both *fractional taxes*★ and concurrent indirect taxes. In October 1297 the eighth and fifth granted in July by a group of magnates, deemed insufficiently representative, was cancelled in favour of a single-rate ninth voted by a full parliament only after Edward made the familiar concession of re-issuing the charters.[20]

Continuing conflict with Scotland led to regular grants of *fractional taxes*★, albeit grudgingly conceded, from 1301 to 1332. The fifteenth granted in 1301 was initially only a twentieth that was increased after Edward agreed to various reforms. In view of the urgent situation, no minimum threshold of liability was set. The fifty-seven wealthiest towns, based on the last assessment, were asked to pay negotiated lump sums and loans were solicited from them in anticipation of the tax collection, a practice that would be repeated in future. Parliament's final grant to Edward I was in 1306; seven others made to his son Edward II in 1307, 1309, 1313, 1315, 1317, 1319 and 1322, at varied rates, added to the latter's unpopularity. In addition to reported resistance to the 1317 levy, complaint was made in parliament in 1319 that the assessors and their clerks had embezzled at least a third of all the aids hitherto voted to Edward II, prompting investigations of corruption in fourteen counties. The tenth and sixth granted in 1322 – the most onerous of his reign – yielded over £42,000, most of which he kept for his own use, since a truce with Scotland was agreed soon after payment of the first instalment.

After Edward III's accession to the throne in 1327, parliament granted him a twentieth for the Scottish war, most of which instead paid his debts to the Bardi merchants. In 1332 parliament voted him a *fifteenth and tenth*★ under a new two-tiered system of administration. Two assessors and collectors appointed in each county delegated under-assessors to make the assessment, receive the money and transfer it back to them for payment into the Exchequer. Complaints of fraud and corruption on the part of the assessors and collectors led, however, to a major investigation by the Exchequer, beginning in 1335. Such corruption may have become endemic among crown tax officials who, it should be noted, received no payment for their services. The historian Mark Ormrod also noted that despite charging different rates, all *fractional taxes*★ prior to 1332 produced similar yields, attributing the phenomenon to the increasing expertise of administrators in undervaluing property.[21] The *fifteenth and tenth*★ granted in 1332 proved to be the last directly-assessed *fractional tax*★ on moveable goods. As we shall see, a new system was devised in 1334.

Separate taxation of the clergy: *papal tenths* and *clerical tenths*

Until the reign of Edward I, the clergy paid land taxes and *tallages*★ along with the laity, but these were not the only fiscal burdens that they bore. Since 1173 the papacy had imposed subsidies periodically on the income from their spiritualities (i.e., income from lands appurtenant to their parish churches), mostly to fund crusades to the Holy Land. Information about these levies is sketchy until the papal fortieth imposed by Innocent III at the end of 1199 – a tax that was assessed on the oaths of the clerics themselves, collected by the bishops and delivered to the papal nuncio Master Philip the notary. The papal twentieth levied in 1217, similarly assessed, provided the basis of subsequent papal levies until the assessment made for the *papal tenth* of 1229. The *three papal tenths* imposed over three years by Pope Innocent IV from 1254 to fund Henry III's intended crusade necessitated a new assessment – the so-called "Valuation of Norwich" (named after the bishop who supervised it) – verified by rural deans. Subsequent valuations for *papal tenths* in 1267 to 1269 and in 1276 proved highly contentious, due mainly to their inclusion of the clergy's temporal possessions, and *papal tenths* were still levied according to the 1254 valuation as late as 1290. In the early part of this period, the English clergy may have paid these taxes without much objection, but as the thirteenth century progressed, they met increasingly in provincial and other clerical councils to consider papal demands and sometimes oppose them. Henry III also began to claim the right to withhold his assent to their imposition. Popes were compelled, therefore, to grant Henry and his successors at least a share of the proceeds if they promised to undertake a crusade, such as occurred with all the *papal tenths* levied between 1267 and 1280.[22]

It was also early in Edward I's reign that the clergy first agreed to pay the king *fractional taxes*★ on their spiritualities. In 1275 they rebuffed him with pleas that they were already paying *papal tenths*, but in January 1280 the clergy of Canterbury province (which included the Welsh dioceses) agreed to grant a fifteenth for two years. Meeting separately in Pontefract weeks later, the clergy of most of York province voted a *clerical tenth*★, establishing a pattern that would be largely repeated for the next 250 years. Usually, but not always, clerical tax grants closely corresponded to lay tax grants made in parliament, after pressure applied by the king's councillors.[23]

These clerical taxes were levied on spiritualities in accordance with the 1254 assessment for *papal tenths*, but clerical resistance to the taxation of temporalities ended after the new assessment (the "*Taxatio*") made in 1291 for the *six papal tenths* imposed by Pope Nicholas IV two years earlier to fund a crusade by Edward I. Presided over by the bishops of Winchester and Lincoln, two separate teams carried out a careful assessment of spiritualities and temporalities, working to detailed papal instructions of what was to be taxed and what was to be exempted – i.e., the income of leper houses, hospitals, poor nuns and the Hospitallers and Templars. Any benefice holder whose total income was less than six marks (or £4) was also exempt, but if a benefice holder derived an income of more than six marks from several benefices, no matter how small the income from each, every separate item of income was assessed. The rector was liable for the whole income of his church, even where a vicarage had been endowed, but the assessors in practice treated the income of each vicar separately, and if his total income was less than six marks, the vicarage escaped taxation. The assessment of temporalities, undertaken mostly by cathedral canons working in dioceses other than their own, was hotly contested as being grossly and arbitrarily overvalued. The *Taxatio* assessment was not used to collect clerical taxes until the moiety (i.e., one-half) granted in 1294, since the assessment was still in progress when the first instalment of the *papal tenths* imposed in 1289 came due. Thereafter it became the assessment according to which clerical and papal taxes were collected for the rest of the middle ages, each *tenth* yielding about £16,000 (£12,000 from the southern province and £4,000 from the north).[24]

The unprecedented level of taxation triggered by Edward I's wars from 1294 to 1297 hit the clergy particularly hard. Firstly, monastic houses with great flocks of sheep bore the brunt of Edward's confiscation of wool, woolfells and hides in the summer of 1294 and greatly increased the new customs duty that he imposed on the forced sale of each sack to benefit his coffers. Collected for three years and yielding in all £110,000, this wool tax ("*maltolt*") had the effect of suppressing the prices paid to the houses by wool merchants. In the same summer Edward ordered royal agents to seize all money and treasure stored in religious houses and churches, on the pretext of searching for clipped coins. In a meeting of both convocations in September he insisted that the clergy pay him a moiety (one-half) of their income for a year, in three payments. Countering fierce resistance from the lower clergy with the threat of outlawry, he forced them to comply, but agreed to exempt benefices worth less than ten marks per annum; the total amount assessed was nevertheless £105,300. In the autumn of 1295 Edward asked the clergy for a third or fourth, but they agreed to only a *clerical tenth*★ over two payments, following difficult negotiations led by Robert Winchelsey, archbishop of Canterbury, who refused a demand for a further subsidy in November 1296.

In response Edward outlawed the entire clergy in early 1297, instructing sheriffs to fine them a fifth of their income. Most submitted to his authority, purchasing letters of protection, but Winchelsey held out until July. When Edward renewed his demand for a subsidy in August, the clergy would not agree, citing the recent papal bull *Clericis Laicos* that forbid taxation of the clergy by secular rulers without papal approval. Edward then forcibly imposed a tax as a national emergency measure, offering them a choice between a fifth of their whole income or a third of their temporalities alone; most opted for the former. In response to his urgent request for another subsidy when the Scots invaded in the autumn, the southern convocation voted a *clerical tenth*★ in November 1297, the lower clergy to pay according to the 1254 assessment only. Being more directly affected, the York convocation granted a fifth, paying some in kind, such as in the provision of horses. The southern clergy ceased payment once the immediate crisis had passed, and when Edward asked for the balance in June 1298, they retorted that no tax could be paid without papal permission.[25]

No further clerical or papal taxes were levied until Pope Boniface VIII's imposition of three *papal tenths* in 1301. With a much-reduced minimum threshold of liability of two marks (26s.8d.), these *tenths* required a new assessment of the previously unassessed minute benefices and a slight revision to the *Taxatio* assessment because of damage to the northern benefices by marauding Scots. Boniface gave half the proceeds to Edward I, who also claimed the rest after the pope's death in 1303. In future, Edward and his successors found the sharing of *papal tenths* a useful arrangement whenever the clergy refused them subsidies. At Edward's request Pope Clement V imposed seven *papal tenths* on his behalf in 1305, collected by Edward's own agents and paid directly to his creditors. Having secured renewal of Clement's grant after his father's death in 1307, the new king Edward II similarly took direct possession of the proceeds, and, indeed, the papacy imposed continuous *papal tenths* largely on his behalf and that of Edward III until 1336. From the onset of the French war in 1337, Edward III was able to persuade the clergy to grant *clerical tenths*★ to him regularly and the imposition of *papal tenths* for English kings ceased.[26] With very few exceptions, all taxes on clerical income thereafter were levied directly by the crown and authorised by consent in convocation.

Lay fifteenths and tenths, clerical tenths, wool taxes and a parish tax

Meanwhile, when the laity granted Edward III a *fifteenth and tenth*★ for the expenses of the Scottish war in 1334 his ministers devised a new means of establishing taxpayers' liability. The king appointed two "chief taxers" for each county (one lay and one cleric) to treat with the most substantial men of the cities, boroughs, vills and ancient demesne, and settle with them an overall amount which their localities should pay, provided that it was not less than the total paid by that locality in 1332. Wherever negotiations failed, the taxers would assess the amount themselves. From the crown's point of view there were manifold benefits to this new "quota system": the slightly increased overall yield would remain stable over time (about £37,000), the tax could be collected more quickly and with much less administrative effort, fraud was more easily detectable and the anticipatory loans (which became a regular feature) would be raised more easily on the strength of the guaranteed yield. It was a further step, moreover, towards familiarising the realm with the need for recurrent taxation. So successful was this form of taxation that it remained in place for 300 years.[27]

Thus it came to pass that the separate systems developed in the thirteenth century for the taxation of the laity and clergy came to resemble each other in their abandonment of continuous assessment in favour of fixed levies, based on the valuations made in 1334 and 1291, respectively. Over time, however, modifications to the fixed levies were required to respond to changed economic circumstances. The earliest of these were deflations in value of some northern ecclesiastical benefices due to Scottish raids. A revaluation in the dioceses of York, Durham and Carlisle, known as the "*Nova taxatio*", had already been made for the levy of *papal tenths* on behalf of Edward II in 1317. Reducing the yield of a *clerical tenth*★ there by £1,600 (nearly a third), it was henceforth employed for the collection of both clerical and papal taxes. A further devaluation in the diocese of York in 1328, after renewed hostilities with Scotland, lowered the yield further.[28]

Edward III's need had only increased, however, by the end of the 1330s and the beginning of the French war. Although he was able to secure grants of multiple units of the fixed-levy taxes on six occasions – *three fifteenths and tenths* in 1337, 1348 and 1352 and *two fifteenths and tenths* in 1344, 1346 and 1373, with the clergy following suit – there was no increase of yield, since the instalments were paid each time at the usual half-yearly intervals. The popularity of the fixed-levy system of the *fifteenth and tenth*★ was enduring, however, with the aristocratic and mercantile classes represented by the members of parliament who voted for taxes. It allowed them to control its assessment locally and by undervaluing their own property, shift the tax burden onto the shoulders of the peasantry. As a result, efforts to levy other subsidies that would tax the wealth of the king's prosperous subjects more effectively were always resisted. The three *fifteenths and tenths* and three *clerical tenths*★ levied in 1337, e.g., were granted in exchange for the cancellation of a fledgling attempt to levy a subsidy of 12*d.* per pound on the lands of both laity and clergy.[29] Other types of taxes, nonetheless, were soon under consideration.

An assembly of wool merchants had already agreed in that same summer to participate in a scheme to seize 30,000 sacks of wool and sell them in Dordrecht on behalf of the king, who was to receive half the profits – anticipated to reach £200,000. Ninety-nine purveyors of wool were appointed from the merchant community to purchase wool compulsorily, operating in separate teams in each county or group of counties. They were to pay set prices for the best wool and bargain a price for lesser quality wool, paying half the amount due within six months of receiving the wool and the other half within the year, the payment guaranteed with their personal bonds. The scheme ran into trouble, allegedly through the corruption of the two lead merchants overseeing it and disputes between the king's representatives and the Dutch merchants, and in February 1338 parliament voted the king half the wool in the kingdom – an estimated 20,000 sacks – to make up the shortfall. There was still a deficit of 17,500 sacks in July, causing a great council to grant a further *wool tax* on both laity and clergy, according to the 1334 and 1291 assessments, at ten stones of wool for every 20s. of assessment paid for the *fifteenth*, and a *pro-rata* amount for the *tenth*. Later it was ordered that those without wool pay with money and the cities of London and York make fine instead. The tax eventually yielded the equivalent of 14,000 sacks.

A variation on this theme of a combination *wool* and *fractional tax*★ followed in the complex *two ninths and fifteenths and subsidy on wool* (payable over two years) granted in parliament in April 1340, when the king's desperate need for money for the French war coincided with a severe depletion in the supply of coin. Modelled on the ecclesiastical tithe, rural inhabitants engaged in arable or pastoral farming were asked to pay a ninth of corn, wool, and sheep in kind ("the ninth sheaf, the ninth fleece, and the ninth lamb") for two years, while town-dwellers paid a ninth of the value of their moveable goods and rural merchants and people living in forests or wastes were taxed at a fifteenth of theirs. Like clerical taxes, the levy would be organised at the parish level and proceeds were expected to reach £100,000 each year. The king appointed assessors to value, collect and arrange for the sale of the goods to local purchasers, at prices higher than their value under the *Taxatio* of 1291. The preferred purchasers, in the first instance, were to be the rectors or farmers of the parish churches, who were to pay in advance of their receipt of the goods, which would be delivered to them by the individual taxpayers. At the lowest level, therefore, the administration of the tax would be as far as possible identical with that employed for the gathering of tithes, and the goods required from each taxpayer would simply represent an addition to those that they contributed to the church. The assessors were to take security for the purchases, but the collection of the money itself was the job of receivers appointed in each county.

Collection of the tax was complicated by the shortage of coin, high prices fixed for the sale of the goods and a general resistance to its novelty. Only £15,000 had been received by the end of 1340 and yet the king had already assigned £200,000 to his creditors in return for their loans. The goods had to be sold in the end for less than their *Taxatio* value and the second year of the tax was replaced by a grant of 30,000 sacks of wool. After the administration of a levy of a further 20,000 sacks of wool (granted by a great council convened while Edward was abroad in 1347) was dogged by resistance and allegations of fraud, *wool taxes* ceased.[30]

The year 1340 also saw the onset of *tunnage and poundage*, an indirect tax on a wide range of imported and exported commodities, but most importantly on tuns of wine (6d. per tun, initially) and sacks of wool (1s. per sack). Originally granted to the king by his council, with the assent of an assembly of merchants, the profits were earmarked to provision English ships with arms to protect them from the French. Although the first grant was in effect from late August to early October, it was renewed ten times over the years 1345 to 1382, increasingly by parliament. From 1386 the tax was virtually permanent, with fixed-term grants that usually dovetailed, at 3s. per tun and 1s. per pound value of merchandise, the rate that became standard thereafter. Henry V, Henry VI and Edward IV received life grants and from 1484 such grants were made in the first parliament of a new king's reign.[31]

The end of the 1340s was marked by the social upheaval that followed the arrival of the Black Death in 1349. A large portion of the population having perished, the surviving labourers demanded higher wages for their work. Consequently, the wealthy complained of being unable to pay the second and third of the three *fifteenths and tenths* granted in 1348. The collectors were instructed to assess labourers' wages retrospectively and collect tax from the labourers for them, but the plan proved unworkable. By the time of the three *fifteenths and tenths* granted in 1352, limits had been set on wages under the Ordinance and Statute of Labourers, enforced by itinerant royal justices, and under the terms of the tax grant, fines collected for violations were assigned for redistribution to indigent vills to help them pay their *fifteenth and tenth** quotas.[32]

Edward III levied only *fifteenths and tenths* and *clerical tenths** in the 1350s and 1360s, but in 1371 his council devised an experimental *parish tax* to fund a new expedition to France. Agreed by parliament and both convocations only under duress, its goal was to raise £100,000, half each to come from the laity and clergy, administered separately. Having estimated that there were 45,000 parishes in England, the council calculated that the target could be achieved by collecting a national average of 22s.3d. from the laity in each parish, with richer communities helping poorer ones meet these quotas. The figure of 45,000 parishes – perhaps derived from the widely-read *Polychronicon* of Ranulf Higden – turned out to be grossly overestimated (the true figure was about 8,600), and the quota due from each parish had to be increased to 116s. The province of Canterbury was expected to raise £45,000 of the £50,000 – two and a half times what they paid for a *clerical tenth**. Benefices were charged one and a half tenths of their income, and, for the first time, benefices that had not been assessed in 1291 – i.e., those owned by more recent foundations such as secular colleges or chantries – were taxed at a tenth of two-thirds of their value. Finally, unbeneficed (stipendiary) clergy paid a tenth of the value of their annual income. Despite considerable resistance and widespread evasion, the eventual yield was around £42,000 from the clergy and £49,600 from the laity. Many of the proceeds, however, had still not been received as late as 1376, and the tax had proved administratively complex.[33] This particular experiment was not repeated, therefore, although another parish-based tax was attempted in 1428.

Poll taxes, income taxes, alien subsidies and benevolences, 1377 to 1504

It was perhaps not so much of a conceptual leap to make from the 1371 tax to the *poll taxes** levied from 1377 to 1381 on individual members of the laity and clergy. The first of these, granted in parliament in February 1377, was a straightforward tax of 4d. on every man and woman over the age of 14, "honest beggars" excepted, for another French campaign. Two men and the constable of each vill (or the bailiff in boroughs) were to make the local assessment and collection, overseen by county commissioners and sheriffs. A return of taxpayers' names to the Exchequer was not required, but some of the hundreds of surviving receipts given to the collectors by the commissioners reveal the number of persons taxed in each vill. The yield was a disappointing £22,560. The clergy also voted to pay a *poll tax** in convocations that met in March and April, to be levied at two rates. Every beneficed cleric or member of the religious orders, of both sexes, was to pay 1s. (or 12d.), and all unbeneficed clerics (over 14 years old), excluding mendicant friars, paid 4d. Most of the extant returns from seven dioceses list the names of the clergy. The total yield from both provinces was estimated at a mere £1,100.[34]

At Edward III's death in June 1377, a minority council governed for his grandson Richard II. Following the laity's grant of two *fifteenths and tenths* in October for an unsuccessful foreign campaign led by Richard's uncle John of Gaunt, duke of Lancaster, parliament refused a further subsidy in October 1378 for the expenses of Richard's coronation. In May 1379, however, they granted a graduated *poll tax**. Using the same administrative apparatus as in 1377, the tax was levied in accordance with a tariff of fifteen separate rates paid by twenty-two social ranks.

The highest was 10 marks paid by the dukes of Lancaster and Brittany, while many of the other ranks were charged according to the values of their estates. Lesser merchants and artisans were taxed, e.g., at one of five rates, ranging from 6s.8d. to 6d. Widows paid at the rates that their husbands would have and married men not in any of the tariff categories paid 4d. for themselves and their wives. Unmarried persons paid 4d. for themselves alone. Clergy paid a comparable tariff of rates for each clerical rank, according to the values of their benefices, offices or monastic estates. Unbeneficed clerks aged sixteen or older paid 4d. Mendicant friars and nuns from monastic houses with an annual income of less than £40 were exempt. The return of taxpayers' names to the Exchequer was required from both the lay and clerical collectors, and full or partial returns survive from fourteen dioceses and nineteen counties. Both levies were beset by widespread underassessment and evasion, and only £22,000 altogether was raised.[35] The crown then returned briefly to more conventional taxation, securing a grant in February 1380 of one and a half *fifteenths and tenths* from the laity and a *clerical tenth** from the clergy. The latter included a tax of 16d. in the mark on two-thirds of the value of unassessed benefices and a *poll tax** of 2s. each from unbeneficed clergy. Returns listing the names of unbeneficed clerks survive from fourteen dioceses, plus the liberty of St Albans abbey.[36]

The most infamous of these *poll taxes** was granted in parliament on 6 December 1380, following a month of debate, to alleviate severe financial difficulties caused by the disruption of the wool and cloth trade in Flanders, impending military campaigns in Scotland and France, and royal debts. At three groats (1s.) from all persons of both sexes over fifteen years of age, it was three times the 1377 rate for a single person and six times that of married couples in 1379. It did, however, mandate that the wealthy of each vill should help the less well-off pay their tax and set limits on how much (sixty groats or £1) and how little (one groat or 4d.) each married couple could be charged. Championed by the chancellor, Simon Sudbury, archbishop of Canterbury, the lay tax was expected to yield 100,000 marks, and was conditional upon a like grant by the clergy, intended to raise 50,000 marks. At his prompting, the southern clergy made their grant the day before the laity gave their consent, with the York convocation following suit in February 1381. It levied two rates: twenty groats (6s.8d.) from beneficed and unbeneficed clerics and office holders of both sexes, and three groats (12d.) from clerks in minor orders, aged sixteen or older (friars excepted). Bishops had discretion as to the rate charged; in Lincoln and London dioceses the unbeneficed and monastic clergy (below the rank of prior) paid an intermediate rate of 3s.4d. Most clerics, however, were assessed to pay 6s.8d.

These ambiguities caused confusion during assessment and collection, leading to widespread evasion, outright refusal to pay and violence against the collectors. Indeed, attempts to collect the second instalment sparked the rebellion in June 1381 known as "the Peasants' Revolt" during which rebels captured and beheaded Archbishop Sudbury. Records of the returns, nonetheless, survive in greater number than from the earlier *poll taxes**.[37] It is little wonder that there were no more lay *poll taxes** for a century thereafter and both laity and clergy were subsequently stinting in their grants of *fifteenths and tenths** and *clerical tenths** to the unpopular Richard II. Following a series of tyrannical measures that included imposing a penal tax on London in 1392 and a coercive forced loan in 1397, Richard was overthrown by his cousin Henry of Bolingbroke, crowned as Henry IV in 1399.[38]

It was in Henry's reign that crown ministers devised the first in a series of experimental taxes on the landed income of the laity. By the fifteenth century landed wealth had clearly become the unit of assessment for the *fifteenth* in many places, although elsewhere both land and goods were taxed. In the north, where a pastoral economy predominated, the tax was levied on livestock. In towns and boroughs, goods and possibly wages were assessed for the *tenth*. Evident everywhere is that many of the wealthy paid little or no tax. To increase yields and tax wealth more effectively the king's ministers tried to levy directly-assessed taxes on wealth and income. That these efforts were resisted by parliamentary knights of the shire and burgesses at every turn is no better illustrated than by the conditions attached to the novel *income tax** granted in March 1404, when the crown was beset by war and rebellions in Wales and Ireland and massively in debt.

Anxious that it did not form a precedent for future grants, the subsidy of £12,000 was agreed by the commons on condition that no mention of it be made on the parliament roll and that all records of the tax be destroyed afterward. The lords made a similar grant (on income of 500 marks or more) some months later, but without the secrecy provisions. Lands held by military tenure were to be taxed at 20s. per knight's fee, with portions of fees to pay on a *pro-rata* basis, and lands held by other forms of tenure, worth 20s. or more annually, to pay a lesser rate of 12d. (or 1s.) per pound (5 per cent). Tenants of land worth less than 20s., who possessed moveable goods valued at £20, would also pay 1s. per pound, but no one would be taxed on both lands and goods. The grant would be cancelled if the planned military campaigns did not take place and the king appointed four war treasurers to receive and disburse the proceeds. Apart from those of the lords, who contributed over £996 in tax, assessments were forbidden to be returned to the Exchequer to prevent the disclosure there of the value of taxpayers' estates.[39] A second subsidy on land, granted in 1411, was levied only on lands or rents worth £20 or more, at the less contentious rate of 6s.8d. per £20 of land (or 2%). Accordingly, only £1,388 was received.[40]

The clergy generally responded to Henry IV's requests for tax grants with *clerical tenths**, but in 1404, to correspond with the lay subsidy, the southern convocation granted their usual *clerical tenth** and an additional subsidy of 2s. per pound from all benefices and offices (worth £5 or more) not assessed for the *Taxatio*. Assessed by the bishops, the unassessed benefices yielded an additional £880. The same subsidy on the unassessed was granted again in 1406, by both convocations, together with a standard *clerical tenth** and a *poll tax** of 6s.8d. from every unbeneficed stipendiary or salaried chaplain – including friars, for the first time. Total proceeds were £3,419 from the south and £627 from the north. The low yield from the latter is perhaps the reason why no further *poll taxes** were levied on the unbeneficed in the north, and on only one further occasion (in 1418) did holders of northern unassessed benefices pay the *clerical tenth**. In the south, however, *clerical tenths** on unassessed benefices were frequent from 1415, and from the reign of Edward IV, were regularly included in grants of *clerical tenths**. Another *poll tax* on unbeneficed chaplains (receiving an annual income of seven marks or more, or stipends of 40s. plus food provision) was levied in the southern dioceses in 1419, along with half a *clerical tenth**. These *poll taxes** targeted the inflated wages of chantry chaplains, whose numbers had swelled since the Black Death. Nominal returns survive from eleven dioceses; the net yield was £1,515.[41]

Attempts to increase the crown's tax revenue had become ever more desperate since the beginning of the fifteenth century. Economic depression, caused primarily by depopulation, was manifest in the decline of the woollen cloth trade, falling rents and a shrinkage of coin; by the mid fifteenth century the economy had fallen into a slump.[42] Accordingly, subsidy yields were on the decrease. Because of impoverishment from the frequent Scottish wars, grants of *clerical tenths** by the northern clergy were made by the late fourteenth century only on condition of specific hardship exemptions – many of them in effect over prolonged periods of time. In 1408 the minimum threshold of liability for benefice holders rose to ten marks annually and lists of exemptions grew ever longer. In the wealthier southern province the liability threshold remained in place until 1425 but claims for hardship exemptions or reductions – usually considered at diocesan level after convocation – were ever more numerous. Convocation also exempted some categories of individuals, such as non-resident incumbents studying at university. The many surviving certificates give details of exemptions, often the result of environmental disasters such as frequent coastal flooding, as well as general economic decay.[43]

Claims for hardship exemptions also of course came from lay taxpayers and collectors – most notably, from destruction and depopulation in the English border counties caused by the revolt of the Welsh rebel leader Owain Glyn Dŵr from 1400 to 1409 – but shifts in population and the distribution of wealth since 1334 required more lasting adjustments to the *fifteenth and tenth*★ quotas.[44] Accordingly, a rebate of £4,000, to be deducted from the overall sum of £37,000, was instituted in the 1433 grant of a *fifteenth and tenth*★, and reapportioned on a *pro-rata* basis to poorer vills, cities and boroughs so that they could meet their quotas. The members of parliament themselves appointed assessors to redistribute the rebates in their counties and draw up schedules of the reductions for the collectors and Exchequer. The rebate was included in all future levies of *fifteenths and tenths* and in 1446 was increased to £6,000. Rebates continued to be assessed after each tax grant, although in 1468 the total rebates apportioned to each county were fixed.[45] About 100 surviving schedules of reductions thus provide rare evidence for shifts in the distribution of wealth.[46]

Succeeding his father in 1413, Henry V required high levels of taxation to fulfil his large military ambitions in France. His solution to the problem of lower tax yields was to levy double *fifteenths and tenths* and *clerical tenths*★ at much accelerated payment dates – effectively doubling the rates. Altogether, he levied ten and one-third *fifteenths and tenths* in his short reing of nine years, and twice raised general public loans, secured on the receipts of these taxes. In 1421 he toured his kingdom, raising further loans (without guaranteed repayment) totalling £36,840 – the bulk of it from his uncle Henry Beaufort, the wealthy bishop of Winchester.[47]

After the accession to the throne of his infant son Henry VI, who proved much less adept in securing tax grants and relied heavily on forced loans,[48] experimental lay taxes on income again came to the fore. The first, granted in 1428, was a tax on both parishes and knights' fee. Rural lay householders paid at one of two rates, based on the 1291 *Taxatio* valuation: 6s.8d. if the church was valued at under ten marks, or 13s.4d. for every ten marks of value (a tenth), if over 10 marks. In cities or boroughs, following new assessments of churches (many of which would not have been assessed in 1291), parishioners of parish churches valued at 20s. or more paid a rate of 2s. per 20s. (also a tenth). Tenants of lands held by military tenure paid 6s.8d. per knight's fee, one-quarter knight's fee being the threshold of liability. Yielding only £12,291, it was deemed a failure. In 1429, together with a grant of one and a half *clerical tenths*★, the southern convocation was compelled to grant a *poll tax*★ on unbeneficed clergy, graduated according to five income brackets, ranging from £5 to £10, that yielded about £968. In 1431, the king's ministers attempted to levy a lay subsidy on income from land on the same basis as the 1411 tax, but at much higher rates (£5 per knight's fee, £1 per £20 of the net annual value) and a lower threshold of liability (one-tenth of a knight's fee, £5 net annual value). It was replaced by a *fifteenth and tenth*★ after fierce resistance and delay during assessment, but assessments from a handful of counties survive.[49]

A far more ambitious tax on all forms of income was granted by the lords and commons in December 1435 to be levied at three graduated rates: (1) annual incomes of £5-£100 taxed at 6d. per pound; (2) incomes of £101-£399 taxed at the same rate for the first £100, but the second £300 at 8d. per pound; and (3) incomes of £400 paid 2s. per pound on their entire income. Lands, goods, wages and annuities were all taxable, while fees paid to their retainers by the nobility and gentry were allowable deductions from their tax liability. The chancellor and treasurer assessed the nobility, but the rest of the taxpayers had to appear before commissioners appointed by the king's council, and nominal returns to the Exchequer were required. The yield was less than £9,000.⁵⁰ In addition to one and a half *clerical tenths*★, the southern clergy granted, for their part, a *poll tax*★ on unbeneficed clergy, at two graduated rates, which yielded £1,214. A final *poll tax*★ on stipendiary clergy (including mendicant friars), at a single rate of 6*s*.8*d*., was included with the grant of a *clerical tenth*★ by the southern convocation in 1449; gross receipts were estimated at £1,193.⁵¹

The last and broadest in scope of Henry VI's *income taxes*★ was the lay subsidy granted in June 1450 in a desperate bid to finance reinforcements in Normandy. It took the same form as the 1435 graduated *income tax*★, but attempted to extend the levy to a larger proportion of the population by lowering the liability threshold on landed income to 20*s*. per annum and £2 of annual wages, and increasing the tax rate in the middle income bracket to 12*d*. per pound. Whereas only landowners of freehold lands had been liable for past *income taxes*★, in 1450 lands held by customary tenures were also taxed, as were estates owned communally (by cities, towns, guilds and other corporations), and also income from offices of £200 annually and over. The assessment and collection process was intensely resisted; it coincided with a major uprising against the government ("Cade's Rebellion"), forcing an increase in the minimum thresholds of liability on land and wages to 40*s*. and £3, respectively, by amendment to the subsidy act in December 1450. Collected by four war treasurers and disbursed to military captains, the proceeds did not reach £7,303.⁵²

Xenophobic feeling against England's large community of alien merchants and craftsmen was particularly strong in England in the 1430s and 1440s, when the English suffered a series of reversals of fortune in France. A 1436 treatise advocated the restriction of their liberties and legislation enacted in 1439 attempted to control the trade of foreign merchants. They could not buy or sell commodities to other aliens inside England, had to be "hosted" by Englishmen, and sell their goods within eight months of arrival. In 1440, the first of a series of *poll taxes*★ on resident aliens (aged over twelve years) granted in parliament imposed an annual tax of 16*d*. on alien householders and 6*d*. on alien non-householders for three years. The names and occupations of all aliens (including the Irish) living in each county were ascertained in inquests held before its justices of the peace, with sheriffs responsible for collecting and accounting for the tax twice annually at the Exchequer. Alien wives of English men and members of monastic communities were exempt, as well as purchasers of letters of denization.⁵³

The *alien subsidy*★ was extended in 1442 for a further two years, the Irish and Channel Islanders being declared exempt, and again in 1449 for four years, when two new higher rate categories of taxpayer were added: alien merchants (6*s*.8*d*. each) and their clerks (20*d*. each). Aliens born under the king's allegiance in Normandy, Gascony and Guyenne were made exempt. The *alien subsidy*★ granted to Henry VI for life in 1453 included two rates on alien merchants, brokers, factors and their attorneys (40*s*., householders; 20*s*. non-householders). After the Yorkist seizure of power in 1461, Edward IV continued to levy it (from 1463) on the grounds that the grant was for the "natural" life of the deposed Henry, but collection ceased after his death in May 1471. Edward was granted an *alien subsidy*★ in his own right in 1483, at much higher rates and with a new category of alien brewers but died before it was levied. His brother Richard III collected it under the same grant in 1484, exempting certain favoured alien merchants, as did his successor Henry VII, under a one-year grant in 1487.⁵⁴ *Alien subsidies*★ never raised much money; evasion was widespread, exemptions frequently purchased, and sheriffs were increasingly disinclined to administer the tax properly, as a team of researchers into alien immigration into England recently found in a systematic investigation of the extant records.⁵⁵

The search for new, more effective lay taxation meanwhile continued. In April 1453, facing a desperate situation in France, parliament granted a novel lay subsidy of 13,000 archers, to be raised proportionally in the counties and funded for six months. It was conditional upon Henry leading a force to France personally; since he never did, the grant was cancelled.[56] Although Edward IV twice tried to levy *income taxes** early in his turbulent reign, he relied on *fifteenths and tenths* and *clerical tenths** until 1472,[57] when he procured a grant of the same 1453 tax for his own French campaign. This time the commons granted a subsidy to pay the wages of 13,000 archers for one year, at the rate of 6*d*. per day – a total of £118,625. Each locality was expected to support its quota of archers, the allocation having been based upon the amount paid there for a *fifteenth and tenth**, but the money was to be raised by a tax of one-tenth of the net income for one year from lands, tenements, rents, fees, annuities, offices, corrodies and pensions, paid by their owners or occupiers, whether held jointly or severally, by any form of tenure, to their own use or by others to their use. There was no minimum threshold of liability and the taxable year began on 1 January 1472. County commissioners would make assessments and appoint collectors to deliver the proceeds to local repositories for deposit until the muster of troops. The return of the assessments to the Exchequer was forbidden. The lords granted their tax separately, to be administered by the archbishop of Canterbury and three other lords, and the clergy made corresponding grants of *clerical tenths**.

Because the grant was of a specific sum of money, parliament was not dissolved upon the subsidy act's passage, but merely prorogued until 8 February 1473, when the commons were due to be informed of the total receipts. By the end of the session (8 April), however, they still did not know the amount and agreed to a *fifteenth and tenth** in order to pay the archers' wages before the king sailed. Only in July 1474 did the information arrive that the proceeds totalled a mere £31,410 14*s*.1½*d*., with returns still lacking from five northern counties. Although the yield was suspiciously close to that of a *fifteenth and tenth**, when one compares the amounts assessed in each county and city with those paid for a *fifteenth and tenth** genuine shifts in the distribution of wealth can be perceived.[58] Assessors may have consistently undervalued taxpayers' income, but they do appear to have carried out assessments. To make up the shortfall, the commons demanded that the delinquent northern counties pay the outstanding £5,383 15*s*. for their quota of archers and apportioned the remaining sum of £51,147 4*s*.7¾*d*. among individuals in the rest of England known to have paid little or nothing. This strategy of targeting individuals reportedly proved too "diffuse and laborious" and the commons agreed to convert the tax into its equivalent in *fifteenths and tenths* (one and three-quarters). On 14 March 1475 Edward IV finally dissolved parliament. He sailed in July with the largest army that had ever invaded France but was bought off by the French almost immediately with a lump sum and life annuity. Popular disturbances followed the return and disbanding of the army, and in October 1475 Edward was forced to remit the final instalment of the *fifteenths and tenths* (three-quarters).[59]

These problems did not deter Henry VII from levying a modified form of this tax in 1489, when seeking £100,000 for an expedition to aid Anne, duchess of Brittany, against the French. The commons granted him £75,000, levied as an *income tax** of one-tenth of a year's net income and 20*d*. on every 10 marks' worth of goods. The remaining £25,000 was to come from the clergy, levied as two *clerical tenths** (*pro-rata*). Although they laid down harsh penalties for refusal to receive the proceeds in the designated repositories, as occurred in 1472, collection problems, an uprising against the tax in Yorkshire, and massive underassessment added up to a total yield of only around £27,000. A *fifteenth and tenth** made up the shortfall.[60]

In 1496 the Scots threatened to invade. Henry VII raised loans, hoping for £120,000, in anticipation of a subsidy grant. Early in 1497 the commons granted two *fifteenths and tenths*, which would yield £62,000, but since that amount fell short of Henry's target, they soon after voted the specific additional sum of £62,000 as an "aide and subsidy" to be collected from landowners with estates worth 20s. per annum or more, or possessors of goods and chattels worth 10 marks or more, according to the discretion of the appointed tax commissioners. With few fixed rules and no appeals procedure, it was arbitrary in practice and proved highly contentious. In Cornwall, it sparked a rebellion and the second instalment was cancelled; the yield reached only £30,735.[61] The southern clergy had made a corresponding grant of £40,000, levied as two *clerical tenths*★, pro-rata (£10,000 of which was cancelled), and the northern clergy a standard two *clerical tenths*★.[62] The final fixed-yield tax levied by Henry VII was a subsidy of £30,000, accepted by him in 1504 in lieu of two (far more intrusive) *feudal aids*★ with the clergy granting corresponding taxes.[63] Fixed-yield subsidies continued to be levied by Henry's son Henry VIII until 1523, when they gave way to directly-assessed subsidies with a much-improved machinery of administration, but after this form of taxation lapsed into institutionalised underassessment, the fixed-yield subsidy returned and predominated for much of the seventeenth century.

Finally, mention should be made of a form of *feudal aid*★ that originated under Edward IV and had a long subsequent history: the *benevolence*. It derived from the notion that it was the king's prerogative to require a contribution from his subjects for the defence of the realm in lieu of military service – an updated form of *scutage*★ – without any form of parliamentary approval. An expression of his goodwill, the subject made the gift freely in return for the king's "benevolence". Edward imposed the first *benevolence* in late 1474 on the wealthier of his subjects for the expenses of his impending French campaign. He began in London with the mayor and aldermen, before extending his solicitation efforts to the citizenry, most of whom gave £4 11s.3d., the equivalent of the wages of half a man, at 6d. per day, for a year. He then toured the countryside in a four-month charm offensive, described by an Italian observer as "pluck[ing] out the feathers of his magpies without making them cry out". Contributors gave promissory notes for their gifts – some of which have survived – but receiving the actual monies proved arduous. Although the general-receiver's account, rendered in May 1475, recorded receipts of £21,656 8s.3d., payments were still being pursued in 1478.[64] Edward's second *benevolence*, imposed in 1481 for a campaign against the Scots, had a strong element of coercion; reluctant donors were reminded that the king could compel them to fight if they refused to contribute. Total receipts were estimated at £30,000, even though northerners mostly provided soldiers instead of money.[65] Ignoring a statute passed in 1484 banning their imposition, Henry VII levied his own *benevolence* in 1491 to finance an expedition to Boulogne, using strong-arm tactics. Promised sums were again slow to materialise – the archbishop of Canterbury's contribution of £1,500 was not received, e.g., until June 1496 – but total proceeds eventually reached £48,498 16s.8d.[66]

As a method of raising money when parliament was stingy with tax grants, *benevolences* were a useful last resort and continued to be imposed by Tudor and Stuart kings; Elizabeth I even collected one from the clergy. In a society where valuation of the property of the king's most prosperous subjects was an intrusion to be avoided at all costs, the *benevolences* and forced loans solicited in the fifteenth century, while seeming unfair abuses of royal power, may have been the only viable way to break through the collusive obstruction of the aristocratic and mercantile classes. They presented an individual, personal approach to the problem of achieving effective taxation of the nation's wealth in order to provide good governance and defend the realm. It was a problem that consistently challenged English royal government throughout the middle ages and would continue to do so in future.

Conclusion

As we have seen, underassessment and evasion were recurrent themes in the history of public taxation in medieval England. The early land-based *gelds*★ and *carucages*★, and the feudal *tallages*★, *scutages*★ and *aids* – generally limited to tenants of the royal demesne – often relied on outdated assessments or negotiated lump sum contributions. The directly assessed *fractional taxes*★ on moveable goods that extended the levies to a wider populace received their initial impetus from the international crusading movement and could only continue to be justified by similarly consequential wars of conquest and defence. They required the consent of taxpayers through representative assemblies, who, from 1225, demanded concessions from the king in return. The reciprocal tax-granting process fuelled the development of parliament as a legislative body, but its primary purpose remained supplying kings with the necessary funds to meet their extraordinary expenditure. In the middle years of Henry III's reign his rebellious barons did refuse his requests, but when in the grip of national emergencies – firstly, from 1294–1297, and again in 1340–1341 – English kings enforced their right to compel subjects to aid them in times of necessity. In 1297, as we saw, this compulsion went as far as outlawing the clergy. English taxpayers grew accustomed to consistently high levels of taxation, but the assessors, drawn from the ranks of local gentry, softened the blow by continually undervaluing property.

The replacement of the directly assessed *fractional tax*★ in 1334 with a negotiated, fixed *fifteenth and tenth*★ in which each locality paid a "quota" provided the king with a guaranteed yield and simplified the tax's administration. By the latter part of the century, however, demographic and economic decline had decreased the yields of both *fifteenths and tenths* and *clerical tenths*★, which encouraged experimental (but deeply unpopular) types of subsidy, such as the 1371 *parish tax* and 1377–1381 *poll taxes*★. In truth, allowing local elites to shift the burden of taxation onto the peasantry after 1334 meant that their representatives in parliament would oppose repeated royal attempts to secure grants of directly assessed taxes on income in the next century. When the king's need for supply was such that he could not be refused, parliament attached conditions such as the appointment of war treasurers to administer the proceeds and the prohibition of the return of assessments to the Exchequer. Through underassessment and evasion, moreover, they ensured that the proceeds fell far short of expectations, all the more evident after the onset of fixed-yield subsidy grants in 1472. It was only by personal interventions that fifteenth-century kings were able to wring substantial contributions from their greater subjects in the form of *benevolences* and loans.

Did the remarkable ability of the late medieval parliament to maintain control and thwart the king's will in this respect constitute a serious challenge to the crown's authority, marking a staging post in the evolution of parliamentary democracy, as past generations of English historians have maintained? Perhaps, but no matter how much the crown was weakened by Henry VI's ineffectual rule and the disruptive Wars of the Roses, parliament was still unable to refuse the king's requests to fund his wars, and at no time before the seventeenth century was it claimed that the king derived his authority from parliament itself. Arguments for an "English exceptionalism" should instead be sought in the combination of historical factors that forged the unique English link between representation and taxation – namely, a long tradition of wide conciliar consultation by its kings, the chronic insecurity of the royal succession that included periods of minority rule and dynastic challengers, strong local administrative structures, and perhaps most crucially, the liability of the English nobility to pay royal taxes with the rest of the kingdom, which gave them a stake in both the institution of parliament and the tax-granting process.[67] It was the historical accident of their confluence that created England's "exceptional" system of medieval parliamentary taxation.

Maureen Jurkowski

Notes

1 HARRISS, *King, Parliament*; MADDICOTT, *Origins*.
2 CLANCHY, *From Memory*, pp. 162–172; BROWN, *The Governance*, pp. 43–60, 100–140.
3 MITCHELL, *Taxation*; WILLARD, *Parliamentary Taxes*; WILLARD, "A Brief Guide"; LUNT, *Financial Relations*.
4 Administered successively by Cambridge University, University of Wales, Bangor, and the University of York: CROOK, "Records"; JURKOWSKI, SMITH and CROOK, *Lay Taxes*, pp. v–xvi; JURKOWSKI, "Clerical Taxation". For the E 179 database: www.nationalarchives.gov.uk/e179/.
5 STRAYER and RUDISILL, "Taxation"; THORNTON, "Taxing".
6 TAIT, "The *Firma Burgi*", pp. 321–360, lists fee-farms paid to 1191; STEPHENSON, *Borough*, pp. 222–224, lists *dona* and aids to 1189; BRIDBURY, "English".
7 REYNOLDS, *An Introduction*, pp. 50–51, 126–129; MARTIN, "The English Borough", pp. 123–144, surveys early borough records; *Sixth Report*, pp. 579–580.
8 HARVEY, "Pavage Grants"; COOPER, *Bridges, Law and Power*, pp. 80–148 (pp. 155–168 list *pontage* grants to 1400); HARRISON, *The Bridges*, pp. 208–213; ALLMAND, "Taxation"; MASSCHAELE, "Tolls and Trade"; MARTIN, "English Borough", pp. 136–137, for the Shrewsbury account.
9 STENTON, *Anglo-Saxon England*, pp. 644–648; CHIBNALL, *Anglo-Norman England*, p. 106n.
10 GALBRAITH, *Domesday Book*, pp. 33–46; GREEN, "Last Century", pp. 241–245. For a full edition: *Domesday Book, A Complete Translation*.
11 JURKOWSKI, et al., *Lay Taxes*, pp. xvi–xvii; GREEN, "Last Century", pp. 241–258.
12 JURKOWSKI, et al., *Lay Taxes*, pp. 4–6, 8–11; MITCHELL, *Taxation*, pp. 121–131, 136–138; TOMKINSON, "The Carucage", pp. 212–216; CARPENTER, *The Minority*, p. 223.
13 JURKOWSKI, et al., *Lay Taxes*, pp. xxiii–xxiv, 26–27, 30–31; MITCHELL, *Taxation*, pp. 237–357; STACEY, "Royal Taxation"; HADWIN, "The Last Royal Tallages".
14 JURKOWSKI, et al., *Lay Taxes*, pp. xix–xxi, 27, 31–32, 35. 42–43. BARRATT, "The Revenue of King John", for the yields of *scutages* levied by John.
15 CHEW, "Scutage under Edward I"; CHEW, "Scutage in the Fourteenth Century"; LEWIS and PALMER, "The Feudal Summons".
16 JURKOWSKI, et al., *Lay Taxes*, pp. xxiv–xxvi; MITCHELL, *Taxation*, pp. 164–165. For the recently edited *scutage* assessment of 1166: *Carte Baronum*, pp. xiii–xxxviii.
17 JURKOWSKI, et al., *Lay Taxes*, pp. xxv, 15, 26, 28–29, 47–48, 73, 129; MC HARDY, "Paying for the Wedding"; *Inquisitions and Assessments*, for the edited 1302, 1346 and 1401 assessments.
18 CAZEL, "The Tax"; LUNT, "The Text"; MITCHELL, *Taxation*, pp. 114–127; JURKOWSKI, et al., *Lay Taxes*, pp. xxvi–xxvii, 1–4, 7–8, 10–11; BARRATT, "Revenue of King John", p. 839; MADDICOTT, *Origins*, pp. 106–109; CAZEL, "The Fifteenth".
19 JURKOWSKI, et al., *Lay Taxes*, pp. 13–21; MADDICOTT, "The Crusade Taxation"; HARRISS, *King, Parliament*, pp. 27–48; STRAYER and RUDISILL, "Taxation", pp. 410–416; WATT, "Was Wales".
20 HARRISS, *King, Parliament*, pp. 49–74; JURKOWSKI, et al., *Lay Taxes*, pp. 22–24.
21 JURKOWSKI, et al., *Lay Taxes*, pp. 25, 29–38; HARRISS, *King, Parliament*, pp. 75–97; MACKMAN, "The 'Unfortunate' Fraudster"; ORMROD, "The Crown", pp. 153–155.
22 LUNT, "Early Assessments"; LUNT, *The Valuation*; LUNT, "Papal Taxation"; LUNT, *Financial Relations*, 1, pp. 187–346.
23 DEIGHTON, "Clerical Taxation"; JURKOWSKI, "Clerical Taxation", pp. 55–71.
24 DENTON, "The Valuation"; JURKOWSKI, "Clerical Taxation", pp. 61–64. Printed edition at *Taxatio Ecclesiastica*; collated edition of *Taxatio* manuscripts by Jeffrey H. Denton, 2014, at www.dhi.ac.uk/taxatio.
25 DENTON, *Robert Winchelsey*, pp. 55–176; LUNT, *Financial Relations*, 1, pp. 346–365.
26 LUNT, *Financial Relations*, 1, pp. 366–412; 2, pp. 75–94; JURKOWSKI, "Clerical Taxation", pp. 55–56, 63.
27 JURKOWSKI, et al., *Lay Taxes*, xxxi–xxxiv, 38; HARRISS, *King, Parliament*, p. 85; WILLARD, *Parliamentary Taxes*, pp. 77–81, 87–91; GLASSCOCK, *The Lay Subsidy*, prints all local quotas.
28 JURKOWSKI, "Clerical Taxation", pp. 56–57; LUNT, *Financial Relations*, 1, pp. 404–407.
29 JURKOWSKI, et al., *Lay Taxes*, pp. xxxiii–xxxiv, 40–42, 46–47, 50–52, 55; DYER, "Taxation"; WILLARD, "Edward III's Negotiations", pp. 727–731.
30 LLOYD, *The English Wool*, pp. 144–153, 200–202; HARRISS, *King, Parliament*, pp. 253–293; JURKOWSKI, et al., *Lay Taxes*, pp. 43–46, 49; *Nonarum Inquisitiones*, prints many of the extant parish assessments.

31 ORMROD, "The Origins" (full list of grants and rates of duty at pp. 211–212).
32 JURKOWSKI, et al., *Lay Taxes*, pp. 51–52; PUTNAM, *The Enforcement*, pp. 106–131.
33 ORMROD, "An Experiment"; *Clerical Poll-Taxes*, pp. xii–xvii.
34 JURKOWSKI, et al., *Lay Taxes*, pp. 56–57; *The Poll Taxes*, edits most surviving returns of all three lay poll taxes; *Clerical Poll-Taxes*, pp. xvii–xviii, 1–70; JURKOWSKI, "Clerical Taxation", p. 64, lists surviving clerical returns.
35 JURKOWSKI, et al., *Lay Taxes*, pp. 58–59 (tariff of lay rates); *Clerical Poll-Taxes*, pp. xviii–xix (tariff of clerical rates), pp. 71–91; JURKOWSKI, "Clerical Taxation", p. 64, lists surviving clerical returns.
36 JURKOWSKI, et al., *Lay Taxes*, pp. 58–60; *Clerical Poll-Taxes*, pp. xxi–xxii; JURKOWSKI, "Clerical Taxation", p. 65, lists surviving returns.
37 JURKOWSKI, et al., *Lay Taxes*, pp. 60–62; *Clerical Poll-Taxes*, pp. xxii–xxiv, 92–174; JURKOWSKI, "Clerical Taxation", pp. 66–67, lists surviving clerical returns; *The Peasants' Revolt*, pp. 168–176.
38 JURKOWSKI, et al., *Lay Taxes*, pp. 68–71; BARRON, "The Quarrel"; *The Church in London*, pp. 39–77; BARRON, "The Tyranny", pp. 1–6.
39 DYER, "Taxation and Communities", pp. 175–185; JURKOWSKI, et al., *Lay Taxes*, pp. xxxvii–xxxix, 74–76.
40 JURKOWSKI, et al., *Lay Taxes*, pp. 78–79; *Inquisitions and Assessments*, p. 6, prints most surviving returns.
41 JURKOWSKI, "Clerical Taxation", pp. 57–58, 67–69, 80–1; JURKOWSKI, "Were Friars"; MC HARDY, "Clerical Taxation", pp. 179–189, lists clerical tax grants from 1401 to 1504.
42 DYER, "England's Economy".
43 JURKOWSKI, "Clerical Taxation", pp. 69–71; HAYES, "'For the State".
44 WATT, "On account".
45 JURKOWSKI, et al., *Lay Taxes*, pp. 89–90, 98–99, 110–111; JURKOWSKI, "Parliamentary and Prerogative Taxation", p. 272, 289 (prints county quotas from 1468).
46 FORREST, "Patterns of Economic Change"; DYMOND and VIRGOE, "The Reduced Population".
47 JURKOWSKI, et al., *Lay Taxes*, pp. 79–84; DOIG, "Propaganda and Truth"; ORMROD, "Henry V".
48 JURKOWSKI, et al., *Lay Taxes*, pp. 84–87, 89–93, 96–102, 104–105, 108–109; KLEINEKE, "The Commission".
49 JURKOWSKI, et al., *Lay Taxes*, pp. 85–86; JURKOWSKI, "Clerical Taxation", pp. 58, 67–69, 80–81; JURKOWSKI, "Were Friars", pp. 132–134; *Inquisitions and Assessments*, vols. 1–6, prints the 1428 and 1431 lay tax assessments.
50 JURKOWSKI, et al., *Lay Taxes*, pp. 91–92; GRAY, "Incomes from Land"; PUGH and ROSS, "The English Baronage"; THRUPP, *The Merchant Class*, pp. 378–388.
51 JURKOWSKI, "Clerical Taxation", pp. 67–69, 80–81; JURKOWSKI, "Were Friars", pp. 140–152.
52 JURKOWSKI, et al., *Lay Taxes*, pp. 102–104; VIRGOE, "The Parliamentary Subsidy".
53 JURKOWSKI, et al., *Lay Taxes*, pp. 94–95; THRUPP, "A Survey"; BOLTON, *The Alien Communities*.
54 JURKOWSKI, et al., *Lay Taxes*, pp. 96, 100–101, 106–107, 120–121; BOLTON, *The Alien Communities*, pp. 47–118.
55 ORMROD, LAMBERT and MACKMAN, *Immigrant England 1300–1550*, pp. 45–51.
56 JURKOWSKI, et al., *Lay Taxes*, pp. 105–106.
57 JURKOWSKI, et al., *Lay Taxes*, pp. 109–111; JURKOWSKI, "Parliamentary and Prerogative Taxation", pp. 273–275.
58 JURKOWSKI, "Parliamentary and Prerogative Taxation", pp. 288–289, prints county totals; "Income Tax Assessments", pp. 121–138, prints partial Norwich assessment.
59 JURKOWSKI, et al., *Lay Taxes*, pp. 111–115; JURKOWSKI, "Parliamentary and Prerogative Taxation", pp. 275–283; MC HARDY, "Clerical Taxation", p. 181, 188.
60 JURKOWSKI, et al., *Lay Taxes*, pp. 122–125; MC HARDY, "Clerical Taxation", p. 181, 189; "Income Tax Assessments", pp. 106–119, 139–156, prints Norwich assessment; HICKS, "The Yorkshire Rebellion".
61 JURKOWSKI, et al., *Lay Taxes*, pp. 126–128.
62 MC HARDY, "Clerical Taxation", p. 182, 189.
63 JURKOWSKI, et al., *Lay Taxes*, p. 129.
64 JURKOWSKI, et al., *Lay Taxes*, pp. 115–117; GRAY, "The First Benevolence"; HARRISS, "Aids, Loans and Benevolences".
65 JURKOWSKI, et al., *Lay Taxes*, pp. 118–120; VIRGOE, "The Benevolence".
66 JURKOWSKI, et al., *Lay Taxes*, p. 125.
67 MC KENNA, "The Myth"; GRUMMITT and LASSALMONIE, "Royal Public Finance", pp. 143–144; MADDICOTT, *Origins*, pp. 376–453.

References

Primary Sources

Carte Baronum, ed. Neil STACY, Pipe Roll Society, new series, 62, 2019.
The Church in London 1375–1392, ed. Alison K. MC HARDY, London Record Society, 13, 1977.
Clerical Poll-Taxes of the Diocese of Lincoln 1377–1381, ed. Alison K. MC HARDY, Lincoln Record Society, 81, 1992.
Domesday Book, A Complete Translation, ed. Ann WILLIAMS and Geoffrey H. MARTIN, London, 2002.
"Income Tax Assessments of Norwich, 1472 and 1489", ed. Maureen JURKOWSKI, in *Poverty and Wealth: Sheep, Taxation and Charity in Late Medieval Norfolk*, ed. Mark BAILEY, Maureen JURKOWSKI and Carole RAWCLIFFE, Norfolk Record Society, 71, 2007, pp. 99–156.
Inquisitions and Assessments Relating to Feudal Aids, 6 volumes, London, 1899–1920.
Nonarum Inquisitiones, ed. George VANDERZEE, London, 1807.
The Peasants' Revolt of 1381, ed. R. BARRIE DOBSON, London, 1970.
The Poll Taxes of 1377, 1379 and 1380, ed. Carolyn C. FENWICK, 3 vols., Oxford, 1997-2005.
Sixth Report of the Royal Commission of Historical Manuscripts, Appendix, Corporation of Wallingford, ed. Henry T. RILEY, London, 1877, pp. 572–595.
Taxatio Ecclesiastica Angliae et Walliae Auctoritate Papae Nicholai IV, ed. Thomas ASTLE, Samuel AYSCOUGH and John CALEY, London, 1802.

Secondary Sources

Christopher T. ALLMAND, "Taxation in Medieval England: the Example of Murage", in *Villes, bonnes villes, cités et capitales. Études d'histoire urbaine (XIIe-XVIIe siècle) offertes à Bernard Chevalier*, ed. Monique BOURIN, Tours, 1989, pp. 223–230.
Nick BARRATT, "The Revenue of King John", in *English Historical Review*, 111, 1996, pp. 835–855.
Caroline M. BARRON, "The Tyranny of Richard II", in *Bulletin of the Institute of Historical Research*, 41, 1968, pp. 1–6.
Caroline M. BARRON, "The Quarrel of Richard II with London 1392-7", in *The Reign of Richard II: Essays in Honour of May McKisack*, ed. F.R.H. DU BOULAY and Caroline M. BARRON, London, 1971, pp. 173–201.
James L. BOLTON, *The Alien Communities of London in the Fifteenth Century: the Subsidy Rolls of 1440, 1483-84*, Stamford, 1998.
Anthony R. BRIDBURY, "English Provincial Towns in the Later Middle Ages", in *Economic History Review*, 34, 1987, pp. 1–24.
Alfred L. BROWN, *The Governance of Late Medieval England 1272–1461*, London, 1989.
David A. CARPENTER, *The Minority of Henry III*, London, 1990.
Fred A. CAZEL, "The Tax of 1185 in Aid of the Holy Land", in *Speculum*, 30/3, 1955, pp. 385–392.
Fred A. CAZEL, "The Fifteenth of 1225", in *Bulletin of the Institute of Historical Research*, 34, 1961, pp. 68–81.
Helena M. CHEW, "Scutage under Edward I", in *English Historical Review*, 37, 1922, pp. 321–336.
Helena M. CHEW, "Scutage in the Fourteenth Century", in *English Historical Review*, 38, 1923, pp. 19–41.
Marjorie CHIBNALL, *Anglo-Norman England 1066–1166*, Oxford, 1986.
Michael T. CLANCHY, *From Memory to Written Record, England 1066–1307*, second edition, Oxford, 1993.
Alan COOPER, *Bridges, Law and Power in Medieval England, 700–1400*, Woodbridge, 2006.
David CROOK, "Records of Lay Taxation in the Public Record Office, London, c. 1200–1700", in *Crises, Revolutions and Self-Sustained Growth, Essays in European Fiscal History, 1130–1830*, ed. W. MARK ORMROD, Margaret BONNEY and Richard BONNEY, Stamford, 1999, pp. 427–435.
Herbert S. DEIGHTON, "Clerical Taxation by Consent, 1279–1301", in *English Historical Review*, 68, 1953, pp. 161–192.
Jeffrey H. DENTON, *Robert Winchelsey and the Crown, 1294–1313*, Cambridge, 1980.
Jeffrey H. DENTON, "The Valuation of the Ecclesiastical Benefices of England and Wales in 1291-3", in *Historical Research*, 66, 1993, pp. 231–250.
James DOIG, "Propaganda and Truth: Henry V's Royal Progress in 1421", in *Nottingham Medieval Studies*, 40, 1996, pp. 167–179.

Christopher Dyer, "Taxation and Communities in Late Medieval England", in *Progress and Problems in Medieval England, Essays in Honour of Edward Miller*, ed. Richard Britnell and John Hatcher, Cambridge, 1996, pp. 168–190.

Christopher Dyer, "England's Economy in the Fifteenth Century", in *The Fifteenth Century*, 13, ed. Linda Clark, Woodbridge, 2014, pp. 201–225.

David Dymond and Roger Virgoe, "The Reduced Population and Wealth of Early Fifteenth-Century Suffolk", in *Proceedings of the Suffolk Institute of Archaeology*, 36, 1986, pp. 73–100.

Mark Forrest, "Patterns of Economic Change in the South-West during the Fifteenth Century: Evidence from the Reductions to the Fifteenths and Tenths", in *Economic History Review*, 70, 2017, pp. 423–451.

Vivian H. Galbraith, *Domesday Book, its Place in Administrative History*, Oxford, 1974

Robin E. Glasscok, *The Lay Subsidy of 1334*, London, 1975.

Howard L. Gray., "The First Benevolence", in *Facts and Factors in Economic History*, ed. Arthur H. Cole, Arthur L. Dunham and Norman S.B. Gras, Cambridge, Massachusetts, 1932, pp. 90–113.

Howard L. Gray, "Incomes from Land in England in 1436", in *English Historical Review*, 49, 1934, pp. 607–639.

Judith A. Green, "The Last Century of the Danegeld", in *English Historical Review*, 96, 1981, pp. 241–258.

David Grummitt, and Jean-François Lassalmonie, "Royal Public Finance (*c.* 1290–1523)" in *Government and Political Life in England and France, c.1300–c.1500*, ed. Chris Fletcher, Jean-Philippe Genet and John Watts, Cambridge, 2015, pp. 116–149.

J. F. Hadwin, "The Last Royal Tallages", in *English Historical Review*, 96, 1981, pp. 344–358.

David Harrison, *The Bridges of Medieval England: Transport and Society 400–1800*, Oxford, 2004.

Gerald R. Harriss, "Aids, Loans and Benevolences", in *Historical Journal*, 6, 1963, pp. 8–13.

Gerald R. Harriss, *King, Parliament and Public Finance in Medieval England to 1369*, Oxford, 1975.

Edward Harvey, "Pavage Grants and Urban Street Paving in Medieval England, 1249–1462", in *Journal of Transport History*, 31, 2010, pp. 151–163.

Rosemary C. E. Hayes, "'For the State and Necessity of the Realm': Clerical Taxation in the Reign of Henry VI (1422-61), A Case Study using the E 179 Database", in *Clergy, Church and Society in England and Wales c. 1200–1800*, ed. Rosemary C. E. Hayes and William J. Sheils, York, 2013, pp. 101–120.

Michael A. Hicks, "The Yorkshire Rebellion of 1489 Reconsidered", in *Northern History*, 22, 1986, pp. 39–62.

Maureen Jurkowski, "Parliamentary and Prerogative Taxation in the Reign of Edward IV", in *Parliamentary History*, 18, 1999, pp. 271–290.

Maureen Jurkowski, "Were Friars Paid Salaries? Evidence from Clerical Taxation Records", in *The Fifteenth Century*, 13, ed. Linda Clark, Woodbridge, 2014, pp. 131–152.

Maureen Jurkowski, "The History of Clerical Taxation in England and Wales, 1173–1663: The Findings of the E 179 Project", in *Journal of Ecclesiastical History*, 67, 2016, pp. 53–81.

Maureen Jurkowski, Caroline L. Smith and David Crook, *Lay Taxes in England and Wales 1188–1688*, London, 1998.

Hannes Kleineke, "The Commission *De Mutuo Faciendo* in the Reign of Henry VI", in *English Historical Review*, 116, 2001, pp. 1–30.

Norman B. Lewis and John J. N. Palmer, "The Feudal Summons of 1385", in *English Historical Review*, 100, 1985, pp. 729–746.

Terrence H. Lloyd, *The English Wool Trade in the Middle Ages*, Cambridge, 1977.

William E. Lunt, "Papal Taxation in the Reign of Edward I", in *English Historical Review*, 30, 1915, pp. 398–417.

William E. Lunt, "Early Assessments for Papal Taxation of English Clerical Incomes", in *Annual Report of the American Historical Association, 1917*, Washington D.C., 1920, pp. 267–280.

William E. Lunt, "The Text of the Ordinance of 1184 Concerning an Aid for the Holy Land", in *English Historical Review*, 37, 1922, pp. 235–242.

William E. Lunt, *The Valuation of Norwich*, Oxford, 1926.

William E. Lunt, *Financial Relations of the Papacy with England*, 2 vols., Cambridge, Massachusetts, 1939–1962.

Jonathan Mackman, "The 'Unfortunate' Fraudster: Thomas de Boulton and the East Riding Lay Subsidy of 1332", in *Monarchy, State and Political Culture in Late Medieval England, Essays in Honour of W. Mark Ormrod*, ed. Gwilym Dodd and Craig Taylor, Woodbridge, 2020, pp. 1–20.

John R. Maddicott, "The Crusade Taxation of 1268–1270 and the Development of Parliament", in *Thirteenth Century England*, 2, ed. Peter R. Coss and Simon D. Lloyd, Woodbridge, 1987, pp. 93–117.

John R. Maddicott, *The Origins of the English Parliament 924–1327*, Oxford, 2010.

Geoffrey H. Martin, "The English Borough in the Thirteenth Century", in *Transactions of the Royal Historical Society*, 5th series, 13, 1963, pp. 123–144.

James Masschaele, "Tolls and Trade in Medieval England", in *Money, Markets and Trade in Late Medieval Europe: Essays in Honour of John H.A. Munro*, ed. Lawrin D. Armstrong, Ivana Elbl and Martin Elbl, Leiden, 2007, pp. 146–183.

Alison K. Mc Hardy, "Clerical Taxation in Fifteenth-Century England: the Clergy as Agents of the Crown", in *The Church, Politics and Patronage in the Fifteenth Century*, ed. Barrie Dobson, Gloucester, 1984, pp. 168–192.

Alison K. Mc Hardy, "Paying for the Wedding: Edward III as Fundraiser 1332-3", in *Fourteenth Century England*, 4, ed. Jeffrey S. Hamilton, Woodbridge, 2006, pp. 43–60.

John W. Mc Kenna, "The Myth of Parliamentary Sovereignty in Late-Medieval England", in *English Historical Review*, 94, 1979, pp. 481–506.

Sydney K. Mitchell, *Taxation in Medieval England*, New Haven, Connecticut, 1951

W. Mark Ormrod, "An Experiment in Taxation: The English Parish Subsidy of 1371", in *Speculum*, 63, 1988, pp. 58–82.

W. Mark Ormrod, "Urban communities and royal finance in England during the later Middle Ages", in *Corona, municipis i fiscalitat a la Baixa Edat Mitjana: Col.loqui*, ed. Manuel Sánchez Martínez and Antoni Furió, Lleida, 1997, pp. 45–60.

W. Mark Ormrod, "The Crown and the English Economy, 1290–1348", in *Before the Black Death: Studies in the 'Crisis' of the Early Fourteenth Century*, ed. Bruce M. S. Campbell, Manchester, 1991, pp. 149–183.

W. Mark Ormrod, "The West European Monarchies in the Later Middle Ages", in *Economic Systems and State Finance*, ed. Richard Bonney, Oxford, 1995, pp. 123–160.

W. Mark Ormrod, "England in the Middle Ages", in *The Rise of the Fiscal State in Europe, c. 1200–1815*, Oxford, 1999, pp. 19–52.

W. Mark Ormrod, Margaret Bonney and Richard Bonney (ed.), *Crises, Revolutions and Self-Sustained Growth, Essays in European Fiscal History, 1130–1830*, Stamford, 1999.

W. Mark Ormrod, "The Origins of Tunnage and Poundage: Parliament and the Estate of Merchants in the 14th Century", in *Parliamentary History*, 28, 2009, pp. 209–227.

W. Mark Ormrod, "Henry V and the English Taxpayer", in *Henry V, New Interpretations*, ed. Gwilym Dodd, Woodbridge, 2013, pp. 187–216.

W. Mark Ormrod, Bart Lambert and Jonathan Mackman, *Immigrant England 1300–1550*, Manchester, 2018.

Thomas B. Pugh and Charles D. Ross, "The English Baronage and the Income Tax of 1436", in *Bulletin of the Institute of Historical Research*, 26, 1953, pp. 1–28.

Bertha Putnam, *The Enforcement of the Statute of Labourers*, New York, 1908.

Susan Reynolds, *An Introduction to the History of English Medieval Towns*, Oxford, 1977.

Robert C. Stacey, "Royal Taxation and the Social Structure of Medieval Anglo-Jewry: The Tallages of 1239–1242", in *Hebrew Union College Annual*, 56, 1985, pp. 175–249.

Frank Stenton, *Anglo-Saxon England*, third edition, Oxford, 1971.

Carl Stephenson, *Borough and Town*, Cambridge, Massachusetts, 1933.

Joseph R. Strayer and George Rudisill Jr., "Taxation and Community in Wales and Ireland, 1272–1327", in *Speculum*, 29, 1954, pp. 410–416.

James Tait, "The *Firma Burgi* and the Commune in England, 1066–1191", in *English Historical Review*, 167, 1927, pp. 321–360.

Tim Thornton, "Taxing the King's Dominions: The Subject Territories of the English Crown in the Late Middle Ages", in *Crises, Revolutions and Self-Sustained Growth, Essays in European Fiscal History, 1130–1830*, ed. W. Mark Ormrod, Margaret Bonney and Richard Bonney, Stamford, 1999, pp. 97–109.

Sylvia L. Thrupp, "A Survey of the Alien Population of England in 1440", in *Speculum*, 32, 1957, pp. 262–273.

Sylvia L. Thrupp, *The Merchant Class of Medieval London*, Ann Arbor, Michigan, 1962.

A. Tomkinson, "The Carucage of 1220 in an Oxfordshire Hundred", in *Bulletin of the Institute of Historical Research*, 41, 1968, pp. 212–216.

Roger Virgoe, "The Parliamentary Subsidy of 1450", in *Bulletin of the Institute of Historical Research*, 55, 1982, pp. 125–138.

Roger VIRGOE, "The Benevolence of 1481", in *English Historical Review*, 104, 1989, pp. 25–45.

Helen WATT, "'On account of the frequent attacks and invasions of the Welsh': The Effect of the Glyn Dŵr Rebellion on Tax Collection in England", in *The Reign of Henry IV, Rebellion and Survival, 1403–1413*, ed. Gwilym DODD and Douglas BIGGS, Woodbridge, 2008, pp. 48–81.

Helen WATT, "Was Wales 'A Joy for Indigent, or Greedy, English Kings or Lords'? A Re-Evaluation of the Subsidies Granted to Richard II in Carmarthenshire and Cardiganshire in 1393", in *Foundations of Medieval Scholarship, Records Edited in Honour of David Crook*, ed. Paul BRAND and Sean CUNNINGHAM, York, 2008, pp. 197–213.

James F. WILLARD, "Edward III's Negotiations for a Grant in 1337", in *English Historical Review*, 21, 1906, pp. 727–731.

James F. WILLARD, "A Brief Guide to the Records Dealing with the Taxes upon Movables 1290–1350", in *Bulletin of the Institute of Historical Research*, 3, 1925, pp. 27–37.

James F. WILLARD, *Parliamentary Taxes on Personal Property, 1290–1334*, Cambridge, Massachusetts, 1934.

15

THE SCANDINAVIAN KINGDOMS

Thomas Lindkvist

The Scandinavian kingdoms

Periodization in Scandinavian history differs from the conventional of Western and Southern Europe. The Middle Ages in Scandinavia begin around 1000. The previous period is often termed the Viking Age or the Late Iron Age and mostly studied by archaeology. The social transformation around 1000 involved the Christianization and the gradual growth of a Church organization. Scandinavia became a province within the Roman church in 1103, with Danish Lund in Scania as see of the archbishop. In 1153, Nidaros became the see of the separate Norwegian church. Sweden's political structure was then instable, but in 1164, Uppsala became an independent archbishopric. This process also involved the establishment of the Christian monarchies and the beginning of a state formation. The three Scandinavian kingdoms were the precursors of the later nation states and originated in roughly the chronological order Denmark, Norway and Sweden. At least the making of a Swedish kingdom was later than the other two. From 1397, the three kingdoms were in a personal union, the Kalmar union, with Denmark as the political centre. In spite of Swedish separatist challenges. it existed until the early 1520s. The beginning of the sixteenth century was a period with important transformations and therefore usually regarded as the end of the Middle Ages and the transition to the early Modern Period. Two centralized states emerged in Denmark and Sweden. Norway was in a personal union with Denmark since the late fourteenth century. The Reformation in the 1520s and 1530s was furthermore the beginning of a great cultural transformation.

The history of taxes and fiscal systems of medieval Scandinavia can be divided into three separate phases: the Late Viking age and the transition to the Middle Ages, the rise of the Christian monarchies during the twelfth and thirteenth centuries and the Kalmar union from the late fourteenth century.

Sources

Fiscal systems and taxation are research topics closely linked with the political history and the origins and the development of the states. This is also one of the main reasons why research about the fiscal systems and taxation in Scandinavia is national. There are few comparative inter-Scandinavian studies, and even less to put the fiscal history into a European perspective.[1] The methodological nationalism is solid within this field of research. The historiography consists of often detailed analyses and the interpretations diverge. Important contributions have been made in different studies of political, agrarian and local history. Many results and observations from previous research can be found in various articles of the comprehensive dictionary of Nordic cultural history (*Kulturhistoriskt lexikon för nordisk medeltid*).

An important study is Erik Lönnroth's study from 1940 about the state power and state finances in medieval Sweden. Since it is an innovative study with a comprehensive discussion concerning the fiscal development of one kingdom and the relations to the political and general economic development it has been seminal for later research. Nils Hybel and Bjørn Poulsen provided 2007 for Denmark a synthesis of fiscal systems in relation to the economic development.[2]

The sources available for studying taxation and fiscal systems are in general scanty and meagre, but also varied and often subject to diverging interpretations. The normative sources, the laws from the twelfth to the fourteenth centuries, have a central place in the discussions. The rights and duties of the kings and their relation to the society are there prescribed. There are extensive regulations concerning taxes and other duties of the population and different communities to the king and crown. Various charters of privileges also have information about taxes.

Medieval fiscal accounts are poorly preserved. Before the sixteenth century there are but a few. The records were often dispersed and divided at shifts of regency, or at other administrative changes. Wars and social unrest, particularly in Sweden, during the fifteenth century, not least during the 1430s, implied the burning and destruction of many castles and the records kept there. A more efficient fiscal administration evolved during the sixteenth century.

In Denmark there are some accounts from fiefs; the oldest known are from 1442 of what peasants paid in a district in Funen. In Sweden accounts are rare before the late fifteenth century. The oldest preserved are those of the North German knight Raven van Barnekow from 1365–1367. From the castle of Nyköping he held fiefs in the provinces Södermanland and Dalarna on behalf of king Albert. The accounts were brought, probably by the duke, to Mecklenburg shortly afterwards. These accounts are valuable since they illustrate the names of different fiscal items and the importance of the extraordinary taxation.

Another detailed account book is from Gotland 1485–1487, when administered by the Danish–Swedish aristocrat Ivar Axelsson Tott. The regular taxes from the island are recorded and they were levied in money from the old established districts and mainly twice a year, in the winter and in the summer.[3]

An important source of a different kind is the *Liber Census Daniæ* (in Danish termed as *Kong Valdemars Jordebog*) consisting of several manuscripts from the reign of king Valdemar II (r. 1202–1241) with the purpose to provide registries over royal incomes and properties. The registers are wide-ranging but the content and topic of the different manuscripts or lists varies. The *Liber Census* is subject of comprehensive, but also intricate research.[4]

There is also an important register or inventory of resources of King Erik from 1413, which was an attempt to conduct a survey or evaluation of the regal incomes in Sweden, usually termed *Erik av Pommerns skattebok* (Erik of Pomerania's tax book) in Swedish and partly preserved in excerpts from the seventeenth century.[5] The knowledge of the formal and normative fiscal framework is far greater than how taxes actually were paid, calculated, and collected.

The source material of urban taxation is fragmentary preserved and the fiscal principles are less known and studied. From Stockholm there are, however, extensive registers of all liable to pay tax from 1460–1468 and some years of the early sixteenth century. These lists have information about taxes and fees from burghers and other inhabitants.[6]

Tributary kingdoms, age of plunder

The political system of the Viking Age differed regionally and partly based upon an external appropriation. The social and political elites controlled emporia or ports of trade, like Birka, and Hedeby. It was also an economy of plunder. Substantial resources to reproduce the position of the political elites originated in acquiring wealth outside the endogenous society. Tributes were taken, sometimes on a regular basis, from foreign peoples and territories. The organizations necessary for external appropriation and warfare promoted increased internal control. A predatory system paved the way for a society based upon a predominantly internal appropriation. A new type of kingship gradually gained ground: a kingship with a greater control over the inhabitants and the material resources of their realm.

Regular tributes were also a way to attach peripheral or oversea areas to the emerging kingdoms. Permanent Norse settlements emerged in Iceland and the Faroe Islands. There were also Viking Age and medieval Norse communities in *i.a.* Greenland, Shetland, and Orkney. The *skattlands* of the Norwegian king were dependencies and tributary lands. *Skattr* (Old Norse) could stand for tax or tribute, but also property in a general sense.[7] The independent commonwealth of Iceland established from mostly mainland Scandinavia from the late ninth century became a part of the Norwegian realm through the agreement called *Gamli sáttmáli* in 1262–1264. In a similar way kings as overlords in the emerging Danish and Swedish realms demanded tributes from oversea territories like Bornholm, Rügen and Gotland.[8]

Present Finland became a part of Sweden from the second half of the thirteenth century, partly thorough crusading warfare. Åbo (Finnish: Turku) became a diocese during the late thirteenth century, castles and a similar administration as in the realm were introduced. A colonization of a Swedish-speaking population took place during mainly the twelfth and thirteenth centuries in the coastal areas, but Finland never had a status of a tributary land.[9]

The pre-Christian realms of Denmark, Norway and the Swedish of the *Svear* in the Lake Mälaren region were thalassocracies; power rested upon the control over the sea. Chiefdoms and petty kingdoms existed in various parts. The emergence of Christian monarchies in general implied an increasing control of people and resources within their realm, including the claims of different duties and rights. This was the foundation for the later medieval taxes. Although of very different kinds and origins, permanent taxes were the basis for a consolidation of more permanent power and political institutions.

The rise of the Christian monarchies

Demesnes

The material resources of the kings and the emerging state power in medieval Scandinavia depended until the middle of the thirteenth century mostly on the incomes from the royal domain. The domain was also of political and economic importance throughout the medieval period. In Denmark and Sweden there was a distinction between the royal domain, *bona regalia*, following the kingship irrespective of what dynasty or kinship group was in power, and the *patrimonium*, the estates belonging to the royal family. The royal domain was in general termed as *Uppsala öd* in Sweden. The origins are unknown, but the term indicated pretentions to be land belonging to the kings at Uppsala in pre-Christian times. There are some references made in the laws to manors or farms in Västergötland and Hälsingland, but otherwise the royal domain was most common in the Svealand provinces around Lake Mälaren.

The domains of *patrimonium* in Sweden were mostly located in the provinces of Östergötland and Västergötland. A special type of farms belonging to the *bona regalia* were those called *husabyar*. They were a kind of administrative centres, possibly for collection of contributions in kind from the population of the districts. They were important up to the twelfth century, but lost gradually in importance and were obsolete by ca. 1250. The *husabyar* were part of the resources following the kingdom and mostly in the Svealand provinces. Roughly, there was one *husaby* for each administrative district.[10]

There was a difference between Western and Eastern Denmark. In the Western parts, notably Jutland, the kings had their *patrimonium*, their ancestral estates. The *kongelev*, the Old Danish term for the *bona regalia*, was most common in the Eastern parts of the realm.[11]

The estates of the crown were, however, not extensive. The farms of the crown before the Reformation were around 5 per cent in Denmark, Norway and Sweden of the total number of farms.[12] This is indicating a rather fragile financial situation of all the Northern monarchies.

The origins of the estates of the *Uppsala öd* in Sweden and the *kongelev* in Denmark is obscure. Land was confiscated or in some other way appropriated during the constant struggles during the formation of the early Christian monarchy. Opposing and defeated factions lost their land. In Norway, the distinction between *bona regalia* and *patrimonium* is known from the later thirteenth century, but it is uncertain if it is older.[13]

Other important royal revenues were fines and certain regnal rights such as the *danarv*, the inheritance following a person with no known heirs. Tolls and minting were also part of the kings' material resources. The kings claimed rights over common land from at least the twelfth century in Denmark and Sweden, which caused social tensions and protests.[14]

Diverging principles and assessment

The fiscal systems varied and were in character highly heterogenic and of different kinds. The motivations and origins varied. The range of regional and local differences were great. The administrative possibilities to calculate taxes and other duties were however limited. Some taxes became permanent, while others were of temporary character. Regardless of this, the taxes could be paid according to different principles during the Middle Ages in all the Scandinavian kingdoms.

There were variations and taxes could be levied in kind, in money, or in labour. Different local customs and social organizations caused adjustments to the demands of the king or the state. In general, there were three different principles of fiscal assessment.[15] A personal principle was a frequent way of collection. Traditions exist about an early tax called *nefgildi*★, literally "nose-tax" and mentioned in the Norse history writing. A tax for every nose, i.e. every person, was introduced in connection with the rise of a kingdom in Norway. The historian Edvard Bull pointed out, that it would have been impossible to impose such a tax during the tenth or eleventh centuries. It contradicts what are otherwise known facts about the political structure with a predominantly external appropriation.[16]

There is also a narrative of the introduction of a tax per nose in Sweden, or at least in the Lake Mälaren region, in pagan times. It was one coin for each nose, but not known from other sources, except by the name of *nefgiald*, a tax from the province of Västmanland 1285. There is no connection with the personal tax mentioned in the Norse literature.[17] A nose-tax, *nefgilde*★ was, according to a later chronicle, introduced in Denmark by King Knud ca. 1085 and caused widespread protests and unrest. This tax was evidently not a regular duty. Nevertheless, personal taxes were considered to be ancient. One tax known mainly from the Swedish province of

Västergötland was the *almæningsöre*, a tax from "all men". It was claimed from every household, but the age of the tax is unknown.

The personal principle meant that a fixed amount was claimed from every individual, in general every free man or peasant household and irrespective of the economic capacity of the individual households. These taxes were at times roughly graded since households could be demanded to pay a "full" or a "half" tax.

There were also collective taxes. A number of individuals or households contributed with a fixed sum. The distribution was according to the economic capacities of the individual households, but the principles of distribution within the communities varied.

Another principal form of assessing taxes and other duties was according to the value of the land. Land measuring systems are the subject of discussion within especially Swedish historiography. During the second half of the thirteenth century, a system based upon the monetary system was introduced in the provinces around Lake Mälaren: the *markland* and its subdivisions. It was used to value the land, but also to calculate the rents of the tenant peasants. Another field of application was the calculation of the taxes. In other areas, especially the Östergötland province, an older organization, the *attung*, the eighth of the rights a village community, became an instrument to calculate rents and taxes.[18]

In Denmark, taxes were evaluated according to *bol*, which was a unit corresponding to a part of the village.[19]

In general, medieval taxes were roughly individual or collective. The individual households or a wider community of several households was responsible for delivering the tax.

Several taxes or duties are also mentioned, but with unknown origins. One of these is the *ættærgæld*, known since the late thirteenth century in Uppland and other provinces. It was a tax paid by a district and distributed equally among the householders. It was thus a combination of the personal and collective principle.[20]

Ledung – military duties and taxes

The emergence of regular and permanent taxes was part of the transformation of all three Scandinavian kingdoms and creating the financial foundation of more advanced polities, making them European monarchies amongst others. The permanent taxes originated as commutation of ancient obligations. The most important military resource of the kings was the *leþunger*★ (Old Swedish; *lething* in Old Danish and *leiðangr* in Old Norse). Henceforward the Modern Swedish term *ledung*★ is used. It was the naval military organization, aimed for both offensive and for defensive purposes. It was also the organization for colonization overseas. The *ledung*★ was an organization to protect the native country from attacks of e.g. Slavonic Vends against Denmark or Baltic pirates against the Swedish East coast.

It was the duty of the free men, i.e. the peasant householders, to provide men, ships and victuals to the king's *ledung*★. The origins and development of this organization is ambiguous and much discussed. Control over a maritime war organization was of course important during the Viking Age and different chiefs and petty kings organized it. The Danish historian Niels Lund claims that the king's *ledung*★ was rather late. The retinues of local lords preceded this centralized royal *ledung*★. During the twelfth century, the king's entitlements were so solid that he could impose upon a free peasantry the duty to participate in military enterprises. In 1170/71 the rules of the *ledung*★ were set out in law, but then mainly as a defensive organization. Other researchers argue that there was an earlier and firm royal control over the *ledung*★.[21]

The military *ledung*★ was gradually transformed to a fiscal *ledung*★, which in Denmark took place mainly during the early thirteenth century; in Sweden during the second half of the thirteenth century. The *ledung**, the military as well as the fiscal, is regulated in detail in many of laws, like the Law of Jutland from 1241 in Denmark and the Law of Uppland from 1296 and from other provinces in the Lake Mälaren region in Sweden. There was a regional difference in Sweden since the *ledung** was mainly levied in that region and along the coast northwards and southwards. From e.g. the province of Västergötland the *ledung** was never demanded as a duty or as a tax.

The military *ledung** was based upon collectives. Different groups had to contribute in various ways with men or provisions, or building ships. When changed into annual taxes and fees the former warships became tax units and laid out on land. The districts were organized, and with a varying terminology, according to the ships that were the basis like the *skeppslag* (community of a ship), *skibreide* (in Norway, ship's fee), or the *hamna* in Sweden and *havne* (rowlock) in Denmark.[22] The collective principle was later replaced by tax based on the land held by individual household. It was in Denmark termed *terra in censu* and the principle introduced in the 1220s in large parts of the Western parts of realm. In Eastern Denmark, like the province of Halland, the collectives of the *havne*s were the fiscal units in the *Liber Census* from 1231.[23]

The general principle was that fines or fees were paid when the military *ledung** was neglected or not required. These fees became permanent and transformed into taxes. There were regional and local varieties concerning practice and terminology. In Sweden they were often termed *skeppsvist* and *ledungslama*.[24]

In Denmark, the oldest *ledung** taxes were *stud* and *kværsæde*. The latter means "remain seated", i.e. something paid when not participating.[25] The *stud*, or *stuth*, was a general fee for support of any kind. *Stud* means support.

The transformation of the *ledung** into a tax was also a great social and military transformation. The military role of the peasantry diminished. The new military system rested upon the cavalry with knights and the castles as strongholds and centres of fiscal administration.[26] It was also the rise of the knightly class, the armour and the mounted horse as the main military instrument of power, an important indication of the adaptation to the European social and political culture. Castles were built in Denmark and Sweden during especially the thirteenth century as administrative centres. The castles with their military garrisons required more resources and the *län* (Swedish) or *len* (Danish and Norwegian) was the fief or area that usually had to sustain and support the military troops and the incipient administration.

Privileges from during the decades around 1300 settled the relations between the aristocracy and the crown in Denmark and Sweden. The term *fræls* means freed, i.e. freed from taxes. Those who could provide military service with a knight and mounted horse became tax-exempt from the permanent taxes, including their tenants. Instead, the *frälse* (aristocracy) made military service with knights and mounted horses. The tenant farmers or peasants were the *landbor* (Sweden), *fæster* (Denmark) or *leiglendingar* (Norway) and they paid a rent to the owner of their land. They were not subordinated and they possessed land, but did not own it.[27] There were therefore two different categories of peasants: the tax-paying peasants (generally termed *skattebönder*) and the tenants.

In Norway the *ledung** had a longer history as a military instrument of power, but could also be converted into a fiscal duty. Disposal over land was requirement to fulfil it as a military or fiscal obligation. As a tax, it was at first demanded in the late twelfth century during a period with civil wars.[28]

Provisions and services

There were other services demanded from the peasantry and the local communities. One of the most important of these duties was the *gæstning* (Old Swedish) or *gisting* (Old Norse). It was the duty of the population to sustain, lodge and feed the king and his comprehensive retinue during their continuous ambulation throughout the realms. Bishops had also a similar right. Others forms of duties, labour service and haulage, were demanded. These duties were also transformed into annual taxes in a similar way as the *ledung*★ was. When not made or requested, a fee was paid. Later, the fee became permanent.

In Sweden, the commutation tax was termed *gengærþ*★. It was most common in the provinces of Västergötland and Östergötland. That region of the realm was the homelands of the Christian monarchy until the middle of the thirteenth century and with the peripatetic form of government. The earliest record is from 1267, when king Valdemar in his privileges to Gudhem nunnery in Västergötland exempted it from this fee.

The commutation was general, but at certain occasions a de facto contribution to the king. The mining farmers at the important mining site of Norberg in Västmanland had, according to the privileges of 1354, to provide a *gengærþ*★ only in case the king, or his deputy, came in person.[29]

In Denmark, different terms were used, in Latin charters often called *servitium noctis*, corresponding to the vernacular *nathold*. Similar to the *nathold* was the *stud* (Old Danish *stuth*), a term frequently used for various taxes and fees. Literally, they were support or contribution to the king. In the *Liber Census*, there was in the province of Halland a distinction between spring contribution and winter contribution. Several astute hypothesis have been put forward by researchers how the tax was calculated and about the various principles. No generally accepted interpretation exists. Evidently, there were many local varieties and different agreements between representatives of the royal administration and the local communities.[30] *Inne* was different kinds of labour duties the king was entitled to; this included i.a. the haulage (*ægt*). *Inne* was a flexible concept, and was sometimes converted into a fee paid in money after negotiations.[31]

Veitsle was a term for an obligation in Norway and connected with the itinerant kingdom. The kings travelled between their central farms and stayed there for shorter or longer periods. In Norway, the notion was widely upheld among the communities that the *veitsle* was a voluntary gift and not a legal obligation. Rents from the royal farms and provisions from the peasantry were collected there. King Håkon Håkonsson (r. 1217–1263) built large halls at some of these central farms in the middle of the thirteenth century.[32]

Urban taxes

The towns that emerged in the Middle Ages had no continuity with the Viking Age emporia and were mostly small towns. Towns with importance to international trade, like Bergen, Stockholm or Visby, were exceptions with at most around 5000–7000 inhabitants. In total, there were around 175 medieval towns. Denmark was the most urbanized kingdom with more than 110 towns established during the medieval period, followed by Sweden with slightly more than 40. There was a special jurisdiction and administration of the towns and special Town Laws existed. The Scandinavian towns were under the control of the monarchies.[33] The king or his representative had the early right to certain fees, such as tolls and other levies related to trade. The sources have scarce and fragmentary information and there were great regional and local differences. In Denmark the *midthsumærsgyald*, "midsummer tax", Latin: *census æstitualis*, was a common and annual duty from a town to the king. The principles of assessment are unknown, but it was probably a collective contribution from the town. The sources are somewhat better concerning the later Middle Ages. The ancient duties merged into a general town tax to the king, *byskat*★ in Danish, *contributio* in Latin. It is at first recorded for Ribe in South Jutland in

1326 and from several other towns at the end of the century. In Denmark, the Latin term *pactus* was used for taxes, indicating an agreement or treaty between the town and the king. The tax was the result of negotiations, at least formally.

There was a similar special town tax, *stadsskatt**, in Sweden during the period of the Kalmar union from the late fourteenth century. It was paid in money and was a collective duty of the entire town. It originated probably during the reign of Margareta, replacing different older duties. According to the inventory of King Erik from 1413, the town tax was paid in money, but also converted by iron and butter.

The town's authorities collected as well several fees and taxes, mainly for financing the town's tax to the crown. The term is the *skotte**, "contribution" or "grant" in Sweden. According to the Stockholm registers from fifteenth century, it was distributed among the individual residents and paid according to wealth and fortune. How it was calculated is, however, difficult to reconstruct. The *skotte** corresponds in Norway to an urban tax called the *bæjargjald**, but no major information can be obtained from the sources.[34]

Extraordinary taxation

The most common permanent taxes were appropriation of the agrarian surplus and emerged during the period up to the thirteenth century. In general, they were based upon commutation of military service, but also of other services to the king. The peasantry's ancient military role declined and the peasants and farmers transformed into taxpayers. The Uppland Law, a provincial code from 1296, defined a farmer or householder as the one who had the capacity to pay *skeppsvist*, *spannmale* and other taxes. If he is not able to do it, he was considered to be a hired and unlanded worker.

These taxes provided the economic basis for the monarchy and incipient state with increasing political and administrative capacities. The royal needs exceeded the resources and extraordinary taxation therefore became necessary and frequent, mostly in order to finance the castles and their garrisons and mercenary troops.

In Denmark, a plough tax was launched, at first at Jutland in 1231 and later in other parts of the realm. The land of one plough had to deliver a fixed tax. It was thus a tax upon what might be a full farm and assessed according to the value of the land. After a revolt in Scania, it was introduced there as well, and considered very burdensome. King Erik Valdermarsson (r. 1241–1250) was therefore named Plovpenning (Plough-Penny).

Later the plough tax became annual in practice, especially during the 1310s. A declaration to abolish it in 1320 was revoked five years later. The tax often caused protests and revolts. In Denmark coronation charters from 1326 and 1376 includes proscriptions for the king to impose of new taxes. The extraordinary taxes became anyhow more frequent and were often termed *bede** in Danish or *petitio* in Latin. They were motivated as requests made by the king and had, at least formally, to be approved by the tax-liable communities.[35]

The extraordinary taxes were recurrent in Sweden during the fourteenth century to meet the military needs. One form of extraordinary taxation was the *gærþ**, roughly translated as "collection of what has to be given". A group of households contributed jointly with products in kind, mostly what was necessary for actual requests. Extraordinary taxation became particularly common during the struggles between the king and his rebellious brothers in 1309–1316. There are unique records of collection of this taxation from a part of the province of Uppland. Each tenant on church land paid six different taxes, three in money and three in kind. Extraordinary taxes were also levied exclusively in money and then often an identical sum from each household. They often caused complaints and resistance among the peasantry.

According to the account rolls of van Barnekow from 1365–1367 the extraordinary taxes were far more onerous than the permanent ones. In one district, Västerrekarne in Södermanland, the regular taxes were in total 194 *marker*, while the extraordinary *gærþs*★ brought in a sum of 233 *marker*.[36]

The extraordinary taxation was temporary, varied and of an arbitrary nature. This caused several political problems, not least since they inflicted the privileges of the church and the aristocracy. The tenants, *landbor*, were liable to the extraordinary taxation. Whether the lords of their land reduced the ordinary rent is unknown. The main political conflict was between the kingship and the privileged groups about the distribution of the rent.

The financial situation of the monarchies was constantly precarious. The taxes and the fiscal system were too inefficient and unmanageable. Loans were necessary and consequently with large parts of the realms mortgaged. The debts of the crown increased significantly. The church often had to admit under pressure that a part of the tithe was at the crown's disposal. In order to pay the loans a heavy extraordinary taxation was indispensable. Negotiations with different communities and corporations followed.

The coronation charter issued in the name of the minor king Magnus Eriksson of Sweden by leading aristocrats and bishops in 1319 stated that extraordinary taxes were always voluntary and approved whenever required. The Swedish Law code of the realm from the middle of the fourteenth century stated that the king should govern over castles and land, the royal domain (*Uppsala öd*), the land of the crown, all royal levies and certain fines. The levies, here termed *ingæld*, literally income, were the permanent taxes. Nevertheless, the law also allowed extra taxes at certain defined occasions, for defence against internal or external enemies, for coronation, election itinerary of the king (the *eriksgata*), or the marriages of royal children. The law also prescribed the approval of these taxes by a group of six representatives of the tax-exempt aristocracy and six of the common peasantry from each legal province. The local *thing* assemblies were in general the arena for negotiations about taxation.

In the royal Swedish testament 1346 the incomes from "Nordanskogs" (North of the Forest: the Svealand provinces) were assigned to pay off the royal debts.

Extraordinary taxation was often paid from all land, including those tax-exempt according to the privileges. The tax-exempt land expanded due to acquisition of land by the aristocracy and spiritual institutions. The land liable to pay the permanent taxes diminished and was another cause to financial deterioration.

In the Finnish part of Sweden, there were other units of taxation and a partly different fiscal system. The *koukku* in Western Finland and the *aatra* in the Eastern parts was a tax named from different types of ploughs (plough and ard). The Swedish term was *krok*. It was possibly identical with the ancient tax units in the Baltic areas south of the Gulf of Finland. Later another unit based upon the household or farm for taxation, in Latin termed as *fumus*, "smoke" (in Finnish *savu* or *suitsu*, in Swedish *rök*) became more frequent. It is mentioned in sources from the first half of the fourteenth century, and later in large areas according to the inventory from 1413. The new tax based upon the personal principle was probably more efficient to the monarchy and state and it resulted as well in a homogeneous fiscal system in the Eastern Finnish part. The late integration of Finland into the realm meant that there were no taxes based upon *ledung*★ and other ancient services to the king. The taxes in Finland were mostly to support the castles and the administration.[37]

The late medieval period: crisis and centralization

The financial problems of the Scandinavian monarchies caused *len* or *län* (the Danish and Swedish terms for fiefs) to be handed over to members of the aristocracy, but also to German and other foreign princes, as mortgages for loans. Political power and administration was decentralized and the authority of the kingdom weakened. The period 1241–1340 has been labelled as one of feudal dissolution in Danish history.[38] By 1340, all of Denmark was under the control of the dukes of Holstein. The king of Sweden paid a redemption for the province of Scania, which in turn caused fatal financial problems.

The attempts of king Magnus Eriksson to strengthen royal power in Sweden was financed by mortgaging *län* and loans, unable to pay back. A German duke, Albert of Mecklenburg became king of Sweden in 1363 when the major part of the realm was under the control of magnates and German princes as mortgage fiefs. Later, after he was disposed in 1389, a Swedish aristocrat was able to redeem what had been mortgaged and he controlled thirteen castles, their *län*, and other resources, making him the de facto regent. The state power and the administration of taxes were privatized.

The reign of Albert was a period with frequent extraordinary taxation and intensified exploitation, and consequently with grievances, complaints and protests. The community of the province of Hälsingland in Northern Sweden complained that a new tax where ten peasants must pay ten marker as commutation of a horse, made them all impoverished.[39]

From the late fourteenth century, the three Scandinavian kingdoms merged into the personal Kalmar union, due to the dynastic alliances and circumstances. A centralization of royal power took place in Denmark during the reign of king Valdemar Atterdag (r. 1340–1375) and his daughter Queen Margareta (r. 1387–1412). Margareta and her successor, Erik (formally king of all three kingdoms 1396–1439), strengthened the position of royal power to get a firmer control over the fiscal resources. The most comprehensive fiscal changes took place in Sweden. Resistance from fractions of the Swedish aristocracy was however fierce and the realm was for long periods ruled by domestic regents and kings.

The financial bases of the state increased with appropriation of land acquired by the aristocracy and spiritual institutions since 1363.[40] The privileges corroded and the land was again liable to permanent duties. The expansion of tax-exempted land stopped. The late decade of the fourteenth century saw new taxes introduced in Sweden. In the year 1403 a certain tax, the fifteen *marker*-aid (in Old Swedish: *marcegiæld*; in Latin: *subsidium marce*) paid in money, was quit after severe and intense protests. The queen regretted in the charter the burden caused by the taxation and introduced instead, a new tax. A group of peasants, two rich and two poor, should deliver specified quantities in kind. Each household had to do sixteen annual labour services.[41] It was an entirely new tax, but legitimized as a reintroduction of the "old taxes" from the days of Saint Erik of the 1160s. The new collective taxes from the early Kalmar union period made in practice the previously frequent extraordinary taxes permanent.[42]

Burdensome temporary taxes led to protests and could be a reason for revolts. After the uprising, led by the wealthy mining farmer Engelbrekt Engelbrektsson in 1434–1435, and the deposition of the union king Erik, the collective tax was reduced with one third; the groups were extended to six peasants. Many castles were systematically destroyed during the war.[43] After the Engelbrekt revolt, the fiscal system was rather stable with few examples of extraordinary taxation. One new and permanent tax was introduced, the *foding*, forage, in Latin often termed *pro equo*, from all the peasants and aiming to maintain a certain number of the officials' horses. This duty was common in late medieval Scandinavia.[44]

In Norway, the ancient *ledung*★ taxes were still important and it was furthermore an important instrument of military power for a longer period than in the other Scandinavian kingdoms. *Víseyrir* were taxes introduced in parts of South-Eastern Norway around 1300, mostly in inland districts that were not subject to the military *ledung*★ duty.[45] There were some extraordinary taxes, but as far as can be deduced from the existing sources not as frequent as in Denmark and Sweden.

The agrarian crisis from the middle of the fourteenth century affected Norway more than the other kingdoms in the North with deserted farms and land. This was partly a consequence of the settlement structure in Norway with many single and often isolated farmsteads. Villages existed in Scandinavia mainly in the plain areas, like Denmark and in large areas of Sweden.

The decline of royal revenues was substantial in Norway. The revenues of the royal domains decreased with possibly 80 per cent, and the taxes with ca. 60 per cent. During the Kalmar Union period the king and the central administration was absent in Norway, and resided mostly in Denmark. Estimates are of course precarious due to the nature of the sources, but at the middle of the thirteenth century, the Danish king had probably at his disposal five to ten as much as his Norwegian counterpart did.[46]

In Denmark, there were several extraordinary taxes during the late Kalmar union period, and demanded in money and in kind to meet the rising military costs during the struggles to uphold the union monarchy in Sweden. The political power in Sweden was in the hands of different fractions of the aristocratic elites challenging the union kings mostly residing in Denmark.

A *skeppsskatt* imposed by King Christian I in 1463 upon all peasants in Sweden led to a revolt into which the archbishop of Uppsala and leading Swedish aristocrats joined. There was a competition for the rights to collect taxes or the land rent from the tenants.

Sweden was, during the period from 1470 to 1520, mostly ruled independently by aristocratic regents, *riksföreståndare*. This was a period with a decentralized fiscal policy. The *län*, fiefs, were in the hands of the aristocracy and the regents controlled a rather confined area, the *fatabur* (literally: storage houses), mostly the area around Stockholm, the rich mining districts of Bergslagen north of Lake Mälaren, and South-Western Finland. The taxes were mostly levied in kind.[47] The Danish fiscal policy was on the other hand increasingly monetarized and centralized.[48]

The early modern state

The early fifteenth century witnessed great changes in Scandinavia and the transformations of the organization of state power and consequently the fiscal systems. The Reformation had political and economic implications. Lands belonging to ecclesiastical and other spiritual institutions were confiscated and the domain at the crown's disposal increased substantially.[49] New and efficient financial foundations of a centralized royal power emerged both in Sweden and in the monarchy of Denmark–Norway.

Both monarchies had great military expenses due to the internal warfare at the end of the Kalmar union. The Danish king relied on foreign, mercenary troops, financed with extraordinary taxes and credit. Heavy loans were therefore a great burden to the fiscal structure of Denmark. When paid off, the king was supposed to live from the ordinary revenues and not inflict the aristocratic privileges.

In Sweden, King Gustav I (r. 1523–1560) established a national kingdom after an uprising against the union king. Norway remained in a personal union with Denmark until 1814. Gustav inherited an ancient and disorganized fiscal system. Most of the fiefs came under the control of the royal administration. In the 1530s central registers, *undervisningar* (instructions) recorded all ancient taxes.[50] The collective principles of taxation ceased and the households became the tax units and with an evaluation of the land. All taxes, also the ancient and forgotten ones, were recorded in cadastres from the 1540s and onwards. The control over what could be demanded as tax increased and consequently the level of exploitation.

The collectiveness of the medieval taxation served to some degree as a bond of solidarity within the peasant communities. The relation between the taxpaying peasant and the crown became very similar to those between tenant and a lord of the land. A tax-paying peasant could fall into arrears and be evicted. Gustav I organized the fiscal system as a centralized feudal estate. Taxes in kind dominated entirely and the revenues brought to special warehouses and were commercialized.[51]

Conclusion

The history of taxes and fiscal systems of medieval Scandinavia can be divided into three separate phases. The Late Viking age and the transition to the Middle Ages was a period with partly external appropriation. Chiefs or local kings took regular tributes from other areas. It was the establishment of i.a. Iceland as a Norwegian *skattland*.

A second phase was the rise of the Christian monarchies during the twelfth and thirteenth centuries and the establishment of a kingship with rights of certain resources within the emerging realms. This included the rights to certain lands, but also the possibilities to levy and muster ships, men and victuals for the warfare organization. The king also acquired rights to certain services, especially during his itineraries. These obligations were commuted into taxes, fees and other forms of fiscal duties. The permanent taxes originated and were based upon land and according to different principles, but with partly diverging developments between the realms.

The political conjectures and the transformation of the military system, including the castles, made these permanent taxes and other royal resources insufficient. The structural inefficiency made extraordinary taxation necessary, as well as several huge loans. Since the taxation had to be negotiated and approved, the political stability deteriorated.

A third phase was the Kalmar union from the late fourteenth century, initially characterized by tendencies towards a more organized and stabilized state power. The state tried to rely on permanent taxes, mostly based upon collectives of households. The administrative incapacities became evident and the state had no survey over the economic resources. The political struggles within the union became increasingly endemic. The beginning of the sixteenth century was the end of the union and the rise of the modern and more efficient state power in Denmark and in Sweden. Following the Reformation, the domains and lands at the disposal of kings and political power expanded. This created a new and steady economic foundation. The Danish king financed the expenses, and the military expenses were prodigious, with loans, which in turn must be repaid with extraordinary taxes. In Sweden, systematic administrative reforms created a firmer and effective control of the individual taxpaying households. The taxation was homogeneous throughout the realm and mostly levied in kind and the income was traded. The many different medieval taxes were transformed into a new and efficient fiscal system and a tax-based state.

Notes

1 An exception is POULSEN, "Kingdoms on the Periphery".
2 LÖNNROTH, *Statsmakt och statsfinans*; HYBEL and POULSEN, *The Danish Resources*; *Kulturhistoriskt lexikon för nordisk medeltid*, see esp. vol. 15, col. 413–441, where the state of previous research about taxation is reviewed in national commentaries by Jakob Benediktsson, Halvard Bjørkvik, Gunvor Kerkkonen, Eva Österberg, and Poul Ramussen.

3 Fritz and Odelman (ed.), *Raven von Barnekows räkenskaper*; Melefors (ed.), *Ivar; Kulturhistoriskt lexikon*, 11, 1966, col. 111–118.
4 Aakjær (ed.), *Kong Valdemars*; Erslev, "Kong Valdemars"; *Kulturhistoriskt lexikon*, 19, 1975, col. 456–460.
5 Odén, *Rikets*, pp. 42–47; Bjurling, *Das Steuerbuck*. The king is in historiography conventionally called Erik of Pomerania. He was born as Bogislav, son to Duke Vartislav of Pomerania, and a niece's son to Margareta, who adopted him as heir.
6 Almquist and Hildebrand (ed.), *Stockholms stadsböcker*.
7 Imsen (ed.), *Taxes*, pp. 115–129, 133–147; Imsen (ed.), *Rex Insularum*; Bjørshol Wærdal, *The Incorporation*; Hastrup, *Culture and History*, pp. 223–237.
8 Blomkvist, "The Skattland" and Poulsen, "Tribute as Part".
9 Huldén, "När kommo svenskarna"; Tarkiainen, *Sveriges Österland*, pp. 44–63, 153–186.
10 Pettersson, "Husabyarna". The *husabyar* are also discussed in Eilergaard Christensen, Lemm and Pedersen (ed.), *Husebyer*, pp. 141–149, 165–172.
11 Andrén, "Städer och kungamakt"; Porskrog Rasmussen, "Danish Crown Lands".
12 Porskrog Rasmussen, "Kronens gods".
13 *Kulturhistoriskt lexikon för nordisk medeltid*, 7, 1962, col.. 664–670. Bjørkvik, "Det norske krongodset"; Dørum, *Romerike*, pp. 69–157, 226–236.
14 Rosén, *Kronoavsöndringar*, pp. 36–50; Holm, "Kampen".
15 Dovring, *De stående skatterna*, pp. 95–139. Lindkvist, "Fiscal Systems".
16 Bull, "Sagaernes beretning", p. 490; Holmsen, *Nye studier*, pp. 84–100.
17 Lönnroth, *Statsmakt och statsfinans*, pp. 265–268.
18 Dovring, *Attungen och marklandet*, pp. 69–84. Lönnroth, *Statsmakt och statsfinans*, pp. 84–108; Andræ, *Kyrka och frälse*, Uppsala 1960, pp. 114–123; Myrdal, "De medeltida jordvärderingarnas historiografi"; Ericsson, *Terra mediaevalis*.
19 *Kulturhistoriskt lexikon*, 2, 1957, col. 55–63.
20 Dovring, *De stående skatterna*, pp. 13–17. *Kulturhistoriskt lexikon*, 20, 1976, col. 599–601.
21 Lund, *Lið, leding og landeværn*. For another standpoint, see *i.a.* Malmros *Vikingernes syn på militær og samfund belyst gennem skjaldenes fyrstedigtning*, Århus 2010, pp. 325–329; Malmros, *Bønder og leding i valdemartidens Danmark*, Århus 2019, pp. 125–130. For the aristocratic origins of the Swedish *ledung*, see Andræ, *Kyrka och frälse*, pp. 64–72.
22 Andersson, "Nordiska distriksbeteckningar".
23 Arup, *Danmarks historie*, 1, København 1935, pp. 281–283.
24 Lönnroth, *Statsmakt och statsfinans*, pp. 108–120; Dovring, *De stående skatterna på jord*, pp. 17–28; Lane, *Kingship and State*, pp. 225–267.
25 Bolin, *Ledung och frälse. Studier och orientering över danska samfundsförhållanden under äldre medeltid*, Lund 1934. Malmros, *Bønder og leding*, pp. 45–53.
26 Elortza Larrea, *A Comparative Analysis*; Elortza Larrea, "The Transformation".
27 Lindkvist, *Landborna i Norden*.
28 Bull, *Leidang*, pp. 13–38; Ersland, "Kongshird og leidangsbonde", p. 55.
29 Bjurling, *Våldgästning*;. *Kulturhistoriskt lexikon*, 5, 1960, col. 256–257.
30 Bolin, "Hallandslistan"; Bolin, *Ledung och frälse*; Stenstrup, *Studier over Kong Valdemars Jordebog*; Hybel and Poulsen, *The Danish Resources*, p. 302.
31 *Kulturhistoriskt lexikon*, 7, 1962, col.. 420–423.
32 *Kulturhistoriskt lexikon*, 19, 1975, col. 632–634.
33 Andersson, *Medeltida urbanisering*, pp. 53–85, 127–139; Andrén, "State and Town"; Corsi, *Urbanization in Viking Age*.
34 *Kulturhistoriskt lexikon*, 11, 1966, col. 614–615; *Kulturhistoriskt lexikon*, 16, 1971, col. 712–722. Mackeprang, "De danske købstæders"; Matz, "Det stadskommunala skottet"; Dahlbäck, *I medeltidens Stockholm*, pp. 50–55, 84–94.
35 Bolin, "Skattpenning och plogpenning"; *Kulturhistoriskt lexikon*, 13, 1968, col. 350–351; Poulsen, "Kingdoms on the Periphery of Europe", p. 112; Venge, *Danmarks skatter*, pp. 195–203; Hybel and Poulsen, *The Danish Resources*, pp. 309–311.
36 Rosén, *Striden mellan Birger Magnusson*, pp. 264–270; Lönnroth, *Statsmakt och statsfinans*, pp. 139–142, 156–167; Andræ, *Kyrka och frälse*, pp. 196–219; Lindkvist, *Landborna i Norden*, pp. 63–66.
37 *Kulturhistoriskt lexikon*, 9, 1964, col. 395; 14, col. 630 and 15, col. 436–441. The most comprehensive study of taxation in medieval Finland is Voionmaa, *Suomalaisia keskiajan tutkimuksia*.

38 CHRISTENSEN, *Kongemagt og aristokrati*, pp. 101–122.
39 LÖNNROTH, *Statsmakt och statsfinans*, pp. 174–176.
40 ROSÉN, "Drottning Margaretas svenska räfst", *Scandia,,* 20, 1950, pp. 169–246.
41 DOVRING, *De stående skatterna*, pp. 51–54; LÖNNROTH, *Statsmakt och statsfinans*, pp. 176–179. ANDRÆ, *Kyrka och frälse*, pp. 198–208; LINTON, *Drottning Margareta – fullmäktig*, pp. 109–111; LINTON, *Drottning Margareta. Nordens drottning*, pp. 137–146.
42 ANDRÆ, *Kyrka och frälse*, p. 202.
43 Concerning the changed conditions of peasants and tenants after the Engelbrekt uprising, see LÖNNROTH, "Stadgorna om landbors", pp. 32–41.
44 *Kulturhistoriskt lexikon*, 4, 1959, col. 451–455.
45 HOLMSEN, "Integreringen av innlandsdistriktenen", pp. 9–19.
46 HOLMSEN, *Norges historie*, pp. 331–353; BAGGE, *Cross and Scepter*, pp. 124–131.
47 HAMMARSTRÖM, *Finansförvaltning*, pp. 39–192; RETSÖ, *Länsförvaltningen i Sverige*, 38–52.
48 POULSEN, "Kingdoms on the Periphery of Europe", p. 116.
49 In Sweden the number of tenant householders on land belonging to the crown (*kronolandbor*) increased from 5,5 per cent of the total number in 1521 to 28,2 per cent in 1560.
50 DOVRING, *De stående skatterna*, pp. 155–190.
51 DOVRING *De stående skatterna*, pp. 155–190; ODÉN, *Rikets uppbörd och utgift*, pp. 10–57; HAMMARSTRÖM, *Finansförvaltning och varuhandel*, pp. 273–317; HALLENBERG, *Kungen, fogdarna och riket*, pp. 133–192; POULSEN, "Kingdoms on the Periphery of Europe", pp. 116–122.

References

Svend AAKJÆR (ed.), *Kong Valdemars Jordebog*, 1–3, Copenhagen, 1926–1943.
Johan AXEL ALMQUIST and Hans HILDEBRAND (ed.), *Stockholms stadsböcker från äldre tid*, 3:1, *Stockholms stads skottebok 1460-1468 samt strödda räkenskaper från 1430-talet och från åren 1460–1474*, Stockholm, 1926.
Hans ANDERSSON, *Medeltida urbanisering*, Lund, 2017.
Thorsten ANDERSSON, "Nordiska distriksbeteckningar i gammal tid", *Namn och bygd*, 104, 2014, pp. 9–16.
Carl Göran ANDRÆ, *Kyrka och frälse i Sverige under äldre medeltid*, Uppsala 1960.
Anders ANDRÉN, "Städer och kungamakt – en studie i Danmarks politiska geografi före 1230", *Scandia*, 49, 1983, pp. 31–76.
Anders ANDRÉN, "State and Towns in the Middle Ages", *Theory and Society*, 18, 1989, pp. 585–609.
Erik ARUP, *Danmarks historie*, 1, Copenhagen, 1935.
Sverre BAGGE, *Cross and Scepter. The Rise of the Scandinavian Kingdoms from the Vikings to the Reformation*, Princeton, 2014.
Halvard BJØRKVIK, "Det norske krongodset i mellomalderen", *Historisk tidsskrift*, 40, 1960–61, pp. 201–231.
Randi BJØRSHOL WÆRDAL, *The Incorporation and Integration of the King's Tributary Lands in the Norwegian Realm c. 1195–1397*, Boston, 2011.
Oscar BJURLING, *Våldgästning och frälse*, Lund, 1952.
Oscar BJURLING, *Das Steuerbuch König Eriks XIII. Versuch einer Rekonstruktion*, Lund 1962.
Nils BLOMKVIST, "The Skattland – a Concept Suitable for Export? The Role of Loosely Integrated Territories in the Emergence of the Medieval State", in *Taxes, Tributes and Tributary Lands in the Making of the Scandinavian Kingdoms in the Middle Ages*, ed. Steinar IMSEN, Trondheim, 2011, pp. 167–188.
Sture BOLIN, "Hallandslistan i kung Valdemars jordebok", *Scandia*, 2, 1929, pp. 191–196.
Sture BOLIN, *Ledung och frälse. Studier och orientring över danska samfundsförhållanden under äldre medeltid*, Lund, 1934.
Sture BOLIN, "Skattpenning och plogpenning", in Sture BOLIN, *Ur penningens historia*, Lund 1962, pp. 133–153.
Edvard BULL, *Leidang*, Kristiania, 1920.
Edvard BULL, "Sagaernes beretning om Harald Hårfagres tilegnelse av odelen", *Historisk tidsskrift*, 5:4, 1920.
Aksel E. CHRISTENSEN, *Kongemagt og aristokrati. Epoker i middelalderlig dansk statsopfattelse indtil unionstiden*, Copenhagen, 1945.
Maria CORSI, *Urbanization in Viking Age and Medieval Denmark. From Landing Place to Town*, Amsterdam, 2020.
Göran DAHLBÄCK, *I medeltidens Stockholm*, Stockholm, 1987.
Knut DØRUM, *Romerike og riksintegreingen. Integreringen av Romerike i det norske rikskongedømmet i perioden ca. 1000–1350*, Oslo, 2004.

Folke DOVRING, *Attungen och marklandet. Studier över agrara förhållanden i medeltidens Sverige*, Lund, 1947.
Folke DOVRING, *De stående skatterna på jord 1400–1600*, Lund 1951.
Lisbeth EILERGAARD CHRISTENSEN, Thorsten LEMM and Anne PEDERSEN (ed.), *Husebyer – status quo, open questions and perspectives. Papers from a workshop at the National Museum Copenhagen 19–20 March 2014*, Copenhagen, 2016.
Beñat ELORTZA LARREA, *A Comparative Analysis of the Transformation of the Scandinavian Military Apparatus from a European Perspective, c. 1035–1202*, unpublished doctoral thesis, University of Aberdeen, 2017.
Beñat ELORTZA LARREA, "The Transformation of Naval Warfare in Scandinavia during the Twelfth Century", *Journal of Medieval Military History*, 2020, pp. 81–98.
Alf ERICSSON, *Terra mediaevalis. Jordvärderingssystem i medeltidens Sverige*, Uppsala, 2012.
Geir Atle ERSLAND, "Kongshird og leidangsbonde" in Geir Atle ERSLAND and Terje H. HOLM, *Norsk forsvarshistorie*, 1, *Krigsmakt og kongemakt 900–1814*, Bergen, 2000, pp. 11–154.
Kristian ERSLEV, "Kong Valdemars jordebog og den nyere kritik", *Historisk tidsskrift*, 4:5, 1875–1877, pp. 56–116.
Birgitta FRITZ and Eva ODELMAN (ed.), *Raven von Barnekows räkenskaper för Nyköpings fögderi 1365–1367*, Stockholm, 1994.
Mats HALLENBERG, *Kungen, fogdarna och riket. Lokalförvaltning och statsbyggande under tidig Vasatid*, Stockholm, 2001.
Ingrid HAMMARSTRÖM, *Finansförvaltning och varuhandel 1504–1540. Studier i de yngre Sturarnas och Gustav Vasas statshushållning*, Stockholm, 1956.
Kirsten HASTRUP, *Culture and History in Medieval Iceland. An Anthropological Analysis of Structure and Change*, Oxford, 1985.
Poul HOLM, "Kampen om det som ingen ejer. Om rettighederne til den øde jord indtil 1241 som baggrund for den tidlige middelalders bondeuro" in *Til kamp for friheden. Sociale oprør i nordisk middelalder*, ed. Anders BØGH, Jørgen WÜRTZ SØRENSEN and Lars TVEDE-JENSEN, Ålborg, 1988, pp. 90–109.
Andreas HOLMSEN, *Nye studier i gammel historie*, Oslo, 1976.
Andreas HOLMSEN, "Integreringen av innlandsdistriktenen i det gammelnorske riket", in *Hamarspor. Et festskrift till Lars Hamre*, ed. Steinar IMSEN and Gudmund SANDVIK, Oslo, 1982, pp. 9–19.
Lena HULDÉN, "När kommo svenskarna till Finland? Trender i en tvärvetenskaplig debatt från slutet av 1800-talet till 1950-talet", in *När kommo svenskarna till Finland?*, ed. Ann-Mari IVARS and Lena HULDÉN, Helsinki, 2002, pp. 15–38.
Nils HYBEL and Bjørn POULSEN, *The Danish Resources. Growth and Recession*, Leiden, 2007.
Steinar IMSEN (ed.), *Taxes, Tributes and Tributary Lands in the Making of the Scandinavian Kingdoms in the Middle Ages*, Trondheim, 2011.
Steinar IMSEN (ed.), *Rex Insularum, The King of Norway and his 'Skattlands' as a Political System c. 1260–1450*, Bergen, 2014.
Lis JACOBSEN et al. (ed.), *Kulturhistoriskt lexikon för nordisk medeltid*, Copenhagen, 1956–1978.
Philip LANE, *Kingship and State Formation in Sweden 1130–1290*, Leiden, 2007.
Thomas LINDKVIST, *Landborna i Norden under äldre medeltid*, Uppsala, 1979.
Thomas LINDKVIST, "Fiscal Systems, the Peasantry and the State in Medieval and Early Modern Sweden", in *Genèse de l'état moderne. Prélèvement et redistribution*, ed. Jean-Philippe GENET and Michel LE MENÉ, Paris, 1987, pp. 53–64.
Michael LINTON, *Drottning Margareta – fullmäktig fru och rätt husbonde*, Göteborg, 1971.
Michael LINTON, *Drottning Margareta. Nordens drottning 1375–1412*, Stockholm, 1997.
Niels LUND, *Lið, leding og landeværn. Hær og samfund i Danamrk i ældre middelader*, Roskilde, 1996.
Erik LÖNNROTH, *Statsmakt och statsfinans i det medeltida Sverige. Studier över skatteväsen och länsförvaltning*, Göteborg, 1940.
Erik LÖNNROTH, "Stadgorna om landbors och bönders skyldigheter under 1400-talet", in *Medeltid. Närbilder från fyra världsdelar*, Stockholm, 1968, pp. 32–41.
Mourtitz MACKEPRANG, "De danske købstæders skattevæsen indtil begyndelsen af det 17. århundrede", *Historisk Tidsskrift*, 7:3, 1900–1902, pp. 150–161.
Rikke MALMROS, *Vikingernes syn på militær og samfund belyst gennem skjaldenes fyrstedigtning*, Århus, 2010.
Rikke MALMROS, *Bønder og leding i valdemartidens Danmark*, Århus, 2019.
Richard MATZ, "Det stadskommunala skottet före 1620", *Historisk tidsskrift*, 86, 1966, pp. 296–312.
Evert MELEFORS (ed.), *Ivar Axelsson Totts räkenskaper för Gotland 1485–1487*, Visby, 1991.
Janken MYRDAL, "De medeltida jordvärderingarnas historiografi", in *Jordvärderingssystem från medeltiden till 1600-talet*, ed. Alf ERICSSON, Stockholm, 2008, pp. 125–138.

Birgitta ODÉN, *Rikets uppbörd och utgift. Statsfinanser och finansförvaltning under senare 1500-talet*, Lund, 1955.
Jonathan PETTERSSON, "Husabyarna – en kritisk forskningsöversikt", in *En bok om husabyar*, ed. Michael OLAUSSON, Stockholm, 2000, pp. 49–63.
Carsten PORSKROG RASMUSSEN, "Kronens gods", in *Danmark i senmiddelalderen*, ed. Per INGESMAN and Jens VILLIAM JENSEN, Copenhagen, 1994, pp. 69–87.
Carsten PORSKROG RASMUSSEN, "Danish Crown Lands AD 1230 – and before?", in *Settlement and Lordship in Viking and Early Medieval Scandinavia*, ed. Bjørn POULSEN and Søren Michael SINDBÆK, Turnhout, 2011, pp. 239–259.
Bjørn POULSEN, "Kingdoms on the Periphery of Europe: The Case of Medieval and Early Modern Scandinavia", in *Economic Systems and State finance*, ed. Richard BONNEY, Oxford, 1995, pp. 101–122.
Bjørn POULSEN, "Tribute as Part of the Financial System of the Medieval Danish King" in *Taxes, Tributes and Tributary Lands in the Making of the Scandinavian Kingdoms in the Middle Ages*, ed. Steinar IMSEN, Trondheim, 2011, pp. 279–292.
Dag RETSÖ, *Länsförvaltningen i Sverige 1434–1520*, Stockholm, 2009.
Jerker ROSÉN, *Striden mellan Birger Magnusson och hans bröder. Studier i nordisk politisk historia 1302–1319*, Lund 1939.
Jerker ROSÉN, *Kronoavsöndringar under äldre medeltid*, Lund, 1949.
Jerker ROSÉN, "Drottning Margaretas svenska räfst", *Scandia*, 20, 1950, pp. 169–246.
Johannes STENSTRUP, *Studier over Kong Valdemars Jordebog*, Copenhagen, 1874.
Kari TARKIAINEN, *Sveriges Österland. Från forntiden till Gustav Vasa*, Helsinki, 2008.
Mikael VENGE, *Danmarks skatter i middelalderen indtil 1340*, Copenhagen, 2002.
Väinö VOIONMAA, *Suomalaisia keskiajan tutkimuksia*, Porvoo, 1912.

16
KINGDOM OF POLAND AND THE GRAND DUCHY OF LITHUANIA

Piotr Guzowski and Urszula Sowina

The medieval and early modern Polish treasury system has been the subject of historians' interest for almost two hundred years,[1] although the sources which make it possible to reconstruct all the basic types of state income, including the amount of tax revenue, date from as late as the turn of the Middle Ages and modern times. Therefore, some researchers take a very cautious approach to building budget models and estimating tax revenue.[2] A very limited set of resources is available from the early and mature Middle Ages; they are primarily chronicle sources. Documentary sources appeared as late as in the fourteenth century. The first tax registers that have survived date from the end of the fifteenth century. Most works so far have focused on selected aspects of the tax system, particular types of taxes or the legal and constitutional context of their introduction in the late Middle Ages.[3] There are also some synthetic studies of the tax system in the early Middle Ages.[4] However, the present state of knowledge in this field cannot be considered satisfactory, and recent years have not brought a breakthrough in Polish historiography in this area; in fact, a crisis can be observed in the research not only into the economic organization of the state in the Middle Ages, but also into the economy in general. This text aims to present the system of public taxes in Poland and Lithuania during the Middle Ages up to the beginning of the sixteenth century, i.e. when Zygmunt I (*Sigismund I*) came to power at the turn of 1506 and 1507, first in the Grand Duchy of Lithuania and then in the Kingdom of Poland. The ruler began fiscal reforms that were typical of modernization of the early modern period.[5]

State taxes in the early Middle Ages (tenth–mid-thirteenth century)

The early medieval Polish state is described in the literature as a system of ducal law (Latin: *ius ducale*) derived from or similar in its initial phase to a chieftainship-type organization. Immunity privileges exempting certain estates from the common law should be recognized as still valid with regard to the fiscal system; they are the findings of the classic studies by Karol Buczek and Karol Modzelewski,[6] who built models of the organization of the Polish state with the retrogressive method – mainly based on later sources. According to these researchers, the first dukes and kings of the Piast dynasty "within settlement complexes created a closed economy system, based in its essence on the redistribution of wealth. According to this system, specific payments were collected from the local population, which were then used to satisfy the needs of the ducal court that moved around the country with the monarch".[7] Among them tributes in the form of agricultural products are usually distinguished (to maintain the ducal court and officials), communication services for the ruler, the obligation to build castles (moats, ramparts), guard (serving in the castle or providing food for the needs of the crew) and in-kind tributes (mainly crafts and livestock) provided by a network of servant settlements.[8] Most of the above-mentioned performances are not treated as treasury revenue, although they undoubtedly relieved the reigning monarch of expenses on transport, communications or construction. The performances were also cared for and managed by the clerical apparatus, territorially based on castellans (Latin: *castellani*) officiating in castles (Latin: *castrum*). The area of their authority was castellum (Latin: *castellum* – "castrum cum pertinentis"), which was both a tribute district and a collection of performances from the district's population to the state.[9] "The castle's branch of economic management was called the chamber (Latin: *camera*)",[10] from the granary and storehouse of possessions. It was headed by managers (Latin: *vlodarii*), in some regions called bailiffs (Latin: *camerarii/camerrarii castrenses*).[11] In the state of the first Piasts they had property administrators to help them. As consideration, the castle clerks were entitled to some or all of the performances from the population for the ruler and the ruler's court.[12] At the central level, the income of the ducal court from tributes coming from particular *castella* was managed by an official called a bailiff or chamberlain.[13]

Karol Buczek pointed out that the proper sources of income for the rulers were tributes, certain regalia (Latin: *regalia* or *iura ducalia*), i.e. performances due to the rulers or their servants, penalties and court fees, and the monarchs' own economy.[14] In the context of this chapter, only the first three categories will be highlighted, although it is worth noting that the elements of the Polish system did not differ from the Western European organization of the royal domain, which was first formed in France in the second half of the eleventh century.[15]

The basic general tax paid by peasants had different names in different regions of the country: plough tax★ (Polish: *poradlne*), ox tax (Polish: *powołowe*) and hearth tax (Polish: *podymne*). It depended on the number of ploughs or cattle (plough tax/ox tax), on the unit of cultivated land (plough tax) and on the house/farm (hearth tax).[16] Until the end of the twelfth century these taxes were paid in kind, in the next century perhaps already in cash or grain.[17] In Greater Poland there was also a tribute paid in cows or oxen imposed on *opole*, an organizational unit representing a neighbourhood community.[18] The castle clerks also collected tributes for grazing animals in the forests, i.e. the so-called *narzaz*, and tributes for the possibility of keeping beehives and hunting in them. Moreover, the local population paid fees for the exemption from the duty of guarding the castle and for the maintenance of the duke and the ducal court travelling around the country (hearth tax and state). Unfortunately, there are no sources available to accurately determine the frequency of all these taxes, although it is usually assumed that they were collected every year.[19] As Karol Modzelewski wrote: "The property structure of the burdens of ducal law in its most widespread version was characterized above all by a patchwork of various objects and duties designed to reliably satisfy the needs of the ruler and the state apparatus".[20] Thus, at its core, the treasury system of the first Piasts was not so much focused on the quantitative maximization of income, but rather on satisfying as many needs of the court, the clerical apparatus and the state as possible.

However, the system was complemented by the second important element of the fiscal system, considered to be regalia: performances related to trade, customs and roads. They involved the collection of market fees, customs duties and tolls, which were probably paid to a greater extent in money. Around the year 1200, there were already at least 200 weekly markets operating in the Polish lands. The castellan and his judge (Latin: *iudex castri*) were responsible for the safety of merchants on the roads and disputes related to trade, but the collection of fees was handled by central officials. *Theloneum forense* was collected by mint workers (Latin *monetarii*) reporting directly to the duke. They were also responsible for enforcing the obligation to use current coinage in trade. Therefore, they were accountable not only for classical minting production (coins started to be minted in Poland at the beginning of the eleventh century), but also for the exploitation of bullion circulation. In turn, *theloneari nostri*, or ducal tax collectors, enforced tolls and duties (Latin: *thelonea*).[21] Originally, tolls and duties were levied on the number of carts and horses or ships and boats, and with time a specification system was introduced: on the quantity and type of goods.[22]

Unfortunately, there are no sources available which would allow us to establish the proportions of the importance of general tributes and the above-described fees related to markets, customs and tolls, as well as other regalia such as mint or mining monopolies, revenues from penalties or the rulers' own economy. Although the literature points to the existence of the duke's/king's own assets, both at the beginning of the state's functioning and during the vast majority of the Middle Ages, no distinction was made between the state (public) treasury and the duke's/king's treasury. The rulers' own economy was connected with agriculture and breeding in the estates inhabited by the duke's peasants (including serfs). The revenue was used both for the direct needs of the court and for various state purposes.

Taxes of the late medieval domain state in Poland

Despite the evolution of the state's structures during the first two hundred years of the Piast dynasty until the end of the twelfth century both the treasury system and the whole economy were hardly monetized, although the rulers discovered a chance to draw income from the cyclic re-coinage relatively early (already in the first half of the twelfth century). A breakthrough in the economic development of the Polish lands was brought about by German colonization, which resulted in changes in the organization of agriculture, the development of cities, and commercialization. This happened in the period when the country was fragmented into districts, when the system of ducal law was eroded due to, among other things, decentralization and disintegration of the state. As Karol Modzelewski wrote: "In the thirteenth century clerical emoluments were individualized; particular tributes or their parts became separate rights of the monarch's court, castellans, castle judges, landlords and deputy castellans responsible for military affairs (Polish: *wojski*, Latin: *tribunus*)".[23] In addition, first the clergy, and with time the nobility and knighthood expanded their own economic base, independent of the ducal law system. Initially, ducal grants and immunity privileges exempting certain estates or people from the ducal law, and with time, the massive reception of the German law and the related legal and economic immunity meant that increasingly new areas came to be excluded from the jurisdiction of the castle and the execution of tributes and services, and the tributes and services themselves were replaced with rent paid to the lord of the land rather than to the duke or the state. Besides, under conditions of commercialization and the emerging market, the system of burdens and services resulting from the natural economy lost its raison d'être.[24] The dukes also modernized the system of organization of their own estates, deriving income from them in a manner similar to other landowners, limiting the jurisdiction of state officials and the fees collected by them from the population and replacing them simply with rent. This increased the revenue from the monarchs' own estates, who saw in the expansion of the domain an opportunity to increase their treasury income. Therefore, they conducted a wide colonization campaign, including the foundation of not only new villages, but also towns under German law. Revenue from the domain was to be supplemented by funds coming from the fiscal exploitation of the growing commodity–money trade, primarily customs duties. These two sources of income, supplemented by income from minting, mines and the salt monopoly, constituted the basis for the treasury of Ladislaus the Short (*Władysław Łokietek*)[25] and Casimir the Great (*Kazimierz Wielki*),[26] i.e. the rulers who rebuilt the Kingdom of Poland after the period of the country's fragmentation. Anna Sucheni-Grabowska, an outstanding researcher of the old Polish treasury system, wrote: "Casimir the Great was not only the last hereditary Polish king in the strict sense of the word, but also the last host and steward of his homeland, who managed it as he wished and was capable of".[27] In the treasury system created by the last Piasts the importance of taxes was limited, and therefore there are no sources available making it possible to thoroughly understand their nature or the amount of the burden. We can assume that in the thirteenth and for most of the fourteenth century the basic general tribute continued to be called the plough tax★ or hearth tax (Latin: *exactio regalis; fumale*). However, it was not levied on hearths/houses or ploughs, as in the early Middle Ages, but on the mansi of settled peasants and was paid in money.[28] Light on the operation of the tax system is shed by immunity documents, which exempted certain estates from the obligation to pay tributes, and above all by privileges issued by the successor of Casimir the Great, Angevin king of Hungary Louis the Great (*Ludwik Węgierski*). While still aspiring to the Polish throne, he issued a guarantee in Buda in 1355 that in the case of taking over the rule in Poland he would be content with collecting only those taxes which the Polish people had been used to paying for a long time.[29] In turn, as he wanted to secure the Polish throne for one of his daughters, he first issued a privilege in 1374, regulating the principles of collecting the plough tax★ from the estates of the nobility, and in 1381 from church estates. From then on, all other taxes could only be collected by the king with the consent of the nobility gathered at assemblies. The decisions of Louis the Great have been the subject of a debate among Polish historians focusing on three elements: whether in the earlier period the plough tax★ was an ordinary tax, chosen annually or exceptionally in times of extraordinary need; what was the rate of this tax during the reign of Casimir the Great and the scale of income coming from it; and whether the privileges of Louis the Great meant a reduction of fiscal pressure and of tax revenue. Traditional historiography holds that Casimir the Great put a number of treasury matters in order by creating, among others, the office of the treasurer of the Kingdom of Poland, i.e. the administrator of all the national income, who also performed the function of court treasurer, hence was responsible directly for the king's financial matters. Thus there was no division between the private treasury of the ruler and the public treasury. It was also believed that the plough tax★ was a basic permanent levy, in the times of Casimir the Great collected every year, or even more often, as an extraordinary tax, negatively perceived by the population as a burdensome payment, which was to be confirmed by the account of the greatest Polish chronicler of the late Middle Ages, Jan Długosz, about 100 years later. This system was to collapse as a result of the privileges of Louis the Great.[30] Meanwhile, Jacek Matuszewski's meticulous analysis of the extant source material has critically verified the results of earlier studies and pointed to new interpretative possibilities. According to this researcher, Ladislaus the Short and Casimir the Great had the right to introduce taxes, or at least to indicate the circumstances which were the basis for their collection. However, there is no evidence that the commonly collected tribute in the form of the plough tax★ was a permanent tax. According to Jacek Matuszewski, it was a tax paid in emergency situations, but imposed relatively often and enforced firmly. Its rate was probably variable and depended on the will and needs of the ruler, which caused understandable resentment among the population. Therefore, the provisions of the privileges of Louis the Great of 1374 and 1381 meant the construction of a new tax system, based on a permanent tax with an unchanging rate. Its establishment was to the advantage of both the subjects and the ruler. The basis for taxation was the acreage of the settled land, cultivated by the peasant population. According to the first document, subjects from noble estates were to pay 2 groschen per year per mansus, and according to the second privilege, subjects from secular clergy estates were to pay 2 groschen per mansus per year and in monastic estates 4 groschen per mansus per year.[31] Jacek Matuszewski estimated the income from this tax at about 8,700 marcs (*grzywna*) per year, which constituted 11 per cent of the average revenue of the treasury at the end of the fourteenth century. This was therefore slightly more than the royal mints brought in (7,000 marcs), but considerably less than the income from royal estates (15,000 marcs), salt and lead mines (25,000 marcs), and customs (23,000 marcs).[32]

It is impossible to estimate the Crown revenue from the tax levied on town dwellers in the late Middle Ages. Also in this case, the first references to the tribute paid by the townspeople are connected with the documents issued by Louis the Great. It can be inferred from the abovementioned privilege issued in Buda in 1355 that taxation was not permanent; tributes were paid at the king's request.[33] Later documents demonstrate that taxes were imposed due to an emergency of the state (e.g. war) or as gifts to celebrate important events in the king's life (e.g. marriage).[34] Thus, in the course of the fifteenth century, two different extraordinary taxes evolved from a single municipal tribute. The first of them was connected with the family celebrations of the ruler and the ruler's children. Initially, it was a subsidy paid at the request of the ruler in the amount determined by the towns themselves (as, for example, in 1423 for the coronation of the fourth wife of king Władysław Jagiełło (*Ladislaus Jagiello*), Zofia Holszańska (*Sophia of Halshany*)). At the end of the fifteenth century it already existed under the name of "coronation" (Latin: *statio pro coronatione, exactio pro coronatione*), and the rates were set by the ruler for individual towns. The earliest extant accounts of this tax date back to 1507 and amount to 2,336 marcs, i.e. a maximum of approximately 4 per cent of the budget revenue estimated at the beginning of the sixteenth century at 60,000 marcs.[35] This tax was levied on the town communities and it was the town authorities that decided how to collect it among the town dwellers.

The second extraordinary tax, non-permanent, paid initially by the towns in response to the "king's request" was the *szos królewski* (royal szos★). As the main and most important direct tax payable to the Crown treasury by royal, church and private (nobility) towns, it was studied thoroughly in 1900 by one of the most eminent Polish historians, Stanisław Kutrzeba.[36] The thorough analysis of sources, as well as nineteenth-century European (including Polish) literature on the subject, makes this study still relevant for present-day comparative studies. The king asked for the collection *szos*★ in exceptional political situations, e.g. in 1404 in connection with the purchase of the Dobrzyń land from the Teutonic Knights pledged earlier by duke Władysław Opolczyk for 40,000 Hungarian florins or in 1410 for the purposes of the war with the Teutonic Order. In the first of the two collections, Cracow alone paid 4,000 florins, which constituted a tenth of the total (4,000 florins = 2,500 *marcs* (Polish: grzywny), with the annual municipal budget not exceeding 1,700 marcs in 1404). In 1410, the amount paid by Cracow was 2,400 marcs (1 *grzywna*/marc = 48 groschen).[37] From 1456 this tax was levied by the Sejm or regional assemblies (Polish: *sejmik*) of Greater Poland (*Wielkopolska*) and Lesser Poland (*Małopolska*). Simultaneously, Cracow lost the right to give or deny its consent for the imposition of *szos*★ on towns. Since then, the decision belonged effectively to the nobility. This led to the considerable weakening of the position of towns in the early modern period, symbolized by the fact that they did not have their representation in the Sejm.[38]

In the middle ages, in the Kingdom of Poland *szos*★ was paid in a lump sum to the king by the municipal authorities. From the early 1420s, it became a tax collected directly from the townspeople in the form of a tax on the value of real estate, movables and debts, usually 2 groschen per 1 marc (per 48 groschen), i.e. more than 4 per cent of the value of the real estate, although there were also higher rates.[39] At the same time it became a mandatory tax levied by the king, losing de facto the character of a voluntary payment.[40] As a result of this change, in addition to the usual collection of the tax by the authorities of a given city (e.g. in Cracow), the king could appoint his own tax collector by a resolution of the Sejm.[41] In general, however, *szos**, calculated according to the above criteria, was collected by the municipal authorities, and then paid to the monarch. The money came from the municipal tax revenues (*perceptae*), including the city *szos** (*census terrestris*), which consisted of three taxes: 1) the main revenue source – a real property tax on properties in the city and the suburbs; 2) a tax on the sale of goods and services; and 3) a personal property tax.[42] The real property tax was the oldest, paid from the moment the town was established. It took the form of an annual cash payment collected by the municipal authorities from real property owners. The tax was imposed on an urban property: *curia, hereditas, area, Erbe, Hof*, or its part, taxed accordingly.[43] It is thought that the city *szos** was an inspiration for the royal *szos**,[44] which transformed from the lump sum tax to the levy paid by individual citizens.[45]

As noted by Kutrzeba, the city *szos* was of German origin[46] because Polish towns were chartered upon the German municipal law (the Magdeburg law, the Chełmno law, the Lübeck law). Due to the legal, organizational and economic similarities, the *szos** in Polish medieval cities can be compared with the equivalent tax paid in Lower Silesian cities such as Wrocław[47] or Świdnica,[48] as well as in urban settlements established by Teutonic Knights, such as Toruń or Chełmno[49] for which the number of written sources is significantly higher than for Polish towns. While the oldest document establishing the rate of *szos** in Cracow comes from 1385[50] (the rate was ½ marc = 24 groschen per each residential 36x72-ells plot near the market square),[51] fourteenth-century Silesian cities have their *szos** tax documented by numerous municipal books of records or separate *szos** records.

According to the tax resolution of 1498, a fee of 1 grosch per wife, children and servants per capita was added to the previous rate.[52] The literature speaks of a parallel between the extraordinary tax paid by the townspeople: the *szos** and the mansus tax* paid by the peasants.[53]

Crucial for the functioning of the state, especially in times of war conflicts, was the extraordinary tax known as a mansus tax* (Latin: *exactio*). As part of this tribute, taxes were levied primarily on land cultivated by peasants (Polish: *kmieć*), i.e. peasants with inherited plots of land, inns, mills, and on an ad hoc basis on gardeners, village mayors, nobility without peasants, Orthodox clergy and vagrants (Polish: *ludzie luźni*). It is assumed that this was an element of the system based on the feudal principle of *consilium et auxilium*, i.e. the obligation to provide advice and assistance to the lord (Polish: *senior*), which existed throughout the entire late medieval Europe.[54] Subjects paying rent within fief dependence were obliged to pay the tax. This tax was usually adopted interchangeably with the proclamation of levée en masse. The parliament, to which the king would turn to remedy the problem, for example a military threat to the state, would decide whether it was better to adopt a tax to organize the army or to request that knights to turn up in person. In special cases it was possible to raise an army and adopt a tax at the same time. In the first half of the century the mansus tax* was imposed only occasionally (1404, 1440, 1447), but in the second part of the century it became a frequent levy (1451, 1453, 1454, 1455, 1456, 1457–1458, 1459, 1463, 1465, 1466, 1468, 1470, 1472, 1474, 1475, 1476, 1478, 1479, 1482, 1484, 1487, 1489, 1490, 1492, 1493, 1496, 1498, 1499, 1501, 1504, 1507), although it remained an extraordinary one. After more than 100 years from the tax reform of Ludwik Węgierski, the importance of the plough tax* decreased and it brought only about 3 per cent of the annual revenue of the treasury of king Casimir IV Jagiellon (*Kazimierz Jagiellończyk*) (1440–1492), yet the revenue from the mansus tax*, regularly levied every two years, kept increasing. Its rates ranged from 4 to 18 groschen per mansus, although the most common rate was 12 groschen per mansus (Latin: *exactio fertonum*). Thus, land was primarily the basis for tax calculation for two basic groups: peasant payers and nobility without peasants. In some years (1456, 1459, 1461, 1470, 1472, 1493, 1504), however, the burden was defined as a percentage of the rents collected on noble, church and municipal estates, and thus bore the features of an income tax. In 1510, the mansus tax★ brought in over 43,000 florins,[55] which amounted to about 40 per cent of the treasury revenue.

In the second half of the fifteenth century, along with the mansus tax★, another extraordinary tax was collected, i.e. liquor tax (Latin: *ducilla*). It was a tax on the production, importation and trade of beer, wine and meads. At the turn of the fifteenth and sixteenth centuries, the basic rate for the dominant spirit on the market, i.e. beer, was 1 grosch per barrel (transport unit). The majority of beer production facilities (breweries and maltings) were located in towns, so a decision was made to link the collection of liquor tax with the town administration in such a way that one-third of the collected tax was to remain at the disposal of the town, which had an official apparatus capable of collecting tax from manufacturers on a regular, quarterly basis.[56] The role of this tax grew over time, and it is estimated that in 1534 it accounted for as much as one quarter of all tax revenue.[57]

In 1498, the risk of the Tatar invasion prompted the parliament to decide to impose an extraordinary tax, which was a poll tax and a land tax at the same time (Latin: *exationes personales atque locales*). All inhabitants of the country (regardless of their social group, including the clergy and the nobility) were obliged to pay it, usually at the rate of 1 grosch per capita, and additionally landowners had to pay one marc per village, and village mayors has to pay 12 groschen. In towns and cities, the tax was imposed also on wives, children and servants at the rate of 1 grosch per person. The main tax-payer, the male head of the household, the one who, according to the old custom", paid 2 groschen per 1 marc of the value of his property, was exempted from the extraordinary poll tax. That "old customary" payment was undoubtedly the royal *szos*★. It was paid as a non-flat rate, proportional to the total value of the tax-payer's property (assessed by the collector on the basis of the payer's sworn statement). Additionally, the extraordinary tax of 1498 was to be paid at the rate of 1 grosch by persons identified in the parliament act as not possessing any property.[58] Prostitutes and Jews were supposed to pay more than the common rate, with the latter paying 1 florin (Hungarian zloty = 30 groschen) per male head of the household and 12 groschen per wife, child and servant.

The fiscal benefits of this tax turned out to be negligible, and the inconvenience of its collection too great for it to become a permanent element of the tax system, and in the following century it was levied only twice: in 1520 and 1590.[59]

A tax on the Jewish population was a much more stable source of revenue. The Jews, settling down throughout the Middle Ages in the Polish and Ruthenian lands that were part of the Kingdom of Poland, formed communities of several to 500–800 inhabitants in 106 larger and smaller towns.[60] According to Hanna Zaremska, the annual amount of the so-called Jewish *szos*★ paid by the Jews was as much as the one-off coronation tax in 1507, that is about 890 marcs, or about 1.5 per cent of the budget revenue of Alexander Jagiellon (*Aleksander Jagiellończyk*) after he ascended to the Polish throne.[61]

At the turn of the Middle Ages and modern times, the above-described ordinary taxes (plough tax★, tax paid by the Jewish population) played a supplementary role in the treasury system of the Jagiellonians after their ascension to the Polish throne. As in the times of Casimir the Great, the most important sources of regular royal income were still the ruler's landed estates, the salt mines of Lesser Poland and the Red Ruthenian breweries, as well as the silver and lead mines in Olkusz, managed directly by royal officials or leased. In the course of the late Middle Ages, customs and toll revenue was reduced as a result of temporary or permanent exemptions granted by the rulers to individual towns, church institutions, individual merchants or the wealthy.[62] In addition, in 1496 the nobility and in 1504 the clergy were exempted from customs duties on the export of products from their estates and the import of goods for their own use.[63] Therefore, starting from the reign of king Casimir IV Jagiellon and the Thirteen Years' War against the Teutonic Order (1454–1466), which was connected with the beginning of the military revolution, a progressive transformation from a domain state to a tax state and the growing importance of extraordinary taxes, such as the mansus tax★, liquor tax, the town szos★, the occasionally imposed coronation tax or incidental poll tax can be observed. As the ruler was unable to convince the parliament to impose extraordinary taxes every year (in the years 1451–1507 they were imposed 31 times), he sought support in times of particular crisis either from the clergy or by taking out loans. On the part of the clergy, from the mid-fifteenth century the support took the form of the so-called synod contribution, i.e. a special tribute paid by the clergy called *subsidium* in some sources, i.e. an allowance, aid, subsidy, or *contributio pro subsidio*, i.e. a contribution to the subsidy. It originated from the papal tithe payment as a church tax, which evolved into a state performance, imposed on the Polish clergy by diocesan or provincial synods at the request of the king, parliament or bishops. There is information about 28 cases of this type of activity between 1454 and 1507. The tax base constituted the value of all the income of the beneficiary, and the amount of the levy ranged from 6 to 24 groschen per 1 marc (48 groschen) of income, i.e. from 12.5 to 50 per cent.[64] As the collection of both ordinary and extraordinary taxes was a relatively time-consuming process, the king took out loans. They usually took the form of loans against a pledge of royal estates or income, which was a convenient solution, but in the long run could have a negative impact on the size of the royal domain and the amount of income that it generated.

Tax collection system and treasury records

The treasury system evolved over the course of the fourteenth and fifteenth centuries, and its final form is known from the so-called statute of King Alexander of 1504 and the tax records of the early modern period. The official in charge of the central treasury in Poland since the fourteenth century had been the Royal Treasurer (Latin: *thesaurarius Regni Poloniae*), who was responsible for all payments and disbursements from royal estates, salt mines, mints and taxes alike. In the middle of the fifteenth century the office of the court treasurer, and thus his deputy (Latin: *vicetesaurarius regis/vicetesaurarius curiae*) evolved; this official was constantly present at the royal court, performing essential accounting functions.[65] Both treasurers had treasury clerks to assist them.

The tax collectors (Latin: *exactores*) of the ordinary tax, i.e. plough tax★, being royal officials, were accountable to the crown or court treasurer. Each voivodeship and land had its own *exactores*, and there were also higher-ranking collectors at the provincial level, such as the collector of the Greater Poland or Red Ruthenia. Usually lower-level land officials and secretaries of the royal chancellery became tax collectors, but sometimes also voivodes and starostas. At the lowest level of the tax collection were the owners of estates, who delivered the money collected from their subjects to the royal collectors, who in turn delivered it to the treasurer or the king.[66]

The imposition and collection of extraordinary taxes created the need for a separate administration system. The decision to levy the extraordinary tax was made by the parliament and in the official letter on taxes (Polish: *uniwersał podatkowy*), i.e. the document specifying the procedure and rules for collecting taxes, the names of tax collectors and tax collection dates in individual lands and voivodeships were indicated. The contents of the official letter on taxes was announced in market squares in towns and in churches. The official letter indicated the general tax collector of a voivodeship or province (Latin: *exactor generalis*), who was responsible for settling accounts with the Sejm and the Royal Treasurer (Latin: *thesaurarius*). He had subcollectors to help him, and they had clerks compiling the documentation. Peasants or their landlords brought taxes to the seat of the starosta, where royal officials and subcollectors were working.[67]

Extraordinary taxes, adopted on a regular basis by parliaments in the second half of the fifteenth century, marked the beginnings of the public treasury, not yet permanent but temporary. Local assemblies of the nobles (*sejmiki*) and the parliament accounted not only for the revenues but also for expenditures. The crown treasurer, with the help of the public treasury clerks, accounted to the parliament for the total receipts from extraordinary taxes. The parliament appointed special commissions to audit the accounts. The audit took place within two years of enactment, as often the tax was enacted in the second half of the calendar year and collected in two instalments over the next twelve months. It took at least three months to collect one instalment, although tax arrears were collected much longer.[68]

The oldest preserved tax registers drawn up by the tax collectors of particular lands or voivodeships date back to the end of the fifteenth century and have a very terse form; they contain a list of localities in a given parish, land or district (Polish: *powiat*) with the number of taxed mansi or another tax base, and sometimes also the amount of dues. More elaborate forms of registers, containing names of the payers, appeared at the beginning of the sixteenth century. The oldest surviving books of receipts issued by treasurers and other officials to tax payers also date from the beginning of this century. This documentation can be found in the form of manuscripts in the Central Archives of Historical Records, in the Crown Treasury Archives: section I – collection books, and section V – receipt books. The archives also contain royal accounts from 1388 onwards, with records of treasury income, including from ordinary and extraordinary taxes, and expenditure. The Central Archives of Historical Records in Warsaw have also preserved the materials from the so-called Crown Metrica in manuscript form, i.e. the chancellery books recording documents issued by the royal chancellery (and containing copies of documents) which include all kinds of instruments related to the treasury, but mostly to the royal domain and other types of income not being taxes.

The treasury system of Royal Prussia

As a result of the 1454–1466 war with the Teutonic Knights, Pomorze Wschodnie (*Eastern Pomerania*) was incorporated into the Kingdom of Poland, with Gdańsk and the former Teutonic capital of Malbork at its helm. As a province under the name of Royal Prussia, the incorporated territories retained their autonomy, had a separate representative body from the Polish one, namely the Prussian estates (Polish: *stany pruskie*) (composed of representatives of the nobility and towns), and a separate treasury, although they were governed by a council subordinate to the Polish king. The treasury system of Royal Prussia in the years 1466–1569 has been described in a synthetic manner by Janusz Deresiewicz,[69] with the majority of the sources coming from the early modern period, when the office of the Prussian treasurer appeared in 1506. Earlier, the treasury functions were performed by the Malbork treasurer, who was assisted by a treasury clerk and tax collectors. As the starostas at the helm of the royal estate complexes in Prussia accounted directly to the king, just like the largest cities,[70] the treasury apparatus was primarily associated with tax collection. A distinction was made between rural collectors, who were usually representatives of the nobility, and town collectors, appointed by local governments. The Duchy of Warmia, governed by the Bishop of Warmia, had a separate collector.⁷¹ Under the Prussian system, taxes were an extraordinary tribute, adopted by the Prussian estates. Direct and indirect taxes were applied. Direct taxes were paid by landowners as a tax on the rents paid by the rural population (usually one-tenth of the amount of rents), but also on protoidustrial facilities. Thus, in the case of the nobility, it was revenue-based, and in the case of the peasant population, it was either land-based (when it came to settled peasants) or poll-based. Peasants paid a maximum of one-quarter of a marc per mansus of the land that they cultivated. At the same time, a tax called *szos*★ was collected on the value of real estate in towns (approximately 0.8 per cent).⁷²

A more important tax was the indirect tax called excise tax (Latin: *cisa*; German: *Maltz-Akcise*) initially imposed on beer, and later on other goods and crops, fish and products of the wood industry. Each time, an official letter on taxes specified the list of taxable goods and the tax rate. The tax was enacted for one year, although sometimes also for several years, e.g. in 1468 for four years.⁷³ Despite the fact that taxes were enacted due to the sudden and large military needs on the war fronts outside Royal Prussia, the Prussian estates sought to limit the ability to spend tax revenue outside the Prussian province. The spending rules were negotiated with the king, who in moments of crisis, with his presence in Royal Prussia enforced decisions suitable for him. Negotiations between the Prussian estates and the king about taxes, however, are part of a system of loans, granted by Prussian towns or representatives of banking families. Loans acquired relatively quickly in Royal Prussia were repaid from funds collected in the province through extraordinary taxes.

Tax system of the Grand Duchy of Lithuania

From 1385–1386 the Grand Duchy of Lithuania was first in a personal union and then in a dynastic union with the Kingdom of Poland. The latter union ultimately transformed into a real union in 1569 and a common state, the Polish–Lithuanian Commonwealth. The institutional changes could not catch up with the dynamic territorial development of the country as a result of the peaceful or military subjugation of a number of Ruthenian principalities by Duke Gediminas (1316–1341) and his successors, hence the country had an archaic structure with a limited bureaucratic apparatus, and the economy was hardly monetized. Therefore, the potential sources available for research into the tax system are limited to copies of documents issued by the chancellery of Lithuanian dukes and recorded in the Lithuanian Metrica. Another issue is that the Lithuanian treasury archives were destroyed in the middle of the seventeenth century, hence there are no surviving medieval tax registers, and the sources related to the ducal domain have been preserved in residual form. Most of these sources were used by Mitrafan Doŭnar-Zapolski in his fundamental and up-to-date work, where he described the economic foundations of the Lithuanian state under the Jagiellons in the early twentieth century.⁷⁴ However, both he and the subsequent scholars taking up the issue of state finance were forced to write primarily about the early modern period.

Undoubtedly, it was not taxes but the economy of the estates belonging to the Grand Duke, war booty, tributes and gifts collected from the conquered and dependent territories that determined the wealth of the Lithuanian treasury. The landed estates of the grand dukes guaranteed a minimum level of monetary income, but also provided supplies for the court and served as collateral for the loans taken out by representatives of the ruling dynasty. They also made it possible to build a specific patron–client system binding the elites of the officials with the monarch through a system of leases, grants and endowments. Other important sources of revenue were the fees imposed on entire towns, on inns operating in them or tolls related to the trade.

Centrally imposed general and direct taxes did not exist in this system, although variously named local taxes were collected, including *pososzczina* (the Smolensk land), *podimszczyna* (the Kyiv land) and *wołoszczyna* (Volhynia). One of them, *serebszczyna*, paid in Lithuania proper and incorporated into the Grand Duchy of Vitebsk and Polotsk lands early, was paid in silver coin. The Lithuanian nobility was exempted from this tax, as well as from the tax called *dziakło* and paid in kind, by a general privilege issued in 1447 by Grand Duke Casimir Jagiellon, who was about to assume the Polish throne. Over time, by the end of the fifteenth century, the nobles of each region were exempted from other local taxes (*pososzczina, podimszczyna, wołoszczyna*).[75]

A nationwide tax in the Grand Duchy of Lithuania was extraordinary. Its collection had to be approved by the nobility, which contributed to the formation of the Lithuanian state representation (the Sejm or parliament) in the following decades. During negotiations, the tax base and tax rates were determined. Over time, this unique burden, collected at times of particular national emergency, came to bear the general name of *serbszczyna*. It was probably first collected in 1473, although more detailed data only come from a tax collected in 1507.[76] It was based on land and was calculated per one *socha*. The imposition of extraordinary taxes contributed to the initial formation of a public treasury, although, by analogy to the Kingdom of Poland, the Grand Duchy of Lithuania did not achieve a complete separation of the public treasury from the private ruler. Yet, in the treasury administration itself a differentiation of offices emerged, probably resulting from the temporary existence of extraordinary tax revenue.

Already during the reign of Casimir Jagiellon there appeared a court treasurer in charge of the duke's personal treasury, and a grand (land) treasurer in charge of a quasi-public or land treasury. The first of these was related to the upkeep of the court, the courtiers performing administrative functions and serving in the court company, and partly to the enlistment of the army.[77] The remaining needs of the state, including the enlisted army, diplomatic service and *jurgielt* (the soldier's pay) were covered by the land treasury. The interaction between the two Lithuanian treasuries evolved in the second half of the fifteenth and in the sixteenth centuries.[78]

Krzysztof Pietkiewicz attempted to estimate the amount of the revenue of the Lithuanian treasury at the time of Alexander Jagiellon (1492–1506). According to him, the largest part of the income – about 34,500 kopas – was provided by the *hospodar*'s domain, while the rest was supplemented by the revenue from the towns (tolls, inns and taxes on towns), the mint, pledges, and the *czołobicie* tax (related to property transfer). This author did not include the income from general taxes in his calculations because their monetary value is difficult to assess, and they were probably partly collected in kind. In total, the average annual budget was to be 60,000 kopas,[79] although this figure should be considered greatly inflated. On the basis of ledger books from the period between 1499 and 1500 the income of the *hospodar*'s treasury can be calculated at the level of 5,000–6,000 kopas,[80] and the known accounts of the land treasurer Jan Abraham Ezofowicz from the years 1511–1514 indicate an average annual income of the land treasury at the level of 15,000 kopas,[81] which in total would yield 20,000 rather than 60,000 kopas of Lithuanian income.

The development of the fiscal system in medieval Poland was connected not only with the formation and transformation of the state and royal authority, but also with the level of commercialization of the economy and the growing importance of money in the society.[82] In the case of the Kingdom of Poland, the processes of modernization of the economy, organization of the state and administration took place earlier than in the Grand Duchy of Lithuania. However, it should be emphasized that the fundamental transformations leading to the formation of the public treasury and the tax state did not occur until the second half of the sixteenth century. As a result, the number of available primary sources for research on fiscal systems in the middle ages is limited, and so is interest in this aspect of state and economic functioning among historians.

Among the few relevant studies on the subject, most concern political and legal aspects of the fiscal system. The practice of tax collection, the management of taxes, and the theory behind the formation of the fiscal system in the late middle ages still await further study and research.

Notes

1 LUBOMIRSKI, *Trzy rozdziały z historii skarbowości w Polsce 1507–1532*.
2 MATUSZEWSKI, "Uwagi wprowadzające – początki skarbowości publicznej".
3 BRZECZKOWSKI, "Ustanawianie podatków nadzwyczajnych w Polsce w XV w."; BRZECZKOWSKI, "Podatki zwyczajne w Polsce XV wieku"; MATUSZEWSKI, *Przywileje i polityka podatkowa Ludwika Węgierskiego w Polsce*; SZULC, "Organizacja poboru podatków pokoszyckich do połowy XVI wieku",; SZULC, "Przeznaczenie a wydatkowane kwot z podatków nadzwyczajnych z dóbr szlacheckich w Polsce w XV wieku"; SZULC, *Uchwały podatkowe ze szlacheckich dóbr ziemskich za pierwszych dwu Jagiellonów*; SZULC, "Sposoby wynagradzania poborców podatkowych w Polsce od schyłku XIV do XVIII wieku".
4 BUCZEK, *Książęca ludność służebna w Polsce wczesnofeudalnej*; MODZELEWSKI, *Organizacja gospodarcza państwa piastowskiego*.
5 WYCZAŃSKI, "Z dziejów reform skarbowo-wojskowych za Zygmunta I"; SUCHENI-GRABOWSKA, *Odbudowa domeny królewskiej w Polsce 1504–1548*; BORODA and GUZOWSKI, "From King's Finance to Public Finance".
6 MODZELEWSKI, "The System of the Ius Ducale"; MODZELEWSKI, "Le système du ius ducale".
7 CIESIELSKA, "Od plemienia do państwa czy od wodzostwa do państwa? Modele procesów państwotwórczych i nowe tendencje w ich badaniu", p. 62.
8 Ibidem.
9 MODZELEWSKI, *Organizacja*, p. 85.
10 MODELEWSKI, *Organizacja*, p. 15.
11 MODELEWSKI, *Organizacja*, pp. 100–104.
12 MODELEWSKI, *Organizacja*, p. 90.
13 MODZELEWSKI, "Skarbowość: okres prawa książęcego (X-XIII w.)", p. 267.
14 BUCZEK, "Skarbowość: Polska".
15 GAWLAS, *O kształt zjednoczonego Królestwa. Niemieckie władztwo teytorialne a geneza społeczno-gospodarczej odrębności Polski*, p. 64, 71.
16 MODZELEWSKI, *Organizacja*, p. 146.
17 BUCZEK, "Skarbowość", p. 206; BUCZEK, "Powołowe- poradlne- podymne".
18 BUCZEK, "Skarbowość", p. 206.
19 MODZELEWSKI, *Organizacja*, p. 147.
20 Ibidem, p. 150.
21 Ibidem, p. 114.
22 BUCZEK, "Skarbowość", p. 205.
23 MODZELEWSKI, "Skarbowość", p. 268.
24 MODZELEWSKI, "Skarbowość".
25 OBARA-PAWŁOWSKA, *Polityka gospodarcza Władysława Łokietka*.
26 GRODECKI, "Początki pieniężnego skarbu państwowego w Polsce"; KACZMARCZYK, *Monarchia Kazimierza Wielkiego*; GAWLAS, "Polska Kazimierza Wielkiego a inne monarchie Europy Środkowej – możliwości i granice modernizacji władzy"; KURTYKA, *Odrodzone królestwo*.
27 SUCHENI-GRABOWSKA, *Odbudowa*, p. 39.
28 BUCZEK, "Powołowe", p. 4.
29 GRODECKI, *Polska piastowska*, p. 563.
30 BARDACH, *Historia państwa i prawa Polski*, p. 470.
31 MATUSZEWSKI, *Przywileje i polityka podatkowa Ludwika Węgierskiego w Polsce*, p. 70, 237.
32 Matuszewski, *Przywileje i polityka*, p. 190; KACZMARCZYK, *Monarchia*, p. 199.
33 MATUSZEWSKI, *Przywileje*, pp. 45–48.
34 KUTRZEBA, *Szos królewski w Polsce w XIV i XV wieku*, pp. 5–6.
35 RUTKOWSKI, "Skarbowość polska za Aleksandra Jagiellończyka", p. 73.
36 KUTRZEBA, *Szos*, p. 14 *and passim*.
37 KUTRZEBA, *Szos*, p. 16.

38 BARDACH, *Historia*, p. 416.
39 KUTRZEBA, *Szos*, pp. 20–21.
40 KUTRZEBA, *Szos*, p. 20.
41 KUTRZEBA, *Szos*, pp. 28–29.
42 KUTRZEBA, *Finanse i handel średniowiecznego Krakowa*, p. 63.
43 GOLIŃSKI, "Działka miejska w śląskich źródłach pisanych (XIII–XVI w.)", pp. 335–337; SOWINA, "Średniowieczna działka miejska e świetle źródeł pisanych", pp. 326–327.
44 GOLIŃSKI, *Wokół socjotopografii późnośredniowiecznej Świdnicy*, p. 29.
45 KUTRZEBA, *Finanse*, p. 63.
46 Kutrzeba, *Finanse*, p. 64.
47 GOLIŃSKI, *Socjotopografia późnośredniowiecznego Wrocławia*.
48 GOLIŃSKI, *Wokół socjotopografii*.
49 JASIŃSKI, *Przedmieścia średniowiecznego Torunia i Chełmna*; Roman CZAJA, *Socjotopografia miasta Elbląga w średniowieczu*, Toruń 1992; Janusz TANDECKI, *Szkice z dziejów Torunia i Prus w średniowieczu i na progu czasów nowożytnych*, Toruń 2008.
50 *Najstarszy zbiór przywilejów i wilkierzy miasta Krakowa*, ed. Stanisław ESTREICHER, Kraków 1936, p. 38, no. 28.
51 GOLIŃSKI, *Wokół socjotopografii*, p. 79.
52 Volumina constitutionum, vol 1. ed. GRODZISKI, DWORNICKA, and URUSZCZAK, p. 87: *Statutum exactionum personalium: uxores pueri et familia ipsorum utriusque sexus et cuiuslibet aetatis a personis per grossum unum solvere teneantur*.
53 MATUSZEWSKI and SZULC, "Opodatkowanie i polityka zastawu miast królewskich w Polsce za Jagiellonów", p. 178.
54 BORODA, "Kmieć łan czy profit? Co było podstawą poboru łanowego w XV i XVI wieku?", pp. 157–158.
55 The Central Archives of Historical Records in Warsaw: Archive of the Crown Treasury 1 (Royal Accounts), manuscript 40.
56 BORODA, "Rynek produkcji piwa i handlu alkoholem w województwie łęczyckim w XVI wieku", pp. 61–62.
57 RUSSOKI, "Czopowe", pp. 132.
58 *Volumina constitutionum*, vol 1. ed. GRODZISKI, DWORNICKA and URUSZCZAK, p. 87: *Statutum exactionum personalium*: "servi, laboratores, socii artificiorum, medici, clerici, begvidae, mixtati et reliqui vagi absque officiis domiciliis et serviciis viventes".
59 WEYMAN, "Pierwsze ustawy pogłównego generalnego w Polsce (1498, 1520) na tle ówczesnego systemu podatkowego", in *Roczniki Dziejów Społecznych i Gospodarczych* 18, 1956, pp. 29–31.
60 GULDON, "Skupiska żydowskie w miastach polskich w XV-XVI wieku".
61 ZAREMSKA, *Żydzi w średniowiecznej Polsce. Gmina krakowska*, p. 265.
62 WEYMAN, *Cła i drogi handlowe w Polsce piastowskiej*.
63 MANIKOWSKI, ŁUKASIEWICZ and KALISZUK, "Cło", p. 103.
64 KARBOWNIK, *Ciężary stanu duchownego w Polsce na rzecz państwa od roku 1381 do połowy XVII w.*, pp. 128–160.
65 KUTRZEBA, *Urzędy koronne i nadworne w Polsce, ich początki i rozwój do roku 1504*, pp. 59–82.
66 BRZECZKOWSKI, *Ordinary taxes*, pp. 49–53.
67 GOCHNA and ZWIĄZEK, "Spatio-temporal aspects".
68 SENKOWSKI, "Materiały źródłowe do genezy skarbu publicznego w Polsce w Archiwum Głównym Akt Dawnych w Warszawie".
69 DERESIEWICZ, *Z przeszłości Prus Królewskich: skarbowość Prus Królewskich od r. 1466–1569*.
70 MOŻEJKO, "Financial Obligations", pp. 181–191.
71 DERESIEWICZ, *Z przeszłości*, pp. 9, 21.
72 DERESIEWICZ, *Z przeszłości*, pp. 18–132.
73 DERESIEWICZ, *Z przeszłości* p. 117.
74 DOŬNAR-ZAPOLSKI, *Dziarżaunaja*.
75 DOŬNAR-ZAPOLSKI, *Dziarżaunaja* p. 567.
76 DOŬNAR-ZAPOLSKI, *Dziarżaunaja*, p. 574.
77 PIETKIEWICZ, *Wielkie Księstwo Litewskie pod rządami Aleksandra Jagiellończyka. Studia nad dziejami państwa i społeczeństwa na przełomie XV i XVI wieku*, p. 188.

78 Pietkiewicz, *Wielkie Księstwo Litewskie*, pp. 187–189.
79 Pietkiewicz, *Wielkie Księstwo Litewskie*, p. 198.
80 Pietkiewicz, "Dwór litewski wielkiego księcia Aleksandra Jagiellończyka (1492–1506)", p. 96.
81 *Lietuvos Metrika*, book 9 (1511–1518), Vilnius 2002, doc. 545, pp. 301–302 and doc. 623, pp. 342–343; Lesmaitis, *Wojsko zaciężne*, p. 136.
82 Gawlas, "Komercjalizacja jako mechanizm europeizacji peryferii na przykładzie Polski".

References

Juliusz Bardach, *Historia państwa i prawa Polski*, vol 1: *do połowy XV wieku*, Warszawa 1964.
Krzysztof Boroda, "Kmieć łan czy profit? Co było podstawą poboru łanowego w XV i XVI wieku?" in *Człowiek wobec miar i czasu w przeszłości*, eds. Marzena Liedke, Piotr Guzowski, Kraków 2007.
Krzysztof Boroda, "Rynek produkcji piwa i handlu alkoholem w województwie łęczyckim w XVI wieku", in *Rynki lokalne i regionalne w XV-XVIII w.*, eds. Krzysztof Boroda, Piotr Guzowski, Kraków 2013.
Krzysztof Boroda and Piotr Guzowski From "King's Finance to Public Finance. Different Strategies of Fighting Financial Crisis in the kingdom of Poland under Jagiellonians Rule (1386–1572)", in *Le crisi finanziarie: gestione, implicazioni sociali e conseguenze nell'età preindustriale: selezione di ricerche. The financial crises: their management, their social implications and their consequences in pre-industrial times: selection of essays*, ed. Giampiero Nigro, Firenze 2016, pp. 451–470.
Tadeusz Brzeczkowski, "Podatki zwyczajne w Polsce XV wieku" in *Acta Universitatis Nicolai Copernici, Historia XVIII – Nauki Humanistyczno-Społeczne*, vol. 128, Toruń 1982, pp. 39–62.
Tadeusz Brzeczkowski, "Ustanawianie podatków nadzwyczajnych w Polsce w XV w.", in *Roczniki Dziejów Społecznych i Gospodarczych* 42, 1981, pp. 77–105.
Karol Buczek, *Książęca ludność służebna w Polsce wczesnofeudalnej*, Wrocław 1958.
Karol Buczek, "Powołowe- poradlne- podymne", in *Przegląd Historyczny* 63, 1972, pp. 1–30.
Karol Buczek, "Skarbowość: Polska", in *Słownik starożytności słowiańskich*, vol. 5, Wrocław 1961, The Central Archives of Historical Records in Warsaw: Archive of the Crown Treasure 1 (Royal Accounts), manuscript 40.
Adrianna Ciesielska, "Od plemienia do państwa czy od wodzostwa do państwa? Modele procesów państwotwórczych i nowe tendencje w ich badaniu" in *Instytucja „wczesnego państwa" w perspektywie wielości i różnorodności kultur*, eds. Jacek Banaszkiewicz, Michał Kara, Henryk Mamzer, Poznań 2013.
Roman Czaja, *Socjotopografia miasta Elbląga w średniowieczu*, Toruń 1992.
Janusz Deresiewicz, *Z przeszłości Prus Królewskich: skarbowość Prus Królewskich od r. 1466–1569*, Poznań, 1947.
Mitrafan Doŭnar-Zapoĺski, *Dziarżaunaja haspadarka Vialikaha kniastva Litouskaha pry Jahielonach*, Minsk 2009.
Sławomir Gawlas, "Komercjalizacja jako mechanizm europeizacji peryferii na przykładzie Polski", in *Ziemie polskie wobec Zachodu: studia nad rozwojem średniowiecznej Europy*, ed. Sławomir GAWLAS, Warszawa 2006, pp. 25–16.
Sławomir Gawlas, *O kształt zjednoczonego Królestwa. Niemieckie władztwo teytorialne a geneza społeczno-gospodarczej odrębności Polski*, Warszawa 2000.
Sławomir Gawlas, "Polska Kazimierza Wielkiego a inne monarchie Europy Środkowej – możliwości i granice modernizacji władzy", in *Modernizacja struktur władzy w warunkach opóźnienia. Europa Środkowa i Wschodnia na przełomie średniowiecza i czasów nowożytnych*, eds. Marian Dygo, Sławomir Gawlas, Hieronim Grala, Warszawa 1999, pp. 5–34.
Michał Gochna and Tomasz Związek, "Spatio-temporal aspects of the extraordinary tax collecting system in Greater Poland (1492–1613)", *Roczniki Dziejów Społecznych i Gospodarczych* 90, 2019, pp. 78–92.
Mateusz Goliński, "Działka miejska w śląskich źródłach pisanych (XIII-XVI w.)", in *Kwartalnik Historii Kultury Materialnej* 63, 1995.
Mateusz Goliński, *Socjotopografia późnośredniowiecznego Wrocławia (przestrzeń-podatnicy-rzemiosło)*, Wrocław 1997
Mateusz Goliński, *Wokół socjotopografii późnośredniowiecznej Świdnicy, część 1*, Wrocław 2000.
Roman Grodecki, "Początki pieniężnego skarbu państwowego w Polsce", in *Wiadomości Numizmatyczno-Archeologiczne* 15, 1933, pp. 1–32;

Roman GRODECKI, *Polska piastowska*, Warszawa 1969.
Zenon GULDON, "Skupiska żydowskie w miastach polskich w XV–XVI wieku", in: *Żydzi i judaizm we współczesnych badaniach polskich*, vol. 2, eds. Krzysztof PILARCZYK and Stefan GĄSIOROWSKI, Kraków 2000, pp. 13–25.
Tomasz JASIŃSKI, *Przedmieścia średniowiecznego Torunia i Chełmna*, Poznań 1982.
Zdzisław KACZMARCZYK, *Monarchia Kazimierza Wielkiego*, Vol. 1: *Organizacja państwa*, Poznań 1939.
Henryk KARBOWNIK, *Ciężary stanu duchownego w Polsce na rzecz państwa od roku 1381 do połowy XVII w.*, Lublin 1980.
Janusz KURTYKA, *Odrodzone królestwo. Monarchia Władysława Łokietka i Kazimierza Wielkiego w świetle nowszych badań*, Kraków 2001.
Stanisław KUTRZEBA, *Finanse i handel średniowiecznego Krakowa*, Kraków 2009.
Stanisław KUTRZEBA, *Szos królewski w Polsce w XIV i XV wieku*, Kraków 1900
Stanisław KUTRZEBA, *Urzędy koronne i nadworne w Polsce, ich początki i rozwój do roku 1504*, Lviv 1903, pp. 59–82.
Lietuvos Metrika, book 9 (1511–1518), Vilnius 2002.
Tadeusz Jan LUBOMIRSKI, *Trzy rozdziały z historii skarbowości w Polsce 1507–1532*, Kraków 1868.
Adam MANIKOWSKI, Juliusz ŁUKASIEWICZ, M. KALISZUK, "Cło", in *Encyklopedia historii gospodarczej Polski*, ed. Antoni MĄCZAK vol. 1, Warszawa 1981.
Jacek MATUSZEWSKI, "Uwagi wprowadzające – początki skarbowości publicznej", in *Studia z Dziejów Państwa i Prawa Polskiego* 8, 2003, pp. 9–18.
Jacek S. MATUSZEWSKI, *Przywileje i polityka podatkowa Ludwika Węgierskiego w Polsce*, Łódź 1983.
Jacek S. MATUSZEWSKI and Tadeusz SZULC, "Opodatkowanie i polityka zastawu miast królewskich w Polsce za Jagiellonów", in *Czasopismo Prawno-Historyczne* 41, 1989.
Jacek S. MATUSZEWSKI, *Przywileje i polityka podatkowa Ludwika Węgierskiego w Polsce*, Łódź 1983
Karol MODZELEWSKI, "Le système du ius ducale en Pologne et le concept de féodalisme" in *Annales Économies, Sociétés, Civilisations 37*, 1982, pp. 164–185.
Karol MODZELEWSKI, "Skarbowość: okres prawa książęcego (X-XIII w.)", in *Encyklopedia historii gospodarczej Polski*, ed. Antoni MĄCZAK, vol. 2, Warszawa 1981.
Karol MODZELEWSKI, "The System of the Ius Ducale and the Idea of Feudalism:(comments on the Earliest Class Society in Medieval Poland)", in *Quaestiones Medii Aevi* 1, 1977, pp. 71–99;
Karol MODZELEWSKI, *Organizacja gospodarcza państwa piastowskiego, X–XIII wiek* (2nd edition), Poznań, 2000.
Beata MOŻEJKO, "Financial Obligations of the City of Gdańsk to King Casimir IV Jagiellon and His Successors in the Light of the 1468–1516 Ledger Book", in *Money and Finance in Central Europe during the Later Middle Ages*, ed. R. ZAORAL, Basingstoke 2016, pp. 181–191.
Najstarszy zbiór przywilejów i wilkierzy miasta Krakowa, ed. Stanisław ESTREICHER, Kraków 1936.
Anna OBARA-PAWŁOWSKA, *Polityka gospodarcza Władysława Łokietka*, Lublin 2014.
Krzysztof PIETKIEWICZ, *Wielkie Księstwo Litewskie pod rządami Aleksandra Jagiellończyka. Studia nad dziejami państwa i społeczeństwa na przełomie XV i XVI wieku*, Poznań 1975, p. 188.
Kszysztof PIETKIEWICZ, "Dwór litewski wielkiego księcia Aleksandra Jagiellończyka (1492–1506)", in *Lietuvos valstybė XII-XVII a.*, Vilnius 1997.
Stanisław RUSSOCKI, "Czopowe", in *Encyklopedia historii gospodarczej Polski*, ed. Antoni MĄCZAK vol. 1., Warszawa 1981.
Jan RUTKOWSKI, "Skarbowość polska za Aleksandra Jagiellończyka", in *Kwartalnik Historyczny* 23, 1909.
Jerzy SENKOWSKI, "Materiały źródłowe do genezy skarbu publicznego w Polsce w Archiwum Głównym Akt Dawnych w Warszawie", in *Archeion* 23, 1954, pp. 29–50.
Urszula SOWINA, "Średniowieczna działka miejska e świetle źródeł pisanych", in *Kwartalnik Historii Kultury Materialnej* 63, 1995, pp. 326–327.
Anna SUCHENI-GRABOWSKA, *Odbudowa domeny królewskiej w Polsce 1504–1548* (2nd ed.), Warszawa 2007.
Tadeusz SZULC, "Przeznaczenie a wydatkowane kwot z podatków nadzwyczajnych z dóbr szlacheckich w Polsce w XV wieku", in *Kwartalnik Historyczny* 100, 1993, pp. 15–26;
Tadeusz SZULC, "Organizacja poboru podatków pokoszyckich do połowy XVI wieku", *Czasopismo Prawno-Historyczne* 40, 1988, pp. 62–83;
Tadeusz SZULC, "Sposoby wynagradzania poborców podatkowych w Polsce od schyłku XIV do XVIII wieku", in *Studia z Dziejów Państwa i Prawa Polskiego* 1, 1993, pp. 91–106.
Tadeusz SZULC, *Uchwały podatkowe ze szlacheckich dóbr ziemskich za pierwszych dwu Jagiellonów (1386–1501)*, Łódź 1991.

Janusz TANDECKI, *Szkice z dziejów Torunia i Prus w średniowieczu i na progu czasów nowożytnych*, Toruń 2008.
Volumina constitutionem, vol 1. Eds. Stanisław GRODZISKI, Irena DWORNICKA, Wacław URUSZCZAK, Warszawa 1996.
Stefan WEYMAN, *Cła i drogi handlowe w Polsce piastowskiej*, Poznań 1938.
Stefan WEYMAN, "Pierwsze ustawy pogłównego generalnego w Polsce (1498, 1520) na tle ówczesnego systemu podatkowego", in *Roczniki Dziejów Społecznych i Gospodarczych* 18, 1956, pp. 29–31.
Andrzej WYCZAŃSKI, "Z dziejów reform skarbowo-wojskowych za Zygmunta I. Próby relucji pospolitego ruszenia" in *Przegląd Historyczny* 43, 1952, pp. 287–304.
Hanna ZAREMSKA, *Żydzi w średniowiecznej Polsce. Gmina krakowska*, Warszawa 2011.

17
RUSSIA FROM THE MONGOL INVASION TO THE DEATH OF IVAN THE TERRIBLE (1242–1584)

Pierre Gonneau

The formation of Muscovy, the ancestor of the Russian Federation, began in 1304 and was completed during the reign of Ivan IV the Terrible (1533–1584). But the roots of the Russian State, and its fiscal organization go back to the period of the Mongol or Tatar[1] lordship over the Russian lands. Our investigation focuses on the three centuries from 1242, when Khan Batu settled in Sarai on the lower Volga (near the city currently known as Volgograd), to 1584. The previous political system known as Kievan Rus', which functioned from ca. 945 to 1240, differed in its geography and institutions and we have only limited information on its fiscal practice. A network of principalities revolving around the city of Kiev was ruled by the Rurikide dynasty, named after its mythic founder, Prince Riurik (his death is traditionally dated in the year 879). The elite and urban population professed the Orthodox faith since ca. 988 when the Russian Church was founded as a metropolitan see of the patriarchate of Constantinople. The metropolitan's residence was in Kiev and the main bishoprics were located in the capitals of the various principalities.

The first Rus', Scandinavian traders-cum-warriors, levied annual tribute (*dan'**) upon their Slavic, Balt and Finnic subjects. The earliest known rate is as "one white squirrel-skin from each household", furs being the most precious commodity (*Russian Primary Chronicle*, AM 6367. AD 859).[2] The prince made rounds (*poliudie*) on his territory, from tribe to tribe, every autumn, as described in Constantine VII's *De administrando imperio* (ca. 948–952).[3] The tribute was collected in kind and consisted mainly of food and furs. In the second half of the tenth century, this kind of "living off the land" policy was replaced by collection of dues at special stations (*pogosty*). Thanks to the Russian–Byzantine treaties (911, 944), a very important part of Kievan revenues came from trips to Constantinople in the spring and the summer, when Rus' merchants sold their wares and purchased toll-free luxury goods. There is still debate on the nature of the economy in Kievan Rus'. Some view it as rural, based upon the domain, others as mainly commercial, deriving its wealth from active exchanges with Scandinavia, Western Europe, Byzantium and Asia. From the tenth century up to the beginning of the thirteenth century, the economy of Kievan Rus' is supposed to have steadily grown and we have some evidence of the emergence of great domains. We also know that Prince Vladimir of Kiev (980–1015) allocated a tenth of his revenues to the local Church of the Tithe. But it is not possible to reconstruct a clear picture of the public taxation system at that time.

The Mongol invasion and submission of Rus' created a new situation that is partially documented, but still leaves much to be discussed. As Muscovy expanded in the fourteenth century, still under the "Tatar yoke", its scribes produced new sources: the testaments of the Moscow grand princes and their treaties with their cousins,[4] primitive forms of cadastres, and a variety of documents produced in monastic scriptoria… Under Ivan III (1462–1505), Muscovy subdued most of its neighbours, formed the first cohesive Russian state and emancipated itself from the Tatar yoke (1480). It developed a kind of bureaucracy and fiscal apparatus. This process of consolidation reached new levels during the rule of Ivan IV the Terrible (1533–1584) who was the first to be crowned tsar in 1547. His reign marked the culmination of the building process of the Russian state. Its fiscal history can be, more or less, reconstructed from available sources. In 1591, the English traveller Giles Fletcher published *Of the Russe Commonwealth*, a seminal book, Chapter 12 of which is called *Of the emperor's customs and other revenues*. Although his data were probably wrong, this account gives us the first global picture of the Russian fiscal system at the end of the long Middle Ages. According to Russia's own chronology, the Middle Ages ends when Muscovy becomes a centralized state under Ivan III (1462–1505) and assumes imperial status under Ivan IV (1533–1584).

The Mongol Tribute in Russia during and after the "Tatar yoke" (1242–1480)

Fundamental notions in Russian administrative and financial practice were borrowed from the Mongols. For example, the terms for "money" (*den'ga*, pl. *den'gi*), "Treasure" (*kazna*), "customs" (*tamozhnia* derived from *tamga**), "courier", or "postal service" (*yam**) derive from either Mongol or Turkic.[5] As soon as they established their "yoke", the Mongols introduced a strict system of taxation in the Russian lands. Already in December 1237, preparing to conquer Ryazan, they demanded "one-tenth of everything" (*The First Chronicle of Novgorod*, AM 6746).[6] From 1242 on, the princes of the Rus' were obliged to journey to the Golden Horde[7], that is to Sarai, to pay their respects to the khan Batu (grandson of Genghis Khan). He confirmed their right to rule by issuing a special charter, called *yarlyk*. The most important among the Russian princes was the grand prince of Vladimir whom the khan appointed as a kind of lieutenant general. Batu and his successors could replace him at will. Russians had to pay dues to the khan and provide him with troops when required. The system was at first directly controlled by the Mongols who proceeded to conduct a census of all the Russian lands (southwestern Rus' in 1245, Suzdalia and Novgorod in 1257–1259, Galicia and Volynia in 1260, Smolensk and northeastern Russia in 1273–1275) based on a decimal system. The population was divided into tens, hundreds, thousands and ten thousands.[8] There is no mention of systematic new census in the fourteenth and fifteenth centuries, which suggests that collection continued on the same basis. Some treaties mention "old scrolls" (*davnye svertki*, DDG n°5, ca. 1367), or "old registers" (*starye deftery*[9] DDG n° 34, 1434; n°38, 1441–1442) on which the tribute continued to be based.

The Khan regularly sent officers called *basqaqs* (Turkic), or *darughachi* (Mongol) to collect the sums. In 1267 the Russian Church was granted full exemption for its clergy and its domains (including peasants tilling the land), provided that clerics "invoke Heaven and request happiness for the Emperor".[10] The grants were translated from the Mongol (in Uighur script) to Old-Russian, probably at the end of fourteenth or the beginning of fifteenth century. The services from which clergymen and their estates were exempt "go far beyond the basic tribute (*dan'**) payments, listing a series of other levies: the *tamga** (customs duty or basic city tax), *popluzhnoe* ("plough money", a tax on tilled land), the *yam*★ and *podvody* (obligations to provide horses, also known in Kievan Rus'), *poshlina* ("traditional duty"), *voina* (obligation to furnish recruits or "soldiers' tax" possibly paid in years when no recruits were drafted), *korm* (subsistence payments), *myt*★ (local duty on goods), and others".[11] These very valuable privileges were part of the religious tolerance policy of the Mongols and a clever way to neutralize a potential force of resistance. Copies of the *yarlyks* pertaining to the status of the Russian Church were kept in Russian translation up to the sixteenth century and shown to Ivan the Terrible to justify the fiscal immunity of the clergy.[12]

Around the end of thirteenth or the beginning or the fourteenth century, collection of the tribute was delegated to the Russian princes, under the supervision of the grand prince of Vladimir. In 1327, Ivan I Kalita of Moscow obtained the title and managed to keep it (except for a short intermission in 1338–1339) and transmit it to his heirs Semen the Proud (1341–1353) and Ivan II (1353–1359). Meanwhile, the seat of the Russian metropolitan was moved first from Kiev to Vladimir-on-the-Kliazma (1299) and finally to Moscow (1328). Muscovy began its ascent, but the territories of Far-Eastern Europe were still divided into rival principalities, and city-states such as Novgorod and Pskov. Between 1380s and 1420 individual principalities began to coin money and collect its own revenues. After 1389, a new division emerged between four main political centres, or grand principalities: Moscow-Vladimir, Tver, Ryazan and Suzdal-Nizhny Novgorod, each one dealing directly with the Horde. As early as 1392, Nizhny Novgorod fell under the control of Moscow, but fought back. With Suzdal it managed to preserve a certain amount of autonomy up to the 1440s. Then, these territories were required to pay their part of the Mongol tribute through Muscovy.[13]

Assuming that the Mongol tribute was annual, George Vernadsky proposed an elaborate estimation of its amount, by combining separate units of calculation. The first ones are units of exploitation: *derevnia* (hamlet or farm) and *sokha* (wooden plow, then a unit of tax assessment). The second ones are units of population corresponding to the Mongol census: *desiatok* (ten men), *sotnia* (a hundred men), *tysiacha* (a thousand men) and *t'ma* (ten thousand men). In town, Mongol agents counted *dvory* (households). Knowing that in 1384 khan Tokhtamysh taxed the whole grand-principality half a ruble (*poltina*) per *derevnia* and knowing that in 1409 emir Edigey considered as a norm one ruble per 2 *sokhas*, Vernadsky concluded that one *sokha* was equal to one *derevnia*. Half a ruble per *sokha* equals 5000 rubles per *tma*. Extrapolating from data of 1549, Vernadsky estimated that the grand-principality of Muscovy had 29 *t'mas*, and concluded that the annual Mongol tribute was worth 145,000 rubles, plus ca. 25,000 rubles from Novgorod under the special tax called black tribute (*cherny bor*★) .[14] If, as Vernadsky, we consider that the ruble weighed 92 grams of silver, the total amounts to 15.6 tons. The sums involved seem very high and these calculations have been much discussed.

The data in the fourteenth and fifteenth century testaments and treaties of Russian princes are incomplete and puzzling. Depending on the documents, Mongol tribute (*vykhod*★, *ordynskaia tiagost*) is apportioned on the basis of 5000 rubles (DDG n°11, 13, in 1389–1390, n°17 in 1401–1402), or 1000 rubles (DDG n°12, in 1389). In 1401–1402 and 1433, the basis is 7000 rubles (DDG n° 16, 29). One of the main questions among specialists has been: is this a real sum, indicating the total amount of the tribute (P. P. Smirnov, K. V. Bazilevich, P.N. Pavlov, M. Roublev) or a conventional one serving as a help for calculation (V.O. Kliuchevskii, V.A. Arakcheev).[15] The documents support the latter view: they often add that if the sum collected is more important or less important, the repartition has to be corrected accordingly. M. Roublev showed that the grand prince of Moscow was free to choose the basis on which the calculus would be made: for certain territories, the tribute would be taken on a conventional sum of 7000 or 5000 rubles, for others, the sum would be only 1000 rubles. Additionally, as later documents show, the grand prince could exempt regions from the tribute for a certain number of years as a gracious concession to a relative or ally (DDG n°24, 1428, DDG n°41, 1445, DDG n°44, 1447). Meanwhile, the onus on the other regions was greater. Suretyship and collective responsibility (*poruka*) existed in Kievan Rus', but they became a systematic tool of government under the Mongols. The *yam*★ postal service, borrowed by the Mongols from the Chinese, was also organized in *poruka* fashion. The population had to provide for post houses, carts, horses, grain storehouses to be set up along the routes.[16] "In all this the Tatars set an example that some of their Russian successors would later follow. As the decades wore on, the Mongols left the practical aspects of tribute collection to their agents, the Russian princes, but the underlying principle of fiscal *poruka* remained inviolable".[17]

Another question is whether the Mongol tribute was collected on an annual basis or only at intervals of seven years. Before Ivan Kalita's death, when the *yarlyk* of the grand prince was not securely in the hand of the Muscovite prince, it seems that the collection was annual and one of the ways to contest the grand prince's rule was to accuse him of keeping part of the tribute for his own profit. Internal feuds within the Horde allowed Russian princes to delay payments in the 1370s and in 1389, Dmitri Ivanovich of Moscow openly discusses the case "if God delivers us from the Horde" (DDG n°11). His testament, in the same year, stipulates more precisely: "If God brings about a change regarding the Horde [and] my children do not have to give Tatar tribute (*vykhod*★) to the Horde, then the tribute (*dan'*★) that each of my sons collects in his patrimonial principality shall be his" (DDG n°12).[18] Nevertheless, Muscovites were exposed to punitive raids when a Tatar ruler reinstated his authority and had to pay hefty sums as a penalty, or in lieu of arrears, such as in 1384 (levy of khan Tohtamysh) or 1409 (levy of emir Edigey). Meanwhile, the grand duchy of Lithuania already acted as a rival of the Golden Horde, although some of its lands, formerly principalities of Kievan Rus', had paid the Mongol tribute.[19]

After Edigey's death (1419), the Horde entered another very instable period and from 1436 it was divided between rival competitors. Later, one can see hordes in the plural among which the main powers were the khanates of Kazan and Crimea. This could help Muscovy to shake the Tatar yoke, and in 1437, Khan Ulug Mehmet offered to abolish tribute in exchange for a safe haven near Muscovite territory. But the Muscovite grand prince Vasili II did not trust him and tried instead to oust his horde, thus breaking the deal. He suffered a first defeat in 1437, and another one in 1445. Taken prisoner, Vasili II had to pay an enormous ransom, estimated at 25,000 rubles by one source and 200,000 (!) by another.[20] Beginning in 1441 or 1442, treaties between members of the Muscovite dynasty mention tributes (in the plural) to different khans (DDG n°38). Moscow paid tribute to Kazan up to 1469 at least and also to the "Great Horde" up to 1476. In the summer of 1480, during what is known as the "Great Standoff" on the Ugra river, Ivan III of Moscow opposed Ahmed Khan who tried to reunite all Mongol hordes and to restore regular tribute on the Russian lands. Ahmed's retreat on November 11th is seen in Russian historiography as the end of Tatar yoke over Russia. At the same time, Muscovy conquered all the vast lands of Novgorod (1478) and the grand principality of Tver (1485). Nevertheless, Ivan III occasionally made payments to the Crimean khan (740 rubles in 1492 and 350 in 1498).[21] In his testament (1504) there are still the following provisions: "And my children, Yuri and his brothers, shall give to my son Vasili,[22] from their patrimonial principalities, as Tatar tributes (*vykhody ordinskie*★) to the Hordes, [namely] to Crimea and to Astrakhan and to Kazan and to Tsarevichev burg and to the other tsars and tsar's sons, who are in the land of my son Vasili, and to the Tatar envoys who come to Moscow, and to Tver, and to Novgorod Nizhny and to Yaroslavl, and to Torusa, and to Ryazan Staraia, and to Perevitsk, the share of Prince Feodor of Ryazan, and for all the expenses of the Tatars (*tatarskie protory*), one thousand rubles".[23] Thus, the Mongol tribute still existed in the beginning of the sixteenth century as a tool of Muscovite diplomacy with Tatars khanates. But its amount was lower than in the past, although the ruble has depreciated to 80 grams of silver.[24] The annexation of Ryazan by Muscovy in 1521 completed the process of the gathering of those Russian lands formerly under the control of the Horde. By conquering Kazan and Astrakhan (1552–1556) Ivan the Terrible abolished all tribute to these khanates, but he was still under threat from the Crimean Tatars who burned down Moscow in 1571. The Russians still paid them "gifts" (*pominki*). As we have seen, before the gathering of the Russian lands was complete, fiscal practice was decentralized. Information about smaller principalities is scarce, but we have a good idea of the situation in Novgorod and in Muscovy.

The Fiscal System in "Republican" Novgorod (1264–1478)

As early as 1136, the citizens of Novgorod acquired the right to choose their prince. The assembly of the free men, known as the *veche*, hired and fired their prince at will, and elected its own magistrates: the *posadnik* (*borchgrave*, or *borgravius* in Latin and German sources), and the *tysiatski* (commander of a thousand, *dux* or *Herzog* in Latin and German sources). The city's archbishop was also elected by the population. Of course, as in Italian city-states local "democracy" was marred by violent rivalries between quarters and great families.[25] There were also harsh social tensions between commoners and the aristocracy of boyars and merchants. During the 1259 census ordered by the Mongols, "the boyars made it easy for themselves and ill for the lesser ones". (*The First Chronicle of Novgorod*, AM 6767).[26] Indeed, although Novgorod was not taken by storm during the Mongol conquest in 1238, it was included into the areas obligated to pay Mongol tribute, under the authority of the grand prince of Vladimir, at that time Alexander Nevsky. Most of the rules governing the local fiscal system were established then: a new treaty was concluded in 1262–1263 between Novgorod, Gotland, Lübeck and "all the Latin nation", ruling the foreign trade, and three treaties between Novgorod and Yaroslav Yaroslavich, Alexander Nevsky's brother and successor (1264–1270) defined their mutual relationship.[27] In fact, they functioned as a template for a contractual regime between prince and town that was to last for two centuries.

Foreign trade was one of the main sources of Novgorod's wealth. Twice a year, a party of Germans and Goths (men from Gotland) came to the city and lived in their respective court (*Nemetski Dvor, Gotski dvor*) that enjoyed the privilege of a consulate, thus avoiding many expenses and taxes on ordinary merchants.[28] They were protected from imprisonment and torture, impoundment of goods, and benefited from suretyship. The Russians went as far as to accepting the German scales for weighting goods.[29] From at least 1191–1192 till the fall of Novgorod (1478) merchants from Gotland and Baltic cities included in the Hanse benefited from this kind of most favoured nations status. Far from cutting Russia off the Western trade, the Mongol domination eased it: by order of khan Mengu Temir, Yaroslav Yaroslavich confirmed to the citizen of Riga (one of outposts the of the Hanse) that he gave them "free passage" through his lands (1266–1271).[30] Unfortunately, we do not have accounts of this foreign trade. Fiscal revenues from weighting, even taxed at a discount price for the Hanseatic partners, were obviously very important. We know that the periods of closure of the German yard, in case of conflict, were short (two years being a maximum) and that peace was restored as soon as possible while Novgorod kept its autonomy. On the contrary, after annexation, Ivan III did not hesitate to impose a total ban on trade in 1494, as an arm-twisting method with the Hanse. This boycott was ended only in 1514, by his son Vasili III.

As overlord of Novgorod, the grand prince of Vladimir, had to swear to "hold Novgorod according to custom" and received only a "gift" (*dar*) from Novgorod provinces; the amount of the toll (*myt**) he received was also fixed.³¹ As the princes of Moscow assumed the function of grand prince of Vladimir, however, they asked more from Novgorod. In 1332, a conflict arose between the city and Ivan I of Moscow about the "silver from the country beyond the Kama" (*serebro zakamskoe*).³² Another source describing the same event says that Novgorodians were refusing to give "the black tribute (*chornyi vykhod**) to the tsar of the Horde".³³ This tax was also known as the "black tax", or "tax on the common people" (*cherny bor**).³⁴ According to V. L. Ianin, *chernyi bor* was taken only on the land of Novotorzhok the eastern part of the Novgorodian lands touching Suzdalia, because the Mongols invaded it in 1238 but got no further; the tax was due by commoners, not by boyars, neither citizens of Novgorod. He also concludes that the tax was due every seven or eight years. When intervals became greater conflict arose and the grand prince could ask for arrears. However, it seems that in the course of the fourteenth and fifteenth centuries collection of the *chernyi bor** was extended to other districts, such as Vychegda and Perm, and even "all the possessions of Novgorod".³⁵ There was a connection between the trips made to the Horde by the grand prince and the collection of *chernyi bor** or *serebro zakamskoe* just before he departed or when he returned in Russia. This was the case with Ivan I in 1322 (he asked for 500 rubles) and in 1339 (he asked for a "second *vykhod**" of 1,000 rubles), with Dmitrii Ivanovich in 1384, Vasili I in 1392 (no sum mentioned). In 1419, Konstantin, younger brother of Vasili I, fled from Moscow and was welcomed by the Novgorodians who offered him *chernyi bor**. This would suggest that *chernyii bor** was a kind of "joyous accession gift" for the prince who had received or was about to receive the *yarlyk*, or for a newly invited prince.

In other circumstances Moscow could exact a sum from Novgorod as a settlement. In 1386, Dmitrii Ivanovich demanded 8,000 rubles from Novgorod in reprisal for acts of piracy on the Volga. The accusation seems true enough, but one cannot help to notice that this happened two years after the punitive Mongol tribute levied by Tokhtamysh on Muscovy. Obviously, Prince Dmitri wanted to replenish his coffers and restore his authority on the merchant city. In 1441, Vasili II "turned his wrath of Novgorod the Great", taking 8,000 rubles, and again 8,500 in 1456. In a charter of 1461 Novgorodian magistrates agreed to a very precise set of conditions dictated by Moscow about the amount of the *chernyi bor** and the fees in kind due to his *chernobortsy* (agents in charge of the tax). The tax fell not only on peasants, but also on artisans and small merchants.³⁶ Ivan III followed the same path as his father. In 1471, he exacted 15,500 rubles.³⁷ After 1478, having liquidated the old "republican" regime of Novgorod, he ordered the deportation of most of the great local families and confiscated half the lands of the more prominent monasteries, to the amount of about 2,9 million acres.³⁸ This allowed him to redistribute this as fief, or service-tenure (*pomest'e*), land held contingent upon service to his person. In the meantime a fiscal system in Muscovite territory proper had been built little by little since the time of Yuri Danilovich (1303–1325) and Ivan I Kalita (1325–1341). Based upon a patrimonial view of the land, it slowly evolved to become a "public taxation" system of sorts.

The Fiscal System and immunities in Muscovy (1303–1584)

The Muscovite medieval taxation system took four main forms: taxes on landowning and persons, taxes on industrial and commercial production, service obligations and judicial fees.³⁹ The owner or the user of the land had to pay first tribute (*dan'**) plus a recension due called "recension squirrel" (*pishchaia belka*), and sometimes a "supplement" (*primet*). In cities, *dan'** was levied on taxable households. There was also a tax on saddles (*sedel'noe delo*) and clothes (*portnoe*).

Although most of the peasants were free till the end of the sixteenth century, people leaving a given community to get married had to pay a "tax of foreign marriage" (*vyvodnaia kunitsa*), while people marrying within the community paid a "marriage tax" (*ubrusnoe*). Newcomers paid a fee for their settlement (*vorotnoe*). Besides, all agents of the prince when in mission had the right to their *korm* or *kormlenie* (feeding, subsistence payment), either in kind or in cash. *Korm* and registration fees were due to agents of justice at every step of the procedure.

The two main commercial duties were two forms of toll. The first one, *myt**, dated from the Kievan period and the new one *tamga** (stamping of goods) had been introduced by the Mongols. The wealthiest merchants paid the *tamga** individually, while lesser merchants were assessed collectively, in associations.[40] Along the way, a great number of other dues existed: *perevoz* (ferry crossing), *mostovoe* (bridge crossing), *poberezhnoe* (landing), *pomernoe, veschee* (measuring and weighing goods), *iavka* (registration tax for foreign merchants not covered by bilateral treaties) and *lavka* (fee for renting a trading stand). After the sale, one had to pay *(v)osmenichee*, that is one eighth of his profits. *Pischee* was the registration on sold cattle and *piatno* (brand) the fee paid when selling horses.

The instruments used in the fabrication of salt (open pan salt making) were subject to various taxes called *ploshki, polovniki, oshitki*. Apiculture was also taxed; beekeepers (*bortniki*) paid dues, and hive owners paid the so-called *podlaznoe*.

Commoners were obliged to transport goods (*povozy*), supplying horses and carts for this purpose (*podvody*). They were also required either to contribute to the postal service (*yam**), or to pay a special tax, called "postal money" (*yamskie den'gi*). War messengers had the right to food (*kormy emliti*), shelter (*nochevati*), and guides (*prododniki*) on the road. The prince could send his fishing and game supervisors (*lovchie*), falconers (*sokol'nichie*), equerries (*koniukhi*) on hunting grounds, rivers and lakes and they had the right to enlist the population. Such obligations were not trivial as is proven by the treaties between the city of Novgorod and his princes, from 1264 to 1456, where these rights were strictly limited. People living in towns and the surrounding areas also had the duty to work on fortifications and repairs (*gorodovoe delo*).

Legal documents did not differentiate between State property or State tax and the private property of the prince or the revenues from his domain. In his testament (DDG n°1, ca. 1339), Ivan I of Moscow wrote: "I bequeath my patrimony (*otchina svoia*), Moscow, to my sons. And lo, I have arranged the [following] distribution (...). And of the city revenues, I give the *osmnichee* to my princess. But my sons shall share the *tamga** and the other city revenues; in the same manner [they shall] also share the *myty**, that which is in the district of each shall be his. And my sons shall share the city quitrent in honey (*obrok medovyi*)".[41] *Otchina*, or *votchina* "is indeed the exact equivalent of the Latin *patrimonium* (...). The language was readily understood in a society in which the patriarchal order was still very much alive, especially among the lower classes (...). Quite naturally, therefore, the testaments of the north-eastern princes, many of which have survived, read like ordinary business inventories in which cities and *volosti* are indiscriminately lumped with valuables, orchards, mills, apiaries or herds of horses".[42] Also, the first clerks redacting acts, were domestics of the prince; the word *d'iak* by which they are known is translated as "secretary", or "state secretary", and in the last quarter of the fifteenth century they became quite important in the nascent Muscovite bureaucracy, but, just like *diakon* (deacon) the term derives from the Greek *diakonos* (servant).[43]

The Black Death pandemic of 1348 had a devastating impact on Russia. It reached Pskov in 1352, Moscow in 1353 where it killed the grand prince Semen the Proud, all of his children, his younger brother and the metropolitan Theognostus. There were periodic flare-ups until 1427.[44] It is estimated that up to a quarter or a third of the population in some areas perished. Simultaneously, under the influence of Saint Sergius († 1392) and his disciples, new coenobitic communities formed in the countryside. Initially pledged to a vow of absolute poverty, the monastic communities soon acquired important lands, some by donation and others through exchanges and purchase. Soon the grand prince of Moscow, his younger brothers and cousins granted them large privileges, for religious reasons of course, but also because they saw these communities as potential agents for the recovery of the economy.[45] These privileges are our main source about Muscovite medieval fiscal system because they give us a precise list of all the existing taxes. Some great lay landlords had similar privileges, but very little of their private archive have survived. We rely mostly on ecclesiastical documentation, because it was kept by monks through the centuries, till Catherine II confiscated it with the lands of the Church in 1764.

The golden age of fiscal and judicial immunity spread from the 1410s to 1462, the generations of Vasili I (1389–1425) and Vasili II (1425–1462). The situation remained the same during this period because of the recurring epidemics and the precariousness of Vasili II's political situation at least until 1453. A privileged domain was termed "white" or "whitened" (*obelennyi*) as opposed to the black lands (*chernye zemli*), submitted to current taxes. The charter or grant (*zhalovannaia gramota**) gave temporary (*l'gotnaia*) or complete (*tarkhannaia*) fiscal exemption and also judicial immunity (*nesudimaia*). The temporary exemption of tribute (*dan'**) and other customs could last for 3, 5 or even 10 years. However, there was often a special article maintaining Church dues (*tserkovnye poshliny*). Judicial immunity forbade any agent of the prince to "set foot" (*vstupatisia*) on the domain, judge the inhabitants and receive a fee. In case of litigation between a man benefiting from an immunity and a commoner, a special joint court (*smestnoi sud*) composed of ecclesiastical and secular judges was formed. Most of the immunity charters excluded cases of high justice such as murder (*dushegubstvo*), and sometimes banditry (*razboi*) and theft with corpus delicti (*tat'ba s polichnym*), that is cases when the thief is caught red-handed. On his accession, a new prince had to confirm his predecessor's charters and could restrict or suppress them, but the privileges could also be abolished by the one who had granted them. In 1456 Vasili II suspended immunities awarded to the Trinity-St. Sergius abbey in the regions of Radonezh, Sol'-Galitskaia and Bezhetskii-Verkh, probably because the monks protested against the arrest of their local landlord and former ally of Vasili II, prince Vasili Yaroslavich, but soon the privileges were restored, probably because the community accepted the arrest.[46] The great monastic estates, such as the Trinity-St. Sergius, enjoyed not only exemption from *myt** and *tamga**, but also the right to brand horses (*piatno*) and protection against "undesirable guests" (*nezvannye gosti*) during market days. They could also ferry goods from their many domains, fisheries and salt production centres free of charge and they had an open road to Novgorod or the White Sea. They also acquired courts and dwelling places (*dvor, podvor'e*) in the main Russian cities.[47]

Ivan III (1462–1505) showed caution when he succeeded his father on the throne by maintaining most of the privileges Vasili II had granted. But the situation changed dramatically in the last quarter of the fifteenth century. When new lands were aggregated to the old Muscovite territory, the need for larger administrative agencies, armed forces and Court were felt. Following the annexation of Novgorod, in 1478, Muscovite administrators began to keep registers of landed property (*pistsovye knigi*) that give us a rough idea of the cadastre, the density of population and the weight of taxation. Land was not measured on the sole basis of area, but divided into good, medium quality and poor and measured in *obzha*. The assessment depended on the quality of the land and the status of its owner. At that time the ruble was divided into 10 *grivny* and 200 *den'gi*.[48] A. Shapiro estimated that at the end of the fifteenth century the amount of *dan'** was 4,7 Muscovite *den'gi* per *obzha*, or one Muscovite *grivna* per *sokha*. The total amount of the fiscal duties was from 25–30 per cent of a peasant's annual production.⁴⁹ Meanwhile, the privileges granted to monasteries were greatly reduced; temporary fiscal exemption became rare and exemption from the *dan'** exceptional. In the summer of 1503, Ivan III seems to have been on the verge of confiscating the lands of the Church, but relented, possibly because he suffered a stroke.⁵⁰

Vasili III (1505–1533) left monasteries more room to manoeuvre. Some of them (such as the Trinity-St.-Sergius or Dormition-St.-Joseph of Volokolamsk) got new lands and recovered certain privileges. S.M. Kashtanov and other Russian specialists saw political motivations behind this leniency: Vasili sought ecclesiastical support against his younger brothers and especially in 1525 when he sent his first wife to a convent to marry Elena Glinskaia, who gave him his long-awaited heir, Ivan the Terrible (1530). Political motivations and rivalries between boyar clans also explains the lax fiscal policy at the time of Ivan the Terrible's minority (1533–1547). Yet, even during this period, forces within Muscovite bureaucracy worked to tighten the reins and obtain greater state revenues. Indeed, the state needed money to pay for fortifications, to coin a stronger ruble (1535), to create a more efficient local criminal police, at least in selected regions (1539) and a new military force of musketeers (the famous *streltsy*, 1550). The reforms were systematized in the 1550s, as Russia mounted a huge military campaign to take Kazan and Astrakhan. This conquest was quickly followed by the long, and finally fruitless, war for Livonia (1558–1582). Meanwhile the Court and the State apparatus had been greatly expanded. Between 1565 and 1572, Ivan the Terrible experimented with a totally new system of government, the *Oprichnina*, ruling from a new capital, and operating his own private army. He could count on some revenues from the English Muscovite Company, created in 1554 and operating under privilege on the newfound route through the Arctic Ocean, the White Sea and the Northern Dvina,⁵¹ but most of the weight fell on the Russian taxpayer.

Ivan the Terrible's government attempted to limit ecclesiastical property and goods and to tax Church holdings. In 1551, the Council of the Hundred Chapters (*Stoglav*, art. 43) stipulated that there would be no more fiscal immunity charters (*tarkhannaia gramota**) and that all such privileges would be confiscated.⁵² Nevertheless, the tsar himself relented and granted some charters to his favourite pious foundations. During the *Oprichnina* period, many noblemen in peril took the cowl (which did not always save their life) and gave their possessions to monasteries. Finally, in June 1584, after Ivan's death, it was once again prohibited to grant any *tarkhannaia gramota**, thus proving that the practice had not ended. The fight to exact money from the Church would keep on until Catherine II's reign.⁵³

The increasing fiscal pressure fell mostly on the commoners' shoulders. By some calculations, payments rose 16 times in the first half of the 1550s in comparison with those at the beginning of the century. They rose again by 32 per cent in the second half of the 1550s and again by 40 per cent between 1561 and 1570. Simultaneously the first measures were taken to prevent peasants and commoners living in towns to leave their place in search for a better fiscal position. Thus began the process that resulted in the enserfment of roughly half the population. More often than not, becoming a fugitive was the only way out.⁵⁴

Russian public taxation system in 1591

In his *Russe Commonwealth* Giles Fletcher made a substantial report about the Russian taxation system which deserves to be quoted almost entirely. Fletcher, who acquired an insider's understanding of the mechanism of Muscovite finances, showed us that Muscovy was still very much viewed as the tsar's private property and that the main goal of the household's steward was "good husbandry". His book distinguishes three main departments responsible for "the receiving of customs and other rents belonging to the Russian crown". "The first is the office of *dvortsovyi*, or steward of the household. The second is the office of the *chetverti* (…), divided into four several parts (…). The third is called *bol'shoi prikhod* or the great income".[55]

Fletcher provided us with British equivalents, not always accurate, but nevertheless very telling. The *dvortsovyi*, or steward of the household, was responsible for the revenues of the *votchina*, which Fletcher translated as "the rents of the emperor's inheritance or crownland". As R. Pipes noted, it is also the exact equivalent of the Latin *patrimonium*. The *votchina* included 36 towns "with the territories of hundreds belonging unto them". Here we see that the old decimal division going back to Kievan Rus and the Mongols yoke remained in force. Tenants paid either "rent money", or "rent duties called *obroki*", that is "certain *chetverti* or measures of grain (…) or of other victual", ranging from meat to "fish, hay wood honey etc". Thus, the primary source of revenues of the Russian state was paid in kind. A fraction was used for the tsar's table, another directly allotted to his noblemen as part of their gratification (*zhalovanie*, a term still used in Russia in the sense of salary) and the surplus was sold for the benefit of the Treasury. There was absolutely no difference from the practices that a gentleman farmer employed on his domain. The *obrok* system, a fixed payment of various kinds, will remain in place on noble land till the nineteenth Century. According to Fletcher, under Ivan the Terrible, the office of the steward of the household yielded a benefit of only 60,000 rubles yearly, because the tsar "kept a more princely and bountiful house than the emperor now doth". Under the more frugal reign of Ivan the Terrible's son, tsar Fedor Ivanovich (1584–1598), the revenues reached 230,00 rubles a year.[56]

The second type of contributions were direct taxes on the land, which qualify as public taxation. According to Fletcher's calculation, they amounted to the double of the first type of revenues, bringing in 400,000 rubles: "The second office of receipt, called the *chetverti* (…) hath four head officers which, besides the ordering and government of the shires contained within their several *chetverti*, have this also as a part of their office, to receive the *tiaglo* and *podat'*, belonging to the emperor, that riseth out of the four *chertverti* or quarters. The *tiaglo* is a yearly rent or imposition raised upon every *vyt'* or measure of grain that groweths within the land, gathered by sworn men and brought into the office".[57] The term *chetvert'* (quarter) is used there both to identify the four fiscal administrations responsible for parts of the Russian territory, and as a measure of surface area. The *vyt'*, a tax unit of land, was equal to 12 *chetverti* of good land of a property measured on a three field basis, 14 *chetverti* of middling land, or 16 to 20 *chetverti* of poor land. The *vyt'* was therefore equal to between 65 and 81 acres.[58]

The third fiscal institution, the *Bol'shoi prikhod*, or Great income, "receiveth all the customs that are gathered out of all the principal towns and cities within the whole realm", for a total sum of 340,000 rubles a year. To this must be added "the yearly rent of the common bathstoves and *kabaki* or drinking houses" (amount not given), plus "a certain mulct or penalty that growth to the emperor out of every judgment or sentence that passeth in any of his courts of record in all civil matters", and a tax on "every name contained in the writs that pass out of these courts", for a total amount of "3,000 rubles a year or thereabouts".[59] Besides, the *Bol'shoi prikhod* kept "the overplus or remainder that is saved out of the land rents allotted to various offices": about 250,000 rubles from the *razriad* "which hath lands and rents assigned unto it to pay the yearly salaries of the soldiers or horsemen that are kept still in pay", or the surplus out of the *streletskii* offices "which has proper lands for the payment" of the *strel'tsy* men or gunners, or the *inozemnyi prikaz* "which has set allowance of lands to maintain the foreign mercenary soldiers", and the *pushkarskii prikaz*, "for the provision of munition, great ordnance, powder, shot, saltpeter, brimstone, lead, and such like". So that the whole sum that groweth to this office of *bol'shoi prikhod* or the great income (as appeareth by the books of the said office) amounteth to 800,000 rubles a year of thereabouts.[60]

As we can see, the *Bol'shoi prikhod* aggregated at least three different kinds of receipts. The first category covered customs duties and indirect taxes on foreign and domestic trade. One can add to them the taxes on bathhouses and drinking houses, considered as public houses. The sale of alcohol was already a State monopoly in Russia. The second category included revenues from justice: fines and registration fees. A third category involved unspent grants that reverted back to the Treasury, for example, parcels of land ordinarily reserved for grants to an indeterminate number of military personnel, but not distributed due to corruption, slowness, or the lack of proper candidates. In time of peace these grants were "paid by halves, sometimes not the half", so there were surpluses, especially during the reign of Fedor Ivanovich, which was exceptionally peaceful. On the contrary, Fletcher tells us, the custom of the great towns "is set and rated precisely what they shall pay for the custom of the year, which needs must be paid into the said office though they receive not so much".[61]

Fletcher recapitulated his data in what seems to be a final account: "The sum that groweth to the emperor's treasury in money only, for every year. 1. Out of the steward's office above the expense of his house 230,000 rubles. 2. Out of the four *chetverti* for soke and head money, 400,000 rubles. 3. Out of the *bol'shoi prikhod* office or great income for custom and other rents, 800,000 rubles. Sum: 1,430,000 rubles clear, besides all charges for his house and ordinary salaries of his soldiers otherwise discharged".[62] But the following paragraph in Fletcher's book provides a glimpse of another fiscal field: what Russia received "in furs and other duties to a great value out of Siberia, Pechora, Perm', and other places, which are sold or bartered away for other foreign commodities to the Turkish, Persian, Armenian, Georgian and Bulgarian merchants". (…) What it maketh in the whole (…) it may be guessed by which was gathered the last year out of Siberia for the emperor's custom, viz., 466 timber of sables, five timbers of martens, 180 black foxes, besides other commodities".[63]

The Russian penetration in Northern Asia had only just begun, but was promising. From the point of view of Fletcher, Russia was acting as a colonial power exacting natural resources while not contributing visibly to the development of the country. Leading specialists think that the sums he mentions are not revenues from customs, but the amount of tribute (*yassak*) levied on the native population.[64]

The figure of 1,430,000 rubles as total revenue of the Russian state in 1591 has been regarded with suspicion. Already in 1891, Sergei Seredonin said that a more likely figure would be 400,000 rubles. Ca. 1667, according to Grigorii Kotoshikhin, a Russian clerk who fled to Sweden where he wrote a well-informed treaty on the government of his country, the income of the Russian state was only two million rubles.[65] Recently, Mikhail Krom acknowledged that Fletcher correctly identified the three main departments responsible for processing revenues of the State, the Great Palace office (*Prikaz bol'shogo dvorca*), the Quarters (*Chetverti*) and the Great income (*Bol'shoi prikaz*) but agreed with Seredonin on the improbability of the sum. In Krom's view, between 1591 and 1667, the territory of the Russian empire had increased and the value of the ruble had fallen four times, yet its revenue were 2 million rubles.[66]

It seems that Fletcher counted some receipts twice, or counted as regular receipts savings that were made only occasionally. Yet he had a fine sense of the precariousness of Muscovite finances. As a typical Elizabethan, he was prejudiced against the wealth of the Church. He knew that the Russian Church was very rich, especially the main monasteries: "of friars they have an infinite rabble far greater than in any other country were popery is professed (…) the number of them is so much the greater not only for that it is augmented by the superstition of the country but because the friar's life is the safest from the oppressions and exactions that fall upon the commons".[67] Therefore, when the State was in dire straits, it had to use the perverse mechanism of extorting from the extortionists. Fletcher gives us a list of the means used to draw back the wealth of the land into the emperor's treasury. Its first item is very striking: "To prevent no extortions, exactions, or briberies whatsoever done upon the commons by their dukes, *d'iaki* or other officers in their provinces, but to suffer them to go on till their time be expired and to suck themselves full, then to call them to the *pravezh*[68] (or whip) for their behaviour and to beat out of them all, or the most part, of the booty (as the honey from the bee) which they have wrung from the commons and to turn it into the emperor's treasury, but never anything back again to the right owners, how great or evident soever the injury be".[69]

This practice had another advantage: it promoted the idea that the tsar did not yet know about the ordinary corruption around him, but in due time would apply his terrible retribution, or *tsarskaia rasprava* and restore justice.

Conclusion

Muscovy was organized as a patrimonial domain and, although it became a centralized State at the beginning of the sixteenth Century, most of its fiscal system remained patrimonial. It kept most of the fiscal organization from the "Tatar yoke" period. Territorial expansion increased fiscal pressure because of the needs of a bigger State administration, court and army. During the seventeenth Century, the State tried to tax Church landowning, mostly between 1649 and 1676, by creating a Monastery chancery (*Monastyrskii prikaz*), but these measures were fiercely resisted by the Church. Muscovite fiscal system remained quite the same until Peter the Great's reforms. They marked the beginning of a new era, with the introduction upon every commoner, free or serf, of the so-called Soul tax (*podushnaia podat'*), or capitation, in 1724.

Notes

1 For the purpose of this chapter, we do not differentiate between the terms Mongol and Tatar. Russian medieval sources call the invaders "Tatars", although Gengis Khan was himself of Mongol stock.
2 *Povest' vremenykh let*, p. 18. *The Russian Primary Chronicle.* p. 59. Russian chronicles used the Byzantine count since Creation, supposed to take place in 5508 BC (AM = anno mundi).
3 CONSTANTINE PORPHYROGENETICUS, *De administrando Imperio*, pp. 56–62.
4 HOWES, *The Testaments*. The original charters are published in DDG. Dates of the documents have been revised by ZIMIN, "O khronologii dukhovnykh", pp. 275–324. See also KUCHKIN "Vnutripoliticheskie dogovory", pp. 34–43; "Izdanie zaveshchanii Moskovskikh, 1 (31) 2008, pp. 95–108, 2 (32) 2008, pp. 129–132, 1 (35) 2009, pp. 93–100, 2 (36), 2009, pp. 110–113, 3 (37), 2009, pp. 132–136.
5 VASMER, *Etimologicheskii slovar'*, 4 vol.; SHIPOVA, *Slovar' tiurkizmov*.
6 NPL = *Novgorodskaia pervaia letopis'*, p. 286; *The Chronicle of Novgorod*, p. 81.
7 The term Horde, from Mongol *Ordu*, means encampment. After the breakup of the Golden Horde, rival Hordes appear, some of them nomad, some of them sedentary, developing into khanates.
8 ALLSEN, "Mongol Census Taking in Rus'", pp. 32–53; MASSON-SMITH Jr., "Mongol and Nomadic Taxation", pp. 46–85.
9 *Defter* in Russian comes from Turkic *daftär* (accounts, register) borrowed from the Greek *diphtera* (skin, book, charter).
10 FENNELL, *History of the Russian Church*, pp. 189–204; SCHURMANN, "Mongolian Tributary" pp. 318, 367–368.
11 DEWEY, "Russia's Debt to the Mongols 1988, pp. 249–270, quote on pp. 261–262.
12 The collection includes copies of *yarlyki* issued by Mengu Temir (1267), Taydula (1347, 1351, 1354), Berdi Beg (1357), Tyuliak (1379), *Pamiatniki russkogo prava*. pp. 463–480.
13 GORSKII, *Moskva i Orda*.
14 VERNADSKY, *The Mongols and Russia*, pp. 214–232.
15 ARAKCHEEV, "Poriadok sbora ordynskogo 'vykhoda'", pp. 17–31; BAZILEVICH, "K voprosu ob istoricheskikh usloviiakh", p. 32; KLIUCHEVSKII, *Sochineniia v 9 tomakh*, t.2, pp. 38–42; PAVLOV, "K voprosu o Russkoi", pp. 74–112; ROUBLEV, "Le tribut aux Mongols", pp. 487–530; "The Periodicity of the Mongol Tribute", pp. 7–15; SMIRNOV "Obrazovanie Russkogo", p. 72.

16 WITTFOGEL and CHIA-SHENG, *History of Chinese Society*, pp. 161–162.
17 DEWEY, "Russia's Debt to the Mongols". See also OSTROWSKI, "The Mongol Origins", pp. 525–542; *Muscovy and the Mongols*.
18 HOWES, *The Testaments*, p. 216.
19 PELENSKI "The Contest between Lithuania", pp. 131–150.
20 *Pskovkie letopisi*, t.1, Moscow; Leningrad, 1941, p. 47 (25.000 rubles); NPL, p. 425 (200.000 rubles).
21 *Sbornik Rossijskogo istoricheskogo obshchestva*, t.41, St-Petersburg, 1884, p. 152, 268.
22 The future Vasili III.
23 HOWES, *The Testaments*, p. 294.
24 ROUBLEV, "Le tribut aux Mongols", p. 519.
25 GRANBERG *Veche in the Chronicles*; BIRNBAUM, *Lord Novgorod the Great*.
26 NPL, p. 82, 310; *The Chronicle of Novgorod*, p. 97.
27 GVNP = *Gramoty Velikogo Novgoroda i Pskova*, pp. 9–13.
28 See below about Muscovite commercial taxes.
29 GVNP n°29, pp. 56–57.
30 GVNP, n° 30, p. 57. In return for their high taxes, the Mongols guaranteed safety on the roads for the merchants. This Mongol peace (*Pax mongolica*) has been compared to the *Pax romana* under the Roman empire, LEMERCIER-QUELQUEJAY, *La Paix mongole*
31 GVNP, n°1, pp. 9–10.
32 NPL, pp. 344–346; *The Chronicle of Novgorod*, pp. 127–128.
33 DORONIN, "Vychegodsko-Vymskaia", pp. 257–271.
34 IANIN, "Chernyi bor v Novgorode", pp. 98–107.
35 NPL, p. 412 AM 6927, AD 1419.
36 GVNP n°21, pp. 38–39.
37 GVNP n°25, p. 44.
38 VESELOVSKII, *Feodal'noe zemlevladenie*, pp. 286–299.
39 English translation of Russian terms are made with the help of HOWES, *The Testaments of the Grand Princes of Moscow*, DEWEY, *Muscovite Judicial Texts*.
40 VERNADSKY, *Mongols and Russia*, pp. 216, 222–223.
41 HOWES, *The Testaments*, p. 182, 184.
42 PIPES, *Russia under the Old Regime*, pp. 40–41. Of course, Kievan Rus' and Muscovy did not know the Roman notion of *fiscus*, whereas the Merovingians kings kept it in mind, while considering their realm as a patrimony, DUMÉZIL, "Le bon temps des rois mérovingiens", pp. 40–49.
43 ZIMIN, "D'iacheskii apparat", pp. 219–286.
44 LANGER, "Plague and the Russian Countryside:", pp. 351–368; GOEHRKE, *Die Wüstungen in der Moskauer Rus'*; BORISENKOV, and PASETSKIJ, *Ekstremal'nye prirodnye iavleniia*, pp. 88–97.
45 During the soviet period a lot of studies were devoted to the immunity policy of the Russian princes, mostly in the context of the ascent of Muscovy, notably by IVINA, "Kopiinye knigi", pp. 5–44; "Troitskii sbornik materialov", pp. 149–163; "Sudebnye dokumenty", pp. 326–356; *Krupnaia votchina; Vnutrennee osvoenie*; KASHTANOV, "Kopiinye knigi", pp. 3–47, "Iz istorii poslednikh udelov", pp. 275–302, *Sotsial'no-politicheskaia istoriia Rossii*; "Ogranichenie feodal'nogo immuniteta", pp. 269–296, "Monastyrskii immunitet", pp. 25–30; "The Centralized State", pp. 235–254, *Ocherki russkoi diplomatiki*; "Po sledam troitskikh", 38, 1977, pp. 30–63, 40, 1979, pp. 4–58, 43, 1982, pp. 4–37, *Finansy srednevekovoi Rusi*; ZIMIN, "Aktovye poddelki", pp. 247–251, "K izucheniiu, pp. 339–428; *Krupnaia feodal'naia*"; GONNEAU, *La Maison de la Sainte Trinité*, pp. 157–185, 236–260.
46 GONNEAU, pp. 171–173. Vasili Yaroslavich died in prison in 1483.
47 GONNEAU, pp. 419–454, KASHTANOV, "La demande des grands propriétaires fonciers", pp. 81–91; VODOFF, "Les transports dans la vie économique", pp. 315–336.
48 KAMENTSEVA and USTIUGOV, *Russkaia metrologiia*, pp. 63–64.
49 SHAPIRO, *Russkoe krest'ianstvo*, p. 106.
50 PLIGUZOV, *Polemika v Russkoi Tserkvi*; GONNEAU, pp. 203–206.
51 WILLAN, *The Early History*; BARON, "The Muscovy Company", pp. 133–155; "Thrust and Parry", pp. 19–40; STOUT, *Exploring Russia*.
52 KOLLMANN, *The Moscow Stoglav*, ch. 43.
53 KROM, *Vdovstvuiushchee tsarstvo*, ch. 8 https://royallib.com/read/krom_mihail/rogdenie_gosudarstva_moskovskaya_rus_xvxvi_vekov.html#40960
54 SMITH, *Documents Relating to the Enserfment of the Peasants*; HELLIE, *Enserfment and Military*.

55 *Rude and Barbarous Kingdom*, p. 158.
56 *Rude and Barbarous Kingdom*, pp. 158–159.
57 *Rude and Barbarous Kingdom*, pp. 159–160.
58 *Rude and Barbarous Kingdom*, p. 159, n.5. The "three-field" measurement was used by Muscovite clerks in their registers. It is still unsure if this means that the landowners were practicing the three-field system, CONFINO, *Systèmes agraires et progrès agricole*, pp. 32–36, 420–421; GONNEAU, *La Maison de la Sainte Trinité*, pp. 67–69.
59 *Rude and Barbarous Kingdom*, pp. 160–162.
60 *Rude and Barbarous Kingdom*, pp. 162–163.
61 *Rude and Barbarous Kingdom*, pp. 161–162.
62 *Rude and Barbarous Kingdom*, p. 163.
63 *Rude and Barbarous Kingdom*, p. 164.
64 FISHER, *The Russian Fur trade*, pp. 108–109.
65 SEREDONIN, *Sochinenie Dzhil'sa Fletchera*, p. 323; PENNINGTON, *Grigorii Kotoshikhin*.
66 KROM, *Rozhdenie gosudarstva*, ch. 8.
67 *Rude and Barbarous Kingdom*, p. 216.
68 DEWEY and KLEIMOLA, "Coercion by Righter (Pravezh)", pp. 156–178.
69 *Rude and Barbarous Kingdom*, pp. 164–165.

References
Sources

The Chronicle of Novgorod 1016–1471, translated from the Russian by Robert MICHELL and Nevill FORBES, London, 1914.
CONSTANTINE PORPHYROGENETICUS, *De administrando Imperio*, ed Gyula MORAVCISK, tr. Romilly James Heald JENKINS, Washington, 1967 (Corpus fontium historiae byzantinae 1).
DDG = *Dukhovnye I dogovornye gramoty velikikh i udel'nykh kniazei XIV-XV vv.*, éd. Lev Vladimirovich CHEREPNIN, Moscow-Leningrad, 1950.
Horace W. DEWEY, *Muscovite Judicial Texts, 1488–1556*, Ann Arbor, 1966 (Michigan Slavic Materials 7)
GVNP = *Gramoty Velikogo Novgoroda i Pskova*, ed. Sigizmund NATANOVICH VALK, Moscow-Leningrad, 1949.
Robert Craig HOWES, ed. *The Testaments of the Grand Princes of Moscow*, Ithaca, Cornell University Press, 1967
NPL = *Novgorodskaia pervaia letopis' starshego i mladshego izvodov*, Moscow-Leningrad, 1950.
Pamiatniki russkogo prava. t.3. *Pamiatniki prava perioda obrazovaniia russkogo tsentralizovannogo gosudarstva XIV-XV vv.*, Moscow, 1955.
Povest' vremenykh let, ed. Dmitrii Sergeevich LIKHACHEV, Moscow-Leningrad, 1950, 2 vol.
Pskovkie letopisi, ed. Arsenii Nikolaevich NASONOV, Moscow-Leningrad, 1941–1955, 2 vol.
Rude and Barbarous Kingdom: Russia in the Accounts of Sixteenth-Century English Voyagers, edited by Lloyd E. BERRY and Robert O. CRUMMEY, Madison-Milwaukee, London, 1968.
The Russian Primary Chronicle. Laurentian Text, translated and edited by Samuel Hazzard cross and Olgerd P. sherbowitz-wetzor, Cambridge Mass. 1953.
TMIAI = *Trudy Moskovskogo istoriko-arkhivnogo Instituta*, Moscow, 1939.
ZOR = *Zapiski Otdela rukopisei gosudarstvennoi biblioteki imeni V.I. Lenina*, Moscow, 1938–1995, 49 vol.

Secondary literature

Thomas T. ALLSEN, "Mongol Census Taking in Rus', 1245–1275", *Harvard Ukrainian Studies*, 5:1 1981, pp. 32–53.
Vladimir Anatol'evich ARAKCHEEV, "Poriadok sbora ordynskogo 'vykhoda' v russkikh zemliax vo vtoroi polovine XV v.", in *Velikoe stoianie na reke Ugre i formirovanie rossijskogo tsentralizovannogo gosudarstva: lokal'nye i global'nye konteksty. Materialy Vserossijskoi s mezhdunarodnym uchastiem nauchnoj konferencii (30 marta-1 aprelia 2017 g., Kaluga)*, Kaluga, 2017, pp. 17–31.
Samuel H. BARON, "The Muscovy Company, the Muscovite Merchants and the Problem of Reciprocity in Russian Foreign Trade", *Forschungen zur osteuropäischen Geschichte*, 27 (1980), pp. 133–155.

Samuel H. BARON, "Thrust and Parry: Anglo-Russian Relations in the Muscovite North", *Oxford Slavonic Papers*, 21 (1998), pp. 19–40.

Konstantin Vasil'evich, BAZILEVICH, "K voprosu ob istoricheskikh usloviiakh obrazovaniia Russkogo gosudarstva", *Voprosy istorii*, 7, 1946, pp. 26–44.

Henrik BIRNBAUM, *Lord Novgorod the Great: Essays in the History and Culture of a Medieval City-State*, Columbus, Ohio, 1981 (UCLA Slavic Studies 2).

Henrik BIRNBAUM, *Novgorod in Focus: Selected Essays*, Columbus, Ohio, 1996.

Michael CONFINO, *Systèmes agraires et progrès agricole: l'assolement triennal en Russie aux XVIIIe – XIXe siècles: étude d'économie et de sociologie rurales*, Paris, 1969.

Horace W. DEWEY and Ann KLEIMOLA, « Coercion by Righter (Pravezh) in Old Russian Administration », *Canadian American Slavic Studies*, 9.2, 1975, pp. 156–178.

Horace W. DEWEY, "Russia's Debt to the Mongols in Suretyship and Collective Responsibility", *Comparative Studies in Society and History*, 30.2, 1988, pp. 249–270.

Pavel Grigor'evich DORONIN, "Vychegodsko-Vymskaia (Misailo-Evtikhievskaia) letopis'", *Istoriko-filologicheskii sbornik Komi filiala AN SSSR*, 4, 1958, pp. 257–271.

Bruno DUMÉZIL, "Le bon temps des rois mérovingiens", *L'Histoire*, n°358, novembre 2010, pp. 40–49.

John FENNELL, *A History of the Russian Church to 1448*, London; New York, 1995.

Raymond Henry FISHER, *The Russian Fur trade, 1550–1700*, Berkeley; Los Angeles, 1943.

Carsten GOEHRKE, *Die Wüstungen in der Moskauer Rus': Studien zur Siedlungs- Bevölkerungs- und Sozialgeschichte*, Wiesbaden, 1968 (Quellen und Studien zur Geschichte des östlichen Europa 1).

Pierre GONNEAU, *La Maison de la Sainte Trinité: un grand monastère russe du Moyen-âge tardif (1345–1533)*, Paris, 1993.

Anton Anatol'evich GORSKII, *Moskva i Orda*, Moscow, 2016.

Jonas GRANBERG, *Veche in the Chronicles of Medieval Rus: A Study of Functions and Terminology*, Göteborg, 2004.

Richard HELLIE, *Enserfment and Military Change in Muscovy*, Chicago, 1971.

Liudmila Ivanovna IVINA, "Kopiinye knigi Troitse-Sergieva monastyrja XVII v.", ZOR, 24, 1961, pp. 5–44.

Ljudmila Ivanovna IVINA, *Krupnaia votchina severo-vostochnoi Rusi kontsa XIV – pervoi poloviny XVI v.*, Leningrad, 1979.

Ljudmila Ivanovna IVINA, "Sudebnye dokumenty i bor'ba za zemliu v russkom gosudarstve vo vtoroi polovine XV – nachale XVI v.", *Istoricheskie zapiski*, 86, 1970, pp. 326–356.

Ljudmila Ivanovna IVINA, "Troitskii sbornik materialov po istorii zemlevladeniia russkogo gosudarstva XVI-VII vv.", ZOR, 27, 1965, pp. 149–163.

Ljudmila Ivanovna IVINA, *Vnutrennee osvoenie zemel' Rossii v XVI v.: istoriko-geograficheskoe issledovanie po materialam monastyrej*, Leningrad, 1985.

Valentin Lavrent'evich IANIN, "Chernyi bor v Novgorode XIV-XV vekov", in *Kulikovskaia bitva v istorii i kul'ture nashei Rodiny (materialy iubilejnoj nauchnoi konferentsii)*, Moscow, 1983, pp. 98–107.

Elena Ivanovna KAMENTSEVA and Nikolai Vladimirovich USTIUGOV, *Russkaia metrologiia*, Moscow, 1965.

Sergei Mixajlovich KASHTANOV, "The Centralized State and Feudal Immunities in Russia", *Slavic and East-European Review*, 49, 1965, pp. 235–254.

Sergei Mixajlovich KASHTANOV, "La demande des grands propriétaires fonciers en objets de consommation en Russie du XIVᵉ au XVᵉ siècle », in *Domanda e consumi, livelli e strutture: nei secoli XIII-XVIII: atti della sesta settimano di studio, 27 IV-3 V 1974*, Florence, 1978, pp. 81–91.

Sergei Mixajlovich KASHTANOV, *Finansy srednevekovoi Rusi*, Moscow, 1988.

Sergei Mixajlovich KASHTANOV, "Iz istorii poslednikh udelov", TMIAI, 10, 1957, pp. 275–302.

Sergei Mixajlovich KASHTANOV, "Kopiinye knigi Troitse-Sergieva monastyrja XVI veka", ZOR, 18, 1956, pp. 3–47.

Sergei Mixajlovich KASHTANOV, "Monastyrskii immunitet v Dmitrovskom udele 1504–1533", in *Voprosy sotsial'no-èkonomicheskoj istorii i istochnikovedeniia perioda feodalizma v Rossii*, Moscow, 1961, pp. 25–30.

Sergei Mixajlovich KASHTANOV, *Ocherki russkoi diplomatiki*, Moscow, 1970.

Sergei Mixajlovich KASHTANOV, "Ogranichenie feodal'nogo immuniteta pravitel'stvom russkogo tsentralizovannogo gosudarstva v pervoj treti XVI v.", TMIAI, 11, 1958, pp. 269–296.

Sergei Mixajlovič KASHTANOV, "Po sledam troitskikh kopiynykh knig XVI v.", ZOR, 38, 1977, pp. 30–63, 40, 1979, pp. 4–58, 43, 1982, pp. 4–37.

Sergei Mixajlovich KASHTANOV, *Sotsial'no-politicheskajjja istoriia Rossii kontsa XV-pervoi poloviny XVI s.*, Moscow, 1957.

Vasilii Osipovich KLIUCHEVSKII, *Sochineniia v 9 tomakh*, t.2, Moscow, 1989, pp. 38–42, *Kurs Russkoj Istorii*. Lekciia XXII.

Jack Edward Jr. KOLLMANN, *The Moscow Stoglav (Hundred Chapters) Church Council of 1551*, Ann Arbor, 1982.

Mixail Markovich KROM, *Rozhdenie gosudarstva: Moskovskaia Rus' XV-XVI vekov*, Moscow, 2018, ch.8 https://royallib.com/read/krom_mihail/rogdenie_gosudarstva_moskovskaya_rus_xvxvi_vekov.html#40960

Mixail Markovich KROM, *Vdovstvuiushchee tsarstvo: politicheskii krizis v Rossii 30-40-kh godov XVI veka*, Moscow, 2010.

Vladimir Andreevich KUCCHKIN, "Izdanie zaveshchanii Moskovskikh kniazei XIV v", *Drevniaia Rus'. Voprosy medievistiki*, 1 (31) 2008, pp. 95–108, 2 (32) 2008, pp. 129–132, 1 (35) 2009, pp. 93–100, 2 (36), 2009, pp. 110–113, 3 (37), 2009, pp. 132–136.

Vladimir Andreevich KUCHKIN, "Vnutripoliticheskie dogovory moskovskikh knjazei XIV veka", *Vestnik Rossiiskogo gumanitarnogo nauchnogo fonda*, 1:50, 2008, pp. 34–43.

Lawrence N. LANGER, "Plague and the Russian Countryside: Monastic Estates in the Late 14th and 15th Century", *Canadian-American Slavic Studies*, 10, 1976, pp. 351–368.

Chantal LEMERCIER-QUELQUEJAY, *La Paix mongole: joug tatar ou paix mongole?*, Paris, 1970.

John Jr. MASSON-SMITH H, "Mongol and Nomadic Taxation", *Harvard Journal of Asiatic Studies* 30 (1970), pp. 46–85.

Donald OSTROWSKI, "The Mongol Origins of Muscovite Political Institutions", *Slavic Review*, 49:4, 1990, pp. 525–542.

Donald OSTROWSKI, *Muscovy and the Mongols: Cross-Cultural Influences on the Steppe Frontier, 1304–1589*, Cambridge, 1998.

Evgenij PASETSKIJ, Panteleimonovich BORISENKOV and Vasilii Mikhailovich PASETSKIJ, *Ekstremal'nye prirodnye iavleniia v russkikh letopis'iax XI-XVII vv.*, Leningrad, 1983.

Pavel Nikolaevich PAVLOV, "K voprosu o Russkoi dani v Zolotuiu Ordu", *Uchenye zapiski Krasnoiarskogo gosudarstvennogo pedagogicheskogo Instituta*, t.13. Seriia istorii i filosofii, vyp.2, 1958, pp. 74–112.

Jaroslaw PELENSKI, *The Contest for the Legacy of Kievan Rus*, Boulder CO, 1998 (East European Monographs 377).

Anne Elizabeth PENNINGTON, *Grigorii Kotoshikhin: O Rossii v tsarstvovanie Alekseia Mikhailovicha: text and commentary*, Oxford – New York, 1980.

Richard PIPES, *Russia under the Old Regime*, Baskerville, 1974.

Andrej Ivanovich PLIGUZOV, *Polemika v Russkoi Tserkvi pervoi treti XVI stoletiia*, Moscow, 2002.

Michel ROUBLEV, "The Periodicity of the Mongol Tribute as paid by the Russian Princes during the fourteenth and the fifteenth centuries", *Forschungen zur osteuropäischen Geschichte*, 15, 1970, pp. 7–15.

Michel ROUBLEV, "Le tribut aux Mongols d'après les testaments et accords des princes russes", *Cahiers du monde russe et soviétique*, vol. 7, n°4, Octobre–Décembre 1966, pp. 487–530.

Herbert Franz SCHURMANN, "Mongolian Tributary Practices of the Thirteenth Century", *Harvard Journal of Asiatic Studies*, 19:3–4 (1956), p. 367–368.

Sergei Mikhailovich SEREDONIN, *Sochinenie Dzhil'sa Flechera "Of the Russe common wealth" kak istoricheskij istochnik*, S.-Peterburg, 1891, p. 323 (Zapiski istoriko-filologicheskago Fakul'teta Imperatorskago Sankt-Peterburgskago Universiteta 27).

Aleksandr L'vovich SHAPIRO, *Russkoe krest'ianstvo pered zakreposhcheniem: XIV-XVI vekov*, Leningrad, 1987.

Elizaveta Nikolaevna SHIPOVA, *Slovar' tiurkizmov v russkom iazyke*, Alma-Ata, 1976.

Pavel Petrovich SMIRNOV, "Obrazovanie Russkogo gosudarstva v XIV–XV vv.", *Voprosy istorii*, 1946, 2–3, pp. 55–90.

Robert Ernest Frederick SMITH, *Documents Relating to the Enserfment of the Peasants in Russia*, Birmingham, 1966 (University of Birmingham. Center for Russian and East-European Studies. Discussion Papers. Series RC/D4).

Robert Ernest Frederick SMITH, *The Enserfment of Russian Peasantry*, Cambridge, 1968.

Felicity Jane STOUT, *Exploring Russia in the Elizabethan Commonwealth: The Muscovy Company and Giles Fletcher*, Manchester, 2015.

Max VASMER, *Etimologicheskii slovar' russkogo iazyka*, 4 vol., Moscow, 1964–1973.

George VERNADKY, *The Mongols and Russia*, New Haven – London, 1953.

Stepan Borisovich VESELOVSKII, *Feodal'noe zemlevladenie v Severo-Vostochnoj Rusi*, t.1, Moscow; Leningrad, 1947.

Vladimir VODOFF, "Les transports dans la vie économique des monastères de la Russie du nord-est au XVe siècle", *Annales de Bretagne et des pays de l'Ouest (Anjou, Maine, Touraine)*, 85, 1978.2, pp. 315–336.

Thomas Stuart WILLLAN, *The Early History of the Russia Company, 1553–1603*, Manchester, 1956.
Karl August WITTFOGEL and Feng CCHIA-SHENG, *History of Chinese Society (907–1125)*, Philadelphia, 1946, pp. 161–162 (Transactions of the American Philosophical Society, n.s. 36).
Aleksandr Aleksandrovich ZIMIN, "Aktovye poddelki Troitse-Sergieva monastyria 80-kh godov XVI v.", in *Voprosy sotsial'no-èkonomicheskoi istorii i istochnikovedeniia perioda feodalizma v Rossii*, Moscow, 1961, pp. 247–251.
Aleksandr Aleksandrovich ZIMIN, "D'iacheskii apparat v Rossii vtoroi poloviny XV-pervoi treti XVI v.", *Istoricheskie zapiski*, 87, 1971, pp. 219–286.
Aleksandr Aleksandrovich ZIMIN, "K izucheniiu fal'sifikatsii aktovykh materialov v russkom gosudarstve v XVI-XVII vv.", TMIAI, 17, 1963, pp. 339–428.
Aleksandr Aleksandrovich ZIMIN, *Krupnaia feodal'naia votchina i sotsial'no-politicheskaia bor'ba v Rossii: konets XV-XVI v.*, Moscow, 1977.
Aleksandr Aleksandrovich ZIMIN, "O khronologii dukhovnykh i dogovornykh gramot velikikh i udel'nykh kniazej XIV-XV vv.", *Problemy istochnikovedenija*, 6 (1958), pp. 275–324.

18
THE BYZANTINE EMPIRE

Anastasia Kontogiannopoulou

Taxation was the basic pillar of Byzantine public finances throughout the existence of the state (fourth to fifteenth centuries). As in all aspects of public life, the emperor controlled economic policy, which was based on a well-organized administrative apparatus. Fiscal policy affected the entire population, whether landowners, tenants of land or merchants, craftsmen, and other professionals. The main purpose of the revenue services was to assess and collect taxes; fiscal revenues mostly covered state expenditures on the maintenance of the administration and the army.[1] In addition to its budgetary nature, taxation functioned as a medium for forming ideas on citizenship, as the ruled perceived the emperor's ideals, ideas, and priorities through his tax policies. Moreover, as a point of communication between the state and the citizens, taxation was also a field where loyalty, resistance and negotiation could be expressed.[2]

The organization and function of the Byzantine fiscal system has been studied thoroughly, with significant emphasis on its transformations over time to adapt to political and economic developments.[3] The taxes were either direct, i.e., taxation of land and the rural population or indirect, taxation burdening commercial transactions. Taxes were paid in three ways: in cash, in kind, and in service. Similarly, there were three main ways to finance administrative and military expenditures: by offering an annual salary (*roga*), or granting financial privileges, or having citizens remunerate an official for his services to them. The political and economic conditions of each period decreed which method would prevail as regards tax collection and government expenditure financing, while the financial administration would be restructured to adapt to the demands of the time.[4]

In the Early Byzantine period (fourth to sixth centuries), the *jugatio-capitatio* system was used to calculate direct taxes. According to this, taxation on both land and people was assessed based on a standard equal unit of account, the *jugum* for land and the *caput* for the workforce and animals. Added up, these units would provide a region's tax value. Land was divided into categories according to its quality and the type of farming it supported (arable land, vineyards, olive groves) and, thus, depending on the circumstances, the *jugum* represented a different amount of land.[5]

In the Middle Byzantine period (seventh to eleventh centuries), the *jugatio-capitatio* system was gradually replaced by one based on the evaluation of individual properties. The land tax was calculated according to the size and quality of the land. The unit commonly used for measuring land was the *modios* (μόδιος),[6] which generally corresponded to one coin for first quality land, half coin for second quality land and one third of a coin for third quality land.

These percentages might vary depending on local conditions and imperial policy. The tax the taxpayer was required to pay corresponded to 1/24 of the value of the land. There were also changes in the way people and animals were taxed during this period. The rural population was categorized according to the amount of land they held and the number of oxen they owned. The main categories were *zeugaratos* (owner of a pair of oxen), *boidatos* (owner of one ox) and *aktemon* (a peasant with neither animals nor real property), and they were taxed based on the means of production available. In general, a *zeugaratos* was equivalent to two *boidatoi* and four *aktemones*. Animals were taxed based on a percentage of their value.[7]

Indirect taxes were levied on trade and real estate transfers. These included cross-border duties and customs duties, which usually corresponded to 10 per cent of the value of imported goods.[8] With some modifications, adapted to the conditions created by the development of large, landed properties and the state economy of privileges the Palaiologoi adhered to, the fiscal system of the Middle Byzantine period was maintained until the late Byzantine centuries.[9]

In this chapter we shall focus on the study of public taxation in Byzantium during the last centuries of the state, a period coinciding with the reign of the Palaiologoi emperors (mid-thirteenth to mid-fifteenth centuries). The major fields to be examined are the organization of the financial administration and the staffing of the fiscal services. Subsequently, we shall study the direct and indirect taxes the emperors imposed. Finally, we shall examine the basic principles of Palaiologan fiscal policy and its influence on the formation of the emperor's relations with his subjects.

Archival documents – such as imperial charters, tax registers, administrative documents, and transactions, as well as treaties with foreign powers – provide useful evidence about the fiscal system of the Palaiologan era.[10] Information about the fiscal policy of the emperors can also be found in the historical works of the period. Georgios Pachymeres,[11] Nikephoros Gregoras[12] and John Kantakouzenos,[13] the main Byzantine historians of the thirteenth and fourteenth centuries, often refer to and comment on tax measures imposed by the emperors. Furthermore, scattered evidence about taxation can be gleaned from the abundant correspondence and other literary sources of the time.[14]

The recapture of Constantinople in 1261 by the forces of Michael VIII Palaiologos (1261–1282) and the restoration of the Byzantine Empire created new financial demands to meet the increased expenses of foreign policy as well as those of the administration.[15] As in the past, land and agricultural activities were the main source of taxation. Duties imposed on commercial activities were a secondary source of revenue, yet the public treasury was faced with diminished profits due to tax exemptions granted to Italian and other Western merchants from the eleventh century on.[16] From the mid-fourteenth century on, civil strife and Serbian and Ottoman expansion caused the gradual decline of the large estates. Consequently, land tax revenues declined and the management of commercial duties took on a new importance for the state's finances.[17] All economic activity revolved around the central financial office, the *vestiarion*, while a large number of fiscal officials were employed in the provinces.

Fiscal administration
The Central Financial Office

In the period under consideration, the *vestiarion* (βεστιάριον) evolved into the principal financial office of Byzantium. The state treasury in the mid-Byzantine period, it also acquired the economic functions of the old *logothesia* (λογοθέσια) during the Palaiologan era.[18] Revenues from taxation,[19] property confiscations[20] and other state financial requirements ended up in the *vestiarion*.[21] Additionally, this is where the central cadastre (θέσις or μεγάλη θέσις) and the *praktika*, compiled by financial officials in the provinces upon the emperor's order (ὁρισμός), were kept.[22] As the state treasury, the *vestiarion* funded the expenses of the administration, the army, the requirements of foreign policy, and other kinds of payments, while there is some evidence that it accompanied the emperor on his travels.[23] Finally, the *vestiarion* was associated with coin minting. There is little information about the staffing of the *vestiarion*. According to Pseudo-Kodinos, the head of the *vestiarion* was the *prokathemenos*, who was responsible for the revenues and expenditures of the service.[24] Another official associated with the central financial administration was the *logariastes* of the *aule* (court), who was apparently in charge of the tax officials tasked with collecting the capital's commercial duties.[25]

Financial officials

State officials were charged by imperial order with registering agricultural land and assessing and collecting direct taxes. In some cases, especially from the second half of the fourteenth century on, when the Serbian and Ottoman expansion into Byzantine territory resulted in an unstable situation in the provinces, this process would take place during the emperor's tour of the provinces. The emperor would then confirm the privileges of any persons whom he or previous emperors had favoured with concessions of land and tax exemptions.[26] In the first half of the fifteenth century, a census would be ordered not only by the emperor, but also, in some cases, by members of the imperial family who, bearing the title of *basileus* or *despot*, ruled the provinces still under Byzantine control. One such census was conducted by order of Emperor John VII (1390) and *Despot* Andronikos in the area of Thessaloniki in 1418 and another by order of *Despot* Demetrios Palaiologos in Lemnos in 1430.[27]

The officials who assessed the agricultural taxes were usually called *energountes* of public functions (ἐνεργοῦντες τὰς δημοσιακὰς δουλείας).[28] The *apographeis* belonged to this category of officials. The duties of the imperial tax assessors were usually complicated and consisted of compiling the *praktika*, i.e., documents which recorded the households of the *paroikoi* under the authority of a property holder (whether state, single individual, or religious institution), the tax that corresponded to each household, any supplementary charges burdening these lands and people, as well as the fiscal privileges accorded to the property holder.[29] The *apographeis* were also frequently called upon to intervene in case of property rights violations and to dispense justice.[30] The purpose of their work was to guarantee the property rights of the landowners, as well as to inform the central tax authorities of the amounts of taxes and tax exemptions that corresponded to each property. The work of the *apographeus* could, as in the past, be carried out by state officials, such as the *domestikoi* of (eastern or western) *themes*,[31] the dukes,[32] and the provincial governors (*kephalai*).[33] The *apographeis* usually bore the title of *sebastos* and thus occupied the lower rank of Byzantine aristocracy. Often coming from provincial circles, they acquired prestige and financial benefits through the position of *apographeus*. As members of the same family often served as *apographeis*, e.g., Theologites, Pharisaios, and Vardales, this resulted in certain families becoming traditionally associated with professions related to financial administration. The *apographeis* sometimes acted alone and sometimes collaborated with other *apographeis*.[34] Land was measured by *geometers* (γεωμέτραι) or *counters* (μετρηταί), who were subordinates to the *apographeis*.[35]

According to Byzantine tradition, other officials collected the taxes; in the sources they are usually referred to as *praktores* or *energountes* or *demosiakoi enochoi*. According to the *entalma praktikon*, the surveyor of a region instructed the *energon* to perform his service in a spirit of justice and selflessness.[36] Nevertheless, *apographeis*, such as the *Sebastos* Nikolaos Theologites[37] and Theodoros Patrikiotes[38] often undertook to collect taxes.

Tax collectors were usually tax farmers (τελῶναι) contracted to collect the taxes for a share of the proceeds. To obtain the office, they submitted bids to the State, indicating the amount of fiscal revenues they expected to collect. They would even give an advance or a guarantee to secure the agreement, while the final amount would be deposited in the state treasury after the taxes were collected. Failure to collect the agreed amount would result in the confiscation of their property.[39] Naturally, the tax collectors did everything they could to collect the amount they had promised the state and to turn a profit themselves. Patriarch Gregory II of Cyprus (1283–1289) referred to the abuses of tax collectors, who farmed out fiscal revenues and profited at the expense of the people.[40] In one case he doubted the honesty of tax farmers during the performance of their duty.[41] Some tax farmers accumulated great wealth, such as Patrikiotes who donated his fortune to John Kantakouzenos to pay for the army in 1341.[42] According to Nikephoros Gregoras, John Vatatzes went from poor to rich thanks to the census service he had undertaken.[43]

Although profitable, the profession was also risky, as there was a chance that the expected amount could not be collected. One such case was that of the tax collector John Theologites who was dismissed from his position, for, among other things, failing to deliver the promised amount.[44] Monemvasiotes, another tax collector, also failed to collect the promised amount and asked Patriarch Gregory of Cyprus to mediate with the *Megas Logothetes* Theodoros Mouzalon for clemency.[45]

The *kommerkiarioi* (or οἱ εἰς τὸ κομμέρκιον τῆς θεομεγαλύντου Κωνσταντινουπόλεως καὶ οἱ εἰς τὰς ἄλλας σκάλας πάσας καὶ χώρας καὶ κάστρα ἐνοχοποιούμενοι κατὰ καιρούς) were responsible for collecting the *kommerkion*, the basic tax on trade.[46] Usually, the *kommerkiarioi* farmed out their services for one year. This is why Pegolotti advised traders to request payment receipts, so as to avoid paying the next functionary the same amount. He also instructed them to offer the *kommerkiarioi* or their subordinates a gift in cash or kind, so as to be treated fairly when their merchandise was taxed.[47]

Starting in the mid-fourteenth century, when the Byzantines turned their interest to commercial activities to take advantage of the great development of trade in the Mediterranean, members of the upper social class engaged in commercial tax farming. One such example is *Megas Doux* Alexios Apokaukos who, in the mid-fourteenth century, in addition to being a high court dignitary, was also a salt pans tenant and tax collector.[48] Other such members of the upper social class were Demetrios Notaras, Theodoros Vatatzes, and Konstantinos Kritopoulos, who, in the fifteenth century, were granted the right to collect the *kommerkion* on wheat, fish, and wine, and the taxes from the sale of slaves, exploitation of saltworks, and minting. Tax farming provided the state with regular revenue and, as a reward for services provided, covered part of the expenses for the function of the administration and defence of the state.[49]

Fiscal system

Direct taxes

All the regular and supplementary taxes that burdened the land, the agricultural production, and the rural population constituted direct taxes. First and foremost was the land tax, which was borne by the landowner.[50] Calculated on the basis of the size and quality of the land, it was paid even if the land remained uncultivated in the context of mutual tax liability.[51] In addition to the land tax, the direct taxes of a property included the tax on dependent peasants (*paroikoî*), which was levied on their person, families, animals, and property. The peasants' total tax liability was called *oikoumenon* and was paid to the landowner biannually (in March and September); he, in turn, paid the state. If the landowner was the beneficiary of an imperial privilege, which granted him tax exemptions, he kept his estate's fiscal income for himself. The peasants also paid the landlord rent, the *morte*, for the land they rented and were obligated to offer him a gift, the *kaniskion*, three times a year.[52]

Supplementary taxes on agricultural activities were an important source of income for the state. Because of their extraordinary character, these charges were burdensome for the rural population and the sources refer to them in negative terms, characterizing them as *epereiai* (abuses), *zemiai* (damages), *dienoxleseis* (coercions), and *katatribai* (disasters).[53] The sources also usually present their imposition negatively (as aggression or oppression) due to the frequent abuses committed by tax collectors during the collection process. Supplementary taxes were usually calculated based on the *oikoumenon* of a property. The sources of the period are full of additional taxes, whose purpose is often hard to decipher.

These were primarily taxes paid for the use and exploitation of common areas or infrastructure. This category includes charges levied on livestock for the use of pastureland, the *ennomion*,[54] the *melissoennomion* (levied on beehives),[55] the *probatoennomion* (on sheep),[56] the *choiroennomion* (on pigs),[57] and the demand of *nomithron* or *nomistron*.[58] *Mandriatikon* was a levy on stalls. The *planene* and the *oreiatikon* were associated with using mountainous areas for grazing, the *balanistron* with pigs grazing in oak woodlands. The *orike* was associated with the right to exploit forest timber, the *strobilaia* with the exploitation of pines forests. A levy on using mills was also burdened the peasants. From the mid-thirteenth until the early fourteenth century, the sources refer to a tax, the *alopia*; its purpose is hard to determine. It might have been a charge levied on fox skins or the fox hunt.[59] Certain charges were associated with fishing, such as *aleia*, which appears in the sources throughout the fourteenth century.[60] The *apostatos* was a levy on fishing grounds, the *bibarion* a levy on fish farms, the *tritomoiria* a levy on catches. The *linobrocheion* was a charge for the use of the place where flax was washed.[61]

The rural population was burdened by supplementary taxes, such as the *oikomodion*, an annual levy in kind that was calculated in proportion to the *telos* of the *paroikoi*. Also, *charagma* and *dimodaion* were extraordinary charges required from certain properties or villages. *Zeugaratikion* and *zeugologion* were taxes that burdened the *zeugaria* of the peasants. Other supplementary taxes were the tax in money named *sitarkia*, the *oinarike*, the *gennematike dosis*, charges on the production of wine and cereals, the *alatotelos*, tax on the salt, the *opheleia* a tax of disputed origin. The *anepignostikion* was a tax levied on foreign or free peasants who were not registered in the public records.[62]

After 1204, the political fragmentation of the Greek peninsula and the Serbian and Ottoman expansion from the mid-fourteenth century on affected the evolution of Byzantine institutions, including taxation. The Latin *prebenda*★, and the Serbian *pozobitze* and *preselitza*★ are taxes derived from the respective tax system.[63] The Ottoman system was probably the source of other charges, such as various tithes, the *dekaton* of *zeugaria*, the *dekaton* of *gennematikes katasporas*, the *dekaton* of *oinou*, as well as the *ospitiakon*, and possibly the *kephalatikion*.[64]

The redemption of the *paroikoi*'s personal obligations to the State or the landowner was usually considered another category of secondary taxes. The *angareia* (ἀγγαρεία) was compulsory and unpaid labour peasants owed the lord. The public *angareia* was usually imposed on property, *paroikoi*, and animals. It encompassed the number of working days the peasants owed the landowner, whether a week, twelve days, or twenty-four days of compulsory labour, or even a number of days determined by local custom. The *angareia* was also imposed on ships, mainly under exceptional circumstances, such as to build a fleet. Beneficiaries of imperial privileges were usually exempted from public *angareiai*. Like other charges, *angareiai* could be redeemed. It is possible that the term *dosis* describes meeting one's *angareia*. *Paroikoi* paid an *angareia* proportional to their financial means.[65]

Paroikoi owed other compulsory services, such as the obligation to transport salt (ἐκφορησις καὶ μετακομιδὴ ἅλατος), transport timber (ξυλάχυρον, ξυλόσυρμα), and bake bread (ψωμοζημία). Some compulsory labour contributions were aimed at repairing and maintaining castles (*kastroktisia*), shipbuilding (*katergoktisia*), and guarding castles and fortresses (*bigliatikon*).[66]

Supplementary taxes include court fines such as *aer*, *phonos*, *parthenophthoria* (corruption of virgins) and *eureses thesaurou* (discovering treasure). The *aer* was a judicial fine, which gradually became a permanent charge calculated on the basis of the paroikoi's *oikoumenon*.[67] *Phonos* was imposed in case of proven murder. Depending on the circumstances and local conditions, a certain proportion of the offender's property would be confiscated by the state. It is worth noting that the state usually kept the proceeds for itself and did not grant landowners any exemption from the tax, at least until the outbreak of the first civil war in the first half of the fourteenth century.[68] *Parthenophthoria* was a judicial fine imposed for rape and other similar crimes. The law of the Isaurian and Macedonian emperors provided that raped women had some rights to the property of the guilty party. Over time, this claim was taken over by the State.[69] *Eureses thesaurou* was the State's right to coin hoards found by individuals. Under the Palaiologoi the *eureses thesaurou* appeared as a state claim on the whole find.[70] The supplementary taxes also included the *abiotikion*, which was a charge on the transfer of the property of anyone who died intestate and childless.[71]

Additional taxes were military in nature and related to the taxpayers' obligation to provide light-armed soldiers for military campaigns. Although a well-known traditional Byzantine military obligation, it could be replaced by monetary payments during the time of the Palaiologoi. Such charges were the payment for recruiting of sailors (*exelasis* of *ploimoi*), of infantry (*exelasis* of *pezoi*), of infantry with pole weapons (*kontaratikion*), of another category of soldiers, the *mourtatoi*, and for recruiting of archers (*dosis toxarion*).[72] From the mid-fourteenth century on, these taxes were not mentioned in the sources because, by then, the Byzantine army consisted mostly of mercenaries. Two military taxes, the *phosiatikon* and the *eureses vasmoulon* associated with the recruitment of *gasmouloi*, existed in the fifteenth century.[73]

Indirect taxes

Indirect taxes, imposed on the circulation and sale of merchandise, on the conclusion of contracts, and on transactions, constituted an important source of income for the state apparatus. The *kommerkion* was the main commercial duty imposed on the circulation and sale of merchandise. Until the mid-fourteenth century, it corresponded to a percentage – ranging between 12.5 and 10 per cent – of the value of the goods. The *kommerkion* applied to both foreign and domestic trade. It was also levied on commercial activity at *panegyreis* (fairs). It is worth noting that the lists of complaints regarding treaty violations that Venice submitted to the Byzantine emperor mentioned the *kommerkion* as a kind of professional tax imposed on Greek sailors working on Venetian ships.[74]

During the Palaiologan period, revenues from the *kommerkion* were limited, due to the tax exemptions from commercial duties granted to the Italian naval cities. Proceeds from customs duties would end up in the treasuries of the Genoese of Galata and the Venetians, who had been granted a full exemption from paying the commercial tax. In the mid-fourteenth century, John Kantakouzenos reduced the Byzantine *kommerkion* to 2 per cent in order to increase

Byzantium's customs duties revenues. This policy, however, led to war with Genoa, as the latter saw its commercial interests affected, and to the defeat of the Byzantine fleet. In the fifteenth century, in an effort to find resources, the emperors created new types of *kommerkia*, such as the flour *kommerkion*, salted fish *kommerkion*, and the ship rental *kommerkion*.[75]

In addition to the *kommerkion*, commercial transactions were burdened with a number of commercial duties, which encompassed duties implemented on the movement of people and merchandise (*diabatikion, poriatikon, embletikion, ekbletikion, exereumatikion*), on means of transport and infrastructure (*antinaulon, naulokatartiatikon, limeniatikon, skaliatikon*), and on various transactions (*pratikion, exoprasia, apaitesis* on cloth, *apaitesis* on wheat transported by ships, *metaxiatikon*).

Other indirect taxes concerned the use of professional spaces (*katathesis, ergasteriakon, kapeliatikon, katagogion*). Indirect taxes also included the *embatikion*, a fee the *paroikoi* paid when signing an agreement with the proprietor of land they intended to cultivate. The purpose of certain indirect taxes, such as the *opsonion*★, remains obscure.[76]

Fees paid to state officials

A major portion of the levies on taxpayers went to state officials or professionals as payment for their services. These fees, the *sportula, suffragia, synetheiai*, and *paramythiai*, dated from the Roman period and represented a charge for issuing certificates, for court decisions, or for other services.

Under the Palaiologoi, these entitlements included the rights of *kephalatikion*, the *doukike* and *katepanike dianome*, the *biologion*, and the *katathesis nomismaton*. In the 1317 chrysobull of Andronikos II regarding the city of Monemvasia, it appears that the *kommerkion, diavatikion*, and *poriatikon* were entitlements due to the governors and financial functionaries, while the *opsonion*★ and the *mageiria* were due to other officials.[77] Some taxes probably constituted payment for services related to the measurement of goods (*gomariatikon, zygastikon, kampanistikon, mesitikon, meniatikon, metriatikon, pachiatikon, gouveliatikon*). This category might also include the *kritikon*, a cash payment to judicial functionaries, which is found in the fifteenth century in the Peloponnese.

In addition to paying for services, taxpayers had to provide traveling state officials with accommodation (*aplekton*) or soldiers with winter lodging (*mitaton*).[78] Under the Palaiologoi, the latter term was used for the compulsory sale of wheat at a low price to the governors of a region (*kephalai*), so that they might benefit from its resale.[79]

The fiscal policy of the Palaiologoi

Under the Palaiologoi, the Byzantine state suffered a significant territorial decline accompanied by a weakened economy and military. To cope with the increased government expenditure, the emperors resorted to a policy of granting privileges to members of the upper social class and to foreign powers, especially Venice and Genoa, as compensation for services provided to the state. These privileges were financial and usually consisted of a tax exemption (*exkousseia*). This policy shared common elements with the Western institution of immunity (*immunitas*), and many scholars have seen in this practice evidence of Byzantine feudalization and the privatization of tax revenues. Recently, however, it has been acknowledged that the Byzantine tax exemption did not have the same characteristics as the Western European institution, since its privileges were fiscal rather than administrative, could be revoked by emperors, and were the main means of rewarding individuals and foreign allies for services provided to the State.[80] In the period under study, the recipients of tax exemptions were the following: a) large proprietors, b) some provincial cities, c) foreign powers. Large estate holders, who were members of the imperial family or state officials, and the Church and large monasteries all held their properties either in full ownership or as *pronoiai*.[81] *Exkousseia* was granted to beneficiaries through an imperial chrysobull in which the state renounced its financial rights over large properties and *pronoiai*. The emperor granted or confirmed tax exemptions and assured the recipients of the privileges that their properties would not be harassed by tax officials.[82]

Granting city dwellers privileges was not a new practice. Starting in the twelfth century, emperors used it to show favour to certain cities and the Nicaean emperors and, subsequently, the first Palaiologoi followed this practice. The privileges usually consisted of confirming the city dwellers' property rights over their real estate and releasing them from fiscal obligations to the state.[83] Such privileges were also granted by imperial chrysobull and usually only in exceptional cases, such as when a city was incorporated into the empire or to reward the inhabitants of a city for services to the emperor. Emperor John III Vatatzes (1222–1254) issued a chrysobull awarding privileges to Thessaloniki in Macedonia when the city was incorporated into Byzantium. Additionally, Kroai, present-day Krujë in Albania, received privileges after its conquest by Michael VIII (1259–1282).[84] The privileges Andronikos II (1282–1328) granted the inhabitants of Monemvasia and Ioannina are better-known examples of this practice. In a series of chrysobulls, he exempted the merchants of Monemvasia from commercial duties and from taxation on real estate they had inherited.[85] The surrender of Ioannina to imperial forces in 1318 was considered a great achievement of the Byzantine emperor who hastened to reward the city of Epirus. In 1319, he issued a chrysobull which exempted the inhabitants of Ioannina from paying the *kommerkion* and any other contributions they made according to local custom.[86] The aim of the privileges granted to city dwellers was on the one hand to confirm Byzantine rule after the cities were incorporated into Byzantium or underwent a crisis and on the other to support the local community. More specifically, the cities' tax exemptions from commercial duties sought to strengthen Byzantine trade in the competitive environment created by the Italian naval cities.

Granting privileges and customs exemptions to foreign powers, especially to Venice and Genoa, was a way to reward them for the services they rendered to the empire, usually naval aid. As these powers were engaged in trade in the Byzantine territories, the privileges they obtained were related to commercial duties exemptions and, especially, the *kommerkion*. The exemption from the *kommerkion* was either complete or partial, while its duration could be temporary, lifelong, or hereditary. Byzantium sought to maintain a balance between the naval cities; therefore, the favor the emperors demonstrated to one or the other depended on political circumstances and the requirements of foreign policy. For their part, the naval powers served their own interests and often took advantage of the internal conflicts of the Byzantines to strengthen their position in the trade of the Eastern Mediterranean. When imperial policy infringed on their privileges, they did not hesitate to come into open conflict with Byzantium, as in the so-called War of the Straits (1350–1352).[87]

The emperor's relationship with his subjects was shaped by this management of privileges and tax exemptions. He emerged as the undisputed distributor of state lands and privileges, granting or revoking them depending on the political situation. A case in point was the practice of conceding privileges and tax exemptions, which the opposing sides employed during the civil strife of the fourteenth century to enlist the support of members of the upper class, reward allies, and punish opponents. For example, in the beginning of the civil war between Andronikos III (1328–1341) and his grandfather Andronikos II, the former tried to obtain the backing of the soldiers-*pronoiarioi* of Asia Minor who had lost their property during the

Turkish expansion in the region in the early fourteenth century. The *pronoiarioi* then moved to the European territories of Byzantium where they either acted as destabilizing elements against the ruling dynasty or were employed as mercenaries.[88] Andronikos III granted them *pronoiai* for their support in the struggle against his emperor grandfather. In 1322, after the end of the first phase of the civil war between the two Andronikoi, the old emperor ordered a land census in Macedonia and Thrace in order to restore order to the distribution of land, which had undergone radical changes due to the young Andronikos' concessions of land to his followers.[89]

During the second civil war of the fourteenth century, the balance of power determined property confiscations and land redistribution. The archives of the Monasteries of Mount Athos, for example, provide information on the confiscation of the property of John Kantakouzenos and his supporters by the regency of John V (1341–1391).[90] According to John Kantakouzenos, Guy Lusignan, the governor of Serres and a relative and supporter of John V, ordered the confiscation of the property of Konstantinos Palaiologos, who had initially sided with John Kantakouzenos. Shortly afterwards, in March 1342, when Konstantinos realized the extent of the destruction of his property, he switched sides and supported the regency.[91] In the same year, the regency of John V awarded John Margarites tax revenues amounting to fifty-five *hyperpyra* in the region of Zichna in Eastern Macedonia, which had been taken from supporters of John Kantakouzenos.[92] The political instability caused all those who received privileges to rush to confirm them after each political change.

In some cases, confiscations concerned the income from *pronoiai* that had been granted to churches and monasteries, as well as property that ecclesiastical institutions held in full ownership.[93] The confiscation of monastic property carried out by John V around 1370 and Manuel II around 1403 to strengthen the military *pronoiai* was one such case. This practice, usually aimed at financing military operations and strengthening the defence of the state, was implemented by the emperors until the first quarter of the fifteenth century.[94]

In addition to the policy of granting privileges and tax exemptions, thus ensuring the beneficiaries would provide services to the state, the emperors resorted to imposing extraordinary taxes to cover increased military and defence expenditures. In 1300 and 1304, Andronikos II took extraordinary tax measures to cover the payroll of the Alanian and Catalan mercenaries. Subsequently, other emperors resorted to extraordinary taxation to meet extraordinary military expenses; this occurred when Andronikos III undertook a struggle against the Turks in 1334/6, and when John VI Kantakouzenos (1347–1454) sought to finance a war against Genoa and the construction of a fleet. After 1404, Manuel II imposed a new tax, the *kokkiatikon*, associated with his effort to meet the expenditure for nourishing the fleet's crew.[95]

Extraordinary taxation was a source of income for the repair and maintenance of fortifications or the construction of new fortifications.[96] Michael VIII's demand that *kastroktisia* be exacted from monastic properties was associated with the emperor's effort to strengthen the state's defenses by building fortresses.[97] In 1428, Emperor John VIII (1425–1448) demanded that the *phloriatikon* and the *kephalaia* – taxes imposed for the above-mentioned purpose – be used for the restoration of the Hexamilion, the barrier-wall that defended the Peloponnesos against an attack from the north.[98] Additionally in 1442, Theodoros Palaiologos, the *Despot* of the Peloponnesos, stipulated that the income from the *abiotikion* would finance the repair of the fortification of Monemvasia.[99] The frequent demand for the *bigliatikon* from the mid-fourteenth century on and its exemption from *exkousseiai* is indicative of the importance of this tax for the staffing and function of the garrisons in the provinces.[100]

In addition, the Palaiologoi resorted to extraordinary taxation to finance the construction of a fleet, something necessary for the state to break free from the naval cities of Italy. One such case was Michael VIII's demand of *katergoktisia* in order to build ships.[101] Independence from foreign maritime forces was also demanded by the rising merchant class, which made its presence felt during the Second Civil War of the fourteenth century. *Megas Doux* Alexios Apokaukos, a member of the regency of John V took a series of measures to strengthen Byzantium's naval power and limit the privileges of Western merchants. Apokaukos imposed a new tax on grain imported from the Black Sea and from areas that once belonged to Byzantium, such as the coast of Asia Minor. Wheat belonged to the class of banned products, whose trade was under the emperor's strict control.[102] The state's protectionist policy extended to the trade of wine and salted fish, which constituted an important source of revenue for the state treasury. Apokaukos banned all foreign traders from the retail sale of wine in Constantinople. He also installed a customs station in Ieron at the northern entrance of the Bosphorus to better control the passage of ships and the collection of commercial duties.[103] Upon assuming the throne in 1347, John VI Kantakouzenos continued this policy, imposing two new taxes on the importation of wheat as well as on the purchase of wine directly from the producers, while reducing the *kommerkion* all merchants in Constantinople paid to 2 per cent.[104] This was followed by protests from the Genoese and the Venetians who saw their commercial interests affected and the Byzantine defeat in the War of the Straits (1350–1352). Despite this defeat, starting in the second half of the fourteenth century, members of the Byzantine upper class, including high-ranking state officials, such as Georgios Goudeles and Nikolaos Notaras, became involved in commercial activities.[105]

After the mid-fourteenth century, when Serbian and Ottoman expansion into Byzantine territory led to the decline of large estates and a reduction in agricultural tax revenues, the state turned its attention to managing trade taxes. In 1418, for example, Emperor Manuel II (1391–1425) imposed a tax on the wine consumed by Venetians in their homes or in taverns. Despite Venetian protests, the tax remained in effect until the following year, when it was limited to wine consumed in taverns. Konstantinos XI (1449–1453), the last emperor of Byzantium, turned to taxing wine and the leather trade in order to strengthen public finances.[106]

From the fourteenth century on, apart from managing direct and indirect taxes, the Palaiologoi were faced with paying taxes to the Ottomans. Andronikos III was the first who was called upon to pay tribute to maintain sovereignty over certain Bithynian cities in Asia Minor.[107] During the reign of John V, Byzantium became an Ottoman tributary state, paying taxes and providing military support. This subjection lasted until the Mongols defeated the Ottomans at the Battle of Ankara in 1402, when Byzantium was temporarily relieved of its burdens and was able to reacquire parts of Macedonia, the Black Sea, the Sea of Marmara, and the Sporades.[108]

The strict tax policy of the Palaiologoi, especially the first members of the dynasty, sought to meet the demands of the state's foreign and domestic policy. The result was intense protests, which manifested in the works of the intellectuals of the time as well as in uprisings. Particular mention should be made of the historian Georgios Pachymeres' criticism of the fiscal policy of Michael VIII Palaiologos, which had catastrophic consequences for the state's eastern provinces as well as for all taxpayers, while allowing some tax officials to enrich themselves at taxpayer expense. Pachymeres compared Michael's policy to that of his predecessors, the Nicaean emperors, John III and Theodore II (1254–1258), whom he presented as paragons. According to the historian, John III had exempted his citizens from taxes and contributed to the needs of the state with income from the exploitation of public lands.[109] Patriarchs also criticized the fiscal policy of the first two Palaiologoi. Patriarch Arsenios Autoreianos (1254–1260 / 1261–1264), who opposed Michael VIII because he had usurped the imperial throne from John IV Laskares (1258–1261), condemned the rising of taxes by the emperor. Patriarchs Gregory II of Cyprus (1283–1289) and John XII Kosmas (1294–1303) protested against the measures imposed on church property and asked Andronikos II to grant citizens relief from the tax burdens.[110] Moreover, Patriarch Athanasios I (1289–1293 / 1303–1309) issued a decree in 1304 asking the same emperor to reduce taxes.[111] In the second half of the fourteenth century, Nikolaos Kabasilas and the Metropolitan of Thessaloniki, Isidoros, protested against the confiscation of ecclesiastical property.[112]

The intellectual Thomas Magistros strongly criticized the tax policy of Andronikos II in his treatise *On the Imperial Office*. Magistros, one of the most important scholars of Thessaloniki in the early fourteenth century, was sympathetic to the merchant class. His work deals with the relationship between ruler and subject. A common line of argument in this work is that the emperor must possess the virtues of justice, generosity, and charity. These must be expressed through concessions to his subjects, such as rendering the *pronoiai* hereditary. Magistros considered that taxation was harmful to the population and opposed the imposition of supplementary taxes. According to him, the emperor must pay for extraordinary expenses from the public treasury. He urged the emperor to protect merchants and enhance the autonomy of the cities.[113] In the second half of the fourteenth century, Georgios of Pelagonia criticized the fiscal policy of John V in his *Life of Saint John the Merciful*. He condemned the political choice of the Palaiologoi to increase taxes and confiscate the property of their subjects and contrasted this practice with the decision of the Nicean emperor John III Vatatzes to distribute money and properties to his subjects.[114]

As mentioned above, the Palaiologoi's strict fiscal policy incited uprisings. The uprisings of the Peloponnesian nobility against the new taxes imposed for the construction of the Hexamilion in the late fourteenth and early fifteenth century are a good example. Work on this large defensive wall began with the appointment of *Despot* Theodoros Palaiologos, son of John V, as Governor of Peloponnesos. The Peloponnesian magnates opposed his measures at the instigation of the circle of the Kantakouzenoi, the previous governors of the region. Furthermore, these reactions continued during the reign of Manuel II.[115]

The resentment and protests of the social groups whose interests were affected by fiscal policy, be it Church and monasteries or landowners and merchants forced the emperors to enlist court rhetoric to support their political choices.[116] Imperial propaganda promoted the ideal of an emperor who ruled on the basis of his personal virtues, which were rewarded by Divine Providence.[117] The scholar Theodoros Metochites, a high official in the court of Andronikos II, responded to his contemporaries' criticism of the emperor's policy in his *Miscellanea* treatise. For Metochites, taxation was necessary for the function of the state and to cover the expenses of the army and the administration. He also considered it useful to recruit foreign mercenaries to defend the empire. Regarding the distribution of wealth, he advocated that the emperor grant privileges to members of the upper social class.[118] Apart from Metochites, the historian Nikephoros Gregoras, a member of the court of Andronikos II, argued in his work that the emperor's tax increases were justified, as they were necessary for the survival of the state and brought the expected results.[119]

Also worth mentioning is the panegyric (*enkomion*) written between 1423 and 1427 by Isidoros of Kiev praising the emperors Manuel II and John VIII Palaiologos. It referred to, among other virtues, the emperor's spirit of justice towards his subjects. This was, in fact, a defence of the economic policy of the two Palaiologoi and a justification for the excessive tax increases, which burdened the entire population of the capital.[120] The scholar-emperor Manuel II himself supported in his letters the necessity of taking fiscal measures and their effect on the local community. The treatises of Georgios Gemistos Plethon on the administration of the Peloponnesos should also be included in this category of texts supporting imperial fiscal policy. The measures Plethon proposed, such as reconstructing the Hexamilion, granting land to soldiers, etc., had already been adopted by the emperors. Therefore, these treatises should be understood as texts that supported imperial policy in the Peloponnesian peninsula.[121]

Court propaganda regarding fiscal policy was part of the wider context of the political ideology of the time, which was based on a more humanitarian approach to the imperial institution. The emperor appeared to rely more on his personal virtues for the exercise of government and less on Divine Providence. Imperial propaganda attributed the decline of the state and the common plights to divine punishment for the sins of the Byzantine people. It was only due to the emperors' virtuous policy that Divine Providence aided Byzantium, such as when the Ottomans were defeated at the Battle of Ankara in 1402, prolonging the life of the state. In the matter of fiscal policy, the assistance of Divine Providence served as an excuse for imposing tax measures.[122]

To summarize, during the turbulent period of the last two centuries of Byzantium, the Palaiologoi were unable to reform the organization of public finances and thus adapt to the challenges of the time and the prospects of international trade. The emperors continued to distribute public resources and fiscal privileges according to the political situation. Their fiscal policy, however, should be described as short-sighted and opportunistic, as it aimed to ensure their political acceptance by serving the interests of the social forces that supported the government at any given time. The administrative and defence function of the state was based on a policy of managing privileges and on the opportunistic shift to extraordinary taxation when the policy of privileges was unsuccessful. The increase in supplementary taxes from the mid-thirteenth to the mid-fourteenth century shows that the state could still use taxation to improve public finances. However, the reduction in the number of direct taxes from the mid-fourteenth and, especially, the early fifteenth century testifies to the devastation of public finances that followed the civil wars as well as to the territorial losses that hindered the smooth operation of taxation. From then on, the only option for improving public finances was the shift to boosting Byzantine trade and imposing commercial duties. However, the new indirect taxes devised in the early fifteenth century primarily served an ideological purpose that strengthened the emperor's image as the distributor of state revenues, rather than a practical one that met basic state needs. Thus, the latter Palaiologoi functioned more as managers of the period of constant crisis, which they were called upon to face, rather than as creators of new financial practices.

Notes

1 Oikonomides, "The Role of the Byzantine State", p. 979; Kontogiannopoulou, "La fiscalité à Byzance", p. 5.
2 Clark, *Taxation*, p. 98.
3 See mainly, Dölger, *Beiträge*; Dölger., "Zum Gebührenwesen der Byzantiner"; Karayannopulos, *Das Finanzwesen*; Ostrogorsky, "Byzance"; Svoronos, "Recherches sur le cadastre"; Lefort, "Fiscalité médiévale"; Oikonomidès, *Fiscalité et exemption*; Kontogiannopoulou, "La fiscalité à Byzance"; Smyrlis, "The Fiscal Revolution".
4 Oikonomides, "The Role of the Byzantine State", pp. 973–980.
5 Karayannopulos, *Das Finanzwesen*, pp. 28–43; Segrè, "Studies in Byzantine Economy". For the measurement of land for fiscal purposes see *Géométries du fisc byzantin*.
6 For the various kinds of *modii* see, Schilbach, *Byzantinische Metrologie*, pp. 56–59.
7 Oikonomidès, *Fiscalité*, pp. 49–51, 67–68.
8 Antoniadis-Bibicou, *Recherches sur les douanes*, pp. 107–122; Oikonomidès, "The Role of the Byzantine State", p. 1050.
9 Kontogiannopoulou, "La fiscalité à Byzance", p. 7 n. 13; Oikonomidès, "The Role of the Byzantine State", pp. 1026–1029; Estangüi Gómez, *Byzance face aux Ottomans*, pp. 30–32, 71–84.
10 We mainly mention the documents from the Monasteries of Mount Athos (in the series Archives de l'Athos: Chilandar, Dionysiou, Docheiariou, Esphigménou, Iviron, Kutlumus, Lavra,

Saint-Pantéléèmôn, Vatopédi, Xénophon, Xéropotamou, and also *Actes de Zographou*, *Actes de Philothée*, *Actes de Chilandar* of Louis Petit and Basile Korablev edition), the documents from the Monastery of Saint-John the Prodrome in Serres (see ed. Guillou, Bénou) and from the Monastery of Saint-John the Theologian in Patmos (see ed. Vranoussi). Also, we notice the documents from the Miklosich-Müller collection (MM), the treaties concluded between Byzantium and foreign powers (see Tafel and Thomas, *Urkunden*; *DVL*; Thiriet, *Régestes*).

11 *Georges Pachymérès*.
12 *Nicephori Gregorae Byzantina Historia*.
13 *Ioannis Cantacuzeni ex imperatoris Historiarum Libri IV*.
14 See mainly the correspondence of Patriarch Gregory II of Cyprus, of Patriarch Athanasios I, of Demetrios Kydones, the literary works of Nikolaos Kabasilas, Thomas Magistros, Theodoros Metochites and others.
15 Laiou and Morrisson, *The Byzantine Economy*, pp. 224–225.
16 Oikonomidès, "The Role of the Byzantine State", p. 1050.
17 For the shift of the aristocracy to commercial activities from the middle of the fourteenth century onwards, see *Acta et Diplomata Graeca Medii Aevi*, p. 374, 378, 384, 463, 543 and *passim*; *Il libro dei conti di Giacomo Badoer*, p. 19, 27, 29, 108, 135, 148, 153 and *passim*; Thiriet, *Regestes*, no 237. Cf. Oikonomidès, *Hommes d'affaires grecs*, pp. 120–123.
18 For *logothetes* and their bureaus (*logothesia*) see Guilland, "Les logothètes".
19 Eustratiades (ed.), Γρηγορίου τοῦ Κυπρίου οἰκουμενικοῦ πατριάρχου ἐπιστολαῖ καὶ μῦθοι, p. 94, 122; Fatouros (ed.), *Die Briefe*, p. 287: "νῦν δὴ τὸ τῆς σῆς φιλανθρωπίας βάρος μέλλει δοκιμάζεσθαι, ὅτε τὸν ἐπὶ ταῖς ἡμῶν ἀμπέλοις φόρον ὅσον δή τινα αὐτὸν τοῖς ταμείοις τοῦ βασιλικοῦ χρυσοῦ ἡμᾶς ἐμβάλλειν νομιεῖς".
20 *Actes de Lavra II*, l. 37–39: "Παρακαλῶ δὲ καὶ τὸν κραταιὸν καὶ ἅγιον ἡμῶν αὐθέντην καὶ βασιλέα ἵνα καὶ ὅπου ἂν ἀλλαχοῦ ἀναφανῇ πρᾶγμα ἐμὸν ἀφαιρεθὲν ἐν τῇ προγεγονυίᾳ ἐκ βασιλικῆς προσταγῆς κατασχέσει τῆς οἰκείας μου, ἄνευ τοῦ εἰσκομισθέντος ἐν τῷ βασιλικῷ βεστιαρίῳ, πᾶν ὁποῖον ἂν καὶ εἴη".
21 One such case were the revenues derived from *euresis thesaurou*, MM V, p. 82: "ἔτι ἵνα γένηται εὕρεσις θησαυροῦ ἐκεῖσε παρά τινος, εἰ μὲν κατὰ ἀλήθειαν ἔνι τοῦτο, ἀναλαμβάνηται αὐτὸ τὸ μέλλον εὑρεθῆναι καὶ εἰσκομίζηται εἰς τὸ θεοφρούρητον βεστιάριον".
22 *Actes de Lavra II*, no 99 (1304).
23 *Actes de Philothée*, no 2 (1284); *Diplomatarium Veneto-Levantinum*, v. I, no 74; *Georges Pachymérès* I, p. 307; *Pseudo-Kodinos*, p. 139, 186 (see also the new edition: Macrides, Munitiz and Angelov, *Pseudo-Kodinos*, p. 110).
24 *Pseudo-Kodinos*, p. 139, 186 = *Pseudo-Kodinos*, ed. Ruth Macrides, J.A. Munitiz, Dimiter Angelov, p. 110).
25 *Pseudo-Kodinos* (ed. Jean Verpeaux), pp. 139, 186–187. For the office of *logariastes* see Guilland, "Études sur l'histoire administrative". For the function of the *vestiarion* during the reign of Andronikos II Palaiologos see Kontogiannopoulou, *Η εσωτερική πολιτική*, pp. 210–215.
26 *Actes d'Esphigménou*, no 14 (1318). Cf. Estangüi Gómez, *Byzance face aux Ottomans*, pp. 366–386.
27 *Actes de Vatopédi III*, no 211 (1418); *Actes de Dionysiou*, no 25 (1430). Cf. Kontogiannopoulou, "Autonomy".
28 MM IV, p. 261; *Actes d'Iviron III*, no 76 (1320).
29 Lefort, "Observations diplomatiques"; Kravari, "L'enregistrement des paysans"; Kontogiannopoulou, "La fiscalité à Byzance", pp. 8–9.
30 *Actes de Xéropotamou*, no 21 (1322–1334); *Actes de Chilandar*, no 103 (1324).
31 Guillou (ed.), *Les archives*, no 5 (1312); *Actes de Vatopédi I*, no 62 (1324).
32 *Actes de Lavra II*, no 89 (1298).
33 *Actes d'Iviron III*, no 76 (1320).
34 *Actes de Dionysiou*, no 20 (1421). For the office of *apographeis* see Kontogiannopoulou, *Η εσωτερική πολιτική*, pp. 215–219.
35 *Actes de Vatopédi II*, no 147 (1375); Schilbach, *Byzantinische Metrologie*; *Géometries du fisc byzantin*, p. 248.
36 Μεσαιωνική Βιβλιοθήκη, v. VI, pp. 641–642.
37 Bénou (ed.), *Le codex B*, v. I, no 161 (1317).
38 Fatouros, *Die Briefe*, p. 287.
39 Kontogiannopoulou, *Η εσωτερική πολιτική*, p. 221.

40 Γρηγορίου Κυπρίου Εγκώμιον εις τον αυτοκράτορα κυρόν Ανδρόνικον τον Παλαιολόγον, p. 386.
41 EUSTRATIADES (ed.), Γρηγορίου τοῦ Κυπρίου οἰκουμενικοῦ πατριάρχου ἐπιστολαῖ, no 134. Patriarch Athanasios I, also, protested against the abuses of tax collectors, see MAFFRY TALBOT (ed.), *The Correspondence*, no 17, 18, 27, 77, 87.
42 *John Kantakouzenos* II, pp. 58–63.
43 *Nikephoros Gregoras* II, p. 741.
44 EUSTRATIADES (ed.), Γρηγορίου τοῦ Κυπρίου οἰκουμενικοῦ πατριάρχου ἐπιστολαῖ, no 116.
45 EUSTRATIADES (ed.), Γρηγορίου τοῦ Κυπρίου οἰκουμενικοῦ πατριάρχου ἐπιστολαῖ, no 117, 118.
46 For *kommerkiarioi* see DUNN, "The Kommerkiarios"; OIKONOMIDÈS, "The Kommerkiarios".
47 Francesco Balducci Pegolotti, *La pratica della mercatura*, ed. Allan Evans, Cambridge, Massachusetts 1936, p. 41. Cf. KONTOGIANNOPOULOU, *Η εσωτερική πολιτική*, pp. 223–224.
48 MATSCHKE, "Commerce, Trade", p. 804.
49 KIOUSOPOULOU, *Emperor or Manager*, p. 106.
50 The notion of tax is presented in the sources by the term *telos* (τέλος) and *kephalaion* (κεφάλαιον). See accordingly *Actes de Philothée*, no 10 (1355); *Actes de Saint-Pantéléèmôn*, no 10 (1311).
51 For the *allelengyon*, the collective tax liability of the peasants, see KAPLAN, *Les hommes*, pp. 439–440.
52 *Actes de Zographou*, no 17 (1320), no 39 (1357). Cf. KONTOGIANNOPOULOU, "La fiscalité à Byzance", pp. 9–10.
53 *Actes de Saint-Pantéléèmôn*, no 10 (1311); GUILLOU (ed.), *Les archives*, no 24 (1329), no 26 (1332).
54 *Actes de Lavra* II, no 104 (1317); *Actes d'Iviron* IV, no 86 (1341).
55 *Actes de Xénophon*, no. 15 (1321); *Actes de Philothée*, no 9 (1346).
56 *Actes de Chilandar*, no 45 (1319); *Actes d'Esphigménou*, no 22 (1346).
57 *Actes de Lavra* II, no 109 (1321).
58 MM, IV, p. 352 (1266); MM, V, p. 83 (1319).
59 For these taxes see *Actes de Chilandar I*, no 43 (1319), Appendix II (1300); *Actes d'Iviron III*, no 70 (1301), 72 (1310), 74 (1316).
60 *Actes de Chilandar*, no 62 (1321); *Actes de Kutlumus*, no 38 (1386).
61 *Actes de Lavra* II, no 104 (1317), 109 (1321).
62 For these taxes and their meaning see, KONTOGIANNOPOULOU, "La fiscalité à Byzance", pp. 27–33.
63 *Prebenda*★ was a levy, basically in kind, on ecclesiastical as well as secular properties. *Pozobitze*★ and *preselitza* were probably levies required for feeding of horses and soldiers. See BEES, "Fragments d'un chrysobulle", p. 486; DÖLGER, *Regesten der Kaiserurkunden*, v. 4, no 2823 (1336); SOLOVJEV and MOŠIN (ed.), *Grčke povelje Srpskih vladara*, no 20 (1348). Also, the *govbeliatikon* or *koubeliatikon* was a supplementary charge of Slavic origin. See *Actes de Vatopédi II*, no 93 (1346); *Actes de Xénophon*, no 29 (1352). Cf. KONTOGIANNOPOULOU, "Φορολογικές πληροφορίες για τη Θεσσαλία από προνομιακά έγγραφα του 13^{ου} και 14^{ου} αιώνα", pp. 172–176.
64 OIKONOMIDÈS, "Ottoman Influence", pp. 5–9.
65 For the *angareia* see mainly, STAVRIDOU-ZAFRAKA, "Η αγγαρεία στο Βυζάντιο".
66 For these compulsory services see KONTOGIANNOPOULOU, "La fiscalité à Byzance", pp. 18–20.
67 *Actes d'Esphigménou*, no 22 (1346); *Actes de Docheiariou*, no 53 (1409).
68 *Actes de Zographou*, no 26 (1327), no 37 (1346).
69 *Actes de Saint-Pantéléèmôn*, no. 10 (1311). Cf. TOURTOGLOU, Παρθενοφθορία και εὕρεσις θησαυροῦ, p. 68.
70 LAIOU, "Le débat sur les droits".
71 LEMERLE, "Un chrysobulle". Cf. KONTOGIANNOPOULOU, "La fiscalité à Byzance", p. 25.
72 *Actes de Lavra* II, no 71 (1259); *Actes de Philothée*, no 3 (1287).
73 *Actes de Vatopédi* III, no 191 (1404), no 206 (1415). For *gasmouloi*, who were offspring of mixed Latin and Greek unions in the late byzantine period see MALTEZOU, "Παρατηρήσεις στο θεσμό της βενετικής υπηκοότητας. Προστατευόμενοι της Βενετίας στον λατινοκρατούμενο ελληνικό χώρο (13^{ος}-15^{ος} αι.)", pp. 10–12.
74 MM V, pp. 165–167 (1317); *Actes de Vatopédi* II, no 109 (1356); in latin *comerclo*: see mainly TAFEL and THOMAS (ed.), *Urkunden*, v. III, no 358 (1268); *DVL*, I, no 73–74, 77–79 (1319–1320).
75 *Nikephoros Gregoras* II, p. 842, 844–867. Cf. GANCHOU, "Giacomo Badoer", pp. 94–95; KIOUSOPOULOU, *Emperor or Manager*, p. 106.
76 VRANOUSSI (ed.), Βυζαντινά έγγραφα της μονής Πάτμου, Α' – αυτοκρατορικά; *Actes de Philothée*, no 3 (1287); *Actes de Lavra* II, no 104 (1317); MM V, pp. 166–167 (1317); *Actes de Lavra* III, no. 118 (1329). For *opsonion*★ see KONTOGIANNOPOULOU, "La fiscalité à Byzance", pp. 39–40, n. 218.
77 MM V, p. 167 (1317).

78 *Actes de Lavra* II, no 71 (1259); *Actes de Vatopédi* I, no 62 (1324).
79 KONTOGIANNOPOULOU, "La fiscalité à Byzance", pp. 40–43.
80 ESTANGÜI GÓMEZ, *Byzance face aux Ottomans*, p. 71.
81 *Pronoia* consisting in the concession of land and its tax revenues to individuals or corporations usually as a way of compensation for their services since the 11th century. The concession was usually for life and was granted by imperial chrysobull, on the basis of which the tax assessors recorded the delimitation of the land (*periorismos*), the peasants who cultivated it, and the buildings that were in it in the so-called *praktikon*. All of these constituted the income (*posoteta*) of the *pronoia*, which was valued in money. The *praktika* were registered with the central financial office and copied into a code, which was called *thesis* or *megale thesis*. In each census, the *praktika* were revised and updated. For the institution of *pronoia* see mainly KAZHDAN, "*Pronoia*"; KARAYANNOPOULOS, "Ein Beitrag zur Militärpronoia"; BARTUSIS, *Land and Privilege*.
82 *Actes de Philothée*, no 3 (1287): "οὐδενὸς ὀφείλοντος ἐπάγειν τῇ κατ' αὐτοὺς τοιαύτῃ σεβασμίᾳ μονῇ ἢ τοῖς προσοῦσιν ὡς εἴρηται κτήμασι καὶ λοιποῖς δικαίοις λύμην ὁποιανοῦν καὶ ἐπήρειαν, μήτε ὁ κατὰ τὴν ἡμέραν κεφαλαττικεύων μήτε ὁ δουκεύων μήτε ὁ ἐπ' ἐξουσίᾳ πάσῃ".
83 KYRITSES, "The 'Common Chrysobulls'".
84 OIKONOMIDÈS, "Andronic II Paléologue".
85 MM V, pp. 154–155 (1284), 165–168 (1317).
86 MM V, pp. 77–84 (1319).
87 *Nikephoros Gregoras* II, pp. 844–867; *John Kantakouzenos* III, pp. 68–80. Cf. KONTOGIANNOPOULOU, *Η εσωτερική πολιτική*, pp. 253–260.
88 *Georges Pachymérès* IV, p. 425, 433, 447.
89 *John Kantakouzenos* I, p. 169. For confiscations of properties during the first civil conflict of the fourteenth century see also *Nikephoros Gregoras* I, pp. 352–353; *John Kantakouzenos* I, p. 119, 287.
90 LEMERLE, "Un chrysobulle d'Andronic II", pp. 428–446.
91 *John Kantakouzenos* II, pp. 196.
92 BÉNOU (ed.), *Le Codex B*, no 206.
93 SMYRLIS, "The State, the Land", pp. 59–61.
94 The emperors Michael VIII, Andronikos II, John VI, and John V effected this policy to meet military expenditure, see *Georges Pachymérès*, III, p. 81, IV, p. 425, 541; *Actes de Vatopédi* I, no 16 (1265); *Actes de Docheiariou*, no 33 (1355); *Actes de Vatopédi* III, no 199 (1408), no 206 (1415). Cf. ESTANGÜI GÓMEZ, *Byzance face aux Ottomans*, pp. 242–254.
95 *Georges Pachymérès*, IV, p. 539; *Nikephoros Gregoras* I, p. 205, 524, II, p. 856, 870. For the meaning of *kokkiatikon* see KATSONE, "Κόκκος σίτου και κόκκος βαφική. Το πρόβλημα ερμηνείας του κόκκου στις βυζαντινές πηγές και η σημασία του για την οικονομία και τη φορολογία", pp. 67–68.
96 MM II, p. 501, where the imposition of extraordinary taxes for the maintenance of the fortress of Constantinople is mentioned.
97 MM IV, p. 332 (1272).
98 LAMPROS, Παλαιολόγεια και Πελοποννησιακά, vol. III, pp. 331–333, vol. IV, pp. 104–105.
99 MM V, pp. 174–175.
100 *Actes de Vatopédi* II, no 114 (1359); *Actes de Vatopédi* III, no 165 (1387), no 213 (1419), no 227 (1442).
101 MM IV, p. 332 (1272).
102 The other barren products were the salt and for a period of time the mastic. For the provisions on their circulation see KONTOGIANNOPOULOU, *Η εσωτερική πολιτική του Ανδρονίκου Β'*, pp. 202–203, 257–260.
103 *John Kantakouzenos* II, p. 522.
104 *Nikephoros Gregoras* II, p. 842.
105 GANCHOU, "L'ultime testament"; MATSCHKE, *Die Schlacht bei Ankara*, p. 175 s.
106 THIRIET, *Regestes*, II, no 1688, no 1705, no. 1757; THIRIET, *Regestes*, III, no 2831, no 2834; *DVL*, II, no 207 (1450).
107 *John Kantakouzenos* I, pp. 446–448.
108 DENNIS, "The Byzantine-Turkish Treaty of 1403".
109 ANGELOV, *Imperial Ideology*, pp. 269–280.
110 *Georges Pachymérès* I, p. 283; IV, pp. 321–327; EUSTRATIADES, Γρηγορίου τοῦ Κυπρίου ἐπιστολαῖ, no 120, 129, 132.
111 ZEPOI (ed.), *Jus Graecoromanum*, vol. I, pp. 533–536. Cf. TOURTOGLOU, "Παρατηρήσεις επί της φερομένης ως Νεαράς 26 του Ανδρονίκου Β' Παλαιολόγου".

112 ŠEVČENKO, "Nicolas Cabasilas", pp. 91–125; LAOURDAS (ed.), Ἰσιδώρου ἀρχιεπισκόπου Θεσσαλονίκης ὁμιλίαι εἰς τὰς ἑορτὰς τοῦ ἁγίου Δημητρίου, no 4. See also, CONGOURDEAU, "Les énigmes du discours".
113 TOMA MAGISTRO, ch. 5, 20, 21, 23–24.
114 HEISENBERG, "Kaiser Johannes Batatzes".
115 DENNIS (ed.), The Letters, no 51, no 68. Cf. NECIPOĞLU, Byzantium, pp. 236–238.
116 The prefaces of imperial documents (prooimia), the imperial panegyrics, funeral speeches, and mirror of princes are considered as the principal genres using court rhetoric to advocate political causes. See Elizabeth JEFFREYS (ed.), Rhetoric in Byzantium, London 2003; ANGELOV, Imperial Ideology.
117 Démétrius Cydonès, vol. I, no 14; Μανουὴλ τοῦ Παλαιολόγου, Ὑποθῆκαι βασιλικῆς ἀγωγῆς, PG, 156, pp. 313–384.
118 Theodori Metochitae, ch. 82–83, ch. 85, ch. 98.
119 Nikephoros Gregoras I, p. 317.
120 Lampros, Παλαιολόγεια καὶ Πελοποννησιακά, vol. III, pp. 132–199.
121 Adolf Ellissen, Analekten der mittel- und neugriechischen Literatur, IV. 2, Leipzig 1860, pp. 41–59, 60–84; LAMPROS, Παλαιολόγεια καὶ Πελοποννησιακά, v. III, pp. 246–265, 309–312; v. IV, pp. 113–135.
122 For a new approach on the function of the imperial propaganda under the last Palaiologoi see ESTANGÜI GÓMEZ, Byzance face aux Ottomans, pp. 449–452.

References

Acta et Diplomata Graeca Medii Aevi, I–VI, ed. Franz MIKLOSICH and Joseph MÜLLER, Vienna, 1860–1890.
Actes de Chilandar, ed. Louis PETIT and Basile KORABLEV, Actes de l'Athos V, *Vizantiyskiy Vremennik*, 17, 1975.
Actes de Chilandar I. Des origines à 1319, ed. Mirjana ŽIVOJINOVIĆ, Vassiliki KRAVARI and Christophe GIROS, Paris, 1998.
Actes de Dionysiou, ed. Nicolas OIKONOMIDÈS, Paris, 1968.
Actes de Docheiariou, ed. Nicolas OIKONOMIDÈS, Paris, 1984.
Actes d'Esphigménou, ed. Jacques LEFORT, Paris, 1973.
Actes d'Iviron III. De 1204 à 1328, ed. Jacques LEFORT et allii, Paris, 1994.
Actes d'Iviron IV. De 1328 au début du XVIe siècle, ed. Jacques LEFORT et allii, Paris, 1995.
Actes de Kutlumus, ed. Paul LEMERLE, Paris, 1988.
Actes de Lavra II. De 1204 à 1328, ed. Paul LEMERLE et al., Paris, 1977.
Actes de Lavra III. De 1329 à 1500, ed. Paul LEMERLE et al., Paris,1979.
Actes de Philothée, ed. Vasilij REGEL, Eduard KURTZ, Basile KORABLEV, Actes de l'Athos VI, *Vizantiyskiy Vremennik*, 20, 1913.
Actes de Saint-Pantéléèmôn, ed. Paul LEMERLE, Gilbert DAGRON, Sima ĆIRKOVIĆ, Paris, 1982.
Actes de Vatopédi I. Des origines à 1329, ed. Jacques BOMPAIRE et allii, Paris, 2001.
Actes de Vatopédi II. De 1330 à 1376, ed. Jacques LEFORT et allii, Paris, 2006.
Actes de Vatopédi III. De 1377 à 1500, ed. Jacques LEFORT et allii, Paris, 2014.
Actes de Xénophon, ed. Denise PAPACHRYSSANTHOU, Paris, 1986.
Actes de Xéropotamou, ed. Jacques BOMPAIRE, Paris, 1964.
Actes de Zographou, ed. Vasilij REGEL, Eduard KURTZ and Basile KORABLEV, Actes de l'Athos IV, *Vizantiyskiy Vremennik*, 13, 1907.
Dimiter ANGELOV, *Imperial Ideology and Political Thought in Byzantium, 1204–1330*, Cambridge, 2007.
Mark BARTUSIS, *Land and Privilege in Byzantium. The Institution of Pronoia*, Cambridge, 2012.
Hélène ANTONIADIS-BIBICOU, *Recherches sur les douanes à Byzance*, Paris, 1963.
Nikos BEES, "Fragments d'un chrysobulle du couvent de Lycousada", in *Mélanges offerts à Octave et Melpo Merlier*, v. 3, Athens, 1957, pp. 479–486.
Lisa BÉNOU, (ed.), *Le codex B du monastère Saint-Jean-Prodrome (Serrès)*, v. I (XIIIe–XVe siècles), Paris, 1998.
Patrick CLARK, *Taxation and the Formation of the Late Roman Social Contract*, PhD Dissertation University of California Berkeley, 2017.
Marie-Helene CONGOURDEAU, "Les énigmes du discours de Nicolas Cabasilas contre les archontes", in *Nea Rhome*, 7, 2011, pp. 169–188.
Démétrius Cydonès, Correspondance, ed. Raymond-Joseph. LOENERTZ, vols. I–II, Vatican, 1956–1960.
George DENNIS, *Byzantium and the Franks, 1350–1420*, London, 1982.

George Dennis, "The Byzantine-Turkish Treaty of 1403", in *Orientalia christiana periodica*, 33, 1967, pp. 72–88.
George Dennis (ed.), *The Letters of Manuel II*, Washington, 1977.
Diplomatarium Veneto-Levantinum sive acta et diplomata res Venetas Graecas atque Levantis illustrantia, a. 1300–1350, ed. Georg Martin Thomas and Riccardo Predelli, vol. I, Venice, 1880, vol. II, ed. Georg Martin Thomas, Venice, 1899.
Franz Dölger, *Regesten der Kaiserurkunden des oströmischen Reiches*, v. 4, Munich, 1960.
Archie Dunn, "The Kommerkiarios, the apotheke, the dromos, the vardarios, and the west", in *Byzantine and Modern Greek Studies*, 17, 1993, pp. 3–24.
Adolf Ellissen, *Analekten der mittel- und neugriechischen Literatur*, IV. 2, Leipzig, 1860.
Raúl Estangüi Gómez, *Byzance face aux Ottomans. Exercice du pouvoir et contrôle du territoire sous les derniers Paléologues (milieu XIVe – milieu XVe siècle)*, Paris, 2014.
Sophronios Eustratiades (ed.), Γρηγορίου τοῦ Κυπρίου οἰκουμενικοῦ πατριάρχου ἐπιστολαῖ καὶ μῦθοι, Alexandria, 1910.
Georgios Fatouros (ed.), *Die Briefe des Michael Gabras (ca. 1290-nach 1350)*, vol. I–II, Vienna, 1973.
Francesco Balducci Pegolotti, La pratica della mercatura, ed. Allan Evans, Cambridge, Massachusetts, 1936.
Thierry Ganchou, "Giacomo Badoer et kyr Théodoros Batatzès, 'chomerchier di pesi' à Constantinople (flor. 1401–1449)", in *Revue des études byzantines*, 61, 2003, pp. 49–95.
Thierry Ganchou, "L'ultime testament de Géôrgios Goudélès, homme d'affaires, mésazôn de Jean V et ktètôr (Constantinople, 4 mars 1421)", in *Mélanges Cécile Morrisson (TM 16)*, 2010, pp. 277–358.
Géométries du fisc byzantin, ed. Jacques Lefort et al., Paris, 1991.
Georges Pachymérès, Relations historiques, vol. I–II, ed. Albert Failler, trad. Vitalien Laurent (CFHB XXIV/1–2), Paris 1984; vol. III–IV, ed. Albert Failler (CFHB XXIV 3–4), Paris, 1999.
Γρηγορίου Κυπρίου Ἐγκώμιον εις τον αυτοκράτορα κυρόν Ἀνδρόνικον τον Παλαιολόγον, ed. Jean François Boissonade, *Anecdota Graeca*, vol. I, Paris, 1829, pp. 359–393.
Rodolphe Guilland, "Études sur l'histoire administrative de l'Empire byzantin. Le logariaste, ὁ λογαριαστής; le grand logariaste, ὁ μέγας λογαριαστής", *Jahrbuch der Österreichischen Byzantinistik*, 18, 1969, pp. 101–113.
Rodolphe Guilland, "Les logothètes. Etudes sur l'histoire administrative de l'empire byzantin", in *Revue des études byzantines*, 29, 1971, pp. 5–115.
Rodolphe Guilland, *Titres et fonctions de l'empire byzantine*, London, 1976.
André Guillou (ed.), *Les archives de saint-Jean-Prodrome sur le Mont Ménécée*, Paris, 1955.
Augustus Heisenberg, "Kaiser Johannes Batatzes der Barmherzige", in *Byzantinische Zeitschrift*, 14, 1905, pp. 160–233.
Il libro dei conti di Giacomo Badoer, ed. Umberto Dorini and Tommaso Bertelè, Rome, 1956.
Ioannis Cantacuzeni ex imperatoris Historiarum Libri IV, vol. I–III, ed. Ludwig Schopen, Bonn, 1828–1832; translation in German Georgios Fatouros and Tilman Krischer, *Johannes Kantakuzenos, Geschichte*, I–II, Stuttgart, 1982–1986.
Elizabeth Jeffreys (ed.), *Rhetoric in Byzantium*, London, 2003.
Michel Kaplan, *Les hommes et la terre à Byzance du VIe au XIe siècle: Propriété et exploitation du sol*, Paris, 1982.
Johannes Karayannopulos, *Das Finanzwesen des frühbyzantinischen Staates*, Munich, 1958.
Ioannes Karayannopoulos, "Ein Beitrag zur Militärpronoia der Palaiologenzeit", in *Geschichte und Kultur der Palaiologenzeit*, ed. Werner Seibt, Vienna, 1996, pp. 71–89.
Polymnia Katsone, "Κόκκος σίτου και κόκκος βαφική. Το πρόβλημα ερμηνείας του κόκκου στις βυζαντινές πηγές και η σημασία του για την οικονομία και τη φορολογία", in *Byzantiaka*, 27, 2008, pp. 47–116.
Alexander Kazhdan, "*Pronoia*. The History of a Scholarly Discussion", *Mediterranean Historical Review*, 10, 1995, pp. 133–163.
Tonia Kiousopoulou, *Emperor or Manager. Power and Political Ideology in Byzantium before 1453*, Geneva, 2011.
Anastasia Kontogiannopoulou, "Autonomy, Apostasy and the Administration of Macedonia and Thrace in the Palaiologan Period (mid-14th – mid-15th century)", in *Travaux et mémoires*, 25/1, 2021, pp. 333–360.
Anastasia Kontogiannopoulou, *Η εσωτερική πολιτική του Ανδρονίκου Β' Παλαιολόγου (1282–1328). Διοίκηση-Οικονομία*, Thessaloniki, 2004.
Anastasia Kontogiannopoulou, "La fiscalité à Byzance sous les Paléologues (13e-15e siècles). Les impôts directs et indirects", in *Revue des études byzantines*, 67, 2009, pp. 5–57.

Anastasia KONTOGIANNOPOULOU, "Φορολογικές πληροφορίες για τη Θεσσαλία από προνομιακά έγγραφα του 13ου και 14ου αιώνα", in *Byzantiaka*, 29, 2010–2011, pp. 164–177.

Vassiliki KRAVARI, "L'enregistrement des paysans dans les praktika byzantins, XIe–XVe siècle", in *Documenti medievali greci e latini. Studi comparativi*, ed. Giuseppe DE GREGORIO, Otto KRESTEN, Spoleto, 1998, pp. 187–201.

Demetrios KYRITSES, "The 'Common Chrysobulls' of Cities and the Notion of Property in Late Byzantium", in *Symmeikta*, 13, 1999, pp. 229–245.

Angeliki LAIOU, "Le débat sur les droits du fisc et les droits régaliens au début du 14e siècle", in *Revue des études byzantines*, 58, 2000, pp. 97–122.

Angeliki LAIOU and Cécile MORRISSON, *The Byzantine Economy*, Cambridge, 2007.

Spyridon LAMPROS, Παλαιολόγεια και Πελοποννησιακά, vol. I–IV, Athens, 1912–1923 (reprint Athens, 1972).

Basileios LAOURDAS (ed.), 'Ισιδώρου ἀρχιεπισκόπου Θεσσαλονίκης ὁμιλίαι εἰς τὰς ἑορτὰς τοῦ ἁγίου Δημητρίου, Thessaloniki, 1954.

Jacques LEFORT, "Observations diplomatiques et paléographiques sur les praktika du XIVe s.", in *La Paléographie grecque et byzantine*, Paris, 1977, pp. 461–472.

Paul LEMERLE, "Un chrysobulle d'Andronic II Paléologue pour le monastère de Karakalla", in *Bulletin de Correspondance Hellénique*, 60, 1936, pp. 428–446.

Ruth MACRIDES, Joseph A. MUNITIZ, Dimiter ANGELOV (ed.), *Pseudo-Kodinos and the Constantinopolitan Court: Offices and Ceremonies*, Birmingham, 2013.

Alice-Mary MAFFRY TALBOT (ed.), *The Correspondence of Athanasius I Patriarch of Constantinople*, Washington, 1975.

Chryssa MALTEZOU, "Παρατηρήσεις στο θεσμό της βενετικής υπηκοότητας. Προστατευόμενοι της Βενετίας στον λατινοκρατούμενο ελληνικό χώρο (13^{ος}–15^{ος} αι.)", in *Symmeikta*, 4, 1981, pp. 1–16.

Klaus-Peter MATSCHKE, "Commerce, Trade, Markets, and Money: Thirteenth-Fifteenth Centuries", in *The Economic History of Byzantium: From the Seventh Through the Fifteenth Century*, ed. Angeliki E. LAIOU, vol. 2, Washington, 2002, pp. 771–806.

Klaus-Peter MATSCHKE, *Die Schlacht bei Ankara und das Schicksal von Byzanz*, Weimar 1981.

Μεσαιωνική Βιβλιοθήκη, vol. I–VII, ed. Konstantinos SATHAS, Venice, 1872–1894.

Nevra NECIPOĞLU, *Byzantium Between the Ottomans and the Latins. Politics and Society in the Late Empire*, Cambridge, 2009,

Nicephori Gregorae Byzantina Historia, vol. I–II, ed. Ludwig SCHOPEN, Bonn 1829, vol. III, ed. Immanuel BEKKER, Bonn, 1834; translation in German Jan Louis VAN DIETEN, *Nikephoros Gregoras, Rhomäische Geschichte*, Stuttgart, 1973–2007.

Nicolas OIKONOMIDÈS, *Fiscalité et exemption fiscale à Byzance (IXe–XIe s.)*, Athens, 1996.

Nicolas OIKONOMIDÈS, *Hommes d'affaires grecs et Latins à Constantinople (XIIIe–XVe siècles)*, Montréal-Paris, 1979.

Nicolas OIKONOMIDÈS, "Ottoman Influence on Late Byzantine Fiscal Practice", in *Südost-Forschungen*, 45, 1986, pp. 1–24.

Nicolas OIKONOMIDÈS, "The Kommerkiarios of Constantinople", in *Byzantine Constantinople: Monuments, Topography and Everyday Life*, ed. N. NECIPOĞLU, Leiden, 2001, pp. 235–244.

Nicolas OIKONOMIDÈS, "The Role of the Byzantine State in the Economy", in *The Economic History of Byzantium: From the Seventh Through the Fifteenth Century*, ed. Angeliki E. LAIOU, vol. 3, Washington 2002, pp. 973–1058.

Nicolas OIKONOMIDÈS, "Andronic II Paléologue et la ville de Kroia", in Οι Αλβανοί στο Μεσαίωνα, Athens, 1998, pp. 241–247.

Pseudo-Kodinos. Traité des offices, ed. Jean VERPEAUX, Paris, 1976.

Erich SCHILBACH, *Byzantinische Metrologie*, Munich, 1970.

Erich SCHILBACH, *Byzantinische Metrologie Quellen*, Thessaloniki, 1982.

Angelo SEGRÆ, "Studies in Byzantine Economy: jugation and capitation", in *Traditio*, 3, 1945, pp. 101–127.

Ihor ŠEVČENKO, "Nicolas Cabasilas 'Anti-zealot' Discourse: A Reinterpretation", in *Dumbarton Oaks Papers*, 11, 1957, pp. 79–171.

Kostis SMYRLIS, "The State, the Land and Private Property. Confiscating Monastic and Church Properties in the Palaiologan Period", in *Church and Society in Late Byzantium*, ed. Dimiter ANGELOV, Kalamazoo, 2009, pp. 58–87.

Kostis SMYRLIS, "The Fiscal Revolution of Alexios I Komnenos: Timing, Scope, and Motives", in *Travaux et Mémoires*, 21/2, 2017, pp. 593–610

Alexandre SOLOVJEV and Vladimir MOŠIN (ed.), *Grčke povelje Srpskih vladara. Diplomata graeca regum et imperatorum Serviae*, London, 1974.

Alkmene STAVRIDOU-ZAFRAKA, "Η αγγαρεία στο Βυζάντιο", in *Byzantina*, 11, 1982, pp. 21–54.

Nicolas SVORONOS, "Recherches sur le cadastre byzantine et la fiscalité aux XIe et XIIe siècles: le cadastre de Thèbes", in *Bulletin de Correspondance Hellénique*, 83, 1959, pp. 1–166 (reprint in *Études sur l'organisation intérieure, la société et l'économie de l'Empire byzantin*, London, 1973).

Gottlieb TAFEL and Georg THOMAS (ed.), *Urkunden zur älteren Handels- und Staatsgeschichte der Republik Venedig mit besonderer Beziehung auf Byzanz und die Levante*, vol. I–III, Vienna, 1856–1857.

Theodori Metochitae Miscellanea philosophica et historica, ed. Christian MÜLLER, Leipzig 1821 (reprint Amsterdam, 1966).

Freddy THIRIET, *Regestes des délibérations du sénat de Venise concernant la Romanie*, I–III, Paris-La Haye, 1958–1961.

TOMA MAGISTRO, *La regalità*, ed. Paola CACCIATORE, Naples, 1997.

Menelaos TOURTOGLOU, "Παρατηρήσεις επί της φερομένης ως Νεαράς 26 του Ανδρονίκου Β' Παλαιολόγου", in Πρακτικά της Ακαδημίας Αθηνών, 70, 1995, pp. 65–87.

Menelaos TOURTOGLOU, Παρθενοφθορία και εύρεσις θησαυρού, Athens, 1963.

Era VRANOUSSI (ed.), Βυζαντινά έγγραφα της μονής Πάτμου, Α' – αυτοκρατορικά, Athens, 1980.

Panagiotes ZEPOI and Ioannes ZEPOI (ed.), *Jus Graecoromanum*, vol. I–VIII, Athens, 1931.

19
MUSLIM WORLDS
Al-Andalus and the early Ottoman state

Ángel Galán Sánchez, Alejandro García-Sanjuán and Kate Fleet

This chapter explores two forms of taxation adopted by Islamic societies in two very different regions, situated at the geographical antipodes of Classical Mediterranean Islam, al-Andalus (eighth–fifteenth centuries) and the expanding Ottoman state of the fifteenth and sixteenth centuries. It is worth recalling that Islam, in its various waves of expansion, from the time of Muhammad and later, with the great conquests that spanned from Persia to the Maghreb in the seventh century, largely took over societies with consolidated fiscal traditions.

Taxation in Muslim societies: general considerations
(Ángel Galán Sánchez)

We must take into consideration that Islam does not separate state and religion, in contrast to the form of Christianity developed in the Roman world, in which the notions of political power and the state were independent from the message of salvation represented by Christ. This has important implications for the development of their respective fiscal systems. As conversions to Islam increased, a process that by the tenth–eleventh centuries was well under way, although with significant regional differences, Muslims became the predominant religious group and the state's needs grew.[1] The small fiscal leeway afforded by the Quran and the taxes inherited from the conquered states, which were only paid by the *dhimmis*,[2] people allowed by Islam to remain in their land and keep their religion after the conquest, fell short of the state's requirements. Initially, the state's treasury needs were covered by the abundant booty, *fay'* or *ghanīma*. Believers were only required to hand over a tithe of their income or crops, the "legal alms" (*zakā*), the beneficiary of which was not a still underdeveloped "State" but needy members of the Community. Therefore, the state's only role was to collect and redistribute these tithes.

As a result of these circumstances, taxation in the Islamic world was characterised by four elements: a) the light taxes that Quran imposed on believers; b) a consideration of taxation as a unitary notion, parallel to that of a unitary Islamic community or *umma*, even though this soon became politically fragmented; c) the uneven needs of the Islamic states that replaced the single *umma*; d) the difficult coexistence, in both economic and political terms, a constant in the history of Islam, of Qur'anic and extra-Qur'anic taxes, the latter of which were, in theory, illegal, but could be temporarily authorised by the community to meet urgent needs.

As such, in the Islamic state, which crystallised gradually, the management of taxation comprised two components.[3] First, institutions which dealt with the *umma*, whose role was to supervise religious activities, the administration of justice, interpersonal relationships between believers (marriages, contracts, etc.), and the free trade of goods, among others. The head of these institutions were "doctors in law" (*fuqahā'*) with judicial and jurisprudential responsibilities, whose legitimacy was largely grounded on their knowledge of Islamic law. Second, "political" authorities outlined the jurisdictional areas of each "magistrate" for instance, by appointing the *qāḍī*, or Muslim judges in a given district and delegating in him, or not, because this was not a universal norm, the appointment of judges for smaller territorial units or specialised cases. For instance, they could appoint a *muḥtasib*, who was entrusted with the smooth operation of the urban market. The key point is that the authority wielded by these officials emanated from their legal-religious knowledge, and this, in turn must be based on the acknowledgement of the *umma*.

However, the practical implementation of this more or less ideal framework was rife with conflict and varied from region to region. From an early stage, the state assumed wide administrative and political–military responsibilities. Caliphs, emirs and sultans (depending on the state model followed in each case) and their officials also appointed tax collectors, provincial governors and army chiefs, leading to a dangerous intersection of both spheres from a fiscal perspective. In this way, the responsibility of the officials in charge of the mints that issued coinage, the main tax-collection instrument in an economy that was, in general, intensively monetised, had close links with a Qur'anic obligation, the payment of *zakā* by the believer. Similarly, military leaders were in charge of another obligation for all Muslims, that of *jihad*, and it must not be forgotten that armies need their pay.

Most times, as the enormous Islamic jurisprudential literature demonstrates,[4] the tension between *umma* and political government fell in favour of the latter, and the religious element tended to dilute, although it came back to the surface time and time again as the catalyser of protest and revolt. In fact, in contrast with the Christian West, taxation, or, rather, the legitimacy of fiscal impositions, was a permanent factor of social contestation. This should not lead us to the hasty conclusion that "fiscal revolts" were consubstantial to Islamic economic systems; rather, they were a central ideological argument to justify both the change of ruler and popular upheaval. An excellent example of this is found in tenth-century Maghreb, with the struggle between the Egyptian Fatimids, who were *Shiites*, and the Caliphs of Córdoba, who were *Sunnis*, for the control of the region. These two major approaches to the interpretation of Islam, which were also internally marked by infinite hues, constantly accused one another of imposing illegal (extra-Qur'anic) taxes (*maghārim*).[5]

These conflicts did not prevent the emergence of a mighty tributary system. Until the thirteenth century, the fiscal systems of Islamic states were more complex and sophisticated than in the Christian West or Byzantium, where to a large extent these relied on the transference of wealth to the privileged groups through territorial concessions. In the fourteenth and fifteenth centuries, European fiscal systems became more diverse, although the earlier statement is still applicable, even if with many more caveats.

The main, but not only, means to increase revenue and address the growing complexity of fiscal management were the following:

- Keeping a separate fiscal system for *dhimmis* (protected subject populations), which was present from the start of the political expansion of Islam. In addition to the inherited fiscal systems, like the Roman-Byzantine and the Persian, to mention only the two most significant, new specific taxes were levied, like the *jizya*, a personal tribute due for the protection afforded by, and at the same time a sing of submission to, Islam. These taxes were crucial for the early Umayyad state, the Egyptian Fatimids and the Córdoba Caliphate, and they were also successfully exploited by the Ottomans with their system of *millet* (nations). Although the existence of a historical "Millet System" is in doubt, especially in the early stages of the Ottoman state, between the fourteenth and sixteenth centuries, the historiographical success of the concept is in itself proof of the need to keep a dual taxation system, for instance in the Balkans.[6]

- The gradual imposition of taxes inherited from the conquered states to Muslims, who were theoretically exempt, as the curve of conversions rose, as shown by the universalisation of the *kharāj*, the land tax, its "Qur'anic" variants and the multiple debates that this triggered.[7]
- The branching of the concept of *zakā*, the Qur'anic tithe, into a wide variety of exactions. These were differently applied in the various medieval Islamic states, differences that not only affected the tax base, or the asset or activity subject to taxation, but also the percentage (between 2 and 10 per cent of the tax base value).
- The community's temporary and voluntary support, an instrument which, not entirely unlike the *pedidos* or *donativos* granted by Western representative assemblies, led to forms of taxation that eventually became permanent. The fiscal consent awarded by the *umma* was a constant in the history of Islam. A good example is the *al-ma'ūna*, a grant that the community awarded the emir should the public treasury not be able to meet military needs, a well-known phenomenon in al-Andalus.[8] In fact, based on the jurisprudence on these *magharim* taxes in al-Wansharīsī's *Mi'yār*, the Granada-born Ibn Manẓūr (d. 1482) demanded this taxation to be strictly conditional, and only to be collected if the public treasury could not guarantee the country's defence. For his part, an eleventh-century quadi from Almería, Ibn al-Farrā', went much further, and asked the ruler to publicly swear at the mosque that the public coffers were empty and that he needed this aid.[9] However, this did not prevent the *almaguana* to turn into a regular tax on land and real estate for all the inhabitants of Nasrid Granada in the fifteenth century. The generalisation of more or less forced, and certainly extra-Qur'anic, corvées for the maintenance in public works (city walls, etc…), or the increase in taxes, which had no Qur'anic base, on commercial transactions are also part of this trend.[10]

In short, as we shall see in detail in the following pages, Islamic states were compelled to develop complex fiscal systems to address their growing needs. The most eloquent expression of this is, perhaps, the Maghrebi Ibn Khaldūn's in the fourteenth century. This Tunisian-born scholar was one of the most important thinkers of his time, and one of the first to point out the role played by public spending and fiscal revenue in bringing about a healthy market. For him, the reasons that could drive a state to increase taxes and impoverish its people were: the need to keep a strong army for defence; the need to pay greedy civil servant's wages; and the expansion of government activity. The conflicts that this caused in the Muslim world are illustrated by a story told by Ibn Khaldūn further down the line. In this story, a qadi stated, to the surprise of his audience, that he would rather draw his pay from the taxes levied on the sale of wine. The qadi argued that, since all taxes were illegal, except for those established by the Quran, "I chose those which do not leave the heart of the payer aching", because wine gives the joy of life, and paying for this causes no heartache.[11]

Islamic fiscal systems and their development in al-Andalus (eighth–fifteenth centuries). An introductory essay *(Alejandro García-Sanjuán)*

As pointed out by Pierre Guichard (1939–2021) nearly 20 years ago, taxation remains one of the most obscure aspects of the history of al-Andalus.[12] With the, by now distant, precedent of Evariste Lévi-Provençal's (1894–1956) pioneering contribution, which focused on the Umayyad period,[13] our understanding of Andalusi fiscal systems is associated with the historiographical renewal triggered by the irruption of the concept of "tributary society". The earliest publications on the matter, in the late 1970s, by authors such as Miquel Barceló (1939–2013) and Pedro Chalmeta,[14] were followed by other works in which these same authors focused on the Umayyad period.[15] Around that time, Pierre Guichard published his works about eleventh–thirteenth-century Valencia, which include his classic monograph *Les musulmans de Valence et la Reconquête (XIe-XIIIe siècles)* (1990–1991), in which he examined Islamic and Mudejar taxation systems.[16] These works pretty much constitute the whole bibliography on Andalusi fiscal systems, with the addition of a number of more recent publications that largely focus on the Nasrid period. It is important to highlight the important recent monograph by Pedro Chalmeta, which is the first synthesis about the socio-economic structure of al-Andalus, the result of over 50 years of intense academic endeavours.[17]

In order to summarize our knowledge on Andalusi taxation systems it is necessary, first, to lay down a series of basic premises. To begin with, it is worth emphasising two fundamental differences between Islamic and European-feudal fiscal systems. The first has to do with the radically different organisation of both societies. In the early 1960s, the Egyptian economists Samir Amin elaborated on the traditional Marxist concept of Asiatic mode of production to define the tributary mode of production, which he then applied to pre-capitalist Islamic societies.[18] A decade later, the British medievalist Chris Wickham re-elaborated the notions "feudal" and "tributary" based on the difference between tribute and rent.[19] These theoretical foundations led to the characterisation, largely by Pierre Guichard, of al-Andalus as a lords-less society, to which we must add Eduardo Manzano's ideas on the concept of "extra-economic coercion" in the collection of taxes, which tends to blur the difference between tributary and feudal societies.[20]

In this way, the characterisation of al-Andalus as a tributary society has crystallised over 50 years of historiographical debate. This characterisation emphasises the different approach of Islamic and Christian societies in the exaction of productive surplus.[21]

The second great difference, which is both qualitative and quantitative, has to do with the evidence available, with the near total absence of archival records for the Andalusi period being the most important factor. This severely curtails all attempts at quantitative analysis, and only Pedro Chalmeta has tried to estimate the volume of revenue exacted by the Umayyad state.[22] As pointed out by Guichard, the study of Andalusi taxation, despite being essential for the understanding of a tributary society "is barely possible, despite the systematic examination of Arabic sources, which are poor and are, in almost every case, frustratingly vague if not irritatingly inaccurate".[23]

Historians have resorted to another two sources of evidence to offset the unavailability of archival documents, but the results have not been entirely satisfactory. First, legal and doctrinal sources, which are especially abundant in Islamic societies, but which have some serious limitations. First, they only become abundant from the tenth century onwards; second, they are substantially normative and theoretical in nature, and they rarely make reference to specific contextual conditions. On the other hand, as pointed out by Guichard a few years ago, the use of Islamic jurisprudence as a source for the study of Andalusi taxation has barely begun.[24] Significant works include Pedro Chalmeta's examination of Ibn al-'Aṭṭār's notarial treatise in the 1980s,[25] and later analyses of the fatwas contained in al-Wansharīsī's *Mi'yār*, beginning with Guichard and Lagardère in the early 1990s[26] and a late publication by Vincent Lagardère. By the same token, Soha Abboud-Haggar explored different collections of jurisprudence from the eleventh–twelfth centuries.[27]

Despite the importance of these works, there is still a long way to go, because the volume of juridical sources edited and translated has increased very significantly over the last twenty years. This applies, for instance, to texts written by a number of Nasrid ulamas and compiled by the Mahgrebi al-Wansharīsī, of which more later. The compilation of the qadi 'Iyāḍ also includes some valuable fiscal information,[28] as does Ibn Rushd's,[29] or the treatise on juridical controversies written by his grandson Averroes, which includes an extensive theoretical section on the *zakā*.[30] These and other juridical sources can potentially expand our understanding of Andalusi fiscal policies.

The second alternative corpus of evidence is constituted by the documents issued by Christian conquerors which, indirectly, reveal aspects of taxation system during the period of Islamic rule. The problems raised by this evidence, which has been used mostly to study the region of Levante from the mid-thirteenth century onwards and the Nasrid period, are sometimes greater than the solutions they provide, as demonstrated by Guichard's analysis of the tax on *almagra*, from the Arabic *al-maghram* (pl. *maghārim*): while in Valencia this seems to have been used to refer to a tax on irrigated *huerta* land, in Granada it was a tax on trade.[31]

The analysis of Islamic taxation can be arranged around three major axes. First, the centralised and state-based nature of the system, which implies the absence of rent lords. Second, the early foundation of the system on a Quranic and prophetic basis. As a result, the legal framework was very solid, but also very rigid, and its adaptation to specific contexts was the source of political and social tension. Finally, its religious nature, which led to the imposition of different taxes on Muslims and non-Muslims, for instance with the *zakā* and the head tax imposed on non-believers in Quran 9:29.

The contradiction between Quranic norms and fiscal reality was not, as pointed out by Guichard, exclusive of al-Andalus, but a constant for all Medieval Islamic regimes.[32] Indeed, the issue posed by extra-Quranic taxes was one of the central problems in the historical evolution of these societies, and the source of many of the social conflicts undergone by them over time. Although this should be clear by now, it is worth insisting again on the need to keep a clear terminological distinction between "extra-canonical" and "illegal" taxation, because in some conditions ulemas were willing to declare the legality of extracanonical taxation.[33]

The Quranic and prophetic foundations

The Islamic fiscal system is confessional, and taxes depend on the religious adscription of each individual, which in practice means distinguishing between Muslims and non-Muslims. In theory, Muslims have to pay the *zakā*, while non-Muslims are allowed to remain in their territory, under the protection of the Islamic authority, with a special legal status, the *dhimma*, which grants them certain rights in exchange for meeting certain obligations. This involves a contractual relationship between the Islamic state and these communities, which is largely based on tribute, because the essential condition for the system to be upheld is the payment of the head tax (*jizya*).

Islámica canónica clásica. Zakā (which is levied on production), jizya (poll tax) and *kharāj* (which is levied on property) stand for the backbone of the classical canonical Islamic taxation system.

The *zakā is* the most important tax in the Islamic fiscal system, payable by all believers above a certain wealth threshold. Its importance also springs from the fact that is an individual religious obligation, being one of the "five pillars of Islam". Like all of these obligations, the *zakā* features frequently in Quran, where the word is found in 35 occasions, along with other terms and verbal forms with the same root.[34]

According to the Quran, the *zakā* is an alms that purifies the soul of the believer by sharing with the needy. For instance, Quran 9:60 defines the following beneficiaries: "Alms are meant only for the poor, the needy, those who administer them, those whose hearts need winning over, to free slaves and help those in debt, for God's cause, and for travellers in need".[35] Owing to its compulsory nature, it was collected by the state, which used it for three main purposes: public works and sustaining the administrative structure and the army. In the real world, therefore, the charitable nature of the tribute was strongly diluted, and compensated by additional voluntary donations by the believers. These charitable donations (*awqāf*, sing. *waqf*) crystallised in a wide variety of real estate possessions, which were theoretically inalienable and enjoyed a special legal status, but their fiscal regime is poorly understood.[36]

The Quran does not specific what assets and rents were subject to the *zakā*, nor the tax rate to be applied, and these details were outlined by the ulamas. Traditionally, the *zakā* is proportional, beginning from a minimum wealth threshold, known as *niṣāb*, which in the case of crops is the equivalent of five *wasaq* and with livestock depends on the type of animal. The *niṣāb* of gold was 20 dinars and that of silver 200 dirhams. The tax rate on agricultural produce, precious metal, minerals and livestock ranged between 2.5 and 20 per cent, depending on the type of asset. Capital (money and jewels) was generally subject to a 2.5 per cent tax, while wages and commercial rents were exempt.

Although the root *kh-r-j* is common in the Quran, the term *kharāj* only features on one occasion (23:72): "Do you [Prophet] ask them for any payment? Your Lord's is the best payment: He is the Best of Providers".[37] It is, therefore, the fiscal concept with a weakest Quranic base, at least compared with the *zakā* and the *jizya*. However, this tribute became consolidated from the eighth and especially the ninth century as a result of the emergence of a corpus of fiscal literature, the so-called *kutub al-kharāj*, that is, the books of *kharāj*. The most important among these are Yaḥyà ibn Ādam's *Kitāb al-kharāj*, a work with the same title by Abū Yūsuf, Ibn Sallām's *Kitāb al-amwāl* and Qudāma ibn Ja'far's *al-Kharāj wa-ṣinā'at al-kitāba*.

The doctrinal and ideological base of this central concept of *jizya* is the Quran, specifically the ninth *sūra*, "the repentance" (*al-tawba*), whose 29th āya contains the only mention in the sacred book of the term, which is the starting point for the characterisation and meaning of the *jizya*. The Quranic text, however, does nothing more than establishing the *jizya*, providing no further details about it, so that the specific conditions, forms and amounts were to be entirely set up by later jurists. Although the ayah points out a direct relationship between *jizya* and *ahl al-kitāb*, the jurists suppressed this confessional restriction from an early date.

The payment of *jizya* plays a central role in the definition of the status of the *dhimma*, as it is the only Quranic obligation imposed on non-Muslims. This prominent role is fully reflected in, and acknowledged by, juridical literature. Owing to its Quranic base, the *jizya* is a primary norm, and its obligatory nature turns it into the axial factor in the articulation of the relationship between Muslims and their protégée communities.

Concerning the communities on which the *jizya* could be imposed, there were two legal doctrines. The more restrictive of these doctrines argued that the *jizya* could only be legitimately applied to the *ahl al-kitāb* and the *majūs*, based on Quranic and prophetic precepts. However, from an early date, important ulemas supported a more universalist view on the tribute. Among these, Abū Yūsuf, a direct disciple of Abū Ḥanīfa, argued for *jizya* to be paid by all polytheists (*jamī' ahl al-shirk*), be then *majūs*, idol, fire and stone worshippers, Sabaeans and Samaritans, but not by apostates of Islam or idolaters of Arabic origin, whose only choice could be Islam or death. The founder of the maliki tradition is among the greatest supporters of the universalist view, as he was in favour of imposing the *jizya* on all polytheists and unbelievers (*jamī' ajnās al-shirk wa-l-jaḥd*), Arabic or otherwise, except for apostates (*murtadd*).[38]

There is a wide consensus about the passive subjects of *jizya*, a head tax on free and healthy adult males. The tax rate was, however more controversial, owing to the existence of three traditions, one of which appealed directly to the prophet and two to Caliph 'Umar. The differences revolve around whether the tax rate was fixed and, if so, in what proportion. The maliki tradition supported the existence of a fixed rate: the work attributed to Malik ibn Anas makes a reference to a saying according to which Caliph 'Umar ibn al-Khaṭṭāb stipulated a rate of 4 dinars for those who handle gold, and 40 dirhams for those who handle silver, and this was the rate applied by maliki ulemas.[39]

The conquest and the early foundations of the fiscal system

The Umayyad caliph's avidity for revenue is a common place in the sources, and we know that the foundations of the Islamic fiscal system were laid down very soon after the arrival of Islam to the Iberian Peninsula.

An early testimony in this regard is the so-called pact of Tudmīr' or Teodomiro, signed in 94/713 by the governor of a Visigothic province situated between the modern provinces of Murcia and Alicante and 'Abd al-'Azīz ibn Mūsà, who was soon after appointed by his father as first valí or governor of al-Andalus. A number of versions of the pact are reproduced in much later sources, which has triggered intense debates concerning the pact's authenticity, originality and reliability. Miquel Barceló argued that the pact was real, but that the versions that have reached us are unauthentic, and that it is difficult to assess how far the adulterations go;[40] Pedro Chalmeta has no doubts that the pact is authentic, based on textual exegesis and "the way it has reached us".[41]

The text contains the earliest reference to the *jizya* in al-Andalus, a tribute that applied to both free men and slaves (*'abd*). The rate, payable in both cash and kind, was as follows: one dinar, four *almudes* of wheat, four of barley, four *qisṭ* of vinegar, one of honey and one of oil. The slave (*'abd*) paid half the rate.[42] According to Barceló (following Hill), the difference was grounded on the fact that, at this early date, the *jizya* was "the term used to refer to the tribute imposed on both people (Christians and Jews) and their land",[43] which means that the distinction between *jizya* and *kharāj* only came later.

The sources name the second valí or governor of al-Andalus, al-Ḥurr 'Abd al-Raḥmān al-Thaqafī (97–100/715–718) as responsible for the earliest collection of the tax, although it seems that the organisation of a more formal system was undertaken only by his successors. The sources speak about three population censuses, during the governorships of al-Samḥ ibn Mālik al-Khawlānī (100–102/718–721), 'Uqba ibn al-Ḥajjāj (117–123/735 or 736–740 or 741) and Yūsuf al-Fihrī (130–138/747–756). As pointed out by Manzano, the exact dates of these censuses are unknown, but the periods in office of the governors that ordered them are significant, and it is plausible to think about 15-year intervals (720, 735 y 750), which parallels the Byzantine indiction.[44]

The Umayyad period

The Umayyad period, the long interval spanning 'Abd al-Raḥmān I's takeover in 756 and the extinction of the dynasty in 1031, has been characterised as a period of growing fiscal consolidation for the Islamic state in the Iberian Peninsula: "throughout the Umayyad period, with the only hiatus of the crisis undergone by the emirate in the late 9th century, state revenue did nothing but grow exponentially".[45]

By the early ninth century, the emirs of Córdoba were collecting 600,000 dinars per year, and 'Abd al-Raḥmān II raised this to over a million. After the crisis brought about by the *fitna*, revenue peaked at 5,800,000 dinars during the reign of the founder of the caliphate, and this is excluding 'Abd al-Raḥmān III's private rents, which amounted to 765,000 dinars. According to Manzano, "although it is risky to give too much credit to the figures conveyed by the narrative sources, there is no reason to doubt these, especially since they come from court-based historians who had access to official documents, and since they agree with the volume of coinage issued, which also presents this kind of exponential growth".[46]

Beyond the overall figures, there is little evidence to assist in the breaking down of this revenue. Barceló tried to reconstruct the basic outlines of the system based on the Almería-born geographer al-'Udhrī's description of the taxation system in place in the cora of Córdoba during the eleventh century. Rural hamlets (*qarya*, pl. *qurà*) were the basic tributary unit for taxes paid in kind, while taxes in cash fell into three major categories: the military tax (*nāḍḍ li-l-ḥashd*), which accounted for nearly 50 per cent of revenue in coin; the territorial tax (*ṭabl*) (45 per cent); and, the *ṣadaqa* or livestock tithe.

The Almería-born geographer does not include the *jizya* in his description, which prevents us from knowing what proportion of the total revenue (*jibāya*) came from this source. However, the text reports that, at that time, almost one third of the hamlets in the cora (213 of 773, that is, 27.75 per cent), were Christian. No information is provided about the rate applied to the *jizya*, so the total amount of revenue raised is also unknown, although Barceló argued that in this period the protected communities were subject to an "unsustainable" increase in fiscal pressure.[47]

Not even the distribution of the revenue between confessions is particularly clear, and Chalmeta's arguments are not altogether convincing. According to him, the fiscal system of the emirate and the caliphate was based on three subjects of taxation: Arabic Muslims, who only paid the *zakā*, which was equivalent to the tithe (*'ushr*) of their production; the *dhimmī*, who paid the *jizya* and the *kharāj*; and the new-Muslim or muladí (*muwallad*), who by converting to Islam had the *jizya* replaced by the *zakā*, but who had to continue paying the territorial contribution, no longer termed as *kharāj*, but as *ṭabl*.[48] Concerning the latter tribute, Chalmeta adds: "it seems difficult to convince the taxpayer that the ideological-juridical-fiscal result of his conversion amounts to nothing but a change in terminology: the *ḫarāj* turned into *ṭabl* and the *ǧizya* turned into *'ušr*. It is likely, therefore, that the new-Muslim assumed the *moral right* to pay the *zakā* (which he could meet by giving alms directly to travellers and the poor), but not the *fiscal obligation* to do so".[49]

Some sources point out that, despite the enormous revenue collected during the caliphate (20 million dinars around 340/951), taxes were not a heavy burden.[50] Concerning expenditure, the sources indicate that, from the reign of 'Abd al-Raḥmān III, one third of revenue was used to maintain the army (*jund*).[51]

The evidence is especially poor concerning commercial transactions, although there is some agreement that this must have been an important source of revenue, accounting for between 12 and and 15 per cent of the total. Felipe Maíllo, however, points out that fraud was widespread, which suggests that commercial activity was even more intense than the sources reveal.[52]

From taifas to the reformist Berber dynasties

The collapse of the political and administrative structure of the caliphate and the beginning of the Christian expansion are the two main factors in the evolution of taxation during the taifa period, when the problem posed by extra-canonical tributes became for the first time truly urgent.

In all fairness, the narrative of a perfectly orthodox Umayyad taxation that dissolves in the *taifa* period probably oversimplifies a much more complex reality, the details of which are beyond us. At any rate, extra-canonical taxes (*magharim*) were being collected in the Umayyad period: in 941, the inhabitants of Tortosa complained to the caliph of the burden posed by these taxes, especially since they lived near the Christian frontier and were exposed to enemy attack, for which reason 'Abd al-Raḥmān III exempted them from the payment of the *zakā* and the *ṣadaqa*.[53]

However, the image of a fully canonical Umayyad fiscal system is reflected in some sources dated to the taifa period. In a famous text that alludes to the military reform undertaken by al-Manṣūr, the last king of the zirīd taifa of Granada, 'Abd Allāh writes about the imposition of special tributes by the *ḥājib* to hire mercenaries:[54]

> Moreover, they were not a warlike people. Al-Manṣūr therefore conceded them the right to concentrate on the cultivation of their land while they in turn willingly agreed to make annual contributions to support troops to act in their stead. And so he imposed taxes on them and had assessments of all their property entered into the registers. Dividing the taxes among them, he fixed a collective sum that was to be paid for the upkeep of the army.

According to the zirid sovereign, until that point the population of al-Andalus had lived in peace (*mu'taminīn*), only subject to the canonical tributes which were, to boot, also spent for the stipulated ends:[55]

> It was left to people's own honesty to pay the alms-tax (*zakā*) due on their property in cash (*nāḍḍ*), produce, or livestock and to distribute such alms among the poor in each town. This matter did not come within the competence of the ruler who was merely concerned with funds for maintaining the army and the government on which all else depende.

As pointed out by Guichard, the fiscal abuses committed during this period led to the emergence of an idealised image of the caliphate. In any case, even if that "golden age" of taxation never existed, its recurrence in texts written in the taifa period "reveals that the ideal of Islamic taxation persisted in the collective consciousness".[56]

The situation of al-Andalus became more precarious after the 1040s, when the Christian kingdoms increased their military pressure and gradually imposed a system of extortion began by Ferdinand I and brought to its maximum expression by his son and heir Alphonse VI. The need to meet the economic demands of the Christian kings forced the taifa rulers to increase the fiscal pressure on their subjects, which severely undermined both their popularity and their legitimacy.

The zirid king's autobiography accurately reflects the scope and seriousness of the problem caused by the extortion policies followed by the Christian monarchs towards the taifa rulers, especially during the reign of Alphonse VI. The enormous damage that the payment of *parias* caused to the political legitimacy of the taifa monarchs is aptly illustrated by a particular decision adopted by 'Abd Allāh. In order to avoid the population reacting negatively to the exaction of *magharim* (sing. *maghram*, extra-canonical taxes), the zirid king decided to meet the three annual payments of *jizya* owed to Alphonse VI, the equivalent of 30,000 *meticales*, with his own private rents, rather than with funds drawn from the public coffers.[57]

Testimonies from two of the most important eleventh-century authors, Ibn Ḥayyān and Ibn Ḥazm, analysed by Guichard and Barceló, respectively, help to further characterise taxation during the taifa period.[58] Ibn Ḥazm, the most conspicuous advocate of Umayyad legitimacy and, at the same time, the harshest critic of taifa rulers, bitterly decried the disarticulation of Umayyad tributary orthodoxy and the imposition of tributes to met the payment of *parias*. In a famous juridical ruling (*fatwà*) he does not hesitate to refer to them as "tyrants" and "highway robbers", denouncing the exaction of illegal taxes and the concession of authorisation for their collection to the Jews. The role played by Jews in the collection of taxes is also prominent in ʿAbd Allāh's memoirs, which claim that the Banū Naghrela viziers "had exclusive control of revenue".[59]

Such was the voracity of taifa kingdoms that they even charged Muslims for a permit to sell wine,[60] an activity declare illegal by all doctrinal sources. As pointed out by Manzano, coming from Ibn Ḥazm's pen, the fiscal orthodoxy of the Umayyads sounds too much like mere "nostalgic propaganda",[61] although allusions to it can also be found in other sources with no legitimist agenda, like emir ʿAbd Allāh himself: "But my subjects (*raʿiyya*) gave me cause for some concern because they were so eager to see the end of non-canonical taxes (*al-maghārim*) and because the attitude of the Almoravids, [who were concerned with] the obligatory alms tax (*zakā*) and the tithe (*ʿushr*), was widely known".[62]

ʿAbd Allāh's reference is highly significant, taking into account that it is set against the background of the arrival of the Almoravids to the Iberian Peninsula. One of the Almoravids central political mottos was the abolition of extra-canonical taxes (*qaṭʿ al-maghārim*). As such, the restoration of fiscal orthodoxy was one of the propaganda tools wielded by the dynasty, along with the reactivation of jihad to contain the Christian expansion and stop the economic extortion suffered by the Muslims.

However, neither the Almoravids nor the Almohads brought about a watershed moment in Andalusi taxation, and their policies were heavily conditioned by their constant struggle with the Christian kingdoms. One of the most important sources for the Almoravid period is Ibn ʿAbdūn's famous treatise of *ḥisba*, written in Seville. The treatise contains some references to taxation. For instance, the mention to the women of *dūr al-kharāj*, which could refer to a brothel fee, is significant, because prostitution was in theory forbidden.[63]

But, perhaps, the most important aspect of Ibn ʿAbdūn's treatise are his references to corruption and fiscal fraud, which are barely mentioned in other sources. Ibn ʿAbdūn severely criticises the public agents involved in tax collection, which suggests that abuses were widespread. His comments target three specific figures. He begins with the crop estimators (*kharrāṣ*, sing. *khāriṣ*), which are termed as miscreants, prevaricators, traffickers, bad fellows and the scum of society, for making a living out of illicit gains and usury. He continues: "they take bribes, they are evil, unjust and perverse. They have no faith, religion, fear or convictions". For this reason, he argues, they should not be let out in the fields without the judge's instructions, and their salaries should be paid by their superior (*raʾīs*) and not by landowners (*ahl al-amwāl*), "as is currently the case". Similarly, he asked for the records with their estimates (*zimām*) to be endorsed with the judge's seal before they are considered valid.[64]

Concerning tax collectors (*qubbāḍ*, sing. *qābiḍ*) Ibn ʿAbdūn argues that they must not use violence, and must collect only what is due. Similarly, he emphasises the use of appropriate weights and measures, "just scales and exact weights", citing several Quranic verses (83:1; 17:35 y 26:182; 25:19). He also points out that collectors must not humiliate anyone, and refrain from brutality, which is a significant clue of actual everyday practices; according to Ibn ʿAbdūn, tax collectors should always operate under the supervision of a judge.[65]

His opinion of the tax-farmers who leased the market rents (*mutaqabbil*) is not much better: they are defined as "the worse kind of creature, like a botfly conceived to harm and do no good, because all his efforts go to make life hard for Muslims". Concerning the collection of "market fees" (*maks*), he insists on the need for the rates to be fixed beforehand and to be put in writing in a document in the possession of the collector (*mushrif*), the judge (*qāḍī*) and the *mutaqabbil*.[66]

The abuses revealed by Ibn ʿAbdūn, who, let us remember, wrote in the Almoravid capital, suggest that the system was very vulnerable to corruption, in terms of both tax evasion (through the payment of bribes to officials and collectors) and extortion to taxpayers by the officials themselves. There is little doubt that this was a major issue, but explicit evidence, beyond Ibn ʿAbdūn's treatise, is extremely scarce. The treatise also reveals the will of the rulers to reduce, if not totally supress, these corruption practices.

The Nasrid period

Nasrid taxation is the most extensively known Andalusi fiscal system, within a general framework characterised by the paucity of the evidence. It is the only period in the history of al-Andalus for which non-Arabic sources are more important than the Arabic ones; based on the capitulation treaty signed with the Crown of Castille, which guaranteed that the conquered population would be subject to the same taxation system in operation prior to the conquest, the study of Mudéjar records (like in the region of Levante and Murcia) has become the main methodology for the understanding of the Nasrid fiscal system. These records mention taxes to which the Arabic sources make little or no reference, such as the tribute on silk production.

Similarly, the wealth of archival documentation available explains why Nasrid taxation is the Andalusi fiscal system with the longest historiographical tradition,[67] including some synthetic approaches.[68] For this reason, the absence of any reference to taxation in the latest monograph on the Nasrid emirate is all the more glaring.[69]

It must be remembered that the use of the term "rents" in these records embraces two different concepts: taxes and the rents yielded by the lease of state property.[70] For instance, the so-called rent of the *hagüela*, *haguela*, *hahuela* or *halhuela* (from the Arabic *ḥawāla*, "commission, transference"), designated the income derived from former Nasrid public property.[71] The Nasrid public coffers fed on taxes and the rental of public property, and the revenue raised by both was spent to meet the same expenses, which sometimes adds to the confusion.

Historiography has paid considerable attention to the general nature of Nasrid taxation, which is fairly similar to that implemented by the taifa kingdoms: a Muslim society under considerable military Christian pressure, which forces the state to frequently buy peace with parias and incur considerable military expense to defend the frontier; this explains the use of the expression of "the emir's harsh taxes" to describe the Nasrid tributary system.

Owing largely to Mudéjar records, Nasrid Granada is virtually the only Andalusi society whose taxation can be broken down in some detail, presenting a more or less broad perspective of the fiscal sytem: *alacer* (tithe on crops); *alfitra* or *alsira* (on property); *almaguana* (on rural property); *açaque* (on livestock); *magrán* (custom duties); *tigual* (fishery fees); *almahuala* (on almonds, grapes and raisins); *hijuela* (on wills), *tartil* (on silk); and, *tarcon* (on *zambra* parties). To this we might add the "talbix", a tax on transhumant livestock which is strongly reminiscent of the Castilian *montazgo*,[72] and the "mucharan", on the export of nuts.[73]

Occasionally, Arabic texts also refer to taxes that are not mentioned in other sources, such as the *kharāj al-sūr*, which aimed to raise funds to build and maintain city walls, but sometimes the information simply complements that conveyed in other texts. The *almaguana*, the main Nasrid tax, has been linked with the *ma'ūna* or *ma'wana*, a tax attested for the first time during the Almoravid period.[74] A fatwa issued by Ibn Manẓūr (d. c. 1483) characterises this tax as an extraordinary tribute on landed property. The fatwa is of great interest from a legal perspective, because it authorises the sovereign to exact extra-canonical taxes under certain conditions, the most important of which is for the tax to contribute to the "commonwealth" (*maṣlaḥa*).[75] This reveals that, in exceptional circumstances, extra-canonical taxes could be legally endorsed and legitimised.

Along with the Castilian records, Arabic texts are a valuable, and often unexploited, source of information. For instance, the section on the *zakā* in al-Wansharīsī's compilation includes texts by Nasrid ulemas (Ibn al-Ḥaffār, Ibn Lubb, Ibn Sirāj),[76] and mentions to taxes on the sale of real estate or on auction sales can also be found. The small number of publications available suggests that these texts have great potential for a better understanding of the Nasrid fiscal system.[77]

Taxation in the early Ottoman state fourteenth to the sixteenth centuries (Kate Fleet)

Not a great deal is known about fiscal practices in the early Ottoman period, largely due to a lack of primary sources. There are very few extant sources for the fourteenth century, and it is only into the sixteenth century that the number increases substantially. Much of what is written about Ottoman fiscal practices in the first centuries of the state's existence thus relies on sources from a later period.

Ottoman taxation was pragmatic, eclectic, displayed much regional variation and had a tax base "of extreme diversity".[78] Many of the taxes levied in the empire were not part of any Islamic tax structure and fell not under the sharia, the religious law, but under the *kanun*, the law issued by the sultan. The *kanun* applied in particular to taxation and land tenure, as well as criminal law, and was based largely on custom and on the law already in place in regions the Ottomans conquered.[79] This dual system allowed for the incorporation of taxes that were actually in contravention of Islamic precepts, such as the tax levied on pigs in the region of Belgrade in 1431,[80] Trikala (Tırhala in north western Greece) in 1501[81] and in the islands of Gökçeada (Imbros) and Thassos (Taşoz) in 1519.[82] This ability seamlessly to absorb local and customary taxes within their legal structure allowed the Ottomans to ensure income for the treasury, to avoid unnecessary economic disruption and, by leaving the tax-paying population largely undisturbed in tax matters, to prevent uprisings against Ottoman authorities.

As Halil İnalcık has noted, "in view of the interests of the treasury the Ottoman administration followed a very liberal policy in maintaining local taxes especially in the first centuries of its history".[83] As the Ottomans advanced, they absorbed the taxes in the regions they conquered and either incorporated them into their own tax system unchanged, or modified and adapted them to their own needs, or abandoned them altogether. They thus absorbed local taxes in Egypt, which they conquered from the Mamluks in 1517, and in the lands they took in eastern Anatolia from the Akkoyunlu and from the Dulkadiroğulları in the early sixteenth century.[84] In Hungary the *sefer filorisi*, introduced originally by Matthias Corvinus, was preserved, representing, for Bruce McGowan, an "excellent example of the Ottoman practice of preserving customary local taxes".[85] Not all taxes were incorporated, however. Two lump sum payments (*kara salgun* and *harac-i timur*) were abolished by the Ottomans in Siverek, as were various other local taxes there.[86]

Many local taxes were absorbed but adapted, former labour services being commuted into cash payments, for example, as was the case with the *çift*★ tax which combined a number of traditional labour services converted into a cash payment.[87] Not all services, however, were converted, for some could be left in place, or required in some locations but not in others where instead a cash payment was levied. On occasion a local tax absorbed in one area could be transferred to another part of the empire, as was the case with the *ispence*★ tax, a pre-Ottoman tax which the Ottomans imposed as a poll-tax on non-Muslim males and which they transferred from the Balkans to areas in eastern and south-eastern Anatolia.[88]

Tax surveys

In order to assess taxable assets, the state conducted periodic surveys of its territories at intervals of between five and 40 years. These cadastral surveys (*tahrir defterleri*) are thought to have begun in the reign of Bayezid I (1389–1402).[89] An Ottoman history, dating from the late fifteenth or early sixteenth century, refers to a certain *subaşı* (an official who was often responsible for law and order) Süleyman conducting a land survey near Bursa probably around 1405.[90] The earliest extant survey is from Albania from 835/1431. It divides the province (*sancak*) of Albania up according to *timar*s (land grants in return for military service), giving for each village within the *timar* the number of households, widows, unmarried men, and the overall production figures.[91] There were two types of survey, detailed (*mufassal*) and summary (*icmal*).[92]

The aim of these surveys was to compile a list of taxable revenue to be assigned to those who held *timar*s.[93] They did not, therefore, include sources of income that were not part of the *timar* system, such as the income of pious endowments (*vakıf*) or income that went not to the *timar* holder but to the centre, such as customs dues or the *cizye*★, a poll tax paid by non-Muslims. Further, the surveys did not record the actual amounts of tax collected in the year in which the survey was made, but the expected amounts of tax based on averages of the last three years. They therefore reflected average values, not actual sums collected. Many surveys began with or included a law code (*kanunname*) for the region covered by the survey. One of the purposes of the *kanunname* was to set out taxes and rates to be applied. The first extant *kanunname* is that in the detailed survey from 892/1487 for the province of Hudavendigar (Bursa) in north western Anatolia.[94]

Tax collection

Tax revenue from the different parts of the empire could either be collected locally or despatched to the central treasury. Much tax income remained in the provinces, never being transferred to the centre, and was therefore not entered (with the exception of the budget from 933–934/1527–1528) into the state budgets, or rather the statements of income and expenditure which was what they were. Mehmet Genç and Erol Özvar have calculated that one might suggest that, very roughly, the figures found in the budgets represent only between 25 and 40 per cent of total state income.[95]

Under the *timar* system, whereby what was granted was not the land, which was retained by the state, but the right to collect tax revenues in return for military service, the holders of *timar*s collected taxes which represented their income. Such assigned taxes were collected in cash, or in kind in the case of tithes on grain, for example. Other local income, destined for the central treasury, could be assigned by the centre to be spent on specific local requirements, such as the payment of castle garrisons or to pay for military provisions. In Caffa, for example, at the end of fifteenth century the government official (*emin*) was to cover the payments to the garrisons in the Ottoman fortresses in the Crimea from the revenues he collected.[96] In Limnos in the late fifteenth century revenue that would normally have been sent to the central treasury or the sultan's own treasury (which received budget surplus and extraordinary revenue, such as the sultan's share of booty, confiscated estates or gifts, and which could function as a reserve treasury), was allocated to cover the costs of the local Ottoman administration on the island.[97] This system, whereby an order (*havale*) was sent from the centre for a specific payment to be made from local revenue, avoided the necessity of transporting coins from often distant parts of the empire to the centre only to be despatched again, potentially even back to where they had come from, to cover local payments. It was thus both more efficient and less risky than funnelling all collected revenue to the centre.

Much agricultural tax was collected by *timar* holders for their own use. Those with large *timar*s used agents to collect the tax or would tax farm it out. Methods of tax collecting could be somewhat rough, for a peasant from the land of Bayezid II's (1481–1512) son Şehzade Korkud complained that he had been beaten up by those collecting the sheep tax and had lost a tooth.[98] Pious endowments had agents, usually called *cabi*, who conducted tax collection. Taxes could also be collected directly by a state employee and then despatched to the central treasury. This applied, for example, to the poll tax (*cizye*★) which was paid by non-Muslim males. Revenue from the imperial domain (*hass-ı hümayun*), made up of revenue from lands that had not been assigned in the *timar* system or income from urban or commercial taxes, was collected either by salaried agents or by tax farmers and sent to the central treasury, unless reassigned for another purpose.

Tax farming was a method commonly used for tax collection, in particular for major sources of revenue such as customs dues, market taxes or taxes on enterprises such as mining. Under this system the right to collect certain taxes was auctioned off, usually for a period of three years. It is not clear when tax farming was introduced but it was in operation under Mehmed II (1444–1446, 1451–1481) and under his father Murad II (1421–1444, 1446–1451). It also seems to have been used under Murad I (1362–1389). It is possible that it was simply taken over by the Ottomans in the regions they conquered, for it was a widely used method of tax collection in operation under the Seljuks, the Mongols, the Byzantines and the various small Turkish *beylik*s (states) in Anatolia in the fourteenth century. Latins, in particular the Genoese, were tax farmers for the Ottomans in the fifteenth century and it is possible that they were acting in this capacity in the late fourteenth century as well.[99]

Tax farming was clearly profitable, but it is impossible to assess any levels of profit as available figures for tax farms tell us only what the tax farm was sold for, not what the tax farmer actually collected. They do not therefore tell us what the actual level of economic productivity was. Apart from being lucrative, tax farming could also be a risky enterprise. Defaulting tax farmers under Mehmed II were executed.[100] Those unable to make payment could also flee, as those tax farming fish traps in Ostrova in the province of Thessaloniki (Selanik) did in 1479.[101] Tax farmers were also vulnerable to having their tax farms taken away from them if a more lucrative bid came along. For the state, tax farming could be advantageous as risk fell not on the state but on the tax farmer. In the early period, when the central government had firm control over the tax farmers, the system was largely unproblematic but later, when the state lost control of them, it was to be a major weakening factor and to provoke much local protest against rapacious tax farmers who used their positions to build up local political power bases.

Tax could also be collected as lump sums (*maktu*★). This was the case, for example, on Mount Athos in the early sixteenth century where the monks paid their taxes as a fixed annual lump sum.¹⁰² Daniel Goffman has suggested that the Ottoman practice of allowing tax-payers in Egypt in the immediate aftermath of the Ottoman conquest in 1517 to pay taxes as *maktu*★ was primarily intended "to create good will in the local population and to grant them some sort of autonomy".¹⁰³ The *cizye*★ was often collected as a *maktu*★ payment, particularly from urban populations or from those on the islands. *Maktu*★ was also used in remote places where collection was more difficult.

Tax-payers

Under sultanic law (*kanun*) a distinction was made between tax-payers and non-tax-payers. Tax-payers (*reaya*) were largely the peasant tax-payers, while non-tax-payers (*askerî*) were made up of those who were granted landholdings by the sultan or who were paid directly from the treasury.

Tax exemption, usually from specific taxes, could be granted to *reaya* for services rendered, such as repairing bridges or roads, or guarding passes, a letter from Bayezid II's son, Şehzade Alemşah, ensuring exemption, for example, for those guarding the Akpınar road in the region of Fethiye (Makri) in modern south west Turkey.¹⁰⁴ Specialist workers could receive exemptions, as the carpenters and stonemasons in the castle of Ayamavra on the island of Lefkas in the Ionian Sea did in 1501¹⁰⁵ or the miners at the Kreševo mine in Bosnia did in 1489.¹⁰⁶ The arrow smith Yani-veled-i Kalavriça was granted exemption in return for providing 400 arrows every year to the castle of Yenihisar in the region of Balybadra in the Peloponnese and for castle repairs he undertook to do.¹⁰⁷

Religious services such as reciting the Koran or repairing a mosque could bring immunity from taxation. Thus, the seventeen people who recited the Koran for the sultan every Friday in İskilip in central Anatolia received exemption from certain taxes in 1501,¹⁰⁸ as did the non-Muslim Gordan veled Peter, due to his repairing of the mosque of Mehmed II in Görice, modern Korça in south eastern Albania.¹⁰⁹ Monasteries too could be granted immunity. Monks of the Gerontos Osiou Leontiou and Panagias Pepelenitsis monasteries in the Peloponnese were granted tax exemption in the early 1460s. The Ottomans here checked and renewed the privileges formerly granted to the monastic communities by the Byzantine authorities.¹¹⁰

The sultan could also grant exemption as he saw fit. Bayezid II granted exemption from *avarız*★ taxes (extraordinary taxes imposed in particular to cover military expenses in time of war and levied per household) to villagers on the *vakıf* of the late Sitti Hatun in Edirne,¹¹¹ and people in two villages in the region of Ohri on the *timar* on Mevlana Sinan Çelebi, Bayezid's late *nişancı* (the head of the chancery), were also exempt from payment.¹¹² A non-Muslim subject, Bigan İklitos from Mizistre (Sparta in modern Greece), described as "a useful and reliable person" who carried out whatever matters the sultan wanted dealing with "with trustworthiness and integrity", was also exempt from *avarız*★ taxes.¹¹³

While immunity from taxation might be granted by the state for one reason or another, it was not always respected and those who had exemption could find themselves being forced to pay, a practice that resulted in complaints to central government. Two non-Muslim subjects (*zimmi*s) who were guards of passes (*derbentci*s) in the region of Samokov (Samakov) in south western Bulgaria complained in 1501 that, despite being exempt, they were being charged *avarız*★ taxes. Noting that an earlier order had already been issued that, provided their work was satisfactory, they were to be exempt, the central government instructed that they were not to be charged.¹¹⁴ A similar case concerned builders and carpenters in Edirne who had been granted immunity from *avarız*★ taxes but were still having to pay them.¹¹⁵

Types of taxes

Taxes levied in the Ottoman empire can be grouped in various ways: type, where they went, who paid them, or their economic nature. They can be classified according to whether they were religiously sanctioned (*tekalif-i şeriye*), customary (*tekalif-i örfiye*) or extraordinary taxes (*tekalif-i divaniye* or *avarız★ akçesi*).[116] Or they can be divided according to recipient and to whether they were collected and used locally, such as the tithe (*öşür*), or were collected and sent directly to the central treasury, as was the case, for example, with the poll tax (*cizye★*).[117] Heath Lowry, basing himself on extensive research on the *liva kanunname*s, refers to "the tripartite nature of the Ottoman tax-paying *re'aya*", that is peasants engaged in agriculture, the urban population, and the semi-nomadic tribes.[118] In her study of Euboea at the end of the fifteenth century, Evangelia Balta divided taxes into three groups: regular and extraordinary taxes levied on people; taxes on rural activities; and revenues from real estate and enterprises.[119]

Metin Coşgel has argued that historians have tended to group Ottoman taxes into ad hoc or purely legal categories rather than dividing them on the basis of their general structure. He instead classifies taxes according to their tax bases which he divides into three major categories: personal taxes, trade taxes and production taxes, a category which he further subdivides into output taxes (levied on and collected as specific percentages of harvested products, such as tithes), input taxes (such as taxes on fruit or vineyards where the assessment was made according to the number of trees or, for honey, on the number of beehives) and enterprise taxes (which were levied as a lump-sum payment on an activity as a whole, such as taxes on shops or manufacturing enterprises).[120]

As the empire was an agricultural one, many of the taxes levied were related to agricultural activity and agricultural taxes represented a major element of state income. The Ottoman treasury did not follow the lunar Islamic calendar in setting the timings of such tax collection but the solar Julian one, which was more suitable in this regard. One of the major agricultural taxes was the tithe (*öşür*), which was levied predominantly on grain and pulses. The rate varied according to location, but was usually 1/10th, though it could be 1/8th or 1/5th of the produce.[121] Taxes were also levied on other agricultural production, such as fruit and vegetables, and other activities such as viticulture and apiculture. If peasants cultivated vegetables or fruit trees for their own consumption, they did not pay tax, but if the produce was cultivated for sale, then tax was levied. Taxes on livestock included the sheep or goat tax (*resm-i ağnam* or *adet-i ağnam*) which was a fixed figure per head, the rate varying region to region. The tax rate for pigs differed under Mehmed II depending on whether the pigs were roaming freely with cows, in which case the rate was one *akçe* (a silver coin) for every two pigs, or were being fattened up for slaughter, in which case the rate was one *akçe* per head.[122]

A major tax paid by the rural population was the *çift resmi★*, which was on the one hand a tax tied to land and on the other to person (individual or household).[123] The amount of land represented by a *çift★* varied region to region and was divided into good, medium and poor land. Both Muslims and non-Muslims could pay the *çift resmi★*, as was the case in Siverek, for example.[124] In other areas, however, where the *ispence★*, a poll tax of 25 *akçe* paid by non-Muslim males, was levied, the non-Muslims paid this in place of the *çift resmi★*. The *ispence★* is known to have been being levied in the later fourteenth century. It appears in the Albanian register in 1431 where it was only paid by married men.[125] In Euboea at the end of the fifteenth century *ispence★* was levied on each non-Muslim household at the rate of 25 *akçe*. A tax, *resm-i bive*, was charged on households of widows at a rate of six *akçe*.[126] Halil İnalcık suggested that *ispence★* was a tax which existed under Stefan Duşan and only entered the Ottoman tax system after the conquest of Thrace in the late fourteenth century.[127] It was paid by both the settled rural population and nomads, and by the urban population.

One of the most lucrative taxes of the empire was the *cizye*★ (Arabic *jizya*), a poll tax levied on non-Muslim men. Under Islamic law it was a poll tax paid by non-Muslim males, but under the Ottomans it was levied not on individuals but on households. As Colin Imber has noted, the *cizye*★ was often "simply a pre-Ottoman tax under a new name".[128] A further example of the divergence between the Islamic poll tax and the Ottoman *cizye*★ is that it could be imposed on Muslims, as was the case with Muslim gypsies in the Balkans.[129]

The degree to which rates of the same tax varied across the empire is striking. In Eubeoa in the late fifteenth century the rates charged on mills, for example, showed considerable variation which Evangelia Balta suggests must have been due to the type of mill and the quantity of the grain it processed.[130] The mill tax in eastern Anatolia in the early fifteenth century at the time of the Ottoman conquest of the region also shows the level of variation that could be found in the same tax in the same region, where the Ottomans either left a local tax unchanged or modified it. Taxes on mills (*resm-i asiyab*) varied according to the type of mill and on whether they worked all year round or only part of the year. In the provinces of Erzincan in 1516 and of Mardin and Harput in 1518 the rate was five *akçe* per month, making an annual tax of 60 *akçe*.[131] While the tax in Arabgir in 1518 was set at 16 Arabgir *kile*s (a measurement of weight), equivalent to eight Istanbul *kile*s, of grain, half of which was to be wheat and half barley,[132] that in the province of Ergani at the same date was converted into a cash payment, for the *kanunname* noted that from every mill that worked throughout the year the rate had been 16 Amid *kile*s of grain, half of which was wheat and half barley, which made 56 Ottoman *akçe* annually.[133] In Sis in 1519 every mill that worked for an entire year was taxed at the rate of 120 Aleppan *akçe*s per annum and those that worked for six months a year the rate was 60 Aleppan *akçe*s.[134] These rates also display another characteristic of the empire, and that is the variety of currencies employed. Different *akçe*s of different weights and values existed across the empire, as did different currencies, the empire effectively functioning in a series of currency zones. The same applied to weights which again varied location to location. The Ottomans could also forego a tax if it had not been the previous practice to impose one. Thus, the *kanunname* of Çirmik in 1518 notes that no *resm-i asiyab* had been charged previously so none was entered in the *kanunname*.[135]

The variety of rates charged for the same tax in different parts of the empire could be considerable, as was the case, for example, with the *çift*★ tax. In Tekfurdağ and Üsküp in 1455 and Malkara in 1456 it was 22 *akçe*, but in Aydın in 1455 it was 30. Later in the century, in 1474, it was 22 *akçe* in Gelibolu, 33 in Hudavendigar in 1487, 37 in Ankara in 1522 but only 22 in Tırhala in 1520 and the same figure in Sofia in 1525. The tax was considerably higher in some parts of the empire: 50 in Harput and Mardin in 1518, 57 in Çorum in 1466 and 57 in Kayseri in 1500.[136]

Such variation also applied to agricultural activities such as apiculture. While the rate for beehives was one *akçe* per hive on Gökçeada and Limnos is 1519,[137] it was two *akçe* in Kayseri in 1500.[138] Producers on Thassos paid both one *akçe* per hive and a tax (*resm-i ağıl*) of two *akçe*s for the land they stood on.[139] This lack of uniformity could lead to confusion or abuse. Peasants in the region of Simav in western Anatolia complained in 1501 that they were being overcharged tax at a rate of two *akçe* per hive, leading the government to issue instructions to ascertain what the registered rate of tax was for beehives in the region, and to ensure that that alone was charged.[140]

The type of taxation employed could also vary. The *kannuname* of Hudavendigar noted that while a tithe on honey had been previously entered into the register, in some places a cash payment was in fact being taken, varying according to productivity and location with two *akçe*s being charged in some regions per beehive and in some places, one *akçe*. It was this arrangement that was now entered into the new register.[141]

Other state income came from taxes on commercial activities, which attracted a range of taxes, including those charged on weighing and for brokerage, on selling and buying, transit tolls, and customs dues. Shops paid a tax, the *resm-i asesiye*, to cover provision of security of shops at night. The rate varied in different parts of the empire. In Mardin the rate was one *akçe* per shop per month. Previously one *akçe* had been levied per month on houses where there were looms working, but this was annulled and instead this was levied on shops in the market.[142] This applied also to Diyarbakır in the 1540 *kanunname*.[143] In Nusaybin the rate, which had been 7.5 *akçe* per month, was reduced to three.[144] In Serres in 1512 shop owners paid one *akçe* per month for shops that were locked at night and were situated within the market. Dyers paid two *akçe* per month, while soap merchants paid one *akçe* per month for their shops as well as providing soap to the value of one *akçe*.[145]

As many of these urban taxes were tax farmed, it is often impossible to work out the bases for the charges, or how much was charged per activity. A further complication is that such taxes were often made up into bundles of different revenues (*mukataa**) which were tax farmed, the lump sum alone being entered in the register. Thus, for example, the annual revenue from the rent of shops in Eğriboz (modern Chalcis, Halkida) appeared together with that from mills which possessed five millstones near Eğriboz which was entered into the register as one lump sum.[146]

Market taxes (*bac*) were levied on goods sold at town markets or at periodic fairs, such as the Şin-Marya fair which appears in the 1431 Albanian register,[147] but not on goods sold in villages,[148] although some transactions in villages could be taxed. Unfermented grape juice sold in all villages on the island of Gökçeada paid at the rate of one *akçe* per *medre* (a unit of liquid measurement).[149] Usually paid by the seller, though sometimes by both seller and buyer, market taxes were imposed according to pack, load, weight or value. In the case of the sale of private property, such as shops and houses or vineyards, mills and orchards, no tax was levied.[150] Rates, which varied across the empire, were set out in detail in the *kanunname*s.

Customs rates, too, were set out for listed goods in the *kanunname*s. Rates varied place to place. It is not known what rates the Ottomans charged in the fourteenth century. The 1387 treaty between Murad I and the Genoese refers only to the Genoese paying according to custom but gives no further details.[151] It seems possible to suggest, however, that the rate was around two per cent on both imports and exports. In the 1430s a customs rate of two per cent was charged at Gelibolu (Gallipoli), Edirne and Samsun on the Black Sea. Under Mehmed II the rate charged on foreigners was five per cent (or sometimes four), while that on Ottoman subjects was four per cent. At the beginning of the reign of Bayezid II the rate was four per cent for foreigners (Venetians and Genoese being specified), two per cent for non-Muslim subjects, and one per cent from Muslim subjects of the empire.[152]

Customs charges could vary depending on whether the person was or was not local to a particular region, as was the case for those importing sheep onto Gökçeada where a local person did not pay. There was no distinction made, however, between locals and non-locals in the case of export of sheep from the island when both paid customs taxes. If a local imported horses or oxen onto the island for his own use, then he was not charged customs tax.[153] A similar distinction is evident in Kilia where in 1484 the customs on cloth was set at three per cent for both buyer and seller, but the buyer, if he was an inhabitant of the town, was not charged.[154]

Such differential rates encouraged the passing off of goods of foreigners or non-Muslims as the goods of Muslims or locals. In 1493 the tax farmer of the customs of Edirne, Mihal Mavrudi, complained to the sultan that merchants were importing cloth but, without entering

Edirne, were selling the merchandise to merchants from the city in order to evade customs. In the order issued instructing that this practice was to be investigated and stopped, it was stated that no Muslim was "to come to an agreement [with an infidel] and enable the infidel's goods to evade [full] customs-duty by claiming that they are his".[155]

Conclusion

Ottoman economic approaches in the early period of the state's existence were essentially pragmatic and revolved around avoiding economic disruption, adopting and adapting methods the Ottomans found in place in areas they conquered and balancing central control against local autonomy.[156] In matters of taxation, the Ottomans absorbed and adapted the local taxes in areas they expanded into. Many of the taxes collected were not transferred to the central treasury but were used locally, either by the *timar* holders to whom the right to collect them had been assigned or for specific local needs to which they were assigned by central government.

Careful to avoid economic disruption wherever possible, the Ottoman government responded in cases where tax practices caused distress to tax-payers and either annulled or amended taxes as necessary. When peasants on Limnos, for example, complained in the early sixteenth century that Ottoman officials had been collecting an annual tax from them in the place of their usual service of coastal defence, this tax was removed for it was causing the peasants suffering.[157] This awareness of the importance of previous practice is also evident in the government response to the complaint of tax-payers on the island of Thassos in the early fifteenth century. Here it had been the custom to levy a tax of one *akçe* per sheep or goat. Instead, however, officials were collecting one animal in every ten. The peasants complained that this was causing them difficulties, and therefore an order was issued to return to "the former custom" and take one *akçe* per head of livestock.[158] Taxes could also be modified due to local conditions in order to avoid causing the tax-payers unnecessary hardship. This was the case, for example, on Limnos in 1489 where, due to the mild climate, rams were never separated from the ewes and thus lambing was not restricted to any particular season. It was therefore agreed not to charge lambs together with the sheep when the sheep tax was collected, as this "would cause the peasants some distress" and instead it was agreed that the peasants would pay one *akçe* per head of sheep, their lambs being excluded from the count.[159] The same applied to the sheep tax on Gökçeada in 1519, where the rate, too, was the same.[160]

Hardship could even win out against taxes approved under the sharia. The *kanunname* of Hudavendigar noted that levying a tithe on vineyards and gardens was allowed under the sharia but that, since this caused hardship for the peasants, the tithe had been converted into a cash payment.[161] This underlines the importance in the early centuries of Ottoman rule of a modus vivendi style of government where former local practice, the importance of regional variation as opposed to a uniform, centrally imposed and controlled system (something in any case impractical in an empire of that size, even before it reached its maximum extent in the mid-sixteenth century), and a dual legal system which gave wide-ranging flexibility to an eclectic system of taxation, characterised the modus operandi of Ottoman government in the first centuries of its existence.

General conclusions *(Ángel Galán Sánchez)*

In these pages, the reader has had the opportunity to see that some elements appear time and time again, although with different emphasis.

The first is the importance of inherited fiscal systems for both examples under examination: al-Andalus and early Ottoman state. The fiscal systems of Islamic states, based on pre-existent taxation structures, did not undergo the sharp caesura that affected the Christian West between the seventh/eighth and thirteenth centuries, even if the notion of the "public", and its fiscal projection, no matter how modest, did not disappear even in this region. Under Islam, fiscal systems generally formed by aggregation, and this made them greatly adaptable to the economic conditions of the different territories on which they settled.

The second is the need to legitimise fiscal exaction and the expense that justified it with *sharía*, Islamic law as developed by a secular legal tradition with multiple doctrinal and regional branches. Beyond the permanent conflict between Quranic and extra-Quranic taxes, Muslims jurists demonstrated considerable exegetic skill in accommodating the taxes paid by Muslims and *dimmíes* under the umbrella of Islam when necessary.[162] The important thing about the adaptability of the legal rulings of *fuqaha* and *ulemas* lies in context, because we must not forget that, despite the shifting kingdoms and dynasties, medieval Islam possessed solid state structures that could barely be partially modified by the, only apparently, confusing comings and goings of ruling families and social groups.

The third seems like stating the obvious. Islamic societies were predominantly agricultural, like all societies in the Middle Ages, and the countryside was the base on which taxation, Quranic or otherwise, mostly rested. However, property structures and agricultural production could vary widely between, say, Mamluk Egypt and Nasrid Granada, and multiple land property regimes co-existed in early Ottoman state. Therefore, the *ideal* model of Muslim and non-Muslim communities subject to a more or less homogenous taxation by their Muslim rulers is little more than a fiction, and there is much work to be done for a more precise understanding of specific tributary models. In addition, we must remember that, to a large extent, Islam expanded into territories inhabited by nomadic or semi-nomadic kinship-based groups. It is possible that Islam was in great measure a lords-less society, but only if we understand the word "lord" merely in the feudal sense.

Finally, Islam, which was characterised by robust urban networks, developed a sophisticated tributary system to tax commercial and craft activities, and detailed lists of taxes and tributes, as well as multiple treatises of *hisbah*, which regulated the operation of markets, are known. In general, these suggest that the most direct, and succulent, sources of revenue for Muslim rulers were often foreign merchants and their transactions.[163] The intense commercial activity that characterises the Islamic world facilitated the implementation of efficient systems to control custom duties and fees on craft and industrial production.

If our two examples are examined in detail, we detect two different paths of evolution. In al-Andalus, fiscal systems evolved continuously from the conquest to the fall of the Nasrid emirate of Granada in 1492. While for the earliest stages the evidence is scarce and unreliable, the arrival of the Umayyads to al-Andalus led to the emergence in the sources of a double taxation system, one for *dimmíes* and another one for Muslims. Concerning the former, the conquering elites were directly involved in tax collection, while the latter were still a minority, and a poor source of revenue. By the time the Umayyads decided to proclaim themselves caliphs in the mid-ninth century, the fiscal system was fully functional and enjoyed full religious legitimacy, as well as having developed tributes like the *jaray*, which taxed the land owned by converted Muslims. The collapse of the caliphate led to two processes of political fragmentation between the first third of the eleventh century and the mid-thirteenth century, alternating with two North African invasions that temporarily unified al-Andalus again. This period can only be understood if we take into account the constant drain on the resources of the fragmented Islamic polities posed by the *parias* demanded by the thriving Christian kingdoms in their southward march, which the heirs of the caliphate were forced to pay to keep their independence. First the Almoravids and later the Almohads arrived with the promise, well disseminated by their propagandists, to end with the tyrannical and unjust taxes levied by the *taifa* rulers, but the fiscal pressure on the population of al-Andalus did not, in fact, diminish. Finally, when the territory of al-Andalus was reduced to Granada, a territory of approximately 60,000 km^2 at its largest, their rulers, under the constant threat of Christian conquest, increased the fiscal pressure and focused the economy on the production of market crops for the Mediterranean and Atlantic markets[164] as a way to obtain revenue with which to buy peace or pay for war. This explains the wide array of Nasrid taxes on commercial transactions and craft activities, for instance on nuts, raisins and silk.

Another important aspect of this evolution is that, from the eleventh century onwards, the number of *dimmíes* (Jews and Christians) in al-Andalus declined. In the late Middle Ages, Granada was a deeply Islamicised society. In fiscal terms, the consequence of this process was twofold. First, the growing sophistication of arguments to increase extra-Quranic taxes, for the needs of the state were real and stubborn. Second, the islamicisation of inherited traits in a complex but well-organised fiscal system; this was a widespread feature in the Islamic world, but was especially conspicuous in Granada.

The Ottomans, for their part, could implement their fiscal system (or fiscal systems) differently, owing to the circumstances that surrounded their imperial expansion. The first difference with al-Andalus is that the dual taxation system did not disappear, but in fact became more prevalent because of the large number of non-Muslim taxpayers. This explains, for instance, the functional conversion of the *yizya*, a head tax on *dimmíes*, into a household tax. Second, in contrast with the relatively homogeneous – in economic terms – Nasrid Granada, the Ottoman expansion over Anatolia, the Balkans and the Mediterranean covered a broad variety of economic conditions, which projected onto the taxes imposed on land ownership and agricultural production; no parallel to this diversity can be found in the Islamic world in the fourteenth and fifteenth centuries, especially with the incorporation of Egypt to the empire in the early sixteenth century. Finally, compared with a small state under constant enemy threat like Granada, where the levying of revenue was a centralised operation, the Ottoman empire could resort to the *timar* to distribute some of the income and expense *in situ*, a highly functional measure given the diversity of inherited fiscal and administrative structures, and reserve for the central government only a proportion of the revenue collected. Although the situation progressively changed during the sixteenth and, especially, the seventeenth century, this also goes a long way to explain the widespread success of tax-farming.

Although the impression that transpires from the pages dedicated to Ottoman state is that, like in every Muslim state the need existed to legitimise taxes through *sharia*, it is easy to see why fiscal conflicts in the Ottoman Empire in the Late Middle Ages, the period covered by this volume, had a minimum Islamic component.

We know a good deal less, except for exceptions like Late Mamluk Egypt and the Ottoman Empire in the sixteenth century for which much fuller records survive, about the amounts collected or the management systems implemented by these states.[165] If I had to synthetise a very long process, I would say that the main outlines are:

a) Built upon a solid tributary foundation, the states sustained a level of income that, compared with those in the West, was enormous, if we are to trust the chronistic sources despite their imprecise nature; b) the frequent fiscal revolts were, in my opinion, evidence of the ability of Muslim states to diversify their tax base and, ultimately, of their administrative capabilities; c) the widespread distinction between the community's treasury (*umma*) – initially derived from the Quranic taxes – and assets owned by pious foundations, and the public treasury, the administration of which corresponded to the political authorities; d) both the public and community treasuries were administered by officials appointed by the government; e) at the most basic administrative level, especially in rural communities, which comprised the vast majority of the population, collection was made possible by the intervention of local agents; f) although juridical doctrines were against this practice, tax-farming became increasingly common, especially from the eleventh century onwards in the intermediate tiers of the system; the route of taxes from their base to the public coffers is one of the less understood aspects of Islamic taxation; e) tributes and taxes reached their destination mostly in coin form, stimulating, as recognised by Ibn Khaldūn, a "world economy" within Islam (the expression is C. Cahen's), despite its shifting political divisions.

I must finish by mentioning a phenomenon that often goes overlooked: the transference of Islamic fiscal models to the Christian world. The best known example is that of Islamic cities conquered by the Christians in the Iberian Peninsula, in Sicily or in the Crusader states. From the eleventh century onwards, Spanish Mudéjar communities offer an excellent illustration of this: e.g. the terms *zequi*, *çequi* or *azaque*, used in various Romance languages in the Iberian Peninsula to refer to a large number of versions of this tax, which affected the possession of livestock or the legal alms paid at the end of Ramadan in the form of a universal head tax; the *zakā al fitr*, the *alfitra* of Romance texts; the survival of the multiple taxes on silk production and export; and, the detailed accounts of the *hawala*.[166] But much more important than this is the transmission of accountancy systems and institutions for the regulation of markets and municipal organisation. Spain offers again a good illustration of this phenomenon (e.g. the Arabic *muhtasib*, for instance, has a Castilian counterpart, the *zabazoque*), which has been thoroughly examined by Pedro Chalmeta. But we also find it in Italy, spurred by the intense commercial relationship between Amalfi and Islamic territories from the ninth century onwards, or the close trade connections with Venice and Genoa throughout the Late Middle Ages. This phenomenon has not been paid nearly as much attention as it deserves. Muslim influence on commercial organisation models and financial instruments, in contrast, is much better known. The chronological limits assumed by this volume prevent us from going so far ahead, but it is likely that the study of the close trade links between Ottomans and central Europe from the first third of the sixteenth to the eighteenth century will come to offer further confirmation to our thesis.

Notes

1 The Ottomans could implement a different fiscal system (or fiscal systems in the plural), because of the circumstances that surrounded their expansion. For the classic conversion curve, see the classic BULLIET, *Conversión to Islam*. For a detailed discussion of his chronological proposal in Syria see ELLENBLUM, *Frankish Rural Settlement*.
2 For the concept of *dimmi*. BOSWORTH, *The Arabs, Byzantium and Islam*.
3 See the still essential LAMBTON, *State and Government in Medieval Islam*
4 See for instance the classic BEN MESHEH, *Taxation in islam*, This book reproduces the work of three jurists dated to the eighth to tenth centuries, which were for centuries at the centre of debate in Sunni law. Especially remarkable is the staying power of the ideas of Yaḥyà ibn Ādam, one of these three jurists, along with Qudāma ibn Ja'far and Abū Yūsuf.
5 BENHIMA, "Normes fiscales et pouvoir califal", pp. 315–323.
6 INALCIK's classic work is still valuable. For a synthesis of his ideas in English see INALCIK, *Essays in Ottoman History*. A recent work that focuses on taxation in KENANOĞLU, "Is Millet System a Reality or a Myth?" pp. 17–38. For the Balkans see the classic BELDICEANU, *Le monde des ottomans des Balkans*.
7 A most interesting economic perspective, beyond the traditional legal approaches, in two works by CAMPOPIANO: "Land Tax Alā l-misāḥa and muqāsama", pp. 239–269; "Land Tenure, Land Tax and Social Conflictuality, pp. 464–499.
8 MOLINA LÓPEZ "Economía, propiedad, impuestos".

9. Lagardère, *Histoire et societé en Occident musulman.*
10. For an excellent summary of this, see Ibn Khaldūn, *Al-Muqadimma*, pp. 517–520.
11. Ibn Khaldūn, *Al-Muqadimma*, pp. 504–505 and 659.
12. Guichard, *From the Arab Conquest to the Reconquest*, p. 184.
13. Lévi-Provençal, *España musulmana*, pp. 17–25.
14. Barceló, "La más temprana organización fiscal de al-Andalus", pp. 231–261; Chalmeta, "Facteurs de la formation des prix", pp. 111–137.
15. Barceló, *El sol que salió por occidente*; Chalmeta, "An approximate picture of the economy of al-Andalus", Jayyusi, *The Legacy of Muslim Spain*, vol. II, pp. 741–758; Chalmeta, "Consideraciones sobre el establecimiento", pp. 103–110; Chalmeta, "Moneda y fiscalidad en la España musulmana", pp. 179–192; Chalmeta, "Fiscalité musulmane: au sujet du *ṭabl*", pp. 217–222.
16. Spanish version: Guichard, *Al-Andalus*
17. Chalmeta, *Historia socioeconómica de al-Andalus.*
18. Amin, *Sobre el desarrollo desigual*
19. Wickham, "The other transition" pp. 3–36.
20. Manzano, *La corte del califa.* pp. 59–61.
21. García-Sanjuán, "El concepto tributario", pp. 81–152.
22. Chalmeta, "Introducción al estudio de la economía", pp. 113–128; Chalmeta, "Balance. Renovación-ampliación del cuestionario", pp. 315–339.
23. Guichard, *Al-Andalus*, p. 325.
24. Guichard, *From the Arab Conquest*, p. 185.
25. Pedro Chalmeta, "Un formulaire notarial", pp. 186–188.
26. Guichard and Lagardère, "La vie sociale et économique", pp. 197–236.
27. Lagardère, "Structures étatiques et communautés rurales", pp. 57–95; Abboud-Haggar, "La fiscalidad en al-Andalus", pp. 23–40.
28. Serrano, *Maḏāhib al-ḥukkām*, pp. 101–104.
29. Ibn Rushd, *Fatāwā*, pp. 503–511, 598–602, 907–909, 994–996, 1412–1413 (consultations about the *zakā*).
30. Ibn Rushd, *Bidāyat al-mujtahid,* vol., I, pp. 364–412; trans. Nyazee, *The distinguished jurist's primer*, vol., I, pp. 283–329.
31. Guichard, *Al-Andalus*, pp. 343–357.
32. Guichard, *Al-Andalus*, p. 338.
33. Jiménez Puertas, "Fiscalidad y moneda en Al-Andalus", pp. 123–143.
34. Badawi and Haleem, *Arabic-English Dictionary of Qur'anic Usage*, Leiden, pp. 399–400.
35. Haleem, *The Qur'an*, p. 121.
36. García-Sanjuán, *Till God Inherits the Earth.*
37. Haleem,, *The Qur'an*, p. 218.
38. Ibn Rushd, *Bidāya,* I, p. 583; Nyazee, *The distinguished*, I, p. 465.
39. Mālik, *Muwaṭṭa'*, vol., I, p. 233; Ibn Rushd, *Bidāya*, I, p. 609; Nyazee, 1994–1996, I, p. 484.
40. Barceló, *El sol*, p. 80.
41. Chalmeta, *Invasión e islamización.* pp. 214–215.
42. Chalmeta, *Invasión*, p. 216, which translates 'abd as "settler".
43. Barceló, *El sol*, p. 39.
44. Manzano, *Conquistadores*, pp. 72–74.
45. Manzano, *Conquistadores*, p. 298
46. Manzano, *Conquistadores*, p. 297.
47. Barceló, *El sol*, pp. 133–134.
48. Barceló, *El sol*, p. 126, defines the *ṭabl* as "the part of the *zakāt* which is not '*ushr*".
49. Chalmeta, "Balance", p. 329.
50. Ibn Ḥawqal, *Kitāb ṣūrat al-arḍ*, pp. 108 and 112.
51. Molina, *Una descripción anónima*, vols, I, pp. 163–164 (Arabic) and II, p. 174 (Spanish); Lévi-Provençal, p. 23.
52. Constable, *Trade and Traders*, pp. 127–128; Maíllo, "De la formación social", pp. 21–30.
53. Guichard, *Al-Andalus*, p. 327.
54. Tibi, *The Tibyān*, p. 44.
55. Tibi, *The Tibyān*, p. 45.
56. Guichard, *Al-Andalus*, pp. 329–330.

57 Tibi, *The Tibyān*, pp. 132–133.
58 Guichard and Premare, "Croissance urbaine et société rurale", pp. 15–30; Barceló, *El sol*, pp. 205–212.
59 Tibi, *The Tibyān*, p. 60.
60 Asín Palacios, "Un códice inexplorado", pp. 38–42.
61 Manzano, *Conquistadores*, p. 462.
62 Tibi, *The Tibyān*, p. 128.
63 Lévi-Provençal, "Un document", p. 241; Lévi-Provençal & García Gómez, *Sevilla,* p. 156.
64 Lévi-Provençal, "Un document", p. 196; Lévi-Provençal & García Gómez, *Sevilla*, pp. 43–46.
65 Lévi-Provençal, "Un document", p. 197; Lévi-Provençal & García Gómez, *Sevilla*, pp. 47–48.
66 Lévi-Provençal, "Un document", p. 220; Lévi-Provençal & García Gómez, *Sevilla*, pp. 104–105.
67 Álvarez de Cienfuegos, "La Hacienda", pp. 99–124; Ladero Quesada, "Dos temas de la Granada nazarí, II: pp. 321–334.
68 Torres Delgado, "La hacienda nazarí", pp. 552–557.
69 Fábregas (ed.) *The Nasrid Kingdom.*
70 Castillo Fernández, "Fiscalidad nazarí", pp. 27–28.
71 Galán Sánchez and Peinado Santaella, "De la madīna musulmana", pp. 197–238.
72 Galán Sánchez, "Acerca del régimen tributario", pp. 379–392.
73 López Beltrán, "Un impuesto sobre la exportación", pp. 95–110.
74 Ladero Quesada, *Granada*, Granada, p. 264.
75 Jiménez Puertas, "Fiscalidad", p. 126.
76 Al-Wansharīsī, *al-Mi'yār al-mu'rib*, vol. I, pp. 363–409.
77 Domínguez Rojas, "La economía", pp. 82–83 y 98.
78 Darling, "Ottoman Fiscal Administration",, p. 164.
79 For a discussion of *kanun*, see, Imber, *The Ottoman Empire*, pp. 244–251.
80 Şahin and Emecen, *II. Bâyezid Dönemine*, no. 41, p. 12.
81 Şahin and Emecen, *Ahkâm Defteri*, no. 41, p. 12.
82 Barkan, *XV ve XVI inci Asırlarda* no. 46, p. 238, 240.
83 İnalcık, "The Problem of the Relationship", no. II, p. 237.
84 Barkan, *Kanunlar*, p. lxiv.
85 McGowan, *Sirem Sancağı*, p. Lxii.
86 Ménage, *Ottoman Historical Documents*, p. 109.
87 İnalcık,, "Osmanlılar'da Raiyyet Rüsûmu", pp. 577–581.
88 Imber, *Ottoman Empire*, p. 240.
89 Lowry, "The role of Byzantine Provincial Officials", p. 262.
90 Kastritsis (ed.), *An Early Ottoman History*, p. 132.
91 İnalcık, (ed.), *Hicrî 835.*
92 For a description of land surveying and *tahrir*s, see İnalcık, "The Ottoman State", pp. 132–139.
93 Lowry, "The Ottoman *Tahrır Defterleri*", pp. 7–8.
94 For an English translation, see Ménage, *Ottoman Historical Documents*, no. 2, pp. 99–104.
95 Genc and Özvar (ed.), *Osmanlı Maliyesi*, vol. 2, p. 11.
96 İnalcık,, *The Customs Register of Caffa, 1487–1490*, p. 99.
97 Lowry, "The Island of Limnos", p. 238.
98 Şahin and Emecen, *Ahkâm Defteri*, no. 107, p. 31.
99 Fleet, *European and Islamic Trade*, pp. 134–140.
100 Gökbilgin, *XV-XVI Asırlarda*, no. 3, p. 135; no. 22, p. 152.
101 Ménage, *Ottoman Historical Documents*, no. 2b, p. 130.
102 Lowry, "A Note on the Population", p. 130.
103 Goffman, "The Jews of Safad", p. 82.
104 Şahin and Emecen, *Ahkâm Defteri*, no. 244, pp. 68–9.
105 Şahin and Emecen, *Ahkâm Defteri*, no. 231, p. 65.
106 Ménage, *Ottoman Historical Documents*, no. 3b, p. 135.
107 Şahin and Emecen, *Ahkâm Defteri*, no. 396, p. 110.
108 Şahin and Emecen, *Ahkâm Defteri*, no. 382, p. 106.
109 Şahin and Emecen, *Ahkâm Defteri*, no. 211, p. 60.
110 Liakopoulos, *The Early Ottoman Peloponnese*, p. 243, 364.
111 Şahin and Emecen, *Ahkâm Defteri*, no. 144, p. 41.

112 ŞAHİN and EMECEN, *Ahkâm Defteri*, no. 202, p. 57.
113 ŞAHİN and EMECEN, *Ahkâm Defteri*, no. 154, p. 43.
114 ŞAHİN and EMECEN, *Ahkâm Defteri*, no. 105, p. 30.
115 ŞAHİN and EMECEN, *Ahkâm Defteri*, no. 254, p. 71.
116 AKDAĞ, *Türkiye'nin İktisadi*, Istanbul, 2010, p. 553.
117 DARLING, "Ottoman Fiscal Administration", p. 162.
118 LOWRY, "The Ottoman *Liva Kanunnames*", p. 52.
119 BALTA, *L'Eubée a la fin du XVe siècle*, p. 2.
120 COŞGEL, "Efficiency and Continuity", pp. 570–573.
121 AKDAĞ, *Türkiye'nin İktisadi*, p. 362.
122 BARKAN, *Kanunlar*, no. 56, p. 393.
123 İNALCIK,, "Osmanlılar'da Raiyyet Rüsumu", p. 581.
124 MÉNAGE, *Ottoman Historical Documents*, no. 4, p. 108.
125 İNALCIK,, *Defter-i Sancak-i Arnavid*, pp. 5, 88–9, 103.
126 BALTA, *Eubée*, pp. 18–19.
127 İNALCIK, "Osmanlılar'da Raiyyet Rüsumu", p. 603. For a detailed discussion, see BOJANIC-LUKAC, "De la nature", pp. 9–30.
128 IMBER, *Ottoman Empire*, p. 244.
129 GINIO, "Neither Muslims nor Zimmis", pp. 117–144.
130 BALTA, *Eubée*, p. 23.
131 BARKAN, *Kanunlar*, no. 37, p. 158; no. 39, p. 165; no. 45, p. 181.
132 BARKAN, *Kanunlar*, no. 43, p. 172.
133 BARKAN, *Kanunlar*, no. 34, p. 150.
134 BARKAN, *Kanunlar*, no. 55, p. 201.
135 BARKAN, *Kanunlar*, no. 40, p. 168.
136 İNALCIK,, "Osmanlılar'da Raiyyet Rüsumu", pp. 584–585.
137 BARKAN, *Kanunlar*, no. 66, pp. 237, 239.
138 BARKAN, *Kanunlar*, no. 17, p. 57.
139 BARKAN, *Kanunlar*, no. 46, p. 240.
140 ŞAHİN and EMECEN, *Ahkâm Defteri*, no. 155, p. 44.
141 MÉNAGE, *Ottoman Historical Documents*, no. 2, p. 102.
142 BARKAN, *Kanunlar*, no. 38, p. 164.
143 BARKAN, *Kanunlar*, no. 31, pp. 134–135.
144 BARKAN, *Kanunlar*, no. 38, p. 164.
145 BELDICEANU, *Recherche sur la ville ottomane*, pp. 266–267.
146 BALTA, *Eubée*, p. 39.
147 İNALCIK, *Defter-i Sancak-i Arnavid*, pp. 89, XXVII.
148 MÉNAGE, *Ottoman Historical Documents*, no. 1, p. 98.
149 BARKAN, *Kanunlar*, no. 46, p. 237.
150 MÉNAGE, *Ottoman Historical Documents*, no. 1, p. 98.
151 FLEET, "The Treaty of 1387", clause 5, p. 15, 17.
152 FLEET, *Trade*, pp. 130–131.
153 BARKAN, *Kanunlar*, no. 46, p. 238.
154 BELDICEANU, *Recherche*, no 10, pp. 164, 165.
155 MÉNAGE, *Ottoman Historical Documents*, no. 2f, p. 132.
156 FLEET, "The Turkish Economy", pp. 254–265.
157 LOWRY, "Limnos", p. 246.
158 BARKAN, *Kanunlar*, no. 46, p. 240.
159 LOWRY, "Limnos", p. 258.
160 BARKAN, *Kanunlar*, no. 46, p. 237.
161 MÉNAGE, *Ottoman Historical Documents*, no. 2, p. 102.
162 This is paralleled by other issues in the history of Islam, such as the alleged Islamic inability to move towards capitalistic societies, a notion against which Maxime Rodinson fought with ardour and intelligence, RODINSON, *Islam et capitalisme*, translated into multiple languages and re-edited in French in 2014. Some of the debates triggered by her work are examined, with uneven success, in HUFF and SCHLUCHTER (ed.), *Weber and Islam*.

163 See for instance the well-known peace treaty between the Mamluk sultan and the Republic of Genoa (1290) in CAHEN, *Orient et Occident*.
164 CONSTABLE, *Trade and Traders* and PICARD, *Sea of the Caliphs*
165 For the fascinating Mamluk period see LOISEAU, *Les Mamelouks* and more specifically see MIURA, *Dynamism in the Urban Society* chapter four pp. 111–135.
166 GALÁN SÁNCHEZ, "An Old society", pp. 495–518 and ABBOUD-HAGGAR "Precedentes andalusíes", pp. 475–512.

References

Soha ABBOUD-HAGGAR "Precedentes andalusíes en la fiscalidad de las comunidades mudéjares", *En En la España medieval*, 31, 2008, pp. 475–512.
Soha ABBOUD-HAGGAR, "La fiscalidad en al-Andalus entre los siglos VIII y XII a través de las recopilaciones de sentencias de Ibn Sahl y de Ibn Qāsim al-Šaʿbī", *Espacio Tiempo y Forma. Serie III, Historia Medieval*, 2015, 28, pp. 23–40.
Mustafa AKDAĞ, *Türkiye'nin İktisadi ve İçtimai Tarihi*, Istanbul, 2010.
María Isabel ÁLVAREZ DE CIENFUEGOS, "La Hacienda de los naṣríes granadinos", *Miscelánea de Estudios Árabes y Hebraicos* 1959, 8, pp. 99–124
Samir AMIN, *Sobre el desarrollo desigual de las formaciones sociales*, Barcelona, 1974.
Miguel ASÍN PALACIOS, "Un códice inexplorado del cordobés Ibn Ḥazm", *Al-Andalus*, 1934, 2, pp. 38–42.
Elsaid BADAWI and Muhammed Abdel HALEEM, *Arabic-English Dictionary of Qurʾanic Usage*, Leiden, 2008;
Evangelia BALTA, *L'Eubée a la fin du XVe siècle. Économie et Population. Les registres de l'année 1474*, Athens, 1989.
Miquel BARCELÓ, "La más temprana organización fiscal de al-Andalus según la *Crónica del 754* (95/713(4)-138/755)", *Faventia* (1979) pp. 231–261.
Miquel BARCELÓ, *El sol que salió por occidente. Estudios sobre el estado omeya de al-Andalus*, Valencia, 2010.
Ömer Lütfi BARKAN, *XV ve XVI inci Asırlarda Osmanlı İmparatorluğunda Ziraî Ekonominin Hukukî ve Malî Esasları. I Kanunlar*, Istanbul, 1943, no. 46, pp. 238, 240.
Nicoară BELDICEANU, *Recherche sur la ville ottomane au XVE siècle. Étude et actes*, Paris, 1973.
Yassir BENHIMA, "Normes fiscales et pouvoir califal au Maghreb au Xe sièclela fiscalité dans l'affrontement idéologique entre Fatimides et Omeyyades », in Florent GARNIER, Armand JAMME, Anne LEMONDE, Pere VERDÉS (dirs.), *Cultures fiscales en Occident du Xe au XVIIe siècle. Études offertes à Denis Menjot*, Presses universitaires du Midi, Toulouse, 2019, pp. 315–323.
Nicoara BELDICEANU, *Le monde des ottomans des Balkans (1402–1566): institutions, société, économie*, Variorum Reprints, London, 1976.
Ahmed BEN MESHEH, *Taxation in islam*, Brill, Leyden, 1967–1969, t. I, II and III.
Dušanka BOJANIC-LUKAC, "De la nature et de l'origine de l'ispendje", in *Wiener Zeitschrift für die Kunde des Morgenlandes*, 68, 1976, pp. 9–30.
Clifford Edmund BOSWORTH, *The Arabs, Byzantium and Islam*, Variorum Reprints, London, 1996.
Richard BULLIET, *Conversión to Islam in Medieval Period*, Cambridge, 1979.
Rodney ELLENBLUM, *Frankish Rural Settlement In The Latin Kingdom Of Jerusalem*, Cambridge Univ. Press, 1998.
Claude CAHEN, *Orient et Occident au temps des croisades*, Aubier Montaigne, Paris, 1983 (appendiz IX). Reed. 2010.
Michelle CAMPOPIANO, "Land Tax Alā l-misāḥa and muqāsama: Legal Theory and Balance of Social Forces in Early Medieval Iraq (Sixth to Eighth Centuries)", in *Journal of the Economic and Social History of the Orient*, 54/2, 2011, pp. 239–269.
Michelle CAMPOPIANO, "Land Tenure, Land Tax and Social Conflictuality in Iraq from the Late Sasanian to the Early Islamic Period (Fifth to Ninth Centuries CE)" in Alain DELATTRE, Marie LEGENDRE and Petra SIJPESTEIJN (ed.), *Authority and Control in the Countryside. From Antiquity to Islam in the Mediterranean and Near East (6th–10th Century)*, Leiden Studies in Islam and Society, Volume 9, Brill, 2018, pp. 464–499.
Javier CASTILLO FERNÁNDEZ, "Fiscalidad nazarí y fiscalidad castellana en Baza a fines de la Edad Media", *Miscelánea Medieval Murciana* 2008, 32, pp. 27–28.
Pedro CHALMETA, "Facteurs de la formation des prix dans l'Islam medieval", *Congreso Internacional sobre la historia del Magreb*, Tunisia, 1979, pp. 111–137.

Pedro CHALMETA, "An approximate picture of the economy of al-Andalus", in KHADRA JAYYUSI, S. (ed.), *The Legacy of Muslim Spain*, Leiden, 1994, 2nd ed., 2 vols., II, pp. 741–758.

Pedro CHALMETA, "Consideraciones sobre el establecimiento de la fiscalidad musulmana (644–750)", *Res Orientales* VI (1994), pp. 103–110.

Pedro CHALMETA, "Moneda y fiscalidad en la España musulmana", in *Moneda y monedas en la Europa medieval (siglos XII–XV). XXVI Semana de Estudios Medievales (Estella, 19 a 23 julio 1999)*, Pamplona, 2000, pp. 179–192.

Pedro CHALMETA, "Fiscalité musulmane: au sujet du *ṭabl*", in *L'Orient au coeur, en l'honneur d'André Miquel*, Paris, 2000, pp. 217–222.

Pedro CHALMETA, *Historia socioeconómica de al-Andalus*. Almería, 2021.

Pedro CHALMETA, "Introducción al estudio de la economía andalusí (siglos VIII–XI)", in Felipe MAÍLLO (ed.): *España. Al-Andalus. Sefarad. Síntesis y nuevas perspectivas*, Salamanca, 1990, 2nd edition, pp. 113–128.

Pedro CHALMETA, "Balance. Renovación-ampliación del cuestionario. Un ejemplo de análisis socio-económico", *Aragón en la Edad Media*, 1991, IX, pp. 315–339.

Pedro CHALMETA, "Un formulaire notarial hispano-arabe du IV/X siècle. Glanés économiques", *Revista del Instituto Egipcio de Estudios Islámicos*, XXIII (1985–1986), pp. 186–188.

Pedro CHALMETA, *Invasión e islamización. La sumisión de Hispania y la formación de al-Andalus*, Madrid, 1994.

Olivia R. CONSTABLE, *Trade and Traders in Muslim Spain: The Commercial Realignment of the Iberian Peninsula, 900–1500*, New York, 1994.

Olivia Remie CONSTABLE, *Trade and Traders in Muslim Spain: The Commercial Realignment of the Iberian Peninsula, 900–1500*, Cambridge Studies in Medieval Life and Thought, Cambridge, 1996.

Metin COŞGEL, "Efficiency and Continuity in Public Finance: the Ottoman System of Taxation", in *International Journal of Middle East Studies*, 37/4, 2005.

Linda DARLING, "Ottoman Fiscal Administration: Decline or Adaption", in *Journal of European Economic History*, 26/1, 1997.

Salud María DOMÍNGUEZ ROJAS, "La economía del reino nazarí a través de las fetuas recogidas en el Miʿyār de al-Wanšarīsī", *Anaquel de Estudios Árabes*, 2006, 17, p. 82–83 y 98.

Kate FLEET, "The Treaty of 1387 between Murad I and the Genoese", in *Bulletin of the School of Oriental and African Studies*, 56/1, 1993.

Kate FLEET, *European and Islamic Trade in the Early Ottoman State*, Cambridge, 1999.

Kate FLEET, "The Turkish Economy, 1071–1453", in *The Cambridge History of Turkey Volume I Byzantium to Turkey 1071–1453*, ed. Kate FLEET, Cambridge, 2009.

Adela FÁBREGAS (ed.), *The Nasrid Kingdom of Granada between East and West (Thirteenth to Fifteenth Centuries)*, Leiden, 2020.

Ángel GALÁN SÁNCHEZ, "Acerca del régimen tributario nazarí: el impuesto del talbix", *Actas del II Coloquio de Historia Medieval Andaluza. Hacienda y comercio (Sevilla, 8–10 abril 1981)*, Sevilla, 1982, pp. 379–392.

Ángel GALÁN SÁNCHEZ and Rafael G. PEINADO SANTAELLA, "De la madīna musulmana al concejo mudéjar: fiscalidad regia y fiscalidad concejil en la ciudad de Granada tras la conquista castellana" in Manuel SÁNCHEZ MARTÍNEZ and Denis MENJOT (eds), *Fiscalidad de Estado y fiscalidad municipal en los reinos hispánicos medievales*, Casa de Velázquez, Madrid, 2006, pp. 197–238.

Ángel GALÁN SÁNCHEZ, "An Old society, Mudejar neighbors. New perspectives", in Adela FÁBREGAS GARCÍA (ed.) *The Nasrid Kingdom of Granada between East and West (Thirteenth to Fifteenth Centuries)*, Leyden Brill, 2021, pp. 495–518.

Alejandro GARCÍA-SANJUÁN, "El concepto tributario y la caracterización de la sociedad andalusí: treinta años de debate historiográfico", in Alejandro GARCÍA SANJUÁN (ed.), *Saber y sociedad en al-Andalus. IV–V Jornadas de Cultura Islámica*, Huelva, 2006, pp. 81–152.

Alejandro GARCÍA-SANJUÁN, *Till God Inherits the Earth. Islamic Pious Endowments in al-Andalus (9th–15th centuries)*, Leiden, 2007.

Mehmet GENÇ and Erol ÖZVAR (ed.), *Osmanlı Maliyesi Kurumlar ve Bütçeler*, Istanbul, 2006, vol. 2.

Eyal GINIO, "Neither Muslims nor Zimmis: the Gypsies (Roma) in the Ottoman State", *Romani Studies*, 14/2, 2004.

Daniel GOFFMAN, "The Jews of Safad and the Maktu System in the Sixteenth Century: a Study of Two Documents from the Ottoman Archives", in *Osmanlı Araştırmaları/Journal of Ottoman Studies*, 3, 1982.

Mustafa Tayyip GÖKBİLGİ, *XV-XVI Asırlarda Edirne ve Paşa Livası Vakıflar – Mülkler – Mukataalar*, Istanbul, 1952.

Pierre GUICHARD, P. and Alfred L. de PREMARE, "Croissance urbaine et société rurale à Valence au début de l'époque des royaumes Taifas, XIe siècle de J.C. Traduction et commentaire d'un texte d'Ibn Ḥayyān", *Révue de l'Occident Musulman et de la Méditerranée*, 1981, 31, pp. 15–30.

Pierre GUICHARD, *Al-Andalus frente a la conquista cristiana: los musulmanes de Valencia, siglos XI–XIII*, Madrid-Valencia, 2001.

Pierre GUICHARD, *From the Arab Conquest to the Reconquest: The Splendour and Fragility of al-Andalus*, Granada, 2006.

Pierre GUICHARD and Vincent LAGARDÈRE, "La vie sociale et économique de l'Espagne musulmane aux XI–XIIe siècles à travers les fatwās du Mi'yār d'al-Wanšarīšī", *Mélanges de la Casa de Velázquez*, 1990, XXXVI/1, pp. 197–236.

Muhammed Abdel HALEEM, *The Qur'an*, Oxford, 2005.

Toby HUFF and Wolfgang SCHLUCHTER (ed), *Weber and Islam*, Transactions Publishers, New Jersey, 1999.

Colin IMBER, *The Ottoman Empire, 1300–1650*, London, 2019.

Halik INALCIK, *Essays in Ottoman History*, Eren, Istanbul, 1998.

Halil INALCIK, "The Problem of the Relationship between Byzantine and Ottoman Taxation", in Halil INALCIK, *The Ottoman Empire: Conquest, Organization and Economy*, London, 1978, no. II.

Halil INALCIK, "Osmanlılar'da Raiyyet Rüsûmu", in *Belleten*, 23/92, 1959.

Halil INALCIK (ed.), *Hicrî 835 Tarihli Sûret-i Defter-i Sancak-i Arnavid*, Ankara, 1954.

Halil INALCIK, "The Ottoman State: Economy and Society, 1300–1600", in *An Economic and Social History of the Ottoman Empire 1300–1914*, ed. Halil INALCIK and Donald QUATAERT, Cambridge, 1994.

Halil INALCIK, *The Customs Register of Caffa, 1487–1490*, ed. Victor OSTAPCHUK, Cambridge, MA., 1996.

Miguel JIMÉNEZ PUERTAS, "Fiscalidad y moneda en Al-Andalus: aportaciones al conocimiento de la evolución del sistema tributario nazarí (siglos XIII–XV)", *Cuadernos de la Alhambra* 2010, 45, pp. 123–143.

Dimitri KASTRITSIS (ed.), *An Early Ottoman History. The Oxford Anonymous Chronicle (Bodleian Library, MS Marsh 313)*, Liverpool, 2017.

IBN KHALDUN, *Al-Muqaddima*, ed. and translation by Elías Trabulse, Fondo de Cultura Económica, Mexico, 1977.

M. Macit KENANOĞLU, "Is Millet System a Reality or a Myth? The Legal Position of the Non-Muslim Subjects and their religious Leaders in the Ottoman Empire", *Türk Hukuk Tarihi Araştırmaları*, 12, 2011, pp. 17–38.

Miguel Ángel LADERO QUESADA, "Dos temas de la Granada nazarí, II: el duro fisco de los emires", *Cuadernos de Historia*, 1969, 3, pp. 321–334.

Miguel Ángel LADERO QUESADA, *Granada después de la conquista: repobladores y mudéjares*, Granada, 1988

Vincent LAGARDÈRE, "Structures étatiques et communautés rurales: les impositions légales et illégales en al-Andalus et au Maghreb (XIe–XVe)", *Studia Islamica* 1994, 80, pp. 57–95.

Vincent LAGARDÈRE, *Histoire et société en Occident musulman au Moyen Âge. Analyse du Mi'yar d'Al-Wansarisi*, Madrid, 1995.

Ann Katharine Swynford Lambton, *State and Government in Medieval Islam. An Introduction to the Study of Islamic Political Theory: The Jurists*, Oxford, 1981.

Evariste LÉVI-PROVENÇAL, *España musulmana hasta la caída del califato de Córdoba (711–1031 de J.C.). Instituciones y vida social e intelectual*, Madrid, 1957.

Evariste LÉVI-PROVENÇAL, "Un document sur la vie urbaine et les corps de métiers a Séville au début du XIIe siècle: le traité d'Ibn 'Abdūn", *Journal Asiatique*, 1934, 224, p. 241.

Evariste LÉVI-PROVENÇAL & Emilio GARCÍA GÓMEZ, *Sevilla a comienzos del siglo XII. El tratado de Ibn 'Abdūn*, Madrid, p. 156.

Georgios LIAKOPOULOS, *The Early Ottoman Peloponnese. A Study in the Light of an Annotated Edition Princepts of the TT10-1/14662 Ottoman Taxation Cadastre (ca. 1460–1463)*, London, 2019.

Julien LOISEAU, *Les Mamelouks XIIIe–XVIe siècle: Une expérience du pouvoir dans l'islam médiéval*, Seuil, Paris, 2014.

María Teresa LÓPEZ BELTRÁN, "Un impuesto sobre la exportación de frutos secos: el mucharan", *Miscelánea de Estudios Árabes y Hebraicos*, 1984–1985, XXXIII, pp. 95–110.

Heath LOWRY, "The role of Byzantine Provincial Officials following the Ottoman Conquest of their Lands", in *IIIrd Congress on the Social and Economic History of Turkey*, ed. Heath LOWRY and Ralph HATTOX, Istanbul, 1990.

Heath LOWRY, "The Ottoman *Tahrır Defterleri* as a Source for Social and Economic History: Pitfalls and Limitations", in Heath LOWRY, *Studies in Defterology. Ottoman Society in the Fifteenth and Sixteenth Centuries*, Istanbul, 1992.

Heath LOWRY, "The Island of Limnos: a Case Study on the Continuity of Byzantine Forms under Ottoman Rule", in *Continuity and Change in Late Byzantine and Early Ottoman Society: Papers Given at a Symposium at Dumbarton Oaks in May 1982*, ed. Anthony BRYER and Heath LOWRY, Birmingham and Washington DC, 1986.

Heath LOWRY, "A Note on the Population and Status of the Athonite Monasteries under Ottoman Rule (Ca. 1520)", in *Wiener Zeitschrift für die Kunde des Morgenlandes*, 73, 1981.

Heath LOWRY, "The Ottoman *Liva Kanunnames* Contained in the *Defter-i Hakani*", in *Osmanlı Araştırmaları. The Journal of Ottoman Studies*, 2, 1981.

Bruce MCGOWAN, *Sirem Sancağı Mufassal Tahrir Defteri*, Ankara, 1983.

Felipe MAÍLLO, "De la formación social tributara ¿y mercantil? Andalusí", *El Saber en al-andalus. Textos y estudios*, III, Seville, 2001, pp. 21–30.

MĀLIK, *Muwaṭṭaʾ*, ed. Muḥammad Fuʾad ʿABD AL-BĀQĪ, Cairo, 1993, 2nd edition, 2 vols., I

Eduardo MANZANO, *Conquistadores, emires y califas. Los Omeya y la formación de al-Andalus*, Barcelona, 2006

Eduardo MANZANO, *La corte del califa. Cuatro años en la Córdoba de los omeyas*. Barcelona, 2019

Victor MÉNAGE, *Ottoman Historical Documents. The Institutions of an Empire*, ed. with additions by Colin IMBER, Edinburgh, 2021, no. 4, pp. 109.

Luis MOLINA, *Una descripción anónima de al-Andalus*, Madrid, 1983, 2 vols., I, pp. 163–164 (Arabic) and II, p. 174 (Spanish).

Toru MIURA, *Dynamism in the Urban Society of Damascus*, chapter four ("Administrative Networks in the Late Mamluk Period: Taxation and Bribery"), Brill, Leyden, 2016, pp. 111–135.

Emilio MOLINA LÓPEZ "Economía, propiedad, impuestos y sectores productivos", in *El retroceso territorial de Al-Andalus. Almoravides y Almohades. Siglos XI-XIII*, t. VIII-2 *Historia de España Menéndez Pidal*, Madrid, 1997.

Christophe PICARD, *Sea of the Caliphs: The Mediterranean in the Medieval Islamic World*, Harvard, 2018.

Maxime RODINSON, *Islam et capitalisme*, Editions de Seuil, Paris, 1966.

IBN ḤAWQAL, *Kitāb ṣūrat al-arḍ*, ed. J. H. KRAMERS, Leiden, 1939

IBN RUSH, *Fatāwā*, ed. al-Mukhtār ibn AL-ṬĀHIR AL-TALĪLĪ, Beirut, 1987, 3 vols.

IBN RUSH, *Bidāyat al-mujtahid wa-nihāyat al-muqtaṣid*, ed. ʿAlī Muḥammad MUʿAWWAḌ and ʿĀdil Aḥmad ʿABD AL-MAWJŪD, Beirut, 1997, 2 vols., I, pp. 364–412; trans. Imran Ahsan Khan NYAZEE, *The distinguished jurist's primer*, Doha, 1994–1996, 2 vols., I, pp. 283–329.

İlhan SAHIN and and Feridun EMECEN, *II. Bâyezid Dönemine Ait 906/1501 Tarihli Ahkâm Defteri*, Istanbul, 1994, no. 41.

Delfina SERRANO, *Maḏāhib al-ḥukkām fī nawāzil al-aḥkām (La actuación de los jueces en los procesos judiciales)*, Madrid, 1998.

Amin T. TIBI, *The Tibyān. Memoirs of ʿAbd Allāh b. Buluggīn, last Zīrid Amīr of Granada*, Leiden, 1986.

Cristóbal TORRES DELGADO, "La hacienda nazarí", in *El reino nazarí de Granada (12-1492). Política, instituciones, espacio, economía. Historia de España Menéndez Pidal, VIII-3*, ed. María Jesús VIGUERA, Madrid, 2000, pp. 552–557.

AL-WANSHARĪSĪ, *al-Miʿyār al-muʿrib*, ed. M. ḤĀJJĪ and others, Rabat-Beirut, 1981–83, 13 vols. I

Chris WICKHAM, "The other transition: from the Ancient World to Feudalism", *Past and Present*, 1984, 103, pp. 3–36.

PART III

Glossary

GLOSSARY

The reader will find here a selection of terms for each region of Part II (the definitions have been written by the authors of the corresponding chapters). This glossary is therefore not exhaustive: it is composed of the most important terms for the tax systems analysed. Some terms are defined at length, whereas other definitions are relatively brief. As for the chapters, the level of detail depends on the historiography and the quality and quantity of extant sources. For more information and additional terms, the reader can also refer to the online glossary: https://medieval-fiscal-glossary.net.

1. Accises (France) — 442
2. Adoa (Sicily) — 443
3. Aides (France) — 443
4. Aides (Burgundian Low Countries) — 443
5. Alberga (Provence) — 444
6. Alcabala (Castile) — 444
7. Alien subsidy (England) — 444
8. Almojarifazgo (Castile) — 444
9. Annates (Church taxation) — 445
10. Assisen (Burgundian Low Countries) — 445
11. Auxilium (France) — 445
12. Avarız (Ottoman) — 445
13. Ayuda (Navarre) — 446
14. Bede (Scandinavia) — 446
15. Bede (German Holy Roman Empire) — 446
16. Bœjargjald (Scandinavia) — 447
17. Bovaje (Aragon) — 447
18. Bor, chernyi bor (Russia) — 447
19. Byskat (Scandinavia) — 447
20. Carucage (England) — 447
21. Cavalcata (Provence and Savoy) — 448
22. Cens (Church Lands) — 448
23. Çift resmi (Ottoman) — 448
24. City szos (Poland and Lithuania) — 448

Glossary

25.	Cizye (Ottoman)	448
26.	Clerical tenth (England)	449
27.	Cloison, droits de (France)	449
28.	*Collecta* (Northern Italy)	449
29.	Colletta (Sicily)	449
30.	Cronsteuer (German Holy Roman Empire)	450
31.	Cuartel (Navarre)	450
32.	Dan' (Russia)	450
33.	Datium (Northern Italy)	450
34.	Datium vini (Northern Italy)	450
35.	Diezmos y aduanas (Castile)	450
36.	Donativum (Sicily)	451
37.	Entrées et issues (Brittany)	451
38.	Équivalent des aides (France)	451
39.	Expedition (Scandinavia)	451
40.	Exuwe (Burgundian Low Countries)	452
41.	Estimum (Northern Italy)	452
42.	Feudal aid (England)	452
43.	Fifteenth and tenth (England)	452
44.	Focagium (Provence)	453
45.	Focatico (Sicily)	453
46.	Fodrum (Northern Italy)	453
47.	Fogaje (Aragon)	453
48.	Fondaco (Sicily)	454
49.	Fouage (Brittany)	454
50.	Fouage (France)	454
51.	Fractional taxes (England)	454
52.	Gabella (Sicily)	455
53.	Gabella (Provence and Savoy)	455
54.	Gabelle (France)	455
55.	Gabelle du sel (France)	455
56.	Gabelles and péages (Dauphiné)	456
57.	Gærþ (Scandinavia)	456
58.	Gate tax (Northern Italy)	456
59.	Geld (England)	456
60.	Gemeiner Pfennig (German Holy Roman Empire)	457
61.	Generalidades (Aragon)	457
62.	Gengærþ (Scandinavia)	457
63.	Gouveliatikon (Byzantine Empire)	457
64.	Gramota (Russia)	458
65.	Güldener Opferpfennig (German Holy Roman Empire)	458
66.	Hearth tax (Church Lands)	458
67.	Hofsteuer (German Holy Roman Empire)	458
68.	Hussensteuer (German Holy Roman Empire)	458
69.	Imposition foraine (France)	459
70.	Imposición (Navarre)	459
71.	Imposicions (Aragon)	459
72.	Income tax (England)	459

Glossary

73.	İspence (Ottoman)	459
74.	Issue (Burgundian Low Countries)	460
75.	Ius exportationis (Burgundian Low Countries)	460
76.	Ius fondaci (Sicily)	460
77.	Ius passuum (Sicily)	460
78.	Judensteuer (German Holy Roman Empire)	460
79.	Ledung (Scandinavia)	461
80.	Lesda (Provence and Savoy)	461
81.	Lezdas (Aragon)	461
82.	Lezta (Navarre)	462
83.	Libra (Northern Italy)	462
84.	Longuellum (Savoy)	462
85.	Losung (German Holy Roman Empire)	462
86.	Macina (Northern Italy)	462
87.	Maktu (Ottoman)	463
88.	Mala pecunia (Burgundian Low Countries)	463
89.	Mansus tax (Poland)	463
90.	Martiniega (Castile)	463
91.	Monedaje (Aragon)	463
92.	Monedaje (Navarre)	464
93.	Moneda forera (Castile)	464
94.	Mukataa (Ottoman)	464
95.	Munus (Right to tax)	465
96.	Myt (Russia)	465
97.	Nefgildi (Scandinavia)	465
98.	Octroi (France)	465
99.	Octroi, octroy (patent) (Burgundian Low Countries)	466
100.	Opsonion (Byzantine Empire)	466
101.	Ongeld (Burgundian Low Countries)	466
102.	Passagia (Sicily)	466
103.	Peajes (Aragon)	466
104.	Pecha (Navarre)	466
105.	Pecha / peita (Aragon)	466
106.	Pedagium portarum (Northern Italy)	467
107.	Plough tax (Poland and Lithuania)	467
108.	Poll tax (England)	467
109.	Portazgo (Castile)	467
110.	Pozobitze (Byzantine Empire)	467
111.	Prebenda (Byzantine Empire)	467
112.	Precaria (Scandinavia)	468
113.	Preselitza (Byzantine Empire)	468
114.	Procurations (Church taxation)	468
115.	Procurations (Church Lands)	468
116.	Quèstia (Aragon)	468
117.	Reichsstadtsteuer (German Holy Roman Empire)	469
118.	Relevium (Sicily)	469
119.	Royal szos (Poland and Lithuania)	470
120.	Salt gabelle (Northern Italy)	470

121.	Scutage (England)	470
122.	Servicio de Cortes (Castile)	470
123.	Servicio y montazgo (Castile)	471
124.	Sisas (Castile)	471
125.	Sisas (Aragon)	471
126.	Skotte (Scandinavia)	472
127.	Stadsskatt (Scandinavia)	472
128.	Subventio generalis (Sicily)	472
129.	Subsidio (Navarre)	472
130.	Subsidy (Dauphiné)	472
131.	Subsidy (Church taxation)	472
132.	Subsidy (Provence and Savoy)	473
133.	Subsidy (Church Lands)	473
134.	Szos (Poland and Lithuania)	473
135.	Tallage (England)	473
136.	Tallia (Church Lands)	474
137.	Tallia (Provence and Savoy)	474
138.	Taille (France, royal tax)	474
139.	Taille (France, municipal tax)	474
140.	Talea (Northern Italy)	475
141.	Tamga (Russia)	475
142.	Theloneum (Sicily)	475
143.	Tenth (Church taxation)	475
144.	Tenth (England)	475
145.	Traite des vins (France)	475
146.	Traites (Brittany)	476
147.	Tratta (Sicily)	476
148.	Ungeld (German Holy Roman Empire)	476
149.	Vacancies (Church taxation)	476
150.	Vykhod (Russia)	477
151.	Wine gabelle (Northern Italy)	477
152.	Yam (Russia)	477
153.	Zwanzigster Pfennig (German Holy Roman Empire)	477
154.	Zehnter Pfennig (German Holy Roman Empire)	478

1. Accises (France)

Municipal indirect taxes on the circulation or sale of merchandises, also called *assises*, or *maltôtes* in the fourteenth century. They developed in Northern France (where they were called *accises*) in the second half of the thirteenth century, and in the South in the mid-fourteenth century, when indirect taxation became the main source for financing urban fortifications until modern times. They were levied by farmers, either at the town gates on merchandise entering or leaving (they were then called *droits de barrage*, or barrier duties), or in shops and markets. The most profitable item was wine, whose retail sale was taxed through the technique of *appetissement* (or *billot* in Brittany, *souquet* in the South), a reduction by about one-tenth of the quantity delivered to the consumer. The second most lucrative item was salt, taxed through an additional duty granted by the king on top of the *gabelle*.

Glossary

2. Adoa (Sicily)

This was a royal direct subsidy based on land rent and applied to seigneurs between the first half of the twelfth century and the second half of the eighteenth. The subsidy was introduced during the Norman kingdom as *servitium pecuniarum* due to the sovereigns alongside *servitium personarum*. Frederick II decided that the *adoa* should have been the cash equivalent to the military aid usually given to the monarch. In 1282, Charles I of Anjou set the amount due: twelve and a half *onze* for every twenty of feudal income; after the Vespri the amount was halved; beginning in 1285, it was decided that the lords should pay three *onze* a month for each man which they should have provided. In 1316, the *adoa* raised 6,000 *onze*; in 1341, 8,000 and at the beginning of fourteenth century, it totalled 20,135 *onze*. The *adoa* was abolished by Alphonse V Trastámara, but was restored by his successors and remained in force throughout the modern era.

3. Aides (France)

This is a generic term to describe various forms of indirect taxation. It usually refers to a tax proportional to the circulation and sale of goods and chattels, either retail or wholesale, also called *gabelles* in the fourteenth century and *impositions* in the fifteenth century. This type of tax was common in various countries in Europe. In France in 1355, the Estates General approved this tax (at a rate of 8 *deniers* per *livre*) across the whole kingdom. It retained its feudal nature ("aid for the ransom" of King John in 1360), and then became a royal tax. The rate stabilised at 12 *deniers* per pound (5 per cent) in 1360, except for the most lucrative goods: wine and salt (see *Gabelle du sel*). The aids on wine (and other alcoholic drinks) were named after their special rate: a stable "twentieth" (5 per cent) for wholesale, and a rate fluctuating in time and space from "thirteenth" to "fourth" for retail. Only the aid on wine retail sales was subject to exemptions for the usual privileged groups: clerics, noblemen, mint officials and some royal officers. The *élus* of fourteenth-century dioceses and fifteenth-century *élections* separately leased to farmers the collection of aids for each particular taxable category of merchandise in their whole districts, or most commonly, in a subdistrict. A variety of products were affected: for consumption (wine, animals), clothing or construction. After starting out as an extraordinary tax, *aides* became an ordinary tax in the north of the French kingdom in 1436, in the south in 1437, and in the centre-west in 1451. To avoid paying it, provinces obtained an *abonnement* (a one-off payment equivalent to the *aides*) from the 1440s onwards.

4. Aides (Burgundian Low Countries)

The term *aides* (in Dutch *beden*) refers to the fact that the prince "asked" for it. This was an extraordinary contribution to princely finances, in addition to the traditional income based on the princely demesne. Apart from some traditional motives (*les cas féodaux*: crusade, ransom, marriage of the prince's daughter, knighthood of the eldest son), it was freely consented by the subjects. Traditionally, its amount was negotiated with the Third Estate, although in several cases, the clergy also participated. This tax was collected by ad hoc receivers, the sum to be raised was financed through indirect taxes in the cities and through direct taxes in the countryside. In principle, it was a non-recurring subsidy and came into use from the thirteenth century onwards. I gradually became by far the most important source of income for the prince.

5. Alberga (Provence)

Alberga, in Provence, was the right for the count, as feudal lord, to be hosted by his vassals under certain conditions. Deriving from early medieval occasional practices of *fodrum* or *gistum*, the Provençal *alberga* was, from the early thirteenth century, collected on an annual basis, either as a fixed amount or as a hearth tax generally rated at 12 pence (*denarii*) per hearth. *Alberga* is occasionally referred to as a *focagium minus*, as distinct from the feudal aid (*quista* or *focagium majus*).

6. Alcabala (Castile)

An indirect royal tax on commercial transactions dating back to the effective rule of Alphonse XI (1325–1350). In 1333, the cities and towns of Andalusia and Murcia ceded the king the collection of *alcabalas* to shoulder the costs of defending the frontier with Granada. The collection of *alcabalas* was extended to the whole kingdom in 1342, after the *Cortes* granted their temporary authorization to pay for the conquest of Algeciras. The temporary award of *alcabalas* continued during the second half of the fourteenth century, during which time the tax rate increased from 3.33 to 5 per cent. Eventually, from 1398, Henry III was able to bypass the authorization of the *Cortes* and turned this tax into an ordinary tribute. Thereafter, *alcabalas*, which by this date taxed 10 per cent of the value of transactions, became the main ordinary royal rent in Castile. The tax was paid by sellers and its collection was outsourced to the highest bidder in each territorial circumscription (*partidos*). Within each circumscription, *alcabalas* were divided by products (in cities and towns) or by village (in more sparsely populated and less economically active towns/villages). In 1495, the system of *encabezamiento* of *alcabalas* was introduced, which involved surrendering the administration of the tax to local councils in exchange for a fixed amount negotiated for a given time period; this system remained in place throughout the Early Modern Age. The *alcabala* was finally suppressed in 1845.

7. Alien subsidy (England)

A subsidy granted by Parliament that was levied annually in England on individual immigrants intermittently from 1440 to 1487 and collected by county sheriffs, it was first instituted when xenophobic feeling against England's large community of foreign merchants and craftsmen was particularly strong. Two rates were initially imposed of 16d. (on householders) and 6d. (on non-householders), with higher rate categories of alien merchants (6s.8d. each) and their clerks (20d. each) added in 1449, which rose in 1453 to 40s. (householders) and 20s. (non-householders). The basic rates increased in 1484 to 6s.8d. (householders) and 2s. (non-householders), respectively, and a new category appeared of alien keepers of brewing houses (20s. each). Spanish, Breton and German merchants were exempt from 1484. *Alien subsidies* were not particularly lucrative, since sheriffs were lax in administering them and exemptions were frequently purchased. Surviving records of inquests held to identify the taxpayers throw some light on immigrant communities, nonetheless.

8. Almojarifazgo (Castile)

A group of rents, rights and indirect taxes inherited from urban fiscal systems from al-Andalus, which were originally administered by a single treasury apparatus. The system was adopted by the Castilian Crown in cities to the south of the Central System, like Toledo, Córdoba, Seville and Murcia, after the territorial conquests of the eleventh to the thirteenth centuries.

Originally, each local *almojarifazgo* comprised multiple items, which varied from place to place: rents on royal real estate properties used for commercial and industrial purposes; censuses on private shops; inspection fees paid on craftspeople and merchants; fees for the use of official weights and measures; fees for the supervision of market activities and the sale of certain goods; rents yielded by suburban properties; tithes on specific products, like olive oil in the district of El Aljarafe, in Seville; duties on gambling houses (*tafurerías*); and, transit tolls on goods (*portazgos* and *pontazgos*), among others. In some cases, these rents were surrendered to the local councils, for instance in Seville. In any case, the main item in the royal *almojarifazgos* was a 10% custom duty on exports and imports. Eventually, these custom duties were taken out of the conglomerate of rents and tributes grouped under the umbrella of the *almojarifazgo*; for instance, from the fourteenth century the *almojarifazgo mayor* of Seville consisted of a custom duty on maritime trade to and from the Atlantic coast of Andalusia. The *almojarifazgo mayor* comprised the following components, which were leased out separately: *almonaima* and *cuenta de mercaderes*, which were custom duties paid on imported goods; the *partido de las mercaderías*, or *alcabala*, which taxed the first sale of imported goods; and the *renta de Berbería*, which was a tax specific to trade with North Africa. In 1498, the *almojarifazgo mayor* of Seville absorbed other *almojarifazgos* in the south and the south-east, for instance those of Murcia and the newly-conquered Kingdom of Granada, which had hitherto been administered autonomously. The collection of the *almojarifazgo* continued into the Early Modern Age.

9. Annates (Church taxation)

A tax received by the papacy, levied on ecclesiastical benefices at the time of the holder's conferral or designation. It could also be called *annualia* or *fructus primi anni* (first fruits), as it was the equivalent of one year's income, once the expenses associated with the upkeep of the benefice had been deducted, and it was only paid once. It was levied on minor benefices; the major ones (bishoprics, abbacies) contributed with other kinds of taxes (common and minor services) that were paid to the pontifical curia. The spread of annates during the fourteenth century was directly related to the spectacular increase in papal reservations on ecclesiastical benefices. As it was a tax paid in situ, the papal collectors were responsible for collecting it in each district. For this, it was necessary to have up-to-date lists including all the recent conferrals of benefices.

10. Assisen (Burgundian Low Countries)

This tax made up the bulk of a city's revenues, in "normal" years up to 80–85 per cent of total urban income. As an indirect tax based on consumption and production which taxed everybody without distinction and not taking into account somebody's purchasing power, it was quite unpopular, hence the unsympathetic denominations in most of the vernaculars (*ongeld, maletôte, mala peccunia*).

11. Auxilium (France)

See Aides.

12. Avarız (Ottoman)

An extraordinary tax that was imposed for a specific reason, such as to cover the costs of a military expedition. The tax was levied by order of the sultan and was directed to the central treasury. Paid by both rural and urban population, it was originally levied per household, but this changed in the late sixteenth century and the household came to be in reality a taxable unit made up of a group of individuals. By the beginning of the seventeenth century, it had become a regularly imposed tax rather than one only levied extraordinarily to cover specific needs. The tax could be levied in kind or in cash, or in the form of a service, such as being oarsmen on galleys. Those performing services such as protecting highways, passes and bridges, building works, and working in enterprises such as salt pans and mines were exempt from paying this tax, while others could be granted immunity from it due to work undertaken.

13. Ayuda (Navarre)

See Subsidio.

14. Bede (Scandinavia)

Terms used for common forms of extraordinary taxes. These were frequent in all the Scandinavian kingdoms during the thirteenth century, and paid in kind, notably products required for military purposes. The term *gærþ*, "collection of what has to be given", which was most frequent in Sweden, indicates that it was owed by a group of householders. Labour services could also be included as a duty. Another form of extraordinary taxes was the *markgäld* (*marcagiæld*, Latin: *subsidium marcæ*) which was paid in money. The term *bede*, "request", which occurred in Denmark, indicates that the tax was, formally, admitted after a royal request. They were royal taxes and a form of direct tax. The principles of collection varied, and are only imperfectly known.

15. Bede (German Holy Roman Empire)

This levy was a manorial taxation attested from the twelfth century. At that time, it was requested on a case-by-case basis, in the form of an aid provided under extraordinary circumstances. Sometimes linked to the seigneurial land power (*Grundherrschaft*, land lordship), sometimes attributed to the ban power, to the ecclesiastical advocate offices or to the feudal system, the *Bede* seems to have been correlated to the assistance duty owed by dependants by virtue of the protection they had access to (*Schutz und Schirm*). This direct taxation expressed mainly in money terms – although not systematically – adopted subscribed forms (ordinary *Bede*) from the thirteenth century. It was collected on fixed dates, one to three times a year, often in May, in the summer and on Saint Martin's Day (hence denominations referring to such a schedule, including *Hornungsbette, Maibede, Erntebette, Martinsbede,* or *Herbstschatzung*). The taxation was based on dependants' property holdings, and on estates, while the basis on which the *Bede* is levied sometimes specified the tax designation (e.g. the *Weinbede*, levied on the vineyard). It was levied throughout the royal domain, noble possessions (*Adelsherrschaften*, and *Territorien*) or towns. In places where communities existed, they were often granted the right to respond collectively to the seigneurial *Bede*, according to the principle of distribution. Some towns were granted permission to use the tax for their own benefit, and if that was the case, clerics were not systematically exempted. In the thirteenth and fourteenth centuries, extraordinary forms of the *Bede* (*Notbede, Gemeine Bede*) were levied in addition to the consolidated *Bede* in seigneurial and princely territories. Gradually, the *Bede* was redesigned and extended to be levied on all inhabitants of a territory as the "aid and tax" (Tyrol, 1315) for the country (*Landssteuer, Landbede*). Various naming conventions were used: *petitio, precaria, exactio, collecta, tributum* in Latin; *Bede*, in Middle High German; also, *Beet, Bet*, a term referring to request (*Bitte*); this type of taxation is known under other terms such as *Schaff, Schatz, Schoss, Geschoss, Tell, Gewerf, Vogtgeld*; it is similar to the French "taille" (land tax).

16. Bœjargjald (Scandinavia)

See Skotte.

17. Bovaje (Aragon)

Two different taxes were known under this name in Catalonia. On the one hand, this was an exaction equivalent to the *rescat de la Pau*, a form of compensation for the victims of feudal violence. From the mid-twelfth century onwards, monarchs were able to collect it and, under the reign of Peter III, turn it into an accession tax, although it became increasingly sporadic until its suppression in the fourteenth century. On the other hand, from 1211, it designated a new direct tax that had to be agreed upon by the estates. It was levied on all the inhabitants of the Principality of Catalonia, regardless of their jurisdictional adscription, and it was meant to fund different military expeditions during the central decades of the thirteenth century. It was, in both cases, a tax of a general character, which was levied, with some exceptions, on personal property and real estate.

18. Bor, chernyi bor (Russia)

"Black tax", or "tax on the common people", an extraordinary tax paid by the Novgorodians in the fourteenth and fifteenth centuries to the Grand-Prince of Vladimir, then of Moscow. It may have been their share of the Mongol tribute or a kind of "joyous accession gift".

19. Byskat (Scandinavia)

Byrka (Danish) and stadsskatt (Swedish) were genera urban taxes paid to the king from the early fourteenth century (Denmark) or late fourteenth century (Sweden). Several ancient fees and obligations were abandoned or merged into these taxes, uniform for most towns. The most important of the older taxes was the *midthsumærsgyald*, "midsummer tax" (latin: *census æstitualis*) in Denmark. All these taxes were collective contributions from a town to the king and distributed according to principles that are not known. They were mostly collected in money, but conversions into various goods did occurr.

20. Carucage (England)

A direct land tax that succeeded the *geld*, it was levied from 1194 to 1224, assessed on each ploughland (or carucate), *i.e.*, the amount of land that could be ploughed by a team of oxen in one year. The first *carucage* charged a rate of 2s. per ploughland in 1194, based on an outdated *geld* assessment. The carucage of 1198 was preceded by a fresh assessment made on the oaths of local officials, overseen by a knight and a clerk in each county. They determined the number of cultivated carucates in each vill, by what form of tenure they were held, the amount of their value and the identity of their owners. Royal justices subsequently held an investigation because underassessment was suspected, and many landholders made fines in lieu of further enquiries. Future *carucages* were only partly assessed; in 1217, the overall hundred totals were apportioned among the vills in at least one locality, and many paid negotiated lump sums or made fine to avoid assessment.

21. Cavalcata (Provence and Savoy)

In Provence, *cavalcata* originally referred to the armed service (*servitium*) owed to the count by his tenants or vassals. From the early thirteenth century, the *cavalcata* was converted into a fixed annual tax, paid by the subjects, either directly to the count or to intermediate lords, in order to finance their own personal obeying to the count's military summons. From the early fourteenth century, the summoning of a *cavalcata generalis* provided for the obligation of a general service warranted by actual defence necessities. Such service could be provided to the count either by actual in-person attendance or by a tariffed compensation fee. As such, it very much resembled the French contemporary *arrière-ban*.

22. Cens (Church Lands)

Paid by monasteries, lords, princes, communes and individuals, a *cens* could have many reasons in the Church Lands (use of estates, seigneurial rights or political privileges). It referred to the idea of rent, paid for the enjoyment of the rights, goods or privileges granted. Quite rare for laymen in 1200, these census grew more numerous in the thirteenth century to gradually collapse in the fifteenth century.

23. Çift resmi (Ottoman)

A tax which was based partly on land and partly on individuals or households. The *çift* tax originated in pre-Ottoman labour services and payments in kind which were converted into a cash payment. It was levied on a peasant family which held a *çift* and was assigned to the *timar* holder as part of his income. By the sixteenth century, it became a land tax paid in cash. The *çift* was a plot of land that could in theory be cultivated by a peasant family and a pair of oxen. The size of the *çift* varied according to the nature of the land, the smallest units being made up of good productive land and the largest by less productive land. The rates of the *çift* tax varied location to location throughout the empire. It was not applied everywhere and Christian peasants in the Balkans paid the *ispence* tax in lieu of the *çift resmi*.

24. City szos (Poland and Lithuania)

A basic, direct tax, collected directly from the townspeople by the municipal authorities; it consisted of three taxes: 1) the main revenue source – a real property tax on properties in the city and the suburbs; 2) a tax on the sale of goods and services; and 3) a personal property tax. The real property tax was the oldest, paid from the moment the town was established. It took the form of an annual cash payment collected by the municipal authorities from real property owners. The tax was imposed on urban property: *curia, hereditas, area, Erbe, Hof*, or its part, taxed accordingly.

25. Cizye (Ottoman)

A poll tax levied on non-Muslim households, in contrast to the practice under Islamic law where it was applied to individuals – non-Muslims males – not households. It was paid directly into the central treasury. The state kept *cizye* registers, the first extant one of which dates from the late fifteenth century, which recorded the names of the heads of each household who were liable to the tax. Groups of taxpayers, such as those on the Aegean islands, frequently paid this tax as a lump sum. It was often in reality the continuation of a pre-Ottoman tax, as was the case in Hungary in the sixteenth century where the Ottomans simply absorbed the Hungarian war tax as *cizye*. Although in theory a tax levied on non-Muslims, it could be applied to Muslims, as was the case with gypsies in the Balkans.

26. Clerical tenth (England)

The main clerical subsidy granted by the northern and southern clergy from 1337 to 1497, it levied a tenth on the income from the clergy's temporal (mainly monastic) and spiritual lands, based on the assessment (the "*Taxatio*") made in 1291 for *papal tenths* imposed by Pope Nicholas IV. Before 1337, the clergy had intermittently agreed to pay variable fractional rates, beginning in 1280, based (from 1294) on the *Taxatio*, if they were not then paying *papal tenths*. The total yield per tenth (about £16,000) declined over time, through destruction wrought by Scottish raids on the northern dioceses, which were devalued by nearly a third in the revised assessment of 1319. In the later fourteenth century, *clerical tenths* began to be levied also on benefices that had not been assessed in 1291. From 1415, these were frequently included in levies of *clerical tenths* in the southern dioceses. Like lay *fifteenths and tenths*, the tax yields of *clerical tenths* could only be increased by levying them in multiples.

27. Cloison, droits de (France)

Municipal indirect taxes raised, by royal or princely grant, to finance the *cloison* or *clouaison* (enclosure) of towns, *i.e.* the creation, restoration or maintenance of their fortifications, from the 1340s to the modern era.

28. *Collecta* (Northern Italy)

The *collecta, colta, fodrum, datum,* or *datium* was the extraordinary direct tax originating from the rule of emperors and lords, which the Communes levied on their citizens and on rural communities. It is documented as such starting in the twelfth century. The terms are synonymous, changing depending on the city. *Collecta* and *colta* (or *colletta*) are the most common, while *datium* and *accaptum* were used in Tuscany, and *fodrum* in Lombardy, where it derived from the *fodrum* due to the Holy Roman Emperors when they travelled to Italy. *Datium*, a synonym of *fodrum*, meant direct tax in Tuscany, while in northern Italy, it meant indirect tax. From the second half of the twelfth century to the first half of the thirteenth century, the *colletta* was collected based on the *estimo* or *libra* (see Estimo). The *estimo* for the countryside *contadi* was assigned to each community and was then divided up at the local level among the hearths, or *foci (fumantes)*.

29. Colletta (Sicily)

This was a direct proportional subsidy based on hearths and applied between the first half of the twelfth century and the second half of the fifteenth. Albeit reserved for landowners since the Norman kingdom, Frederick II was the first sovereign to organise the withdrawal system in 1231. It became annual, even though it was considered an extraordinary levy. In 1238, the amount collected raised 102,000 *onze* and in 1242, to 60,800 *onze*. During the Angevin reign the request of *collecte* was added to the *sovvenzione generale*. The latter was due annually and the *collecte* formed an additional amount levied in exceptional circumstances. These taxes were formally abolished by Alphonse of Aragon who replaced them with the *focatico*. In reality, he decided also to ask for *collecte* for war emergencies: the sovereign and the Parliament imposed three of them in 1450, and two *collecte* were due in 1456.

30. Cronsteuer (German Holy Roman Empire)

An extraordinary tax on estates, payable by Jews on the occasion of royal or imperial coronation. It took the name of *Cronsteuer* from the fifteenth century. The taxation was described as a payment by the Jews to secure the protection of the new ruler in the fifteenth century. It may correspond to the *Dritter Pfennig*, the "third penny" and thus could amount to one-third of the estate value. In a 1463 charter, this taxation is defined as the redemption price whereby the Jews "save their lives" which the king of the Romans had the power to take away. Also named *Judenkrönungsteuer*.

31. Cuartel (Navarre)

This term came to replace *ayuda* from 1377, designating the satisfaction of a royal demand with the concession by the *Cortes* of a direct tax. The word *cuartel*, therefore, refers to the king's request, because originally the Crown left the councils to decide the collection method. Originally, the *cuartel* was one quarter of the annual *ayuda* of 40,000 florins, although soon the king began asking for more than four *cuarteles* per annum. By the fifteenth century, *cuartel* (*cuarteles*) had totally replaced the word *ayuda*. Also called *quarter* or *quarteron*.

32. Dan' (Russia)

Princely tribute. Direct tax. Existed from the beginning of the Kievan period (ninth century). First paid in kind (mostly furs, various produces of the land), later in money. This was the main direct tax on revenues during the Middle Ages. During the Tatar yoke (1242–1480), it was integrated with the Mongol tribute (*vykhod*). Replaced by the capitation (*podushnaia podat'*) by Peter the Great in 1724.

33. Datium (Northern Italy)

See Collecta.

34. Datium vini (Northern Italy)

See Wine gabelle.

35. Diezmos y aduanas (Castile)

Tithes and custom duties: indirect 10 per cent tax on imports and exports collected by the kings of Castile in districts where *almojarifazgos* did not apply. Their collection dates back to the reign of Alphonse X, when the *Cortes* held in 1268 established the network of coastal and overland posts for the collection of custom duties. This network was revised in 1351. Concerning overland trade, the duties were collected in the dry ports situated at the frontiers with Navarre and the Crown of Aragon (bishoprics of Calahorra, Osma, Sigüenza, Cuenca and Cartagena). In the Cantabrian Sea and on the Galician coast, these royal custom duties were known as "tithes of the sea" (*diezmos de la mar*), and in 1469, they were ceded to the aristocratic lineage of the Velascos.

36. Donativum (Sicily)

Introduced in 1446, the *donativum* (donation) was a type of taxation resulting from the negotiation between the King of Aragon and the Sicilian parliament. The latter granted the monarch an economic subsidy, which was to be paid in a few years, in exchange for the approval of a list of demands on various matters. Unlike the extraordinary *subventio generalis*, the *donativum* was part of the regular revenue of the Crown, as the parliament paid the amount due in annual instalments. At the beginning of the sixteenth century, it was allocated as follows: two-fifths each one for the demesnial and the baronial estates, and one-fifth for the ecclesiastical estate. In turn, each parliamentary branch autonomously distributed the quotas to be paid by each of its members, with the municipalities allowed to raise incomes both through duty tolls and hearth taxes. The so-called *deputati* (deputies) were entrusted with the *donativum*'s collection on behalf of the parliament.

37. Entrées et issues (Brittany)

Princely indirect taxes, also called *devoirs de ports et havres*, on the maritime import and export of merchandise, instituted in 1365 and still in use in modern era. Their rate, made uniform in 1397 and reformed in 1422, was expressed per capacity unit, per item unit or *ad valorem*; it was different for the import or export of a said item. Collection was made in the ports of the duchy by specialised agents, first under the local authority of domain officials, then progressively under the direct control of the Treasurer and *receveur général* and the Chamber of Accounts from the 1420s onwards. In the second half of the fifteenth century, the duchy's coast was divided into six general farms. Many clerics, noblemen and ports were exempt for products intended for their own use.

38. Équivalent des aides (France)

A royal tax (also called *composition* in the fourteenth century), consisting of a flat sum, granted by some provinces instead of aids from 1362 to modern times. It was a direct tax, voted by local Estates and raised alongside the *taille* by many Massif Central lands and Normandy from the 1450s. It was extended to the countryside of northern France, where there were no Estates, in the 1460s as a mere supplement to the *taille*. Languedoc also paid a special *fouage* instead of aids from 1362 to 1367, but after the restoration of aids in 1437, a different formula was established. From 1443 on wards, a fixed grant instead of aids was collected through an indirect taxation designed by the Estates, and different from the royal taxes it replaced, on meat (except poultry), fish and wine retail sales. The collection was leased for three years to farmers by the Estates, then royal commissioners from 1455 onwards, at three levels: the province, the seneschalty and the diocese.

39. Expedition (Scandinavia)

See Ledung.

Glossary

40. Exuwe (Burgundian Low Countries)

See Issue.

41. Estimum (Northern Italy)

The *estimum/estimo* and the *libra/allibramento* were assessments of wealth carried out in order to levy an extraordinary direct tax or a forced loan. The terms *estimo* and *libra* were first documented around the middle of the twelfth century when they were both in use. They were probably two different methods of assessment. In the twelfth century, the *estimo* is found in Genoa, Pisa and Piacenza, but this is merely what has survived in documentation and it is possible that it was more widespread. The *estimum/libra* was a more equitable method of distribution than the levy *per focum* (*focatico*, or hearth tax). There is little evidence of the criteria used to implement the *focatico*, which was present in the imperial and communal *fodrum* in the twelfth century. An overall estimate of wealth was established after written declarations had been submitted by the individual taxpayers (in twelfth-century Pisa and perhaps Genoa), the heads of families (perhaps starting in the thirteenth century) and also, in Venice, the *fraterne*. The calculation was carried out by communal officials. Although it is impossible to generalize or provide dates, it was perhaps during the thirteenth century that an extension of the *estimo* to a greater number of cities was accompanied by a direct tax (*colletta* or *fodro*) demanded based on a figure (*estimo* figure) assigned to each person registered on the *estimo*. The figure was assigned by locally-appointed commissions pursuant to rules that were established from time to time. The two terms *estimum* and *libra* therefore became essentially synonymous (although not everywhere): levying the *estimum ad libram* meant taxing on the basis of financial capacity to pay. In northern Italy, the term *estimum* was more widespread, while *libra* was used in central Italy and *talea* in Piedmont. This practice, which sped up the collection procedure, was already in use for the direct taxation of the countryside *contadi*, where it probably originated. In the event of necessity, several successive taxes could be levied, and the coefficient used with respect to the estimated figure could be varied in *denari* (or *soldi* and *denari*) *per lira* (or 100 lire) of the *estimo* (e.g. 2 *denari per lira* of the *estimo*, 6 *denari per lira*). When analytical declarations were collected in the register (starting in the thirteenth century) they were called *catasti*. The term *estimo* also refers to the tax to be paid.

42. Feudal aid (England)

Initially a direct tax required from vassals to assist their feudal lord in exigent circumstances, the *feudal aid* persisted as a form of royal taxation into the Later Middle Ages, when it became a subsidy granted by Parliament. It could be legitimately demanded of a lord's tenants to pay the expenses of knighting his eldest son or of marrying his first-born daughter, but the exactions had to be reasonable and moderate, according to the size of the vassal's fee, so as not to diminish his social position. The basis of assessment of *feudal aids* evolved over time and kings increasingly abused the rules for levying them. The early *feudal aids* tended to be levied as *scutages*, *gelds* or *tallages*, but in 1306 a *feudal aid* to knight the future Edward III took the form of a *fractional tax* on moveable goods and a *feudal aid* levied in 1333 even solicited contributions from the clergy by personal letters.

43. Fifteenth and tenth (England)

The main lay subsidy granted in Parliament from 1334 to 1624, it was originally based on an assessment of the moveable goods of individual taxpayers in 1332, when a tax of a fifteenth part of goods was levied in rural communities and a tenth part in urban areas and on tenants of the king's ancient demesne. In 1334, however, each community instead negotiated with royal commissioners the overall amount of its contribution, which was to exceed what it had paid in 1332. It was then free to levy the tax however it wished provided that the same quota was raised in all subsequent levies. The total overall yield was about £37,000 until 1433 when a rebate of £4,000 (increased to £6,000 in 1446) was introduced to be redistributed from richer to poorer vills to help them meet their quotas. Royal governments increased the yield by levying the tax in multiples. By the fifteenth century the basis of assessment in many areas appears to have been landed wealth or wages instead of goods.

44. Focagium (Provence)

Focagium or *quista*, in Provence, refers to the general feudal aid. Required by the count from his vassals under certain circumstances, *focagium* was a form of extraordinary taxation, although it might be quite frequently levied (approximately two dozen times in the first half of the fourteenth century). The four main occasions were the knighting of a son, the marriage of a daughter, the payment of the lord's ransom and his crusading aid. A fifth and a sixth forms of aid, for the count's visit to the emperor his overlord and for the purchase of a valuable piece of feudal land, were also levied in specific areas of the county. Occasionally referred to as a *subventio* (in 1269), a *tallia* (in 1274) or a *collecta* (in 1287), the feudal aid was more generally known as a *focagium* because it was levied as a hearth tax, at the usual rate of six shillings (*solidi*) per hearth. The levying of such feudal aids, from the mid-fourteenth century, gradually merged into the collection of general subsidies. See also *alberga*.

45. Focatico (Sicily)

This was a royal direct tax introduced by Alphonse V of Aragon during the Parliament of Saint Lorenz in 1443. It was enforced until the second half of eighteenth century. Initially, the king decided to ask for one ducat per hearth in exchange for one *thomolo* of salt; in this way he thought of forfeiting more than four hundred thousand ducats. After the first review of the number of hearths the amount dropped to two hundred and thirty thousand ducats. The officers who managed tax districts were named *percettori*, they received the money from the *taxatores* operating in the cities. During the reign of Alphonse the fixed rate fluctuated somewhat and it was unpopular. Hence Alphonse's successor, Ferrante decided, unsuccessfully, to abolish the *focatico* to replace it with the proceeds of indirect taxes.

46. Fodrum (Northern Italy)

See Collecta.

47. Fogaje (Aragon)

It functioned as a mechanism for the distribution of different taxes of a general scope, together with the subsidies approved by the Estates' assemblies, based on the number of *fuegos/focs* (hearths, *i.e.*, households) in urban and rural communities. The resulting figure determined the sum of the contribution, which was usually distributed among the town's neighbours through a tax levied on real estate and personal property. In Catalonia, this form of distribution, which depended on the number of households, was consolidated around 1360, with the first counting of *focs*, also known as *fogatjament* (a previous tally from 1358 did not include royal communities). Between then and the beginning of the sixteenth century, there were five *fogatjaments*, with the tally of 1378 being especially used, and in force until 1496 with only partial updates. In Aragon, the *fogajes generales* were developed in parallel to Catalonia, with six documented tallies. The two oldest ones are those of 1362 and 1367, although they are only preserved in fragments. Those of 1405 and 1495 are especially note-worthy, since they include information about the whole kingdom. The usage of these types of registers is less well documented in Valencia, although it is generally considered that they were applied in similar terms as in Catalonia and Aragon. The first extant Valencian *fogatge* dates from 1510.

48. Fondaco (Sicily)

See Ius fondaci.

49. Fouage (Brittany)

A princely direct tax, whose general features were those of the royal *fouage*. It was granted by the local Estates to the duke from 1365 until modern times. It was collected by special *receveurs* at the diocese or sub-diocese level.

50. Fouage (France)

A royal direct tax, whose rate was expressed as an amount per *feu* (hearth). This formally makes it a proportional tax, but the rate was actually used to divide the total amount between communities according to their number of hearths, so the *fouage* was in fact a mix of proportional and distributive tax. Each town or country parish divided its collective share between taxable heads of hearth, with the instructions that "the mighty should support the feeble". Individual contributions were thus supposedly proportionate to economic capacity: taxpayers did not bear a uniform burden. Beginning in 1342, *fouage* was regularly levied in Languedoc, then spreading to the north, first at a regional level. From 1363 onwards, general *fouages* were raised everywhere for the defence of the kingdom, with a rate half as high for the countryside as for towns. Charles V abolished them on his deathbed in 1380, and they were was replaced by the royal *taille*. *Fouage* did not apply to clerics (including university members), noblemen, royal households and mint officials, some royal officers and destitute people. It was levied by collectors mandated by the local community and transferred to the *receveur des aides* of the diocese.

51. Fractional taxes (England)

Direct taxes that were first collected by the military orders in France and England in 1166 to support crusading states in the Holy Land, fractional taxes came to predominate in England in the thirteenth century because they yielded much larger sums than traditional feudal taxes. In their earliest form they taxed both land revenue and moveable goods, but from 1225, when they became subsidies granted in Parliament, only moveable goods were taxed. They resembled ecclesiastical tithes in taking the value of a fractional part of a taxpayer's goods, but the rates varied with each tax grant. Two separate rates were usual from 1294, with urban taxpayers and tenants of the royal ancient demesne paying a higher rate than residents of (poorer) rural communities. The *fifteenth and tenth* levied in 1332 was the last assessed fractional tax, because in 1334 the sums due from each locality were instead negotiated with royal commissioners and were henceforth fixed at these "quotas".

52. Gabella (Sicily)

In late-medieval Sicily, the *gabella* (also named *cabella* or *cassia*) was an indirect tax on the production, circulation, and consumption of various products. The monarchs entrusted each demesnial municipality with its own, specific royal *gabelle* (ranging from butchering to dyeing and transits), which had different regulations and tolls. They also included custom duties, which amounted to about 3 per cent of the value of imports and exports. On behalf of the monarchs, the *magister secretus* and his network of officers annually farmed out the demesnial cities' excise incomes in return for immediate and higher profits. If needed, the *credencerii* directly managed the *gabelle* on behalf of the Crown. At the same time, the urban centers autonomously administered their own municipal *gabelle*, which served the purpose of funding local administrations (e.g., for the maintenance of walls). In case of need, extraordinary *gabelle* could be levied for raising incomes for subsidies and *donativi*, such as the ad hoc toll on food stuff known as *maldinaru*.

53. Gabella (Provence and Savoy)

Gabella is a general term describing various forms of indirect taxes established by municipal authorities and levied on the local commercial exchanges of various commodities, most generally basic foodstuffs such as wine, wheat and cereals, or meat and poultry. Such taxes might be locally described by a variety of terms, either general (*reva*), specific to one commodity (*soquetus*, levied on wine), or referring to their percentage of their tariff (*dezenum trezenum, trentenum* and so forth). A specific variety of *gabella* levied on the extra-local salt traffic (*gabella salis*) was a major source of revenue monopolised from an early period (twelfth century) by princely authorities.

54. Gabelle (France)

The word *gabelle* is derived from the Arabic root *qavala* used in al-Andalus, before being adopted in Italy in the twelfth century and in the Kingdom of France in the mid-thirteenth century. An indirect tax, it refers primarily to a tax on consumption and was later applied exclusively to the sale and consumption of salt in France in the fourteenth and fifteenth centuries. Royal warehouses controlled salt transaction and levied a high tax.

55. Gabelle du sel (France)

A royal indirect tax on salt retail sales, instituted in 1341, and in use until 1790. In the north, it was collected in monopolistic salt warehouses (*greniers à sel*), run by *greneticrs*, where merchants were compelled to deposit their stock and consumers to purchase it. Beginning in 1363 or 1370, a quantity of salt was divided between local communities according to the number of their hearths, then between their heads of hearth, to fix the minimal quantity each one had to buy.

The southern limits of this system were the Loire Valley and northern Massif Central. The *gabelle* was replaced by a *composition* (flat sum) in Artois, a *quart du sel* (salt fourth) in Poitou and a *quint du sel* (salt fifth) in Auvergne. In Languedoc, the *gabelle* was collected in *greniers* set along the coast near salt marshes, whose stock was sold in retail within ten *lieues* or in wholesale to merchants who resold it inland. In the south-east, the *tirage à la part du royaume* held a monopoly on salt sales on the western bank of the Rhône and the lower Saône valley, and the *tirage à la part de l'Empire*, co-organised by the king and the Count of

Provence in 1398 at the latest, on the eastern bank; the *gabelle* was collected in port *greniers*. From 1448 onwards, both *tirages* were leased out to farmers.

56. Gabelles and péages (Dauphiné)

Princely indirect taxes raised on the transit of merchandise, by land or waterway, along the main trade roads of Dauphiné: the Rhône valley, the valleys of Isère and Durance to Italy through the Alps, from the thirteenth century until modern times. In contrast to *péages*, collected in a single place, the *grandes gabelles* were levied at different points of a fiscal area: those of Viennois and Valentinois along the Rhône, those of Romans around lower Isère, those of Briançonnais along the Durance road. The collection was carried out by officials until the 1350s, then leased out to farmers. Local lords also levied seigniorial *péages*.

57. Gærþ (Scandinavia)

See Bede.

58. Gate tax (Northern Italy)

By the thirteenth century, the term *gabella*, synonym of *datium* and *tholoneum*, referred to all taxes, even direct taxes, except for those based on the *estimo*. The prevailing meaning was that of indirect tax. Among the taxes on the circulation of goods, the most frequent were the gabelles on merchandise in transit, tolls, *ripatici* (mooring), *pontatici* (bridge tolls), customs clearance, and entry and exit from cities (*gabella delle porte*). It is difficult to date the gate tax, as is generally the case for tolls and *ripatici*, fair and market rights, which in some cases were documented starting in the tenth century when they were collected by bishops. In addition to the gate tax, in much more recent times, a duty on merchandise was also collected in the cities. It is possible that a separate merchant duty originated from a division of the gate tax, in order to distinguish the commodities that came from the countryside from goods imported by merchants. Merchant duties were calculated based on values set out in product rate lists. There were also duties on individual products or raw materials. In some cities in the Veneto, the name of the duty (*stadera*) stemmed from the monopoly of weights and measures because some goods were taxed by weight. Gate and merchant duties were among the largest portions of urban revenues.

59. Geld (England)

Originally devised as a tribute to placate Danish invaders of the tenth century, this general land tax was a direct tax levied by Anglo-Saxon and post-Conquest kings until 1162 to raise money for their extraordinary expenditure. The unit of assessment in most of southern England was the "hide", defined as the amount of land sufficient to support a very large family group, varying in size according to the fertility of the soil and prevailing local customs. It was assessed in Kent by the "sulung" and in the north by the "carucate" (or ploughland) – i.e., the amount of land that could be ploughed by a team of oxen in a year. In East Anglia, rather than basing the tax on individual assessments, a set rate of £10 was levied on each hundred (an administrative unit estimated at 100 hides), to which each vill contributed. The normal *geld* rate was 2s. per hide, and the few surviving "*geld* rolls" record the number of hides in each hundred liable to pay.

60. Gemeiner Pfennig (German Holy Roman Empire)

Gemeiner Pfennig, communis denarius; the term refers to both the currency (*Pfennig*, penny) and the money tax; the adjective *gemein* expresses the common and universal dimension. This tax was an attempt at a universal direct tax throughout the Empire: a four-year extraordinary tax, which combined a capitation tax, an estate tax and an income tax, with variations according to estate value and social status. There were precedents in 1422 and 1427 with the *Hussitensteuer** (*Hussengeld*). The *Gemeiner Pfennig* was established in 1495 at the Diet of Worms and was meant to fund wars (against the Turks and against France) as well as new imperial institutions. The levy was only effective in the period 1497–1499. Other such attempts were made in the sixteenth century.

61. Generalidades (Aragon)

Indirect taxes created within the framework of the *Cortes Generales* of Monzón of 1362 and 1363. In the following two years they came under the control of the *Diputaciones del General* and, on their behalf, the commissions that emanated from the Estates gathered in the *Cortes* of Aragon, Catalonia (including Majorca), and Valencia. These taxes were divided in two main groups: the first consisted of the levies on the production, commercialization, and circulation of textiles; the second was levied on the entry and exit of goods through border enclaves. In Catalonia and Valencia both groups were applied through the *dret de la bolla*, the *segell de cera*, and the *drets d'entrades i eixides*, in the former, and the *tall del drap* and the *tretes* in the latter. Conversely, in Aragon, this type of tax was limited to custom duties. These exactions became permanent with the emission of public debt from 1365 (in Catalonia) or in the following decades (Aragon and Valencia), and served as the principal source of income for the *Diputaciones del General* until the eighteenth century.

62. Gengærþ (Scandinavia)

Term used mainly in Sweden for the commutation tax for the duty to provide support to the kings, but also (for example) to bishops, during their travels. *Veitsle* was the corresponding term for an obligation used in Norway and connected with the itinerant kingdom. The kings travelled between their central farms and stayed there for longer or shorter periods. In Denmark, different terms were used, in Latin charters often called *servitium noctis*, corresponding to the vernacular *nathold*. Similar to the *nathold* was the *stud* (Old Danish *stuth*), a term frequently used for various taxes and fees. Literally, they were support or contributions to the king. *Inne* referred to different kinds of labour duties that the king was entitled to; this included the haulage (*ægt*). *Inne* was a flexible concept, and occasionally converted into fees usually paid in money.

These were all royal taxes. They were direct taxes based upon the land, sometimes upon an evaluation of the land but could be levied by collectives or by households. There is only slight information about the collection of these taxes.

63. Gouveliatikon (Byzantine Empire)

Also *kouveliatikon*, an additional agricultural tax that appears in the sources in the mid-fourteenth century. The term probably derives from the Slavic word *kouvelion*, which means grain container as well as hive. The tax, therefore, was probably imposed on grain or hives.

64. Gramota (Russia)

Letter (of the alphabet), letter (document), charter. The adjective explains the nature of the privilege: *dannaia* is a charter of donation, *nesudimaia* a charter of judicial immunity, *tarkhannaia* a fiscal immunity charter, and a *zhalovannaia* granted various fiscal exemptions. *Gramoty* were issued all along the Russian Middle Ages and even in the Modern Era.

65. Güldener Opferpfennig (German Holy Roman Empire)

This was an annual poll tax on Jewish adults, brought in by Emperor Ludwig of Bavaria in 1342 under the term *Guldin Pfennig*. The emperor l it on every Jew and every widowed Jewess over twelve years of age who possessed an estate of more than twenty guilders. It amounted to one guilder, due annually "as a ground rent for their body" (Leibzins). The payment was promoted as a guarantee for better protection of the Empire for the Jews and was due at Christmas. Various names: *Goldener Opferpfennig*, *Goldener Pfennig*, *Guldenpfennig*, etc.

66. Hearth tax (Church Lands)

Named *fodrum, focaticum, focularia, affictus, fumantaria*, in the various provinces of the Church, it appears in the sources around 1200 as a tax normally set at 26 *denarii* by hearth. It had ancient imperial origins, as many social categories and large cities were then already exempt. The reconstitution of the sovereign's rights after the wars against the Staufen transformed it into a fixed tax, sometimes called *cens*. It then disappeared during the fifteenth century when tax simplifications were carried out.

67. Hofsteuer (German Holy Roman Empire)

This tax was due to the king in lieu of the "droit de gîte" (*Gastung*, board and lodging for the king). There is evidence that as early as the ninth century, bishops and counts owed lodging to the king and his itinerant court. The population was then called upon to contribute to the costs and to food supplies. The obligation to lodge and fund the needs of the court continued over time for churches, royal towns, and later imperial town, as evidenced for example by the urban law of the town of Haguenau, a place standing as palatial residence (1164). In 1274, after ecclesiastical princes refused to offer such board and lodging, Rudolf I generalised the taxation to all the towns of the Empire during the Nuremberg court assembly (March 1274), "for the upkeep of the Empire". The forms issued under the royal mandates urged for the payment of the tax, sometimes by threatening to use the pledging system, sometimes by promising to guarantee urban privileges.

68. Hussensteuer (German Holy Roman Empire)

This taxation is also referred to as *Hussengeld* and various periphrases. It was a general composite direct tax levied at imperial scale in 1422 and 1427 to finance the crusade and the war against the Hussites. Direct taxes named likewise appear to have been levied in free and imperial towns in 1431.

69. Imposition foraine (France)

This royal indirect tax was levied as compensation on any merchandise, subject to the 5 per cent aids, leaving the collection area to be sold outside, at the same rate *ad valorem*. It was established by 1362–1363 and was still in use in modern times in lands of *langue d'oil*. In Languedoc, it was replaced in 1443 by a flat sum (still called *imposition foraine*) leased along with the *équivalent des aides*, and suppressed in 1512. Its collection was leased by *élus* to farmers who levied it on merchants where they bought their stock. If not paid on departure, it is due in Paris (at half rate) or at special collection places at the limits of the aids zone, the *ports et passages*. Parisian goldsmiths paid it only when back in the capital, on the basis of their sworn statement. Some seaports and neighbouring countries were exempt as were foreign merchants who left the kingdom with goods they had brought in, but were unable to sell.

70. Imposición (Navarre)

An indirect tax of 5 per cent of the value on all commercial transactions carried out in the kingdom's markets. In 1363, the *imposición* emerged as an occasional tax, directly administered by the king and granted by the *Cortes*. After 1372, the *imposición* gradually became an ordinary tribute, and its administration was leased out to major mercantile companies. In the fifteenth century, the Crown decided to subdivide the tax-farming arrangements by region, market and product. This led to the widespread use of the expression "*imposiciones*" instead of "*imposición*" (and later "*alcabalas*").

71. Imposicions (Aragon)

See Sisas.

72. Income tax (England)

Any one of a series of experimental subsidies on income granted in Parliament between 1404 and 1504, which taxed landed income primarily with the aim of generating greater yields and taxing wealth more effectively than *fifteenths and tenths*. The earlier such taxes (in 1404, 1428 and 1431) assessed different rates according to type of tenure, but such distinctions were no longer made in 1435 and 1450, when graduated rates according to level of income were charged, and wages, fees of office and income from communally-owned land were taxed. The income taxes of 1472 and 1489 levied a tenth of all income, but the subsidy grants were tied to overall quotas which had to be made up by *fifteenths and tenths* when they fell short. The terms of the fixed-levy taxes on income of 1497 and 1504 were only vaguely formulated, and like the other income taxes that preceded them, marked by gross underassessment and disappointing yields.

73. İspence (Ottoman)

A poll tax of usually 25 *akçe*, although higher and lower amounts could be levied in different parts of the empire, paid by non-Muslim males. It was paid by Christian peasants in the Balkans in place of the *çift resmi*. Originally a tax that existed before the Ottomans and was taken over by them after their conquest of the Balkans, it was paid by both the settled rural population and nomads, and by the urban population. In the sixteenth century the Ottomans introduced it into eastern and south-eastern Anatolia. It was usually included in the income of the *timar* holder and was paid in cash.

74. Issue (Burgundian Low Countries)

Direct taxation levied on all goods, movable and immovable, which parted from the hands of somebody belonging to a given community (in almost all cases a city) into the hands of somebody from outside. This could be caused by death (and thus via the person's bequest), a marriage outside the city or a simple removal. As such, it did not limit a strangers' right to transfer his or her goods, but it placed a limit on his right to acquire goods. Also named *exuwe* or *ius exportationis*.

75. Ius exportationis (Burgundian Low Countries)

See Issue.

76. Ius fondaci (Sicily)

This was an indirect proportional tax applied on circulation both by lords and by the sovereign, between the first half of the twelfth century and the second half of the eighteenth. Although during the Norman kingdom there were some warehouses for goods, only in 1231 did Frederick II decide to organize and control the system of storage of merchandise. He appointed officers called *fundicari* who were to levy the tax on everything going to the market, except animals and goods subject to other taxation. Very often the *ius fondaci* was combined with the *ius dohane* and it was called *maggior fondaco*. During the Angevin period, it was farmed out. Between the thirteenth and fourteenth centuries the rate stabilized at around 2–2.5 per cent of the selling price of the goods. It declined to 1 per cent in 1469 thanks to the policies of Ferrante of Aragon, who sought to encourage trade.

77. Ius passuum (Sicily)

This was an indirect proportional tax on circulation, both seigneurial and royal, applied between the twelfth century and the second half of eighteenth. Probably of Lombard origin, its name at the beginning was also *theloneum*. The tax was levied on persons and goods crossing the border. During the reign of Charles I of Anjou, the officers named *passagerii* were to levy the amount required according to a precise tariff, whereas the *custodes passuum* performed police functions. In 1282 there were 25 *passi* at along the kingdom's borders, between Sperlonga and the River Tronto. During the fourteenth century, they became more numerous because of the many feudal concessions and they spread throughout the kingdom. To promote trade, in 1466, Ferrante of Aragon made a reform, to reduce the number of *passi* and to abolish those that were illegal.

78. Judensteuer (German Holy Roman Empire)

A direct tax in money, owed by the Jews, by virtue of sovereign rights. In 1236, a complaint accusing the Jews of ritual murder of children was brought before the royal court by figures close to the Abbot of Fulda. After investigation, Emperor Frederick II rejected the accusation. However, he extended the status that the Privilege of Worms (*Wormser Privileg*) had granted to the Jews of Worms (1090) to the whole German Empire. The Jews therefore became *servi camere nostre*, meaning "serfs of our chamber", and as a result, were placed under the direct tutelage and theoretical protection of the ruler, while becoming a source of funds for the Royal Treasury. The first evidence of the *Judensteuer* appears in the imperial tax list of 1241/1242, showing that the amounts paid by the Jews represented almost 16% of the total money collected (857 marks). Among other sovereign rights, the Golden Bull of 1356 granted electors the right to keep Jews and to levy customs and revenues on them. Thus, from the thirteenth century onwards, the *droit de régal* over the Jews *de facto* fell out of the hands of the king, to the benefit of princely or municipal powers.

79. Ledung (Scandinavia)

Ledung (or *lething* in Old Danish) was the naval organisation in all the Scandinavian kingdoms and a duty of all men to participate in warfare by providing manpower, victuals and ships (named *leiðangr* in Old Norse, *lepunger* in Old Swedish, and *expeditio* in Latin). It evolved from a fine when neglected into a permanent tax. This transformation took place during the first half of the thirteenth century in Denmark and at the end of the century in Sweden. It was a lengthier process in Norway since it was an important military instrument of power for a longer period there. There were different terms for taxes connected with the *ledung*. The principles of assessment varied. It could be based upon collectives of householders or a territory. The *ledumgslame* was a commutation of military service, while the *skeppsvist* was the substitute for provisions. In Denmark, the *kværsæde* was a tax or fee for remaining at home, when the *ledung* was summoned. In parts of inland Norway the *víseyrir* was introduced around 1300, thus in districts without an original military *ledung* duty. All these were royal taxes. They were direct taxes based on the land, sometimes on an assessment of the land, but they could be levied by collectives or by households. There is only slight information about the collection of these taxes.

80. Lesda (Provence and Savoy)

Lesda or *leyda* was an indirect tax in the form of economic duties levied on the entry or exit of goods into towns or villages or on their sale on the local marketplace. In Provence, *lesda* applied only to goods exchanged between local inhabitants and foreign buyers or dealers. When applying more generally to goods sold on local weekly markets, *lesda* was hardly distinguishable from other forms of *gabelle*. In many Sabaudian towns, the right to levy *leyda* was granted by the prince through franchise charters, and the term usually refers to a tax on goods sold at the local market.

81. Lezdas (Aragon)

This diverse set of indirect taxes was levied by the royal treasury and some lay and ecclesiastical lords on the trade and circulation of merchandise in urban centres and road enclaves. With precedents dating back to the eleventh century, the terminology and exact features of the tax varied by location over the following centuries. The tax differed according to the place of collection (the *portazgos* or *pontajes*), the use of official measures (*mesuratges*), the act of transportation (*peajes*), and their legality (*lezdas*). In the royal towns of Catalonia, they were usually grouped into *lleudes, passatges*, and *mesuratges*. Despite the supervision of royal officers, they tended to be the subject of infeudations and alienations, thus giving rise to a highly complex mosaic of levies that were collected or leased separately. In addition, because of the granting of royal exemptions to different communities, their payment was somehow limited.

82. Lezta (Navarre)

Local tax on sales collected for the Crown in some town markets. The nature of *leztas* was described in the local charters of market and fair towns from the second half of the twelfth century. They were especially common in the southern half of the kingdom. The main *leztas* taxed the sale of meat, fish and livestock, between the late twelfth and the early fourteenth centuries. Other specific *leztas* applied to other products.

83. Libra (Northern Italy)

See Estimum.

84. Longuellum (Savoy)

In the Pays de Vaud during the fourteenth and fifteenth centuries *longuellum* referred to an indirect tax on wine sold within cities (various spellings, including *unguellum* in Latin or, in the vernacular, *onguel*, *ungelt* among others). Originally a seigneurial tax, it was mostly conceded for the fortification needs of the cities. Similar taxes on wine, mainly allocated to cities for the fortifications, can be found under various names in other territories of the County of Savoy: such as *commune* (Faucigny and Maurienne) or *trézain* (Bresse) and *gabella grossa* (Piedmont, even though this tax was also imposed on the sale of meat and circulation of cloth). See also Ungeld.

85. Losung (German Holy Roman Empire)

The *Losung* was a property tax levied by the government of the royal and imperial town of Nuremberg, starting from 1302/1303. It was administered by the tax and financial administration (*Losungsstube*), the *Losung* Chamber. As time went on, the *Losung* was collected at more regular intervals, becoming yearly from the second half of the sixteenth century onwards. The collection was based on a prior tax oath. Every resident of Nuremberg had to assess his or her dues according to taxation principles laid down by ordinance. The tax was composite and included both a capitation and taxation of movable assets and land holdings. Registers were used to draw up the list of taxpayers called to take the oath, and therefore to make payment.

86. Macina (Northern Italy)

The *macina*, under its various local names (including the *gabella dei mulini*), was a gabelle that was perhaps introduced in the mid-thirteenth century based on the ancient lordly right over mills. Nevertheless, it was also found in locations where this common right did not exist. It involved the grain that was brought to mills for grinding. In the city it was a personal tax, whereas in the countryside it was calculated by number of *bocche* (mouths). It could be paid by the millers, who recouped the amount from their customers. In Florence, at the time of Giovanni Villani's chronicle, a *gabella* was paid on flour sold at the market, together with the milling *gabella*. It was one of the most hated taxes because it directly influenced the cost of bread and foods made with flour. It increased or decreased according to financial needs and political interests and could occasionally be levied on wheat only to lighten the burden (as in fourteenth-century Milan). The tax revenue from the *macina* was among the highest.

87. Maktu (Ottoman)

This was payment of tax as a lump sum. It was applied in areas where collection was difficult or areas which were inaccessible, and was used by communities to pay, for example, the *cizye*. The system had advantages for the state since it made collection easier and, by agreeing a fixed sum with the tax-paying community, ensured a non-fluctuating income. Conversely, it diminished state control and meant that were the population to increase, this would not be reflected in the tax income, thus representing a loss of revenue. For the tax-paying community the system offered autonomous control over apportioning the tax among its members and protected it from any exactions by tax collectors. If the population declined, however, the per capita level of tax necessarily increased.

88. Mala pecunia (Burgundian Low Countries)

See Assisen.

89. Mansus tax (Poland)

This was a direct and extraordinary tax paid by peasants, village mayors, millers, inn-keepers, gardeners and nobility without peasants. Initially, it was imposed very infrequently. In the second half of the fifteenth century, it was levied regularly every two years, with parliamentary approval. Its rates ranged from 4 to 18 groschen per mansus, although the most common rate was 12 groschen per mansus (Polish: *łanowe, pobor*; Latin: *exactio, exactio fertonum*).

90. Martiniega (Castile)

This was a direct tribute paid on Castile on Saint Martin's day (11 November) by non-privileged groups in recognition of seigniorial authority. Its origins, predating the thirteenth century, are reminiscent of old seigniorial levies on peasant communities. This was one of the earliest royal tributes to expand outside the *realengo* estates after the reign of Alphonse VIII of Castile. However, even if the rent ledgers for 1292 indicate that this tribute was still a substantial item of taxation in quantitative terms, by the fourteenth century, the royal *martiniega* had become a residual and obsolete figure, being set at a flat rate that lost value with the depreciation of the *maravedí* (the unit of account). In many seigniorial territories, the rents went to the lord (secular or ecclesiastical), as attested by the references to *martiniegas* included in the *Libro Becerro de las Behetrías*, dated to 1352. In some territories, tributes similar to the *martiniega* were known under different names (such as *infurción* or *marzazga*). The collection of this tribute continued into the Early Modern Age.

91. Monedaje (Aragon)

Tax paid to the king to keep the value of the currency stable. In 1205, Peter II imposed it in Catalonia and Aragon as an extraordinary and general service which was levied on personal property and real estate. In Aragon, Valencia, and Majorca, its payment became regular throughout the thirteenth century. In the Kingdom of Aragon, James I collected various *monedajes* as extraordinary taxes approved in the estates' assemblies and, in 1236, he turned it into a periodical tax, which was collected every seven years in the area of influence of the currency minted in the city of Jaca, together with the County of Ribagorza, Lleida, and Tortosa. In Valencia, after the minting of royal currency in 1247, the *monedajes* were similarly regularised in a parliament in 1266, also for periods of seven years. In Majorca, the Valencian royal currency was in force between 1247 and 1301, when James II of Majorca created his own monetary system, together with a new tax to guarantee its value. In the case of Catalonia, this tax was associated with the *bovaje* and, after 1258, there were no extra taxes needed to keep the value of Barcelonian currency stable.

92. Monedaje (Navarre)

Subsidy that aimed to "rescue" the issue of coinage from the king. Issuing coinage was an exclusive royal right established in the *Fuero General de Navarra*, which enabled negotiation between the king and the kingdom at the beginning of the reign to decide upon the issuing of coinage or the collection of an alternative tax. It is one of the earliest subsidies known in Navarre, and it was formulated as a quota-based direct tax. The collection of at least five *monedajes* is attested from 1265 to1390. Therefore, although it emerged early, it was only used rarely, and it was superseded by the imposition of direct tax in the second half of the fourteenth century.

93. Moneda forera (Castile)

Direct tribute collected by the Kings of Castile every seven years and on their accession to the throne, and paid by the non-privileged inhabitants of Castile (*pecheros*) who were above a certain wealth threshold. The origin of this tax lies with the donations awarded to the Kings of León (from 1202, at the latest) and Castile (perhaps from as early as 1197) for giving up their prerogative to alter the content and legal value of coinage. However, from the reign of Alphonse X (1252–1284) until the suppression of the tribute in 1724, the *moneda forera* was an ordinary tax which recognized the "king's sovereignty" and which did not require the approval of the *Cortes*. In the fifteenth century, it involved a single payment of 8 *maravedíes* per taxpayer in Castile and the *Extremaduras* and 6 *maravedíes* in the territories of the former Kingdom of León. Nobles, clergymen and taxpayers whose assets (bed, linen and weapons excepted) were below 120 *maravedíes* were exempt. The administration of this tax was leased out to financial companies, although they were supervised by council officials in charge of censuses (*empadronadores*) and collection (*cogedores*).

94. Mukataa (Ottoman)

Was a term used both for a bundle of revenues and for tax farming. Such revenues went to the central treasury and made up a significant part of the central budget. They could be composed of a single revenue stream, for example, customs dues or taxes on commercial transactions such as the tax collected on weighing goods, or made up of a range of different taxes, such as taxes on candle-making factories and tanneries combined with market taxes charged on sales. *Mukataa*s could also be made up of revenue from state monopolies, such as salt production or mints. Such revenues were usually farmed out but could also be collected by a state agent (*emin*).

95. Munus (Right to tax)

The term *munus* is mentioned in the final book of the Digest (D. 50. 16. 18). The word developed in Rome and came to mean a "requisition of service". The *munera civilia seu publica* were distinct from the *municipalia munera*. The cost of a "public service" was passed on to individuals due to insufficient local resources. In the first category, a distinction was made between personal and asset-based *munera*. The former referred to an individual in a personal, physical and intellectual role, without any expenditure. The latter, by contrast, required a financial contribution. There were mixed *munera* for personal activity incurring expenditure. Canon scholars were particularly interested in the term *munus*. Sinibaldo Fieschi (Innocent IV) in the early thirteenth century, and then Panormitanus in the first half of the fifteenth century used this term to moot the establishment of public charges and taxes. They defined people's obligations in relation to the coercive power of the law, custom, or the authority of a sovereign invested with public power. Theologians and canon law scholars were especially interested in *munera patrimoniala*. Panormitanus made a distinction between *munera mere patrimonialia* (a tax on property independent of the person), *capitatio* (a tax on a person independently of property), and *collecta* (a tax on a person relative to the size of their assets). Richard de Mediavilla suggested defining *munera realia* or *patrimoniala* as a payment resulting from the right to ownership, thus distinguishing between taxation of the property itself and taxation of the person owning it. This thinking by theologians was a response to a growing desire to define taxation in terms of property rather than people. Thinking about *munera* also owes a significant debt to Bartolo (1317–1357). Taking as his starting point the general definition in the *Digest* relating to normative authority (D., 50, 16, 214), he arrives at a much narrower conception of *munera personalia, patrimonialia e mixta*. Learned jurists used this three-part classification as a framework to structure their thinking. These three elements were the functional categories in which the vernacular terminology of taxation and new fiscal measures were placed.

96. Myt (Russia)

Toll and custom duties in general on bridges, roads, and rivers. Dated back to Kievan Rus', and kept by the Muscovite fiscal system.

97. Nefgildi (Scandinavia)

Literally "nose-tax" or "nose-fee", a duty for every nose, *i.e.* every person. It was a usual term for taxes based upon the personal principle, i.e. the same amount from every person or household. It is mentioned in Norse literature and its introduction was connected with the rise of a kingdom, but this is considered unlikely by modern scholarship. In Norwegian laws, it was a term for compensation for a killing. There is also a narrative of the introduction of a tax per nose in Sweden (*nefgiald*), or at least in the Lake Mälaren region, in pre-Christian times. It was said to be one coin for each nose but is not known from other sources. The term *nefgiald* was a household tax from the province of Västmanland noted in 1285. There is no connection with the personal tax mentioned in Norse literature. In 1085, King Knud ("the Holy") introduced a nose-tax, *nefgilde*, in Denmark, which caused social disturbance. This tax was evidently not a regular duty.

98. Octroi (France)

Any indirect tax the king, or the duke in Brittany, granted a town the right to raise for a specific purpose during a limited, but renewable time of one or more years (*octroi* means "grant").

Thus, it is a municipal tax by destination, though a royal or princely tax by its legal basis. The first documented case of royal *octroi* dates back to ca. 1260, but they became widespread in the 1340s and 1350s to finance the creation or restoration of urban fortifications, and thereafter their maintenance until modern times. They were collected by municipal farmers.

See also Accises, Cloison, droits de.

99. Octroi, octroy (patent) (Burgundian Low Countries)

Sum paid by the city as a recognition of the prince's competence to allow the city to levy indirect taxes or to change their rate. This sum could be rather important (the princes sought to upgrade it to a certain percentage of the indirect tax) in the case of a small and therefore politically lightweight city, or on the contrary almost trivial and purely symbolic in the case of a politically influential big city.

100. Opsonion (Byzantine Empire)

Fiscal demand mentioned between other indirect taxes in the imperial charters granting privileges and tax exemptions. During the middle Byzantine period (seventh to eleventh centuries), *opsonion* was related to supplying the army. Under the Palaiologoi, *opsonion* was mentioned as imposition on the boats, as financial aid to a person, and as a fee paid to state officials.

101. Ongeld (Burgundian Low Countries)

See Assisen.

102. Passagia (Sicily)

See Ius passuum.

103. Peajes (Aragon)

See Lezdas.

104. Pecha (Navarre)

Rural rent (or census) which in Navarre was distinguished from other taxes and exactions because it implied and flagged the servile condition of the taxpayer. The dependence of peasants was expressed in the dispositions that forbade them from abandoning their lords' land or failing to pay the *pecha*, along with other civil (concerning inheritances, for instance) and penal rules. The rent had no fiscal nature, but the *pechas* collected in royal possessions turned them into the main source of revenue for the Navarre Crown until the mid-fourteenth century.

105. Pecha / peita (Aragon)

See Qüestia.

106. Pedagium portarum (Northern Italy)

See Gate tax.

107. Plough tax (Poland and Lithuania)

A direct tax, paid by peasants, initially based on the number of ploughs or the unit of cultivated land. Until the end of the twelfth century the tax was paid in kind. In the thirteenth and for most of the fourteenth century, the basic general tax levied on the mansi of settled peasants and paid in money. Its rate was established by royal privilege in 1374 for the estates of the nobility and in 1381 for the church estates. Since then, it was the only tax that could be collected by the king without the consent of the nobility gathered at assemblies (Polish: *poradlne*; Latin: *exactio regalis*).

108. Poll tax (England)

A subsidy granted by parliaments and convocations of clergy, levied on individual lay and clerical taxpayers, who paid per head (poll). Edward III levied the first poll tax in 1377, on both laymen and clergy, at a single rate. His son Richard II levied the second one in 1379 according to a tariff of rates, graduated according to status and income bracket, and the third in 1381, at triple the rates of the 1377 tax, which was widely evaded and sparked a violent riot against the king. Unbeneficed clergy – not otherwise liable for clerical taxes – also paid poll taxes in 1406, 1419, 1429, 1435 and 1449. Returns to the royal Exchequer of the names of those liable to pay were required for all except the 1377 lay tax, and many survive today.

109. Portazgo (Castile)

Indirect tax on the transit of goods collected at the local level in the Crown of Castile; many *portazgos* were created in the eleventh and twelfth centuries. Although according to Alphonse X's *Partidas* they belonged to the king and only he could create new *portazgos*, total or partial exemptions became common between 1157 and 1369 to stimulate internal trade, especially during the reign of Alphonse X (1252–1284). From the thirteenth century and, especially, from the ascension of the Trastámara dynasty to the throne in 1369, it was common for the Crown to surrender these tolls to council and seigniorial *haciendas*, which continued charging *portazgos* into the Early Modern Age. In this way, by 1429 *portazgos* barely accounted for 0.23 per cent of the Crown's ordinary revenue.

110. Pozobitze (Byzantine Empire)

The term is mentioned in a chrysobull of Tsar Stefan Dušan (1331–1355) in favour of the Monastery of Lykoussada in Thessaly. *Pozobitze* is probably related to *pozob* and *pozobisma*, which is mentioned in Serbian documents and in documents from the Monastery of Lavra in Mount Athos accordingly. It was probably derived from the Serbian word *zob*, which means oats and constituted a demand in kind for nourishing the horses of the ruler and other high dignitaries.

111. Prebenda (Byzantine Empire)

The term is mentioned in the middle of the fourteenth century between other tax exemptions in chrysobulls from the region of Epirus and Thessaly. *Prebenda* is not related to the Byzantine fiscal system, as it is not mentioned in Byzantine fiscal treatises or other fiscal sources. It was more probably associated with the homonymous institution of the Latin Church, denoting the income derived from ecclesiastic property and received by high church dignitaries or tenants of the property. *Prebenda*, also had a secular nature, as it was demanded by state authority in Kerkyra and Crete under Latin occupation. From Kerkyra, it was probably transferred to Epirus and Thessaly under the Orsini's authority.

112. Precaria (Scandinavia)

See Bede.

113. Preselitza (Byzantine Empire)

The term is mentioned in a chrysobull of Tsar Stefan Dušan (1331–1355) in favour of the Monastery of Lykoussada in Thessaly. *Preselitza* is probably associated with *priselica*, which is mentioned in Serbian documents from Mount Athos Monasteries. It has been argued that this charge constituted a demand for the maintenance of the army or a collective payment for the damages caused by thieves in a village community. In the case of Thessaly, the first interpretation seems more convincing, in view of the region's capacity for furnishing the army with supplies.

114. Procurations (Church taxation)

A tax demanded by bishops and archdeacons – personally or through delegates – from the parish rectors in their bishopric or respective demarcation every time they made a visit to inspect the state of the churches and the performance of the religious services associated with worship. It was also named a visitation or right of visit. Initially required in kind to pay travelling and accommodation expenses – a sort of hospitality tax – over time it was demanded in cash, in accordance with rates established by Pope Benedict XI (bull *Vas electionis*, 1336). Papal legates, and the popes themselves, could also demand it on their travels around Christendom. In the second half of the fourteenth century, the Avignon Papacy viewed the reservation of episcopal procurations as a new way of increasing the amount of money paid into its treasury. Collecting them, half procurations generally, was a task entrusted to the papal collectors.

115. Procurations (Church Lands)

A feudal custom integrated by the ecclesiastical hierarchy, the *procuratio* allowed the prelates visiting the clerics under their jurisdiction to demand hospitality. Commuted into a tax, it was also levied in the thirteenth century in the Church Lands, but not in a uniform manner. In the provinces of Latium formerly subject to the pope, it was collected when a new rector arrived in the province and paid by the lay and religious communities. In the Duchy, therefore, it was referred to as the *adventus novi rectoris*. In the "new provinces", March, Romagna and the Duchy, only the clergy contributed. This tax disappeared in the fifteenth century.

116. Quèstia (Aragon)

This tax was known under different names but had common features throughout the territories of the Crown of Aragon. It was a communally imposed tribute, which was levied among the neighbours and landowners of a specific locality. In Catalonia, it received the name of *quèstia*, and it became widespread in the royal estates under the reign of Peter II (1196–1213). It later acquired an almost annual periodicity, which forced continuous negotiations between the monarch and the Catalan towns (the larger cities received tax exemptions between the end of the thirteenth and the beginning of the fourteenth centuries). Until 1340, it was mostly assimilated to the granting of subsidies. From then on, it remained as an increasingly fossilised resource that was often subject to alienations. In Valencia, they were called *peites*, and were similarly the object of frequent negotiations between the Crown and the royal towns from the mid-thirteenth century until 1330, when the annual sum each town had to pay was finally determined (the capital city of Valencia was exempt from 1286). In Aragon, it received the denomination of *pecha*. Its process of consolidation had begun in the first half of the thirteenth century and, by the end of the same century, the annual sum levied on the communities was already well established. In all three peninsular territories of the Crown, the tax was usually collected through *tallas*, which were an important stimulus for the development of local administrations.

117. Reichsstadtsteuer (German Holy Roman Empire)

Starting from the thirteenth century onwards, at least, communities in royal towns (*königliche Städte*) or in towns where the ruler was the solicitor (*Vogt*) paid an annual tribute to him, by virtue of his protection and that of the Empire. Initially, the payment was akin to the seigneurial *taille* (land tax, *Bede*) owed to the lord/ecclesiastical advocate (and king), and was referred to by various terms, including *bede, precaria, stiura, collecta imperio praestanda* (1219), or *exactiones sive precarias imperatoribus et regibus* (1274). The common feature to these taxes is the fact that they were labelled royal or imperial. The payment soon attracted privileges that granted the municipalities concerned a collection right and the authorisation to respond globally to the royal urban tax. The first overall view of the *Reichsstadtsteuer* dates back to a parchment list of 1241/1242 (*MGH Constitutiones* III, p. 2 ff). From the fourteenth century onwards, rulers frequently channelled the revenues of the *Reichsstadtsteuer* through pledges granted to third parties for several years. Thus, under Frederick III, Frankfurt was the only town whose imperial urban tax went directly and regularly to the Treasury. In the fifteenth century, this tax was considered "customary" by the towns, which often paid it in two instalments, on requisition and with a receipt. It became a symbol of belonging to the Empire and of having a direct link with the ruler (*Reichsunmittelbarkeit*). Imperial towns ensured that the receipts remained under the imperial seal. The fiscal link with the royal authority was maintained as long as the imperial immediacy lasted, which means it may have endured until the end of the old empire (1806). Free towns, in contrast, did not want to have to pay the *Reichssteuer*.

118. Relevium (Sicily)

This was a royal direct tax applied on the inheritance of fiefs between the first half of twelfth century and the second half of the eighteenth. Frederick II regulated the payment system of the *relevio* which was already introduced by the Normans. The sovereign decided that it corresponded to half the value of the annuities of the year prior to the death of the feudal lord. The *relevio* had to be paid both for the populated fiefs and for those uninhabited, it was calculated subtracting the sum paid in the form of *adoa* and was collected by the provincial officers called *giustizieri*. During the reign of Charles I of Anjou, the revenues amounted to two thousand *once*. Alphonse of Aragon charged the *percettori* of the collection of *relevio*, whereas the *regia camera della Sommaria* had to do the checks and draw up the necessary documentation.

119. Royal szos (Poland and Lithuania)

The main and most important direct tax payable to the Crown treasury by royal, church and private (nobility) towns. Initially, it was of an extraordinary nature, levied on cities in exceptional political situations. Later, it became a tax paid by townsmen based on the value of their real estate, movables and debts, usually 2 groschen per 1 marc (per 48 groschen), *i.e.*, more than 4 per cent of the value of real estate. From the mid-fifteenth century, it was levied by the Sejm or sejmiks of Greater Poland and Lesser Poland without the participation of town representatives, as a required tribute.

120. Salt gabelle (Northern Italy)

From the eleventh century onwards, governments throughout the Mediterranean held monopolies on the sale of salt. The salt *gabella*, introduced in the second half of the thirteenth century, combined business, a sales monopoly, and an obligation to buy at a political price. In many cities and, generally, in the countryside *contadi*, distribution was organised in a compulsory manner, with the obligation to collect certain quantities that were calculated based on the *estimo* or using mixed criteria, the number of *bocche* (mouths) and the *estimo*. During the first half of the fourteenth century, the salt trade became a personal business for the lords of the Po Valley, the Visconti of Milan, the Della Scala of Verona, and the da Carrara of Padua. In Veneto and in Tuscany, the obligation seems to have applied only to the countryside, while in the city, salt was still sold under a monopoly. In the countryside of Florence it was levied based on the *estimo*, but in the city, as in Lucca, it was limited to sale under a monopoly. In the mid-fourteenth century, Siena transformed salt into a direct tax, both for citizens and for inhabitants of the countryside. In the Visconti-Sforza State, the salt *gabella* was the most profitable asset.

121. Scutage (England)

A direct tax known by 1100, it was a payment to commute military service due to the king by his tenants-in-chief, who held their lands by military tenure. The lands were valued in knights' fees, each fee being the amount of land considered adequate to support one knight on military service. When the king issued a summons for the feudal host, each tenant-in-chief had to appear personally with his full complement of knights, but if he did not, he was expected to pay *scutage* after the campaign to reimburse the king for his expenses in hiring replacements. The rising cost of armour, warhorses and mercenaries' wages from the late twelfth century meant that *scutage* rates, charged per knight's fee, had quadrupled by the mid-thirteenth century, and the subdivision of knights' fees with the passing of generations made it more complicated to levy. From 1279, tenants-in-chief not obeying a summons paid both a fine before a campaign and *scutage* after it. Its unpopularity led to its abolition in 1340.

122. Servicio de Cortes (Castile)

Economic subsidy negotiated with, and granted to, the king by the procurators of the *Cortes* of Castile. The *servicio* was granted to meet specific eventualities, and their legitimacy rested on their purpose being conducive to the "commonwealth" of the kingdom; these purposes were set down in detail in the documents (*otorgamientos*) in which the concession was recorded. From this perspective, the *servicio de Cortes* was a form of economic *auxilium*, and therefore was not fiscal in nature. The request of *servicios* began during the reign of Alphonse X in 1269, although some precedents existed; the practice soon took hold and remained in full force throughout the Early Modern Age. At first (between the reigns of Alphonse X and Alphonse XI), the amount granted was calculated as a given number of *monedas*. However, after the awarding of *alcabalas* to Alphonse XI by the *Cortes* held in 1342, and until 1398, *servicios* comprised a number of *monedas* and the *alcabala* for the duration of the concession. After the collection of *alcabalas* by the Crown became an ordinary affair, no longer requiring the authorization of the *Cortes*, and until 1476–1477, the *servicios* authorized by the assembly were constituted by a certain number of *monedas* and a total amount (*pedido*) divided proportionally between the towns and cities by population, using general censuses, like the one carried out in 1409, as a reference; these censuses, however, soon became obsolete, and led to tributary inequalities and complaints. Between 1478 and 1498, the Catholic Monarchs abstained from requesting *servicios de Cortes*, which were replaced by an "ordinary contribution" negotiated with the *Hermandad General*. The tax, generally implemented in the form of *sisas* over staples, was administered by the cities. When the *Cortes* began granting *servicios* again in 1500, the collection method used by the *Hermandad* (setting a fixed sum by province and subdividing this sum among the towns and cities in the province), was followed.

123. Servicio y montazgo (Castile)

A group of royal indirect taxes that imposed toll duties on transhumant stock-keeping, collected in obligatory transit points for the flocks. In fact, the *servicio y montazgo* was a mixed tribute formed by the merge of two independent figures by Alphonse XI in 1343: first, the *servicio* on transhumant livestock, imposed by Alphonse X in 1269 in recognition of the protection that the Crown afforded this activity; the amount payable by the owner of the flock depended on the number of animals; and second, *montazgos*, appropriated by the Crown in 1343, which were toll duties paid by the flocks entering woodland and grazing areas; in this case, the payable amounts depended on the region in which these grazing areas were located. In the fifteenth century, the *servicio y montazgo*, the regulation of which was very complex owing to the multiple variables at play, was leased out to financial companies that arranged collection in multi-year periods, beginning on St John's Day (24 June).

124. Sisas (Castile)

Indirect *ad valorem* tax on staples, such as meat, wine and fish, collected by Castilian councils following a royal temporary authorization. They were aimed to endow councils with resources to cover their own needs or to meet the council's obligations with the royal *Hacienda* (the *Hermandad*'s *contribución ordinaria* between 1478 and 1498; *servicio de Cortes* after 1500). The creation of local taxes on consumption is attested in Castile as early as the thirteenth century, although the collection of these extraordinary *sisas* by the councils increased substantially during the reign of Isabella I (1474–1504), and continued into the Early Modern Age.

125. Sisas (Aragon)

Indirect taxes levied by municipal administrations, especially in towns and cities, on the consumption, commercialisation and circulation of a wide array of products. Notwithstanding a few precedents from the late thirteenth century, these taxes began to expand as a fiscal resource, granted by the king to local corporations, in the 1320s and 1330s, and were definitively consolidated in the 1350s and 1360s. They were usually grouped into different lots and then leased out. The most important were those which were levied on basic necessities, such as cereal, meat, wine, and fish. With different *ad valorem* rates, they were also imposed on the trade of these foodstuffs, but also raw materials, manufactured goods, and other kinds of merchandise, as well as real estate, financial instruments or the entry of people, animals, goods and even ships into cities. Also named *imposicions*.

126. Skotte (Scandinavia)

Taxes collected by the town's municipal authorities and urban taxes known from the fifteenth century. According to the extensive Stockholm *skotte* registers from the 1460's, it was paid individually. The principles of assessment varied, but were based on fortune. Named *boejargjald* in Norwegian.

127. Stadsskatt (Scandinavia)

See Byskat.

128. Subventio generalis (Sicily)

This was a royal subsidy imposed on hearths applying a system of distribution of taxable amounts. The term was introduced by Charles I of Anjou in order to emphasise the fact that the contribution, which was levied on all owners of non-feudal assets, was a subsidy for the kingdom. Although it was an extraordinary income, the *subventio* was collected every year at the end of September. At court, the officers called *rationales* prepared the tax coupons (*cedole*) showing the amount owed by each *università* (city) and periodically updated. The officers of provincial districts (justiciars) had to organise the collection of the subsidy, and the funds collected were physically taken from the citizens by the *taxatores* and *collectores*. The tax coupons were issued every year until at least 1338. The last surviving coupon dates back to 1320 referring to all the provinces of the kingdom: the total revenue was almost 40,000 *onze*.

129. Subsidio (Navarre)

Subsidies or petitions granted to the king by the *Cortes*, in the form of either direct or indirect taxes. The word *ayuda* connotes the voluntary nature of the tax, that is, that it was granted to the king, rather than imposed by him. In order to emphasize this voluntary nature of the tax, sometimes it was referred to as "*ayuda graciosa*". Most often, the word "*ayuda*", which was particularly common in the second half of the fourteenth and the fifteenth centuries, was used to allude to the collection of direct taxes.

130. Subsidy (Dauphiné)

A princely direct tax, whose general features are those of the royal *fouage*. It was granted by the local Estates to the dauphin from 1357 to the modern times. It was called *don gratuit* in the early fifteenth century, and *aide* in the second half of the century. It was collected by ordinary officials in the frame of castellanies or *mandements*.

131. Subsidy (Church taxation)

The generic term that was usually given to the demand for money, at the behest of bishops or popes – in this case, going by the name of charitable subsidies – or of secular institutions. These payments were always considered extraordinary, depending on the reasons or purposes put forward for them in each case. Ecclesiastical subsidies would only be those that directly affected the clergy, in other words, treating clergymen as taxpaying subjects; they should therefore be distinguished from other demands that were passed on to the vassals of the Church. The sum of money demanded in each subsidy could be imposed by whoever demanded it, or rather be the result of negotiations between the parties involved; once it had been established, the overall sum had to be distributed differently among the bishoprics according to their resources to pay. Throughout the fourteenth century, coinciding with a greater proliferation of tenths transferred to monarchies, these subsidies could be paid at the same rate as tenths, through the establishment of apportionments among the beneficed clergy in each diocese.

132. Subsidy (Provence and Savoy)

A subsidy was an extraordinary contribution to princely finances, over and above any form of traditional taxation. It was characterised by its freely consented and non-recurring nature (in theory at least) and its overarching nature, overriding customary tax exemptions benefitting privileged groups of society. Subsidies came into general use from the late thirteenth century onwards. During the fourteenth and fifteenth centuries, subsidies were debated and granted through the assemblies of estates. Also called *subsidium, donum, or donum gratiosum*.

133. Subsidy (Church Lands)

In the eleventh century, the popes used this term to request occasional and extraordinary assistance from a part of the clergy. In the Church Lands in the thirteenth century, it therefore unsurprisingly concerned clerics with a benefice. Not until Cardinal Albornoz did the lay communities begin to pay subsidies, first exceptionally, then regularly, on a State and provincial basis. The term became very widespread in the fifteenth century, undoubtedly due to its flexibility: a tax levied regularly, whose rate was variable, and which said nothing about the use of its proceeds. Always negotiated with the representatives of each city, who could choose already in the fourteenth century between direct or indirect taxation to finance the sum they had to pay, it became the flagship tax of the Papal State in modern times.

134. Szos (Poland and Lithuania)

See City szos and Royal szos.

135. Tallage (England)

A direct tax that evolved in the second half of the twelfth century from the traditional levies that manorial lords imposed annually on their unfree tenants before the Conquest, in which lords and tenants agreed a lump sum without a formal assessment. As only occasional impositions on the free men of the king's boroughs and tenants of his rural demesne, royal *tallages* differed, but the amount paid was similarly negotiated by his officials. The arbitrary nature of *tallages* was a factor in their frequent imposition by Henry II, Richard I, John and Henry III, especially between 1237 and 1269, when Parliament withheld its consent to the more lucrative *fractional taxes*. John, and Henry III in particular, demanded large sums as *tallages* from the Jews. The later *tallages* levied by Edward I in 1304 and Edward II in 1312 were at least partly assessed in the manner of *fractional taxes*. They were abolished by law in 1340.

136. Tallia (Church Lands)

The term *tallia militum* became common in the Church Lands from the 1270s onwards. Fifty years earlier, the pope considered it was an *insolite exactio*. It actually replaced the term *stipendia militum*, which referred to the sum paid by each community in lieu of military service owed with a specified number of knights. Ordered and collected by the rector throughout the fourteenth century, it disappeared there after, because of tax simplification policies, but mathematically absorbed by the subsidy.

137. Tallia (Provence and Savoy)

Tallia was a general term describing diverse forms of direct taxes. In its earliest form, it might be a personal tax of feudal origin (especially in Savoy). In its most general meaning, it was a distributive tax established by municipal authorities in order to provide for common expenses, either in the form of a fixed amount applying to each hearth (*capagium*) or of a proportional tax based on revenue or on fixed (mainly land) assets. Such taxes were extraordinary, inasmuch as they applied to specific purposes, but they might be collected on a regular, such as weekly (*tallia dominicalis*) basis. Such taxes were in general use throughout the late medieval period.

138. Taille (France, royal tax)

A royal direct tax, also called *aide* until the reign of Charles VI, and even as late as the fifteenth century in the South. Its main difference with the *fouage*, which it replaced in 1384, is that it was not defined by a rate per hearth. It was in use until 1790. The *taille* was granted by local or general Estates, or ordered by the king. It was a distribution tax, whose amount was divided at successive levels by *généraux* and *élus* according to the number of hearths of each territory, down to the town or country parish, which fixed each head of hearth's contribution with respect to his economic capacities, "the mighty supporting the feeble". In the North, this appraisal relied on public assessments; in the South, where written records of private property were available, the *taille* took the shape of a *taille réelle* (a tax on real assets). Exempt categories were the same as for fouage, in addition to some towns and the members of the *francs-archers* militia instituted in 1448.

139. Taille (France, municipal tax)

A municipal direct tax, also called *collecte* or *quête* (collection) in the North until the fourteenth century, *comu* (common tax), *dimergue* (Sunday tax) or *prêt* (loan) in the South, in use from the twelfth century to modern times. In the thirteenth century, Languedoc cities drew up inventories and assessments of taxpayers' personal and immovable property, written up in *livres d'estime*, to provide themselves with an accurate taxation basis. In the fourteenth century, such records (often called *compoix* from the 1350s) became widespread south of a line from Bordeaux to Dijon. The southern taxpayer's share then typically combined an amount set according to his assessed wealth through the technique of *allivrement* (proportionate calculation) with a *capage* or *personal* (per-head amount). Northern towns relied on lists of taxpayers with their occupations and set individual shares more roughly. The *taille* was collected by a receiver usually appointed for each levy by the municipal government.

140. Talea (Northern Italy)

The *talea* (*taglia*) was an extraordinary direct tax levied in the *signorie*. Use of this term arose after the diffusion of the terms *colletta* and *fodro*, spreading outside of the areas of ancient lordships, like Piedmont. It was primarily linked with the *signorie* of northern Italy during the fourteenth century. The *taglia* was always a distribution tax. In the regional states, once the amount was established, it was demanded by the lord city by city. The city's accounting offices then divided the city's *taglia* from that of the *contadi*, where it was divided among rural communities. Smaller towns were taxed individually if they were autonomous from the cities. Another extraordinary direct tax under the *signorie* was the *subsidium*, which was frequent during the fourteenth and fifteenth centuries. As with the *taglia*, the prince had to justify the reason for his demand without any differences regarding the methods of the levy with respect to the *colletta* or *fodro*. *Taglie* and *subsidia* disappeared in the *Terraferma* during the Venetian age.

141. Tamga (Russia)

As toll, fee for pre-sale stamping of goods. An indirect tax introduced by the Mongols (1242) under the *pax mongolica* system that guaranteed total safety to merchants. Kept by the Muscovite fiscal system.

142. Theloneum (Sicily)

See Ius passuum.

143. Tenth (Church taxation)

An ecclesiastical income tax originating in the twelfth century to finance the crusades in the Holy Land. Although it was usually transferred to secular rulers, it continued to be a papal tax; only popes could authorise its imposition on the clergy in each kingdom for the length of time deemed appropriate in each case. As the name indicates, it was levied on a tenth of the annual income of every clergyman or religious institution, although the imposition of other percentages (twentieths, fortieths, etc.) was occasionally resorted to. With a view to collecting the tenths, it was necessary to have inventories available of the existing ecclesiastical benefices in each bishopric, along with their corresponding valuation: the "tenth rate" was the equivalent of the net income of each benefice, to which the corresponding quota of 10 per cent was applied. Cardinals and military orders were exempted from paying it, as were certain religious orders and the poorest benefices.

144. Tenth (England)

See Fifteenth and tenth.

145. Traite des vins (France)

A royal indirect tax raised, as a compensation, on wines leaving the collection area of aids to be sold outside, at the same rate *ad valorem*. It was the equivalent of *imposition foraine* for wine taxation. It was also referred to by its rate, with mention of export to distinguish it from the aid it replaced (for instance, "thirteenth of wines brought to Flanders and thereabouts" in Rouen in 1361). It appeared in 1361 and was still in use in modern times.

Its collection was leased by *élus* to farmers, who levied it in seaports or at the last bridge across the river before the boundaries of the tax area. Major farms were those of the wine exporting regions, such as Anjou (by the River Loire), Poitou and Saintonge (by sea).

146. Traites (Brittany)

Princely taxes on the land export of merchandise, instituted between 1365 and 1387 and still in use in modern times. They were mainly levied in the eastern part of the duchy on three categories of goods: "dead things", grains and live animals. Their rate was fixed either per weight unit, item unit or *ad valorem*.

Their collection on "dead things" was leased out by local *receveurs ordinaires* to farmers for each particular taxable category of merchandise. From the mid-fifteenth century, the *traites* of grains and live animals were directly leased by the Treasurer and *receveur général* of the Duchy.

147. Tratta (Sicily)

Since the Swabian age, the royal court sold ad hoc licences (*tratte*) for exporting grain and legumes from Sicily through the payment of a custom duty known as *ius exiturae*. Wheat was by far the main export and the most profitable product of the realm. Whereas a *salma* of wheat corresponded to a single *tratta*, a *salma* of barley or legumes corresponded to two *tratte* (a *salma* was equivalent to ca. 3.3 hectolitres and ca. 2.75 hectolitres, respectively in the eastern and western parts of the island). The central officer known as *magister portulanus*, who administered the ports and grain warehouses of the island, managed the sale of *tratte*. Although their price (roughly between 3 and 4 *tarì* per *tratta*) varied significantly in connection to the production of and the demand for grain – and wheat in particular – those custom duties generated a variable, but substantial ordinary income, amounting to about 10,000 *onze* per year.

148. Ungeld (German Holy Roman Empire)

In the Upper Rhineland and Switzerland, especially in the 1470s, some forms of the *Ungeld* were referred to as *Böser Pfennig* (bad penny), which is also reflected in the term *Ungeld*. Historiography generally equates the *Ungeld* with an excise duty, a term more commonly used in the middle and northern parts of the Holy Roman Empire. The *Ungeld* was referred to as *Angal* in French-speaking areas in the north-east of the County of Burgundy. This was an indirect taxation of royal origin levied by the ruler and by enfranchised towns or territorial lords. Initially, it was extraordinary and was often associated with costs for fortifications or roads and bridges. The *Ungeld* was levied on consumption or trade. In its earliest forms, it was levied on the consumption of wine or on milling (*Mahlungeld*), and could be extended to other food products. The *Weinungeld* (wine *Ungeld*) was usually paid by managers of drinking establishments, taverns, and inns or by traders on the market. The German term, *Ungeld*, used to designate the levy dates back to the beginning of the thirteenth century. A modern form of the *Ungeld* remained in place in Switzerland until 1887. See also Longuel.

149. Vacancies (Church taxation)

This term referred initially to the ecclesiastical benefices that became vacant, whether due to the death of the holder or his transfer to another benefice. By extension, it eventually referred to the appropriation, by the papacy, of the incomes generated by a benefice during the period of time it remained vacant. It was a type of tax frequently associated with the payment of annates.

150. Vykhod (Russia)

Mongol tribute. A direct tax (1242–1480). Collected first by agents of the Khan (*basqaqs*), then by agents of the Grand Prince of Vladimir, who remitted the amounts collected to the Golden Horde. Since 1389, Muscovite princes attempted to keep the amount for themselves. After the fall of the Tatar yoke (1480), a lower *vykhod* was still levied to finance relations with Tatar khanates.

151. Wine gabelle (Northern Italy)

The duty on wine was one of the greatest sources of income for a city. A public right of tavernkeepers and wine merchants appears in documentation in the twelfth century (in Piacenza and Pisa). In some cities, towards the middle of the thirteenth century, people could pay for a licence to sell wine produced in other people's vineyards. After the harvest, the *imbottato (imbottatura)* was collected on the spot. This was a tax based on a calculation of the quantity of must in the barrels, but we do not know how it was carried out. A tax was then paid on wine transported for sale upon entry into the city (wholesale, by the wagon); the tax was also paid when passing through customs stops along the way. The "retail" or *ad spinam* wine duty concerned wine served in taverns. In the 1260s, the Communes of Lombardy, Venice and probably elsewhere held a monopoly on the retail sale of wine, setting the number of taverns, which were assigned to licensees. The direct management of taverns ended around the beginning of the fourteenth century, when the retail duty on wine was contracted out. In Tuscany, this contact was taken on by the tavernkeepers' guild. In Venice, the tavernkeepers could only buy wine retail from the commune. The wine duty was levied when the barrel was filled and the tax was calculated by the jug, based on the quality. The glass was then stamped to ensure the correct quantity.

152. Yam (Russia)

Courier, postal service. Indirect tax based upon service duty, then paid in money (*yamskie den'gi*). Introduced by the Mongols (1242) to keep safe and quick communication all over their vast empire. Kept by the Russians for the same reason. Around the capital (Sarai for the Golden Horde, Moscow for the Russians from the end of the fifteenth century), post stations (*yamskie slobody*) were built and eventually grew into suburbs.

153. Zwanzigster Pfennig (German Holy Roman Empire)

This was a money levy with a tax rate of one-twentieth of an estimated amount.

1. Crusade or defence of Christianity tax levied on the income of the clergy
The clergy was repeatedly subjected to a "Zwanzigster", a twentieth. Thus, in 1215, all clerics were asked to pay this portion of their ecclesiastical income as part of the crusade effort for three years. The collection was performed by agents of the Holy See. The demand was renewed at the Council of Lyon in 1245. To finance the Council of Basel and the war against the Hussites, the conciliar assembly also considered raising a twentieth (half a tithe) of the ecclesiastical revenues secured by the diocesan clergy.

2. One-fifth extraordinary tax

The twentieth penny was also an extraordinary tax that was commonly encountered in territorial contexts, such as in Bavaria, in the Palatinate elective principality, or in the Tyrol. It represented a tax rate of 5 per cent on the estimated estate. It was not necessarily motivated by the crusade.

154. Zehnter Pfennig (German Holy Roman Empire)

The penny generated other variations such as the *Zehnter Pfennig* or tenth penny. These should be differentiated from the *Zehnt*, which refers to the tithe, or the crusade *Zehnt* (*Saladinzehnt* of 1188, *Lyoner Kreuzzugszehnt* of 1274, etc.), which corresponded to the *decima* or tithe. The tenth penny was an extraordinary tax of necessity levied in several territories for one or several years. In 1408, the high county (*Obergrafschaft*) of Katzenelnbogen was a collection place for a tenth penny. The tenth penny could also be claimed by municipalities. The *Zedler* or *Zehnter Pfennig* levied in Hildesheim in 1342, for example, was a municipal tax payable by the citizens and justiciables (*Dingpflichtigen*) on the basis of their landholding. Likewise, from the beginning of the fourteenth century, the tenth was a 1/10 inheritance tax owed by the citizens or residents of Hamburg. In Frankfurt or Wetzlar, the *Zehntpfennig* or *10. Pfennigsgeld* was paid by Jews who wanted to leave the town. It should be noted that the duration and frequency of collection gave rise to other denominations derived from *Pfennig* (penny), such as the *Wochenpfennig* (weekly penny). The town of Basel levied this type of extraordinary tax in 1446, on a weekly basis, and for a period of 13 weeks. It was a mixed tax that combined capitation for the less fortunate and a tiered levy system based on estates.

INDEX

Note: For practical reasons, the index has been divided into three sections: names of persons, geographical places, and taxation terms. Modern authors are to be found under their family name. Medieval people are indexed under their first name. Taxation terms that are marked with a ★ also appear in the glossary (p. 439). The glossary has not been indexed.

Abboud-Haggar, Soha 411
'Abd al-'Azīz ibn Mūsà (governor of Al-Andalus) 414
'Abd Allāh 416
'Abd al-Raḥmān I (first emir of Córdoba) 415
'Abd al-Raḥmān II (emir of Córdoba) 415
'Abd al-Raḥmān III (emir then caliph of Córdoba) 415–16
Abū Ḥanīfa 413
Abū Yūsuf 413, 429n4
Abulafia, David 156
Adalbert (archbishop of Hamburg-Bremen) 272
Adrian VI (pope) 220n107
Ahmed Khan (khan of the Great Horde) 375
Albert of Mecklenburg (king of Sweden) 349
Albizzo Guidi dei Franzesi 37, 245
Albrecht VI of Habsburg (duke of Austria) 284
Aleksander Nevsky 376
Alexander III (pope) 81, 182
Alexander Jagiellon 362, 366
Alexios Apokaukos 392, 398
al-Ḥurr 'Abd al-Raḥmān al-Thaqafī (governor of Al-Andalus) 414
Al-Manṣūr (last king of the zirid taifa of Granada) 416
Alphonse III (king of Aragon) 318
Alphonse V (king of Aragon) 87, 102–3, 155–6, 163–4, 169–71
Alphonse VI (king of Leon and Castile) 123, 416–17
Alphonse VII (king of Leon) 120, 123
Alphonse VIII (king of Castile) 123, 129

Alphonse IX (king of Leon) 123
Alphonse X (king of Castile) 123–4, 126–32, 140–1, 145–6
Alphonse XI (king of Castile) 127, 129–34, 142–3, 146
Alphonse of Poitiers (count of Toulouse) 242–3
al-Samḥ ibn Mālik al-Khawlānī (governor of Al-Andalus) 414
al-'Udhrī 415
al-Wansharīsī 410, 411, 419
Amari, Michele 156
Anacletus II (antipope) 155
Anderson, Perry 26
Andrew of Hungary (duke of Calabria) 162
Andronikos II (Byzantine emperor) 395–7, 399, 401n25, 403n94
Andronikos III (Byzantine emperor) 396–8
Andronikos Palaiologos (despot of Thessaloniki) 391
Anne de Beaujeu 235
Anne of Brittany (queen of France) 237
Anzilotti, Antonio 213
Arakcheev, Vladimir Anatol'evich 374
Ardant, Gabriel 26
Aristotle 33, 56–7, 61, 63
Arsenios Autoreianos (patriarch) 398
Arthur (son of Henry VII of England) 318
Astesanus of Asti 62
Athanasios I (patriarch) 399, 401n14, 402n41

Balde 65
Baldwin, John 226

Balta, Evangelia 423
Banū Naghrela 417
Barbadoro, Bernardino 178
Barceló, Miquel 411, 414–15, 417
Bartolo da Sassoferrato 185
Batu (khan of the Golden Horde) 372–3
Bauer, Klemens or Clemens 213, 217n8, 220n98
Bayezid I (Ottoman sultan) 420
Bayezid II (Ottoman sultan) 421–2, 425
Bazilevich, Konstantin Vasil'evich 374
Below, Georg von 25
Benedict XI (pope) 80
Benedict XII (pope) 203
Benedict XIII (pope) 76
Benno II (bishop of Osnabrück) 272
Berthold (abbot of Guebwiller) 275
Bertrand du Guesclin 135, 231
Bianchini, Ludovico 156
Biche see Albizzo Guidi dei Franzesi
Biel, Gabriel 55
Bigan İklitos 422
Biget, Jean-Louis 23
Bisson, Thomas N. 26
Blanche (daughter of Henry IV of England) 318
Blasco II Alagona 169
Blockmans, Wim 28–9
Bois, Guy 26
Boniface VIII (pope) 65, 73, 80, 86, 209, 218n52, 218n53, 227–8, 323
Boniface IX (pope) 213
Bonney, Richard 2, 29–31
Bonsignore di Gregorio 218n45
Borrelli de Serres, Léon-Louis 25, 224
Bowsky, William 27, 178
Brayson, Alex 30
Bresc, Henri 156, 168
Broussolle, Jean 27
Brown, Elizabeth A. R. 224
Buchholzer-Rémy, Laurence 20
Buczek, Karol 356–7

Caffaro 180
Çag de la Maleha 130
Cahen, Claude 429
Calixtus III (pope) 87, 220n94
Caravale, Mario 214, 220n98
Carocci, Sandro 4, 29, 157
Casimir III the Great (king of Poland) 359
Casimir IV Jagiellon (king of Poland) 361, 363, 366
Catherine de Foix (queen of Navarre) 138
Catholic Monarchs (kings of Castile and Aragon) see Isabella I (queen of Castile) and Ferdinand II (king of Aragon)
Causse, Bernard 81
Cesare Borgia 204
Chalmeta, Pedro 411–12, 414–15

Charlemagne (Holy Roman emperor) 177
Charles I (king of Hungary) 161
Charles I of Anjou (count of Provence, king of Naples and Sicily) 155, 160–2, 164, 167, 182, 185, 188, 294, 296
Charles II (king of Navarre) 137–7, 146
Charles II of Anjou (king of Naples) 161, 183, 296
Charles IV (Holy Roman emperor) 277–8
Charles IV (king of France) 82, 229
Charles V (Holy Roman emperor) 194, 284
Charles V (king of France) 66, 230–1, 233, 236, 240, 243–6
Charles VI (king of France) 66, 225, 231
Charles VII (king of France) 62, 67, 232–6, 241, 243, 245–6
Charles VIII (king of France) 64, 281, 229, 232, 234–7, 246
Charles (duke of Lorraine) 280
Charles of Blois (duke of Brittany) 237
Charles the Bold (duke of Burgundy) 235, 255, 260–1
Chénon, Emile 25
Chevalier, Bernard 38, 56, 225, 245
Chomel, Vital 225
Christian I (king of Denmark) 350
Cicero 58, 68
Clamageran, Jean-Jules 25, 224, 245
Clanchy, Michael 225
Clauzel, Denis 27
Clement III (pope) 74
Clement IV (pope) 81, 218n50
Clement V (pope) 246, 323
Clement VII (pope) 214–15
Collavini, Simone 4, 29
Conrad IV (Holy Roman emperor and king of Sicily as Conrad I) 132, 159–60
Conrad of Lichtenberg (bishop of Strasbourg) 275
Constantine VII (Byzantine emperor) 372
Conti, Elio 27
Coşgel, Metin 423

Declareuil, Joseph 25
del Treppo, Mario 156, 165, 172
Delumeau, Jean 204
Demetrios Kydones 401n14
Demetrios Notaras 392
Demetrios Palaiologos (despot of Lemnos) 391
Denton, Jeffrey. 73, 80, 315
Deresiewicz, Janusz 364
di Martino, Giuseppe 156
Dino Rapondi 261
Dmitri Ivanovich (prince of Moscow) 375
Dognon, Paul 224
Doŭnar-Zapolśki, Mitrafan 365
Dupont-Ferrier, Gustave 25, 224

Index

Edigey (emir of the White Horde) 374–5
Edward I (king of England) 64, 83, 317–23
Edward II (king of England) 317–18, 321, 323–4
Edward III (king of England) 82, 231, 243, 317–21, 323–6
Edward IV (king of England) 325, 328, 330–2
Edward the Black Prince 318
Edward the Confessor (king of England) 316
Eleanor (daughter of Edward I) 318
Eleanor (sister of Edward III) 318
Elizabeth I (queen of England) 332
Engelbrekt Engelbrektsson 349
Enguerrand de Marigny 37
Enzo (son of Frederick II) 206
Epstein, Stephen 156, 172
Erik of Pomerania (king of the Scandinavian kingdoms) 341
Erik Valdermarsson (king of Denmark) 347
Esmein, Adhémar 25
Espinas, Georges 25
Eugene IV (pope) 87
Evrart de Trémaugon 66

Falkes de Bréauté 317
Faure, Claude 212
Favier, Jean 5, 7, 27–8, 88n3
Fawtier, Robert 25
Fedor Ivanovich (tsar of Russia) 381–2
Fengler, Georg 27
Feodor of Ryazan 375
Ferdinand I (count of Castile and king of Leon) 120, 122, 416
Ferdinand I (king of Aragon) 169
Ferdinand II (king of Aragon) 120–1, 134, 136, 143, 170
Ferdinand III (king of Castile) 120–1, 123, 129
Ferdinand IV (king of Castile) 132
Ferrante I (king of Naples) 163–5
Fletcher, Giles 380–2
Font Rius, Josep Maria 25
Foulque de Puyricard 208
Francesco Balducci Pegolotti 392
Francesco di Marco Datini 21
Francesco Guerra Ventimiglia 169
Francesco II Sforza (duke of Milan) 192
Francesco Lucani 63
Francis I (king of France) 68, 80
Frederik I Barbarossa (Holy Roman emperor) 177–82, 218n36
Frederick II (Holy Roman emperor) 81, 155, 159–60, 177, 182, 185, 203, 206, 218n49, 273–4, 318
Frederick III (king of Sicily) 168, 171

Galeazzo Maria Sforza (duke of Milan) 194
Garcia de Valdeavellano, Luis 25
Gardi, Andrea 204, 215

Garnier, Florent 25, 79, 225
Gediminas (Grand duke of Lithuania) 365
Genç, Mehmet 420
Genet, Jean-Philippe 28, 56
Genghis Khan, 373, 383n1
Georgios Gemistos Plethon 399
Georgios Goudeles 398
Georgios of Pelagonia 399
Georgios Pachymeres 398
Gervase of Canterbury 319
Gian Galeazzo Visconti (duke of Milan) 177, 184, 194
Gil de Albornoz (cardinal) 203–4, 211–13, 216, 220n89
Giles of Rome 63–4
Ginatempo, Maria 4, 29, 178, 184, 188, 194, 196n1
Giovanni Antonio Orsini (prince of Taranto) 163, 166
Giovanni Bertachini 63, 65
Godefroid de Fontaines 64
Goffman, Daniel 422
Gonçalves, Iria 26
Goody, Jack 225
Gordan veled Peter 422
Gratian 60–1, 65
Gregory II of Cyprus (patriarch) 401n14
Gregory IX (pope) 75
Gregory X (pope) 75
Gregory XI (pope) 212, 214, 219n89
Grigorii Kotoshikhin 382
Grohmann, Alberto 27
Guerreau, Alain 40
Guichard, Pierre 411–12, 416–17
Guillaume de Bénévent 211
Guillaume de Rochefort 64
Gustav I (king of Sweden) 350–1
Guy Lusignan 397

Håkon Håkonsson (king of Norway) 346
Harriss, Gerald Leslie 26, 51, 314
Henneman, John Bell 26, 224
Henry I (king of England) 316, 318
Henry II (king of Castile) 133, 135
Henry II (king of England) 59, 81, 316–19
Henry III (king of Castile) 133, 135
Henry III (king of England) 61, 160, 316–22, 333
Henry IV (king of Castile) 134–6, 143
Henry IV (king of England) 82, 318, 327–8
Henry V (Holy Roman emperor) 318
Henry V (king of England) 82, 325, 329
Henry VI (Holy Roman emperor) 181, 203, 316, 319, 325, 333
Henry VI (king of England) 234, 329–30
Henry VII (king of England) 314, 318, 330–2
Henry VII (king of Sicily and Germany) 273
Henry VIII (king of England) 87, 332

Henri de Gand 79
Henri de Gauchi 63
Henry Beaufort (bishop pf Winchester) 329
Henry of Bolingbroke 327
Henry the Lion (duke of Saxony and Bavaria) 272, 274
Hilton, Rodney 26
Honorius III (pope) 61, 75, 209, 218n49
Hubert de Burgh 319
Humbert II (dauphin de Viennois) 239
Humbert, Françoise 27, 40
Hybel, Nils 341

Ianin, Valentin Lavrent'evich 377
Ibn 'Abdūn 417–18
Ibn al-'Aṭṭār 412
Ibn al-Farrā 410
Ibn al-Ḥaffār 419
Ibn Ḥayyān 417
Ibn Ḥazm 417
Ibn Khaldūn 410, 492
Ibn Lubb 419
Ibn Manẓūr 410, 419
Ibn Rushd 412
Ibn Sallām 413
Ibn Sirāj 419
Imber, Colin 424
İnalcık, Halil 423, 429n6
Innocent II (pope) 182
Innocent III (pope) 74–5, 203, 205, 322
Innocent IV (pope) 33, 322
Innocent VI (pope) 77
Isabeau of Bavaria (queen of France) 232
Isabella I (queen of Castile) 121, 134, 136, 143
Isenmann, Eberhard 56, 270
Isidoros of Kiev (metropolitan of Thessaloniki) 399
Ivan I Kalita (Grand prince of Moscow) 374, 377–8
Ivan II (Grand prince of Moscow) 374
Ivan III (Grand prince of Moscow) 373–7, 379–80
Ivan IV the Terrible (tsar of Russia) 372–3
Ivar Axelsson Tott 341
'Iyāḍ 412

Jacob von Sirck (archbishop of Trier) 288n48, 289n60
Jacques Cœur 37
Jacques de Révigny 61
Jacques Legrand 63
James I (king of Aragon) 80, 100
James II (king of Aragon) 100, 168
James III (king of Majorca) 16
James VI (king of Scotland) 318
Jan Długosz 359
Jean Bodin 68–9

Joanna I (queen of Naples) 162–3, 166, 297
Joanna II (queen of Navarre) 137–8
João de Avis (king of Portugal) 135
John I (king of Aragon) 169
John I (king of Castile) 133, 135
John II (king of Castile) 134–6
John II (king of Navarre and Aragon) 102, 144–5
John II the Good (king of France) 66, 230–1, 244
John III Vatatzes (Byzantine emperor) 396, 398–9
John IV Laskares (Byzantine emperor) 398
John IV of Montfort (duke of Brittany) 237–9
John V (Byzantine emperor) 397–9, 403n94
John V (duke of Brittany) 238
John VI Kantakouzenos (Byzantine emperor) 390, 392, 394, 396–8
John VII (Byzantine emperor) 391
John VIII (Byzantine emperor) 397, 399
John XII Kosmas (patriarch) 398
John XXII (pope) 77, 209–10
John (duke of Calabria) 298
John (king of England) 316–20
John Margarites 397
John of Freiburg 62
John of Gaunt (duke of Lancaster) 326
John the Fearless (duke of Burgundy) 254, 259, 261
John Theologites 392
John Vatatzes 392
Juan de Albret (king of Navarre) 138
Julius II (pope) 204
Justinian (Roman Emperor) 56, 180, 182

Kantorowicz, Ernst 299
Kashtanov, Sergei Mixajlovich 380
Kazimierz Jagiellończyk *see* Casimir IV Jagiellon
Kazimierz Wielki *see* Casimir III the Great
Kerhervé, Jean 26, 225, 239
Kirchgässner, Bernhard 27
Kliuchevskii, Vasilii Osipovich 374
Knapton, Michael 178
Knox Mitchell, Sidney 315
Knud IV (king of Denmark) 343
Konstantin Dmitrievich 377
Konstantinos Kritopoulos 392
Konstantinos Palaiologos 397
Konstantinos XI (Byzantine emperor) 398
Körner, Martin 27
Kotoshikhin, Grigorii Karpovich 382
Krom, Mikhail Markovich 382
Kuchler, Winfried 26
Kutrzeba, Stanisław 360–1

La Roncière, Charles Marie de 178
Labrousse, Ernest 25
Ladero, Miguel-Angel 26
Ladislaus Jagiello (Grand Duke of Lithuania and King of Poland) 360

Index

Ladislaus the Short (King of Poland) 359
Le Goff, Jacques 7, 23
Leguay, Jean-Pierre 27
Lemonde, Anne 225
Leopold V (duke of Austria) 319
Lévi-Provençal, Evariste 411
Lönnroth, Erik 341
Lot, Ferdinand 25
Louis VI (king of France) 226
Louis VII (king of France) 81, 226, 319
Louis VIII (king of France) 227, 319
Louis IX (king of France) 81, 160, 227–8, 242–3
Louis X (king of France) 65, 228
Louis XI (king of France) 58, 63–4, 67, 225, 234–6, 239, 241, 245, 261
Louis XII (king of France) 67
Louis (dauphin of France, son of Charles VI) 240
Louis IV of Bavaria (Holy Roman emperor) 77
Louis of Male (count of Flanders) 254
Louis the Great (king of Hungary) 359–60
Ludovico Sforza il Moro (duke of Milan) 192, 194–5
Ludwig of Bavaria (duke of Upper Bavaria and count palatine of the Rhine) 276–7
Ludwik Węgierski *see* Louis the Great
Lund, Niels 344
Lunt, William 315
Luzzato, Gino 178
Lyon, Brice 25

Maddicott, John 314
Magnus Eriksson (king of Sweden) 348–9
Maíllo, Felipe 415
Manfred (king of Sicily) 155, 160
Manuel II (Byzantine emperor) 397–9
Manzano, Eduardo 411, 414–15
Marcel II (pope) 215
Margaret (daughter of Henry III of England) 318
Margaret (daughter of Henry VII of England) 318
Margaret of Anjou (queen of England) 298
Margaret of Male (duchess of Burgundy) 254
Margareta (queen and regent of the Scandinavian kingdoms) 347, 349, 352n5
Maria (princess of Navarre and queen of Aragon) 138–9
Martin I (king of Aragon) 155, 169
Martin IV (pope) 206
Martin V (pope) 213, 279
Martin Perez 33
Master Philip the notary 322
Matilda (Countess) 219n61
Matilda (daughter of Henry I of England) 318
Matilda (daughter of Henry II of England) 318
Matthew (saint) 21
Matthias Corvinus (king of Hungary and Croatia) 419
Matuszewski, Jacek 359–60

Maximilian I (Holy Roman emperor) 235–6, 258, 263, 281
McFarlane, Kenneth Bruce 25
McGowan, Bruce 419
McHardy, Alison 315
Mehmed II (Ottoman sultan) 421–3, 425
Menjot, Denis 32, 38, 225
Menzinger, Sara 180
Michael VIII Palaiologos (Byzantine emperor) 403n94
Mihal Mavrudi 425
Miller, Edward 26
Milon de Châtillon 205
Mitchell, Sidney Knox 26
Modzelewski, Karol 356–8
Molho, Anthony 27, 178, 191
Mollat, Michel 27, 88n3
Monaco, Michele 204
Monemvasiotes 392
Montaguti Estragués, Tomás de 25
Mouche *see* Mucciatto Guidi dei Franzesi
Moxó, Salvador de 27
Mucciatto Guidi dei Franzesi 37, 245
Mueller, Reinhold C. 178
Murad I (Ottoman sultan) 421, 425
Murad II (Ottoman sultan) 421

Napoléon III (French emperor) 224
Nicholas IV (pope) 73, 209, 322
Nicholas of Gorran 61
Nicole Oresme 33, 230
Nikephoros Gregoras 392, 399
Nikolaos Kabasilas 399, 401n14
Nikolaos Notaras 398
Nikolaos Theologites 392
Nobili, Paolo Gabriele 184
Nuglish, Adolf 277

Oldradus de Ponte 62
Ormrod, Mark 2, 29–30, 315, 321
Otto I (Holy Roman emperor) 272
Otto III (duke of Lower Bavaria, king of Hungary and Croatia) 277
Owain Glyn Dŵr 329
Özvar, Erol 420

Partner, Peter 77, 204, 213–14, 217n12, 219n89, 220n98
Paul II (pope) 87
Paul III (pope) 215
Pavlov, Pavel Nikolaevich 374
Percy, William A. 160–1
Peter I (king of Castile) 132–3, 142
Peter II (king of Aragon) 100, 107
Peter III (king of Aragon) 155, 167
Peter IV the Ceremonious (king of Aragon) 82, 101–3, 138–9

Peter the Great (tsar of Russia) 383
Petronila (queen of Aragon) 97
Petrucci, Armando 22
Petrus de Ubaldi 63
Pharisaios 391
Philip I (prince of Taranto) 163
Philip II (king of Spain) 217n15, 260, 263
Philip II (prince of Taranto) 163
Philip II Augustus (king of France) 226, 236
Philip III (king of Navarre) 137–8
Philip IV the Fair (king of France) 23, 59–60, 62, 65, 73, 227–31, 236–7, 243, 245–6, 321
Philip VI (king of France) 65, 82, 229–30, 243
Philip the Bold (duke of Burgundy) 254, 259, 261
Philip the Good (duke of Burgundy) 254–5, 259–61, 263
Philippe de Beaumanoir 61, 242
Philippe de Commynes 21, 261
Pierre Antiboul 65
Pierre Choinet 63
Pierre d'Estaing 220n100
Pierre de Beaujeu 235
Pierre II (count of Savoy) 294
Pierre Landais 237–8
Pietkiewicz, Krzysztof 366
Pipes, Richard 381
Pirenne, Henri 256, 264n13
Post, Gaines 299
Poulsen, Bjørn 341
Prestwitch, Michael 26
Pseudo-Kodinos 391

Qudāma ibn Ja'far 413, 429n4

Ramon Berenguer IV (count of Barcelona) 97
Ranft, Andreas 27
Raniero Capocci (cardinal) 206
Ranulf de Glanville 318
Ranulf Higden 326
Raven van Barnekow 341
Raymond de Turenne 298
Raymond of Penyafort 33, 60, 62
Reginald (count of Guelders) 318
Rehoboam (son of Solomon) 58
Reinhard, Wolfgang 204
René I of Anjou (king of Naples) 163, 298
Rey, Maurice 26, 225
Richard I (king of England) 316–20
Richard II (king of England) 82, 318, 326–7
Richard III (king of England) 330
Richard de Mediavilla 60–2, 66
Rigaudière, Albert 25, 225
Rinaldo Malavolti 218n45, 52, 219n60, 64
Riurik 372
Robert I of Anjou (king of Naples) 165, 183, 298
Robert Winchelsey 323
Rodinson, Maxime 432n162

Roger II (king of Sicily) 155–8
Roger of Lauria 168
Rosen, Josef 27
Roublev, Michel 374
Roustit, Yvan 28
Rudolf of Habsburg (king of Germany), 275
Rudolf IV (duke of Austria) 275
Rupert (duke of Bavaria) 318
Rupert of the Palatinate (king of Germany) 277–8

Sacchetti, Franco 186
Sakellariou, Eleni 156
Samaran, Charles 27, 88n3
Sánchez Martínez, Manuel 32, 101, 225
Sancho III (king of Pamplona) 120
Sancho IV (king of Castile) 132
Sancho VI (king of Navarre) 125, 146
Sancho VII (king of Navarre) 125–6, 146
Sander, Paul 27
Sassu-Normand, David 225
Say, Léon 25
Schumpeter, Joseph A. 7, 25–6, 29–30
Scordia, Lydwine 79
Şehzade Alemşah 422
Şehzade Korkud 421
Semen the Proud 374, 378
Ser Lapo Mazzei 21
Seredonin, Sergei Mikhailovich 382
Sergius (saint) 378
Sesma Muñoz, José Angel 26
Shapiro, Aleksandr L'vovich 379
Sieveking, Heinrich 178
Sigismund I (king of Poland) 356
Sigismund of Luxembourg (Holy Roman emperor) 277, 279
Simiand, François 25
Simon Sudbury (archbishop of Canterbury) 327
Simone Boccanegra (doge of Genoa) 190
Sitti Hatun 422
Sixtus IV (pope) 220n94
Sixtus V (pope) 215
Smirnov, Pavel Petrovich 374
Solomon 58
Spont, Alfred 224
Steel, Anthony B. 25–6
Stefan Dušan 423
Stephen (king of England) 316
Strayer, Joseph Reese 28, 224
Sucheni-Grabowska, Anna 359

Tabbagh, Vincent 78
Terrasse, Véronique 241
Theobald I (king of Navarre) 126, 137
Theobald II (king of Navarre) 126, 137
Theodoros II (Byzantine emperor)
Theodoros Metochites 399, 401n14
Theodoros Mouzalon 392

Theodoros Palaiologos (despot of Peloponnesos) 397, 399
Theodoros Patrikiotes 392
Theodoros Vatatzes 392
Thomas Magistros 399, 401n14
Thomas of Melbourne 239
Tilly, Charles 28–9
Titone, Fabrizio 171
Todeschini, Giacomo 192
Tokhtamysh (khan of the Blue Horde) 374, 377
Tommaso Portinari 261
Tracy, James 263
Trasselli, Carmelo 156
Tudmīr' (Teodomiro) 414
Turull Rubinat, Max 25

Ulrich (duke of Wurttemberg) 289n65
Ulug Mehmet (khan of the Golden Horde) 375
'Umar ibn al-Khaṭṭāb (Rashidun caliph) 414
'Uqba ibn al-Ḥajjāj (governor of Al-Andalus) 414
Urban IV (pope) 73
Urban V (pope) 77
Urban VI (pope) 212

Valdemar Atterdag (king of Denmark) 349
Valdemar II (king of Denmark) 341
Vallerani, Massimo 183
Van Nieuwenhuysen, André 26
Van Werveke, Hans 27
Vardales 391
Vasili I (Grand prince of Moscow) 377, 379
Vasili II (Grand prince of Moscow) 375, 377, 379
Vasili III (Grand prince of Moscow) 376, 380
Vasili Yaroslavich 379, 384n46
Verger, Jacques 76

Verhulst, Adriaan 25
Vernadsky, George 374
Vernus-Moutin, Isabelle 225
Vidal, Jacques 225
Viollet, Paul 25
Vladimir (Grand prince of Kiev) 372–4, 376–7
Vogeler, Goerg 285
Vuitry, Adolphe 25, 224

Waley, Daniel 204, 208, 218n52, 218n55
Walter of Geroldseck (bishop of Strasbourg) 275
Waquet, Jean-Claude 6, 30
Weber, Max 25
Wickham, Chris 2, 4–5, 26, 411
Willard, James 315
William I (king of England) 316
William I (king of Sicily) 159
William II (king of England) 316
Władysław Jagiełło see Ladislaus Jagiello
Władysław Łokietek see Ladislaus the Short
Władysław Opolczyk 360
Wolfelin (Schultheiss of Haguenau) 273
Wolff, Philippe 28
Wurms, Nikolaus 21

Yaḥyà ibn Ādam 413, 429n4
Yani-veled-i Kalavriça 422
Yuri Danilovich (Prince of Moscow) 377
Yūsuf al-Fihrī (governor of Al-Andalus) 414

Zaremska, Hanna 362
Zofia Holszańska (wife of king Ladislaus Jagiello) 360
Zygmunt I (king of Poland) see Sigismund I

Places

Åbo 342
Abruzzo 157, 162, 164, 165
Acquapendente 206
Agincourt 232
Aix-en-Provence 297, 303
Al-Andalus 6, 120, 408–19, 426–9
Alarcos 123
Albania 420, 422–3, 425
Alcalá de Henares 128
Alcamo 169
Alcántara 125
Alcoi 110
Algeciras 131, 133
Aljubarrota 135
Almadén 129
Almería 410, 415
Alpont 108
Alsace 273–5, 277; lower Alsace, 273

Alzira 36, 108
Amalfi 165, 429
Amiens 231, 241–2
Amsterdam 255, 264
Anatolia 419–22, 424, 428
Ancona (city, March) 203, 205–8, 210, 212–13
Andalusia (district, region) 120, 124, 129, 130, 132–4, 141–2
Angri 165
Ankara 398, 400, 424
Ansbach 282
Ansbach-Bayreuth (principality) 289n68
Ansbach-Kulmbach (principality) 283
Antwerp 255, 264
Aosta see Valle d'Aosta
Apulia 155, 158, 162–4, 172
Aquila 157, 167

Index

Aragon (county, kingdom, crown) 6, 18, 25–7, 32, 37, 61, 80–7, 97–120, 124, 126, 130, 135–6, 138–9, 143–4, 155–7, 163–4, 167, 169–72, 296, 298
Arezzo 179, 183
Ariano 158
Arles (kingdom) 294–5
Arras 19, 235, 241–2, 255, 259, 263–4
Artois 241, 254–5, 259–60, 262, 265n41
Assisi 207, 211–12
Asti 259
Astrakhan 375–6, 380
Asturias (kingdom) 120
Asturias and Leon (kingdom) 122
Athens 58
Atri 165
Augsburg 272–3, 277–8, 281, 288n47, 288n50, 288n57
Auray 237
Austria 274, 278
Avignon 18, 62, 73, 75–9, 84, 86, 160, 203, 210–11, 214, 294, 298, 303
Ayamavra 422
Aydın 424

Baden 279
Balkans 410, 420, 424, 428, 429n6
Balybadra 422
Barcelona (city, county, bishopric) 18, 28, 31, 85, 97, 100, 102–4, 106–9, 155, 157, 192, 294
Basel 19, 272, 280
Basque country 126
Bassano 36
Bavaria 276–8; lower 277; upper and lower 281, 289n74
Bavaria-Landshut (duchy) 272, 276, 285
Bavaria-Munich (duchy) 276
Beauvais 205
Belforte 217n27
Belgrade 419
Bergamo 184
Bern 19, 272
Bernedo 126
Berre 296
Bettona 209
Bezhetskii-Verkh 379
Birka 342
Black Sea 425
Bohemia 288n48
Bologna 117–79, 182–3, 185–8, 192, 196n1, 211
Borgo San Sepolcro 183
Bornholm 342
Bosnia 422
Bourges 232–3
Brabant 254–6, 258, 260, 262–3, 264n13
Brandenburg 277–8, 288n41, 288n48

Brescia 189, 193, 194
Breslau *see* Wrocław
Bresse 300, 304–5
Brignoles 296
Brisach 273, 280
Brittany (duchy) 6, 18, 26, 224–5, 237–41, 244–5
Bruges 19, 255, 257, 259, 261, 263, 264n12
Brunswick-Luneburg (duchy) 285
Brussels 255
Buda 359–60
Bulgaria 422
Burgos 141–3
Burgundian Low Countries 6, 32, 254–4, 301
Burgundy (duchy) 18, 20, 26
Bursa 420
Byzantine empire 6, 389–400

Calabria 155, 158, 161
Calais 19, 230, 241, 261, 263
Calatayud 108
Calatrava 128–9
Cambrai 254–5
Camerino 217n27, 217n28
Campagna 203, 207, 210, 212–13, 215
Cannara 207
Canterbury 314–15, 319, 322–3, 326–7, 331–2
Capitana 164
Capua (principality, city) 158, 167
Cariñena 103
Carlisle 324
Cascia 211
Castellabate 161
Castellammare 165
Castelló de Plana 108, 110
Castile (county, kingdom, crown) 6, 16–17, 19, 27, 36–8, 81, 87, 98, 101–3, 106, 109, 120–5, 127–37, 139–40, 142–3, 145–6, 418
Castile and Leon (kingdom) 120–4, 126–7, 140
Catalonia (principality) 6, 15, 17, 36, 81, 97–119, 296
Catania 169–71
Cerdanya 97
Cervera 25, 36, 103, 107, 109–10
Chablais 300, 305
Chalcis *see* Eğriboz
Chambéry 299, 304–5
Champagne (county) 126, 137, 233
Chełmno 361
Chieri 178, 259
Chillón 129
Church Lands 3, 6, 203–17
Çirmik 424
Colmar 273, 284
Cologne 19, 33, 272–3, 276, 280–1, 283–4, 288n48, 289n76
Como 189, 192

486

Index

Comtat Venaissin 203, 208, 210–13, 220n107, 303
Constance 27, 74, 84, 86, 180–1, 273
Constantinople 372, 390, 398, 403n96
Córdoba 125, 129, 141–2, 409–10, 415
Cornwall 317, 331
Corsica 97
Çorum 424
Cracow 360–1
Crécy 230
Cremona 186, 188, 189, 192, 196n1
Crimea 375–6, 421
Cuenca 141
Cullera 36
Cutrofiano 166
Cyprus 78

Dalarna 341
Dauphiné 6, 203, 224–5, 236, 239–41, 245, 294
Denmark (kingdom) 18, 32, 340–51
Dijon 18, 20, 27, 40, 242, 244, 248n55, 255, 261
Diyarbakır 425
Dordrecht 324
Dortmund 19, 288n41
Douai 19, 25, 263
Draguignan 302
Drente 255
Drôme 224
Duisburg 19
Durham 324

Edirne 422, 425–6
Eğriboz 425
Egypt 419, 422, 427–8
El Aljarafe *see* Seville
Elsinore 18
Elvas 22
Emilia-Romagna 177, 192, 196n1
England (kingdom) 3, 6, 8n22, 15, 18, 26–67, 73–5, 80–2, 86–7, 160, 228–30, 234, 265n28, 298, 314–33
Epirus 396
Erfurt 280
Ergani 424
Ericeira 22
Erzincan 424
Estella 126, 144
Euboea 423
Evreux (county) 137
Extremaduras 122–3

Fabriano 208, 218n33
Fano 205
Faroe Islands 342
Faucigny 304
Fermo 205, 211
Ferrara 178
Fethiye 422

Finland, 342, 348, 350
Flanders 18, 27, 34, 228–9, 243, 254–64, 265n28, 265n33, 265n35, 265n41, 321, 327
Florence 27, 172, 177–8, 181, 184, 186–9, 191–5, 196n1, 197n56, 212, 261
Foligno 207
Forcalquier *see* Provence
Fraga 108
France (kingdom) 3, 6, 18–21, 23, 25, 27, 31, 36–8, 55–69, 73–5, 77, 80–2, 86, 98, 136–7, 160, 203, 212, 214, 224–46, 254, 261, 265n28, 281, 294–5, 319, 326–31
Franche-Comté 254
Franconia 277–8
Frankfurt 289n68
Freiburg im Breisgau 272, 280
Freiburg im Üchtland 272, 284
Fresneda 108
Friesland 255
Fulda (bishopric) 289n69

Galata 394
Galicia (kingdom) 130, 133, 135, 373
Gallia Cispadana 204, 214–15
Gallipoli *see* Gelibolu
Gandia 36, 108
Gascony 234, 243, 315, 319–21, 330
Gdańsk 364
Gelderland (duchy) 285
Gelibolu 425
Gelre 255
Geneva 18, 304–5
Genoa 19, 30, 172, 178, 180–1, 189–92, 195, 196n1, 262, 395–7, 429, 433n163
Germany 88n4, 230, 273, 276; *see also* Holy Roman Empire
Ghent 27, 257–9, 263, 264n12, 264n13
Gibellina 169
Girona 97, 110
Gmünd 274
Gochsheim 282
Gökçeada 419, 424–6
Görice 422
Goslar 288n41
Gotland 341–2, 376
Granada (emirate, kingdom) 121, 128, 130, 132–3, 136–7, 410, 412, 416, 417, 427–8
Great Britain 73
Greenland 342
Groningen 255
Gubbio 216
Guebwiller 282
Guipúzcoa 129
Guyenne 330

Haguenau 276
Hainault 254–5

Halland 345–6
Hälsingland 342, 349
Hamburg 19
Harput 424
Hattin 319
Hedeby 342
Heidelberg (bishopric) 282
Hesse 276
Hispaniae (Roman province) 123
Holland 254–5, 260, 263, 265n13, 265n34
Holstein 349
Holy Roman Empire 236, 239, 270–86, 294–5
Hudavendigar 420, 424, 426
Hungary 6, 419
Hyères 296

Ibiza 107
Iceland 342, 351
Iesi 205
Île-de-France 232–3, 242
Ille-et-Vilaine 224
Imbros *see* Gökçeada
Imola 218n54
Ioannina 396
Ireland 315, 320–1, 328
Isenburg-Büdingen 289n69
Isère 224
Italy 19, 23, 27, 30, 32, 36, 55–69, 74–5, 77, 157, 170–1, 173, 174n47, 178, 185, 203–17, 255, 295, 299, 301; Northern Italy 177–98; Southern Italy 155–8, 161, 164–7, 171–2, 174n70; *see also* Naples and Sicily

Jutland 343, 345–7

Karlstein Castle 279
Kayseri 424
Kaysersberg 273
Kazan 375–6, 380
Kent 316
Kiev 372, 374–5
Kilia 425
Konstanz *see* Constance
Korça *see* Görice
Kreševo 422
Kroai (Krujë) 396
Kulmsbach 282

La Mancha 120, 125
La Ribera (district) *see* Seville
Laguardia 126
Lake Mälaren 342–5, 350
Landshut 276
Languedoc 15, 17, 23, 224–5, 227–35, 242–3, 295
Lateran 75, 79–80
Latium 77

Lausanne 304
Lecce 167
Leipzig 288n47
Lemnos 391
Leon (city, district, kingdom) 120, 123–4, 132, 134, 140–2
Levante 412, 418
Liège 34, 254–5, 258
Liguria 177, 196n1
Lille 18, 27, 255
Limburg 254–5
Limnos 424, 426
Lincoln 322, 327
Linz 274
Lisbon 22
Lithuania (Grand Duchy) 356–67, 375
Livonia 380
Lleida 106
Loire-Atlantique 224
Lombardy 63, 74, 177, 182, 184, 187, 189–90, 192, 196n1, 259, 300
London 255, 315, 317, 319, 325, 327, 332
Los Arcos 126
Loulé 22
Low Countries *see* Burgundian Low Countries
Lübeck 19, 283, 287n33, 288n41, 361, 376
Lucca 178, 181, 184, 187, 189–91, 261
Lucera 161
Lucerne 27
Lund 340
Lüneburg 27
Luxembourg 260
Lyon 75, 85, 227, 248n55

Macedonia 394, 396–8
Mâcon 248n55
Madrid 141
Mainz 272–3, 281, 283, 288n48
Majorca (city, kingdom) 6, 97–119
Makri *see* Fethiye
Malbork 364
Malines 254
Malkara 424
Mallorca *see* Majorca
Manfredonia 167
Manosque 302
Manresa 109
Mantua 178
Mardin 424–5
Marseille 302
Mechlin 255, 262
Mecklenburg 289n68
Melfi 159
Menorca 107
Meran 285
Messina 169–70

Index

Milan (city, duchy) 177, 179, 181–9, 192–5, 196n1, 261, 299, 300
Millau 17, 19
Mizistre 422
Modena 178
Molfetta 166
Mondovì 304–5
Monemvasia 395–7
Monopoli 165
Monroyo 108
Monte San Vito 218n36
Montemor-o-Novo 22
Monticelli 181
Montmélian 299
Montpellier 243
Monzón 103–5, 109
Moscow 373–80, 383, 384n45
Moscow-Vladimir (principality) 374
Munich 272, 276
Murcia (city, kingdom) 19, 124–5, 129, 141–2, 414, 418

Najac 19, 242
Namur 254–5
Nantes 237, 239
Naples (kingdom) 136, 155–7, 162–5, 172, 236, 297
Navarre (kingdom) 6, 18, 120–2, 124–7, 135, 137–40, 144–6
Navas de Tolosa 122
Netherlands 69
Nice 294, 297
Nicopolis 261
Nicosia 171
Nidaros 340
Norberg 346
Normandy 139, 226–7, 231–4, 242, 265n28, 319, 330
Norway 32, 340–51
Norwich 75
Novara 189
Novgorod 373–9
Novotorzhok 377
Nuremberg 27, 278–80, 282–4, 288n47
Nusaybin 425
Nyköping 341

Ohri 422
Olite 144
Olkusz 362
Orkney 342
Orvieto 208
Osimo 205, 218n 33, 40
Osnabrück 19
Osona 97
Östergötland 343–4, 346
Ostrova 421

Öttingen 279–80
Outre-Seine-et-Yonne 233–4
Overijssel 255
Oviedo 142

Pairis (abbey) 273
Palatinate 288n48
Palermo 155, 157, 168–71
Palma 108
Pamplona (city, kingdom) 18, 120, 122, 126, 144
Papal State *see* Church's lands
Paris 19, 28, 56, 59, 137, 203, 224, 226, 228–34, 244, 255, 261
Parma 204, 214
Partanna 169
Patrimony of St Peter 203, 205–10, 212–13, 218n52, 219n60; *see also* Church Lands
Pavia 19, 181, 189
Pechora 382
Peloponnese 395, 397, 399–400, 422
Perevitsk 375
Périgueux 18
Perm' 377, 382
Perugia 22, 27, 183, 211–12, 215
Pesaro 205
Pescara 165
Piacenza 19, 181–2, 189, 196n1, 204, 214
Picardy 242
Piedmont 177–8, 182–3, 188–9, 196n1, 197n7, 259, 294, 300, 304–5
Pinerolo 178, 196n1
Pisa (city, republic) 172, 178, 180–1, 189–91, 196n1
Pistoia 179
Poitiers 66, 211
Poitou 319
Poland (kingdom) 32, 74, 356–67
Pomerania (Eastern) 364
Pomorze Wschodnie *see* Pomerania (Eastern)
Pontefract 322
Porto 22
Portugal (kingdom) 6, 75, 82–3, 85, 87, 120, 130, 133, 135
Principato 162
Provence (county) 6, 18, 212, 243, 294–305
Provins 19, 241, 243
Pskov 374, 378

Radonezh 379
Raiano 165
Randazzo 169
Ravenna (exarchate) 203
Regensburg 273, 280–1, 288n47; bishopric 276
Reims 19, 233
Rennes 27, 248n83
Reus 36, 110
Rhineland 273, 275
Rhodes 79

Index

Ribagorza (county) 120
Ribe 346
Rieti 209
Riga 376
Rimini 215
Rivoli 299
Rocca Contrada 219
Roccabotte 165
Rodez 20
Romagna 203, 208, 210, 218n55
Roman Empire (Western) 1
Romans 240
Rome 6, 58, 63–4, 77, 83, 177
Roncaglia 180
Rouen 231, 234
Rouergue 19, 231
Rouffach 275
Roussillon (county) 136
Rügen 342
Russia 6, 32, 372–83
Ryazan 373–6

Sabina 203, 219n57
Saintes-Maries-de-la-Mer 303
Saint-Flour 18, 25, 36
Saint-Maurice 299
Saint-Palais 126
Salon-de-Provence 302
Salzbourg 280
Samokov 422
Samsun 425
San Cernin *see* Pamplona
San Feliu de Guíxols 36
San Martino 161
Sangüesa 126
Sarai 372–3
Sardinia 82, 97, 100–1, 107
Savigliana 299
Savoy (county, duchy) 6, 18, 22, 294–305
Saxony 278; elector 288n48; Upper and Lower 288n47
Scania 340, 347, 349
Schaffhausen 20
Schönau (monastery) 282
Sciacca 171
Scotland 321, 324, 327
Segovia 141
Selanik *see* Thessaloniki
Selestat 273
Senigallia 215
Sennfeld 282
Serres 397, 401n10, 425
Sessa Aurunca 167
Seville 16–17, 19, 123, 125, 129, 130, 141–2, 417
Shetland 342
Shrewsbury 315
Siberia 382

Sicily (kingdom) 6, 18, 81, 97, 101, 155–60, 163, 165, 167–73, 173n10, 177, 182, 185, 273, 296, 429; Sicily *citra farum* 155, 160, 165, 171; Sicily *ultra farum* 155, 171
Siena (city, republic) 19, 21, 178, 181, 184–5, 187–9, 191, 196, 196n1
Silesia 278
Simav 424
Şin-Marya 425
Sisteron 303
Siverek 420, 423
Smolensk 373
Södermanland 341, 348
Sofia 424
Sol'-Galitskaia 379
Soleto (city, county) 166
Soria 141
Soultz 275
Spain 69; *see also* Aragon; Castile; Navarre
Sparta *see* Mizistre
Spello 212
Speyer 272–3
Spoleto (city, duchy) 203, 205–8, 210–12
Sporades 398
Stein 274
Stockholm 341, 346–7, 350
Strasbourg 272–3, 275, 278, 283
Suzdalia 373, 377
Suzdal-Nizhny Novgorod (principality) 374
Svealand 342–3, 348
Swabia 275, 277, 288n47
Sweden 32, 340–51
Świdnica 361
Switzerland 294–5
Syracuse 169

Taranto (principality) 163, 166
Tarascon 303
Tarifa 131
Tarragona 80
Taşoz *see* Thassos
Tekfurdağ 424
Terni 207, 219n57
Terra di Lavoro 161–2
Terraferma 178, 189, 193–5, 196n6, 197n56, 198n75
Terranova 168
Thassos 419, 424, 426
The Hague 255
Thessaloniki 391, 396, 399, 421
Thrace 397, 424
Thuringia (landgraviate) 285
Tiber valley 203, 218n52
Tırhala *see* Trikala
Tirol 274, 289n78
Todi 211
Toledo (kingdom, city) 1, 121, 123, 125, 129, 130, 134

Index

Tolfa 214
Tortosa 104–5, 416
Toruń 361
Torusa 375
Toulon 302
Toulouse 27, 229, 242
Tournai 254, 263
Tours 67
Transierra 122
Trier 281, 288n48
Trikala 419
Tsarevichev 375
Tudela 126, 138, 144–5
Tunis 81
Turin 178, 196n1
Turku *see* Åbo
Tuscany 30, 63, 177–9, 183, 185, 187, 189, 191, 194, 196n1, 196n4, 198n83, 203
Tver (principality) 374–5

Úbeda 141
Ulm 282–3
Umbria 177
Uppland 344–5, 347
Uppsala 340–3, 348, 350
Urbino 206
Üsküp 424
Utrecht 254–5

Val di Noto 168
Valencia (city, kingdom) 6, 17, 23, 36, 83, 97–119, 130, 192, 243
Valladolid 141, 142
Valle d'Aosta 294, 300
Valls 110
Valnerina 205
Vannes 237
Västergötland 342–6
Västerrekarne 348
Västmanland 343, 346
Vatican 73
Vaud (Pays de) 304–5
Veneto 177–8, 184, 188, 192, 196n1
Venice (city, republic) 30, 172, 177–8, 181, 186–95, 196n1, 196n4, 197n48, 255, 261–2, 394–6, 429; *see also Terraferma*

Vercelli 305
Verona 181, 186, 188, 192, 193, 196n1, 197n42
Viana 22, 144
Vic 109
Vicari 169
Vicenza 36, 192–3
Vienna 287n33
Vienne 76
Vila do Conde 22
Villeneuve (Chablais) 304
Vilvoorde 255
Visby 346
Viterbo 208
Vizcaya (state, province) 123, 139
Vladimir (principality) 373–4, 376–7
Volgograd 372
Volynia 373

Wales 73, 315, 320–1, 328
Warsaw 364
Weingarten (monastery) 289n65
Wetterau 277
Wetzlar 276
Wimpfen (convent) 282
Winchester 322, 329
Wootton hundred 316
Worms 271–3, 281, 283, 289n64, 69
Wrocław 19, 280, 361
Würzburg 283

Yaroslavl 375
Yenihisar 422
York (city, diocese, province) 80, 82, 314, 322–5, 327
Yorkshire 331
Ypres 19, 259, 264n12
Ytalie (*regnum*) 177, 195

Zamora 141
Zaragoza (city, province) 80, 97, 100, 103–9
Zeeland 254–5, 260, 263
Zichna 397
Zollino 166
Zurich 19

Taxation terms

aatra see koukku
açaque 418
accises★ 241
addizionali 187
adiutoria de festis 205
adiutorium★ 159
adoa★ 159, 161–2, 168

ættærgæld 344
affictus 206, 210, 212–13, 218n38, 218n40, 219n57
affictus fumantie 208
aide aux quatre cas 226
aides★ 210, 212, 245, 257, 259, 261, 265n33; *see also donum*

Index

ajude 108
alacer 418
alatotelos 393
alberga★ 296
albergarias 181, 205–6
alcabala vieja 133, 142
alcabala★(Castile) 16, 27, 127, 132–7, 142, 145; *alcabala*★ (Navarre) 138–9, 144, 145
aleia 393
alfitra (alsira) 418, 429; see also *zakat al fitr*
alfolíes 129, 134, 142
alien subsidy★ 326, 330; see also subsidy (England)
al-ma'ūna 410
almadrabas 129
almaguana 410, 418–19
almahuala 418
almojarifazgo★ 17, 124, 129–30, 133–4, 142
almojarifazgo mayor de Sevilla see *almojarifazgo*
almonaima see *almojarifazgo*
almotacenazgo 142
almudies 142
alopia 393
anepignostikion 393
angareia 393
annates★ 73, 76–7, 82, 86–7
Anschlag 280
Anubda 122
appatis see *patis*
arcas 109
arrière-ban 8n31
assisum see duty on trading 55
auxilium 7, 123, 127, 300; see also *servitium*
avarız★ 422–3
ayuda★ 7, 138–9; see also *subsidio*
azaque see *zequi*

bac 425
bakers' tribute 144
balanistron 393
banalities 57
banna 205–7, 209
baratteria 186, 188
barra 142
barrage 242, 244
Bede★ (German Holy Roman Empire) 270–3, 275; (Scandinavia) 347
beden see *aides*
benevolence 332–3
bibarion 393
Bierpfennig 284
billot 244
biologion 395
blanca 144
boateria 181
bocche 187
bovatge★ 100, 110
bracciatici 179

Brauermalzpfennig 284
Bürgermalzpfennig 284
butchers' rents 144
byskat★ 346

cabella (cabella dohane maris) 168; *(cabella figulorum)* 168; *(cabella platee someriorum)* 168; see also *gabella*
cabeza de pecho 131
cabeza de pecho de los moros 131, 133
capage 243
capagium 302
capitations 8n34
carapito 144
carati 193
carneraje 98
carreggio 194
carucage★ 316–17, 332
carucate 316
cassia 168, 171
cassia propter guerram 168
castellano 137
castellaría 122
catasto 178, 182, 184, 193–4
cavalca degeneral 8n31
cavalcata★ 296–7
cena de ausencia 99; *de presencia* 99
cens★/*census* 57, 205–6, 208–10, 213, 295
censal 36, 105, 107–9, 144
census æstitualis see *midthsumærsgyald*
census see ground rent
census terrestris (Poland) see *szosm*
çequi see *zequi*
chapiteles 126
charagma 393
chernybor★ 374, 377
choiroennomion 393
chornyi vykhod★ 377
çift resmi★ 420, 423–4
cisa see excise tax
cizye★ 420–4; see also *jizya*
clerical tenth★ 322–4, 326–33
cloision★ 244
collecta★ 55, 60, 63; *collecta*★ (Northern Italy) 179, 181–2, 190; *collecta* (Church Lands) 218n40, 218n49; *collecta* (German Holy Roman Empire) 273; *collecta* (Savoy) 305
collecta fumantium 218n40
colletta★ (Sicily) 159–60, 162, 164, 168–72; *colletta* (Northern Italy) 179, 183–5, 190; *colletta* (Churchland) 208
colta 181; see also *collecta* (Northern Italy)
common penny see *Gemeiner Pfennig*
commun 304
commune 305
compere 189–90
complainta 300
comu see *taille*★

Index

conducho 123
corambres 144
cornado 144
coronatge 101–2
corredurίa de oreja 144
corredurίas 143–4
coutumes 237
crues de taille★ 235–6
cuarteles★ 137–9, 144–5
cuenta de mercaderes 130; see also *almojarifazgo*
cugidas see *echas*
culmagium 300
curaria 181
custom duties 126, 129–31, 134, 137, 145, 157–60, 162, 164–8, 172, 185–6, 189–91; see also toll
czołobicie 366

dacia comunis 218n40
dadia delle lance 193
dan'★ 372–3, 375, 377–80
danegeld 1
dateria 214
datia (Sicily) 164, 165, 167, 172; *datia* (Northern Italy) 179, 183, 185, 191
dazio 181; *dazio della carne* 187; *dazio sul pane* 180, 195
decima (Church tithe) 180, 195; *decima* (Northern Italy) 193; see also tithes
decimum 190
dekaton 393
derecho de montaracίa 141
derecho de vecindad 141
derechos de italianos y alemanes 111
desè 110
devoirs d'entrée et issue★ 239
dezenum 302
diavatikion 395
dienst 279
diezmo★ 130
diezmos de la mar see *diezmo*
dimodaion 393
doblamiento de la barra see *portazgo*★
dogana del bestiame 213–14
dogana delle pecore 164
dogana delle tratte 213
donativos 138, 410
donativum★ 162, 167
donum, dona 300–1, 315, 318
dotzè 110
doukikedianome 395
Dreizigsten Pfennig 276
dret del segell de cera 104
drets d'entrades i eixides 104
Dritten Pfennig 273
droit de haut passage 229
droit de rève 229

ducilla 362–3
duty on trading 55, 59

echas 144
embatikion 395
empréstitos 135
ennomion 395
ergasteriakon 395
Ertragssteuer 279
estimum★ 178–88, 190–5
exactio/exaction 55, 60; *exactio* (Poland) see *mansus tax*
exactio regalis see plough tax (Poland)
excise tax 158–60, 162, 164–8, 171–2, 365
exuwe see *issue*

ferrerίas 129
feudal aid★ 317–19, 332
fifteen *marker*-aid 349
fifteenth and tenth★ 322, 324–6, 329, 331, 333
fishing (levy on) 167
fitto 207
focagium 300
focatico★(Sicily) 163–5, 172, 179; *focatico* (Northern Italy) 179; *focatico/focaticum* (Church Lands) 206–10, 212–13, 215, 218n52
focularia 207
fodrum★ 179, 181–4, 192; *fodrum* (Church land) 205–8, 217n19; see also *alberga*
fogatge 17
foglietta on wine 215
follias 205–7
fondaco dei Tedeschi 190; see also *fundaci*★
fonsadera 123–4
foranίas 144
forced loans 123, 134–5, 156, 172, 178, 182–4, 190–3, 195; see also *auxilium* and *prestanze*
fortieth 74
fouage★ 18, 66–7, 226, 229, 231, 237–40
fractional taxes★ 317, 319–22, 332
fumale see plough tax (Poland)
fundaci★/*ius fundici* 159, 163
funzioni fiscali 164–5

gabella buchirie 171
gabella 7, 17, 33, 55, 63–6; *gabella*★ (Sicily) 162, 168–71, 174n47; *gabella* (Northern Italy) 179, 185–92; *gabella* (Church land) 215; *gabelle*★ (France) 230, 231, 239, 244; *gabelle* (Burgundian Low Countries) 259; *gabella*★ (Provence and Savoy) 296, 299, 302, 304; *gabella* on contracts 187; *gabelle delle porte* 186; see also gate tax★
gabelle du sel★ 229
gærþ★ 347–8
gæstning 345
gate tax★ 179, 186

Index

geld★ 316–19, 332
geldkauf 36
Gemain Steuer 277
Gemeiner Pfennig (common penny) 281–3, 286, 289
generalidades★ 101, 103–5, 111
gengærþ★ 346
gennematikedosis 393
Gewerf 272–3, 275
gietum 305
gisia 168
gisting 345
gîte 226
gomariatikon 395
goubeliatikon 395, 402n63
gramota (*tarkhannaia* and *zhalovannaia*)★ 379–80
grandes tailles★ 232
Grosse Hilfe 281
ground rent 55, 60
guaitas 218n40
guidagium see safe-conduct tax
Güldener Opferpfennig★ 279

hagüela/hahuela 418
harac-i timur 420
hearth tax (Sicily) 163–4, 168–71, 174n47; *see also focatico* (Sicily); hearth tax★ (Church land) 206, 210, 216, 217n19; hearth tax (Poland) 357–9, *see also* plough tax (Poland)
hijuela 418
hofsteuer★ 276
hospedaje 123
Hunderster Pfennig 279
Hussengeld/Hussensteuer 276, 280, 288n50

imbottato/imbottature 187, 194, 197n48
imposicions★ (Aragon) 18, 107–11; *imposición*★ (Navarre) 138–9, 144
imposition foraine★ 230
imprestiti 190
income tax★ 326–7, 330–1
infurciones 122, 123
ingæld 348
inne 346
introgiumvini 304
ispence★ 420, 423
issue★258, 265n39
iudaica 131
iugaticum 181
iura fisci 158
ius anchorage 158
ius buczerie 158
ius decime et tareni 174n46
ius exiture★ 159, 162, 168, 172
ius fundici see *fundaci*★
ius passorum★ 164
ius relevi 174n46

ius statere 158
iuvaticum 179

jizya 409–10, 412–15; *see also cizye*★
Judensteuer★ 274–5, 278
juros 134–7

kampanistikon 395
kapeliatikon 395
kara salgun 419
kastroktisia 394, 397
katagogion 395
katathesis 395
katepanikedianome 395
kephalaia 397
kephalatikion 393, 395
Keuteakzise 284
kharāj 412, 415, 419
kleine Hilfe 281
kokkiatikon 397
kommerkion 392, 394–6, 398
korm 374, 378
koukku 348
kritikon 395
krok see *koukku*

land tax (Poland) 362; (Byzantine) 389–93
Landschatzung 284
Landsteuer 274
ledung★ 344–9
ledungslama 345
leiðangr see *ledung*
lesda/leyda★ 295, 299, 304
lething see *ledung*
leþunger see *ledung*
leva 305
lezdas/lleudes★ 99
leztas★ 126, 144
libra 181–3
linobrocheion 393
liquor tax 362–3
loans see foced loans
lods et ventes 237
longuellum★ 304
losung★ 280, 282, 288n58

macina★ 186–7, 194
mageiria 395
maghārim 409–10, 412, 416–17
magrán 418
Mahlungeld 275
maktu★ 420–1
mala pecunia 35
maldinaru 171
maltolt see wool tax
maltôte★ 19, 228, 243; *see also accise* and *ongeld*
maltz-Akzise see excise tax

494

Index

Malzpfennig 284
mandriatikon 393
mansus tax★ 361–3
marcegiæld see fifteen *marker*-aid
maridatges 101–2
market rights 179–80, 185
martiniega★ 122–3
marzazga 122–3
medio diezmo de lo morisco see diezmo★
melissoennomion 393
mena see castellaría
meniatikon 395
menusel 142
merchant duties 179, 186; *see also curaria* and tolls
mesitikon 395
mesuratges 98
metriatikon 395
midsummer tax *see midthsumærsgyald*
midthsumærsgyald 346
mines (monopoly on) 1, 27, 129
moneda 16–17, 124, 132, 134–6
moneda forera★ 122, 124, 131–2, 145
monedaje★ (Aragon) 100, 110; *monedaje* (Navarra) 122, 126, 137–9, 145
monopoly *see* mines; royal; sale of staples; salt; soap and taverns
montazgo 131, 140–1, 418; *see also servicio y montazgo*
mucharan 418
mukataa★ 425
munus★ 5
murage 315
myt★ 374, 377–9

nāḍḍ li-l-ḥashd 415
narzaz 357
nathold 346
nefgilde★ 343
nomithron 393
nosetax see nefgilde
Notbede 276
novella cavalleria 101
novitas 296

octroi★ 235, 243–4, 257
oikomodion 393
oinarike 393
olive oil (tithe on) 130
onera et exactions 182
onera rusticana 179
ongeld★ 257; *see also Ungeld*
onus 188
onzè 110
opheleia 393
opsonion★ 395
oreiatikon 393
orike 393

oshitki 378
ospitiakon 393
öşür 423
ox tax 357

pachiatikon 395
padrones 17
papal tenth 322–4
paramythiai 395
parias 128
parish tax 326, 333
paroikoi 395
partido de las mercaderías 130; *see also almojarifazgo*
patent *see octroi*
patis 233, 237
pavage 315
peaje/peatge 126
pecha★ 4, 98–9, 110, 122, 125, 137, 145
pechas encabezadas 125; *see also pecha*★
pecho de los judíos 131; *see also cabeza de pecho*
pechos y derechos ciertos 122–3
pedagium see toll
pedido (Castile) 123, 135; (Navarre) 138, 139, *see also donativos*
peita 98, 106, 110
personal see capage
peso del concejo 142
peso del rey 142
peso y cuchares 142
pesquerías 129
petitum see pedido (Castile)
phloriatikon 397
pipage 238
planene 393
plaustri ferrati 188
ploshki 378
plough money *see popluzhnoe*
plough tax★ (Poland) 357, 359, 361–3
ploughland *see carucate*
podimszczyna 366
podushnaia podat' 383
podvody 374, 378
podymne see hearth tax (Poland)
pogosty 372
poll tax (England★) 326–30, 333; (Poland) 362–3; (Ottoman Empire) 420–21, 423–24
polovniki 378
pontage 315
pontajes 98
ponteis 209
pontonagium 299
popluzhnoe 374
poradlne see plough tax (Poland)
poriatikon 395
portazgo★ 98, 142–3
poshlina 374
pososzczina 366

powołowe see ox tax
pozovitze 393, 402n63
praestationes 55
prebenda/prebendal★ 393, 402n63
precaria 274, 276
preselitza★ 393, 402n63
prestanze 183–4, 191, 193, 195; *see also* forced loans
primicias 139
Princeps namque 8n31
probatoennomion 393
procurations★ 205–6, 208, 210, 213
proteccion 99

qaṭʿ al-maghārim 416
quattrino on meat 215
quayage 315
quema 102, 111
queste 17
quèstia ★98, 102, 106, 110; *see also pecha* and *peita*
quindennia 87
quinto real 102
quista★ *see focagium*

redelme 110
redempcio d'host 99
rediezmo 126, 139
regalia 236–7
Reichsstadtsteuer★ 274–5; *see also precaria*
Reichssteuer 274, 278, 283n 285; *see also precaria*
relevio★ 161
relief 226
renta de Berbería 130; *see also almojarifazgo*
renta de las medidas 142
rentas menudas 130; *see also almojarifazgo*
repartimientos 141, 143
resm-i ağıl 424
resm-i asesiye 425
resm-i asiyab 424
reva/rèves 17, 302
ripatica 179, 185, 190
rivagium 304
rodas 142
Römermonat (Roman Month) 283
royal monopolies 159

ṣadaqa 415–16
safe-conduct tax 55, 60
Saladin tithe *see* tithes
sale of foodstuffs (monopoly on) 57
sale of staples (monopoly on) 142
salinarium 60
salt (monopoly on) *see alfolíes*
salt *gabelle*★ 186, 187–9
salt tax 164, 183, 188
saltpans 129, 134, 142

scutage★ 317–19, 332
secrezie (lease) 160, 162, 168–70, 172
serebszczyna 366
servicio★ (Castile) 127, 131–6, 141, 143, 145; (Navarre) 139
servicio y medio servicio 131, 135; *see also servicio*★ (Castile)
servicio y montazgo★ 127, 129, 131, 134
servitium 123; *see also auxilium*
servitium noctis see nathold
servitium pecuniarum/personarum see adoa★
sisas★ 84, 100–1, 108–11; *sisas*★ (Castile) 133, 136, 139, 142–3, 145; *sisas*★ (Navarre) 126, 139, 144, 145
sitarkia 393
situados 134–5
skattr 342
skeppsskatt 350
skeppsvist 345, 347
soap (monopoly on) 142
soldadas 128
soquet/souquet 17, 244, 302
soul tax *see podushnaia podat'*
sportula 395
St Martin tax 278
stadsskatt★ 347
Stadtsteuer 274, 276–8, 281, 284
Steura/stiura 276
stipendium 55
Strafgeld 277
strobilaia 393
stud 345–6
subsidy★ (ecclesiastical subsidies) 77, 79–82, 86–8, 127, 137, 322–3, 363
subsidio★ (Navarre) 7, 137–40; subsidy (Sicily) 159–61, 164, 166, 168–9, 174n45; subsidy★ (Church land) 210, 213, 215, 217, 219n70, 219n79, 220n107; subsidy (France) 229–30, 232, 235, 237, 240, 245; *subsidium/subsidy*★ (Provence and Savoy) 295–7, 299–301, 305, 307n47, 307n52, 307n53; subsidy (England) 314, 319, 321, 324–6, 328–33; subsidy (Poland) 360; *subsidium* (to the emperor) 181
subsidium marce see fifteen marker-aid
subvención 138
subventio★ 160–2, 166–7, 171
suffragia 395
sulung 316
sussidio see subsidy
synetheiai 395
szos (city★ and royal★) 360–3, 365

ṭabl 415
tafurerías 141
taglia/talea★ 183–4, 193–5, 305; *talea salis* 188

Index

taille★ 4, 17–19, 21, 60, 63, 66–7, 226, 232–3, 235–6, 241–2, 244–5; taille des gens d'armes 234–5; taille du roi 234; see also grandes tailles
talbix 418
tallage★ 55, 317–18, 322, 332
tallia 55, 60; talla (Aragon) 106–7, 110; talla (Navarre) 144; tallia★ (Church land) 208, 210–13, 218n55, 219n64; tallia (Burgundian Low Countries) 258; tallia★/talliagium (Provence and Savoy) 300, 302, 305; tallia dominicalis 302; tallia judeorum 296; tallia militum 208
tallo 144
tamga★ 373, 378–9
tansa 193
tarcon 418
tartil 418
tassa generale 163; tassa (or tassa mensualis) 193; tassa dei cavalleggeri 215
taverns (monopoly on) 187
tax on the common people see cherny bor
taxa equorum 194
taxatio 75, 87
tekalif-i divaniye 423
tekalif-i örfiye 423
tekalif-i şeriye 423
tenth★ 59, 73–5, 77, 80–2, 85–8, 210
tercias 83
tercias reales 127, 134–5; see also tithes
teysia domorum 300
theloneum 179, 185, 274, 299; theloneum forense 358; see also tolls
thelony 55
tierras 128
tigual 418
tithes 110, 127, 130, 142, 215, 227, 230, 325, 346, 363, 373, 393, 408, 410, 415, 417, 418, 420, 423, 424, 426; see also diezmos; öşür; redelme; Zwanzigster Pfennig; ecclesiastical tithes 3, 73, 83, 85; islamic tithe 130; Saladin tithe 74, 81, 227, 319
tolls 55, 99, 123, 126, 131, 136, 140–2, 157–8, 162, 164–8, 179, 183, 185–6, 206–7, 209, 219n57, 239, 299

traites★ 239
tratta★ 164, 168–9, 172
trezenum 304
tribute 55, 60; see also dan', chornyi vykhod, and vykhod
tribute on hearths 144
tritomoiria 393
tunnage and poundage 325
twentieth (on the Jews) 215, 220n107

Ungeld★ 7, 35, 272–5
'ushr 415, 417, 430n48

vacancies 76–7, 79, 87
vectigal 7
veinteno 139
veitsle 346
vintè 110
vintenum 302
víseyrir 349
voina 374
vykhod★ 374–5, 377

wine gabelle★187, 190; see also foglietta and longuellum★
wołoszczyna 366
wool tax 323–5

yam★ 373–5, 378
yantar 123, 124

zakā 408–10, 412–13, 415–17, 419, 430n29, 430n48
zakat al fitr 429
zappatici 179
zequi 429
zeugaratikion 393
zeugologion 393
zinskauf 36
Zwanzigster Pfennig★ 276, 280
zygastikon 395

Printed in the United States
by Baker & Taylor Publisher Services